# THE ENCYCLOPEDIA OF
# CLASSIC CARS

# THE ENCYCLOPEDIA OF CLASSIC CARS

GENERAL EDITOR
## KEVIN BRAZENDALE

THUNDER BAY
P·R·E·S·S

First published in the United States in 1999 by
Thunder Bay Press
An imprint of the Advantage Publishers Group
5880 Oberlin Drive, San Diego, CA 92121-4794
www.advantagebooksonline.com

Library of Congress Cataloging-in-Publication Data

The encyclopedia of classic cars / general editor, Kevin
Brazendale. -- Rev. and updated ed.
   p. cm.
   Includes index.
   ISBN 1-57145-182-X
   1. Antique and classic cars--Encyclopedia. I. Brazendale,
Kevin.

  TL9.E5235 1999
  629.222'03 21--dc21
99-044936

Conceived and produced by Amber Books Ltd
Bradley's Close, 74–77 White Lion Street,
London N1 9PF

Editorial Consultant: John Tipler

Printed in Italy - Nuova GEP, Cremona

  2 3 4 5   00 01 02 03

This revised and updated edition is based on material previously published by Orbis
Publishing Ltd, in 1992 as part of the reference set *The Encyclopedia of Supercars*.

# Contents

# Contents

# Introduction

**Y**ou see it ticking over at the traffic lights. It appears in your rearview mirror, closing in on a fast main road. It glides past you in the outside lane on the motorway. Or maybe you seek it out at the auction or the race circuit paddock. It's your favourite supercar, the one that gives you that frisson, exciting enough to make your hair stand on end, and send shivers down your spine. It's your ultimate motoring masterpiece, an object of desire and you lap up every scrap of information about it. Pictures on the wall and models in the cabinet. It's intriguing, perhaps because of historical provenance, some magnificent sporting exploit, or simply a manufacturing idiosyncrasy. You may have more than one favourite. They are undoubtedly supercar classics, and the chances are, they're in this book.

But just what makes a supercar? It's going to be rare, exotic in some way, with an exalted pedigree, extremely capable in its own particular niche, and possibly a flawed design. Its performance will be better than state-of-the-art for its time, and above all, its styling will clinch the issue. It's a combination of all these factors that defines a classic. The accepted time span of twenty years doesn't need to have elapsed for a car to qualify for an entry here, as it's possible to predict what some of the future classics will be from the moment they turn a wheel.

If styling and mechanical design are the criteria, where does the love affair start? Probably on the drawing board, since we commonly excuse a host of mechanical flaws provided their cladding is perceived as stylish. Great engineers were always prominent; men like Vittorio Jano, Ferdinand Porsche, and Wilfredo Ricart. But the car stylist was rather taken for granted until the 1950s when individuals like Harley Earl, Frank Spring and Nuccio Bertone became widely known. The men who design the cars we salivate over at motor shows, the cars we'd long to have standing in our own driveways, seem to have been enthusiasts first and foremost, and draughtsmen and design engineers by trade. To produce great designs, they had to be passionately addicted to their subject, as well as having a sound grasp of what went on underneath the bodywork.

## Coachbuilders

In the early days, the preoccupation was simply with the need to clad the mechanicals in some sort of practical fashion, so that the electrics and the occupants didn't get soaked. The original coachbuilders naturally knew more about the craft of building horse-drawn vehicles, so vehicle bodies were simply applied to the chassis of a horseless carriage. Right up to the 1950s in the luxury and sporting market, it was customary to buy a rolling chassis from the chosen manufacturer and have a specialist coachbuilder fit one of his hand-built bodies. Broken down into its fundamentals, the car consists of four wheels, an engine, somewhere for its driver to sit and a receptacle for its fuel. Styling is merely a matter of how you deal with the dressing of the bare bones. Probably the first car with distinctive styling was the Mercer Raceabout of 1908. Its designer was Finlay Robertson Porter, and it set the standard for a generation of sporting cars, with sweeping mudguards and running-boards from front to back. It had twin seats with fuel-tank behind and a neat functional cover over the bonnet. Other cars of the period had the same element, but the 75 mph Mercer had that extra panache, that elemental austerity that makes great styling.

The great stylists have always lavished their talents on the sporting end of the vehicular spectrum, because speed has always had a romantic fascination, and can be further glamorised by extravagant styling. Sports car builders operate, invariably, on relatively short production runs, and this is also true of major manufacturers who offer models aimed at the sports market. They can call upon a well-known stylist or styling house to give their sports model a distinctive look.

If the Mercer represented the sporting side of the market in 1910, the Hispano Suiza Alfonso of 1913 was the flagship of the slightly more restrained Grand Tourers. Although Marc Birkigt designed the mechanical engineering side of the Hispano Suiza, it was clad in a variety of bodies from a number of coachbuilders.

## Romantically Decadent

The mass-production Fords and Morris cars in the early years of the 20th century were rather at odds with the romantically decadent Art Nouveau, the rustic Arts and Crafts movement, and the fripperies of late Victoriana

*Below: Claimed to be the most successful model ever produced by Aston Martin, the DB7 has the styling that gets noticed. Styled by Ian Callum, formerly of Carrozzeria Ghia of Turin, it has distinctive styling.*

*Above: This BMW Z3 2.8 Roadster was first publicized in the James Bond movie, Goldeneye. It was more widely available than its predecessors and while it looked superb with the roof off, some thought it detracted from its appearance when fitted.*

that gripped western society. The art world was being turned upside down by the Cubists and other modernist groups like the Futurists, the latter venerating the motor car as the symbol of the dynamic new age. Fiat's Lingotto factory with its rooftop, banked-bend racetrack was designed by Matte Trusco, a Futurist architect. These obsessions inevitably gave rise to the earliest supercars, notably Mercedes Benz, Isotta Fraschini, Marion, Fiat, Nazzaro, Itala, National, Vauxhall, Pierce-Arrow and Peugeot.

Not surprisingly, the evolution of the automobile body style languished until after World War I. One of the main effects of the Great War was the establishment of production lines to meet the insatiable demand for basic weaponry and munitions. Motor manufacturers like Rolls Royce and Hispano Suiza provided their engines for aircraft and military vehicles. The war produced few significant technological advances, turbocharging in aircraft proving a notable exception. Put coldly, it was an industrial exercise, all about building a great many identical machines and components. But if the pre-war decade and the period of hostilities had yielded little in terms of aesthetics, the 1920s saw vehicle styling really begin to take off, to the point where it became an integral part of automotive marketing. It was the racing machines that led the way, with their quest for streamlined shapes to push back the frontiers of speed.

Probably the foremost innovator was Ettore Bugatti, whose 1923 'tank' bodied grand prix cars were clad in all-enveloping bodywork, which had an aerofoil configuration. Whereas today we know all about reverse lift and the downforce generated by inverted aerofoils, Bugatti didn't, and the Type 30 body, shaped in cross-section like the wing of an aircraft, was decidedly unstable around its 120 mph top speed. In addition, it was considered to be unattractive, so Bugatti abandoned it in favour of the pretty, low-slung Type 35 that followed in 1924 and was also innovative as the first car to have cast alloy wheels with integral brake drums. Bugatti's chief rivals at the time were Ballot, Sunbeam and Fiat, and of course Bentley, who was following a very different course. The Bentley sports-racing cars of the 1920s, described by Bugatti as the 'fastest trucks in the world', were brutish and archaic in comparison with the light and attractive French creation. Yet on the racetrack, they were hugely successful. More brutal still was Mercedes-Benz's SSLK, designed by Ferdinand Porsche in 1929. Less aggressive were models from Lagonda and Vauxhall, whose 30/98 preceded the company's General Motors take-over and subsequent subordination to stylist Harley Earl.

In the 1920s and 1930s, the Bauhaus, Le Corbusier, Art Deco and De Stijl were big in Europe, while Jazz and Hollywood ruled in the USA. The Bugatti Type 35 and the Alfa Romeo 6C 1750 of 1929 exemplify the best in European car styling during the 1920s, while the Cord, Lincoln Zephyr and Chrysler Airflow were the Stateside hits of the 1930s. If you wanted something a bit special rather than off the production line, you ordered a chassis and power unit from your favourite maker, and selected a design from the stylist. The coachbuilder then made a model in wood, and perhaps even a full-scale mock-up, in order to give a good idea of what the finished article would look like. When all was approved, the vehicle would be assembled,

and off you went. In broad terms, the styling process is virtually unchanged today, except for different mediums for the model, like clay, which was introduced in the late 1920s by Harley Earl, or plaster, plasticine and, more recently, glass-reinforced-plastic (GRP), and wind-tunnels and computer-aided-design (CAD), to develop the designer's original ideas.

## Extravagant Bodies

Between the two World Wars, the French stylists were dominant in Europe. The rich and fashionable were traversing the globe, and in Europe in particular it was the thing to do to motor down to the Côte d'Azure, the French Riviera. To do this in style, the 1930s fast set turned to the supercars of the day, and very soon these Grand Routieri were to be seen speeding southward to the sea and the sunshine. A number of excellent French coachbuilders came to prominence: Saoutchik, Faget Varnet, Franay, Pourtout, Figoni et Falaschi, all producing the most delightfully elegant and sometimes extravagant car bodies. Bugatti, Delage, Delahaye, Hotchkiss, Salmson, and Talbot provided the leading French chassis. Their appeal was strictly limited to the wealthiest market. The cars tended to be heavy and uneconomical because of their overly heavy chassis and bodywork. Two classic cars from a very different mould spelled the end for the Grand Routier exotics. The first was the light, monocoque front-wheel-drive Citroën Light 15, and the second the contemporary Peugeot, which had excellent road-holding and offered economical and comfortable motoring in considerable style, even in 1934. The Citroën, above all, showed the writing was on the wall for the luxurious leviathans, but the end really came with World War II and the

*Below: The Mercedes-Benz SLK was another classic car to die for. The unique folding steel Vano roof was stowed in the boot, and could be erected at the touch of a button.*

occupation of France. After hostilities ceased, many of the coachbuilders tried to get going again with their pre-war designs, but of course, times had changed not only in the automobile market, but also the availability of raw materials.

Mass-market designs in Europe like Standard's Vanguard, were heavily influenced by the USA, although in the specialist sector, the mantle was swiftly taken up by Italians like Ghia and Pininfarina. The war fostered major developments in aerodynamic, mechanical and metallurgic technology, and it seemed as if a pent-up wave of creativity was about to break in the buoyant atmosphere of liberated Italy. It didn't happen in Britain, doomed to a decade of stylistic mediocrity thanks to an economy devastated by five years of war. Many of Britain's factories may have survived, but industry was moribund, and in a climate of enforced austerity, functionality abounded, from Utility furniture to Land Rover. The one bright spot was Sir William Lyons' Jaguar XK120. Even the small French manufacturers forsook their native designers for Italy, and certainly by 1950, the big manufacturers like Peugeot and Renault were aware of the marketing advantages of being able to identify a prominent Italian stylist as having penned one of their models. Quite an accolade given that Pininfarina inititially produced only three or four designs a month. His Lancia Aurelia B20, launched at the 1951 Turin Show and in production from 1953, had a softness of line heralding a new sense of proportion for the 1950s, certainly in Europe. First of the new-look sporting machines was another Pininfarina effort, the alloy-bodied Cisitalia 202, a light, fresh design which influenced a further generation of coupés.

### Journey into Space

Rational styling in the 1950s, where aesthetics were paramount, belonged to the Italian styling houses of Pininfarina, Touring Superleggera and Ghia. In the USA, things became increasingly outrageous due to the obsessions of the principal stylists – Harley Earl, Bill Mitchell, Dutch Darrin and Raymond Loewy – first with jet fighters and then space rockets. In the mass market, stylistic changes were done as a matter of course as a means of selling more cars. In Britain, the market followed the USA and Italy in diluted form, while there was a more realistic attitude toward aerodynamics in the Frank Costin and Colin Chapman-designed Lotus sports-racing and Vanwall grand prix cars. British laurels in international sports-car racing were won by Jaguar with its curvaceous C- and D-Type cars, followed by Aston Martin's DB-Rs, while Lotus spearheaded the small-capacity classes.

The great British conceptual breakthrough came in 1959 with Alex Issigonis' Mini, which fitted in with other elements of trendy design exemplifying the pop culture. The popular climate revolved around youth culture, and there was a significant wealth explosion, providing greater disposable income for car buying. In terms of vehicle design, the Mini fostered a new generation of small front-wheel-drive town cars, and popularised the front-drive layout that Citroën had taken for granted for twenty years. At the glamorous end of the market, it was again the Pininfarina Ferraris, Malcolm Sayer's E-Type Jaguar, and slightly down-market from those, the Lotus Elan that epitomised desirable sports styling. It was a time of extravagant colour schemes, directly influenced by the fashion houses in swinging London. In the USA, the 'pony' car took off with the Ford Mustang in 1964, and the Corvette got steadily meaner-looking. As the

decade sprinted on, supercars like the Bertone studio's Lamborghini Miura and the Eric Broadley-derived Ford GT40 captured the imagination. It was about this time that the very word supercar was coined. Proper sports-racers like the GT40, Ferrari 250LM and 330 P3/4, plus Broadley's own Lola T70, and the Porsche 906, were the stylistic benchmark cars. You can see their styling cues resurfacing in 1999 in Julian Thomson's fabulous Lotus Elise. Porsche's own succession of 906, 907, 908 and 917 is a clear example of how such a design progresses, traceable right down to the 962s racing in 1989. During the 1960s and 1970s, tyre technology progressed through competition development to such an extent that the wide tyres seen on the racers became a regular feature of the road-going supercar.

### Household Names

A great many anonymous bread-and-butter designs are 'styled-by-committee' – the Ford Capri was a good example – insofar as there was input from a number of draughtsmen working in the design department, and the management hierarchy also had its say. However, men like Earl, Loewy and Mitchell were virtually household names in the USA, and by the 1970s, the same was starting to become true in Europe. Stylists like Giugiaro and Gandini had served their time with the old houses of Ghia and Bertone, and were busy setting up studios of their own. Giugiaro's Ital Design consultancy was chiefly responsible for the spate of angular, wedge-shaped cars so popular with the British in the early 1970s. Best examples of the wedge design are the Lotus Excel and long-running Esprit. A stunning show-car every year doesn't pay the rent, even if it does enhance the showcase, and these men followed in the footsteps of their peers by producing styles for major manufacturers. There ensued a progression of logical but unexciting Eurobox hatchbacks, which embraced competition-derived aerodynamic aids in order to look interesting, so that city-centre chic demanded spoilers, air dams and side skirts on cars that gasped for breath at 100 mph. Cars such as Uwe Bahnsen's jelly-mould Ford Sierra took interesting styling into the popular market, and the uncompromising Audi Quattro popularised turbocharging and four-wheel-drive: now there was a supercar for everyday use. A few niches further down were Pininfarina's Peugeot 205 the Renault 5 GT Turbo and the Uno Turbo, popular 'designer' cars, in so far as they were crisp, rationalised urban-tiger shapes. While supercars were in the super-tax bracket as far as values were concerned, these pocket rockets were at least widely affordable, and the same was true of their more proletarian classic equivalents.

Modern car styling is tempered by the all-powerful market forces, and at the turn of the millennium we fluctuate almost annually from retro to futuristic designs according to perceived fashions or as manufacturers try to outdo their rivals. Thus we may be tempted by classically influenced cars like Walter da Silva's Alfa Romeo 156 or Ford's New Edge models exemplified by the excellent Focus. To some eyes they may be mere family saloons, but whichever way your fancy takes you, their innovative top drawer styling makes them classics of the future.

*Below: This Porsche 911 Carrera was launched in 1997. With its stunning styling cues, it looks every inch the classic car.*

*The initials stand for Auto Carriers, the name the company chose in 1907: it was previously known as Autocars and Accessories Ltd.*

# AC Cars Ltd

A professional combination of engineer and butcher sounds unlikely, but it was just such a pairing that led to the formation of AC: engineer John Weller's first car, built in 1903, was financed by butcher John Portwine. This car was too expensive, so in the following year the team developed a cheap commercial three-wheeler known as the Auto-Carrier, a kind of back-to-front tricycle with a box over the front axle. It was as Autocars & Accessories Ltd that Weller and Portwine produced these and a passenger-carrying variant known as the AC Sociable. A name change to Auto-Carriers Ltd came in 1907, followed by a move to the company's best-known home in riverside Thames Ditton in 1911, but it was not until S.F. Edge became chairman, on the departure of Weller and Portwine in 1922, that AC Cars Ltd finally arrived.

The first AC four-wheeler appeared in 1913, an aluminium-bodied two-seater with a four-cylinder Fivet engine, but of more note was John Weller's overhead-camshaft inline-six. This was first shown in 1919, and remained in production in two-litre form right through until 1963. Competition success came in the 1920s, but the company found itself in voluntary liquidation on the retirement of Edge in 1929, being revived in 1931 by brothers William and Charles Hurlock.

A range of coupés, convertibles and saloons followed, all with a sporting pedigree, but there was plenty of diversification, most notably in the shape of the invalid cars made for many years from the early 1950s. This was the AC heyday, with famous models like the Ace, Aceca, Cobra and Greyhound in production.

The Cobra-based 428 of 1966 was not a success and perhaps marked the beginning of the end for AC. The mid-engined 3000ME sports two-seater first appeared in 1973, but did not get into production until 1979 and only 68 had been built by 1984, when the rights were sold to AC (Scotland) Ltd, a new company which closed in the following year.

The AC name was kept alive by Brian Angliss, whose Autokraft company built Cobras, known as the AC Mk IV. For 1986 he developed a new high-tech Ace, and Ford bought AC in 1987 with a view to putting this into production. However, the Ford buyouts of Jaguar and Aston Martin killed the project. In 1999 they were still making the Cobra, now known as the AC Superblower and the Ace.

*Although never a big company, AC produced vehicles as wildly different as invalid carriages and the potent Cobra, the fearsome 427-cu in version of which is shown here. Despite its poor aerodynamics it could reach 160 mph.*

## AC Ace 1954-1964

The Ace came out of a realisation by AC that it could not afford to replace its ageing saloon range with anything to match the burgeoning competition. A demonstration of one of John Tojeiro's lightweight sports-racers impressed AC's management, who bought the car in the summer of 1953 and set about building a roadgoing version. By the time the Motor Show opened at Earls Court in October, the Tojeiro had taken on a fresh look, and alongside it on the stand was the fruit of its modification, the AC Ace, created in record time.

Like the Tojeiro, the Ace was based on a twin-tube main chassis, with multiple lightweight tubes forming a frame for the aluminium convertible bodywork, in Italian *superleggera* style. Suspension was independent all round, with transverse leaf springs, lower wishbones and telescopic dampers. Drum brakes all round in early cars gave partial way to front discs in 1957, while the rack-and-pinion steering of the Tojeiro and the first ground-up Ace proved geometrically troublesome and was supplanted for production by an old-style steering box.

Power was provided by the old-faithful AC two-litre straight-six, initially with 85 bhp but eventually with 102. Mounted well back in the chassis for good weight distribution, this drove the rear wheels through a four-speed Moss gearbox.

Primarily a road car, low weight and exceptional handling brought the Ace immediate competition success, and it was a racer, Ken Rudd, who first used Bristol's BMW-based two-litre six, an engine that became a factory option in 1956, together with a Bristol gearbox. Overdrive was also offered with both engines in this year.

In 1961 production of the Bristol engine ceased, so AC turned to Ford's 2.5-litre Zephyr/Zodiac six, which was offered in various states of Ruddspeed tune, ranging from 90 to 170 bhp.

Detail changes during the Ace's life were many, but it remained substantially unaltered until its demise in 1964, with nearly 700 examples built.

### Ace variants

#### Aceca

A two-seat coupé version of the Ace was based on a modified chassis and running gear and powered by AC, Bristol or Ford engine; built between 1954 and 1963

*Introduced in 1953, the Ace was based on a design by John Tojeiro. It featured independent suspension and aluminium bodywork.*

## Ace-Bristol

Primarily offered for competition use and powered by a hand-built six-cylinder Bristol engine whose design was acquired from BMW after World War II; also used Bristol gearbox

*The interior boasted leather upholstery and a very comprehensive set of instruments.*

## Ace 2.6

Introduced, with Ford power, when the Bristol engine was withdrawn and produced alongside other versions right up to the end. This was much cheaper than Bristol variants

### Specification (AC engine)

**Engine:** inline-six, overhead cam
**Bore × stroke:** 65 mm × 125 mm
**Capacity:** 1991 cc
**Maximum power:** 85 bhp
**Transmission:** four-speed manual gearbox driving rear wheels
**Chassis:** twin longitudinal steel tubes with cross-bracing
**Suspension:** independent, with transverse leaf springs, lower wishbones and telescopic dampers
**Brakes:** drums
**Bodywork:** aluminium-alloy open two-seater, multiple-steel-tube framing
**Maximum speed (approx):** 100 mph (161 km/h)

*The Ace was powered by various engines during its career, the AC and Bristol two-litre fours, and a Ford Zephyr straight-six. This is the Bristol engine, which produced 130 bhp at 5750 rpm.*

---

# AC Cobra 1962–present

Ace production was on the wane when American racer-turned-entrepreneur Carroll Shelby approached AC in 1961 with the aim of beefing up the car and transplanting a meaty Ford V8 into it. A deal was quickly struck and Ford agreed to supply modified versions of its 4.2-litre (260-cu in) V8.

Shelby's prescribed changes were quickly carried out at Thames Ditton, and February 1962 saw the first car running in the States. It would have been easy just to drop the V8 into the cavernous engine bay, but instead the structure was stiffened and the transmission and suspension beefed up to match engine weight and power.

The Jaguar E-type-style Salisbury limited-slip differential came complete with inboard rear discs, although these were quickly moved outboard in production. A Borg-Warner four-speed gearbox transmitted the V8's 260 bhp.

The track was widened and the wheel arches flared to match and give the Cobra its distinctive sleek yet muscular appearance. Performance was staggering (top speed up to 150 mph!)

*This far more flamboyant badge showed the influence of Carroll Shelby on the staid AC company.*

and this was immediately reflected on the race tracks of America. With this success came greater Ford involvement, new developments being fed back to the Thames Ditton factory, from where engineless cars were shipped.

The American racing programme brought a multitude of special body

styles to what was by late 1962 the Cobra 289, with its 4.7-litre V8 and rack-and-pinion steering, but the most sensational variant was yet to come. The AC name

had been dropped in the US by the time the Mk III arrived in January 1965.

The 289 continued, but now there was a 427 as well, with a seven-litre engine

*Above: Adding a hardtop made the Cobra more effective on the world's tracks. This is a '64 Le Mans.*

*Below: The classic Cobra is the 289, the name referring to the size of the 4.7-litre V8 engine in cubic inches.*

and generally well over 400 bhp on tap. This Mk III Cobra had a new and much stiffer chassis, coil spring suspension and strengthening in just about every area. Bodywork of the 427 was stretched to house huge wheels and tyres.

With the coming of the Mustang, Ford lost interest in this beast, and production ceased in 1966. In England, AC produced its own coil-sprung 289 until 1968, but without the Cobra name.

One of the all-time classics seemed to have passed, yet the design was perpetuated by Brian Angliss, founder of Autokraft at Brooklands, who reached an agreement to use the AC badge. In the late 1990s the Cobra resurfaced as the AC Superblower, as aggressive and purposeful as ever.

## Cobra variants

### Cobra Mark II
Same basic specification as the original car, but fitted with a 289-cu in (4.7-litre) Ford V8. The most common version of the Cobra in Europe

### Cobra 427
Very much modified and stiffened variant of the Mk III, equipped with a 427-cu in (7-litre) V8 and capable of more than 160 mph

### AC 428
Cobra 427 chassis, fitted with brand new steel coupé or convertible body, styled by Frua of Turin. Produced entirely by AC, with no Shelby involvement, between 1966 and 1973

### Cobra Mark IV
Improved version produced by Autokraft from 1975 on, with thicker chassis tubes, ventilated disc brakes, five-speed gearbox and luxury trimming

### Specification (Mk II 289)
**Engine:** V8, overhead valve
**Bore × stroke:** 102 mm × 73 mm
**Capacity:** 4735 cc
**Maximum power:** 300 bhp
**Transmission:** four-speed manual gearbox driving rear wheels
**Chassis:** twin longitudinal steel tubes with cross-bracing
**Suspension:** independent, with transverse leaf springs, lower wishbones and telescopic dampers
**Brakes:** discs
**Bodywork:** aluminium-alloy open two-seater, with multiple-steel-tube framing
**Maximum speed (approx):** 138 mph (222 km/h)

*Left: The 427 badge refers to the engine size in cubic inches; in European terms, that is 6998 cc. Power was over 400 bhp.*

*Above: Least successful of the Cobra variants was the 428. It was built in both coupé and convertible versions. Styling was by Frua of Turin.*

*Below: Considerable modification was needed to fit the big, heavy 427-cu in V8 into the Cobra. The chassis was greatly stiffened to cope with the extra power, and the wheel arches flared dramatically.*

*Bottom: The Cobra driver could monitor every engine function, thanks to the array of dials that included speedo, tachometer, oil pressure, amps, water temperature and oil temperature.*

# AC Greyhound 1960-1963

Realising that it was always going to be difficult to make money out of the small numbers of Aces and Acecas on order and in response to gentle public demand, AC decided to spread its net by introducing a four-seater.

As with the Aceca before it, the new Greyhound was evolved from the Ace rather than designed completely anew. Prototype work was carried out around stretched Aces and Acecas so that plenty of development miles could be put in before the new design was finalised.

The transverse leaf springs were replaced by coils to allow the engine to be moved forwards and the passenger compartment extended even further than the 10 inches that the extra wheelbase facilitated. At the back, the coil springs were accompanied by a new semi-trailing arm arrangement, again to release interior space.

The round tubes of the main chassis became square for the Greyhound, and gained an additional reinforcing network, while the body gained additional support from an outrigger arrangement. Rack-and-pinion steering was standard, as were disc front brakes and aluminium rear drums.

As ever, the bodywork was handcrafted in aluminium sheet, the flowing lines giving an obvious continuation of the Aceca theme. Luggage now sat in its own compartment with a bottom hinged lid and the luxurious interior featured reclining front seats and respectable room for rear passengers. The 16-inch wheels were wider than on the Ace or Aceca, but they reflected those cars' sporting appeal in their spoked, centre-lock nature.

Power came mostly from variants of the Bristol engine, including one with a 2.2-litre capacity, although there were a few cars with the old AC six. With a kerb weight of only just over a ton, the Greyhound could manage around 105 mph, but that low weight meant that handling characteristics were sensitive to passenger load changes.

*The Greyhound marked AC's return to the sporting four-seater saloon market. It was powered by the Bristol or AC two-litre six-cylinder overhead-cam engines rather than the big V8s used in the Cobras.*

A good car the Greyhound might have been, but it was too expensive to sell in large quantities and was discontinued in 1963 with fewer than 100 built.

## Specification

**Engine:** inline-six, overhead cam
**Bore × stroke:** 66 mm × 96 mm
**Capacity:** 1971 cc
**Maximum power:** 105 bhp
**Transmission:** four-speed manual gearbox driving rear wheels
**Chassis:** twin longitudinal steel tubes with reinforcement
**Suspension:** independent, with coil springs, telescopic dampers, lower front wishbones and semi-trailing rear arms
**Brakes:** front discs, rear drums
**Bodywork:** aluminium-alloy four-seat coupé, with multiple-steel-tube framing
**Maximum speed (approx):** 105 mph (169 km/h)

# AC 3000ME 1979-1984

AC appeared to have moved into a new age with a bang when it exhibited a new mid-engined coupé, the 3000ME, at the London Motor Show of 1973, but that bang soon turned into a phut, with production delays coming thick and fast. As one show exhibit followed another, the ME became something of an in-joke in the motoring press, and it was not until 1979 that the first production cars finally left the Thames Ditton factory.

The idea was a good one, based on another show exhibit, the Diablo, bought in by AC from Peter Bohanna and Robin Stables in the same way as the Tojeiro had sired the Ace 20 years earlier. Austin Maxi power in the Diablo gave way to a Ford three-litre V6 mounted transversely behind the two seats and driving the rear wheels via a chain and a Hewland five-speed gearbox.

A first for AC was the so-called monocoque chassis, in essence a massive steel platform providing a home for a stylish glassfibre body and mountings for the suspension. Following racing traditions, double wishbones featured at each end, with coil spring/damper units. Rack-and-pinion steering was controlled through an adjustable column and disc brakes sat inside alloy wheels at each corner.

Inside, the ME was neatly and professionally finished, with adequate room for two occupants, and the whole design had great appeal and potential. Unfortunately, however, after all those years of development, the AC really did not perform well enough to match a price tag that put it into the same market as the far more refined Lotus Esprit and the Porsche 924 Turbo. It could manage 130 mph or so, but it was still unrefined and the handling was questionable.

Only 68 cars were made in five years before the project was sold to an independent new company, AC (Scotland) Ltd, which built about 30 more examples before itself foundering amid ambitious plans for a replacement, which came to nothing.

## Specification

**Engine:** V6, overhead valve
**Bore × stroke:** 94 mm × 72 mm
**Capacity:** 2993 cc
**Maximum power:** 140 bhp
**Transmission:** five-speed manual gearbox driving rear wheels
**Chassis:** platform 'monocoque'
**Suspension:** independent, with coil springs, telescopic dampers and double wishbones
**Brakes:** discs
**Bodywork:** glassfibre two-seat coupé
**Maximum speed (approx):** 135 mph (217 km/h)

*An incredibly long development process meant that the AC 3000ME was lagging behind the opposition when it finally appeared in 1979. The design was hampered by AC's inadequate resources. Matched against rivals such as the Lotus Esprit, it was poor value.*

# Abarth & Cie

**C**arlo Abarth was an Austrian born in 1908 who had to wait until after World War II to gain real fame in the motor industry, although he had been producing performance exhaust systems since the 1920s. Abarth's career really took off when he met Ferry Porsche in Italy after World War II and became involved in helping Porsche to produce the Cisitalia racing cars. When Cisitalia expired from financial problems, Abarth took over the racing department under the patronage of a wealthy driver, Carlo Scagliarini. This proved profitable enough for Abarth to form his own company in 1950.

Abarth's speciality was in extracting a lot of power from small engines, and being based in Italy, that basically meant tuning Fiats. His first car, shown at the 1950 Turin Motor Show, used a one-litre Fiat four-cylinder engine that in normal spec produced just 35 bhp. Once Abarth had finished tuning it, it was capable of powering his small car at over 110 mph.

The most familiar Abarths were the modified Fiat 500 and 600s, with their rear engines tuned to such a degree that the rear engine cover was permanently propped slightly open to improve cooling!

The company did produce complete cars as well as modifying production Fiats; the great majority were race or record-breaking cars. The record-breakers had aerodynamic bodies designed by Pininfarina, and Abarth was shrewd enough to use motoring writers as drivers to gain the maximum publicity for his company.

Although Abarth's main allegiance was to Fiat, he built a number of cars in the 1950s and 1960s based on the French company Simca's 1300- and 1500-cc four-cylinder engines which, like the Fiat fours, could be tuned to good effect. There was a very brief flirtation with Alfa Romeo, but this did not meet with Fiat approval and Abarth did not pursue it. The Fiat relationship grew stronger – after 20 years Abarth could boast of more than 6,000 race wins with Fiat-powered cars. Fiat were sufficiently impressed to take over Abarth in 1971 so that the Abarth name could be given to their fastest-tuned road cars, cars such as the raucous and impressive Strada Abarth of the 1980s.

*Above: In conjunction with the Milan-based coachbuilders Zagato, Abarth built a bewildering number of stylish coupés based on the rear-engined Fiat 500s and 600s of the 1950s and 1960s. This is one of the most unusual.*

*Left: Abarth turned to Pininfarina for his record-breaking cars, such as this 750-cc from 1957.*

## Abarth Bialbero 1959-1964

'Bialbero' means twin-cam, and the term was a general one given to a long range of Abarth GTs built during the 1950s and 1960s that grew and grew in power as both capacity and engine tuning was increased.

The 1960 Abarth Bialbero was a GT racer, based on the humble Fiat 600D's floorpan and retaining its simple suspension system of a transverse leaf spring at the front with double wishbones and trailing arms and coil springs at the rear. The suspension was uprated to deal with the considerably increased power.

That power came from a greatly modified Fiat four-cylinder engine. The modifications involved increasing its capacity to nearly one litre, increasing both the bore and stroke. The compression ratio was increased to 10:1, twin Weber 36 DCL4 carburettors were fitted and a twin-cam cylinder head grafted onto the engine. The result was a dramatic increase in power that saw 84 bhp produced at 7,000 rpm. That was enough to give the tiny car 123-mph performance. Such performance could only be achieved with a very light car and an aerodynamic design: at little over 1,200 lb the Bialbero was light indeed, and its shape was one of Italian coachbuilder Zagato's slipperiest designs. By 1960, however, Abarth had moved production from Zagato's Milan base to Corna, a small factory in Turin.

### Specification (1960)

**Engine:** inline four-cylinder, twin-cam
**Bore × stroke:** 65 mm × 74 mm
**Capacity:** 982 cc
**Transmission:** four-speed manual
**Chassis:** Fiat 600 floorpan, tubular frame
**Suspension:** independent with transverse wishbone front and coil springs rear
**Brakes:** discs front, drums rear
**Bodywork:** alloy two-seater coupé body
**Maximum speed:** 123 mph (200 km/h)

*The Bialbero's shape and good power-to-weight ratio made it a very successful racer, with a top speed of over 120 mph from only one litre. This example is racing at Riverside in California.*

# Alfa Romeo

*Curious bonnet mascots enjoyed a vogue in the 1920s, so manufacturers brought out their own designs.*

*The 'Romeo' was added in 1915 when Nicola Romeo took over the ailing ALFA company.*

*'Milano' appeared on the Alfa badge until the company built a new factory in the south of Italy to produce the Alfasud range.*

*The Alfa Romeo badge shows a serpent swallowing a child; it comes from the coat-of-arms of the city of Milan.*

Amazingly, one of the most famous names in motoring, Alfa Romeo, came about because of the sales failure of the locally assembled French Darracqs in Italy. It was in 1906 that Alexandre Darracq tried selling two underpowered cars through SAID (Società Anonima Italiana Darracq) and just three years later that the company went bankrupt. In 1910, ALFA was formed (Anonima Lombardi Fabbrica Automobili) from the ashes of SAID, and an ex-Fiat designer by the name of Giuseppe Merosi was taken on to manufacture cars more suited to the rough, hilly Italian roads.

ALFA were just starting to make headway in the growing Italian market when production was transferred to the war effort (sales had grown from 20 in 1910 to over 200 in the first six months of 1915). The company flourished, but ALFA's bank was pessimistic about the car market during the war and wanted someone else to stake a claim. That someone was wealthy mining engineer Nicola Romeo, who took over as

Managing Director and the company changed from ALFA to Alfa Romeo.

After the war, during which tractors and general engineering equipment were built, the company was left with parts for more than 100 cars, which gave them a head start on the opposition. Sales in the 1920s were initially slow, but the RL series turned the company's fortunes around, as did the success of the racing P2.

With designer Vittorio Jano's arrival and part-time racer Enzo Ferrari running the company's racing team, Alfa Romeo flourished in the 1930s with exotic six- and eight-cylinder road cars and racers that set standards by which others were judged.

The company survived World War II – just – and their pre-war racer, the Alfetta, dominated early post-war Grand Prix racing. Road car production was still definitely upmarket until the classic four-cylinder twin-cam engine was developed by Dr Orazio Satta Puliga in 1950.

Although Alfa Romeo dabbled with larger cars throughout the 1950s and 1960s, it was the four-cylinder cars, the Giuliettta of 1954 and then the Giulia of 1962, that became the company's backbone. Racing centred on saloon and sports car in this period with much success, before a couple of abortive attempts at Formula 1 in the 1970s and 1980s.

After being under Government control since 1933, Alfa Romeo was sold to Fiat in 1988, becoming the 'sporting car' arm of the huge Turin empire. The company enjoyed a renaissance in the late 1990s with stylish new models like the 156 saloon.

*Alfa Romeo's greatest pre-war supercar was undoubtedly this, the 8C 2900, powered by a supercharged three-litre straight-eight twin-cam.*

## Alfa Romeo 6C 1750 1929-33

The event that most helped to turn Alfa Romeo's fortunes around was the addition of ex-Fiat designer Vittorio Jano to the fold; Enzo Ferrari, later a works driver and team manager with Alfa Romeo, assisted in Jano's moving across the Po valley from Turin to Milan. Jano's first effort took over from where he had left off at Fiat with the sweet little eight-cylinder 805 racer: in Alfa form, this was to become the P2, which won the inaugural World Championship in 1925. The GP machine then spawned the road-going 1500 after two cylinders and the supercharger had been shorn from it and a single overhead cam replaced the two of the racer.

The second camshaft reappeared in 1928 on the 1500 Sport and this developed the following year into the 6C 1750, but with just one camshaft again. However, the 1750 in Sport guise *did* use twin-cams, while the Gran Sport had the addition of a supercharger. It was the last-mentioned that was to be the classic of the range, and some 257 were built.

The 1750's engine actually displaced

*This 1930 Gran Sport version of the 6C 1750 has a supercharged engine with a twin-lobe Alfa supercharger running at engine speed. The red headlight covers are original.*

1752 cc, and it featured hemispherical combustion chambers (just like the famous Alfa fours to this day). This gem of an engine sat in a C-section ladder frame and suspension was by semi-elliptic leaf springs all round. It handled well and had good performance, courtesy of 85 bhp, but most importantly it looked right, especially with classic two-seater tourer bodywork by Zagato.

As well as being a success on the road, the cars excelled on the track in tuned, 102-bhp trim. Campari and Romponi won the 1929 Mille Miglia in a 1750 and the lantern-jawed maestro, Tazio Nuvolari, won the same event the following year. The *Flying Mantuan* beat team-mate Achille Varzi, after a last-minute pass that involved Nuvolari switching off his headlamps so as not to alert Varzi and darting through on a downhill night-time stretch!

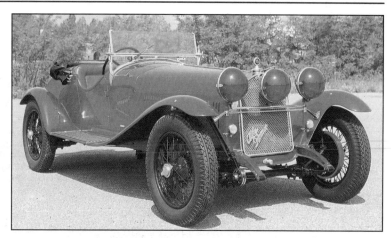

### Specification (Super Sports)

**Engine:** inline six, twin cam
**Bore × stroke:** 65 mm × 88 mm
**Capacity:** 1752 cc
**Maximum power:** 85 bhp
**Transmission:** four-speed
**Chassis:** pressed steel, five cross-members

**Suspension:** non-independent with semi-elliptic leaf springs all round
**Brakes:** rod-operated drums
**Bodywork:** to choice.
**Maximum speed (approx):** 95 mph (152 km/h)

## Alfa Romeo 8C 2300 1931-34

The next obvious stage in Jano's work at Alfa Romeo was to turn the successful six-cylinder 1750 into an eight-cylinder machine. The six had been developed from a two-litre eight by the slicing off of two cylinders, so the new engine would naturally be a reversal of that process, wouldn't it? No; what Jano did was take a further two cylinders off the six and then double it.

This wasn't as strange as it at first seemed. Jano figured that having two shorter crankshafts, joined by twin helical gears, would cut down whip and vibration; one gear drove the camshafts, while the other looked after turning the Roots supercharger or 'blower'. The internal dimensions were the same as the little 1750s, giving the 1931 8C 2300 2336 cc and some 138 bhp.

The beautifully sculpted engine, with its distinctively finned inlet plumbing, sat in a chassis similar to that of the 1750, and was available in two lengths, *corto* (short) and *lungo* (long), although they were commonly known as Mille Miglia and Le Mans.

Even in standard form the 8C 2300 could top 115 mph (185 km/h) and by the time it had been updated by the works team, run by Enzo Ferrari, it was considerably more potent. The works cars differed in that they were larger, at 2556 cc, and had magnesium blocks in place of the standard aluminium ones (remember, each car had two). In this form, the engine produced 180 bhp, enough to give a top speed of more than 135 mph (217 km/h).

*Above: This 1931 Scuderia Ferrari Zagato-bodied short-wheelbase 8C 2300 was raced by Enzo Ferrari himself in 1931, and by Nuvolari two years later to win the 1933 Mille Miglia.*

*Right: Before World War II Enzo Ferrari ran Alfa Romeo's racing team, and his prancing horse emblem appeared on all Scuderia Ferrari Alfas. It was first used by an Italian fighter ace of World War I.*

Success was immediate: in its various forms, the car won the Targa Florio in 1931, the Mille Miglia in 1932, 1933, 1934 and 1935 and the Le Mans classic four times from 1931 to 1934. The most incredible result, however, was the 1-2 in the European Grand Prix at Monza in 1931, for it meant that a design which had started almost a decade before as a Grand Prix car was once again in the Blue Riband class after its intermediate road-car developments.

### Specification

**Engine:** water-cooled inline eight, twin cam
**Bore × stroke:** 65 mm × 88 mm
**Capacity:** 2336 cc
**Maximum power:** 138 bhp
**Transmission:** four-speed manual gearbox driving rear wheels
**Chassis:** two outer longitudinal members and cross members
**Suspension:** non-independent, semi-elliptic leaf springs, adjustable friction dampers and live rear axle
**Brakes:** finned alloy drums
**Bodywork:** two- or four-seater open sports
**Maximum speed (approx):** 112 mph (180 km/h)

*Above: 8C 2300s came with different bodies; this one is by Touring of Milan. This car once finished fifth in the Le Mans 24 Hours, and was later driven by Mike Hawthorn.*

# Alfa Romeo 8C 2900

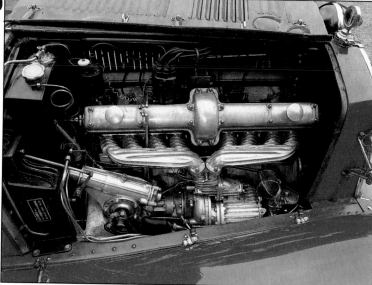

*Above: The picture shows the aerodynamic front of a racing 8C 2900.*

*Left: The 8C 2900's straight-eight had the camshaft drive in the middle to minimise camshaft flexing.*

During the 1920s and 1930s, Alfa Romeo mixed parts not only between models but between their racers and roadsters too. The fabulous P3 Grand Prix car, which had evolved from the 8C 2600 Monza, dominated racing for only one year in 1932 before the company ran out of money and the cars were laid up in storage. Their engines were removed from mothballs, enlarged from 2.6 litres to 2.9 and then fitted to a modified chassis from the austere 6C 2300. The result was the fabulous 8C 2900B of 1937, of which there were just 20 short-chassis versions and a mere 10 *lungo* examples.

This car was to mark the zenith of pre-war sports car development. Its 2905-cc straight-eight twin-cam engine was fed by two downdraught carburettors and two superchargers, one for each inlet manifold on the motor's siamesed four-cylinder blocks. In spite of its extra capacity over the P3, a lower state of tune meant that the 2900 motor had 35 bhp less, but this was still an impressive 180 bhp, which gave the car a top speed of 115 mph in road trim. In racing guise, the 8C 2900 was phenomenal: as well as winning the 24-hour race at Spa in 1938, 8C 2900s took the first three places in that year's Mille Miglia. A special aerodynamic coupé body was built on a 2900 chassis for Le Mans, and this Alfa Romeo was all of 115 miles ahead of the

second-placed runner after 18 hours before a puncture delayed it.

The best coachbuilders of the time, notably Touring of Milan, clothed the 8C 2900s in very attractive bodywork and this run of 30 machines became the most exotic cars ever manufactured by the Milanese company and a fitting swan-song for Vittorio Jano, who was soon to be pensioned off by Alfa as being too old. He then went on to work for Lancia and Ferrari, with great success.

## Specification

**Engine:** inline eight supercharged twin cam
**Bore × stroke:** 68 mm × 100 mm
**Capacity:** 2905 cc
**Maximum power:** 180 bhp
**Transmission:** four-speed
**Chassis:** box section

**Suspension:** twin trailing arms and coil springs front with swing axles and transverse leaf spring rear
**Brakes:** drums all round, hydraulically operated
**Bodywork:** two-seater sports
**Maximum speed (approx):** 115 mph (185 km/h)

*Below: In 1938 Alfa Romeo fitted aerodynamic bodywork to the 8C 2900 for the Le Mans 24 Hours, where it led for 18 hours. That was no surprise, as the engine was derived from that used in the P3 Grand Prix car.*

# Alfa Romeo Disco Volante 1952-53

It was because flying saucers were much in the news in 1952 that Alfa Romeo's racing version of their 1900 was dubbed *disco volante*: the rounded body of one of the two open versions featured a sharp-edged waistline that gave the car the profile. The single closed coupé version had the same distinctive feature.

These three original cars were powered by slightly overbored versions of the 1900's four-cylinder, twin-cam engine, leaving its capacity at just over 1997 cc to allow it to compete in the

two-litre class. With its 158 bhp, the Disco Volante was certainly competitive, but its distinguishing bodywork, although excellent for air penetration, didn't provide a great deal of stability. Ultimately, the open cars weren't successful on the tracks and were pensioned off for the year, while the solitary coupé with its even more striking Touring-designed body never raced at all.

Heavily revised, the cars reappeared in 1953, but this time there were four: one with the four-cylinder motor and the other three sporting six-cylinder engines based on the 1900 four but with two more cylinders added. Only one actually had the sharp-edged bodywork of its predecessors, but the Disco Volante name seemed to stick for the whole series of cars, which ran first at

*'Disco Volante' translates as 'flying saucer'. In 1952, when the Disco Volante was introduced, flying saucers were much in the news and the name stuck.*

*The Disco Volante's shape was slippery, but it generated too much lift for a racing car.*

2955 cc and then in overbored form at 3495 cc. Again, racing success was sparse, but Fangio managed to win the AGIP Supercortemaggiore-sponsored Grand Prix at Merano with one when the much-fancied Lancias all retired; alas it wasn't the 'Disco Volante-bodied' car.

## Specification (1953)

**Engine:** inline six, twin cam
**Bore × stroke:** 88 mm × 98 mm
**Capacity:** 3576 cc
**Maximum power:** 260 bhp
**Transmission:** five-speed
**Chassis:** tubular space frame
**Suspension:** independent with double wishbones and coil springs front and de Dion axle with coil springs rear
**Brakes:** drums all round
**Bodywork:** aerodynamic open or coupé two seater
**Maximum speed:** (approx) 150 mph (241 km/h)

# Alfa Romeo Giulietta Sprint Speciale 1957-62

Alfa Romeo was certainly one of *the* supercar manufacturers in the 1930s, but the recession and World War II hit the company really hard; the 1950s were to see the company going for quantity rather than exotic-car quality.

In terms of motive power, the crafted six- and eight-cylinder engines were too expensive to mass produce, but salvation came with Dottore Puliga's new engine for the company. It had all the classic design elements of the Jano motors, but it was a compact four-cylinder unit, ideal for mass production. It featured an alloy cylinder head with hemispherical combustion chambers and twin camshafts to operate the valves, and remains in production, in essentially the same basic form, to this day.

This engine powered the Giulietta when it appeared in 1954. The Giulietta was available as a saloon, a convertible and two types of coupé, the most attractive of which was the 1957 Sprint Speciale, or SS, as it became known.

The SS was based on a shortened Giulietta floorpan and was clothed in swooping rounded coachwork by Bertone. It was low, sleek and very attractive, and also very fast. Even though its engine was of a mere 1290 cc, tuning had taken the power up from the 53 bhp of the saloon to no less than 100 bhp which, allied to an all-up weight of 2,128 lb and a crisp five-speed gearbox, gave a top speed of 125mph (201 km/h).

With double-wishbone front suspension and a well set-up live axle rear, the SS had handling to match and it was hardly surprising that the car had much success in racing, albeit in private hands.

## Giulietta variants

### Giulietta
Mainstream small saloon produced by the company from 1955. It featured an all-alloy 1290 cc, 53 bhp engine. Car's success turned Alfa Romeo into mass-

production manufacturer. Production ended in 1965.

### Giulietta Sprint
The coupé version of the Giulietta actually appeared before the saloon in late 1954. Styled by Bertone, the Sprint had considerably more power than the saloon, at 80 bhp.

### Giulietta Spider
1955 saw the arrival of the convertible Giulietta Spider, with styling by Pininfarina rather than Bertone. It featured the same engine as the coupé but had slightly better performance due to its lighter weight. Alfa Romeo have produced a convertible every year since the Spider's introduction.

### Giulietta Ti
This tuned version of the base saloon had some 74 bhp. It became the most popular of the range and outsold the rest of them put together, even though it wasn't launched until 1961. Over 50,000 were produced between 1961 and 1964 – with just one being built in 1965!

*Above: The 125-mph Bertone-styled Giulietta Sprint Speciale is now one of the most sought-after Alfas. With a high compression ratio of 9.7:1, its 1.3-litre twin-cam produced 100 bhp. 1,366 were built between 1957 and 1962. The Sprint Speciale treatment was then applied to the later Giulia.*

*Left: The Giulietta SZ was styled by Zagato, built between 1960 and 1962 and raced with great success.*

## Specification (1957 SS)

**Engine:** inline four twin cam
**Bore × stroke:** 74 mm × 75 mm
**Capacity:** 1290 cc
**Maximum power:** 100 bhp
**Transmission:** five-speed manual
**Chassis:** monocoque
**Suspension:** independent front, with coil springs and double wishbones; live rear axle with coil springs, trailing arms and triangular locating member
**Brakes:** hydraulically operated drums (last 30 cars had discs on front only)
**Bodywork:** Bertone, built on racing variant of Giulietta chassis
**Maximum speed (approx):** 125 mph (201 km/h)

# Alfa Romeo GTA

Giorgetto Giugiaro of Ital Design has penned many of the world's most exotic sports cars, but it was during his time at Bertone that he came up with one of the true post-war classics, the Alfa Romeo GTV coupé. Just as the Sprint Speciale was the sports coupé version of the Giulietta, so the GTV (Gran Turismo Veloce) was the sports version of the larger Giulia. In its 11-year life, between 1965 and 1976, the body housed 1.3, 1.6, 1.8 and 2-litre Alfa twin-cams.

By the GTV's launch, Alfa Romeo were once again well into racing with their Autodelta team run by ex-Ferrari engineer Carlo Chiti. Until then, Autodelta were campaigning exotic little coupés, but Alfa wanted to race a car more identifiable with their mainstream products, and so built a batch of 500 lightweight GTVs called GTA (the 'A' standing for *allegerita* – lightened). The cars used the same basic specification as the GTV, with wishbone front suspension (with a novel adjustable front control arm) and live rear axle, but the GTAs were rather more spartan inside and had aluminium body panels in place of some of the steel ones. The car weighed some 700 lb less than the GTV.

Autodelta performed miracles with

**1965-69**

*Above: The roadgoing 1750 GTVs of 1967-72 can be distinguished by their four headlights.*

The GTA's racetrack success came from its lighter, alloy body coupled with a twin-plug version of the 1.6-litre twin-cam.

the engine: in 'standard' GTA guise, the 1570-cc engine pumped out 115 bhp, while the team's own racers had twin-plug-head motors that produced 170 bhp, enough to propel the cars to a top speed of almost 140 mph (225 km/h). There was even a supercharged version

of the car, called the GTA-SA, and one with a reworked Giulietta 1290-cc motor with 165 bhp. The magic worked, and GTAs were triple European Touring Car Champions from 1966 to 1968. The larger 1985-cc GTA took the title in 1970 and the GTA Junior won in 1972.

## Specification

**Engine:** inline four twin cam
**Bore × stroke:** 78 mm × 82 mm
**Capacity:** 1570 cc
**Maximum power:** 115 bhp
**Transmission:** five-speed manual
**Chassis:** monocoque
**Suspension:** independent front with coil springs and wishbones; live rear axle with coil springs and triangular locating bracket
**Brakes:** servo-assisted discs
**Bodywork:** alloy coupé
**Maximum speed (approx):** 115 mph

# Alfa Romeo Montreal 1970-76

After a successful foray with road-based cars, Alfa Romeo entered the world of sports-prototype racing in 1967 with the 33, a V8-powered car with an engine similar to the design Carlo Chiti had used on the doomed ATS Formula 1 and road-car project a couple of years before. The 33s were reasonably successful, but they didn't dominate sports-car racing until an all-new flat-12 engine was adopted in the early 1970s.

Meanwhile, Bertone had exhibited a stunning coupé at the Expo '67 show in Montreal and Alfa, following the fashion of the company in the 1920s and 1930s, decided to put the car into production in 1970 using a version of the old 33 V8 engine – albeit suitably detuned. This was the Montreal.

The car's motor was as exotic as any from Lamborghini or Ferrari: it was an all-alloy 90-degree V8, with twin chain-driven overhead camshafts per cylinder bank, it had dry-sump lubrication (necessary for a racer but extravagant for a road car), electronic ignition and the unfortunately temperamental Spica mechanical fuel injection. Unfortunately, it only had 2593 cc and it really couldn't compete with its illustrious supercar rivals in outright performance. However, a top speed of 137 mph (220 km/h) and a standing-start kilometre time of just over 28 seconds were not to be sneezed at.

Surprisingly, the Montreal still used a live rear axle, albeit a light one that reduced unsprung weight and didn't upset the car's handling. But it was neither fish nor fowl, without real sports-car performance or real 2+2 accommodation. Alfa were happy to produce the car in small numbers, however, selling around 500 per year between 1970 and 1977 when

*Above: The Montreal used a modified version of the GTV's floorpan and running gear, coupled to a quad-cam V8 derived from the sports racing Alfa 33. It was quite a tribute that the four-cylinder GTV's chassis could cope with so much extra power and torque so easily.*

*Right: Stylist Bertone claimed this was an aerodynamic aid, but it was purely for effect.*

production ceased. As a diluted racer, though, it was a worthy successor to the 8C 2300 and 2900 series four decades before.

## Specification

**Engine:** V8, four cam
**Bore × stroke:** 80 mm × 64.5 mm
**Capacity:** 2593 cc
**Maximum power:** 200 bhp
**Transmission:** five-speed
**Chassis:** monocoque
**Suspension:** independent front with double wishbones and coil springs; live rear axle with lower trailing and upper radius arms, coil springs and anti-roll bar
**Brakes:** ventilated discs
**Bodywork:** coupé 2+2 (Bertone)
**Maximum speed (approx):** 137 mph (220 km/h)

# Alfa Romeo GTV6 1981-86

Although introduced only in 1981, the GTV6 was really an old car; it used the chassis and most of the running gear from the four-cylinder twin-cam range that dated from the early 1970s. That meant it had the same rear transaxle and de Dion axle.

The major difference was the installation of Alfa's tremendous 2.5-litre, which was first used in the Alfa Six saloon. The fuel-injected all-alloy V6 used a single cam per cylinder bank operating the inlet valves direct and the exhausts via rockers. Power output was 160 bhp from 2492 cc, and that was enough to give a top speed of almost 130 mph. The bigger engine also gave far better in-gear acceleration than the two-litre twin-cam versions.

Various changes were made to the chassis to equip it for the bigger and more powerful V6: things like a twin-plate clutch, uprated transmission and brakes, and larger wheels and tyres with five-rather than four-stud fixings. In theory, the gear change to the rear-mounted transaxle was improved for the GTV6, but in reality there was little difference. Overall, however, the car's excellent performance made up for such details.

### GTV6 variants

#### GTV6 Callaway Turbo
The American Callaway company, based in Connecticut, began by turbocharging VWs and then moved on to the GTV6, fitting twin turbos to transform its performance. Offered in the USA only

### Specification (GTV6)
**Engine:** V6, overhead-cam
**Bore × stroke:** 88 mm × 68.3 mm
**Capacity:** 2492 cc
**Maximum power:** 160 bhp
**Transmission:** five-speed manual, rear-mounted
**Chassis:** monocoque
**Suspension:** independent front with wishbones and torsion bars; de Dion rear axle with coil springs
**Brakes:** disc, inboard at rear
**Bodywork:** two-door coupé
**Maximum speed:** 129 mph (208 km/h)

*Right: The bonnet bulge is the quickest way of telling that this is the powerful 130-mph V6 GTV6, rather than the four-cylinder twin-cam GTV.*

# Alfa Romeo SZ 1990–91

Under the ownership of Fiat, Alfa Romeo went from strength to strength in the late 1980s, with healthy sales and good designs. Fiat's strategy for Alfa was to turn it back to the manufacture of sporting cars and sports racers and, with this in mind, the company set out to produce a sporting *tour de force* in the form of the SZ, commonly referred to as the 'Zagato' and affectionately known at the factory as *il mostro* (the monster). With a production run of just 1,000, Alfa Romeo wanted to follow in the footsteps of Porsche and Ferrari with their limited-edition specials.

They started with a 3-litre 75 saloon floorpan as a base and modified it by widening the track and then fitted a composite glassfibre two-seater body that was designed to turn heads. Alfa's own design team did the work on the car, rather than Zagato (who actually built them) and Alfa management kept rejecting the plans until they found one that was dramatic enough. Their reasoning was that as aerodynamics played an ever-more important role in car design, those designs were getting too similar: they didn't want that for the ES 30.

The car's engine was a modified version of the 75/164 unit, being an all-alloy V6 displacing 2959 cc which produced 210 bhp and drove the rear wheels through a five-speed transaxle, again as used on the 75. Because of the SZ's light weight and good aerodynamics (in spite of its brick-like appearance), it had a top speed of just over 150 mph (241 km/h), with acceleration to match.

Alfa Romeo produced the car as a limited edition of just 1,000, and they were all sold immediately. *Il mostro* proved that Alfa Romeo was back at the top end of the sports-car market and it paved the way for the 3.0-litre GTV V6 that came on the market in 1998.

### Specification
**Engine:** V6, single overhead camshaft per bank of cylinders
**Bore × stroke:** 93 mm × 72.6 mm
**Capacity:** 2959 cc
**Maximum power:** 210 bhp
**Transmission:** five-speed manual, rear-mounted
**Chassis:** Alfa 75 floor pan
**Suspension:** independent front with struts, transverse links, anti-roll bar, rear de Dion axle, converging rods, Watts parallel links, coil springs and anti-roll bar
**Brakes:** vented discs, inboard-mounted at rear
**Bodywork:** composite body
**Maximum speed:** 152 mph (245 km/h)

*Above: Despite its bizarre looks the SZ, more commonly known as the Zagato, is an aerodynamic design, capable of over 150 mph from 210 bhp. With the Zagato Alfa Romeo wanted to outdo Ferrari's Testarossa in producing the most dramatic design possible for their limited edition of 1,000 cars.*

## Alfa Romeo 155 Supertouring 1992-1996

The Alfa 155 was introduced at Barcelona in January 1992, powered by a range of engines including 1.8 twin-cam, 2.0-litre Twin-Spark, and 2.5-litre V6, and the four-wheel drive Q4 version. From the outset, the 155 was a major force in tackling the burgeoning Super Touring category that was developing into a series of national championships all over the world.

The original 155-based competition car was developed in 1992 as the GTA and based on the Q4. Alfa Corse built a front-drive version to comply with FIA Class 2 regulations. A budget of £5m was available to contest the BTCC in 1994, and driver pairings were ex-F1 star Gabriele Tarquini and Giampiero Simoni.

The 155 Super Touring engine consisted of components from a variety of Fiat corporate sources. The cast iron block came from the 164 VM Turbo, the alloy head from the 155Q4 – basically an Integrale 16-valve – and peak torque arrived at 7000 rpm, with 290 bhp available at the mandatory 8500 rpm limit. It was slowed by massive Brembo eight-piston calliper ventilated 15 in discs at the front and four-piston callipers at the rear, with carbon metallic pads. Gas pressurised Bilstein dampers complemented Eibach springs and MacPherson struts at the front, with fabricated steel trailing arms at the rear. The 155's mechanical specification extended to a TAG 3.8 multi-point sequential and programmable fuel injection system with digital electronic ignition. The single 70-litre fuel cell was housed below floor level in the boot, filled through a carbon fibre funnel.

Wheels were 18 in (45.7 cm) diameter x 8.25 in (21 cm) wide Speedline-cast MIM using Michelin covers. Inside, the 155 Super Touring was a combination of austerity, structural rigidity and

hi-tech laboratory. The bare metal was criss-crossed with the bars of the roll cage, and characterised by the digital rev counter, minimal switchgear and on-board computer, the sequential shift for the Hewland six-speed gearbox, suede-rimmed Momo wheel, Sparco seat and plumbed-in fire extinguisher system

When the 155s walked away with the victory on their first appearance in the 1994 BTCC there were howls of protest about their aerodynamic additions. These consisted of a two-position front splitter and big rear boot spoiler, evolved in the Fiat wind tunnel in order to eliminate lift and generate downforce. To appease the protestors the front splitter was retracted and rear wing extensions omitted, but Tarquini still took the BTCC title.

### Specification

**Engine:** Abarth-built four-cylinder 16-valve twin-cam
**Bore x stroke:** 86 mm x 86 mm
**Capacity:** 1998 cc
**Maximum power:** 280 bhp
**Transmission:** Hewland six-speed sequential
**Chassis:** seam-welded Abarth prepared monocoque
**Suspension:** front, MacPherson struts; rear, trailing links, coil springs and dampers all round

*Left: Alfa's 155 Supertouring 2.0 Twin-Spark, based on the road-going model, was also available with the 2.5-litre V6. Later versions benefited from race-derived technology.*

## Alfa Romeo GTV V6 3.0 1995 to present

Two new models with refreshingly different styling were introduced in 1995, based on the same platform with shared drivetrains and bodywork extending back as far as the windscreen. They were Alfa's new Spider and GTV, one a sports car, the other a coupé, and naturally the latter's closed body ensured that it was a different car ergonomically as well as on the road. The more rigid structure of the closed body meant there was none of the scuttle shake that affected the Spider on a bumpy road. The shared styling included distinctive twin headlights and a steep groove along their rounded flanks, ending in the GTV in a high sawn-off tail. The luxuriously appointed two-plus-two cabin featured a large, steeply raked rear window incorporating a third stop light at its base.

Both models featured radically different multi-link rear suspension from previous Alfas as well as the revised quick steering rack of the later 155, and their original specification included the 16-valve, 2.0-litre Twin-Spark engine. But the piece de resistance was the 24-valve, 3.0-litre five-speed model that came out in 1998. Performance was a blistering 220 bhp, providing a 149 mph (240 km/h) maximum and 0–62 mph (0–100 km/h) in 6.7 seconds, which needed to be treated with some circumspection in view of the GTV's front-

wheel drive transmission. There was a valid argument that the 2.0-litre Twin-Spark was quite adequate, but the aural delights provided by the 3.0-litre model won the day. Inside the GTV's cabin, creature comforts included an automatic climate control system with pollen filter, while upholstery and trim could be specified in blue, white or red Momo

leather. The Spider version was strictly a two-seater, and was available in non-UK markets with the V6 engine.

### Specification

**Engine:** V6, single cams per bank, 24-valves
**Bore x stroke:** 93 mm x 72.6 mm
**Capacity:** 2959 cc

**Maximum power:** 220 bhp
**Transmission:** five-speed
**Chassis:** monocoque
**Suspension:** front, independent MacPherson struts, lower wishbones, anti-roll bar; rear, independent, double wishbone with upper triangle, twin lower links, coil springs, dampers, anti-roll bar

*Right: The GTV and its Spider sibling, the product of Fiat's Centro Stile design studio, were among the best looking sports cars in the 1990s.*

# Allard Motor Co.

*Above: In 1952 Sydney Allard became the only man to win the Monte Carlo Rally in a car of his own make. He did it in a 4.4-litre V8 P-type like this earlier 1950 model.*

*Right: Allard's most famous model was the J2X. It was little more than a large American V8 engine on wheels, but it was a surprisingly competitive sports car.*

Sydney Allard owned a Ford dealership in South London and was a keen trials participant in the 1930s. He built a dozen high-performance Ford-engined cars between 1937 and the outbreak of World War II two years later, using V8s in nine of them and Lincoln Zephyr V12s in the rest.

In 1945 Sydney Allard formed the Allard Motor Co., and it enjoyed considerable success with Ford V8-engined saloons, tourers and sports cars. Cadillac, Oldsmobile and Chrysler engines were sometimes used in addition to the Ford and Mercury V8s, particularly for the American market, where Allards were popular.

In 1952 Allard became the only man to win the Monte Carlo Rally in a car of his own manufacture – that was a P-type 4.4-litre Ford Mercury V8-engined saloon. Unfortunately that great performance did little to help

sales, which peaked at 432 in 1948. The arrival of the Jaguar XK120 provided competition that the crude Allards could not deal with, although, ironically, the XK's twin-cam engine was used in various Allards in the 1950s.

In the early 1950s Allard tried to break into the lighter sports car market with the Palm Beach, a model fitted with Ford Zephyr and Consul engines. Palm Beach production ended in the mid-1950s and then Allard tried his hand at building dragsters and tuning Ford Anglias (known as Allardettes). After Sydney's death in 1966, under Alan Allard the firm then concentrated on superchargers and turbochargers.

In the 1980s the Allard Motor Co. was reborn in Mississauga, Canada, marketing the Chrysler V8-powered J2X2 in limited numbers.

## Allard K1 1946-49

*Right: One of the main characteristics of the early post-war Allards, like this 1947 K1, was their crude swing-axle front suspension, shown to perfection on the racetrack.*

*Below: The last of the K-types was the rather more conventional K3, which featured de Dion rear suspension and could be ordered with the six-cylinder Jaguar twin-cam engine.*

The K1 was the first of Sydney Allard's post-war sports offerings. It was designed to use as many Ford parts as possible, which made sense in post-war Britain where most things were in short supply. The stamped steel frame was made for Allard but everything else was Ford: the leaf springs, the axles, transmission and brakes. The Fords of the day used a solid front axle; Allard's friend, suspension expert Leslie Bellamy, transformed that into the most basic of independent front suspension designs by

cutting it in two and pivoting it.

Allard was a great believer in performance, and fitted the only V8 he could easily get his hands on, which was the English Ford, a simple side-valve L-head device that produced 85 bhp from its 3622 cc. Performance figures were never published for the K1 but fairly decent performance was possible, particularly in the K1s that were fitted with the alternative Canadian-built four-litre Mercury side-valve V8 that could manage 100 bhp.

### Allard K1 variants

**K2**
Produced between 1950 and 1952, the K2 was an improved K1 with such details as coil springs for the front axle. Four engines were available, all V8s

**K3**
Complete contrast in looks – the K3 was an attractive sports car, although still very spartan and basic, with de Dion rear suspension, 61 of which were built between 1952 and 1954. Wheelbase was six inches shorter than the K2. Jaguar twin-cam engine was available

### Specification (K1)

**Engine:** V8, side-valve
**Capacity:** 3622 cc
**Maximum power:** 85 bhp at 3,600 rpm
**Chassis:** pressed steel channel section
**Transmission:** three-speed manual
**Suspension:** independent front with split axle and transverse leaf spring; live rear axle with transverse leaf spring
**Brakes:** drums
**Bodywork:** wood frame with steel panels
**Maximum speed:** N/A

# Allard J2/J2X 1950-54

The stark, uncompromising, almost ugly J2 and J2X are the Allards that most people remember. The design was based on Allard's one-off Steyr-Puch powered hillclimb car, hence its simple bodywork. Not only the bodywork was simple; the car's mechanical make-up was crude in the extreme. The front suspension was independent, it's true, but that independence was achieved by having a Bellamy divided solid axle that pivotted in the middle.

Rear suspension was a little more sophisticated than the front, as a de Dion axle was used. The essence of these Allards was a large V8 engine with the minimum of bodywork to slow it down and, although they don't look like it to modern eyes, the cars were considered to be streamlined. The exposed cycle mudguards, however, would create drag rather than help the car through the air. That wasn't a great problem as the Allards had power to spare, thanks to their large Cadillac or Mercury V8 engines, and even with the big V8s fitted the J2s were never more than 2,600 lb.

Sydney Allard drove a J2 at Le Mans in the 1950 24-hour race. He confounded all the critics and finished in an excellent third place at an average speed of 87.75 mph (141.2 km/h).

*Above and right: The Canadian-built J2X2 carried on Allard tradition into the 1980s, with Chrysler V8 power.*

*Below: Sydney Allard drove a J2 like this to an incredible third place in the 1950 Le Mans 24 Hours.*

## Specification

**Engine:** Cadillac V8
**Capacity:** 5420 cc
**Maximum power:** 160 bhp
**Transmission:** three-speed manual
**Chassis:** pressed steel channel section
**Suspension:** independent front with divided axle; de Dion rear axle
**Brakes:** drums
**Bodywork:** open two-seater sports
**Maximum speed (approx):** 110 mph (177 km/h)

# Allard Palm Beach 1952-57

*Above: The prettiest of all Allard sports cars, the low-powered Palm Beach was not a sales success, even when given Jaguar twin-cam power.*

The Palm Beach was a total contrast to the J2 in that it had attractive styling almost in the AC Ace class. Under the skin it was just as basic as the J2, however, with the same Bellamy divided front-axle design. That was changed during the car's production span from 1952 to 1957 to a more conventional tor-sion-bar independent system.

Although the Palm Beach looked attractive and was, at £1,200 rather than £2,000, far cheaper than the J2, sales were not good. That may have been due to the more ordinary powerplants fitted. These were English Ford four- and six-cylinder engines rather than big American V8s, and gave less dramatic performance. Later in its career the Palm Beach was given the 3.4-litre six-cylinder Jaguar twin-cam, but production ended in 1957, making the Palm Beach the last car that Allard made.

## Specification

**Engine:** Ford inline four-cylinder
**Bore × stroke:** 79.4 mm × 76.2 mm
**Capacity:** 1508 cc
**Maximum power:** 47 bhp
**Transmission:** three-speed manual
**Chassis:** tubular ladder frame
**Suspension:** independent front with Bellamy divided axle; live rear axle
**Brakes:** drums
**Bodywork:** convertible
**Maximum speed (approx):** 80 mph (129 km/h)

# Alpine (Automobiles Alpine)

*Above and left: The last Alpine was the sophisticated but still rear-engined GTA. The stylised 'A' was the only Alpine badge.*

*Right: Best known of all the Alpines was the A110, a highly successful rally car in the 1960s and a desirable road car.*

Shortly after World War II Jean Redele, a Renault dealer in Dieppe, began tuning Renault 4CV models for his own enjoyment and use in competition. He won an Alpine cup in 1954 and the 750-cc class in the demanding Mille Miglia three years in a row, from 1952-54.

The following year he formed his own company to begin building Renault-based sports cars. The first was the A106 Mille Miles, a glassfibre-bodied model styled by Michelotti. As larger Renault engines became available Redele fitted them, and there was soon a choice of coupé or roadster bodywork.

By 1960 production had risen to around 100 per year, a figure that had grown to around 500 per year a decade later when Alpine were given responsibility for Renault's competition programme. Monte Carlo and World Rally Championship victories followed, and Renault took over Alpine in the mid-1970s. Renault competition cars were still called Alpines and an A442 won the Le Man 24 Hours in 1978.

Alpines were road cars as well as rally cars, and the A110s were produced with a range of engine sizes before being replaced by the A310, which maintained the rear-engine and glassfibre body tradition. The final incarnation of the GTA was the A610, which went out of production in 1996. Alpine continued to make the Renault Sport Spider until 1999, Espace body shells and the Megane Cabriolet.

## Alpine A110 1963-1974

*Above and left: Pronounced negative camber was an obvious feature of the A110, intended to overcome the drawback of the swing-axle rear suspension. The four-cylinder Renault engine has twin Weber carbs.*

The A110 was introduced in 1963 as a development of the A108, and carried on the same basic configuration of a rear-mounted Renault engine and swing-axle rear suspension.

The body, designed by Marcel Hubert, was made of glassfibre and carried on a distinctive tubular steel backbone chassis. The range of engines used in the A110 over the years was enormous, starting at only 956 cc and culminating at 1796 cc in the more powerful rally versions. Between those extremes came capacities of 1100, 1150, 1300, 1470 and 1600 cc.

The first A110s used the running gear from the contemporary small Renault saloon, the rear-engined R8, but Redele made certain changes to overcome the limitations of that design, for example introducing the extreme negative camber on the rear wheels to compensate for the simple swing-axle rear suspension. He also developed his own five-speed gearbox; the earliest Alpines had just a three-speed Renault unit.

The light but strong A110 was a very successful rally car, so much so that they finished 1-2-3 in both the Coupe des Alpes in 1969 and the 1970 Monte Carlo Rally. The ultimate A110 rally car was the 170-bhp 1796-cc version, which was good enough to take the World Rally Championship for Renault and Alpine in 1973, over 10 years after the car was introduced.

The road-going A110s could not boast the same performance, but the most popular version, with a twin Weber carburettor 1300-cc engine, could achieve over 120 mph (193 km/h) from 90 bhp.

### Specification (1963 Tour de France)

**Engine:** inline four-cylinder twin-cam
**Capacity:** 1108 cc
**Maximum:** 100 bhp
**Transmission:** four-speed manual
**Chassis:** tubular steel backbone
**Suspension:** independent with double wishbones front and swing axle rear
**Brakes:** discs
**Bodywork:** glassfibre coupé
**Maximum speed (approx):** 135 mph (217 km/h)

# Alpine A310 1971-1984

The 310 was a far more modern-looking machine than the A110 when it was introduced in 1971, but the basic mechanical layout was repeated. The A310 also featured a glassfibre body, steel backbone chassis and rear-mounted Renault engine.

The first engine fitted was a 1.6-litre four-cylinder, based very closely on that used in the contemporary Renault 16TX saloon. That was really not powerful enough for what was meant as a more upmarket car than the A110. The solution was to fit the Renault 2.6-litre overhead-cam V6. With a power output of 150 bhp, that was enough to give the sleek A310 a top speed approaching 140 mph (225 km/h) with an excellent 0-60 time of 6.4 seconds.

A310 production was never huge, although the car did stay in production for 13 years. Its most obvious rival was the evergreen Porsche 911, which shared its

rear-engined layout; but somehow, despite its excellent performance, the 310 lacked the charisma of the longer-established German car.

## Specification

**Engine:** V6, overhead-cam
**Bore × stroke:** 88 mm × 73 mm
**Capacity:** 2664 cc
**Maximum power:** 150 bhp
**Transmission:** five-speed manual
**Chassis:** steel backbone
**Suspension:** independent all round with double wishbones and coil springs
**Brakes:** discs
**Bodywork:** 2+2 glassfibre coupé
**Maximum speed:** 137 mph (220 km/h)

*Right: The A310 maintained the same rear-engine layout as the A110, but was designed as a more upmarket sports car rather than a rally car.*

# (Alpine) Renault GTA Turbo 1985-present

*Left: The sleek GTA Turbo was as slippery as it looked, having a Cd of 0.28, the lowest coefficient of drag of any contemporary sports car. Power came from a 2458-cc turbo V6 engine producing 200 bhp, enough for a top speed of 155 mph.*

tained, as was the use of glassfibre panels for the bodywork, but the GTA Turbo was altogether a more advanced car than the 310: for example, the glassfibre was bonded to the steel structure to produce a stiff steel/glassfibre monocoque construction.

Performance was improved as much as the car's looks, partly because the new shape was the most aerodynamically efficient on the sports car market and because Renault had extracted 200 bhp from the 2458-cc turbo V6. That was enough to give a top speed of 155 mph (249 km/h) and 0-60 acceleration in only 6.3 seconds.

Annoyingly for Renault, the improvements that had made the car a worthy 911 rival, and at far lower cost, still did not overcome the disadvantage of the humble Renault name in the eyes of potential customers, leaving the GTA Turbo one of the most underrated sports cars in production.

With the GTA, the Alpine range became more Renault than Alpine. Renault wanted a sports car that could compete with the Porsche 911 on the world market, and accordingly updated the concept of the A310.

The plan was to have a sports car that could sell in large numbers in the North American market, but when Chrysler bought Renault's stake in American Motors the scheme was overtaken by events. The rear-engine theme was re-

*Left: Although very well equipped, the interior was criticised for being too close to Renault production saloons. But one of its best features was the steering-wheel-mounted radio controls.*

## Variants

### GTA

The normally aspirated version has larger, 2849-cc V6 and 160 bhp, giving top speed of 140 mph (225 km/h)

## Specification (GTA Turbo)

**Engine:** V6, overhead-cam, turbo
**Bore × stroke:** 91 mm × 63 mm
**Capacity:** 2458 cc
**Maximum power:** 200 bhp
**Transmission:** five-speed manual
**Chassis:** steel backbone
**Suspension:** independent all round with double wishbones and coil springs
**Brakes:** disc
**Bodywork:** 2+2 glassfibre coupé
**Maximum speed:** 155 mph (249 km/h)

# Alvis Car Co.

*Right: The Alvis name had no meaning; it was chosen simply because it sounded good. The Silver Eagle was Alvis' six-cylinder model of 1929. Its engine provided the basis for the Speed 20 of the 1930s.*

*Below: The last Alvis model produced was the superb TD21, with its elegant body designed by the Swiss coachbuilders Graber. It was powered by a three-litre straight-six engine (as were all Alvis cars from 1950 onwards).*

A lvis was founded in Coventry in 1919 by T.G. John (who was formerly with both Armstrong-Whitworth and Siddeley-Deasy) and G.P.H. De Freville, the importer of the French DFP cars.

The name Alvis meant nothing at all; it was coined simply because it sounded good in any language. The cars were good, too, Alvis always building models of better than average quality and performance. The most famous among the early cars was the 12/50, designed by Captain G.T. Smith-Clarke, who had moved from Daimler to become Alvis chief engineer in 1923; he was responsible for most of Alvis' subsequent models. By that time Alvis already employed over 350 people.

By 1932 Alvis had sold approximately 9,000 cars, including 155 of the pioneering front-wheel-drive types that were built between 1928 and 1930. Although variations on the light-car theme were continued, with Alvis in competition with Lea-Francis and Riley, after the Depression of the 1930s Alvis decided to get into the smaller-volume grand touring market dominated by Bentley and Lagonda. They developed two- and three-litre cars, culminating in the 4.3, produced between 1937 and 1940. Alvis were among the first to introduce synchromesh on all gears and independent suspension, as early as 1934.

During the 1930s, with rearmament under way, aero engines and military vehicles became increasingly important to Alvis and the company concentrated on military production after the war.

Post-war car production resumed with variations on the 12/50, 12/60 and 12/70 theme, with the TA14 and TB14 models.

From 1950 Alvis started their one-model policy, based on a three-litre chassis with hydraulic brakes and independent front suspension. The best known of these had elegant bodywork designed by the Swiss coachbuilders Graber. The three-litre lasted two years after Alvis were taken over by Rover in 1965. Plans for a mid-engined grand tourer did not progress past the prototype stage, and Alvis then concentrated on military vehicle production.

*Left: An Alvis Speed 20 from 1936. The Speed 20 was introduced in 1932 with a 2.5-litre six-cylinder overhead-valve engine. By the time this particular car was built the engine size had increased to 2762 cc, the chassis had been greatly strengthened and independent front suspension fitted.*

*Right: A wire wheel from a 12/50. The red Alvis badge lived on after car manufacture ended in 1967, to be seen on military vehicles such as armoured cars.*

## Alvis 12/50 1923-32

Designed by G.T. Smith-Clarke, the 12/50 had a pushrod overhead-valve four-cylinder engine with a capacity of 1496 cc. The engine was Alvis' first overhead-valve design and was fitted first in the alloy sports-bodied 10/30 chassis. The prototype was good enough to lap the Brooklands track at 86 mph. The production version, the 12/50, appeared in 1923, available in two chassis lengths – the SA and SB.

In 1925 a larger-engined 12/50 was offered, with a 1598-cc version of the four-cylinder overhead-valve engine. That same year it was also given the considerable advantage of four-wheel braking.

For 1926 the design of the 12/50 was modified and two types were produced, the TE touring chassis of 1645 cc and the

TF sports chassis of 1496 cc. Their enginess were identical except for the larger 1645-cc's longer stroke. The new models also had a redesigned and stronger chassis with an improved steering mechanism, while the old cone clutch had been replaced by a more modern single-plate design.

In 1929 the 12/50 was dropped from the range as Alvis had introduced a six-cylinder model, but it was revived, in 1645-cc form, the next year, and it continued in production until 1932. The twin-carb version introduced alongside it was designated the 12/60.

Judged on the criteria of performance and durability, the 12/50 was one of the great vintage sports cars; it looked to the future too, its engine being used in the later front-drive model.

*Above: The 12/50 was produced in various forms. This is a typical upright Tourer from 1928 with the 1645-cc four-cylinder overhead-valve engine.*

### 12/50 variants

**12/70**

After a lapse in four-cylinder car production, the 12/70 appeared in 1937, featuring a conventional semi-elliptic sprung chassis and a larger engine of 1842 cc

**TA/TB14**

A post-war revival of the 12/70, almost 3,500 of which were built in the 1940s. There was a twin-carb version of the TB14 but only 100 were built

### Specification (12/50)

**Engine:** inline four-cylinder, overhead-valve
**Bore × stroke:** 68 mm × 103 mm
**Capacity:** 1496 cc
**Maximum power:** 50 bhp
**Transmission:** four-speed manual
**Chassis:** pressed steel channel section
**Suspension:** non-independent with semi-elliptic leaf springs all round
**Brakes:** drums all round
**Bodywork:** choice of eight styles
**Maximum speed (approx):** 70 mph (113 km/h)

*Right: A sporting alloy-bodied 12/50 from 1932 – the last year this model was produced.*

# Alvis 12/75 Front-Wheel Drive 1925-30

Only a year after Alvis' victory in the Brooklands 200-mile race in 1923 their 16-valve racer was already uncompetitive, and designers Smith-Clarke and Dunn had to do something drastic to regain their edge.

They experimented with supercharging, but decided that a new front-wheel drive layout would be a better proposition as it would allow them to build a lighter racer. Light weight was guaranteed by the use of a chassis made from duralumin alloy. The car was powered by a 12/50 engine turned back to front so that it could drive the front wheels, and the front suspension was a curious arrangement of two tubes linked by four vertical supports and carried on two transverse quarter-elliptic springs per side.

The design was compact as well as light, being a mere 36 inches high, and the combination was enough to give a top speed of over 100 mph around Brooklands. Alvis were inspired to produce two straight-eight front-wheel-drive racers for the 1.5-litre formula, and although these cars were very fast (capable of over 120 mph) their development problems had not been overcome before the demise of the 1.5-litre formula.

Alvis' next move was to produce the Front-Wheel Drive for road use in the form of the 1482-cc car of 1928. That was available in supercharged form (at £625) and was normally aspirated. Both raced successfully, at Le Mans and the Ulster Tourist Trophy.

### Specification (1928 12/50)

**Engine:** inline four-cylinder, overhead-cam
**Bore × stroke:** 68 mm × 102 mm
**Capacity:** 1482 cc
**Maximum power:** 50 bhp
**Transmission:** four-speed manual
**Chassis:** pressed steel channel section
**Suspension:** independent front with quarter-elliptic leaf springs; dead rear-axle with quarter-elliptic leaf springs
**Brakes:** drums all round (inboard at front)
**Bodywork:** to order
**Maximum speed (approx):** 85 mph (137 km/h)

*Above: Alvis pioneered front-wheel drive in Britain, for racing and then road use. Note the unusual transverse quarter-elliptic front suspension.*

# Alvis Speed 20 1932-36

*Left: There was a wide range of bodies available for the Speed 20. Some were uninspiring, but this is undoubtedly the most elegant.*

As part of Alvis' journey up-market, a six-cylinder Silver Eagle was available from 1929. In its 1931-33 guise it had a capacity of 2511 cc, and this engine, in tuned 87-bhp form, was used in the Speed 20 sports model unveiled at the 1931 Scottish Motor Show.

The original SA type had beam axles, but in 1934 the SB was introduced with in-dependent front suspension and the firm's new four-speed gearbox – making the Speed 20 one of the first cars to feature synchromesh on all forward ratios. The SC of 1935 and SD of 1936 had engines enlarged to 2.8 litres and 98 bhp to cope with the increasing weight of the bodies fitted to the chassis by various coachbuilders. Many attractive styles of Speed 20 were built, both open and closed, nearly all of which featured large chromed Lucas P100 headlamps. The model accounted for 1,165 sales and was raced with limited success. Road tests of the time spoke of hard sus-

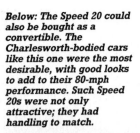

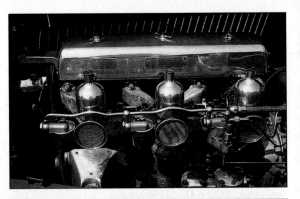

pension but excellent roadholding, due in part to the low overall height of the chassis and resultant low roof line.

## Speed 20 variants

### 3.5-litre SA
Short-lived version of the Speed 20, produced in 1936, fitted with a 3571-cc engine and capable of 95 mph

### Speed 25
Replacement for the Speed 20 using the 3571-cc engine developing 110 bhp; 536 built between 1937 and 1940

### 4.3-litre
Enlarged-engine version of the Speed 25, available in short- or long-chassis form and all capable of over 100 mph

## Specification (Speed 25)
**Engine:** inline six-cylinder, overhead-valve
**Bore × stroke:** 83 mm × 100 mm
**Capacity:** 3571 cc
**Maximum power:** 110 bhp
**Chassis:** pressed steel with cruciform cross-member
**Suspension:** independent front; live rear axle with semi-elliptic leaf springs
**Brakes:** drums all round
**Bodywork:** to order
**Maximum speed (approx):** 95 mph (153 kmh)

*Below: The Speed 20 could also be bought as a convertible. The Charlesworth-bodied cars like this one were the most desirable, with good looks to add to their 80-mph performance. Such Speed 20s were not only attractive; they had handling to match.*

*Right: Power for the Speed 20 was provided by a straight-six overhead-valve engine derived from the 2148-cc six used in the Silver Eagle of 1929. For the Speed 20, capacity was increased to 2.5 litres. The later 3.5-litre version produced 110 bhp and gave the Speed 25 of 1937 a top speed of 95 mph.*

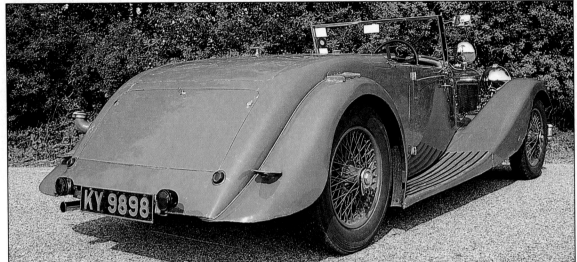

# Alvis 3-Litre 1950-67

In 1950, the year that designer Smith-Clarke finally retired after over 25 years with Alvis, his final creation appeared at the Geneva Motor Show. It had a 2993-cc six-cylinder engine that weighed only 50 lb more than the 1892-cc four-cylinder unit previously offered. The TA/TB/TC 21 series that it originally powered were traditionally British coach-built cars, but in 1951 Graber fitted a model with more European-looking coachwork. Several more were built in this form before Alvis persuaded British firms to copy the style for the TC108G/TD21 of 1956-63. One thousand and ninety-eight examples of this series were built compared with 2,105 of the former TA/TB/TC types, the last of which had been the attractive TC21/100 'Grey Lady'.

As production fell, so prices rose, to make Alvis one of the most exclusive of all marques. Alvis tended to build its entire chassis requirements in just a few weeks each year between more lucrative batches of military and aviation equipment. Only 458 examples of the final TEC/TF21 were produced in 1963-67, which, like their predecessors, came in sports saloon or drophead coupé form, still based on Graber ideas. These late cars had quadruple headlamps and a power output of 130 bhp, later increased to 150 bhp. They had all-round Dunlop disc brakes (also on the Series II TD) and could have ZF five-speed manual gearboxes or automatic transmission. The very latest, in July 1967, was fitted with a 5.4-litre Chevrolet V8.

## Specification (1962 TD21)
**Engine:** inline, six-cylinder
**Bore × stroke:** 84 mm × 90 mm
**Capacity:** 2993 cc
**Maximum power:** 120 bhp
**Transmission:** ZF five- or three-speed automatic

**Chassis:** box-section steel chassis
**Suspension:** independent front with double wishbones and coil springs; live rear axle with semi-elliptic leaf springs
**Brakes:** discs front and drums rear
**Bodywork:** Graber-designed four-seater
**Maximum speed (approx):** 106 mph (171 km/h)

*Above: The TD21 was the last of the Alvis line. The original design dated back to 1955, the work of the Swiss coachbuilders Graber. That basic design lasted until Alvis stopped building cars in 1967. It was powered by a 120-bhp straight-six engine giving a top speed of 106 mph.*

# American Motors Corporation

*Left: The most adventurous sports model built by American Motors was the powerful V8 AMX, here making its motor show debut in 1968.*

**A**merican Motors Corporation came about in 1954 as a result of the merger of Nash and Hudson. The former owned the old Rambler business, which in 1950 had been revived as a brand name for the group's compact cars. From 1958 all AMC cars were known as Ramblers, apart from the little Austin A40-based Metropolitan.

The architect of AMC's growth was George Romney, a great believer in compact cars long before they became fashionable in America. However, after he left to concentrate on a political career as Governor of Michigan, AMC decided to tackle the high-performance field, typified by the Ford Mustang, Chevrolet Camaro and Plymouth Barracuda, with a fastback called the Marlin in 1966. While it was not a commercial success it spawned the Javelin a couple of years later, plus its AMX derivative.

These helped to put AMC on a more profitable footing, and with the firm's acquisition of the Kaiser Jeep Corporation in 1970 it gained a foothold in the leisure and industrial markets. In 1978 Renault took control of AMC and the out-and-out sports models disappeared by the mid-1970s, to be replaced by such cars as the Matador with an option of 'X' sports trim. In 1987 Renault's 46 per cent share of AMC was bought by Chrysler, with control of AMC effectively passing to Chrysler.

The Javelin seemed a very good gamble by American Motors; there was clearly significant growth in that area of the market, as the Mustang and Camaro's enormous success proved. And although AMC could not boast anything like the track record of Ford or Chevrolet, their car had much going for it. It was roomier than the opposition and there was little wrong with its styling.

Clearly that wasn't enough, however, and American Motors took to the track to try to win the car some credibility. They hired the up-and-coming Roger Penske to run the team and one of America's finest drivers, Mark Donohue, and in 1970 Donohue won the prestigious Trans-Am race series for AMC with the distinctive red, white and blue Javelin. AMC had built only 40,675 Javelins in 1969 but that was down to only 28,000 the next year despite Donohue's success. AMC's performance gamble had failed and although the Javelin derivative, the AMX, was a sporty car, AMC turned to different forms of niche marketing in later years with cars like the failed wide-bodied compact Pacer and the more successful four-wheel-drive Eagle.

*Above: American Motors went racing with the Javelin in Trans-Am competition, with great success. This one is on the track at Bridgeport in 1989.*

# AMC AMX 1968-74

*Left: The Javelin was AMC's Mustang and Camaro rival, with up to 280 bhp from its V8 engine.*

The first car to be sold as an AMC rather than a Rambler was the Javelin, a four-seater sports coupé, which went into production in August 1967. It was joined by the two-seater AMX in February 1968. This gave AMC candidates in the fast-growing pony and muscle car markets. Their image was aided by competition in Trans-American road racing, and for serious sport (as well as use by boy racers) a Rallye-Pac was available. This included additional dials – a tachometer, a speedo with 140-mph dial – and, more importantly, revised suspension and shock absorbers. The engines offered were 145-bhp 3.8-litre sixes or V8s of 4.8 or 5.6 litres developing 200 to 280 bhp. Transmission was by three-speed automatic or three- or four-speed manual gearboxes, and there were front disc brakes. For its swansong, the AMX in 1974 could be bought with power disc brakes, handling pack and 6.6-litre V8 four-barrel carburettor that developed around 300 bhp. Earlier there had even been some 'Design Editions', notably the Cardin Javelin with 'coutured' interior.

## Specification

**Engine:** V8, overhead-valve
**Bore × stroke:** 85 mm × 83 mm
**Capacity:** 4752 cc
**Maximum power:** 225 bhp
**Transmission:** three-speed automatic or four-speed manual
**Chassis:** X-braced frame
**Suspension:** independent front with double wishbones; live rear axle with semi-elliptic leaf springs
**Brakes:** disc front, drums rear
**Bodywork:** coupé
**Maximum speed:** 120 mph (193 km/h)

# Amilcar

**T**his Parisian marque gained its name from the two original backers, Emil Akar and Joseph Lamy, who formed the company in 1921 and became, respectively, managing and sales directors. The first Amilcars were high-performance cyclecars, built to a design that had originated with Edmond Moyet, a colleague of Jules Salomon at Citroën. Lamy had worked with Salomon at Le Zebre, and Akar was a rich grocery store owner.

Amilcars were soon being made at the rate of five per day and winning in competitive events almost from the outset. Amilcar's racing record was excellent and the cars very popular. In 1933 the company built 50 of the C6 racer for homologation for the Le Mans 24 Hours, and these were raced by private owners. Amilcars set records too; a twin-cam version set a 24-hour record averaging 84 mph.

The most famous types, commencing with the CC model, all had engines of only about one-litre capacity, but in ultimate twin-cam form they could propel the tiny Amilcar at over 130 mph. Amilcars were the most prolific of the many French light sporting types available in the 1920s and around 15,500 are believed to have been constructed of all types, including some more general touring E, G, J and L types.

From 1925 Amilcar offered a diminutive inline eight-cylinder CO model

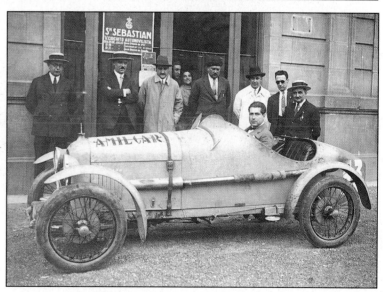

*Above: An 1100-cc four-cylinder Amilcar is seen prior to weigh-in for the 1927 Guipuscoa 12-hour race at San Sebastian in Spain.*

that was developed into the C6, the ultimate Amilcar. The Depression saw the birth of the light sports car in Britain, exemplified by MG, but the virtual end of it in France. Thereafter, between 1934 and 1937, Amilcar made 1.25- to two-litre four-seaters and larger cars in the 1934-37 period, powered by Delahaye engines. Lamy and Akar had left in the late 1920s, and the final cars produced following the takeover by Hotchkiss were called Amilcar Compounds. Only about 700 of these late-1930s models were built, all being remarkable for their combination of aluminium monocoque construction with front-wheel drive and all-round independent suspension. Their engines, however, were of a mere 1200-cc capacity.

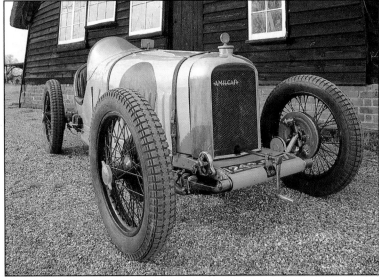

*Above: Racing Amilcars, like this 1926 supercharged CO, were effective because of their lightness and good power-to-weight ratio.*

*Left: A CS of 1926 could boast 23 bhp from its one-litre engine and a top speed of 60 mph.*

*Right: The Amilcar name was an amalgamation of some of the letters of its founders' names: Emil Akar and Joseph Lamy.*

# Amilcar CC 1921-24

*Below: The ultimate model in the Amilcar line was the C6. It was a development of the CO shown top right, with a wider, two-seat, chassis; its price in England was £725 in 1927. Capable of over 130 mph, the C6s were successful racing cars, winning first time out at the Grand Prix de Provence at Miramas in 1926.*

*Right: Power for the C6 came from a one-litre straight-six twin-cam engine equipped with a Solex carburettor and Roots-type supercharger to give 62 bhp at 5,600 rpm. Unlike the CO, the C6's engine had plain, rather than roller, bearings.*

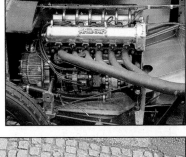

## CC variants

### C4
Elongated CC able to accommodate more spacious bodywork, and with a 1004-cc engine to maintain above-average performance

### CGS
The Gran Sport, and a serious competition car with 1074-cc 30-bhp engine and four wheel brakes, also made as CGS3 to seat three

### CGSS
A *surbaisse* (lowered) version of the above and fitted with a supercharger to boost output to 40 bhp

### C6
An out-and-out racing car but produced in series; it had a twin-overhead camshaft 1100-cc six-cylinder engine developing 83 bhp

## Specification (C6)

**Engine:** inline six-cylinder, twin-cam with Roots supercharger
**Bore × stroke:** 56 mm × 74 mm
**Capacity:** 1094 cc
**Maximum power:** 62 bhp
**Transmission:** four-speed manual
**Chassis:** steel channel section with cross-members
**Suspension:** non independent with rigid axles; semi-elliptic leaf springs front, quarter elliptics rear
**Brakes:** drums all round
**Bodywork:** alloy sports
**Maximum speed (approx):** 130 mph (209 km/h)

The first of the famous Amilcars was more of a small car in miniature than the typical blacksmith-made concoction of motorcycle parts that had been common in France. Le Zebre and Citroën designer Jules Salomon is credited with the four-cylinder water-cooled side-valve 903-cc engine that initially developed only 18 bhp but gave a good power-to-weight ratio owing to the CC's scaling a

mere 960 lb. With two people aboard, the CC was good for 50 mph at a time when few 1.5-litre cars could sustain this speed. It had three forward gears and no differential was needed in the back axle because of its narrow track. The differential-less back axle permitted the foot brake and hand brake to occupy only one drum each, yet at the same time act on both rear wheels. The chassis was

carried on quarter-elliptic springs all round and early models even had a wooden front axle, but that was soon replaced by metal. Current between 1921 and 1924, the CC and its CS and C4 derivatives accounted for a remarkable sales total of around 6,000 cars. Versions were built in both Germany and Austria and parts were exported to Italy, where the Amilcar-Italian was produced.

# Armstrong-Siddeley

T his staunchly British company was the result of a merger in 1919 between Armstrong-Whitworth and John Siddeley's Coventry-based Siddeley-Deasy Motor Manufacturing Co, both of whom had produced cars prior to World War I. The first Armstrong Whitworth commercials were made just after the turn of the century, and its first car appeared in 1906. Armstrong-Whitworth paid £419,750 for Siddeley-Deasy to form the Armstrong-Whitworth Development Co Ltd, and Armstrong-Siddeley Motors Ltd was its subsidiary. Siddeley-Deasy had built the Siddeley Puma aircraft engines during the war, and carried on doing so after the merger.

The first car to roll off the line was the Thirty, a coach-built, five-seater powered by a 30 hp, 4.9-litre, six-cylinder overhead-valve engine. Armstrong-Siddeley's coachwork with its imposing V-shaped radiator grille attracted customers of the calibre of the Duke of York (later King George VI) and the Duke of Gloucester. In 1922, when the workforce numbered 3,000, a smaller 18 hp, 2.3-litre model came out, with a 14 hp, 1.8-litre, four-cylinder, flat-rad car two years later. Being more accessible to

was roughly 3,000 units a year. By now, the marque was well established in the luxury segment, and its reputation was bolstered by minor successes in the Alpine Trials and RAC Rallies – nine were entered in the 1934 event. A Twenty was campaigned in the Monte Carlo Rally by S.C.H. (Sammy) Davies in the 1930s. The Siddeley Special of 1933 was a direct challenge to Rolls-Royce and Daimler's grasp on the upper echelons of that market, a luxury car powered by a 4.9-litre, six-cylinder engine that was made of the Rolls-Royce developed Hiduminium alloy. However, only 235 Specials were sold between 1933 and 1937 despite their 95 mph (153 km/h) top speed and elegant good looks.

J. D. Siddeley was knighted in 1932 and was later created Baron Kenilworth for contributions to the aero-engine industry. The company merged with Hawker Engineering in 1935 to form the Hawker-Siddeley Aircraft Co, and major products were the Lynx and Cheetah seven-cylinder radials, and the Tiger fourteen-cylinder radial. In World War II, Hawker-Siddeley controlled Armstrong-Whitworth, Hawker, A.V. Roe and Gloster Aircraft.

a wider market, this car sold at the rate of 4,000 units a year by 1926. Bottom-of-the-range model between 1922 and 1924 was the Stoneleigh light car, powered by a 9 hp vee-twin engine, and early versions featured a central-driving position with two passengers seated behind.

In 1926 John Siddeley re-gained his independence, forming the Armstrong-Siddeley Development Co Ltd having bought back his business from Armstrong-Whitworth for £1.5 million. The deal included the aircraft manufacturing side of the business, so that Siddeley's holding company now controlled Armstrong-Whitworth Aircraft Ltd, Armstrong-Siddeley Motors Ltd and, later on, the aircraft manufacturer A. V. Roe Ltd.

Military contracts in the 1920s included 350 hp tank engines for Vickers, and the 4 x 4, four-wheel steer Italian Pavesi tractor made under license. In 1929 Armstrong-Siddeley productionised the Wilson epicyclic gearbox, a precursor of modern automatic transmission, and trading as Self-Changing Gears Ltd, these gearboxes were bought by AC, Daimler, Invicta, Lagonda, Riley and Talbot.

Armstrong Siddeley's model range of the 1930s consisted of the 1.5-litre 12/6, 1.9-litre 15/6, 2.8-litre Twenty and the 4.9-litre Thirty, and output

*Above: Armstrong Siddeley initially named their cars after fighter and bomber aircraft produced by Hawker, Avro and Armstrong Whitworth. This 18 hp Typhoon dates from 1949.*

*Right: The elegant chrome radiator-grill of 1949 Armstrong Siddeley Hurricane is a typical example of the attention paid to detail. Completely up-to-date in styling, the designs for the Hurricane were drawn in-house by Cyril Siddeley.*

## Armstrong Siddeley Hurricane 1945-1952

Alongside its extensive aircraft engine production programme, Armstrong Siddeley unveiled its post-war car range in May 1945, just as the war in Europe ended. Two body styles were available initially, the Hurricane drophead coupé and the Lancaster saloon model, both powered by the 2.0-litre, six-cylinder engine that was used previously in the Sixteen of 1939. Contemporary styling with sweeping curves characterised the designs, drawn in-house by Cyril Siddeley, elder son of J.D. Siddeley, while some chassis and engineering design work was by W.O. Bentley and Donald Bastow. Col. Siddeley once remarked that if it was necessary to remove one's hat to get into a car, then that vehicle must be a sports car. You could keep your hat on with an Armstrong Siddeley. The engines were, if anything, more sporting than the cruciform chassis they powered. Two more new models soon followed, and these were the Typhoon fixed-head coupé and Whitley four-light saloon, powered by the same engine, which was enlarged to 2.3 litres in 1949 when it produced 78 bhp. Transmission was via a Rootes-made four-speed synchromesh gearbox, the first time for 13 years that Armstrong Siddeleys had been available with a gearbox other than the Wilson pre-selector box.

**Specification**
**Engine:** six-cylinder in-line
**Bore x stroke:** 65 mm x 100 mm
**Capacity:** 1990 cc
**Maximum power:** 78 bhp

*Above: Exuding elegance and luxury, this 1947 Hurricane D/H Coupé is a beautiful model of the brand. Contemporary styling and sweeping curves were typical of the designs produced at this time by Cyril Siddeley.*

**Transmission:** Rootes-type four-speed
**Chassis:** steel girder section, coach-built body
**Suspension:** front, torsion bar independent; rear, leaf-springs

## Armstrong Siddeley Sapphire 1953–1960

While the Hurricane and Typhoon, Lancaster and Whitley were all named after fighter and bomber aircraft produced by Hawker, Avro and Armstrong-Whitworth, the model launched in 1953 didn't follow the tradition. This was the Sapphire, intended as a replacement for the four 2.0-litre models, but being somewhat larger and more palatial, the 'town carriage' was intended as a competitor for the segment occupied by Jaguar and Daimler. The 150 bhp hemi-head engine was designed by Freddie Allard, and the twin-carb Sapphire was found in Autocar and Motor road tests to be faster than the Mk VII Jaguar to 50 mph (80 km/h), tying at a 100 mph (160 km/h) maximum. But while the four post-war Armstrong Siddeley models had sold some 12,570 units between 1945 and 1953, the 3.4-litre, Sapphire saloon and its 4.0-litre successor, the Star Sapphire sold 8,187 units. The company probably blundered by introducing the 234 and 236 models instead of updating the Sapphire. But by this time Jaguar was just too well entrenched to be ousted, and in 1960 the parent Bristol Siddeley decided that production of Armstrong Siddeley cars was no longer viable. The last Star Sapphires left the production line in June 1960, and the art-deco Sphinx bonnet mascot became history. Armstrong Siddeley produced aero engines until 1983.

**Variants**

**Station Coupé**
The two-seater Station Coupé and three-seater Utility Coupé were stylish pick-up trucks that looked like the standard Hurricane car up to the B-pillar, but had a rounded truck roof, and a tonneau-covered cargo hold occupied the rest of the chassis. Made in small numbers, most went to Australia. A Graber-bodied prototype Coupé was made in 1949, powered by an experimental 3.0-litre aluminium engine.

**Specification (Star Sapphire)**
**Engine:** straight-six, in single or twin carb format
**Bore x stroke:** 97 mm x 90 mm
**Capacity:** 3990 cc
**Maximum power:** 145 bhp with twin carbs
**Transmission:** Borg Warner fully automatic
**Chassis:** separate steel girder with coach-built body
**Suspension:** front, torsion bar independent; rear, leaf-springs

*Below: As Armstrong Siddeley sought to encroach on territory occupied by Daimler and the burgeoning Jaguar concern, it came out with the luxurious Sapphire model in 1953.*

# Arnolt Motor Co.

**C**hicago car dealer S.H. (Wacky) Arnolt introduced a sports-racing car based on an MG T series chassis in the early 1950s. He is, however, best remembered for his Arnolt Bristols. He imported two-litre Bristol chassis with their powerful BMW-derived engines and fitted them with a variety of bodies designed by the Italian stylist Bertone. These included sports, tourers and GTs. Prices started from $4,000. Arnolt Bristols achieved considerable success in competition, and were also sold for normal touring.

Fred Wacker, driving one of the first Arnolt Bristols, was joint victor (with Ted Boynton, Frazer Nash) of the Sports Car Club of America E modified National Championship in 1954, and the cars were regular class winners at Sebring. Arnolt himself died in 1960 and production ended in 1964 after 340 cars had been built during the marque's 10-year existence.

*Above: The Bertone-designed alloy-bodied Arnolt Bristol is seen prior to the London Motor Show of 1953. Engine and running gear were Bristol.*

## Arnolt Bristol 1954-64

*Right: In 1955 Arnolt introduced the coupé version of his Bristol-based car. The design was again by Bertone; only two are known to have been built. Price in the USA was $6,000, including Borani wheels.*

Chicago car dealer 'Wacky' Arnolt was also a vice president of Italian stylists Bertone, and he had employed Bertone to rebody an MG TD to form the Arnolt MG. Consequently it was to Bertone that Arnolt turned when he wanted a body for his new sports car based on the Bristol 404 chassis and much of the running gear from the earlier 403 such as the gearbox and the brakes.

The chassis was sent to Bertone and the finished design was ready for 1954. Bertone designed both a roadster and a closed coupé (only two of which were produced) but the cars were really intended for club racing and the stripped-down standard version, which cost as much as $3,994 even back in 1954, was quite spartan. The Deluxe model offered winding windows and a top.

Production was complicated (and consequently expensive) in that the rolling chassis were sent from England to Bertone in Italy and the finished cars from

Italy to the United States.

Thanks to its 130 bhp and good power-to-weight ratio, the Arnolt Bristol was a successful racer – its first competition success came as early as 1955 with a two-litre class win in the Sebring 12 Hours in Florida, a victory which was repeated the following season.

### Specification
**Engine:** inline six-cylinder, overhead-valve
**Bore × stroke:** 66 mm × 96 mm
**Capacity:** 1971 cc
**Maximum power:** 130 bhp
**Transmission:** four-speed, overdrive
**Chassis:** Bristol, fabricated steel

**Suspension:** independent front with transverse leaf spring and double wishbones; live rear axle with torsion bars
**Brakes:** drums all round
**Bodywork:** sports or coupé
**Maximum speed (approx):** 107 mph (172 km/h)

# Aston Martin

*Above: After the wealthy gear- and tractor-maker David Brown acquired Aston Martin in 1947, his name appeared on the badge. It stayed there until 1972.*

*Right: The 'Martin' in Aston Martin comes from the surname of the company founder Lionel Martin. 'Aston' commemorates Lionel Martin's great success at his local Aston Clinton hill climb.*

**L**ike many small firms building sports cars, Aston Martin had a chequered early career. Lionel Martin was a wealthy car enthusiast who made a few hybrid competition cars before launching in 1923 the Aston Martin (named after his success in the Aston Clinton hill climb).

Fewer than 20 people had built a total of around 50 cars by the mid-1920s, but production gradually increased after W.S. Renwick and A.C. Bertelli acquired the company, showed their new overhead-camshaft model at the 1927 London Motor Show and moved into a factory at Feltham. Various backers came and went, but thanks to a successful competition programme the 1½-litre Aston Martin gained an international following.

In 1936 a new two-litre overhead-cam engine was introduced, the work of Bertelli and Claude Hill, and around 140 cars equipped with it were built before the outbreak of war in 1939.

In 1947 gear- and tractor-maker David Brown acquired both Aston Martin and Lagonda, and W.O. Bentley-designed Lagonda 2.6-litre engines were soon found in all models. The Aston Martins acquired the famous DB initials, denoting David Brown, and from 1955 were built in the Tickford factory at Newport Pagnell.

Aston Martin's pre-war sporting tradition was carried on after the war. In 1949 Aston Martin entered a Lagonda-powered car at Le Mans – without any success, however. That car later entered production as the DB2. The 1949 setback did not put off Aston Martin – the company competed at every Le Mans 24 Hours from 1931 to 1964 – and the next racer produced was the DB3 of 1954. The DB3S with its sophisticated de Dion rear suspension was designed by the ex-Auto Union designer Eberan von Eberhorst, who had moved to Britain and worked on the Aston Martin as well as the ERA racers.

The successor to the DB3S finally brought the company some real success, the DBR winning the Le Mans 24 Hours in 1959, driven by Carroll Shelby of AC Cobra fame and Roy Salvadori. The DBR went on to take the World Sports Car Championship in 1959.

The DB4 of 1959 had a new engine designed by Tad Marek and the last DB was the DBS, which became the V8 after David Brown withdrew from the company in 1972. Various changes of ownership followed, culminating in the Ford takeover in late 1987.

In later years Aston Martin could no longer afford large-scale racing efforts, although there were a few abortive attempts on Le Mans in the late 1970s and early 1980s before the Aston Martin Nimrods brought respectability.

*Above: Aston Martin's early success was gained by this model, the 1½-litre International.*

*Below: The Ulster was a more powerful version of the International, capable of 100 mph.*

*Above: A rare badge indeed. The 'Z' is the characteristic trademark of the Italian coachbuilder Zagato, who produced the most strikingly beautiful body to have been seen on any Aston Martin in the shape of the DB4 GT Zagato of 1960.*

*Right: A 1953 Aston Martin DB3S sports racer. Only 19 were built, powered by a three-litre twin-cam and featuring de Dion rear suspension. It was designed by the ex-Auto Union designer Eberan von Eberhorst.*

# Aston Martin 11.9HP International 1927-35

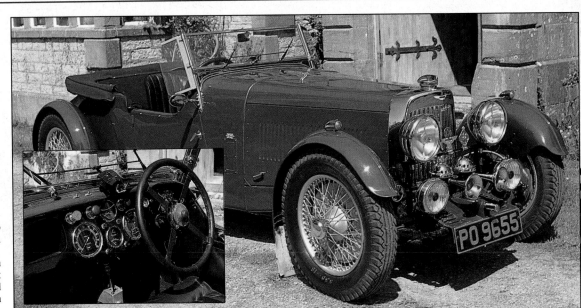

The first of the successful joint Bertelli designs (A.C. Bertelli designed the 1½-litre overhead-cam dry-sump engine and E. Bertelli the bodywork) was introduced in 1927. The International stemmed from two competition cars that were part of the batch of 19 made after the 1927 Motor Show in London.

As many as 81 Internationals were built between 1929 and 1932 and in the latter year came the International Le Mans, 12 of which were made. These had proprietary Moss gearboxes and ENV bevel rear axles in place of the earlier worm type, which had given the Aston its distinctive low lines. The Le Mans model, with its lowered radiator and outside exhaust, went on to sell 72 in the next two years. There were also 20 more formal 12/50 models produced.

The 11.9HP range was one of Aston Martin's most popular and earned great praise from *Autocar*, which observed that it was "One of those cars which makes the heart of the enthusiast rejoice, not only because the lines of the little machine suggest the joys of the open road but because the whole chassis has that indefinable air of breeding."

## International variants

### International Mk II
In short-wheelbase 70-bhp form this was perhaps the best of the 1½-litre cars; 56 were made, along with 61 of

the 80-mph long-wheelbase models

### Ulster
A 100-mph sporting two-seater, still with the classic Bertelli engine; 24 were built between 1934 and 1936

## Specification (1929 11.9HP)

**Engine:** inline four-cylinder, twin-cam
**Bore × stroke:** 69 mm × 99 mm
**Capacity:** 1481 cc
**Maximum power:** 70 bhp
**Transmission:** four-speed manual
**Chassis:** pressed steel
**Suspension:** non-independent with semi-elliptic leaf springs and friction dampers
**Brakes:** drums all round
**Bodywork:** two-seater sports
**Maximum speed (approx):** 84 mph

*Above: A Mk II version of the International, from 1934. It is a four-seat tourer built on the longer wheelbase and capable of 80 mph.*

*Inset: Every single instrument necessary is present on the dashboard. Note how the gear lever sprouts from its miniature four-slot gate.*

# Aston Martin DB2 1950-53

There was a DB1, but only 15 were built, from September 1948 to May 1950. It was based on a final pre-war design called the Atom and had a completely new pushrod overhead-valve engine.

The DB2 of 1950 was far more successful and used the Bentley-designed 2.6-litre twin-cam engine that had been acquired along with the Lagonda firm. Just over 400 were sold, of which a quarter were convertibles.

This was the first Aston Martin model to have the option of a more powerful tuned 125-bhp engine. The improved model was termed the Vantage, as have been all factory-tuned Astons since then.

The DB2's chassis was a development of the DB1's multi-tube affair and the car retained the trailing-arm independent front suspension seen on the earlier car. The body was all alloy and the whole front section hinged forward for good engine access, just like the later E-type

Jaguars of the 1960s.

The DB2's competition record was quite respectable. In 1950 John Wyer ran a team at Le Mans, winning the Index of Performance and finishing fifth. That was followed up by a class win in the Mille Miglia in 1952.

## Specification

**Engine:** inline six-cylinder, twin-cam
**Bore × stroke:** 78 mm × 90 mm
**Capacity:** 2580 cc
**Maximum power:** 125 bhp
**Transmission:** four-speed manual
**Chassis:** square tubular steel spaceframe
**Suspension:** independent front with trailing arms, coil springs and anti-roll bar; live rear axle with trailing arms, Panhard rod and coil springs
**Brakes:** drums all round
**Bodywork:** alloy two-seater coupé
**Maximum speed:** 110 mph (177 km/h)

*Above: The DB2 was a development of the DB2 prototype racer that ran at Le Mans in 1949, with a multi-tube chassis and a 2.5-litre twin-cam engine designed by the famous W.O. Bentley. Only 49 DB2 convertibles were built.*

*Left: The interior of the DB2 improved as time went on, but even this 1952 example is still a bit spartan; the speedo reads (rather optimistically) up to 140 mph.*

*Right: The fixed-head DB2 was designed by Aston Martin stylist Frank Feeley. The body is alloy and the whole front section tilts forward for good engine access.*

# Aston Martin DB2/4 1953-57

Just under 800 DB2/4s were built, between 1953 and 1957. The 2/4 denoted the car's capacity to carry four people in a 2+2 arrangement.

The DB2/4 was powered by Aston's six-cylinder inline twin-cam engine, a powerplant that was enlarged to 2992 cc during 1954. This engine was usually known as the three-litre and developed 140 bhp. That output rose to 165 bhp with factory tuning.

With the transfer of production from

Feltham to the Tickford factory at Newport Pagnell most coachwork was done by this firm, although a few Mk II versions were built as sports tourers by, appropriately enough, Touring of Milan. All used hand-beaten alloy for their body panels and had the traditional British feature of centre-lock wire wheels.

## Specification (Mk II)

**Engine:** inline six-cylinder, twin-cam
**Bore × stroke:** 83 mm × 90 mm

**Capacity:** 2992 cc
**Maximum power:** 140 bhp
**Transmission:** four-speed manual
**Chassis:** square tubular steel spaceframe
**Suspension:** independent front with trailing arms; live rear axle with coil springs
**Brakes:** drums all round
**Bodywork:** alloy coupé
**Maximum speed (approx):** 120 mph (193 km/h)

*Above: The DB2/4 was a four-seat development of the DB2 although, rather curiously, the wheelbase was unchanged from the two-seater, at 99 inches. It was powered first by the 125-bhp 'Vantage' 2.5-litre, then by the larger 2.9-litre 140-bhp twin-cam. The DB2/4 also has the distinction of being the world's first sporting hatchback, years ahead of the E-type Jaguar.*

## Aston Martin DB4 1958-63

Everything about the DB4 was new; it was the first Aston Martin to have a pressed-steel platform chassis, replacing the previous square-tubular arrangement, and there was a new engine built specifically for it. An in-house design by Tadek Marek, it was inspired by the Jaguar twin-cam, but unlike the Jaguar engine it was all alloy. Even in its lowest state of tune it produced 240 bhp from the 3.7 litres. That extra power required a new four-speed David Brown gearbox.

The body design was new too, as was the construction. Aston Martin designer Frank Feeley had left the company and the DB4 was styled by Touring of Milan. They were responsible for the *Superleggera* (literally 'superlightweight') construction of alloy panels over a latticework of small-diameter tubes.

In the course of the DB4's five-year production run various improvements were made, such as the addition of overdrive, while, from 1961, there was a more powerful Vantage variant with 266 bhp.

### DB4 variants

#### DB4 GT Zagato

A lightweight sports racer with a 302-bhp twin-cam six was followed by the lighter and more powerful (314-bhp) DB4 GT Zagato with more rounded bodywork by Touring's rival; the Zagato could reach 153 mph, but a mere 19 were built

*Above: The DB4's interior is a recognisable development of that of the DB2 shown on the previous page.*
*Right: Power for the DB4 came from a 3669-cc twin-cam six that developed as much as 266 bhp.*

*Above: The DB4 was styled in Italy by Touring of Milan, who used their unique Superleggera body construction of lightweight alloy panels over a tubular framework.*

*Below: Only 19 of the 153-mph DB4 GT Zagatos were built – the most desirable Astons of all.*

### Specification (DB4 GT)

**Engine:** inline six-cylinder, twin-cam
**Bore × stroke:** 92 mm × 92 mm
**Capacity:** 3669 cc
**Maximum power:** 302 bhp
**Transmission:** four-speed manual
**Chassis:** fabricated steel platform
**Suspension:** independent front with double wishbones and coil springs; live rear axle with coil springs
**Brakes:** discs all round
**Bodywork:** *Superleggera* coupé
**Maximum speed (approx):** 142 mph (229 km/h)

## Aston Martin DB5/6 1963-70

*Right: The DB5 sprang to fame as James Bond's car in the film Goldfinger (that much-modified and machine-gun equipped car still exists, incidentally). From the rear it's clear how the DB5 could be converted into the 2+2 DB6, which appeared in 1965.*

*Below: Under the DB5's bonnet was a 3995-cc version of the Aston twin-cam straight-six, which produced 282 bhp. Vantage versions produced 325 bhp. Note the Superleggera badge on the bonnet.*

Essentially the mixture as before, the DB5 became famous as the car used by James Bond in *Goldfinger*. It had put on weight compared with the DB4, however, and was given a larger, four-litre 282-bhp engine to overcome the extra mass.

The DB6 could almost be termed a 2+2 version of the DB5; its 3.75-in longer wheelbase allowed two small rear seats to be fitted. In other respects the DB6 was mechanically similar, with the four-litre twin-cam six, a ZF five-speed manual transmission and a Watts linkage to keep the live rear axle under control.

Although the whole of the DB4/5/6 line looked similar, the DB6 was different under the skin in having dispensed with the *Superleggera* body construction in favour of conventional alloy body panels and a steel platform chassis. A close look showed that the DB6 had a more upright windscreen and that the rear-end treatment was different; the curved lines of the DB5 had given way to a sharply cut-off square tail with a small lip spoiler.

### DB5/6 variants

#### DB5 Volante
Convertible version of the DB5, available with a steel hardtop; 123 were produced compared with the 886 production total of the coupé

#### DB5 Vantage
Tuned version of the DB5, with almost 50 bhp more (325 bhp at 5,750 rpm)

#### DB6 Volante
Convertible version with same power output as normal DB6; 140 were built, compared with 1,321 coupés

#### DB6 Vantage
Tuned version with 325 bhp at 5,750 rpm, a top speed of 148 mph and a 0-60 time of 6.5 seconds

### Specification (DB5)

**Engine:** inline six-cylinder, twin-cam
**Bore × stroke:** 96 mm × 92 mm
**Capacity:** 3995 cc
**Maximum power:** 282 bhp
**Transmission:** four-speed manual, ZF five-speed manual or three-speed auto
**Chassis:** steel platform
**Suspension:** independent front with double wishbones, coil springs and anti-roll bar; live rear axle
**Brakes:** discs all round
**Bodywork:** *Superleggera* construction with alloy panels
**Maximum speed:** 141 mph (227 km/h)

# Aston Martin V8 1972-88

The V8 was a development of the last of the DB line, the DBS, which lacked the perfect lines of the DB4 and DB5. Apart from that it was the mixture as before, the main differences being the replacement of the faithful old six-cylinder engine with a new all-alloy V8 that first appeared in the DBS in 1970. It was a four-cam design by Tadek Marek and its capacity was over five litres.

Not surprisingly, with nearly 360 bhp, it gave the DBS and V8 staggering performance, and the chassis was revised to help the car cope. The track was widened and the live axle finally gave way to the superior location offered by a de Dion system. Gone, along with the live axle, in the V8 was any vestige of Italian involvement, as the design was by William Towns.

## V8 variants
### V8 Volante
As usual, Aston Martin produced a convertible version of the V8 which, from 1986, could be bought with the tuned Vantage engine

*Above: The V8 Volante convertible was introduced in 1978, ending an eight-year spell when no open Astons were built.*

### V8 Vantage
With around 360 bhp you would not expect there to be a need for a tuned version, but Aston produced one with over 400 bhp and a top speed verging on 170 mph
### Zagato
Following on the tradition of the DB4 GT Zagato, Aston turned to the Italian coachbuilders for a striking variation on the V8 theme in 1986

## Specification (Vantage)

**Engine:** V8, quad-cam
**Bore × stroke:** 100 mm × 85 mm
**Capacity:** 5340 cc
**Maximum power:** 406 bhp
**Transmission:** five-speed manual
**Chassis:** steel platform
**Suspension:** independent front with double wishbones and coil springs; de Dion rear axle with trailing arms, Watts linkage and coil springs
**Brakes:** ventilated discs all round
**Bodywork:** alloy 2 + 2 coupé
**Maximum speed (approx):** 170 mph (274 km/h)

*Below: Each Aston Martin quad-cam V8 is assembled by one man, who signs the engine personally.*

*Above: The blanked-off grille shows that this is the V8 Vantage, Britain's premier supercar, a 406-bhp, 170-mph heavyweight.*

*Below: In 1986 Aston went back to Zagato for a limited-edition version of the Vantage to brighten up an old design.*

# Aston Martin Virage 1988–95

*Below: The Virage was styled by two British designers John Heffernan and Ken Greenley. It had a V8 engine four valves per cylinder. It was superseded by the V8 Coupe in 1996.*

*Above: Wood and leather luxury; the only way to finish what is still, despite the use of modern light alloy construction in the chassis, a traditional British supercar.*

This distinctively British supercar was styled by John Heffernan and Ken Greenley, and made its first appearance at the 1988 Motor Show in London. The name derives from the French for a bend or corner. Following the normal Aston tradition, the Virage was joined in 1991 by a drophead Volante version.

Both are powered by a new version of the 5340-cc V8 with four valves per cylinder, which develops 330 bhp, and the even more impressive torque output of 350 lb ft. Manual or automatic versions are offered, the latter being able to reach 60 mph from rest in around six seconds, a fine achievement considering that the Virage, like the V8 before it, is no lightweight. Nor does its weight stop it from reaching a top speed of 155 mph. A new chassis incorporating light alloys was designed in conjunction with the aerospace experts at Cranfield Institute of Technology. The de Dion axle was also lightened with the use of special materials, but despite that, and the use of the hand-beaten alloy body panels, the Virage was a true British heavyweight.

## Specification

**Engine:** V8 quad-cam, 32-valve
**Bore × stroke:** 100 mm × 85 mm
**Capacity:** 5340 cc
**Maximum power:** 330 bhp
**Transmission:** five-speed manual
**Chassis:** light alloy and steel platform
**Suspension:** independent front with double wishbones and coil springs; de Dion rear axle
**Brakes:** ventilated discs all round
**Bodywork:** alloy coupé
**Maximum speed (approx):** 155 mph (249 km/h)

## Aston Martin DB7 1994-present

By 1999 Aston Martin could claim that its DB7 was the most successful model it had ever produced, as it was selling at a greater rate than any previous model in the company's 86 year history. Launched in 1994 with an £84,950 price tag, the 2,000th DB7 left the Bloxham final assembly plant in July 1998, beating the previous record of 1,850 units set by the DB6 between 1965 and 1970.

The Aston Martin DB7 was styled by Scottish designer Ian Callum, who was previously senior designer with Carrozzeria Ghia of Turin. The DB7 was available in 2 + 2 Coupé and Volante cabriolet versions, both powered by an all-alloy 335 bhp 3.2-litre, (Eaton) supercharged six-cylinder in-line 24-valve engine. There was a choice of close-ratio five-speed all-synchromesh manual gearbox or four-speed electronically controlled automatic. Top speed was 165 mph (265 km/h) and 0–60mph (0–96 km/h) was covered in 5.5 seconds.

The DB7 was built on a steel floorpan, with steel body panels and composite front wings. Suspension consisted of double wishbones, incorporating anti-dive geometry, coil springs, monotube dampers and anti-roll bar at the front, with double wishbones, longitudinal control arms, coil springs, monotube

*Right: Styled by Ian Callum, the 3.2-litre supercharged DB7 was regarded as possibly the sleekest Grand Touring car in the world.*

dampers and an anti-roll bar at the rear. A Teves anti-lock braking system was also fitted, and it was shod with low profile Bridgestone tyres, specially developed for the DB7. Both versions were equipped with twin air bags, side impact beams, full on-board diagnostic equipment and, as you'd expect, a comprehensive range of luxury and safety features, like climate control, six-speaker stereo, cruise control, Connolly hide upholstery, deep pile carpet with a burr walnut fascia panel and centre console unit.

### Specification

**Engine:** supercharged 24-valve in-line six-cylinder
**Capacity:** 3239 cc
**Maximum power:** 335 bhp
**Transmission:** five-speed manual, optional four-speed automatic
**Chassis:** monocoque
**Suspension:** independent front by double wishbones, coil springs, monotube dampers and anti-roll bar; independent rear by double wishbones, longitudinal control arms, coil springs, monotube dampers and an anti-roll bar
**Brakes:** front, ventilated steel discs with alloy four-pot calipers; rear, ventilated steel discs with sliding aluminium calipers and drum handbrake
**Bodywork:** two door coupé or convertible with 2 + 2 seating

## Aston Martin Vantage, V8 Coupé and Volante 1993-present

In 1999, Aston Martin's three V8-engined models were the range-topping 550 bhp twin-supercharged Vantage and the 350 bhp normally aspirated V8 Coupé and Volante drop-top models. These were built at Newport Pagnall while the DB7 was made at Bloxham. Each Aston took 15 weeks to make, and the prices reflected the level of craftsmanship involved. The Vantage cost almost £190 K, while the other two V8 models were just short of £150 K and £170 K respectively.

The Vantage appeared in 1993, and its unsupercharged siblings came out in 1996 and 1997. Power unit was the 32-valve 5.3-litre all-alloy V8 with twin cams per bank, fitted with twin Eaton superchargers and liquid intercoolers in the case of the Vantage, which powered it to 186 mph and from 0–60 mph in 4.6 seconds. The V8 Coupé and Volante cabriolet were capable of reaching 60 mph in less than 6.0 seconds and has a maximum speed in excess of 150 mph. All units were equipped with an Alpha Plus electronic engine management system linked to a three-way catalyst for operation with unleaded fuel. The Vantage used a six-speed manual gearbox, while the other two were normally specified with four-speed electronically controlled automatic transmission. The Volante had a longer wheelbase, providing increased luggage space and rear legroom, incorporating revised suspension geometry and damper settings. All body panels were hand-made in aluminium, with ten

*Left: Aston's Vantage was an imposing vehicle. Beneath the radiator grille was a a large air intake that supplied the 350bhp quad-cam supercharged V8 motor.*

Connolly hides used in upholstering the Astons' luxury interiors. Each car received a minimum of twelve coats of paint, and each engine bore the name of its builder.

### Specification (V8 Coupé)

**Engine:** all alloy quad cam 32 valve V8
**Capacity:** 5340 cc
**Maximum power:** 350 bhp
**Transmission:** four-speed automatic, with sport and touring modes
**Chassis:** monocoque
**Brakes:** front, ventilated steel discs with AP Racing four-pot aluminium calipers; rear, ventilated steel discs with sliding aluminium calipers. Bosch four channel ABS
**Suspension:** independent front by double wishbone, co-axial spring damper units with anti-roll bar; rear, de Dion axle located by four longitudinal radius arms and transverse Watt's linkage. Coaxial spring damper units
**Body:** two-door coupé with 2 + 2 seating

### Variants

**Aston Martin Shooting Brake**
Introduced in 1992, priced at £165 k, powered by 350 bhp 5.3-litre V8, similar specification to V8 Coupé. High-performance 600 bhp 'works prepared' models made to special order using race-spec components developed for the DB7 GT 'Project'.

# ATS (Automobili Turismo Sport)

*Above: The one thing that ATS did get absolutely right was the design; it was just about perfect in line and proportion. The vents ahead of the rear wheels are for cooling the mid-mounted V8 engine.*

T his was one of the most short-lived of all Italian exotic car producers, lasting only from 1962 to 1964. In many ways the company was intended to be another Ferrari, producing both Formula 1 cars and the most desirable of high-performance road cars. It was a wildly optimistic scenario; where Ferrari had built up relatively gradually (and in an era when there was far less Grand Prix opposition), ATS were attempting to do everything at once.

The omens had looked good in one sense in that the core personnel for ATS had actually come from Ferrari after the so-called 'palace coup' in 1962, when a number of Ferrari's top men, including the renowned and rotund engineer and designer Carlo Chiti, left the company.

On the Formula 1 side ATS took over the Scuderia Serenissima, which had been founded in Bologna by Count Volpi di Misurata and Jaime Ortiz-Patino in 1962. Serenissima had run out of money when their chief backer Volpi withdrew. Under Carlo Chiti, ATS built a Formula 1 car and even managed to get top-flight drivers like the American Phil Hill and Italian Giancarlo Baghetti to drive – with a total lack of success.

Not content with Formula 1, ATS even entered two cars in the Targa Florio in 1964, again without success; but although road car production finished in 1964, race car production continued until 1969.

## ATS 2500 GT 1963-64

Judged purely on criteria like appearance, style and power (which, after all, are crucial in the high-performance expensive coupé market), the ATS coupé should have succeeded. It seemed to have everything. The body was extremely attractive, and the mid-engine configuration promised handling as good as the car's looks.

Power came from an overhead-cam V8, which could be fitted either with quadruple Weber carburettors or Lucas fuel injection and produced around 245 bhp. That gave a claimed top speed of 160 mph, but the design was never given the development its advanced specification demanded; and even though Serenissima's original backer Count Volpi reappeared on the scene to take over road car production again, producing the 2500 GT as a Serenissima, it was never a success. Serenissima did improve the car, giving it a quad-cam V8, but a lack of power was never the GT's failing.

### Specification

**Engine:** V8, twin-cam
**Bore × stroke:** 76 mm × 68 mm
**Capacity:** 2467 cc
**Maximum power:** 240 bhp
**Transmission:** five-speed manual
**Chassis:** tubular steel space frame
**Suspension:** independent with double wishbones and coil springs front and rear
**Brakes:** discs all round
**Bodywork:** alloy two-seater coupé
**Maximum speed (approx):** 160 mph (257 km/h)

*Right: The front view of the 2500 GT emphasises the extremely low bonnet line. That was made possible by having a mid-mounted rather than the traditional front-mounted engine. When the 2500 GT appeared in 1963 it was one of the first mid-engined cars in the world, predating the Lamborghini Miura of the mid-1960s.*

# Auburn Automobile Company

T he Eckhart Carriage Co. of Auburn, Indiana, moved on to motor cars under the name Auburn in 1903. Auburn's cars were 'assembled' machines with a variety of 'bought-in' engines.

After the Eckhart family withdrew at the end of World War I the firm was acquired by a syndicate that included William Wrigley Jr of chewing gum fame. A successful car salesman named Errett Lobban Cord was brought in to revive its prospects, and by astute marketing and stock purchase at depressed levels in the mid-1920s he became president when aged only 32.

A period of empire-building led to Cord owning Auburn and Duesenberg, creating his own Cord marque and buying proprietary engine maker Lycoming along with the Limousine Body Co. of Kalamazoo, as well as other long-time suppliers to Auburn.

Errett Cord went over to eight cylinders at Auburn and, using a formula later employed by SS Jaguar, produced very good-looking cars assembled from cheap components at remarkably low prices.

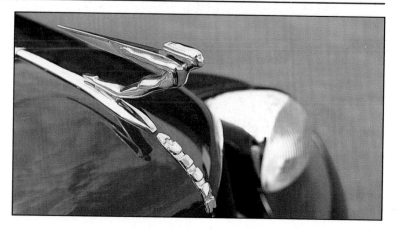

The Speedsters in particular created an important niche, especially after Mercer abandoned production (leaving only Stutz making a similar car, for three times the cost of an Auburn). Over 22,000 Auburns were built by 5,000 employees in 1929, but apart from a peak year in 1931 of just over 28,000 cars it was downhill all the way once the Depression hit.

Even a V12 failed to stem the tide, despite being offered at around a quarter of the price of V12 models from Cadillac, Lincoln and Pierce Arrow.

A last-ditch attempt to avert disaster came with Harold T. Ames, Duesenberg's president, brought in to control day-to-day management in the absence of E.L. Cord, who was concentrating on other parts of his empire. With Ames came August Duesenberg as chief engineer and Gordon Buehrig as stylist. Their 1935 models included the beautiful Type 851 Speedster, but it came too late and 1936 marked the end of Auburn.

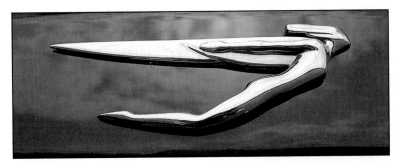

*Above: Auburn's winged flying lady emblem was used both in profile, as here, and as a three-dimensional bonnet mascot.*

# Auburn Speedster 1928-33

*Below: The Auburn Speedsters of the late 1920s were based on a Duesenberg design, the Model X. There was no copyright problem to worry about as both Auburn and Duesenberg were then part of the same company, along with Cord, engine makers Lycoming and various other companies. The Speedsters were robust as well as elegant and capable of over 100 mph.*

*Left: A V12 Speedster from 1930. The vast majority of the Auburn Speedsters were powered by a straight-eight side-valve engine but the V12, introduced in 1930, shared exactly the same chassis and body.*

The first of Auburn's distinctive boat-tailed Speedsters appeared in 1928, the work of Count Alexis de Sakhnoffsky; it was deliberately patterned on the original Duesenberg Model X Speedster designed by Al Leamy. They were mechanically simple, powered by Lycoming straight-eight engines. The 8-88 (the first 8 standing for eight-cylinder and the 88 for its power output) was powered by the 4523-cc engine, which had shown its power and reliability by averaging 63.4 mph over 1,000 miles in 1927.

The 8-115 was the more powerful, 115-bhp version of the Lycoming straight eight, and that extra power helped the Speedster to an excellent top speed of 108 mph. Later that year Wade Morton set a 24-hour record at 84.7 mph in the 8-115, so the cars were certainly not all show and no go. Minor changes were made to power outputs in 1929, to produce the 8-90 and 8-120, and again in 1930 to produce the 8-95 and 8-125.

## Auburn Speedster variants

### Auburn Cabin Speedster

A streamlined alloy-bodied model of 1929 with twin wicker aircraft seats, cycle wings and an overall height of just 58 inches. Styled by Wade Morton, it was killed off by the Depression

### Auburn 12-160 Speedster

A V12 engine was added to the line in 1932. It developed its 160 bhp from 6.4 litres and could achieve a top speed of 117 mph. It was dropped from the range in 1934 but the engine lived on in LaFrance fire trucks

## Specification (8-88)

**Engine:** inline eight-cylinder, side-valve
**Bore × stroke:** 76 mm × 121 mm
**Capacity:** 4523 cc
**Maximum power:** 88 bhp
**Transmission:** three-speed manual
**Chassis:** pressed steel channel
**Suspension:** non-independent with rigid axles front and rear with semi-elliptic leaf springs
**Brakes:** drums all round
**Bodywork:** speedster
**Maximum speed (approx):** 100 mph (161 km/h)

# Auburn 851/852 Speedster 1935-36

The 851 of 1935 was styled by Gordon Buehrig with a deep sloping radiator, teardrop wings, a tiny two-seat cockpit behind a vestigial windscreen and splendidly flamboyant chrome side exhaust pipes. The luggage compartment could only be reached through a hatch on the side, perfect for golf clubs. Each 851 bore a plaque stating what speed the famous record breaker of the times Al Jenkins had achieved in that particular car; it had to be a speed over 100 mph in each case. Such performance was possible thanks to the Schwitzer Cummins supercharger turning at six times engine speed to help generate over 150 bhp from 4½ litres.

The 851 had the desirable feature of a two-speed rear axle ("LOW ratio means terrific acceleration and power... HIGH ratio gears you up for speeds up to 100 mph with low revs and consequent low running costs," as Auburn's publicity blurb put it). The 851 was a genuine performance car, once averaging 102.9 mph for 12 hours.

The 852 of 1936 was little changed; by this time Auburn was running out of money and total 851/852 production amounted to little more than 500. Despite being killed off by the Depression, the design has stood the test of time very well, numerous companies having built replicas in recent years.

## Specification (851)

**Engine:** inline eight-cylinder, side-valve
**Bore × stroke:** 78 mm × 121 mm
**Capacity:** 4586 cc
**Maximum power:** 150 bhp
**Transmission:** three-speed manual with dual ratio rear axle
**Chassis:** pressed steel channel
**Suspension:** non-independent with rigid axles front and rear with semi-elliptic leaf springs
**Brakes:** drums all round
**Bodywork:** speedster
**Maximum speed (approx):** 105 mph (169 km/h)

*Left: The straight-eight engine that powered the 851 and 852 Speedsters was a 4.6-litre side-valve design built by Lycoming and producing 150 bhp.*

*Below: An 851 Speedster from 1935. Thanks to its Schwitzer Cummins supercharger it could top 100 mph; indeed, every 851 was guaranteed to exceed the magic figure, and was given a plaque to prove it.*

# Audi Automobilwerk GmbH

It is generally considered by many people that the Audi company is a product of the post-war period – this is most certainly not the case. The original Audi Automobilwerk GmbH was formed in Zwickau in 1910 by August Horch. Horch had been a one-time employee of Benz & Cie, where he rose to become plant manager for motor car construction, but being of a restless disposition he found a wealthy backer and set out on his own.

His first company was called A. Horch & Cie. It was formed in 1899 and immediately commenced production of an advanced design of motor car, which soon gained an exceedingly good reputation for silence and reliability. By 1907 Horch was working on a six-cylinder engine with a roller-bearing crankshaft and overhead inlet valves. Unfortunately, by this time he was experiencing difficulty in retaining control of his company, and responded by leaving and forming a rival concern. He was prevented from using his own name and so adopted the Latin translation of his surname, Horch – i.e. Audi.

Output consisted of large expensive cars, and by 1929 Horch had left and the company was being run by Jorgen Rasmussen – who had built up DKW. In 1932 four motor manufacturers in Saxony – Audi, DKW, Horch and Wanderer – amalgamated to become Auto Union, which was to become a major force in pre-war Grand Prix racing. Audi had very little to offer this group apart from its name. Production was transferred to the neighbouring Horch factory, where two front-wheel-drive models, the UW and 225, were produced until 1939. At the end of World War II a new factory was built at Düsseldorf, for the production of DKW-Auto Union cars. Production concentrated upon a front-wheel-drive three-cylinder.

In 1958 Mercedes Benz took over financial control of Auto Union. In 1964 Volkswagen obtained the majority of the Auto Union shares, and eventually the name was dropped in favour of Audi. Audi thus became the only one of the four founding members of the original Auto Union to survive. In 1998 it bought the supercar maker Lamborghini.

*Above: The rings in the Audi badge represented the four companies that together made up Auto Union. Audi was one; the others were DKW, Horch and Wanderer, none of which survived as independent marques.*

*Left: The new Audi referred to was the 920 model introduced just before the start of World War II with a 3.2-litre 75-bhp engine.*

*Left: In 1988 Audi introduced a new range-topping model, the V8. To many people's disappointment it looks almost indistinguishable from the more humble 200 model, but is an impressive performer, with a 32-valve, 250-bhp 3.6-litre V8.*

*Above: Audi's 40-bhp 3.5-litre Type C became known as the Alpensieger in 1912, to mark its success in the Austrian Alpine trials. It completed the trials without a single penalty point. Bodywork was alloy and the top speed 60 mph.*

## Audi 100 S Coupé 1969-74

By the late 1960s Audi was once again a recognised name, and the company's reputation as a producer of solid, reliable vehicles continued to grow. Their first post-war sporting car was the 100 S Coupé, which laid the groundwork for their current sporting image.

Introduced at the 1969 Frankfurt Motor Show, it was based on the original 100 saloon that had been announced twelve months previously. The original 1.7-litre engine was enlarged to 1871 cc, and the pushrod-operated overhead valve engine was fitted with a twin-choke Solex carburettor. It had a high, for its time, compression ratio of 10.2:1. Front-wheel drive was retained from the saloon, which assisted in providing the model with extremely good road manners. Perhaps its biggest attraction was the well-streamlined two-door fastback body, which contemporary reports likened to an Aston Martin DBS – unusually it was not a 2+2, but provided

full four-seater accommodation, with a large area for luggage. Truly a Grand Tourer in the originally accepted meaning of the term.

The coupé was expensive, especially so in Great Britain, where it competed directly with the Triumph Stag and BMW 2002 tii. Towards the end of its production run, in 1976, it was faced with the Ford Capri Ghia 3000, which was considerably quicker and £1,300 cheaper.

It was Audi's clever combination of excellent handling, smooth ride and brisk performance that made up its undoubted appeal in its day.

### Specification

**Engine:** inline four-cylinder, overhead-valve
**Bore × stroke:** 74 mm × 84 mm
**Capacity:** 1871 cc
**Maximum power:** 112 bhp
**Transmission:** four-speed manual

**Chassis:** unitary
**Suspension:** independent front with double wishbones and anti-roll bar; beam rear axle with trailing arms, torsion bars, Panhard rod and anti-roll bar
**Brakes:** disc front (inboard mounted), drums rear

**Bodywork:** four-seater coupé
**Maximum speed (approx):** 115 mph (185 km/h)

*Below: The 100 S Coupé was strikingly similar to the Aston Martin DBS but was far cheaper, with only a four-cylinder engine rather than a V8.*

# Audi A4 Quattro Supertouring 1996-1998

*Left: Audi put its extensive experience of successful four-wheel drive competition to good use with the A4 model, which Frank Biela drove to victory in the British Touring Car Championship in 1996.*

Audi's reputation for building successful four-wheel drive competition cars was rooted in world-class rally sport until 1995, when it trounced the opposition at the one-off Touring Car World Cup race at Paul Ricard circuit with the 4 x 4 Audi A4. Its arrival on the scene at the British Touring Car Championship the follow-ing year lifted the level of competition to yet another high. There would, however, be a rein kept on high-tech apparatus such as the sophisticated electronic dif-ferentials that had been criticised on the continent. The operation was run by Audi Sport UK under Richard Lloyd and John Wickham, with drivers Frank Biela and John Bintcliffe at the helm. The Audi A4s' spectacular early successes were tempered by the imposition of weight penalties, so that by the middle of 1996, the A4s were carrying an extra 95 kg (2.18 lb) more than a front-wheel drive competitor with a 30 kg (68 lb) penalty. Many people saw this as a swingeing punishment for its clear traction advan-tage, while others were of the opinion that weight penalties should be given on a handicapping basis to the most suc-cessful drivers. However, Audi were no strangers to weight penalties, having had them imposed in TransAm racing in the USA. It proved no deterrent to the final outcome of the Championship, however, and Biela took the honours in 1996. The ballast factor was reduced by 30 kg (68 lb) at mid-season in 1997 and the performance of both A4s improved dramatically.

Like all Super Touring cars of the pe-riod, the A4 was built according to a strict set of regulations. Its four-door sa-loon body was seam-welded and a steel roll-cage welded in place to further stiffen the chassis. It was powered by a four-cylinder 16-valve dry-sump en-gine, installed longitudinally, with Audi six-speed sequential gearbox, and per-manent four-wheel drive transmission featuring Torsen centre diff, viscous locking front diff and multi-plate rear diff, and Löbrö three-arm sliding univer-sal jointed half shafts.

For 1999, Audi's road-going S4 quat-tros were powered by six-cylinder twin-turbo 30-valve engines, capable of 155 mph (249 km/h), with electronic brake-force distribution (EBD), elec-tronic differential lock (EDL), traction control and electronic ABS.

## Specification
**(1996 A4 Supertouring)**

**Engine:** four-cylinder 16-valve
**Bore** x **stroke:** 85 mm x 88 mm
**Capacity:** 1998 cc
**Maximum power:** 296 bhp
**Transmission:** six-speed sequential, permanent 4 x 4
**Chassis:** seam-welded monocoque with aerodynamic embellishments
**Suspension:** independent front and rear by double wishbones, coil springs, adjustable gas dampers, anti-roll bars

# Audi TT Coupé 1998 to present

The Audi TT Coupé quattro was the re-sult of a styling exercise shown at the 1995 Frankfurt Show, and was launched in May 1998. Its compact, near-symmet-rical lines and rotund cabin top gave it a distinct appearance that integrated well with the rest of the Audi model range. The TT Coupé quattro was based on the Mk IV Golf floorpan, and was available with a choice of two 1.8-litre, four-cylin-der, in-line, 20-valve engines with alloy head and iron block, and the 225 bhp turbocharged model with two intercool-ers had a top speed of 150 mph (243 km/h). Transmission was via a six-speed gearbox and electronically-con-trolled hydraulic clutch, and the traction, provided by its permanent four-wheel drive, enabled it to cover 0–62 mph (0-100 km/h) in 6.4 seconds. The nor-mally aspirated model was good for 180 bhp, and capable of reaching 62 mph (100 km/h) in 7.4 seconds and a top speed of 140 mph (225 km/h).

Suspension was by McPherson struts at the front, and side parallelogram sus-pension at the rear, allied to disc brakes with ABS and electronic brake force dis-tribution (EBD). The TT Coupé ran on cast aluminium wheels (7J x 16 in or 7.5J x 17 in) shod with 205/55 R16 or 225/45 ZR 17 tyres. The TT's functional, yet stylish, cabin featured a combination of aluminium, Alcantara and leather up-holstery and trim, and two front head/ thorax airbags in the seat backs pro-tected the upper body and head region, augmented by pyrotechnic front seat belt restraints. The TT was built to 96/27/EC side impact and European frontal crash regulations, and a tubular steel construction acted as an additional cross bracing of the door post to give the body shell additional rigidity. The TT's ergonomics included a folding mechanism in the rear seat bench that enabled the rear back rest to be half split or completely folded down to pro-vide a flat cargo deck, potentially dou-bling the available luggage space.

## Specification

**Engine:** four-cylinder 20-valve
**Bore x stroke:** 81 mm x 86.4 mm
**Capacity:** 1,781 cc
**Maximum power:** 225 bhp
**Transmission:** six-speed manual, permanent 4 x 4
**Chassis:** monocoque
**Suspension:** front, MacPherson struts, coil springs, lower wishbone, anti roll bar; rear, double wishbones, coil springs, anti-roll bar

*Right: The compact four-wheel drive TT Coupé took Audi into a different market niche and it was as sure-foot-ed and as powerful as its specifica-tion suggested.*

## Audi Quattro 1980–91

Audi really set the motoring world alight in 1980 when they introduced the first series-production four-wheel-drive car. Jensen had manufactured the four-wheel-drive FF model in 1966, but this was only produced in limited numbers.

During the course of a winter testing session in Finland, Audi engineers were surprised when their sophisticated front-wheel-drive designs were continually shown up by a utilitarian, four-wheel-drive, off-road Volkswagen Iltis – a military specification vehicle based on Audi 80 components – and the decision was taken to build the Quattro.

The company's management of the period – in fact the Volkswagen board – required a great deal of convincing that this revolutionary form of transmission would sell in the required quantities. That it did so reflected well on the chief engineer at the time, Ferdinand Piëch, who staked his reputation on the specification. Audi, from its earliest association with DKW and Auto Union, had been pioneers of automotive transmission. Fortunately Audi were in a good position to fulfil the design requirements. The turbocharged version of the 2.2-litre five-cylinder engine was easily persuaded to produce 200 bhp. Some of the transmission parts came directly from the Iltis, and the body was based on the contemporary Audi coupé which was announced shortly afterwards. During the initial development of the design it was hoped to manage without an inter-axle differential – in fact at high speed its absence was quite acceptable – but tyre wear on slower corners made the use of one imperative. This was the principal difficulty with the early development of the design.

Despite its very definite front-weight

*Left: The five-cylinder turbo Audi Quattro used a permanent four-wheel-drive system in a modified version of the Audi Coupé bodyshell with distinctive flared wheel arches.*

*Below: In 1983 Audi homologated the Quattro Sport, the shorter version of the Quattro, with a four-valve-per-cylinder version of the straight-five turbo and 300 bhp.*

bias the Quattro immediately turned into an almost unbeatable rally car. In its first year, 1981, it took Hannu Mikkola to third place in the World Championship for Drivers, and the next year Audi became World Rally Champions with Michelle Mouton second in the Driver's Championship.

Over the next decade Audi brought out a whole range of quattro (with a small 'q') versions of their normal saloons and the Quattro itself was improved by the addition of a four-valve-per-cylinder version of the inline five, producing 220 bhp and a top speed of 141 mph.

### Specification

**Engine:** inline five-cylinder, overhead-cam, turbo
**Bore × stroke:** 79.5 mm × 86.4 mm
**Capacity:** 2144 cc
**Maximum power:** 200 bhp
**Transmission:** five-speed manual with permanent four-wheel drive
**Chassis:** unitary with front subframe
**Suspension:** independent with MacPherson struts and anti-roll bars front and rear
**Brakes:** discs all round
**Bodywork:** coupé
**Maximum speed (approx):** 136 mph (219 km/h)

*Above: Although the Quattro's straight-five turbo was powerful it was a long and fairly heavy engine, giving the car a decided front weight bias. That was one of the car's few drawbacks.*

*Above: Shortening the Quattro to produce the Quattro Sport resulted in a lighter and faster model, but one far more difficult to control. Some of that comes across in this picture of action from the Pike's Peak hillclimb in the USA.*

# Austin-Healey

*Right: Austin-Healey was created in 1952 when Austin adopted a Donald Healey latest sports car design.*

*Left: First product of the Austin-Healey partnership was the 100, later termed the 100/4 after the later six-cylinder 100/6 appeared.*

**W**hen Donald Healey conceived a new Healey 100 model with Austin engine and transmission, to replace the old Riley-engined Healeys, he had no plans for a production tie-up with Austin. When the car was launched in 1952, however, BMC's chairman Leonard Lord was so impressed that he immediately offered to take it over, to rename it the Austin-Healey 100, and to make it in large numbers.

The marque was relatively short-lived, and its career spanned BMC's (and Britain's) dominance of the series-production world sports car market. The first cars were delivered in 1953, and the last were built in 1970.

From beginning to end of this 17-year life, all Austin-Healeys were designed by the Healey business in Warwick, UK, manufactured either at the Austin factory in Birmingham or at the MG factory at Abingdon, and marketed through the worldwide BMC organisation. The vast majority of all Austin-Healeys were sold in North America.

Works-sponsored Austin-Healeys were raced and rallied with great success, the 'Big Healey' in particular being a formidable rally car.

There were only two types, or generations, of Austin-Healey. The original 100 gradually evolved over a 15-year period – to end its days as the 3000 Mk III – and was always based on the running gear of large Austins like the A90, A105 and A99 saloons. The second-generation model was a small sports car, the Sprite, which used running gear from the Austin A35 saloon.

The Sprite, announced in 1958, was such a success that, when the time came for a restyle, BMC decided to sell the improved car as an Austin-Healey Sprite *and* an MG Midget. Although an 'Austin-Healey' version of the 1967 MGC was once proposed, this was never produced.

After the foundation of British Leyland in 1968, however, management began reducing the number of different cars in the range. The result was that the Austin-Healey marque was killed off, whereas the 'MG Midget' version of the Sprite carried on for another nine years.

The Healey family then formed an alliance with Jensen, to produce the Jensen-Healey sports car in the 1970s. In the late 1980s, attempts to revive both the Austin-Healey models (as the Mk IV and the Frog Eye respectively) met with only limited success.

*Above: The grille of a 100-Four has upright slats. Only the '100' appears on the grille, as '100-Four' was only applied retrospectively.*

*Above: The 100 was re-engined in 1956 and given a 2.6-litre six-cylinder Austin engine, bringing a name change, to 100-Six.*

# Austin-Healey 100 1952-56

The original Healey 100 was designed as a successor to the various Riley-engined Healeys that had been in production at Warwick since 1946. It was originally intended to be a cheaper car than those it would replace, and to ensure this Donald Healey and his designer son Geoffrey arranged to use engine, transmission and front suspension units from the current Austin A90 saloon car.

The chassis was a sturdy layout with box-section members to which many basic body panels were also welded on assembly. To simplify things, and to keep the height down, this featured a rear axle which was positioned *above* the line of the side members. The result was a low-slung car that really needed more ground clearance and more wheel movement.

The style, by Healey's own designers, was a sleek and curvaceous two-seater roadster, with a fold-down windscreen. There was an optional removable hardtop. Although considerably developed, this style was retained to the end of the career of the Big Healey, as it came to be known to distinguish it from the smaller

Sprite, which came 15 years later.

The original type, known as the 100 BN1, had a three-speed gearbox with overdrive operating on top and second gears – effectively giving the car a five-speed transmission. One curious feature about the three-speed gearbox was that the gear lever sprouted from the side of the transmission tunnel, having been adapted from a column-shift gearbox.

Three years after its launch, the BN1 was updated to the BN2 type, principally by the fitment of New BMC 'C-Series' four-speed gearbox and hypoid-bevel rear axle units. A year later, however, the car was completely redesigned, with a six-cylinder engine, and became the 100-Six. Final assembly was at Long-bridge; 14,662 four-cylinder Big Healeys were built.

## Austin-Healey 100 variants

### 100M

'M' meant 'Modified', for this was a tuned version of the BN2 type, with 110 bhp, stiffened-up suspension, and a special paint-job; many components

had been proved on 100S models, and most of the 1,159 cars built were conversions of BN2s, produced by Healey at Warwick

### 100S

Healey's own 'Special Test cars' were the 'works' race and record cars used in 1953 and 1954, but a production run of 50 100S models was made at Warwick in 1955; these cars had 132 bhp, a four-speed gearbox, four-wheel disc brakes, and aluminium body skin panels

## Specification (100/4 BN1)

**Engine:** inline four-cylinder, overhead-valve
**Bore × stroke:** 87.3 mm × 11 mm
**Capacity:** 2660 cc
**Maximum power:** 90 bhp
**Transmission:** three-speed manual gearbox with overdrive, rear-wheel drive
**Structure:** steel chassis, box section side members
**Suspension:** independent front, coil springs; beam axle rear, leaf springs
**Brakes:** drums front and rear
**Bodywork:** steel open two-seater, optional hardtop
**Maximum speed:** 103 mph (166 km/h)

*Left: The 100 was powered by the four-cylinder Austin A90 engine, fitted with twin SU carburettors to give 90 bhp from its 2.7 litres. That was enough to give a top speed of over 100 mph.*

*Below: The shield shape of the grille is the quickest way to identify the 100. The basic shape stayed in production for 15 years.*

# Austin-Healey 100-Six and 3000 1956-67

The first major redesign of the 'Big Healey' was put on sale in 1956. The wheelbase was slightly lengthened, to give more cabin space, occasional rear seats were added, and at the same time the new six-cylinder-engined 'C-Series' power unit (with 102 bhp) was also adopted. This was the original 100-Six Model.

This new BN4 type was smoother, but no faster, than the ousted four-cylinder car, and was much criticised for this. To improve matters, BMC launched the 117-bhp BN6 type at the end of 1967. Before long a two-seater version was also reintroduced as an option.

From late 1957, too, final assembly was moved to the MG sports car factory at Abingdon, and for the next decade a whole series of further-developed cars were produced on that site.

The 100-Six became the muscular 3000 in 1959, the first true convertible (as opposed to a roadster) car followed three years later, and the final important styling changes came two years after that. Sales continued at the rate of 4,000-5,000 cars a year throughout this period, but in the end an avalanche of new safety regulations from the USA killed off the 'Big Healey'. A proposed 'Mk IV' version, with the BMC/Rolls-Royce four-litre engine, never passed the prototype stage. No fewer than 57,360 six-cylinder cars were produced in 12 years.

## 100-Six and 3000 variants

### 3000 Mk I
In 1959 the 3000 took over from the 100-Six, complete with 124-bhp/2912-cc engine and front-wheel disc brakes; as before, built as two-seater or 2+2

### 3000 Mk II
Took over from the Mk I in 1961, this time with a three-SU/132-bhp engine; later cars had a new gearbox casing and true 'centre change' layout

### 3000 Mk II Convertible
In 1962, this was the 'Big Healey's' first and only external restyle, featuring a wraparound screen and wind-up door windows; engines reverted to two SU carbs and 131 bhp; all were 2+2s

### 3000 Mk III
Launched in 1964, combining 148 bhp, the 'Convertible' style, and a restyled fascia; except for first cars, also built with radius arm (instead of Panhard rod) rear axle location

## Specification (3000 Mk III)

**Engine:** inline six-cylinder, overhead-valve
**Bore × stroke:** 83.6 mm × 88.9 mm
**Capacity:** 2912 cc
**Maximum power:** 148 bhp
**Transmission:** four-speed manual gearbox, optional overdrive, rear-wheel drive
**Chassis:** steel box section side members
**Suspension:** independent front, coil springs; beam axle rear, leaf springs
**Brakes:** discs front, drum rear
**Bodywork:** steel open 2+2 seater
**Maximum speed:** 121 mph (195 km/h)

*Above: The first six-cylinder Austin-Healey was the 100-Six, with a 2.6-litre overhead-valve straight-six engine producing 102 bhp. It was built between 1956 and 1959.*

*Left: Early 100-Six models like this one were 2+2s; a pure two-seater was added later. The typical Austin-Healey bucket seats held driver and passenger in place perfectly.*

*Right: Last of the six-cylinder Austin-Healey line was the 3000 Mk III of 1964-67. It was an excellent performer, thanks to its 148-bhp straight-six.*

# Austin-Healey Sprite 1958-70

To follow up the success of the original Austin-Healey, BMC asked the Healey family to design a new small sports car, this time choosing developed versions of the engine, transmission and front suspension of the tiny Austin A35 saloon.

The result, launched in 1958, was the original Sprite, which combined small size and brisk performance with simplicity and an appealing character. As originally designed it was to have had foldaway headlamps, but these were turned down on cost grounds. Instead the headlamps stood proud of the sloping bonnet, and naturally the new car was nicknamed 'Frog Eye' (or, sometimes, 'bug eye'). On this car the entire front end – bonnet, grille *and* front wings – lifted up to give engine bay access. There was no exterior access to the stowage space in the tail.

Original cars had hard suspension with built-in rear axle steer caused by the use of quarter-elliptic leaf springs, and struggled to beat 80 mph, but this was only the beginning. Ten years later the Sprite could reach 95 mph, the handling was more predictable, the interior better trimmed (but still strictly two-seater), and there was a near-identical MG Midget derivative.

The only major change in looks came in 1961, when the car was given a conventional front end, with headlamps at the front corners, a separate opening bonnet, and a squared-up tail, complete with opening boot lid. In the meantime, the A-Series engine had been enlarged, and peak power had gone up to 65 bhp.

48,999 'Frog Eyes' and 80,360 restyled Sprites were produced from 1968-71.

### Sprite variants

### Sprite Mk II and Mk II 1100
The first (and only) major restyle of the car, in 1961, with conventional front wings and bonnet opening, stowage access via a boot lid; first with 46 bhp, later with 1098 cc/56 bhp and front disc brakes;

*Left: The original 'Frog Eye' Sprite of 1958 was an instant success. It was simple, being based on the Austin A35 engine and running gear, and consequently cheap. Handling was excellent for the time, making up for its lack of performance.*

also new MG Midget was 'badge engineered' version of this type

### Sprite Mk III and Mk IV

Mk III of 1964 had wind-up windows, half-elliptic leaf rear suspension and 59 bhp, whereas Mk IV of 1966 had 1275 cc/65 bhp, both faster and more civilised than before; MG Midget 'clones' also made; last made in 1970, though 1,022 'Austin'-badged Sprites followed in 1971

### Specification (Mk I)

**Engine:** inline four-cylinder, overhead-valve
**Bore × stroke:** 62.9 mm × 76.2 mm
**Capacity:** 948 cc
**Maximum power:** 43 bhp
**Transmission:** four-speed manual gearbox, rear-wheel drive

**Chassis:** steel unit-construction body/chassis assembly
**Suspension:** independent front, coil springs; beam axle rear, leaf springs
**Brakes:** drums front and rear
**Bodywork:** steel open two-seater, optional hardtop
**Maximum speed:** 80 mph (129 km/h)

*Right: The 'Frog Eye' Sprite's interior. In addition to a speedo and rev counter there was a temperature gauge and oil pressure gauge, but a heater was an optional extra. The indicators were worked by the top small switch exactly in the centre of the dashboard. The windscreen was completely flat and the bolt-on side screens were Perspex.*

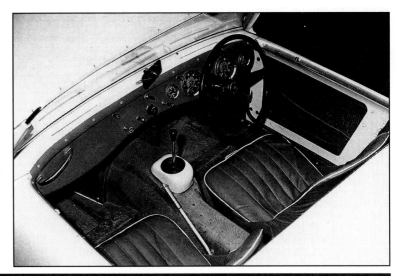

# Austro-Daimler

**A**ustria's most famous car was born in 1899, when Daimler of Germany set up a factory in Vienna to make their own cars. At first the Austrian Daimlers were straight copies of German types, and no special design work was involved.

All this changed in 1905, when Ferdinand Porsche became Austro-Daimler's technical director, and a year later the company also became financially independent of the German parent. With the combative Porsche in charge of the design team until 1922, Austro-Daimler produced a series of impressive sporting cars.

Early 'Porsche' Austro-Daimlers were strictly conventional machines, but worldwide fame arrived in 1910 with the birth of the famous 'Prince Henry' sports car. After World War I had been spent building military machines (including petrol-electric 'road trains'), the company then released the new AD and ADV types, which had overhead-cam six-cylinder engines. Dr Porsche then conceived the Sascha, which was a 1½-litre *voiturette* racing car.

Austro-Daimler's backers vetoed the Sascha, which caused Porsche to abandon his prestigious post. After his departure (to Daimler, in Germany), Austro-Daimler's technical reputation was underpinned by Karl Rabe and the ADM type (built from 1923 to 1928), which was a fine sports and touring car.

Another Austrian concern, Steyr, forged links with Austro-Daimler in 1929, and after both companies had suffered badly in the Depression a full merger took place in 1934. After Rabe moved out, to join his old boss in Stuttgart in the 1930s, the marque gradually ebbed away. The last Austro-Daimler car, the eight-cylinder ADR8, was built in 1936. After that, Steyr-Daimler-Puchs were smaller, cheaper models.

*Left: Austria is hardly renowned for its carmakers, and Austro-Daimler owed its existence to Daimler of Germany. Its finest creation was the ADM range of the 1920s, like this 1925 example.*

## Austro-Daimler Prince Henry 22/80 1910-14

This sports car was specifically designed to compete in the famous 'Prince Henry' reliability trial in Germany in 1910, and after it won convincingly it was put into limited production.

Like the famous Mercedes cars of the day (which were made by Daimler of Germany, though by 1910 there was no connection between the two firms), it was a big sporting car, and ran on a wheelbase of 118 in.

Although the general layout was conventional, with front-mounted engine, separate centre gearbox and rear-wheel drive, the Prince Henry had a very advanced engine, with overhead-camshaft valve gear, and it also remained faithful to chain drive to the rear wheels,

*Right: The limited-production Prince Henry was a monster car, with a big 5.7-litre overhead-cam four-cylinder engine, and was one of the last models to keep faith with the outmoded chain drive.*

which was already considered old hat by other designers. Porsche, for his part, did not think that shaft drive was yet reliable enough – though later types were produced with shaft drive.

### Specification (1911 22/80)

**Engine:** inline four-cylinder, overhead-camshaft
**Bore × stroke:** 105 mm × 165 mm
**Capacity:** 5715 cc

**Maximum power:** 95 bhp
**Transmission:** four-speed manual
**Chassis:** steel frame, with channel-section side members
**Suspension:** non-independent beam axle and semi-elliptic springs front; live

rear axle with cantilever leaf springs
**Brakes:** drums front and rear
**Bodywork:** aluminium and steel open four-seater tourer
**Maximum speed (approx):** 80 mph (129 km/h)

## Austro-Daimler Sascha 1919-26

The Sascha got its name from Count 'Sascha' Kolowrat, who financed this 90-mph sports racer designed by Ferdinand Porsche after the Austro-Daimler board lost interest.

Kolowrat was a wealthy industrialist and keen racer, and he realised the worth of the Porsche design with its light alloy twin-cam engine. The engine had such advanced features as screw-in cylinder liners, alloy pistons, dry-sump lubrication and dual ignition. As for the chassis, it was ahead of its time in having brakes on all four wheels.

The Sascha's best performance came in the 1922 Targa Florio, when Alfred Neubauer drove one of the 1100-cc models to a fine second place overall, beaten only by a 4.5-litre GP Mercedes. In addition, two of the remaining Saschas took first and second in the Touring Car class.

There was a larger, 1.5-litre version, but this could not rival the 1100-cc car's success rate that had seen it chalk up 43 wins in 1922.

### Specification

**Engine:** inline four-cylinder, twin-cam
**Bore × stroke:** 68 mm × 75 mm
**Capacity:** 1100 cc
**Maximum power:** 45 bhp
**Transmission:** four-speed manual
**Chassis:** pressed steel
**Suspension:** non-independent with semi-elliptic leaf springs and beam axle front, live axle and cantilever leaf springs rear
**Brakes:** drums all round
**Bodywork:** two-seater sports
**Maximum speed (approx):** 90 mph (145 km/h)

*Right: One of Ferdinand Porsche's most interesting early designs was the Sascha. It was light, nimble and fast, thanks to the advanced Porsche-designed 1.1-litre twin-cam four-cylinder engine. Its output of 45 bhp was excellent for the time, and enough to turn the Sascha into a class winner in the 1922 Targa Florio.*

## Austro-Daimler ADM 1923-26

*Left: The ADMII of 1925 was powered by a 2.5-litre straight-six. The staid looks of this car mask the fact that it had an advanced twin-cam engine. A sports model was built on the same chassis.*

Just before Dr Porsche left Austro-Daimler he inspired the design of a new range of ADM models, which were originally based on a lengthy 136-in wheelbase, and which used six-cylinder, inline twin-overhead-camshaft engines. The engine was a visual masterpiece, for it had an aluminium cylinder block, and vertical shaft drive to the overhead cams.

The original cars had a distinctive radiator style, more rounded than the Prince Henry type, complete with Austro-Daimler badging cast into the top, along with the well-known arrow motif.

ADMI became ADMII in 1925, when the car was also sold in sports form, and after 1926 it became ADMIII (also known as the 19-100 model) with a three-litre engine.

### ADMI variants

**Austro-Daimler ADMII**
This type appeared in 1925, a sports-type version of the original ADMI
**Austro-Daimler ADMIII**
From 1926 the ADM engine was enlarged to three litres, at which point the power output of the sports version rose to 100 bhp, top speed to 100 mph

### Specification (ADMI 1924)

**Engine:** inline six-cylinder, twin-cam
**Bore × stroke:** 70 mm × 110 mm
**Capacity:** 2540 cc
**Maximum power:** 75 bhp
**Transmission:** four-speed manual
**Chassis:** steel with channel-section side members
**Suspension:** non-independent with beam axle and semi-elliptic leaf springs front, live rear axle with cantilever leaf springs
**Brakes:** drums front and rear
**Bodywork:** choice of open touring, saloon or limousine types
**Maximum speed (approx):** 70 mph (113 km/h)

# Autocostruzione Societa per Azione

**A**utocostruzione Societa per Azione, or ASA, was a very short-lived supercar maker founded in 1962 to exploit a baby Ferrari prototype built with Enzo Ferrari's approval in 1958 and nicknamed the 'Ferrarina'. The car, which some likened to a scaled-down Testa Rossa, was exhibited at the 1961 Turin Show. Its styling attracted a lot of favourable comment but Enzo Ferrari was adamant that his company was not going to build it, and it had to find a home elsewhere.

Various racing drivers, including Baghetti and Bandini, were involved with the ASA company, the finance for which came from the Oronzio de Nora petro chemical business. It took until 1964 to get the ASA into serious production, and then only at the rate of one per week.

Most of the engineering of the car was the work of Ferrari engineer Giotto Bizzarini who was also responsible for the 145-mph Bizzarini GT Strada 5300 produced between 1963 and 1969. Bizzarini, it appeared, could turn his hand to anything. The ASA could hardly have been a greater contrast to the GT Strada 5300 in engine terms; the Strada used a big cast-iron pushrod American Chevrolet and the ASA a tiny twin-cam.

Diminutive sporting cars like the ASA were difficult to sell by the late 1960s, and after only 32 cars had been sold in the company's best market, the USA, production ended in 1966/7. That was despite the boost the ASA management hoped would come from running two 1292-cc six-cylinder cars at Le Mans in the 1966 24 Hours. At most 75 cars had been built, and final plans to make larger engined six-cylinder cars came to nothing.

## ASA 1000 GT 1962-67

Though Pininfarina bodied the original Ferrarina, it was Bertone who styled the GT and its ultra-rare roadster sisters. All were powered by four-cylinder twin-overhead camshaft 1032-cc engines developing 97 bhp at a remarkable 7,000 rpm. There was a four-speed synchromesh gearbox with overdrive on third and top. Suspension featured a live rear axle with coil springs and wishbone independent front suspension. The car weighed only 1,720 lb. That, combined with an aerodynamic shape honed in a wind tunnel, meant it was capable of 113 mph and a typical touring fuel consumption of better than 30 mpg.

### Specification

**Engine:** inline four-cylinder, twin-cam
**Bore × stroke:** 69 mm × 69 mm
**Capacity:** 1032 cc
**Maximum power:** 97 bhp
**Transmission:** four-speed manual with overdrive
**Chassis:** tubular spaceframe
**Suspension:** independent front with double wishbones and coil springs, live rear axle with trailing arms and coil springs
**Brakes:** discs all round
**Bodywork:** coupé
**Maximum speed (approx):** 113 mph (182 km/h)

*Right: Tiny the ASA 1000 GT may have been, but its interior was as fully equipped as any contemporary Ferrari, with such things as an oil temperature gauge to go along with the usual speedo, rev counter, water temperature and oil pressure gauges, and wood-rim wheel.*

*Above: The ASA 1000 GT was styled by Bertone with the mechanical design by Bizzarini. It was small and light enough, despite having only an 1032-cc engine (albeit one with 97 bhp), to be able to reach 113 mph. This particular example was auctioned by Christie's in England in 1990 for an amazingly low figure, reflecting just how few people are aware of the marque.*

# Avanti Motor Corp.

T he origins of this marque lay with Studebaker, an American carmaker based in South Bend, Indiana, USA. Studebaker, which had been in the motor industry since 1902, remained stubbornly independent many years before finally joining with Packard in 1954.

Although Studebaker did not make sports cars, by the 1950s their conventional models were smartly styled by the extrovert Raymond Loewy, some of the coupés being impressively sleek.

By the early 1960s Studebaker-Packard was in financial trouble and, in a last-gasp attempt to produce a prestige product, unveiled the Avanti coupé in 1962. It was very fast, and by North American standards it was unconventional (it was only the second North American production car to use glassfibre bodywork), but it could not long delay Studebaker's bankruptcy, which followed in 1964.

The Avanti therefore went into hibernation, only to be revived in 1965. Ex-Studebaker dealers Nate Altman and Leo Newman bought the surviving tooling, and started up again in a corner of the old factory, fitted a Chevrolet V8 engine instead of the original unit, and called the reborn car the Avanti II.

Production was always limited, for there was no attempt to set up a dealer chain, and there was no advertising. Fewer than 200 cars a year were sold throughout the 1970s and early 1980s, and only the single coupé style was on offer. Even though finances were always precarious, and management changed several times, the Avanti marque refused to die, and eventually staggered on into the 1990s.

*Above: The original Raymond Loewy Studebaker Avanti design dates back to 1962, but, extraordinarily, it lives on into the late 1990s.*

As with Britain's Morgan, the 1990 Avanti was recognisably the same as the one built 30 years earlier, though most individual parts had been changed. By 1990 assembly had moved to Youngstown, Ohio, and production had risen to 250 cars a year. Cabriolet *and* four-door saloon versions had been added to the range, and the latest fully de-toxed five-litre Chevrolet V8 engine produced 172 bhp.

Then, as before, the Avanti had a tiny 'cult' corner of the market, which it seemed sure to keep in the future.

## Avanti II 1965-present

The Studebaker Avanti, launched in April 1962, had dropped out of production in 1964, but was revived as Avanti II at the end of 1965. Except that the V8 engine was changed from a 4.7-litre Studebaker to 5.3-litre Chevrolet, there was little difference between the two models.

The chassis was a shortened (109-in wheelbase) version of the Lark Convertible's frame, and featured front disc brakes, stiffened suspension with front and rear anti-roll bars, and power-assisted steering.

The body was a close-coupled four-seater coupé, made entirely from GRP (glass-reinforced plastic, or glassfibre), lower, smoother and visually more restrained than the average American car of the period.

The most noticeable styling details were the complete lack of a front intake grille and the short, well-rounded, tail. Although there was only one model of Avanti II at first, the customer could choose any colour, any trim material, and any combination of these, just so long as he would pay, and be prepared to wait.

Although the exterior style might have been basically suitable for a European car, the interior style was unmistakably North American, with a flamboyant, fully-equipped instrument panel, glitzy steering wheel, and squashy seats.

Although Steve Blake bought the company in 1982 from Arnold Altman (brother of the founder) and took the old car further upmarket (the interior, in particular, looked much more restrained than before), *total* Avanti II production did not exceed 2,500 until 1983. By this time, too, the cars had five-litre engines, were invariably equipped with automatic transmission, the weight had gone up to meet the latest safety legislation, and the Avanti was not really as fast as it looked.

After a Cabriolet version had been introduced in 1985 Blake ran out of money, but once again the concept was rescued by new management. Assembly moved out of the century-old building at South Bend to Youngstown, and in 1989 a longer-wheelbase four-door saloon version was put on sale.

### Avanti II variants

#### Cabriolet
Mechanically identical to the latest coupé, the Cabriolet arrived in 1985, sharing the same chassis and running gear; top speed was about 118 mph

#### Saloon
This was introduced for 1989, on a longer (116-in) version of the chassis, but with similar running gear. Front and rear styling was unchanged, but the cabin was longer, with four passenger doors and a more spacious rear seat

*Above: Avanti II production branched out in 1985 when the Cabriolet was introduced, based on the same running gear as the coupé. This is the 1991 model as exhibited at the Detroit Show.*

*Left: Even in 1991 the coupé's lines are recognisably those of the original Loewy design.*

### Specification (1966 version)
**Engine:** Chevrolet V8, overhead-valve
**Bore × stroke:** 101.6 mm × 82.55 mm
**Capacity:** 5355 cc
**Maximum power:** 300 bhp
**Transmission:** four-speed manual, or automatic
**Chassis:** separate steel frame, box-section side members
**Suspension:** independent front with wishbones and coil springs, live rear axle with semi-elliptic leaf springs and tubular dampers
**Brakes:** discs front, drums rear
**Bodywork:** glassfibre 2+2
**Maximum speed:** 135 mph (217 km/h)

# Ballot (Moteurs Ballot)

**B**allot manufactured cars for a relatively short period, from 1919 to 1932, in fact; but the company had been in existence for some time before that. From 1905 the brothers Edouard and Maurice Ballot had been making engines, both marine and automotive: the marine element was strong, as demonstrated in the use of an anchor in the Ballot badge, while their car engines were good enough to be supplied to the likes of Delage.

The trigger that began car manufacture was a decision to enter the 1919 Indianapolis 500, and a car was designed (by ex-Peugeot designer Ernest Henry) and built in just 101 days. For the next few years Ballot built advanced and successful four-cylinder sports racing cars until deciding to build a more affordable model, the 2LT (2-Litre Tourer). That was then developed into the somewhat more sporty 2LTS. The four-cylinder model

*Left: The anchor on the Ballot badge hints strongly at Ballot's nautical involvement. In fact, the company made marine engines long before they began car production in 1919.*

was to be discarded in favour of a two-litre (1991-cc) straight-six for 1927 but never went into production. Instead Ballot produced a straight-eight in the form of the RH, with a 2618-cc engine, subsequently enlarged to 2874 cc and then 3054 cc, but the heavy RH was not a success.

Like many other companies, Ballot ran into trouble in the Depression and were taken over, by Hispano-Suiza.

## Ballot straight-eight 1919

*Left: The superb five-litre straight-eight twin-cam Ballots were designed to win the 1919 Indianapolis 500, but wheel failure brought disaster.*

Ballot's first car was a superb model. Four five-litre straight-eights were built for the 1919 Indianapolis 500 and their engines were an engineering masterpiece by the famous ex-Peugeot designer Ernest Henry.

The design was basically two of Henry's 2.5-litre Grand Prix twin-cams joined on a common alloy crankcase. It was a long-stroke design with a bore of 74 mm and stroke of almost double that, at 140 mm, to give a displacement of 4816 cc. Four-valve technology was understood even in 1919 and the Ballot had 32 valves, the four-per-cylinder being operated by twin chain-drive overhead cams. Given the specification the output of 130 bhp at 3,000 rpm might seem low to our eyes, but was excellent at the time.

The five-litre really should have won its debut race at Indianapolis, but it was discovered to have the wrong final drive ratio for the circuit, and in a desperate effort to overcome that, smaller-diameter American wire wheels were fitted. The new wheels proved too weak for the car's performance and they collapsed after just 26 laps. Although the biggest-engined Ballot raced on over the years, its career was dogged by ill fortune and it never achieved what its specification suggested it should.

### Specification
**Engine:** inline straight-eight, twin-cam
**Bore × stroke:** 74 mm × 140 mm
**Capacity:** 4816 cc
**Maximum power:** 130 bhp
**Transmission:** four-speed manual
**Chassis:** pressed steel with cross-members
**Suspension:** non-independent with semi-elliptic leaf springs and friction dampers front and rear
**Brakes:** drums front and rear
**Bodywork:** alloy racer
**Maximum speed (approx):** N/A

# Bentley Motors Ltd

Walter Owen Bentley was born in 1888, started his career as an apprentice in the Great Northern Railway workshops in Doncaster, and entered the motor trade in 1910. From 1912 he started importing French DFP cars to Britain. During World War I he designed successful aero engines – then in 1919 he set up his own company, Bentley Motors Ltd.

Together with his brother (H.M.) and designer F.T. Burgess (who had developed the pre-war racing Humber models), W.O. set out to build a fine sports car. Basing his company on a new factory in North London (backing onto the corners of the Edgware Road and the then still incomplete North Circular Road), he soon developed the 3-litre. The first cars were delivered in 1921.

Bentley Motors was always short of working capital, and because the cars were expensive sales were slow. Looking back, it is amazing to see that the independent Bentley concern built cars only from 1921 to 1931 – and that there were only five models, all inter-related.

In almost every case, however, the cars were beautifully built, fast for their day, and soon established a motor-racing record. The first (three-litre) engine, inspired by the pre-war Peugeot and Mercedes racing designs, had an overhead cam and four valves per cylinder.

To supplement the 3-litre, Bentley then introduced the 6½-litre in 1925, this having a six-cylinder engine with different valve gear operation. The 4½-litre model of 1927 used a four-cylinder version of this unit, the 8-litre of 1930-1931 was a 'final statement' of six-cylinder development, and the short-lived 4-litre of 1931 was really a smaller, cheaper, version of the 8-litre, with an odd inlet-over-exhaust-valve six-cylinder engine that bore no relation to previous Bentley designs.

The Bentley was the epitome of 'vintage' motoring in the 1920s, and its reputation as a road car was underpinned by the exploits of the 'works' racing team. 3-litre types won the Le Mans 24 Hours, in 1924 and 1927, a 4½-litre car won in 1928, and a Speed Six 6½-litre won in 1929 and 1930. By that time Bentley had a firm grip on the French classic event, and retired while on top.

In a decade Bentley ran through several tranches of capital, rarely making profits. Playboy-turned-racing-driver Woolf Barnato financed the company after 1926 and became its chairman, but eventually declined to support its losses. In 1931 the Receiver was called in and, after a sordid courtroom battle, Bentley's assets were taken over by Rolls-Royce.

Except in name only, there was no connection between the W.O. Bentley cars, and the 'Rolls-Bentley' which first appeared in 1933.

Since 1933, every Bentley has been a car designed by Rolls-Royce. Up to 1939 Bentleys (colloquially known as 'Rolls-Bentleys') were built at Derby, but after World War II production was concentrated in Crewe.

Thus it was that pre-war 'Derby' Bentleys were related to Rolls-Royce 20/25 and 25/30 types; Mk VI, S-Series, T-Series and Mulsanne models were close to the Rolls-Royce Silver Dawn, Silver Cloud, Silver Shadow and Silver Spirit families.

Until 1939 all such Bentleys, dubbed 'The Silent Sports Car', were fitted with coachwork by specialists. From 1946 there was always a 'Standard Steel' four-door saloon body, fitted at Crewe, in the range but until the late 1960s a proportion were also produced with special body styles.

Technical advance was steady, but at times behind general trends. The 1930s cars were fast, but lacked independent front suspension. Automatic transmission came in 1952, but cars still had separate chassis, drum brakes and beam rear axles until 1965.

*Top: The winged Bentley badge appeared in various colours; 'Red Label' cars were the Speed models, while 'Green Label' cars were the Super Sports models.*

*Above: The engine was the heart of all pre-war Bentleys before the Rolls-Royce takeover. This is a 6½-litre from the Speed Six, built from 1926 to 1930. Even before this time Bentley engines had four valves per cylinder.*

*Left: The tall, imposing radiator grille was a Bentley hallmark. This one is from a Speed Six; Bentley made no concession to aerodynamics, relying on sheer power instead.*

The most exciting Bentleys were the special editions, such as the Continental coupés of 1952-55 and – from the late 1960s – the drophead and coupé versions of the T-Series. Even so from 1945 to 1980 a Bentley became more and more like a Rolls-Royce; as a consequence, sales dropped steadily away. Then, for the 1980s, there was a change in marketing strategy. First of all the company introduced a turbocharged model, the Mulsanne Turbo, then the Bentley Eight and the better roadholding of the 'R' specification.

Rolls-Royce and Bentley were taken over by Volkswagen in 1998. BMW will supply engines until 2002 for the Rolls Royce, and until the Bentley Arnage goes out of production. It is the intention to switch names in 2003 with VW preceding the Bentley brand and a new Rolls-Royce Motors being set up by BMW.

## Bentley 3-litre 1921-28

The first Bentley 3-litre chassis, a partly-completed mock-up, was shown in November 1919. *The Autocar* tested a prototype in 1920, and first deliveries took place in September 1921. The car remained in production until 1928, by which time 1,691 cars of all types had been produced.

The 3-litre was a rugged design whose only innovation was a massive and beautifully detailed four-cylinder engine, which had been inspired by pre-World War I racing designs. The overhead camshaft valve gear was driven off

the nose of the crankshaft by a vertical shaft and gears, and there were four valves per cylinder. Bentley enthusiasts like to point out, with a smile, that 'four-valve' technology eventually percolated to family cars more than 60 years later....

*The first Bentley model was the four-cylinder 3-litre. It was capable of nearly 80 mph from its overhead-cam four-valve-per-cylinder engine; 1,691 cars were built in all.*

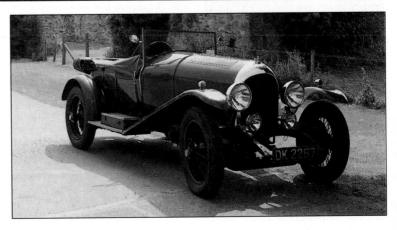

The chassis was a conventional 'ladder style' design, with hard leaf spring suspension of the axles, and rod operation of the big drum brakes. The gearbox was separately mounted, with the change speed lever and the handbrake on the right side of the driver's seat. Bentley was so confident that there was a five-year warranty for the running gear.

The first model was the Short Standard chassis, on a 117.5-in wheelbase that sold for £1,100 (body extra). This was soon followed by the Long Standard (130.5-in wheelbase, £895 chassis price), and eventually by the Supersports (108-in wheelbase, £1,050). Important sub-types were the TT Replica, and the Speed Models.

Most 3-litres had blue radiator badges (hence the title 'Blue Label'), but Speed Models were 'Red Labels', and Super Sports models were 'Green Labels'.

*This is a short chassis variant on the 3-litre chassis, a Red Label Speed model built by Vanden Plas and dating from 1926, two years before 3-litre production ended.*

Sales fell away after the mid-1920s, and stopped after the 4½-litre model became available.

### Bentley 3-litre variants
**Super Sports**

Introduced in 1925 and available for two years, this was the 'Green Label' model, an 85-bhp version of the car, built on the shortest, 108-in wheelbase, with a top speed of 100 mph

### Specification

**Engine:** inline four-cylinder, overhead-cam
**Bore × stroke:** 80 mm × 149 mm
**Capacity:** 2996 cc
**Maximum power:** 70-85 bhp
**Transmission:** four-speed manual
**Chassis:** separate steel frame with tubular and pressed cross-members
**Suspension:** non-independent with beam axle and semi-elliptic leaf springs front, live rear axle with semi-elliptic leaf springs
**Brakes:** drums front and rear
**Bodywork:** choice of open four/five-seater, sports, saloon, or limousine
**Maximum speed (approx):** 80 mph (129 km/h)

# Bentley 4½-litre 1927-31

The 4½-litre Bentley went on sale in 1927, six years after the original four-cylinder Bentley (the 3-litre), and was an enterprising amalgam of 3-litre and 6½-litre features.

Like the 3-litre (which it soon replaced), the 4½-litre had a four-cylinder engine, but its engine included several 'six' features, including the same bore and stroke. It retained the original 3-litre-type camshaft drive, but had a reinforced crankshaft, and used the 6½-litre's connecting rods and pistons.

As with the 3-litre, there was a choice of wheelbase length – 117.5 in or 130.5 in – with a developed version of the 3-litre frame being used, and coachbuilders produced a variety of different styles, both open and closed, sporting or touring, behind the 'black label' radiator.

All in all there were 713 4½-litre chassis, including 50 of the charismatic 'Blower' type; only nine cars had the short-wheelbase chassis.

*Bentley built over 700 4½-litres between 1927 and 1931; this open version dates from 1928.*

### Bentley 4½-litre variants

**Supercharged ('Blower') model**
This car was inspired by racing driver Sir Henry Birkin, the engine being supercharged and modified by Amherst Villiers. Although W.O. Bentley disapproved of the work, he was persuaded to lay down 50 such cars, built between 1929 and 1931

### Specification

**Engine:** inline four-cylinder, overhead-cam
**Bore × stroke:** 100 mm × 140 mm
**Capacity:** 4398 cc
**Maximum power:** 105-110 bhp
**Transmission:** four-speed manual
**Chassis:** separate steel frame with tubular and pressed cross-members
**Suspension:** non-independent with beam axle and semi-elliptic leaf springs front, live rear axle with semi-elliptic leaf springs
**Brakes:** drums front and rear
**Bodywork:** choice of open four/five-seater, sports, saloon, or limousine
**Maximum speed (approx):** 90 mph (145 km/h)

*Left: One of the 4½-litres is seen at Le Mans in 1928; Barnato's car won the French classic at an average speed of 69.11 mph.*

*Below: The 4½-litre engine was an overhead-cam 16-valve four producing a maximum of 110 bhp.*

*Bottom: The most famous variation on the 4½-litre car was the supercharged 'Blower' Bentley; only 50 were built.*

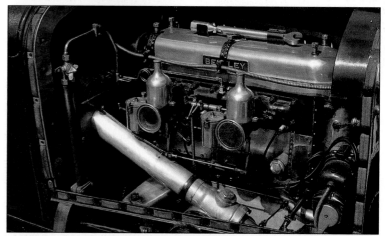

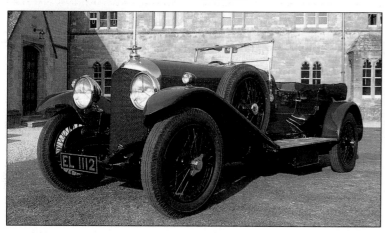

## Bentley 6½-litre 1926-30

The six-cylinder Bentley was developed as a truly high-speed machine, and in limousine form was a potential competitor to the Rolls-Royces and Napiers of the day. Although its chassis followed the same general design as that of the 3-litre, the engine was different in many ways.

The 'six' was, of course, much more bulky than the 'four', and its single overhead camshaft was driven by a clever but complex triple eccentric at the rear of the block – W.O. had clearly remembered something from his railway train days. Compared with the 3-litre four, the six had a bigger cylinder bore and a shorter stroke. It was a stronger and ultimately more tuneable engine, which became very successful indeed in long-distance motor racing events.

Sales began in 1926, and continued to 1930. A total of 545 cars was made, of which 182 were the even faster and more sporting Speed Six chassis. In four years no fewer than five different wheelbase lengths were offered, and total prices (including bodywork) varied between £1,975 and £2,780.

*Bentleys were bodied by all the famous coachbuilders of the day. This Speed Six is the work of the English firm Barker, and is a very rare design indeed – Barker's creations were normally far more staid than this one, which was photographed in California.*

### 6½-litre variants

#### Standard
This was announced in 1925, before the arrival of the Speed Six, on a choice of three wheelbases, with a 147-bhp version of the engine; most of these chassis had spacious saloon bodies

#### 8-litre
The magnificent 8-litre had a massive new chassis frame, on a choice of 144-in or 156-in wheelbases, but the running gear was really modified from the 6½-litre model; only 50 cars were made in 1930 and 1931, most with lofty saloon bodies, but the top speed was a genuine 100 mph

### Specification
**Engine:** inline six-cylinder, overhead-cam
**Bore × stroke:** 100 mm × 140 mm
**Capacity:** 6597 cc
**Maximum power:** 160 bhp
**Transmission:** four-speed manual
**Chassis:** separate steel frame with tubular and pressed cross-members
**Suspension:** non-independent with beam axle and semi-elliptic leaf springs front, live rear axle with semi-elliptic leaf springs
**Brakes:** drums front and rear
**Bodywork:** choice of open four/five-seater, sports, saloon, or limousine
**Maximum speed (approx):** 90 mph (145 km/h)

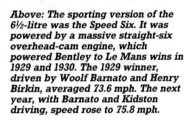

*Above: The sporting version of the 6½-litre was the Speed Six. It was powered by a massive straight-six overhead-cam engine, which powered Bentley to Le Mans wins in 1929 and 1930. The 1929 winner, driven by Woolf Barnato and Henry Birkin, averaged 73.6 mph. The next year, with Barnato and Kidston driving, speed rose to 75.8 mph.*

*Left: Most Bentleys had conservative and heavy closed saloon bodies; the more elegant open versions, like this Vanden Plas Speed Six, are the exception. The instrumentation was truly comprehensive.*

*Top: This 8-litre was once W.O. Bentley's own car. It is a 1930 model with Mulliner body. Despite the upright styling the huge eight-litre engine could power it to over 100 mph.*

*Above: This was Bentley director and racing driver Woolf Barnato's own Speed Six, built for him by Gurney Nutting to Barnato's own brief. The sloping roof meant that there was room for only one rear seat, which was mounted sideways!*

# Bentley 3½-litre 1933-37

*In 1936 the Bentley 3½-litre evolved into the 4¼-litre model. Both were powered by overhead-valve Rolls-Royce engines, as Rolls-Royce had by now taken over Bentley. This convertible is easily the most elegant of the range.*

The first Bentley to be designed by Rolls-Royce appeared in October 1933, on a separate chassis, and powered by a much-modified version of the Rolls-Royce 20/25-hp engine. Road tests showed that it could exceed 90 mph, which made it a very fast car by 1930s standards.

As with all Rolls-Royces of the period, there was no such thing as a standard body style. Instead the company delivered complete rolling chassis to a coachbuilder, where client and specialist agreed on a body style to be employed. Naturally there were favoured builders – notably Park Ward, Gurney Nutting and H. J. Mulliner – but everything from a sleek four-seater tourer to a five-seater limousine could be found. Chassis prices started at £1,100, complete cars costing up to £1,500.

Weights crept up over the years, so from 1936 a 4¼-litre engine was offered

to counter this. From 1938 the gearbox ratios were changed to give higher gearing – and the model became known as the 'overdrive' type. Production of about 2,500 cars ran out in 1939, just as World War II was beginning.

## Bentley 3½-litre variants

### 4¼-litre and 'Overdrive' 4¼-litre
The 4¼-litre was introduced in 1936, as a natural evolution of the 3½-litre, with a

4257-cc engine, but the same basic chassis and wide choice of body styles as before; the 'Overdrive' model followed in 1938, with different (higher) gear ratios.

## Specification

**Engine:** inline-six, overhead-valve
**Bore × stroke:** 82.5 mm × 114.3 mm
**Capacity:** 3669 cc
**Maximum power:** not revealed
**Transmission:** four-speed manual

gearbox, rear-wheel drive
**Chassis:** separate steel frame, channel-section side members
**Suspension:** beam axle front with semi-elliptic leaf springs, live rear axle with semi-elliptic leaf springs
**Brakes:** drums front and rear
**Bodywork:** by specialist coachbuilders, open or closed, sporting, touring or limousine
**Maximum speed (approx):** 92 mph (148 km/h)

# Bentley Mk VI 1946-51

Before the war, Rolls-Royce set out on a rationalisation policy. The result was that cars were assembled at Crewe from 1945. Henceforth all types had to share the same basic engine and chassis and, for the first time, there was to be a 'Standard Steel' body shell, a four-door saloon style, though coachbuilt shells were still available at higher cost.

Most of the running gear, including independent front suspension, was new, though the engine and transmission were direct evolutions of those laid down in the late 1930s.

Cars of the Mk VI type were built for nine years, though an enlarged (4½-litre) engine appeared in 1951. The body was given an extended tail in 1952 for the R-Type, along with GM-type Hydramatic automatic transmission.

More than 9,000 of this family were produced, but among many special styles the most exciting was the R-type Continental, with a lower, lighter and sleeker body style, of which a mere 208 were built.

## Bentley Mk IV variants

### R-type Continental
From 1952 the 4½-litre Mk VI was given long-tail bodywork, along with optional four-speed automatic transmission; R-type Continentals had this chassis, but low and sleek two-door coupé styles, mostly by H. J. Mulliner

## Specification (original Mk VI)

**Engine:** inline-six, overhead-inlet, side exhaust valve
**Bore × stroke:** 88.9 mm × 114.3 mm
**Capacity:** 4257 cc

*Above: This 1951 example of the 4.2-litre six-cylinder Mk VI has bodywork by the Swiss coachbuilder Graber, better known in Britain for his later Alvis designs.*

**Maximum power:** not revealed, but approx 132 bhp
**Transmission:** four-speed manual gearbox, rear-wheel drive
**Chassis:** separate steel frame, channel section side members
**Suspension:** independent front, coil springs, live rear axle with semi-elliptic leaf springs
**Brakes:** drums front and rear
**Bodywork:** steel four-door saloon, other styles from coachbuilders
**Maximum speed (approx):** 100 mph (161 km/h)

*Above: The Bentley R-type Continental had a distinctive sloping rear. The sleek body design was by Mulliner and the car could reach 120 mph.*

*Below: This unique sedanca de ville body on the Mk VI chassis was built for the Maharajah of Mysore in 1949.*

# Bentley S-Series 1955-65

Rolls-Royce introduced a new generation of cars in 1955, retaining the engine and transmission of the R-types but using a new chassis and a bulky new body style, on a slightly shorter wheelbase.

The S-Series Bentley was almost identical to the Rolls-Royce Silver Cloud, but at least there were special body styles, and S-type Continentals as well. When a brand new aluminium V8 engine appeared in 1959 the Bentley became SII, and when a four-headlamp nose style was added in 1962 the family progressed to SIII.

Along the way manual transmission disappeared, power-assisted steering and air-conditioning arrived, and in the end more than 7,500 cars of this type were produced.

## Bentley SII variants

### SI model

The original type, built from 1955 to 1959, had a 4.9-litre six-cylinder engine, producing about 178 bhp

*Right: Although the S-type Bentleys were built on the same chassis as the Rolls-Royce Silver Cloud, Bentleys had the advantage of body styles like this Continental version of the SI, from 1956. It was powered by a 4.9-litre straight-six overhead valve engine producing around 178 bhp.*

### SIII model

Except for a four-headlamp front style and a 220 bhp engine, this 1962-1965 model was essentially much the same as the SII

## Specification

**Engine:** V8, overhead-valve
**Bore × stroke:** 104.1 mm × 91.4 mm
**Capacity:** 6230 cc
**Maximum power:** not revealed, but approx 200 bhp
**Transmission:** four-speed automatic transmission, rear-wheel drive

**Chassis:** separate steel frame, box section side members
**Suspension:** independent front, coil springs, live rear axle with semi-elliptic leaf springs

**Brakes:** drums front and rear
**Bodywork:** steel four-door saloon, other styles from coachbuilders
**Maximum speed (approx):** 115 mph (185 km/h)

# Bentley T-Series 1965–91

For 1966 and beyond, Rolls-Royce introduced a radically new design, their first based on a steel monocoque structure, their first with all-independent suspension (which also featured self-levelling), and also their first with disc brakes. Only the V8 engine and automatic transmission were carried over from the old models. The style was big and square, though dignified and impressive, the character a long way from the sporting Bentleys of the 1930s.

The design changed very gradually in 15 years, with a 6.7-litre engine, a modern GM automatic transmission, and

rack-and-pinion steering all being adopted. In 1980 the T-Series gave way to the new Mulsanne, which retained the same 'chassis' under a new style.

From the late 1960s there were special two-door coupé and drophead types, these being renamed to become the Corniche in 1971.

## Bentley T-Series variants

Mulliner/Park Ward two-door types were introduced in 1966, with two-door coupé/convertible styles on the standard underpan; they were

renamed Corniche in 1971, the convertible becoming the Continental in 1984.

## Specification (1965 T1)

**Engine:** V8, overhead-valve
**Bore × stroke:** 104.1 mm × 91.4 mm
**Capacity:** 6230 cc
**Maximum power:** not revealed, but approx 200 bhp
**Transmission:** four-speed automatic

transmission, rear-wheel drive
**Chassis:** steel unit-construction body/chassis assembly
**Suspension:** independent front, coil springs, independent rear with semi-trailing arms and coil springs
**Brakes:** discs front and rear
**Bodywork:** steel four-door saloon, some other styles from coachbuilders
**Maximum speed (approx):** 115 mph (185 km/h)

*Below: This T-Series Bentley drophead Corniche was introduced in 1971, built on the same floorpan as the standard Bentley saloon. Power came from a 6.2-litre overhead-valve V8 engine.*

# Bentley Mulsanne 1980–98

When Rolls-Royce introduced the Silver Spirit in 1980, the badge-engineered Bentley equivalent was named the Mulsanne. The basic 'chassis' platform as before was retained, but this time covered with a more curvaceous body shell.

Two years later the revival of Bentley began, first with the introduction of the turbocharged Mulsanne Turbo model, and later with the R (R standing for roadholding) suspension pack. The Bentley Eight (mechanically the same, but with the simpler equipment) helped round out a more interesting range.

The old Corniche carried on, becoming the Continental from 1984, by that time having the same 'chassis' as the Mulsanne. As part of the drive to make the Bentley image more sporty, the rather wallowing ride inherited from its Rolls-Royce parent was dramatically stiffened in the more powerful Turbo R model, producing a car that could be hustled around corners at undignified speed. The Mulsanne was superseded in 1998 by the Arnage, powered by a new 4.5-litre V8 turbo engine developed by BMW and Cosworth.

### Bentley Mulsanne variants

#### Turbo, Eight and Turbo R

The Mulsanne Turbo, introduced in 1982, had a turbocharged 298-bhp version of the Mulsanne's V8; the Eight, introduced in 1984, was a simplified version of the original Mulsanne; the Turbo R was even more powerful than the Turbo (333 bhp), and had firmer and more sporty handling characteristics

### Specification (Turbo)

**Engine:** V8, overhead-valve
**Bore × stroke:** 104 mm × 99 mm
**Capacity:** 6750 cc
**Maximum power:** 298 bhp
**Transmission:** three-speed automatic transmission, rear-wheel drive
**Chassis:** steel unit construction body/chassis assembly
**Suspension:** independent front, coil springs; independent rear, coil springs
**Brakes:** discs front and rear
**Bodywork:** steel four-door saloon
**Maximum speed (approx):** 135 mph (217 km/h)

*Until the Arnage appeared in 1998, fastest of all Bentley Mulsanne and Turbo range was the Turbo R variant, with a top speed of over 140 mph.*

# Bentley Continental R 1991–present

Launched at the 1991 Geneva Show, the new Bentley Continental R was the first Bentley for almost 40 years that was distinctly a Bentley rather than a Rolls-Royce in disguise.

The original Continental R was a very desirable limited-edition model produced initially only for export, 208 of which were built between 1952 and 1955. In the 1990s, the name and image seemed ripe for revival. The Continental R took over six years to design and produce following the successful showing of a concept coupé at Geneva in 1985, but is mechanically very similar to the existing Turbo with the same Turbo R engine. Differences such as the greatly improved aerodynamics give a top speed of 145 mph. That is electronically governed – potentially the Continental R is even quicker than that, with a manufacturer's quoted figure of 6.6 seconds for the 0-60 mph dash, despite a truly massive

*Above: The Continental R's two-door coupé body improves on the brick-like aerodynamics of the Turbo R, and top speed is an artificially limited 145 mph.*

kerb weight of 5340 lb. The Sedanca Coupé joined the Continental range in 1998.

### Specification

**Engine:** V8, overhead-valve
**Bore × stroke:** 104 mm × 99 mm
**Capacity:** 6750 cc
**Maximum power:** 333 bhp
**Transmission:** four-speed automatic
**Chassis:** steel unit construction body/chassis
**Suspension:** independent with wishbones, coil springs, anti-roll bar and electronically controlled dampers front; semi-trailing arms, coil springs, anti-roll bar and electronically controlled

dampers rear; automatic levelling system
**Brakes:** discs front and rear
**Bodywork:** steel two-door coupé
**Maximum speed (approx):** 145 mph (233 km/h)

*Bentley followed fashion in giving the Continental R bulged wheel arches to accommodate wider, 255/60 ZR16, tyres. Continental T was a faster derivative, at 170 mph.*

# Benz & Cie

T hree pioneers – Benz, along with Daimler and Otto – were the most important personalities behind the birth of motoring in the 1880s. Otto invented the four-stroke engine which still bears his name, but it was Carl Benz and Gottlieb Daimler, both of them German, who independently invented the motor car itself. Even so, their businesses did not get together, to found Mercedes-Benz, for another 40 years.

By the 1880s the railway already provided an excellent form of mass transportation, but for individual travel there was only the horse or horse-drawn carriage.

Then, in Germany, came the inventions that were to change the world. Carl Benz, an accomplished engineer, set up his own business in Mannheim in the 1870s, and in the same period Dr Nikolous Otto refined Etienne Lenoir's internal combustion engine to produce the 'four-stroke cycle'.

Benz, quite separately from Gottlieb Daimler (who lived in Cannstatt), started designing his first car, a tricycle, in 1883-84, a crude device that made its first faltering test runs in 1885. It was regularly seen on the streets of Mannheim in 1886 and was first exhibited at the Munich Exhibition in 1888, and the first replicas were sold a short time afterwards.

The original tricycle was miraculous because it worked, though no-one could have claimed it to be fully developed or fully reliable. It was, however, the world's first 'horseless carriage', and was vitally important because of that. In the next 30 years Benz grew to become one of Europe's most important carmakers. Although Carl Benz carried on building gasoline-driven stationary engines in the 1890s, he soon started making four-wheel cars, the Victoria and the Velo models of the 1890s being two of the world's first series-production models. By 1900 Benz was making 600 cars a year.

Benz, however, had become complacent. Rival manufacturers began to produce better, more forward-looking designs, so sales of belt-driven Benz models sagged. At the time, too, Carl Benz's refusal to enter his cars in motor racing harmed the company's image. By 1903 sales were down to 172 cars in a year, a new Parcifal model had flopped, and a new start had to be made.

In the next few years a series of modern Benz models appeared, spearheaded by the use of new engines and shaft-driven transmissions. This was the period in which Hans Nibel (later to become the top engineer at Mercedes-Benz) joined the company as the chief engineer. Carl Benz and his sons left the business that he had founded in 1906, yet he lived on, distinguished and well regarded, until 1929.

At the end of the 1900s, however, Benz reverted to chain final drive, but only for their very powerful cars (Grand Prix cars in 1908, and the 'Blitzen' Benz which followed it) where shaft drive was not yet considered reliable enough to cope.

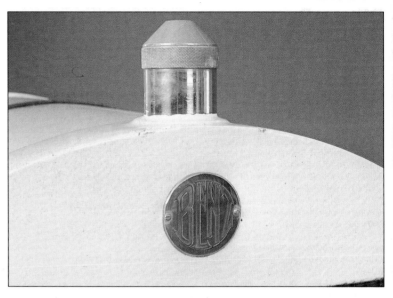

*An early Benz badge. Later examples incorporated a laurel wreath around the name to commemorate Benz's racing successes.*

The Blitzen Benz was a magnificent monster, in every respect, a sort of supercar of which any manufacturer would be proud. By 1909 standards its 120-mph top speed was quite phenomenal, creating as big a stir as would a 250-mph car in the 1990s.

Between 1908 and 1914 Benz produced no fewer than 23 different four-cylinder-engined models, some with shaft drive, some with chain drive.

During World War I, Benz were kept busy producing trucks and related vehicles, along with a variety of six-, eight- and 12-cylinder aeroplane engines. After the war, though, the Mannheim-based company was hampered by labour problems, and Germany's economy was in ruins.

Strangely enough, the most famous Benz-engined car of this period was a 'special' – the *Chitty-Chitty-Bang-Bang* Brooklands race car, which combined an old Mercedes chassis with an 18.9-litre six-cylinder Benz aero engine!

In the early 1920s both Benz and Daimler (who built Mercedes cars) saw that they would have to co-operate if they were to survive. Germany was in a terrifying inflationary spiral, which destroyed all sensible investment programmes. Talks began in 1923, an 'Agreement of Mutual Intent' was signed in May 1924, and a final merger took place in June 1926.

Almost immediately Benz and Daimler (Mercedes) began to bring their engineering, styling and images together. Although the vee-profile Benz radiator was chosen for the next generation of Mercedes-Benz cars, now it was topped by a three-pointed (Mercedes) star, and technical direction came from Stuttgart.

## Benz Tricycle 1885

*The world's very first car. Three wheels were used because no suitable steering arrangement existed for a two-wheel axle. Power came from a mid-mounted 1.5-bhp single-cylinder engine which gave a top speed of 10 mph.*

Carl Benz's first-ever 'horseless carriage' was what we would now call a mid-engined machine. Because Benz was inventing an entirely new mode of transport (and he did not then know what his contemporary, Gottlieb Daimler, was planning), he chose a three-wheeler layout, with a single front wheel. Historians agree that this was the first-ever petrol-driven machine to go out on the public highway – in Germany in 1885.

Except for the use of an internal combustion engine, the Benz Tricycle was unlike the vast majority of other cars that evolved from it. Besides its three-wheeler layout, its engine was behind and under the seats, and had chain- *and* belt-drive transmission.

Benz chose a three-wheeler layout, with a single front wheel, because he could not solve the problems of providing twin steered front wheels: the horse-drawn carriages of the day used axles pivoted in their centre, which was not practical for this purpose, since steering efforts would have been enormous. Naturally, solid tyres were used.

This original car had a single-cylinder engine lying horizontally ahead of the line of the rear wheels, all in unit with the single-speed transmission. It was a long-stroke design that revved only to 250 rpm (a speed well below the idling speed of modern cars), and had an exposed crankshaft and surface-type carburettor.

The car was started off from rest by operating a belt-control lever, but there was only one speed, and on a good day, with the engine working well, the Benz sometimes reached 10 mph. There was a single bench seat perched high above the engine, with no weather protection of any type.

Nevertheless, the concept was developed further, and several replicas were sold in the next few years. The Benz was not important for what it did, but for what it promised.

### Specification

**Engine:** single-cylinder, side-valve
**Bore × stroke:** 116 mm × 160 mm
**Capacity:** 1691 cc
**Maximum power:** 1.5 bhp
**Transmission:** single-speed manual gearbox, rear-wheel drive
**Chassis:** separate tubular frame
**Suspension:** front by full-elliptic springs; beam axle rear, full-elliptic leaf springs
**Brakes:** drums at rear, no front brake
**Bodywork:** open-top two-seater
**Maximum speed (approx):** 10 mph (16 km/h)

## Blitzen Benz 1909-14

The Blitzen was one of a whole series of massive-engined racing cars produced by Benz before World War I. Like its predecessors, which had raced in early Grands Prix, it featured a heavy four-cylinder engine, and chain drive to the rear wheels.

The Blitzen (Lightning) was typical of the fastest cars of this period. It was not a very large car (its wheelbase was only 109 in), but it weighed about 2,800 lb. The chassis was a simple ladder-style frame, with the lofty four-cylinder engine set well back. The body, which featured a beak-like proboscis above the radiator, looked too narrow to accommodate two people, but there was just space for a riding mechanic to perch alongside the driver.

The 21.5-litre engine revved to 1,600 rpm, but produced 200 bhp, and this was quite enough to push the car up to 120 mph in speed trials and on one occasion up to 141 mph. No known shaft drive could deal reliably with this sort of power, so final drive to the rear wheels was by a pair of massive exposed chains.

At the time the Blitzen was definitely the fastest car in the world, for it took a land speed record in 1909 and again in

1914. Blitzen models were occasionally driven on the road, but it was really only comfortable on race tracks or record strips.

### Specifications

**Engine:** inline-four, overhead-valve
**Bore × stroke:** 185 mm × 200 mm
**Capacity:** 21500 cc
**Maximum power:** 200 bhp
**Transmission:** four-speed manual

gearbox, rear-wheel drive
**Chassis:** separate steel frame, channel-section side members
**Suspension:** beam front axle with semi-elliptic leaf springs, live rear axle with semi-elliptic leaf springs
**Brakes:** drums at rear, no front brakes
**Bodywork:** aluminium open-top two-seater
**Maximum speed (approx):** 140 mph (225 km/h)

*Undoubtedly the greatest supercar of its time, the Blitzen (Lightning) Benz was well named. It was capable of enormous speeds for the day, thanks to its 21.5-litre aero engine. That made it fast enough to hold the world land speed record on two occasions, in 1909 and 1914, managing a maximum of 141 mph at Daytona.*

# Bitter-Automobile

S pecialist marques are few and far between in Germany, so Bitter, founded by Erich Bitter in 1973; deserves attention. Bitter came from nowhere; before he began car manufacturing he had no previous experience as an engineer or as a businessman.

He had been a successful bicycle racer in the 1950s, a racing driver and Coca-Cola salesman in the 1960s – and then the owner of some profitable motor accessory shops.

In 1969 he began importing Abarth parts and Intermeccanica cars from Italy. This was a mistake; the Intermeccanica was fast, but poorly-made, so he abandoned this enterprise and looked for ways to build cars of his own. By sheer persistence and force of personality he interested Opel in his ideas, the result being that an Opel dream car eventually went into production with a Bitter badge. According to all the normal tenets around which companies owned by GM should have operated, this was not possible, but as long as Opel could see no direct competition from the cars they seemed to be happy to take his business.

The original Bitter CD that went into production during the depths of the 1970s energy crisis was based on the Opel Diplomat platform. Since that car had never been a success for Opel, one can now see why the management was so interested in the Bitter!

The style was sleek and Italianate, a heady mixture of 'concept by Opel', and practical realisation by Frua of Italy. Like all such cars of the period it had a long shark-like nose with flip-up headlamps, and bore a slight resemblance to the Maserati Ghibli and Indy models of the period. With 2+2 seating, and with all Diplomat features retained, it was an exciting, though expensive, autobahn-cruiser in its day. The Diplomat had been a very underrated car, its Opel badge counting against it when compared with its Mercedes and BMW rivals, despite the fact that its chassis was quite sophisticated, with a de Dion rear axle for example. The Bitter treatment gave it the prestige element it so clearly lacked.

The successor to the CD was the SC, a massive coupé on a 106-in wheelbase which Bitter claimed to have styled himself. Like the CD it was based on a large Opel platform (this time the new Senator), and in due course three different types – coupé, convertible and saloon – were produced.

Sales were restricted, but from a peak of around 150 cars a year in the mid-1980s these fell rapidly away before the end of the decade. The company was in serious financial trouble by 1986, but recovered after Kjell Qvale had injected capital; Qvale later withdrew.

*The only badge found on Bitter cars is the chrome name of the company founder, Erich Bitter, who created his own marque in 1973.*

By the late 1980s Erich Bitter had big ideas, negotiating for larger financial backing and for enhanced distribution. An Opel Manta-based car was shown, but almost immediately dropped. Then, to replace the SC models, the Type 3 range was previewed at the Frankfurt Show in 1987, though series production did not begin before the 1990s. It was intended for production at the rate of up to 2,000 cars a year, supposedly at the Steyr-Daimler-Puch factory in Austria, but this was clearly not possible without huge financial investment.

The new car, still Opel-based, was certain to be very expensive – by 1989, when production had not yet begun, it was forecast to cost £33,000 – and at first it was to be backed by Isuzu, of which GM was a major shareholder. Then, after Isuzu withdrew and a promising USA distribution deal was lost, Bitter had to start again, reducing his sights considerably.

That was a shame, because the car was to have the 204-bhp 24-valve twin-cam Opel engine. This engine was Opel's very latest, combining the age-old bore and stroke of the old unit (as used in the Bitter SC) with a modern four-valves-per-cylinder layout.

## Bitter SC 1979-88

The SC was launched at Frankfurt in 1979, as a direct replacement for the popular CD model. In its original form it used the latest Opel Senator platform, complete with six-cylinder engine and a choice of transmissions, and before the end of its run a long-stroke 3.85-litre version was also developed.

Bitter claimed to have styled the new SC himself, but professional help from Italy was certainly involved along the way. The original car was a two-door coupé, rather like the current Ferrari 400, though a cabriolet option was added in 1981 and a longer four-door saloon in 1985. A larger (long-stroke) engine option came on stream for 1984.

Big ideas for enlarging sales by marketing these cars through GM dealership, not only in Europe but in the USA, came to nothing. At their peak, sales approached 150 cars a year, which was certainly not enough to frighten any other supercar manufacturer in Europe.

At this rate of assembly, it was reasonable that shells should be made in Italy, and some cars were assembled by Steyr-Daimler-Puch.

### Specification

**Engine:** inline-six, overhead-cam
**Bore × stroke:** 95 mm × 69.8 mm
**Capacity:** 2969 cc
**Maximum power:** 180 bhp
**Transmission:** five-speed manual gearbox or three-speed automatic transmission, rear-wheel drive
**Chassis:** steel unit construction body/chassis assembly
**Suspension:** independent front, coil springs; independent rear with coil springs and semi-trailing arms
**Brakes:** discs front and rear
**Bodywork:** steel four-seater coupé, cabriolet or saloon
**Maximum speed (approx):** 130 mph (209 km/h)

*Left: Power for the Bitter SC came from Opel's inline six-cylinder overhead-cam engine. Early examples were 2.7 litres; this is the later, stretched 3.85-litre engine, enough to push the car to nearly 140 mph.*

*Although Erich Bitter claimed to have styled the SC himself, there's surely some Italian influence in the stylish Opel Senator-based coupé.*

# Bizzarrini SpA

iotti Bizzarrini was a prolific engineer who started his working life as a teacher at Pisa University in Italy, next joined Alfa Romeo's experimental department, and later moved on to Ferrari. His work at Ferrari included developing the famous 250 GTO.

After leaving Ferrari and setting up his own business, Bizzarrini designed the Chevrolet-engined Iso Grifo and Iso Rivolta cars which were launched in the early 1960s, before progressing to the design of the original Lamborghini V12 engine.

After a personality clash with Renzo Rivolta, Bizzarrini decided to design and build his own car in Livorno, first showing his original A3C GT Strada in 1963. With Iso's agreement, this car used many Iso Grifo components, including the suspension components – the rear end was a properly-located de Dion layout – but the body style was even lower, much lighter, and the car was really meant for racing.

Because their interior trim was rather stark and they lacked refinement and creature comforts, very few A3Cs were sold, and the model made very little impact in sports car racing. Giotti Bizzarrini therefore decided to try again, moving much further down market, with the GT Europa 1900, which had Opel running gear, a new platform chassis and all-independent rear suspension. Even though these cars were much cheaper than the A3C and had very creditable performance, they sold very slowly indeed. Bizzarrini's reputation might have been high, but the business always struggled to make profits, and it closed down in 1969.

*Left: The Bizzarrini badge of a bird inside a stylised gearwheel is an unusual sight, as total Bizzarrini production was very limited. An extremely talented engineer, Giotti Bizzarrini was better known as the designer of the 250 GTO Ferrari and the Lamborghini V12 than as a car manufacturer.*

*Above: The Bizzarrini Manta of 1968 was based on a modified Iso Grifo Competizione with a tubular chassis. It was not a production model and was more significant in Giorgetto Giugiaro's career than Bizzarrini's, being Giugiaro's first prototype as an independent designer.*

*Left: When this car first appeared it was badged as an Iso rather than a Bizzarrini and ran in the 1964 Le Mans 24 Hours, where it finished 14th, averaging 106.75 mph. It formed the basis for the production Bizzarrini, the GT Strada 5300 coupé.*

## Bizzarrini A3C GT Strada 1965-67

Because he had spent so much time developing the Iso Grifo coupé for the Milan-based company, Bizzarrini's first design under his own name, the A3C, was effectively a special lightweight derivative of the Iso Grifo coupé, but with even more power, even lower styling and a less completely trimmed interior.

Like the Grifo the A3C had a fabricated steel platform chassis, with a wide track, firm springing and with Grifo-type de Dion rear suspension. It also used an even more highly-tuned version of the Chevrolet V8 engine, backed by a heavy-duty gearbox. The body style was by Bertone, and total height was a mere 44 in.

Perhaps the power output claims were over-optimistic, and perhaps the style was not as aerodynamically efficient as it appeared, for the car's top speed was only 145 mph.

Paradoxically, the A3C's commercial failure now makes it more collectable.

### Specification

**Engine:** V8, overhead-valve
**Bore × stroke:** 101 mm × 82.55 mm
**Capacity:** 5354 cc
**Maximum power:** 365 bhp
**Transmission:** four-speed manual gearbox, rear-wheel drive
**Chassis:** separate steel platform chassis frame
**Suspension:** independent front, coil springs; de Dion rear, coil springs
**Brakes:** discs front and rear
**Bodywork:** light alloy two-seater coupé
**Maximum speed (aprox):** 145 mph (233 km/h)

*Above: The Bizzarrini GT Strada 5300 was produced in very limited numbers. Although capable of 145 mph, its American Chevrolet Corvette V8 engine rather unfairly reduced its supercar status.*

# BMW (Bayerische Motoren Werke)

*Above: The famous blue and white quartered BMW badge was meant to represent a whirling propeller, as BMW made aero engines before they turned their hand to producing cars in 1928, some 17 years after the company was founded.*

*Right: Two generations of BMWs: a 328 convertible from 1936, and an Alpina-tuned 5-Series car from the 1980s. BMW's sporting approach turned from producing outright sports cars like the 328 to the current production of sporting saloons and coupés.*

The BMW company was founded in 1911, and initially produced aero engines rather than motor cars; in fact, the well-known blue and white trademark represents a spinning aircraft propeller. The first name of the company was Gustav Otto Flugmaschinenfabrik München – literally translated as Gustav Otto Munich Aircraft Works. Gustav Otto was the son of the inventor of the Otto cycle – or the four-stroke petrol engine.

Business prospered, thanks in no small part to World War I, and by 1918 the company name was changed to the familiar BMW – but the only motors being manufactured were liquid-cooled aircraft engines.

It was not until 1928 that car production was contemplated, and by then BMW was already well known as a producer of motorcycles. In that year the company acquired Dixi-Werke at Eisenach, who were already licensed to produce the British Austin Seven – contrary to popular belief BMW did not produce the car as a Dixi, but as a BMW.

In 1933 BMW took the step that was to establish their international reputation when they introduced an entirely new range of cars with six-cylinder engines. Initially the engine size was only 1175 cc, but soon it was increased to 1500 cc – but the company resisted the then current practice of producing excessively large vehicles. In 1934 the 315/1 was introduced, with a further development of the six-cylinder concept; the 1475-cc engine developed 40 bhp, it had hemispherical combustion chambers, and was fitted with three carburettors. A factory team was victorious in the Alpine Trial of that year, and this victory resulted in the British Frazer Nash (AFN) concern being appointed UK concessionaires.

The 328 sports car followed in 1936. During World War II the company concentrated on aircraft engine production, actually producing a jet engine in 1943 with 800-lb thrust. They also manufactured a 41.8-litre, 14-cylinder radial engine that developed 1,800 bhp. War reparations forced the factory to be restructured in 1946 (it went on to make EMW cars in East Germany), and only the manufacture of agricultural machinery and small motorcycles was permitted. In the mid-1950s BMW acquired the licence to build the Isetta bubble car from Italy; at the opposite extreme they also developed a luxury sports car. The company narrowly averted liquidation during this period, but was saved by the introduction of the 1800 range in 1963. From this point on, success followed success.

## BMW 328 1936-40

When it was introduced in 1936, nobody quite appreciated how far advanced the 328 was. BMW have always been the masters of understatement, and the great majority of their new vehicles have been evolutionary, developments of an existing range. Such was the 328. It was only in 1934 that the company produced its first all-new vehicle in the form of the small straight-six-engined 315; this was rapidly developed through the 319, 320 and 326 models, but these were mere portents of things to come!

The 328 was the beginning of a new era. Its style and performance were 20 years ahead of its time. The new car utilised the 326's cylinder block, but was fitted with a revolutionary aluminium cylinder head with inclined overhead valves operated by a complicated series of push-rods and rocker arms from the original low-mounted camshaft. The effect was to provide the advantages of an overhead camshaft design with hemispherical combustion chambers, without having to go to the expense of designing a new engine.

Providing the engine was not over-revved, it worked extremely well. Unfortunately it suffered, although this was not apparent at the time, from being manufactured from inferior-quality materials, as German high-quality metals at that time were directed towards armaments. It was only after the cessation of hostilities in 1945, when the design was adopted by Bristol, that its true potential was developed, and by the end of production in 1961 the power had been increased enormously, peaking at 125 bhp.

*The 328 engine was an advanced 80-bhp straight-six two-litre overhead-valve unit.*

The 328 was fitted with a classic two-seater body with what was to become the traditional twin-oval, or nostril, grille. Flowing wings and rear wheel spats caused traditional enthusiasts to gasp at the loss of their beloved cycle mudguards. It is generally accepted that the lines of the 328 influenced the styling of the Jaguar XK120, when it was announced in 1948.

### Specification

**Engine:** inline six-cylinder, overhead-valve
**Bore × stroke:** 66 mm × 96 mm
**Capacity:** 1971 cc
**Maximum power:** 80 bhp
**Transmission:** four-speed manual
**Chassis:** steel ladder frame with tubular side members
**Suspension:** independent front with transverse leaf springs; live rear axle with semi-elliptic leaf springs
**Brakes:** drums all round
**Bodywork:** two-seater sports
**Maximum speed (approx):** 100 mph (161 km/h)

*Above: Compared with the traditional British sports cars of the 1930s, the BMW 328 was quite advanced, with a certain measure of streamlining to the body. It was a good performer too, being capable of 100 mph. A streamlined racing version was also developed, which won the 1940 Mille Miglia at an average speed of 103.6 mph. A total of 400 cars and 69 chassis was built in all.*

*Above: Right-hand-drive models were imported into Britain by the Frazer Nash company, which also produced the model after World War II when BMW production had stopped.*

## BMW 507 1956-59

*Below: The 507 convertible was one of BMW's most attractive designs. Unfortunately it was extremely expensive, much too expensive to sell in the numbers anticipated on the US market, despite its performance, which saw a top speed of 124 mph.*

*Left: The 507 was powered by a 3.2-litre 150-bhp pushrod overhead-valve V8 engine.*

To say that BMW were in a state of confusion after the war in 1945 would be an understatement. Bear in mind that war reparations had led to their factories being dismantled, and that they were forbidden to produce anything other than agricultural equipment and motorcycles from pre-war spares for a number of years. It is therefore surprising that in 1955 they announced an entirely new luxury sports car – but that is exactly what happened. But, of course, it was shrewdly aimed at the American market.

The 507 was to all intents and purposes the post-war successor to the 328, and was developed by Fritz Fiedler, the brilliant BMW engineer, who had also been responsible for the earlier model. The basis for the new car was the 502 saloon, for which an entirely new V8 engine had been developed. This was enlarged to 3.2 litres and fitted to a new chassis, which was supplied with a stunning open two-seater body. The BMW nostril air intakes were laid on their side, giving the car a wide, flat front. Behind this was an ex-

ceptionally well-styled (by Albrecht Goertz) and voluptuous body with prominent wings but subtle curves.

Unfortunately the 507 was not a sales success. The Americans had anticipated a production rate in the thousands, at modest cost, in order that the car be pitched midway between the Mercedes-Benz 300SL and the British Triumph and MGs. BMW could not produce them that way. Only 252 cars were manufactured; and they were far too expensive.

### Specification

**Engine:** V8, overhead-valve
**Bore × stroke:** 82 mm × 75 mm
**Capacity:** 3168 cc
**Maximum power:** 150 bhp
**Transmission:** four-speed manual
**Chassis:** steel box section with tubular cross members
**Suspension:** independent front with wishbones, torsion bars and anti-roll bar; live rear axle with radius rods, transverse A-arm and torsion bars
**Brakes:** drums all round
**Bodywork:** two-seater sports
**Maximum speed (approx):** 124 mph (200 km/h)

## BMW 2002 1966-75

BMW reorganisation really got under way in the early 1960s, after half of the aero-engine business had been disposed of to MAN. BMW were then able to get their motor-car act together by the middle of the decade. The company's fortunes were largely restored by the 1800-2000 range, which had been sufficiently successful to make BMW the second most profitable German automobile manufacturer, behind Mercedes-Benz.

The 2002, announced in mid-1968, is the model by which the company was best known in recent years. The basis of the car was the 1600 two-door body shell, which had been introduced in 1963; it was strictly functional, but neat and attractive. To this was fitted a 1990-cc single-overhead-camshaft engine. The 2002 provided a remarkable combination of performance, roadholding and ride comfort. It was also exceptionally refined for a cylinder design. A typical BMW interior treatment was provided; the company did not consider that thick-pile carpets or elaborate walnut veneer trim was necessary on a car of this type. It was plain but of high quality, with no suggestion of spurious luxury. As the years went by a wide range of versions of the 2002 became available, including a turbo, a convertible and an estate car.

The turbo was by far the most interesting. It was the first European production turbo car when it appeared in 1973. That was over 10 years after Chevrolet had turbocharged their rear-engined Corvair to produce the Corvair Monza Spyder. Nevertheless, the BMW predated the Saab 99 Turbo by five years.

Where the most powerful of the normally aspirated 2002s produced 130 bhp, the blown car had an impressive 170 bhp, thanks to the single KKK turbo. To cope with the extra power the brakes were uprated, the suspension stiffened and larger tyres fitted. Turbo cars were obviously far less refined then, and the 2002 suffered bad turbo lag and had a narrow power band. Despite its performance (0-60 in 6.6 seconds and 130 mph top speed), it was not a great sales success and only 1,672 were built, between 1973 and 1974.

*Left: There was no mistaking the 2002 Turbo. It was distinguished from the more ordinary 2002 models by the flared wheel arches and the spoiler on the boot lid, intended to keep the powerful BMW's back wheels firmly on the ground.*

*Below: The 2002 Turbo was Europe's first production turbocharged car and an exciting performance package. Power output from the two-litre engine was boosted to an impressive 170 bhp, which was enough to give a top speed of 130 mph.*

### Specification (2002 Turbo)

**Engine:** inline four-cylinder, overhead-cam, turbo
**Bore × stroke:** 89 mm × 80 mm
**Capacity:** 1990 cc
**Maximum power:** 170 bhp
**Transmission:** four-speed manual
**Chassis:** unitary
**Suspension:** independent with McPherson struts front and semi-trailing arms rear
**Brakes:** discs front, drums rear
**Bodywork:** two-door saloon
**Maximum speed (approx):** 130 mph (209 km/h)

## BMW CSL 1971-75

It wasn't until BMW's four-cylinder coupé version of the two-litre cars was stretched, and then given a six-cylinder engine, that BMW had a car of real style. Suddenly the proportions were perfect, and there was sufficient power to match the looks. Initially the six-cylinder coupés had a 2494-cc six, producing 150 bhp, but that was substantially increased with the 2.8 litres and 170 bhp of the 2800 CS in 1968.

The first three-litre car appeared in 1971, with fuel injection and 185 bhp. By now the car had discs brakes all round rather than just at the front. The ultimate development of the range was the 3.0 CSL, the L standing for lightweight. Weight had been pared off the car by the use of alloy body panels replacing the original steel. BMW fitted their factory racing CSLs with some outrageous aerodynamic aids, principally a big rear wing mounted on three struts, and met with great success on the racetrack, taking the European Touring Car Championship. The fastest of the injected coupés was good for 140 mph but only 1,039 lightweights were built, including those with the larger, 3153-cc engine.

Considering that the car's styling dates back to the 1960s it has aged remarkably well; it led to the 6-Series coupés, which were still in production in the late 1980s.

### Specification

**Engine:** inline six-cylinder, overhead-cam, turbo
**Bore × stroke:** 89 mm × 80 mm
**Capacity:** 2985 cc
**Maximum power:** 206 bhp
**Transmission:** four-speed manual, rear-wheel drive
**Chassis:** unitary
**Suspension:** independent with McPherson struts front and semi-trailing arms rear
**Brakes:** discs all round
**Bodywork:** two-door pillarless coupé
**Maximum speed (approx):** 139 mph (224 km/h)

*Forerunner of the 6-Series coupés, the CSL was a lightweight alloy-bodied coupé with a three-litre straight-six engine producing 206 bhp and giving a top speed of almost 140 mph. The factory racers were a dominant force in the European Touring Car Championship.*

## BMW M1 1980-81

The origins of the M1 (which stood for mid-engined car no. 1) can be traced back to 1971 when BMW built an experimental gullwing turbo car. When BMW decided to homologate a mid-engined car for endurance racing, they turned to the gullwing. Giorgetto Giugiaro was given the job of turning the experimental car into a viable road car, and he dispensed with the gullwing doors. Power came from a straight-six, but with a twin-cam head and four valves per cylinder, which produced 277 bhp.

The M1 was a curiously homeless device; originally it was intended to have Lamborghini build the car in Italy, but they couldn't cope and it was eventually farmed out, the glassfibre body being made by Trasformazione Italiana Resina, the multi-tube chassis by Marchesi, assembly at Ital Design, with the suspension and drivetrain being added by Baur in Stuttgart. It was subject to all manner of delays and the M1 was not launched until the 1978 Paris Show. By this time there was only one season left in the endu-

rance regulations for which the car had been conceived. It did run at Le Mans for a few seasons; on one memorable occasion in the rain, the German endurance specialist Hans Stuck showed what its excellent handling could achieve, but when the rain stopped the M1 dropped back.

M1s were run in the 'Procar' series as back-up to the Grands Prix in one season, but that simply led to a number of badly-damaged cars, as the Grand Prix drivers had a fairly cavalier attitude towards them. Production ended in 1981 after only 450 had been built, the limited numbers making the mid-engined BMW a much sought-after collector's car.

### Specification

**Engine:** inline six-cylinder, twin-cam
**Bore × stroke:** 93 mm × 84 mm
**Capacity:** 3453 cc
**Maximum power:** 277 bhp
**Transmission:** five-speed manual
**Chassis:** fabricated sheet steel and tubular spaceframe

**Suspension:** independent with double wishbones and coil springs front and rear
**Brakes:** discs all round
**Bodywork:** glassfibre two-seat coupé
**Maximum speed (approx):** 163 mph (262 km/h)

*BMW's first supercar was the mid-engined M1, originally designed for endurance racing but later built as an exclusive road car. It used a spaceframe tubular chassis, a glassfibre body and a 277-bhp 3.5-litre straight-six.*

## BMW Z1 1989–90

Following the launch of the 507 in 1955, it was 32 years before the company launched another sports car. The Z1 roadster, introduced in 1987, was sensational in its own way, the most unusual feature being the retractable doors, which may be left down with the car in motion.

The extraordinary factor about this car was that, originally, it was conceived as a product of BMW Technik, a group of BMW engineers who had been briefed to investigate future materials and techniques without worrying about production constraints. As a vehicle for new technologies, the Z1 excelled. It had an all-plastic body, novel rear suspension and those innovative doors. They were designed to drop down into deep side sills operated by electric motors and toothed belts. Even the German Ministry of Transport accepted them as being safe because, when dropped into the bodywork, they provided exceptional chassis stiffness. The injection-moulded thermoplastic body was stress-free and all the panels were quickly removable.

The rear suspension was unusual in that the rear wheels were located by a new and very accurate system known as the 'Z' axle. Two lateral arms controlled the wheels in the vertical plane, while a massive trailing link curved round the tyre from a pivot in line with the hub. Camber changes and bump steer were eliminated but there was a degree of passive steering; toe-out was introduced to give crisper turn-in as lateral forces rose, minimising the risk of throttle-off oversteer. It provided superb handling, was lightweight and was an extremely simple design. The engine and gearbox came from the well-established 325i.

*Right: The 140 mph Z1 was powered by the 325i six-cylinder engine. The doors moved up and down rather than opening in the conventional way.*

### Specification

**Engine:** inline six-cylinder, overhead-cam
**Bore × stroke:** 84 mm × 75 mm
**Capacity:** 2494 cc
**Maximum power:** 171 bhp
**Transmission:** five-speed manual
**Chassis:** steel floorpan
**Suspension:** independent with coil springs and struts front, double transverse arms and coil springs rear
**Brakes:** discs all round
**Bodywork:** thermoplastic two-seat convertible
**Maximum speed (approx):** 140 mph (225 km/h)

*Right: The Z1 was the only BMW produced with a body made from injection-moulded thermoplastic.*

# BMW 840 Ci Sport 1992-present

Top of the range throughout most of the 1990s was the enduring 8-series, which followed conveniently in the wake of the old 6-series and 3.0 CS of the 1970s. The big 2 + 2 coupé was taut and responsive, belying its weight, and it could be driven with verve through corners thanks to prodigious grip and a modicum of passive rear steer. The 840 Ci was the successor to the short-lived V12-engined 850 Ci and around £15,000 cheaper into the bargain. Alongside the basic 840 Ci was the 840 Ci Sport, which provided a full sports pack including front air dam, rear apron diffuser and 'M'-style exterior door mirrors. Both variants were originally powered by a 4.0-litre V8, subsequently raised to 4.4-litres. This 32-valve V8 engine was governed by a Motronic engine management system and produced 286 bhp, the same as its 4.0-litre predecessor, but with a five percent increase in torque. This enabled the 840 Ci to go from 0–62 mph (0-100 km/h) in 7.1 seconds and on to an artificially governed maximum speed of 155 mph (249 km/h). Overall fuel consumption was 21.6 mpg. Transmission was via a five-speed automatic gearbox that featured BMW's intelligent Adaptive Gearbox System (AGS). AGS could read the road, learn its driver's requirements and adapt its behaviour to suit, and worked in conjunction with semi-automatic Steptronic Control. It was all whistles and bells, the 8-series. Automatic stability and traction control (ASC) was also standard, which prevented the driven wheels spinning on slippery roads, as well as an elasto-kinematic rear axle design unique at the time in a production car. Electronically adjustable dampers allowing the driver to switch between sports or comfort handling were also available.

Inside the cabin, the 8-series was equipped with an information system on the centre console that provided the driver with data such as distance, range, outside temperature and average fuel consumption. Other standard features included aerodynamic heated rear view mirrors, leather upholstery, metallic paint, radio cassette system and 12 speakers, six disc CD player, ski bag, alloy wheels and anti-theft alarm system with remote control. The 8-series was always going to be an exclusive model, with anticipated sales as low as 100 units per year.

## Specification
**Engine:** V8, four valves per cylinder
**Bore** x **stroke:** 82.7 mm x 92.0 mm
**Capacity:** 4398 cc
**Suspension:** independent, with electronic traction control
**Brakes:** discs all round with ABS
**Chassis:** monocoque
**Body:** two-door coupé

*Above: The cabin of the 8-series BMW was upholstered predominantly in leather, with dashboard instrumentation laid out in a traditional fashion.*

*Below: The 4.3-litre V8-engined 840i was BMW's top-of-the-range model for the 1990s, and the pillar-less coupé's two-plus-two configuration is evident here, as are the closed headlight pods that characterised the car's low frontal area.*

## BMW Z3 Roadster 1995 to present

Like Dustin Hoffman's Alfa Romeo Spider in *The Graduate*, the BMW Z3 sprang to prominence as Pierce Brosnan's car in the 1995 James Bond film *Goldeneye*. It also caught the wave of resurgent sports car popularity that swelled in the early 1990s, as some went modern like Alfa and MG, and some went traditional like Fiat and Porsche. BMW's Z3 was aggressively retro, front engined with rear wheel drive, blending traditional hairy-chested roadster styling with modern technology; that's to say, old-model 3-series BMW. The base-model Z3 ran on Z-line 7J x 15 alloy wheels with 205/60/Ri 5 tyres, and was powered by the 140 bhp 1.9-litre four-cylinder engine, giving a top speed of 127 mph with 0–62 mph acceleration in 9.5 seconds. And while the Z1 roadster of 1988 was a low-volume high-price affair, the Z3 was much more widely available. The 1.9-litre four-cylinder model was priced at £21,480 in 1998, not much different to the MGF or top of the range Caterham. The Z3 was far from spartan however, and its hood could be lowered or raised from inside the car in a matter of seconds from its recess behind the seats.

There were two other versions of the Z3 Roadster, all produced in the USA at BMW's Spartanburg, South Carolina plant. The 2.8-litre six-cylinder and the 321 bhp, 3.2-litre six-cylinder M roadster, introduced in 1998 and powered by the engine from the M3 Evolution. Both models were available with a 5-speed manual or 4-speed automatic transmission. These were the high performers, and enabled BMW to compete in all areas of the roadster market over a price span of £21,000 to £40,000. The Z3 2.8 rode on 16-inch Z-star alloy wheels with 225/50 ZR x 16 tyres, and used a lightweight, all-aluminium, 24-valve 2.8-litre straight-six engine, producing 192 bhp and reaching a top speed of 135 mph and accelerating from 0–62 mph in 7.1 seconds.

The Z3 specification included rack and pinion steering and disc brakes, vented at the front, with ABS and switchable traction control. The six-cylinder car was distinguished from the four by a front apron with larger air intakes, wider

*Above: The M Roadster used an electronically controlled 3.2-litre engine, making it capable of 155 mph and 0–62 mph in 5.4 seconds. Suspension and brakes were uprated, while body and trim were cosmetically enhanced.*

rear wheel arches, 16-inch alloy wheels, and an electrically-operated hood. Seats too were electrically-adjustable and available in nine leather colours matching the eight body-paint options.

The Z3 range was augmented in February 1998 by the BMW M roadster, powered by the 321 bhp 24-valve 3,201 cc straight-six M3 power unit. Engine monitoring was by BMW's MS S 50 Digital Motor Electronics, capable of performing 20 million calculations per second, and the M-roadster could accelerate to 62 mph in 5.4-seconds and an artificially controlled top speed of

155 mph, yet still yield an overall fuel consumption of 25.4 mpg. Suspension consisted of single joint, spring strut axles at the front and semi-trailing arms at the rear with coil springs and dampers. The M roadster had firmer damping and harder springs than the other Z3 models, similar to the M3 set-up, with fade-free compound disc brakes at the front with floating friction ring on an ultra light aluminium support. The M roadster was slightly lower than its siblings, with re-styled front and rear bumpers and front air dam and four tailpipes, while cosmetic changes in-

cluded white indicator lenses, relocated rear number plate and restyled side grilles.

### Variants

#### The M-Coupé

Like it or loathe it, the two-seater M-Coupé was a bold if somewhat cramped stylistic evolution on the Z3 theme. Precedents included Volvo P1800, Gilbern, Scimitar GTE, Elite, Harrington Alpine, Dove TR4, etc. The M-Coupé was launched in October 1998 and powered by the same engine as the M3 and M roadster, with similar suspension package.

#### Specification (M-roadster)

**Engine:** straight-six, 24-valves
**Bore x Stroke:** 91 x 86.4 mm
**Capacity:** 3,201 cc
**Suspension:** independent front, by single-joint spring-strut with displaced caster, track control arms and MacPherson struts; independent rear by semi-trailing arms with anti-roll bars, coil springs and dampers all round
**Brakes:** discs all round with ABS
**Chassis:** monocoque
**Body:** 2-door two-seat roadster

*Left: Built in South Carolina, the Z3 Roadster was an ostentatious blend of retrospective and classic design cues, driven by an up-to-the-minute BMW powertrain.*

# Bond

S harps Commercials of Preston, in Lancashire, started building fragile and tiny motorcycle-engined three-wheelers designed by Laurie Bond in 1949. This vehicle, which was always called the Bond Mini-car, matured and sold well until the early 1960s, when the company decided to start building four-wheel cars.

Through its parent company, the Loxhams garage group, Bond then made a deal with Triumph to build a car based on Herald, Spitfire and Vitesse components. Not only did this car, the Equipe GT, have Triumph's approval and carry the same warranty, but it was sold through some Triumph dealerships.

Bond was clever, and never overreached himself technically. The car's running gear was pure Triumph, and much of the inner bodywork was also sourced from Triumph, but most of the body skin was in rot-proof glassfibre, the styling being neat and instantly recognisable.

As Triumph's Herald family moved steadily up-market, so did Bond's. To follow the Equipe, Bond produced the Equipe 2-litre, this time using the Vitesse 2-litre chassis and engine. The first 2-litre was a coupé, but

*Designer Laurie Bond started by producing small motorbike-engined three-wheelers in 1949. The pinnacle of his, and the company's, career was producing four-wheel sports cars like the Equipe shown here.*

after one year Bond also launched a smart convertible version of the same style.

In the same period Bond also developed a new type of three-wheeler – the 875, with a rear-mounted Hillman Imp engine and rear suspension – but after Reliant bought the company in 1969 four-wheeler assembly rapidly ran down, and the Preston works was closed in 1970.

Reliant launched the three-wheeler Bond Bug, a very trendy two-seater, in 1970, but this was almost pure Reliant, and died off in 1974. The life of the sporting Bond four-wheeler was a mere seven years.

## Bond Equipe GT and 4S 1963-70

The original Bond was designed with the help and encouragement of Standard-Triumph. Triumph supplied a Herald chassis into which the Spitfire's engine and front disc brake assemblies had been fitted. Bond also took a number of Herald body components, including the bulkhead/scuttle, doors and floorpan, along with a Vitesse fascia, but the sloping bonnet and the fastback coupé superstructure were by Bond, and made from glassfibre. It was a sporty-looking car, badged as a GT.

The original GT sold well but had no outside access to the boot area, and needed to be changed for general appeal. From October 1964, therefore, the GT 4S took over, this being a developed type with four instead of two headlamps and a separate locking boot compartment. 4S, by the way, meant four-seater, for there was more space in the cabin. Before long this car could be

bought with optional wire wheels (Spitfire type), and the later 67-bhp Spitfire engine was standardised.

Then, in the spring of 1967, the 4S was given the latest 75-bhp Spitfire 1.3-litre engine and was then built in that form until 1970, when all Bond car production closed down. In all, 2,949 four-cylinder Equipes were produced.

### Specification (GT)

**Engine:** inline-four, overhead-valve
**Bore × stroke:** 69.3 mm × 76 mm
**Capacity:** 1147 cc
**Maximum power:** 63/67 bhp
**Transmission:** four-speed manual gearbox, rear-wheel drive
**Chassis:** separate steel frame, with box-section side members
**Suspension:** independent front, with coil springs, independent rear with transverse leaf springs and swinging half axles

**Brakes:** discs front, drum rear
**Bodywork:** steel and glassfibre four-seater coupé
**Maximum speed (approx):** 90 mph (145 km/h)

*The Equipe was formed by fitting a glassfibre coupé body over the Triumph Herald's separate backbone chassis, equipped with a Triumph Spitfire engine.*

## Bond Equipe GT 2-litre 1967-70

*When Triumph produced the six-cylinder Vitesse, Bond used that as a basis for their own six-cylinder version. Like the earlier four-cylinder car it used a glassfibre body. Top speed was 102 mph.*

Just as the Triumph Vitesse and GT6 were logical extensions of the Herald/Spitfire theme, so the Bond Equipe GT 2-litre was an obvious additional model to the Equipe range. It was launched in the autumn of 1967, and built for three years until Bond car production closed down.

The chassis/running gear was basically that of the Vitesse 2-litre (which basically meant that a six-cylinder engine and all-synchromesh gearbox went into a strengthened Herald chassis). The frame was modified somewhat and, although the same composite type of body construction was used, the exterior styling was different, with a more integrated front and more sweeping tail. This time, too, overdrive was optional, and the 2-litre could exceed 100 mph.

In their advertising, Bond posed the question: "Is this the most beautiful car in the country?", but didn't bother to argue the point. More seriously, they improved the car in late 1968 by fitting the new lower-wishbone type of GT6/Vitesse

rear suspension, offered a convertible style as an option, and called it the 2-litre Mk II.

The 2-litre's problem was not its style, nor its specification – both of which were liked – but its price, for it was also more costly than Triumph's Vitesse 2-litre. A total of 1,431 2-litres were produced.

### Specification

**Engine:** inline-six, overhead-valve
**Bore × stroke:** 74.7 mm × 76 mm
**Capacity:** 1998 cc
**Maximum power:** 95 bhp
**Transmission:** four-speed manual gearbox, optional overdrive
**Chassis:** separate steel frame
**Suspension:** independent front with coil springs, independent rear with transverse leaf springs and swinging half axles
**Brakes:** discs front, drum rear
**Bodywork:** steel and glassfibre four-seater coupé or convertible
**Maximum speed (approx):** 102 mph (164 km/h)

# Bricklin Vehicle Corporation

**M**alcolm Bricklin made and lost several fortunes before he decided to make and sell his own cars. By the early 1970s he had already built up, and sold, a Handyman hardware store chain in the USA, had bought and sold thousands of motor scooters, and had set up a USA import network for tiny Japanese Subaru cars.

In 1971 he moved to Scottsdale, Arizona, set up the General Vehicle Corporation, and set about developing his own car. The original project was for an inexpensive four-cylinder machine, but the definitive design was a front-engined two-seater coupé, with a 5.9-litre American Motors V8 engine.

Except for the use of gullwing doors and acrylic/glassfibre body panels, the design was mainly conventional – with a live rear axle, and drum rear brakes. There was only one body style – a fastback coupé.

Bricklin himself, although a 'super salesman', had neither the financial backing nor the factory in which to build the cars. By 1973, however, he had secured funding from the government of the eastern Canadian province of New Brunswick, and the car actually went on sale in the summer of 1974. By that time Bricklin had secured 247 dealers all over North America, and the workforce was 750.

It must have been unsettling for all concerned to see the American Motors engine ditched in favour of a Ford V8 only months after launch, and right from the start there were serious dealer and customer complaints over the poor quality and unreliability of the cars.

After little more than a year, during which the car's price had jumped from $7,490 to $10,000, the project collapsed. The New Brunswick backers were already owed $20 million, the dealer network was collapsing, and demand had dried up.

It was a messy end to a project that had looked so promising at first. Looking back from the 1990s, incidentally, it is possible to see many similarities between the Bricklin and DeLorean projects, though Malcolm Bricklin was never connected with the later machine.

## Bricklin SV-1 1974-75

*Above: There was only one Bricklin model, the SV-1. The car was produced at a time when increased car safety was a crucial issue; SV stood for Safety Vehicle. The clumsy styling hid a massive roll-over hoop and gullwing doors, and the whole structure was designed to be immensely strong. Power came from a variety of big American V8s, giving a top speed of over 120 mph; 2,897 cars were built in all.*

According to the Bricklin philosophy, this car was to have unique safety features, hence the model name SV-1 (SV standing for Safety Vehicle). Although the SV-1 used standard North American car hardware, its chassis was massively strong, and incorporated a solid roll-hoop behind the seats, tied to extremely strong windscreen pillars and screen rail by a T-bar.

This was worthy, but conventional, stuff. The only truly unique feature was the body shell, whose panels were actually of acrylic resin backed by glassfibre. This was not only corrosion-resistant, but also it was claimed that scratches could be removed, and the original lustre restored, by sanding and buffing the surface. The acrylic panels, naturally, were self-coloured.

When it was in motion the SV-1 coupé looked conventional enough, but at rest it certainly caused a lot of attention when doors were opened or closed. As with the original Mercedes-Benz 300SL, and as with the DeLorean which followed, the SV-1 had lift-up gullwing doors,

hinged in the centre of the roof, and operated by a combination of electric motors and hydraulics. In the original design these sometimes took up to 10 seconds to actuate fully, but as a retrofit a specialist substituted an air system which reduced that time to two seconds.

Since the car was North American, and meant to appeal to customers in that continent, it was a Chevrolet Corvette-sized two-seater. In many ways it had the mid-1970s Corvette character and performance, with sexily curved styling, hidden headlamps, and a rumbling V8 engine. Unlike the Corvette, though, there was no long-established dealer chain, and the workforce had no previous experience of building cars.

The original engine deal with American Motors was unscrambled at the end of the 1974 model year, after 780 cars had been produced; 144 of them had manual gearboxes, the rest were automatics. After that, all cars were fitted with Ford V8s and automatic transmission. Although the 1976 model year cars went into production after the summer

holidays, Bricklin went into receivership in September 1975, and the project died after 2,897 cars had been made. In later years an owners' club was founded, Bricklin International – an organisation which has located more than 1,500 surviving cars.

### SV-1 variants

#### 1975 and 1976 models

The original 1974 cars had been fitted with an American Motors V8, and Chrysler transmission. Later cars were fitted with a 100 × 87.5-mm, 5752-cc, 175-bhp Ford V8 and Ford automatic transmission; manual transmission was not available. Top speed was approximately 118 mph. There were no styling changes

### Specification (1974 model)

**Engine:** V8, overhead-valve
**Bore × stroke:** 103.63 mm × 87.38 mm
**Capacity:** 5896 cc
**Maximum power:** 223 bhp
**Transmission:** four-speed manual gearbox or three-speed automatic transmission, rear-wheel drive
**Chassis:** steel 'base unit' body/chassis assembly
**Suspension:** independent front with double wishbones and coil springs; live rear axle with semi-elliptic leaf springs
**Brakes:** disc front, drum rear
**Bodywork:** glassfibre/acrylic panelled two-seater coupé, gullwing doors
**Maximum speed (approx):** 122 mph (196 km/h)

# Bristol Cars Ltd

**T**he birth of Bristol owed a lot to the acquisition of 1930s BMW designs as the 'spoils of war' in 1945. In many respects the first Bristols were developed BMWs, though the design was then progressively anglicised over the years.

The original cars were built at Bristol by the Bristol Aeroplane Co., with H.J. Aldington of Frazer Nash (who had been the BMW 'go-between') also involved. By the 1960s Anthony Crook had become closely involved in management, and he eventually became sole owner of the company.

Throughout their near 50-year life, Bristol have utilised only one basic chassis design and two different types of engine. They have never needed a dealer chain, for production was always at a steady trickle and relied on personal contact with wealthy clients. The last body-style change was in the mid-1970s, and there were no major technical changes after that. Like Morgan, Bristol had found a successful image, and were determined to stick with it.

In 1999, Bristol was still producing the Blenheim 2, a two-door coupé based on the Britannia, with exemplary build-quality.

*Above: The coat of arms of the city of Bristol was adopted for the Bristol badge.*

*Above: A more stylised version of the badge appeared on the later V8-engined Bristols.*

## Bristol 400 1947-50

*Above: The radiator grille on the early Bristols, such as this 1949 402 drophead, was reminiscent of BMW's pre-war design. That was appropriate, as Bristol began by using a development of BMW's straight-six two-litre engine.*

*Below: The Bristol two-litre engine used the same complicated valve gear as the BMW. Over the years Bristols increased in power output, from the original 80 bhp to as much as 125 bhp.*

*Above: The Bristol 400 was an aerodynamically efficient design, as you would expect from an aircraft-manufacturing company.*

The first Bristol was an amalgam of BMW ideas – improved and surprisingly harmonious. The chassis drew on BMW 326 ideas, the body was reminiscent of the Autenreith 327 coupé, and the engine was a straight copy of the sporting 328 unit. The engine itself had a unique 'cross-pushrod' arrangement, which married a single side-mounted camshaft, opposed valves in part-spherical combustion chambers, with pivots and 'cross-pushrods' to actuate the valves on one side of the head.

The chassis layout of the 400 was already well developed when the car went into production, and its basic form was to be retained for all Bristols built until the 1990s. Independent front suspension featured a transverse leaf spring (which was eventually changed for the 407) while the rear axle was accurately located by radius arms and sprung on torsion bars.

All 400s were two-door saloon styles,

with a radiator grille much like that of BMW. The engines produced 80 bhp, which was enough to give a 90 mph top speed. Rack-and-pinion steering, and carefully developed chassis, gave the cars exceptional roadholding for their day. A total of 700 cars was built.

All these cars, plus the 401s and 403s which followed, were hand-built, and expensive. They were the direct ancestors of the next generation of Bristols, launched in the mid-1950s.

### Bristol 400 variants

#### Bristol 401

This model, built between 1949 and 1953, used the same rolling chassis as the 400, with an 85-bhp version of the engine, and a new, roomier and more aerodynamically efficient bodyshell styled by Touring of Milan. It was the direct ancestor of the 403, which replaced it. About 650 examples of this 93-mph machine were built.

#### Bristol 402

Built between 1949 and 1951, this was a drophead coupé version of the 401. Early cars were made by Pininfarina. Only 25 were built.

#### Bristol 403

The 403 looked identical to the 401, but had a 100-bhp engine and a top speed of almost 100 mph. Total production was 300 cars, built between 1953 and 1955.

### Specification (1947 Bristol 400)

**Engine:** inline six-cylinder, overhead-valve
**Bore × stroke:** 66 mm × 96 mm
**Capacity:** 1971 cc
**Maximum power:** 80 bhp
**Transmission:** four-speed manual gearbox, rear-wheel drive
**Chassis:** separate steel platform frame
**Suspension:** independent front with transverse leaf spring; live rear axle with torsion bars
**Brakes:** drums front and rear
**Bodywork:** steel and aluminium four-seater saloon
**Maximum speed (approx):** 91 mph (146 km/h)

*Above: The Bristol 404 was the short-wheelbase version of the 405, capable of over 100-mph performance.*

*Right: Like all Bristols, the curved bodywork was made from aluminium alloy rather than steel.*

The first of the new-generation Bristols was actually the 404 coupé of 1953, but the most numerous type was the 405 saloon which was launched a year later. The 405 was the first (and, as it transpired, the only) four-door Bristol ever built, and its smooth style featured an engine air intake inspired by that of the vast Brabazon airliner. Vestigial fins were surely there for decoration only.

Other interesting details included the stowing of the spare wheel in one front wing, and the battery and other electrical gear on the opposite side. There was

more power than in the 403 – 105 bhp compared with 100 bhp – but the car was no heavier than before. In four years, 294 cars were produced.

### Bristol 405 variants

#### Bristol 404

Built on a shorter-wheelbase version of the 405 chassis (96 in instead of 114 in), this was effectively a two-door, two-seater version of the 405, available with either 105-bhp or 125-bhp engines. The top speed of the 125-bhp version

## Bristol 405 1954-58

was about 120 mph, but as the type was very expensive (£3,543 in 1953), only 40 cars were built, between 1953 and 1956.

#### Bristol 406

The 406 took over from the 405 in 1958, and was produced until 1961. Based on the same chassis as the 405, but with a 68.7-mm × 99.6-mm, 2216-cc, 105-bhp engine, and disc brakes all round,

under a new saloon body style with only two passenger doors. This new body was really the progenitor of all Bristols up to and including the Type 411 of the 1970s. A few cars were styled by Zagato.

### Specification (1954 Bristol 405)

**Engine:** inline six-cylinder, overhead-valve
**Bore × stroke:** 66 mm × 96 mm
**Capacity:** 1971 cc
**Maximum power:** 105 bhp
**Transmission:** four-speed manual gearbox with overdrive, rear-wheel drive
**Chassis:** separate steel platform frame
**Suspension:** independent front with transverse leaf spring; live rear axle with torsion bars
**Brakes:** drums front and rear
**Bodywork:** steel and aluminium four-seater saloon, or drophead coupé
**Maximum speed (approx):** 105 mph (169 km/h)

## Bristol 407 1961-63

With the 406 the Bristol engine had reached its limits, so for the 1960s the designers completely revised the style. The new 407 featured a modified version of the long-established chassis and a lightly-modified 406 body, while a big Chrysler V8 engine, and its matching automatic transmission, were chosen to power the car; this was matched by four-wheel disc brakes, and revised front suspension.

Prices were still very high, but as the Bristol had now become a 122-mph car there were sufficient customers to keep the business ticking over. The 408, 409, 410 and 411 types were all linear developments of this car.

### Bristol 407 variants

#### Bristol 408, 409 and 410

These were all improved versions of the 407. The 408 had minor changes, the 409 had a slightly enlarged (5211-cc) engine, and the 410 had further minor changes, including power steering. The 410's top speed was 130 mph.

#### Bristol 411

The 411 was a further linear development of the 407 theme. The 1970 model had a 335-bhp, 107.95-mm × 85.72-mm, 6277-cc engine, the final version having a 264-bhp 6.5-litre engine. The 335-bhp car had a top speed of 138 mph.

### Specification (1961 Bristol 407)

**Engine:** V8, overhead-valve
**Bore × stroke:** 98 mm × 84.1 mm
**Capacity:** 5130 cc
**Maximum power:** 250 bhp
**Transmission:** three-speed automatic transmission, rear-wheel drive
**Chassis:** separate steel platform

*Above: Looking a little like a cross between a Jensen and an Aston Martin DB6, this is actually the rare Zagato-bodied version of the Bristol 408. The sleek bodywork helped give a top speed of over 120 mph.*

*Right: By the time of the 407 and its 408, 409, 410 and 411 derivatives, the six-cylinder engine had been pensioned off in favour of powerful Chrysler V8s in various displacements, with up to 264 bhp.*

**Suspension:** independent front with coil springs; live rear axle with torsion bars
**Brakes:** discs front and rear
**Bodywork:** steel and aluminium four-seater saloon
**Maximum speed (approx):** 122 mph (196 km/h)

## Bristol 412 1975–present

The 412 was the first new Bristol body style since 1958, and featured a rather craggy Zagato shape with definite creases along the side panels. The first cars to be shown were convertibles, but less than a year later what was called a 'convertible saloon' (with a permanent roll-over 'Targa' bar) was added.

The basic layout was as for the old 411 type, which was soon to be dropped. By this time Bristol, like Aston Martin, had tired of being 'out-claimed' on engine power ratings by the Americans, so for the 412 and later cars the power output was never even revealed.

Another new body style followed for the 603 of 1976, both these shapes eventually continuing into the 1990s.

### Bristol 412 variants

#### Bristol 603, Britannia, Brigand and Blenheim

Yet another new style on the long-established chassis, this time with a fastback coupé theme and the 5.9-litre engine. Renamed for 1983, as Britannia (with normally-aspirated engine) or Brigand (with turbocharged engine). All cars were built in very small

numbers. Top speeds were around 150 mph for the turbocharged cars, but none was ever road tested. The 603 was built from 1976 to 1983, while the Blenheim was still in production in the late 1990s.

#### Bristol Beaufighter and Beaufort

These used the 412-style body combined with a turbocharged 5.9-litre engine. The Beaufort was the full convertible version.

### Specification (1975 Bristol 412)

**Engine:** V8, overhead-valve
**Bore × stroke:** 110.3 mm × 85.7 mm
**Capacity:** 6556 cc
**Maximum power:** not revealed
**Transmission:** three-speed automatic transmission, rear-wheel drive
**Chassis:** separate steel platform
**Suspension:** independent front with coil springs; live rear axle with torsion bars
**Brakes:** discs front and rear
**Bodywork:** steel and aluminium four-seater convertible or convertible saloon
**Maximum speed (approx):** 140 mph (225 km/h)

*Top: Developed from the 412, the Bristol Britannia was powered by a 5.9-litre version of the excellent Chrysler overhead-valve V8.*

*Above: The style of the 412 body was retained with the Bristol Beaufighter, which used a turbocharged version of the V8.*

# Brough Superior Cars Ltd

*Left: The Brough Superior name was made by producing the so-called 'Rolls-Royce' of motorcycles before World War II. Brough's move into the car business was a far less successful venture.*

George Brough, an ardent self-publicist, made his name in the 1920s and 1930s with the manufacture of a series of fine vee-twin-engined motorcycles. These were so well-made, so fast, and so special that a *Motor Cycle* journalist dubbed them the "Rolls-Royce of Motor Cycles".

Early in the 1930s Brough began to dabble with the idea of selling motor cars, and eventually took the plunge in 1935 with the Straight Eight model. Brough's practical idea was to have complete Hudson rolling chassis shipped over from the USA, to have them bodied by Atcherly of

Birmingham, and to hype them as being exclusive and built to the same standards as Brough motorcycles.

In the polite atmosphere of the 1930s the motoring press let him get away with his gushing claims, in which the words 'special' and 'unique' were often applied to completely ordinary features. The performance of the cars, however, *was* outstanding: their top speed of 90 mph was excellent for its day.

Down in Cobham, Railton were also selling cars that were effectively rebodied Hudsons, and made strenuous objections to their supplier over this new car, so that in a matter of months Brough were obliged to re-engine the car with a different, six-cylinder, Hudson design.

Because prices were high, sales were slow, and when George Brough produced the Type XII in 1938, there were no takers. Thus discouraged, he gradually closed down his operation, spent the war building precision machinery for the government, and never again revived his car *or* his motorcycle business.

## Brough Superior Straight Eight 1935-36

Compared with the Brough Superior motorcycle, the first Brough car was not nearly so special. The original Brough Superior was introduced in May 1935. Its chassis and running gear were those of the contemporary American Hudson, though 12-volt electrics were fitted; braking was by cable-operated bendix, and the suspension was simple and soft, using leaf springs all round. Its bodywork – a smart cabriolet – was by W.C. Atcherley of Birmingham. Virtually no final assembly needed to take place at the Brough factory, which was in Nottingham.

*Left: Brough did not actually make their cars, nor did they make instruments, despite this sign.*

The Hudson chassis was a modern design, featuring a side-valve straight-eight cylinder engine. The engine was so smooth, and produced such generous torque, that Hudson supplied only a three-speed gearbox. It was a powerful engine – 125 bhp – enough to give this £695 car a top speed of at least 90 mph. Incidentally, to make the engine look like a more modern unit, Brough fitted an aluminium 'cam cover', which certainly fooled a few people!

Only 25 of the original cars were sold, at which point Railton (who also bought their running gear from Hudson) made such a fuss that Hudson stopped supplying eight-cylinder engines. Only six months after launch, therefore, Brough were forced to fit six-cylinder Hudson engines instead. Even so, the supercharged version was as powerful as the original 'Eight', so there was no loss of performance.

## Straight Eight variants

From the end of 1935, a six-cylinder Hudson-engined version of the design was made available. The engine measured 76 mm × 127 mm and had 3497 cc. It developed 90 bhp in normally-aspirated and (for £755) 125 bhp in supercharged form. In all other technical respects the car was like the original 'Eight'. Four-door saloon and two-seater sports versions were also offered. Approximately 50 cars were constructed before production closed down in 1939.

### Specification (Straight Eight)

**Engine:** inline eight-cylinder, side-valve
**Bore × stroke:** 76 mm × 114 mm
**Capacity:** 4618 cc
**Maximum power:** 125 bhp
**Transmission:** three-speed manual gearbox, rear-wheel drive
**Chassis:** separate steel frame, channel-section side members
**Suspension:** beam front axle with semi-elliptic leaf springs; live rear axle with semi-elliptic leaf springs
**Brakes:** drums front and rear
**Bodywork:** convertible four-seater
**Maximum speed (approx):** 90 mph (145 km/h)

*Right: The Brough Superior Straight Eight was basically an American Hudson chassis and engine, rebodied by W.C. Atcherley of Birmingham.*

# Brough Superior Type X11 1938

This was a fascinating design which progressed no further than a single completed prototype. George Brough tried to outflank his major opposition – Railton – with an even more impressive car. This time the chassis design was his own, the massive and impressive sports saloon style was by Charlesworth of Coventry, and the engine was supplied by Ford USA, being a side-valve Lincoln Zephyr V12 which was actually less powerful than the original eight-cylinder Hudson, and which was mounted low down in the frame.

Brough certainly had big ideas for this 18 ft-long car, as it was priced at £1,250 (cheaper than a Rolls-Royce, but not by much). Once the car had been built, however, Brough discovered all manner of development problems, notably connected with keeping the engine cool, and with the chassis being too flexible. By this time, in any case, Brough's entire car business was fading away, and the ambitious Type XII never went into production.

## Specification

**Engine:** V12, side-valve
**Bore × stroke:** 69.85 mm × 95.25 mm
**Capacity:** 4378 cc
**Maximum power:** 112 bhp
**Transmission:** three-speed manual gearbox, rear-wheel drive

**Chassis:** separate steel frame with box-section side members
**Suspension:** beam front axle with semi-elliptic leaf springs; live rear axle with semi-elliptic leaf springs
**Brakes:** drums front and rear
**Bodywork:** steel four-seater saloon
**Maximum speed (approx):** 90 mph (145 km/h)

*Right: Power for the stillborn Type XII came from an American Lincoln V12 side-valve engine of 112 bhp.*

*Below: The Charlesworth-bodied Type XII never went into production.*

# Bugatti

E ttore Bugatti was an Italian, born in Milan, who learned his craft at Prinetti and Stucchi before going on to work for Baron de Dietrich. Having developed several fine cars for the Baron, Bugatti then moved on to work with Mathis in Strasbourg, and then to Deutz in Cologne.

During this period Bugatti spent his spare time designing a small car (the Type 10), and in 1909 he moved into a disused factory in Molsheim, in eastern France, to start the Bugatti business.

Over the next 30 years the Bugatti concern, which was ruled autocratically by Ettore throughout, produced a series of successful racing, sporting and touring cars. Bugatti settled on one basic chassis design, where the frame formed part of the suspension. The frame actually deflected more than the springs, which were very stiff. Rear suspension was by quarter-elliptics which faced *forward* from the tail of the frame. Bugatti kept this design through thick and thin.

He was much criticised for that, for his rigid refusal to consider using six-cylinder engines, and (in sporting circles) for his tardy adoption of supercharged engines and twin overhead-camshaft cylinder heads. No matter – the cars were usually very light, reliable, and could be speedily adapted for many different types of racing.

Some Bugatti lovers insist that there was only ever one *basic* type of

*Left: One of the most evocative of pre-war badges, and a powerful name even today. The 'EB' on top of the badge stands for founder Ettore Bugatti, who founded the company back in 1909 and died in 1947.*

Bugatti, though engines and chassis were scaled up or down according to their market. Certainly, Bugatti was slow to change. The archetypal Type 13 Brescia was in production for 16 years, the original two-litre 'Eight' spanned 13 years, and the Type 35 and its derivatives were campaigned from 1922 to 1935. The Brescia-type four-cylinder chassis was dropped in 1926, and the original single-cam straight-eight cars then took over from 1922 until the end of the decade.

By the late 1920s Ettore Bugatti's reputation was at its height, for his cars were winning races all over the world. He moved his Molsheim-made production cars up-market, making them much larger and more powerful than ever, and developed fascinating peripheral products such as aeroplane engines and railcars.

His most sensational product was the enormous Type 41 Royale, which he hoped to sell to European royalty, and he prepared to build 25 such cars. Royalty, though, was not interested, and in the end only six cars were ever built.

His other eight-cylinder cars – notably the Types 46, 50 and 57 – had smaller engines, less elephantine details, and were all popular and successful. Even so, by the early 1930s Bugatti's racing reputation was past its peak. The cars were seen to be technically backward, and they were beginning to sell only on their sporting reputation.

The introduction of several finely-detailed twin overhead-camshaft engines (for racing *and* for road-car use) restored much of the image, and the use of redundant Royale engines in SNCF (French Railways) railcars was a real talking-point. The Type 57 (1934-39) was also a fine car, in spite of lacking independent front suspension and many other newly-accepted technical advances.

Because Molsheim was in eastern France, close to the German border, it had to stop making cars as soon as World War II broke out. After 1945 only sporadic and half-hearted attempts were made to start building Bugattis again, and the marque expired in the early 1950s. In the early 1990s a short-lived Bugatti 'supercar' known as the EB110 GT was introduced under the patronage of Romano Artioli.

*Above: With a Bugatti scheduled to go into production in 1992, Giugiaro produced his ID90 styling exercise for Bugatti's consideration.*

## Bugatti Type 13

**1910-26**

This was really the first Bugatti 'production car', a small, lightweight, but carefully detailed, design. Original cars ran on a wheelbase of 78.7 in, which persisted into the mid-1920s, though longer-wheelbase versions were also produced. The Type 13 established Bugatti chassis features – such as the use of reversed quarter-elliptic leaf springs to support the rear axle – which were used on every subsequent model.

The original cars had an overhead camshaft operating two valves per cylinder, but post-World War I cars had an enlarged engine with a unique layout, where four valves per cylinder were operated by 'banana-shaped' tappets. The Type 13 got its famous name of Brescia by winning a big race in 1921 in that Italian town.

Although the chassis frame was fairly flexible, the springs themselves were rock-hard. The steering was precise and the engine was free-revving. In every way the Brescia was a very loveable little car, and almost 2,000 of all types were eventually built.

### Bugatti Type 13 variants

**Bugatti Types 15 and 17**
The first cars had 1357-cc engines and two valves per cylinder; the Types 15 and 17 were built with longer wheelbases, which allowed more roomy coachwork. Production ran from 1910 to 1920.

*Above and above right: The Type 13 was a light 1496-cc sports model. The Brescia tag came from its success in the 1921 Brescia event.*

**Bugatti Types 22 and 23**
These were essentially the same as current Type 13s, but with longer wheelbase chassis, built from 1913 to 1926.

### Specification (1910 Type 13)

**Engine:** inline four-cylinder, overhead-cam
**Bore × stroke:** 69 mm × 100 mm
**Capacity:** 1496 cc
**Maximum power:** not revealed
**Transmission:** four-speed manual gearbox, rear-wheel drive
**Chassis:** separate steel frame, channel-section side members
**Suspension:** beam front axle with semi-elliptic leaf springs; live rear axle with reversed quarter-elliptic leaf springs
**Brakes:** drums rear, and transmission drum
**Bodywork:** aluminium open two-seater
**Maximum speed (approx):** 75 mph (121 km/h)

# Bugatti Type 30 1922-26

The Type 30 will always be famous, not only because it was the first-ever eight-cylinder Bugatti, but also because its engine was the first of many successful 1991-cc units to be raced in the 1920s, and provided the inspiration for the Type 35 range. It was also the very first Bugatti to have four-wheel brakes, although only the front ones were hydraulically-operated. The rear brakes were still cable-activated.

In one way the Type 30 was directly descended from the Brescia, for it originally used a Type 23 chassis and suspension. The engine, however, was the very first of the 'slab-style' units, and had three valves per cylinder (one inlet, two exhaust), actuated by rockers from the single overhead camshaft.

Bugatti naturally developed racing cars from this design – but in the 1920s it was often difficult to work out which Bugatti was meant to carry out which function! In all, 600 Type 30s were produced in less than four years.

## Bugatti Type 30 variants

### Bugatti Types 35 and 39
This famous strain of racing Bugattis evolved from the Type 30, but on a shorter (95-in) wheelbase and with tiny, narrow and starkly-equipped racing bodies. Type 35s used two-litre engines, Type 35As used de-tuned engines, Type 35Bs and 35Cs had supercharged engines and 35Ts had 2262-cc 'blown' engines. The Type 39 replaced the Type 35, as a 1.5-litre model, and the Type 39A was a 'blown' version. There were other special race cars.

### Bugatti Type 51
This Grand Prix car, produced between 1931 and 1935, was a replacement for the Type 35, but with a twin-cam eight-cylinder engine. It was a long way from Type 30 engineering, but the lineage was clear.

Above: A Bugatti Type 30 from the second year of production, 1923, is pictured in Australia. The Type 30 was the first production Bugatti to have a straight-eight engine, starting a trend that lasted until the end of Bugatti in 1951.

## Specification

**Engine:** inline eight-cylinder, overhead-cam
**Bore × stroke:** 60 mm × 88 mm
**Capacity:** 1991 cc
**Maximum power:** 104 bhp
**Transmission:** four-speed manual gearbox, rear-wheel drive
**Chassis:** separate steel frame, channel-section side members
**Suspension:** beam front axle with semi-elliptic leaf springs; live rear axle with reversed quarter-elliptic leaf springs
**Brakes:** drums front and rear
**Bodywork:** aluminium open two- or four-seater
**Maximum speed (approx):** 90 mph (145 km/h)

Above: The most famous of all racing Bugattis – the Type 35. Developed from the Type 30, it made its Grand Prix debut at the 1924 French GP at Lyons when Bugatti brought along seven cars and 45 tonnes of spares. The Type 35 won countless races up to 1930.

Left: The famous 'horseshoe' radiator was featured on Bugattis into the early 1950s.

Right: Power for the Type 35 came from a straight-eight overhead-cam 2.3-litre engine. Thanks to the combination of its three-valve-per-cylinder layout and Roots-type supercharger, power output was as much as 150 bhp.

## Bugatti Type 37 1926-30

### Bugatti Type 37 variants

The Type 37A was a Grand Prix derivative with a supercharged engine, the Type 40 had a de-tuned version of the normally-aspirated engine, and the Type 40A had a 72-mm × 100-mm, 1623-cc version of that engine.

### Specification (Type 37)

**Engine:** inline four-cylinder, overhead-cam
**Bore × stroke:** 69 mm × 100 mm
**Capacity:** 1496 cc
**Maximum power:** not revealed
**Transmission:** four-speed manual gearbox, rear-wheel drive
**Chassis:** separate steel frame, channel-section side members
**Suspension:** beam front axle with semi-elliptic leaf springs; live rear axle with reversed quarter-elliptic leaf springs
**Brakes:** drums front and rear
**Bodywork:** aluminium open two-seater, some with closed coachwork
**Maximum speed (approx):** 95 mph (153 km/h)

*Below: The Type 37A was an out-and-out racer. It had a supercharged 1496-cc engine rather than the normally-aspirated unit in the Type 37.*

To replace the long-running Brescia model, Bugatti mated the 95-in wheelbase Type 35 chassis with a three-valve 1.5-litre four-cylinder engine, which had many of the same features as Bugatti's modern eight-cylinder engine (see Type 30 entry). Although it carried over the bore and stroke of the Brescia engine there was no connection between one engine and the other.

The result was the Type 37 model, sold (normally-aspirated) as a high-performance sports car or (supercharged, as the Type 37A) as a Grand Prix car. By the late 1920s at least 10 cars were being built every month, and a total of 270 were pro-

*Above: In its sports-car guise, the Type 37 could have headlights and covered wheels.*

duced by 1930, when assembly ended.

The coachwork was almost pure racer, very slim and with the famous horseshoe-shaped radiator up front. It was, if you insisted, a two-seater, but a large driver with active elbows left little space for his passenger. Weather protection was virtually nil.

Because of the exciting noises which emanated from the eight-cylinder engine, and the attractive styling, this was a charismatic Bugatti to own.

## Bugatti Royale Type 41 1927-33

Ettore Bugatti intended the massive Type 41 as a car for kings, which explains why it was soon nicknamed the Royale or the Golden Bugatti. As it happens, the Type 41 never received a single order from royalty, nor even from a Head of State, the result being that only six cars were built in a six-year period, three of these for use by the Bugatti family themselves.

Everything about the Royale was enormous – from its 170-in wheelbase and its 5,600-lb weight to its huge engine. Naturally there were no shared parts with any other Bugatti motor car, though the general layout of the chassis was familiar to enthusiasts.

The massive eight-cylinder engine was evolved from a 16-cylinder aeroplane engine design produced in the mid-1920s. The prototype Royale unit was of 14726 cc, but production cars merely displaced 12763 cc. The three-speed gearbox was in unit with the rear axle; second gear was direct, and third was very definitely a *Grand Routier* type of 'overdrive'.

When new, a Royale cost nearly three times as much as a Rolls-Royce Phantom II, which easily made it the most expensive car in the world. Happily for posterity, all six cars have survived, some having been rebodied more than once, and those which change hands command fabulous amounts of money.

*Right: A star of the famous Schlumpf collection, the Coupé Napoleon-bodied Royale was designed and built at the factory rather than by an outside coachbuilder.*

### Specification

**Engine:** inline eight-cylinder, overhead-cam
**Bore × stroke:** 125 mm × 130 mm
**Capacity:** 12763 cc
**Maximum power:** 300 bhp
**Transmission:** three-speed manual gearbox, rear-wheel drive
**Chassis:** separate steel frame, channel-section side members
**Suspension:** beam front axle with semi-elliptic leaf springs; live rear axle with two sets of quarter-elliptic leaf springs
**Brakes:** drums front and rear
**Bodywork:** six individual styles, some cars later rebodied
**Maximum speed (approx):** 100 mph (161 km/h)

*Right: The 1932 Kellner-bodied Royale was designed for the owner/driver but remained unsold for years.*

*Above: The enormous Royale was powered by a massive 12.8-litre straight-eight overhead-cam engine producing 275 bhp and giving 100-mph performance.*

# Bugatti Type 44 1927-30

*Above: This three-litre eight-cylinder Type 44 has an open four-seater body made by the Dutch coachbuilders Van Vooren.*

The new Type 44, introduced at the end of 1927, was the largest-engined Bugatti so far to go on sale. Its eight-cylinder engine had nine plain crankshaft bearings, its overhead camshaft was driven from the *centre* of that crankshaft, and it was a much smoother, more flexible and more refined design than any previous Bugatti.

The chassis, on a 123-in wheelbase, had many familiar Bugatti details, and was intended to support roomy (and sometimes flamboyant) touring-car bodywork. Descriptions like 'docile' and 'steam-engine torque' have often been applied to the Type 44, which was a remarkably well-mannered machine for its day. Its successor, the Type 49, was a similar sort of car.

## Bugatti Type 44 variants

### Bugatti Type 49
This was another touring Bugatti which replaced the Type 44, using the same chassis, but with a 72-mm × 100-mm, 3257-cc version of the same engine. It was the last of the single-cam eight-cylinder types, built from 1930 to 1934. A typical top speed was 81 mph. This model was eventually replaced by the new Type 57.

### Specification (Type 44)
**Engine:** inline eight-cylinder, overhead-cam
**Bore × stroke:** 69 mm × 100 mm
**Capacity:** 2991 cc
**Maximum power:** not revealed
**Transmission:** four-speed manual gearbox, rear-wheel drive
**Chassis:** separate steel frame, channel-section side members
**Suspension:** beam front axle with semi-elliptic leaf springs; live rear axle with reversed quarter-elliptic leaf springs
**Brakes:** drums front and rear
**Bodywork:** aluminium open or closed four- or two-seater
**Maximum speed (approx):** 85 mph (137 km/h)

# Bugatti Type 46 1929-36

Here was a true Bugatti luxury car, with a near 12-ft wheelbase, a brand-new 5.36-litre eight-cylinder engine, and great refinement. Except for the Type 41 Royale, which doesn't really count, the Type 46 was the largest-engined Bugatti car of all time.

Like all other Bugattis, it had a simple chassis design, rock-hard suspension, and that famous radiator style. Like the Royale, it also had its three-speed gearbox in unit with the rear axle. The engine was a massive single-cam 'eight' which looked like that of smaller Bugattis but was completely different in detail from any other, though it shared the same 130-mm stroke as the Royale.

Touring cars had 'unblown' engines, but the 46S (Sport) which followed had a supercharger, although that model was soon displaced by the new twin-cam Type 50 unit. In many ways it was the forerunner of the Type 50, and has sometimes been described as a 'mini-Royale'. Reputedly it was Ettore Bugatti's favourite model – nearly 400 were produced in seven years.

### Specification
**Engine:** inline eight-cylinder, overhead-cam
**Bore × stroke:** 81 mm × 130 mm
**Capacity:** 5360 cc
**Maximum power:** 143 bhp
**Transmission:** three-speed manual gearbox, rear-wheel drive
**Chassis:** separate steel frame, channel-section side members
**Suspension:** beam front axle with semi-elliptic leaf springs; live rear axle with reversed quarter-elliptic leaf springs
**Brakes:** drums front and rear
**Bodywork:** aluminium open or closed, four-seater
**Maximum speed (approx):** 88 mph (142 km/h)

*Below: Ettore Bugatti's favourite Bugatti – the 5.4-litre eight-cylinder Type 46. Nearly 400 were built in seven years.*

## Bugatti Type 50 1930-34

The Type 50 was the first Bugatti luxury car to have a big, torquey, and powerful twin-overhead-camshaft engine. It effectively replaced the short-lived Type 46S, and the twin-cam engine layout was reputedly an inspired copy of the American Miller racing cars that had raced at Monza in 1929.

Once adopted, this general layout was used for all current and projected Bugatti engines. It is difficult to decide whether this should be described as a touring style which could be super-tuned for racing, or vice versa – perhaps it's enough to say that the same engine was used in the Type 53 and Type 54 racing cars in the early 1930s!

*Left: Not the normal body for a hill-climb car. . . This closed Type 50 saloon was capable of nearly 110 mph thanks to its 200-bhp straight-eight engine.*

Except for the engine itself, the rest of the rolling chassis was identical with that of the Type 46. Because of the large and roomy chassis platform, these cars were usually treated to sumptuous, beautifully detailed and expensive body styles, and this might explain why only 65 Type 50s were ever sold.

### Bugatti Type 50 variants

#### Bugatti Types 53 and 54
The Type 53 four-wheel-drive racing car of 1932 and the Type 54 GP car (1931-34) both used developed versions of the Type 50's engine, with up to 300 bhp in this supercharged form.

### Specification (Type 50)
**Engine:** inline eight-cylinder, twin-cam
**Bore × stroke:** 86 mm × 107 mm
**Capacity:** 4972 cc
**Maximum power:** 200 bhp
**Transmission:** three-speed manual gearbox, rear-wheel drive
**Chassis:** separate steel frame, channel-section side members
**Suspension:** beam front axle with semi-elliptic leaf springs; live rear axle with reversed quarter-elliptic leaf springs
**Brakes:** drums front and rear
**Bodywork:** two- or four-seater, open or closed, various styles
**Maximum speed (approx):** 110 mph (177 km/h)

*Left: Like many other Bugattis, the Type 50 was bodied by a variety of coachbuilders. This one has the distinctive curved front door line that denotes the work of the Paris coachbuilders Saoutchik.*

## Bugatti Type 57 1934-39

There is no doubt that the Type 57 was Bugatti's most successful single design, for it was in production for five years, was sold in various different types, and is avidly sought after by today's collectors. In all, 710 such cars were built.

Designed almost entirely by Ettore's son, Jean Bugatti, it used a twin-cam development of the well-proven 3.3-litre 'eight' first seen in the Type 44/Type 49 models. However, this unit featured camshaft drive by a train of gears from the tail of the crank, and up the back of the block. The gearbox, though still without synchromesh, had constant-mesh gears, and if Jean had got his way (he didn't!) it would also have had independent front suspension.

For Bugatti there were many innovations in this car, including telescopic dampers, dry-sump lubrication in the Type 57S, rubber-mounted engines and hydraulic brakes on later cars, and extremely low and attractive styling on a

*Left: Some of the most attractive bodies appeared on the Type 57 chassis, like this two-seater by Van Vooren.*

*Below: The Type 57SC engine was a supercharged twin-cam 3.3-litre straight-eight with as much as 230 bhp. Standard engines had 140 bhp.*

*Left: Only three of the famous Atlantic coupés were built, on the Type 57S chassis; they are now among the most valuable cars in the world.*

117.5-in wheelbase. The most desirable of all, no question, was the Type 57SC, which had a supercharged engine and a top speed of 120 mph.

## Bugatti Type 57 variants

### Bugatti Type 59

The Type 59 Grand Prix car (1934-36) used a developed version of the Type 57 engine. In supercharged form it produced 230 bhp.

### Bugatti Type 101

The Type 101 was built in 1951-52, marking Bugatti's return to car production after the war. In effect it was the rolling chassis of the Type 57 with its 135 bhp (normally-aspirated) or 188 bhp (supercharged) engine, with a choice of gearboxes which included the electrically-controlled Cotal unit. Body styles were full-width in shape, but awkwardly tied to the old Bugatti 'horseshoe' grille. These cars were hugely expensive, and unsuccessful. Only 10 cars were sold.

## Specification (Type 57S)

**Engine:** inline eight-cylinder, twin-cam
**Bore × stroke:** 72 mm × 100 mm
**Capacity:** 3257 cc
**Maximum power:** 135 bhp
**Transmission:** four-speed manual gearbox, rear-wheel drive
**Chassis:** separate steel frame, channel-section side members
**Suspension:** beam front axle with semi-elliptic leaf springs; live rear axle with reversed quarter-elliptic leaf springs
**Brakes:** drums front and rear
**Bodywork:** two- or four-seater, open or closed, various styles
**Maximum speed (approx):** 120 mph (193 km/h)

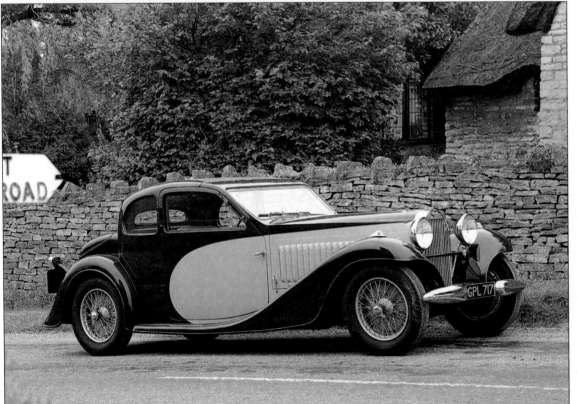

*Left: A Type 57 with Ventoux bodywork from 1934 with the distinctive raked flat windscreen.*

# Buick

*Right and below: Two examples of Buick's changing role within General Motors. Designed to be less expensive than Cadillacs, they still had to be different from Oldsmobiles – made by another GM division. That was not always easy when both divisions stressed comfort and a certain level of luxury. The 364-cu in 250-bhp 1957 Century (right) is typical of Buick designs of the era, while the 206-bhp 3.3-litre supercharged V6 Bolero (below) shows that Buick's thinking in the 1990s is directed towards performance as well as luxury.*

T he original Buick concern was set up in Detroit, USA, by David Dunbar Buick in 1903, but it became one of the founding members of General Motors in 1908.

Under Alfred P. Sloan, General Motors soon established a logical 'pecking order' of all its makes, with all different marques being fully integrated. The result was that Buick began building high-quality cars, slightly less expensive and usually slightly less powerful than General Motors' flagship, Cadillac, but slightly more up-market than Oldsmobile. This situation, once established, has continued right through to the 1990s.

In the 1920s Buick was noted for building six-cylinder cars, but a series of large and well-equipped straight-eight models dominated the 1930s and 1940s; the company's first V8 did not arrive until 1952. Buick's role within GM was carefully mapped out – it was to offer luxury, good equipment and comfort, but performance and sporty motoring were never stressed.

By the early 1960s most Buicks were ultra-powerful cars, with big V8 engines, though a V6 was launched in 1961 and would still feature in the line-up nearly three decades later. Then, in 1963, GM gave the stodgy image a big shake-up by launching the smart and stylish Riviera.

This was the first of several rakish GM cars to carry the Buick badge, which helped lift the marque's annual production from 400,000 (1962) to 666,000 (1970). Buick's standing in the USA improved dramatically in this period, for in 1960 it had been the ninth best-selling marque; by 1970 it was up to fifth place and retained that position thereafter.

Like most GM marques, Buick sales suffered badly in the economy-conscious 1970s and in the 'down-sizing' period that followed. In the early 1980s the styling of all Buick cars was shared with Oldsmobile and Pontiac, and there was danger of their identity being lost.

To counter this, however, GM decided to give Buick a performance boost. In the mid-1980s the Regal Coupe was given an ultra-powerful variant, the Grand National model (which was a synthesis of old and new, with a traditional saloon body and a new-generation turbocharged V6 engine), while in the late 1980s the engineers and enthusiasts finally got their way, with the introduction of the smart Reatta sports coupé.

Although it would take time to completely change Buick's image – the North American buying public is very conservative in its tastes – new styles, more aerodynamic shapes and aggressive marketing were all intended to do just that. Industry-watchers began to look forward to the 1990s with renewed interest.

## Buick Riviera 1963-67

At the end of the 1950s General Motors toyed with the idea of re-introducing the La Salle marque (which had disappeared in 1940). This scheme was eventually dropped, but GM stylists were then encouraged to produce a new 'personal luxury' car to match the latest four-seater Ford Thunderbird.

Using a new 117-in wheelbase chassis, the new car, which was given the name Buick Riviera, was 14 in shorter than other 'full-size' Buicks. The fixed-head coupé style, by Bill Mitchell's team, was sleek and attractive, with a touch of British 'razor-edge' about its detail.

Even so, by European standards it was a very large car. *Autocar*'s test car of 1965 weighed in at 4,370 lb, was 17 ft 6 in long, and could manage only 11 mpg. On the other hand it was fast – with its seven-litre engine the top speed was 122 mph, and it could accelerate to 100 mph in 21.1 seconds – and in the standing-start quarter-mile sprint it was almost as fast as Jaguar's E-type.

In that indefinable way that certain cars grab attention, and make headlines, the Riviera was an immediate success in the USA. The 1963 allocation of 40,000 cars was soon sold out, while in 1964 37,658 cars were sold. In 1965 the body shell was given a facelift, featuring headlamps normally hidden behind the front grille, while tail lights were integrated into the rear bumper, and a further 34,586 cars were delivered.

By that time the most powerful engine was a 360-bhp monster, and there was a modern three-speed automatic transmission, the result being a car that was extremely attractive to affluent middle-class American customers. Even though the Riviera featured only two doors, it had a generously packaged four-seater cabin, a shallow but massive boot, and a great deal of style.

*Above: The 1984 Buick Riviera T-type range, designed to be more European in feel, showed what GM could do in the way of advanced electronic engine control systems, fuel injection and turbocharging.*

European road-testers agreed that it was one of the best handling American cars so far built, although its suspension was still soft by European standards. The major drawback, as with all such American cars of the period, was the drum brakes, which could easily be persuaded to fade after heavy use.

The second-generation Riviera, built from 1965 to 1967, was another fine car, larger, heavier and more massive, with even larger engines to compensate. Amazingly, it sold for a mere $4,424 in 1966 – it was no wonder that sales soared to 45,000 a year in this period.

Thereafter the Riviera style was rationalised with Oldsmobile and Cadillac shapes, and the magic evaporated. It was some years before a truly individual Buick appeared once again.

### Buick Riviera variants

#### Buick Riviera Coupe (1965-71)
The second-generation car had a slightly longer wheelbase, and a much more massive two-door coupé body style. The seven-litre engine was dropped for 1966, but a new type of seven-litre V8 returned for 1967; this was enlarged to no less than 7.5 litres and 370 bhp for 1970. 1968 models were restyled yet again, but the 119-in wheelbase chassis was retained. By 1971, after annual facelifts, the body shell was being shared with a Cadillac Coupe de Ville, and the original unique character had gone, although the Riviera name persisted into the 1980s.

### Specification (1963-65)

**Engine:** V8, overhead-valve
**Bore × stroke:** 106.36 mm/
109.5 mm × 92.5 mm
**Capacity:** 6969 cc
**Maximum power:** 325 bhp
**Transmission:** two-speed (later three-speed) automatic transmission, rear-wheel drive
**Chassis:** separate frame with box-section side members
**Suspension:** independent front with wishbones and coil springs; live rear axle with coil springs
**Brakes:** drums front and rear
**Bodywork:** four-seater fixed-head coupé
**Maximum speed (approx):** 122 mph (196 km/h) with 360-bhp engine option

*Below: One of Mitchell's best Riviera designs was the controversial 'boat-tailed' version from the early 1970s.*

# Buick Grand National 1983-87

During the 1970s and early 1980s Buick produced an enduring middle-size range of rear-drive cars carrying the Century model name on saloons and estate cars; the specialised version of this model was the six-seater coupé, called Regal.

In the late 1970s there were several V6 and V8 engine options, while a 4.3-litre diesel was also made available for those who put economy before performance.

In 1983 Buick once again decided to boost its performance, and launched a special version of the Regal. This model, dubbed Grand National – not after the British horse race, but after the NASCAR series in the USA – still used GM's long-established 90-degree V6 engine, but it was fitted with a Garrett turbocharger

*Above: Buick's turbocharged 200-bhp Regal Grand National was an exercise in sporting extroversion; the 1987 model saw a power increase to as much as 245 bhp.*

and twin exhausts. The result was 200 bhp with masses of torque.

At the same time the Grand National was given special cast-alloy wheels, wickedly 'understated' styling (including bumpers in body colour), and the engine was linked to a four-speed automatic transmission. The result was a tyre-stripping extrovert sports coupé that could reach 125 mph.

For 1987 the engine was further boosted, with fuel injection and an intercooler, to produce 245 bhp, this giving the Grand National a potential top speed

of around 135 mph if the tyres could stand the strain.

But there was more to come. For 1988 the Regal was to be completely redesigned, around a front-wheel-drive installation, and there was to be no place for a turbocharged engine. For the last months of its life, therefore, a 'final edition' Regal, the GNX, was launched. This kept the same angular style as before, but its engine was once again tweaked, this time with a larger turbocharger and a more efficient intercooler.

With no less than 300 bhp under the bonnet, and revised location to keep the rear axle in place, the GNX could sprint to the quarter-mile in 13.4 seconds, by which time it was already doing 104 mph and still accelerating.

Only 500 of these wide-tyred, thundering, GNXs were produced – but what a way to end a long-running series!

### Specification (1983)

**Engine:** V6, overhead-valve
**Bore × stroke:** 96.52 mm × 86.36 mm
**Capacity:** 3791 cc
**Maximum power:** 200 bhp
**Transmission:** four-speed automatic, rear-wheel drive
**Chassis:** separate steel frame
**Suspension:** independent front with coil springs; live rear axle with coil springs
**Brakes:** discs front, drums rear
**Bodywork:** five-seater coupé
**Maximum speed (approx):** 125 mph (201 km/h)

# Buick Reatta 1988-91

For many years Buick's bosses had wanted to produce a sporting car, but were always turned down by General Motors' top management. Buick, they were told, made luxury cars – it was Chevrolet and Pontiac that were allowed to build sporting cars for GM.

Even so, Buick nagged and nagged... but it was not until the mid-1980s that approval was finally given for Buick to build a two-seater. The result, unveiled early in 1988, was the Reatta, whose smooth styling was as smart as anything that had so far emerged from Britain, Italy or Japan.

The Reatta was a compact, limited-production car, based on the platform and transverse engine/front-wheel-drive installation of cars like the Buick Somerset and Pontiac Grand Am. It broke every possible mould at GM by being a two-seater coupé, pure and simple. No-one tried to justify it as a 'commuter car', or with any other weasel words – here was a Buick that was a sports coupé, and which would stand or fall on that image.

Although the Reatta's shape was in-

*Right: The 1988 Buick Reatta two-seater coupé was based on a shortened Riviera platform, and marked GM's return to the domain of mid-size coupés. This front-wheel-drive car replaced the veteran rear-wheel-drive Regal range, but retained 'Buick' external features.*

dividual enough, there was a touch of Porsche, Toyota and Mazda RX-7 about the styling. Under the skin, however, the Reatta was pure corporate GM, late-1980s style, for the roots of the V6 engine were in the early 1960s, and the package with the four-speed automatic transmission, allied to MacPherson strut front suspension, was all very familiar.

It was a neatly detailed style (the Cd was 0.34), well-equipped, and able to sprint to 60 mph in about 10 seconds. Buick claimed the top speed as 125 mph, and unlike the Grand National there were four-wheel disc brakes and all-independent suspension to make this a true sporting car.

By 1991 a cabriolet had been added to the range, and peak power had risen to 173 bhp.

### Specification (1988)

**Engine:** V6, overhead-valve
**Bore × stroke:** 96.52 mm × 86.36 mm
**Capacity:** 3791 cc
**Maximum power:** 165 bhp
**Transmission:** four-speed automatic transmission, front-wheel drive
**Chassis:** unitary body/chassis assembly
**Suspension:** independent front with

MacPherson struts and coil springs; independent rear with transverse leaf springs
**Brakes:** discs front and rear
**Bodywork:** two-seater coupé and convertible
**Maximum speed (approx):** 125 mph (201 km/h)

# Cadillac Car Co.

**T**he name 'Cadillac' was taken from the officer in the French army who founded the city of Detroit in 1701. There were two personalities behind the foundation of the Cadillac Car Company in 1902: William H. Murphy (who had originally backed the young Henry T. Ford), and Henry Martyn Leland, a brilliant designer whose engines were to be used in the cars. The marque was independent only until 1909, when it became a member of the fledgling General Motors Corporation. By that time it had already brought the art of interchangeable parts manufacture to a high level – something proved by a three-car strip-and-rebuild demonstration at Brooklands in 1908, which earned the marque the RAC's Dewar Trophy.

It took years for General Motors to shake themselves into shape, but once Cadillac's four-cylinder engine had been displaced by a brand-new V8 (the world's first series-production V8) the marque became the most prestigious in GM's stable. From that day to this, almost every ambitious American businessman aims to buy a Cadillac, then another, then another...

Almost by definition, Cadillac sales were more limited than those of other GM makes such as Buick, Oldsmobile and particularly Chevrolet. Cadillac prices were the highest in the corporation (but so was its prestige), and because production volumes were limited GM often chose to 'test-market' their innovations at this level before adding them to the more humble Chevrolets or Pontiacs.

The original V8 Cadillacs were sold from 1914 until 1927, to be followed by a brand-new V8, more powerful and more efficient than before. Between the wars Cadillac's styling was always conservative, and relied on coachbuilders like Fleetwood and Fisher to produce an amazing variety of bodies – some open, some closed, some of truly gargantuan proportions.

The most technically exciting Cadillacs of this period were the related V12 and V16 models, both of which appeared in 1930, a year in which the North American economy was rapidly sinking to its knees. These, naturally, sold very slowly indeed, but their reputation was immense – and in some quarters Cadillac were praised for continuing to "believe in America".

Along the way GM introduced La Salle in 1927 as a smaller companion to Cadillac, but this marque died out in 1940. Cadillac itself progressed steadily before World War II, selling 66,130 cars in the 1941 model-year. Along the way, buyers saw the introduction of four-wheel brakes (1923), synchromesh gearboxes (1928), servo-assisted brakes (1932), independent front suspension (1934), hydraulic brakes (1937) and finally automatic transmission for 1941.

Body styles changed only gradually, becoming steadily more rounded through the 1930s. 'Turret-top' construction (very bulbous, with flowing

*Above: The Cadillac V16 badge. The world's first production V16 was announced by Cadillac in 1930.*

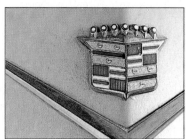

*Above: Cadillac's coat of arms. The company was named after Antoine de la Mothe Cadillac.*

front and rear wings) made its debut in 1935, and by 1941 the cars had faired-in headlamps and wide-mouth grilles.

The next big advances, in engineering and in styling, would follow in the late 1940s. Once World War II was over, GM quickly re-converted their factories to peacetime production, and the first 1,000 cars, to '1942-model' standards, were assembled before the end of 1945. While work went ahead on new models, a series of developed versions of pre-war types were produced in 1946 and 1947. It was not until the autumn of that year that the first true 'post-war' Cadillac went on sale.

Since then, Cadillac's policy has always been successful – and crystal-clear. General Motors designated Cadillac as the most prestigious of all their different marques, so these cars were the largest, the best-equipped and the best-assembled of all. Oldsmobile and Buick were just below Cadillac in GM's 'pecking order', which meant that major components such as basic body shells and chassis were sometimes shared with them. GM's designers, however, were sufficiently experienced to be able to hide most of this!

From 1945 to 1975 a Cadillac always had its own type of V8 engine, though when the smaller Seville came on the scene this used an Oldsmobile engine. For many years there were only two basic series – the Series 60 cars, on wheelbases in the 126-in to 130-in range, and Series 75 cars, on longer wheelbases.

For 1948 there was the first post-war style, then the true post-war V8 engine followed for 1949, power steering was standardised for 1954, a completely new body style followed in the same year, and the famous

*Below: From the 1930s through to the 1970s Cadillac had the benefit of one of the world's most famous designers, Bill Mitchell, pictured here. This massive Eldorado convertible was one of Mitchell's late 1960s designs.*

rear fins grew ever larger, year after year, until 1959. Thereafter they were gradually trimmed back.

Cadillac was so successful by that time that they introduced a new front-wheel-drive car, the Eldorado coupé, the first time for many years that Cadillac production lines had dealt with more than one set of running gear.

In the 1970s new exhaust-emission and safety legislation hit hard at Cadillac, and from the mid-1970s GM progressively began to 'down-size' their cars, making them smaller, lighter, less powerful *and* more fuel-efficient. The first evidence of this was the Seville, which was a conventional front-engine/rear-drive car at first (but a front-wheel-drive car from 1980 onwards).

At the end of the 1980s Cadillac produced the Allanté, a Pininfarina-built cabriolet/coupé that sold slowly. In the late 1990s the company produced a 'world car' in the Seville STS, designed to compete in the Lexus segment. It was the most powerful front-drive car in the world.

*Left: Although Cadillacs are now mechanically virtually indistinguishable from the other General Motors models, that was not the case in the 1930s, when Cadillac built this model – the luxurious V16. Not all had such elegant 'boat-tail' bodies, however.*

# Cadillac Eight 1927-35

The second-generation Cadillac V8 was launched in 1927. This was a slightly larger (341-cu in, 5.6-litre) engine, with side-by-side connecting rods, a larger bore and shorter stroke than before, and with power up to 90 bhp. There was a smaller (303-cu in) version of the engine in the new GM La Salle cars and, like its predecessor, this was such a fine design that it remained basically unchanged until 1935.

The rest of the chassis was strictly conventional at first, but from the autumn of 1928 Cadillac produced another world innovation – the synchromesh gearbox, adding synchro to bottom gear for 1932. Apart from this, Cadillac offered a stun-

ning range of bodies – some open, some closed, some for owner-drivers, some to be chauffeur-driven. Around 18,103 were sold in 1929 (immediately before the Wall Street Crash), and 10,717 in 1931 when the Depression was at its worst. Prices, in the meantime, had been cut to stimulate business – from around $3,400 in 1928 to about $3,000 in 1931.

Body styles changed slowly, but persistently, becoming more rounded for 1932, and even more bulbous for 1934.

## Cadillac Eight variants

For 1930 the engine grew to 353 cu in (and up to 135 bhp by 1935), while for

1934 the Eight became the Type 355D, complete with a new, shorter chassis, and independent front suspension by what Cadillac called "knee action". Once again GM were using their most expensive car to usher in changes that were to be progressively applied to other models. By that time prices were down to $2,600 or $2,700, but only 3,065 cars were sold in the first year.

*Below: A 1928 Cadillac Eight. Eights of this vintage benefitted from chief engineer Seaholm's 'new' V8, which superseded the original 1914 design and eliminated the annoying vibrations that had characterised it.*

## Specification (1928)

**Engine:** V8, side-valve
**Bore × stroke:** 84.1 mm × 125.4 mm
**Capacity:** 5585 cc
**Maximum power:** 90 bhp
**Transmission:** three-speed manual gearbox, rear-wheel drive
**Chassis:** separate steel frame with channel-section side members
**Suspension:** non-independent with beam axle front and semi-elliptic leaf springs; live rear axle with semi-elliptic leaf springs
**Brakes:** drums front and rear
**Bodywork:** steel, open or closed
**Maximum speed (approx):** 75 mph (121 km/h)

# Cadillac V16 1930-37

The world's first-ever V16 passenger car was unveiled in 1930, immediately *after* the Wall Street Crash had sent America's industry into a serious Depression. The car, however, had been conceived in 1927, and Cadillac were determined to make a success of it.

The chassis was conventional in every way, but the 45-degree overhead-valve V16, a 165-bhp 7.4-litre unit, was a magnificent creation that was further tuned, to give 185 bhp, for 1934 and onwards. Cadillac's aim, simply, was to produce the world's smoothest and most advanced power unit – one that, incidentally, had to fight for a tiny market against Marmon's even more advanced V16, and a number of V12s from rivals such as Packard and Lincoln.

Amazingly, no fewer than 3,250 V16s were sold in 1930 and 1931, at prices from $5,350 (two-seat roadster) to $8,750 (town cabriolet); no fewer than 33 different body types were offered!

Prices were twice those of V8 Cadillacs, but kept in check by sharing many chassis components with other models, notably the closely-related V12, but the V16 was still an awfully slow seller. Only 296 cars were built in 1932, 125 in 1933, 60 in 1934, 50 in 1935, 52 in 1936 and 49 in 1937.

For 1938 the original V12/V16 engines were discontinued, and Cadillac intro-

*Right: This 1931 Fleetwood Cadillac V16 was built for the Maharajah of Tikari, hence the right-hand drive.*

*Below: More-modern formal bodywork was also featured on the V16.*

*Inset below: Engine displacement of the V16 was 7.4 litres.*

duced a new 135-degree side-valve V16, a 431-cu in design with side-valve heads that produced 185 bhp; only 508 such cars were built in three years, and these were Cadillac's final V16s.

## Cadillac V16 variants
### Cadillac V12
The V12 was launched a few months after the V16, also with a 135-bhp (later 150-bhp) 45-degree engine obviously derived from the V16, with the same suspension and running gear but on a slightly shorter wheelbase. There was a wide choice of coachbuilt bodies, and prices tended to be at least $1,000 less than the V16. Nearly 11,000 V12s were sold in seven years.

### Specification (1930 V16)
**Engine:** V16, overhead-valve
**Bore × stroke:** 76.2 mm × 101.6 mm
**Capacity:** 7413 cc
**Maximum power:** 165 bhp (later 185 bhp)
**Transmission:** three-speed manual gearbox, rear-wheel drive
**Chassis:** separate steel frame with channel-section side members
**Suspension:** non-independent front with beam axle and semi-elliptic leaf springs; live rear axle with semi-elliptic leaf springs
**Brakes:** drums front and rear
**Bodywork:** steel open or closed five- to seven-seater
**Maximum speed (approx):** 90 mph (145 km/h)

# Cadillac Series 60 and Series 75 1949-53

Immediately after World War II Cadillac's cars were only slightly improved 1941 examples, and the same basic model was built until 1947. The 1948 cars featured a completely new body style, and a year later this style was joined by a brand-new overhead-valve V8 engine; this was the engine used in sports cars such as the Allard and the Cunningham in the early 1950s.

Cadillac built strongly on this base during the next few years. The body styles, by Harley Earl and Bill Mitchell, featured the industry's first tailfins, reputedly inspired by the Lockheed Lightning P-38 fighter plane, while the engine was a light high-compression V8 (200 lb lighter than the obsolete unit!), of a type that inspired many copies in Detroit's next decade.

The separate chassis had independent front suspension and was available in two wheelbases – 126 in and 133 in – with the option of automatic transmission in no fewer than 13 co-related body styles from GM's Fisher Division. Prices started at $2,788, and top speeds were over 100 mph.

As so often in the past, the Cadillac was Detroit's best-selling luxury car, and in the last year before a completely new body style was introduced 90,000 cars were built. Even so, demand for Cadillacs soared even further in years to come.

## Specification (1949)

**Engine:** V8, overhead-valve
**Bore × stroke:** 96.8 mm × 92.2 mm
**Capacity:** 5422 cc
**Maximum power:** 160 bhp (later models up to 210 bhp)
**Transmission:** three-speed manual gearbox or four-speed automatic, rear-wheel drive
**Chassis:** separate steel frame with box-section side members
**Suspension:** independent front with coil springs; live rear axle with semi-elliptic leaf springs
**Brakes:** drums front and rear
**Bodywork:** steel open or closed five-seater, various styles
**Maximum speed:** 100 mph (161 km/h)

*Above: With the Series 75, Cadillac's designers launched fins onto the American market. These were merely embryonic to begin with, but later grew to huge dimensions. The 75 was otherwise conventional with (in the case of this 1953 model) a 210-bhp 5.4-litre V8 driving the rear wheels.*

# Cadillac Eldorado 1966-78

By the 1960s much of Cadillac's advanced engineering work was shared with Oldsmobile, so when that company introduced a new front-wheel-drive car, the Toronado, a similar Cadillac soon followed.

The new Eldorado, launched in 1966, was a massive front-wheel-drive four-seater coupé, sharing all its running gear with the Toronado except for having a different engine size, and a rather 'sharper' version of the same long-bonnet/short-boot body style.

The big 340-bhp V8 engine was mounted in the conventional position under the bonnet, but the Hydramatic automatic transmission was alongside and below the engine itself. There was chain drive from engine to transmission, and the front wheels were driven.

In other ways, in fact, the Eldorado was 'mainstream-Detroit', with a perimeter-type chassis frame, power-assisted everything, and a great deal of typically Cadillac style.

Cadillac retained the same basic design for 12 years, a period during which the car got longer and heavier, but less powerful as emissions regulations bit hard. A convertible style was added for

*Right: Despite its huge dimensions and weight, the Eldorado was actually a front-wheel-drive model based on the Oldsmobile Toronado. Power came from a 340-bhp V8 with chain drive to the three-speed Hydramatic automatic transmission, resulting in a top speed of 120 mph.*

1971 (but dropped again after 1976), while the wheelbase went up by 6.3 inches for 1972. The engine was enlarged from 429 cu in to 472 cu in for 1968, then to 500 cu in for 1970, and then reduced to 425 cu in for 1977 and 1978. Peak power (1970) was 400 bhp; this had dropped to 180 bhp by 1977. Annual sales started at 17,900, but more than 51,000 were sold in 1973, the peak of the car's popularity.

The major change came in 1979, when the Eldorado was completely redesigned, and made much shorter and 800 lb lighter than before.

In 1982 Cadillac introduced a more 'European' version, the Touring Coupé, with black trim, wider tyres and alloy wheels. This changed look was short-lived, however, and the Eldorado soon returned to normal.

### Specification (1967)

**Engine:** V8, overhead-valve
**Bore × stroke:** 104.9 mm × 101.6 mm
**Capacity:** 7031 cc
**Maximum power:** 340 bhp
**Transmission:** three-speed automatic, front-wheel drive
**Chassis:** separate steel frame with box-section side members
**Suspension:** independent front with torsion bars; 'dead' beam rear axle with semi-elliptic leaf springs
**Brakes:** drums front and rear
**Bodywork:** steel five-seater coupé
**Maximum speed (approx):** 120 mph (193 km/h)

*Above: The 1972 Eldorado was built on a wheelbase that had been extended by 6.3 inches. Power came from a 500-cu in V8 producing nearly 400 bhp.*

# Cadillac Seville 1975-79

In the 1960s and 1970s Cadillacs had been getting bigger, heavier and faster. By 1970 a typical Caddy had 375-400 bhp, was well over 18 ft long, and weighed about 5,000 lb. Then, in the first of many 'down-sizing' moves at General Motors, Cadillac took a big gamble and introduced the Seville. This was 2 ft shorter and 1,000 lb lighter than other Cadillacs, with a fuel-injected 180-bhp 5.7-litre engine which they bought in from Oldsmobile; 16-20 mpg was possible.

The stylists, led by Bill Mitchell, aimed the Seville squarely at the Mercedes-Benz type of market: the new car was the size of an S-class, and had handsome but angular styling, based on an existing GM X-body 'compact' shell. The Cadillac grille up front, the discreet badging all round, and some very glossy advertising all helped to establish the image.

Even though it was smaller, it was loaded with every normal Cadillac fitting, including automatic transmission, power-adjustable seats, glitzy trim, air conditioning, and self-levelling of the leaf-spring rear suspension. Road-testers soon christened it the best-handling Cadillac of all time, and it began to sell fast. More than 43,000 were built in 1976, 45,000 in 1977, 57,000 in 1978 and 53,000 in 1979.

Surprisingly, there were no major facelifts during the car's four-year life, and the only major mechanical innovation was the introduction of a 120-bhp 5.7-litre diesel engine option in 1978 and a 125-bhp version in 1979. This made 30 mpg possible, but only about 12,000 diesels found their way into the showrooms.

The second-generation Seville of 1980 was an entirely different machine, with front-wheel drive, with the choice of a V6, a diesel V8, or two petrol V8s. The Seville STS of 1999 was the most powerful front-wheel drive car in the world.

*Right: In the mid-1970s GM's vice-president of design, Bill Mitchell, decided it was time for a 'down-sized', more European, Cadillac. The result was this car – the Seville. It was as much as two feet shorter and 1,000 lb lighter than the other full-size Cadillacs. Unlike the earlier Eldorado, the Seville was a conventional rear-drive design with a 5.7-litre V8.*

### Specification (1975)

**Engine:** V8, overhead-valve
**Bore × stroke:** 103.05 mm × 85.98 mm
**Capacity:** 5737 cc
**Maximum power:** 180 bhp
**Transmission:** three-speed automatic, rear-wheel drive
**Chassis:** steel unit-construction body/chassis assembly
**Suspension:** independent front with coil springs and wishbones; 'dead' beam rear axle with semi-elliptic leaf springs and self-levelling system
**Brakes:** discs front, drums rear (rear discs for 1977)
**Bodywork:** steel five-seater saloon
**Maximum speed (approx):** 115 mph (185 km/h)

*Above: In the early 1980s Cadillac changed the Seville's styling to incorporate the strange 'bustle back', misguidedly intended as a reminder of the more elegant styles of the 1930s.*

## Cadillac Allanté 1987-91

In an effort to compete on equal terms with the increasingly popular 'luxury imports', Cadillac took the bold step of commissioning Pininfarina of Turin to design a two-seater roadster. Introduced as a 1987 model, the Allanté was based on a shortened Eldorado chassis with its 170-bhp, 4.1-litre V8 driving the front wheels.

The Allanté's main claim to fame was the length of its production line. Pininfarina designed, engineered and set up to produce the bodies in a new plant at San Giorgio Canavese. From there they were shipped by Boeing 747 to Detroit and thence to Cadillac's Hamtramck plant for power-trains to be installed and assembly completed. Cadillac could thus claim that they had a car designed and built in Italy, justifying a price near to the Mercedes SL (judged its closest competitor) and much higher than any other series-production Cadillac.

$54,000 was too expensive for the US market, which did not regard the car as a serious alternative to the European exotics. Sales were much less than planned, the 'air bridge' had to be reduced from three Jumbos a week to one, and the car was up-rated with a bigger, 200-bhp 4.5-litre engine and improved equipment in a further attempt to justify its ever-increasing price.

### Specification (1987)

**Engine:** V8, overhead-valve
**Bore × stroke:** 87.8 mm × 76.96 mm
**Capacity:** 4082 cc
**Maximum power:** 170 bhp
**Transmission:** three-speed automatic transmission, front-wheel drive
**Chassis:** steel unit-construction body/chassis assembly
**Suspension:** independent front with coil springs; 'dead' rear axle with coil springs
**Brakes:** discs front and rear
**Bodywork:** two-seater roadster
**Maximum speed (approx):** 130 mph (209 km/h)

# Caterham Cars Ltd

Caterham's story really begins with another car company, Lotus. Lotus produced the first Seven sports car model in 1957, developing it into the Series 2 in 1960, and the Series 3 in 1968. In almost all cases these cars were provided in component form, for home assembly, so that taxes would not have to be paid.

Lotus then went up-market with the modernised S4, which was still mainly supplied in kit form. This model actually remained in production until 1973 and used many glassfibre panels.

In the meantime a group of enthusiasts set up a sports car garage business in Caterham (in the southern suburbs of London), logically enough calling it Caterham Car Sales. This soon took on a Lotus dealership, and remained faithful to the marque in spite of many business problems over the years. Graham Nearn, a director who came to control Caterham, eventually became the sole UK distributor for Sevens, and in the early 1970s, when Lotus lost interest in this car, he bought all the rights from the factory.

At first Caterham built a few S4 types, but in 1974 the obsolete Lotus Seven S3 was re-introduced, was renamed Caterham Super Seven, and has been selling successfully ever since. The early-1990s model has the same basic design as that first produced in 1968, but many improvements have been made along the way.

Demand actually rose as the design grew older, with more and more export markets being opened in the 1980s.

As with the Morgan, 20 years may have brought no obvious styling changes, but under the skin almost every mechanical component has been renewed. By the late 1990s, output was around 600 cars a year, a quarter of which were fully built, the rest sold as kits or in component form.

*Right: Caterham's Super Seven Sprint badge is a clever reworking of the almost triangular Lotus shape, to remind people of the car's origins.*

*Below: In 1974 Caterham re-introduced the obsolete Lotus Seven S3 as the Caterham Super Seven, and they have been selling variations of this model ever since.*

# Caterham Super Seven 1974-present

It was in 1974 that the Super Seven was introduced; it was the Lotus Seven S3 reborn, and has been evolving ever since.

The Seven has been described as the fastest four-wheeler motorcycle in the world, for every version has had the same sort of characteristics. A Seven was a machine for driving, not for living-room comfort. It had a hard ride and inch-sensitive steering, rather than soft suspension and complete insulation of the driver from the road.

It was always a very starkly-built machine. The outline of the multi-tube chassis was visible in the engine bay *and* in the cockpit, the weather protection was not totally efficient (and when erect the hood was so constricting that it was almost impossible to get in or out of the car for any but the smallest of people). There were no doors, virtually nowhere to stow anything, and because the car was so small it always felt vulnerable when used in heavy traffic.

Bodywork was in thin-gauge aluminium, and featured long sweeping wings over the front wheels, and cutaway sides to the cramped cockpit. The front wheels were almost totally exposed, and the Seven's aerodynamic qualities must have been even worse than those of the Morgan.

The original Caterham Super Sevens used Ford four-speed gearboxes, Triumph Herald steering, and Ford Escort rear axles. Over the years (sometimes because of supply problems as parts became obsolete, sometimes in a genuine attempt to upgrade the product) five-speed boxes, BL Morris Ital rear axles and BL Mini steering racks appeared. The cockpit was enlarged in 1981, and de Dion rear suspension finally arrived in 1985.

### Caterham Seven Variant

#### C21

Launched in 1994, with an all-enveloping alloy body, extended Seven spaceframe, productionised with GRP bodies and available with normal Caterham powertrains. Still austere motoring.

### Caterham Seven – different engines

Apart from the Ford 1600 GT, the Caterham has been sold with many different engine options including:

Lotus-Ford Big Valve twin-cam (1558 cc/126 bhp)
Lotus-Ford Vegantune twin-cam (1598 cc/126 bhp)
Vegantune VTA twin-cam (1598 cc/130 bhp)
Ford 1300 GT overhead-valve (1297 cc/72 bhp)
Ford 1600 GT Caterham Sprint overhead-valve (1598 cc/110 bhp)
Ford 1600 GT Caterham Supersprint overhead-valve (1598 cc/135 bhp)
Ford-Cosworth BDR 16-valve twin-cam (1598 cc/155 bhp)
Ford-Cosworth BDR 16-valve twin-cam (1698 cc/170 bhp)
GM 16-valve twin-cam (1998 cc/175 bhp, top speed 126 mph)

### Specification (1974 1600 GT Caterham Sprint engine)

**Engine:** inline-four, overhead-valve
**Bore × stroke:** 80.96 mm × 77.62 mm
**Capacity:** 1598 cc
**Maximum power:** 110 bhp
**Transmission:** four-speed (later five-speed) manual gearbox, rear-wheel drive
**Chassis:** separate multi-tubular steel chassis
**Suspension:** independent front with coil springs and wishbones; live rear axle with coil springs (de Dion rear from 1985)
**Brakes:** discs front, drums rear
**Bodywork:** aluminium open two-seater sports
**Maximum speed:** 110 mph (177 km/h)

*Above: The interior of the Caterham Seven remains stark, but has been made more inviting over the years.*

*Below: A powerful engine with up to 175 bhp inside a very light alloy body – that's the explanation for the Caterham Seven's success.*

*Below: The latest Caterham Super Seven is available with various engines, ranging from the 110-bhp Ford 1600 GT through a 135-bhp 1700 to the two-litre Vauxhall 16-valve twin-cam which gives 125-mph performance.*

# Chevrolet

The original Chevrolet car was inspired by William C. Durant, but was designed by American racing driver Louis Chevrolet. It was intended to be the cheapest, simplest and most numerous car to be built by the General Motors Group in Detroit.

The first Chevrolet was launched in 1912, as a $650 machine with a four-cylinder engine. Before long the marque became a major rival to Ford's Model T, and by the late 1920s it had become the USA's best seller.

From that day to this, Chevrolet has been the largest and most powerful of General Motors' marques. Most of the time, with most of their models, Chevrolet have supplied family-car motoring to millions of Americans. From time to time, though, they have stepped intriguingly out of line, with cars like the Corvette, the rear-engined Corvair 'compact' car, and in more modern times with very small family cars, some of which have actually been re-badged Japanese models!

In absolute terms very few Chevrolets have been exciting cars, but millions have been spacious, reliable, cheap-to-run machines. Chevrolet engines, in particular, have often been strong, lusty, and very tuneable, to such an extent that many found their way into Grand Touring or sports cars.

In the 1990s, as in the 1950s, 1930s or 1920s, Chevrolet remains the most important marque within General Motors.

*Above: The famous Chevrolet 'bow-tie' emblem appeared on the Corvette, along with a chequered flag.*

*Left: Chevrolet are most famous worldwide for the Corvette; this is a 1972 LT1 with the 330-bhp V8.*

*Below: The Camaro is almost equally famous; this is a 175-bhp V8-engined 1981 Z28.*

## Chevrolet International Six 1928-32

Once Chevrolet had been completely integrated into General Motors, it was pitched as a head-on competitor with Ford. With this in mind, the new International Six model appeared in 1928, a design which formed the basis of all successful Chevrolets of the 1930s.

This car was important because it was twice as powerful as its predecessor. Not only that, but it also had a smooth overhead-valve six-cylinder engine, whereas Ford made do with four cylinders and side valves. Although it was utterly conventional in design, this unit was an important 'building block' for Chevrolet's future. It was always affectionately known as the 'Stovebolt Six', because of the ¼-in fixing bolts used throughout the construction.

This was the car which brought trouble-free motoring to Depression-torn American buyers, and as a result Chevrolet soon became market leaders. Masters and Standards took over in 1933, and 'knee-action' independent front suspension followed in 1934, but old-type

beam-axle chassis were still available until 1940. The 'Stovebolt' six-cylinder engine was modified, remodified and updated over the years, but the last of a much-changed line was not produced until 1953, a quarter of a century after the original 'Stovebolt' had appeared.

### Specification (1929)

**Engine:** inline-six, overhead-valve
**Bore × stroke:** 84.1 mm × 95.25 mm
**Capacity:** 3175 cc
**Maximum power:** 46 bhp
**Transmission:** three-speed manual gearbox, rear-wheel drive
**Chassis:** separate steel frame with channel-section side members
**Suspension:** non-independent front with beam axle and semi-elliptic leaf springs; live rear axle with semi-elliptic leaf springs
**Brakes:** drums front and rear
**Bodywork:** steel two- or four-seater, open or closed, various styles
**Maximum speed (approx):** 60 mph (97 km/h)

*Above: The International Six was the car that gave Chevrolet an edge over Ford as it had an overhead-valve six rather than a four-cylinder engine.*

# Chevrolet Corvette 1953-55

The very first Corvette showed what could be done by using mostly existing off-the-shelf Chevrolet saloon car components for the front and rear suspension. The engine too was a modified existing unit, the old 'Blue Flame' straight-six. Raising the compression ratio and fitting triple Carter carburettors increased power output to a quite respectable 145 bhp, which was enough to give the Corvette a good 0-60 mph acceleration time of 11 seconds. To begin with, the straight-six was allied to only a two-speed automatic but a conventional manual gearbox soon made an appearance, and when the Corvette was given a V8 engine to replace the six the model became a real sports car.

## Specification (1953)

**Engine:** straight-six, overhead-valve
**Bore × stroke:** 90 mm × 100 mm
**Capacity:** 3860 cc
**Maximum power:** 145 bhp
**Transmission:** two-speed automatic with torque converter
**Chassis:** separate X-braced steel frame
**Suspension:** independent front with wishbones, coil springs and anti-roll bar; live rear axle with semi-elliptic leaf springs
**Brakes:** drums front and rear
**Bodywork:** glassfibre two-seater convertible
**Maximum speed (approx):** 105 mph (169 km/h)

*Left: The very first Corvette appeared in 1953 and was built in very small numbers to begin with, only 300 being made in the first year. By the time of this 1955 example, the car still looked the same, but the original straight-six engine had given way to Chevrolet's new 265-cu in (4.3-litre) V8, in slightly modified trim to produce 195 bhp.*

*Above: The Corvette pioneered glassfibre construction among major manufacturers and this Chevrolet publicity shot was used to demonstrate the new material's light weight.*

*Below: In 1953 the Corvette was startling different from normal Chevrolet family saloon production.*

# Chevrolet Corvette 1958-62

By 1958 the second generation of Corvettes had been out for three years and was revamped with a new four-headlight treatment, and made both longer and wider.

Power came from a range of V8 engines with outputs from 230 bhp to 290 bhp in the fuel-injected versions. The most popular version, however, was the base 283-cu in engine but even that offered very respectable performance.

The suspension and chassis were still essentially those of the first car, with a simple live rear axle. The car offered great performance and, compared with its more mundane rivals, a surprising number of civilised features, such as optional power windows and air conditioning.

To show that the car could be a serious competition car as well as a sports car, Briggs Cunningham took a team of Corvettes to Le Mans and one finished an excellent eighth overall at an average speed of 97.2 mph.

### Specification (1958)

**Engine:** V8, overhead-valve
**Bore × stroke:** 98.4 mm × 76 mm
**Capacity:** 4639 cc
**Maximum power:** 230 bhp
**Transmission:** four-speed manual or three-speed automatic
**Chassis:** X-braced separate steel frame
**Suspension:** independent front with coil springs and wishbones; live rear axle with semi-elliptic leaf springs
**Brakes:** drums front and rear
**Bodywork:** glassfibre two-seater coupé or convertible
**Maximum speed (approx):** 120 mph (193 km/h)

*Right: The 1958 model, somewhat wider than its predecessor, can be identified by its four headlights.*

*Below: V8 power for the 1958 cars ranged from 230 bhp right up to 290 bhp from the 283-cu in engine.*

*Left: By 1958 Corvette styling had become wonderfully flamboyant, inside and out; the speedo reads to 160 mph . . .*

# Chevrolet Corvette Sting Ray 1963-67

Significant changes were made to the Corvette for the 1963 model year. The body was completely restyled by GM designer Bill Mitchell and followed the lines of his one-off Stingray racer. It was one of his very best designs, the only surprise being that this Corvette generation was so short-lived, lasting only until 1967.

The other really important change was the introduction of independent rear suspension, replacing the old live axle. To save space a transverse leaf spring was used at the rear rather than coil springs. That started a tradition maintained to this day.

Although rivals like the E-type Jaguar had appeared on the American market with the great advantage of disc brakes,

the Corvette's performance still had to be restrained by large drums, although you could have sintered metal linings to help stop what was a very quick car. Disc brakes finally made their appearance on the 1965 models.

Both coupé and convertible versions were built, with the open cars outselling the coupés by almost two to one by 1965.

*Right: The Sting Ray generation of 1963-67 was inspired by GM designer Bill Mitchell, shown here with the convertible and coupé versions. Coupés and convertibles were built in almost equal numbers to begin with, but the convertible soon became the more popular model.*

**Specification (1963 L84 engine tuning)**

**Engine:** V8, overhead-valve wih fuel injection
**Bore × stroke:** 101.6 mm × 82.5 mm
**Capacity:** 5360 cc
**Maximum power:** 360 bhp
**Transmission:** three- or four-speed manual, or three-speed Powerglide automatic
**Chassis:** separate steel frame
**Suspension:** independent all round with wishbones and coil springs front; transverse leaf spring and five links rear'
**Brakes:** drums front and rear with optional sintered linings
**Bodywork:** glassfibre two-seater coupé or convertible
**Maximum speed (approx):** 145 mph (233 km/h)

*Above: By 1965 convertibles were outselling coupés by almost two to one (15,376 to 8,186). Most, including this one, were powered by the 327-cu in (5.3-litre) V8, which produced anything from 250 bhp to 375 bhp when fuel injection was fitted.*

*Left: When the 1963 Corvette convertible was introduced it cost just $4,037 (actually less than the coupé). For that money you got a 250-bhp V8 as standard equipment along with a three-speed transmission, but the option list was enormous and included everything from an AM-FM radio to power steering and a limited slip differential.*

# Chevrolet Corvette 1984-present

When a new model appeared in 1984 the Corvette was long overdue for a change; the previous model had run from 1968 and was looking, and feeling, outdated. The new car was a major redesign, though keeping the usual Corvette features of a glassfibre body and big front-mounted V8 engine.

The suspension and chassis, however, were major steps forward, the Corvette being given a far more sophisticated system at the rear with a five-link independent affair. Curiously a transverse leaf spring, albeit a lightweight plastic composite one, was used at the front as well as the rear. Suspension components were beautifully worked in cast alloy and the Corvette had definitely been moved up-market.

Early versions were criticised for their bone-hard suspension setting which, although it brought fantastic levels of handling, was simply too painful to bear for long. Such faults have long been ironed out, and the latest in the line can stand comparison with its European rivals. A facelift in 1997 updated its appearance to match.

**Specification (1984)**

**Engine:** V8, overhead-valve
**Bore × stroke:** 101.6 mm × 88 mm

*Right: When the 'coke-bottle'-shaped Corvette which ran from 1968 was finally replaced in 1984, the style was greatly improved. Although the V8 engine was retained, the chassis (along with the handling and roadholding) was improved out of all recognition. In 1986 a convertible version was introduced, and it was the convertible that received the Callaway turbo conversion treatment. Top speed of the Callaway shown here was, just as the number plate claims, 194 mph...*

**Capacity:** 5735 cc
**Maximum power:** 205 bhp
**Transmission:** four-speed manual (with overdrive on three ratios) or four-speed automatic
**Chassis:** separate backbone frame with 'birdcage' superstructure supporting body
**Suspension:** independent all round with wishbones and transverse plastic leaf spring front; five-link rear system with transverse plastic leaf spring
**Brakes:** discs front and rear
**Bodywork:** glassfibre two-seater coupé
**Maximum speed (approx):** 140 mph (225 km/h)

# Chevrolet Corvette ZR1 1989-present

In some ways the ZR1 was a total departure from the Corvette tradition; in other ways it was more of the same. Like all the other Corvettes since 1955 it had a big V8 engine, but the essential difference was the valve gear. This V8 had four overhead camshafts operating four valves per cylinder and was designed by Lotus (now a GM-owned company). The new engine, termed the LT5, was an engineering tour de force. Of all-alloy construction, it featured the novelty in an American V8 of 'wet' cylinder liners. Although it was still of 350-cu in displacement, the bore and stroke dimensions were changed to give a shorter stroke. The compression ratio, at 11.25:1, was higher than at any time since the 1960s, and other advanced features included distributorless ignition via four direct firing coils.

Chevrolet were at pains to ensure that the rest of the car lived up to the new exotic engine, and incorporated electronically-adjustable suspension with three settings – soft, conventional and Z51, i.e. the performance or competition setting. Suspension settings vary automatically according to speed.

Just as innovative was the transmission; the previous and not particularly successful manual overdrive gearbox was replaced by a six-speed manual version made by ZF. All told, the ZR1 was technically the most advanced Corvette ever made by Chevrolet.

## Specification (1989)

**Engine:** V8, quad-cam
**Bore × stroke:** 99 mm × 93 mm
**Capacity:** 5737 cc
**Maximum power:** 385 bhp
**Transmission:** six-speed manual
**Chassis:** separate steel frame with 'birdcage' structure supporting body
**Suspension:** independent front with wishbones, transverse plastic leaf spring and anti-roll bar; five-link rear system with transverse plastic leaf spring and anti-roll bar
**Brakes:** discs front and rear
**Bodywork:** glassfibre two-seater coupé
**Maximum speed (approx):** 175 mph (282 km/h)

*Above: At first glance, there is little to differentiate the Corvette ZR1 from the rest of the range. The crucial difference, however, was under the glassfibre skin, where the traditional pushrod 5.7-litre V8 had been replaced by a quad-cam engine with the Lotus cylinder-head design.*

*Left: The addition of the Lotus-designed four-valve-per-cylinder quad-cam top end increased the Corvette's power output dramatically, up to 385 bhp, giving it fearsome acceleration and a top speed of 175 mph.*

# Chevrolet Camaro 1967-70

The Camaro was, along with the mechanically similar Pontiac Firebird, GM's answer to the incredibly successful Ford Mustang. Under the sporty body was essentially the ordinary mechanical make-up of the Chevy II sedan. That meant a simple rear suspension of live axle and semi-elliptic leaf springs, and robust front-mounted straight-six and V8 engines. A performance option was not long in coming, in the shape of the 1968 Z28 which included a 4.9-litre V8 and heavy-duty suspension. Even more impressive was the SS 350 (Super Sport) of 1968, with 5.7 litres and 300 bhp.

## Specification (SS 350)

**Engine:** V8, overhead-valve
**Bore × stroke:** 102 mm × 88 mm
**Capacity:** 5733 cc
**Maximum power:** 300 bhp
**Transmission:** three-speed automatic or four-speed manual
**Chassis:** unitary with separate front subframe
**Suspension:** independent front with wishbones and coil springs; live rear axle with semi-elliptic leaf springs
**Brakes:** discs front, drums rear
**Bodywork:** coupé or convertible
**Maximum speed:** 130 mph (209 km/h)

*Right: More humble than a Corvette, but still highly desirable, is this SS 350 version of the 1968 Camaro with a 300-bhp 5.7-litre V8.*

# Chevrolet Camaro Z28 1982-present

In the late 1970s and early 1980s General Motors were busy 'down-sizing' their large and inefficient designs, and the Camaro's turn came in 1982.

The basic concept was still the same – a front-mounted engine and a live rear axle – but the styling was far cleaner. Although the range of engines ran from a puny four-cylinder producing only 92 bhp there were six- and eight-cylinder models on offer. Top of the range was the performance model, still called the Z28. It was powered by a five-litre V8 producing 190 bhp along with 240 lb ft of torque. As the Z28 was smaller and lighter than its predecessor the relatively low-powered V8 was not a problem, and the fastest Camaro could manage a 0-60 mph time near seven seconds. It had handling to match, although to begin with that was achieved with overly hard suspension settings.

## Specification (1984)

**Engine:** V8, overhead-valve
**Bore × stroke:** 95 mm × 88 mm
**Capacity:** 4999 cc
**Maximum power:** 190 bhp
**Transmission:** five-speed manual or four-speed automatic
**Chassis:** unitary
**Suspension:** independent front with wishbones and coil springs; live rear axle with trailing arms and coil springs
**Brakes:** discs front and rear
**Bodywork:** four-seater coupé
**Maximum speed (approx):** 128 mph (206 km/h)

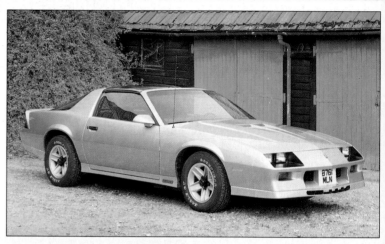

*Right: In common with most American cars of its generation, the Chevrolet Camaro was 'down-sized' in the early 1980s to become a lighter, more fuel-efficient design. The cast-iron V8 engine along with rear-wheel drive was retained. By late 1990s it was also available with a V6 engine. A much-needed face lift updated its appearance.*

*Below: The fastest model in the Camaro range is often termed the Z28. The 1984 version was powered by a five-litre engine producing only 190 bhp but making up for that with 240 lb ft of torque, to give 0-60 mph acceleration in under seven seconds.*

# Chevrolet Corvair 1959-69

During the 1950s Chevrolet, like its rivals in Detroit, set out to build a range of smaller, more compact, cars. Led by Ed Cole and inspired by cars like the VW Beetle, the engineers developed a rear-engined car where the engine was an air-cooled 2.3-litre flat-six, and this duly went on sale in 1959, with prices starting at $1,984. First-generation (1959-64) models were built with 80, 95, 110 and 150-bhp engines.

The second-generation Corvair had smoother, sleeker styling, and completely redesigned suspension. Engines developed 95, 110, 140 or 180 bhp.

If only the car had been reliable, and if only it had handled predictably, all would have been well, but problems allied to its over-steering habits soon brought criticism. When Ralph Nader's book *Unsafe at Any Speed* erupted onto the market, it was the beginning of the slide for this innovative car.

The handling problems that Nader's book drew attention to on the early cars were only a problem if owners neglected something as simple as maintaining the correct specified tyre pressures. They were markedly different front to rear, with 15 psi front and 26 psi rear, and made an

*Left: The Corvair was Chevrolet's ultimately disastrous attempt to market a rear-mounted flat-six-engined compact saloon car.*

enormous difference to the car's behaviour.

Original Corvairs were family cars, but the Monzas and (later) turbocharged Monza Spiders were exciting sporting models which soon attracted a following. Although later-generation Corvairs were much better cars, the public rejected them, and sales dropped inexorably until 1969, when the model was dropped.

### Specification (1960)

**Engine:** flat-six, overhead-valve
**Bore × stroke:** 85.7 mm × 66 mm
**Capacity:** 2287 cc
**Maximum power:** 80 or 95 bhp
**Transmission:** three-speed manual gearbox (later optional four-speed manual) or automatic transmission
**Chassis:** unitary
**Suspension:** independent front with wishbones and coil springs; rear swing axles with coil springs
**Brakes:** drums front and rear
**Bodywork:** four-seater coupé or saloon
**Maximum speed (approx):** 84 mph (135 km/h)

*Right: By 1969 the Corvair coupé was a sleek design, with the original handling problems resolved to the extent that it could cope with up to 180 bhp.*

# Chevrolet Vega 1970-77

For the 1970s Chevrolet developed a new type of 'compact' car, completely different from the Corvair, this time with a front-mounted overhead-cam four-cylinder engine, and called the Vega. The style was a straight crib from Fiat's 124 Sport coupé, but the chassis was strictly conventional. Prices, for 1971, started at $2,090.

In 1975 and 1976 the Cosworth Vega was produced, with a 122-cu in 16-valve twin-cam Cosworth engine. Only 3,507 examples were built, for the car cost $5,916, twice as much as the standard model.

Vegas sold well until corrosion and unreliability problems became known, and sales gradually tailed off until 1977. The main problem lay in the engine, which used the then-novel system of pistons running direct in an alloy block that was acid-etched to reveal a layer of silicon crystals on which the pistons ran. The cylinder head, however, was made of iron and there were problems of block distortion and extreme bore wear.

Nevertheless, in 1974, at the height of the energy crisis 'scare', 456,000 cars were produced.

### Specification (1971)

**Engine:** inline-four, overhead-cam
**Bore × stroke:** 88.9 mm × 92.1 mm
**Capacity:** 2286 cc
**Maximum power:** 90 or 110 bhp
**Transmission:** three- or four-speed manual gearbox, or automatic transmission
**Chassis:** unitary

**Suspension:** independent front with wishbones and coil springs; live rear axle with coil springs
**Brakes:** discs front, drums rear
**Bodywork:** four-seater saloon, hatchback or estate car
**Maximum speed (approx):** 95 mph (153 km/h)

*Below: The 2.3-litre Chevrolet Vega's fame stems from its being another milestone in GM's quest to conquer the compact market.*

# Chrysler Corporation

**W**alter P. Chrysler came to the motor industry via a job with the American Locomotive Co. of Pittsburgh. After becoming works manager at Buick in 1910, he left in 1919, and was then persuaded to 'turn round' Willys, then Maxwell. After this he set up his own Chrysler company, which launched its first model in 1924.

Using the old Chalmers plant in Detroit to build cars, and distributing them through the Maxwell dealer network, he soon established Chrysler in the market place, building strictly middle-class, middle-price machines for the first decade.

By the late 1920s Chrysler had moved up to fourth place in the sales league, and by 1930 Chrysler was emulating General Motors in acquiring other companies. Dodge was bought in 1928, while Plymouth was set up as a 'budget-price' operation, and another new marque, De Soto, also appeared as a slightly down-market Chrysler. By this time the Chrysler Corporation was the third largest group behind General Motors and Ford, a slot which it occupied for the next 60 years.

During the 1930s Chrysler flirted with disaster by producing the Airflow range, whose style was awful even though the engineering was sound. One result was that Chrysler itself slipped back to 10th place in the American sales pecking order, a position it kept for the next half-century.

The marque then settled into a complacent middle-class niche in the Chrysler Corporation's line-up. Its cars were larger and more costly than the Plymouths and Dodges, but less grand than the Imperials which emerged as Chrysler's 'top marque' in the mid-1950s. At this level Chrysler competed happily with marques like Buick and Oldsmobile, leaving most innovation to other marques in the group.

Even so, Chrysler also benefitted from innovations like the mighty 'Hemi' V8 engines, the fast and glitzy 300-Series sporting coupés and, of course, from the gas-turbine car projects.

*Above: Chrysler moved into the 1990s with striking designs like this 1990 concept car – the 300, based on the Dodge Viper running gear.*

*Below: It was cars like the four-cylinder front-wheel-drive LeBaron which kept Chrysler in business in the early 1980s.*

Like Cadillac and Lincoln, of course, Chrysler cars grew ever-larger in the 1950s and 1960s, with fins growing, then fading away. Other cars in the group, like the Dodge Charger, and the Plymouth Road Runner Superbird, made all the headlines, but Chrysler carried on as the most stable of marques.

As the American motor industry hit hard times in the 1970s, Chrysler struggled to stay alive, but after the arrival of Lee Iacocca in 1978 fortunes turned. Chrysler was prominent in Europe in the 1990s with its Neon saloon, Voyager MPV, the Jeep all-terrain models and, more relevant, the Dodge Viper and GTS coupé supercars. In late 1998 it merged with Daimler-Benz to form Daimler Chrysler.

# Chrysler Model 70 'Six' 1924-28

The very first Chrysler-badged car was a solid, conventional, but good-value machine which was intended to compete head-on with other middle-class American cars. Walter Chrysler's own reputation was such that it was sure to get a good reputation, and before long it began to sell well.

The '70' model name came from the use of a sturdy 68-bhp six-cylinder engine; the fact that top speed was also at least 70 mph was coincidental. The mechanical design was conventional, except that it used hydraulic braking at a time when most American cars used rods and cables.

No fewer than 32,000 of these cars were sold in the first year (mainly through Maxwell dealerships), and 43,000 followed in 1925. Sales continued to rise rapidly, so that by 1927 the Chrysler marque sold 200,000 cars. It was a good start for what would be a very eventful career.

## Specification (1924)

**Engine:** inline six-cylinder, side-valve
**Bore × stroke:** 79.4 mm × 120.6 mm
**Capacity:** 3580 cc
**Maximum power:** 68 bhp
**Transmission:** three-speed manual gearbox, rear-wheel drive
**Chassis:** separate steel frame with channel-section side members
**Suspension:** beam axle front with semi-elliptic leaf springs; live rear axle with semi-elliptic leaf springs
**Brakes:** drums front and rear
**Bodywork:** two- or four-seater, open or closed, various styles
**Maximum speed (approx):** 70 mph (113 km/h)

*Right: One of the few exceptional points about the six-cylinder Chrysler 70, apart from its excellent quality, was the use of hydraulic, rather than mechanical, brakes in the mid-1920s.*

# Chrysler Airflow 1934-37

The Airflow was apparently inspired by the shape of United States Air Force planes of the period, but this did it no good in the market place. The streamlined Airflow model qualifies as one of the great motoring flops of all time. In 1934 10,839 cars were delivered, and only 30,673 cars were sold in over four years; a closely related De Soto model fared no better. This damaged Chrysler's finances very severely, and ensured that no such hasty experiments were repeated for many years to come.

Mechanically and structurally the Airflow was a fine car, for it featured an early form of unitary body/chassis construction, and there was a powerful eight-cylinder engine up front. The rest of the running gear was conventional – beam axle suspension front and rear, and the usual Detroit choice of body styles on no fewer than four different wheelbases – 123, 128, 137.5 and 146 in.

Chrysler had two major problems in trying to sell this car – one was that it was launched before ample supplies were available in the showroom, but the more important was that the public found its front-end style hideous. No amount of fiddling and retouching could change this situation, so the model was dropped – just as Lincoln produced its own version of the style (the Zephyr).

## Specification (1934)

**Engine:** inline eight-cylinder, side-valve
**Bore × stroke:** 82.5 mm × 114.3 mm
**Capacity:** 4893 cc
**Maximum power:** 130 bhp
**Transmission:** three-speed manual gearbox, rear-wheel drive
**Chassis:** unitary body/chassis assembly
**Suspension:** beam axle front with semi-elliptic leaf springs; live rear axle with semi-elliptic leaf springs
**Brakes:** drums front and rear
**Bodywork:** five-seater saloon or coupé, various styles
**Maximum speed (approx):** 90 mph (145 km/h)

*Below: The Airflow was a brave attempt by Chrysler to market an aerodynamically-efficient saloon. The company succeeded in making the car aerodynamic, but the public hated its styling and there were few customers, despite the fact that the Airflow was a good car.*

# Chrysler 300 1954-65

After World War II Chrysler's cars were large and fast, but conventional, so the arrival of the original 300 model was a real surprise. Styled by Virgil Exner's team, and inspired by a series of Ghia show cars, the 300 used the standard Chrysler chassis of the period, but combined a sleek four-seater hardtop coupé style with Chrysler's already famous 'Hemi' V8 engine.

This engine, which had already proved itself in racing sports cars such as the Cunningham, featured part-spherical combustion chambers, and in its original 300 form was a 300-bhp 5.4-litre unit. The 300 could top 130 mph, which easily made it the USA's fastest production car. Priced at $4,110 in 1955 (most Chryslers cost around $3,000-$3,500), the 300 was exclusive and over the years became *very* desirable.

The 300 was based on other Chrysler body shells – the original was really a New Yorker shell with an Imperial front end – and changed every year. The series went

from 300 in 1955, through 300D in 1958, all the way to 300L in 1965, when it was finally dropped. By 1962 the seven-litre 300H engine was rated at 405 bhp.

Only 1,725 such cars were made in the first year, and only 17,007 in 10 years. Convertibles were available from 1957 to 1962.

## Specification (1955)

**Engine:** V8, overhead-valve
**Bore × stroke:** 96.77 mm × 92.2 mm
**Capacity:** 5425 cc
**Maximum power:** 300 bhp
**Transmission:** three-speed manual gearbox or automatic transmission, rear-wheel drive
**Chassis:** separate steel frame
**Suspension:** independent front with coil springs; live rear axle with semi-elliptic leaf springs
**Brakes:** drums front and rear
**Bodywork:** five-seater hardtop coupé
**Maximum speed (approx):** 130 mph (209 km/h)

*Above: The limited-edition Chrysler 300B appeared in 1956, based on the New Yorker body shell. It was powered by a 354-cu in (5.8-litre) V8 producing 340 bhp in standard form with an optional output of 355 bhp.*

*Left: Logically enough, the 300C appeared the year after the 300B, in 1957. In the space of just one model year fin size had grown quite dramatically. Engine size had increased too, with a 392-cu in (6.4-litre) V8 producing 375 bhp as standard or 390 bhp as an option.*

# Chrysler TC Maserati 1986–93

To enliven the image of the marque, Chrysler's Lee Iacocca consulted Alejandro De Tomaso of Maserati over the building of a special convertible which used Chrysler's well-proven transverse-engine front-wheel-drive package. The only Maserati input was to be the style of the interior, and assembly of the production cars, the rest being pure Chrysler.

This car was aimed at the Mercedes-Benz SL market, and there were two engines – one a 174-bhp version of the existing turbocharged 2.2-litre four, the other a 16-valve twin-cam turbo version with the Maserati-developed cylinder head.

Production began only at the end of the 1980s and in spite of attempts to inject Italian glamour into the range, sales were very slow. The fact that the body shell was like that of the Le Baron did not help, for this made the TC model less than exclusive.

*Right: The Chrysler Maserati was the wrong sort of collaboration: instead of an exotic Maserati engine in a solid US body, it was a 2.2-litre Chrysler engine in an Italian-made body shell . . .*

## Specification (1991)

**Engine:** inline four-cylinder, twin-cam
**Bore × stroke:** 87.5 mm × 92 mm
**Capacity:** 2213 cc
**Maximum power:** 205 bhp
**Transmission:** five-speed manual gearbox or three-speed automatic transmission, front-wheel drive
**Chassis:** unitary body/chassis assembly
**Suspension:** independent front with coil springs; beam rear axle with coil springs
**Brakes:** discs front and rear
**Bodywork:** 2 + 2 seater, optional hardtop
**Maximum speed (approx):** 140 mph (225 km/h)

# Cisitalia (Consorzio Industriale Sportiva Italia)

**P**iero Dusio was an Italian enthusiast, who raced with honour in the 1930s. Building up a large business in the 1940s, he became a wealthy industrialist. He used the fortune he earned during World War II to open a factory in Turin and to finance a motor business, where he planned to produce a whole variety of cars. He had already built a prototype machine (which he called Cisitalia – after his businesses) in 1939, but the post-war car was a fresh start. Cisitalia, incidentally, was short for Consorzio Industriale Sportiva Italia, a conglomerate which sold anything from textiles to sporting goods and racing bicycles.

In fact Dusio had great ambitions, for he planned to produce budget-price sports cars *and* single-seater racing cars. The single-seaters, like the sports cars, used Fiat 1100 components. Since they cost only £1,000 and offered 100-mph performance they were very popular in European motorsport for a couple of years. Although 48 such cars were sold, an attempt to promote a one-make Cisitalia formula was short-lived.

Dusio also set his sights on building a Grand Prix team, so with a large slice of his wartime profits he commissioned Porsche to design such a car, the Type 360 single-seater; Dusio's friend Tazio Nuvolari was earmarked to drive it when it was race-ready. At the time, Cisitalia's racing manager was a man called Carlo Abarth, who later went on to achieve fame with his own products.

The Porsche-designed car was a magnificent concept, featuring a mid-mounted flat-12 engine of up to 300 bhp, and selective four-wheel drive, but was not completed before Dusio's money ran out, and never actually raced. A few years later it was completed, and tested, but was never used in anger.

The sports car project was altogether more serious, and successful, and there is no doubt that the coupés, styled by Pininfarina, were extremely elegant, and set standards for the next few years at least. The clean lines of this car earned it a place in the New York Museum of Modern Art in 1947.

Theoretically the 1.1-litre-engined sports car should never have been competitive in motor racing, but the legendary Tazio Nuvolari (by then in his 50s, and in poor health) did not believe this. In the Mille Miglia of 1947, where weather conditions were appallingly wet, he led most of the way. It was only towards the end of the race, when waterlogged electrics caused problems, that the game little machine was overhauled by a 2.9-litre Alfa Romeo, but the Cisitalia still finished second.

Unhappily for Dusio, and for Italy, the marque's success was short-lived. No more sports cars were built after 1948, and in 1950 the Italian businesses were closed down, and Dusio moved to Argentina, in the vain hope of gaining state backing.

It was a mistake. Returning to Italy in 1952, he dabbled with Fiat 1100-cc-powered successors to the original car, but these were never successful. At the same time a prototype 2.8-litre Cisitalia sports car was also shown. This car was claimed to have 160 bhp, and a top speed of 137 mph, which should have made Ferrari sit up and think. It was powered by a four-cylinder overhead-cam BPM marine engine and gearbox (could anything be less suitable for a high-performance car?), and de Dion rear suspension was fitted. Nothing ever came of this, as only one prototype was made.

By the end of the 1950s Cisitalia was reduced to 'customising' or rebodying Fiat-based cars, and the business finally folded in 1965. For better or worse, Cisitalia will only ever be remembered for the stillborn Grand Prix car, and the pretty little 1.1-litre sports model.

*Below: This striking, befinned aluminium-bodied coupé was photographed in Buenos Aires in 1946. After building single-seater racers with some success, Piero Dusio turned his attention to two-seater sports cars.*

## Cisitalia Type 202 1946-50

Cisitalia was far too small to design its own engines and transmissions, so for the Type 202 production car Dusio had to use the running gear of a major Italian carmaker. Should this be from Fiat, Alfa Romeo, or Lancia? To keep the price within bounds, Fiat 1100 parts were chosen. Over the years there have been several different Fiat 1100s, but in this case the donor car was the Type 508C model of 1937-48, which was in large-scale production in Turin.

The further link with Fiat was that Dusio asked engineer Dante Giacosa to design the Type 202 sports car for him on a freelance basis. Giacosa's reputation was already on the rise (he was later to become Fiat's highly-regarded technical chief in the 1950s and 1960s), so the Type 202 was a workmanlike effort. The basis of the design was a multi-tubular chassis frame, by no means a pure spaceframe, but rigid, easy to produce, and not requiring expensive tooling. The

tubes, incidentally, came from existing stocks, which had been purchased to build racing bicycles. The car had transverse-leaf independent front suspension from the Fiat 500 'Topolino' and a Fiat 1100 rear axle.

The 1.1-litre engine normally produced 50 bhp, but for racing it was possible to squeeze 65 bhp out of it, yielding a top speed of around 110 mph. Bodies were always produced by Italian coachbuilders, notably Pininfarina and Frua,

*Left: Designed by Pininfarina, the 1946 202 Gran Sport's superb lines earned it a place in New York's Museum of Modern Art as "one of the best automotive designs of all time". Only 153 were built, along with 13 cabriolets.*

some with open tops and some in what is now recognised as a classic fastback coupé style.

Accurate production figures are not available, but it is thought that 100 coupés, 60 convertibles and up to 50 other types were finally sold.

### Cisitalia Type 202 variants

In the 1950s further developed versions were badged Type 33 DF Voloradente, with 70 bhp (introduced in 1954; about 100 cars were built), and then Type 35 DF1250, with enlarged Fiat engines of 1248 cc/72 bhp (1956), but these cars had all faded away by 1958.

### Specification (1946)

**Engine:** inline four-cylinder, overhead-valve
**Bore × stroke:** 68 mm × 75 mm
**Capacity:** 1089 cc
**Maximum power:** 50 bhp
**Transmission:** four-speed manual gearbox, rear-wheel drive
**Chassis:** separate multi-tube frame
**Suspension:** independent front with transverse leaf springs; live rear axle with semi-elliptic leaf springs
**Brakes:** drums front and rear
**Bodywork:** aluminium two-seater, open or closed
**Maximum speed (approx):** 100 mph (161 km/h)

# Citroën (Société Anonyme Automobiles Citroën)

*Left: Andre Citroën first made his name as the inventor of 'double chevron' helical gearing, hence Citroën's insignia.*

*Below: The 2CV, conceived as "four wheels under an umbrella", originated in the 1930s but war held its production back until 1948.*

**A** ndré Citroën, once managing director of the French Mors car concern, and the inventor of double-helical gearing, set up his own factory in Paris in 1917, and launched the first Citroën car, the Type A, in 1919.

After more than a decade of producing conventional (and forgettable) cars, he then threw his company into the advanced *traction avant* project, producing a car which combined front-wheel drive, easy servicing, good looks and a unit-construction shell into a harmonious whole.

The financial strain, however, was enormous, Citroën himself died shortly afterwards, and the Michelin tyre company took a controlling interest. After World War II Citroën introduced the 2CV, followed the Traction Avant up in 1955 with the DS19, and for decades never produced a simple car where a more complex one would do the job instead.

This was always a financially risky strategy, and finally Michelin was obliged to sell out to Peugeot in 1974. It took years for the two companies to integrate fully, but by the late 1980s every new Citroën project was matched by a parallel Peugeot car, and most of the individuality finally disappeared. By this time, Peugeot-Citroën had become the largest and most prosperous French motoring group – its combined plant and production putting it ahead of the other French giant, Renault.

*Above: When Citroën acquired a controlling interest in Maserati the result was the 142-mph SM, which coupled Citroën hydro-pneumatic suspension and styling with 2.7-litre, fuel-injected, quad-cam Maserati V6 power. The SM was innovative in other ways, with fully-powered disc brakes all round and novel swivelling headlamps. A three-litre automatic version was subsequently released in France. Production ran from 1970 to 1975.*

*Left: This competition Citroën ZX was a product of the Peugeot amalgamation. Effectively a rebodied Peugeot T16, it took Ari Vatanen to victory in the 1991 Paris-Dakar 'raid'.*

# Citroën Type A 1919-22

Logically enough, the original Citroën was dubbed Type A, and was really the first mass-produced French car. It was cheap, well equipped, and had full weather protection as standard, which made it an attractive proposition for post-World War I French motorists.

Technically the Type A was mainly conventional, for it had a flexible separate chassis, a side-valve engine, and a three-speed gearbox. Suspension of the beam axles, however, was by paired

*Above: Launched in 1919, the Type A was the first Citroën and more conventional than later designs. It was among the first French cars to enter volume production. Shown here is a 1920 right-hand-drive example.*

quarter-elliptic leaf springs, not cheap and almost certainly influenced by Bugatti methods, though the cars' prices were entirely different.

As many as 30,000 Type As were

ordered before deliveries began, and many were used as taxis in Paris, which worked wonders for publicity for the marque. At any rate the radiator grille, complete with carefully profiled surround, was distinctive in itself.

### Specification (1920)
**Engine:** inline four-cylinder, side-valve
**Bore × stroke:** 65 mm × 100 mm
**Capacity:** 1327 cc
**Maximum power:** 18 bhp

**Transmission:** three-speed manual gearbox, rear-wheel drive
**Chassis:** separate steel frame with channel-section side members
**Suspension:** beam front axle with quarter-elliptic leaf springs; beam rear axle with quarter-elliptic leaf springs
**Brakes:** drums at rear only, with transmission drum brake
**Bodywork:** open four-seater
**Maximum speed (approx):** 45 mph (72 km/h)

## Citroën 11CV Traction Avant 1934-57

When Citroën launched a new front-wheel-drive car (hence the *traction avant* name) in 1934, it caused a sensation. Nothing like it had ever been seen before, especially from Citroën, whose previous models had been utterly conventional. Not only the front drive, but the rakish styling and the wide-track stance, gave the car a rare distinction.

The very first car had a 32-bhp/1.3-litre engine, and was clearly underpowered, but this was enlarged to 36 bhp/1.6 litres within a year, and the definitive 1911-cc unit soon followed. A 3.8-litre V8 version, shown in 1934, never went into production. Once the 1.9-litre 11CV had become established, Citroën stuck to it through thick and thin, adding a six-cylinder version in 1938, and mildly restyling the tail in the early 1950s. There was also a two-seater Roadster version for a time.

The Traction Avant's charm was not in its performance, which was not outstanding, but in its roadholding and its character. An exceptional car would be needed to replace it, and this arrived in 1955, in the shape of the DS19.

In all, 708,339 11CVs were produced.

### Citroën 11CV variants

**Citroën 15CV**

The 76-bhp/2866-cc six-cylinder 15CV model, introduced in 1938, was produced until 1957. This had a top speed of more than 80 mph, and was used as a proving model for the DS19's hydro-pneumatic suspension in 1954 and 1955.

*Right: Development costs of the Traction Avant caused financial ruin for Citroën but the cars were sensational. Extraordinarily advanced for their day, using front-wheel drive, unitary construction, all-independent torsion-bar suspension and an overhead-valve engine with removable cylinder liners, they offered outstanding roadholding, ride and character combined with ease of servicing. As well as a four-door saloon, a drophead two-door style (right) was produced.*

*Right: Right-hand-drive versions of Citroën's Traction Avant for the British market were produced at their works in Slough. This is a 1954 'Big 15'.*

### Specification (1945)

**Engine:** inline four-cylinder, overhead-valve

**Bore × stroke:** 78 mm × 100 mm

**Capacity:** 1911 cc

**Maximum power:** 56 bhp

**Transmission:** three-speed manual gearbox, front-wheel drive

**Chassis:** unitary body/chassis assembly

**Suspension:** independent front with torsion bars; beam rear axle with torsion bars

**Brakes:** drums front and rear

**Bodywork:** four-seater saloon or two-seater tourer

**Maximum speed (approx):** 75 mph (121 km/h)

*Left: A 1953 'Light 15'. Between the series' launch in 1934 and its phasing out over two decades later in 1957, engines offered ranged from a 1.3-litre four-cylinder to a 2866-cc straight-six. A prototype 3.8-litre V8 never entered production.*

# Citroën DS 1955-75

*Left: Among the more interesting variants of the DS was this two-door cabriolet bodied by Henri Chapron.*

### Citroën DS variants

**ID19**

The ID19 (introduced in 1956) had 66 bhp at first, with a conventional gear change, and simpler equipment.

**DS21/DS23**

The DS21, with 100-bhp/2.2-litre engine, was produced from 1965; the DS23 (115- or 130-bhp/2.35-litre engine) followed in 1972.

### Specification (1955 DS19)

**Engine:** inline four-cylinder, overhead-valve
**Bore × stroke:** 78 mm × 100 mm
**Capacity:** 1911 cc
**Maximum power:** 75 bhp
**Transmission:** four-speed manual gearbox, front-wheel drive
**Chassis:** unitary body/chassis assembly
**Suspension:** independent front and rear, each with hydro-pneumatic springs
**Brakes:** discs front, drums rear
**Bodywork:** four-/five-seater; saloon, estate car or cabriolet
**Maximum speed (approx):** 85 mph (137 km/h)

Citroën's first new post-war design was the sleek and advanced DS19, DS standing for *Déesse* (Goddess). The DS19, with its less complex ID19 derivative, was a direct replacement for the long-running 11CV Traction Avant, and was an extremely advanced machine indeed. In 1955 it was certainly the world's most technically complex production car, and even in 1975, when it was dropped, it was still a remarkably modern car.

Not only was it very beautiful, with a long shark-like nose, a roomy interior and smooth lines, but also it had front-wheel drive, power-operated self-levelling hydro-pneumatic suspension, an hydraulic gear change, power brakes and power steering. There were also ride-height adjustments and the ride itself was very soft and 'long', the whole car being ideal for French roads.

The original four-door saloon was eventually joined by an even longer and more versatile seven-seater estate car, and for individualists there was also a cabriolet by Henri Chapron. The original car needed more power, but over the years a new engine, later enlarged and finally with fuel injection, made up for this shortcoming.

Many other sub-derivatives, with different power outputs and different equipment, were also built. A smoother nose restyle arrived in 1967, with swivelling (steering-linked) headlamps on some models. There was fuel injection from 1969, a five-speed gearbox from 1970, and an automatic transmission option from 1971. Complication increased, rather than decreased!

In 20 years more than 1.4 million of these cars were built before the range was succeeded by the new CX family. DSs are now becoming collectors' cars but are still suitable for everyday use.

*Below: The DS, when launched in 1955, was another ground-breaking car, most obviously for its aerodynamic styling and self-levelling suspension. This is a 1972 D-Super.*

# Citroën SM 1970-75

For a few years Citroën had control of Maserati of Italy. One tangible result was the development of the SM coupé, a large, self-indulgent, four-seater coupé which allied a Maserati V6 engine to a DS-inspired chassis, transmission and suspension.

The original concept had a great deal to commend it. None of Citroën's own engines was bigger than four cylinders and the advanced Maserati engine suited Citroën's even more advanced chassis. The engine featured four overhead camshafts and produced 170 bhp from 2670 cc, then a very respectable power output. The engine was also used successfully in Maserati's own mid-engined Merak, and

although it had to haul around a weighty 3,200 lb in the Citroën SM it was still good enough to give the very aerodynamic SM a top speed of 135 mph. Fuel injection replaced carburettors in 1972 (giving an extra 7 bhp), and fuel injection allied to a bigger, 2974-cc, engine was available from 1973.

The SM was full of Citroën ingenuity; it had six headlights, with one pair turning along with the steering to light the way around corners. The power steering was lightning-fast with only two turns lock-to-lock. In almost every way this car was twice as complex as the DS, its underbonnet aspect being nightmarish. It retained all the usual DS characteristics of

*Above: The Citroën/Maserati hybrid, the SM, was produced from 1970 to 1975. It was a sophisticated, fast and technologically innovative car with a very respectable performance. The later, fuel-injected, three-litre examples could top 140 mph, thanks to greater power and effective aerodynamics.*

ride and handling, allied to a 135 mph top speed, but it was never a profitable car to build, and a combination of the energy crisis and Citroën's takeover by Peugeot combined to kill it off after 12,920 cars had been produced. All had left-hand drive. The last few hundred cars were assembled by Ligier in Vichy.

## Specification (1970)

**Engine:** V6, double overhead cam per cylinder bank
**Bore × stroke:** 87 mm × 75 mm
**Capacity:** 2670 cc
**Maximum power:** 170 bhp
**Transmission:** five-speed manual gearbox, front-wheel drive
**Chassis:** unitary body/chassis assembly
**Suspension:** independent front with high-pressure hydro-pneumatic springs; independent rear with hydro-pneumatic springs
**Brakes:** discs front and rear
**Bodywork:** four-seater coupé
**Maximum speed (approx):** 135 mph (217 km/h)

# Citroën CX 1974-89

*Above: The car that succeeded the legendary DS series had to be special. Citroën called it the CX (alluding to its even more aerodynamically-efficient shape) and brought it onto the market in 1974.*

Citroën's replacement for the famous DS range was launched in 1974, and dubbed the CX. It was not quite such a futuristic car as the DS had seemed, but it was still technically advanced, and it had a very spacious interior. Like the DS, too, it had a very smooth shape, and was instantly recognisable as a Citroën.

The CX was in production from 1974 to 1989, and although there were only ever three body styles – a four-door saloon (two wheelbase lengths), and a long-wheelbase five-door estate car – these were offered with a quite bewildering choice of four-cylinder engines.

The least powerful engine was a 66-bhp/2.2-litre diesel type, while the largest and most powerful were the 2.5-litre turbo petrol engines, producing 168 bhp. Because Citroën had been taken over by Peugeot, some engine designs were Citroën's and some were Peugeot's. It was a confusing period!

All these cars had long shark-like noses, a fastback style which looked as if it should be a hatchback, but wasn't, a concave-profile rear window, and all the usual Citroën fittings such as hydro-pneumatic self-levelling suspension, and power-operation for almost everything.

In every case the engine was transversely mounted, driving the front wheels, and in most cases there was a choice of five-speed manual or three-speed automatic transmission.

The least powerful versions felt large and cumbersome, but the most powerful types, notably the GTi and the GTi Turbo, were fast, agile, and well-suited to the sweeping main roads and auto-routes of France. The GTi was produced between 1977 and 1984, during which time its engine developed from 128 bhp/2347 cc to 138 bhp/2473 cc, and was available with manual or automatic transmission. Both the GTi and the GTi Turbo which followed were fast and sleek cars, with a soft ride and seemingly endless reserves of grip. Like other big Citroën's their full-power steering was almost totally without feel, and brake pedal travel was very short indeed, for it was easy to prod too hard and squeak the tyres. Even so there were hundreds of thousands of people who loved the idiosyncrasies of such a Citroën, and forgave it everything. The CX range was replaced by the less extrovert XM, which lasted through the 1990s.

## Specification (1984 CX GTi Turbo)

**Engine:** inline four-cylinder, overhead-valve
**Bore × stroke:** 93 mm × 92 mm
**Capacity:** 2473 cc
**Maximum power:** 168 bhp
**Transmission:** five-speed manual gearbox, front-wheel drive
**Chassis:** separate steel frame with box-section side members
**Suspension:** independent front and rear, each with hydro-pneumatic springs
**Brakes:** discs front and rear
**Bodywork:** five-seater saloon
**Maximum speed (approx):** 125 mph (201 km/h)

*Below: The GTi Turbo was the most powerful and fastest car in the CX range. With a blown and injected 2.5-litre engine coupled with the marque's well-proven hydro-pneumatic suspension, it was a fine long-distance tourer.*

## Citroën BX 1982–95

The Citroën BX model was launched in 1982, and filled a yawning gap in the product line between the smaller GS and large CX models.

Citroën could probably not have afforded to develop the BX had they not merged with Peugeot years earlier. There was one entirely new range of four-cylinder engines, and all other petrol or diesel engines were modified versions of modern Peugeot units.

Like every other modern Citroën of this period, the BX had front-wheel drive, self-levelling hydro-pneumatic independent suspension, and a great deal of quirky character. Like the larger CX range, an estate car version was avail-

*Left: With the BX, launched in 1982, Citroën (now owned by Peugeot) acquired the mid-sized contender they had so badly lacked. The GTi 16V was a genuinely quick car, with 155 bhp and a top speed of 130 mph.*

able, but the style was quite angular, though still aerodynamically smooth.

By the time the range of engines was fully developed, they stretched from a 55-bhp/1.1-litre petrol unit to a 16-valve twin-cam 155-bhp/1.9-litre design, and of course there were various petrol- or diesel-powered options.

The fastest and most sporty types were called GTis, and used 1.9-litre versions of the Peugeot-designed XU9 overhead-camshaft engine. This was the engine used as the basis of the famous turbocharged Peugeot 205 Turbo 16 rally car unit (which could produce a reliable 450 bhp), so clearly there were great reserves of strength in the castings.

The eight-valve, single-cam GTi 8V arrived in 1986, with a fuel-injected 122-bhp/1905-cc engine and a top speed of 120 mph; two years later, a four-wheel-drive version featuring three differen-tials and a torque split of 53 front to 47 rear was launched. The most powerful version was the GTi 16V, with 155 bhp and 130 mph top speed. The BX range was replaced by the Xantia in 1995.

### Specification (1987 BX GTi 16V)
**Engine:** inline four-cylinder, twin-cam
**Bore × stroke:** 83 mm × 88 mm
**Capacity:** 1905 cc
**Maximum power:** 155 bhp
**Transmission:** five-speed manual gearbox, front-wheel drive
**Chassis:** unitary body/chassis assembly
**Suspension:** independent front and rear, each with hydro-pneumatic springs
**Brakes:** discs front and rear
**Bodywork:** four-seater hatchback
**Maximum speed (approx):** 130 mph (209 km/h)

# Cizeta Automobili

**M**any countries find it difficult to build even one supercar, but in Italy that never seems to be a problem. By the 1970s the city of Modena had become the supercar capital of the world, for Ferrari, Maserati *and* Lamborghini cars were all conceived, and built, close by.

Was there really space for another marque, for a new and unknown car to enter the exclusive 200-mph club? Claudio Zampolli, an Italian Ferrari dealer living in Los Angeles, USA, thought there was. To realise his dream, he got backing from Giorgio Moroder (the singer/composer), hired Marcello Gandini to shape his car, and contracted Tecnostyle to design the engine. A new company, Cizeta Automobili srl, was set up in Modena, and the target was to build 100 cars a year by the mid-1990s. However, by this time the project had faded away.

*Right: Is this the supercar to make the superlatives run out? The Cizeta's transverse V16 engine certainly puts it in a class of its own.*

## Cizeta-Moroder V16T 1991–95

The V16T's pedigree was impressive – the Tecnostyle engineers had previously worked for Lamborghini, and Zampolli himself had previously worked in the development shops at Lamborghini – and there was no shortage of enthusiasm for such cars in the Modena area.

Cizeta showed their first car in January 1989, and it caused an immediate sensation. The style was wide, flat, wickedly attractive and – as the pundits soon realised – similar in some ways to the new Lamborghini Diablo. Quite clearly, Zampolli was aiming to outdo both Lamborghini and Ferrari, for his prototype, called the Cizeta-Moroder V16T, seemed to offer more of everything than either the Countach or the Testarossa.

The engine was mid-mounted and drove the rear wheels. That was conventional enough – until people realised that it was a transversely mounted and massive six-litre V16 unit, for which no

*Above: Marcello Gandini styled it, and Tecnostyle engineered its six-litre, 560-bhp V16 engine – the 200-plus-mph V16T was created expressly to take on the very best.*

less than 560 bhp was claimed. The engine layout explains the 'V16T' (for *Transversale*) title of the new car.

For obvious reasons this hugely powerful engine was the most impressive feature of the car. No other car-maker was producing a V16 unit – the last production V16s had been made by Cadillac in the 1930s – and none could offer this sort of power.

The Gandini body style was in light aluminium, clothing a multi-tube frame, and was a big and excitingly detailed design. Under the skin there was a ZF five-speed transmission to the rear drive, and the rear wheels needed 13-in wide rims and 335/35-section tyres to cope with the engine's power.

As one might expect, this made the car very wide (6 ft 9 in) and heavy, but with all that horsepower the performance wasn't in doubt. From the start, Zampolli claimed a top speed of 204 mph for his magnificent creation. In this market it was vital to be the biggest, most powerful, fastest – and, hopefully, the best – so it was significant that the V16T promised to be Italy's, if not the world's, fastest car.

The journalists allowed to try the prototype at an early stage were astonished to find that it delivered almost everything promised. It was flexible at lower speeds, had colossal acceleration, and – by two-seater supercar standards – was comfortable and very well-appointed.

When the car was launched, it was hoped that production would begin in 1989, with 25 cars being built, and with a further 40-60 to follow in 1990. However, it took longer than this to get the car ready

for sale. The body was redesigned, new financial backers had to be found, and production targets were eventually reduced to an exclusive 10 cars a year.

### Specification (1991)
**Engine:** V16, double overhead cam per bank of cylinders
**Bore × stroke:** 86 mm × 65 mm
**Capacity:** 5995 cc
**Maximum power:** 560 bhp
**Transmission:** five-speed manual gearbox, rear-wheel drive
**Chassis:** separate steel multi-tubular frame
**Suspension:** independent front and rear, each with wishbones and coil springs
**Brakes:** discs front and rear
**Bodywork:** aluminium two-seater
**Maximum speed (approx):** 204 mph (328 km/h)

# Clan Motor Company

*Above: Based on Hillman Imp mechanical parts (engine, transmission and running gear), the Clan Crusader was unusual for its glassfibre monocoque. Lotus and Rochdale were the only other carmakers to have used this form of construction.*

**U**ntil Nissan started assembling cars in Washington, UK, in the late 1980s, the only previous car to have been assembled there was the intriguing little Clan sports car. The difference could not have been more complete. Nissan built thousands of cars every week, but Clan built only 315 cars in three years.

The career of the Clan can be summed up very easily. It was one of the nicest, most integrated and neatly-styled specialist cars of the 1960s and 1970s. Unfortunately, because it was a 'kit' car, initially intended to be sold tax-free as a partly-assembled machine, it was badly hit by the new British VAT laws which came into force in 1973. Within months of that, sales had fallen away, and Clan was forced out of business.

Paul Haussauer was a bright young development engineer at Lotus in the 1960s, who had worked on cars like the mid-engined Europa, and had a long-standing love affair with the original Lotus Elite.

At the end of the 1960s he broke away to design and market his own car, and chose to emulate the Lotus Elite by using a reinforced glassfibre monocoque, something which no carmaker other than Lotus and Rochdale had ever attempted. Having decided that Lotus cars were becoming too large, too fast and too expensive, he proposed to build a two-seater sports coupé which would cost considerably less. After casting around for the best possible commercial and financial deal, Haussauer chose a new small factory at Washington, near Newcastle-

upon-Tyne, and prepared to make limited numbers of his innovative new sports coupé in kit form.

Like the Lotus Europa which he knew so well, Haussauer wanted to produce a car with the engine behind the seats, driving the rear wheels. Naturally he could afford to design and manufacture special running gear, so he surveyed the British motor industry for the most suitable units.

The new car was given the name of Clan Crusader (Crusader, because this was a crusade to develop a different kind of car for the enthusiast).

In the autumn of 1973, unhappily, sales finally dried up, and Clan was forced to close its doors. The factory's equipment, including the body moulds, was eventually all sold off to clear the company's debts.

In the years which followed, usually without the knowledge of Haussauer himself, several attempts were made to get the Crusader back into production, at places as far apart as Cyprus and Northern Ireland, and with several different engines, including the flat-four Alfasud unit. None of these projects got beyond the 'pilot-build' stage. So far, the inventive Haussauer has never been able to get back into carmaking.

## Clan Crusader 1971-73

The mechanical design of the Crusader was based on the entire running gear of the rear-engined Sunbeam Imp Sport/ Sunbeam Stiletto. This car had a light-alloy rear-mounted engine of only 875 cc, allied to a four-speed all-synchro-mesh gearbox and final drive, all enclosed in a light-alloy casing.

There was independent front suspension taken, like the engine, from the Imp. This was allied to delightfully direct rack-and-pinion steering, while the rear suspension (all integrated into the Chrysler engine/transmission package) was by semi-trailing arms and coil springs.

Even though the engine was located behind the line of the rear wheels, it was light and low, so the chassis was very well-balanced. Like the cars from which it was derived, it produced very agile roadholding and delightful road manners.

The glassfibre monocoque was small (the car was only 12 ft 6 in long, and weighed a mere 1,275 lb), but it was crisply styled, with a permanent coupé fastback roof, and partly-recessed 'frog-eye' headlamps.

Even though it used mass-produced running gear, the new Crusader was still quite costly when launched in 1971. In basic form it was priced at £1,118, or £1,410 when purchase tax had been paid on a fully-assembled car. A sun roof and cast-aluminium wheels were optional extras.

This compared with a mere £928 for an MG Midget, or £1,470 for a 2½-litre fuel-injected Triumph TR6. By definition, therefore, the Crusader was never likely to be a fast-selling car.

Price apart, though, the Crusader was a very appealing package, for it combined a 100 mph top speed with overall fuel economy of around 40 mpg. It looked very smart indeed (the glassfibre

body shell finish was particularly good), and was a very spacious two-seater.

Testers were surprised by the relative refinement of the tiny Crusader, and a limited 'works' rallying programme by a 998 cc-engined version soon showed that it was solidly built, but the high price meant that Haussauer was always struggling to generate enough sales.

### Specification (1971)
**Engine:** inline four-cylinder, overhead-cam, rear-mounted

**Bore × stroke:** 68 mm × 60.4 mm
**Capacity:** 875 cc
**Maximum power:** 51 bhp
**Transmission:** four-speed manual gearbox, rear-wheel drive
**Chassis:** glassfibre unitary body/chassis assembly, reinforced with steel sections
**Suspension:** independent front with wishbones and coil springs; independent rear with semi-trailing arms and coil springs
**Brakes:** drums front and rear

*Above: Rear- rather than mid-engined, the Clan was nevertheless nimble, thanks to the low weight of its aluminium Imp power unit. Although noted for the quality of finish of its GRP bodywork, it could never look like anything but a kit car, and with the advent of Value Added Tax it became too costly for the UK market.*

**Bodywork:** glassfibre two-seater coupé
**Maximum speed (approx):** 100 mph (161 km/h)

# Continental

american car enthusiasts get very excited, and very pernickety, over the difference between a Continental and a Lincoln Continental. There *were* differences, sometimes small, but to collectors and fanatics, they mean a lot.

Lincoln was taken over by Ford in 1922, and the very first Lincoln Continental was launched in 1940. After World War II Lincolns were always the fastest, largest and most expensive of all cars built by Ford, but they still could not quite get on terms with GM's Cadillac.

The original Lincoln Continental, built between 1940 and 1948, had been such a success that dealers continued to nag away for a successor. Early in the 1950s they got their wish: the Lincoln-Mercury Division put William Clay Ford, Henry Ford II's younger brother, in charge of a new 'Special Products Division' and directed him to design a special new car.

The new car was to use the same basic running gear as other modern Lincolns, but was to have a new chassis and a brand-new body style. More importantly, it was to be called Continental Mk II, and the name Lincoln was never even mentioned.

This meant that the Ford-owned line-up would soon become: Ford (at the lower end of the market), Edsel (from late 1957, a little bit up-market), Mercury (more expensive still), Lincoln (the Cadillac competitor), and Continental (at the exclusive top of the tree).

*Left: In an effort to outdo Cadillac, Ford tried to give the Continental marque even more prestige and exclusivity than their existing Lincoln Division. This is a 1956 Continental Mk II.*

# Continental Mk II 1956-58

Like the original Lincoln Continental, the Mk II was meant to be an expensive, exclusive, four-seater coupé, with space and function taking something of a back seat to style and image.

The Mk II was graced with a new chassis, designed by Harley F. Copp's engineers, which had a 126-in wheelbase, and had side members which dipped low between front and rear axles, so that there could be sensible passenger headroom under a low roof line.

Front and rear suspensions were as in other Lincolns, very softly damped, and not at all sporting, while the engine was a brand-new high-output six-litre V8, rated at 285 bhp, which put Lincoln on a par with, but not ahead of, Cadillac. Three-speed automatic transmission was standard, as was power-assisted steering. The Continental, it seemed, was meant to give high performance with absolutely no effort on the part of the driver.

The style of the car, known in the USA industry as a hardtop coupé, was sleeker and more pure in detail than that of any other Lincoln. It had an enormously long bonnet and a vast engine bay in which even the huge 368-cu in engine had a lot of space, though the cabin was best described as a 'close-coupled' four-seater.

A measure of the Mk II's presence is that it was 18 ft 2.5 in long, and weighed 4,825 lb . . . without passengers. Here was a car which brandished its opulence to the world. Potential customers were asked to sit cosily together so that the overall shape could flaunt itself. It was a fast car, for sure, but the penalty was in poor fuel economy; Mk IIs rarely beat 10 mpg.

Once launched in the autumn of 1955, it was greeted as an all-time great design – until pundits looked at the price. The original Mk II cost no less than $9,695, at a time when the average price of other Lincolns was around $4,500, and a Cadillac Eldorado cost about $6,500.

Few rich Americans, it transpired, were ready to pay so much money for this beautiful machine, especially as it was a

new and 'unknown' make. The result was that only 1,325 cars were sold in the 1956 model year, and after the price was raised to $9,966, a miserly 444 Mk IIs found buyers in 1957.

A cheaper Continental was produced in 1959, but after that Continental was dropped as a separate marque – killed off by a combination of price and the misguided strategy of trying to turn a model name into a distinct car division.

## Specification (1956)

**Engine:** V8, overhead-valve
**Bore × stroke:** 101.6 mm × 92.96 mm
**Capacity:** 6030 cc
**Maximum power:** 285 bhp
**Transmission:** three-speed automatic transmission, rear-wheel drive
**Chassis:** separate steel frame
**Suspension:** independent front with wishbones and coil springs; live rear axle with semi-elliptic leaf springs
**Brakes:** drums front and rear
**Bodywork:** four-seater hardtop coupé
**Maximum speed (approx):** 110 mph (177 km/h)

*Above: The Mk II's 368-cu in (6030-cc) overhead-valve V8 was powerful for its day, with a claimed output of 285 bhp. It drove the rear wheels through a three-speed automatic transmission.*

*Below: 'If you've got it, flaunt it' must have been the Continental motto – although its cabin was not huge, the 1956 Mk II was more than 18 feet long and weighed over two tons.*

# Cord

rrett Lobban Cord was running a car dealership in Chicago in 1924 when he was approached by Auburn of Indiana, to help put the ailing car company back on its feet. After negotiating a bonus-for-profits deal he joined Auburn, and soon made it profitable again.

Within a year he had taken control of Auburn, and soon enlarged his empire by buying up Duesenberg (of Indianapolis), American Airlines, the Lycoming engine business, and several other enterprises including, for a time, Checker of New York taxi fame! At the time he had ambitions to make his Indiana-based group of companies into a real rival to the much bigger companies in and around Detroit. Other entrepreneurs had similar ideas, but history now tells us that none of them made it.

By 1928 he controlled assets worth $11 million, spread over several factories, and as the United States seemed to be in an economic boom he decided to branch out with another marque of car. As well as making Auburns in Auburn, and Duesenbergs in Indianapolis, he also decided to build a new marque called the Cord, using both of those plants.

The enterprising Cord picked up expertise and hardware in the best places – hiring Harry Miller and Cornelius Van Ranst to design the car, while specifying that they should use a Lycoming engine.

To launch a new marque at any time was difficult enough, but to launch

*Above: E.L. Cord started by taking control of Auburn, in Indiana, in 1925, and later acquired both Duesenberg of Indianapolis and the Lycoming engine business before starting to make Cord cars in 1929.*

it immediately before the Wall Street Crash of 1929 was 'mission impossible'. Not even the imaginative use of front-wheel drive, and startlingly sleek styling, could do the trick, so the Cord L-29 was dropped after only three years, when only 3,468 cars had been sold. Within three more years second-hand examples were worth no more than $150. . .

Although Cord himself left the USA in 1934 (rather than face SEC [Security and Exchange Commission] investigations over financial dealings), he kept control of his business group for a time. In the meantime, he decided to try again with the Cord marque name, though the car he chose had originally been conceived in another corner of his empire, by August Duesenberg, to be badged as a Duesenberg.

For Cord the car was retouched by Gordon Buehrig, and had not only front-wheel drive and a specially designed Lycoming V8 engine, but also astonishingly advanced styling. Unhappily, this venture too seemed to be doomed from the start. Not only was there a shortage of investment capital but also the project ran late, and frustrated customers had to be sent tiny models at Christmas 1935 to help them remain patient.

The new Model 810/812 Cords, like the previous L-29s, were technically fascinating, but completely unprofitable. Cord himself sold his group in 1936, and following his departure the last Model 810/812 was built in 1937. His enterprises rapidly fell apart, for the entire Auburn-Cord-Duesenberg group went into receivership in 1938. The last Cord

was made in 1937, the last Auburn had already been built in 1936, and the final Duesenberg was sold in 1937.

Cord himself was a great survivor, retiring to Nevada; there he concentrated on new businesses dealing in radio and TV, and lived on until 1974. Even so, in all those years he never again tried to break into the car market. E.L. Cord, at least, got out (with $4 million) while he was still ahead of the game. Many less financially prudent tycoons fared much worse.

The coffin-nosed Model 810/812 was always charismatic to car enthusiasts (although few of them backed their words with orders, and cheques!), so the concept took ages to die. After the group had folded, the design was taken up by Hupmobile, who converted the running gear to rear-wheel drive with a Hupmobile engine, restyled the nose, and launched it as the Skylark – and then swiftly ran out of money after a few hundred cars had been made. Graham, who operated in the same factory in Detroit and had agreed to supply bodies to Hupmobile, then picked up the dregs, made more changes, put their own engine under the famous bonnet, and launched the Graham Hollywood. This car, too, failed, after only 1,859 cars had been produced.

You could argue that the end for the short-lived Cord marque really came in 1941, rather than 1937, though the heritage was pretty tenuous by that time.

# Cord L-29 1929-32

For his first car, E.L. Cord commissioned race car engineer Harry Miller to develop the L-29. Cord's opinion was that advanced engineering features, clearly advertised, would sell his cars, and the fact that the L-29 was launched at almost *exactly* the wrong time (just before the Wall Street Crash) did not deter him.

Although the L-29 used an existing engine – a modified version of the Lycoming straight-eight which was already being fitted to another E.L. Cord car, the Auburn Custom Eight – it was a brand-new and exciting design. Because American motor car engineering tended to be strictly conventional, the most important technical feature was that the L-29 had front-wheel drive – making it North America's very first front-drive production car. Incidentally,

**Left: Cord's L-29 was extraordinary because it had front-wheel drive; it was the first such American car in volume production and made its debut five years before Citroën in Europe launched the Traction Avant.**

**Below: The L-29 was a big car, with a 5275-cc Lycoming straight-eight engine and 137.5-in wheelbase.**

it was launched five years before Citroën came along to astonish the European motor industry 'establishment' with the legendary *traction avant* model.

The chassis itself was conventional enough, but the engine was effectively turned round, so that its clutch end faced forward and drove a three-speed front-drive transaxle ahead of it. In many ways this was an evolution of the layout used in Miller's 1927 Indianapolis 500 race cars. The use of this system also meant that a more advanced front suspension was needed, so Miller chose a de Dion layout, where the solid cross-tube was suspended on no fewer than four forward-facing quarter-elliptic leaf springs.

Unfortunately the combination of a high price, an unknown marque, and a growing reputation for unreliability hit hard, just at a time when the richer American buyers were cutting back.

The L-29 was not a very fast car; it had a very long wheelbase (137.5 in), weighed around 4,600 lb, and because of its 'barn-door' aerodynamics the standard product struggled to reach 80 mph. It was apparently difficult to handle, especially on any kind of loose surfaces, which made the driver work very hard indeed.

Only 1,700 L-29s were sold in the 1930 model year, a mere 1,433 followed in 1931 (when the prices had been cut by $700-$800), and a further 335 were produced in 1932.

## Specification (1929)

**Engine:** inline eight-cylinder, side-valve
**Bore × stroke:** 85.7 mm × 114.3 mm
**Capacity:** 5275 cc
**Maximum power:** 125 bhp
**Transmission:** three-speed manual gearbox, front-wheel drive
**Chassis:** separate steel frame with channel-section side members
**Suspension:** de Dion front axle with quarter-elliptic leaf springs; beam rear axle with semi-elliptic leaf springs
**Brakes:** drums front and rear
**Bodywork:** two- or four-seater, various styles
**Maximum speed (approx):** 80 mph (129 km/h)

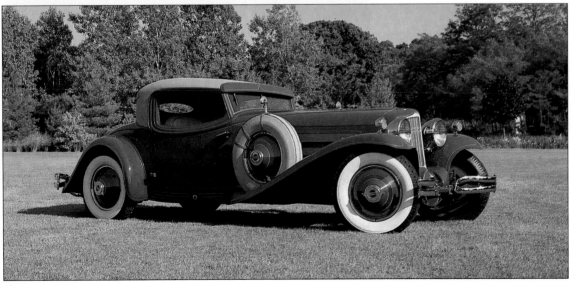

# Cord 810 and 812 1935-37

Three years after Cord had abandoned the unsuccessful L-29, the company tried again, this time with the sensationally styled Model 810. This car, whose body style had been developed by Gordon Buehrig, looked magnificent, and the smooth shape, with what became known as its 'coffin-nose', hid a mass of interesting technical features. There are Americans who still insist that this was one of the most beautiful cars of all time.

Like the L-29, the Model 810 had front-wheel drive, but its layout was completely different in detail. First conceived in 1933 to be badged as a Duesenberg, it had been revamped by Cord engineers before its launch. This time the body/chassis unit was an early example of unitary construction (very expensive to tool-up – which laid the seeds of yet another Cord financial disaster), though the general L-29 layout of front-wheel drive, with engine behind the transmission, was retained. Front suspension was by transverse leaf spring, with massive trailing lower links to hold the wheel in place.

It was a much more compact layout, for the engine was only half the length of the old L-29 type, the wheelbase was 12.5 in shorter, and the new car was about 700 lb lighter. This, truly, was 'down-sizing' with

*Right: Different under the skin from previous Cord models, the 810 and 812 used unitary construction and had an electro-pneumatic gearshift. Supercharged versions in 1937 were genuinely fast.*

*Below: With no distinct radiator grille, hidden headlamps and overall styling quite unlike any other car of its day, Cord's 810/812 series was even more radical than the L-29.*

a vengeance – 40 years before General Motors invented the phrase.

For this model the engine was a specially designed V8, made by Lycoming with an odd arrangement of valve gear and porting, while the transmission had four forward gears, allied to a complex selector system, with a tiny lever and 'gate' on a steering-column stalk, and electro-vacuum operation.

The style was magnificent and, even in later years, quite unmistakeable. More rounded than many other American cars, the Model 810 hid its headlamps under flaps in the front of the wings, there was really no separate radiator grille as such, and a series of styling strakes swept around the engine cover, continuously, from front door to front door.

For the 1937 model year, Cord offered the Model 812, which was the same basic

car as the Model 810, but also offered the option of an engine equipped with a Schwitzer-Cummins supercharger. This allowed peak power to be boosted from 115 bhp to no less than 190 bhp. These cars had chrome-plated external exhaust pipes protruding from the sides of the bonnet – a very flamboyant touch which aped both the Mercedes-Benz SSK models of the late 1920s and the Auburn 851 Speedster (which was another car from the Cord stable of the 1930s period).

In tip-top trim a Model 812 was good for up to 110 mph, and was an exciting 'Grand Touring' car by any standards.

Unfortunately, both models were commercial disasters, for Cadillac prices were being asked for unproven machinery. Only 1,174 Model 810s were produced in the 1936 model year. Even after

the supercharged Model 812 had appeared there was no upsurge in sales, and a mere 1,146 cars were produced. The end came after less than two years and with just 2,320 cars produced.

## Specification (1935 810)

**Engine:** V8, overhead-valve
**Bore × stroke:** 88.9 mm × 95.25 mm
**Capacity:** 4729 cc
**Maximum power:** 115 bhp
**Transmission:** four-speed manual gearbox, front-wheel drive
**Chassis:** unitary body/chassis
**Suspension:** independent front with transverse leaf spring; beam axle rear with semi-elliptic leaf springs
**Brakes:** drums front and rear
**Bodywork:** four-seater, various styles
**Maximum speed (approx):** 90 mph (145 km/h)

# Cunningham

**C**incinnati-born Briggs Cunningham was a wealthy man who took up motorsport in the 1940s, and soon became one of North America's most successful sports car entrants.

His first foray at the Le Mans 24 Hours came in 1950, when his team entered two virtually standard Cadillacs, one of them with a hideous open body, rapidly nicknamed 'Le Monstre'. These cars finished 10th and 11th – a remarkable achievement – so the enthusiastic sportsman then directed his team to produce better and more special cars for future years.

The very first Cunningham car of 1950-51 – the C1 – used a Cadillac V8 engine, gearbox and back axle, while the second car – the C2 – used a Chrysler V8, and had a special chassis frame. For the 1951 Le Mans race the Cunningham team constructed three C2 cars, still with Cadillac running gear, around the basis of chassis frames with large-diameter tubes, but with Ford cross-members. Front suspension was by coil springs and wishbones, and rear suspension by de Dion.

Although the C2s did not finish at Le Mans in 1951, one of them held second place for some time. Thus encouraged, Briggs Cunningham decided to launch a roadgoing sports car, based on the C2's layout, which was to become the C3. This was the first, and the only, Cunningham to be sold to the general public.

*Above: Although Briggs Cunningham began building a limited run of roadgoing models, his real efforts were directed at making cars for the racetrack, Le Mans in particular. This 1953 example is 331 Chrysler-powered.*

## Cunningham C3 1953-55

The C3, like its predecessor, was Chrysler-powered. It was also an expensive car, intended to sell in small numbers to wealthy enthusiasts. It was, in fact, meant to out-Ferrari anything that could be built in Italy at the time.

The principal selling feature of the C3 was the sleek, closed coupé body, which was shaped *and* manufactured by Vignale in Italy. Like its obvious Ferrari rivals of the early 1950s, the C3 was a beautiful machine, rather large for a two-seater, but carefully and delicately shaped.

The manufacture of each car took a great deal of time. The rolling chassis was completed at Cunningham's small factory in Florida before being shipped out to Vignale in Italy. The hand-crafted body shell was then produced, fitted out, and trimmed, before the completed car was returned to the USA – or to its customer somewhere else in the world.

The C3 was, of course, a very expensive car. When officially launched in the USA in 1953 it was priced at $10,000, considerably more than the $4,000 being asked for a Cadillac coupé. Nor was it profitable to build – Cunningham later admitted to having lost a lot of money on every car built. If only the C3 had been more successful, Cunningham might have carried out their plans to produce a longer-wheelbase version, in four-seater sports saloon form, which would have been a truly magnificent car.

Mechanically, the C3 used the same basic chassis as the Cunningham race cars, though there was no de Dion rear suspension. Instead the road car used a Chrysler live rear axle, sprung on coil springs, and located by radius arms. The engine was the mighty new Chrysler 'Hemi' unit, which pushed out no less than 223 bhp.

The C3 was a blindingly fast and desirable machine, but because of its high price it was destined to sell very slowly. By 1955, when Briggs Cunningham reluctantly closed down the project, only 19

*Left: Unlike the C2 racer from which it was derived, the C3 did not have a de Dion rear end. Instead, it used a coil-spring Chrysler live axle located by parallel trailing arms.*

*Right: Cunningham's cars were by now Chrysler 'Hemi'-powered. The 331-cu in overhead-valve V8 with hemispherical combustion chambers was one of the toughest engines of its day. In roadgoing form it developed between 220 and 235 bhp.*

closed coupés and nine convertible versions of the same car had been built. Perhaps it did not help that the $10,000 price had actually been raised to $11,500 in 1955.

Latter-day American pundits have christened the C3 "one of the all-time greats" – and certainly it is much rarer, and therefore more exclusive, than almost any European supercar of the period.

### Specification (1953)
**Engine:** V8, overhead-valve
**Bore × stroke:** 96.8 mm × 92.1 mm
**Capacity:** 5425 cc
**Maximum power:** 223 bhp
**Transmission:** three-speed manual gearbox or four-speed automatic transmission, rear-wheel drive
**Chassis:** separate steel frame with tubular members and fabricated stiffenings

*Above: The handsome C3's Florida-built rolling chassis was bodied and trimmed by Vignale in Italy.*

**Suspension:** independent front with coil springs; live rear axle with coil springs
**Brakes:** drums front and rear
**Bodywork:** aluminium two-seater coupé
**Maximum speed (approx):** 130 mph (209 km/h)

# Daimler

A lthough Daimler is now renowned as a British company, the origins of the marque were in Germany, where Gottlieb Daimler designed the world's first four-wheel car, in the 1880s. In Germany Daimler soon produced the Mercedes marque, and its story will be told in a later A-Z entry.

The first British Daimlers were produced in Coventry in 1896, and were licence-built German designs. The next few years were marked by extraordinary upheavals of directors, finances and policies, with that notorious rogue Harry Lawson at the bottom of everything, and a confused series of models, the largest being a 10½-litre machine.

By 1910, however, Lawson had gone, stability had returned, the BSA Group had bought the company, and Daimler had established a stable policy. The object was to make dignified, well-built, and – by definition – costly machines, for sale to the upper crust. It was a policy which served Daimler well until the 1930s.

The first sleeve-valve-engined Daimlers were announced in 1909, and until the 1930s all new models used the same type of valve gear, but there were many different units. Smooth, silent, but rather oil-consuming, these engines helped to give Daimler their refined image, though the characteristic blue smoke haze which followed the cars everywhere wasn't quite so uplifting.

Daimler's reputation was helped immeasurably when the British (and other) royal families chose the cars for personal and ceremonial travel. Looking back, it is difficult to realise that although Rolls-Royce might indeed have been the "Best Car in the World" (to quote a later advertisement), it was Daimlers which were more often chosen by the real aristocracy.

Until the late 1920s the 'vintage' Daimlers had six-cylinder engines, but in 1926 the first of the huge and magnificent V12-engined Double Six models was introduced, as a flagship. This was something which made Rolls-Royce sit up and think, even more than before. Double Sixes sold only in small quantities, but their prestige, and their technical interest, were immense.

Private car assembly closed down soon after war broke out in 1939, but

*Above: Although of German lineage, the Daimler marque was taken up by British royalty and aristocracy in the 1920s and 1930s. For years Daimler sleeve-valve engines left a blue oil haze on every state occasion.*

although the works were badly bombed in 1940 and 1941 the company survived and prospered.

Sir Bernard Docker was Daimler's chairman immediately after World War II, and until 1955 he presided over a turbulent decade in the company's history. Several different policies seemed to be pulling the firm in several directions at once, for at one time it built expensive cars, armoured vehicles and buses!

Suddenly, in 1960, Sir William Lyons of Jaguar bought Daimler from the BSA Group, and within a few years had integrated it with Jaguar's products. There were two hybrid cars in the 1960s – one being the 2½-litre saloon (Daimler engine/Jaguar structure), the other the DS420 Daimler Limousine (Jaguar running gear and platform/Daimler styling) – but for the 1970s and beyond, all Daimlers became badge-engineered, slightly up-market, Jaguars.

In recent years all Daimler cars have been assembled at Jaguar's principal factory, and in 1998 the range included the Super V8, Jaguar's flagship model.

## Daimler Double Six 1926-37

By the 1920s Daimler's six-cylinder-engined cars were being outpaced by the Rolls-Royce 40/50 models, so to counter this the company evolved a series of magnificent sleeve-valve V12 engines, each of which used many existing six-cylinder components. Thus the original '50' model had a 7.1-litre engine which used many components (including complete cylinder blocks) from the existing 25/85 model.

These cars were all called 'Double Sixes' because in many ways they *were* doubled six-cylinder engines, with two sets of carburettor, ignition and cooling systems, one for each bank of cylinders.

The cars were vast, stately, dignified, and almost entirely silent, which made them ideal for sales to the aristocracy, and to royalty in Britain, where Daimler had a monopoly of the business despite the rivalry from Rolls-Royce.

Four different types of Double Six were made in 11 years, on different-length chassis, but all at prices exceeding £2,000. The original 50 was joined by the smaller, 3744-cc-engined 30 in 1928, but for 1931 these cars were displaced by the 30/40 and 40/50 models (5296-cc and 6511-cc), which had fluid-flywheel/preselector transmissions. A handful of poppet-valved 6.5-litre models was built in the mid-1930s, originally for King George V and Queen Mary. Very few Double Sixes survive today.

### Specification (1927-30)

**Engine:** V12, sleeve-valve
**Bore × stroke:** 81.5 mm × 114 mm
**Capacity:** 7136 cc
**Maximum power:** 150 bhp
**Transmission:** four-speed manual gearbox, rear-wheel drive
**Chassis:** separate steel frame with channel-section side members
**Suspension:** beam front axle with semi-elliptic leaf springs; live rear axle with semi-elliptic leaf springs
**Brakes:** drums front and rear
**Bodywork:** five- to seven-seater, saloon/limousine/landaulette styles by coachbuilders
**Maximum speed (approx):** 80 mph (129 km/h)

*Above: Despite a displacement of just over seven litres, the massive sleeve-valve V12 produced just 150 bhp.*

*Below: This example had its chassis modified by Reid Railton in 1930 to have 'underslung' suspension. The cabriolet body was built by Corsica.*

## Daimler SP250 1959-64

Following Daimler's management upheaval in the 1950s the engineers not only designed a brace of modern V8 engines, but also a sports car which they hoped would rival the Triumph TR and Austin-Healey 3000 types. The result was the SP250.

To cut corners a Triumph TR3 car was bought, torn apart, and studied, so perhaps it was inevitable that the new Daimler's chassis should be almost a 'TR-clone'; in fact it had the same front suspension, and a straight copy of that car's gearbox.

The engine was a lightweight, high-revving V8, designed by an ex-motorcycle engineer, Edward Turner. It was conservatively rated at 140 bhp, which was quite enough even in standard form to give the car a 120 mph top speed. Daimler hoped that an automatic transmission option would attract transatlantic customers, but this plan misfired.

To keep down tooling costs, and to shorten the time lag between design and production, the rather strangely-styled shell was made from glassfibre, which was notable for its rear fins and low snout. At the time this made the SP250 one of the very few glassfibre-bodied sports cars in the world, alongside the Chevrolet Corvette and the Lotus Elite.

When the car was previewed, Daimler called it the 'Dart', but Dodge of the USA (who held trademark rights) objected, and production cars therefore had to be called SP250s. Previewed in the spring of 1959, but not put on public sale until October 1959, the SP250 had barely got into its stride when Jaguar took over the business.

Jaguar's Sir William Lyons hated the style, and despised the build quality of the cars, so in spite of a series of design updates the SP250 was dropped in 1964. Only 2,650 cars were built, but because of the corrosion-resistant body shell many have survived into the 'classic' era. The engine lived on in the Jaguar-derived 2½-litre saloon.

### Specification

**Engine:** V8, overhead-valve
**Bore × stroke:** 76.2 mm × 69.85 mm
**Capacity:** 2548 cc
**Maximum power:** 140 bhp
**Transmission:** four-speed manual gearbox or optional automatic transmission, rear-wheel drive
**Chassis:** separate steel frame with box-section side members
**Suspension:** independent front with coil springs; live rear axle with semi-elliptic leaf springs
**Brakes:** discs front and rear
**Bodywork:** glassfibre open two-seater, optional hardtop
**Maximum speed (approx):** 120 mph (193 km/h)

*Above: Idiosyncratic styling, a TR3-clone chassis and poor build quality handicapped the SP250 but its Edward Turner-designed lightweight V8 engine was an undeniable strength.*

*Below: Daimler called their 2.5-litre sports car the 'Dart' when it was introduced at the 1959 New York Motor Show but, after finding that Dodge owned rights to the name, settled for the designation SP250.*

## Daimler V8 250 1962-69

Having taken over Daimler in 1960, Jaguar then made haste to develop a hybrid 'Daimler-Jaguar' model which would sell in considerable numbers and hopefully make the business profitable once more. The result was the 2½-litre saloon (renamed V8 250 for 1968 and 1969), which married a Daimler engine to a Jaguar structure.

The basis of the new car was Jaguar's handsome Mk II saloon, a curvaceous 15-ft long four-door saloon normally fitted with the Jaguar XK twin-cam engine. In this case, however, it was fitted with the smaller of the two Daimler V8 engines, of the type being used in the SP250 sports car, and the car was given a rounded version of the familiar fluted Daimler grille.

*Left: After Jaguar's acquisition of Daimler came the 2½-litre saloon, a logical hybrid of Jaguar's Mk II body/ chassis with Daimler's V8 engine, different trim and a fluted grille.*

The new 2½-litre Daimler cost £1,571 at a time when the Jaguar Mk II 2.4 cost £1,348 and the Mk II 3.4 £1,463, but the Daimler had automatic transmission as standard, and had several special touches of trim and equipment.

The 2½-litre was a much quicker car than the 2.4, with a 110 mph top speed, and with the same nimble road-holding of other Mk II models, but its character and 'image' were firmly aimed at less sporting drivers. Even so, it sold very well – *much* better than any previous post-war Daimler, no matter of what engine size – and it enjoyed a good reputation.

Despite its popularity at the time, the V8 250 has not enjoyed the 'minor classic' status now given to the similar-bodied Jaguars. 17,620 V8 250s were produced in seven years before the car was displaced by the first of the purely 'badge-engineered' Daimlers, the XJ6-based Sovereign.

## Specification (1962)

**Engine:** V8, overhead-valve
**Bore × stroke:** 76.2 mm × 69.85 mm
**Capacity:** 2548 cc
**Maximum power:** 140 bhp
**Transmission:** four-speed manual gearbox, optional overdrive, optional automatic transmission, rear-wheel drive
**Chassis:** unitary body/chassis assembly
**Suspension:** independent front with wishbones and coil springs; live rear axle with quarter-elliptic leaf springs
**Brakes:** discs front and rear
**Bodywork:** four-seater saloon
**Maximum speed (approx):** 110 mph (177 km/h)

*Right: Like the SP250, the Daimler-Jaguar saloon used the compact, relatively light 'baby Hemi' Turner V8. A free-revving, over-square design, it produced 140 bhp with no strain.*

# Darrin

In the late 1940s Howard A. ('Dutch') Darrin was a famed coachbuilder and designer, hired by Kaiser-Frazer to style this new marque of car. At the same time he worked on sports cars of his own design, first producing a one-off convertible.

In the early 1950s he decided to produce his own car, the result being the DKF-161 model of 1954. Not only was this a startling-looking open-top two-seater, but it also used a glassfibre body shell (something only adopted, to this point, by Chevrolet for the new Corvette), and it was fitted with sliding, rather than hinged, doors.

The DKF-161 had a chequered history. It went on sale in Kaiser-Frazer's factory at Jackson, Michigan, badged as a Darrin, but soon officially became a Kaiser-Darrin. Production came to a halt when Kaiser-Frazer

closed down, but Darrin himself bought up the last 90 units, re-engined them, and carried on selling them until 1957.

The Darrin's problems were closely connected to those of Kaiser-Frazer, who were in deep financial trouble by the early 1950s. The car's original selling price of $3,668 was high, and once Kaiser-Frazer went into decline, so did the Darrin. When the main Willow Run plant was sold off to General Motors, and Kaiser-Frazer merged with Willys, the sports car project was abandoned.

American sports car buyers, in any case, had been strangely reluctant to buy a car which was lauded so highly by the enthusiastic motoring press, and the project gradually faded away. Although Darrin went on to design a smaller car, powered by a German DKW engine, this was soon abandoned.

## Darrin DKF-161 1953-57

Although Darrin's creation had spectacular lines, it was based on the humble Kaiser 'Henry J' chassis, to which a six-cylinder Willys engine had been fitted. Because this was an American car of the 1950s it was felt, rightly, that the style and the visual appeal of the car were more important than its chassis.

In any case, as Kaiser-Frazer was backing this car, and it was to be built in one of that firm's factories, it had to use as many 'corporate' parts as possible. The result was a car which, in North American terms, was more show than go.

The body style was quite beautiful, especially by the standards of garish Eisenhower America. The very first show cars had a divided-glass screen, but production cars had a one-piece curved screen. The style was long, low and graceful, with a tiny front grille and nicely integrated bumpers.

The most startling feature, of course, was the use of sliding passenger doors, something which had never before been used (and has never been repeated) on a · passenger car. The doors were arranged to open by sliding *forward* inside the front wings, which gave absolutely unhampered access to the driving compartment. This was 'Dutch' Darrin's own invention, which he patented in 1948. The original patents mentioned

solenoids, switches and application to a four-door saloon, but for the sports car the linkage was altogether more simple.

The doors moved to and fro on rollers; in old age these gave a great deal of trouble, especially when the slides became encrusted with dirt, or especially if the body shell itself were distorted after an accident.

The Darrin always faced an uphill battle for acceptance. It had no established pedigree, and although it was a lot lighter than Chevrolet's new Corvette it was also a lot less powerful.

On the other hand the instrument layout was comprehensive, the interior was well-equipped, and although a sweeping hardtop option was available most owners settled for what was known as the 'Landau' soft top, where the hood could be rolled back from the screen rail, but the frame and rear protection remained in place.

The Darrin was on sale only for a short time – production began in the autumn of 1953, and ended in the summer of 1954 – and the car was available only in four colours – Champagne, Pink Tint, Red Sail and Yellow Satin.

In the end a total of 435 cars was produced but around 100 of these were still unsold when production stopped. 'Dutch' Darrin himself bought most of them, and

*Above: The Darrin was a graceful car by the standards of its time, but the nose treatment was strange. Its sliding doors were a unique feature.*

sold them through his own Los Angeles showrooms over the next two years. A few were retro-fitted with 304-bhp Cadillac V8 engines, and were reputed to be capable of about 140 mph.

## Specification (1953)

**Engine:** inline-six, overhead-inlet-valve
**Bore × stroke:** 79.37 mm × 88.9 mm
**Capacity:** 2637 cc
**Maximum power:** 90 bhp
**Transmission:** three-speed manual gearbox, optional overdrive, rear-wheel drive
**Chassis:** separate steel frame with box-section side members and cross-members
**Suspension:** independent front with coil springs; live rear axle with leaf springs
**Brakes:** drums front and rear
**Bodywork:** glassfibre two-seater, optional hardtop
**Maximum speed (approx):** 100 mph (161 km/h)

# DB (Deutsch and Bonnet)

Deutsch and Bonnet began building 'specials' based on the running gear of the famous *traction avant* Citroëns in 1938, using a tiny factory at Champigny-sur-Marne in France. Production began again after World War II, with the first competition cars using Panhard-Dyna components following in 1948.

By the early 1950s much competition success had been gained, both with single-seater racing cars and with sports-racing machines. This led DB to launch a backbone-framed production sports car in 1952, a car which was made in several different forms until 1961. To do this a commercial supply partnership was set up with Panhard of Paris. The first cars had aluminium bodywork, but from the mid-1950s glassfibre was adopted instead.

Once established with a successful, limited-production, design in the 1950s, DB never hastened to replace it. Ultimately, however, Deutsch left the partnership, leaving René Bonnet in sole control.

Within months Bonnet had dropped the Panhard connection, and began to produce new-style GRP-bodied cars based on Renault running gear, which were more properly known as Bonnets. There were several types – the Djet had a mid-mounted engine and rear drive, while the Le Mans and Missile models had front engines and front-wheel drive – an intriguing mixture.

In 1964, however, DB was taken over by Matra, and the cars assumed that name, though the same factory was retained. The last Matra-badged example was produced in 1968, after which Matra concentrated on more up-market cars, first with Ford Germany, then Simca, and latterly with Renault co-operation.

*Right: This Deutsch and Bonnet Rally Coupé is seen at the 1954 Monte Carlo Rally. At that time the DBs were front-wheel-driven by a Panhard-Dyna flat-twin engine installed complete with transmission, final drive and front suspension. Panhard's torsion-bar rear suspension was also a feature. In the early years of production the bodywork was hand-crafted from aluminium; the little coupés were compact, light and easy to handle.*

## DB Coach 1953-61

The first DB road car was based on a steel backbone chassis frame, to which the entire Panhard-Dyna front-wheel-drive air-cooled flat-twin engine, transmission, final drive and independent front suspension installation was bolted, with the same car's torsion-bar rear suspension also being used.

For the first couple of years the bodywork was laboriously constructed from aluminium sheeting, but from 1955 DB followed the example of Chevrolet's Corvette by using moulded glassfibre sections instead.

A whole variety of engine sizes and tunes was available, for DB had decided that the customer was important, and his or her wishes should always be honoured. The standard car, therefore, used very lightly modified Panhard-Dyna engines (with 55 bhp from 851 cc), but with various competition classes in mind it was possible to ring the changes between 610-cc and 1.3 litres. The smallest version was the 610-cc engine, which produced only 30 bhp, and meant that the smart coupé sometimes looked a lot faster than it actually was. The 1.3-litre version produced 65 bhp and had a top speed of more than 100 mph.

From 1954 it was even possible to order supercharged versions of the

*Left: A 1958 Panhard-powered DB is pictured at Silverstone in 1961. By now the cars were glassfibre-bodied.*

engine, and early-type disc brakes also became optional from 1955.

The original coupé was called the Coach, but eventually became known as the Rally. It was small and light – although the standard two-seater was 160 inches long it weighed only 1,290 lb – and the front-wheel-drive layout contributed to its nimble handling.

## Specification (1953)

**Engine:** flat-twin, overhead-valve
**Bore × stroke:** 85 mm × 75 mm
**Capacity:** 851 cc
**Maximum power:** 48 bhp or 56 bhp
**Transmission:** four-speed manual gearbox, front-wheel drive
**Chassis:** separate steel backbone
**Suspension:** independent front with transverse leaf springs; beam rear axle with torsion bars
**Brakes:** drums front and rear
**Bodywork:** aluminium (glassfibre from 1955) two-seater coupé
**Maximum speed (approx):** 96 mph (154 km/h)

*Right: This HBR5 DB coupé was driven by Deviterne and Laillier at Le Mans in 1957 and retired after eight hours.*

# Bonnet Djet 1962-68

Once the Deutsch and Bonnet partnership had been dissolved in 1961, René Bonnet hastened to produce a new line of cars, which had Renault R8 engines, transmissions and other components.

Compared with the original Coach and Rally models, the transformation was complete. DB-based cars had used front-wheel drive and air-cooling, while the new cars, christened Djet, had mid-mounted water-cooled engines and rear-wheel drive.

In the next few years Bonnet carried out an active sports car racing programme, and although they were often beaten by Jean Redele's extraordinarily successful Alpine-Renaults these were fast and exciting machines.

There was a world of difference between the Bonnet Djets and the Alpine-Renaults. In the case of the Djet, the four-cylinder engine was mid-mounted – ahead of the line of the rear wheels, but behind the seats – whereas in the Alpines the engines were *rear*-mounted, overhung behind the line of the wheels. The Djets, therefore, traded off passenger cabin space against the advantage of better handling and response.

The Djet's chassis was a simple, but sturdy, steel backbone layout, and supported an all-independent suspension by coil springs and wishbones. The engine itself could be supplied in standard Renault R8 guise, but there was an option of the Renault-Gordini tune, which meant that there was a completely different cylinder head, which featured part-spherical combustion chambers along with a different camshaft grind and exciting high-revving possibilities.

The Djet's body style was neat and stylish, with a very large rear window which also covered the engine bay. Like the Alpine-Renault, the Djet was designed for function before comfort, so it was neither a quiet nor a peaceful car to

*Right: After the partnership with Deutsch dissolved in 1961, René Bonnet produced the Djet sports car, with a mid-mounted Renault engine. Matra took over Bonnet in 1964 but the car, fitted with power units producing up to 1255 cc and 103 bhp, continued to be built at the Champigny-sur-Marne works until 1968.*

drive. On the other hand, it was light, powerful and agile, which made it very suitable for European sports car racing and long-distance rallies of the period.

Several variants were produced, including the Djet 55 model with a larger, 95-bhp, Renault-Gordini engine. From 1966 the most powerful model had the Renault-Gordini 1300 engine. This was a 1255-cc unit with 103 bhp, and it was matched by a five-speed Renault gearbox.

Even after Matra took over Bonnet in 1964, sales of the Djet – renamed the Matra Jet – continued unabated. From 1967, however, Matra produced its own Ford-engined M530A sports coupé, and the last of the true Bonnet cars was built at the original Deutsch and Bonnet works at Champigny-sur-Marne in 1968.

## Specification (1963 Gordini)

**Engine:** mid-mounted inline four-cylinder, overhead-valve
**Bore × stroke:** 70 mm × 72 mm
**Capacity:** 1108 cc
**Maximum power:** 72 bhp
**Transmission:** four-speed manual gearbox, rear-wheel drive
**Chassis:** separate steel tubular backbone chassis
**Suspension:** independent front and rear, each with wishbones and coil springs
**Brakes:** discs front and rear
**Bodywork:** glassfibre two-seater coupé
**Maximum speed (approx):** 100 mph (161 km/h)

# Automobiles Delage

L ouis Delage was a former employee of Turgan-Foy, then of Peugeot – both of them being pioneering French carmakers – who set up his own car-manufacturing business in 1905.

Almost immediately he was smitten with motor racing, seeing it as an ideal way to boost his new company's image, and his cars won their first event in 1908. Even before World War I he began designing Grand Prix machines, and his obsession with racing became a huge financial commitment in the 1920s.

Even so, Delage was a modest little company in its formative years; it was only the profits made by producing munitions for the French war effort which enabled the firm to branch out in the 1920s.

During this period Louis Delage not only saw the versatile D1 models put on sale, and the Type GL produced, abortively, as competition for Hispano-Suiza cars, but he also hired the noted racing expert Albert Lory to design two magnificent Grand Prix engines – first a complex two-litre V12, and then a very successful 1½-litre straight-eight. In the mid-1920s Delages were *the* best Grand Prix cars, for they regularly beat both Bugattis and Alfa Romeos. During these years Delage also built massive cars which managed to capture the world land speed record, which stood in 1924 at over 143 mph.

In the 1930s the extravagant Delage moved his company even further up-market, and inspired the birth of the magnificent eight-cylinder D8

models, all of which were fast, and many of which featured stunningly attractive body styles by French coachbuilders like Letourner et Marchand, or Figoni & Falaschi.

Above all, the D8 range had style, inspiring the saying: "One drives, of course, an Alfa Romeo, one is driven in a Rolls-Royce, but one gives only a Delage to one's favourite mistress."

The D8, however, was always an expensive car, and even though a six-cylinder version (logically called the D6) appeared in 1931, sales slumped badly in the 1930s. Delage himself never adjusted to the straitened economic circumstances, and eventually quarrelled bitterly with his co-directors about the company's future.

Eventually Delage was obliged to sell out to Delahaye of Paris, a more prosperous French concern, in 1935, whereupon Delage himself was forced out of the company which he had founded 30 years earlier.

The Delage company then found itself submerged within Delahaye, a 1937 plan to build cars in the UK was abandoned, and from then on most Delage models were really badge-engineered Delahayes. The last 'Delage' was built in 1954, the year in which the Delahaye/Delage operation was taken over by Hotchkiss, who demonstrated very little interest in maintaining either car production or the Delage name.

Delage himself lived on for many years, eventually becoming very poor, and died having lost all contact with the motor industry.

*Above: Delages were fitted with various elegant radiator mascots – the one above is from the 1924 boat-tail model. The radiator shell's overall shape remained consistent over the years, although its details and proportions varied.*

*Inset left: Another elegant and distinctive Delage was the 1929 DMS, the sporting version of the D1-derived DM, powered by a 3174-cc overhead-valve straight-six engine.*

*Left: Like their celebrated 1930s successors, a number of 1920s Delages had unusual and attractive coachwork. One such car was this Labourdette boat-tail model, dating from 1924.*

# Delage AH 12/14HP

The Delage 12HP, introduced in 1912, marked the company's transition from producing single-cylinder designs to building 'proper' cars.

Before the development of the 12HP, Delage had been in existence for only seven years, having started car production with light cars powered by that staple of the French car industry – the de Dion-Bouton single-cylinder engine. Delage were rewarded for their courage in starting production on Friday the 13th as the early cars were soon in demand on the emerging French market, helped by their successes in light-car racing.

One of the secrets of Delage's fortuitous start was the hiring of their chief designer from Peugeot, a point noted by contemporary journalist Phillipe Marot: "Although this company is new, its head is a veteran of the motor industry, who for several years has been chief of design and testing with one of our great manufacturing companies."

That same head of design was in place when Delage introduced their first four-cylinder design, in 1908, in the form of the 1763-cc Type H. That was followed by other four-cylinder cars, leading up to the 12HP of 1912, and using a variety of proprietary engines – de Dion-Bouton,

Chapuis-Dornier and Ballot.

The distinction of the AH 12/14HP model lay in its having the very first Delage-designed engine, a four-cylinder unit of 2292 cc. It was a simple 'T-head' side-valve design built by Malicet & Blin rather than Delage themselves. It was not outstandingly powerful, producing just 24 bhp from its 2.3 litres. Depending on what body was fitted to the conventional beam-axle and leaf-spring chassis, that meant a maximum speed in the region of 45 mph, which was probably

fast enough for a machine with the customary rear brakes only.

The AH brought a new designation to the Delage catalogue; a Grand Sport runabout was listed and then shortly afterwards a six-cylinder version was made available.

## Specification (1913)

**Engine:** inline four-cylinder, side-valve
**Bore × stroke:** 75 mm × 130 mm
**Capacity:** 2292 cc

*Left: The two-main-bearing, side-valve engine of the early four-cylinder Delage models was a typical light-car power unit of its day. It was a long-stroke design, intended more for slogging along than revving hard, and its power output was modest.*

**Maximum power:** 24 bhp
**Transmission:** four-speed manual gearbox, rear-wheel drive
**Chassis:** separate steel frame with channel-section side members and five channel-section cross-members
**Suspension:** non-independent with beam front axle and semi-elliptic leaf springs; live rear axle with semi-elliptic leaf springs
**Brakes:** rear drums
**Bodywork:** various styles, particularly two-seater roadster and four-seater torpedo tourer
**Maximum speed (approx):** 45 mph (72 km/h)

*Below: One of the more popular cars in the Delage series produced immediately before World War I was the 12HP four-cylinder model, seen here in its roadster form.*

## Delage D8 1930-35

There's no doubt that the D8s were the most glamorous of all Delage road cars. Conceived at the end of the 1920s, when any prudent manufacturing concern would have opted for more modest new models to keep it afloat through difficult economic times, the glorious D8 was one of the most desirable high-performance cars to be built anywhere in Europe.

Unlike a Rolls-Royce, or even a Hispano-Suiza, a Delage D8 was not a discreet car. Every example made was intended to appeal to flamboyant customers – the sort of people who wanted to keep reminding the world that they were wealthy, and that they enjoyed spending their money.

The D8 was a car specifically designed for what was truly 'Grand Touring'. The early 1930s was a period when many French main roads had been brought up to good condition, when there were very few speed limits, and at the same time there was very little traffic on the roads.

The typical Delage D8 journey would encompass an early start from Paris, a long-legged cruise down the RN7, lunch along the way, and arrival on the French Riviera at the end of the day. Naturally the car would then be parked outside a glossy Nice or Cannes hotel for a time, among other models of the same type.

The original D8 chassis was a conventional ladder-type layout, with semi-elliptic leaf-spring suspension and with cable-operated brakes. To accommodate the spacious coachwork, it was available with a choice of wheelbases – 130 in or 143 in – and complete cars sometimes weighed 4,400 lb.

The engine, however, was an efficient eight-cylinder four-litre unit with five crankshaft bearings, which produced 120 bhp at the very start of its develop-

*Below: The D8 was a car of great presence and style, not aimed at a shy or retiring clientele. This is a 1930 Chapron-bodied example.*

ment. Even with the unaerodynamic coachwork fashionable at the time, the top speed was nearly 100 mph.

Although a sober observer would have concluded that to introduce such an expensive eight-cylinder car after the Depression had already begun was folly, Delage carried on developing the design, with not cheaper, but more and more fanciful derivatives. There were lowered chassis frames, tuned engines, better suspension and more rakish coachwork, the collective result being

cars which rapidly acquired exotic status, but equally rapidly lost most of their value when the market collapsed.

Later D8s of all types had centre-lock wire wheels, along with synchromesh gearboxes, hydraulic brakes and transverse leaf-spring independent front suspension. The D8 120 (a car created by Delahaye after the merger) also had a Cotal electromagnetic gearbox. These were the last of the true Grand Touring Delages, for all the later cars were really modified Delahayes.

*Above: The D8 was powered by an overhead-valve straight-eight producing upwards of 120 bhp and giving it near-100-mph capability.*

### Delage D8 variants

#### Delage D8 Grand Sport
The D8 Grand Sport had improved front-axle location, with more rakish coachwork on the original chassis. A specially-bodied version achieved 110 mph for 24 hours at Montlhèry.

#### Delage D8S and D8SS
The D8S and D8SS models used specially-lowered chassis frames, engines tuned to 145 bhp, and had higher gearing to guarantee a top speed of more than 100 mph. One rare version of the D8SS was also available with a shorter wheelbase of 122 in and two-seater bodywork.

### Specification (1930 D8)
**Engine:** inline eight-cylinder, overhead-valve
**Bore × stroke:** 77 mm × 109 mm
**Capacity:** 4050 cc
**Maximum power:** 120 bhp
**Transmission:** four-speed manual gearbox, rear-wheel drive
**Chassis:** separate steel frame with channel-section side members, and tube and pressed cross-braces
**Suspension:** non-independent with beam front axle and semi-elliptic leaf springs; live rear axle with semi-elliptic leaf springs
**Brakes:** drums front and rear
**Bodywork:** various styles; sports, touring and saloon shells
**Maximum speed (approx):** 95 mph (153 km/h)

# Automobiles Delahaye

Left: Delahaye's logo (here on a Type 135 Competition) was stylish but understated, unlike their cars.

Below: The Delahaye Type 135 was fast, handled well, and – thanks to a range of attractive bodies from a variety of coachbuilders – caught the public's imagination. This 1947 model was clad by Vanden Plas.

Until 1890 Emile Delahaye had been chief engineer of a Franco-Belgian railway rolling-stock concern before taking over a machine shop in Tours. After taking time to test, and experiment, Delahaye produced his first car in 1894. In 1898 he moved his new business to Paris, and was well established in the French motor industry by the end of the 19th century.

Early success in town-to-town motor racing led to a series of big-engined cars being produced before World War I, but even by this time Delahaye himself had retired from business. By 1906 the firm's destiny was guided by Charles Weiffenbach, a notable character who remained in charge until the 1950s.

The first shaft-drive Delahaye was built in 1906, a V6-engined car was launched in 1911, and before long a series of sturdy trucks came onto the market. It was trucks, rather than private cars, which were to support the fortunes of Delahaye.

During World War I the Delahaye company built thousands of trucks, aircraft components, stationary engines and rifles, and throughout the 1920s the business produced a whole range of cars variously described as 'stodgy', 'uninspiring' or even as 'dull and non-performing'.

Then, in 1933, the mood changed, with the company announcing its first high-performance car for many years – the Superluxe, offered with a choice of interrelated four- or six-cylinder engines. At the same time an even faster version was launched, the 18 Sport.

Before long the famous 3.5-litre Type 135 had evolved from the Superluxe, this eventually becoming available with 130-bhp or 160-bhp

engine tunes. Here was timely competition for Delage's gorgeous D8 range, a series which was the backbone of Delahaye production until the Germans occupied France in 1940.

But there was more. Delahaye took over Delage in 1935 and imposed their technical will on that firm, so that Delage badges and grilles were put onto a variety of lightly-modified Delahaye models. Delahaye, in fact, were so buoyant at this time that their chief engineer, Jean Francois, was encouraged to produce the Type 145 single-seater racing car, complete with 4½-litre V12 engine, and there was even time for a handful of Type 165s (which were really detuned and road-equipped Type 145s) to be produced in 1939.

After World War II, during which trucks were reluctantly built for use by the German forces, Delahaye Type 135 cars went back on sale in 1946. The Type 175S, introduced in 1946, was a large, fast, and (in economic terms) almost totally irrelevant 4½-litre machine, while the Type 235 of 1952 was really no more than a restyled 135.

By this time, however, the demand for these expensive – and, frankly, outdated – cars was slipping badly, and production of the Jeep-like VLR for the French army only postponed the inevitable.

Charles Weiffenbach sold out to Hotchkiss in 1954, whereupon production of Delahaye cars immediately ceased, and the Paris factory concentrated solely on truck production. Even then there was but a brief reprieve for the once illustrious marque, for the honoured name of Delahaye was dropped in 1956 – it did not seem suitable, somehow, for a truck range, and car production was never resumed.

## Delahaye Type 135 1935-52

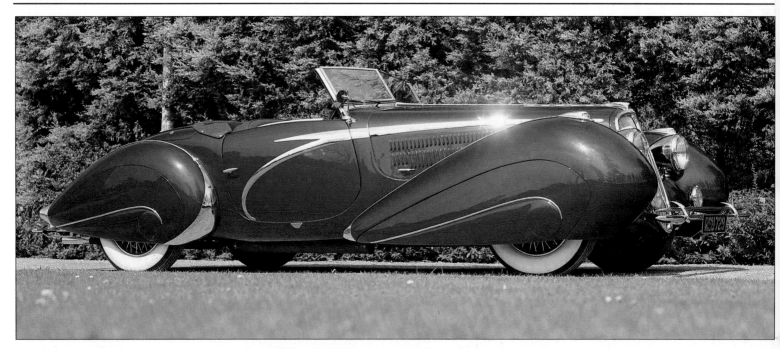

The new Superluxe range was offered with a choice of 2.1-litre four-cylinder or 3.2-litre six-cylinder engines, with manual or Cotal electromagnetic gearboxes, all in a modern chassis with transverse-leaf independent front suspension.

The most startling change, however, was to the styling, for the coachwork applied to these new models had real style, and undeniable attraction – the first time for more than a decade that Delahayes had been easy on the eye.

Almost immediately Delahaye mounted a publicity stunt at Montlhèry, where one of the cars broke 18 world and international speed and endurance records. Soon afterwards a similar car won an Alpine Coupe in the French Alpine trial.

All this, incidentally, was achieved using a very conventional-looking six-cylinder engine. In fact the new range was introduced without making an enormous investment in facilities, for the units were developments of types already in production for the company's commercial vehicles.

The most important, and most exciting, version of all the Type 135s was the Competition model, which was launched in 1936, and given a 3.5-litre engine which developed no less than 160 bhp. Remember that the post-war 3.4-litre Jaguar XK engine needed twin overhead camshafts to produce the same power, and you will realise why the sparkling Delahaye 135 Competition caused such a stir. It was a fast car which handled well, and seemed to have no vices.

Almost as soon as they had gone on sale, Type 135 Competition models made their mark in motorsport, with cars finishing second, third, fourth and fifth in the French sports car Grand Prix of 1936. A few months later another car won the Monte Carlo Rally of 1937, and Messieurs Mongin and Paul finished second in the Le Mans 24 Hours. The crowning glory came in 1938 when Chaboud and Tremoulet won Le Mans at 82.35 mph.

*Above: Type 135 coachwork was sometimes truly wild, as on this extravagantly swoopy 1938 example by Figoni and Falaschi.*

Almost every Type 135 looked very fast, and certainly very desirable, yet apart from the stark Competition versions the bodies always seemed to offer a great deal of comfort and refinement. Even after World War II the Type 135 was still popular enough to be put back on sale (albeit with engines reduced in power output), and in the early 1950s it gracefully gave way to the Type 235 for the last two years of Delahaye private car production.

*Below: Launched in 1936, the Type 135 Competition had a 160-bhp development of the overhead-valve straight-six. This is a Le Mans replica.*

### Delahaye Type 135 variants

#### Delahaye Type 235

Type 135 production, with a post-war engine rated at 110-130 bhp (because post-war fuels were not as high-grade as those of the late 1930s), continued until 1952. At this point Delahaye replaced the old car with the Type 235, which was really the same chassis with new styling, and with an engine further tuned, to produce 152 bhp. Even though this car was obsolete in some respects – mechanically-operated drum brakes should have been consigned to history years earlier – it was very fast; the cars lapped Montlhèry at 112 mph, and the straight-line top speed was more than 120 mph – impressive performance by the standards of the time.

Fewer than 400 135/235 types were sold in the 1950s, and the end of production was inevitable.

### Specification (1936 Type 135 Competition)

**Engine:** inline six-cylinder, overhead-valve
**Bore × stroke:** 84 mm × 107 mm
**Capacity:** 3557 cc
**Maximum power:** 160 bhp
**Transmission:** four-speed manual gearbox, optional Cotal electromagnetic transmission, rear-wheel drive
**Chassis:** separate steel frame with box-section side members, and pressed and tubular cross-braces
**Suspension:** independent front with transverse leaf springs; live rear axle with semi-elliptic leaf springs
**Brakes:** drums front and rear
**Bodywork:** various styles; sports, touring or saloon coachwork
**Maximum speed (approx):** 110 mph (177 km/h)

*Above: After World War II, production of the Type 135 resumed, initially with its power unit detuned to suit the new low-octane petrol. In 1952, though, Delahaye relaunched the model as the Type 235, with completely new styling and a 152-bhp engine – this car was really fast, topping 120 mph.*

# Delahaye Type 165 1939

Jean François' Type 165 was an indulgence which Delahaye could afford only because the company's private-car reputation was so high, and its truck sales (and profits) were underpinning everything else.

The Type 165 was developed from the Type 145, which was Delahaye's cheap and cheerful answer to German supremacy in late-1930s Grand Prix motorsport. Designed in 1936, and launched in 1937, it almost immediately proved to be incapable of matching the performance of those 600-bhp machines from Mercedes and Auto Union.

The Type 145 was fast enough, however, to win a special French government prize of a million francs for achieving 91.1 mph over a 125-mile endurance course at Montlhèry.

A so-called 'road car' derivative, with an entirely different frame, without de Dion rear suspension, and with a single-plug 165-bhp version of the V12 engine, was then announced in 1939. It was also the first-ever Delahaye to use hydraulic brakes, and the engine was fitted with crankshaft roller bearings and dry-sump lubrication. Only a few cars were produced before the outbreak of war made Delahaye concentrate on more serious projects.

This roadgoing version was not revived after the end of the war.

*Right: The V12-engined Type 165 was an ambitious derivative of Delahaye's Grand Prix car.*

## Specification
**Engine:** V12, overhead-valve, single block-mounted camshaft
**Bore × stroke:** 75 mm × 84.7 mm
**Capacity:** 4490 cc
**Maximum power:** 165 bhp

**Transmission:** Cotal electromagnetic gearbox, rear-wheel drive
**Chassis:** separate steel frame
**Suspension:** independent front with coil springs; live rear axle with semi-elliptic leaf springs

**Brakes:** drums front and rear, hydraulically-operated
**Bodywork:** aluminium two-seater roadster
**Maximum speed (approx):** 115 mph (185 km/h)

## Delahaye Type 175S 1946-51

The Type 175S was launched at the Paris Salon (motor show) of October 1946, the first outbreak of joy and glitter in the world's motor industry since the grim end of World War II. In a show dominated by economy cars and re-vamped designs from the late 1930s, the new Delahaye was an astonishing sight.

Delahaye historian J.R. Buckley described it as "almost fabulous", while *The Motor* merely called it "striking". There was general agreement that it was an ambitious design, especially at a time when French buyers were conspicuously short of money. Delahaye, on the other hand, were actively planning to sell these cars overseas, for this car was available with right- and left-hand drive.

The vehicle was available with a choice of wheelbases and the new chassis design featured the odd combination of Dubonnet independent front suspension, and a de Dion rear end, where the axle tube passed through the side members of the frame itself. Hydraulic brakes were standard.

The engine was a seven-bearing development of the famous old Type 135 'six', this time with a much-enlarged cylinder bore. Displacing 4.5 litres, it produced 125 or 140 bhp, depending on the tune, and it was always backed by the

*Below: The Type 175S, launched in 1946, made a tremendous impact amid the post-war austerity. This is a Figoni-bodied 1949 triple-carburettor version.*

French Cotal electromagnetic gearbox.

Several extraordinary body styles were sold on this chassis, some of them in dreadful taste, but all showing that an excess of purchasing power did not guarantee the discreet good taste really needed in such machines.

The Type 175S (and its sister car, the Type 180) was a fast car in a straight line, but its suspension was too soft. By almost any standard, except those of technical appeal, it was a commercial failure. Between 100 and 150 such cars were produced in five years, and a Delage-

*Above: Delahaye gave the Type 175S, a de Dion rear end and an independent front, along with a Cotal gearbox.*

badged version of the same car never actually went on sale.

### Specification (1946)

**Engine:** inline six-cylinder, overhead-valve
**Bore × stroke:** 94 mm × 107 mm
**Capacity:** 4455 cc
**Maximum power:** 125 bhp or 140 bhp
**Transmission:** four-speed Cotal

electromagnetic gearbox, rear-wheel drive
**Chassis:** separate steel frame with box-section side members and pressed cross-braces
**Suspension:** independent front with coil springs; de Dion rear axle with semi-elliptic leaf springs
**Brakes:** drums front and rear
**Bodywork:** various styles; aluminium and steel, open or closed, up to five seats
**Maximum speed (approx):** 110 mph (177 km/h)

# DeLorean Motor Company

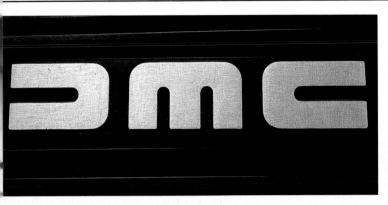

*Left: DMC, or the DeLorean Motor Company, was conceived and orchestrated by John Z. DeLorean.*

*Below: There was only ever one DeLorean model – the DMC-12, built in Belfast from 1980 to 1982.*

T he DeLorean Motor Company project was conceived in the corridors of power at General Motors in the 1970s, came to fruition in Northern Ireland in the early 1980s, and collapsed ignominiously amid a welter of debts and financial chicanery in 1982. For students of business it was an object lesson in poor product planning, over-ambitious manufacture, and appalling mismanagement of funds.

John DeLorean was a charismatic engineer who had clawed his way rapidly up through the American General Motors hierarchy in the 1960s and 1970s. After being chief engineer at Pontiac he then went on to be general manager of Chevrolet, before becoming GM's vice-president of car and truck production in 1972.

Soon after this, though, it all went wrong. John DeLorean insists that he resigned, but many industry observers say he was sacked. The result was the same: in 1973 DeLorean left GM, and soon decided to start his own business.

In 1974 DeLorean began scheming his rear-engined sports coupé, a car that he hoped would dominate that particular market sector in North America. The next four years were spent finding somewhere to build it – on DeLorean's financial terms. After touting the project around countries like Puerto Rico and the Republic of Ireland, DeLorean eventually persuaded the British government to back him, with a new factory to be built at Dunmurry, near Belfast.

Lotus was hired to convert an impractical dream into a fully-developed car which was not only practical to build, but which could meet and pass all the regulations facing cars in North America. This job was achieved in less than two years, the first pre-production cars were built in December 1980, and the DMC-12 officially went on sale in the middle of 1981. Build quality was suspect at first, but this was expected to improve as the new

Belfast-based workforce got used to building cars. At first every car was destined for North America, with European sales due to begin in 1983.

Within months it was clear that product quality was poor and – worse – that the *actual* demand for a specialised car like this was a lot lower than John DeLorean had boasted that it would be. Original forecasts had talked about selling 25,000 DMC-12s a year, which would have meant producing 600 cars a week in Belfast. The financial break-even point was thought to be 10,000 cars a year – or 200 cars per week.

Although DeLorean initially claimed that there were long waiting lists for the new car in 1981, and that second-hand prices were well over list, the truth is that the stainless-steel-skinned machine was almost unsaleable.

By June 1981 40 cars a day were being built, and by November 1981 that rate had doubled, to 80 cars a day, but the business remained well short of financial viability, and the premises were still under-used. The collapse came suddenly, in February 1982 – only eight months after the first shipments had been made to North America – when the British government refused to provide any more financial support, the company ran out of cash, and the receivers were called in. The last cars were built in the autumn of 1982.

Only about 8,000 DMC-12s were produced, and the last of these cars took ages to sell.

## DeLorean DMC-12 1981-82

*Left: John DeLorean insisted that his car should be rear-engined, to compete with Porsche's 911. The DMC-12 was underpowered and ungainly.*

The original DMC-12 project featured a rear-engined car with an Elastic Reservoir Moulding (ERM) plastic monocoque, with styling by Giugiaro, with lift-up 'gullwing' doors and with un-painted stainless-steel skin panels. The rear-engine position was inspired by that of the Porsche 911, which was the most important rival the DeLorean would have to oust if it were to be successful.

That was in 1974. By the time the car had been made ready for production it

had been restyled, a more conventional steel backbone chassis frame had been installed, and a glassfibre body shell formed the base for the stainless-steel panelling. The engine was completely different too! Only the general shape, the eye-catching door articulation, the rear- (*not* mid-) engined layout, and DeLorean's personal belief in his project, remained.

The first prototype, built in 1976, had a Citroën CX engine/transmission, but was

underpowered, while the second proto-type of 1977 had a 2.66-litre Renault/ Volvo V6 engine. The project did not even begin to look practical until it was taken over by Lotus at the end of 1978, whose brief was to make a practical, pro-duceable, motor car out of an almost completely un-engineered concept.

Lotus completed their task in less than two years. Because there was no time for major mistakes to be rectified, the general layout of the rolling chassis was closely based on that of the existing mid-engined Lotus Esprit; the major differ-ence, however, was that the bulky V6 engine was hung out into the tail of the car, which ensured a very tail-biased weight distribution.

The chassis, the performance and the handling were as good as could be ex-

pected (given DeLorean's insistence on the rear-engine position), for the car had been given wider rear tyres than the fronts, and Lotus had used all their expertise to tame the 35/65 per cent rear weight bias. Even so, a distinguished British tester, Michael Scarlett, later described the car as feeling "unfami-liarly spooky.... you can't disguise the effects of a high rear-based polar moment.... I think now, as I have always thought, simply that it was silly to build and try to sell a rear-engined sports car."

The burden of American regulations meant that only 132 bhp was available from 2.85 litres, and that the DMC-12 weighed 2,850 lb. The result was that the car *looked* much faster than it was – "all show, but no go..." was one comment at the time. *Road & Track*'s testers recorded a top speed of a mere 109 mph, and 0-60 mph in about 10.5 seconds (this made it no faster, say, than a Triumph TR7) – which explains why DeLorean was developing a turbocharged version of the PRV V6 engine when the receivers were called in.

Although DeLorean planned to introduce European-specification versions of the DMC-12, and also talked of producing a four-seater saloon model, both these projects were abandoned after the company went into liquidation in 1982.

All in all, the DeLorean DMC-12 was a more attractive talking-point, and a more attractive 'showroom car', than it was a practical proposition.

*Below: All DeLoreans had the same body finish, with satin-look stainless-steel skinning over a glassfibre shell. Although attractive, it marked easily and wasn't popular.*

### Specification (1981)

**Engine:** V6, single overhead camshaft per cylinder bank
**Bore × stroke:** 91 mm × 73 mm
**Capacity:** 2849 cc
**Maximum power:** 132 bhp
**Transmission:** five-speed manual gearbox or three-speed automatic transmission, rear-wheel drive

**Chassis:** separate steel backbone
**Suspension:** independent front with wishbones and coil springs; independent rear with coil springs
**Brakes:** discs front and rear
**Bodywork:** glassfibre two-seater coupé with stainless-steel skin panels
**Maximum speed (approx):** 109 mph (175 km/h)

# De Tomaso Automobili

*Above: Alejandro De Tomaso is an Argentinian who formed an interest in Italian thoroughbred cars when he raced Maseratis in Buenos Aires in the mid-1950s. He started his European business in Modena in 1959.*

*Left: The distinctive De Tomaso logo is apparently a symbol of the ancient Egyptian goddess Isis.*

A lejandro De Tomaso is a hot-blooded and resourceful Argentinian whose first links with Europe were when he raced Maseratis in Buenos Aires in 1956. After leaving Argentina (mainly, it is said, because he had consorted with the wrong political leaders) he married a rich American girl, Elizabeth Haskell. In 1959 he set up shop in Modena, Italy.

For the first few years his business built a succession of racing cars, and De Tomaso regularly amazed the motoring world by showing a series of prototypes at the Turin Motor Show. Most of these cars were never seen again, and none of them ever seemed to go onto the market.

Nevertheless, the first steps towards building series-production machines came in the 1960s, first with the Cortina-engined Vallelunga, followed by the brutally-fast Mangusta.

Along the way, however, in 1967 De Tomaso took control of Ghia, the famous coachbuilding concern, then forged links with another coachbuilder, Vignale, and produced the Pantera as a simple supercar for Ford-USA to sell through their Lincoln-Mercury dealers. Suddenly his was not a small 'back-street' concern, but an impressive mini-conglomerate, which made his rivals sit up and think.

Underpinned by this large potential market, De Tomaso also launched the Deauville four-door saloon, and the Longchamp 2 + 2 coupé, which shared the same design structure, mechanical layout and suspension installations. Having been a one-product, small-time concern in the 1960s, De Tomaso was suddenly rivalling Ferrari and Maserati.

This, however, was the De Tomaso marque's high point, for by 1974 a

*Above: Say 'De Tomaso' to most people and the model they think of is the Pantera – a match for the mid-engined Italian exotics in looks, handling and performance, but designed to be marketed by Ford-USA and powered by a pushrod iron-block V8. The GT5 model shown dates from 1982.*

combination of the energy crisis and a poor product quality reputation led to Ford dropping all support for the Pantera. Before 1974 the Pantera was selling at the rate of thousands a year – later on, De Tomaso was lucky to sell 100 such cars in a year.

Lesser mortals would have seen their companies fold up, and would have gone bankrupt, but not De Tomaso. Undaunted by his huge setback, De Tomaso carried on making his three main models (Pantera, Deauville and Longchamp), sold Ghia and Vignale to Ford, then proceeded to buy up Maserati and Innocenti. He also took control of Benelli and Moto Guzzi (the famous Italian motorcycle concerns).

The conglomerate was not only alive and well, but becoming more impressive by the hour. Maserati, after all, was one of the most distinguished Italian marques, while Innocenti was a large company building tens of thousands of British Leyland Mini-based cars every year.

This meant that De Tomaso, as a separate marque, was left to wither on the vine, and no new models – only revised versions of the old – were produced in the 1980s. By the 1990s a renaissance was in place, courtesy of Bruce Quale (son of Kjell) who funded production of new models through his successful Californian car distributorship. The Gandini-styled Mangusta 2 went on sale in mid-1999 and a new Pantera was scheduled for launch in 2003.

# De Tomaso Mangusta 1967-71

As with several other De Tomaso cars of the 1960s, the Mangusta had a complicated birth owing to De Tomaso's connections with Carroll Shelby and Ghia. In both cases a project was abandoned, and De Tomaso benefitted.

On the one hand, De Tomaso had been playing around with a backbone-framed Ford V8-powered sports-racing project for Carroll Shelby. This was the 5.7-litre 70P, where the engine was mid-mounted, and mated to a ZF gearbox/transaxle. On the other hand, Giorgetto Guigiaro, then chief designer at Ghia, had produced a stunning coupé body style for Piero Rivolta at Iso.

In 1966 both projects lapsed, and the ever-resourceful De Tomaso brought them together. The mid-engined car, the chassis frame of which was a beefed-up version of that used in the Vallelunga, was given a 4.7-litre version of the US-sourced Ford engine, and mated to a developed version of the rejected Ghia body – the result was the De Tomaso Mangusta.

Why 'Mangusta'? Pique, and Latin pride were involved in the choice. 'Mangusta' is the Italian word for mongoose; Carroll Shelby's team raced Cobras – and, as any lover of jungle lore knows, a mongoose is the sworn enemy of the cobra. . . .

The first prototype, revealed in 1966, had a glassfibre body, but when the Mangusta went into production a year

*Above: Looking beyond the gaudy paintwork of this racetrack example, the Mangusta's styling can be seen as an outstanding example of the work of the young Giorgetto Giugiaro, then leading designer at Ghia. Later, Tom Tjaarda, from the same studio, would design the Pantera.*

later it was given a Ghia-built steel body with some aluminium panels. Although it was trimmed and fitted out like a typical Italian supercar of the period, the Mangusta was really a tamed racing car, for it had a very unbalanced weight distribution (68 per cent of the weight was over the rear wheels), a cramped cabin with a windscreen very close to the driver's head, and an interior which got very hot when the engine was working hard.

Like the Vallelunga, the Mangusta had what felt to be a rather flexible backbone frame, and there were many doubts about the precision of its handling, though no-one ever complained about the performance.

The body style, of course, was stunning, one feature being the way that the huge engine lid/rear suspension cover was in two pieces, hinged along the spine, so that these lifted up like monstrous insect's wings.

With a lot of detailed development (something which De Tomaso rarely gave to his cars) the Mangusta could

have been sensational. As sold, however, it was a car that could feel frightening in wet conditions, and would begin to feel distinctly nose-light at high speeds.

Only 400 Mangustas were built in four years.

## Specification (1968)

**Engine:** V8, overhead-valve
**Bore × stroke:** 101.6 mm × 72.9 mm
**Capacity:** 4727 cc
**Maximum power:** 305 bhp
**Transmission:** five-speed manual gearbox, rear-wheel drive
**Chassis:** separate steel backbone with fabricated tubular and pressed subframes
**Suspension:** independent front with wishbones and coil springs; independent rear with coil springs
**Brakes:** discs front and rear
**Bodywork:** steel/aluminium two-seater coupé
**Maximum speed (approx):** 155 mph (249 km/h)

*Above: One of the most distinctive elements of the Mangusta design was the way in which all the rear bodywork lifted up, in two sections pivoting at the centre like an insect's wing covers, to allow access to the engine.*

# De Tomaso Deauville 1971-88

Alejandro De Tomaso himself is a resilient character, who has never been shy about picking up other people's great ideas and adapting them to his own use. The classic example of this was his Deauville saloon, which appeared in 1971.

Although the running gear was typical of De Tomaso at that period, the body style was, to be honest, almost a line-for-line copy of Jaguar's new XJ6 saloon. Its wheelbase was slightly shorter, but its tracks were wider. It was eight inches shorter and claimed to be 350 lb lighter.

De Tomaso wanted to provide his own alternative to the XJ6, with a more exotic name, a more glamorous reputation, but

less complex running gear. For that reason he settled on the same Ford V8 engine that he had chosen for the Pantera, with a choice of ZF manual or Ford-USA automatic transmissions. Even so, Ghia (which built the structures) designed a solid unit-construction shell, and there was double-wishbone independent suspension at front and rear.

It was a smart car, a fast car, and an elegant car with excellent road manners, but it never sold in large quantities. De Tomaso never established a viable dealer chain in any market outside the USA – and the Deauville was never sold in the States.

Like the cars made by Iso, with whom

De Tomaso competed in the early 1970s, the Deauville's very simplicity (and the known provenance of its Ford-USA engine) told against it. Compared with a Ferrari or a Lamborghini, the sound and character, were wrong. The result was a car the *maximum* annual rate of production of which was 46 (in 1972), and by the end of the 1970s only 208 cars had been built.

Even so, the Deauville was still listed

*Below: The Deauville was a typical De Tomaso under the skin, with double-wishbone suspension all round and 5.8-litre V8 power, but looked like Jaguar's XJ series.*

until 1988, by which time the engine had been de-rated to 270 bhp, and about 350 cars had been sold. If the Longchamp had not been developed from the Deauville, using a shorter-wheelbase version of the structure, and the Maserati Kyalami had not evolved from the Longchamp, the Deauville would have died years earlier.

There was a further twist to this complicated relationship, too. Maserati developed the Quattroporte III out of the Kyalami, this being a four-door saloon with a Deauville-like floorpan, a wheelbase only one inch longer than the Deauville, and with the same suspension installations.

**Specification (early 1970s)**
**Engine:** V8, overhead-valve
**Bore × stroke:** 101.6 mm × 88.9 mm
**Capacity:** 5769 cc
**Maximum power:** 330 bhp
**Transmission:** five-speed manual
gearbox or three-speed automatic
transmission, rear-wheel drive
**Chassis:** steel unit-construction body/
chassis assembly
**Suspension:** independent front and
rear, each with wishbones and coil
springs
**Brakes:** discs front and rear
**Bodywork:** steel five-seater saloon
**Maximum speed (approx):** 137 mph
(220 km/h)

*Right: De Tomaso intended the
Deauville to be more distinctive and
luxurious than its British lookalike,
with less complexity.*

# De Tomaso Longchamp 1972-89

If the Deauville was De Tomaso's answer
to the Jaguar XJ6, then the Longchamp,
launched in 1972, was his answer to the
Mercedes-Benz 450SLC. Like the
450SLC, the Longchamp was a sturdily-
built coupé, with a compact 2 + 2 cabin; it
was the sort of car a rich businessman
would buy for regular long-distance
travel, while convincing himself that he
could *just* get four people into it for family
outings.

Like the Deauville, the Longchamp's
structure was built by Ghia before being
delivered to De Tomaso in Modena for
completion. The Longchamp was a very
close technical relative of the Deauville.
It used a shorter-wheelbase version of
the Deauville's underpan – the difference being a mere seven inches – and

shared the same Ford-USA V8 engine,
the same choice of transmissions, and the
same suspension assemblies.

Like the Deauville, this was a fast car in
the long-established Italian-American
'mongrel' tradition, for power was by a
bomb-proof American V8, covered with
Italian styling flair and topped off with the
usual idiosyncrasies.

There is no doubt that the Longchamp
was one of Alejandro De Tomaso's
favourites. Soon after he had completed
the takeover and rescue of Maserati, the
first new model from that famous old
marque was the Kyalami, which was a
facelifted Longchamp into which the
Maserati four-cam V8 engine had been
inserted. The Maserati Quattroporte III
was a further development of that theme.

Although a cabriolet version of the
coupé was launched in 1980, by which
time the power of the engine had been
reduced to 270 bhp, Alejandro De
Tomaso had already lost interest in the
further development of the Deauville
and Longchamp models, as he was completely occupied with the rejuvenation of
Maserati. The Longchamp soldiered on,
being made at the rate of no more than 20
or 30 cars a year, until 1989, but was never
replaced.

*Below: If the Deauville was a
pastiche of the Jaguar XJ6, the
Longchamp was the spitting image of
the Mercedes 450SLC. The thinking
behind it was the same.*

**Specification (1974)**
**Engine:** V8, overhead-valve with single
block-mounted camshaft
**Bore × stroke:** 101.6 mm × 88.9 mm
**Capacity:** 5769 cc
**Maximum power:** 330 bhp
**Transmission:** five-speed manual
gearbox or three-speed automatic
transmission, rear-wheel drive
**Chassis:** steel unit-construction body/
chassis
**Suspension:** independent front and
rear, each with wishbones and coil
springs
**Brakes:** discs front and rear
**Bodywork:** aluminium/steel 2 + 2
coupé, or cabriolet
**Maximum speed (approx):** 149 mph
(240 km/h)

# De Tomaso Pantera 1971-90

To replace the Mangusta, De Tomaso designed a brawny new car, the Pantera ('Panther'), and unveiled it at the New York Motor Show in March 1970. The real significance of this was that a miraculous deal had been concluded with Ford in the United States.

In a complicated arrangement that eventually involved the sale of the Ghia business to Ford, the American colossus agreed to market the new Ford-USA-engined supercar through its Lincoln-Mercury dealers in the USA.

The Pantera was specifically designed to be sold in larger quantities than the Mangusta had ever been, and had a simple but robust unit-construction steel body/chassis unit. The mid-engined style was by Tom Tjaarda at Ghia, this being a brutally-impressive two-seater shape which hid the same type of engine/transmission assembly as had been used in the Mangusta.

The big difference, however, was that the Pantera had a much better chassis, mainly designed by Giampaolo Dallara, with more favourable weight distribution than the old Mangusta (there was only 57 per cent of the weight over the rear wheels), while there was a good deal more space for the two passengers and their luggage, and air conditioning was standard.

The Pantera handled much better than the Mangusta, but still suffered from many niggling problems, such as a harsh ride, a very noisy interior, and an engine which tended to overheat in traffic. It was, however, a shatteringly fast car, and many customers forgave it everything because of that.

Ford supplied a larger-capacity version of the engine than the Mangusta had had, but in a lower state of tune, so that there would be more reliability without any loss of performance.

The Pantera started well, with no fewer than 2,506 cars being built in 1972 and 1,604 in 1973, but poor product quality, and the effects of the energy crisis, caused Ford-USA to withdraw their support in 1974. Pantera production, having peaked sharply in the early 1970s, sagged to fewer than 50 cars a year by the end of that decade.

Along the way there were several different varieties of Pantera. There were four different levels of engine tune in

Europe, and five in the USA. However, the same monocoque and style were used, nominally by Ghia, but originally built by Vignale, and later by Maggiore.

In 1971 the USA-market Pantera was sold with 330 bhp, 310 bhp or 280 bhp. In 1972, tightening emission-control regulations had reduced this choice to 285 bhp and 266 bhp. For 1973 and 1974, only the 266-bhp version was available.

In Europe during the 1970s the original Pantera L had 300 bhp, but the GT3 version had 330 bhp, the GTS (complete with flared wheel arches) had 350 bhp, and the extremely rare GT4 was advertised with 500 bhp. In the 1980s, in common with the Deauville and the Longchamp models, the engine was advertised at 270 bhp, and a GT5 version was also listed. In every case a Ford V8 engine of 5.8 litres was retained.

De Tomaso built a single 'Pantera 290', a car fitted with a 210-bhp version of the Ford-UK three-litre V6 engine, but this car was never put into production.

In the 1980s De Tomaso was happy to sell 50 cars a year, using unchanged facilities, and a style which had not really altered since 1970. By this time the structures were being supplied by Embo of Modena, and the 'cottage industry' feel had returned to the business. Essentially the same Pantera, in fact, was built until 1990, when a revised model took over.

De Tomaso claimed to have built 9,500 Panteras, of which 6,500 were produced in the first five years.

*Above: The GT4 was built to Group 4 racing rules, with a version of the Ford V8 that put out something like 500 bhp. Some examples found their way onto the road.*

*Left: Inspired by the competition GT4, the 1976 GTS brought a power boost to the roadgoing Pantera and introduced spoilers, bonnet vents and blacked-out lower panels.*

## Specification (1971)

**Engine:** V8, overhead-valve
**Bore × stroke:** 101.6 mm × 88.9 mm
**Capacity:** 5769 cc
**Maximum power:** 330 bhp
**Transmission:** five-speed manual gearbox, rear-wheel drive
**Chassis:** steel unit-construction body/chassis assembly
**Suspension:** independent front with wishbones and coil springs; independent rear with coil springs
**Brakes:** discs front and rear
**Bodywork:** steel two-seater coupé
**Maximum speed (approx):** 159 mph (256 km/h)

*Below: By no means the most understated or elegantly styled version of the Pantera, the GT5, introduced in 1982, came with bulbous, add-on-style arch extensions over wider wheels, plus linking sill mouldings, and brought with it the option of a pylon-mounted rear wing.*

## De Tomaso Pantera 1990–92

Twenty years after it had originally been launched, the Pantera was treated to a significant redesign for the 1990s, though De Tomaso still expected to sell only about 40 new-style Panteras every year. The latest car was shown at Turin in April 1990, and sales began at once.

The basic layout, and the basic technical structure, was unchanged, but the exterior was reworked by Marcello Gandini, becoming more rounded without destroying the familiar lines. There were bulging wheel arches, a tiny spoiler just ahead of the base of the rear screen, and a very large transverse rear spoiler which grew, Ferrari F40 style, out of the rear bodywork.

Under the smoother skin there was still a mid-mounted Ford-USA V8, smaller but no less powerful than before, for it was a much-modified fuel-injected Mustang five-litre unit which De Tomaso tuned to produce 305 bhp. A twin-turbo 450-bhp version has subsequently been offered. Larger (17-in) wheels were fitted, along with bigger disc brakes to match. The steering was still without power-assistance.

The cabin had also been revised; as ever, the pedals were heavily offset to clear the wheel arches. Air conditioning was standard.

Like the original version, the 1990s Pantera was a ferociously fast car, with

enough character to make it stand out from its contemporaries. By this time, however, the 1960s design heritage showed through very strongly, for the car lacked many of the high-tech features that were standard in the latest Ferraris. De Tomaso did not mind who knew this, however, stating: "We want to have a really exclusive car. We would like to make the Pantera for 300 years. The market will decide. . ."

*Below: The Pantera 450 was the last gasp of the Italian American hybrid supercar, with a twin-turbo version of the 302 V8 developing 450 bhp.*

### Specification (1990)
**Engine:** V8, overhead-valve, single block-mounted camshaft
**Bore × stroke:** 101.6 mm × 76.2 mm
**Capacity:** 4942 cc
**Maximum power:** 305 bhp
**Transmission:** five-speed manual gearbox, rear-wheel drive
**Chassis:** steel unit-construction body/chassis assembly
**Suspension:** independent front with wishbones and coil springs; independent rear with coil springs
**Brakes:** discs front and rear
**Bodywork:** steel two-seater coupé
**Maximum speed (approx):** 168 mph (270 km/h)

# Dino

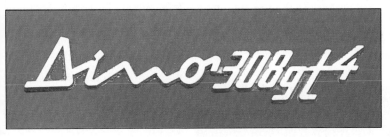

*Above and right: Perhaps to immortalise the name of his dead son, maybe to protect the classic Ferrari image, Enzo Ferrari insisted on badging his first V6 and V8 cars of the late 1960s/early 1970s as a separate Dino marque.*

The Dino marque was an offshoot of Ferrari, and came into existence for two reasons, both of them connected with the use of a V6 engine.

One was that Enzo Ferrari wanted to use the V6 engine to commemorate the name of his son Dino, who had died while still a young man. The other was that, until then, *all* Ferrari road cars had V12 engines, and Ferrari himself was not willing to let his name be used on a different type of car – one that was not only smaller, but that cost a great deal less.

It was all something of a charade, and a short-lived charade at that, for Dino, as a marque, had a life of only nine years. In any case, every Ferrari enthusiast knew the Dinos as little Ferraris. The famous Italian concern persevered for a time, but gave in without a struggle in the mid-1970s, when the successor to the 246GT was badged as a Ferrari.

The 'Dino' name was originally applied to a family of Ferrari V6 racing engines, a multi-faceted series which came to be used in many racing and sports cars from 1957 to the mid-1970s. Designed by Vittorio Jano, the V6 engine eventually found a home in the original 206GT road car in 1967.

If Ferrari had not needed a new Formula 2 racing car in 1966, there might never have been a Dino road car. However, as the rules demanded that 500 engines for road cars be built within a 12-month period, Ferrari struck a deal with Fiat.

It was agreed that Fiat would tool-up for, and manufacture, the engine in significant numbers, use it in one of their own cars, and then supply engines back to Ferrari for use in a road car as well. Confusingly enough, the Fiat *and* Ferrari road cars were both called Dino. . .

Within a short time, in any case, Dinos came to dominate the scene at

Maranello, for they were made in greater numbers than the 'real' Ferraris of the period. Several thousand V6-engined cars were produced – and even more front-engined Fiat-badged cars – before a second-generation Dino came along.

By the mid-1970s Ferrari had realised that the game was up, for they could convince no-one that Dino *was* a separate marque. When the 308GTB was launched as a direct successor to the 246GT in 1975, it was given a Ferrari badge, and even the 308GT4 officially became a Ferrari a year later.

*Below: Not only was the V6 engine of Ferrari's Dino partly built by Fiat, it was also used in Fiat's own Dino Spider (here) and coupé.*

# Dino 308GT4 1973-80

When it was launched in 1973, the 308GT4 was a very controversial car. Not only was it the very first Ferrari road car to use a V8 engine, but it was also the first to have body styling by Bertone.

The V8 engine, in fact, went on to become one of the all-time great Ferrari power units (it was still in use, in much-developed form, in the early 1990s). Ferrari's contract with Bertone, however, was never repeated, so the 308GT4 became the only Ferrari-made car to have Bertone styling.

Bertone were given a very difficult design problem to solve, for Ferrari had decided to offer a 2+2 package on a stretched version of the 246GT's chassis, something which meant that the propor-

tions would be less than ideal, and the rear seat space minimal.

Bertone did their best, but the result was a car with less sweeping, more chiselled, lines than Ferrari/Dino lovers were used to, and one with a rather awkward, elongated, cabin.

The chassis, however, was still a masterpiece, for the lengthened frame and the suspensions of the Dino 246GT had been treated to a brand-new 2.9-litre 90-degree V8 engine. Although this used the same bore and stroke as the existing 4.4-litre 12-cylinder Ferrari engine, everything else was new, including the use of belt-driven overhead camshafts.

Like the 246GT, the 308GT4 was a fast

*Above: Power for the 308GT4 came from a 90-degree four-cam V8 displacing 2927 cc and turning out about 255 bhp in European tune. The same engine was to be used in the popular 308 and 328 models.*

and well-balanced car, with a top speed of 154 mph, 0-100 mph acceleration in about 18 seconds, and impeccable road manners. It remained in production for seven years, with 2,826 GT4s of all types produced.

More importantly, its running gear formed the basis of the Ferrari 308GTB, which was launched in 1975, and of the Mondial, which arrived in 1980.

### Dino 308GT4 variants

#### Dino 208GT4

The 208GT4 was an Italian-market version of the car, built from 1975 to 1980. For Italian car taxation reasons, it was given a 66.8-mm × 71-mm, 1991-cc version of the engine, which produced 170 bhp. The top speed was claimed to be 137 mph.

#### Ferrari Mondial

The Ferrari Mondial, launched in 1980, was the successor to the 308GT4, but had a longer wheelbase, and a more sensual body style by Pininfarina.

### Specification (1973 308GT4)

**Engine:** 90-degree V8, quad-cam
**Bore × stroke:** 81 mm × 71 mm
**Capacity:** 2927 cc
**Maximum power:** 255 bhp
**Transmission:** five-speed manual gearbox, rear-wheel drive
**Chassis:** separate multi-tubular steel frame
**Suspension:** independent front with wishbones and coil springs; independent rear with coil springs
**Brakes:** discs front and rear
**Bodywork:** steel 2+2 coupé
**Maximum speed (approx):** 154 mph (248 km/h)

*Above: The 308GT4 departed from two Ferrari traditions. The mid-engined 2+2 was their first roadgoing V8 and Bertone, not Pininfarina, were given the tricky job of styling it. A Dino at first, in 1976 it became a Ferrari.*

# DKW (Deutsche Kraftfahrzeug Werke)

J orgen Rasmussen originally made his name by building motorcycles in Berlin, calling them DKWs, where DKW was the initials of Deutsche Kraftfahrzeug Werke. These bikes, however, were more familiarly known as *Das Kleine Wunder* ('The Little Wonder').

The DKW motorcycle already had a good reputation before Rasmussen decided to start building cars as well. The first DKW four-wheeler was launched in 1928 on a conventional front-engine/rear-drive chassis, but with a two-cylinder, two-stroke, 584-cc engine and bodywork assembled almost entirely from wood and fabric.

DKW's real breakthrough came in 1931, when it introduced a front-wheel-drive chassis, the very first to be built in volume anywhere in Europe. There were two types – the 490-cc F1 and the 584-cc F2 – both of which featured a transversely-mounted two-stroke engine and independent front suspension. It was a technically-advanced layout which set high standards for other makers to aim at for the next decade at least; not unnaturally, it led to several imitators and (in post-war years) to blatant copies being made.

In the meantime, Rasmussen bought up Audi, and followed it with Horch and Wanderer, the result being the formation of the Auto Union combine. Auto Union became famous for making hugely powerful mid-engined racing cars in the 1930s, but in commercial terms it was also the second-largest German carmaker of the 1930s.

During World War II, Auto Union factories concentrated on building aero engines, and after the war the factories all found themselves behind the Iron Curtain, in the Eastern Bloc. The result was that the DKW design was taken up by the new authoritarian regimes and renamed the IFA (the Polish version was called the Syrena), while DKW was obliged to start up again in Düsseldorf.

The first true post-war DKW was the Sonderklasse, which used a pre-war three-cylinder engine. This helped underpin Auto Union's future – and after Mercedes-Benz took financial control in 1956, its security was completely assured.

Even though the combine had been founded in the 1930s, the 'Auto Union' badge did not appear on a car for many years. In a change of policy no doubt encouraged by Mercedes-Benz, the badge reappeared in the 1950s. From 1958 to 1962, up-market versions of DKWs, with larger and more powerful engines, and some with smart coupé bodies, were sold as Auto Union 1000s.

DKW, in the meantime, continued to expand, with the popular Junior range, the F11, the F12 and the larger F102 types, until there was yet another financial and policy upheaval. In 1964, Volkswagen bought the controlling financial interest from Mercedes-Benz. The first post-war Audi car appeared in 1965, and after 1966 the DKW name was dropped, and the Düsseldorf factory closed down.

DKW, therefore, is now remembered as the predecessor of the modern Audi range.

*Below: The Sonderklasse was the first new DKW to be produced after World War II, albeit with pre-war three-cylinder power. This is a 1954 model.*

## DKW F1500 1931-54

DKW's first-ever front-wheel-drive car was the F1500, launched in 1931. It was a technically advanced car with all-independent suspension, a transversely-mounted two-stroke 500-cc engine, and a weight of around 1,000 lb.

This design later inspired the birth of three-cylinder DKWs and Auto Unions (though these all had longitudinally-mounted engines), and it was also the important direct influence on the layout of the original Saab 92.

The chassis itself was a flexible 'ladder type', but there was independent front *and* rear suspension, by double transverse leaf springs and swinging half-axles. Testers agreed that this gave a better ride than conventional cars which retained beam axles, especially on unmade roads.

However, to keep it cheap, the designers gave this DKW a weird dashmounted gear change lever, cooling was only by thermosyphon (no water pump), there was a six-volt electrical system with a dynastarter, and bodies were simply made from wood and fabric structures.

The original car was small, on an 82.5-in wheelbase, but the later Reichklasse/Meisterklasse versions ran on longer wheelbases, and had larger and more powerful engines. By the end of the

1930s, the range included 'Luxus' models, which looked like the larger Audi and Horch cabriolets.

Like several other German concerns, DKW found some of its production plant trapped behind the Iron Curtain after 1945, but the old-type cars continued to be made at Ingolstadt until 1954. Although these were not quick cars – a natural cruising speed was no more than 45-50 mph – the engine was smooth and refined.

The new three-cylinder Sonderklasse appeared in 1953, and this car led to the first post-war Audis.

### Specification (1934 Meisterklasse)

**Engine:** inline twin-cylinder, two-stroke
**Bore × stroke:** 76 mm × 76 mm
**Capacity:** 684 cc
**Maximum power:** 20 bhp
**Transmission:** three-speed manual gearbox, front-wheel drive
**Chassis:** separate steel ladder frame with channel-section side members
**Suspension:** independent front and rear, each with transverse leaf springs
**Brakes:** drums front and rear
**Bodywork:** wood and fabric two- or four-seater, open or closed
**Maximum speed:** 53 mph (85 km/h)

*Above: F1500s were innovative front-drive cars. This is a 1934 Meisterklasse.*

*Below: This late-1930s development set the style for post-war DKWs.*

## DKW Sonderklasse 3/6 1953-61

The long-awaited 'post-war' DKW did not appear until 1953, when it was seen to be a logical development of the 1930s theme. In a way though, the wheel had gone full circle, for Saab had copied the DKW for its original car, whereas DKW appeared to have copied the Saab 93 for its running gear. The truth was that the three-cylinder/two-stroke concept had first run in the early 1940s, but its introduction had to be held back for years to allow DKW to regain its feet after World War II.

The Sonderklasse was altogether

larger than the 1930s cars, not only because of its larger engine, but also because it had a conventional steel unit-construction body/chassis. It was a genuine four-seater, with a generously wide rear seat, and was renowned for its excellent handling and – for its engine size – sparkling performance in 40-bhp form. Like many other cars of this period, it had a steering-column gear change, though this did not stop it becoming a very effective rally car, especially where the handicapping system worked in its favour.

*Left: Autocar drove this coupé in 1954, saying that its roller-bearing-crank two-stroke triple "revels in being driven hard and . . . appears to have an indefinite rev limit".*

The rounded style was typical of West German cars of the period – in some ways it even had a resemblance to the large BMWs of the 1950s, though there was no business connection between the two companies.

Before long the 'badge-engineering' ploy, which had already afflicted British and American car groups, was also applied to this car, for soon there was a 981-cc 55-bhp Auto Union 1000 version of the Sonderklasse, and a coupé version of that. By the early 1960s, the DKW badge was losing favour relative to Auto Union, and when Audi was revived it disappeared altogether.

*Above: A Sonderklasse runs in the 1954 Daily Express Trophy meeting.*

### Specification (1955)

**Engine:** inline three-cylinder, two-stroke
**Bore × stroke:** 71 mm × 76 mm
**Capacity:** 896 cc
**Maximum power:** 34 bhp
**Transmission:** four-speed manual gearbox or optional 'Saxomet' semi-automatic transmission, front-wheel drive
**Chassis:** steel unit-construction body/chassis
**Suspension:** independent front with transverse leaf spring; beam rear axle with transverse leaf spring
**Brakes:** drums front and rear
**Bodywork:** steel two- or four-door four-seater saloon
**Maximum speed:** 74 mph (119 km/h)

# Dodge

J ohn and Horace Dodge were early shareholders in Ford, but began building cars carrying their own name in 1914. After producing a series of tough, but unexciting, cars – known as 'dependable Dodges', the company was taken over by Chrysler in 1928, reputedly for $175,000,000.

It was all part of Chrysler's master plan. In a very short time, the marque had been integrated into a group comprising Chrysler, De Soto, Dodge and Plymouth. Engines, chassis and bodies were often shared, for this was 'badge-engineering' at its height.

For many years, Dodge's only distinction in the Chrysler Group was its different trim (and price) level. In the 1950s, however, new V8 engines, publicised as 'Red Ram' units, gave it a performance image, cars were entered successfully in motorsport, and Dodge's reputation changed markedly.

In the 1960s a new compact, the Dodge Dart, made many friends, as did GT versions of the car, but the zenith came rather later that decade, when cars like the Dodge Charger – one of North America's archetypal 'muscle cars' – and especially the racing Charger Daytona, made

headlines with their NASCAR successes.

As with most other marques in the North American motor industry, Dodge had a very stable existence, with well-established dealerships, coast to coast. The marque consistently occupied sixth or seventh place in the sales league, usually finishing behind its stablemate Plymouth, but occasionally nudging ahead.

The Challenger coupé of 1970 came too late to make a big impact on the Mustang/Camaro/Firebird market, which was already past its peak, and this was really Dodge's last fling in the 'high performance' market for many years. In the 1970s, the Chrysler Corporation as a whole had a troubled time, but Dodge kept afloat by once again making a series of conventional family machines (which led some to recall the 'dependable Dodge' theme of the 1920s).

By the 1980s, Chrysler Corporation cars had been down-sized considerably, front-wheel drive took over almost completely, and Dodge came roaring back with the Daytona Coupe family. In the 1990s, as in the 1930s, Dodge was one of the most important marques in the North American motor industry.

*Right: Shaking off their old-time 'dependable' epithet, through the 1960s Dodge cultivated a macho performance image, the most extreme manifestation of which was the spectacularly bewinged Charger Daytona, a 'homologation special' built for NASCAR high-speed oval racing. Its 'Hemi' V8 produced over 500 bhp in competition tune, and this model (with its Plymouth Superbird badge-engineered sibling) ruled the series until handicapped out of contention, winning 38 out of 48 major races in 1970. One Daytona qualified at 200 mph for a race at Alabama's Talledega Speedway.*

## Dodge Custom Royal 1954-59

The revitalisation of Dodge's post-war image began in 1952, with the launch of the new 'Red Ram' V8, but this was rated at only 140 bhp, and was capable of a lot more than that. Like Chrysler's 'Hemi', of which it was really a scaled-down version, it had hemispherical combustion chambers, and potentially excellent breathing.

The first of the Royal family appeared in 1954, running on a 120-in wheelbase, and this was followed within months by

*Below: By 1959 the Custom Royal offered engines up to a 6.4-litre, 345-bhp V8, which made the car fast despite its weight of 3,800 lb.*

the even better-equipped, and more powerful, Custom Royal series.

Like all Chrysler cars of this age and price class, the Custom Royal ran on a separate chassis which featured independent front suspension by torsion bars. The styling, sharpened up for 1955, was by Virgil Exner's team, had a wraparound windscreen, and already featured small tail fins, which were to grow larger in subsequent model years.

The original 1955 model had a 4.5-litre/183- or 193-bhp V8 engine, while in 1956 the same car had the choice of a 218-bhp/4.5-litre or 260-bhp/5.3-litre engine. The 1957 cars ran on a slightly longer wheelbase than before, with large tail

fins, and there were two further 'facelift' years before the last Custom Royal of all was built in 1959. By that time the largest and most powerful engine offered was a 6.4-litre V8, available with 320 or 345 bhp.

The Custom Royal came in several styles, but the most glamorous were the two-door hardtop coupé and the closely-related convertible models. By this period, Chrysler had also developed a four-door hardtop coupé which had no centre pillar, so that the cabin felt almost completely open when all the side windows were wound down.

Like other such luxurious American cars of the period, the Custom Royal was large, heavy (up to 3,800 lb), glitzily

equipped, and fiercely fast in a straight line. As one astute American observer put it, there was power-assistance for everything except the ashtray. . .

By European standards the usual failings were to be found in the braking (which was poor, if used persistently), and the handling – but there was no doubt that American buyers loved the cars. 89,304 Custom Royals were sold in the 1955 model year, 49,292 in 1956 and 55,149 in 1957. Dodge had a poor year in 1958, when only 25,112 Custom Royals were sold, this total sagging even further, to 21,206, in 1959.

### Specification (1957)

**Engine:** 90-degree V8, overhead-valve
**Bore × stroke:** 93.73 mm × 96.52 mm
**Capacity:** 5328 cc
**Maximum power:** 260 bhp
**Transmission:** three-speed manual gearbox or optional automatic transmission, rear-wheel drive
**Chassis:** separate steel frame with box-section side members
**Suspension:** independent front with torsion bars; live rear axle with semi-elliptic leaf springs
**Brakes:** drums front and rear
**Bodywork:** five-seater saloon, hardtop, coupé or convertible
**Maximum speed:** 110 mph (177 km/h)

# Dodge Charger 1966-70

In 1964, Ford's Mustang started a compact performance car trend which other manufacturers hastened to match. From Chrysler the first competitor was the Plymouth Barracuda, but Dodge produced the Charger coupé in 1966, and immediately set new standards.

During the next four years, the Charger was sold only as a big and spacious five-seater coupé, but as the strongest of its engine options was a 7.0-litre 425-bhp 'Hemi' unit, it also had colossal performance.

The original Charger ran on a 117-in wheelbase, and shared many body panels with the latest Coronet model, but had its own unique touches, including a grille with hidden headlamps, and an enormous choice of V8 engines. In 1966, for instance, the five different power options spanned 230 bhp/5.2 litres and 425 bhp/7.0 litres, there also being a choice of transmissions and suspension settings.

Even with the middle choice of a 6.3-litre/325-bhp engine, the Charger could sprint to 60 mph in less than nine seconds, and approached a top speed of 120 mph. In 425-bhp form it was a bellowing, tyre-stripping extrovert which the youth of America took to its heart.

The second-generation Charger, of 1968-70, ran on the same floorpan, had an equally wide choice of V8 engines (in no fewer than seven power ratings), but had a smoother, more attractive, and quite wickedly seductive coupé style. Dubbed a styling sensation when new, the car still looks attractive in the 1990s, and it combined outstanding performance (135 mph with the right gearing and the most meaty engine), surprisingly nimble handling, and enormous showroom appeal.

The Chargers which followed in the 1970s were less attractive, less specialised, and less successful. The great days of the Charger, no question, were in the first four years when 53,132 of the original-shape cars, and about 50,000 of the second-generation models, were sold.

## Specification (1969 'Hemi' 426)

**Engine:** V8, overhead-valve
**Bore × stroke:** 107.95 mm × 92.25 mm
**Capacity:** 6974 cc
**Maximum power:** 425 bhp
**Transmission:** four-speed manual gearbox or three-speed automatic transmission, rear-wheel drive
**Chassis:** steel unit-construction body/chassis assembly
**Suspension:** independent front with torsion bars; live rear axle with semi-elliptic leaf springs
**Brakes:** drums front and rear
**Bodywork:** steel five-seater hardtop coupé
**Maximum speed (approx):** 135 mph (217 km/h)

*Above: Pitched against the Mustang, the Charger was somewhat overweight and unwieldy, but from the start in 1966 (as here) it was undeniably fast.*

*Above: The 1969 Charger 500 was a limited-production NASCAR special.*

*Below: Originally an awkwardly slabby-looking fastback coupé, the Charger was rebodied in this more elegant 'semi-fastback' style in 1968.*

# Dodge Charger Daytona 1969

At the end of the 1960s, North America's prestigious NASCAR racing formula was dominated by Ford. Dodge had ambitions to upset this, and produced an astonishing 'racing special' version of the 'Hemi'-engined Charger. This car, the Charger Daytona (and its lookalike sister car, the Plymouth Road Runner Superbird), was the result.

Although it was based on the normal Charger shell, the Daytona derivative had a much more aerodynamic body shape, with a long and smooth droop-snoot nose fixed to the front members, and with a huge rear stabiliser wing supported on struts, 25 inches above the rear decking. It was much longer than the standard car – more than 19 feet long – and weighed 3,800 lb in standard form.

Two engines were available. Most of the 'street' cars were fitted with Chrysler's massive 'wedge-head' 7.2-litre 375-bhp V8, though the alternative intended for full race-car use was the expensive 7.0-litre 'Hemi' unit which produced 425 bhp in standard form.

For NASCAR racing, Dodge squeezed a lot more power from the 'Hemi' engine – more than 500 bhp – and because the sensationally-shaped car developed about 20 per cent less drag it had a much higher top speed. It qualified for a race at Talledega Speedway in Alabama at 200 mph, and beat the old track record at Rockingham, North Carolina, by the huge margin of 17.775 mph.

To meet the racing regulations, Dodge had to produce more than 500 cars, so they did just that – they built 505 cars, at a price of $8,000 each. As a 'homologation special', this type was built only in one year – 1969.

Unless it broke down, and until it was handicapped out of contention by NAS-CAR's officials, the Charger Daytona was virtually unbeatable as a race car. Along with its Plymouth-badged sister car, it won 38 of 48 major NASCAR races in 1969 and 1970.

*Below: Two engines were offered in the Charger Daytona: the competition-oriented 426-cu in 'Hemi' and the 'Magnum' 440 (here), rated at 375 bhp.*

## Specification

**Engine:** V8, overhead-valve
**Bore × stroke:** 107.95 mm × 92.25 mm
**Capacity:** 6974 cc
**Maximum power:** 425 bhp
**Transmission:** four-speed manual gearbox, rear-wheel drive
**Chassis:** steel unit-construction body/chassis assembly
**Suspension:** independent front with torsion bars; live rear axle with semi-elliptic leaf springs
**Brakes:** drums front and rear
**Bodywork:** steel and glassfibre four-seater
**Maximum speed:** 150 mph (241 km/h)

*Right: With its smoothed and extended bodywork, the Daytona developed 20 per cent less drag than the ordinary Charger and in full competition trim could achieve 200 mph on the banked oval NASCAR tracks. Its added nose cone made it more than 19 feet long, and its tail-wing pylons rose 25 inches above the rear deck.*

# Dodge Challenger 1970-74

*Left: Conceived as a direct rival to Ford and GM 'pony cars', the Challenger went on sale in 1970 with coupé and convertible body styles and a variety of engine options from a 3.7-litre slant-six to the 7.2-litre (440-cu in) 'Magnum' V8. The R/T series ('R/T' for Road and Track) offered a range of performance and cosmetic equipment not available on the regular Challenger models.*

The Chrysler Corporation was slow in reacting to the enormous success of Ford's Mustang, and GM's Chevrolet Camaro/Pontiac Firebird cars. To match these, the archetypal 'pony cars', Chrysler developed a matched pair of models – the Dodge Challenger and the new-generation Plymouth Barracuda – which were smaller and lighter than the Chargers.

Although the Challenger used a brand-new unit-construction body style – sold either as a coupé or as a convertible – it hid a choice of familiar running gear, including the usual choice of V8 and slant-six engines, and torsion-bar front suspension.

The Challenger was a smart and smoothly-styled car which looked almost too much like the latest Mustang for its own good. Two different Challenger lines were produced at first – the Basic and the R/T types. 'R/T' stood for 'Road and Track', these cars having more power and better equipment than the less expensive types.

In four model years the Challenger

*Below: Although a good-looking car, the Challenger did not enter the market until the Mustang and Camaro had been established for a number of years, and it failed to make a major sales impact after a promising initial showing.*

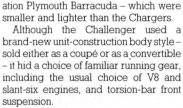

was available with no fewer than 12 different engine specifications. There was one six-cylinder engine (a 3.7-litre/110- or 145-bhp unit), the rest being V8s ranging from a 5.2-litre/150-bhp package to the famous 7.0-litre/425-bhp 'Hemi'. The best-performing/best-handling package

was probably found in those cars with the 5.56-litre/240- or 275-bhp, or the 6.27-litre/275- or 335-bhp installations.

The Challenger looked sportier than it was, for it was a heavy car (most Challengers weighed in at between 3,200 and 3,400 lb) which had rather soft and wallowy suspension. Unhappily for Dodge, too, it soon acquired a reputation for doubtful quality.

The 'pony car' boom was already past its peak before the Challenger came onto the market, so its first-year sales achievement of 83,000 (against 190,000 Mustangs) was creditable enough. Even so, sales dropped to 28,000 in 1971, and continued to fall away. After 1974, when only 16,400 cars were sold, the line was laid to rest.

## Specification (1970 R/T)

**Engine:** V8, overhead-valve
**Bore × stroke:** 109.73 mm × 92.25 mm
**Capacity:** 7202 cc
**Maximum power:** 375 bhp
**Transmission:** four-speed manual gearbox or three-speed automatic transmission, rear-wheel drive
**Chassis:** steel unit-construction body/chassis assembly
**Suspension:** independent front with torsion bars; live rear axle with semi-elliptic leaf springs
**Brakes:** drums front and rear
**Bodywork:** steel four-seater coupé or convertible
**Maximum speed (approx):** 130 mph (209 km/h)

# Dodge Daytona Coupé 1983–94

*Left: 'Shelby' means performance to American drivers, and the 1987 Daytona Shelby Z lived up to its name, with a 176-bhp turbocharged 2.2-litre four-cylinder engine (right).*

By the late 1970s the Chrysler Corporation was in big financial trouble. Having left Ford, following a well-publicised row with Henry Ford II, Lee Iacocca joined Chrysler in 1978 to head up a remarkable recovery programme, and return the group to profitability.

One cornerstone of this strategy was the launch of Chrysler's all-new front-wheel-drive 'K-car' platform – one so versatile that it was used under saloons, estates and (in the case of Dodge) sporting coupés too. The 'E-body' which followed was just as useful.

Two new families of Chargers and Daytonas appeared in the autumn of 1983 and, with regular attention in the form of facelifts and decorative changes, were

still being built in the early 1990s. Unlike the glory days of the 1960s, however, the 1984-model Charger was merely a warmed-over coupé version of the Omni saloon (itself a derivative of the Talbot Horizon), whereas the Daytona was a sleeker and more specialised machine altogether, which took the 'E-body' as its base.

Like most modern Chrysler Group cars of the 1980s, the Daytona featured a transversely-mounted four-cylinder engine, with front-wheel drive. All American cars had been 'down-sized' considerably in recent years, with this smart four-seater running on a 97-in wheelbase and weighing a mere 2,650 lb.

At first the new Daytona was available with 2.2 litres and fuel injection (100 bhp), or with a turbocharged 144-bhp engine. American buyers took some time to grow accustomed to a car which handled, and particularly steered, so much better than the 1970s generation of heavy sports coupés, but the Daytona soon made its mark.

In 1984 the alternative to the 144-bhp turbocharged engine was a 100-bhp normally-aspirated unit. For 1986 an 87.5-mm × 104-mm/2501-cc/101-bhp engine became available, and in 1987 the Turbo model gained an intercooler and 176 bhp (as the Shelby Z). Yet by 1991 the turbo engine had been changed to 2.5 litres/155 bhp, and a new normally-aspirated Mitsubishi-designed 91.1-mm × 76-mm/2972-cc/143-bhp engine option was also available.

Like previous sporty Dodges, the Daytona also had a sister car in the Chrysler Corporation range – the Chrysler Laser, which shared the same basic body style, front-wheel-drive layout, and choice of normally-aspirated or turbocharged 2.2-litre engines.

Because Chrysler needed to rebuild their finances they were in no hurry to make these important cars obsolete, thus enabling enthusiasts to know them better and better with every year. Although there was a facelift towards the end of the 1980s, the early-1990s models looked

very similar to the originals, while there was a wider and torquier range of four-cylinder engines. The real innovation for the 1990s, however, was the addition of the Mitsubishi-designed 3.0-litre V6.

### Specification (1984 Turbo)

**Engine:** inline four-cylinder, transversely-mounted, overhead-camshaft
**Bore × stroke:** 87.5 mm × 92 mm
**Capacity:** 2213 cc
**Maximum power:** 144 bhp
**Transmission:** five-speed manual gearbox or three-speed automatic transmission, front-wheel drive
**Chassis:** steel unit-construction body/chassis assembly
**Suspension:** independent front with struts and coil springs; beam rear axle with coil springs
**Brakes:** discs front, drums rear
**Bodywork:** steel four-seater hatchback
**Maximum speed:** 120 mph (193 km/h)

# Dodge Viper V10 1992–present

Such was the reaction to Chrysler's Dodge concept car of 1989 that it was decided to turn it into a production sports car. Previewed as a proper road car in 1990, it is expected to go on sale in 1992.

In almost every way but its looks, the Viper is a 1990s successor to the AC Cobra. It is a brawny, open-topped two-seater sports car that puts performance, noise and broad-shouldered all-American appeal ahead of refinement, comfort and silence.

The base of this enormously powerful sports car is a tubular chassis frame, with power provided by a front-mounted, truck-derived, V10 overhead-valve engine. The car itself is low, wide and carefully shaped, so with 400 bhp available it is no wonder that the top speed is claimed to be 188 mph. Not only does this car outsprint any production Chevrolet Corvette, but it also has the legs to beat many 12-cylinder-engined Ferraris, at least in a straight line.

Neither Dodge, nor any other company in the Chrysler Corporation, has ever produced a car with such startling performance as this. It was inspired by Chrysler's newly-appointed president, Bob Lutz – himself a car nut with much European motor industry experience – and has almost everything going for it.

The vast eight-litre engine bellows when unleashed, and needs a massive six-speed gearbox to link it to the rear wheels. With so much power on tap,

there is a constant battle of torque against tyre grip, and the glassfibre body has to be very carefully profiled to cut the tendency to lift at high speeds. The Viper is as extrovert as a 12-cylinder Italian supercar is silky.

A coupé version known as the GTS, with its distinctive double-bubble roof was introduced in 1996. A Viper GTS-R won the GT2 class at Le Mans in 1998, driven by Bell, Donohue and Drudi.

*Right: An outrageous modern reincarnation of the Cobra concept, the V10-engined Viper was unveiled in 1990. Production of about 5,000 cars a year was intended.*

### Specification (1990)

**Engine:** V10, overhead-valve
**Bore × stroke:** 101.6 mm × 98.6 mm
**Capacity:** 7990 cc
**Maximum power:** 400 bhp
**Transmission:** six-speed manual gearbox, rear-wheel drive
**Chassis:** separate steel frame with tubular main and bracing members
**Suspension:** independent front and rear, each with coil springs
**Brakes:** discs front and rear
**Bodywork:** glassfibre two-seater roadster
**Maximum speed:** 188 mph (303 km/h)

# Duesenberg

N orth American historians agree that Duesenbergs were the finest cars ever built in the United States. Even though the marque was only in existence for 16 years, and was only independent for the first five of those years, its cars were excellent, and are enduring classics.

The story began with Frederick Samuel Duesenberg, who was born in Germany in 1876, emigrated to the United States as a child, and adopted Iowa as his home state. After building and racing bicycles, along with his brother August he designed the Mason car, then the Maytag, before starting to build engines for racing cars.

Duesenberg racing cars grew in prestige after World War I, for a Duesenberg engine powered a successful world land speed record car in 1919, and in 1921 a Duesenberg racing car won the first post-war Grand Prix, in France. Duesenbergs also won the Indianapolis 500 three times in the 1920s.

To build expensive road cars, the brothers then set up the Duesenberg Motor Company in Indianapolis, Indiana, launching the $6,500 Model A in 1921. This was America's first production straight-eight, and was technically advanced, but although it was a brilliant design the brothers were never good businessmen, and after fewer than 500 cars had been built they sold up to that extrovert 'empire-builder' – Errett Lobban Cord.

E.L. Cord was intent on building a prestigious version of GM and Duesenberg joined Cord, Auburn, Checker and the Lycoming aero-engine concerns. Cord inspired the birth of the Model J, which had an eight-cylinder engine built to Duesenberg designs by Lycoming. This was succinctly described as the "product of Fred Duesenberg's engineering genius, and E. L. Cord's money" – an accurate summary of the rest of the marque's life.

The magnificent Model J was soon followed by the even more complex – and costly – Model SJ, but as the American economy was then on its knees, in mid-Depression, it is no wonder that such cars were extremely difficult to sell.

For a time, Cord's empire could stand the losses – under his control,

Duesenberg never made profits, but was only kept in existence as a prestige marque – but after Fred Duesenberg himself was killed in a car accident while driving one of his own SJs, the end was inevitable.

Lycoming delivered the last engine in 1935, but sales were so slow that the Duesenberg staggered on until the entire Cord empire collapsed in 1937.

Attempts were made to revive the Duesenberg in later years – August Duesenberg designed a (stillborn) new car for new backers in 1947, and replicas on Dodge truck chassis were produced in the 1970s – but the *real* Duesenbergs died in the Cord financial crash of 1937. Little more than a thousand authentic Duesenbergs were made, most of which survive to this day as priceless collectors' cars.

*Above: The Duesenberg Murphy Special, driven by Jimmy Murphy, took the honours at the 1922 Indy 500. Murphy had earlier won the 1921 French GP.*

*Inset below: Rights to the Duesenberg insignia passed to E.L. Cord in 1926.*

*Below: This is a Springfield-bodied 1926 Duesenberg Model A.*

# Duesenberg Model A 1921-26

The Duesenberg Eight (the 'A' was adopted later, as a bastardisation of 'Eight') was launched in 1921, and immediately signalled the brothers' intention to build a superbly-engineered road car. Although it had a conventional chassis layout, its engine was magnificent, and its detailing as carefully crafted as possible.

The new car pandered to the richest and most sporting North American clients, who wanted effortless performance without having to row the car along using the gear lever, and also acres of elegant space inside their automobiles, and were willing to pay for exclusivity.

Model As, like the Model Js and SJs which followed, were therefore distinguished by a series of coachbuilt body shells which were lofty, uncompromisingly 'vintage', but beautifully made and equipped, even if their actual style was not sensationally modern.

The new car's engine was an overhead-camshaft straight-eight – the first such type to be sold to the general public – which had been detuned, developed and refined from the brothers' latest race unit. It made extensive use of aluminium – even pioneering the use of aluminium pistons in North America – yet it only had three crankshaft main bearings.

While the new car had hydraulic brakes, high performance in great style and comfort (85 mph was a very creditable top speed in those far-off days), and great reliability, it took time to establish itself. It was difficult to persuade wealthy buyers that this was not a noisy, smelly, detuned racing chassis.

Fewer than 500 cars were sold in five years before the Duesenberg brothers sold out to E. L. Cord, and the Model A was dropped while a sensational new Duesenberg, the Model J, was being prepared.

*Above: A Duesenberg Eight, or Model A, from 1925-26. The Duesenberg engine, a detuned and developed version of the company's racing power unit, was the first overhead-cam straight-eight to be used in a volume-production car.*

*Below: This Duesenberg Roadster, bodied by Millspaugh & Irish, was priced at the not-inconsiderable sum of $6,500 new in 1925. It had hydraulic brakes and a 4261-cc engine quoted as producing 88 bhp, and could reach around 90 mph.*

## Specification (1921)

**Engine:** inline eight-cylinder, overhead-camshaft
**Bore × stroke:** 73 mm × 127 mm
**Capacity:** 4261 cc
**Maximum power:** 90 bhp
**Transmission:** three-speed manual gearbox, rear-wheel drive
**Chassis:** separate steel frame with channel-section side members, and tubular and pressed bracings
**Suspension:** non-independent with beam front axle and semi-elliptic leaf springs; live rear axle with semi-elliptic leaf springs
**Brakes:** drums front and rear, hydraulically operated
**Bodywork:** various styles, open or closed
**Maximum speed (approx):** 85 mph (137 km/h)

# Duesenberg Model J 1928-36

When E.L. Cord described his new Model J as "the world's finest car", this was not mere hype. By almost any measurement – and this included comparison with the latest machinery from Rolls-Royce, Hispano-Suiza and Mercedes-Benz – it was a superb machine.

The Model J took the philosophy of the original Model A a leap further, for it combined a conventional chassis, an advanced, ultra-powerful and splendidly-detailed engine, and a wide choice of impressive body styles in a way that no other North American concern could hope to match. There was a choice of wheelbases – 142.5 in or 153.5 in – though one extrovert evangelist ordered a car on a 178-in wheelbase, and called it the Throne Car.

The chassis, complete with semi-elliptic leaf springs at front and rear, hydraulic brakes and a three-speed gearbox, was conventional enough, but the 6.9-litre engine was quite simply the best in the world. Not only was it a straight-eight, but it also had a twin-overhead-camshaft cylinder head, with four valves per cylinder. Here, in 1928, was a

*Below: Whether or not it was truly "the world's finest car", the Duesenberg Model J was unquestionably a worthy rival to models from established prestige marques such as Rolls-Royce, Bugatti, Mercedes-Benz and Hispano-Suiza. This 1929 model had a Murphy body.*

layout which would still not be adopted by many other prestigious concerns up to 60 years later.

Lycoming, another Cord subsidiary, built the engines, for which no less than 265 bhp was claimed. This was double the power claimed for *any* other American car at the time, and doubters should be reminded that this car, when fitted with lofty special coachwork, and weighing more than 5,000 lb, could reach an astonishing top speed of 116 mph.

Add to this the fact that the chassis price alone was $8,500 at first ($9,500 by 1931), the bodies were magnificent, and complete cars rarely seemed to cost less than $17,000 at a time when the best Cadillacs retailed for a mere $7,000, and one sees that this was one of the most expensive, and exclusive, production cars of all time.

The miracle is that the Model J, and its supercharged derivative the Model SJ, continued to sell, slowly but steadily, throughout the Depression. By 1936, when the last of all was built in Indiana, 470 cars with a mouth-watering selection of body styles (all incorporating that noble front grille) had been sold. At that time, without question, it was the best American car ever made.

### Duesenberg Model J variants

#### Duesenberg Model JN and SJN

Ten examples of the JN were built in 1935 and 1936. This featured a 153.5-in wheelbase, and smaller (17-in) road wheels. Two of these cars had supercharged SJ-type engines, so logically were called SJNs.

*Right: A Model J running chassis alone cost $8,500 or more, and a complete car like this 1930 example was nearly three times the price of a Cadillac. Despite this, the model sold steadily, admittedly in small numbers, throughout the Depression; perhaps those who could afford one in the first place were insulated from such trifling economic ups and downs. Even with substantial coachwork, the Model J could reach 116 mph.*

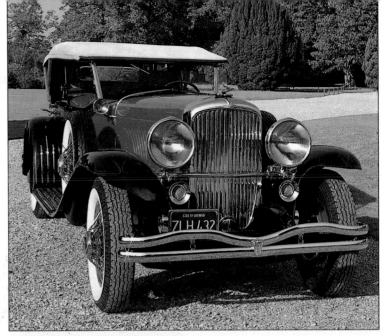

*Below right: The magnificent 6.9-litre straight-eight engine had two overhead camshafts and 32 valves. Even without a blower it delivered 265 bhp, double the power of any other American car of the time.*

### Specification (1928 Model J)

**Engine:** inline eight-cylinder, twin-overhead-camshaft
**Bore × stroke:** 95.25 mm × 120.6 mm
**Capacity:** 6876 cc
**Maximum power:** 265 bhp
**Transmission:** three-speed manual gearbox, rear-wheel drive
**Chassis:** separate steel frame with channel-section side members and tubular bracing
**Suspension:** non-independent with beam front axle and semi-elliptic leaf springs; live rear axle with semi-elliptic leaf springs
**Brakes:** drums front and rear
**Bodywork:** various styles, open or closed
**Maximum speed:** 116 mph (187 km/h)

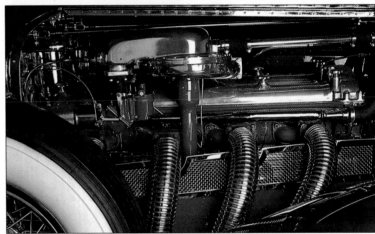

# Duesenberg Model SJ 1932-35

If the Model J were rightly described as "the world's finest car", how was Duesenberg to advertise the SJ, which was more powerful, faster than ever, more expensive, yet always as well-built? The SJ was the *crème de la crème*, for its centrifugal supercharger, used to boost the engine's peak power to 320 bhp, gave the car a potential top speed of at least 130 mph, and made it impossible for so-called rival cars to keep up. In modern terms, the equivalent would be the launch of a

car which was just as capable as any Ferrari or Lamborghini, yet had a top speed of at least 250 mph.

E.L. Cord had the audacity to launch this car in 1932, when American business was still in the depths of the Depression, and advertised it with a chassis price of $11,750, and a probable complete-car cost of about $19,000.

The SJ was an extrovert machine in every way. Because of the bulk of the supercharger installation under the bon-

net, the standard exhaust system could not be used, so Duesenberg brought the exhaust out through the side of the bonnet in four chromed flexible downpipes.

Because of this feature, body styles were even more exotic than on Model Js, some being the sleekest roadsters, often with duo-tone paintwork to contrast with that glittering array of the exhaust system. (In fact, the external piping became a frequently-selected option on non-supercharged Model Js as well, so

appearances could be deceptive).

In character, there was nothing to touch the SJ. An exhaust cut-out was fitted, which allowed the car either to purr like a Cadillac, or to bellow like a massive racing car. It steered well, had vacuum-assistance for the brakes to keep everything in check, and it behaved with a general air of refinement.

Only 36 such cars were built in four years, and almost all have survived. Today they are literally priceless. When the SJ was new it was unbeatable, and even today there are those who say that it still stands supreme.

### Duesenberg Model SJ variants

#### Duesenberg Model SSJ

Two extra-special SSJs were produced, on a very short (125-in) wheelbase, and equipped with sports-car coachwork. Both went to film stars – one to Gary Cooper, the other to Clark Gable.

*Left: Duesenberg Model Js were comprehensively equipped and beautifully finished in every detail, as this close-up of a dashboard shows. A speedometer reading to 150 mph must have looked outlandish in its time but was by no means an affectation, for with a supercharged 320-bhp version of the straight-eight engine the car genuinely had the ability to go well beyond 130 mph.*

## Specification (1932 Model SJ)

**Engine:** inline eight-cylinder, twin-overhead-camshaft
**Bore × stroke:** 95.25 mm × 120.6 mm
**Capacity:** 6876 cc
**Maximum power:** 320 bhp
**Transmission:** three-speed manual gearbox, rear-wheel drive
**Chassis:** separate steel frame with channel-section side members and tubular bracing
**Suspension:** non-independent with beam front axle and semi-elliptic leaf springs; live rear axle with semi-elliptic leaf springs
**Brakes:** drums front and rear
**Bodywork:** various styles, open or closed
**Maximum speed:** 130 mph (209 km/h)

*Right: If a regular 116-mph Model J seemed a touch sedate, you could choose an S-for-supercharged 130-mph version from 1932. This is a 1933 roadster with a Walton body.*

# Edsel

**F**ord Detroit's Edsel project is a perfect example of the wrong product arriving at the wrong time. Although this new range of cars had been subject to a great deal of pre-launch research and planning, it appeared at a time when the public was turning away from Edsel's market sector. The Edsel was a huge failure in some ways, but it set records in others – Ford admitted that it had cost them a colossal amount of money.

By the mid-1950s there were Fords, Mercurys and Lincolns in the Ford group. At this point, the company decided to produce a further range, pitching it into the lower-medium price bracket, where it would cost more than a Ford, but less than a Mercury.

The project, originally known only as the 'E-car', went ahead at breakneck speed, from 1955 to August 1957, by which time two different model ranges were launched. To save time, and to save vast expense on tooling, Ford decided to base the cars on Ford chassis and Mercury body shells, with V8 engines under the skin.

The Edsel name was chosen after a great deal of market research, when all manner of unsuitable names were suggested. Edsel was the Christian name of the second Ford in the long-running hierarchy – Henry Ford I's son, and Henry Ford II's father.

Edsel had died in the 1940s, and it was Ford president Ernie Breech who first suggested using his name for the new car. Many thought it controversial, others considered it unsuitable – and one PR man angrily suggested that this would cost the marque 200,000 sales. As it turned out, this might have been an under-estimate.

The Edsel was aimed squarely at a market area already dominated by Pontiac, Buick and Dodge, but immediately after launch this sector began to slip backwards. The market fall, coupled with an early reputation for doubtful build quality, and the fact that many found the new Edsel style ugly, dealt the new car a heavy blow.

The figures tell their own story. Only 63,110 Edsels – Ford-based Rangers and Pacers, Mercury-based Corsairs and Citations – were sold in the 1958 model year, so Ford panicked and changed the range for 1959, using only a single Ford chassis, increasing the choice of engines but chopping the choice of models. This didn't help, and only 44,891 1959 models were sold.

For 1960 a radically-revised Edsel was launched, based on the new sleek Ford Fairlane/Galaxie style, but Ford had already decided to pull the plug on the marque. A mere 3,008 1960-model Edsels were built, the last actually rolling off the lines before the end of calendar year 1959.

As author Robert Lacey commented, "The Edsel died because it was ugly, because it tended to go wrong, and because it was introduced in the depths of a recession."

*Left: In an era when macho car culture was rampant and typical American cars were loaded with phallic symbolism, the unmistakable Edsel frontal treatment – euphemistically described as resembling a horse-collar – was idiosyncratic and, facing the prejudices of the predominantly male buying public, a marketing blunder. The grille shown here is from a 1959 Corsair.*

# Edsel Ranger and Pacer 1958-59

At launch there were two sizes of Edsel – two models used the 118-in-wheelbase Ford Fairlane chassis, and two others used a 124-in Mercury chassis.

The smaller pair of Edsels were called Ranger and Pacer – the Pacers being slightly better-equipped, and a little more expensive. Prices, in general, were about $500 less than comparable Mercurys.

Under the skin, the running gear was totally conventional, except that a powerful 5.9-litre V8 engine was standard. The car had a cavernous interior and soft, long-travel front suspension, giving the sort of ride which Detroit thought ideal for rough-and-ready city streets, and for long-distance travel. There was no

question of sporty handling, but there were no doubts about the performance, either. A 303-bhp Edsel Pacer was fast and more agile than other types, although fuel economy was poor – 10-12 mpg was normal, but this was typical of many other American cars of the period.

In 1958 there were seven types of Rangers and six Pacers, but no choice of engines. The chassis and the body shells were closely based on contemporary Ford designs.

For 1959 the range was tightened up, with only four Rangers but no Pacers on offer, and a wheelbase two inches longer. For the first time there was the option of a 3.65-litre/145-bhp six-cylinder

engine, along with 4.8-litre/200-bhp and 5.4-litre/225-bhp V8s as well as the existing 5.9-litre/303-bhp V8.

It was the styling of the cars which caused such a furore. Although broadly based on the latest Ford Fairlanes – which is to say that they had steep, wrap-around windscreens, sharply sculptured lines and complex rear wing shapes, the Rangers and Pacers also had unique 'horse-collar'-style grilles, and narrow horizontal tail lamp clusters.

Where automatic transmission was fitted, it was controlled by 'Teletouch' buttons recessed into the centre of the steering wheel. The speedometer was a rotating drum. It was a car which put features above handling, and styling

above engineering – and the American public rejected it.

Within no more than a year, the Edsel jokes, and the rejection of the marque, had begun. In one climactic sequence in the 1980s film *Peggy Sue Got Married*, where a middle-aged woman is projected back in time to become a teenager again, she greets her father's proud purchase of an early Edsel with disdain. He doesn't understand – but before long he would.

*Below: Initially there were four Edsel models (plus station wagons) and the two more down-market types used the 118-in Ford Fairlane chassis. This one is a 1958 Pacer.*

## Specification (1958)

**Engine:** V8, overhead-valve
**Bore × stroke:** 103 mm × 88.9 mm
**Capacity:** 5920 cc
**Maximum power:** 303 bhp
**Transmission:** three-speed manual gearbox with optional overdrive, or automatic transmission with rear-wheel drive
**Chassis:** separate steel frame with box-section reinforcing members
**Suspension:** independent front with wishbones and coil springs; live rear axle with semi-elliptic leaf springs
**Brakes:** drums front and rear
**Bodywork:** steel five/six-seaters; saloon, coupé and estate styles
**Maximum speed:** 110 mph (177 km/h)

# Edsel Corsair and Citation 1958-59

The larger of the original Edsels were called Corsairs and Citations – the latter being more expensive, better-equipped, and also available in convertible form.

Except that these cars ran on Mercury chassis, with modified Mercury bodies, with monstrously powerful 345-bhp engines, the Rangers and Pacers had the same styling features at front and rear, and the same range of fittings inside the cabin. Almost everything possible was power-assisted.

There were two Corsairs and three Citations on a 124-in-wheelbase Mercury-based design in 1958. For 1959 this chassis was dropped, and both Corsairs

and Rangers were built on a new 120-in platform. 1959 Corsairs were available with the 5.4-litre/225-bhp V8, or the 5.9-litre/303-bhp V8.

In 1958, sales had been very slow indeed – only 9,191 Corsairs and 8,577 Citations were sold – so for 1959 the Citation and Pacer were dropped, and the Corsair badge was applied to the up-market version of the 120-in-wheelbase Ranger model. In that year the 'horse-collar' grilles became slimmer, yet just as obvious, but sales fell further, to just 8,653 cars.

Thereafter the Corsair name was dropped, only two years after it had been launched. It would reappear, four years later, on a British Ford.

*Above left: Based on a 124-in Mercury chassis and powered by a 345-bhp 410-cu in V8, the Corsair and Citation models topped the 1958 Edsel range. Citations, like this convertible, had fancier trim than Corsairs.*

*Above right: In 1959 engines were down-sized and a six-cylinder was introduced as an option on the Ranger. The Pacer and Citation were dropped, and both Ranger and Corsair were now based on a 120-in Ford chassis, although the Corsair had a 332-cu in V8 engine as standard against the Ranger's 292-cu in unit. The convertible version was available only as a Corsair.*

## Specification (1958)

**Engine:** V8, overhead-valve
**Bore × stroke:** 106.4 mm × 94 mm
**Capacity:** 6724 cc
**Maximum power:** 345 bhp
**Transmission:** three-speed automatic transmission, rear-wheel drive
**Chassis:** separate steel frame with box-section reinforcing members
**Suspension:** independent front with wishbones and coil springs; live rear axle with semi-elliptic leaf springs
**Brakes:** drums front and rear
**Bodywork:** steel five/six-seaters; saloon, coupé or convertible
**Maximum speed:** 110 mph (177 km/h)

# Elva

After World War II, Frank Nichols opened a garage in Bexhill-on-Sea, Sussex, specialised in sporting machinery, and eventually began designing cars of his own.

The first car was a CSM Special (this name came from his garage – Chapman Sports Motors), but in the 1950s Nichols founded a new company called Elva Engineering, the name Elva being a romantic contraction of the French phrase 'elle va' – 'she goes'!

The first Elvas were racing sports cars with multi-tube chassis frames, which achieved a great deal of success in British and North American events.

From 1958, however, Nichols also began selling a neat MG-engined roadgoing sports car called the Courier, which was an immediate success in export markets, and soon went on sale in the UK as a kit car, which meant that prices could be reduced as no taxes had to be paid.

Although Nichols then expanded his racing car activities by producing mid-engined Formula Junior single-seaters, his business was never profitable. The original company went into voluntary liquidation in 1961,

to be replaced by Elva Cars (1961) Ltd, and from 1962 this company made an agreement with Trojan Ltd of Purley, in Surrey, for the Courier to be assembled there.

Nichols then sold out to Trojan in 1964, but stayed on to design the sensationally beautiful BMW-powered 160XS sports car, of which only three examples were built, after which he severed all his links with the marque which he had founded, and returned to the motor trade in Sussex.

Having been re-engineered in 1962, the Courier pottered on with only minor improvements, and Trojan finally lost interest in it. The project was sold to Ken Sheppard Customised Sports Cars (in Radlett) in 1966, where the last cars of all were built in 1968.

*Below: In their early years, Elva's commercial success meant they could afford to build racing cars like this Formula Junior, while selling road cars in kit form. When VAT was introduced in Britain, kit cars lost their great pricing advantage, and many kit carmakers did not survive for long.*

## Elva Courier 1958-68

Elva's first and only roadgoing sports car was launched in 1958, and like most of its contemporaries it used proprietary mechanical components.

The new car, which Frank Nichols called the Courier, had been inspired by enquiries from his agents in the USA. Because his manufacturing facilities were limited, he based the car on a simple ladder-style chassis frame which had main side members made of 2½-in diameter steel tubes, and cross-bracing of 1¼-in tubing, with additional super-structure braces.

The engine and gearbox came straight from the MGA, while the rear axle was that of a Riley 1.5 saloon. Front and rear suspensions were of Elva design, there were MGA-type Lockheed drum brakes, and Morris Minor-type rack-and-pinion steering.

The prototype had an aluminium body shell, but all production cars had glass-fibre bodywork, the shells being constructed in Nichols' own premises. The style was a neat and simple two-seater open sports layout, with a side profile looking rather like that of the Triumph Spitfire, but pre-dating it by four whole seasons. It was a compact car, weighing a mere 1,550 lb, and had a top speed of

around 100 mph.

About 700 cars had been made by the end of 1961, when production came to a halt for a time. Whereas the first Courier, built in 1958, had a 1.5-litre/72-bhp engine, 1.6-litre/80-bhp and 1.6-litre/86-bhp power units were introduced in 1960 and 1961. Production began again at the Trojan works by the end of 1962, this time with a 1.8-litre MGB engine, front-wheel disc brakes, and coil-spring independent rear suspension. Compared with the earlier cars, this Courier had a lot

more performance, for it had 95 bhp instead of 72 bhp, yet weighed the same.

On the Series III model, introduced in 1963, a 1.5-litre 78-bhp Ford engine was listed as an option, but very few such cars were built. The Series IV replaced the Series III in the mid-1960s, with few changes.

For a time a 1.5-litre Ford Cortina GT engine and gearbox assembly were optional, but few cars were so equipped, as the MG engine was much better known in export territories, where most

Couriers were sold.

Even though the Elva project changed hands several times in the 1960s, and was based in several factories, very few further changes were ever made to the design, and the last cars of all were produced in 1968.

*Below: There were many British specialist carmakers in the 1950s and 1960s. The Elva Courier was one of the best models of its type, with elegant lines and good performance.*

*Left: The Courier used mass-produced engines, like the MGB unit or Ford's 1.5-litre pushrod engine, but Elva's own independent suspension gave their cars good roadholding.*

### Specification (1963 Series III)

**Engine:** inline four-cylinder, overhead-valve
**Bore × stroke:** 80.3 mm × 88.9 mm
**Capacity:** 1798 cc
**Maximum power:** 95 bhp
**Transmission:** four-speed manual gearbox, optional overdrive, rear-wheel drive
**Chassis:** separate tubular steel frame
**Suspension:** independent front and rear, each with coil springs
**Brakes:** discs front, drums rear
**Bodywork:** glassfibre two-seater open sports
**Maximum speed (approx):** 110 mph (177 km/h)

# Excalibur Automobile Corporation

From 1964 to 1990 North America's most famous maker of pastiche machinery concentrated on cars which originally took the late-1920s Mercedes-Benz SSK roadsters as their role models, and later moved forward to ape 1930s types instead. For more than a quarter of a century they brought old-style looks, which hid modern North American running gear, to customers willing to pay a lot of money to be different.

Excalibur of Milwaukee was founded by David and William Stevens, who were the sons of the noted industrial designer Brooks Stephens. The new/old car came about because the brothers' father had been a consultant to Studebaker in the early 1960s, had been unimpressed by that company's mundane offerings, and had hoped to persuade the management to back his idea of a flashy image-changing roadster.

Early in 1964 the first car was built, on the basis of a Studebaker Lark Daytona convertible chassis, with an Avanti-type supercharged V8 engine, and was put together in just six weeks. At the last minute, however, Studebaker withdrew their support, so the Stevens family decided to go it alone, relaunched the car as an Excalibur in April 1964, and started building machines on the Lark chassis.

The car's secret was in its looks, styled by Brooks Stevens, which were a sweeping approximation of the late-1920s Mercedes-Benz SSK roadster. To match the company's name (which refers to the legendary sword of Arthurian tales) the model's massive and proud grille was complete with its own sword-in-a-circle badge, but the lines were unmistakably Teutonic, and it is a miracle that the German concern never sued.

The first cars weighed a mere 2,100 lb, and cost $7,250 – at a time when the Chevrolet Corvette cost $4,250 – so the combination of an unknown firm, quirky styling and high prices ensured that sales would always be low.

For 1966, Excalibur dropped the Studebaker engine in favour of Corvette power, one or other of the engines from this model then being retained for the rest of the marque's life, while for 1970 a specially-designed chassis frame took over from the original Studebaker unit.

For the next 20 years the Excalibur marque pottered on, sometimes making as many as 300 cars a year, sometimes fewer than 100 a year, but there always seemed to be enough custom to keep the small company alive. Series II gave way to Series III for 1975, when the style changed to something more akin to a late-1930s Mercedes-Benz 540K; the long-wheelbase Series IV arrived for 1980, and by the end of that decade the line had progressed to Series V, with an enormous limousine option.

Although Excalibur battled hard to keep abreast of North American legislation and changing fashion, they eventually ran out of customers willing to pay such very high prices. The end came in 1990, when the business ran out of money and finally folded.

*Below: At a casual glance, this Excalibur Roadster might well be a classic Mercedes, except that Mercedes' three-pointed star has been replaced by Excalibur's own 'sword' motif. The car has a two-piece windscreen – note that the windscreen wipers are of the old-fashioned 'clap hands' type, but later Excaliburs had one-piece screens and parallel wipers.*

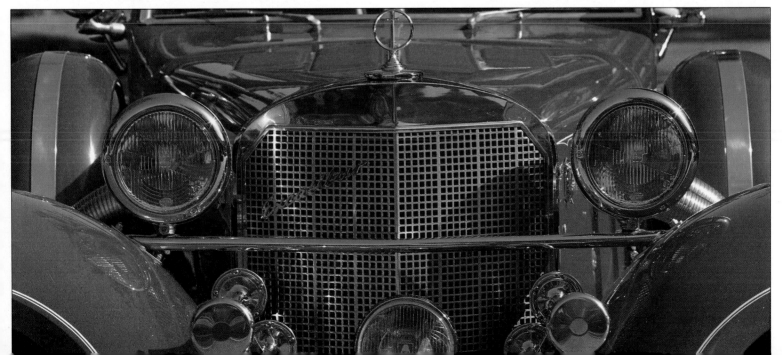

## Excalibur Series I 1965-69

The original Excalibur was a starkly-styled roadster which tried to ape the late-1920s Mercedes-Benz SSK sports car, while running on a 1960s-type Studebaker chassis with fat wheels and tyres.

The Lark Daytona chassis itself was surprisingly suitable for this purpose, as its main side rails were not set too far apart, which allowed an appropriately slim body to be mounted on it. Power – sheer brute power – in the original Series I cars, built in 1965, came from the same supercharged 4.7-litre/290-bhp V8 engine which had been optional on the short-lived Studebaker Avanti, there being a choice of manual or automatic transmission behind it.

Even so, much detail re-engineering was done, especially on the position of the steering column and pedals, while spring and damper rates were altered, and the front suspension geometry was also changed considerably.

The first few cars had aluminium bodies, but Excalibur soon converted to glassfibre for the main production run. The style featured cycle-type wings, there was an engine-turned dashboard with Studebaker Hawk-style instruments, and the bucket seats were also modified Studebaker items.

The body style featured exposed, flexible exhaust manifold pipes, Excalibur actually purchasing these from the West German concern that had originally made them for Mercedes-Benz! The radiator grille looked almost exactly like that of the Mercedes-Benz model, except that there was no three-pointed star.

By 1966 the range was expanding. A more completely equipped roadster, with full-length wings and running boards, and a four-passenger 'phaeton' were both added, while a 5.3-litre Chevrolet Corvette engine and choice of transmissions took over from the Studebaker items. A 400-bhp version of the Chevrolet engine was optional in 1967 only, and a 435-bhp option was offered in 1968 and 1969.

Before the Series I bowed out in 1969, Excalibur also added optional air conditioning, variable-ratio power steering, and a tilt steering wheel, while options included steel-belted radial-ply tyres, a hardtop, and the latest, three- rather than two-speed, Turbo-Hydramatic automatic transmission.

All in all, 168 Series I SSKs, 59 Roadsters and 89 Phaetons were produced.

### Specification (1966 Series I)

**Engine:** V8, overhead-valve
**Bore × stroke:** 101.6 mm × 82.55 mm
**Capacity:** 5355 cc
**Maximum power:** 300 bhp
**Transmission:** four-speed manual gearbox or two-speed automatic transmission, rear-wheel drive
**Chassis:** separate steel frame with box-section side members and reinforcements
**Suspension:** independent front with coil springs; live rear axle with semi-elliptic leaf springs
**Brakes:** discs front, drums rear
**Bodywork:** glassfibre open two-seater, or four-seater 'phaeton'
**Maximum speed:** 125 mph (201 km/h)

*Above: Excalibur's SSK echoed the lines of Mercedes' SSK roadster, made in the late 1920s. The original car had six cylinders which fed into three outside exhaust pipes on the right-hand side of the car. When Brooks Stevens designed the Excalibur SSK, he decided to keep the three-pipe look. As the Excalibur had a V8 engine, it had outside exhausts on both right and left sides, and the four cylinders on each bank had to feed into the three pipes.*

*Below: The SSK and the Roadster were produced from 1965 to 1969, and 265 were built altogether. This is the Roadster, which had the same mechanical specification as the SSK, but was fitted with full-length wings and running boards. The car was an uncompromising two-seater, but it became a sought-after status symbol in the wealthy American market, where there are always buyers who want something different and are prepared to pay for it.*

*Right: Excalibur originally made their bodies from aluminium, and then went over to glassfibre. In both cases, the body was unstressed and so the chassis had to cope with all of the loads. Having a separate chassis, which carried all of the mechanical components, made it relatively easy for Excalibur to fit a variety of bodies – the wheelbase gradually got longer as Excalibur's cars became more spectacular.*

# Excalibur Series II and Series III 1969-80

**Top: The Phaeton's body extended backwards beyond the line of the axle, giving spacious rear seats.**

**Above: The styling of the Roadster gradually changed, with the wings becoming fuller and more curved.**

**Below: There would be no mistaking this car if you saw it coming in your mirror! All Excaliburs had a similar frontal appearance, with an old-style grille but modern wide tyres. This is a Phaeton with the hood raised and the side screens in place.**

After five successful years with their first car, Excalibur produced the Series II, which had an entirely new box-section chassis frame, designed by David Stephens, which used Chevrolet Corvette suspension components. This had a slightly longer wheelbase than before – 111 inches, compared with 109.

Although this was still an old-style pastiche car, the engineering was more modern than before, for the latest machine had independent front *and* rear suspension, there were four-wheel disc brakes, an enlarged and torquier Corvette V8, and a choice of the latest GM manual or automatic transmissions.

Like the original, this was an extrovert machine which offered Corvette-like performance, stability and handling, in an intriguing old-look visual package. The Series II was 400 lb heavier than the Series I model, while prices were considerably higher than ever before – the 1970 SSK cost $12,000, and by 1974 the slightly more modernised SS Roadster was listed at $17,000, but this did not deter the wealthy few.

342 Series II cars were sold before the Series III model took over in 1975. The Series III chassis was merely a modified version of the Series II; it took into account Federal safety and emissions regulations, and was complete with a detoxed 215-bhp 7.4-litre 'big-block' Chevrolet Corvette engine. The Series III cars were clothed in an updated style, with a far heavier and more plushly-equipped body that was visually much closer to the late-1930s Mercedes-Benz 540K coupé. In the last year of its life, the Series III was equipped with another 350-cu in/5.7-litre Corvette engine, by this time de-rated to 180 bhp.

By this time, like Britain's Morgan, the Excalibur had taken on its own character, so henceforth it would be unfair to compare it with any other car, past or present. Even though Series III prices rocketed from $18,900 in 1975 to $28,600 in 1979, there was no shortage of customers. Excalibur must have offered something unique, for the same performance *and* running gear were available for a third of the price from Chevrolet!

No fewer than 1,141 Series III cars were produced.

## Specification (1970 Series II)

**Engine:** V8, overhead-valve
**Bore × stroke:** 101.6 mm × 88.4 mm
**Capacity:** 5733 cc
**Maximum power:** 300 bhp
**Transmission:** four-speed manual gearbox or three-speed automatic transmission, rear-wheel drive
**Chassis:** separate steel frame with box-section side members and cross-bracings
**Suspension:** independent front with coil springs; independent rear with transverse leaf spring
**Brakes:** discs front and rear
**Bodywork:** glassfibre open two-seater, optional hardtop, or optional four-seater 'phaeton'
**Maximum speed:** 150 mph (241 km/h)

## Excalibur Series IV and Series V 1980-90

Even so, the SS Roadsters and four-seater Phaetons continued to the bitter end of Excalibur, which came in mid-1990.

### Specification (1981 Series IV)

**Engine:** V8, overhead-valve
**Bore × stroke:** 95 mm × 88.4 mm
**Capacity:** 5013 cc
**Maximum power:** 155 bhp
**Transmission:** three-speed automatic transmission, rear-wheel drive
**Chassis:** separate steel frame with box-section side members
**Suspension:** independent front with coil springs; independent rear with transverse leaf spring
**Brakes:** discs front and rear
**Bodywork:** glassfibre two-seater, optional four-seater
**Maximum speed:** 110 mph (177 km/h)

The biggest change in Excalibur's history came with the launch of the Series IV in February 1980. Although the new car's basic engineering was much as before, this was a much larger and more luxurious machine than ever.

Compared with the Series III, the Series IV had a 13-in longer wheelbase which promised much more interior passenger accommodation, the body waistline had been raised, and wind-down glass was fitted to the doors. The lines, though still faintly redolent of 1930s Mercedes-Benz models, now had their own distinct character, with long and sweeping wings and running boards, rather angular cabins if the optional hardtop were fitted, and with a great deal of all-American glitz in evidence.

Roadsters had rumble seats (dickey seats in British terms), while the four-seater Phaeton had a fully power-operated soft-top. To keep abreast with emission standards, the cars had smaller, but more fuel-efficient, 305-cu in/five-litre Chevrolet V8 engines. Four-speed automatic transmission was adopted for 1983.

This was the basic style of Excalibur which was to be built throughout the 1980s, though after the middle of the decade there was a rash of larger and heavier new derivatives, which must surely have contributed to the company's eventual failure.

Excalibur tried to expand the appeal of their cars from an annual production rate of about 100 cars, by adding new body types, and by stretching the robust chassis.

The Series V type took over in 1985, with style and equipment changes, while from 1988 there were three choices of engine – 305 cu in/198 bhp, 350 cu in/248 bhp or 454 cu in/233 bhp. In 1987, two new long-wheelbase types, the Royale and Limited four-door saloons, were introduced (148-in and 171.6-in wheelbases respectively) while from late 1988 there was also a monstrous car called the Series V Grand Limousin, which rode on a vast 204-in wheelbase, weighed 5,700 lb, and had four doors and eight seats. Despite all this activity, only 125 cars were sold in 1989.

*Below: One of the biggest Excaliburs of all was the four-door Sedan, which had a wheelbase of a full 12 feet and an overall length of nearly 19 feet. This car first appeared in 1987, the year after Brooks Stevens' original Excalibur company had become bankrupt but had been rescued by the Acquisition Company of Illinois.*

# Facel Vega

*Above: The Facel II typified Facel Vega's products – solid and elegant, with an international feel.*

*Right: Facel Vega's badge echoed the art deco style of earlier decades, but their cars always looked modern.*

F rance was always the spiritual home of the *grand routier* – the car which had sleek lines, high performance, and the ability to swish effortlessly from city to city without stressing its occupants. In the 1950s and 1960s Facel Vega of Colombes made the definitive example of that great tradition.

*Forges et Ateliers de Construction d'Eure et de Loire* (FACEL for short) was set up by Jean Daninos in 1938, originally to produce large tools and press dies for the aircraft industry. During World War II, under German occupation, the company produced wood-gas generators for cars and trucks, but by the 1950s it had become a mass-manufacturer of car body shells for models as diverse as the Simca 8 Sports Coupé, the Ford Comète and the Panhard Dyna. At the same time it dabbled with special body styles on other cars, notably the Bentley R-type of the early 1950s.

After the Panhard Dyna contract ended, Daninos moved swiftly to fill his factories by producing a massive new car which he called the Facel Vega FVS. In this model he combined a tubular chassis frame with a pressed-steel coupé body style, but bought in engines and automatic transmissions from Chrysler-USA, and commissioned a new (truck-based) manual gearbox from Pont-à-Mousson.

The FVS was launched in 1954. It was considered large, heavy and ponderous, but the car, picked out with stainless-steel brightwork, attracted attention and had lavish equipment to make up for its lack of agility. It was an immediate, if small-scale, success. This Chrysler-engined theme was to be continued for the next decade, supplying the rich as well as those who wanted something without the complication of Italian 'supercar' engineering, but with the space of a large Mercedes-Benz model, and which yet was different from almost every other type of car.

All would have been well for Facel if Daninos had not then decided to produce a smaller-engined car which he intended to produce in larger numbers. The result of this plan, the Facellia, was neatly packaged, attractive, and with obvious styling links to the larger cars, but was badly let down by a very unreliable engine; this eventually cost so much to put right that the company failed.

Pont-à-Mousson, Hispano-Suiza and Mobil-France all poured in extra finance during 1962 to keep the company afloat, but this was not enough, and a receiver was appointed before the end of that year. During 1963 the troublesome Facellia engine was dumped, a Volvo P1800 unit was fitted in its place, and there were hopes for a recovery.

Unhappily, it was not easy for Facel Vega to restore their previous reputation, and although a new management team under Paul Badre took over in September 1963 the receiver only gave them 12 months to work the miracle.

Although the last models they made were the best cars ever developed by this French concern, they simply did not sell, and Facel SA finally went into liquidation for good before the end of 1964. Jean Daninos' dream of *la gloire, pour la France* had lasted for no more than a decade.

# Facel Vega FVS Coupé 1954-59

The original Facel Vega FVS was launched in 1954, and immediately established the technical pattern of all the large cars that Facel built during the next 10 years. Daninos' technical team chose components and techniques with which they were familiar, which explains the use of a separate chassis frame with tubular side and bracing members, plus a great deal of extra bracing by channel-section pressings.

The massive steel body was produced entirely in the Facel workshops with a style inspired by the Ford Comète and Simca Sports Coupés already being assembled at Colombes. The nose was bluff, vertical and would always be recognisable in future years, for there was an 'egg-crate' grille flanked by a pair of grille 'ears', while the headlamp/side-lamp assemblies had a vertical aspect.

The two-door cabin provided wide but rather compact four-seater accommodation, there was a well-equipped dash, and the windscreen was a simple, modest, curved affair – the exaggerated wrap-around style was yet to come! The interior was often described as like that of a 'classy private aeroplane', for the dash was well-stocked with instruments.

Power was by Chrysler's modern 'Hemi' V8, and there was a choice of Chrysler Torqueflite automatic transmission, or a Pont-à-Mousson four-speed manual gearbox.

The result was a heavy (3,600 lb), but formidably fast machine which was very expensive, and very exclusive.

Facel rarely sold more than three or four Vega FVS cars a week, which gave Daninos plenty of opportunity to update the specification when he felt like it. The car benefitted from North America's ongoing horsepower race, for no fewer than four sizes of Chrysler engines were fitted in five years, the increases in power being matched by the fitment of power steering, disc brakes and radial tyres.

The original body style was modified in 1956, with a pronounced Detroit-style wrap-around windscreen, this being re-tained until 1959 when the second-generation model, the HK500, was introduced. By that time the FVS weighed in at a sturdy 4,100 lb.

The Chrysler engine was enlarged to 4768 cc in 1956, to 5407 cc in 1957, and to 5801 cc in 1958; final power output was 325 bhp. Power steering became optional in 1957. Disc brakes, front and rear, were available from 1957. A four-head-lamp nose was standardised in 1957.

The HK500 of 1959-62 was a further development on the FVS theme. Another variant, the Excellence, was a four-door saloon which used a lengthened version of the FVS/HK500 chassis and running gear.

Facel Vega ownership was not for the poor, nor for the modest. It helped to be rich (fuel consumption was rarely better than 12-14 mpg), to have several other cars (service was difficult to find, especially outside France), and to be flamboyant. Whether Daninos had intended it that way or not, the FVS was an extrovert coupé, for extrovert people.

A mere 403 of these cars were produced in five years.

## Specification (1954-55)

**Engine:** V8, overhead-valve
**Bore × stroke:** 92 mm × 84.93 mm
**Capacity:** 4528 cc
**Maximum power:** 180 bhp
**Transmission:** four-speed manual gearbox or three-speed automatic transmission, rear-wheel drive
**Chassis:** separate steel frame with tubular side and bracing members
**Suspension:** independent front with coil springs; live rear axle with semi-elliptic leaf springs
**Brakes:** drums front and rear
**Bodywork:** steel four-seater coupé
**Maximum speed:** 120 mph (193 km/h)

*Below: Early FVSs had conventional windscreen pillars.*

*Bottom: Later models were redesigned with Facel's trademark, the rearward-curved pillar.*

# Facel Vega Excellence 1958-64

Once the FVS was safely launched, Jean Daninos pushed ahead with expansion of his range of cars, showing a four-seater prototype at the Paris Motor Show in 1956 and 1957, before sales began in 1958.

This new type, badged 'Excellence', was not only a lot longer and heavier than the two-door types, but it also had an unusual type of pillarless four-door construction, where the front doors hinged at the front, and the rear doors at the rear, which meant that they closed onto each other. All but the last eight cars had the familiar HK500-style wrap-around wind-screen and pronounced tail fins.

Sadly, the layout of the body shell almost guaranteed that its torsional stiffness was poor, and there were many reported cases of fully-loaded cars with doors which refused to close or, once closed, refused to open again.

Although the Excellence had a magnificent 'presence', it was not a great success. Daninos had hoped to sell these cars to heads of state and government figures, not to mention tycoons all over the world, and although a few such names appear on the sales ledgers, few made any impact on the motoring world.

Between 1958 and 1964, 152 Excellences were built, of which 63 were sold in the USA.

*Below: The Excellence shared its unusual door layout with the Lincoln Continental of the 1960s – the forward-opening rear doors made it easy to step gracefully into the rear compartment. Despite its great size and weight, the Excellence was still a genuine high-performance car, thanks to its 355-bhp engine.*

## Specification (1958)

**Engine:** V8, overhead-valve
**Bore × stroke:** 107.95 mm × 85.85 mm
**Capacity:** 6286 cc
**Maximum power:** 355 bhp
**Transmission:** three-speed automatic, rear-wheel drive
**Chassis:** separate steel frame
**Suspension:** independent front with wishbones and coil springs; live rear axle with semi-elliptic leaf springs
**Brakes:** discs front and rear
**Bodywork:** four-seater coupé and saloon
**Maximum speed (approx):** 130 mph (209 km/h)

# Facel Vega HK500 1959-62

The HK500 – the reason for the new model name was never explained – was launched in 1959, as a direct successor to the original FVS type.

By comparison with the FVS, on which it was based, the HK500 had a much larger and more beefy Chrysler engine, previously optional items like the disc brakes and the power-assisted steering were standardised, and there seemed to be even more fixtures and fittings on the wall-to-wall wooden fascia panel.

Although the HK500 was not nearly as agile as the Italian supercars of the day, it was still a tremendously fast and impressive machine. Few cars could match its 140-mph top speed, or its ability to sprint to 100 mph from rest in a mere 21 seconds.

In many ways, the HK500 was a motoring magic carpet which, at sensible cruising speeds, whispered along without stressing the engine, or the driver. In three years 4,539 HK500s were sold,

*Left: The HK500 resembled the FVS Coupé but had a lot more power.*

*Below: Facel Vegas had hints of American styling, but the cars were never over-adorned with chrome.*

*Right: The forward slant of the radiator grille gave the car a crouching, urgent appearance, like a sprinter waiting for the gun.*

before the Facel II took over. The new model, produced from 1962 to 1964, used the HK500's running gear, but had a new body style.

## Specification (1959)

**Engine:** V8, overhead-valve
**Bore × stroke:** 107.95 mm × 85.85 mm
**Capacity:** 6286 cc
**Maximum power:** 360 bhp
**Transmission:** four-speed manual or three-speed automatic, rear-wheel drive
**Chassis:** separate steel frame with tubular main members and mainly tubular bracing members
**Suspension:** independent front with coil springs; live rear axle with semi-elliptic leaf springs
**Brakes:** discs front and rear
**Bodywork:** steel four-seater coupé
**Maximum speed:** 140 mph (225 km/h)

# Facel Vega Facellia 1959-63

*Above: Still recognisably a Facel Vega, the Facellia was much smaller than its stablemates.*

The second-generation Facel was a much smaller car than the Chrysler V8-engined cars which had founded the dynasty. This time Jean Daninos planned to produce a smaller sports car that would sell in larger numbers.

His major mistake was to attempt to produce a car with a specially-designed and unproven engine. This was a marketing somersault. Larger Facel Vegas, and several other marques, used proprietary engines and sold perfectly well, but Daninos was not satisfied with this strategy. This time he wanted to produce an all-French car.

Accordingly, he commissioned a brand-new 1.6-litre twin-cam four-cylinder engine. The first schemes came from Harry Mundy, then *The Autocar's* technical editor, but one-time chief engine designer at Coventry-Climax, although the definitive design was by ex-Talbot engineer Carlo Marchetti.

The Facellia was really a smaller re-statement of the original Facel design using entirely different components, with a tubular chassis frame, and a steel

body the styling of which looked like that of the larger HK500 model. Compared with that car, the wheelbase was eight inches shorter, the tracks four inches narrower, and it weighed only 2,520 lb.

The engine's parts, and four-speed gearbox, were manufactured by Pont-à-Mousson, but assembly was at Facel's own premises.

If only the new car had been reliable, it might have been a success, for Daninos was projecting assembly of 3,500 cars a year by 1961 and 5,000 a year in 1962. Its performance was on a par with cars like the Triumph TR4 and the Alfa Romeo Giulia Spider; it had good roadholding, and (once the disc brakes were standardised) it was safe and secure in all departments.

Launched in 1959, the Facellia was a lot more expensive than its competitors – it cost no less than £2,509 in the UK, at a time when the 1.6-litre MGA cost a mere

*Above: Facel Vega ambitiously decided to design their own high-performance twin-cam power unit for the Facellia, but it never proved reliable. Later versions of the Facellia were fitted with more reliable units with easily obtained spare parts, like Volvo's proven four-cylinder engine and Austin-Healey's trusty six.*

£940 – which meant that it sold very slowly.

The Facellia soon suffered massive engine unreliability problems – piston burning was a major fault – and because the bad news spread rapidly, sales virtually dried up. Fewer than 500 such twin-cam-engined cars were actually sold.

This was the major factor which plunged Facel SA into receivership, and re-engining the car with a Volvo P1800 engine and gearbox (as the Facel III), or with a reduced-capacity six-cylinder Austin-Healey 3000 unit (as the Facel Six) merely postponed the end until 1964.

### Facel Vega Facellia variants

#### Facel Vega Facel III
In 1963 the Facellia gave way to the Facel III, which was basically the same design with structural changes, and fitted with a four-cylinder, 84.1-mm × 80-mm, 1778-cc/90-bhp Volvo P1800 engine; 619 Facel IIIs were built in 1963 and 1964.

#### Facel Vega Facel Six
In 1964 a few Facel Six models were produced, these being Facel IIIs fitted with a six-cylinder, 82.5-mm × 88.9-mm 2851-cc/150-bhp Austin-Healey 3000 engine; 26 were produced.

### Specification (1962 Facellia)

**Engine:** inline four-cylinder, twin-cam
**Bore × stroke:** 82 mm × 78 mm
**Capacity:** 1647 cc
**Maximum power:** 115 bhp
**Transmission:** four-speed manual gearbox, rear-wheel drive
**Chassis:** separate steel frame with tubular side and bracing members
**Suspension:** independent front with wishbones and coil springs; live rear axle with semi-elliptic leaf springs
**Brakes:** discs front and rear
**Bodywork:** steel 2 + 1-seater roadster or hardtop
**Maximum speed:** 114 mph (183 km/h)

# Facel Vega Facel II 1962-64

After eight successful years with the FVS and HK500 models, Facel replaced them with the Facel II – the ultimate statement of the Chrysler-engined 2+2 theme.

Mechanically, the Facel II was very similar to the late-model HK500, except that in manual-transmission form the engine was equipped with two four-barrel Carter carburettors, and produced a whopping 390 bhp (gross). Although manual and automatic transmissions were both still available, most customers seemed to prefer the automatic version, with which the engine produced a mere 355 bhp, though performance was still startling.

Although the basic dimensions of the car, including the 104-in wheelbase, the two-door four-seater layout, and the provision of only a coupé style, were not changed and much of the original coachwork was retained, Facel had completely restyled the cabin and the doors.

The outmoded 'dog-leg' windscreen pillars had been discarded in favour of a more restrained layout, there was increased glass area, and there was a more angular look to the pillars and the roof panel. Not only that, but there had also been a comprehensive front restyle, and because the roof was lower, the overall frontal area was less than before.

The Facel II was a massive and heavy car, but one which could deliver quite astonishing point-to-point average speeds, for the straight-line acceleration was matched by finger-light steering, and safe four-wheel Dunlop disc brakes. The only snag was that Michelin did not really guarantee their tyres for more than 120 mph at continuous ratings. . .

Because of the smaller Facellia's problems, however, this was nearly the end for the big-engined Facels, and the Facel II sold only slowly. By this time, too, there were other American V8-engined Euro-USA cars on sale, most of them considerably cheaper than the French machine.

*Above: The bulging bonnet concealed Chrysler's mighty 383-cu in V8, which was subsequently fitted in other European cars like the Jensen Interceptor and the Bristol 411.*

*Left: An airline pilot would have felt at home on the Facel II's flight deck. Facel's recipe for their GT cars was simple – European 'leather and walnut' coachbuilding combined with American brute horsepower.*

*Below left: Probably the best-looking car that Facel Vega built, the Facel II still seems smart and modern.*

## Specification (1962)

**Engine:** V8, overhead-valve
**Bore × stroke:** 107.95 mm × 85.85 mm
**Capacity:** 6286 cc
**Maximum power:** 390 bhp (manual) or 355 bhp (automatic)
**Transmission:** four-speed manual gearbox or three-speed automatic transmission, rear-wheel drive
**Chassis:** separate steel frame with tubular main members and tubular cross-bracing
**Suspension:** independent front with coil springs; live rear axle with semi-elliptic leaf springs
**Brakes:** discs front and rear
**Bodywork:** steel four-seater coupé
**Maximum speed:** 133 mph (214 km/h) (automatic) or 149 mph (240 km/h) (manual)

# Ferrari

*Above: Enzo Ferrari's first road car was not even known as a Ferrari; it was the straight-eight 1.5-litre 815 built by his Auto-Avio Costruzioni company shortly before World War II.*

*Above and below: Ferrari used the best of Italy's coachbuilders such as Milan-based Touring; the superleggera on the badge refers to their 'super lightweight' form of construction. Pininfarina (originally Pinin Farina) has bodied the vast majority of production Ferraris.*

T he world's most glamorous make of car was founded by a man who had already spent two decades working for other Italian concerns. It was only when he started his own business that his name took on a magical aura.

Born in 1898, Enzo Ferrari worked for Alfa Romeo between the wars, first as a racing driver, then as a preparation specialist. Scuderia Ferrari built and ran the 'works' Alfa Romeo team in the 1930s, but before World War II broke out, Enzo Ferrari went his own way.

Auto-Avio Costruzioni di Ferrari Enzo came into existence in Modena in 1939, but the first car to carry his name – and the famous 'prancing horse' badge – was not built at the Maranello factory (quite close to Modena) until 1947. At first Ferrari was only interested in motor racing, but built and sold a few roadgoing cars to finance that obsession.

For the rest of his long life, many insist, Ferrari only treated the road cars as an unavoidable nuisance, for he kept his hands on the racing team until the absolute end. Ferrari is the *only* racing team to have taken part in every Grand Prix formula, and is still the make by which other racing teams measure their worth.

Once established, Ferrari expanded inexorably. In the early 1950s, Ferrari built fewer than 50 road cars a year. By the early 1970s, annual output passed the 1,000 mark, and by the 1980s Ferrari was selling around 2,500 cars every year. This was thought to be the sensible limit for such cars, and production was set to be pegged at fewer than 4,000 a year into the 21st century.

For the first 20 years, *all* Ferrari road cars had 60-degree V12 engines of one type or another. In the next 20 years, there was a great deal more

*Below: Any company that begins production with a V12-engined car is surely destined for greatness, and that was the case with Ferrari. Like Enzo Ferrari's first car, the 166 (shown here in 'Barchetta' and coupé form) was notable for the small displacement of its engine; the V12 was only a two-litre unit and that explained the '166' name – it was the displacement of each of the Ferrari's tiny 12 cylinders. The body was styled by Touring of Milan.*

*Left: Every Ferrari is noteworthy, but the company history has been dotted with cars that are outstanding even by Ferrari standards. The Testa Rossa ('red head') is a perfect example. Confusingly, the Testa Rossa name referred to both the inline four-cylinder and the more exotic V12-engined cars. The 1958 250 Testa Rossa shown here was powered by a three-litre V12 and was an immensely successful sports-racing car, winning both the Le Mans 24 Hours and the Sports Car World Championship in 1958.*

*Below: If anything this car, the 250 GTO, is even more famous than the Testa Rossa. In theory it was just a development of the roadgoing 250 GT SWB, but in reality it was a purpose-built racing car with superior aerodynamics to the SWB, designed to win long-distance sports car races as varied as the Targa Florio and Le Mans. Like the Testa Rossa it was powered by a three-litre V12, and was capable of over 170 mph. The GTO was built in very small numbers, making it one of the most sought-after Ferraris ever built.*

ariety; V6s, V8s and V12s, and turbocharged units came along in great rofusion, although each was high-output, high-revving, and extremely igh on the adrenalin scale.

Ferrari's design philosophy has gone through several different phases, ach being a logical progression. From 1947 to 1964 every Ferrari road ar had a front-mounted V12 engine, with rear-wheel drive, and a live ear axle. All used the same characteristic type of chassis frame, with val-section tubes, and little pretence of high-tech engineering. In the arly days, many different coachbuilders provided bodies, but by 1960 ininfarina was the favoured stylist and Scaglietti the company's builder f such shells.

After 1964, the cars were progressively given independent rear uspension, some with rear-mounted transmissions. The first mid-engined errari road car went on sale in the late 1960s, though this was also the eriod when Ferrari tried to establish the fiction of a new marque – the Dino – to avoid marketing a V6 car as a Ferrari.

The major business change came in 1969, when Ferrari sold half of his business to Fiat, although this did not destroy the nature of the cars. From the mid-1970s there was only one front-engined car left in the range, and by the 1980s the same old design was staving off the inevitable. As the 1990s opened, Ferrari produced nothing but mid-engined cars.

Enzo Ferrari died in 1988, whereupon Fiat took control of the company. At that point Ferrari had not produced a four-wheel-drive car, had only recently adopted ABS braking and was still only dabbling with advanced electronic systems. With new models trickling out of Maranello on a regular basis throughout the 1990s, Ferrari remained the definitive supercar marque, having produced more classics than any other manufacturer.

*elow: As elegant as any Ferrari but more attainable than many, this is the errari Dino, which appeared in 1967 and was produced up to 1973. Orginally arketed as a Dino rather than a Ferrari, Enzo Ferrari's attempt to create a eparate marque was never convincing and the cars are now regarded as erraris. The Dino marked several firsts for Ferrari: it was his first mid-ngined road car and the first without a V12, having a two-litre and then 2.4-tre V6.*

*Below: Until the likes of the Lamborghini Diablo appeared on the scene in 1990 there was nothing on the road to touch this car, the Ferrari F40. It was introduced in 1987 with an intercooled twin-turbo three-litre V8 producing a massive 471 bhp. That was enough for determined drivers to see a genuine 200 mph. It was developed from the 288 GTO, which Ferrari had created to contest Group B racing in the 1980s. That formula was stillborn and the 288 GTO never raced, but it did give us the F40, which was intended to be the nearest thing to a racing car practical for road use, echoing road/competition Ferraris of old.*

# Ferrari 166 Inter, 195 Inter and 212 Inter 1948-53

In the first few years, Ferrari's road cars were always less important than the racing cars. Ferrari never built car bodies, and in every case the engineering of the engines and transmissions was markedly superior to that of the chassis.

The original Ferrari road car was the 166 Inter, of which 38 examples were built from 1948 to 1951, on a 93-in wheelbase. In effect, this chassis was a detuned version of the early Ferrari racing car, though the road-car aspect gradually emerged in the years which followed. Immediately, this car established an early Ferrari quirk – the model name indicated the swept volume of one

*Above: Ferrari's first production car, the two-litre V12 166, was produced with various different body styles. This is the Spyder Corsa, built in 1948. The cycle wings and lights were easily removed, and the 166 could thus be transformed into a competitive Formula 2 car. Very few Spyder Corsa models were built.*

*Below: The 166 Inter was powered by a detuned single-carburettor version of the two-litre V12 engine, with nearer 110 bhp rather than the 160 bhp of the competition 166 MM or Mille Miglia.*

*Below: Infinitely more attractive than the Spyder Corsa were the Touring-designed 166 MM Barchetta and 166 Inter. They were produced in sufficient numbers to be considered Ferrari's first production models, a total of 83 of all types being built between 1948 and 1953.*

cylinder, expressed in cubic centimetres.

This car set the layout, if not the performance standards, for all Ferraris of the next decade, for it had a beautifully detailed front-mounted V12 engine, designed by Gioacchino Colombo, allied to a five-speed gearbox, in an almost agriculturally-simple tubular chassis frame. Front suspension was by a transverse leaf spring and wishbones. Worm-and-sector steering, and a heavy live rear axle suspended on leaf springs, with radius arms for location, completed the mechanical assemblies.

Cars were completed, to order, by a variety of Italian coachbuilders, all being

o-seaters, some with open 'Barchetta'
orts car styling, some with closed
upé bodywork. Even at this stage,
achbuilders' names such as Pinin
arina, Allemano, Vignale and Touring
ecame linked with Ferrari.

The 166 Inter had 110 bhp (only 90 bhp
some examples) and looked faster
an it was, for the top speed was little
ore than 100 mph, although purchasers
ho loved the architecture of the V12
gine, and the sounds it made, did not
orry too much. The car had enormous
aracter and great exclusivity – the fact
at the steering was heavy, the brakes
ere doubtful from high speeds, and the

*ight: Sixteen Touring-bodied
archettas were produced for the 212
addition to the 31 made for the 166
M; the difference between 166 and
2 models was merely the engine
ze. The Barchetta ('little boat') body
as made in alloy over a steel frame.*

*bove: Power for the 212 came from a stretched version of the original all-
lloy 1.5-litre Colombo-designed V12. It was built with greater displacements
mind and in the 212 that rose to 2562 cc, while power output was 150 bhp at
500 rpm.*

*Above: There was little luxury about the interior of the 212 Barchetta, with its
painted metal dashboard. The seats were leather-trimmed, however, and the
instruments were as attractive as anyone could wish, with contra-rotating
speedo and tachometer.*

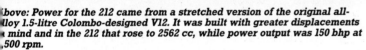

*Left: The Touring Barchetta
pioneered the company's famous
superleggera construction. That
consisted of a tubular steel
framework of small-diameter tubing
carrying a non-structural lightweight
alloy body. It was just one of a
number of body styles fitted to the
166, 195 and 212 range. There were
also coupés, berlinettas, cabriolets
and spyders from Ghia, Pinin Farina
and Vignale, among others. In all, 216
examples of the 166, 195 and 212 were
built in various guises.*

roadholding did not match the promise
of the engine, was usually forgotten. This,
after all, was a Ferrari!

The 166 Inter was joined by the 2.3-
litre/130-bhp 195 Inter for 1951 only; this
was really a larger-engined version of
the same car on a 98.4-in wheelbase, and
27 such machines were produced. At the
same time, the 2.6-litre/140-bhp 212 Inter
joined the range, this time using a
100.4-in wheelbase. By this time, too,
Ghia was one of the favoured coachbuilders, and the general standard of
'fixtures and fittings' was gradually improving.

After 100 212s of all types had be[en]
produced, the car was phased out
October 1953, to be replaced by the 2[
Europa.

### Ferrari 212 Inter variants

#### Ferrari 212 Export
The 212 Export was a higher-powere[d]
version of the 212 Inter, with a 170-bhp
version of the engine, and with a
shorter, 90.6-in, wheelbase.

*Left: The 195 Inter was introduced i[n]
1950 and ran to 1952. Twenty-seven
were produced in berlinetta and
coupé form, and were powered by a[
2341-cc version of the overhead-cam
alloy V12 engine. The greater
displacement accounted for the nam[e]
change – 2,341 divided by 12
equalling 195 . . .*

*Below: Although Pininfarina came t[o
dominate Ferrari body design,
Vignale bodied some cars very
successfully, such as this 1952 mode[l
(shown here in action at Silverstone[
before going out of favour.*

*Right: The large egg-crate grille
design, shown here on a 212, was to
become a familiar Ferrari feature for
some years. The five-speed 212 had a
top speed of around 150 mph.*

### Specification (1948 166 Inter)
**Engine:** 60-degree V12, single
overhead camshaft per bank of
cylinders
**Bore × stroke:** 60 mm × 58.8 mm
**Capacity:** 1995 cc
**Maximum power:** 110 bhp
**Transmission:** five-speed manual
gearbox, rear-wheel drive
**Chassis:** separate steel frame with
tubular main and bracing members
**Suspension:** independent front with
wishbones and transverse leaf spring;
live rear axle with semi-elliptic leaf
springs
**Brakes:** drums front and rear
**Bodywork:** light-alloy two-seater, open
sports or closed coupé
**Maximum speed (approx):** 115 mph
(185 km/h)

# Ferrari 340 America 1951-55

In the early 1950s, Ferrari was at its most inventive, with new engine designs flooding out of Maranello, and a host of slightly different exclusive road car models tumbling after them. The original America family – which was so clearly aimed at rich American buyers – was a classic case in point.

Ferrari decided to build a normally-aspirated Grand Prix car for 1950, with a large-capacity V12 engine which could

*Above: In 1953 Ferrari entered a team of four cars in the Carrera Panamericana in Mexico, one of the toughest of all road races. This is a 340 Mexico driven by American Phil Hill. Another Ferrari, driven by Maglioli, averaged an amazing 138 mph on a couple of stages.*

*Right: The 340 Mexico was powered by a 4.1-litre V12 with a compression ratio of 8.5:1 producing 280 bhp at 6600 rpm in race trim. It did boast a five-speed transmission but in other respects the Vignale-styled car was crude, with one owner saying that it ". . . steers like a truck and rides like a brick wagon . . ." It was, however, very fast as it weighed a mere 2200 lb, giving an excellent power-to-weight ratio of under 8 lb per horsepower – better than the modern Testarossa.*

be built in various capacities up to 4.5 litres and also used for sports car racing in models like the 340 Mexico and MM, and the later 375 MM. Inevitably, a detuned version of the new unit was soon developed, making its road-car appearance in the 340 America of 1951.

The new engine was designed by Lampredi, and was altogether larger, and heavier, than the original 'Colombo' type. For a big new road car, therefore, it was necessary to alter the established Ferrari chassis, so for the 340 America the wheelbase became 104 in and the side members passed under the line of the back axle. Except for the size and power of the engine, the running gear was virtually shared with that of the 250 Europa which followed.

The original Americas were rare, costly and handbuilt machines, for only 22 were produced in 1951 and 1952, of which only eight were true road cars.

*Above: The 340 America was introduced in 1951 and was an immediate success; a Vignale-bodied berlinetta similar to this one won the 1951 Mille Miglia, driven by Villoresi and Cassani, ahead of Bracco and Maglioli's Lancia and another Ferrari. Ghia and Touring built 14 cars in addition to the 11 Vignale examples.*

Each had a specially-crafted coachbuilt two-seater body by Touring, Ghia or Vignale, and there were berlinetta, coupé and barchetta styles available.

The 342 America of 1952-53 which took over from the 340 America retained the same basic chassis, but had wider wheel tracks, and a robust new four-speed transmission. These were the first 'big' Ferraris to be available with left-hand drive, and were purely touring cars rather than civilised versions of racing sports cars. Only six such cars were produced, one of them having a 4.5-litre engine.

By this time Ferrari had discovered that its America model could be matched, in straight-line acceleration at least, by powerful V8-engined American cars, so a great effort was needed. The result was the very quick 375 America, which was produced from 1953 to 1955.

Except for the difference in engine sizes, the 375 America and the 250 Europa were almost identical. By any standard the 375 America was monstrously fast and powerful, for its Lampredi V12 had been enlarged to 4522 cc, and rated at 300 bhp.

Once again, production was tiny, for only a dozen 375 Americas were ever built, each with its own individual coachwork, this time by Pinin Farina or Vig-

*Left: The 340s appeared in numerous guises and were bodied by a variety of coachbuilders. This is a Vignale-bodied 340 MM from 1953; 'MM' stood for Mille Miglia, commemorating Ferrari's victory in the 1953 Mille Miglia with a 340 Vignale-bodied spider driven by Giannino Marzotto. In theory the winning car had a 4.1-litre V12 engine, although there were suggestions that the larger 4.5-litre V12 power unit had surreptitiously been fitted to Marzotto's car.*

nale. The 375's successor, revealed in 1956, was the 410 Superamerica.

All the Americas were big, heavy, searingly fast, expensive and – above all – exclusive. Most of the 40 cars built have survived; many of these have been extensively restored, and on the rare occasion that one is sold it commands an astonishingly high price.

## Ferrari 340 America variants

### Ferrari 342 America

The 342 America of 1952-53 used the same basic running gear as the 340 America, but had a four-speed gearbox, and its 4.1-litre V12 engine was de-rated to 200 bhp. The last car of all was fitted with a 4.5-litre engine. A mere six were built.

*Above: Vignale's spider body echoed the style of the earlier Touring Barchettas.*

*Below: This 375 dates from 1953; it's a competition spider MM with the 4522-cc V12 producing 340 bhp and a wheelbase four inches longer than that of the 340 models.*

### Ferrari 375 America

The 375 America, built from 1953 to 1955, had a reinforced chassis on a 110.2-in wheelbase, an 84-mm × 68-mm 4522-cc/300-bhp version of the big V12 engine, and retained the sturdy four-speed gearbox of the 342 America. One car had a 4.9-litre engine.

*Below: This slightly strange mixture of curves, straight lines and fins is Michelotti's (while working for Vignale) berlinetta treatment of the 340 Mexico, examples of which were built for the second Carrera Panamericana. The 4.1-litre V12s were driven by Ascari, Villoresi and Chinetti, with Chinetti finishing third behind two Mercedes 300 SLs driven by Karl Kling and Hermann Lang.*

## Specification (1952 340 America)

**Engine:** V12, single overhead camshaft per bank of cylinders
**Bore×stroke:** 80 mm×68 mm
**Capacity:** 4101 cc
**Maximum power:** 220 bhp
**Transmission:** five-speed manual gearbox, rear-wheel drive
**Chassis:** separate steel frame with tubular side members and cross-bracings
**Suspension:** independent front with wishbones and transverse leaf spring; live rear axle with semi-elliptic leaf springs
**Brakes:** drums front and rear
**Bodywork:** aluminium two-seater
**Maximum speed (approx):** 140 mph (225 km/h)

*Above: Roadgoing 375 America models had 300-bhp 4.5-litre V12 engines and various body styles; this version is by Pinin Farina.*

# Ferrari 250 Europa 1953-54

*Above: The 250 Europa was essentially similar to the America range but with significantly smaller engines. Instead of the 4.1- or 4.5-litre 12s of the Americas, the Europa had three-litre version producing 'only' 00 bhp at 6,000 rpm. Although very ew were built, they did appear in oth coupé and cabriolet form with inin Farina and Vignale bodies.*

Designed to replace the 212 Inter, the 250 Europa was in many ways the twin sister of the America models, with similar coachwork but smaller engines, and sold at a reduced price.

These were the first Ferrari road cars to use modified three-litre versions of the second-generation Ferrari V12 engine, the 'Lampredi' unit, which still had a 60-degree layout, but was altogether more bulky. This was originally a Grand Prix racing engine in 1950, and in 4.1-litre form had already been specified for the original 340 America model of 1951.

Except for the heavy but powerful engine and a strengthened chassis on a lengthy (110.2-in) wheelbase, the 250 Europa had the same basic mechanical layout as earlier Ferraris. In many ways, though, this was a more practical road

car, for it had a much more roomy cockpit, the fatter tyres not only gave better grip but also a better ride, while the coachwork (mainly Pinin Farina 2+2-seater coupés, though two Vignale styles were also fitted) was smoother and more luxuriously appointed than before.

This was another very rare Ferrari – only 21 Europas were built in a 12-month period – and it should not be confused with the famous and long-running 250 GT models, which took over in 1954.

## Specification (1953)

**Engine:** V12, single overhead camshaft per bank of cylinders
**Bore×stroke:** 68 mm×68 mm
**Capacity:** 2963 cc
**Maximum power:** 200 bhp
**Transmission:** four-speed manual gearbox, rear-wheel drive
**Chassis:** separate steel assembly with tubular main and bracing members
**Suspension:** independent front with wishbones and transverse leaf spring; live rear axle with semi-elliptic leaf springs
**Brakes:** drums front and rear
**Bodywork:** light-alloy two-seater, open or closed styles by various coachbuilders
**Maximum speed (approx):** 135 mph (217 km/h)

# Ferrari 250 GT 1954-62

ne respected Ferrari-watcher escribed the 250 GT family as 'The eart of the Legend', and indicated how errari road-car sales mushroomed hile it was on sale: "Thirty-five cars ere produced in 1954 . . . In 1964, when e career of the 250 GT had ended, the nnual production of *gran turismo* Ferra-s was about 670 units. Thus in 10 years errari had multiplied by 20 its produc-on of touring vehicles, and without oubt the success of the 250 GT was a rimary factor . . ."

Quite simply, after five years of dilet-nte production of road cars, of thrash-g about from theme to theme, and after great deal of self-indulgence, Ferrari ad settled on the correct formula. Ex-ept for one feature, every element of e 250 GT had already been seen at aranello, but this was a cohesive and evastatingly attractive mechanical ssembly.

The original 250 GT, called the

*Above: Coachbuilders Boano produced this coupé version of the 250 GT from 1956 to 1958. This is a 1957 model with the three-litre, 220-bhp V12. Later Ellena coupés had higher roof lines.*

Europa, made its bow at the Paris Salon in October 1954. Like all previous Ferraris, the new 250 GT had a sturdy chassis frame with main members built of oval tubes; it was, however, the very first Ferrari to have coil-spring independent front suspension.

The engine was the definitive version of the original 'Colombo' design, with a capacity of 2953 cc and output of 240 bhp. It was flexible, torquey, sang gloriously round to 7,000 or even 8,000 rpm, and was in every way a sensual mechanical creation which made wonderful sounds.

Although the chassis, the sound, and

*Left: After a 250 GT won the 1956 Tour de France, the 'Tour de France' label was unofficially given to the coupés, which were bodied by Zagato, Pinin Farina and Scaglietti.*

the amazing performance were the basic ingredients of every car in the 250 GT family, body styles changed several times in almost a decade. All were Pininfarina designs, Ferrari having settled on Pininfarina (the named had changed from Pinin Farina in 1958, incidentally) to style its bodies.

The build-up was steady, but unstoppable. The 250 GT Europa, built in 1954 and 1955, used a modified version of the 375 America style, and 36 cars were made. From 1956 to 1958, a different style was produced by Carrozzeria Boano of Turin, which was later renamed Carrozzeria Ellena; about 130 models were produced.

The variety seemed endless. There were about 40 Pinin Farina-bodied Cabriolets built between 1957 and 1958, then around 350 of the classic Pininfarina

Coupé of 1958-60.

Pininfarina then went on to refine the drop-head theme in two ways. The first was a lighter car called the Spyder California, which had a 250-bhp engine. Later cars had the shorter wheelbase of the Berlinetta, and 280 bhp; there were 47 longer-wheelbase and 57 shorter-wheelbase types. The second was the Series II Cabriolet, also with 250 bhp, some 210 of which were produced from 1959 to 1962.

Each style led logically to the next, and experienced Ferrari fanatics can 'date' each body shell by the details of its headlamp treatment, by its profile in side

*Above: Confusingly, the 250 GT Spyder California looked very similar to the standard Pininfarina Cabriolet; this is a 1959 Scaglietti-built California.*

### Ferrari 250 GT Coupé
The 250 GT Pininfarina-built Coupé (1958-60) had an entirely new body style, being rather longer and more angular than the Boano/Ellena types.

### Ferrari 250 GT Spyder California, 250 GTE 2+2 and Lusso
The 250 GT Spyder California (bodied by Scaglietti) was more closely linked to the Berlinetta than to other 250 GTs,

view, or by its lamp layout or fascia.

All this activity led to two outstanding members of the family – the short-wheelbase 250 GT Berlinettas, and the sensationally sleek 250 GT Lussos.

*Above and inset: This is a 250 GT Tour de France. The 'fastback' styling with louvres was not common to all the TDF berlinettas.*

being lighter and (from late 1959) having a shorter wheelbase, and 280 bhp. The 250 GTE 2+2 and Lusso were both derived from this line.

## Specification (1955 250 GT)
**Engine:** V12, overhead-camshaft
**Bore×stroke:** 73 mm×58.8 mm
**Capacity:** 2953 cc
**Maximum power:** 240 bhp
**Transmission:** four-speed manual gearbox, rear-wheel drive
**Chassis:** separate steel frame with tubular main and cruciform members
**Suspension:** independent front with wishbones and coil springs; live rear axle with semi-elliptic leaf springs
**Brakes:** drums front and rear
**Bodywork:** aluminium two-seater coupés and cabriolets by Pinin Farina
**Maximum speed (approx):** 150 mph (241 km/h)

## Ferrari 250 GT variants

### Ferrari 250 GT Boano and Ellena
From 1956 to 1958 the 250 GT Boano and Ellena coupés took over from the original production type, the Europa coupé of 1954-55, with a lower, sleeker style, and a low oval snout in place of the Europa's rounder type.

### Ferrari 250 GT Cabriolet
The first series of Cabriolets, of 1957-58, had wide shallow grilles and cowled headlamps, with distinctive rear haunches kicking up behind the doors. The second series (1959-62; 250 bhp, and 210 built) had similar bodies, this time with exposed headlamps.

*Below: More than 30 years after they were created, the elegant, balanced lines of the Spyder California are almost impossible to fault.*

# Ferrari 410 Superamerica 1956-59

Ferrari's 410 Superamerica of 1956 was developed with two aims in mind – to be the ultimate Ferrari road car, and the fastest car in production.

Compared with the last of the America series (the 375 of 1953-55), the new 'super-Ferrari' had been extensively redesigned. Although it retained the same wheelbase as the 375 America, the new 410 Superamerica had yet another new design of chassis, this time with the coil-spring independent front suspension which had recently been adopted for the new 250 GT family.

The engine was the largest and most powerful yet fitted to a Ferrari road car – 4.9 litres of V12 and 340 bhp made it a monster by any standards. The engine had already distinguished itself in the 1954 Le Mans 24 Hours, where Gonzales' 375 Plus won the race outright.

As with the previous America types, each Superamerica was individually sold and built, so a variety of luscious two-seater styles – open or closed – was produced, nine being Pinin Farina coupés. Only 15 Series I cars were produced, the most impressive of all being the Superfast shown at the Paris Salon in October 1956.

Series II Superamericas took over in 1957, the important change being the use of a shorter wheelbase (102 in instead of 110 in), the 8-in reduction giving a smaller cabin. Only eight cars were produced in 1957; six of them were the now-familiar Pinin Farina coupé, one was another stunning 'Superfast' before the type temporarily died out.

After a year in which Ferrari concentrated on building up the 250 GT line, the Superamerica was reintroduced, this time as the 'Lampredi' 4.9-litre/400-bhp Series III type, on the same wide-track, 104-in-wheelbase chassis as the last of the Series IIs. The prototype had Pininfarina lines which signalled the way the four-seater 250 GTE would look in two years' time, and was followed by just 14 other examples in 1959, all of them being derivatives of this famous style, some with open headlamps, but some with cowled lamps.

The Series III was quite astonishingly fast, for a three-year-old car was tested by *Road & Track* in 1962, and recorded a top speed of 165 mph. Without doubt, the Series III was the world's fastest car at the time – it also offered sumptuous styling, and was extremely rare.

*Above: The louvred rear side panel was a feature of the 1959 Pininfarina-bodied 410 Superamerica.*

*Below: The very first Superamerica was this Superfast, the star of the 1956 Paris Motor Show. It looked fast and, with a 4.9-litre V12 producing 340 bhp at 6,000 rpm, it was as quick as its looks suggested, capable of a top speed of around 160 mph and 0-60 mph acceleration in just over five seconds.*

*Above: The 410 Superamerica was something of a departure for Ferrari, being the first of his road cars to have coil-spring front suspension. It was powered by an engine larger than any previous Ferrari powerplant, a 340-bhp 4.9-litre V12 giving 160-mph performance. This is a 1957 Pinin Farina example; other models were built by Ghia and Boano.*

## Specification (1956 Series I)

**Engine:** V12, single overhead camshaft per bank of cylinders
**Bore×stroke:** 88 mm×68 mm
**Capacity:** 4963 cc
**Maximum power:** 340 bhp
**Transmission:** four-speed manual gearbox, rear-wheel drive
**Chassis:** separate steel frame with tubular side members and cross-braces
**Suspension:** independent front with wishbones and coil springs; live rear axle with semi-elliptic leaf springs
**Brakes:** drums front and rear
**Bodywork:** aluminium two-seater
**Maximum speed:** 160 mph (257 km/h)

## Ferrari Testa Rossa 1956-61

*Above and right: Testa Rossa bodywork changed considerably over time. By 1960 it had lost its dramatic pontoon styling in favour of this more conventional body. This was an aerodynamic improvement and one that paid off on the long Mulsanne straight at Le Mans as the V12 Testa Rossa won the 24-hour race in 1960, driven by Olivier Gendebien and Paul Frere at an average speed of 109.17 mph, ahead of another Ferrari.*

Ferrari could be confusing in their use of model names as well as numbers, and the Testa Rossa is a fine example. The current Testarossa is all one word while the original racing car from the mid-1950s was two words, meaning 'red head' after the red-painted cam covers.

The first Testa Rossa, the 500 TR, used a light-alloy four-cylinder two-litre twin-cam engine producing a maximum of 190 bhp at 7,400 rpm. The engine was mounted in a Pininfarina-designed open two-seater alloy sports body built by Scaglietti. Chassis design was conventional except for the use of coil springs at the front rather than a leaf spring.

It was an immediate success on the racetrack, and on 24 March 1956 won at Sebring. Another victory, earned by Mike Hawthorn and Peter Collins, came at the Supercortemaggiore Grand Prix at Monza, and the 500 TR enjoyed a successful racing career in the USA.

Far better known than the 500 TR is the V12 Testa Rossa, the 250 TR, with its unique, distinctive pontoon-styled body by Scaglietti. That the shape was aerodynamically effective seemed to have been demonstrated at the 1958 Le Mans 24 Hours when the 250 TR driven by Olivier Gendebien and Graham Hill won at an average speed of 106.18 mph, but in fact the pontoon body was later discarded because of its poor aerodynamics. The Testa Rossa went on to take the Sports Car World Championship in 1958 with wins at Buenos Aires, Sebring and the Targa Florio in addition to Le Mans.

The Testa Rossa's great performance was given by a compact short-stroke V12

*Below: The most distinctive 250 TR (Testa Rossa) appeared first in 1958 with this wonderful Scaglietti-bodied design, which was intended to decrease frontal area and provide streamlined cover for the front wheels. Under the exotic bodywork was a three-litre V12 with no fewer than six Weber 38 DCN downdraught carburettors.*

f only three litres which produced a maximum of 300 bhp at 7,500 rpm when ...ed by its six Weber DCN carburettors. ...uring the course of the 1958 season the ...ar was restyled to be more aerodynamically effective and sensible mechanical ...hanges were made, with the fitting of ...isc rather than drum brakes. These ...hanges were not enough to keep the ...0 TR competitive in 1959, however, and

*Above and right: Top speed of the 300-bhp 250 TR ranged between 123 and almost 170 mph, depending on which out of no fewer than six final drive ratios was specified.*

*Below: Later 250 TRs had more sophisticated independent rear suspension, rather than the de Dion rear axle used on the early cars.*

...nreliability dogged the cars.

The Testa Rossa's career wasn't ...nded there, though, as further develop...ent (with independent rear suspension ...ather than de Dion) made the car good ...nough to win the 1960 Le Mans with ...endebien and Paul Frere leading from ...e second to the final hour. A further Le ...Mans success in 1961 helped the car

clinch the Sports Car World Championship again, and the Testa Rossa finished its career as one of the truly great sports racers.

By the end of its life, Ferrari engineer Carlo Chiti had helped produce a car that looked rather different from the first 250 TR, but it's the earlier pontoon-bodied car that lives in the memory.

*Below: The Testa Rossa's great performance was helped by its very lightweight alloy body.*

*Above: The V12 in the Testa Rossa dictated a complex multi-pipe exhaust system running exposed outside the bodywork.*

## Ferrari Testa Rossa variants

### Ferrari 330 TR/LM
This used a four-litre V12 390-bhp engine fitted in the last of the Testa Rossa bodies and it earned the TR its fourth Le Mans victory in five years, winning the 1962 event, again driven by Hill and Gendebien.

### Specification (1959 250 TR)
**Engine:** V12, overhead-cam
**Bore × stroke:** 73 mm × 58.8 mm
**Capacity:** 2953 cc
**Maximum power:** 300 bhp
**Transmission:** four-speed manual
**Chassis:** tubular steel frame
**Suspension:** independent front with wishbones and coil springs; de Dion rear with coil springs
**Brakes:** discs front and rear
**Bodywork:** open alloy two-seater
**Maximum speed (approx):** 168 mph (270 km/h)

# Ferrari 250 GT SWB 1959-63

SWB stood simply for short wheelbase, but such is the magic of Ferrari that even SWB now seems exotic when added to a Ferrari model name.

The SWB tag was appropriate, as the new model was some 5.7 inches shorter in the wheelbase than the standard 250 GT (now retrospectively known as the long-wheelbase car). The change in dimensions clearly suited Pininfarina, who were inspired to create some of their most elegant and integrated designs. Looking at a 250 GT SWB, it is hard to fault the lines from any angle.

Although a roadgoing car, the SWB was intended for competition too; in which case you would have specified the all-alloy body (which was some 200 lb lighter) rather than the standard steel affair. But to confuse the issue, even the standard steel shell featured alloy bonnet, doors and boot lid to lighten the load on the tubular steel chassis.

The Pininfarina body was not the only thing that was new when the SWB made its debut at the Paris Salon in 1959. The SWB was the first Ferrari to feature disc brakes and changes had also been made to the familiar V12 engine. The spark plugs had been located in a mild cylinder-head redesign which also featured coil – rather than hair-spring – valve springs and helped increase power output to 280 bhp at 7,000 rpm from its three litres. That was enough power to give the SWB near-150-mph

*Above: Perfectly balanced, a 250 GT SWB corners at Brands Hatch ... but this one is not being driven at full race speed.*

*Top: From the side, the shorter wheelbase of the SWB is apparent; it was some 5.7 inches less than on the previous 250 GT and helped produce a far more integrated design.*

performance (depending on the choice of body and of final drive ratio – and there was a choice of no fewer than six of those, ranging from 3.44:1 to 4.57:1).

Acceleration off the line was affected by those same choices, but the best that could be achieved was in the region of

*Above: Even under heavy cornering loads like this, the 250 GT SWB's rear wheels stayed vertical because the rear suspension system was still the traditional live axle. It was a simple, almost crude, system in which springing and location was by semi-elliptic leaf springs.*

*Below: Like most Ferraris of its era, the 250 GT SWB had a selection of final drive ratios, which affected its top speed. That could be as high as 150 mph. The same selection determined acceleration, the lowest ratio allowing 0-60 mph in around 6.5 seconds.*

*Above: Power for the SWB came from the over-square three-litre overhead-cam V12, with 280 bhp at 7,000 rpm.*

*Right: The scoop on the bonnet is surprisingly small for the volume of air that the 250 GT SWB's three thirsty downdraught Weber carburettors would consume at full throttle . . .*

*Below: This classic interior features a typical alloy wood-rim steering wheel and large, clear dials.*

*Below: The SWB's body was a combination of alloy and steel panels, the mixture of which depended on whether or not the car was a competition model. The angled vents on each wing are a distinctive SWB styling feature.*

6.5 seconds from 0-60 mph, which was impressive indeed for the late 1950s. Between 1959 and 1963 Scaglietti built no fewer than 166 Berlinetta SWBs.

## Ferrari 250 GT SWB variants

### Ferrari Spyder California

There had been a Spyder California before the SWB appeared, one built on the previous long-wheelbase chassis. The first built on the short-wheelbase chassis appeared in 1960 and Spyders were produced up to 1963, 57 being built in that time.

## Specification (1959 250 GT SWB)

**Engine:** V12, overhead-cam
**Bore × stroke:** 73 mm × 58.8 mm
**Capacity:** 2953 cc
**Maximum power:** 280 bhp
**Transmission:** four-speed manual
**Chassis:** tubular steel frame
**Suspension:** independent front with wishbones and coil springs; live rear axle with semi-elliptic leaf springs and parallel trailing arms
**Brakes:** discs front and rear
**Bodywork:** steel/alloy coupé
**Maximum speed (approx):** 150 mph (241 km/h)

# Ferrari 250 GTE 2+2 1960-63

Ferrari's first series-production four-seater (which was more properly rated as a 2+2 by those who had to ride in the back seats. . .) first appeared in public as the course car at the 1960 Le Mans 24 Hours.

After a great deal of careful planning and the relocation of the familiar three-litre V12 engine to a position eight inches further forward (the seats, pedals and steering column also moving forward to suit), Ferrari and Pininfarina managed to produce an extremely attractive style on the existing 102.2-in wheelbase, although the wheeltracks were wider and an entirely different chassis frame was provided to accommodate all this.

Mechanically, therefore, the 250 GTE was familiar to Ferrari watchers, except that a Laycock electrically-operated overdrive was added to the four-speed gearbox. The problem, never really solved, was that the two components shared the same oil, but really needed different types to work properly.

The new body style was a miracle of packaging, for it was a mere 12 in longer, and 2.4 in wider, than the existing two-seater coupé. It was also, some say, the most attractive Ferrari yet produced –

*Right: An array of instruments was supplied to monitor every possible engine function on the 250 GTE.*

Pininfarina had excelled themselves with a design which this time was built on Pininfarina's own premises.

But would a four-seater Ferrari sell? Some observers thought not. They were wrong, for the 250 GTE 2+2 was an instant success. So many orders were received that the existing two-seater coupé had to be dropped to make factory space for it. In three years, no fewer than 950 examples were built, which made it much the most successful Ferrari built to that date.

Even so, Enzo Ferrari was not content with a mere three-year career for this body. He intended to get the most out of this successful 2+2 style, the result being that he launched the 330 America before the end of 1963, and replaced the 250 GTE 2+2 with the 330 GT 2+2 in 1964.

By any standards, this Ferrari was a great success, for 500 Mk 1s and 575 Mk 2s were produced in less than four years. Its successor, unveiled in the autumn of 1967, was the even larger 365 GT 2+2.

### Ferrari 250 GTE variants

#### Ferrari 330 America
Late in 1963 an interim 330 America car was produced, matching the 77-mm × 71-mm, 300-bhp, 3967-cc V12 engine to the existing style; only 50 were produced.

#### Ferrari 330 GT (Mk 1)
The 330 GT (Mk 1) took over from the 250 GTE in 1964, complete with a 3967-cc engine, and a restyled (four-headlamp) nose and tail; 500 were built.

*Left: Like all 250s, the GTE had a three-litre V12. Ultimate power was not a consideration in the GTE, and the engine was tuned to deliver 240 bhp, less than in the sporting models.*

*Below: The styling on the 250 GTE was relatively sombre and restrained, but well-balanced. Although a 2+2, it was little longer than Ferrari's two-seater coupés.*

### Ferrari 330 GT (Mk 2)
The 330 GT (Mk 2) kept the same engine, this time matched to a five-speed gearbox, with centre-lock aluminium wheels and optional power steering, plus a two-headlamp nose style; 575 were produced.

### Specification (1960 250 GTE 2+2)
**Engine:** V12, overhead-cam
**Bore × stroke:** 73 mm × 58.8 mm
**Capacity:** 2953 cc
**Maximum power:** 240 bhp
**Transmission:** four-speed manual gearbox and overdrive, rear-wheel drive
**Chassis:** separate steel frame with oval tubular section side members and cruciform braces
**Suspension:** independent front with wishbones and coil springs; live rear axle with semi-elliptic leaf springs
**Brakes:** discs front and rear
**Bodywork:** steel 2+2-seater coupé
**Maximum speed:** 150 mph (241 km/h)

## Ferrari 400 Superamerica 1960-64

were all very fast, expensive and self-indulgent machines and, as forecast by the model name, most were sold to American buyers. Standard cars could reach 150 mph, but at least one car, enlarged to 4.6 litres, was clocked at 180 mph by *Road & Track* magazine.

Except that the wheelbase was lengthened to 102.2 inches from the end of 1962 on the last 23 cars, the Type 400 was mechanically little changed in five years, for compared with the three-litre types it was only a small part of the business at Maranello. Most of the extra length seems to have been concentrated behind the seats, to provide more accommodation.

The last of these truly large-engined Ferraris was the 500 Superfast, which took over from the 400 SA in 1964. Yet again it was an amalgam of existing Ferrari features, though with a unique 104.3-in wheelbase (it was easy to alter tube lengths in this simple chassis design), and with yet another unique engine.

*Left and below: The 400 came after the 410 Superamerica; that's the sort of confusion that occurs with Ferrari's model-numbering system, which relates only to engine size – in this case a four-litre V12.*

Even though they sold only in small numbers, Ferrari were always wedded to the idea of marketing amazingly powerful, ultra-large-engined cars. The America and Superamerica models of the 1950s had surely not been commercially successful – but Ferrari decided to repeat the trick for the 1960s.

The first of the new-generation cars was the Type 400 Superamerica, which first appeared at the Brussels Salon in January 1960. Although it carried forward a famous Ferrari model name, it was technically very different, and for the first time ever its model name did *not* reflect the capacity of one cylinder.

This time the rolling chassis was based on the current 250 GT layout and had a surprisingly shorter wheelbase – 95 inches – but the engine was a new V12. Mechanically, in fact, there were many obvious links with the 250 GTE/330 GT.

As the largest-yet derivative of the original 'Colombo' engine (which had started life in 1947 as a 1.5-litre unit), the 400 Superamerica's engine displaced no less than 3967 cc – the combination of a 77-mm bore and a 71-mm stroke, both the largest yet seen in this basic cylinder block. This was a considerably smaller and lighter engine than the 4.9-litre engine of the deposed Type 410, the whole car being lighter than before.

The power output was quoted at 340 bhp – not as much as that of the Series III Type 410 Superamerica which it replaced, but probably just as effective on the road. As on the latest three-litre Ferraris, this engine was coupled to an overdrive transmission.

Most of the 48 cars were built with what is now known as Pininfarina 'Aerodinamico' coupé bodywork, but there were many individual differences between cars, and a few specially-built cars were dubbed 'Superfast'. These

*Below: After the 400 Superamerica came the 500 Superfast, which appeared in 1964 – a variation on the same theme with an even larger, five-litre, V12.*

The Superfast's physically larger V12, although having a familiar displacement of 4963 cc, was really an amalgam of 'Lampredi' and 'Colombo' features – but there was no doubting its performance, for it was rated at 400 bhp (like the last of the Type 410 SAs), and produced a top speed of up to 170 mph.

The first 25 cars had the four-speed-plus-overdrive transmission, while the last 12 had the latest five-speed transmission, but no overdrive. Every car built between 1964 and the summer of 1966 had the same wonderfully sleek Pininfarina style of two-seater coupé body, with a nose like that of the final 330 GT model, and a long tail which was a smoothed-out derivative of the Coupé Aerodinamico version of the Type 400 SA.

At the time, this very exclusive Ferrari model was probably the fastest road car on sale anywhere in the world.

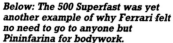

*Below: The 500 Superfast was yet another example of why Ferrari felt no need to go to anyone but Pininfarina for bodywork.*

*Top and above: The 500 Superfast could have such a long, sloping rear as there were no back-seat passengers to worry about.*

*Above: Longer than the 400 Superamerica, the 500 Superfast was still only a two-seater coupé.*

## Ferrari 400 Superamerica variants

### Ferrari 500 Superfast

This car took over from the 400 Superamerica in 1964, using the same longer-wheelbase chassis, and a smoothed-out version of the Pininfarina coupé body. Its engine was a different and larger 88-mm × 68-mm V12, of 4963 cc, producing 400 bhp. The last 12 cars had a new five-speed gearbox as used in the 330 GT.

### Specification (1960 400 Superamerica)

**Engine:** V12, overhead-cam
**Bore × stroke:** 77 mm × 71 mm
**Capacity:** 3967 cc
**Maximum power:** 340 bhp
**Transmission:** four-speed manual gearbox and overdrive, rear-wheel drive
**Chassis:** separate steel frame with oval tubular main and cruciform bracing members
**Suspension:** independent front with wishbones and coil springs; live rear axle with semi-elliptic leaf springs
**Brakes:** discs front and rear
**Bodywork:** steel and aluminium two-seater coupé or cabriolet
**Maximum speed:** 150 mph (241 km/h)

## Ferrari 250 GTO 1961-64

*Left and below: No fewer than six downdraught Weber carburettors were needed to feed the 250 GTO's three-litre V12. This example is luxuriously trimmed in leather.*

*Above: A GTO at speed. The three air vents in the nose are open here to allow more air to cool the tightly packaged V12. Top speed, depending on gearing, was as high as 170 mph.*

The GTO was developed from another set of initials, the SWB, but while it was clear that SWB meant 'short wheelbase' there was confusion about GTO. Some claimed it stood for *Gran Turismo Omologato;* in other words, the title referred to the fact that this was the homologated racing version of the 250 GT SWB.

Although the SWB was fast, its aero-dynamics could have been better and the GTO's design overcame that problem. The body, built on the SWB chassis, was designed by Bizzarrini with the aid of a wind tunnel, which produced the low nose and high tail. The surprising thing about the GTO was that Ferrari managed to persuade the racing authorities that the car was an evolution of the SWB and not the virtually new design that it appeared to be.

Curiously, a live rear axle was re-tained but at least it was well located, with parallel trailing arms and the addi-tion of a Watts linkage to improve loca-tion. Power came from the Colombo-de-signed three-litre V12, dry-sumped to permit a low bonnet line.

With 300 bhp on tap and superior aerodynamics, the GTO could exceed 170 mph on a long enough straight and the car was an immediate success on the track, winning the Manufacturers' title in the Sports Car World Championship in its first season, 1961, then again in 1963 and 1964.

The GTO's track record was impres-sive indeed, with class wins in the Sebr-ing 12 Hours, Targa Florio, Spa 1000 km, and Le Mans, where it also finished second overall in 1962 and 1963.

Ferrari never intended the GTO to be used as a road car, despite its having suf-ficient equipment (bar a speedo) to be easily made legal.

*Below: The GTO's longer, lower, nose was Ferrari's successful attempt to make his sports-racing cars more aerodynamically efficient than the 250 GT SWB.*

In all, 40 GTOs were built – well short of the 100 that should have been required to homologate a car so different from the 250 GT SWB.

## Ferrari 250 GTO variants

### Ferrari GTO four-litre

As the GTO was a racing, rather than a production, model there were differences from car to car, depending on the state of development at the time. There were many detail changes, but the most significant model difference was between the original three-litre cars and the four-litre (3967-cc) models. There were only three four-litre cars built, with 390 bhp at 7,500 rpm. They can be identified by a large, unsightly power bulge in the bonnet.

### Ferrari GTO/64

By 1964 the GTO needed wider wheels and tyres to remain competitive. This necessitated a redesign which lacked the dramatic lines of the original style.

*Above: The 330 LMB derivative was quicker than the 250 GTO, as it had the GTO's aerodynamics with more power – 400 bhp at 7,500 rpm.*

*Below: Engine-cover detailing was old-fashioned on the GTO, with a curious combination of leather straps and chrome.*

*Above and below: The distinctive nose treatment of the GTO was used with only subtle variation on the later, larger-engined, four-litre 330 LMB.*

## Specification (1962 250 GTO)

**Engine:** V12, overhead-cam
**Bore × stroke:** 73 mm × 58.8 mm
**Capacity:** 2953 cc
**Maximum power:** 300 bhp
**Transmission:** five-speed manual
**Chassis:** tubular steel frame
**Suspension:** independent front with wishbones, coil springs and anti-roll bar; live rear axle with semi-elliptic leaf springs, trailing arms and Watts linkage
**Brakes:** discs front and rear
**Bodywork:** aluminium alloy two-door coupé
**Maximum speed (approx):** 170 mph (274 km/h)

# Ferrari 250 GT Berlinetta Lusso 1962-64

Ferrari's most beautiful 250 GT road car, the Lusso ('luxury') was also the most numerous, for 350 were produced between 1962 and 1964. It was an eagerly-awaited car because the previous 250 GT Coupé had been dropped in 1960. For more than two years, therefore, the only closed road cars available to Ferrari customers had been the steel-bodied, short-wheelbase Berlinetta (really a slightly detuned racing car) and the larger 250 GT 2+2.

The Lusso (the *official* name of which was actually 250 GT Pininfarina Berlinetta 1963) was the sleekest Ferrari road car yet put on sale. Earlier cars had been impressive and attractive, but somehow brutal; the new car was so smooth that many felt tempted to stroke its flanks for the sheer pleasure of the experience.

In many ways the Lusso was a civilised version of the short-wheelbase Berlinetta, or the 250 GTO, for it used the same type of compact, 94.4-in-wheelbase chassis, allied to disc brakes, yet had a 250-bhp version of the famous three-litre V12 engine and a four-speed gearbox. It was, of course, a 150-mph machine, and handled in the same way as other contemporary three-litre Ferraris – but in this case it was the body style which made the headlines.

Here was a car which had a smoother and simpler nose than any previous Ferrari; there was one long sweep of wing line from front to rear, and at the rear there was a panoramic rear window – the largest yet used on a Ferrari – allied to a sharply cut-off 'Kamm' tail. The ensemble, built by Scaglietti (as many future Ferraris were to be), was irresistible. By a considerable margin, it sold better than any other two-seater 250 GT type.

What could be better than a Lusso? It would have to be an amazing machine. That successor duly appeared in the shape of the 275 GTB of 1964.

## Specification (1962)

**Engine:** V12, overhead-cam
**Bore × stroke:** 73 mm × 58.8 mm
**Capacity:** 2953 cc
**Maximum power:** 250 bhp
**Transmission:** four-speed manual gearbox, rear-wheel drive
**Chassis:** separate steel frame with oval-section tubular side members and cruciform braces
**Suspension:** independent front with wishbones and coil springs; live rear axle with semi-elliptic leaf springs
**Brakes:** discs front and rear
**Bodywork:** steel two-seater coupé
**Maximum speed:** 150 mph (241 km/h)

*Above: The 250 GT Berlinetta Lusso is arguably the most beautiful of all Ferraris, let alone the huge 250 GT range. It was lower and sleeker than the SWB type.*

*Below: The small chrome overriders below the headlamps provide a distinctive finishing touch to the Scaglietti-built Pininfarina design of the Berlinetta Lusso.*

*Left: The cut-off tail, with its raised lip for downforce, was a useful feature in a car capable of 150 mph thanks to its 250 bhp.*

*Below: Perfect bodywork hid a straightforward tubular frame chassis, live rear axle and three-litre V12 with four-speed gearbox.*

## Ferrari 250 LM 1963-66

This was a departure for Ferrari, being their first mid-engined 'production' sports-racer. It was never homologated, so always ran in prototype classes.

In fact the 250 LM was developed from the 250 P ('P' for prototype) of 1963. That was an out-and-out racer with the same V12 as used in the Testa Rossa and an output of 310 bhp at 7,500 rpm. As its dry weight was a mere 1,520 lb it was blindingly fast, with a maximum speed of 178 mph.

The 250 P's competition debut came in the USA at the Sebring 12 Hours; it was a successful debut, too, as John Surtees and Ludovico Scarfiotti drove it to victory, ahead of another two 250 Ps in second and third spots. That was no fluke, as the car's performance in the Le Mans 24 Hours later in the year proved. This time with Lorenzo Bandini partnering Scarfiotti, the 250 P won at an average speed of 118.5 mph. The combination of the V12's power and the nimble handling brought about by the car's mid-engined configuration made it extremely competitive.

Ferrari had always intended to produce a dual-purpose road/competition version of the 250 P, and this was first shown in October 1963 at the Paris Motor Show as the 250 LM. The 250 P's distinctive rear wing had become the rear of the 250 LM's closed cockpit, but otherwise the cars looked similar. When the 250 LM went into limited production, however, the rear side roof section was extended and air intakes for the mid-mounted V12 fitted over the rear wings.

Although in theory the 250 LM appeared to be a usable road car, in reality it was built for racing, and had a very successful record to prove it, both in Europe and the USA, winning 10 major races in 1964.

*Above: Ferrari's mid-engined 250 P (for prototipo) won at Le Mans in 1963. Until then Ferrari had relied on front-engined Grand Touring cars, like the legendary 250 GTO and the 330 LM, for races like Le Mans, Sebring and Daytona.*

*Below: Ferrari built the 250 P to fight back against Ford, who were developing the GT40 to win at Le Mans. A mid-engined Ferrari had won the Formula 1 Championship in 1961, convincing Ferrari of the correctness of the layout.*

Its greatest hour came in the 1965 Le Mans 24 Hours. It was a surprise victory, as the car was lying a lowly 14th after eight hours. But by the 11th hour the car, driven by Jochen Rindt and Masten Gregory, had moved to third place, and that became second during the next hour. The lead was taken from the 21st to the last hour and the Rindt/Gregory car won, averaging an excellent 121.07 mph and leading home a Ferrari 1-2-3.

The first 250 LM was powered by Ferrari's 2953-cc V12 engine with the same 300-bhp output as the 250 TR Testa Rossa; the difference was that the V12 was mid-mounted. Later 250 LMs used the 3.3-litre V12 with an improved output of 320 bhp at 7,500 rpm.

The engine was held in the car's tubular steel frame, and mounted behind the cabin with the transmission to the rear of the car.

By this stage virtually every Ferrari was styled by Pininfarina and the 250 LM was no exception, although it's arguable whether Pininfarina really came to grips with a mid-engined layout.

LM construction was by Scaglietti and a total of 32 cars was built over a period of three years from 1963 to 1966.

## Specification (1965)

**Engine:** V12, overhead-cam
**Bore × stroke:** 77 mm × 58.8 mm
**Capacity:** 3286 cc
**Maximum power:** 320 bhp
**Transmission:** five-speed manual
**Chassis:** tubular steel frame
**Suspension:** independent front and rear, each with coil springs and wishbones
**Brakes:** discs front and rear
**Bodywork:** alloy two-seater sports coupé
**Maximum speed (approx):** 160 mph (257 km/h)

*Below: The mid-mounted 3.3-litre V12 gave the 250 LM enough performance to hold its own with supercars made 25 years later. It can accelerate from 0-100 mph in about 12 seconds – roughly the same as the latest Porsche 911 Turbo.*

*Above: The racing regulations of the time stated that the 250 LM had to be a dual-purpose car – as well as racing, it had to be able to carry two people (although it would only ever race one-up) and it needed to have enough ground clearance to be suitable for road use.*

*Below: An all-time classic. Although it's 30 years old, the 250 LM's specification reads like a modern supercar – mid-mounted V12, limited-slip differential, disc brakes all round, double-wishbone suspension and coil springs front and rear. It's rather more exclusive, though – just 32 were made.*

# Ferrari 275 GTB 1964-68

When the time came to replace the marvellously successful 250 GT Lusso, Ferrari did it with a much more advanced design – the 275 GTB. Here, for the very first time on a Ferrari road car, was a chassis with independent rear suspension, and with the gearbox in unit with the rear axle.

The result was a car closer to being a roadgoing racing car than any model which Ferrari had sold in recent years. It was very fast (the top speed was well over 150 mph), it had very nimble handling, and it also had a Pininfarina body which combined all the best visual styling 'cues' of the 250 GTO and 250 GT Lusso.

Although the chassis frame was new, it was still built up of a mixture of oval-section and other tubes, strictly in a 'ladder-style' layout, and retained the familiar 94.5-in wheelbase. The engine was a further development of the V12 used in the long-running 250 GTs, though with a larger cylinder bore, dry-sump lubrication and more mid-range torque. Normally it was supplied with three carburettors and 280 bhp, but a six-carburettor/320-bhp engine was also available.

Apart from the all-independent suspension, the real technical advance was provided by a new transaxle, where the five-speed gearbox was in unit with the chassis-mounted rear differential. This improved the weight distribution, and also allowed more space for the passengers. The clutch was still bolted to the engine flywheel, while the propeller shaft was originally a slim, solid-section member, with a central steady bearing.

The Pininfarina style was wickedly attractive, featuring a smoothly detailed nose with cowled headlamps, a short cabin with rather restricted glass area, and a GTO/Lusso-like cut-off tail with a transverse spoiler.

Original cars had what later became known as the short-nose body, but from late 1965 a longer nose was featured. At the same time the engine and rear-mounted transmission were joined together by a stout torque tube.

As with most such Ferraris, the 275

GTB was merely the start of a series of cars. At the end of 1966 the original coupé gave way to the 275 GTB/4, which had a twin-cam version of the same 3.3-litre engine. The heads themselves had already been used, and well-proved, in Ferrari racing-sports cars of the late 1950s; the result was an even more sporty engine which produced 300 bhp, and gave the car a top speed of at least 160 mph.

This was the chassis that smoothly provided Ferrari's road cars with up-to-date suspension to match their engines and their styling. The 365 GTB/4 Daytona which followed was an even more sensational machine.

A total of 250 'short-nose' 275 GTBs, 205 'long-nose' GTBs, and 280 GTB/4s was produced in four years.

## Ferrari 275 GTB variants

### Ferrari 275 GTB/4
This was the second version of the 275 GTB, with twin-cam cylinder heads and 300 bhp.

### Ferrari NART Spyder
Commissioned by Luigi Chinetti of the USA, this was a convertible version of the 275 GTB/4, but only nine cars were produced.

### Ferrari 275 GTS, 330 GTS and 365 GTS
These were convertibles using the same basic chassis and suspension layout as their GTB counterparts.

## Specification (1964 275 GTB)

**Engine:** V12, overhead-cam
**Bore × stroke:** 77 mm × 58.8 mm
**Capacity:** 3286 cc
**Maximum power:** 280 bhp
**Transmission:** five-speed manual gearbox, rear-wheel drive
**Chassis:** separate steel frame with oval tubular main members and cross-braces
**Suspension:** independent front and rear, each with wishbones and coil springs
**Brakes:** discs front and rear
**Bodywork:** steel two-seater fastback coupé
**Maximum speed:** 153 mph (246 km/h)

*Above: This later 'long-nose' GTB has a slightly smaller radiator air intake than the earlier 'short-nose' cars. The longer nose improved aerodynamic efficiency, although the car was already very fast.*

*Above: Three Weber twin-choke carburettors supplied fuel for the standard engine. A 320-bhp competition version, with six carburettors, was also available.*

*Below: In this classic instrument layout, matching speedometer and rev-counter flank water temperature and oil pressure gauges, with the minor instruments over to the left.*

*Below: The rear-mounted gearbox gave the 275 GTB an almost 50/50 weight distribution. This even balance, along with the independent rear suspension, produced good handling and roadholding.*

# Ferrari 275 GTS Spider 1964–66

When Ferrari introduced the 275 GTB, the company also commissioned Pininfarina to design *and* produce an alternative convertible spider version. This car was a direct replacement for the 250 GT Spyder California, and eventually led to the development of two further types – the 330 GTS, and the 365 GTS, which finally died in 1969.

Mechanically, the 275 GTS was identical to the 275 GTB, except for the use of old-style wire-spoke wheels, but the body style was entirely different, with visual links to the new 330 GT. It was much less of a high-speed 'racing' road car, and more of a high-speed open-top tourer. Naturally, it was popular in North America, where most of the 200 cars built in two years were delivered.

Ferrari then produced the 330 GTS from 1966 to 1968. This was a typically resourceful 'Ferrari cocktail', for the chassis was as before, the engine was the same 300-bhp/four-litre V12 as then currently used in the 330 GT four-seater, while the modified nose style was almost the same as that to be found on the new 330 GTC coupé, and the 275 GTB's cast-alloy road wheels were standardised.

Just 100 such cars were produced before yet another derivative, the 365 GTS, took over for 1969. This was yet another 'mix-and-match' product, for this time the engine was the same 320-bhp/4.4-litre V12 as used in the 365 GT 2 + 2. The only styling change was the elimination of cooling louvres in the flanks, and the fitment of new louvres in the bonnet top to reduce underbonnet temperatures.

*Below: The wide air intake, with a centrally-mounted 'prancing horse' badge, was typical of Ferrari's road cars in the mid-1960s. Note that, although the car has right-hand drive, the windscreen wipers are still set up for left-hand drive.*

By this time, though, American interest in such an old-fashioned style of Ferrari had waned, and only 20 cars were built. These were the last Pininfarina-built convertibles to be offered by Ferrari for some time.

*Right: The sloping bonnet and raised rear wings are the hallmarks of a 1960s Pininfarina design. Pininfarina's Fiat 1500S and Fiat 124 Spider had the same features.*

*Below: Earlier versions of the GTS had 14-in Borrani wire wheels, with 185-section tyres. The wheels were changed during 1965 to light-alloy units.*

## Ferrari 275 GTS variants

### Ferrari 330 GTS
Using the same chassis and basic styling, this car had a 77-mm × 71-mm, 3967-cc/300-bhp V12 engine, and cast-alloy road wheels.

### Ferrari 365 GTS
Still using the same basic chassis and body style, this derivative had an 81-mm × 71-mm, 4390-cc/320-bhp engine.

## Specification (1964 275 GTS)
**Engine:** V12, overhead-cam
**Bore × stroke:** 77 mm × 58.8 mm
**Capacity:** 3286 cc
**Maximum power:** 280 bhp
**Transmission:** five-speed manual gearbox, rear-wheel drive
**Chassis:** separate steel frame, ladder-style, with oval tubular main and bracing members
**Suspension:** independent front and rear, each with wishbones and coil springs
**Brakes:** discs front and rear
**Bodywork:** steel two-seater style by Pininfarina
**Maximum speed:** 145 mph (233 km/h)

## Ferrari 365 California 1966-67

Although only 14 of these cars were made, they are an ideal indication of the way Ferrari could mix and match all their mechanical components, commission Pininfarina to produce yet another stunning body style, and offer a new model. This time the intention was to replace the 500 Superfast, but with an open car.

Mechanically, the 365 California used the same rolling chassis, suspension and transmission as the last of the 500 Superfast types, but reverted to a smaller engine, this being an enlarged version of the V12 already being fitted to 330 GT road cars. Power-assisted steering was standard, while the 330 GT's alloy wheels were optional.

The only true novelty was the body style, and even that had the same basic nose and front panels as the 500 Superfast. Behind the screen, though, it was a gracious two-seater cabriolet layout, with long indents/scoops let into the doors, and with a sharply cut-off tail.

One thing that was certainly not sharply cut off, though, was the front of the car, even though Ferrari had decided that the extremely high per-

*Below: One of the last Ferraris with a live rear axle, the California had a dramatic Pininfarina body.*

formance of the 365 California dictated the use of four headlamps rather than the standard two. That was achieved by placing the main beams behind two circular flaps which were, at first glance, almost unnoticeable, thus preserving the smooth lines of the nose. The clean lines of the 365 California helped its performance too; in its day it was the fastest production convertible in the world, in addition to being the rarest.

It was the final model of this *very*-limited-production line, the last of which was delivered in July 1967.

### Specification (1966)

**Engine:** V12, single overhead camshaft per bank of cylinders
**Bore × stroke:** 81 mm × 71 mm
**Capacity:** 4390 cc
**Maximum power:** 320 bhp
**Transmission:** five-speed manual gearbox, rear-wheel drive
**Chassis:** separate steel frame with oval tubular main and bracing members
**Suspension:** independent front with wishbones and coil springs; live rear axle with semi-elliptic leaf springs
**Brakes:** discs front and rear
**Bodywork:** steel two-seater cabriolet
**Maximum speed (approx):** 150 mph (241 km/h)

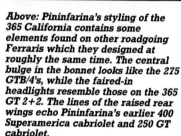

*Above: Pininfarina's styling of the 365 California contains some elements found on other roadgoing Ferraris which they designed at roughly the same time. The central bulge in the bonnet looks like the 275 GTB/4's, while the faired-in headlights resemble those on the 365 GT 2+2. The lines of the raised rear wings echo Pininfarina's earlier 400 Superamerica cabriolet and 250 GT cabriolet.*

*Below: The California was Ferrari's luxury two-seater model for 1966; the 365 GTB/4 (Daytona) would fill the same role two years later. One of the rarest Ferraris, total production amounted to just 14 Californias, of which only two had right-hand drive. The California was luxuriously equipped – it was even fitted with air conditioning so that with the hood up, the interior could be kept cool.*

# Ferrari 330 GTC 1966-68

Here was a perfect example of the way that Ferrari could – and did – mix-and-match various features in their production-car range. At the beginning of 1966 there was a big marketing gap between the 275 GTB two-seater coupé and the 330 GT 2+2 four-seater saloon, so Ferrari decided to fill it with an intermediate model. The result was the 330 GTC.

The basis of the new car was the chassis, suspension and transmission of the existing 275 GTB – complete with 94.5-in wheelbase, and rear-mounted five-speed transaxle – matched to the four-litre engine of the 330 GT 2+2 saloon.

The body shell, by Pininfarina (where the production cars were also assembled), was all-new, being a two-seater coupé with a larger cockpit than that of the 275 GTB. There was some commonality with other Pininfarina styles, for the nose was near-identical with that of the 330 GTS or the 500 Superfast, the tail was similar to that of the 330 GT 2+2, and the cabin, though shorter, was also like that of the 330 GT 2+2.

Like every other Ferrari of the period, the 330 GTC was a very fast car, and it was also an intriguing mixture of 275 GTB handling characteristics with the practicality of the 330 GT 2+2. It was also a quieter and more civilised car than the 275 GTB.

Between 1966 and the end of 1968 Ferrari sold 600 of these cars, compared with a mere 150 of the larger-engined 365 GTC in 1969 and 1970.

The 330 GTC's replacement, another short-lived Ferrari model, was the 365 GTC/4 which ran only from 1971 to 1972.

*Above: The driver has a full set of instruments, dominated by the large matching speedometer and rev counter. The interior is luxuriously trimmed in leather. Note the open gate at the base of the gear lever, with a slot for each gear position.*

*Left: Although the overall shape of the GTC is broadly similar to the later, single-headlight 330 GTS, there are detail differences, such as the GTC's smaller rear side windows, shorter nose and flared wheel arches.*

*Below: The GTC's double-wishbone suspension keeps all four wheels parallel to the car's vertical axis, but the soft suspension, set up for fast road use, allows a fair amount of body roll.*

## Ferrari 330 GTC variants

### Ferrari 365 GTC
This car took over from the 330 GTC from 1968 to 1970. The engine was an 81-mm × 71-mm V12 of 4390 cc/320 bhp – the same as that used in the 365 GT4 2+2. Except for the repositioning of engine-bay cooling vents – in the bonnet instead of in the sides of the front wings – there were no visual changes. It had a top speed of 151 mph (243 km/h).

## Specification (1966 330 GTC)

**Engine:** V12, single overhead camshaft per bank of cylinders
**Bore × stroke:** 77 mm × 71 mm
**Capacity:** 3967 cc
**Maximum power:** 300 bhp
**Transmission:** five-speed manual gearbox, rear-wheel drive
**Chassis:** separate steel frame with oval tubular main and cross-bracing members
**Suspension:** independent front and rear, each with wishbones and coil springs
**Brakes:** discs front and rear
**Bodywork:** steel two-seater coupé
**Maximum speed:** 143 mph (230 km/h)

*Right: For the 365 GTC, Ferrari fitted air vents in the bonnet, not in the front wings.*

## Ferrari 365 GT 2+2 1967-71

Ferrari's first four-seater model, the 250 GTE/330 GT 2+2 family, had sold very well between 1960 and 1967, so its replacement, the 365 GT 2+2, had to be good to avoid disappointing the clientele.

This new car was launched in 1967, and proved to be one of the largest and heaviest Ferraris of all. Like the cars it replaced, the body was styled and constructed by Pininfarina, and was a long, graceful 2+2 coupé, with a nose rather like that of the 500 Superfast, and a cut-off tail which echoed other Ferraris of the period.

It was extremely well-equipped, with air conditioning as an option, with self-levelling rear suspension and – for the very first time on a Ferrari – with power-assisted steering.

Under the graceful skin, however, there was yet another amalgam of well-developed Ferrari components. Like the old 250 GTE/330 GT 2+2 models, the chassis ran on a 104.25-in wheelbase, but the rear suspension was independent, as in the 275 GTB. To confuse matters further, however, the five-speed gearbox was mounted up front, in unit with the engine, and there was a new rear axle design.

The engine was the latest statement of single-overhead-cam V12 engineering and, at 4.4 litres, produced 320 reliable horsepower. That made it the most powerful Ferrari road car on sale (the 365 California had just been discontinued) and explains why it could achieve more than 150 mph even though it weighed more than 3,500 lb and could carry four passengers.

Before long, however, Ferrari used this engine in the 365 GTS and the 365 GTC, and once the Daytona came into production with an engine of the same capacity, there was a remarkable degree of continuity across the range.

Those who never drove the 365 GT 2+2 were ready to criticise it as too large and too heavy to be a 'genuine' Ferrari. Those who *did* drive it were invariably captivated. To quote the eminent French journalist Jose Rosinski: "...all brutality has been carefully banished. But miraculously the vehicle has not by any means been emasculated or even corrupted..."

While the 365 GT 2+2 was in production, it represented more than 50 per cent of all Ferrari road-car assembly, which shows how successful a model it was; 800 were produced.

*Below: Pininfarina managed to give the 365 GT 2+2 habitable rear seats and a decent-sized luggage boot, but some enthusiasts say that the result, with its long rear overhang, is a less balanced design.*

*Above: Cromodora alloy wheels were the standard fitment, but Borrani wire wheels were available as optional extras.*

*Below: There was adequate leg room in the back when the front seats were pushed forward, but rear head room was limited.*

### Specification (1967)

**Engine:** V12, single overhead camshaft per bank of cylinders
**Bore × stroke:** 81 mm × 71 mm
**Capacity:** 4390 cc
**Maximum power:** 320 bhp
**Transmission:** five-speed manual gearbox in unit with engine, rear-wheel drive
**Chassis:** separate steel frame with oval tubular main and cross-bracing members
**Suspension:** independent front and rear, each with wishbones and coil springs
**Brakes:** discs front and rear
**Bodywork:** steel two-door four-seater coupé
**Maximum speed:** 152 mph (245 km/h)

*Left: Ferrari and Pininfarina designed the 365 GT 2+2 for Grand Touring, which means comfort as well as speed. The car had power-assisted steering and brakes, electric windows, leather upholstery and was fully carpeted. Air conditioning was an optional extra.*

# Ferrari 365 GTB/4 Daytona 1968-73

After the 275 GTB and GTB/4 ranges had been in production for four years, they were dropped to make way for an absolutely phenomenal new model – the 365 GTB/4 Daytona. There is no question that this was the best, the fastest and the most beautiful front-engined Ferrari road car ever built.

'Daytona' was really only an unofficial title. It appeared because Ferrari had completed an astonishing 1-2-3 line-abreast finish in the Daytona 24-hour race in 1967, and because sales of the new model were likely to be concentrated in the USA – the word Daytona never appeared on the bodywork of the car, nor in the sales brochures!

The 275 GTB/4 had been a remarkably fast and glamorous berlinetta – yet the Daytona was better in all respects. Not

*Above: One of the world's most desirable cars. Many Daytona Spyders started life as coupés.*

only was it Pininfarina's finest front-engined two-seater style for Ferrari, but it had a top speed of at least 170 mph.

Its basis was the same chassis as that of the 275 GTB/4, which is to say that it had wishbone independent front and rear suspension, a five-speed gearbox located in unit with the rear axle, and a rigid torque tube connecting the engine to the transaxle. There was a new type of five-spoke cast-alloy road wheel, and ventilated disc brakes took the place of the 275 GTB/4's solid discs, but in every case the heritage of the design was obvious.

The heart of the Daytona was the

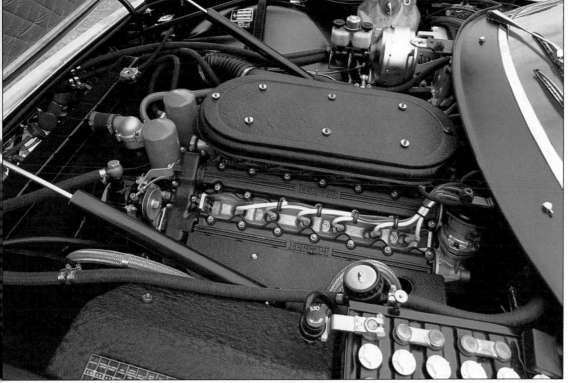

*Above: All the ingredients for Grand Touring are here: plenty of room for two, lots of instruments, and a 'prancing horse' badge ...*

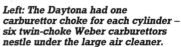

*Left: The Daytona had one carburettor choke for each cylinder – six twin-choke Weber carburettors nestle under the large air cleaner.*

4390-cc engine which, although of a familiar capacity, was new in almost every way. Like that of the 275 GTB/4, it had twin cams per cylinder bank, and there was dry-sump lubrication, but it was much larger – 4390 cc instead of 3286 cc – and produced an extremely impressive 352 bhp at 7,500 rpm, and the even more impressive peak torque figure of 318 lb ft at 5,500 rpm.

The Pininfarina style featured a long shark-like nose, a small cabin set well back on the chassis, a sweeping roof line, two seats, and a small luggage compartment. The headlamps were hidden behind glazed panels at first, for European sale. USA models (and cars for all markets, in due course) had flip-up headlamps instead.

Everyone who could afford to buy a Daytona made haste to do so – the result being that in less than five years 1,284 coupés were sold. Dismissed by some as a 'truck' – there was no power steering, and the tide was running against front-engined two-seaters – the Daytona exhilarated everyone by its performance.

*Autocar* tested a UK-market car in 1971 and suggested that it was the fastest road car in the world, quoting a 171 mph top speed, 0-60 mph acceleration in 5.4 seconds, 0-100 mph in 12.6 seconds, and 0-150 mph in a mere 31.5 seconds. Who cared if the fuel consumption was a greedy 14 mpg? In 1971 the Daytona cost only £9,582!

## Ferrari 365 GTB/4 variants

### Ferrari 365 GTS/4

This was the open Spyder version of the Daytona, which – because it offered open-top motoring – became even more desirable in the classic-conscious era of the late 1980s. Far fewer Spyders than coupés were made; only 122 were produced between 1969 and 1973.

Technically this car was identical to the coupé, except for the use of wire-spoke wheels. In recent years, incidentally, a considerable number of coupés have been 'recreated' as Spyders, theoretically to make them more valuable. This only applies to people who do not know the difference between the real thing and a conversion. Learned books by Daytona fanatics make the differences very clear. . .

*Above: From mid-1971, the Daytona had retractable headlights in place of the original faired-in units. This Daytona has been fitted with flared wheel arches and wide wheels for racing.*

*Below: At home on fast, sweeping bends, the Daytona is a well-balanced car for fast cornering, thanks to the heavy gearbox being fitted in unit with the differential at the rear of the car.*

## Specification (1968 365 GTB/4 Daytona)

**Engine:** V12, quad-cam
**Bore × stroke:** 81 mm × 71 mm
**Capacity:** 4390 cc
**Maximum power:** 352 bhp
**Transmission:** five-speed manual gearbox in unit with rear-mounted differential, rear-wheel drive
**Chassis:** separate steel frame with oval tubular main and cross-bracing members
**Suspension:** independent front and rear, each with wishbones, coil springs and anti-roll bar
**Brakes:** discs front and rear
**Bodywork:** steel two-seater fastback coupé
**Maximum speed (approx):** 170 mph (274 km/h)

*Below: The Daytona was quite big for a two-seater. In order to keep the weight down, the doors, bonnet and boot lid were made from aluminium. Even so, the complete car weighed over one and a half tons with its steel chassis and body shell.*

# Ferrari 365 GTC/4 1971-72

In some ways the 365 GTC/4 has become the 'forgotten Ferrari', for it was on sale for less than two years, and although 500 such cars were built and sold it always seemed to be overshadowed by the 365 GTB/4 Daytona.

To put the 365 GTC/4 in context, therefore, it was effectively the replacement for the 330 GTC/365 GTC model, between the two-seater Daytona and four-seater 365 GT4 2+2. Actually, because the new 365 GTC/4 occupied the production line recently vacated by the 365 GT 2+2, in fact (if not in marketing terms) it replaced that model too.

For this car, there was yet another amalgam of current Ferrari technical features. The Daytona chassis and all-independent suspension were retained, but the gearbox was in unit with the engine, not the rear axle, although a torque tube still connected front to rear.

Yet another variation on the 4390-cc V12 engine theme was chosen, this time with inlet ports down the 'V' between the twin overhead camshafts in each bank, and three horizontal twin-choke Weber carburettors mounted on the outer edge of each bank of cylinders (which reduced the overall height of the unit), with wet-sump lubrication and with a quoted power output of 340 bhp.

Features lifted from the 365 GT4 2+2 included the air conditioning, the power-assisted steering and the self-levelling rear suspension, though the ventilated disc brakes were shared with the Daytona.

The body style, by Pininfarina, who also built the production shells, had some themes shared with the Daytona, but had a stubbier nose with a characteristic 'ring' front bumper, as well as smoother sides and, of course, a roomier cabin.

Like the Dino 308 GT4, this car was rather snubbed by certain snobbish 'classic' Ferrari enthusiasts for a time, but there can be little wrong with a 2+2 seater that could beat 150 mph and sold 500 in such a short time. In fact this was the very last of the large 2+2 Ferrari road cars, for future models would either be pure two-seaters (the Boxer) or full four-seaters (the 365 GT4 2+2/400 GT types).

*Above: There were twin retractable headlights on each side as well as auxiliary driving lights. In some markets, the front number plate was fitted higher, partly obscuring the radiator grille and the classic 'prancing horse' badge.*

*Below: For the 365 GTC/4, Ferrari were able to lower the bonnet line by moving the carburettors from the centre of the 'V'. Six sidedraught Webers were fitted – three per bank – on the outside edge of the cylinder heads.*

## Specification (1971)

**Engine:** V12, quad-cam
**Bore × stroke:** 81 mm × 71 mm
**Capacity:** 4390 cc
**Maximum power:** 340 bhp
**Transmission:** five-speed manual gearbox, rear-wheel drive
**Chassis:** separate steel frame with oval tubular main and cross-bracing members
**Suspension:** independent front and rear, each with wishbones, coil springs and anti-roll bar
**Brakes:** discs front and rear
**Bodywork:** steel 2+2-seater fastback coupé
**Maximum speed (approx):** 150 mph (241 km/h)

*Below: In terms of styling, the 365 GTC/4 forms an evolutionary link between the earlier 365 GTB/4 Daytona and the later 365 GT4 Berlinetta Boxer.*

## Ferrari 365 GT4 2+2 1972-85

The diehards might not like to admit it, but in the 1960s Ferrari had built a series of extremely successful four-seater cars. Accordingly, when the 365 GT 2+2 came to the end of its useful life in 1971, a successor was assured.

The new car, the 365 GT4 2+2, was launched at the Paris Motor Show in October 1972, and its basic design continued through several derivatives until the mid-1980s. Even then the model was changed yet again, continuing as the 412 until the end of the 1980s.

With a body styled and manufactured by Pininfarina in Turin, this new car replaced the 365 GTC/4 on the assembly lines at Turin and at Maranello, even though they were different types of car.

Although there was very little difference between the titles of the two full four-seater cars – 365 GT 2+2 compared with 365 GT4 2+2 – and their chassis had many similarities, the body styles were utterly different. Although the new car was the most generously proportioned four-seater yet marketed by Ferrari, and had a longer 106-in wheelbase, it was still only a two-door car, and it was actually six inches shorter than the 365 GT 2+2 which it replaced. As a comparison, it is worth noting that it was almost exactly as long as the Jaguar XJ6 saloon of the period.

Its shape was the most angular yet seen on a Ferrari road car, but with a neatly profiled nose, and a cut-off tail which followed the Daytona style. The wheels were of the latest five-spoke alloy

type, like those on the Daytona and 365 GTC/4.

The new car's chassis and running gear were based on those of the displaced 365 GTC/4 in all respects except the wheelbase, which was two inches longer. The engine retained its six horizontal carburettors (which allowed Pininfarina to produce a low bonnet line), and the five-speed gearbox was in unit with the engine, the whole being tied to the chassis-mounted rear differential by a sturdy torque tube.

In time, the car became progressively more 'touring' and less 'sporting'. The second-generation type was the 400 model of 1976, really the same car, but with a longer-stroke, 4.8-litre, engine, and – for the very first time in any Ferrari – the option of automatic transmission! Heresy to the diehards, but by the end of the 1970s, more than 80 per cent of these models were being fitted with the automatic option.

The third-generation type was the 400i of 1979, complete with Bosch fuel injection and a rather detuned (for emission-reduction purposes) 310 bhp. Because this car was slower than its predecessors, and was beginning to look old-fashioned, it sold only slowly until 1985 when it was displaced by the much-modified 412.

*Right: The low, sloping nose with its faired-in headlights was reminiscent of the earlier 365 GTB/4 (Daytona) two-seater.*

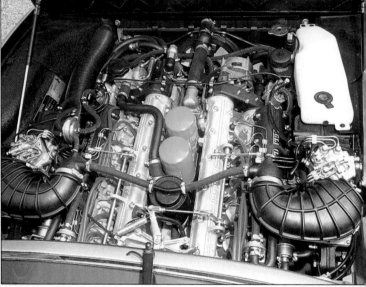

*Below: Compared with the 365 GT 2+2, the 365 GT4 2+2 was more spacious, with two inches more shoulder room in the front and four inches more in the back. The boot was also over one cubic foot bigger. Even so, the 365 GT4 2+2 was more than seven inches shorter and 1½ inches lower than the 365 GT 2+2.*

*Right: The V12, four-camshaft, engine was fitted with six sidedraught carburettors, like those on the 365 GTC/4, which helped to keep the bonnet line low. All of the powerplant's 320 bhp was needed to propel the heavy car (it weighed 1¾ tons) from a standstill to 60 mph in around seven seconds.*

*Above: Outwardly similar to the 365 GT4 2+2, the 400 series had a slightly larger engine – 4.8 litres compared with 4.4.*

*Below: Many enthusiasts were horrified when Ferrari offered automatic transmission, but the automatic model sold well.*

*Above: Like many Ferraris of the period, the 365 GT4 2+2 and 400 GT had five-spoke alloy wheels. The 365 GT4 2+2 was fitted with 215 × 15 tyres.*

*Below: The 400 series can be distinguished from the 365 GT4 2+2 by the small air dam under the nose of the car, which improved the aerodynamics.*

## Ferrari 365 GT4 2+2 variants

### Ferrari 400, 400 GTi and 400i Automatic

The original 365 GT4 2+2 model survived until 1976. It was replaced by the Ferrari 400 in the same year. That was essentially the same car, but with a larger, 4.8-litre, engine. The 400 models became 400i in the autumn of 1979, with Bosch fuel injection instead of six Weber carburettors, and 310 bhp. A total of 1,807 cars of the '400' family was produced in nine years.

### Ferrari 412

This was a substantial redevelopment of the original design, with an enlarged version of the V12 engine.

### Specification (1972 365 GT4 2+2)

**Engine:** V12, quad-cam
**Bore × stroke:** 81 mm × 71 mm
**Capacity:** 4390 cc
**Maximum power:** 320 bhp
**Transmission:** five-speed manual gearbox, rear-wheel drive
**Chassis:** separate steel frame with oval tubular main and cross-bracing members
**Suspension:** independent front and rear, each with wishbones, coil springs and anti-roll bar
**Brakes:** discs front and rear
**Bodywork:** steel two-door four-seater saloon
**Maximum speed (approx):** 152 mph (245 km/h)

## Ferrari 365 GT4 BB Berlinetta Boxer 1973-76

To replace the 365 GTB/4 Daytona, Ferrari had to produce something quite amazing, and when a new car finally appeared nobody was disappointed. At a stroke, Ferrari's front-V12-engined heritage was consigned to the history books, for the new machine had a flat-12 engine mounted behind the cabin, driving the rear wheels. This car, in fact, appeared five years after Lamborghini had launched the trend-setting V12 Miura.

The new car, called the 365 GT4 BB – but universally known as the Boxer – was previewed in 1971, and finally went on sale in 1973. Except that its new engine used some internal elements of the Daytona's, it was completely new. Ferrari had drawn on all their racing sports car experience to produce a two-seater road car with flashing acceleration, good looks and enormous character – yet it also had full air conditioning as standard, and had an engine which was 'clean' enough for the car to be sold in the USA. The fact that it had very little stowage space for luggage was cheerfully shrugged off by enthusiasts.

As always with a Ferrari of this period, there was a complex tubular frame with all-independent suspension, this time with rack-and-pinion steering. The use of a 4.4-litre flat-12 engine explains the name Boxer (after the behaviour of opposing banks of pistons and connecting rods), but although the bore, stroke, capacity, pistons and connecting rods were the same as those of the old Daytona engine, the rest of the unit was completely new, and slightly more powerful than before.

The flat-12 engine was positioned ahead of and above the transmission and final drive, which (according to accomplished drivers who could sense such things) made the handling uneasy when the car was pushed hard. That apart, the mid-engined Ferrari supercar was a phenomenal machine, which could easily beat 170 mph (even if the factory's

*Above: Dramatic when it was introduced at the 1973 Paris Motor Show and still just as striking today, the Boxer was one of Pininfarina's most successful designs.*

*Right: Retractable headlights kept the nose line low and improved the car's aerodynamics. The inlet admits cooling air to the front-mounted radiator.*

*Below: The Boxer was equipped with a single, pantograph-type windscreen wiper, designed to vary the angle of the wiper blade so that it swept as much of the screen as possible.*

### Ferrari 365 GT4 BB variants

#### Ferrari BB 512

This derivative took over from the original type from late 1976 and was built until 1981, with an 82-mm × 78-mm, 4942-cc/340-bhp engine, allied to some minor style changes to improve the aerodynamics. The top speed was actually reduced, to 163 mph.

#### Ferrari BB 512i

The third version of the Boxer model took over from the BB 512 from 1981 to 1984. It had a fuel-injected engine, which still produced 340 bhp.

### Specification (1973 365 GT4 BB)

**Engine:** flat-12, quad-cam
**Bore × stroke:** 81 mm × 71 mm
**Capacity:** 4390 cc
**Maximum power:** 360 bhp
**Transmission:** five-speed manual gearbox, rear-wheel drive
**Chassis:** separate steel frame with box-section main and cross-bracing members
**Suspension:** independent front and rear, each with wishbones, coil springs and anti-roll bar
**Brakes:** discs front and rear
**Bodywork:** steel, aluminium and glassfibre two-seater coupé
**Maximum speed (approx):** 170 mph (274 km/h)

*Above: The engine cover of the BB 512 had more cooling slats than that of the preceding 365 GT4 BB. Underneath the boxes are the air filter covers.*

*Below: The Boxer is strictly a two-seater. Both right- and left-hand-drive cars had the gear change on the left of the central tunnel.*

original claims of 188 mph were never matched by independent testers).

Even after the 365 GT4 BB became the BB 512, with a more docile 4.9-litre engine (which produced *less* power than the original 4.4-litre unit), it was still a specialist car for skilled drivers, and quite definitely the peak of Ferrari road cars in the 1970s.

*Below: Both the 365 GT4 BB and 512 BB had four triple-choke carburettors, giving one carburettor choke per cylinder.*

*Below: Ferrari never officially raced the Boxer, but some private teams modified their cars for long-distance racing.*

# Ferrari 308 GTB and 308 GTS 1975-85

When the much-loved Dino 246 GT (which was *not* badged as a Ferrari) was replaced by the Dino 308 GT4, everyone bemoaned the loss of such a compact, lithe, and exciting mid-engined two-seater, and wondered whether there would ever be another one.

Less than two years later they could breathe a sigh of relief, for Ferrari unveiled a splendid new two-seater based on 308 GT4 running gear. This was the Ferrari 308 GTB.

The 308 GTB was the start of a long-running and successful dynasty, for it and its derivatives were made for the next 16 years, the numbers built breaking all previous Ferrari records. The original 308 GTB was a two-seater coupé with glassfibre bodywork, but fewer than 200 such cars were built before Scaglietti changed to a conventional steel shell and added a steel Spyder version (with a removable roof panel) called the 308 GTS.

The new 308 GTB ran on the same wheelbase as the old Dino 246 GT (which was 8.3 inches shorter than the contemporary Dino 308 GT4, which was supposedly a 2+2-seater), but had a wider track, and was fitted with the same transverse quad-cam V8 engine and integral transmission as the Dino 308 GT4.

The style was very similar indeed to that of the Ferrari Boxer, which had recently gone on sale, but was distinguished by the scoops in the doors which channelled air into the engine bay. The 308 GTB was faster than the Dino 246 GT – 154 mph rather than 148 mph – and

*Right: The 308 GTS (Spyder) had a lift-off roof panel which stowed behind the seats.*

rushed up to its cruising speeds even faster, yet it had lost none of the excitement, and none of the sheer pleasure of driving first seen in the Dino.

No fewer than 2,897 308 GTBs and 3,219 GTSs of the original type were built between 1975 and 1981, with the later four-valves-per-cylinder derivatives being even more successful. The 308 was also the basis for the later 328 models with larger, 3.2-litre, V8 engines.

## Ferrari 308 GTB and 308 GTS variants

### Ferrari 308 GTBi and 308 GTSi
These derivatives took over from the original 308 GTB in 1981 and 1982, with a fuel-injected engine producing 214 bhp. There were 494 GTBis and 1,743 GTSis built.

### Ferrari 308 GTBi and 308 GTSi Quattrovalvole
As the *quattrovalvole* tag denoted, these had new four-valves-per-cylinder heads, and took over from the 308 GTi from 1982 to 1985. There was a significant increase in peak power, which was quoted as 240 bhp. The top speed was approximately 155 mph. No fewer than 748 GTBi QVs and 3,042 GTSi QVs were built in three years.

The 308 Quattrovalvole models were replaced by the essentially similar 328 models in 1985.

## Specification (1975 308 GTB)
**Engine:** V8, quad-cam
**Bore × stroke:** 81 mm × 71 mm
**Capacity:** 2926 cc
**Maximum power:** 255 bhp

**Transmission:** five-speed manual gearbox, rear-wheel drive
**Chassis:** separate steel frame with tubular main and cross-members
**Suspension:** independent front and rear, each with wishbones, coil springs and anti-roll bar
**Brakes:** discs front and rear
**Bodywork:** two-seater coupé; glassfibre until 1977, steel thereafter
**Maximum speed:** 154 mph (248 km/h)

*Below: Many private owners have raced their GTBs – this car is competing at Silverstone. The car's layout, with its mid-mounted engine and gearbox, gives it good balance and quick response.*

*Below: The 308 GTB was the first of a series of Pininfarina-designed, V8-engined Ferraris. The air scoops in the doors were featured on other Pininfarina designs, including the Ferrari F40.*

BUT 503Y

## Ferrari Mondial 8 1980-89

Seven years after Ferrari had introduced the Bertone-style 308 GT4, it was replaced by the Pininfarina-styled Mondial 8. Ferrari traditionalists breathed again, for they had never accepted the use of Bertone – all Ferraris, they reasoned, should be shaped by Pininfarina.

Naturally, it was a close mechanical relative of the 308 GTB two-seater. Like the 308 GT4, the new Mondial 8 was a 2+2-seater, but a more practical one than before. The name Mondial (meaning world) revived the name of a Ferrari racing-sports car of the mid-1950s.

To make sure that the cabin was more spacious and habitable, Ferrari had lengthened the wheelbase by four inches (which made this the longest of all types produced on this mid-V8-engined chassis). The new car was also wider than its forebears.

There were two important problems, however. One was that the proportions of the car looked slightly awkward (one writer suggested that the Mondial was "too long for its width. . ."); the other was that this was the first V8-engined Ferrari to have a completely de-toxed engine, with fuel injection.

With only 214 bhp, this was one of the least powerful Ferraris to be produced for many years, and although it was still a fast car compared with most other marques, it seemed to struggle once past the 130-mph mark. Surprisingly enough, it

*Above: The Mondial was styled, like most modern Ferraris, by Pininfarina, and perhaps the grille treatment for the mid-mounted engine's air intake was the inspiration for the exaggerated side strakes that were later to appear on the Testarossa.*

*Below: The open version of the Mondial was the Cabriolet 3.2. This was introduced in 1985 and featured a larger-displacement engine than the original Mondial of 1980, with 3.2 litres rather than 2.9. That increased the top speed to nearly 150 mph.*

*Left: Mondial means world, and to equip the Mondial for a world market the car was fitted with an injected engine that could meet any country's emissions regulations. In addition to electronic fuel injection, the transversely-mounted V8 engine boasted four camshafts and, in its original form, a power output of 214 bhp.*

sold no better than its Bertone-styled predecessor, the 308 GT4.

Like its short-wheelbase relatives – the 308 GTB and 308 GTS – the Mondial benefitted from the arrival of four-valve cylinder heads in 1982, and from a more powerful 3.2-litre engine in 1985. It was eventually replaced by the longitudinal-engined Mondial t in 1989.

In the first two years a total of 703 original-type Mondials was produced.

## Ferrari Mondial 8 variants

### Ferrari Mondial Quattrovalvole and Mondial Cabriolet Quattrovalvole

These derivatives were built from 1982 (Cabriolet from 1984) to 1985, replacing the original Mondial 8. The engine featured four-valves-per-cylinder heads, and produced 240 bhp. The top speed was 146 mph. The Cabriolet derivative retained 2+2 seating. Production was 1,144 Mondial QVs and 629 Mondial QV Cabriolets.

### Ferrari Mondial 3.2 and Mondial Cabriolet 3.2

When the two-seater 308 GTB was upgraded to 328 GTB, the Mondial followed suit, with an 83-mm × 73-mm, 3185-cc/270-bhp engine, which raised the top speed to 148 mph. These cars were built from 1985 to 1989.

## Specification (1980 Mondial 8)

**Engine:** V8, quad-cam
**Bore × stroke:** 81 mm × 71 mm
**Capacity:** 2926 cc
**Maximum power:** 214 bhp
**Transmission:** five-speed manual gearbox, rear-wheel drive
**Chassis:** separate steel frame with tubular main and cross-bracing members
**Suspension:** independent front and rear, each with wishbones, coil springs and anti-roll bar
**Brakes:** discs front and rear
**Bodywork:** steel and aluminium 2+2-seater
**Maximum speed:** 138 mph (222 km/h)

*Above: The mid-engined Mondial in full flight. Even with its original three-litre quad-cam V8, the car was good for a top speed of almost 140 mph. This example is a later Quattrovalvole (i.e. four valves per cylinder) model. The extra valves helped boost power output to 240 bhp and the top speed past the 145-mph mark.*

*Right: Despite some criticisms, the Mondial was a perfectly acceptable styling solution to the problem of making a successful mid-engined 2+2 design. The long bonnet gives no hint of the mid-engined configuration.*

*Left: The leather-trimmed Mondial interior retains such traditional Ferrari features as a large analogue instrument panel and the long, chromed gear lever operating in its equally shiny exposed gate.*

*Below: The engine hatch nestles between the two 'flying buttresses' of the rear roof line which from the side successfully conceal the car's mid-engined layout.*

## Ferrari Testarossa 1984–91

To replace, and improve on, the much-loved Berlinetta Boxer, Ferrari developed the amazing Testarossa, a mid-engined two-seater coupé which set new standards for every other carmaker in the world.

Not only was the car beautiful, it was also effective. In the right hands, it was both docile and spine-chillingly fast. After giving it red-painted cylinder heads, Ferrari were also proud to re-surrect another famous racing name of the late 1950s – *Testarossa* (the Italian for red head). Confusingly the current-generation car is the third Testarossa, but the first two (the four- and 12-cylinder cars from the 1950s) were Testa Rossas (two words) . . . for no apparent reason.

Apart from its performance, the Testa-rossa's attraction was its style. Although based on a slightly lengthened version of the Berlinetta Boxer's chassis, the Testa-rossa was a more angular car, with a deep line of strakes and sail panels at each side, starting in the doors and blending into the rear wings, which were there to encourage air to enter the engine bay and the twin electric fan-assisted radiators, one on each side of the car.

The car itself was quite traditional under that striking bodywork, being a latticework of square- and rectangular-section steel tubes. The chassis differed from a conventional (albeit old-fashioned) arrangement in that the engine was fitted to a rear subframe which could be detached from the car to give perfect access to the big flat-12 unit, should major work be required. The engine's position, towards the rear of the Testarossa, produced a somewhat rear-biased weight distribution – one reason why the rear suspension featured a double-wishbone system with twin coil spring/damper units per side. The car's rearward weight bias was further tamed by the different tyre sizes, which gave the rear as much grip as possible – the front wheels were fitted with 240/45 tyre, while the rears had wider 280/45 tyres.

*Above: As its name indicated, the Testarossa had red heads, or cam covers, although they were less obvious that the old V12-engined car, as the recent model had a flat-12 unit. The tops of the induction system were painted red as compensation. The engine displaced five litres and produced almost 400 bhp thanks to the combination of four cams, four valves per cylinder and Bosch fuel injection.*

*Left: From head-on, the great width of the Testarossa is emphasised. At just under 80 inches it's wider than a contemporary Rolls Royce and the rear track is almost a foot wider than the front, in an attempt to tame the rear-biased bulk of the powerful flat-12 engine. To provide adequate rear vision, the driver's wing mirror (complete with aerodynamically efficient stalk) is mounted on an extended arm halfway up on the front screen pillar.*

*Below: To make the Testarossa's high performance usable at night, each pop-up headlamp pod contains twin halogen lights. With the lights up, the Testarossa's ultra-low nose line is highlighted. That was easy to achieve, as the bonnet contains neither the engine nor the radiator; the mid-mounted engine is equipped with two water radiators, one on each side with their cooling air fed through those unmistakable side strakes.*

It was a wickedly attractive machine which hid the same basic mechanical layout as the beloved Boxer, a mid-mounted flat-12 engine which was fitted above and ahead of the transmission. For the Testarossa application, however, the 4.9-litre engine had been given four valves per cylinder (which meant 48 valves in all), Bosch fuel injection, and a totally reliable 390 bhp. Even so, because it was quite a large car, with no more than averagely-efficient aero-dynamics, it could 'only' just exceed 170 mph; the days of the '200-mph Fer-rari', it seemed, were a long way away. When you realise that the Testarossa tips the scales at over 3,600 lb, that top speed appears all the more impressive, as does the 0-60 mph acceleration time of 5.2 seconds and the car's ability to reach 100 mph in just 11.4 seconds and 140 mph in under 25 seconds.

Here was a car that did everything very quickly, very safely, and in great style.

## Specification (1984)

**Engine:** flat-12, quad-cam
**Bore × stroke:** 82 mm × 78 mm
**Capacity:** 4942 cc
**Maximum power:** 390 bhp
**Transmission:** five-speed manual gearbox, rear-wheel drive
**Chassis:** separate steel frame with oval- and square-section main and bracing members
**Suspension:** independent front and rear, each with wishbones, coil springs and anti-roll bar
**Brakes:** discs front and rear
**Bodywork:** steel and aluminium two-seater coupé
**Maximum speed:** 170 mph (274 km/h)

*Above: Although the Testarossa followed the mechanical layout of its predecessor, the Berlinetta Boxer – which meant that the engine was actually mounted above the transmission at the rear – the Testarossa is not as high at the back as you might think. The flat-12 design of the engine means such a layout is a practical proposition, and as the engine is of all-alloy construction it does not disturb the weight distribution to an unacceptable degree, despite some of the engine being behind the rear axle line.*

*Right: The Testarossa's rear lights are housed behind a grille which echoes the styling treatment seen on the side of the car for the engine cooling vents. The black area on the rear deck of the car is a large grille through which the hot air from the engine bay is extracted. For engine access the whole rear deck, including the 'flying buttresses', lifts up from the front.*

*Below: On the track it's possible to exploit all of the Testarossa's 390 bhp and high performance. There, with no speed limits to worry about, the Testarossa can reach 170 mph and sprint to 60 mph in 5.2 seconds, going on to achieve 100 mph in just 11.4 seconds. That's despite the car tipping the scales at over 3,600 lb – a weight that would be even greater except for the use of many alloy body panels.*

# Ferrari 288 GTO 1984-85

In the early 1980s a new international racing formula – Group B – was launched. Although more applicable to rallying, it was also thought to be a potentially important racing formula.

Ferrari were attracted to this idea, and immediately laid plans to produce a 200-off 'homologation special', which looked like the existing 308 GTB, but which was very different under the skin. The result was the 288 GTO.

In the end, Group B never took off in racing, so the 288 GTO never raced. Even so, not 200 but 272 of these machines were produced, many of which went straight into storage as 'instant classics' for investment purposes.

In retrospect, this new car is seen as the very first of a whole series of V8-engined Ferraris which have a longitudinally-positioned engine, rather than the transversely-mounted engine of the original 1970s design.

Compared with the 328 GTB, which it resembled very closely, the 288 GTO had a 4.4-in longer wheelbase and a wider track. The engine was a 2.85-litre turbocharged version of the familiar 90-degree V8 which produced an impressive 400 bhp, and was married to a new five-speed gearbox. Tests proved that the standard car could exceed 180 mph, which made it the fastest Ferrari road car so far put on sale, and a worthy carrier of the celebrated 'GTO' badge.

To keep the weight down and the strength up, the body shell was an intriguing mixture of glassfibre, Kevlar, Nomex and aluminium honeycomb. This certainly worked, for the 288 GTO weighed 2,557 lb – 227 lb less than the normal 328 GTB. However, even though it was originally intended to be a racing-

sports car, it was well-equipped in a way that could be called business-like rather than luxurious.

## Specification (1984)

**Engine:** V8, quad-cam
**Bore × stroke:** 80 mm × 71 mm
**Capacity:** 2855 cc
**Maximum power:** 400 bhp
**Transmission:** five-speed manual gearbox, rear-wheel drive
**Chassis:** separate steel frame with oval tubular main and cross-bracing members
**Suspension:** independent front and rear, each with wishbones, coil springs and anti-roll bar
**Brakes:** discs front and rear
**Bodywork:** glassfibre, Kevlar, Nomex and aluminium honeycomb two-seater coupé
**Maximum speed (approx):** 180 mph (290 km/h)

*Above: With 400 bhp from its 2.9-litre quad-cam turbo engine, the GTO would have been a formidable proposition on the racetrack. Unfortunately the formula for which it was developed, Group B, was outlawed before the GTO could race.*

*Below: The 180-mph GTO can be distinguished from the 328 by the side vents behind the rear wheel and by the split-rim wheels themselves, which are larger than those on the 328. The bodywork is a mixture of composite materials.*

*Below: At first glance it's hard to distinguish the 288 GTO from the far more common 328 GTB, but in fact the GTO has both a longer wheelbase and a wider track as well as far more power.*

# Ferrari 412 1985-89

More than 12 years after Ferrari had launched the 365 GT4 2+2, the fourth generation of this family, the 412, was introduced. Although this still looked similar to the style which had been on the market since 1972, it had been retouched in many ways. In particular it became the very first Ferrari, in fact the very first Italian car of any type, to have ABS anti-lock braking as standard.

Except in detail, the graceful two-door Pininfarina body style was not changed. The engine, however, was enlarged yet again. A one-millimetre increase in bore size, giving 4942 cc, and other changes allowed the peak power to be pushed back up to 340 bhp, which was where it had been until exhaust-emissions limitations took their toll in the late 1970s; later a 325-bhp version, complete with exhaust catalyser, became available.

Coincidentally, the bore, stroke and engine capacity were now exactly the same as those of the current Testarossa. The major difference, of course, was that the 412 had the very last of a long line of 60-degree V12s, while the Testarossa had a horizontally-opposed or 'boxer' 12-cylinder unit.

As before, there was a choice of manual or automatic transmission but – how times had changed! – automatic was now looked upon as normal, with the manual transmission as the option.

*Right: The 412's external styling hardly differed from that of the original 1972 365 GT4 2+2 but automatic transmission was now the norm, with a five-speed manual optional, and ABS brakes were fitted.*

## Specification (1985)

**Engine:** V12, quad-cam
**Bore × stroke:** 82 mm × 78 mm
**Capacity:** 4942 cc
**Maximum power:** 340 bhp
**Transmission:** five-speed manual gearbox or three-speed automatic transmission, rear-wheel drive
**Chassis:** separate steel frame with tubular main and bracing members
**Suspension:** independent front and rear, each with wishbones, coil springs and anti-roll bar
**Brakes:** discs front and rear
**Bodywork:** steel four-seater saloon
**Maximum speed:** 155 mph (249 km/h)

*Right: In 1985 a slight increase in engine size gave the 412 an output of 340 bhp.*

# Ferrari 328 GTB and 328 GTS 1985-89

Ten years after the company had launched its best-selling car, the 308 GTB, Ferrari finally gave it a larger engine, along with some notable styling improvements to keep the design fresh.

The most obvious difference was in the bumper arrangement front and rear; the sharper front profile of the 308 was lost in the 328's deeper wrap-around front, and a similar treatment appeared at the rear. It did make the car seem that bit bulkier than the 308 but the overall design was more co-ordinated. The 328 was, in fact, larger than the 308 but only by a minuscule amount, the wheelbase being a fraction of an inch longer.

Technically, the 328 GTB and 328 GTS models were like the 308 GTB and GTS Quattrovalvole models except for the use of a 270-bhp/3185-cc V8 engine. The greater displacement had been achieved by increasing the bore by 2 mm and lengthening the stroke by 2.6 mm. It was the extra engine size alone that led to an increase in power (up to 270 bhp) as there were no other differ-

*Right: The 328 GTB and GTS were introduced together in 1985. On the surface, changes from the 308 series were insignificant – the most noticeable was the adoption of body-colour bumpers.*

ences – the Bosch K-Jetronic injection was retained, for example. The overall gearing was also left the same, giving the new car a top speed of about 153 mph. The front and rear bumpers were colour-matched to the rest of the car, the front spoiler was standard (it had been optional on the previous model), and there were subtle but satisfactory revisions to the instrument layout, and to the trim and furnishings.

With production running at the rate of about 2,500 cars a year, the 328 GTB and GTS might not have been the most affordable of cars, but they were demonstrably popular. A reflection on how well the cars sold in hotter climes was the fact that the majority of the models produced were lift-off-roof GTS types.

This was the last of the transverse-engined V8 cars, for in 1989 they were superseded by the new 348 tb model with its engine mounted longitudinally.

## Specification (1985 328 GTB)

**Engine:** V8, quad-cam
**Bore × stroke:** 83 mm × 73.6 mm
**Capacity:** 3185 cc
**Maximum power:** 270 bhp
**Transmission:** five-speed manual gearbox, rear-wheel drive
**Chassis:** separate steel frame with oval tubular main and bracing members
**Suspension:** independent front and rear, each with wishbones, coil springs and anti-roll bar
**Brakes:** discs front and rear
**Bodywork:** steel two-seater coupé
**Maximum speed (approx):** 153 mph (246 km/h)

*Above: At the front, a spoiler – previously optional equipment – was now a standard fitment. The GTS (shown here), with its open-roof capability, proved more popular than the fixed-head GTB.*

*Below: Now displacing 3185 cc from a bore and stroke of 83 mm × 73 mm, the 328's mid-mounted V8 (the last fitted transversely in a Ferrari) produced 270 bhp at 7,000 rpm and 223 lb ft of torque at 5,500 rpm.*

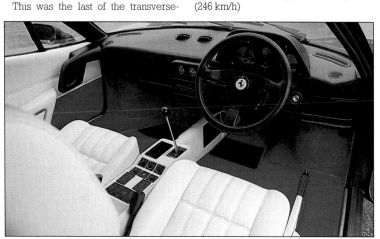

*Above: Although still clearly akin to the cabin of the 308 GTB a decade earlier, the 328's interior was revised in a number of ways, including a better dash layout with clearer instrumentation.*

*Below: The 328 GTS was recognisably descended from the first of Ferrari's transverse-engined two-seaters – the 206 and 246 Dinos of the late 1960s. Over the years, the swoopy, curvaceous lines of the Dino had given way to the rather sharper styling of the 328.*

F 474 MPK

## Ferrari F40 1987–92

Fittingly, the F40 was the last new model to be developed, and revealed, in Enzo Ferrari's long lifetime. In 1986, the company's founder directed that a special model be produced to commemorate the 40th anniversary of the birth of the famous marque. The result, launched in the summer of 1987, was the sensational F40 – the fastest and most powerful Ferrari road car of all.

F40 stands for 'Ferrari 40th Anniversary' – and what a way to make a celebration! By using a wide-track version of the chassis and running gear of the 288 GTO limited-edition car, but further tuning the engine to give an astonishing 478 bhp, the engineers produced a fully road-legal machine with a claimed top speed of 201 mph.

The body shell, on the other hand, was a totally new Pininfarina style, simpler but no less beautiful than that of the 288 GTO, functional to a fault, and very much a case of a road-racing car which had been mildly detuned and civilised for road use. There seemed to be slots and ducts everywhere – including long, thin outlets behind the front wheels, which seemed guaranteed to spray water on the doors in wet-weather motoring – and the ensemble was rendered unforgettable by the use of a very large transverse spoiler above the tail.

Had so many of these cars not been delivered in the first two years of the model's life, the claims would have been considered unbelievable, but owner

*Above: If the 288 GTO was a competition-oriented development of the 308 GTB, the F40 took the concept a league further on, as the result of a project initiated by Enzo Ferrari to commemorate his company's 40th anniversary.*

*Below: The F40 was the nearest thing possible to an off-the-shelf road-equipped sports-racing car.*

*Above: Instead of a near-vertical window and a louvred deck as an engine compartment lid, on the F40 the rear window itself (a huge plastic moulding) formed the engine cover, with a generous set of vents encouraging hot air to be drawn out by the peripheral flow.*

*Below: The F40, closely derived from the GTO Evoluzione, was a case of function dictating form, almost without compromise. Its numerous spoilers, ducts and vents, as well as its purposeful overall shape, were finalised in Pininfarina's wind tunnel*

*Left: Inside the F40 there were few concessions to comfort, with much bare carbonfibre and Kevlar-reinforced panelling on view, but air conditioning was fitted.*

*Below: Under the louvred plastic, that twin-turbocharged, four-cam, 32-valve, 90-degree V8 produced 478 bhp at 7,000 rpm and 425 lb ft of torque at 4,000 rpm from 2936 cc.*

ter owner took their cars out for the first ne, came back in a state of high excitement, and confirmed that the permance, the handling, and the sheer haracter were everything that had een claimed.

Originally, Ferrari stated that a mere 0 F40s would be built in three years, ut within a year that figure had been oubled to 900, and by mid-1991 the tar-et had become open-ended. Every rich errari owner, it seemed, rushed to der an F40, but many were disap-ointed, while others made haste to 'lay own' these cars as investment objects or future sale.

Given suitably brutal treatment off the e, it took a mere 4.5 seconds to reach mph, 8.8 seconds to reach 100 mph nd, staggeringly, just 18.5 seconds to et to 150 mph. It was no wonder the cky few owners were so impressed.

That performance was helped by the 40's low kerb weight of just over 400 lb, which gave the car a power-to-eight ratio equalled by very few other adgoing cars, at under 5 lb/hp. That as thanks to a superb V8 engine. It may ave displaced fractionally under three tres, but its huge power output, pro-uced at a high 7,000 rpm, was impres-ve indeed. The engine was all-alloy, an xotic creation in Silumin with shrink-tted alloy liners in the block. The top nd featured twin belt-driven camshafts or each bank of cylinders, operating ur valves per cylinder. The compres-ion ratio was a lowly 7.7:1, but that was xplained by the use of a pair of water-ooled IHI turbochargers with Behr tercoolers to increase their efficiency, lowing at up to 16 psi.

The F40 was succeeded – briefly – y the F50, produced from 1996 to 1997, vhich was virtually a road-going ormula 1 car.

*ight: Much of the F40's technical nd performance edge came from the ightness of its body structure, which sed panelling formed from arbonfibre and Kevlar composite naterials to an unprecedented legree.*

## Specification (1987)

**Engine:** V8, quad-cam
**Bore × stroke:** 82 mm × 69.5 mm
**Capacity:** 2936 cc
**Maximum power:** 478 bhp
**Transmission:** five-speed manual gearbox, rear-wheel drive
**Chassis:** separate steel frame with oval tubular main and bracing members
**Suspension:** independent front and rear, each with wishbones, coil springs and anti-roll bar
**Brakes:** discs front and rear
**Bodywork:** glassfibre, carbonfibre and other composite materials; two-seater coupé
**Maximum speed (approx):** 200 mph (322 km/h)

*Right: Very much an F40 'trademark', the distinctive, pylon-mounted tail aerofoil would never have conformed to real racing regulations, but that was irrelevant on what was a street car conceived to give its buyers the flavour of a racer.*

## Ferrari Mondial t 1989-present

Although the new 348 tb *was* new in all respects – engine, chassis and body style – its longer-wheelbase 2 + 2 cousin, the Mondial t, was not quite as pure a design. In effect, the new Mondial had a new engine and transmission shoe-horned into the same wheelbase as the old Mondial 8, had a modified chassis and used a lightly-modified version of the old car's Pininfarina style.

The technical changes, therefore, were a lot more significant than the re-touched styling would suggest. As described in the 348 tb entry, the famous V8 engine had been enlarged, further developed, and made more environmentally 'green' for the 1990s.

Like the 348 tb, the Mondial t had its engine longitudinally mounted, quite a lot lower in the chassis than before, and had the transmission behind the final drive. Because the Mondial t was heavier than the 348 tb, and had to carry up to four people, the overall gearing was lower.

The Mondial's long-wheelbase tubular chassis was modified to support the re-located engine and transmission. The brakes had anti-lock as standard, there were three driver-controllable damper settings, and the rack-and-pinion steering had power assistance – all features which made the latest Mondial a very different car from its predecessor.

Like the original Mondial, the 1990s Mondial t was more of a 'touring' than a 'sporting' Ferrari, though there can be few cars in the world which 'toured' in such a fast, glamorous or individual way.

### Specification (1989)

**Engine:** V8, quad-cam
**Bore × stroke:** 85 mm × 75 mm
**Capacity:** 3405 cc
**Maximum power:** 300 bhp
**Transmission:** five-speed manual gearbox, rear-wheel drive
**Chassis:** separate steel frame with oval tubular and bracing members
**Suspension:** independent front and rear, each with wishbones, coil springs and anti-roll bar
**Brakes:** discs front and rear
**Bodywork:** steel 2 + 2-seater; coupé or cabriolet
**Maximum speed (approx):** 150 mph (241 km/h)

*Above: Available in either closed Mondial t or convertible Mondial t Cabriolet form, the 1989 Ferrari 2 + 2 had its midships engine mounted longitudinally, with a transverse five-speed gearbox aft of the differential.*

*Right: Whether hard- or soft-top, it was definitely what you would call an 'occasional' four-seater; as can be seen here, rear-seat leg room is very restricted.*

*Below: With 300 bhp, obtained at 7,200 rpm, from its Bosch fuel-injected, 3405-cc quad-camshaft V8, the Mondial t had a good turn of speed, although its maximum was limited to about 150 mph by the lower gearing needed for its potential four-passenger capacity.*

## Ferrari 348 tb and 348 ts 1989-94

The 308 GTB/328 GTB range had been running for more than 15 years before Ferrari finally replaced it. First to appear was the Mondial t, in 1989, but a new two-seater, the 348 tb, was launched a few months later. Like the ousted range, it was meant to provide pure, high-speed, two-seater enjoyment, and it was intended for a long production life.

In every way, this was Ferrari's restatement of the mid-engined 308 GTB/328 GTB theme, but it was a roomier, more civilised, yet technically more advanced, car than before. Its Pininfarina styling was strongly reminiscent of the current Testarossa, for there were brakes and air intakes in the flanks of the doors to channel air into the cooling radiators, which had been moved to the engine bay.

There was a horizontal theme across the tail, with the same plain nose style. As with the old cars, there were to be two types, the 'b' standing for berlinetta or closed coupé, the 's' standing for spider, or Targa-top model.

Compared with the last of the 328 GTBs, the 348 tb had a 4-in longer wheelbase and, like the 288 GTO and F40 cars which had preceded it, the engine was longitudinally mounted, with the gearbox behind the final drive. Although the chassis was longer than before, the engine was five inches lower, which

meant that the handling was improved.

Ferrari claimed that the revised chassis was 59 per cent stiffer than before; otherwise it was familiar, with coil-spring independent suspension at front and rear, and rack-and-pinion steering, though there was still no power assistance. Anti-lock braking was standard.

The 3.4-litre engine was a further development of the famous V8 which had originally been used in the Bertone-styled 308 GT4 of 1973. Like its immediate predecessors, it had four valves per cylinder, but was now capable of running on unleaded fuel. Even so, it produced 300 bhp, a 30-bhp improvement on the 328 GTB.

*Above: The 348 tb is the heir to the original 308, but in the 15 years that separate the two models, changing conditions have dictated a rather different, and larger, design, the 348 tb being longer and wider and having a longer wheelbase.*

*Below: A sign of the times: the V8 engine used in the 348 (which can trace its ancestry back to the early 1970s) can run on unleaded fuel. With four valves per cylinder, the 3.4-litre V8 produces 300 bhp at 7,000 rpm, along with 224 lb ft at 4,000 rpm.*

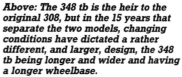

*Left: The 348 tb's gearbox is mounted on the end of the engine in conventional fashion, unlike the under-engine system used on the Boxer and Testarossa, for example. That arrangement gives a low centre of gravity and contributes to the car's excellent handling.*

*Below: The Testarossa-style side treatment was carried over to the 348 tb. It serves the same purpose: to cover the large vents on the side feeding air to the V8's side-mounted radiators. This is a more restrained treatment, however, as the rear of the 348 tb is nowhere near as wide.*

Along with its bigger sister car, the Mondial t, the new model was meant to be Ferrari's staple throughout the 1990s, with plans being laid to produce about 2,500 every year. As you would expect, this was a very fast car indeed, with all the charisma that a Ferrari badge brings. Britain's weekly magazine *Autocar & Motor* wrote: "The car has a passion and an energy matched by few others, a charisma that is peerless. . .".

Apart from the mere fact that it was a Ferrari, there were other extremely desirable aspects to the 348, such as real performance from as low as 1,000 rpm all the way past the 7,500 rpm red line. Rev the engine past its 4,200 rpm torque peak towards 5,000 rpm and the power unit was transformed, lacking nothing in comparison with the most exotic V12s in Ferrari's past. The high speeds the powerful V8 gave were matched by immensely reassuring stability.

But was time beginning to catch up with Ferrari? This time there were complaints about seating, ride and noise levels and there is no doubt that Honda's clinically-competent NSX had raised the standards of the world's mid-engined supercars. In 1994 the 348 was replaced by the excellent F355 available as Berlinetta, GTS and Spider.

## Specification (1989)

**Engine:** V8, quad-cam
**Bore × stroke:** 85 mm × 75 mm
**Capacity:** 3405 cc
**Maximum power:** 300 bhp
**Transmission:** five-speed manual gearbox, rear-wheel drive
**Chassis:** separate steel frame with tubular main and cross-bracing members
**Suspension:** independent front and rear, each with wishbones, coil springs and anti-roll bar
**Brakes:** discs front and rear
**Bodywork:** steel two-seater coupé or Targa-top spider
**Maximum speed (approx):** 170 mph (274 km/h)

*Above: Certain elements of Ferrari interiors have stayed constant over the years, such as leather-covered seats and the exposed chromed gear lever gate. Standard equipment includes air conditioning (even on this cabriolet model), central locking and power-operated windows.*

*Below: The 348 was produced in two forms the tb coupé and the ts convertible cabriolet models. The 348 ts had a removable lift-off roof section which was stowed in the boot when not required. Its replacement, the 355 Berlinetta cost just under £100,000 in 1999.*

*Above: A 348 tb accelerates away; its large torque output helps give it an excellent 0-60 mph acceleration time of 5.6 seconds. Its in-gear acceleration is just as impressive, 50-70 mph taking 7.6 seconds. The penalty for such performance is not great, either, as fuel consumption is over 21 mpg.*

*Below: Ferrari interiors have become more modern over the years and their layout more rational. That's been at the cost of individuality, however, as the fascia here could have come from any one of a number of manufacturers. Unfortunately, too, seat adjustment and lumbar support could both be better.*

## Ferrari 550 Maranello 1997-present

By the late 1990s, Ferrari's interpretation of the 12-cylinder berlinetta theme was manifest in the 550 Maranello. It was classically styled by Pininfarina with front engine and rear drive layout, with a faultless two-seater coupé body. A measure of its prowess in action can be gauged by the fact that it was 3.2 seconds a lap faster round Ferrari's Fiorano test track than the mid-engined 512BB.

Its regular GT shape belies 4,800 hours of wind tunnel tests that resulted in a drag coefficient of 0.33 Cd, partly achieved by giving it a flat underbelly. Fixed front light clusters were incorporated in the bonnet to improve aerodynamics and wind noise during night driving, with foglights incorporated into the front bumper. Door windows were flush with the bodywork and fitted with an automatic opening and closing device. The 550 bodyshell was built round a tubular steel frame with the light aluminium alloy bodywork welded on, using a special alloy known as Feran, which allows aluminium to be welded to steel.

The 550 Maranello was powered by an all-aluminium 485 bhp, 4.5-litre, V12 engine, with four valves per cylinder, using a Bosch Motronic M5.2 ignition/injection system. Aluminium Nikasil-coated cylinder liners were fitted, along with titanium con rods and Mahle forged aluminium pistons, while dry sump lubrication was used. Ferrari developed a particular type of variable geometry intake for the 550 Maranello engine to en-

*Below: The 550 Maranello Berlinetta was significantly quicker around the test track than the 512 BB, which was testimony to Ferrari's chassis engineering skills, as well as the coupé's wind-cheating aerodynamics.*

*Right: Where every sports car enthusiast dreams of sitting: the cockpit of the 550 Maranello, where there is nothing superficial or extraneous.*

hance torque and power features. Particular attention went into the design of the exhaust system, incorporating variable back pressure that improved torque in average load conditions as well as enhancing engine efficiency at high speeds with a full load. A transaxle differential unit incorporated the six-speed gearbox for better weight distribution.

To keep the car as light as possible, weight-saving measures included drilled brake discs, aluminium callipers and stub axles, and magnesium wheels. The 30-gallon fuel tank was also in aluminium and mounted ahead of the rear axle. The 550 Maranello had independent suspension on all four wheels by wishbones at the front, and transverse parallelogram structure and upper wishbones at the rear, plus aluminium gas dampers with coaxial coil springs and anti-roll bars both front and rear. The front track was wider than the rear to maximise turn-in potential, and the front suspension geometry provided an anti-dive effect under braking. Damper settings could be adjusted by the driver, using a switch on the fascia, in normal and sport modes, and depending on which mode was selected, the system intervened by cutting off the torque delivered by the engine or, co-ordinated by the ABS system, by braking the two rear wheels independently. This was the first active anti-wheel spin system that could be controlled by the driver. The Formula 1 derived braking system was developed with Brembo, and consisted of four-piston callipers front and

rear with ventilated discs and special pads, while a four-channel ABS incorporated electronic brake proportioning. This prevented the driven wheels from spinning by a combination of the rear brakes and engine management system. ZF rack and pinion steering was fitted, incorporating speed-sensitive Servotronic power assistance.

The 550 Maranello was fitted with five-spoke magnesium alloy Speedline wheels measuring 8.5 x 18 in front and 10.5 x 18 in rear, and was available with four different types of tyre, all produced specially for the car. Homologated sizes were 255/40 ZR 18 front, 295/35 ZR 18 rear, as Bridgestone Expedia S02, Good Year Eagle GS Fiorano, Pirelli P Zero, or Michelin MXX 3 Pilot.

The cockpit was every bit as you'd expect a grand touring Ferrari to be, with wraparound leather-upholstered

contours and the traditional alloy gear knob. The driving position had eight settings, five of which were electrically assisted and the pedals were fitted with drilled light alloy racing supports. Instrumentation was by LCD analogue dials, and the air conditioning unit incorporated a radiation sensor for more accurate cabin temperature regulation. Top speed was 199 mph (320 km/h), with 0–60 mph (0-196 km/h) achieved in 4.3 seconds.

### Specification
**Engine:** all aluminium V12
**Bore** x **stroke:** 88 mm x 75 mm
**Capacity:** 4562 cc
**Suspension:** independent front and rear by wishbones, coil springs and dampers, anti-roll bars
**Body:** aluminium panels on steel monocoque frame

## Ferrari 456M, GT and GTA 1993-present

*Above: The 456M was a front-engined, rear-drive Berlinetta, and was an evolution of the 456GT that came out in 1993, with improvements to aerodynamics and greater comfort within the cabin.*

*Below: The aerial view of the 456M demonstrates the classic proportions of its Pininfarina-styled aluminium-panelled body.*

Continuing the fine tradition of the 2 + 2 Ferrari Berlinetta, the 456M was itself an evolution of the Pininfarina-styled 456GT (the M stands for Modified) and the upgrading consisted of aerodynamic improvements, better cabin comfort and ergonomics. The 456GT was launched in 1993, followed by the GTA version with automatic transmission in 1996. In 1998 the 456M was unveiled, in both manual GT and automatic GTA form, featuring a one-piece carbon fibre bonnet with retractable headlights and more rounded front bumper with in-

tegral spoiler. The front air intake was modified to provide improved engine cooling and brake air intakes, incorporating fog lights in the aperture. The rear bumper with integral spoiler was also new, while the interior of the car was totally re-designed.

The 456M was based around a tubular steel frame, clad in light aluminium alloy panels that were welded to the steel chassis with an intermediate material known as Feran. The door windows were flush fitting and featured an automatic sealing device, while new weather strips between windows and body enhanced the aerodynamics. New struts improved access to the boot. Access to rear seats was improved by increasing front-seat travel and, as befitted a sophisticated grand tourer, the front seats were part constructed from a new special foam rubber with five-position electrical controls and position memory.

The 456M was powered by the 65-degree V12 engine, developing 436 bhp at 7,250 rpm, managed by a Bosch Motronic M5.2 system. The GT's six-speed transaxle gearbox and ZF limited slip differential unit was connected to the engine via a driveshaft supported by three bearings and housed in a steel pipe. The GTA version was fitted with four-speed automatic transmission with torque converter monitored by a Bosch Motronic MS.2 ECU.

The suspension system was independent all round, with upper and lower wishbones, aluminium gas-dampers with coil springs and anti-roll bars front and rear. Further sophistications included a self-levelling system at the rear, plus anti-dive front suspension geometry. An ECU managed the cali-

bration variation of each shock absorber via four motors, and the driver could select either Normal or Sport mode. Traction control was achieved by an ASR system that detected skidding through the ABS and the engine management system, integrated through a CAN line. This system was unprecedented in offering three different control options, operated by a switch on the dashboard. The 456M was equipped with four ventilated discs with aluminium callipers and 4-channel ABS, integrated with ASR and EBD (rear electronic braking corrector). The rack and pinion steering was allied with a Servotronic, speed-sensitive power-steering system.

*Below: The GTA version of the 456M appeared in 1996, equipped with four-speed automatic transmission.*

### Variants

The 456M could be further personalised with the Carrozzeria Scaglietti options list. Introduced in 1997, this scheme offered a number of possibilities for 456M, F355 and 550 Maranello models, including body colour options, coloured seat upholstery, travel accessories including a battery-charger with special connector in the engine compartment.

### Specification (456M)
**Engine:** all aluminium V12
**Bore x stroke:** 88 mm x 75 mm
**Capacity:** 4562 cc
**Suspension:** independent front and rear by wishbones, coil springs and dampers, anti-roll bars
**Body:** aluminium panels on steel monocoque frame

# Fiat (Fabbrica Italiana Automobili di Torino)

*Right: Fiat actually stands for Fabbrica Italiana Automobili di Torino, a company founded in 1899 by Giovanni Agnelli, Count Carlo Biscaretti di Ruffia and Emanuele Bricherasio. Fiat's first car appeared in 1899. Designed by Aristide Faccioli, it had a twin-cylinder engine of only 663 cc (the level of displacement Fiat were still using in the 1960s) and two gears.*

*Above and below: In the mid-1950s Fiat brightened their image enormously by building this one-off gas turbine-powered car. The mid-mounted engine produced no less than 300 bhp at 22,000 rpm, giving an estimated top speed of 157 mph. The car actually achieved over 135 mph at Turin Airport. The hole at the rear exhausts the residual thrust from the gas turbine engine.*

F iat was founded in 1898 and rapidly became Italy's largest carmaker, a position it retains to this day. The company has been the most powerful Italian industrial group for at least 70 years, for it also makes trucks, aircraft and railway rolling stock.

The firm's roots include the short-lived Ceirano concern, which was founded in 1898 by Giovanni Battista Ceirano and started by making Welleyes bicycles before their first small Welleyes car. Ceirano was taken over by the fledgling Fiat company, along with some of its staff who went on to become famous names in the motor industry in their own right – people such as Vincenzo Lancia and Felice Nazzaro. Also part of the package was the designer Faccioli; he designed the first Fiat, which was similar to the tiny two-gear 663-cc Welleyes machine, apart from having horizontal cylinders.

Fiat's first front-engined model was the work of Fiat's new designer Enrico and appeared in 1902. It was along Mercedes lines, with a 4.2-litre four-cylinder engine.

Although the company went on to make its name and fortune by building cheap transport, in the early days Fiat produced some large and luxurious models, cars such as the 60HP of 1905, with a huge 10082-cc four-cylinder engine. Four cylinders had given way to six by 1911, with an even bigger engine of over 11 litres. By this time there was sufficient demand to produce Fiat's first small mass-produced model, the Tipo Zero of 1912.

Fiat were involved in racing from the earliest days, and with considerable success. The early racers followed the then-fashionable practice of using very large-displacement engines which produced their power at low and reliable engine speeds. Today such devices are condemned as dinosaurs, but at the time they were sensible enough; their reign came to an end before World War I thanks to the success of the four-valves-per-cylinder, twin-cam Grand Prix Peugeots with far smaller engines, but originally there was little to choose between the approaches. Although Fiat adopted Peugeot's practice of small, high-revving engines, the company had withdrawn from Grand Prix racing completely by 1927. The exit was a dramatic one, however, as the 1927 Milan Grand Prix at Monza was won by a Fiat 806 complete with a 1.5-litre V12 with three overhead camshafts and two 'V's of six cylinders, producing no less than 185 bhp at 8,500 rpm.

Before that event, Fiat had already made road car production their main concern, and after World War I they introduced the small 1.5-litre side-valve 501, which did much to put Italy on wheels as some 45,000

*Left: The Fiat badge changed considerably through the course of the company's history as some attempt was made to keep up with the changing fashions. Originally, full stops were used between the letters (F.I.A.T.) but they were dropped at the end of 1906. The letters FIAT were always used – sometimes in an embossed brass plate, often within a circle, sometimes in a long rectangle, and very occasionally in an upright rectangle as here on this example from a 1960s Fiat 600 economy model.*

In the more austere immediate post-war years Fiat production was not terribly exciting. In the 1950s and 1960s, the company produced cars like the rear-engined 500s and 600s (marking a change from the first Topolino, which was a front-engined design) and the 1100 and 1200 family cars, and steadily grew to an enormous size. Accordingly, it could afford to build a series of attractive and popular sports cars, some of which were engineers' indulgences (like the tiny V8-engined 8V), others of which sold very well indeed (like the sporting derivatives of the 124 family saloon), while at least one was produced for almost altruistic reasons. That was the Fiat Dino, which was essentially a way of providing a sufficiently high production volume to homologate the Ferrari V6 Dino engine (which Fiat went on to produce in iron-block form).

Fiat's high point in advanced design, and in the sports car realm, came in the 1970s with two mid-engined, rear-drive models – the Fiat X1/9 and the Lancia-badged Monte Carlo. The X1/9 marked a considerable advance over Fiat's previous small sports models, the 850 Spider and Coupé, which had pushrod overhead-valve engines of under one litre. Despite the popularity of the X1/9, such models were only built as a sideline compared with the bulk of Fiat production, which concentrated on small front-wheel-drive cars.

Early in the 1980s Fiat decided to pull out of the sports car business, but that did not mean an end to two of their most popular designs; the X1/9 lived on as the Bertone X1/9, built by the coachbuilders who designed the original model. A similar arrangement saw the front-engined Spider 2000 convertible stay in production, built by its coachbuilders Pininfarina.

Despite withdrawing from sports car production directly, Fiat were still heavily involved in motorsport, and their major contribution to the sporting and supercar scene in modern times has been the rescue of several famous marques which might otherwise have disappeared altogether. Since the 1950s Fiat have absorbed Abarth, Lancia, Ferrari and finally Alfa Romeo, while also taking a majority shareholding in De Tomaso (which also meant control of Innocenti and Maserati at one stage). The only significant firm to escape the Fiat net was Lamborghini, which eventually became a part of Chrysler – there was clearly no way both Ferrari and Lamborghini could be accommodated within the same company framework. Fiat's sporting interests were fully covered by the businesses under their control, and were exercised in a most rational manner. Lancia were given full responsibility for World Championship rallying after Fiat themselves withdrew, and cars like the Stratos and the later four-wheel-drive Lancia Deltas enjoyed huge success. Lancia were also involved in endurance racing (with less impressive results), while Ferrari took sole charge of Formula 1 Grand Prix racing. With Alfa Romeo it had a marque with sufficient panache in building sports saloons to challenge the international touring car scene. Fiat acquired Maserati, and new model launches in the 1990s, introducing the coupé, Barchetta and Bravo lines, served to strengthen its position in the market place.

were built up to 1926. Then, in the mid-1920s, came the 509 with an even smaller, 990-cc, overhead-camshaft engine. That was the first in a series of 'baby cars' which have figured in Fiat's history ever since.

The greatest Fiat success stories of the between-war years were the 508 Ballila, with a 25-bhp one-litre engine, and the first Fiat 500, the Topolino, introduced in 1936. The Ballila proved popular enough to be produced under licence in Germany, Czechoslovakia, Poland and France, while the Topolino (Mickey Mouse) showed what could be done with just 570 cc. With independent front suspension, hydraulic brakes and synchromesh it was advanced indeed for such a cheap and cheerful design. The first model continued to be built until 1948.

*Above: Like Alfa Romeo (who Fiat now own), Fiat always incorporate a laurel wreath around the outside of their badge. That dates back to 1922 and the second Italian Grand Prix (the first to be held at Monza). A Fiat 804-404, driven by Pietro Bordino, won at an average speed of 86.9 mph and the laurel wreath commemorates that famous victory.*

*Right: Although Fiat's success has always been based on providing economical and affordable transport for the masses, the company has not ignored motorsport, sports car or the hot hatchback market. The Uno Turbo produced 118 bhp from its 1372-cc fuel-injected turbo-engine giving it a top speed of 126 mph along with a 0–60 mph acceleration time of 8.3 seconds.*

# Fiat 1100S 1947-51

Fiat's first post-war sports car, although launched in 1947, was really conceived in 1932 when the original Type 508 Ballila was announced. This was the first small Fiat for many years, and it was the first to use a new type of four-cylinder engine.

The Ballila Sport was introduced in 1933, an overhead-valve version of the engine followed a year later, and the 508C MM model raced in the Mille Miglia of 1938. This had a remarkable style, which was at least a decade ahead of the rest of the industry.

After Dante Giacosa became Fiat's technical director in 1945, a flood of new models was designed, one being the 1100S. The chassis and running gear of the new car were those of the existing 1100 saloon (which had been launched in 1939), while the style made it a direct descendant of the 508C MM coupé.

The chassis itself, though sticking with channel-section side members and a rigid rear axle, used coil-spring and wishbone front suspension, while the 1.1-litre engine was both reliable when standard, and powerful when tuned for racing. The body shell, which was built for Fiat by Savio, was a smoothly-detailed two-seater coupé. One of the very first to have aerodynamic styling, it had no bumpers, and was equipped with rear wheel spats.

The 1100S was a splendid little car, for it could achieve 93 mph with a standard power output of 51 bhp, and several race-tuned cars proved their point in the heat of competition. Only 401 were built, however, before the Pininfarina-styled 1100ES took over in 1950.

Mechanically this was the same as before, but although it was heavier and bulkier, it was an occasional four-seater – and it was remarkably attractive. Those pundits who insist that the Lancia Aurelia GT was the prototype of all post-war Grand Touring cars should look instead at the Fiat 1100ES, where all the same styling cues are evident.

## Fiat 1100S variants

### Fiat 1100ES
The 1100ES Pininfarina coupé was produced in 1950 and 1951, with a 2+2 body style. Only 50 were built.

## Specification (1947 1100S)
**Engine:** inline four-cylinder, overhead-valve
**Bore × stroke:** 68 mm × 75 mm
**Capacity:** 1089 cc
**Maximum power:** 51 bhp
**Transmission:** four-speed manual gearbox, rear-wheel drive
**Chassis:** separate steel frame with channel-section side and cross-bracing members
**Suspension:** independent front with coil springs; live rear axle with semi-elliptic leaf springs
**Brakes:** drums front and rear
**Bodywork:** aluminium two-seat coupé
**Maximum speed:** 93 mph (150 km/h)

*Above: Although the 1100S could trace its ancestry back to before the war, the bodywork was very advanced for the time. This is a 1950 ES example with a coupé body designed by Pininfarina.*

*Below: The smooth lines of the original Savio-built coupé helped give the 1100S a top speed of 93 mph, despite a lowly power output of only 51 bhp from its overhead-valve 1089-cc engine.*

*Below: In addition to the Savio and Pininfarina designs, Fiat's small coupé was also bodied by Zagato, who could be guaranteed to come up with striking designs, often giving a far greater impression of speed.*

## Fiat 8V 1952-54

Two noted motoring historians have assessed the 8V thus: Michael Sedgwick described it as a case of "technicians thinking aloud", while Graham Robson saw the car as "Fiat's designers indulging themselves". The 8V, in other words, was never a serious series-production project, but it was produced to show the world how Fiat could, and just *might*, produce a great sports car in the future.

The *Otto Vu*, as it was called in Italian, was one of those rare new cars, in that it really *was* new, from end to end. None of the chassis, suspension, or engine components had previously been seen on a private car, while the style was unique, striking, and very attractive.

At the heart of the car was a narrow-angle, 70-degree, V8 engine with three crankshaft bearings and with the spark plugs outboard of the cylinder heads. This unit had originally been projected for use in an up-market version of Fiat's new 1900 saloon, but was never used in that application. The narrow angle was necessary for the engine to fit inside the slim engine bay of the 1900. It had no connection with any other Fiat engine, either previously designed or to be used in the future, and in standard form it produced 105 bhp. A tuned version brought the power output up another 10 bhp, to give a maximum of 115 bhp.

The basis of the structure was a twin-tube frame, to which the car's body was later welded. The front suspension was conventional by contemporary Fiat

standards, but the rear suspension was a real advance, for it was independent, with a chassis-mounted differential. The secret here was that the differential was 'lifted' from Fiat's latest Campagnola 4×4 model.

A study of the style showed this to be a frustrated race-car design, rather than a completely practical road-car layout. The shape, a smooth and sinuously-detailed two-seater fastback with four headlamps, was by Rapi, and had a cabin so narrow that the passenger's seat was set back, out of line with the driver's seat, by several inches, so that the driver could have space to work the controls.

By the standards of the day the 8V was a very fast car, for it could reach nearly 120 mph under normal conditions. It was not until the 1960s that Fiat produced a car which could outrun it. Fiat's problem was that they had no desire to make large numbers of these cars (there was no production tooling for the V8 engine, for example), so they priced the car at 2.85 million lire, a prohibitive cost which was well over twice that of the 1400 saloon.

After the first 34 cars had been built, Fiat altered the nose style, removed the rear wheel spats, and provided the four headlamps in slanted 'Chinese' location. Unhappily, this fascinating limited-production car (only 114 were produced) was never further developed by Fiat, although Siata used the running gear in the Siata 208.

### Specification (1952)

**Engine:** V8, overhead-valve
**Bore × stroke:** 72 mm × 61.3 mm
**Capacity:** 1996 cc
**Maximum power:** 105 or 115 bhp
**Transmission:** four- or five-speed manual gearbox, rear-wheel drive
**Chassis:** separate steel frame with tubular side members, welded to body on assembly
**Suspension:** independent front and rear, each with wishbones and coil springs
**Brakes:** drums front and rear
**Bodywork:** steel two-seater coupé
**Maximum speed (approx):** 120 mph (193 km/h)

*Above: Both the engineers and the stylists were permitted a degree of self-indulgence with the 8V, which was never intended for volume-production. Under the skin it was more like a racing machine than a roadgoing product; on the outside its streamlined contours echoed the features of contemporary jet aeroplanes. This is a 1953 Ghia-bodied example.*

*Below: Seen here at the 1952 Paris Motor Show, the car looked sleek and modern in the mostly still-austere post-war climate. Under its curvaceous front end was a brand-new two-litre V8 engine.*

# Fiat 1200 Cabriolet 1959-63

At the Geneva Motor Show of 1959, Fiat produced a successor to the 1200 Spider which was as shapely as the 1200 had been lumpy, and as versatile as the old type had been single-purpose. The new models, spearheaded by an OSCA twin-cam-engined option, were very competent sports cars indeed.

The new range was coded Fiat 118, and was to be built with a choice of pushrod or twin-cam engines. Like the earlier types, the new cars were monocoques, using a slightly modified Fiat 1100/1200 saloon underpan, topped off with a two-seater open-top shell at the Pininfarina factory. This time, however, the models were also styled by Pininfarina, and all

were produced with permanent cabriolet soft tops.

Although it was built up on the same floorpan and basic chassis, compared with the obsolete *Trasformabile* style of the mid-1950s, the new Cabriolet was 8.4 inches longer and two inches wider. It had a smooth profile, complete with a conventional curved (not wrap-around) windscreen, and there were glass wind-up windows in the doors.

In many ways these Fiats were the MGAs of the Italian motor industry, for they were smart-looking cars which used mainly 'mainstream' components. Their reputation was rescued by the use of a pleasing shape, and by a sporting, if

not a racing, character.

These cars were to be built, in various forms, for seven years, and during this time there was always a choice of engines – one a Fiat pushrod overhead-valve unit, the other a limited-production twin-cam which OSCA of Bologna had designed, but which Fiat always manufactured.

The original choice was of the old-type 1200 Gran Luce engine (58 bhp) or a 1.5-litre twin-cam (80 bhp), but the 1500S became a 1600S (with 90 bhp) in 1962, while the 1200 was replaced by a new type of 1.5-litre/72-bhp pushrod engine in 1963. The 1600S was rare (only 3,089 were built), and it had a top speed of nearly 110 mph.

Even at this stage, Fiat were still learning all about sports cars. In seven years, nearly 40,000 cars in this range were produced – not nearly as many as models like the Triumph TR3 or the MG MGA, but a great success by Fiat's standards. When the time came to develop another generation, based on the 124, Fiat did not hesitate.

*Left: Although based on the floorpan of the mundane Fiat 1100 saloon, the 1959-on Cabriolets were handsomely styled two-seaters with bodywork designed and constructed by Pininfarina.*

*Below: With power ranging from 58 bhp to 90 bhp, the Fiat Cabriolets covered a wide performance range. The quickest, 1600S, version had a 1.6-litre OSCA-designed twin-cam engine and a top speed of around 110 mph. This is a 1963 1500.*

## Fiat 1200 Cabriolet variants

### Fiat 1500 Cabriolet

The 1500 Cabriolet took over from the 1200 Cabriolet from 1963 to 1966, with a 77-mm × 79.5-mm, 1481-cc/72-bhp engine, front disc brakes and a top speed of 91 mph.

### Fiat 1500S Cabriolet

The 1500S Cabriolet was the first to use the twin-cam OSCA-designed engine, this being a 78-mm×78-mm, 1491-cc/80-bhp unit. Front disc brakes were fitted from late 1960. Top speed was 105 mph.

### Fiat 1600S Cabriolet

The 1600S was introduced in 1962 and lasted until the range was replaced in 1966. It was rare, with only just over 3,000 built, but quite desirable with its 90-bhp engine and a top speed of well over 100 mph.

## Specification (1962 1600S)

**Engine:** inline four-cylinder, twin-cam
**Bore × stroke:** 80 mm × 78 mm
**Capacity:** 1568 cc
**Maximum power:** 90 bhp
**Transmission:** four-speed (later five-speed) manual gearbox, rear-wheel drive
**Chassis:** steel unit-construction body/chassis assembly
**Suspension:** independent front with wishbones and coil springs; live rear axle with semi-elliptic leaf springs
**Brakes:** discs front and rear
**Bodywork:** steel two-seater, optional hard top
**Maximum speed:** 110 mph (177 km/h)

## Fiat 2300S and 2300 Coupé 1961-68

Although Fiat have never been very successful at designing and marketing large-engined cars, they did well with the 2300S and 2300 Coupés of the 1960s. Styled by Ghia on the apparently unpromising base of the square-rigged 1800/2100 four-door Fiat saloons, these cars were distinctive, and made a good name for themselves.

By this time, Fiat were adept at turning a saloon car 'chassis' into something much more sporting, and this big six-cylinder car was no exception. The platform – literally – of the design was that of the existing saloon, while the superstructure was styled and manufactured by Ghia of Turin.

This car, in fact, started life as a private-venture design by Ghia, but after Fiat saw it at the Turin Motor Show in 1960 it was officially adopted by the factory, and went on sale a year later. Because it was a substantial platform, on a 104.3-in wheelbase, there was ample room for a four-seater cabin, although the body Ghia produced had a very smart two-door coupé shape.

The engine was Fiat's modern straight-six 2.3-litre unit, which was offered in two tunes – as a 136-bhp 2300S, or as a 105-bhp 2300 with lower overall gearing. Most people, as you would guess, chose the 136-bhp version, which gave a top speed of 121 mph, this speaking well of the aerodynamic efficiency of what was quite a large car.

The 2300S was actually dubbed the 'poor man's Ferrari' at one time, for it made all the right sort of noises, though in fairness its character, style and furnishings were never up to Ferrari standards. Neither, for that matter, was the price asked!

Fiat have never released production figures for the 2300, but Ghia once boasted of producing up to 15 a day. More than 20,000 must surely have been built before assembly ended in 1967.

*Below: Powered by a 2279-cc six-cylinder engine, the 2300 Coupés of the 1960s were elegant, spacious two-door four-seaters offering a good deal of style and sophistication at relatively down-to-earth prices. Seen here is the more powerful and popular S model.*

*Above: The 2300S had the more powerful, 136-bhp, version of the pushrod straight-six.*

The 2300 Coupés were the last models designed for Fiat by Ghia (who were soon to be taken over by Ford), as Fiat switched to Pininfarina for the 2300's successor, the 130 Coupé.

### Specification (1961 2300S)

**Engine:** inline six-cylinder, overhead-valve
**Bore × stroke:** 78 mm × 79.5 mm
**Capacity:** 2279 cc
**Maximum power:** 136 bhp
**Transmission:** four-speed manual gearbox, rear-wheel drive
**Chassis:** steel unit-construction body/chassis assembly
**Suspension:** independent front with wishbones and torsion bars; live rear axle with semi-elliptic leaf springs
**Brakes:** discs front and rear
**Bodywork:** steel four-seater coupé
**Maximum speed:** 120 mph (193 km/h)

*Below: Even stripped for the racetrack, the Ghia coachwork looks distinguished.*

# Fiat 850 Coupé and Spider 1965-73

FMO 123K

## Specification (1965 850 Coupé)

**Engine:** inline four-cylinder, overhead-valve
**Bore × stroke:** 65 mm × 63.5 mm
**Capacity:** 843 cc
**Maximum power:** 49 bhp
**Transmission:** four-speed manual gearbox, rear-wheel drive
**Chassis:** steel unit-construction body/chassis assembly
**Suspension:** independent front with wishbones and transverse leaf spring; independent rear with coil springs
**Brakes:** discs front, drums rear
**Bodywork:** steel four-seater coupé
**Maximum speed (approx):** 87 mph (140 km/h)

*Left: Although its 843-cc four-cylinder engine was tail-mounted, the little Coupé had attractive, well-proportioned lines, styled by Fiat's in-house design team, now led by Mario Felice Boano.*

When Fiat's new 850 saloon appeared in 1964, it looked a most unlikely candidate for conversion for sports-car motoring. In 1965, however, Fiat proved just how resourceful they were, by launching the 850 Coupé and 850 Spider.

The 850 saloon was really no more than a grown-up 600, which is to say that it had a steel monocoque four-seater saloon body shell, with all-independent suspension, and a small but high-revving four-cylinder engine, mounted in the tail and driving the rear wheels.

On this unpromising base, Fiat then produced two sporting derivatives, one of them a Coupé with 2+2 seating, the other a smart little two-seater open sports car. The Coupé was styled in-house by Fiat's own specialists, who were now being led by Mario Felice Boano, and the Spider by Giorgetto Giugiaro at Bertone.

Fiat manufactured their own Coupé body shells, but Spider manufacture (plus painting and trimming) was completed by Bertone themselves, at the Grugliasco factory in the outskirts of Turin. The 850 Spider was in good company, for it took shape alongside the Ferrari-engined Fiat Dino Coupés.

The two cars looked, and were, rather different, but both had the same sort of urgent, bustling character which, allied to competitive prices, made them sell very well indeed. By comparison with the Spider, the Coupé was almost a conventional car; the Spider, on the other hand, had smart and rounded lines, looking faster than it actually was. The rear engine position provided excellent traction, and the light weight helped to make the cars nimble, all of which added up to an appealing package.

The original models were replaced by the 'Sport' types in 1968, which meant that the engines were enlarged and made more powerful. By the time production ended in 1973, a total of 342,873 Coupés and 124,660 Spiders had been built.

The 850 Coupé's replacement was the 128 Coupé, which was not really such an appealing car, while the Bertone-styled Spider gave way to the excellent mid-engined X1/9.

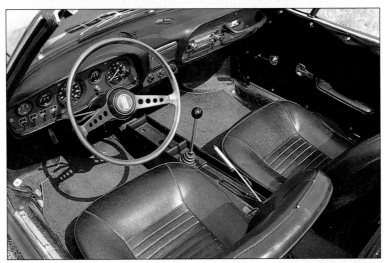

*Left: Both Coupés and Spiders were relatively small cars, so their interiors were necessarily somewhat cramped. Apart from a typical 1960s Italian long-armed/short-legged driving position, though, they were comfortable and convenient, with a neat and well-integrated fascia design incorporating a passably comprehensive array of clearly-legible dials and minor controls worked by the then-trendy banks of toggle switches.*

*Below: Unlike the Fiat-built Coupé, the 850 Spider was designed, assembled and trimmed by Bertone, whose chief stylist at that time was Giorgetto Giugiaro, later to win fame with his own studio, Ital Design.*

# Fiat 124 Sport Coupé and Spider 1966-82

When Fiat replaced their long-running 1100 family car with a new mass-production model, the 124, it was natural that there should be new sporting derivatives of this design. The result was the long-running 124 Sport Coupé and Spider models. By any standards, particularly in terms of numbers sold, these were an enormous success.

Like previous middle-sized Fiat sports cars, these new models were based on the underpan of the 'donor' saloon. The 124, though strictly conventional, had a modern 'chassis' and suspension layout and – even more importantly – it used a new powertrain family of which twin-cam engines were integral members, and for which five-speed gearboxes were already available.

As with the 850 models, Fiat decided to produce two rather different types of two-door sporting 124. The Coupé would be a four-seater 'in-house' design using a standard-length underpan, while the Spider would run on a 5.4-in shorter wheelbase, and would have a two-seater roadster body, styled and manufactured by Pininfarina.

Power for these cars was originally by a 1.4-litre twin-cam rated at 90 bhp, but it was already known that the engine

*Right: For the 124 Sport, as with the 850, design and construction of the Spider were both entrusted to an outside styling house – in this instance, Pininfarina.*

would stretch readily to 1.8 litres and – with difficulty – all the way to two litres. The future for this design looked very promising.

The Coupé was a smart and practical car which combined brisk performance with style, comfort, and a great deal of stowage capacity, whereas the Spider was a roomy open-top two-seater with the accent on dash, and on hood-down motoring. The combination was near-irresistible, and the cars sold in large numbers right from the start.

Over the years the twin-cam engine was enlarged first to 1.6 litres, then to 1.8 litres, with the Coupé being facelifted (or, more accurately, 'noselifted') on each occasion. Few changes, on the other hand, were made – or needed – on the Spider, which had the same timeless appeal, and much the same performance, as the MGB.

The 1.6-litre Coupés were introduced in 1969, with an 80-mm × 80-mm, 1608-cc/110-bhp engine, and a top speed of 112 mph. The 1.8-litre models, from 1972,

had an 84-mm × 79.2-mm, 1756-cc/118-bhp power unit. The Coupé was finally dropped in 1975, nine years after launch, and after 279,672 cars had been built, but the Spider carried on.

The Spider became a two-litre model in 1978, with an 84-mm × 90-mm, 1995-cc/87-bhp engine, later 103 bhp, normally-aspirated or turbocharged, for North American sale only.

A total of 178,439 Fiat-badged Spiders had been built before Fiat took a corporate decision to get out of the sports car business in 1982. Pininfarina, who already built, painted and trimmed the monocoques, then took over complete assembly, and after that the car carried on in production as a 'Pininfarina Spider' until the late 1980s.

*Left: Fiat styled and built the 124 Sport Coupé themselves; Coupés and Spiders were all powered by a free-revving, belt-driven, twin-cam four-cylinder engine. Early versions had single headlamps and the 90-bhp/1438-cc engine; this is a 110-bhp/1608-cc model from 1971.*

*Below: Pininfarina continued producing the Spider into the late 1980s. Shown is a 1982 Canadian-market two-litre Turbo, fitted by the North American importers with a small IHI turbocharger to achieve an output of 120 bhp.*

## Fiat 124 Sport Coupé and Spider variants

### Fiat 124 Abarth Rallye
From late 1972 to 1975 Fiat produced the 124 Abarth Rallye as a 'homologation special' for motorsport. It had a 1756-cc/128-bhp engine, independent rear suspension by coil springs, many glassfibre skin panels, and a glassfibre hard top. Top speed was 118 mph, and 1,013 cars were made.

### Fiat 124 Spider Turbo
A two-litre 120-bhp Turbo was sold in North America in 1981 and 1982.

### Pininfarina 124 Spider Europa
A 122-bhp European version of the two-litre Spider was launched in 1982.

## Specification (1966 124 Sport)
**Engine:** inline four-cylinder, twin-cam
**Bore × stroke:** 80 mm × 71.5 mm
**Capacity:** 1438 cc
**Maximum power:** 90 bhp
**Transmission:** four-speed or five-speed manual gearbox
**Chassis:** steel unit-construction
**Suspension:** independent front with wishbones and coil springs; live rear axle with coil springs
**Brakes:** discs front and rear
**Bodywork:** steel two-seater
**Maximum speed:** 106 mph (171 km/h)

# Fiat Dino Spider and Coupé 1966-73

Fiat's Dino was conceived because Ferrari had a problem – one that only Fiat's massive manufacturing capability could solve. In the mid-1960s, Ferrari wanted to race in a new Formula 2 category. To do so, the company wished to use its well-developed aluminium V6 'Dino' engine. The new Formula 2 rules required a minimum of 500 of these engines to be fitted to cars in a 12-month period. At the time, Ferrari could neither build so many engines, nor sell so many cars.

After negotiations, Fiat agreed to manufacture the engines, and to develop their own sports cars for them. The Ferrari engines, however, were only ever used in one type of Fiat, for the V6 engine used in the later Fiat 130 models was completely different.

Except for their use of the 65-degree V6 quad-cam engines, there was no technical link between the front-engined Fiats and the mid-engined Dino 206 and 246 types. The front-engined Fiat Dinos were built in two guises – a Pininfarina Spider two-seater, and a longer-wheel-base Bertone 2+2 Coupé – both of them using a new pressed-steel underpan and

*Right: Enzo Ferrari gave his V6 mid-engined road car the name of his late son, Dino; it was natural that Fiat should also use the name when making the same V6 engine and using it in their own cars.*

suspension layouts.

The Spider was a short and curvaceous machine, while the Bertone Coupé was a longer and less exuberant car. Because of the engine they used, both had urgent and very sporty characters – and both were very fast.

The original two-litre Fiat Dinos were developed in a great hurry, and the miracle is that they were both very desirable cars. In truth the originals were a real mish-mash of componentry, with very little new design. The front suspension was derived from the 125 saloon, the gearbox was a modified 2300S unit, and the axle was a 2300-type beam. The rear suspension was not as simple as that description makes it sound, however. Granted, it was a live axle, but the semi-elliptic leaf springs were wide mono-filament types which gave reasonable

location while the damping system featured double dampers per side, one on each side of the leaf spring. The axle also had the sophisticated touch of a limited-slip differential. The handling and roadholding produced by this system was excellent, as was the performance – even from just two litres, as the engine would spin around to

8,000 rpm and the standing kilometre could be covered in 29.5 seconds.

The Spider went on sale before the end of 1966, while the Coupé followed during 1967. The first 500 cars were completed quickly to allow Ferrari to race their new Formula 2 cars – but it was all for nothing. The new racing category was utterly dominated by the Cosworth FVA engine, which meant that Ferrari's haste was in vain.

When the 2.4-litre iron-block version of the engine appeared in 1969, Fiat built

*Left: There were two distinct Fiat Dino styles: an open two-seater and a closed 2+2 model. The attractively curvy Pininfarina-bodied Spider seen here was first on the market, in late 1966. Using a version of the Ferrari-designed two-litre V6 detuned slightly to produce 160 rather than 175 bhp, it had a maximum speed of close to 130 mph.*

*Below: In 1967 came the release of Bertone's less striking but still handsome Dino Coupé, built on a slightly longer wheelbase to provide a four-seat, or at least 2+2, option. Like the Spider, it gained the heavier but more powerful and considerably torquier 2.4-litre engine in 1969, along with a stronger ZF gearbox and independent rear suspension.*

an even better Dino. Behind the engine there was a new five-speed ZF gearbox, while there was also independent rear suspension using a modified Fiat 130 saloon layout.

By this time, however, the Ferrari-built mid-engined Dino 246 GT had come onto the market, and made most of the headlines. The result, therefore, was that far fewer Fiat Dino 2400s than Dino 2000s were sold. In seven years, a total of 7,651 Fiat Dinos were built – 4,833 with two-litre engines, and 2,818 of the later 2.4-litre cars.

## Fiat Dino variants

### Fiat Dino 2400

From late 1969, an extensively redesigned family of Dino 2400 models went on sale. The second-generation car had an iron-block 92.5-mm × 60-mm, 2418-cc/180-bhp engine and a different five-speed gearbox; independent rear

suspension by coil springs replaced the original leaf-spring four-damper live axle system. The top speed was 130 mph, while the extra torque helped acceleration.

## Specification (1966 two-litre)

**Engine:** V6, quad-cam
**Bore × stroke:** 86 mm × 57 mm
**Capacity:** 1987 cc
**Maximum power:** 160 bhp
**Transmission:** five-speed manual gearbox, rear-wheel drive
**Chassis:** steel unit-construction body/ chassis assembly
**Suspension:** independent front with wishbones and coil springs; live rear axle with semi-elliptic leaf springs
**Brakes:** discs front and rear
**Bodywork:** steel two-seater Spider (Pininfarina) or four-seater Coupé (Bertone)
**Maximum speed (approx):** 125 mph (201 km/h)

*Above: Although both Fiat Dino designs were good-looking, the Pininfarina two-seater soft-top version was perhaps the bolder of the two. Its more bulbous, muscular lines seemed to give a stronger hint of its Ferrari connection.*

*Below: Early Dinos used the 1987-cc version of the quad-cam V6; 500 were built quickly so Ferrari could qualify it for racing. When the engine block was made in iron instead of aluminium in 1969, capacity grew to 2418 cc and output to 180 bhp.*

*Above: The Fiat Dino's dash was typical of those in Italian sports models of the time, with large speedometer and tachometer dials in twin binnacles viewed through the aluminium-spoked wheel.*

*Right: Although notably different in looks and styling flavour, the Pininfarina (foreground) and Bertone Dinos had some things in common, like the four headlamps set into the grille.*

# Fiat 130 Coupé 1971-77

Although Fiat's large Type 130 saloon of the 1970s was a very plain design which did not sell at all well, it gave rise to an extremely elegant large coupé. Except for its Fiat-like tendency to rust away rather severely if neglected, the 130 Coupé was a fast, impressive and altogether attractive four-seater.

The 130 saloon was launched in 1969, and under its very upright four-door saloon steel monocoque was a brand-new 60-degree V6 engine (a totally different engine from the Dino unit), a choice of manual or automatic transmission, disc brakes all round and all-independent suspension. The original 130 was not fast enough, and seemed to have few impressive features, but the Pininfarina-styled two-door Coupé that followed it was a different proposition altogether.

For this car, the engine was enlarged from 2.9 litres to 3.2 litres and 165 bhp, which meant that the car was capable of nearly 120 mph. Its attraction was in its styling, and its character. In some ways, perhaps, it is slightly too square-rigged to stand the test of time, but from all angles it still looks good, and there is ample space in the cabin for four full-sized adults to travel in comfort. Pininfarina also built one four-door saloon version of this style – cynics asked why Fiat did not put it on sale instead of their own lumpen creation!

The V6 engine was a fine design by Fiat's resident genius, Aurelio Lampredi (yes, the same Lampredi who had designed a V12 engine for Ferrari in the late-1940s), and featured single-overhead-camshaft valve gear, driven by a cogged belt from the crankshaft. It was not meant to be as sporting an engine as the Ferrari Dino unit – and was not fitted to any other type of Fiat.

The 130 Coupé was always quite an expensive car, which explains why sales were limited, but in a six-year life Fiat sold a total of 4,491, most of them with Borg-Warner automatic transmission.

## Specification (1971)

**Engine:** V6, overhead-cam
**Bore × stroke:** 102 mm × 66 mm
**Capacity:** 3235 cc
**Maximum power:** 165 bhp
**Transmission:** five-speed manual gearbox or three-speed automatic, rear-wheel drive
**Chassis:** steel unit-construction body/chassis assembly
**Suspension:** independent front with wishbones and coil springs; independent rear with coil springs
**Brakes:** discs front and rear
**Bodywork:** steel four-seater coupé
**Maximum speed** 116 mph (187 km/h)

*Left: You might not guess from its broad, flat panel expanses and, arguably, stark overall look that the Fiat 130 was styled by Pininfarina – a firm better known for creating rippling, rounded and more sensuous shapes at that time. Nonetheless, the crispness of the big Fiat coupé's styling made it look light for its size and earned the car much admiration.*

*Below: Based on the mechanics of a dull and unwieldy-looking four-door saloon, the 130 Coupé was powered by an Aurelio Lampredi-designed 60-degree V6 engine entirely unrelated to the 65-degree Dino V6. The 130 engine, which had a single overhead camshaft per bank, driven by toothed belts rather than chains, was enlarged from 2.9 to 3.2 litres for use in the Coupé, giving an output of 165 bhp with plenty of torque. Five-speed manual transmission was available, but most examples were sold with a three-speed automatic.*

## Fiat X1/9 1972-88

When Fiat developed the new front-engine/front-wheel-drive 128 family car, they toyed with the idea of developing a Spider derivative. Bertone, one of their most trusted styling consultants, thought differently, and proposed a mid-engined car instead.

The result, unveiled in 1972, was the Fiat X1/9, a pretty little Targa-topped two-seater which sold remarkably well for more than 15 years. In all that time, the car received only one styling facelift, one change of name, and one major mechanical updating

In many ways, this car was the inspiration for the Lancia Monte Carlo, which was a larger car but had the same basic layout, the same advantages, and the same drawbacks.

The compact little monocoque of the X1/9 was all-new, but most of the running gear was lifted from the 128, or modified from that design. The secret was to mount the transverse engine/transmission package of the 128 behind the cabin, where it could drive the rear wheels.

Although the original car was only 151 inches long, it was a miracle of packaging. Because the fuel tank and the spare wheel were mounted behind the seats, there was space for a luggage container up front; there was also another one in the tail, behind the engine itself. The roof panel could be removed and either left at home or stowed under the front 'bonnet'.

The X1/9 (the title was also its project code at Fiat) was such a pretty little car that it was unkindly dubbed a 'hairdresser's special', which was unfair to a fine chassis which handled very well indeed. At first, as a 1.3-litre four-speed car, it could not quite reach 100 mph, but from 1978, with 1.5 litres and a five-speed

*Right: The compact, mid-engined X1/9 proved an amazingly long-lived model, remaining on sale for 16 years after its 1972 launch.*

gearbox, it was more than a match for cars like the MGB or the Triumph Spitfire.

Ten years after its launch, by which time Fiat had produced more than 150,000 X1/9s, Bertone took over total assembly and the car was given a 'Bertone' badge. By this time, though, the car was well past its peak, and sold only slowly until 1988, when the last examples of all were produced.

### Fiat X1/9 variants

#### Fiat X1/9 1500

From late 1978, the X1/9 became the X1/9 1500, with an 86.4-mm × 63.9-mm, 1498-cc/85-bhp engine, a five-speed gearbox, and a top speed of 106 mph.

The X1/9 1500 officially became a 'Bertone' model in 1982, but was mechanically unchanged until the end of production in 1988.

### Specification (1972 1.3-litre)

**Engine:** inline four-cylinder, overhead-cam
**Bore × stroke:** 86 mm × 55.5 mm
**Capacity:** 1290 cc
**Maximum power:** 73 bhp
**Transmission:** four-speed manual gearbox, rear-wheel drive
**Chassis:** steel unit-construction body/chassis assembly
**Suspension:** independent front and rear, each with struts and coil springs
**Brakes:** discs front and rear
**Bodywork:** steel two-seater coupé, with removable roof panel
**Maximum speed:** 99 mph (159 km/h)

*Above: Just out of shot in this interior view is the 'Nuccio Bertone' plaque on the dashboard. Fiat themselves stopped manufacturing the Bertone-designed X1/9 10 years after it was introduced, but the coachbuilder took over assembly and the car remained on the market until 1988, with only cosmetic changes.*

*Below: The X1/9 underwent few major mechanical revisions. In 1978 its transverse, mid-mounted single-overhead-cam engine was enlarged from 1290 to 1498 cc and a five-speed gearbox was added. Engine power, which suffered from 1970s emission restrictions, climbed to 85 bhp on later models with the addition of fuel injection.*

OLX 288W

# Fiat 131 Abarth Rallye 1976

Fiat made an entry into world-class rallying in 1969, and soon laid master plans to produce 'homologation specials' which would be outright winners against cars like the Lancia Stratos and the Ford Escort RS1800. The 124 Abarth Rallye sports car of 1972 was the original, but this was only an interim model. For 1976, and to meet Group 4 regulations, Fiat developed the very specialised 131 Abarth Rallye.

Although outwardly similar to the Fiat 131 – Fiat's 'Ford Cortina' of the period – it was very different under the skin, and production was limited to a mere 400 cars, the minimum which the sporting regulations required. Instead of steel, many body panels were in lightweight glassfibre, and the driveline was unique to the Abarth.

At the rear, the standard 131's rigid rear axle was discarded in favour of the 124 Abarth Rallye's independent rear suspension layout. Both rear and (modified) front suspension were laid out to be adaptable for loose-surface or tarmac rallies.

The engine was a long-stroke development of the celebrated mid-sized Fiat twin-cam unit, this time with the 16-valve head which had been evolved for the 124 Abarth Rallye, and although it only developed 140 bhp in 'road car' trim, another 90 bhp was available for rally use. It was backed by a Colotti-developed five-speed gearbox.

The entire batch of 400 cars was built in a matter of months during 1976, with two-door monocoques manufactured by Bertone. Compared with the standard 131, the Abarth derivative had flared wheel arches (to accommodate ultra-wide racing tyres), front and rear spoilers, and a multitude of air intakes and ducts, some of which were blanked-off on the road cars.

Like Ford's Escort RS1800, the 'road car' version of the 131 Abarth Rallye fell between several stools, for it was neither shatteringly fast, nor quiet and civilised, and was not good value for money. In fully-prepared form, however, it rapidly became an effective rally car, with which Fiat won the World Championship for Makes in 1977, 1978 and 1980.

Very few unmodified road cars survived, such was the enthusiasm of customers to turn their cars into full-blooded competition machines, but those which do remain have enormous character and exude special-purpose breeding from every pore.

## Specification

**Engine:** inline four-cylinder, twin-cam
**Bore × stroke:** 84 mm × 90 mm
**Capacity:** 1995 cc
**Maximum power:** 140 bhp (road car), or up to 230 bhp (rally car)
**Transmission:** five-speed manual gearbox, rear-wheel drive
**Chassis:** steel unit-construction body/chassis assembly, glassfibre body panels
**Suspension:** independent front with wishbones and coil springs; independent rear with semi-trailing arms and coil springs
**Brakes:** discs front and rear
**Bodywork:** steel four-seater saloon, with glassfibre panels
**Maximum speed (approx):** 118 mph (190 km/h)

*Left and below: As a rally contender in the late 1970s the 131 Abarth Rallye was superbly successful, winning the manufacturers' title for Fiat three times in the four years from 1977. Both these pictures are from the 1977 RAC Rally: left is the Alen/Kivimaki car and below the Chequered Flag-sponsored Lampinen/Andreasson entry.*

# FIAT Barchetta 1995-present

Launched in spring 1995, the Barchetta put Fiat back on the sports-car map that it had last occupied two decades earlier with the 124 Spider. Its charming classically-inspired lines were the work of Fiat's Centro Stile in Turin. In the UK, it was only available to special order, in left-hand drive only. The front-wheel drive Barchetta was powered by a new 1,747 cc four-cylinder twin-cam engine with 16-valves and variable valve timing, producing 130 bhp at 6,500 rpm and a top speed of 124 mph (200 km/h) and going from 0–62 mph (0-100km/h) in 8.9 seconds.

The term Barchetta means 'little boat', and was first coined for the Ferrari 166S made by Touring Superleggera in 1948, which recalled Fiat's own 509 SM of the 1920s that featured a wooden boat-like body. Retro touches in the Barchetta of the 1990s included faired headlamp pods and chromed door-opening levers embedded in the outer door panels. The boot lid was sunk into the sheet steel without visible hinges, achieved by hand-crafted brazing, and the stylish rear end included recessed rectangular rear-lights and a deep lateral gash on the underside incorporating twin, chrome, exhaust tail-pipes. The hood was manufactured in PVC and folded away into a well behind the seats and covered by a body-coloured metal

*Right: The Barchetta – 'Little Boat' – was a tempting prospect for anyone looking for a production sports car. It boasted a full specification that included ABS, power steering and fire prevention system. The body incorporated a host of intriguing period details that were innovative yet classic, such as the headlight fairings and chromed door handles.*

cover. An air-bag was standard fitment in the three-spoke steering wheel.

The Barchetta was equipped with ventilated discs at the front, and a four-channel ABS system was standard on UK versions. Suspension was independent all round, with MacPherson struts and an anti-roll bar at the front with trailing arms, coil springs and gas dampers, an anti-roll bar and a rigid H-frame consisting of a transverse tubular element and two pressed steel rails at the rear. Power steering was also standard equipment.

The Barchetta also featured passive safety features, including programmed crumple zones reinforced against frontal impact, side-impact bars in the doors, a windscreen reinforced by a tubular hoop that offered some roll-over protection, and a deformation-resistant cockpit. There was also a Fire Prevention System (FPS) with inertia switch, fuel pump

cut-out and fuel shut-off valve.

## Specification

**Engine:** four-cylinder 16-valve
**Bore** x **stroke:** 82 mm x 82.7 mm
**Capacity:** 1747 cc
**Maximum power:** 130 bhp
**Transmission:** five-speed manual
**Chassis:** monocoque
**Suspension:** front, independent by MacPherson struts, lower swinging arms anchored to subframe, coil springs, anti-roll bar; rear, independent by trailing arms anchored to subframe, coil springs, anti-roll bar
**Brakes:** discs all round, 4-sensor ABS

## Variants

### Barchetta 'Ltd'

The Limited Edition version was available in 1998 in two colour co-ordinated versions: Stelvio Green with tan leather interior and a matching hood, or Steel Grey metallic with a red leather interior. Steering wheel, gear lever, door inserts and interior door handles were leather-covered, and it ran on 15-in alloy wheels and 195/55 tyres. Additional features included front foglights, titanium-coloured air vents and instrument surrounds, electric mirrors and aerial.

# FIAT Coupé 1995-present

The Fiat Coupé was unveiled in 1995, and was one of the forerunners of a new generation of stylish coupé models that included the Alfa GTV, Porsche Boxster, BMW Z3 and Audi TT. Its original and innovative design was the product of Fiat's in-house Centro Stile, and took the company back into territory it had last occupied in the 1960s and 1970s with the 124 Sport Coupé. By 1996, the Coupé had been fitted with Fiat's new five-cylinder 20-valve engines in place of their original four-cylinder 16-valve units. In turbocharged 20-valve form, it was the fastest production model that

Fiat Auto had ever built. A Limited Edition version, based on the 20v Turbo with a six-speed gearbox, became available in August 1998.

The normally aspirated Fiat Coupé 20v developed over 150 bhp at 6,700 rpm and 137 lb/ft torque at 3,750 rpm, while the Coupé 20v Turbo yielded 220 bhp at 5,750 rpm and 228 lb/ft of torque at a low 2,500 rpm. The normally aspirated Coupé 20v was capable of 132 mph (212 km/h), with 0–62 mph (0-100 km/h) acceleration in 8.9 seconds, while the Coupé 20v Turbo could do 155 mph (249 km/h) and make

0–62 mph (0-100 km/h) in 6.5 seconds. With 110 bhp per litre, it was one of the fastest 2.0-litre production cars available in the late-1990s, and undercut most of its competitors price-wise by a considerable margin.

It also scored better ergonomically, in that the back seats were useable and boot space was realistic for a young family. The cabin also provided climate control.

From 1998 the normally aspirated engine was equipped with variable geometry inlet manifolding (VIS) and a new Bosch Motronic ME 3.1 injection/ignition

system, which raised power output over 150 bhp at 6,700 rpm. The Bosch Motronic system on the Turbo model included 'gear recognition' and, where appropriate, limited turbocharging boost in first and second gears to prevent excessive wheel spin. Viscodrive traction control was also standard equipment. The Coupé 20v Turbo benefited from a more powerful braking system developed with Brembo that combined one-piece aluminium four piston fixed calipers, thicker, larger diameter ventilated discs, and pads with an increased friction surface.

## Specification (Coupé 20v Turbo

**Engine:** five-cylinder 20-valve, transverse, front-mounted
**Bore** x **stroke:** 82 mm x 76 mm
**Capacity:** 1998 cc
**Maximum power:** 220 bhp
**Transmission:** five-speed
**Chassis:** monocoque
**Suspension:** front, independent by MacPherson struts, transverse lower wishbones anchored to auxiliary cross beam, coil springs, anti-roll bar; rear, independent, with trailing arms anchored to a subframe, coil springs and anti-roll bar
**Brakes:** ventilated discs all round, 4-sensor anti-lock ABS

*Left: The blossoming of the coupé in the mid-1990s spawned a number of new designs. It was undoubtedly the best value in terms of performance and ergonomics – there was good rear-seating and boot space.*

# Ford Motor Company

**Above: The Ford symbol of today differs little from the script on this 1911 Model T Tourer radiator.**

**Below: Cars like this Model A were Ford's mainstays before the sensational V8s arrived in 1932.**

H enry Ford built his first experimental car – the Quadricycle – in a workshop behind his home in Detroit in 1896, but this was well before he set up his own business.

After working for Edison, then for the Detroit Automobile Co., he founded the Ford Motor Company Ltd in 1903. Early Fords were large, hand-built and expensive, but the breakthrough to fame came in 1908 with the launch of the Model T.

With the Model T, Ford set out to build a 'people's car'. By selling the cars at the lowest possible price in only one mechanical specification, he wanted to "put America on wheels". At the Highland Park factory he also developed the novel moving assembly line, which reduced production costs even further.

The result was that more than 15 million Model Ts were built between 1908 and 1927, Ford became the USA's market leader, and fame was assured. But Henry Ford himself was an eccentric who rarely listened to his advisers. Even though the Model A, and the V8-engined cars which followed, were great cars, the company clashed with the trade unions, and gradually fell behind General Motors in the sales battle in the 1930s.

The Model A had been the successor to the famous Model T, an incredible car but one carried on in production far too long. As it represented a new beginning for Ford, the new car was called the Model A. It was thoroughly up-to-date, with four-wheel brakes and a three-speed gearbox, and it established some notable firsts, not only for Ford but among mass-production cars. It was the first mass-produced car to have a safety-glass windscreen, the first to feature hydraulic dampers and it was also the first to boast a station-wagon derivative as a production model.

The Model A was an instant success. In the first 16 months of production, over a million cars were sold. That was a record that was to stand until another Ford, the Escort, outperformed it 57 years later.

After the Model A came the less successful AB and then the far more important V8, known as "Ford's last mechanical triumph". It shared the chassis of the AB, including that model's substandard brakes, and despite the sort of teething problems that were inevitable given its rapid development programme, the flat-head V8 went on to be the mainstay of Ford production through the 1930s. By this stage American cars, the V8s included, were given annual styling changes, demonstrating that Ford had learnt one lesson from the stagnant Model T.

Henry Ford came close to bankrupting his company before he died in the 1940s. His son Edsel never had a chance to stabilise the business before he too died, so it fell to Henry Ford II to sweep into power after World War II and revitalise the firm.

**Left: The Model T established for ever the Ford marque's reputation as a mass-producer of unsophisticated but cheap vehicles. Launched as Henry Ford's 'people's car' in 1908, it was the first model built on a moving assembly line and, with total production reaching more than 15 million, remained the world's best-selling car until overtaken by the VW Beetle. This is a 1911 Model T Tourer.**

**Below: Ford-USA used this badge on the 1956 Thunderbird.**

By this time Ford were also making Mercury and Lincoln models, and had large subsidiary companies in Europe and other continents. For the next 30 years, expansion was steady and consistent.

For much of the time Ford concentrated on supplying cheap family transport, which resulted in US sales climbing from 468,000 in 1946 to 1.5 million by 1959, and on to two million by 1970. Throughout this period Ford fought – and sometimes won – the battle as North America's best-selling company, but in general they were in a secure second place.

By this time, therefore, the company could indulge itself, with cars like the two-seater Thunderbird of the 1950s, the phenomenally successful Mustang of the 1960s, and with models varying in size from the 1.6-litre Pinto of the early 1970s to the 7.0-litre Galaxies and Torinos of the 1960s.

Ford, like GM and Chrysler, suffered badly from the energy crises of the 1970s and 1980s and were obliged to down-size their cars, to make their engines smaller and less powerful, and – in general – to make them less sporting. Like their competitors, Ford also forged links with a Japanese company (in this case, Mazda) and turned to building front-wheel-drive machines in huge numbers.

In the course of the 1980s, Ford made great strides in their US car designs. The company moved on from producing clumsy and conventional models like the LTD, one of the last of the full-size American sedans, through down-sized but still overly conventional types like the Fairmont family car, to almost European-looking models. This trend started with a revolution in the Thunderbird line in the early 1980s, when the car went from being one of the more grotesque examples of American styling to a smooth aerodynamic shape that remains recognisable in today's production car. The Tempo was another example of Ford's growing commitment to the 'aero' look.

Although the company had turned away from its 'Total Performance'

*Above: This Tempo was typical of the new aerodynamic but anonymous-looking 1980s Ford-USA designs; it was firmly in the traditional Ford mould of affordable family transportation but was smaller than earlier Ford saloons.*

image in the 1970s and 1980s as the fuel crises bit hard, that couldn't keep Ford down, and more exciting performance models were produced – cars like the turbocharged Mustang SVO and a rejuvenated Mustang GT. Ford also turned to Japan for a performance option in one of their current-generation cars, the smoothly-styled Taurus, using a specially-commissioned Yamaha V6 to power the Taurus SHO to 135 mph.

The most exciting Ford-designed products were usually sold as Lincolns (the Continental types), but during the 1980s there was a more direct link with Ford of Europe, which led to USA-style Escorts and European-style Escorts starting from the same base. Fords sold in the USA were sometimes built overseas – a classic example being the late 1980s Probes and Capris, which were effectively reshaped Mazdas – but new American styling themes also led to the birth of the smooth and successful Taurus range.

*Below: In the mid-1960s Ford's Mustang was the model that inspired the term 'pony car' and gave impetus to a new category of high-performance saloon-derived models less massive than the alternative 'muscle cars'.*

# Ford Model T 1908-27

Before the VW Beetle swept all before it in the 1970s, the Ford Model T could simply be described as the world's best-selling car. In 19 years well over 15 million were produced, mostly in Detroit, USA, but also assembled from Detroit-supplied parts at factories in the UK and elsewhere.

The Model T was developed to satisfy Henry Ford's belief that American people wanted reliable and basic transportation, not necessarily with beautiful styling. In some ways the Model T was archaic – in its chassis, and particularly its suspension – but in other ways it was needlessly complicated – the epicyclic gearbox and controls, for instance.

There were two vital factors which contributed to the Model T's huge popularity – one was that it was always very cheap to buy, and the other (closely related) was that Ford built up a huge service network of dealers to keep the cars on the road. In both respects, this was unique for the period.

The transverse leaf-spring suspension allowed the chassis and wheels to articulate easily over the often unmade roads of rural America, but the handling and steering precision suffered accordingly. The side-valve engine was robust and torquey, but the transmission was quite unlike any other built into American cars of the day. The 'clutch' pedal was really the gear change lever, neutral position was held by keeping this pedal halfway

*Below: Even for its day, the Model T's construction was spidery, but its simple ladder-type chassis and other vital parts were unusually robust, thanks to the use of vanadium-steel alloys newly developed by Ford's metallurgist, Childe Harold Wills. This Speedster dates from the height of Model T production in 1922.*

down, low gear was engaged by pushing the pedal all the way down, and direct-drive top gear was engaged by releasing it completely.

Prices began at $850 in 1909, but as production built up rapidly the price fell, so that by 1916 it was down to a mere $350. Production began modestly, at 10,000 cars in 1909, but in 1923 no fewer than two million Model Ts were produced in a single year. Production was such that at one point a third of all the cars in the world were Model Ts.

At one stage the Model T was the best-selling car in Britain as well as the USA, the car being built at the Trafford Park plant in Manchester which opened in 1911.

The famous aphorism credited to Henry Ford – "You can have any colour you like, as long as it's black" – was never strictly true; in addition Ford also offered many different body styles.

Although Henry Ford had shown a keen early interest in motorsport, racing fearsome-looking racers like his 999, he saw the Model T's role as cheap, reliable transport rather than as a platform for racing. That didn't stop people from creating cheaper versions of the popular raceabouts (such as the Stutz Bearcat and Mercer Raceabout) on the Model T chassis.

Chevrolet overtook Ford in the mid-1920s, because the Model T had been allowed to continue for too long, and its sales sagged towards the end.

*Right: The Model T engine was a side-valve inline-four, with cylinders cast in unit with the upper crankcase, and a detachable head. Relatively understressed, it was reliable, and flexible enough to permit use of an epicyclic transmission with only two gear ratios.*

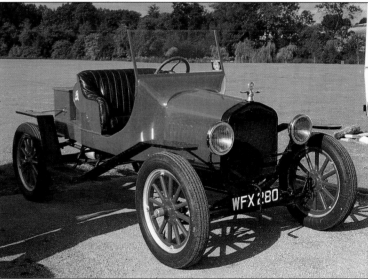

*Above: There was little variation in the mechanical specification of the Model T, and components were almost entirely interchangeable from year to year – this was deliberate policy, to ensure ease of servicing and constant availability of parts – but the 'Tin Lizzie' was offered in a wide variety of body styles with both two and four seats. Shown here is a 1922 Speedster Special. The Speedsters were all adaptations of existing Model Ts rather than factory models.*

## Specification (1908)

**Engine:** inline-four, side-valve T-head
**Bore × stroke:** 95.2 mm × 101.6 mm
**Capacity:** 2896 cc
**Maximum power:** 20 bhp
**Transmission:** two-speed manual (epicyclic) gearbox, rear-wheel drive
**Chassis:** separate steel frame with channel-section main members
**Suspension:** non-independent with beam front axle and live rear axle, each with transverse leaf springs
**Brakes:** drums on transmission, and at rear
**Bodywork:** steel two- and four-seaters, open and closed; various styles
**Maximum speed (approx):** 45 mph (72 km/h)

# Ford V8 1932-42

Ford's second great car, another trend-setter, was the famous 'flat-head' V8-engined range of the 1930s. Although in Ford terms this had a strictly conventional chassis layout, its engine set significant new standards for the American motor industry.

From the 1990s we look back at the simple 'flat-head' (side-valve) V8 and wonder what all the fuss was about, but this was precisely what caused such a sensation in the early 1930s. Although Detroit was already using V8s in Cadillacs (and straight-eights in Buicks), the new Ford engine was the very first V8 to be offered in a lower-priced car.

The original V8 Ford was a re-engined Model A, put on sale in 1932. These cars, with a huge choice of body styles, were not only fast, but were also tremendous bargains, for prices started at a mere $460.

The first cars were neither totally reliable, nor modern-looking, so it is generally agreed that the definitive V8s arrived in 1933 and 1934. For 1933 there was an increase in wheelbase – from 106.5 inches to 112 inches, and a new range of body styles, with more flowing lines.

For 1934 the old side-valve four-cylinder engine option was dropped completely, and for the rest of the decade *all* Fords were powered by the V8. Before long the same engine found its way into British Fords, and enlarged and more powerful versions would be used in Detroit-made Fords until 1953, by which time it was pumping out 110 bhp.

The 1930s cars themselves progressed slowly, though. There was yet another new styling theme for 1935, a smaller-capacity (2.2-litre, producing 60 bhp) version of the V8 was launched in 1936, and all-steel saloon bodies were used from 1937 onwards. Yet another new look

arrived for 1938 – this time with a more streamlined shape than ever before, and before the outbreak of war Ford had also introduced the slightly more expensive Mercury range.

Throughout this period Ford was the market leader in the USA, selling 931,000 cars in 1936 and 942,000 cars in 1937; the torquey attraction of the V8 had a lot to do with this.

## Specification (1933 Model 40)

**Engine:** V8, side-valve
**Bore × stroke:** 77.8 mm × 95.25 mm
**Capacity:** 3622 cc
**Maximum power:** 65 bhp (later 85 bhp)
**Transmission:** three-speed manual gearbox, rear-wheel drive
**Chassis:** separate steel frame with channel-section side members
**Suspension:** non-independent with beam front axle and live rear axle, each with transverse leaf springs
**Brakes:** drums front and rear
**Bodywork:** steel two- and four-seaters, open and closed; various styles
**Maximum speed (approx):** 78 mph (126 km/h)

*Above and below: Starting with the 1932 type sometimes known as a 'Model B', Ford's new 1930s cars brought the V8 engine into the popular domain for the first time. Opinions differ as to whether the 1933 or 1934 V8s were more handsome. The two were very similar, but on the 1933 design the distinctive, heart-shaped, V-sectioned radiator grille had a concave curvature when seen from the side. Above is a 1933 V8 Cabriolet; below a 1934 Roadster.*

# Ford Thunderbird 1954-57

Although Ford have now had a Thunderbird model continuously on sale for nearly half a century, the most famous of all was the original two-seater sporting model of 1954-57.

The first Thunderbird took shape in 1953, and was publicly launched in 1954, as the first 'sporting' Ford, and their first two-seater for many years. Quite clearly, it was Ford's response to the new Chevrolet Corvette – and in the important 'two-seater years' it was commercially more successful. A total of 53,166 examples was produced in three model years, from 1954 to 1957.

Like many European sports cars, before and since, the Thunderbird had a unique chassis and body style which hid a multitude of normal saloon model parts – in this case from Mainlines and Fairlanes. The steel shell, however, was unique, had crisp styling, and was available as an open roadster or with an optional lift-off hard top.

By the standards of the day the wraparound windscreen, the hooded headlamps, the bonnet scoop, and the embryonic fins were all typical. The car, although only a two-seater, was quite large (it was 185 inches long) and weighed nearly 3,500 lb, so it was clearly not in the same market sector as Triumph TRs and Austin-Healey 100s of the period.

On the other hand, with a choice of V8 engines producing between 200 bhp and 300 hp, and with a choice of manual or automatic transmission, the Thunderbird was a head-on competitor to the Chevrolet Corvette. Ford's planners thought that the style, the equipment and the line-up of options were more important than precise roadholding and steering, which explains why this car never appealed to European enthusiasts.

Later on, one of Ford's advertising punchlines was: "Ford has a better idea" – and, with the new Thunderbird, they obviously had. Even so, market research suggested that there would be still larger demand for a more spacious model.

For 1958, therefore, Ford produced a new four-seater Thunderbird model, a larger and heavier car in what Detroit was pleased to call the "personal coupe" style, and every subsequent Thunderbird has been a four- or five-seater.

## Specification (1955)

**Engine:** V8, overhead-valve
**Bore × stroke:** 96.5 mm × 87.4 mm
**Capacity:** 5113 cc
**Maximum power:** 225 bhp
**Transmission:** three-speed manual gearbox or three-speed automatic transmission, rear-wheel drive
**Chassis:** separate steel frame with box-section main and bracing members
**Suspension:** independent front with wishbones and coil springs; live rear axle with semi-elliptic leaf springs
**Brakes:** drums front and rear
**Bodywork:** steel two-seater, optional hard top
**Maximum speed:** 113 mph (182 km/h)

*Above: Ford held a contest to name their Corvette competitor and chose 'Thunderbird' – a magical totem of the Pueblo Indians.*

*Below: Unlike its GM rival, the Thunderbird had a V8 engine from the start: 292 cu in at first, with a 312-in (5113-cc) option in 1956.*

*Below: The original Thunderbird, designated a 1955 model though launched in late 1954, was, like the Corvette, really a response to the sales threat posed by overseas sports cars like Jaguar's XK120. Bigger tail fins came in 1957, and the T-bird survived as a two-seater only until 1957.*

## Ford Fairlane 500 Skyliner 1957-58

Ford's Fairlane was the name chosen for what Detroit called the 'standard-size' class of cars in the mid-1950s. Launched in 1954, there was a choice of 11 models at first, with six-cylinder and V8 engines.

In addition to the standard engines, there were also 4.8-litre V8s with 205 or 212 bhp, 5.1-litre engines with 245 bhp, and 5.4-litre V8s of 240 bhp, 265 bhp or 300 bhp. At first this was a strictly conventional model range, aimed to sell car-for-car against the Chevrolets of the day.

In mid-1957 Ford permitted themselves an indulgence by launching the Fairlane 500 Skyliner derivative, the unique feature of which was a retractable steel hard top. When the top was erected, the Skyliner looked exactly like a two-door hard-top coupé, but operating a complicated sequence of electric motors and hydraulic controls saw the long rear boot lid open up, the front end of the roof fold down under the rest of the hard top, after which the massive hard top itself folded down into the boot and the boot lid closed over it!

This meant, of course, that there was little useful boot space for luggage. This scheme had originally been proposed for use on a Continental, but was taken up by the Ford Division when the short-lived Continental marque died off. The Skyliner idea was fascinating and (when reliable) beautifully detailed in operation, but naturally it was expensive. For example, in 1957 the Victoria hard-top coupé (which looked the same) sold for $2,339, whereas the Skyliner cost $2,942. Nevertheless 20,766 were sold in 1957, and 14,713 in 1958, before the same basic body style was donated (for just one season) to the new Galaxie model, where a further 12,915 were produced.

### Specification (1957)

**Engine:** V8, overhead-valve
**Bore × stroke:** 91.95 mm × 83.82 mm
**Capacity:** 4453 cc
**Maximum power:** 190 bhp
**Transmission:** three-speed manual gearbox or automatic transmission, rear-wheel drive
**Chassis:** separate steel frame with box-section side and bracing members
**Suspension:** independent front with wishbones and coil springs; live rear axle with semi-elliptic leaf springs
**Brakes:** drums front and rear
**Bodywork:** steel five-seater, retractable hard top
**Maximum speed (approx):** 110 mph (177 km/h)

*Above: Ford's 1957 'standard-size' Fairlane range included the novel Skyliner, with a steel roof that could be folded automatically into its boot. When the hard top was retracted, as here, it looked much like an ordinary convertible.*

*Below: In 1959, when Ford launched the Galaxie, they transferred the Skyliner name and concept to the new model for its first year. Seen here in mid-operation, the folding mechanism was ingenious but made some impact on luggage space . . .*

# Ford Falcon Futura Sprint 1963-65

Ford introduced their Falcon 'compact' car in 1959, a basic family car smaller, lighter, cheaper and more economical than any existing Ford. This was to meet the then-current American demand for more practical cars. However, as with all such model ranges, the Falcon gradually grew up, became more powerful, and lost its original 'economy' tag.

By the early 1960s Ford had embraced a 'Total Performance' marketing policy, which saw their cars and engines entered in motorsport all round the world. One result was a short-lived USA-funded rallying programme, for which the Falcon Futura Sprint was developed.

The first Futura was a 1961 model, which was a two-door version of the Falcon saloon, intended to beat Chevrolet's Corvair Monza, but only available with six-cylinder engines. The 'homologation special' developed for rallying was the Futura Sprint which followed for 1963. Not only did this have a 4.2-litre/164-bhp V8 engine (the same as used on early AC Cobras, Ford Mustangs and Sunbeam Tigers), but also firmed-up suspension and racks of optional equipment. This completely transformed the Futura's performance, and – more importantly – its image.

Ford very nearly won the 1963 Monte Carlo Rally with that car, and went on to win other international rallies, so for 1964 the Futura Sprint was made even better, with a restyled and more craggy body, and yet more options. The homologated extra equipment (which was almost impossible to buy unless one was actively

involved in motorsport) included glass-fibre body panels, engine tune-up kits, and front-wheel disc brakes.

Once again the car narrowly failed to win the Monte Carlo Rally, but went on to become a very successful racing saloon car, particularly in the British Touring Car Championship. The last of the Futura Sprints had a 200-bhp/4.7-litre engine as standard, which could be super-tuned to more than 300 bhp for racing; these aggressive-looking coupés won many events in the mid-1960s.

By this time, however, Ford-USA had launched the Mustang, which meant that the Futura Sprint was left to die away, which it did in 1965. There were 15,081 1963-model Futura Sprints, 18,108 1964 types, and a mere 3,106 1965 models.

## Specification (1964)

**Engine:** V8, overhead-valve
**Bore × stroke:** 96.5 mm × 72.9 mm
**Capacity:** 4260 cc
**Maximum power:** 164 bhp
**Transmission:** three-speed or four-speed manual gearbox or three-speed automatic transmission, rear-wheel drive
**Chassis:** steel unit-construction body/chassis assembly
**Suspension:** independent front with wishbones and coil springs; live rear axle with semi-elliptic leaf springs
**Brakes:** drums front and rear
**Bodywork:** steel four-seater hard-top coupé or convertible
**Maximum speed (approx):** 100 mph (161 km/h)

*Above: Introduced in late 1959 for the 1960 model year, the Falcon was three feet shorter than 'full-size' Fords of the time, and the up-range Futura variant (added in two-door sedan form in 1961) was the choice for a fast version.*

*Below: In 1963 Futura Sprint hardtops and convertibles were introduced, bringing V8 power into the Falcon range as part of Ford's 'Total Performance' policy. Seen here is a soft-top 1964 Sprint; the 'wire' wheels were only covers.*

## Ford Mustang 1964-73

The Mustang not only changed the face of Ford-USA, but for a time it also changed the face of motoring in North America. Not only was it the first 'young and sporting' car to be put on sale by Ford-USA in the 1960s, but it also invented a whole new class of car – the 'pony car' – for the young-at-heart to buy.

Ford's new high-performance/sporting strategy was already established before the Mustang was launched in mid-1964, but this was no accident. Ford's Lee Iacocca wanted to offer a new type of car to the young motorists he was trying to impress – one which was small (by USA standards), and one the specification of which could virtually be decided by the customer. The result was a car available in near-infinite variety, and in four distinctly different shapes in the 1964-73 period.

The original Mustang used many Falcon components (this was an unpromising beginning, for the Falcon was a dumpy 'economy compact'), and had a very simple 'chassis' with semi-elliptic leaf-spring rear suspension, but it had a new and racy style, with a lengthy bonnet, a compact cabin, and a short tail (or 'deck' as the Americans called it).

The original-style Mustang, built until 1966, was available in coupé, convertible or fastback styles on a 108-in wheelbase. The 1966-68 Mustang had a reskinned body shell, but the same basic underpan and running gear.

The 1968-70 model again ran on the same underpan, but had a new and smoother body style, while the 1970-73 version ran on a lengthened (109-in) wheelbase, with a choice of longer, wider, smoother and heavier bodies, in hard-top, fastback and convertible forms.

Right from the start it was available with six-cylinder and V8 engines, with coupé or convertible body styles, manual or automatic transmission, and a raft of dress-up kits. Before long, disc front brakes became optional, a fastback body style became available, different-size road wheels, power-assisted steering and all manner of extras appeared –

*Above: Shown in 1962, the first Mustang prototype, designed by Gene Bordinat and Roy Lunn, was a radical two-seater sports car with mid-mounted V4 power. Lee Iacocca, then Ford's president, vetoed it for being too adventurous.*

but an independent rear suspension kit proposed for racing was abandoned at the preview stage.

The result was not only a car which was cheap to buy and to run, but also one on which money could be spent to make it a successful race and rally car – 400,000 Mustangs were sold in the first year, and the car won the Tour de France. Carroll Shelby (of Cobra fame) produced several GT variants (covered in the 'Shelby' section of this A-to-Z).

The first million cars were sold within two years, but after that Ford's opposition, General Motors, had developed the competing Camaro and Firebird models, and sales fell away. There is no doubt, however, that the Mustang set every standard for the new 'pony car' category, so as it grew larger, heavier

*Left: When it appeared in 1964 the Mustang was a conventional front-engined, rear-drive car. Still exciting enough for automotively conservative America, it was a huge success, originating an entirely new market niche and catching other US carmakers off guard. Top engine option was initially a solid-lifter 289-cu in V8 producing a claimed 271 bhp.*

*Below: Until 1967, restyling was mild: this is a 1966 hard-top model.*

and more powerful in the late 1960s its opposition followed suit.

By the early 1970s, however, the Mustang had become less of a sporting car and more of a virility symbol for its customers. Environmental pressures then began to mount, and as safety legislation proliferated, the Mustang lost its way, so for 1974 it was replaced by the Mustang II, a much smaller, simpler, slower, very ugly and altogether less interesting design.

Although in retrospect the Mustang II was a less desirable car than the original, the buying public didn't see it that way, and the first year's sales of the Mustang II matched those of the original car. That was thanks to its more fuel-efficient performance – the Mustang II's launch coincided with the first 'energy crisis' of the 1970s.

Between 1964 and 1973 almost three million Mustangs were built, in hard-top, convertible, fastback, Mach 1 and Grande versions.

Like many other American cars of the period, the Mustang was available with a bewildering variety of engines.

In nine years no fewer than eight different straight-six engines, and 18 different V8s were available – and this ignores the very special Shelby derivatives.

The extremes were a 2.8-litre six-cylinder, rated at 101 bhp, and a five-litre V8 rated at 375 bhp. Most popular engine options were 4.7-litre, 5.0-litre and 5.7-litre V8s, variously rated from 200 to an impressive 330 bhp.

## Specification (1964 V8)

**Engine:** V8, overhead-valve
**Bore × stroke:** 101.6 mm × 72.9 mm
**Capacity:** 4727 cc
**Maximum power:** 271 bhp
**Transmission:** four-speed manual gearbox or three-speed automatic transmission, rear-wheel drive
**Chassis:** steel unit-construction body/chassis assembly
**Suspension:** independent front with upper and lower wishbones and coil springs; live rear axle with semi-elliptic leaf springs
**Brakes:** drums front and rear
**Bodywork:** steel four-seater coupé or convertible
**Maximum speed (approx):** 116 mph (187 km/h)

*Inset above: A mustang is a small wild horse, hence the term 'pony car' for the sporty-looking but affordable concept Ford created.*

*Above: Perhaps the Shelby versions of the 1967-68 models were the best-looking Mustangs of all. This GT 350 had a 315-bhp 302-cu in V8.*

*Above: Some Mustangs were powered by big-block V8s, and in 1969 the mighty 'Boss 429' was offered: officially rated at 375 bhp but able to produce well over 500 bhp.*

*Below: 1970 Mustangs were not greatly different from 1969 models. This GT 500 was another Shelby-badged big-block car.*

## Ford Torino 1967-76

By the late 1960s Ford were proud of their 'Total Performance' image and cars like the Mustang, the result being that they also produced more sporting, more powerful, and very fast larger cars. The sleek Torinos were offshoots of the 'full-size' Fairlane models.

The Fairlane was a conventional car which had been launched in the early 1960s, but the new generation for 1966 had long and sleek lines and, naturally, was available in many varieties. For the 1968 model year a new car called the Torino (the Italian for Turin) appeared, this being a more sporty version of the basic Fairlane design.

Torinos were big cars which ran on a 116-in wheelbase, and weighed about 3,300 lb, and were available as coupés, convertibles, fastbacks and hard-tops at first, some of them with V8 engines offering well over 300 bhp. For the slightly older generation who did not want to be restricted to Mustangs, these were heady offerings which sold very well.

Then, for 1969 and 1970, Ford traded on their links with Carroll Shelby by offering a real 'muscle car' called the Torino Cobra. This was Ford's answer to the Plymouth Road Runner, and came with a choice of 7.0-litre V8 engines offering between 335 and 375 bhp. Even in standard form the cars could scorch up to 100 mph in about 15 seconds, top speed was well above anything the USA's law-upholders could ignore, and the Cobra GT was a formidably successful car in NASCAR racing.

Even so, by 1971, the short-lived fashion for such extrovert 'muscle cars' was fading, so there were no more tyre-stripping Cobras after this time. The Torino family, in any case, suffered badly from the onset of emission controls and other legislation, so those turn-of-the-decade fastbacks, complete with louvred rear windows, fat tyres and exotic colour combinations, became collectors' pieces in later years.

### Specification (1969 Cobra GT)

**Engine:** V8, overhead-valve
**Bore × stroke:** 110.7 mm × 91.2 mm
**Capacity:** 7022 cc
**Maximum power:** 335 bhp
**Transmission:** four-speed manual gearbox or three-speed automatic transmission, rear-wheel drive
**Chassis:** steel unit-construction body/chassis assembly
**Suspension:** independent front with upper and lower wishbones and coil springs; live rear axle with semi-elliptic leaf springs
**Brakes:** discs front, drums rear
**Bodywork:** steel four/five-seater fastback coupé
**Maximum speed (approx):** 135 mph (217 km/h)

*Above: Initially the name 'Torino' was used for the top trim level in the Fairlane range. It gradually became a type in its own right.*

*Below: The Torino was a full-size American car (i.e. huge!); this 1971 Squire station wagon was available in eight-passenger form.*

*Right: Torino Cobra models with 428 and 429 V8s producing 500-plus bhp were formidable opposition for the Dodge Daytonas and Plymouth Superbirds in NASCAR racing; one of America's most famous and successful Indy and NASCAR drivers, A. J. Foyt (inset), drove one.*

*Below: The Fairlane name was dropped entirely for the 1971 model year and a Torino GT model appeared. Identifiable by its divided grille, it was a sportier version of the luxury Brougham.*

## ord Mustang III SVO 1983-86

rd's second-generation Mustang of '3-78 sold well enough, but was ither fast nor visually attractive. The rd-generation car, launched in 1978, d more rakish lines but, for a time, still ffered from a lack of performance. ter types, particularly the SVO model d V8-engined types, made up for the ficit.

At a time when more and more North nerican cars were turning to the 'Euro-an' transverse-engine/front-wheel-ive layout, the Mustang III (like Ford-rope's long-running Capri) stuck stub-rnly to the classic front-engine/rear-ive layout. By the early 1990s, when it d been on sale for 13 years, it had been ilt in four-seater coupé, hatchback and nvertible types, with a variety of four-linder, V6 and V8 engine types.

The original sharp-nosed/hard-edged le was subtly restyled in the late 1980s, that the nose had a more rounded pro-. By that time the original choice of gines – 2.3-litre/88-bhp 'four' or 3.8-e/120-bhp V6 – had expanded to in-lde a series of low-revving five-litre s, the most powerful producing bhp.

The first, and – in character – the most citing derivative of the Mustang III is the SVO type of 1983-86. The SVO ronym stood for 'Special Vehicle erations', denoting a car which had en developed by Ford Motorsport oremo Mike Kranefuss's department. While the basic 2.3-litre overhead-mshaft 'Lima' engine – which was a ose design relative of the European nto' unit – was retained, it was fitted h fuel injection and a turbocharger ed to an air cooler, the result being a quey, 200-bhp output (in its final year) which the Sierra Cosworth would have en proud. This engine was backed by Borg-Warner close-ratio five-speed arbox (as used in the Sierra Cos-rth).

*low: Multi-port fuel injection, an -to-air intercooler and a close-tio Borg-Warner five-speed arbox with a Hurst linkage helped ve the 200-bhp SVO performance e that of earlier 'real' Mustangs.*

Although the SVO Mustang was no faster than the V8-engined types, it had a more urgent, European-style, character, which helped raise the model's image at a critical time. By the late 1980s, however, Ford had reverted to providing high performance by more conventional means.

### Specification (1986)

**Engine:** inline-four, single overhead camshaft, turbo
**Bore × stroke:** 96.04 mm × 79.4 mm
**Capacity:** 2301 cc
**Maximum power:** 200 bhp
**Transmission:** five-speed manual gearbox, rear-wheel drive
**Chassis:** steel unit-construction body/chassis assembly
**Suspension:** independent front with wishbones and coil springs; live rear axle with coil springs
**Brakes:** discs front and rear
**Bodywork:** steel four-seater coupé
**Maximum speed (approx):** 125 mph (201 km/h)

*Above: Ford's third-series Mustang ran from the 1979 model year. Although bland-looking, it was a big improvement on the ugly second series. The SVO was launched in 1983.*

*Below: Unlike fast, V8-powered, Mustangs of old, the SVO (which stood for Special Vehicle Operations, the Ford division that created it) had a turbocharged four-cylinder engine.*

## Ford Mustang GT 1983–94

Although Ford had moved away from their performance image during the 1970s, the 1980s saw a steady return to cars with respectable, if not stupendous, performance. That move was demonstrated with the long-lived Mustang GT model.

In 1983 its five-litre pushrod overhead-valve V8 produced 175 bhp at just over 4,000 rpm, which was not a great power output given the displacement. For 1984 an HO ('High Output') version was announced, with power increased to 205 bhp at 4,400 rpm. The next year saw 210 bhp listed for the HO as the trend progressed. By 1991, when really only popular demand was keeping the old-fashioned rear-drive car in production, output had risen to 228 bhp, by which time the engine had been given multi-point electronic fuel injection to complement the revised cylinder heads and manifolds that had appeared in 1987.

There were styling changes to the exterior too, of course; they were inevitable in the American scheme of things,

despite the fact that no fundamental r visions to the body were considered f such an old design. The most notab changes came in 1987 when an attem was made to give the Mustang a se blance of the 'aero' look of Ford's othe newer, models. That had to be done wi add-on panels, which gave a rather fus look to the car.

Even in the 1990s, though, the ca chassis was essentially as simple as th of the 1983 car (which in turn was ve little more sophisticated than the pr ceding models). The 1983 model ha anti-tramp bars on the four-link live re axle, uprated dampers and alloy whee shod with Michelin's advanced TI radials. That was enough to tame wh power was available, and the GT was enjoyable if somewhat old-fashioned to drive. Into the 1990s Ford continue to follow the obvious solution of uprati tyre specification to improve the Mu tang's handling and roadholding, a moved on from the TRXs to convention modern high-performance radials lower-profile 225/55 guise. Such mir changes seemed to work, as the Mu tang GT maintained its appeal, outselli its Pontiac Trans Am and Camaro Z rivals.

### Specification (1990)

**Engine:** V8, overhead-valve
**Bore × stroke:** 101.6 mm × 76.2 mm
**Capacity:** 4942 cc
**Maximum power:** 228 bhp
**Transmission:** five-speed manual
**Chassis:** steel unit-construction body/ chassis assembly
**Suspension:** independent front with wishbones and coil springs; live rear axle with trailing links, anti-roll bar an coil springs
**Brakes:** discs front and rear
**Bodywork:** steel four-seater coupé
**Maximum speed (approx):** 135 mph (217 km/h)

*Above: HO ('High Output') variants of the 302-cu in V8 were available in the GT after the 1984 model year. Late versions like this, with multi-point injection, produced 228 bhp.*

*Below: The Mustang III's coil-sprung live axle was located by a four-bar linkage, and the GT version had the benefit of SVO-type handling aids such as a rear anti-roll bar.*

*Below: Externally, late-model GTs have had the dubious benefit of som very strange and tacky-looking bodywork add-ons, but the basic shape and structure has remained from the first of the third-series Mustang of 1978-79.*

# Ford Taurus 1985–92

During the 1970s, Ford's design reputation stagnated, as the company produced a series of rather angular and conventionally-engineered models, but for the 1980s the company decided to become technically more adventurous, and to produce more graceful styles.

The Sierra-like Tempo was the first such model, the Thunderbird soon followed suit, then in 1985 the new twins – the Ford Taurus and the Mercury Sable – appeared. These smoothly-shaped machines had obviously been influenced by the same hand that had formed the European Granada/Scorpio types, and certainly changed the face of Ford-USA.

The basic layout featured transversely-mounted engines, all-independent suspension, and front-wheel drive, with the usual generous amount of space and carrying capacity, but at first these were no more than mid-market family cars which gave General Motors a real fright.

The original Taurus was built with a choice of 2.3-litre, 88-bhp four-cylinder or 3.0-litre, 140-bhp V6 engines. By 1991 the 'base' engine power had risen to 106 bhp, the 3.0-litre engine produced 141 bhp, and there was also a 3.8-litre V6 producing 141 bhp.

In the meantime, Ford also signed an engine design deal with Yamaha of Japan, the result being the SHO model, where SHO stood for 'Super High Output'. The new Yamaha engine was a high-revving three-litre V6 unit, with four valves per cylinder and twin overhead camshafts per bank – which completely transformed the character of the Taurus.

The Mercury Sable was based on the same basic design, with different levels of trim and equipment. There was no SHO version of the Sable. Both types were built on the same production line.

With a claimed top speed of 142 mph and with 0-60 mph acceleration in around seven seconds, the SHO was clearly an extraordinary car by Ford-USA standards, especially as the handling balance and the weighting of the power-assisted steering had been altered to suit.

Even so, American buyers had to be educated to use the rev range (the Yamaha unit peaked at 6,200 rpm, and could spin round to 7,000 rpm) to get the best out of the car, and the company was clearly aiming for business from those who would normally buy a large-engined BMW or Audi model.

By almost any standards, the SHO was the most refined performance car Ford-USA had so far produced.

## Specification (1988 SHO)

**Engine:** V6, twin overhead camshafts per bank of cylinders
**Bore × stroke:** 89 mm × 80 mm
**Capacity:** 2986 cc
**Maximum power:** 223 bhp
**Transmission:** five-speed manual gearbox, front-wheel drive
**Chassis:** steel unit-construction body/chassis assembly
**Suspension:** independent front with MacPherson struts; independent rear with transverse and longitudinal links and torsion bars
**Brakes:** discs front and rear
**Bodywork:** steel five-seater saloon
**Maximum speed (approx):** 142 mph (229 km/h)

*Below: Ford's front-wheel-drive, all-round independently-suspended Taurus was launched in 1985. The new model, with its up-to-date engineering and aerodynamically-efficient styling, marked a major design shift, slotting into the range in place of the big, traditional, rear-wheel-drive LTD.*

*Above: In the Taurus, SHO stood for 'Super High Output' in the form of a quadruple-camshaft three-litre Yamaha V6 engine delivering more than 220 bhp.*

*Below: With uninhibited use of the free-revving Japanese four-valves-per-cylinder engine, the SHO would deliver sparkling performance, with a top speed of over 140 mph.*

## Ford Probe 1988–93

*Left: In either turbocharged 2.2-litre four-cylinder or naturally-aspirated three-litre V6 form, the Probe could reach 130 mph. With finely-developed all-independent suspension, it made fast and satisfying driver's car.*

### Ford Probe variants

#### Ford Probe GL

The GL version had a normally-aspirated variant of the 2.2-litre engine developing 111 bhp; this car had rear drum brakes. Top speed was around 110 mph.

#### Ford Probe LX

The LX version, announced in 1990, had a 60-degree V6 overhead-valve engine with 89-mm × 80-mm bore and stroke, 2986 cc and 147 bhp. It had the same performance as the GT.

### Specification (1988 GT)

**Engine:** inline four-cylinder, single overhead camshaft
**Bore × stroke:** 86 mm × 94 mm
**Capacity:** 2184 cc
**Maximum power:** 147 bhp
**Transmission:** five-speed manual gearbox or four-speed automatic transmission, front-wheel drive
**Chassis:** steel unit-construction body/chassis assembly
**Suspension:** independent front with MacPherson struts; independent rear with MacPherson struts, twin control arms, trailing arms and anti-roll bar
**Brakes:** discs front and rear
**Bodywork:** steel four-seater hatchback coupé
**Maximum speed:** 130 mph (209 km/h)

Ford's long-standing links with Mazda (in which it has a financial stake) were made even closer by the launch of the Probe sports hatchback in 1988. In many ways this car was a rebodied Mazda, for the platform, suspension and front-engine/front-drive installation were based on those of Mazda cars built at Flat Rock, Arkansas, USA.

When conceived, the new Probe was intended as a successor to the long-running Mustang III, but in the end it was launched to run alongside that old design. Perhaps the thought of introducing a transverse-engined front-wheel-drive car with a 'Mustang' model name proved too much for the traditionalists at Ford?

The developed version of the 626/MX-6 platform and running gear was topped by a smooth new coupé/hatchback body style. Because the Probe was built on a wheelbase of 99 inches, there was space for four close-coupled seats – the result being the sporty but practical package which North Americans flocked to buy.

Compared with the Mazdas, the handling and steering had been refined, so that this felt like a true sports car, with a great deal of character. Even the GL 'base' model had a top speed of more than 110 mph, but the more powerful turbocharged GT model could rush up to 130 mph.

When Ford introduced a normally-aspirated V6-engined version for 1990 (using the same engine as that fitted to Taurus saloons), the same performance was available without fuss and clamour.

*Below: Neither more nor less than a rebodied Mazda 626, the Probe was expected to be Ford-USA's replacement for the Mustang III, but the rear-drive model ran on by popular demand.*

# Ford Thunderbird Super Coupe 1989-present

The latest-generation Ford Thunderbird was introduced in the mid-1980s and featured a far more stylish, aerodynamic shape than any previous Ford-USA car. Its slippery lines soon made it a candidate as a successful base for Ford's NASCAR programme, while the road cars had an interesting version in the form of the 2.3-litre Turbo Coupe. That featured a special four-link rear axle system with two hydraulic dampers mounted longitudinally between the axle and body, supplementing the usual dampers.

The Turbo Coupe was a good performer, but not sufficiently good to wean Americans away from V8s for high performance, so Ford decided on another variation of the forced-induction theme, switching to a supercharger rather than a turbo for the Super Coupe of the 1990s. That featured a 3.8-litre pushrod V6 with alloy cylinder heads and an intercooled Roots-type supercharger boosting at a maximum charge of nearly 12 psi. That was enough to increase output to 210 bhp at 4,000 rpm, along with 315 lb ft of torque at only 2,600 rpm, giving V8-type engine characteristics from a smaller V6.

The blown engine was coupled to either a five-speed manual gearbox or four-speed automatic and the performance was excellent, with a top speed approaching 140 mph. To cope with that extra performance, the old Turbo Coupe's curious rear suspension system had been discarded in favour of a more advanced independent system featuring lower wishbones and upper control arms along with an anti-roll bar and coil springs.

*Below: For many years the celebrated Thunderbird name had been applied to 'personal luxury' models adapted from prosaic sedans like Lincolns and LTDs, but it at last regained a performance image with the 1989 Super Coupe option. This was powered by a 210-bhp intercooled, supercharged (not turbocharged) 3.8-litre V6 engine and had handling to match.*

## Specification (1990)

**Engine:** V6, overhead-valve, supercharged
**Bore × stroke:** 96.52 mm × 86.36 mm
**Capacity:** 3791 cc
**Maximum power:** 210 bhp
**Transmission:** five-speed manual or four-speed automatic
**Chassis:** integral steel body/chassis assembly
**Suspension:** independent front with upper and lower wishbones and anti-roll bar; independent rear with wishbones, anti-roll bar and coil springs
**Brakes:** discs front and rear
**Bodywork:** steel two-door coupé
**Maximum speed (approx):** 137 mph (220 km/h)

*Above: After the all-new 1983 Thunderbird, there were reskins in 1987 and in 1989, bringing all-independent suspension, plus a blown V6 on the Super Coupe.*

*Below: When it appeared for the 1983 model year, the radically restyled T-bird ushered in a new trend in American automobile styling: the clean, sharp, fewer-frills 'aero' look.*

# Ford of Europe

H enry Ford's famous American enterprise had been running in the United States for eight years before he opened the first of his overseas subsidiaries, Ford of Britain.

That was in 1911, the first assembly factory being at Trafford Park, Manchester. Other European companies like Ford-Germany (1925), Matford (France, 1934) and Ford-France (1947) eventually joined in, each with its own management team, and its own distribution network. Ford-UK built a vast new factory at Dagenham, on the Essex marshes.

Until the 1930s all European-built Fords were of American design – such as the Model T, the Model A and the V8 – and used a lot of American-supplied parts, but a family of specially-developed European small cars based on a new 8-hp and 10-hp design arrived in the 1930s, and large expansion followed.

Until the 1960s Ford-UK, Ford-Germany and Ford-France designs were different and the companies were independent of each other, but by the 1970s an integrated Ford of Europe organisation had been set up, and product design had been integrated. Later, Ford also moved into Spain, for the start of the front-wheel-drive Fiesta project.

In the 1960s Ford began to move steadily ahead of their opposition in Britain. Where the General Motors subsidiary Vauxhall was stagnating in terms of model design, Ford's policy of updating their models on a more regular basis paid off and brought them to a position of supremacy in the

*Above: Ford of Europe have been using a standard badge (a reproduction of the script used on early Model Ts set on a blue oval) and sharing an increasingly uniform product range over the past two decades.*

1980s. The basis of that success was in cars like the first Cortina, introduced in 1962 and reskinned whenever necessary to keep the design appearing fresh. The first revamp, with a more angular body style, came in 1966, to be followed by the 'Coke-bottle' Mk 3 look and then back to a sharper-edged design. In other words, Ford did whatever was necessary to keep a very conventional design appearing fresh and interesting. The same approach was followed with the Escort range, although, at least with the Escort, Ford changed to front-wheel drive with the third-generation car, while the Cortina's replacement was the rear-drive Sierra, albeit with more advanced aerodynamic styling.

*Above: European Ford divisions once had quite separate ranges. The Anglia 105E, with its quirky back-slanted rear window, was a 1950s British design. Integration started in the 1970s and the Capri – a European translation of the 'pony car' concept – was among the first models with a common body shell. The RS3100 (right) was a genuinely quick 'homologation special', using a development of the British 'Essex' V6 engine in conjunction with improved suspension and brakes.*

*Below: When Ford's bid to buy motor racing success in the form of Ferrari failed, they built their own GT40 Le Mans winner in Britain, where endurance-racing expertise was greater.*

*Above: After producing a succession of interesting sports saloons in the 1970s (many based on the rally-winning Escorts), in the early 1980s European Fords lacked a real performance image. This changed again with fast Sierra developments like this 1987 Cosworth RS500.*

Almost every Ford-Europe model has been mass-produced, but in the 1960s Ford also began to aim for motorsport supremacy, and developed a series of fast, sporting and more specialised limited-production cars.

The first of these was the Lotus Cortina of 1963, a design which matched a twin-cam Lotus engine to a Cortina; this was actually assembled for Ford by Lotus. Within two years it had become a proven winner in races and rallies. As a successor, Ford then produced the Escort Twin-Cam, which used the same powerplant, and followed up with a whole series of sporting Escorts. Like the Lotus Cortina, these soon began winning races and rallies all round the world.

At the same time the company dipped into its USA experience with the Mustang, and produced a smaller, European, equivalent – the Capri. As with the Mustang this was produced and sold in bewildering variety, the most exciting models of which were the V6s and the specialised RSs.

In the early 1980s the flow of exciting new cars died away for a time, but in the next few years a series of exciting models appeared, notably the Escort RS Turbo and the Sierra RS Cosworth.

Although Ford made many headlines by building the *very* limited-production RS200, a mid-engined four-wheel-drive car developed too late for the short-lived Group B rally category, its most successful very fast road car so far has been the Sierra Cosworth. By the early 1990s this had already progressed through various derivatives – hatchback and saloon, the latter with two- or four-wheel drive – and had also inspired the birth of the smaller, lighter, and faster Escort RS Cosworth.

By the early 1990s cracks were beginning to appear in the Ford operation. In Britain, the company had come under fierce attack from a totally revitalised Vauxhall. However Ford staged a major comeback with their 'New Edge' designs, including the Ka, Focus, Puma and Cougar. The Mondeo saloon was a consistent midfield runner in the British Touring Car Championships during the second half of the decade.

*Below: Since the beginning of the 'four-wheel-drive era' in the late 1970s other makes have taken the honours in top-notch international rallying, but with cars like this Escort Cosworth, Ford had a competitive presence on the dirt at the beginning of the 1990s.*

# Lotus Cortina Mk 1 1963-66

Until the 1960s, Ford-UK cars had a stodgy image, but that all changed when Walter Hayes arrived as the company's Director of Public Affairs, and a wide-ranging motorsport programme was initiated.

One of the first moves was to persuade Colin Chapman of Lotus to co-operate with the company, the result being the original Lotus Cortina. This married the new Lotus-Ford twin-cam engine to the light two-door Cortina body shell, making sure that the suspension was suitably modified, and that a number of aluminium body panels took over from the standard steel items.

The car was launched in 1963, with assembly concentrated at the Lotus factory at Cheshunt, Hertfordshire. Almost immediately it started winning saloon car races, but it also acquired a reputation for unreliability as a road car. The main problem was that Lotus's own rear suspension, which featured radius arms and coil springs instead of leaf springs, placed heavy loads on the rear axle and encouraged it to leak away its oil.

From 1965 it was re-engineered, using Ford's own Cortina GT rear suspension (leaf springs and radius arms), and a totally steel body shell. In this 'Mk 1½' guise it was no less effective than before.

By the time the original-shape Lotus Cortina went out of production in the summer of 1966, a total of 2,894 cars had been built. Its successor, the Lotus Cortina Mk 2, was heavier, and not quite as fast, but it benefitted from all the effort put into the original car and sold better.

### Lotus Cortina Mk 1 variants

#### Lotus Cortina Mk 2
The mass-production Cortina Mk 2, with new styling, was announced in 1966 and appeared a few months later, in 1967. The Mk 2 was mechanically similar to the Mk 1, but was assembled by Ford at Dagenham, rather than by Lotus at Cheshunt; 4,032 were produced between 1967 and 1970.

*Below: The Lotus-powered Cortina achieved immediate success in various branches of motorsport.*

*Above and right: Using a Ford four-cylinder block, Lotus built a powerful twin-overhead-camshaft engine. Ford then used it in a sporty version of their new Cortina family saloon with revised suspension.*

### Specification (1963 Mk 1)
**Engine:** inline four-cylinder, twin overhead camshafts
**Bore × stroke:** 82.55 mm × 72.8 mm
**Capacity:** 1558 cc
**Maximum power:** 105 bhp
**Transmission:** four-speed manual gearbox, rear-wheel drive
**Chassis:** steel unit-construction body/chassis assembly with aluminium panels
**Suspension:** independent front with MacPherson struts; live rear axle with 'A'-frame link and coil springs
**Brakes:** discs front, drums rear
**Bodywork:** steel and aluminium two-door four-seater saloon
**Maximum speed (approx):** 106 mph (171 km/h)

# Ford GT40 1965-68

After Ford-USA's attempt to buy Ferrari stalled in 1963, Ford decided to mount their own ambitious racing sports car programme, and to beat Ferrari by making an assault on the Le Mans 24 Hours.

To do this, a design team was set up in the UK, at Slough. After buying Eric Broadley's services, and his Ford V8-engined Lola racing-prototype, Ford appointed John Wyer (ex-Aston Martin) to run the programme. The result was the GT40, first seen in 1964.

At first the cars were built purely as racing-prototypes, but for 1965 it was decided to put them on sale as limited-production machines, the Mk Is to race and – if anyone were so inclined – the Mk IIIs for a few rich men to use as road-going toys.

The name GT40 was chosen, quite simply, because the car's height was 40 inches. Under its brutally aggressive glassfibre skin the car used a heavy steel monocoque. Naturally, the engine was behind the cabin. On the prototypes Ford used a Ford-USA 4.2-litre V8 engine allied to a Colotti transmission, but all the production cars used 4.7-litre engines and ZF transmissions.

Ford eventually needed re-engined (seven-litre Mk II) versions of these cars to win at Le Mans in 1966, and entirely different designs (the Mk IV, or J-car) to win in 1967, but much-developed versions of the GT40s won at Le Mans in 1968 and 1969. In race form, their top speed was around 200 mph.

Production began at Slough early in 1965, with most of the cars being built over the next three years. Only a handful

of fully road-equipped Mk IIIs was sold, but detuned racing cars often appeared on the open roads, where they proved to be enormously fast, if afflicted by poor cockpit ventilation, poor all-round visibility, and by a marked dislike for driving slowly in heavy traffic.

All in all, 124 cars were built, of which 12 were prototypes and 10 were Mk IVs. Ford identify 94 as 'production cars', of which seven were Mk IIIs, and 31 Mk Is were equipped to 'road car' specification.

In the 1970s the value of a GT40 dropped to very low levels, but in the classic-conscious 1980s it soared.

*Above: Basing their design on a Lola prototype, Ford built a GT to beat Ferrari at Le Mans.*

*Below: Ford GTs triumphed in the endurance classic four times running; this car won in 1968.*

*Right: With Gurney-Weslake cylinder heads, the V8's output rose to over 400 bhp.*

*Below: Most roadgoing GT40s had engines with milder cams. The GT40P (here) still used quad-twin-choke carburation, which allowed about 335 bhp; later Mk III road cars were further detuned with only a single four-barrel carburettor, giving 306 bhp.*

## Specification (1965)

**Engine:** V8, overhead-valve, mid-mounted
**Bore × stroke:** 101.6 mm × 72.9 mm
**Capacity:** 4737 cc
**Maximum power:** 380 bhp (335 bhp on 'road cars')
**Transmission:** five-speed manual gearbox, rear-wheel drive
**Chassis:** steel unit-construction body/chassis assembly
**Suspension:** independent front and rear, each with wishbones and coil springs
**Brakes:** discs front and rear
**Bodywork:** glassfibre two-seater coupé
**Maximum speed (approx):** 170 mph (274 km/h)

# Ford Escort Twin-Cam 1968-71

Originally intended as a 'homologation special', to allow the car to be used in motorsport, the Twin-Cam later became a limited-production road car. Ford Motorsport produced the Escort Twin-Cam by shoehorning most of the Lotus Cortina running gear into the smaller body shell of the new Escort family car. Production began in a small way at the Halewood Escort factory in 1980.

The result was a car that was lighter, faster, more nimble and more versatile than the Lotus Cortina had ever been, and it led to the development of a whole series of sporting, or RS (Rallye Sport), Escorts in the next few years.

Like the Lotus Cortina, the Escort Twin-Cam had an urgent character, with an engine that barked and gobbled through its twin-choke Weber carburettors. What was new, however, was the roadholding, which actually tended to tail-out oversteer, making the car enter-

taining for the enthusiasts, but rather tiring to drive on straight main roads.

As a standard road car the Twin-Cam was perhaps too noisy, too low-geared, and too sparsely trimmed to be satisfactory, but as the basis of a competition car it was ideal. Before long, Ford had produced race and rally cars with up to 170 bhp, with five-speed gearboxes and with four-wheel disc brakes, which were outright winners in all forms of motorsport, all over the world.

Even so, the Twin-Cam only had a limited life, for Ford had already commissioned the design of a new 16-valve twin-cam engine from Cosworth. This, the BDA, was even more flexible, even more versatile, and even more tuneable than the Lotus-Ford engine had ever been. Once it was slotted into the car, from 1970, the days of the Twin-Cam were clearly numbered, and the last of all was built in 1971.

## Ford Escort Twin-Cam variants

### Ford Escort RS1600

In 1970 Ford re-engined the Twin-Cam, using a newly-designed 1.6-litre Cosworth BDA 16-valve twin-cam engine. In standard form this engine produced 120 bhp; at first it had a cast-iron cylinder block, but an aluminium block was introduced in 1972. Race-prepared cars had two-litre versions.

The RS1600 was Ford's famous rally-winning car of the early 1970s, but when the restyled Escort Mk 2 was announced in 1975, it was replaced by the Escort RS1800.

*Left: Lotus's twin-cam engine was good but the RS1600's Cosworth-designed 16-valve BDA (here) was a revelation, producing 120 bhp even in standard form.*

*Below: The Mexico was a tame, 1600 pushrod-engined spin-off.*

*Above: The Twin-Cam was a minor sensation, ripping through the opposition in motorsport, particularly rallying. It was a tough act to follow, but the RS1600 (shown here) had even more performance and quickly took over its role.*

## Specification (1968 Twin-Cam)

**Engine:** inline four-cylinder, twin overhead camshafts
**Bore × stroke:** 82.55 mm × 72.8 mm
**Capacity:** 1558 cc
**Maximum power:** 106 bhp
**Transmission:** four-speed manual gearbox, rear-wheel drive
**Chassis:** steel unit-construction body/chassis assembly
**Suspension:** independent front with MacPherson struts; live rear axle with semi-elliptic leaf springs
**Brakes:** discs front, drums rear
**Bodywork:** steel two-door four-seater saloon
**Maximum speed (approx):** 113 mph (182 km/h)

# Ford Escort RS2000 1973-80

After the Escort Twin-Cam had gone on sale, Ford turned to the idea of making special 'Rallye Sport' cars in a new Advanced Vehicle Operations factory at Aveley. The first cars to be assembled there were Escort RS1600s, but it was the later cars – Mexicos and RS2000s – which sold in the largest numbers.

The Mexico was really a re-engined Twin-Cam/RS1600, with the same dull but reliable 'Kent' engine as was already used in Capri and Cortina 1600GTs. The RS2000 was, however, a different machine in many ways. Ford wanted it to be more of an 'executive' model rather than a sports saloon, which explains why it was fitted with the same 100-bhp two-litre overhead-camshaft 'Pinto' engine as the Capris and Cortinas, an engine matched on this occasion by a German-built gearbox and back axle.

The original-shape car (the Mk 1) of 1973 and 1974 was more refined and more civilised than the RS1600, but a little slower. It was also the last type of Escort RS model to be built at AVO, which closed down at the end of 1974.

All the Mk 2 Escort RS models, including the RS2000 Mk 2 of 1976-80, were built at Saarlouis, in West Germany. This last car was faster and better-equipped than the original version, and was distinguished by a unique 'droop-snoot' nose which included four headlamps. With 110 bhp, it was no slower than the RS1800 'homologation special', and was a smart and refined high-speed machine which sold very well indeed. Not only

was it quick and easy to drive, but it also handled well, was a practical four-seater, and was easily repaired and serviced by every Ford workshop, in contrast to its exotic rivals.

Many Ford enthusiasts would insist that it has never properly been replaced – for the early 1990s type of RS2000 is a very different car indeed. Accurate Ford figures have never been released, but it seems certain that between 10,000 and 15,000 such cars were produced in four years.

*Right: The Mk 2 RS2000 could be distinguished from earlier examples by the twin headlights. The Mk 2 Escort shell was a sharper-edged design than the first Escorts, although it followed the original car in basic design, with strut front and live-axle rear suspension.*

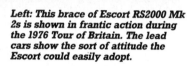

*Below: More 1976 Tour of Britain action. The 110-bhp overhead-cam two-litre RS2000 Mk 2 was a popular rally car, thanks to its power, its robustness, and the fact that it was easy to drive quickly.*

*Left: This brace of Escort RS2000 Mk 2s is shown in frantic action during the 1976 Tour of Britain. The lead cars show the sort of attitude the Escort could easily adopt.*

## Ford Escort RS2000 variants

### Ford Mexico
The original Mk 1 Mexico was built from 1970 to 1974, with an 80.97-mm × 77.62-mm, 86-bhp/1599-cc overhead-valve engine, and a top speed of 100 mph. The Mk 2 Mexico was produced from 1976 to 1978, now with the 1600 Pinto engine and a power output of 95 bhp.

### Ford RS1800
This was a Mk 2-styled model produced from 1975 to 1977, with an enlarged version of the 16-valve BDA engine. Bore and stroke were 86.75 mm × 77.62 mm, giving 1835 cc and a power output of 115 bhp. Production was very limited. This was the car used so successfully by the 'works' rally team, and by hundreds of private owners, and it is still winning in the 1990s.

### Specification (1980 Mk 2)
**Engine:** inline four-cylinder, single overhead camshaft
**Bore × stroke:** 90.8 mm × 76.95 mm
**Capacity:** 1993 cc
**Maximum power:** 110 bhp
**Transmission:** four-speed manual gearbox, rear-wheel drive
**Chassis:** steel unit-construction body/chassis assembly
**Suspension:** independent front with MacPherson struts; live rear axle with semi-elliptic leaf springs
**Brakes:** discs front, drums rear
**Bodywork:** steel two-door four-seater saloon
**Maximum speed (approx):** 109 mph (175 km/h)

# Ford Capri 3-litre 1969-81

Ford-UK watched carefully while Ford-USA made such a success of the launch of the Mustang in the mid-1960s, and decided to repeat the trick. The result was a close-coupled four-seater coupé, codenamed 'Colt', which was eventually unveiled in 1969 as the Capri.

The Capri had long-bonnet coupé body styling, and a very cramped four-seater cabin, and was sold in several guises, with a variety of trim packs, engine sizes, and transmission options. The 3-litre version, using the V6 Zodiac engine, went on sale at the end of 1969.

At first the 3-litre qualified as a 'point-and-squirt' machine, for the handling was not well-balanced and it was easy to provoke wheelspin, but progressive developments made it a better car. The gearbox ratios were improved, engine output was increased, and the rear suspension was redesigned. The Capri range included many different engine sizes and transmission options, but no other mass-production type was as fast or as sporting as the 3-litre. The wide choice of engines stretched from 1.3 litres to 3.1 litres, using four-cylinder, V4 and V6 layouts.

The Capri 3-litre was always exceptional value by current British standards for such performance cars, and sold very well indeed. In 1974 the body style was changed considerably, becoming smoother outside, roomier inside and with a hatchback feature. Later cars, particularly those with the Ghia trim pack, were more refined and more civilised.

The 3-litre was still selling steadily in 1981 when it was finally displaced by the fuel-injected 2.8i model. In 17 years a total of 1.9 million Capris of all types were produced, though Ford never revealed how many of these had 3-litre engines.

## Specification (1970 Mk 1)

**Engine:** V6, overhead-valve
**Bore × stroke:** 93.7 mm × 74.2 mm
**Capacity:** 2994 cc
**Maximum power:** 128 (later 138) bhp
**Transmission:** four-speed manual gearbox or three-speed automatic transmission, rear-wheel drive
**Chassis:** steel unit-construction body/chassis assembly
**Suspension:** independent front with MacPherson struts; live rear axle with semi-elliptic leaf springs and telescopic dampers
**Brakes:** discs front, drums rear
**Bodywork:** steel two-door 2+2-seater coupé
**Maximum speed (approx):** 120 mph (193 km/h)

*Left: Late-model three-litre Capris were hard to differentiate from their 2.8i replacement. This is an 'X-pack' version, boasting wider alloy wheels than the standard car.*

# Ford Capri RS2600 1970-74

The first Capri RS2600 was developed by Ford-Germany as a 'homologation special' which could be used in saloon car racing, but over the years it became more civilised and better-equipped. Compared with mass-production Capris, the RS2600 had a fuel-injected 2.6-litre engine, and the earliest cars also had Perspex side windows, a number of glassfibre body panels, rudimentary bumpers and wide-rim alloy road wheels. An RS2600 could easily be identified by its quadruple circular headlamps and its quarter-bumpers. It was only available in left-hand-drive form.

By the time the car was in what passed for series-production (in Cologne), many 'comfort' features had once again been standardised, but the RS2600 was always a lot lighter and more agile than the other smaller-capacity V6 cars from the same factory. Although these Capris were really detuned racing cars, they still had four seats.

Not only did the car achieve its object in motorsport – for Capris won the 1971 and 1972 European Touring Car Championships – but it also made many friends in Europe, where flat-out performance on autobahns and autostradas was needed. It also inspired the birth of the Capri RS3100 of 1973-74, a British-built car which used the British (Essex), as opposed to the German (Cologne), Ford V6 engine.

Nearly 4,000 RS2600s were produced in about four years, which meant that it qualified easily for the racing category it dominated in the early 1970s.

*Below: The RS Capris were raced to good effect in European Touring Car Championship events, although much modified as here.*

*Above: The rear wing and four-spoke alloy wheels show that this is a rare RS3100 with 3091 cc rather than the standard three-litre V6. It was built as a homologation exercise.*

## Ford Capri RS2600 variants

### Ford Capri RS3100

This car was produced in the last few months of Capri Mk 1 production, as a 'homologation special', to allow Ford to use a developed version with a quadcam 3.4-litre Cosworth GA engine. In standard form the RS3100 used a 95.19-mm × 72.4-mm, 148-bhp/3091-cc engine. Only about 200 were built.

## Specification (1970 RS2600)

**Engine:** V6, overhead-valve
**Bore × stroke:** 90 mm × 69 mm
**Capacity:** 2637 cc
**Maximum power:** 150 bhp
**Transmission:** four-speed manual gearbox, rear-wheel drive
**Chassis:** steel unit-construction body/chassis assembly
**Suspension:** independent front with MacPherson struts; live rear axle with semi-elliptic leaf springs
**Brakes:** discs front, drums rear
**Bodywork:** steel two-door 2+2-seater coupé
**Maximum speed (approx):** 130 mph (209 km/h)

# Ford Capri 2.8i 1981-86

Ford set up its Special Vehicle Engineering department in 1980 with the avowed intention of raising the image of Ford cars. Rod Mansfield headed the design team, and their first product was the Capri 2.8i.

Starting from the basis of the Capri 3-litre, whose big V6 had admirable amounts of low-speed torque but was heavy and had a reluctance to rev highly, SVE substituted the 2.8-litre version of

*Below: By the time the 2.8i was introduced, the Capri had been refined into a fast sports coupé with entertaining handling and a top speed in excess of 125 mph. The injected V6 engine gave 160 bhp.*

the German engine used in the old RS2600 model, made sure that it had fuel injection, and matched it to a better-balanced chassis with 7-in wide alloy road wheels. The structure and basic style of the existing Capri 2 were not changed, with the compact four-seater cabin and the hatchback feature retained.

The resulting car went on sale in 1981 and immediately began to outsell all forecasts, especially in the UK, where 4,000 cars a year were sold in the early 1980s. It was very well-received by the pundits, for its handling was the most agile ever achieved by a Capri, and it was also the fastest proper roadgoing Capri ever put on sale.

Although the Capri should have been moving towards the end of its career, Ford continued to improve the 2.8i model. There was a five-speed gearbox from late 1982. The car was renamed 2.8i Special in 1984, when a limited-slip differential was standardised, and a final short run of cars was produced in 1986, specially-trimmed and called Capri 280s.

The last Capri of all, a 280, was built in December 1986.

*Below: Last flowering of the long Capri line was the limited-edition 280, which was mechanically identical to the 2.8i. The interior was more luxuriously trimmed.*

## Specification (1981)

**Engine:** V6, overhead-valve
**Bore × stroke:** 93 mm × 68.5 mm
**Capacity:** 2792 cc
**Maximum power:** 160 bhp
**Transmission:** four-speed manual gearbox (later five-speed), rear-wheel drive
**Chassis:** steel unit-construction body/chassis assembly
**Suspension:** independent front with MacPherson struts; live rear axle with semi-elliptic leaf springs
**Brakes:** discs front, drums rear
**Bodywork:** steel two-door four-seater hatchback
**Maximum speed (approx):** 127 mph (204 km/h)

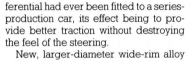

# Ford Escort RS Turbo 1984-90

The third-generation Escort, introduced in 1980, was the first to have a transverse-engine/front-wheel-drive layout. As with all such modern cars, the new car was sold in various forms, with a number of different engines.

For some years the most powerful Mk 3 Escort was the XR3i, which had a 105-bhp/1.6-litre CVH overhead-camshaft engine, but once again it was a motorsport requirement which led to that being surpassed and the Escort RS Turbo being developed.

Ford's SVE department finalised the installation of a turbocharger on the CVH engine (the turbo had to be tucked tightly between the engine and the front grille), and also fitted an FF-type viscous-coupling limited-slip differential. This was the first time such a dif-

*Below: The six-spoke alloy wheels and ultra-low-profile tyres were a feature of the fastest of the Mk 3 Escorts, the 126-mph RS Turbo.*

ferential had ever been fitted to a series-production car, its effect being to provide better traction without destroying the feel of the steering.

New, larger-diameter wide-rim alloy wheels, front and rear aerodynamic spoilers, and redeveloped suspension settings all helped to make this into an effective little sports saloon. With a top speed of more than 125 mph, it was comfortably the fastest Escort so far produced.

Every one of the 1984-86 cars built was a three-door hatchback, and all were white – Ford must have been delighted when a British magazine dubbed the Turbo 'White Lightning'.

After about 9,000 of the original type had been produced, Ford introduced a facelifted range of Escorts, which became familiarly known as 'Mk 4s'. The Escort RS Turbo version of that car shared all the facelift features – modified front styling, a different fascia, and other touches – along with the familiar turbo-

charged engine, but with higher gearing, a softer ride and a full choice of body colours.

In 1990, the entire Escort range was replaced by a new model, culminating in the Escort Cosworth that, was successful on the international rally scene. Cosworth Focus was destined to carry the mantle into the new millennium.

*Above: Bonnet louvres were incorporated in the RS Turbo's bonnet to allow for the greater engine-bay temperatures.*

## Specification (1984)

**Engine:** inline four-cylinder, single overhead camshaft, turbo
**Bore × stroke:** 79.96 mm × 79.52 mm
**Capacity:** 1596 cc
**Maximum power:** 132 bhp

**Transmission:** five-speed manual gearbox, front-wheel drive
**Chassis:** steel unit-construction body/chassis assembly
**Suspension:** independent front with MacPherson struts; independent rear with struts and coil springs
**Brakes:** discs front, drums rear
**Bodywork:** steel three-door four-seater hatchback
**Maximum speed (approx):** 126 mph (203 km/h)

## Ford RS200 1985-86

In the early 1980s a new set of regulations – called Group B – was applied to World Championship rallying, and several manufacturers developed special cars to meet these rules. Ford's contender, conceived in 1983, but not available until 1985, was the RS200.

For a car to qualify for Group B, only 200 examples had to be built, and because this was not likely to be a profitable project Ford produced precisely that number. It was totally different from every other Ford product, for design was in the hands of Ford Motorsport, with consultancy advice from race-car designer Tony Southgate.

The two-seater coupé style was developed by Ford's Ghia subsidiary, the engine was a BDT (a development of the famous BDA first seen in the Escort RS1600 and Escort RS1800 models), transmission design was by FF Developments (and included *three* viscous-coupling differentials), while assembly was carried out in a redundant Reliant factory in the Midlands.

Like all competitive Group B cars, the RS200 had a turbocharged engine mounted behind the seats, and drove all four wheels. The chassis was a complex 'tub' made from steel, carbonfibre and Kevlar, with all-independent suspension which was adjustable for height, while there was a two-seater cabin with very little stowage space and rudimentary ventilation.

Intended for use in top-flight rallying, the RS200 left a lot to be desired as a normal road car, for it was noisy and uncivilised, with a fierce clutch and an engine which tended to overheat in heavy traffic. On the other hand it had superb roadholding and traction, with performance on a par with that of contemporary V8 Ferraris.

Because Group B was cancelled prematurely, the RS200 could never reach its full potential as a rally car, but rallycross types were extremely successful in the next few years. Road-

*Right: Because of the demise of Group B rallying, the RS200's career in international rallying was short; this action is from the 1986 Manx Rally.*

equipped cars became collectors' items in the investment boom of the late 1980s, and a high proportion are kept for 'high days and holidays' in the early 1990s.

### Ford RS200 variants

#### Ford RS200 'E'

At the end of 1986 Ford also homologated an 'Evolution' version of the RS200, specifically for use in motorsport. The most important change was to the engine. Although looking like that of the normal RS200, and having the same basic architecture, it was effectively an all-new design, by Brian Hart Ltd, and was larger, with a greater swept volume, and far more powerful.

Compared with the 1.8-litre engine, this was a 2137-cc unit, developing 500 bhp in 'standard' form. For motorsport it was easily tuned to 600 bhp in 1986, but later developments allowed up to 700 bhp to be produced.

A total of 22 such cars was built in 1987 and 1988, and other RS200s were later converted to 'E' specification after production had ceased.

### Specification (1985 RS200)

**Engine:** inline four-cylinder, twin overhead camshafts, turbo
**Bore × stroke:** 86 mm × 77.62 mm
**Capacity:** 1803 cc
**Maximum power:** 250 bhp
**Transmission:** five-speed manual gearbox, four-wheel drive
**Chassis:** separate steel/carbonfibre/Kevlar frame
**Suspension:** independent with double wishbones and twin coil spring/damper units front and rear
**Brakes:** discs front and rear
**Bodywork:** glassfibre two-door two-seater coupé
**Maximum speed (approx):** 140 mph (225 km/h)

*Below: With its rally career blighted, the remaining RS200s were sold off as exclusive roadgoing supercars.*

*Below: More 1986 Manx action, with Mark Lovell driving. The RS200 was a car of enormous potential that would have brought Ford considerable international success. Later developments indicated that the RS200's engine was capable of producing as much as 700 bhp.*

*Below: The wing was a very necessary aerodynamic aid to maximise rear downforce.*

# Ford Sierra RS Cosworth 1986–92

To take advantage of the latest Group A rules governing international motor racing in the 1980s, Ford developed a 'homologation special' version of the mass-produced Sierra. The 5,000 examples of the original four-seater/three-door type, called the Sierra RS Cosworth, sold out in a matter of months, and several other versions were extremely successful in the years that followed.

Although based on the three-door body shell of the normal Sierra, the RS Cosworth type was visually different, and completely redesigned under the skin. The engine was a two-litre turbocharged Cosworth unit, coupled to a robust five-speed Borg-Warner gearbox, while there was a large, but completely functional, 'duck-tail' spoiler across the rear.

The result was a civilised 150-mph sports hatchback whose engine could be tuned to well over 300 bhp for motorsport. In standard form the engine was docile, the interior well-equipped, the ride pliant and the roadholding excellent. The car also gained the distinction of being one of the most regularly stolen vehicles in the UK!

The Sierra RS Cosworth set new standards in saloon car racing and, in its further-tuned RS500 Cosworth form, was so dominant that entire championships had to have their rules rewritten to give any other make a chance.

The second-generation car, which was launched in 1988, married the same running gear to the latest four-door Sierra saloon body shell, making it a more understated machine, but the third-generation car (introduced in 1990), looking the same but having a four-wheel-drive transmission, was the most capable of all.

This Cosworth 4×4 was the model chosen by Ford Motorsport to make its serious assault on World Championship rallying in the early 1990s, and it was also used as the basis for the exciting Escort RS Cosworth, which was previewed in 1990.

All the engines for this family of Sierras were designed, developed *and* manufactured by Cosworth Engineering.

*Right: Like the RS200 before it, the first RS Cosworth was a homologation exercise, but in this case 5,000 of the near-150-mph car were built.*

## Ford Sierra RS Cosworth variants

### Ford Sierra RS500 Cosworth

In mid-1987 precisely 500 special versions of the three-door car were produced for Ford by Aston Martin Tickford at Bedworth, Coventry, with 224-bhp engines and various aerodynamic add-ons. This was the version that would produce more than 550 bhp in Group A racing trim, and win hundreds of saloon car races.

### Ford Sierra RS Cosworth (four-door notchback)

In 1988 and 1989, Ford produced approximately 14,000 cars that combined the original running gear with the normal Sierra four-door 'notchback' saloon style.

### Ford Sierra RS Cosworth 4×4

In 1990 Ford married the XR4×4's four-wheel-drive installation with a 220-bhp version of the Sierra RS Cosworth engine, in the four-door 'notchback' saloon style. This was a direct replacement for the rear-drive car. The first 5,000 cars were completed before the end of July 1990.

## Specification (1986 three-door RS Cosworth)

**Engine:** inline four-cylinder, twin overhead camshafts, turbo
**Bore × stroke:** 90.8 mm × 76.95 mm
**Capacity:** 1993 cc
**Maximum power:** 204 bhp
**Transmission:** five-speed manual gearbox, rear-wheel drive
**Chassis:** steel unit-construction body/chassis assembly
**Suspension:** independent front with MacPherson struts; independent rear with semi-trailing arms and coil springs
**Brakes:** discs front and rear
**Bodywork:** steel three-door four-seater hatchback
**Maximum speed (approx):** 145 mph (233 km/h)

*Above: The Cosworth was powered by a two-litre turbocharged twin-cam engine. In the motorsport form shown here it could produce far more power than the 204-bhp version in the original Cosworth.*

*Left: The first Cosworth was made using the hatchback Sierra body. Later, after the Sierra Sapphire-booted version of the Sierra was built, a Cosworth four-wheel-drive model was developed for international rallying.*

*Below: The distinctive black livery of an RS500. The RS500 was a limited edition of 500 cars produced for homologation purposes for Group A racing. The roadgoing RS500 produced another 20 bhp more power than the original Cosworth.*

*Above: The RS Cosworth's rear wing was almost as flamboyant as that on the Porsche Turbo, and just as necessary, given the Ford's performance.*

## Ford Cougar 1998-present

The Cougar replaced the poor-selling Probe as Ford's top-line coupé model, and expanded its late-1990s New Edge theme that already included the Ka super-mini, Puma small coupé, and Escort replacement, the Focus. Based on the Mondeo floorpan, the Cougar was available with Ford's proven 2.0-litre 16-valve Zetec, developing 130 bhp, or the 170 bhp 2.5-litre V6 24-valve Duratec drivetrains with five-speed MTX75 manual gearbox. The V6 could do 0–60 mph (0-96 km/h) in 8.1 seconds with a maximum speed of 140 mph (225 km/h), while the 2.0-litre model ran out at 130 mph (209 km/h) with 0–60 mph (0-196 km/h) coming up in 9.1 seconds. Automatic transmission was optional, while ventilated discs and ABS were fitted as standard, with electronic brake-force distribution and dual-mode traction control on the V6.

The Cougar inherited the Mondeo's suspension and steering systems, although virtually every item that influenced dynamic performance was re-calibrated. Up front, the suspension was independent by MacPherson struts with angled coil springs and damper units, and lower wishbones (A-arms) mounted on vertical bushes. The suspension arms, anti-roll bar and steering rack were mounted on a separate perimeter front sub-frame. At the rear was Ford's 'Quadralink' system with strut-type coil springs and damper units, two transverse and one trailing arm each side, incorporating passive rear-wheel steering, plus a rear anti-roll bar. Steering was via variable-rate power-assisted rack-and-pinion system, and the Cougar was shod with 205/60 x 15 tyres for the 2.0-litre model and 215/50 x 16 for the 2.5-litre version. Alloy wheels were standard on the V6 model.

The cabin included electrically adjustable bucket seats, along with standard driver and passenger airbags, load-limiting seat belts and sèmi-deformable steering column, head-and-chest combination side airbags. In the rear, accommodation was reasonable, given the constraints of the coupé design. A large tailgate provided access to the boot, and split-fold rear seats increased its carrying capacity. Other as-sets included air conditioning, air filtration system, CD auto-changer, and power tilt/slide sunroof.

The Cougar was designed by Darrell Behmer and engineered in Europe at Ford's Small and Medium Vehicle Centre – then headed by Richard Parry-Jones – by a multi-national team based in the UK, Germany and the USA under the direction of Chief Programme Engineer Martin Lunt. The first renderings were approved in 1994, and its drag coefficient was a reasonable 0.32 Cd. The manufacturing process was extremely thorough. It involved a 24-stage paint and body protection programme, including pre-coating with zinc for all exterior panels, phosphate spray coat, electro-coat filler, wet-on-wet enamel topcoat, comprehensive wax injection of cavities, PVC and wax underbody coating, plus stone chip protection. Attention was paid to sealing flanges with rust-inhibiting adhesive and thick PVC sealing beads. Plastic liners were fitted in the front wheelarches, with textile wheelarch liners in the rear, and anti-scuff strips on inner doorsills and rear load sill completed the picture.

*Above: The most dramatic incarnation of Ford's late-1990s 'New Edge' styling was the Cougar coupé, featuring sharp lines, narrow angles and shallow radius curves. It was a quantum leap from the lacklustre Probe. Power came from 2.0 Zetec or 2.5-litre Duratec V6 engines, while ST24-type suspension meant handling was good. Interiors were spacious and comfortable, if tending towards plastic, which was a legacy of their US origins.*

### Specification (V6 model)

**Engine:** V6 Duratec
**Bore x stroke:** 82.4 mm x 79.5 mm
**Capacity:** 2544 cc
**Maximum Power:** 170 bhp
**Transmission:** five-speed manual
**Chassis:** monocoque
**Suspension:** front, independent by MacPherson struts, lower wishbones, coil springs and dampers; rear, 'Quadralink' trailing arm system, coil springs and dampers, anti-roll bar
**Brakes:** ventilated discs front and rear
**Bodywork:** steel, two-door coupé

# Ford-Australia

A merican-type Ford Model Ts were first assembled in Australia in 1925; the first major local content, in the form of Australian-designed bodies for Model As, came a few years later. Until the 1960s all Australian Fords were really Ford-USA designs with minor differences.

By the 1970s Australian Fords were individually designed, but still followed North American trends, and there were interesting hybrids like Cortinas with 4.1-litre six-cylinder engines.

Later the LTDs and Falcon XDs, which were totally Australian designs, used styling similar to those of European Granadas, but in the 1980s Ford's links with Mazda led to more and more Japanese influence on the cars. Late-1980s Lasers were modified Mazda 323s, and Telstars were Mazda 626s; the only all-Australian Ford was the large Falcon/Fairmont/Fairlane type.

Ford Australia's outstanding new car of the 1980s was the Capri sports car, which was based on Mazda 323 engineering. The Tickford-tuned Falcon engine XR6 was the bargain sports saloon of the 1990s.

*Above: Like other branches of the multinational combine, Ford-Australia nowadays use the oval badge with classic script.*

## Ford Capri 1989–96

Ford-USA began to dabble with the idea of producing a compact new sports car in the early 1980s, and exhibited a Ghia 'barchetta' concept car at various European motor shows. Then, as so often happens at Ford, changes of policy led to this car being abandoned, but in its place a cabriolet derivative of the Mazda 323 evolved instead.

Ford had forged financial links with Mazda of Japan in the 1970s, and gradually began to use Mazda components and expertise in developing its smaller models. The new Capri, which was assembled by Ford-Australia, and sold in the USA as a Mercury Capri, was a perfect example.

The Mazda 323, originally launched in 1980 alongside the new front-wheel-drive Ford Escort, was heavily revised in 1985, and became a third-generation

type in 1989. As a typically efficient transverse-engine/front-wheel-drive model it provided an ideal platform for the new Ford sports car, once the wheelbase had been shortened by two inches.

There were two versions of the 16-valve engine, one with fuel injection, the other with both injection and turbocharging. Engines and transmissions were modified versions of those already being used in Mazda 323s and in the closely-related Ford Laser; these were sent to Australia from Mazda in Japan. The body style featured rounded lines including a slim and finely detailed nose, though there was no connection with the little Mazda MX-5 (which used the same engine, but had rear-wheel drive).

Exterior styling, complete with pop-up headlamps, was by Ford's Turin-based Ghia design house, while the interior

was by Ital Design. This meant that the neat little car had the right sort of pedigree to appeal to sports car buyers all over the world.

The new Capri's launch was rather mysteriously delayed until 1989, and although sold in Australia as a Ford, it was marketed in the USA as a Mercury model. Although it looked the part, and was a fast little car, the Capri's character was originally more 'sporting' than 'sports', which may explain why Ford did not sell it in Europe.

### Specification (1989)

**Engine:** inline four-cylinder, twin-cam
**Bore × stroke:** 78 mm × 83.6 mm
**Capacity:** 1598 cc
**Maximum power:** 105 bhp (or 136 bhp with turbocharger)
**Transmission:** five-speed manual

gearbox or four-speed automatic transmission, front-wheel drive
**Chassis:** steel unit-construction body/chassis assembly
**Suspension:** independent front with MacPherson struts; independent rear with MacPherson struts, longitudinal and transverse control arms and anti-roll bar
**Brakes:** discs front and rear
**Bodywork:** steel 2+2-seater cabriolet, optional hard top
**Maximum speed (approx):** 125 mph/201 km/h (with turbocharged engine)

*Below: This is actually a US Mercury version, but it's the same as the Aussie Ford under the skin: a neat front-wheel-drive sports car with turbo twin-cam power.*

# Franklin Automobile Company

**I**f Franklin had not always built its cars with air-cooled engines, insisting that this was the only technically efficient way to arrange things, it would now be a forgotten American marque.

The miracle is not that Franklin produced a few air-cooled-engined cars, but that the engines were so large (and therefore needed a lot of cooling) and that Franklin stayed in business for so many years. More than 150,000 air-cooled Franklins were built between 1902 and 1934.

In many ways the early cars seemed to be different for the sake of being special – Franklins were the last cars, it seems, to use wooden rather than steel chassis frames, and they hung on to the use of carriage-style full-elliptic spring suspension years after the rest of the world's motor industry had abandoned them.

All manner of air-cooled types were on sale in the early years, but by the 1920s the cars built at Syracuse, New York, all had inline six-cylinder engines, with large fans to provide a sufficient blast of cooling air.

Aviators who flew behind air-cooled engines were often persuaded to buy Franklins (no doubt some financial inducement was offered . . .), which explains why an 'Airman' model was introduced in 1927, and why Charles Lindbergh was the very first owner.

Franklin sales reached their peak (of around 14,000 cars a year) in 1929, just before the American Depression hit hard. For the 1930s two new ranges were then developed – one with a brand-new supercharged six-cylinder engine, the other a supercharged V12.

For Franklin, however, the combination of the Depression, high prices, and unfashionable engineering led to a sharp drop in sales. The V12 was the wrong car for this money-tight period, and the last Franklins of all were produced in 1934.

*Below: Franklin's cars were bound to suffer when the post-1932 V8 Fords proved so popular and the Depression bit hard at the same time, but their big air-cooled engines made them very distinctive. Shown is a 1931 Franklin Airman convertible.*

## Franklin Six 1929-34

Even as the Depression struck North America like a whirlwind, Franklin introduced its new 140-series cars, which had conventional chassis, but featured a brand-new engine.

The latest Franklin Six had a super-charged air-cooled engine, with a large fan flexibly mounted on the nose of the crankshaft, and there was a new design of a false front 'radiator' with thermostatically-controlled shutters to regulate airflow over the cylinders. The cooling air was ducted, and blasted across the cylinders, rather than along the engine from front to rear – hence the name 'side-blast engine' which was bandied around.

Although the cars sold very slowly, they were available with a big choice of body styles, open and closed, formal and sporting, though all had the same type of front end. Prices were cut, and specifications simplified, as the 1930s progressed, but not even the introduction of the Olympic range of 1933 could lift the business.

It was a brave, but ultimately unsuccessful, project. In five years total production of Franklin Six cars with this engine was 12,090. Three of those cars were owned by famed flyers Charles Lindbergh, Amelia Earhart and Orville Wright.

*Below: This is an Airman Six Sedan from 1932. Its 'side-blast' air-cooled straight-six engine displaced 4.5 litres and was rated at 100 bhp.*

### Franklin Six variants

#### Franklin Airman
The output of the Franklin Six's six-cylinder engine was raised to 100 bhp for 1931 and the subsequent years. The mechanically similar Airman models were introduced in 1932.

#### Franklin Olympic
In 1933-34 Franklin also produced the Olympic, the result of collaboration with Reo, using Reo's Flying Cloud chassis and Franklin's six-cylinder engine.

### Specification (1930)
**Engine:** inline six-cylinder, overhead-valve
**Bore × stroke:** 88.9 mm × 120.65 mm
**Capacity:** 4494 cc
**Maximum power:** 95 bhp
**Transmission:** three-speed manual gearbox, rear-wheel drive
**Chassis:** separate steel frame with channel-section main members
**Suspension:** non-independent with beam front axle and leaf springs; live rear axle with leaf springs
**Brakes:** drums front and rear
**Bodywork:** steel four/five-seaters, various styles
**Maximum speed:** 80 mph (129 km/h)

# Frazer Nash (A. F. N. Ltd)

**A**rchie Frazer-Nash was a partner in the GN cyclecar business, which went out of business in the early 1920s, but as he was still convinced of the basic merits of that car's layout – which featured chain drive to the rear wheels – he started another car marque, calling it Frazer Nash.

Or was it Frazer-Nash? Should there be a hyphen or not? This has caused controversy among enthusiasts and historians over the years, particularly as the company's advertising sometimes did, and sometimes did not, use it! We've chosen to use 'Frazer Nash' as that was the last title used in the 1950s.

Frazer Nash was always a very small concern, the sports cars being hand-built throughout their careers. Prices were high, specifications were individually variable for each customer, and in many ways the cars' general features were outside the mainstream for the period.

Between 1924 and 1956 only two basically different types of 'Nash were produced – the 'Chain Gang' types before World War II, and the Bristol-engined types after it. There was no technical connection between them.

All the pre-war types were what are affectionately known as 'Chain Gang' models, with gearboxes featuring a series of cogs and chains which could be clutched into or out of engagement as required. Production of these cars began at Kingston-upon-Thames in 1924, but the factory moved to Isleworth in 1926, where – as A. F. N. Ltd – it stayed.

Archie Frazer-Nash, though technically competent, was not a prudent businessman, and sold out to H. J. Aldington in 1936, who was much more capable. Under the Aldington family's control the 'Chain Gang' survived into the late 1930s, by which time A. F. N. was also importing BMWs.

Plans for post-war cars were laid in 1945, and involved links with the Bristol Aeroplane Co., and the distinguished BMW engine designer Dr Fiedler. Commercial links were shortly unscrambled, but all post-war Frazer Nash cars used the Bristol development of the pre-war BMW engine. Technically the post-war cars were more up-to-date than the 'Chain Gangs' had ever been, but as they were extremely expensive they sold very slowly.

A. F. N. picked up the British Porsche franchise in the mid-1950s, and Frazer Nash car assembly ceased soon afterwards. A project to build a BMW V8-engined car, to be called the Continental, was abandoned after a single prototype had been built.

*Above: Pre-war Frazer Nashes all had primitive but effective chain-and-dog transmission.*

*Below: Post-war models, like this Le Mans Replica, were developed from BMWs.*

*Below: 1920s and 1930s Frazer Nash cars used several different engines. This 1930 Vitesse had a 1496-cc Meadows overhead-valve four.*

## Frazer Nash TT Replica 1932-38

The GN ancestry showed up strongly in every 'Chain Gang' Frazer Nash – the typical TT Replica included – for there was always a very simple chassis frame with straight side members, near-rigid cantilever-type leaf springs at front and rear, very hard suspension, and direct steering.

A propeller shaft linked the engine to the (intermediate) rear axle itself, but a series of chains, running on different-sized dogs, then provided the final drive. This chain-drive transmission was so simple that critics often used to disbelieve its efficiency. Because all cogs and chains were exposed to the elements they needed frequent cleaning and oiling. Breakages were common, but repairs were simple. Because of the layout there was no torque-splitting differential, the 'solid' rear axle having a narrow track which gave superb traction.

Over the years the basic layout changed very little, the major advances – and differences – being in the supply of engines, bodies and model names. A total of 17 early cars were fitted with Plus Power engines, and about 215 with Anzani engines. From 1933, 27 cars had Blackburne engines, and 27 'Gough' (Frazer Nash) engines were fitted, starting in 1934.

Frazer Nash models were often named after earlier sporting successes, which explains the arrival of the Shelsley, Boulogne, Colmore, Ulster and TT Replica models. The most numerous of all styles was the TT Replica – 85 cars built in six years – though the most familiar engine was undoubtedly the Anzani, which was used on the vast majority of cars built from 1925 to 1929. Only a few

models used the Blackburne engine which, in supercharged racing form, could produce up to 150 bhp. The TT Replica normally featured the 1496-cc Meadows engine, but a twin-cam unit could be ordered.

### Specification (1932)

**Engine:** Meadows inline four-cylinder, overhead-valve
**Bore × stroke:** 69 mm × 100 mm
**Capacity:** 1496 cc
**Maximum power:** 62 bhp
**Transmission:** four-speed manual gearbox by chains, rear-wheel drive
**Chassis:** separate steel frame with channel-section side members and tubular bracing
**Suspension:** non-independent with beam front axle and live rear axle, cantilever leaf springs all round
**Brakes:** drums front and rear
**Bodywork:** aluminium two-seater open sports car on ash frame
**Maximum speed (approx):** 87 mph (140 km/h)

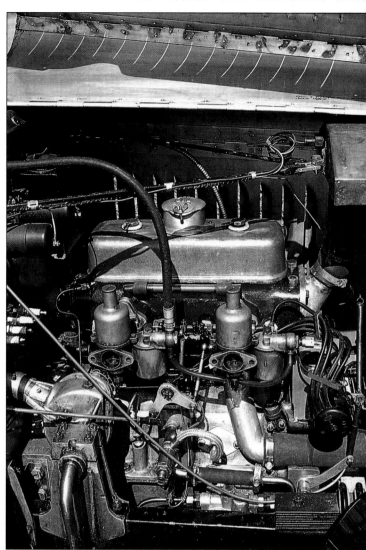

*Right: A 1496-cc overhead-valve unit developing around 55-65 bhp, the Meadows inline-four was a popular choice among pre-war independent carbuilders lacking the resources to make their own engines. Equipped with twin SU carburettors, it was the usual fitment in the Frazer Nash TT Replica.*

*Below: Frazer Nash introduced the TT Replica model in 1932. Instead of the Meadows, it could be fitted with a twin-overhead-camshaft six-cylinder Blackburne engine.*

# Frazer Nash Le Mans Replica 1950-51

ans for post-war Frazer Nash cars were
d in 1945 and 1946, after the Aldington
mily had arranged for BMW's Dr Fie-
er and his modern 328 engine design
come to Britain. Redesigned and
dated BMW engines and body styles
came the basis of the first post-war six-
linder Bristol models.

In the original scheme the Bristol
eroplane Co. and Frazer Nash were to
are more running gear and chassis
mponents than the production cars
entually did. The engines and trans-
ssions, however, were beautifully and
refully built by Bristol, while Frazer
ash cars were hand-built, as ever, at
eworth.

All post-war Frazer Nash cars were
sed on a simple, but rigid, chassis
me which was built almost entirely
m large-diameter steel tubes. The
riations, from year to year, involved
fferent tunes of the two-litre Bristol
igine, and different model names, the
e Mans Replica being one of the best-
membered.

The majority of all post-war Frazer
ash cars were equipped with a 'cigar-
yle' narrow two-seater body featuring
rcle-type front wings. The original cars
ere known as High Speed models, but
llowing a stirring performance in the
rst post-war Le Mans 24 Hours they
ere quickly renamed Le Mans Repli-
s. Of the 83 Bristol-engined cars built
m 1948 to 1956, around 60 had Le Mans
eplica-derived bodies.

The Le Mans Replicas, in common
ith all Frazer Nash cars, had well-
eveloped chassis which handled ex-
emely well. The engines, though
aving very long strokes, revved freely,
id the construction quality was always
rst-rate.

Time, and fashion, however, slipped
way from Frazer Nash, such that
emand dried up in the mid-1950s.

*elow: Broadly the same mechanical
esign was offered with various
ngine tunes and different bodies,
uch as this racing Mille Miglia type.*

### Frazer Nash Le Mans Replica variants

The original name for cars with Le Mans Replica coachwork was the High Speed or Competition model.

The Mk II Le Mans Replica had de Dion rear suspension.

Between 1948 and 1956 the same post-war design of chassis was offered with various tunes of Bristol engine, in various guises, including the Fast Tourer (a full-width-style roadgoing sports car), the Mille Miglia (a full-width model, for racing and road use) and the Sebring (a full-width racing-sports car, with de Dion rear suspension; only three were built).

The last Frazer Nash of all was the Continental coupé prototype, which used a similar type of chassis and suspension to the de Dion-suspended Sebring model, but had a 1950s-style BMW V8 engine and gearbox. Only one car, completed in 1957, was built.

### Specification (1950 Le Mans Replica)

**Engine:** inline six-cylinder, overhead-valve
**Bore × stroke:** 66 mm × 96 mm
**Capacity:** 1971 cc
**Maximum power:** 110/120/125 bhp, to order

*Above: The Le Mans Replica, shown at the 1952 Goodwood 9 Hours race, used a Bristol-built two-litre BMW engine.*

**Transmission:** four-speed manual gearbox, rear-wheel drive
**Chassis:** separate steel frame with tubular main and bracing members
**Suspension:** independent front with transverse leaf spring; live rear axle with torsion bars
**Brakes:** drums front and rear
**Bodywork:** aluminium two-seater open sports car
**Maximum speed (approx):** 110 mph (177 km/h)

# Gilbern Sports Cars Ltd

G iles Smith and Bernard Frieze were enthusiasts who started by building 'specials'. Frieze was German-born and had studied engineering in his youth. After working for another maker of glassfibre-bodied cars he decided to branch out on his own – and built a special shell for Giles Smith, a local enthusiast.

The two then got together, and decided to break into the sports car business on their own account. They went on to make history by founding the only car company to design and build complete cars in Wales. 'Gilbern' was a blend of their first names – GILes and BERNard.

The first Gilbern was simply called the GT, and was based on a multi-tubular frame clothed in a neat but undistinguished body style. Like many cars of its day, it was available with a choice of proprietary engines, and was sold in kit form to avoid the payment of British Purchase Tax.

The GT was so popular that Gilbern was inspired to produce a more modern car, the Genie, which was larger, faster, and altogether more expensive than the original GT. This Ford V6-engined car was also sold in kit form, was renamed Invader in 1969, progressed to Mk II two years later, and became the Mk III in 1972.

When Britain joined the EEC in 1973, Value Added Tax (VAT) took over from Purchase Tax, and was applied to *all* car purchases, whether in built-up or kit form. Gilbern could no longer sell its cars when they were so much more expensive than their opposition, and in spite of the injection of new finance the business finally folded in 1974.

*Above: The Gilbern GT had a certain historic importance, as the first car to be designed and built entirely in Wales. Initially it came with a choice of BMC and Coventry Climax engines.*

## Gilbern GT 1960-67

This, the original Gilbern, was a simply-engineered car which relied almost totally on proprietary components for its running gear. Launched in 1960, it had a multi-tubular chassis frame with square-section tubes (which was by no means of pure 'spaceframe' design), and a glass-fibre body shell in 2 + 2 coupé style.

Almost every mechanical fitting to this chassis – front suspension, rear axle, and steering – was from current MG or Austin-Healey models. In the beginning there was a wide choice of engines – 948-cc BMC, 1489-cc BMC, and the Coventry Climax 1098-cc FWA type. The small BMC engine could also be sup-plied in supercharged form, an option in Austin-Healey Sprites of the period.

This was altogether too confusing for the customers – and too difficult for Gilbern itself to manage – so from 1962 the current 1.8-litre/95-bhp MGA (later MGB) engine was standardised instead, and sales improved. The GT's main attraction was always that it was sold in partly-finished 'kit' form, to avoid British Purchase Tax having to be paid, though it was never any faster and certainly no more refined than the MGs and Triumphs of the day.

Nevertheless, at its peak, Gilbern built more than 150 GTs in a year, with total production approaching 600 cars. When the larger Genie appeared, the GT gradually disappeared, for there was no space at the Llantwit Fardre factory for two different cars to be manufactured.

### Specification (1960, MGA engine)

**Engine:** inline four-cylinder, overhead-valve
**Bore × stroke:** 75.4 mm × 88.9 mm
**Capacity:** 1588 cc
**Maximum power:** 80 bhp
**Transmission:** four-speed manual gearbox, rear-wheel drive
**Chassis:** separate steel frame with tubular side and cross-bracing members
**Suspension:** independent front with wishbones and coil springs; live rear axle with coil springs
**Brakes:** discs front, drums rear
**Bodywork:** glassfibre four-seater coupé
**Maximum speed (approx):** 94 mph (151 km/h)

*Below: From the 1962 model year the BMC 1.8-litre inline-four was made standard in the GT, giving 90-mph-plus performance. This replaced a range of other BMC overhead-valve engines and an overhead-cam Coventry Climax unit.*

## Gilbern Genie 1966-69

Gilbern's second model was the Genie, later redeveloped and renamed the Invader, which relied on the meaty Ford-UK V6 engine and its related gearbox. Developed in something of a hurry in 1966, this car almost immediately took over from the GT model.

Like the GT in concept, although entirely different in detail, the Genie had a multi-tubular chassis frame, and a glass-fibre body shell, and it was sold either in fully-built or partly-complete kit form. It was larger and more spacious than the GT had been.

As with the GT, the running gear was an amalgam of proprietary bits – Ford engine and gearbox, MGB front suspension, and MGB rear axle. The car was pushed into production during 1966-67, and was soon being criticised for its lack of roadholding, and its general lack of refinement, though it was undoubtedly fast, with a top speed of at least 115 mph.

In the next few years Gilbern tried hard to improve the design, and the newly-named Invader of 1969 was better in many ways, especially in the roadholding department. Gilbern then decided to attack the Reliant Scimitar GTE market by launching an estate-car version of the Invader.

Gilbern was already struggling to survive when VAT was imposed in 1973 on all car sales, and this new impost finished it off. About 280 Genies and 600 Invaders were produced.

### Gilbern Genie variants

### Gilbern Invader

The Invader was a development of the Genie, with similar mechanical and styling details. The Invader I arrived in 1969, with style and suspension improvements, the Mk II took over in

*Below: The Invader's styling was clearly influenced by Bertone's Alfa Romeo GTV.*

1971 for a year, then finally came the 1972-73 Invader III, which had a Ford Cortina front suspension and rear axle. There was also an Invader estate.

### Specification (1972 Invader III)

**Engine:** V6, overhead-valve
**Bore × stroke:** 93.7 mm × 72.4 mm
**Capacity:** 2994 cc
**Maximum power:** 141 bhp
**Transmission:** four-speed manual gearbox, rear-wheel drive
**Chassis:** separate steel multi-tubular frame
**Suspension:** independent front with coil springs; live rear axle with coil springs
**Brakes:** discs front, drums rear
**Bodywork:** glassfibre four-seater coupé or estate car/hatchback
**Maximum speed (approx):** 115 mph (185 km/h)

*Above: This was the Invader in kit form in 1970, a year after it had superseded the Genie. It was fast, thanks to its Ford V6 power unit.*

*Below: An estate version of the Invader was produced in an attempt to capture some of the Reliant Scimitar GTE's market.*

JMT 266K

WVK 700H

# Ginetta Cars Ltd

Ginetta was set up by the four Walklett brothers in 1957, and was based at Woodbridge, in their native Suffolk. In earlier years, however, the Walkletts had run an agricultural and construction-engineering business. All were avid motor racing enthusiasts, their first automotive project being the building of a 'special' based on pre-war Wolseley Hornet components, named Ginetta G1.

At the time the mystery (which has never been solved) was how and where the name Ginetta originated. None of the Walklett family has ever explained – one may only assume that it was a girl's name.

The first 'own-design' Ginetta, penned by Ivor Walklett and styled by Trevor, was the G2 of 1958-60, a stark, open two-seater sports car, and in the next decade this was followed by a series of competently engineered and attractively styled two-seaters.

In those years every Ginetta was a kit car, for completion by the customer at home, the vast majority being intended for circuit racing. By Ginetta standards the G4 of the 1960s was the first series-production model, and was so successful that it was re-introduced in considerably modified form in the 1980s.

Ginetta Cars moved to Witham in Essex in 1962, and it was from there that the first single-seater race car – the mid-engined G8 – was introduced. The G10 was a short-lived front-engined road car which used a number of MGB body and glass components, but the car which convinced British enthusiasts that Ginetta was a serious carmaker was the Rootes Sunbeam Stiletto-engined G15 road car, which arrived in 1968.

After other racing Ginettas had appeared, the G15's successor was introduced in the form of the front-engined G21 Coupé, a smart medium-sized machine of TVR or Reliant class, which would have sold better had it not been so expensive. By this time Ginetta had expanded so much that it took on new premises at Sudbury in Suffolk, but this venture lasted for only two years, after which the business shrank and returned to Witham.

The imposition of VAT on British cars rendered G15s and G21s uncompetitive in the marketplace, so after the G21 was discontinued in 1978 Ginetta concentrated on making competition cars, while dabbling with a variety of road cars. The G26, first seen in 1984, was a Capri-sized four-seater hatchback (using Ford Cortina components); but the spiritual successor to the G15, the mid-engined G32, was not previewed until 1986, and did not actually go on sale until 1990.

By this time Ginetta's business had attracted the attention of an entrepreneur, Martin Phaff, who took control at the end of 1989. Before the G32 went into production, Ginetta moved to a new factory at Scunthorpe. In 1990 the G32 was joined by the Rover V8-engined G33, though this was fundamentally redesigned before being prepared for sale in 1991.

In 1998, the G4 and fabulous mid-engined G12 sports racer were being made by Dare UK, while Ginetta itself was still producing the G27 from its Sheffield base. A new model was unveiled at the 1999 Motor Show.

*Right: Few of the 1950s and 1960s kit car manufacturers survive, but Ginetta is an exception, and many would say that the company is making its best-ever cars in the 1990s.*

*Below: Ginetta's first design was the G2, a no-frills open two-seater sports car along similar lines to early Lotuses.*

*Above: The G10 was a roadgoing sports car with Ford V8 power.*

*Below: The successful little G4 was revived in the 1980s.*

## Ginetta G4 1961-66

*bove: Club-racing G4s were often ble to outmanoeuvre more powerful rs, as here in 1963.*

*Below: Its glassfibre body and spaceframe chassis gave the G4 light weight and good handling.*

Ginetta's first really successful model was the G4, i.e. only the fourth 'production' model from the tiny Suffolk-based company.

Designed by one of the four Walklett brothers, Ivor, the G4 first appeared at the 1961 Racing Car Show. It was designed to be sold in kit form rather than as a made-up car because of the great tax advantages then allowed kits. Like its rather more ugly predecessors it featured a tubular steel spaceframe, on this model cut away at the sides to allow for doors. The front suspension was a very effective twin wishbone and coilspring design taken directly from that most popular of donor cars, the Triumph Herald, while the live rear axle was from the Ford Anglia. With the standard Ford Anglia 105E engine (a 997-cc pushrod overhead-valve design with good tuning potential), the car retailed for only £499. For another £16 it could be supplied with the larger, 1350-cc, engine from the Ford Classic.

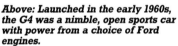

*Above: Launched in the early 1960s, the G4 was a nimble, open sports car with power from a choice of Ford engines.*

With its low weight and low centre of gravity the G4 had good roadholding, handling and performance, making it a very successful club racer. The factory raced a disc-braked G4 very successfully, and in club races driver Chris Meek frequently beat larger GT cars like the E-type Jaguar and AC Cobra. The racing G4 had a 1600-cc engine and independent rear suspension and the latter modification was made available for the ordinary roadgoing cars.

The G4 was almost forgotten when Ginetta moved on to more overtly roadgoing cars like the G15 and G21 but in the early 1980s the factory, now based in the small Essex town of Witham, decided the time was right for a re-introduced and slightly restyled G4 with a variety of power options. Unfortunately this proved to be a miscalculation, but the appearance of the similar-looking G33 in the early 1990s showed the concept was right – all that was needed was far more power.

### Specification (1965)

**Engine:** inline four-cylinder, overhead-valve
**Bore × stroke:** 81 mm × 73 mm
**Capacity:** 1498 cc
**Maximum power:** 90 bhp
**Transmission:** four-speed manual
**Chassis:** tubular steel spaceframe
**Suspension:** independent front with wishbones, coil springs and telescopic dampers; live rear axle with 'A' bracket, trailing arms, coil springs and telescopic dampers
**Brakes:** discs front, drums rear
**Bodywork:** glassfibre two-seater sports
**Maximum speed (approx):** 120 mph (193 km/h)

## Ginetta G15 1968-74

After building a series of attractive racing cars, and producing a few road cars, Ginetta began selling the smart little G15 sports car in 1968. This combined the entire rear-mounted engine/transmission/rear suspension of the modern Rootes 'baby' car, the Imp, with a smart rounded two-seater coupé style.

The basis of the G15 was a tubular chassis frame, to the rear of which was grafted the Sunbeam Stiletto/Imp Sport power pack. This featured a light-alloy overhead-cam engine of 875 cc which had evolved from a racing Coventry Climax design, and which was laid over at an angle of 45 degrees to reduce the overall height of the package. Front suspension was essentially by Triumph Spitfire wishbones and coil springs, and the body, by Trevor Walklett, was a neatly-detailed two-seater coupé, manufactured from glassfibre.

This little car was sold completely built-up, or in partly-assembled form as a kit car. Because it only weighed about 1,100 lb, it was fast, nimble, and extremely agile. Like the Rootes Imps from which its running gear was derived, the G15 had a very free-revving engine, an urgent character, and light controls allied to cheeky road manners.

In 1972 assembly of G15s moved to the new factory at Sudbury where, at the peak, up to six G15s were being built every week. In 1973, however, Britain joined the EEC, VAT became payable on all cars and components, and there was no longer any advantage in Ginetta offering the G15 as a kit.

*Below: The G15 was popular: over 800 were produced.*

Demand for G15s slumped in 1973; all cars were fully built-up after April, and the last cars of all were produced in 1974. More than 800 G15s had been built in six years.

### Specification (1968)

**Engine:** inline four-cylinder, single overhead camshaft
**Bore × stroke:** 68 mm × 60.4 mm
**Capacity:** 875 cc
**Maximum power:** 55 bhp
**Transmission:** four-speed manual gearbox, rear-wheel drive
**Chassis:** separate steel frame with tubular main and bracing members
**Suspension:** independent front with wishbones and coil springs; independent rear with semi-trailing arms and coil springs
**Brakes:** drums front and rear
**Bodywork:** glassfibre two-seater coupé
**Maximum speed (approx):** 94 mph (151 km/h)

*Above: A neat-looking coupé, the G15 used the Hillman Imp's rear-mounted engine, transmission and rear suspension.*

*Below: Most G15s had the 875-cc Imp Sport engine, with twin Stromberg carburettors, producing about 55 bh*

# Ginetta G21 1973-78

Following the successful launch of the rear-engined G15, and the rapid build-up of Ginetta as a road car manufacturer, the company next developed a second, entirely new, road car design, which it called G21.

The G21 was considerably larger than the G15, being a front-engined 2+2-seater, and it had rather a confused birth. The prototype, unveiled at the London Motor Show of 1970, was advertised as having a choice of 1.6-litre or 3.0-litre Ford-UK engines, along with independent rear suspension for one type, and a live rear axle for the other.

By the time the car actually went into production in 1973, it had been redesigned, this time with a choice of 1.7-litre Chrysler-UK engines, and with a live rear axle to reduce costs. This Chrysler link was logical, since Ginetta was already taking substantial numbers of engines for the G15 from the same company.

The 3.0-litre V6 Ford engine option remained, but very few were ever sold, and that alternative was soon abandoned, leaving the G21 available with 85-bhp or 93-bhp Rapier engines.

By the time G21 deliveries began in 1973, production of G15s was already tailing off, so for the next five years the East Anglian concern was able to concentrate on the front-engined G21. Customers soon learned that this was an honest, rugged, and intrinsically simple machine, with a tubular chassis which featured steel backbone members, and a compact 2+2 cabin.

The G21 was much faster than the G15 had ever been, for in 93-bhp form it had a top speed of 117 mph, which speaks volumes for the aerodynamic efficiency of the Walklett-inspired style.

In five years a total of 150 G21s was produced.

## Specification (1973)

**Engine:** inline four-cylinder, overhead-valve
**Bore × stroke:** 81.5 mm × 82.55 mm
**Capacity:** 1725 cc
**Maximum power:** 85 bhp or (optional) 93 bhp
**Transmission:** four-speed manual gearbox and overdrive, rear-wheel drive

**Chassis:** separate steel frame with tubular main and cross-members with 'backbone' bracing
**Suspension:** independent front with wishbones and coil springs; live rear axle with radius arms and coil springs
**Brakes:** discs front, drums rear
**Bodywork:** glassfibre 2+2 coupé
**Maximum speed (approx):** 117 mph (188 km/h) with 93 bhp

*Below: The G21 was one of Ginetta's most attractive designs and was, like all Ginettas, an in-house creation by the Walklett brothers. It was powered by either a four-cylinder Hillman engine or the Ford Essex three-litre V6, but very few of the V6 models were built.*

# Ginetta G32 1989–92

The spiritual replacement for the G15, though only in general layout and character, was the G32 sports car. This model first appeared, in early prototype form, at the British Motor Show in 1986, but it did not actually go on sale until the beginning of 1990.

The G32 was literally the 32nd project undertaken by the Walklett family since the company was founded, and its design was influenced by the reception given to Toyota's mid-engined MR2 of 1984 (which was itself influenced by the Fiat X1/9 of the 1970s).

This, therefore, was the first mid/rear-engined Ginetta with a transversely-mounted engine and integral gearbox to go on sale, though it was not the first such Ginetta to be designed. A broadly similar G25 coupé had been shown at the Motorfair in 1983, but had never gone into production.

*Right: The G32 was the spiritual descendant of Ginetta's rear-engined G15, being their first mid-engined production car. It was first shown at the 1986 British Motor Show, production following four years later.*

As ever, Ginetta had to look around for a proprietary engine to power its new car, and – like Fiat – chose a modified version of a front-wheel-drive car's power pack. The G32 had a Ford CVH engine and its related five-speed gearbox, as fitted to the existing Ford Escort XR3i and Fiesta XR2i models. Many suspension and steering components were also 'found' in the Ford corporate parts bin.

Like the G15 before it, the G32 was a small (148-in long) and agile two-seater. At 1,940 lb, it was a lot heavier than the G15 had ever been, but it was a much more roomy and better-equipped car,

*Left: The G32's separate tubular steel chassis meant that it was easy to develop a convertible version.*

*Below: With the engine behind the driver the G32's bonnet line was low, and incorporated pop-up lights.*

with a top speed of around 110 mph. was the first car for which Ginetta ever achieved National Type Appro and it raised the company's image position in the market place.

## Specification (1989)

**Engine**: inline four-cylinder, single overhead camshaft
**Bore × stroke**: 80 mm × 79.5 mm
**Capacity**: 1598 cc
**Maximum power**: 110 bhp
**Transmission**: five-speed manual gearbox, rear-wheel drive
**Chassis**: separate steel frame with tubular main and cross-bracing members
**Suspension**: independent front with struts and coil springs; independent rear with coil springs
**Brakes**: discs front and rear
**Bodywork**: glassfibre two-seater cou
**Maximum speed (approx)**: 112 mph (180 km/h)

# Ginetta G33 1991–97

Having re-established itself in Scu thorpe, got the little G32 into productic and been refinanced by new own Martin Phaff, Ginetta decided to have bit of fun, and produced the ultra-spo ing new G33 two-seater, which was pr viewed at the British Motor Show of 19 Substantially redesigned in the mont which followed, it was ready for sale 1991.

The aim of the G33 was to be the hig est-performance Ginetta road car produced. For true-blue sports car e thusiasts the combination of the 200-bl aluminium Rover V8 engine, low a light two-seater bodywork, and

*Left: The G33's instruments include an 8,000-rpm tachometer, and a combined oil and water temperature gauge in a neat binnacle.*

claimed top speed of around 150 mph as irresistible. For export only, there was an optional engine – the Ford Sierra RS Cosworth unit, a two-litre turbocharged four-cylinder engine of 90.8 mm × 77 mm, producing 220 bhp.

Comfort, refinement and passenger space all took a back seat here, for the G33 was all about brute performance, tail slides and tyre-stripping acceleration where it was appropriate, and – in a Ford – enjoyment. Ivor Walklett, as usual, had designed the car around a multi-tubular chassis frame, while Mark Walklett (Trevor's son) had styled the low, wide, but sensuously curved open two-seater.

The windscreen was small and very swept back, the side windows could be fixed in place or removed (but could not be retracted), while there was a twin-headrest feature behind the cabin to provide a unique profile. There was a limited-slip differential, but the 195/50 ZR 16-in tyres still had to struggle to keep control of the Rover engine's very lusty torque output.

Priced at £18,187 when launched in 1991, it was the sort of machine that would sell to a large number of enthusiasts, sometimes as a second or even a third car, but definitely as an indulgence.

## Specification (1991)

**Engine:** V8, overhead-valve
**Bore × stroke:** 94 mm × 71 mm
**Capacity:** 3946 cc
**Maximum power:** 200 bhp
**Transmission:** five-speed manual gearbox, rear-wheel drive
**Chassis:** separate steel frame with multi-tubular main and bracing members with pressed-steel reinforcements
**Suspension:** independent front and rear, each with wishbones and coil springs
**Brakes:** discs front and rear
**Bodywork:** glassfibre two-seater open roadster
**Maximum speed:** 150 mph (241 km/h)

*Right: Power for the G33 came from a stretched, four-litre, version of the old Rover 3.5-litre V8, with fuel injection and a power output of 200 bhp, giving 150-mph performance.*

*Below: The smooth, rounded contours of the G33 were the work of Mark Walklett, son of one of the original Walklett brothers, Trevor, and echoed the early G4.*

# Glas (Hans Glas GmbH)

*Left: The 2600 V8 was the most ambitious project undertaken by the small Glas company, and was ultimately instrumental in its downfall. The car's attractive styling was the work of the Italian coachbuilders Frua.*

T he original Hans Glas company built agricultural machinery in Dingolfing, Bavaria, Germany, and its first motor vehicle was the Goggo motor scooter of 1951. Thereafter evolution was steady, for the four-wheeler 250-cc Goggomobil appeared in 1955, while the first family-sized Glas, a one-litre model called the 1004, appeared in 1962.

For a relatively small company Glas had great ambition, but it also had one great fault – it allowed its model range to become too large and over-complicated, and always seemed reluctant to drop an old model.

It was already accepted as a serious carmaker in the 1960s, not only because the Italian styling house Frua had supplied the smart S1004

range of coupés, convertibles and saloons, but also because the engine of this car was the very first to use cogged-belt drive to its overhead camshaft, ahead of a technically advanced company like Fiat.

In the next phase the one-litre engine was enlarged to 1.2 litres, and when that engine size was enlarged to 1.3 litres it was time to show new Frua-styled coupés and convertibles, the 1300GT types.

New model followed new model, for a newly-engineered 1.5-litre Ghia styled four-door saloon was previewed in 1963, but went into production a year later with a 1.7-litre version of that engine, as the Glas 1700.

Not content with this complicated line-up, Glas then forged ahead and introduced a real flagship in 1965, the 2600 V8. This was an elegant 2 + 2 coupé, styled by Frua on a special platform-type chassis, which was intended to sell at a price between the Porsche 912 and 911 models.

Even though the big V8 was a good-looking and competently-engineered machine, Glas found it difficult to establish it in the marketplace. By this time, the family-owned Glas business was in financial trouble, for the only model which appeared to be genuinely profitable was the old Goggomobil mini-car.

After a brisk period of negotiation with BMW, whose Munich headquarters was not too far away, BMW took control in 1966 for DM91 million. Within a year many old Glas models were dropped, while the smart 1300GT, 1700GT and 2600 V8 models were redeveloped and given BMW badges.

This, however, was only a short-term strategy, for BMW closed down all Glas manufacture by 1969. Three years later the Dingolfing factory had been completely rebuilt and expanded, chosen as the home of the new 5-Series BMW, and was to go on to be larger than the Munich factory during the 1980s.

## Glas 2600 V8 1965-67

The elegant Glas 2600 V8 was a sensational new model at the Frankfurt Motor Show of 1965, for it was by far the largest and most powerful Glas-badged car so far produced. Running on a new platform chassis, which featured de Dion rear suspension, it had Frua styling which looked remarkably like that of certain contemporary Maserati models, in which Frua had also had a hand. It was no wonder that the German motoring press christened it the 'Glaserati'.

The heart of the car was a 2.6-litre 90-degree V8 which was effectively, though not in fact, two Glas 1300GT four-cylinder blocks and overhead-cam cylinder heads on a common crankcase. There was a separate reinforced-rubber cogged belt from the crankshaft, to drive each camshaft, and even though this engine exhibited a number of obvious compromises it worked well, and was very powerful.

The 2600 V8 had a fine chassis, whose ride and handling was helped along by the use of de Dion rear suspension and self-levelling Boge dampers.

All would have been well if Glas had not suffered great financial traumas at this time (which were partly due to the cost of putting this exotic machine onto the market), and a mere 71 Glas-badged 2600s were produced before BMW took over.

As a final fling, BMW approved the upgrading of the car to a full 3000 V8, with an enlarged and more powerful engine,

at which point it also acquired BMW identity, with the famous badges on the bonnet, wheel covers and rear panel. This 1967 BMW-Glas 3000 had a 78-mm × 78-mm/2982-cc engine, developing 160 bhp. Top speed was claimed to be 125 mph – a good selling-point to GT purchasers – and 400 cars were built. However, with BMW's own 2800CS Coupé on the way, there was no long-term future for this car, which was finally dropped in the summer of 1968.

### Specification (1965)
**Engine:** V8, single overhead camshaft per bank of cylinders
**Bore × stroke:** 75 mm × 73 mm
**Capacity:** 2576 cc
**Maximum power:** 140 bhp
**Transmission:** four-speed manual gearbox, rear-wheel drive
**Chassis:** steel unit-construction body/chassis assembly
**Suspension:** independent front with wishbones and coil springs; de Dion rear axle and leaf springs
**Brakes:** discs front and rear
**Bodywork:** steel and aluminium four-seater coupé
**Maximum speed (approx):** 125 mph (201 km/h)

*Below: The 125-mph 2600 V8 was elegant enough to compete with rival BMW and Mercedes models but lacked the other companies' glamour and reputation.*

# Gordon-Keeble

In the 1950s John Gordon (managing director) and Jim Keeble (designer) had been involved in the design and manufacture of the Peerless sports coupé, which was renamed the Warwick in its final years. It was their final project work on the Warwick – the installation of a large-capacity Chevrolet V8 engine – which provided the germ of an idea for a new car.

Working together, the two conceived a new and larger coupé, this time a full four-seater, which was provisionally titled the Gordon. As before, this had a glassfibre body shell, but unlike the Peerless/Warwick design, this not only used an American V8 engine, but it also featured graceful styling by Bertone of Italy. In fact it was the first of several British/Italian/USA hybrids of the 1960s, others including the Jensen Interceptors and the Bristol 407-412 family.

It took four years for the prototype to progress to production, even at a limited rate. By this time the company had been renamed Gordon-Keeble, with financial assistance from George Wansborough (earlier involved in the Jowett firm), and a factory was acquired at Eastleigh, near Southampton. From the very outset Gordon-Keeble's problem was that, to generate sales, the car had to be sold too cheaply, making the business unprofitable. When the price was raised, sales dropped away.

The company then went into liquidation after fewer than 100 of these 135-mph machines had been made. Harold Smith (Motors) Ltd, London-based motor traders, then took over, renamed the unchanged car a Gordon-Keeble 1T, and attempted to sell it at an even higher price, but without success.

Finally, in 1967, the assets were bought by a mysterious American called De Bruyne. His company, based at Newmarket in East Anglia, attempted to revive the car under the new 'De Bruyne' name, showed it at the New York Motor Show alongside another ambitious mid-engined project, but neglected to take its ideas any further than this.

Although Jim Keeble set up another business to service and maintain existing Gordon-Keeble cars, this was really the end of the project, but, because the cars had glassfibre bodies and easily-repaired chassis frames, a great proportion of those built are still in existence.

*Above and below: In essence, Gordon-Keeble produced just one model. It was a hybrid design, a British car styled by Bertone with a Chevrolet V8. Despite advantages like its stylish glassfibre bodywork and de Dion rear suspension, customers were not willing to pay an adequate price.*

## Gordon-Keeble GK1 1964-65

The original prototype of what became the Gordon-Keeble GK1 was designed by Jim Keeble in 1960. The basis of the design was a multi-tubular chassis frame, using square-section tubes. Power came from a 4.6-litre/230-bhp Chevrolet V8 engine, and the body shell (styled and built by Bertone of Italy) was built of steel panels. This was one of the very first European cars to use four headlamps – in this case with the paired lamps mounted with an oriental slant.

Other technical features included the use of de Dion rear suspension (the Peerless/Warwick cars had also used this layout), there were four-wheel disc brakes, and the Chevrolet engine was matched to an American Borg-Warner gearbox.

After it had been built, and revealed, the project marked time for a while, principally because there seemed to be no way of getting steel bodies built at an affordable price. Eventually it was decided to have the bodies built of glassfibre, giving more viable unit prices, and on that basis the car was relaunched.

Production cars had a larger and more powerful Chevrolet engine, bigger and more effective disc brakes, and used chassis frames built at Eastleigh, while body shells were produced by Williams & Pritchard in London.

Road-test reports were flattering, for this was a car which looked attractive, was very fast and comfortable, and was to be sold at a very appealing price. At the time, the 135-mph top speed and the general combination of quality and 'image' was almost but not quite a match for that offered by Aston Martin, Bristol and Jensen.

The car sold steadily at its original price of £2,798, but this was not profitable. When the price was raised to a more realistic £3,626 in 1965, sales virtually stopped. This was the point at which Harold Smith (Motors) Ltd took over, when the price rose again to £3,989, later increased to £4,058.

Even after two changes of model name – the last to 'De Bruyne' – the 1967 car was the same as that first sold in 1964. A grand total of 99 Gordon-Keebles of all types was sold.

### Specification (1964)

**Engine:** Chevrolet V8, overhead-valve
**Bore × stroke:** 101.6 mm × 82.55 mm
**Capacity:** 5355 cc
**Maximum power:** 300 bhp
**Transmission:** four-speed manual gearbox or three-speed automatic transmission, rear-wheel drive
**Chassis:** separate steel frame with multi-tubular layout
**Suspension:** independent front with wishbones and coil springs; non-independent rear with de Dion axle and coil springs
**Brakes:** discs front and rear, servo-assisted
**Bodywork:** glassfibre four-seater coupé
**Maximum speed (approx):** 136 mph (219 km/h)

*Below: A big, handsome coupé with a deep wrap-around windscreen overlooking its long bonnet, the GK1 was identifiably a Bertone styling job. Long, and just low enough to look elegant without cramping interior space, it was also a mover, thanks to a 5.4-litre Chevy V8.*

*Above: The GK1 was among the first cars to adopt 'twin' headlamps – unfortunately, their slanted pattern compromised the purity of its lines.*

*Below: Apart from some exposed screw-heads, the GK1's fascia was impressive, with an array of clear instruments and a barrage of toggle switches.*

# Donald Healey Motor Co. Ltd

bove and below: After working for Riley and Triumph before World War II
d then for the Rootes Group on armoured vehicle design during the war,
hen peace came Donald Healey soon set up a facility to produce his own
arque of car. Working from a corner of a works where concrete mixers were
ade, with the help of a friend, Vic Leverett, and ex-Rootes colleagues A. C.
mpietro, Ben Bowden and James Watt, he began producing a number of
dels, using the powerful, reliable, and conveniently available 2.4-litre Riley
gine in a Sampietro-designed chassis. This is a 1947 prototype; the same
adlight treatment was later used on the Healey Silverstone.

low: This photograph, taken in 1948, shows Donald Healey himself with one
the first models he put into production, a Westland. The car had the four-
linder twin-camshaft Riley 2.4 power unit (producing about 100 bhp),
iling-arm front suspension and a live rear axle. Its use of rear coil springs
s unusual in an era when semi-elliptic leaf springs were common.

onald Healey was already a formidable figure in the British motor industry when he founded his own concern in 1946. In the 1920s and 1930s he had become a successful rally driver (he won the Monte Carlo Rally in 1931), while from 1934 to 1939 he directed the technical development of Triumph cars until that company's bankruptcy intervened.

As World War II neared its close, he tried to revive the Triumph name, but eventually set up the Healey company in a corner of premises rented from Benfords of Warwick, a concern which was then producing concrete mixers. For the new generation of cars a chassis was designed by A. C. Sampietro, until Healey secured supplies of engines and transmissions from Riley of Coventry, a company with which he had always maintained happy links.

Healey's small firm was quite incapable of building body shells, so in the next few years the problem was not to sell the cars, but to find coachbuilders to produce the shells for them. In one respect, at least, this has made life easier for historians, as most Healey models were simply named after whichever coachbuilder provided the shells. Commercial life in the British motor industry was difficult for everyone in the 1940s, not least because of the problems of securing steel supplies, and of overcoming high taxation on UK-delivered cars, but the Healey business prospered on its export sales, which attracted priority of supply.

The Riley engines were both powerful and reliable, which meant that Healey cars could exceed 100 mph – a quite exceptional speed for the late 1940s. This, coupled with the undoubted charisma of the company's founder, helped to build the cars' reputation in double-quick time. Healey himself was still an active racing driver, and made sure that his cars competed with honour in famous long-distance races like the Le Mans 24 Hours and Mille Miglia.

The business grew so rapidly that new premises had to be built for the 1950s. After Donald Healey encountered George Mason (the president of the US car-builders Nash Kelvinator), the result was the birth of the Nash-Healey, and further commercial expansion.

By the early 1950s, in fact, supplies of Riley running gear were running down, so the use of Nash and (to a limited degree) Alvis running gear was a timely substitute. In 1952, however, Healey began the development of a new, simpler and cheaper-to-build car which used an Austin engine, transmission and front suspension components. A single prototype, titled the Healey 100, was prepared for display at the London Motor Show of October 1952, where the design was snapped up by Len Lord (the chairman of BMC, the corporation that included the Austin brand).

The result was the birth of the Austin-Healey marque, for which the production cars were always assembled by BMC. As a consequence, the last Healey car was built in 1954.

## Healey Westland, Elliot, Duncan and Sportsmobile 1946-50

The first-generation Healeys were designed in 1945 and 1946, around a rugged 'top-hat'-section chassis frame which used a complex trailing-arm type of independent front suspension. Using his contacts in the motor industry in Coventry, Donald Healey also obtained supplies of 2½-litre engines, gearboxes and rear axles from Riley.

Although Riley had been taken over by Lord Nuffield's Nuffield Organisation in 1938, its engineering was still unique. The engines, in particular, were advanced (though heavy) four-cylinder units with twin camshafts mounted high in the cylinder blocks, and with part-spherical combustion chambers. The chassis itself was designed within the limits of the simple tooling available at the Westland company in Hereford, but was so solid and so durable that its basic design was not altered in the next eight years.

Donald Healey was a gifted stylist who knew what he wanted, but could not draw it himself. His associate Ben Bowden therefore schemed the smart and curvaceous lines of the next two cars,

and the chassis came to be clothed with open tourer bodies by Westland and two-door saloons by Elliot of Reading.

Following the launch of the Silverstone Healey also produced the Duncan and Sportsmobile models, to give even greater variety to the production lines of this small factory. The Duncans were built by a Norfolk-based business and featured a low-nosed two-door style. The saloons were of pillarless construction, and there was a stark two-seater Duncan sports car as an alternative to the Silverstone. Finally there was the Sportsmobile, one of the less attractive Healey styles, which sold only slowly. This car could carry four passengers and possessed a large boot, but it had rather severely upright nose styling.

Production totals ran to 64 Westlands, 101 Elliots, 23 Sportsmobiles and 39 Duncans. These types were superseded by the Tickford and Abbott models in 1950.

*Above: Healeys were soon racing for a living: this is an Elliot in the International Trophy race at Silverstone in 1953.*

### Specification (1946 Elliot)

**Engine:** inline four-cylinder, overhead valve
**Bore × stroke:** 80.5 mm × 120 mm
**Capacity:** 2443 cc
**Maximum power:** 104 bhp
**Transmission:** four-speed manual gearbox, rear-wheel drive
**Chassis:** separate steel frame with box section main and bracing members
**Suspension:** independent front with coil springs; beam rear axle with coil springs
**Brakes:** drums front and rear
**Bodywork:** aluminium on wood framing, two- or four-seater
**Maximum speed (approx):** 102 mph (164 km/h)

*Above: Healey began producing various models with virtually the same chassis but differing bodies; this is a 1952 Duncan.*

*Below: One of the least popular variants of the 1946-50 Healey range was the open four-seater Sportsmobile 'Dropflow Coupé'.*

# Healey Silverstone 1949-50

After launching the first production cars – Westland, Elliot and Sportsmobile – Healey turned to constructing a lightweight, out-and-out sports car using the same basic chassis design. The result was the launch of the Silverstone two-seater, a car which was not only competitive in motorsport at the time, but which has become highly desirable as a collector's car in more recent years. The car took its name from Britain's newly-developed motor racing circuit.

Mechanically the Silverstone had the same chassis and powertrain as the other Healeys, though the engine/gearbox assembly was moved back in the frame by eight inches, there was a front anti-roll bar, and the rear suspension was firmed up with stiffer springs.

The aluminium bodywork was made as light and compact as possible, by fitting a 'cigar-style' shell and cycle-type front wings (which could be removed for racing, where the regulations allowed this). The windscreen could be retracted, the headlamps were hidden away *behind* the radiator grille bars, and the spare wheel was housed in a 'letter-box' opening in the tail, where it also acted as a convenient – and effective – rear bumper.

Equipped in this way, the Silverstone was around 200 kg (450 lb) lighter than earlier Healey models, which meant that it was an agile and successful competition car, for the ruggedness of the chassis was not impaired. The Silverstone was only in production for a short time, during which 105 cars were produced.

*Right: The Silverstone – built on substantially the same chassis as previous Healeys – was an uncompromising sports two-seater, lightweight and with its engine moved back for better balance. Its spare tyre served as a rear bumper.*

## Specification (1949)

**Engine:** inline four-cylinder, overhead-valve
**Bore × stroke:** 80.5 mm × 120 mm
**Capacity:** 2443 cc
**Maximum power:** 104 bhp
**Transmission:** four-speed manual gearbox, rear-wheel drive
**Chassis:** separate steel frame with box-section side and bracing members
**Suspension:** independent front with coil springs; beam rear axle with coil springs
**Brakes:** drums front and rear
**Bodywork:** aluminium open two-seater
**Maximum speed (approx):** 100 mph (161 km/h)

*Below: The Silverstone was made as light as possible, with removable cycle-type wings, concealed headlamps, a retractable windscreen and a minimal, track-style body. It made a fine competition car. Only 105 were built and now the model is a very desirable collectors' item.*

## Healey Tickford and Abbott 1950-54

*Right: When the 'second-generation' Healeys arrived, again models took their names from the outside coachworks that built their bodies. This is a 1951 Tickford. Its lines were an improvement on the earlier saloon models, but were still a little clumsy.*

What were really the 'second-generation' Healey touring cars – the Tickford and Abbott types – took over from the Westland/Elliot range in 1950. The new models were more modern and better-equipped but, on average, they were also 300-350 lb heavier than the cars they replaced.

The Tickford was a smart two-door four-seater sports saloon, the body shell of which was built by Tickford at Newport Pagnell, while the Abbott was its drop-head coupé sibling, built by Abbott of Farnham. Compared with the originals, the style had been made less bulbous, slightly more crisp in detail, and with more equipment and plusher furnishings.

Technically the new cars were the same as the old at first, but from late 1951 a new type of transmission was standardised, with a hypoid rear axle and open propeller shaft replacing the old torque-tube design. These were among the most successful of the Riley-engined Healeys, for 241 Tickfords and 77 Abbotts were produced between 1950 and 1954.

### Specification (1951 Abbott)

**Engine:** inline four-cylinder, overhead-valve
**Bore × stroke:** 80.5 mm × 120 mm
**Capacity:** 2443 cc
**Maximum power:** 104 bhp
**Transmission:** four-speed manual gearbox, rear-wheel drive
**Chassis:** separate steel frame with box-section main and bracing members
**Suspension:** independent front with coil springs; beam rear axle with coil springs
**Brakes:** drums front and rear
**Bodywork:** wood-framed drop-head coupé panelled in aluminium
**Maximum speed (approx):** 104 mph (167 km/h)

*Right: A firm called Abbott of Farnham provided the coachwork for the new drop-head model, so it became the Healey Abbott. From 1951 onwards, as with this example, a new, hypoid-type rear axle was installed with an open propshaft instead of a torque tube.*

*Below: Logically enough, the Tickford – a two-door sports saloon – was bodied by Tickford in Newport Pagnell. Like the Abbott, it still used the lusty Riley 2.4-litre power unit.*

# Nash-Healey 1950-54

Having met Nash Kelvinator president George Mason on board the *Queen Elizabeth* in 1949, Donald Healey was quick to set up a co-production deal with him, for cars to be sold exclusively in the USA. The result, made public less than a year later, was the Nash-Healey, which combined the existing Healey chassis with Nash mechanical components, all clothed in a smart new 'full-width' sports-tourer shell.

The new car was successfully tested, in prototype form, by finishing fourth overall in the Le Mans 24 Hours race of 1950. The production car was displayed on the Healey stand at the London Motor Show in October 1950.

The basic Healey chassis and trailing-arm front suspension were retained, but this time there was a six-cylinder Nash engine, as fitted to that company's big saloon cars, modified to produce 125 bhp at first, and supplied complete with a three-speed gearbox and overdrive installation. The body, initially produced by Panelcraft of Birmingham, was a smart three-seater roadster (there was a bench front seat) with grille, bumpers, headlamps and other embellishments produced by Nash and shipped over from the USA for assembly. All production was earmarked for the US market, and there were no official sales in the UK.

The Nash-Healey weighed about 2,400 lb – which made it heavier than the Silverstone but considerably lighter than the new Tickford and Abbott touring models. With a top speed of 110 mph, and the ability to reach 60 mph in 9.5 seconds, its performance approached

that of the Jaguar XK120.

From 1952 the car was modified, this time to have a Farina body shell of similar design to the original. Healey now supplied longer-wheelbase (108 inches instead of 102) rolling chassis to Italy and Farina completed the cars, which were then shipped over to the USA for sale. At approximately the same juncture the Nash engine was enlarged to 4138 cc, to give 135 bhp.

Total production of all Nash-Healeys was 506 cars. This, however, was not the end for the original UK-built Nash-Healey shell, which was used in slightly modified form for the Alvis-engined Healey Sports Convertible which made its bow at the end of 1953, and (unlike the Nash-engined type) *was* available for sale in the UK. It featured a Panelcraft body but a different grille, and was fitted with a 84-mm × 90-mm six-cylinder Alvis engine of 2993 cc and 106 bhp. The top speed was 100 mph (161 km/h). Just 25 of these cars were produced.

*Above: The Nash-Healey was developed in less than a year after Healey agreed to build it, using the existing Healey chassis with Nash mechanicals.*

## Specification (1950)

**Engine:** inline six-cylinder, overhead-valve

**Bore × stroke:** 85.7 mm × 111.1 mm

**Capacity:** 3848 cc

**Maximum power:** 125 bhp

**Transmission:** three-speed manual gearbox with overdrive, rear-wheel drive

**Chassis:** separate steel frame with box-section side and bracing members

**Suspension:** independent front with coil springs; beam rear axle with coil springs

**Brakes:** drums front and rear

**Bodywork:** aluminium three-seater, optional hard top

**Maximum speed (approx):** 110 mph (177 km/h)

*Above: Early Nash-Healeys had Panelcraft bodies but later ones, like this 1953 example, were sent as rolling chassis to Pinin Farina for finishing.*

*Below: Initially the model was propelled by a 3848-cc, 125-bhp Nash straight-six but this was upgraded to 4138 cc, with more torque and 10 extra horsepower.*

# Hispano-Suiza

F or linguists the very name of this company should spell out some of its complexities, for it indicates Spanish and Swiss components. There was, however, a further complication, for before long a major part of Hispano-Suiza's operations was also located in France!

The link with all these countries was Marc Birkigt, a Swiss-born engineer who had already designed the very first Spanish-built car (the La Cuadra) before founding SA Hispano-Suiza in Barcelona in 1904. This business prospered so well that a French concern was set up in 1911 to build the Spanish-designed cars under licence.

Then matters became complicated, for Hispano-Suiza also went on to produce excellent aircraft engines during and after World War I, and before long both the Spanish and French companies were renowned as high-quality producers of many other types of engineering products.

In Spain, a country which was considerably less prosperous than France at the time, Hispano-Suiza produced cars of its own design before World War I, but moved on to making French-designed Hispanos from 1919. Less mechanically-complex derivatives of those cars followed in the 1930s. Hispano-Suiza of Barcelona survived the Spanish Civil War in the 1930s, and carried on making cars until 1944 – having built around 6,000 cars of all types.

The French side of the business was always more glamorous to car enthusiasts, because of the models it produced. The first post-World War I design was the legendary H6B, a car equally as well-engineered as the contemporary Rolls-Royces, which enjoyed a similarly high reputation for many years.

After this the Hispano-Suiza marque, probably unfairly, became known as a French, rather than a Spanish, carmaker, this reputation being underpinned in the 1930s when the fabulous Type 68 V12 range appeared. There was little question that these *were* the world's finest cars of the period – Rolls-Royce, Bentley or Cadillac notwithstanding –

*Above: Although the nationality of the firm might have been tricky to pin down, there was never any doubt about the engineering quality, or the prestige, of the illustrious Hispano-Suiza marque.*

but relatively so few were made that few modern enthusiasts have ever been able to sample their charms.

In 1938 the Bois-Colombes factory of Hispano-Suiza France stopped building cars, to concentrate once again on making aircraft engines for the fast-growing military fleets of Europe, and the marque was never revived. In France about 2,600 cars had been produced.

In the 1930s, incidentally, Hispano-Suiza took over Ballot, the French carmaker, but closed that company's production lines soon afterwards.

## Hispano-Suiza Alfonso XIII 1911-14

Like many other fledgling car companies, Hispano-Suiza used motorsport to generate favourable publicity, and was certainly encouraged by the Spanish monarch, King Alfonso XIII, when he put up a trophy for a *voiturette* race at Sitges in 1909.

In that event a team of Hispanos looked to be possible winners, but all were forced to retire with mechanical problems. The team fared better in the Coupe de l'Auto races at Boulogne, and in 1910 revised machines not only finished third at Sitges, but won outright at Boulogne.

Soon after this, Birkigt decided to build near-replicas for sale to customers, retaining the same basic chassis and mechanical layout, but fitting an enlarged engine, of 3.6 litres instead of 2.6 litres. He named his new sports car in honour of the Spanish king and motoring enthusiast, Alfonso XIII.

The result was one of the world's very first production sports cars, a compact two-seater. Although it was neither small nor delicately engineered, it was seen as a very advanced machine for its day, and had a top speed of around 80 mph, which was very exciting indeed for this period. Later, less 'sporting' but equally successful derivatives were added.

It was renowned for its ease of control, and had a very torquey long-stroke

*Right: Inspiration for sporting Hispanos came from the Spanish monarch, so this car was named after him, Alfonso XIII.*

engine which made it an easy car to drive on winding roads. Its wheelbase was short – 104 inches for two-seaters, 106 inches for four-seaters or those with closed coachwork – and it was relatively light, which made a change from other battleship-heavy and huge-engined sports cars of the period.

*Left: A torquey 3.6-litre four-cylinder engine made the Alfonso XIII fast and controllable.*

## Specification (1911)

**Engine:** inline four-cylinder, side-valve
**Bore × stroke:** 80 mm × 180 mm
**Capacity:** 3620 cc
**Maximum power:** 64 bhp
**Transmission:** three-speed or four-speed manual gearbox, rear-wheel drive
**Chassis:** separate steel frame with channel-section side members
**Suspension:** non-independent with beam front axle; live rear axle with semi-elliptic leaf springs
**Brakes:** drums on transmission and rear wheels
**Bodywork:** wood-framed aluminium two- or four-seater
**Maximum speed (approx):** 80 mph (129 km/h)

# Hispano-Suiza H6B 1919-38

he first French-designed Hispano-uiza, the H6B, was launched at the Paris alon in 1919, and immediately set new tandards in automotive design. Not only n its engine, but in its chassis, the H6B as one full step ahead of anything that ad previously been seen.

The chassis was conventional enough, xcept that there was a new type of echanically-actuated brake servo vhich, driven off the gearbox, was so fficient that Rolls-Royce eventually took ut a licence and used such a device for e next 40 years.

To anyone who was already familiar vith Hispano-Suiza's aero engines there vas nothing startling about the engine, ut for motor cars any unit which com-ined aluminium cylinders, removable teel liners, overhead-camshaft valve ear and a fixed cylinder head was in-eed a novelty.

Here was an 85-mph car built with reat flair – and care – so that it set tandards which marques like Rolls-oyce and Cadillac had to struggle to iatch. The H6B was not a particularly uiet or refined car, but it did everything sked of it with such assurance that it was ewed as the best of its day.

Not surprisingly, Birkigt then pursued 'one-chassis' policy for many years. The milar H6C ('Boulogne') model followed 1924, and derivatives known as the ype 56bis were produced at Hispano-uiza's Spanish factory in the 1930s. It was ot until the new V12 Hispano-Suiza ppeared that the H6B drew back into e shadows, though sales continued, owly, throughout the 1930s.

Total H6B production was about 2,200 ehicles, while 264 H6Cs were also pro-uced. Curiously, to modern eyes, the 6B was built under licence by the Cze-hoslovakian firm Skoda from 1924 to 27.

## Hispano-Suiza H6B variants

### Hispano-Suiza H6C Boulogne
The H6C Boulogne was a sporty version of the H6B, which evolved from cars that won the Coupe Boillot races at Boulogne in 1921, 1922 and 1923. Such machines had engines enlarged to 110 mm × 140 mm/7983 cc.

### Hispano-Suiza Type 56bis
The Type 56bis was another version of this design, built by Hispano-Suiza in Spain at their Barcelona plant.

## Specification (1919)

**Engine:** inline six-cylinder, overhead-cam
**Bore × stroke:** 100 mm × 140 mm
**Capacity:** 6597 cc
**Maximum power:** 135 bhp
**Transmission:** three-speed manual gearbox, rear-wheel drive
**Chassis:** separate steel frame with channel-section side members
**Suspension:** non-independent with beam front axle; live rear axle with semi-elliptic leaf springs
**Brakes:** drums front and rear; later models had the industry's first brake servo
**Bodywork:** aluminium and steel, on wooden frames; styles by various coachbuilders
**Maximum speed (approx):** 85 mph (137 km/h)

*Below: Resplendent in extraordinary tulip-wood coachwork, this is a 1924 H6C, with the eight-litre engine. The car was once raced by the wealthy Andre Dubonnet.*

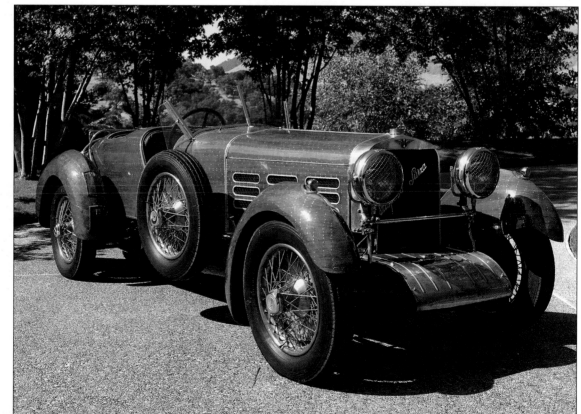

## Hispano-Suiza Type 68 V12 1931-38

*Right: A superb high-speed tourer, the 9.4-litre Type 68 V12 was a magnificent car, hand-built for the very rich only.*

Marc Birkigt planned to replace the successful H6B model with an even more astonishing machine, the Type 68, for which he designed a magnificent 9.4-litre V12 engine. He was only partly successful, for the old H6B model refused to die, and was built alongside the new V12 to the end.

As before (with the H6B), the company drew on its own aero engine in designing the V12, though the overhead-cam valve gear was dropped in favour of conventional (and much quieter) overhead-valve operation. The new Type 68 V12 was really an update of a similar aero engine which Birkigt had designed during World War I.

The V12 car, when announced in 1931 (when the European Depression had sunk to new depths), was a magnificently built – and magnificently priced – machine, hand-built for the very rich. The longest of the available wheelbase choices was a magisterial 158 inches – longer than, say, a complete Ford Escort of the 1980s.

Except for the Type 41 Bugatti Royale, it was by far the most expensive French production car, and was probably the fastest saloon/limousine being built anywhere in the world. It could certainly match the new-fangled Cadillac V16 in every respect, even though it made do with only a three- rather than a four-speed manual transmission.

As you might expect, the Type 68 only sold in small quantities, even after the company produced a version with an enlarged 11.3-litre 250-bhp engine (which was also used for French rail cars of the period), but throughout the 1930s these models set standards which were probably unmatched across the automotive spectrum. Between 1931 and 1938 a mere 76 V12s were produced, which explains why Hispano-Suiza was happy to drop the model when demand for its aero engines perked up again as the pre-World War II arms race accelerated and the French air force expanded.

### Specification (1931)

**Engine:** V12, overhead-valve
**Bore × stroke:** 100 mm × 100 mm
**Capacity:** 9424 cc
**Maximum power:** 190 bhp or 250 bhp
**Transmission:** three-speed manual gearbox, rear-wheel drive
**Chassis:** separate steel frame with channel-section side members
**Suspension:** non-independent with beam front axle; live rear axle with semi-elliptic leaf springs
**Brakes:** drums on front and rear, servo-assisted
**Bodywork:** steel or aluminium on wooden framing; two-, four- or six-seater styles from various coachbuilders
**Maximum speed (approx):** 100 mph (161 km/h)

*Below: As the V12 was announced in mid-Depression, it was no surprise that it sold in small numbers. Most of the engines were of 9424-cc capacity but there was even a version displacing 11.3 litres, with a power output of around 250 bhp rather than the 190 bhp of the smaller engine. This is a Type 68B convertible.*

# Holden

olden was originally a specialist coach-building company, starting in 1885 as Holden and Frost of Adelaide. Its first car was based on a 1914 Lancia chassis, and by 1920 it had evolved into Holden's Motor Body Builders Ltd, while the original firm did the leather trimming. Meanwhile, General Motors' Australian operation had itself grown out of Motor Exports Co, founded in 1918, and in 1926, GM took over Holden for £1.1m. The bulk of Holden's work was building bodies for General Motors' Chevrolet and Buick brands, as well as a small number of Hudson, Essex, Chrysler, De Soto, Plymouth, Willys, Graham, Reo and Studebaker. One of the most distinctive designs was the Sloper, a two-door fast back coupé built on US Buick, Chevrolet, Oldsmobile, Pontiac and European Clyno, Fiat, Morris, Singer and Vauxhall chassis between 1935 and 1941, which was ahead of the game stylistically. But these cars were indigenous to Australia, and rarely seen in Europe or the USA. They weren't restricted to cars either, as a new plant came on stream in 1936 at Melbourne to make Bedford, Chevrolet and General Motors truck bodies. Holden made a whole raft of commercial and civilian vehicle bodies during World War II, ranging from Chevrolet staff cars and ambulances to fuel bowsers and gun tractors.

Post-war production resumed on Chevrolet and Vauxhall car chassis, but Holden's managing director, Sir Lawrence Hartnett, was committed to the concept of an all-Australian car that was midway between the dimensions of US and British vehicles. The plan was backed by General Motors in Detroit as well as Australian banks and government. The first prototype appeared in 1946 and the first production Holden car rolled off the line in November 1948. This was the 48/215, a four-door unit-construction saloon powered by a 2.2-litre six-cylinder overhead-valve engine. The last bodies to be built on American chassis were made in 1948 and on Vauxhalls as late as 1952, although Bedford truck chassis were fitted out up to the late-1950s.

The utility version of the 48/215 joined the range in January 1951 and, by 1953, 100,000 units had been sold by May 1953.

In 1956 the FE model came out, a full-width six-seater saloon running the same engine and transmission until 1960 when engine capacity went up to 2.3 litres, 75 bhp with the FB series. Holden outsold all other makes in Australia in 1950, and was never topped until 1982, when it was ousted by Ford. Volumes from the main Fisherman's Bend plant were up to a million units by October 1962, and the two millionth Holden was built in March 1969. Bodies were made at the original Woodville factory and there were also assembly plants at Pagewood in New South Wales, The Valley in

Brisbane, Mosman Park in Perth, and Birkenhead in South Australia. A new body plant came on stream at Elizabeth, South Australia, in 1963, and another factory, at Acacia Ridge, Queensland was opened in 1964.

In 1967 the model range was extended to include the small Torana HB, which was a restyled Vauxhall Viva, and the 5.0-litre Chevrolet V8 HK model at the top end of the range appeared the following year. Holden began making its own 4.1- and 5.0-litre V8s in 1969. The Monaro coupé was available with an all-Australian V8 and 5.3-litre Chevrolet 327 unit, and eventually with the 7.4 litres Chevrolet 454, which bested Ford's 289 Falcon in touring car racing. During the Monaro's production life, from 1968–1976, some 41,000 units were made. The Torana LH series was in production from 1974 to 1979, and was available with four-, six- or eight-cylinder engines, ranging from a 1.9-litre Opel four to a 5.0-litre V8. The Gemini that superseded the Torana was essentially an Isuzu version of the Vauxhall Chevette. Another non-Australian Holden was the Commodore, introduced for 1979, powered by four-, six- or eight-cylinder engines from 1.9 to 4.1 litres, and it became Australia's top-selling car until overtaken by the Ford Falcon.

Such was the global influence of General Motors' empire that panels from the Camira estate car were exported to the UK in the 1970s and 1980s for the Vauxhall Cavalier estate. Holden engines powered certain Vauxhalls, including Cavaliers and Swedish market Opels, since Swedish and Australian emission regulations were similar.

There were a number of joint ventures with Japanese manufacturers including Nissan and Isuzu. Top of the range in the late 1980s was the Commodore with 3.0-litre ohc Nissan or 5.0-litre GM V8 engines.

A decade on, and Holden Special Vehicles had been set up and had engaged Tom Walkinshaw's Oxfordshire, UK-based TWR to produce Supertouring machines, including the HSV 5.0-litre Manta, 5.7-litre GTS and 5.7-litre Grange. Top of the range Holdens were the 5.0-litre Statesman and Caprice in the Commodore range.

*Above: As you might expect, the Holden General of 1961 shows strong similarities to contemporary four-door Vauxhall and Opel models. These were the days when for three decades Holden outsold all other makes in Australia.*

*Right: Utility vehicles – or Utes – are popular in Australia and Holden's contribution to the genre was this big-engined be-winged VS Maloo pick-up from 1998 (above). It was a product from its Special Vehicles division, like the VT Commodore GTS (below). This model was fitted with aerodynamic paraphenalia so that it didn't take off when reaching its 150 mpg (243 km/h) top speed.*

# Holden VR HSV GTS 215i 1994-present

A fine example of a Holden Special Vehicles' product was the 1994 VR Commodore GTS 215I, capable of doing 0–62 mph (0–100 km/h) in 6.6 seconds, making it one of the quickest accelerating production cars ever made in Australia. With a 150 mph (243 km/h) top speed, it was the fastest Australian production car – ever. The GTS 215i was powered by a new fuel injected 5.7-litre Holden 'stroker' V8 engine, coupled to a Borg Warner T56 six-speed

transmission with Hydratrak limited slip differential. Peak torque was 475 Nm at 3,600 rpm, and power output was 215 bhp at 4,800 rpm, with the redline at 5,500 rpm and limiter just beyond that. A nose-heavy weight bias implied that the Commodore GTS 215i was an understeering car, but its engine was so responsive that it could be controlled on the throttle. The clutch was a hybrid cable and hydraulic system, while brakes were curved vane ventilated

discs with two-piston callipers at the front and single piston callipers at the rear, with ABS as standard. It was shod with 235/45ZR 17 Bridgestone Expedia S-01 tyres.

## Specification

**Engine:** V8, 16-valve, rear drive
**Bore x stroke:** 102.0 mm x 88.0 mm
**Capacity:** 5710 cc
**Compression ratio:** 8.5:1
**Chassis:** monocoque, four-door

**Suspension:** front, independent by struts, coil springs, dampers, anti-roll bar; rear, independent by semi-trailing arms, coil springs, dampers, anti roll bar

*Below: The VR HSV GTS 215I was certainly hot property in 1994. The Commodore super-tourer was the quickest production car in Australia, powered – naturally – by a fuel-injected 5.7-litre V8 motor allied to a Borg Warner six-speed gearbox.*

# Holden Commodore VN Group A 1991-present

The VN Commodore was the ultimate development of the VN series for homologation to Group A racing spec. Just 302 of the projected 500 units were made, and the last one rolled out of Holden Special Vehicles on 8th March 1991. Most of the development work was done by the factory, and individual race teams applied whatever customising they required. The body's aerodynamic package was developed at the MIRA wind tunnel in the UK, and it had the doubtful honour of being the most expensive Holden to date. Among the extensive modifications to the body-work – which was not as outrageous as the VL Batmobile – were rear wheel arches widened to accommodate racing tyres. Drag co-efficient was said to have been less than 0.30 Cd, compared with the 0.34 Cd of the standard VN. Like most Holden high-performance models, the VN Group A started life as a Berlina because there were fewer luxury items to replace when the special sports interior with its Group A steering wheel were fitted at the HSV workshops.

The VN Commodore differed from its mass-produced siblings in a number of other ways, most of which had to do with its competition persona. At that point, no other Australian production car had run

with a 17 inch wheel and 45 profile tyre combination, and its totally redeveloped 215 bhp Group A-spec V8 engine was coupled to a six-speed ZR1 Corvette gearbox, developed by ZF in Germany, using a Chevrolet bell-housing and high torque AP racing clutch. The engine shared the VL Group A SV's twin throttle bodies, rather than the other HSV high-performance V8s that used the regular fuel injection system. Virtually every component was modified in some way, and included large diameter push rods and valve lifters, heavy duty valve springs, special cast aluminium rocker covers and Group A plenum chamber, revised camshaft with steel sprockets and heavy duty double row timing chain, special rubber camshaft drive chain damper, racing pistons, crankshaft and con-rods, a lighter 7 kg flywheel, and heavy duty main and big end bearings. A high pressure electric fuel pump with large capacity fuel tank and stone shield completed the drivetrain picture, and it was capable of doing 0-62 mph (0–100 km/h) in 6.2 seconds, with a top speed of 155 mph (250 km/h).

The Commodore's archaic live axle rear suspension was beefed up with higher rate coil springs, which were also fitted on the front end, plus spe-

cially tuned anti-roll bars and Bilstein dampers all round. It was retarded by heavy duty ventilated discs all round with the twin piston front callipers of the SV5000.

They were normally painted deep red – known as Durif Red – but a couple of special metallic black versions were of-

fered as prizes for the Toohey's 1000 Bathurst promotion in 1991. Another two were finished in Alpine white. The first few units were built with air-conditioning and not climate control. Racing driver Win Percy drove chassis number 016 as his personal road car, registration WIN 1

*Below: In 1998, the most recent evolution of Holden's HRT racing cars was the Mobil-sponsored VT Commodore V8, driven in the Australian Supercar series by Craig Lowndes and Greg Murphy.*

# Honda Motor Company Ltd

The world's largest and most successful motorcyle manufacturer also decided to start making cars in the 1960s, and by the early 1990s had grown to become Japan's third-largest car company, with annual sales approaching 1.5 million a year.

In terms of technical interest, in the first 30 years of the marque, the two most important cars were both two-seaters – the S800 and the NSX.

Honda started in a small way by producing a series of small front-engined sports cars (which culminated in the S800 series of the late 1960s), then began to develop more and more transverse-engined, front-wheel-drive family cars, gradually spreading up from the small, to the small/medium, then to the medium-sized categories.

Throughout the 1970s and into the 1980s, model after model succeeded earlier versions at great speed – ranges of Civics being accompanied by ranges of Accords, then by ranges of Prelude coupés too. At the same time the various market niches were ruthlessly filled, which led to the birth of saloons like the Ballade, hatchbacks like the Quintet, and eventually to complete series of different cars – hatchbacks, saloons, coupés and estates – all based on the same versatile platforms.

Technical (and eventually financial) links were forged with Rover in the 1980s, these leading to the birth of the joint Honda Legend/Rover 800 project, to the first Honda V6 engines and, in the USA, to the launching of the new Acura brand. As with other large Japanese concerns, only time seemed to limit the number of new cars which could be put on sale, as the company continued to expand steadily throughout the decade.

By 1990 Honda had not only opened up a manufacturing plant at Swindon in the UK, but it also unveiled its first supercar, the mid-engined NSX, which set out to match the Ferrari 328/348 models, and succeeded most competently. Honda was so profitable, so technically confident, and still possessed such an inbuilt attitude of motoring enthusiasm at top management level, that it was able to introduce the Beat sports car by using outwardly humble 'city-car' components.

Like Toyota and Nissan, however, Honda's main thrust was in the making of carefully-developed and manufactured family cars.

*Above: From the company's first steps with four-wheelers in the early 1960s, Honda produced models with a sporty slant as well as more mundane everyday transport. In contrast to some Japanese firms, which were at first content to copy European designs, behind the 'H' symbol there was always an emphasis on technical innovation.*

*Below: Undoubtedly the first true Japanese supercar, the NSX must be the pinnacle of Honda's achievement in roadgoing cars so far.*

## Honda S800 1966-70

The S800 was the fourth and the most successful derivative of the original small two-seater sports car which Honda had previewed in 1962.

The very first Honda car, appearing in 1962, was the ancestor of the S800, having a tiny 360-cc engine. This was soon followed, in 1963, by a 500-cc version. These were both sighting shots for the S600 which appeared in 1964, with an engine of 54.5 mm × 65 mm and 606 cc giving 55 bhp. This car looked similar to the later S800. Because the company was already well-versed in building complex and high-revving motorcycles, Honda was happy to produce the S800 with a phenomenally high-revving four-cylinder engine.

Honda's first sports car was a fascinating design in many ways. The even smaller-engined cars on which the S800 was based used double-chain drive to the rear axle, the chain cases acting as locating trailing arms for the axle. By the time of the S800, that system had been replaced by a more conventional live axle. There was still nothing conventional about the engine, however, as that featured some superb (and expensive) engineering. Like the pre-war Bugattis it used roller, rather than plain, bearings and was a chain-driven double-overhead-cam design. Unlike the old Bugattis, however, Honda's miniature engine, which featured a carburettor for each cylinder, could rev as high as 9,000 rpm without the least complaint. Not surprisingly, the considerable output from such a small engine could only be achieved if the revs were kept up.

Structurally the S800 was simple

*Right and below: The dinky little S800 was styled in much the same vein as its European rivals, particularly the British Sprite/Midget and Triumph Spitfire. Its engine was far more sophisticated, however.*

enough; its separate box-section chassis frame was topped by a two-seater body shell with rather less than adequate space in the cabin, for at this stage Japanese designers were not paying much attention to the greater bulk of typical Europeans and Americans.

The car was competitive with, but did not exceed the performance of, equivalent-sized (but larger-engined) British cars such as the Triumph Spitfire and the Sprite/Midget models, and let itself down badly with a very hard ride, a rapidly-earned reputation for unreliability and a tendency for the body to rust away if neglected.

In addition to the open two-seat sports car, there was a closed coupé version which sold just as well as the convertible but lacked something of the open car's appeal.

It was important to realise, however, that this was only a first-generation car, that the Japanese were rapid learners, and that future products would be more competitive – as the world now certainly knows.

*Above: The tiny twin-cam four produced 70 bhp from just 791 cc.*

### Specification (1966)

**Engine:** inline four-cylinder, twin overhead camshafts
**Bore × stroke:** 60 mm × 70 mm
**Capacity:** 791 cc
**Maximum power:** 70 bhp
**Transmission:** four-speed manual gearbox, rear-wheel drive
**Chassis:** separate steel frame with box-section main side and bracing members

**Suspension:** independent front with wishbones and torsion bars; live rear axle with trailing arms and coil springs
**Brakes:** discs front, drums rear
**Bodywork:** steel two-seater convertible or coupé
**Maximum speed (approx):** 94 mph (151 km/h)

# Honda CRX 1987–92

Honda's original front-drive Civic hatchback appeared in the early 1970s, but by the mid-1980s the latest-generation Civic was being made in a bewildering variety of shapes. One, introduced in 1984, was the stubby fastback 2 + 2-seater sporty type called the CRX. From 1987 the second-generation CRX went on sale – faster, sleeker and technically more complex than ever before.

This car, in many ways, pointed the way to the cars MG and Triumph *should* have been building by that time if those marques had not been killed off by the parent company. The underpan/platform, suspension and steering were all developed from those of the Civic 'base car', while the 16-valve twin-cam engine was a high-revving high-tech version of Honda's modern four-cylinder unit; thus 130 mph was available from a car only fitted with a 1.6-litre engine.

The style was a neat, smoothly-detailed and adequately roomy 2+2-seater coupé/hatchback, with a spacious driving compartment and small rear seats.

Like many such Japanese cars the CRX had an advanced, high-revving, engine (8,000 rpm could habitually be used in the intermediate gears), but there was also a version of the unit known by the acronym 'VTEC'; those initials indicated that it had a variable valve timing and lift electronic control system, to optimise power output throughout the rpm range.

The VTEC system was far better at maximising power rather than torque as the torque output was, at 106 lb ft, more in line with engine displacement. But as the engine revved so cleanly, the VTEC approach was fully justified and pro-

duced sparkling acceleration figures; the 0-60 mph time, for example, was only eight seconds.

In many ways this was an uncompromising machine, for it lacked power-assisted steering, and had hard suspension, but it served to demonstrate the effective way in which the Japanese could tailor the specification of their mechanical 'building blocks' so carefully to a particular model's requirements. The end result was a true sports car with sparkling performance and such excellent well-balanced handling that its front-wheel drive was hard to detect. The late 1990s saw the Integra-R coupé powered by the 1.8-litre, 9,000 rpm V.TEC engine.

*Above: Honda cleverly occupied diverse market niches by fitting various engine/body combinations to the Civic platform; most notable was the CRX coupé, especially post-1987.*

## Specification (1990 VTEC)

**Engine:** inline four-cylinder, twin overhead camshafts
**Bore × stroke:** 81 mm × 77 mm
**Capacity:** 1595 cc
**Maximum power:** 150 bhp
**Transmission:** five-speed manual gearbox, rear-wheel drive
**Chassis:** steel unit-construction body/chassis assembly

**Suspension:** independent front with coil springs; independent rear with longitudinal and transverse control arms and coil springs
**Brakes:** discs front and rear
**Bodywork:** steel 2 + 2-seater hatchback
**Maximum speed (approx):** 130 mph (209 km/h)

*Below: Compared with many hot hatchback rivals, the CRX was uncompromisingly sporty in character, with quite stiff suspension, but it performed and handled superbly. CRX Challenge entries needed little work to make them race-worthy.*

## Honda NSX 1990-present

By the late 1980s Honda had not only graduated to building large-engined cars, but had established a fine reputation for itself in the USA. The decision to create a mid-engined supercar was merely one of a series of moves which confirmed Honda's status in the world.

The new NSX was previewed in 1989, but went on sale during 1990. Although carrying unmistakable rounded, long-tailed styling of its own, the NSX was clearly in the school of mid-engined Ferraris, for although it was slightly longer (but lighter) than the 348 tb it was about the same width, with a similar package, and a very similar performance.

Cynics who suggested that the NSX did not have the 'soul' or the 'charisma' of

*Right: Honda had one objective with the NSX: to build a better supercar than the Europeans.*

a Ferrari were only correct if this could be translated as meaning a lack of silly failings, a lack of temperament, and the possession of an irritating competence in everything from performance to equipment to quality.

To build this car, Honda prepared a completely new production facility in Japan, took six years to develop the car (which is a very leisurely schedule by Japanese standards) and arranged to power it with a 274-bhp 3.0-litre quad-cam engine which was only distantly related to other Honda V6s used in the Legend and Rover 800 models.

Not only was the NSX a very fast car, with a top speed of around 160 mph, but it also had excellent roadholding, a sumptuously-equipped two-seater cabin, along with features like ABS brakes, an automatic transmission option (which

American buyers clearly wanted), air conditioning, cruise control, and all manner of fittings thought to be unnecessary by Ferrari and others.

It was no wonder that, in its road test, *Autocar & Motor* commented: "The NSX

offers a fantastically fresh and different face wrapped up in a specification as exotic as a Ferrari's. . .".

Within months of its launch, production of the NSX had to be doubled to meet demand. At the end of the decade the plaudits were as lavish as ever.

*Below: Honda created a quad-camshaft 24-valve VTEC-equipped three-litre V6 for the NSX; though untemperamental, it has titanium con-rods, will rev safely to 8,000 rpm and produces 274 bhp.*

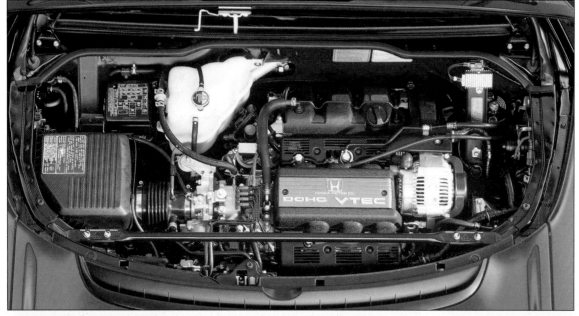

### Specification (1990)

**Engine:** V6, twin overhead camshafts per bank of cylinders
**Bore × stroke:** 90 mm × 78 mm
**Capacity:** 2977 cc
**Maximum power:** 274 bhp
**Transmission:** five-speed manual gearbox or four-speed automatic transmission, rear-wheel drive
**Chassis:** steel unit-construction body/chassis
**Suspension:** independent with wishbones and coil springs front and rear
**Brakes:** discs front and rear
**Bodywork:** aluminium-panelled two-seater coupé
**Maximum speed (approx):** 159 mph (256 km/h)

*Below: Unique among supercars for its very docile nature, the NSX can nonetheless sprint from 0-60 mph in 5.2 seconds.*

## Honda Beat 1991–95

*Right: Honda's stubby, cute little Beat was the fun car everybody wanted to drive when it appeared in 1991 – but it was for Japan only.*

If a 1991 model from a Japanese manufacturer has a top speed of only 84 mph, can it qualify in any way as a supercar? If that top speed is electronically limited, if the car's price is a mere £6,000 and if the car is a tiny-engined sports model with bags of youth appeal it certainly can. . .

Previewed in 1991, Honda's new Beat sports car showed all the signs of becoming a cult object in the following months, for it was chunky, cheeky, high-revving, and overflowing with the 'fun factor' which many Japanese cars had lacked in the past.

Pundits made haste to compare it with the original S600/S800 cars of the 1960s, though in truth it was an entirely different type of car. Its secret was a transverse mid-mounted *three*-cylinder engine/transmission package, a reworked version of that fitted to the front-engined Honda Today city-car, in a machine with an overall length of a mere 130 inches and a weight of 1,676 lb.

Like the S800's, the Beat's engine thrived on high revs, and Honda billed the little car as the world's first mass-produced mid-engined fully-open sports car. It proposed to produce 3,000 Beats every month. Because the car was so small, and because there was so little stowage room, cynics giggled and refused to take it seriously.

They were wrong. The little Beat handled well, was lively up to its governed top speed of 84 mph, and would certainly be a 100-mph machine if that electronic leash were slipped off.

### Specification (1991)
**Engine:** inline three-cylinder, single overhead camshaft
**Bore × stroke:** 66 mm × 64 mm
**Capacity:** 656 cc
**Maximum power:** 64 bhp
**Transmission:** five-speed manual gearbox, rear-wheel drive

**Chassis:** steel unit-construction body/chassis
**Suspension:** independent with coil springs front and rear
**Brakes:** drums front and rear
**Bodywork:** steel two-seater sports
**Maximum speed (approx):** 84 mph (135 km/h)

# Horch Motorwagenwerke AG

The company that was once Mercedes-Benz's closest rival in the luxury car market was started by August Horch, in Cologne-Ehrenfeld, in 1899. From 1904 the company was located at Zwickau. Before the end of the decade, however, the founder disagreed with his associates over model policy, left the company, and founded Audi in a new factory in the same town.

At first Horch produced a variety of models with a wide range of four-cylinder engines. In the 1920s, however, a series of prestige cars with larger engines was produced, inspired by the newly-appointed chief engineer, Paul Daimler (son of the famous Gottlieb, one of the founders of the world's motor industry).

The first of the straight-eight Horchs was the Type 300, which had twin-overhead-camshaft valve gear, this being followed later in the 1920s by other eight-cylinder twin-cams called the 305 and 306, while the Type 350/375 models of 1928 had a four-litre 80-bhp version of the straight-eight engine.

After Paul Daimler left, two more cars which he had influenced – the 400 and 405 – appeared, then the first true 'post-Daimler' Horch was the all-new single-cam 450 of 1930. This not only had a choice of wheelbases, but also the option of three different engine displacements, and was built until the end of the 1930s.

From 1932 Horch became a member of the new German Auto Union combine (which also included Audi, DKW and Wanderer), and the famous mid-engined Auto Union Grand Prix cars were actually constructed at the Horch works at Zwickau.

Yet more prestige models continued to flow out of the Horch factory in the 1930s, and historians have found it extremely difficult to keep track of type numbers, for various cars were built with different wheelbases and engine sizes. In the late 1930s, as an example, Horch was producing straight-eights with overhead-cam valve gear and 66-degree V8s with side valves. Engine sizes varied from 3.5 litres to five litres, and power outputs from 75 bhp to 120 bhp. Yet annual production of 'eights' never exceeded 500 cars a year.

The most notable – but rare and complex – 1930s Horchs were the massive V12-engined 600/670 models, and the eight-cylinder 850s.

Somehow Horch was able to sell these cars at lower prices than equivalent Mercedes-Benz types, and the company prospered until World War II broke out. Along with the 'Grosser' Mercedes, the large Horchs were used as staff cars by German military and Nazi officials.

After the end of the war the old Horch factory found itself behind the Iron Curtain, in East Germany, so there was no chance of large and luxurious Horchs coming back onto the market. Eventually the factory sank to producing the dreary two-stroke Trabant, although traces of Horch heraldry remained at the works when it closed down in 1991. The name, however, is still owned by the Auto Union combine, though it has not been used again on a production car.

*Below: Seen embossed on the radiator surround of one of the superb 1930s V12s, the Horch emblem signified a convincing alternative to the powerful, luxurious pre-war Mercedes range.*

## Horch 670 1931-33

The straight-eight overhead-cam Horch of the 1920s was a fine car, but it did not quite have what it took to wean customers away from Mercedes and by 1929 only around 16 were sold, with none the following year. The company's solution to that problem was to hire a new designer, Fritz Fiedler (who was later responsible for the famous BMW 328). Fiedler came up with a very ambitious plan, particularly considering the state of Europe's economy at the time. He decided a luxury V12 was the solution, and the first car was completed in time for the 1931 Paris Motor Show in October. There it caused a sensation, not because of its specification but because Horch's body designer, Herman Ahrens, had created an extremely attractive style for the two-door Cabriolet 670 model (the four-door Pullman body was a far more staid and

formal design). Ahrens' flowing lines were perfectly proportioned and made the vast car look smaller in pictures than it was.

Unfortunately the body was too heavy for the power available, despite the fact that the car was powered by a V12 engine. Fully loaded, the Cabriolet weighed as much as two and a half tons. That V12 was a conservative pushrod design (although it did boast hydraulic tappets and a crankshaft damper for quiet running). It had seven main bearings and a control on the dashboard so that the driver could increase the oil flow to those bearings when the car was travelling near its top speed.

The black-enamelled engine produced just 120 bhp at 3,500 rpm from a little under six litres. The torque output, however, was excellent and the big car

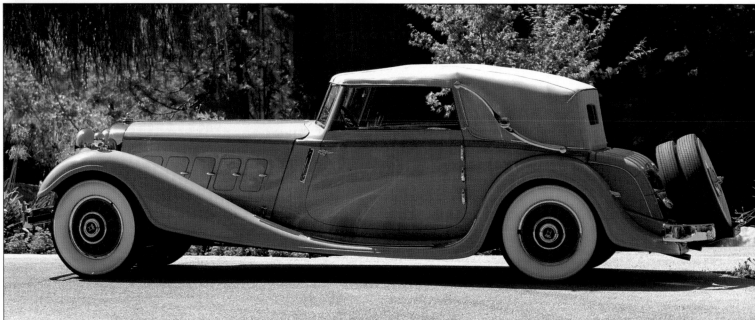

*Above: The Horch 670 was larger and heavier than its elegant, sweeping lines made it look.*

could accelerate smoothly from 15 mph in top to reach its maximum speed, which was only 80 mph.

The ZF four-speed gearbox boasted synchromesh on the top three gears and top gear was effectively an overdrive, with a ratio of 0.67:1. That was somewhat negated by the bulk of the car, as the engine really couldn't pull that high a ratio. As compensation, however, the V12 Horch handled very well, particularly considering its simple beam-axle and semi-elliptic leaf-spring suspension front and rear. The handling was better than its braking performance; the V12's original drum brakes found the task of stopping well over 5,000 lb of car too much for them, although brake size was increased to 16-in diameter in 1933. By that time the writing was on the wall for

the Horch. Precise production figures are unknown but probably only 54 V12 were built, of which four survive today. Luckily, all are the most attractive two door Cabriolet models. One forms part of the huge (predominantly Bugatti) Schlumpf Collection and another, the one shown here, belongs to a collector in the United States.

### Specification (1931)

**Engine:** 60-degree V12, overhead-valve
**Bore × stroke:** 80 mm × 100 mm
**Capacity:** 5990 cc
**Maximum power:** 120 bhp
**Transmission:** four-speed manual gearbox, rear-wheel drive
**Chassis:** separate steel frame with channel-section side members
**Suspension:** non-independent with beam front axle and live rear axle, each with leaf springs
**Brakes:** drums front and rear
**Bodywork:** steel on wood framing; many four-/six-seater styles
**Maximum speed (approx):** 80 mph (129 km/h)

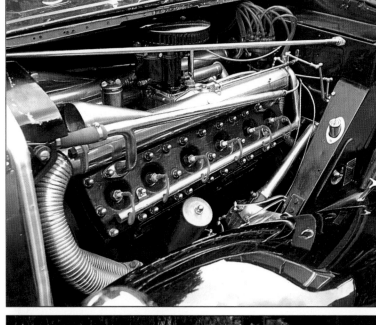

*Left: Horch built a six-litre 60-degree V12 for the 670. Smooth and refined rather than massively powerful, it produced 120 bhp, but its torque output was impressive.*

*Below: Various four- and six-seater bodies were fitted to the 670-series chassis. This 1932 Cabriolet must have been among the most attractive. The total built of all the different types was little more than 50.*

# Horch 853 1936-39

After the extravagances of the twin-overhead-camshaft straight-eight were abandoned, Horch started again in post-Daimler times with a more restrained 'eight', this time with an engine designed by Fritz Fiedler (who went on to work with BMW and – after World War II – with Bristol).

By the time this design reached its zenith, cars carrying it were using box-section frames with independent front suspension. The single-overhead-camshaft engines themselves were solid creations, with 10 crankshaft bearings, and the gearboxes had synchromesh, backed with overdrive.

The first 'Fiedler eights' were fitted to

*Below: Under the Horch 853's stylish cabriolet-type body were independent front suspension and a de Dion rear axle.*

the 450 of 1930, but the more well-known models so equipped were the 850s and 950s of the late 1930s, which had five-litre units with 100 bhp or even 120 bhp and, being not overbodied or too heavy, were also fast and elegant machines. A few of these cars were sold in the UK, where their performance matched that of cars like the Bentley and Lagonda, but at rather lower prices. Only British patriotism (and a rising phobia over all things German) saw them sell so slowly.

The most sporting of all was the 853 of 1936-39 (950 of which were built), for this had a smart sports cabriolet body (similar in some aspects to the Mercedes-Benz 540K) which hid a chassis with an independent front end and de Dion rear suspension. Although these cars weighed about 5,000 lb, speeds of up to 90 mph were possible, achieved in great style, albeit with poor acceleration.

### Horch 853 variants

#### Horch 850, 851 and 951

More 'touring' versions of this basic design included the 850, 851, and 951, with longer wheelbases, less power and heavier coachwork (all but the 951 had beam-axle rear suspension). Some cars had a gargantuan 149-in wheelbase chassis.

### Specification (853 Cabriolet)

**Engine:** inline eight-cylinder, overhead-valve
**Bore × stroke:** 87 mm × 104 mm
**Capacity:** 4946 cc
**Maximum power:** 120 bhp
**Transmission:** four-speed manual

*Above: The Horch 853, here, was the top-priced Auto Union model of its time. Its five-litre straight-eight produced 120 bhp.*

gearbox with overdrive, rear-wheel drive
**Chassis:** separate steel frame with box-section side members plus cruciform cross-bracing
**Suspension:** independent front with transverse leaf springs; de Dion rear with leaf springs
**Brakes:** drums front and rear
**Bodywork:** steel on wood framing; many four-/six-seater styles
**Maximum speed (approx):** 90 mph (145 km/h)

# Hotchkiss

*Below: The crossed cannons on the Hotchkiss insignia hinted at the company's main trade, which was armaments manufacture. The French firm took its name from its American founder.*

The original Hotchkiss company (set up by Benjamin Berkeley Hotchkiss, an American) was a French arms concern which turned to making cars when military business slumped. The two activities carried on side-by-side until 1914, when machine-gun manufacture naturally took priority

A new factory was built at this time, later managed by the Englishman Harry Ainsworth. After the war and throughout the 1920s a series of worthy but mechanically dull four-cylinder cars was produced. As far as motoring enthusiasts and historians were concerned, the interesting breakthrough came in 1928 when the first modern Hotchkiss six-cylinder car, the Model AM80, was put on sale. Ainsworth carried on directing the fortunes of the Hotchkiss combine well into the post-war era, although his tenure was over before Hotchkiss car manufacture ceased.

The robust six-cylinder engine, designed by Bertarione of GP engine design fame, was to be Hotchkiss's staple unit for the next two decades, and in the first place the '80' part of the model title denoted the cylinder bore dimension in millimetres. The faster varieties, such as the 686 and 686GS, soon made their name in long-distance rallies (winning the Monte Carlo several times) and their reputation was almost, but not quite, bracketed with that of other French *Grand Routier* marques such as Delage and Delahaye.

By the end of the 1930s Hotchkiss was not only still in the armaments business, but it was producing nearly 3,000 cars a year. In automotive terms, however, the design was stagnating. That was even more noticeable after the war, for the pre-war cars were continued into the late 1940s and early 1950s with little attempt to replace them or bring them up to date. There were facelifted versions of the 'big six'-engined models in 1951 (called the 2050 and 2050GS) but these could only provide a short-lived postponement of the inevitable.

The only commercial way for Hotchkiss to stay alive was a merger with another company, and this was duly accomplished in 1952, when Delahaye took over. The result was that after 1954 Hotchkiss concentrated on making trucks, and the famous carmaking name was buried. Even so, Hotchkiss trucks were built until 1970, along with American Jeeps which were manufactured under licence, while the company also sold Leyland trucks in France.

## Hotchkiss 686 1936-54

The first of the modern generation of six-cylinder Hotchkisses, the AM80, was launched at the Paris Salon in 1928, and set standards from which the later, more powerful, 686 models were developed. The 686 had a solid but strictly conventional chassis, with beam axles at front and rear, which had evolved from that of the sporting AM80S of 1933. By this time it had cruciform bracing to the frame and Bendix cable-operated brakes.

The engine was a sturdy straight-six, with a seven-bearing crankshaft and pushrod overhead-valve operation, and it was backed by a four-speed synchromesh gearbox. Depending on the application, the engine could have as little as 100 bhp in single-carburettor form or as much as 125 bhp in 'Paris-Nice' and 'Grand Sport' guises.

The 686s came in various shapes and sizes, on no fewer than four wheelbases, while there were many different body styles. The most exciting version of all, the GS or Grand Sport, was sold as a roadster, a sports saloon and as a fixed-head coupé, had a top speed of more than 100 mph, and was a most accomplished and successful rally car.

During the life of this series the Hotchkiss won the Monte Carlo Rally no fewer than five times, which proved that it was fast and nimble as well as large and heavy. About 1,500 such cars were produced in 1939.

The mechanical design had gradually improved during the 1930s – hydraulic brakes coming in during 1936. Independent front suspension and an optional Cotal gearbox appeared from 1948, followed by a facelift to the 2050/2050GS.

*Right: In the inter-war years Hotchkiss built the AM series, which gained a new overhead-valve 2.2-litre engine in 1926.*

types in 1951 – but the basic design remained unaltered until 1954.

### Hotchkiss 686 variants

#### Hotchkiss AM80 and AM80S
The AM80 was built from 1929 to 1933 and was the original Bertarione-engined six-cylinder Hotchkiss, with an 80-mm × 100-mm, 3015-cc/70-bhp engine, and a top speed of about 72 mph. There was also the AM73, which had a 73-mm × 100-mm engine, while the AM80S used the later 3485-cc power unit.

#### Hotchkiss 615 and 680
The Type 615 of 1935 and the 680 of

1936-39 both used the original three-litre engine in the 686 3½-litre chassis.

#### Hotchkiss 620
The 620 was the 1934-35 predecessor of the 686, with the 100-bhp version of the 3½-litre engine.

#### Hotchkiss 2050 and 2050GS
After World War II, the 2050 and 2050GS types were produced; these were facelifted 686s.

### Specification (1936 Grand Sport)
**Engine:** inline six-cylinder, overhead-valve
**Bore × stroke:** 86 mm × 100 mm

**Capacity:** 3485 cc
**Maximum power:** 125 bhp
**Transmission:** four-speed manual gearbox, rear-wheel drive; Cotal gearbox optional after 1948
**Chassis:** separate steel frame with channel-section side members
**Suspension:** non-independent with beam front axle and live rear axle, each with leaf springs; from 1948 the cars were given independent front suspension, by coil springs
**Brakes:** drums front and rear
**Bodywork:** aluminium and steel on wood framing; various two and four-seater styles
**Maximum speed (approx):** 100 mph (161 km/h)

# HRG Engineering Co. Ltd

**M**essrs Halford, Robins and Godfrey combined forces in 1935 to set up a tiny sports car business based at Tolworth, on the south-western outskirts of London. The result was the birth of the HRG – always affectionately known as the 'Hurg' – a car which remained on sale, visually unchanged, for the next 20 years.

Each of the three partners had considerable sports car experience before they joined together – Major 'Ted' Halford was an engineer and Brooklands racing driver who had also worked on the Vale sports car, Guy Robins had been involved in the making of Trojan cars, and Ron Godfrey had been the 'G' of the GN cycle car concern, in partnership with Archie Frazer-Nash. One of their most important associates, who was closely involved in the design of a new car, was Stuart Proctor.

There was some GN and – by inference – some Frazer Nash influence in the design of the HRG chassis, which was simplicity itself. Like the Frazer Nash, this featured forward-facing quarter-elliptic springs to locate the front axle, and rearward-facing springs to support the rear axle. Unlike the Frazer Nash, however, the HRG had a conventional gearbox and shaft drive. Meadows and Singer engines were used.

Although the cars always offered good (if not exceptional) value for money, they could only be built by hand, and carefully at that, which explains why production was always very limited. The records show that it normally took about five months to completely build a car – three months for the rolling chassis, and two more for the body.

Peak pre-war production was 11 cars (in 1937), then – in spite of material and power shortages – a dizzy 67 in 1947, but by the 1950s

the design was seen as out of date, and production of the old-style 'square-rigged' car fell to four in 1954 and ended after 1956.

The company, though small, was never short on enterprise, which explains the production of 45 'Aerodynamic' models in the post-war period (these had full-width styling on the original narrow frame), the development of an advanced twin-overhead-camshaft version of the Singer engine in the 1950s, and a final dabble with Ford- and Vauxhall-engined prototypes in the 1960s.

*Below: HRG took its name from the initials of the firm's three instigators – Halford, Robins and Godfrey. They set up their sports car business at Tolworth, south-west of London, in 1935.*

## HRG 1100, 1500 and Aerodynamic 1935-56

The car which founded, supported and, in the end, closed the life-cycle of HRG was launched in 1935, although deliveries did not actually begin until 1936. Like the ageing Frazer Nash, like the MG and Singer sports cars, and like the new Morgan 4/4, it was a traditionally-styled two-seater which put sport before comfort, and character before space and high-tech equipment.

The basis of the car was a slim and simple chassis with channel-section side members, and a 103-in wheelbase. The cantilever leaf springs – which pointed forward at the front, backwards at the rear – were so hard that it was once said that if an HRG wheel was seen to deflect, then there must be a serious frame failure somewhere!

The light-alloy body was narrow, but distinctively styled, with cycle-type wings. It had the minimum of weather equipment, the steering was direct, and the car soon earned a reputation as a precise-handling machine which was extremely versatile in all forms of motorsport.

The first cars – the original 1500s – used 69-mm × 100-mm/58-bhp, 1496-cc Meadows engines, but these power units were introduced at the end of their development (Frazer Nash was about to discard them, too), so in 1937 HRG began to supply cars fitted with a more modern overhead-cam Singer engine and gearbox. This unit had slightly more power than the Meadows, but the difference in performance was negligible, top speed in any case being limited by poor aerodynamics.

As an alternative, in 1938 the car became available with the smaller Singer 60-mm × 95-mm/38-bhp 9-hp engine, of 1074 cc, this running on a 99.5-in wheelbase but otherwise looking the same. Although this 1100 car sold only slowly (49

*Above: Eric Thompson built this Monaco-bodied HRG for Le Mans, and it won the 1.5-litre class.*

were built between 1938 and 1950), it was still an attractive sports car, with a top speed of 78 mph.

After World War II, the car continued much as before, except that a full-width 'Aerodynamic' model was put on sale from 1945 to 1949. This shared the same chassis and running gear as the long-stroke Singer 1500-engined car, but had a light-alloy body shell with fully-enveloping wings and was heavier than the traditional style.

The latest short-stroke Singer 1.5-litre engine (73-mm × 89.4-mm/1497-cc) took over in 1953, and hydraulic brakes were offered at the very end of production, but there were no visual changes to report.

Total production was 16 Meadows-engined cars, 109 long-stroke Singer-engined 1500s, 49 1100s, 45 Aerodynamic 1500s and finally just 12 short-stroke Singer-engined 1500s.

### Specification (1937 Singer 1500)

**Engine:** inline-four, overhead-camshaft
**Bore × stroke:** 68 mm × 103 mm
**Capacity:** 1496 cc
**Maximum power:** 61 bhp
**Transmission:** four-speed manual gearbox, rear-wheel drive
**Chassis:** separate steel frame with channel-section side members
**Suspension:** non-independent with beam front axle and leaf springs; live rear axle with leaf springs
**Brakes:** drums front and rear
**Bodywork:** aluminium on wood frame; two-seater sports car
**Maximum speed (approx):** 86 mph (138 km/h)

*Below: A full-width Aerodynamic body became an option in 1949, using standard running gear.*

*Below: The standard HRG looked traditional; Singer engines replaced Meadows units in 1937.*

# Hudson

T he Hudson marque was founded in 1909 by Howard Earle Coffin and Roy Dikeman Chapin, who were chief engineer and sales manager respectively at Olds, and the Hudson was named after their principal backer, a millionaire who owned a Detroit department store.

The 6-40 that came out in 1914 was the lightest six-cylinder car in the USA, and it gave Hudson an enduring reputation for good performance. Output was 10,260 units, making Hudson the most prolific maker of six-cylinder cars in the world. From this point, it also began to build more fully-enclosed saloon cars than rival firms, sourcing its bodies from Biddle and Smart of Amesbury, Massachusetts.

An associate company, Essex cars, started up in 1917 in a disused Hudson plant, and the two manufacturers merged in 1922 when output was roughly the same from both factories. In 1926 Hudson opened a $10 million factory that made 1,500 bodyshells a day, making it more self-sufficient, and annual output was 110,000 Hudsons to 160,000 Essex, a combined tally that placed Hudson-Essex third in the sales league tables behind Ford and Chevrolet. The Depression brought a collapse, resulting in Essex models being badged as Terraplanes.

Meanwhile, Hudson brought out a 3.5-litre straight-eight engine in 1930, which remained in production until 1952, and which was fitted by Brough Superior and Railton. Hudsons were themselves popular in Britain and assembled at the rate of 2,000 a year in west London.

Both Terraplane and Hudson were successful in competition, winning the American Automobile Association stock car hillclimb record in 1933, but fickle finances caused the Terraplane name to be dropped in 1938. When Hudson introduced coil sprung independent front suspension in 1940, the cars were touted as 'America's safest'. During World War II Hudson made a variety of aircraft components, Invader marine engine and Oerlikon cannon in its Detroit arsenal.

Hudson's most stylish model ranges were introduced after the war. Chief designer Frank Spring drew the 'Step-Down' model that was launched in 1948, so-called because the rear of the chassis continued on the outside of the wheel arches with the floor pan set below the chassis. Bodies and chassis were welded together in semi-unit construction, and the Step-Down model was powered by the straight-eight engine and later on the Super Six was fitted in the Pacemaker derivative. The Hornet came out in 1951, using the new 145 bhp side-valve six-cylinder engine which proved successful in competition, although the big six was an anachronistic design and the majority of US car-makers were fitting V8s.

Annual sales galloped to 150,000 units by 1950, but three years on Hudson was facing losses of $10m as sales fell back to 33,000 units. Even the introduction in 1953 of a new compact model, the 3.3-litre Jet, didn't win many new customers.

By this time, Hudson was ripe for another merger, and in 1954 amalgamated with Nash in the wealthy American Motors Corporation. However, that was effectively the end of Hudson as a significant force in the industry, as its products became badged Nashes. They were built at Kenosha, Wisconsin, and powered by Jet, Hornet or Packard V8 engines, and sales actually picked up in 1955. The Hudson badge was also applied to compact Ramblers and a version of the Austin Metropolitan and from 1958 the cars were called Ramblers. Although no further Hudson cars were made, the Detroit plant continued to build military vehicles such as the 4 x 4 Mighty Mite, and was finally absorbed into AM's General armaments division.

## Hudson Hornet 1951-1954

Hudson was busy building air frames for planes like the B29 Superfortress during World War II, along with other military contracts, and Frank Spring's 1941 design for the semi-unit-construction 'step-down' line had to wait until 1948 to go into production. The series began with the entry-level Pacemaker, moving up to the Super Six, Hornet, Wasp, Super Wasp and top-of-the-range Commodore, and eventually more than 142,000 'step-down' Hudsons were built. Special editions included the Super Wasp Hollywood hardtop Coupé, and Commodore Brougham. Power plant was the tried and tested 4.2-litre straight-eight, but a new 145 bhp 5.0-litre straight six was introduced in the Hornet in 1951, and this was very successful in US stock-car racing. The step-down series was engineered by Sam Frahm and Reid Railton, and the model was so-called because the car's rear floor-pan was sunk below the chassis. There were chassis outriggers on either side of the back wheels – outside the wheelbase – which allowed the body line to be much lower towards the rear of the car than was normally the case. The low centre of gravity contributed to the car's success on the race circuits, while the long, low-slung curved body was one of the most graceful of all US models of the early 1950s.

*Right: The 1951 Hornet styled by Frank Spring, with engineering input from Sam Frahm and Reid Railton, was notable for its 'step-down' chassis. The rear floorpan and body panels were fixed at a lower level than normal.*

Designer Frank Spring had studied engineering in France and had worked at the Murphy Body Company in the 1920s before joining Hudson as Design Director in 1931. He was a real car enthusiast, owning a Type 30 and a Type 35 Bugatti, and given to flying himself around in an autogyro or riding his BMW motorcycle. Spring's design team was responsible for interiors as well as exteriors, and all materials were ready to hand at the Hudson Tech Center. At the time the Commodore was designed, Hudson's design department used plaster to make the scale models, despite the fact that most stylists used clay. The disadvantage of plaster was that once the model was made, it was very difficult to go back to it to incorporate detail changes, and it was at design stage that one of the Hudson's problems was built in. The issue was cooling, and Spring's original design called for a high frontal grille, which would have allowed better air flow to the radiator, but the management vetoed it in favour of a low opening. Another stylistic quirk was the Hudson's diminutive rear window – just 11 inches high, and modelled on the Buick Sedanette of 1942. However, the Hudson step-down range was innovative with body colour, pioneering the use of metallic pigments and two-tone paint schemes. Typically, there was lashings of chrome trim, and Hudsons invariably wore whitewall tyres and full-width exterior sun visors across the windscreen.

### Specification (Hornet)

**Engine:** straight six
**Capacity:** 5.0-litre
**Chassis:** steel frame with rear outriggers welded to bodyshell
**Body:** four-door saloon, two-door cabriolet
**Suspension:** independent front by coil springs and dampers; rear, semi-elliptic leaf springs

# Innocenti

I nnocenti of Italy rocketed to fame all round the world with their Lambretta motor scooters in the 1950s, before deciding to enter the car business in the 1960s. It was carefully done – at first the cars were licence-built, but their own models soon came.

The first Innocenti cars of 1961 were kit-built BMC A40 Farinas, with front-wheel-drive BMC 1100s and Minis soon added to the range. Right from the start, however, Innocenti was also determined to produce more distinctive machines, the first being the Sprite-based Spider. Pressings for these cars came from Officine Stampaggi Industrial (OSI).

By the end of 1960s Innocenti had expanded considerably. The newly-formed British Leyland (which had absorbed BMC) saw the company as a simple way to break into the Italian market, and made a successful takeover bid in 1972. For a short time the business was run by Geoffrey Robinson, the Leyland nominee who later went on to become Jaguar's controversial chairman in the mid-1970s.

The most important new British Leyland Innocenti of this time was the Bertone-styled Mini, but after the British group's financial traumas (and subsequent nationalisation) Innocenti itself was sold to Alejandro De Tomaso, and integrated into his De Tomaso/Maserati/Moto Guzzi empire.

The product range was then rationalised by killing off older BMC-based model assembly, and for a time Innocenti prospered on Bertone Mini sales, with the cars renamed De Tomaso Minis from 1976. De Tomaso eventually tired of dealing with the British, struck a new deal with the Japanese, and ditched Mini front-wheel drive in favour of three-cylinder Daihatsu drivelines from 1982. Innocenti was completely absorbed by Fiat in 1990, ending its short independent history.

*Left: Innocenti's adaptation of the Mini brought refreshing contemporary looks and a useful rear hatch to BL's small car, years before the British produced the Metro. But while linear styling went out of fashion, the Mini just kept running.*

# Invicta Cars

I n the 1920s there was a place – albeit a small place – in the British market for expensive, limited-production, sporting cars. To feed this market, Noel Macklin got together with Sir Oliver Lyle to found Invicta in 1925, and this tiny Cobham (Surrey)-based company produced high-priced vintage-style cars until the late 1930s. Invicta then went into hibernation until after the war, when an attempt was made to revive it with a new design, but this was short-lived.

Macklin, who had previously been connected with Eric Campbell and Silver Hawk cars, wanted to produce a British car with an American feel – one that would have a big and flexible engine, and would be easy to drive, but which would be hand-built according to the best British traditions.

Invicta, being small, could not afford to make any of its own running gear, so every car was a classic 'assembled model' using proprietary engines, transmissions and axles. The secret of the early Invictas' character was the use of the torquey and reliable, large Meadows six-cylinder engines, which provided something that the mid-1930s Blackburne-engined 1½-litre model could not match.

From the early 1930s Macklin became more and more involved in a

*Left: This Pegasus radiator mascot was an interesting detail on a 1949 Invicta Black Prince. The expensive and over-complicated Black Prince brought the end to Invicta car production.*

*Below: Seen at a recent historic cars race meeting at Silverstone, this is Bob Wood's 4½-litre Invicta S Type from 1931. It was the low-chassis, sport-orientated model.*

new motoring enterprise – the Railton (using Detroit-manufactured running gear), which was also made at Cobham after Invicta assembly was moved to London. This meant that the driving force behind Invicta disappeared, for not even a supercharged version of the Blackburne-engined cars could preserve the image.

Three new Invictas – 2½-, three- and four-litre-engined cars – were launched in 1937, but enthusiasts soon realised that these were nothing more than disguised French Darracqs, and the project died at birth.

After World War II a reborn Invicta concern launched an ambitious new twin-cam six-cylinder car, the Black Prince, but this was horribly expensive and the project foundered after only 25 had been made.

*Above: Violet Cordery drives a new 4½-litre Invicta in the renowned Coupe Boillot competition at Boulogne in 1928.*

# Invicta 4½-litre 1929-35

The definitive 4½-litre Invicta arrived in 1929, four years after the first Meadows-engined cars went on sale. Like previous types it was very expensive – a typical chassis price was about £1,000, which was very close to that of the 20/25 Rolls-Royce – which ensured that sales were very limited.

All 4½-litres were ruggedly simple machines, with hard leaf-spring suspension at front and rear, large-diameter wheels and heavy steering, but they were faster than most, for the top speed of a typical saloon was between 80 and 85 mph.

The most sensational, though very rare, model was the low-chassis S Type sports car, which had rakish looks, flashing performance, and a well-deserved reputation for its limited roadholding. It was one of the fastest – though one of the most feared – supercars of its day.

Even so, this 100-mph Invicta was good enough to win many races and rallies, most notably the 1931 Monte Carlo when driven by Donald Healey. The frame, supposedly inspired by that of the 1920s-type Delage Grand Prix car, was very rigid, and passed *under* the line of the

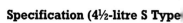

rear axle, which ensured that there was very limited wheel movement. The body style – all sharp edges, and rivets along the bonnet, allied to external exhaust pipes – was the sort of thing that *Boy's*

*Own Paper* fantasies were made of.

In four years only 77 S Types were produced, though most have survived to this day. The engine, incidentally, was taken up by Lagonda for use in its own 4½-litre model, a car which was built until the outbreak of war in 1939.

## Meadows-engined Invicta variants

Every Invicta built from 1925 to 1931 used one or other version of the famous Meadows six-cylinder engine.

The first-ever Invicta was the 2½-litre model with a 69-mm × 120.6-mm/2692-cc engine, running on a 112-in wheelbase. This was sold from 1925 to 1927.

Next was the three-litre model with a 72.5-mm × 120-mm/2972-cc/95-bhp engine, on the same wheelbase, but with a 120-in wheelbase option; production spanned 1926-30.

The definitive 4½-litre model arrived in 1929 and was built through to 1935. The first type was the NLC, the 'Tourer' Invicta on a long, 126-in, wheelbase, but from 1930 there was a choice of A Type (high-chassis, reduced-specification) and S Type (low-chassis, ultra-sporting) models.

*Above: With its external exhaust pipes, the Invicta S Type looked just as fast as it was. The low-chassis S Type had a frame – purportedly modelled on that of 1920s Delage Grand Prix cars – that passed under the rear axle, limiting suspension travel; roadholding was reputedly quite limited.*

## Specification (4½-litre S Type)

**Engine:** inline six-cylinder, overhead-valve
**Bore × stroke:** 88.5 mm × 120.6 mm
**Capacity:** 4467 cc
**Maximum power:** 115 bhp; later S Types up to 140 bhp
**Transmission:** four-speed manual gearbox, rear-wheel drive
**Chassis:** separate steel frame with channel-section side members and tubular bracings
**Suspension:** non-independent with beam front axle; live rear axle with semi-elliptic leaf springs
**Brakes:** discs front and rear
**Bodywork:** aluminium on wood-framing, two-seater
**Maximum speed (approx):** 95 mph (153 km/h)

*Above: The front suspension of the S Type used a forged 'T'-beam axle with a dropped centre section.*

*Below: This is a handsome Salmons-bodied version of the 4½-litre S Type from 1934.*

## Invicta 12/45 1931-33

Invicta reacted promptly to the financial traumas of the Depression by putting a smaller-engined model on sale. A Blackburne 1½-litre-engined car was offered as an alternative to the massive 4½-litre car. The original, normally-aspirated car was dubbed 12/45 – RAC horsepower and claimed brake horsepower respectively – but a year later a Powerplus supercharged derivative known as the 12/90 was added to the range.

Invicta's problem was that it knew nothing about building small-engined cars, so the new car still had a strong separate chassis on a 118-in wheelbase, which ensured that it was heavy and needed low gearing to give reasonable acceleration.

Even the supercharged 12/90 model struggled to beat 70 mph, and rarely exceeded 23 mpg. Like its larger-engined relatives, the Blackburne-engined car felt sporting, and looked the part, but few were prepared to pay the £535 asked for such performance at a time when Riley, Triumph and SS prices were at half that level. Only about 50 such cars were built.

### Specification (1931)

**Engine:** inline six-cylinder, overhead-camshaft
**Bore × stroke:** 57 mm × 97.7 mm
**Capacity:** 1498 cc
**Maximum power:** N/A
**Transmission:** four-speed manual gearbox or Wilson preselector transmission, rear-wheel drive

**Chassis:** separate steel frame with channel-section main side members
**Suspension:** non-independent with beam front axle and leaf springs; live rear axle with semi-elliptic leaf springs
**Brakes:** drums front and rear
**Bodywork:** steel on wood framing, four-seater saloon or tourer
**Maximum speed:** 75 mph (121 km/h)

*Above: The smaller Invicta's designation referred to the RAC horsepower rating and the claimed brake horsepower of its Blackburne 1498-cc six-cylinder engine. As well as the 12/45, there was a supercharged 12/90, but even this was not fast, for the chassis was heavy.*

## Invicta Black Prince 1946-50

During World War II, Invicta allowed designer William Watson's muse to run riot, the result being that in 1946 an impossibly overcomplicated new car, dubbed the Black Prince, was launched. If it had been proposed by a company of – say – Jaguar's size, it *might* have succeeded, but for a small company like Invicta it was an impossible dream.

Except for the hopelessly underdeveloped transmission system, the Black Prince could have been a successful car, if Invicta had only had the resources to iron out all the bugs, and if the price had been a lot lower.

The chassis frame was a solid new design, with independent suspension by longitudinal torsion bars and wishbones at front and rear. The engine was a brave new twin-cam seven-bearing three-litre

'six' by Henry Meadows which, in a few years, would not only be overshadowed, but also overpowered, by Jaguar's XK twin-cam six.

The car's Achilles heel was the Brockhouse 'hydro-kinetic turbo transmitter', which was essentially a massive torque converter that offered infinitely variable ratios between 4.27:1 and 15:1. There was a solenoid-operated reverse gear which gave endless trouble in the early stages, and of course the pick-up was not as crisp as with a normal manual-transmission car.

Charlesworth were contracted to build the smart bodies, but went bankrupt, whereupon Airflow Streamlines and Jensen tried to pick up the pieces. The main problem was that the car was heavy – more than 3,900 lb – and very ex-

pensive at £3,890. Nevertheless, production was planned to take place at the rate of 250 cars a year.

However, the project failed, for at the time this was Rolls-Royce money for an undeveloped car, so customers were very thin on the ground.

The Black Prince was a ponderous but interestingly-engineered car which deserved a better fate. The few survivors have usually been re-engined with Jaguar XK power, and matching gearboxes.

### Specification (1946)

**Engine:** inline six-cylinder, twin overhead camshafts
**Bore × stroke:** 81 mm × 97 mm
**Capacity:** 2998 cc
**Maximum power:** 120 bhp

**Transmission:** Brockhouse hydro-kinetic automatic transmission, rear-wheel drive
**Chassis:** separate steel frame with box-section side and cruciform members
**Suspension:** independent with wishbones and torsion bars front and rear
**Brakes:** drums front and rear
**Bodywork:** aluminium four-door four-seater saloon, or two-door drop-head coupé
**Maximum speed (approx):** 90 mph (145 km/h)

*Below: Invicta's Black Prince, with its fault-prone torque-converter drive, was a case of a small company's ambition exceeding its capabilities.*

# Iso

There was a world of difference betweeen the first two Iso models. The second car was a Chevrolet V8-powered supercar, while the first had been a tiny 40-mph 236-cc bubble-car called the Isetta.

Iso started in the 1940s by building motorcycles, then turned to producing the Isetta from 1953 to 1955. This was really no more than a grown-up scooter, with a tiny motorcycle-type engine, and was built in Milan for only three years, though licence-built Isettas were produced by BMW (West Germany), VELAM (France) and Trojan (UK). The last Isetta-derived machines were produced in 1964.

Starting again on its own in 1962, Iso then set out to produce fast, large-engined cars, with chassis developed for them by ex-Ferrari GTO engineer Giotto Bizzarrini, power by Chevrolet, and bodies styled by Italian coachbuilders. These became classic examples of Euro-American 'mongrels' – those which mixed Detroit engineering with proprietary transmissions, but with home-grown structures. Gordon-Keeble in Britain and Facel Vega in France followed the same path in the 1960s.

Iso's assembly plant was in Milan, but because its cars were always expensive, and the bodies hand-built by craftsmen at Bertone and Ghia, sales were limited. Tradition counts for a lot at these price and performance levels, which partly explains why Iso struggled to make its name in the world, though the mixed technical parentage of the cars cannot have helped.

Iso's guiding force was Renzo Rivolta; his supercar plans were ambitious, for the Rivolta four-seater of 1962 was soon joined by the Grifo two-seater of 1963, the Fidia four-door four-seater of 1967 and finally by the Lele two-door 2+2 of 1969. All shared the same basic platform chassis and running gear, but each had its own distinctive style.

During this period Giotto Bizzarrini terminated his consultancy with Iso, and moved off to Livorno to produce his own cars, which were remarkably close in design to the Grifo coupés which he had also created.

Renzo Rivolta died in 1966, and control of his company passed to his son Pierro. For a time the business prospered, but misfortune followed misfortune in the early 1970s. First of all the company made an unwise

*Above: Even if Renzo Rivolta didn't settle on a standard insignia for his company, the Iso script was consistent and the firm's Milan origin was invariably referred to.*

*Below: A heraldic griffon on a Grifo, this is from the very fast seven-litre version of the two-seater hybrid supercar.*

move to sponsor Formula 1 cars (the Iso-Marlboro car, an early Frank Williams enterprise, was a failure), then it was hit hard by the effects of the 'energy crisis' of 1973-74.

By this time, too, potential customers were becoming bored with the same old styles – the Grifo, after all, had not changed in looks for more than a decade – which meant that sales dried up. The result was that the company closed its doors at the end of 1975, and it was not until 1988 that a new start was made with the Grifo 90. The results of this new enterprise are still awaited.

*Below: Big, muscular and beautifully proportioned – this was one of the most desirable Isos, a 427-cu in Grifo seven-litre from 1970.*

## Iso Rivolta 1962-70

*Right: Bubble-cars apart, the first Iso was the Rivolta, a handsome Bertone-designed four-seater coupé. This one was at the 1966 London Motor Show.*

Like all Isos of the 1960s and 1970s, the first car of this pedigree, the Rivolta, was based on a rugged steel platform chassis, which had de Dion rear suspension. The engine and automatic transmission units were provided by Chevrolet, though the manual gearbox was supplied by ZF of West Germany.

The Rivolta's steel body shell was a two-door four-seater saloon, which was not only styled by Giorgetto Giugiaro (it was one of his early efforts for Bertone) but also constructed by Bertone of Turin. There were two types at first – IR300 and IR340 – the different numbers approximately referring to the gross horsepower that was on offer.

The style resembled the Gordon-Keeble in some ways, which is predictable, as Bertone also shaped that car at about the same time, though the Rivolta had but two headlamps, and rather more fussy detailing around the nose and flanks.

Like all subsequent Isos, the Rivolta was a fast, high-geared and somehow muscular machine, with an altogether different character from the Ferraris, Maseratis and (later) the Lamborghinis with which it attempted to compete. It rumbled where its rivals thrummed, and it cruised where its rivals raced – but it was nevertheless a very fast car indeed for the early 1960s.

A total of 797 Rivoltas was produced in eight years.

### Specification (1962 IR300)
**Engine:** V8, overhead-valve
**Bore × stroke:** 101.6 mm × 82.55 mm
**Capacity:** 5359 cc
**Maximum power:** 300 bhp
**Transmission:** five-speed manual gearbox or automatic transmission, rear-wheel drive
**Chassis:** separate steel platform chassis frame
**Suspension:** independent front with wishbones and coil springs; de Dion rear axle with coil springs
**Brakes:** discs front and rear
**Bodywork:** steel two-door four-seater saloon by Bertone
**Maximum speed (approx):** 140 mph (225 km/h)

## Iso Grifo 1963-75

Although the original Rivolta was often criticised for having rather staid styling, the second Iso derivative of this design, the Grifo coupé, was a startlingly attractive, and brutally effective, machine.

Once again the style was by Bertone, but this time the car was lower, wider, and strictly a two-seater coupé, with a 8-in-shorter-wheelbase version of the Rivolta's platform chassis. Only the style was new for, under the skin, the suspension, engines and transmissions were all like those fitted to the Rivolta saloons.

Except for a 'nose job', over the years the Grifo's looks were barely altered, although a variety of more and yet more powerful Chevrolet V8s were eventually offered; a five-speed manual gearbox was also available. All the cars were tremendously fast – the rare seven-litre or 7.4-litre types could certainly exceed 170 mph – which meant that in performance, if not in image, these were definite

*Above: Grifo, Italian for griffon, is the name of a powerful hybrid creature of mythology – appropriate for a blend of svelte Italian style and American V8 musclepower.*

*Below: With a wishbone front/de Dion rear chassis engineered by Bizzarrini, as well as lines created by the young Giugiaro, then working at Bertone, the Grifo handled as well as it looked.*

MNM 121G

*Above: Most Grifos used the 327-cu in Corvette-type Chevrolet small-block V8.*

*Below: In 1971 the Grifo was given an aerodynamically slick but less distinctive nose.*

rivals to Ferrari's V12 Daytona.

Early Grifos had a four-headlamp nose, with a conventional radiator grille opening, but later cars were restyled to have pop-up headlamps and a more wind-cheating snout.

Although cars like the Grifo can be criticised for their hybrid nature and the use of an unsophisticated American pushrod V8 engine, the Grifo's chassis certainly bore comparison with anything its exotic Italian rivals were sporting at the time, and despite the big front-mounted engine the weight distribution was neutral. The Grifo's welded re-inforced steel platform chassis was very stiff and held an excellent suspension system consisting of the traditional un-equal-length wishbones allied to a rear de Dion system located by radius arms, with a Watt linkage giving extra side-ways location. The de Dion suspension also allowed the use of inboard-mounted disc brakes, which had the advantage of

saving on unsprung weight. The fro brakes, naturally, were also discs.

In spite of the huge performance, t Grifo was not as successful as its rival 504 cars were sold in its 10-year life.

## Specification (1963)

**Engine:** V8, overhead-valve
**Bore × stroke:** 101.6 mm × 82.55 mm
**Capacity:** 5359 cc
**Maximum power:** 365 bhp
**Transmission:** four-speed manual gearbox or automatic transmission, rear-wheel drive
**Chassis:** separate steel platform chassis frame
**Suspension:** independent front with wishbones and coil springs; de Dion rear axle with coil springs
**Brakes:** discs front and rear
**Bodywork:** steel two-door two-seater coupé by Bertone
**Maximum speed (approx):** 161 mph (259 km/h)

# Iso Fidia 1967-75

With the Rivolta (two-door four-seater) and the Grifo (two-door two-seater) models already on sale, Pierro Rivolta decided to expand the range still further. The third type to be produced, on the same basic chassis as before, was the S4, soon renamed Fidia.

There were two basic innovations – one was that the Fidia was a four-door four-seater saloon, the other was that the style was by Ghia – and the wheelbase was six inches longer than that of the Rivolta. Advertised as having the "four fastest armchairs in the world", the Fidia had a strange 'cow-hipped' side profile, allied to four rectangular headlamps, but

the interior was spacious and featured full air conditioning.

Compared with the Rivolta, the Fidia was larger, better-equipped, and more luxurious, while unlike the Grifo it was an executive express rather than a super-car, but it was never a fast seller. In spite of being made available with all the

engine and transmission options, only 1 cars were sold in seven years.

At the very end of the run a few ca were fitted with 5.8-litre Ford (instead Chevrolet) V8 engines.

## Specification (1967)

**Engine:** V8, overhead-valve
**Bore × stroke:** 101.6 mm × 82.55 mm
**Capacity:** 5359 cc
**Maximum power:** 300 bhp
**Transmission:** four-speed manual gearbox or automatic transmission, rear-wheel drive
**Chassis:** separate steel platform chassis frame
**Suspension:** independent front with wishbones and coil springs; de Dion rear axle with coil springs
**Brakes:** discs front and rear
**Bodywork:** steel four-door four-seater saloon by Ghia
**Maximum speed (approx):** 133 mph (214 km/h)

*Left: Though ungainly-looking, the Ghia-styled Fidia was a luxurious four-door cruiser.*

## so Lele 1969-75

he fourth and final variation on the Biz-
arrini-designed Iso chassis theme was
e Lele, a two-door 2+2-seater rather
diosyncratically styled by Bertone. This
as effectively a replacement for the
riginal Rivolta (which was dropped
on after the Lele was launched), and
sed the same wheelbase.

Compared with its contemporary, the
dia, the Lele was an ultra-fast cruiser, a
al sporting coupé, radiating status and
performance image. In its styling it was
strange car, with rather sharply-
etailed lines, an overhanging prow,
rtly hooded headlamps, and – as be-
ame fashionable – a dropped waistline
yle aft of the windscreen pillars.

It was a very successful amalgam of
alian and American engineering, pro-
ding effortless performance (at
0 mph the engine was only running at a
tle over 3,000 rpm) with a comfortable
de matched to viceless handling

helped by the de Dion rear suspension.

In all 317 Leles were sold before Iso
production closed down in 1975, the last
cars having Ford V8 engines instead of
Chevrolets.

### Specification (1969)

**Engine:** V8, overhead-valve
**Bore × stroke:** 101.6 mm × 82.55 mm
**Capacity:** 5359 cc
**Maximum power:** 300 bhp
**Transmission:** four-speed manual
gearbox or automatic transmission,
rear-wheel drive
**Chassis:** separate steel platform
chassis frame
**Suspension:** independent front with
wishbones and coil springs; de Dion
rear axle with coil springs
**Brakes:** discs front and rear
**Bodywork:** steel two-door 2+2-seater
coupé by Bertone
**Maximum speed:** 132 mph (212 km/h)

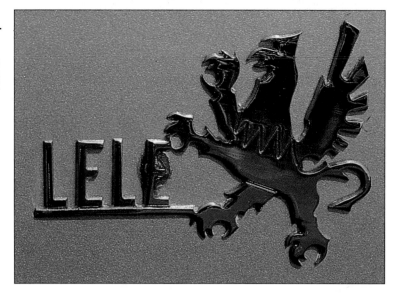

*Above: Perhaps as a reminder of its celebrated sibling, though it looked completely different, Iso's Lele coupé still bore a fierce-looking Grifo-type beast beside its nameplate.*

*Below: Don't be fooled by the rocker covers; all the big Isos had American V8s. There was a switch from GM to Ford, though, and this Lele had a 351-cu in Ford 'Cleveland' unit.*

*bove: A two-door 2+2-seater sports oupé, the Lele was, in effect, a eplacement for the original Iso ivolta, but it didn't sell in large umbers.*

*Below: With its strange detailing and a heavily-overhung, bustle-like rear end, the Lele was not one of Bertone's most impressive body designs.*

# Iso Grifo 90 1991

More than a decade after the previous generation of Iso Grifos and Rivoltas had died out, the marque reappeared unexpectedly. Previewed in 1991, the Grifo 90 was a totally new supercar that echoed the character of the old Grifo.

Like the old cars the Grifo 90 prototype was powered by a Chevrolet Corvette V8, this time extensively modified by the American Callaway company (which developed the Aston Martin Virage's quadcam V8) complete with turbocharging and backed by the massive ZF six-speed gearbox which was also used in the Corvette.

The new tubular-framed car was conceived by Pierro Rivolta and former general manager Pierro Sala in 1988. Two famous Italian consultants were responsible for the design – Gian Paolo Dallara for the chassis and running gear; Marcello Gandini for the striking two-seater coupé body. Significantly, they chose to produce a *front*-engined car, even though the car would have to compete against mid-engined cars like the revised Ferrari Testarossa and the Lamborghini Diablo.

The decision to make the Grifo 90 front-engined was a deliberate policy rather than just the easy way out. The old Grifo's fame had been in its being one of the most successful of Italian-American muscle car hybrids and it was that image that Pierro Rivolta (son of the company founder Renzo Rivolta, who had died back in 1966, leaving Pierro in charge) intended to preserve. The outstanding handling and performance of front-engined cars like the ZR-1 Corvette and

**Below: The Grifo 90 was the work of Countach designer Marcello Gandini, although changes required by Piero Rivolta were included in the finished prototype.**

**Above: The front-engined Grifo 90 has a drag coefficient of just 0.31, which should help produce a top speed of over 180 mph, given the 440 bhp produced from its Callaway-modified 5.7-litre V8.**

the Dodge Viper, or Panoz of the late 1990s had shown that there was no absolute need for all supercars to be mid-engined.

The Grifo 90's wide tracked rivalled that of a Ferrari Testarossa, at 63.5 inches for the front and 62 inches at the rear. That coupled with double-wishbone and coils spring suspension at the font, a four-link rear system and huge Pirelli P Zero tyres made the revived Iso very hard to unstick. The Grifo 90 had its fair share of modern technology despite its front-engine layout; self adjusting dampers were part of the package while traction control, not to mention Valeo's electronic clutch, would probably have been found on the production cars, scheduled to appear in 1993. Output was expected to be in the region of 200 per year, assuming potential buyers were not put off by the price being over the £100,000 mark, appreciably more than its most obvious rival, the XZR-1.

The new car was not fully developed when it was launched, but with a claimed top speed of 186 mph, and such respected engineers in the development team, it showed all the signs of being a great competitor in the Italian tradition. It never made it into production.

## Specification (1991 prototype)

**Engine:** V8, overhead-valve
**Bore × stroke:** 101.6 mm × 88.4 mm
**Capacity:** 5733 cc
**Maximum power:** 440 bhp
**Transmission:** six-speed manual gearbox, rear-wheel drive
**Chassis:** separate steel chassis frame with tubular main and bracing members
**Suspension:** independent with wishbones and coil springs front and rear
**Brakes:** discs front and rear
**Bodywork:** aluminium two-seater coupé
**Maximum speed (approx):** 186 mph (299 km/h)

# Isotta-Fraschini

Cesare Isotta and Vincenzo Fraschini first joined forces in Milan, Italy, in 1899 to import French cars. The first car built by them, launched a year later, was a thinly-disguised Renault.

The first totally Italian-designed Isotta-Fraschinis appeared in 1903 (following some already-proven Mercedes engine layouts), and before long the company was concentrating on making large and fast cars. By 1906 Isotta-Fraschini was already Italy's second-largest carmaker, behind Fiat. Lorraine-Dietrich took over in 1907, but two years later the company regained its independence.

In the pre-World War I era, Isotta-Fraschini had a rather different image from that which gained them fame in the 1920s as builders of large, almost always chauffeur-driven, luxury cars. In 1905 Isotta's brilliant engineer Giuseppe Stefanini was joined by Giustino Cattaneo. One of their first projects was Stefanini's Tipo D, a 100-bhp racer with a monstrous overhead-cam engine of 17203 cc, which competed in the 1905 Coppa Florio. In 1908 an Isotta-Fraschini actually won the Targa Florio (averaging 35.38 mph over the eight-hour race), driven by Vincenzo Trucco, with one of the Maserati brothers, Alfieri, as riding mechanic.

By the end of World War I Isotta-Fraschini not only held a fine reputation for building classy cars, but also for producing military machines, marine engines and aero engines. Prototypes of a completely new range of cars – the Tipo 8 – were assembled during the war, and from 1919 the company embarked on a confident 'one-model' policy, using a sturdy overhead-valve eight-cylinder engine. It was a policy that proved successful, at least until the 1930s.

The Tipo 8 was big, powerful and expensive, and was originally intended as a chauffeur-driven machine to match illustrious competition from Rolls-Royce and Hispano-Suiza. At first it was a little too ponderous to shape up, but after it was joined by the 8A and the 8ASS during the 1920s the marque's image improved even further.

However, after luxury car sales suffered during and after the Depression of the early 1930s, Isotta-Fraschini proposed a merger with Henry Ford in the USA. This alliance foundered, allowing the Tipo 8 family to die away, and the company then elected to concentrate on building aero engines before merging with the Caproni group in 1933.

After World War II Isotta-Fraschini attempted re-entry to the motor industry by designing the technically interesting rear-engined 8C Monterosa car, but a great many changes were needed between the prototype and the first production cars. Only a few 8Cs were actually sold before the factory was closed in 1949 by order of the Italian government, which controlled it. The name was then acquired by Breda, the armaments concern, but no further Isotta-Fraschini cars were produced.

*Above: Actor Rudolph Valentino (here with two-tone shoes) was a keen Isotta-Fraschini owner and gave the company an invaluable marketing edge in North America, where the cars sold well.*

*Left: Any one of a number of mascots could be mounted on the radiator caps of prestige cars like the Isotta-Fraschini. This one is from an 8A.*

*Below: Isotta-Fraschini's best-known model was the large and imposing Tipo 8, produced in the 1920s. This is a Farina-bodied 8A Torpedo from 1920 with a six-litre straight-eight engine.*

## Isotta-Fraschini Tipo 8 1919-35

The new Tipo 8, designed by Giustino Cattaneo, Isotta-Fraschini's long-time technical chief, had been developed during World War I, and went on sale in 1919, with the world's first series-production straight-eight engine. In many ways it was American in concept – not surprisingly, for Isotta-Fraschini had great sales ambitions for that continent. The Tipo 8 was a large and heavy car, with solid engineering, a very flexible power unit, and a three-speed gearbox with central change. The intention was for such cars to be almost exclusively chauffeur-driven.

Although it was neither as refined nor as fast as its more established competitors, the Tipo 8 sold well at first, with customers including Rudolph Valentino, actress Clara Bow, boxer Jack Dempsey, and newspaper tycoon William Randolph Hearst.

Later derivatives, with larger engines and more power, were more desirable, the 8A and 8ASS types being the best-known and (these days) the most sought-after models; these had a choice of 133-in or 145-in wheelbases, which ensured that they were stately and very heavy. Total production of all between-wars Isotta-Fraschinis was about 1,350, of which 950

were 8A types. The 8B came on the scene far too late to make an impression, and fewer than 30 were sold.

*Above: This rather staid and formal bodywork was typical wear for the Tipo 8 range.*

*Below: The 8ASS was the ultimate development of the 8; this one has superb convertible bodywork.*

### Isotta-Fraschini Tipo 8 variants

#### Isotta-Fraschini Tipo 8A and 8ASS

The Tipo 8A took over in 1925, with a 95-mm × 130-mm engine of 7372 cc and 110/120 bhp, servo-assisted brakes, and more suitable gear ratios. The similar-engined 8ASS followed, as a more specialised Hispano-matching sports version, this having 135 bhp and a claimed top speed of 104 mph.

#### Isotta-Fraschini Tipo 8B

The third-generation type was the 8B of 1931, which had a new and stiffer chassis, the same 135-bhp 7.4-litre engine, and (from 1932) the option of a Wilson four-speed preselector transmission. A four-speed synchromesh gearbox was standardised in 1934.

*Above: The Tipo 8's engine was a simple overhead-valve, long-stroke design giving 80 bhp.*

### Specification (1919 Tipo 8)

**Engine:** inline eight-cylinder, overhead-valve
**Bore × stroke:** 85 mm × 130 mm
**Capacity:** 5902 cc
**Maximum power:** 80 bhp
**Transmission:** three-speed manual gearbox, rear-wheel drive
**Chassis:** separate steel frame with channel-section side members
**Suspension:** non-independent with beam front axle and leaf springs; live rear axle with semi-elliptic leaf springs
**Brakes:** drums front and rear
**Bodywork:** steel on wood framing, open or closed; various four- or five-seater styles by coachbuilders
**Maximum speed (approx):** 70 mph (113 km/h)

## Isotta-Fraschini 8C Monterosa 1947-49

*Right: Isotta-Fraschini's last fling was quite unlike any of their previous cars. Under the Zagato-designed body was a rear-mounted three-litre V8, and the 8C also featured rubber suspension and pre-selector transmission.*

Isotta-Fraschini attempted a comeback in 1947 with the launch of the Tipo 8C Monterosa, designed by Fabio Rapi and Alessandro Baj. Once again, this was a fast car intended for sale to North American buyers, which explained its looks if not its technical layout.

The name Monterosa has allegorical connections, for Monterosa is the highest peak of the Alps between Italy and Switzerland – and Isotta-Fraschini wanted this car to be seen as the peak of automotive achievement.

There was absolutely no connection with previous Isotta-Fraschinis, or with any other Italian car, for in prototype form the Monterosa was a big six-seater with a steel platform chassis, a V8 engine mounted in the tail to drive the rear wheels, a preselector gearbox with overdrive, and rubber suspension. The radiators were also in the rear compartment. In many ways this was totally alien to the old Isotta-Fraschini image; consider, for instance, the public reaction

had Rolls-Royce attempted to introduce such a machine!

The body style (by Zagato) was long, smooth, but not quite graceful enough, with a touch of Rolls-Royce or Mercedes-Benz in the front grille area, and Lancia Aprilia/Alfa Romeo – or even Tatra – about the tail.

Although the new car looked dramatic, and technically fascinating, it had to be considerably redesigned before sales began; the engine was enlarged from 2.5 litres to 3.0 litres (and the 103-bhp peak improved to 115 bhp), a front-mounted radiator became necessary, and the rubber-suspension layout was

abandoned in favour of coil springs.

The handling was reported to be remarkably neutral, and the top speed was supposedly over 100 mph, but we will never know if the Americans would have warmed to this esoteric design, as the Italian government pulled the plug on the project in 1949, closing the state-owned business, and transferring it to the Breda armaments combine.

The Americans, in fact, were very conservative buyers at this stage (as the fate of the advanced Tucker Torpedo illustrated) so the rear-engined Isotta-Fraschini might have had a very difficult task if the company had persevered.

### Specification (1947)

**Engine:** V8, overhead-valve
**Bore × stroke:** 78 mm × 78 mm
**Capacity:** 2982 cc
**Maximum power:** 115 bhp
**Transmission:** four-speed preselector gearbox with overdrive, rear-wheel drive
**Chassis:** steel platform chassis, with body welded in place
**Suspension:** independent with coil springs front and rear
**Brakes:** drums front and rear
**Bodywork:** steel four-seater saloon
**Maximum speed (approx):** 100 mph (161 km/h)

# Itala

**A**fter leaving the Ceirano carmaking company, which he had founded in Turin in 1901, Matteo Ceirano joined forces with Guido Bigio to set up Itala in 1904. The restless Ceirano only stayed with his new enterprise until 1906, however, leaving his partner to run the business until he died in 1913.

Early Italas followed the latest fashion for sporty cars, which had been set by Mercedes of Germany. This meant that rather flexible chassis were given impressive and sporty coachwork, powered by a selection of large-capacity, low-revving four- or six-cylinder engines.

Itala soon established its reputation around Europe, not only with competition success, but with Royal patronage, and – most notably of all – by the amazing drive by Prince Scipione Borghese to win the Peking-Paris marathon of 1907. The Prince drove a four-cylinder Itala over the 8,000-mile course, during which it proved totally reliable and left the de Dion and Spyker opposition well behind.

The biggest Italas of all were the six-cylinder 11.1-litre and 12.9-litre models introduced in 1908; these sold well enough for Itala to report an annual production total of 720 cars in 1911. The 'big is beautiful' philosophy was not always a success, however, for Itala's attempts to produce Hispano-Suiza aeroplane engines for use by the Italian air force during World War I ended in failure.

In the 1920s Itala's fortunes stagnated for a time, as motorists were no longer interested in buying old-fashioned, large-engined, cars. A change of policy then led to ex-Fiat engineer G. C. Cappa being hired to develop new, smaller-engined, machines.

The result, unveiled in 1924, was the completely new Tipo 61, which had a two-litre six-cylinder engine, and this model kept Itala rather tenuously afloat for a few years. Financial problems persisted, however, and eventually the state-owned IRI concern (the Reconstruction Finance Corporation, which also controlled Alfa Romeo's destiny) stepped in to shore up the business.

Despite this help, Itala's fortunes fell away, and attempts to redesign and improve the Tipo 61, into the Tipo 65 and finally the Tipo 75, were failures. The last Itala of all was produced in 1934, after which the business was closed down.

The remnants of the company were absorbed by Fiat in 1935, but Fiat never revived the Itala name.

*Above and below: Itala made its name producing huge-engined racers like this 1907 example, with a massive 16.7-litre engine producing 120 bhp.*

## Itala 35/40HP (Peking-Paris) 1907

In 1907 the French newspaper *Le Matin* laid down a challenge to Europe's emerging motor industry. It enquired, in large letters: "Will anyone agree to go this summer from Peking to Paris by motor car?" That's a fairly major undertaking in the 1990s, let alone the first decade of the century, and the winning car was a truly exceptional machine.

It was a 35/40HP Itala built specifically for Prince Scipione Borghese and suitably modified for the epic journey. It was powered by a large, 7.4-litre, four-cylinder engine featuring cylinders cast in pairs and a bore and stroke of 130 mm × 140 mm. The valves were symmetrical and thus interchangeable, ignition was by low-tension magneto, and the engine was designed to run on the lowest grade of fuel. Surprisingly to modern eyes, the transmission used a four-speed manual gearbox and a disc clutch (replaced in Moscow . . .). Despite its projected journey across huge tracts of roadless desert heavily loaded, the Itala set off with just the standard radiator and cooling system but did not suffer from overheating.

The suspension was typical of the time, being two beam axles located and sprung by semi-elliptic leaf springs. Broken springs (and spokes) were some of the very few problems this extraordinarily tough car suffered during thousands of miles from Peking, through Mongolia and the Gobi desert, Russia and eastern Europe. At the end of the trip, the engine was still in good condition and the gearbox found to have "not the slightest trace of wear". Even the tyres, made specially for the trip by Pirelli in a larger size and flatter profile than normal, stood up well to the journey, lasting around 2,500 miles each.

The success of the Peking-Paris car did wonders for the company's reputation, and the basically similar models produced in the next few years were quite popular. The year after the Peking-Paris marathon, Itala introduced the 12.9-litre model. The main differences were the six- rather than four-cylinder engine and a longer-wheelbase chassis. No dampers were fitted (requiring the springs to be very stiff, to prevent the car from permanently oscillating as it went down the road) and there were brakes only on the rear wheels and transmission, confusingly controlled by separate pedals. The usual bodywork was almost as spartan as that of the Peking-Paris car, and in most cases proved just as durable.

### Itala 35/40HP variants

#### Itala 11.1-litre
The 11.1-litre used the same chassis and running gear as the 12.9-litre but had a smaller-displacement version of the six-cylinder engine.

### Specification (1908 12.9-litre)
**Engine:** inline six-cylinder, side-valve
**Bore × stroke:** 140 mm × 140 mm
**Capacity:** 12930 cc
**Maximum power:** 75 bhp
**Transmission:** four-speed manual gearbox, rear-wheel drive
**Chassis:** separate steel frame with channel-section and side members
**Suspension:** non-independent with beam front axle and leaf springs; live rear axle with semi-elliptic leaf springs; no dampers front or rear
**Brakes:** drums on transmission and rear wheels
**Bodywork:** various styles by coachbuilders
**Maximum speed (approx):** 70 mph (113 km/h)

*Above: The Mandarin governor of Urga enjoys a ride in the 7.4-litre Itala (the first car he had ever seen) during the Peking-Paris epic of 1907. The short trip frightened his escort, who thought he was being kidnapped!*

*Below: A determined C. Clutten drives his 1908 12-litre six-cylinder side-valve Itala around Silverstone in 1961. Its considerable power and weight were restrained by only rear-wheel and transmission brakes.*

## Itala Tipo 61 1924-32

*Right: The Itala Tipo 61 was virtually the end of the line for Itala. With features like an aluminium-alloy cylinder head, overhead valves and four-wheel brakes, it was far more advanced than Itala's pre-war monsters, but sales were disappointing, ending in 1932.*

To revive the company's fortunes after World War I, Itala hired Fiat's G. C. Cappa to design an all-new car – one which would be more appropriately sized and engineered to meet 1920s fashions. The result was the Tipo 61, a range which persisted to the end of Itala production in the 1930s.

The Tipo 61 was a conventional two-litre machine with not only a smooth seven-bearing engine, but also an aluminium cylinder block with overhead valves. By this time, too, there were four-wheel brakes and the advanced feature of torque-tube drive from the gearbox to the rear wheels.

From 1926, the Tipo 61 was fitted with a friction-drive brake servo, which made it the technical equal of the large and exquisitely engineered Hispano-Suiza and Rolls-Royce cars of the day.

The Tipo 61 was a handsome, though rather lofty, touring car in the best Italian traditions of the day, but sales were never sufficient to make Itala profitable. Not even the twin-cam Tipo 65 sports car which followed, nor the 'last-gasp' 2.3-litre Tipo 75, could do that.

### Itala Tipo 61 variants

### Itala Tipo 65
The Tipo 65 of 1928-1930 was a more sporting derivative, using a twin-overhead-camshaft version of the two-litre Tipo 61 engine, and had a new chassis frame in which the rear axle tubes passed through the chassis-frame side members. More than 80 mph was claimed for this technically interesting car; 150 Tipo 65s were built.

### Itala Tipo 75
The Tipo 75 of 1932 was a revised version of the Tipo 61, this time with a long-stroke 2309-cc/70-bhp version of the pushrod engine. This was the last Itala of all.

### Specification (1924)
**Engine:** inline six-cylinder, overhead-valve
**Bore × stroke:** 65 mm × 100 mm
**Capacity:** 1991 cc

**Transmission:** four-speed manual gearbox, rear-wheel drive
**Chassis:** separate steel frame with channel-section main side members
**Suspension:** non-independent with front beam axle and leaf springs; live rear axle with semi-elliptic leaf springs
**Brakes:** drums front and rear
**Bodywork:** various styles by coachbuilders
**Maximum speed (approx):** 60 mph (97 km/h)

# Jaguar Cars Ltd

**A**lthough the first Jaguar-badged car was not built until 1945, the company's origins stretch back into the 1920s, to Blackpool, and to a small motorcycle sidecar business.

In the beginning a small business owned by William Lyons and William Walmsley produced Swallow sidecars, but special bodies for cars soon followed, and the company then moved to Coventry. The first SS car came along in 1931, and there was a new range of cars called SS-Jaguars in 1935. All were personally styled by Lyons himself.

William Walmsley left the company in 1935, and SS Cars 'went public' in the same year. William Lyons then continued as the majority shareholder until he retired in 1972.

The 'SS' part of the title was dropped in 1945 (by that time the initials suggested Hitler's wartime forces rather than a car company), and all cars have been Jaguars since then. The company, which had settled in Foleshill, Coventry, in 1929, needed a larger factory in the 1950s, and took over an old ex-government 'shadow factory' in 1951-52. This was the famous Browns Lane, Allesley, plant which is still company headquarters.

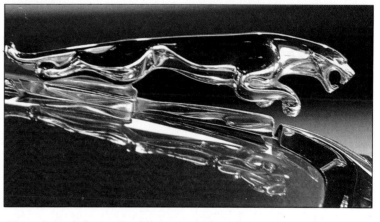

*Above: Jaguar's famous leaping cat mascot has all the elegance that Jaguar's Sir William Lyons gave to his cars in the 1950s and 1960s.*

*Above and right: Before World War II Jaguar were known as SS Cars; that changed after the war. The most famed pre-war model was the SS100.*

Jaguar's post-war reputation grew rapidly on the back of the cars' styling, the modern twin-cam XK engine, and excellent sports models like the XK120. By the mid-1950s Jaguar had also built the C-type and D-type racing-sports cars, which won the Le Mans 24 Hours no fewer than five times in seven years.

In the 1960s the company expanded rapidly, by taking over other concerns, and the model range grew complex. The company itself absorbed Daimler in 1960, and Coventry Climax in 1963, along with Henry Meadows and Guy Motors.

The original monocoque 2.4-litre saloon eventually spawned the famous Mk II types, the S-types and the 420, while Jaguar also found time to produce the sensational E-type sports car and the gargantuan Mk X saloon. Along the way, annual production soared from 10,000 in 1955 to 25,000 by the mid-1960s.

Sir William Lyons (knighted in the 1950s) sold out to BMC in 1966, which meant that Jaguar became a part of British Leyland in 1968. The ultra-refined XJ6 model was launched in 1968, and the magnificent V12 engine followed in 1971. Production leapt to 32,500 in the early 1970s, but after that the company became embroiled in the British Leyland tragedy, with quality and company image sagging alarmingly.

Jaguar, therefore, became part of a state-owned company from 1975, and for a time its future looked to be very bleak indeed, but once Sir Michael Edwardes arrived as BL's chairman a more logical approach to business followed.

Things improved in the 1980s, with the arrival of Sir John Egan as a dynamic new chairman, with a new six-cylinder AJ6 engine

*Above: Perhaps the most famous of all Jaguars, the E-type offered an unrivalled combination of 150-mph performance and value for money.*

coming onstream in 1973, and with Jaguar being 'privatised' again in 1984. A new generation XJ6 saloon was launched in 1986, but the company once again struck financial difficulties and was taken over by Ford in 1989. This had the desired effect of placing Jaguar on a secure footing, enabling it to launch the V8-engined XJ series, the all new XK8 sports car and the S-type saloon in the late 1990s.

*Below: With the XJ220 going on limited sale in 1992, Jaguar entered the supercar market with the world's fastest production car. Just 350 were made.*

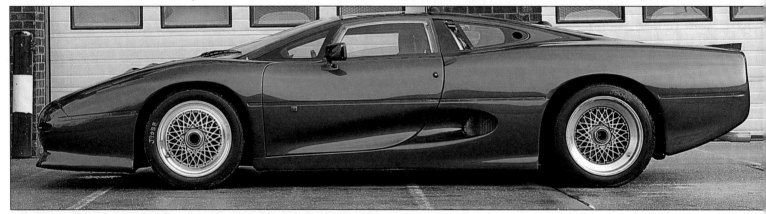

# Jaguar Mk V 1949-51

If Pressed Steel had not quoted such a long time to prepare the tooling of the new Mk VII's body shell, the Mk V might never have been produced. It was an interim model, Jaguar's first post-war design, and was produced in a great hurry, to link Jaguar's pre-war styling with the all-new cars yet to come.

The Mk V used a new chassis frame, complete with torsion-bar independent front suspension on a 120-in wheelbase, which had been designed for use in the

Mk VII. Instead of the new twin-cam engine, however, it used developed versions of the pushrod 2½-litre and 3½-litre six-cylinder units which SS-Jaguar had developed in the late 1930s.

To clothe this running gear, William Lyons styled two shells – one a four-door saloon, the other a two-door drop-head coupé – which were intriguing updates of the SS-Jaguar theme, still with partly-exposed headlamps, and with every traditional SS-Jaguar styling 'cue', including

the flowing wing lines and the tiny sausage-shaped rear window. The cars were wider, more roomy and subtly squatter than before, but the links with the past were still evident.

In its habits, too, the Mk V was an interim creation, for it combined pre-war elegance with modern ride and handling, as the chassis was a close relation of that produced for the sensational new XK120 sports car. On the one hand the Mk V could be cruised at 80 mph, and on

the other it had a very sedate middle class character, with the interior even smelling of 'club-land'.

The Mk V was in production for only 2 months, but in that time 9,492 saloons and 1,001 drop-head coupés were produced. More than 80 per cent of these cars used the larger 3½-litre engine.

## Specification (1949)

**Engine:** inline six-cylinder, overhead-valve
**Bore × stroke:** 82 mm × 110 mm
**Capacity:** 3485 cc
**Maximum power:** 125 bhp
**Transmission:** four-speed manual gearbox, rear-wheel drive
**Chassis:** separate steel frame with box section side members
**Suspension:** independent front with wishbones and torsion bars; live rear axle with semi-elliptic leaf springs
**Brakes:** drums front and rear
**Bodywork:** steel four-door/five-seater saloon, plus wood-and-steel two-door drop-head coupé
**Maximum speed (approx):** 91 mph (146 km/h)

*Left: Jaguar's first post-war model, the 125-bhp 3.5-litre Mk V, was a slightly uneasy blend of pre- and post-war design.*

## SS100 1936-39

*Above: One of the last, this 1939 SS100 had a 3.5-litre six. By that time the model had proved its potential in races and rallies.*

Although the public never took to the short-lived SS90 of 1935, with its short-wheelbase version of the SS1 chassis and side-valve engine, the SS100 which followed it was a different matter. Between 1936 and 1939 this two-seater sports car was enormously popular.

Although it used the same basic body shell as the SS90, the SS100 was given a brand-new chassis, which was effectively a shorter-wheelbase version of that developed for the new SS-Jaguar saloon car range. Like its predecessors, it had beam axles front and rear, hard springing, and heavy steering.

Compared with almost any other British sports car of the period, the SS100 offered remarkable value for money. Even in its original form, with a 102-bhp 2.7-litre overhead-valve engine, the new car could exceed 90 mph. This in itself was not remarkable for the period, but the price – a mere £395 – most certainly was.

The SS100 had rakish styling, which featured long, sweeping front wings and a compact (some would say cramped) cockpit. It looked every inch the fast sports car it undoubtedly was. Naturally the styling was by William Lyons himself.

There were many different reactions to the SS100. The most vocal, which was encouraged by rival manufacturers who had a lot to lose, was that this was a vulgar new model made by a company which had no experience or tradition of building sports cars. Good performances in sprints and rallies soon put a stop to *that* attitude. The SS100 was good enough for Ian Appleyard to win the first of several Coupe des Alpes in the post-war Alpine Rally.

Another, more favourable, reaction was to treat the SS100 as a real sports car breakthrough, representing excellent performance value for money. Certainly when the 3½-litre version arrived, priced at £445, with an engine which had 125 bhp and which propelled the car at 100 mph, there were absolutely no complaints about its speed.

At this time, though, the SS-Jaguar marque was still struggling to throw off its undeserved "Jew's Bentley" label, so the SS100 never sold as well as its performance suggested it might. Even so, it was such an exciting-looking car that survivors became enormously valuable in later years.

Production of SS100s ended just before war broke out in 1939, by which time 198 2½-litre types and 116 3½-litre versions had been produced. Only 49 of these cars were exported – and all of those had right-hand drive.

*Above: The cockpit was not spacious, but SS100 buyers had other priorities. Note the optional aero screens (left), which marginally increased top speed – and the sensation of it.*

*Above: The car's high power-to-weight ratio and low centre of gravity gave superb performance.*

### Specification (1936)

**Engine:** inline six-cylinder, overhead-valve
**Bore × stroke:** 73 mm × 106 mm
**Capacity:** 2664 cc
**Maximum power:** 102 bhp
**Transmission:** four-speed manual gearbox, rear-wheel drive
**Chassis:** separate steel frame with channel-section main side members
**Suspension:** non-independent with beam axle and semi-elliptic leaf springs front; live axle with semi-elliptic leaf springs rear
**Brakes:** drums all round
**Bodywork:** wooden-framed aluminium two-seater open sports
**Maximum speed (approx):** 92 mph (148 km/h)

## Jaguar XK120 1949-54

It is amazing, but true, to recall that although the XK120 was designed as a short-term project it, along with its descendants, became successful the world over during a production life of 12 years.

The original XK120 model was hastily produced in 1948 on a shortened version of the MK V's chassis, to provide a showcase, and a mobile test-bed, for the brand-new range of XK twin-cam engines. At first Jaguar intended to produce two versions of the car, but the two-litre four-cylinder engine (for the 'XK100' model) never went into production.

By the standards of 1948, the XK120 was a huge leap into the future. Not only was it beautiful, but it was also very fast, it had the world's first production twin-cam engine, and it offered remarkable value for money. Today, of course, we might laugh at its heavy steering and dodgy brakes, but in its day it was an accomplished race and rally car.

That was helped by the front suspension design, which was a wishbone and torsion-bar affair, rather more modern than the traditional cart-sprung rear axle with which the XK120 was fitted. Its motor racing success started in 1950 with a win in the Tourist Trophy in Northern Ireland and very nearly a victory in the Le Mans 24 Hours. In 1951 it did win the RAC Rally (a less demanding affair then than today) and repeated the feat in 1953.

The first 240 production cars had wooden-framed bodies with aluminium panelling, and deliveries began in mid-1949, but a completely tooled all-steel body followed in 1950, after which production accelerated rapidly. Because of its remarkable looks and performance, the XK120 was a huge success in the USA, even though it was soon found to overheat in hot climates and heavy traffic.

XK120s were heavy to drive and had cramped cockpits, but like all other Jaguar sports cars they had enormous character and great sensual appeal. In five production years a total of 12,078 cars was built, of which nearly 8,000 were two-seater open Roadsters.

*Above: Inspiration for the XK120 came from BMW's 328; compare this picture with that on page 1087.*

### Jaguar XK120 variants

### Jaguar XK120 Fixed Head Coupé
This was produced between 1951 and 1954 and featured a very elegant, rounded hard top incorporated into the design. In right-hand-drive form it was the rarest of all the XK120s, with fewer than 200 being built.

### Jaguar XK120 Drophead Coupé
In addition to the original Roadster which was intended to be an open car and nothing more, Jaguar introduced a Drophead version which had a hood to give all-weather motoring. The Drophead was introduced in 1953 and ran until 1954.

### Jaguar XK120 SE
The SE stood for Special Equipment, the main ingredient of which was the more powerful engine, which had higher-lift cams and a lighter flywheel to produce 180 bhp rather than the 160 bhp of the standard engine.

### Specification (1949)
**Engine:** inline six-cylinder, twin-cam
**Bore × stroke:** 83 mm × 106 mm
**Capacity:** 3442 cc
**Maximum power:** 160 bhp
**Transmission:** four-speed manual, rear-wheel drive
**Chassis:** steel ladder-type frame with cross-members
**Suspension:** independent front with wishbones and torsion bars; live rear axle with semi-elliptic leaf springs and lever-arm dampers
**Brakes:** drums front and rear
**Bodywork:** wood-framed aluminium two-seater, followed by choice of steel Roadster, Fixed Head Coupé or Drophead Coupé
**Maximum speed (approx):** 120 mph (193 km/h)

*Above: The XK120 was produced as an open car, but the Fixed Head Coupé showed how successfully a roof could be incorporated.*

*Below: The Roadster was the first and most popular of the XK120 range, even though there was no provison for a convertible roof.*

# Jaguar XK140 1954-57

Jaguar could have got away with not changing the XK120's name to XK140, as the later car was merely a straightforward evolution of the later mostly-steel-bodied XK120. In fact the car was initially known at the factory as the XK120 Mk 4. The most significant difference was that the engine was moved forward by three inches. Jaguar thought it acceptable to trade off the adverse change in weight distribution (the straight-six XK engine was a heavy unit) for much-needed extra cabin room, and the improved leg room was much appreciated. The rear was re-modelled with a shorter boot lid and there were detail changes such as heavier bumpers front and rear (the XK120 had started out with just overriders at the rear), which was a reflection on the fact that the majority of cars were sold in the American market. In addition the rear lights were made larger and the front grille was a heavier design.

There were mechanical changes to complement the cosmetic alterations, and the major differences in this area were the switch to the more precise rack-and-pinion-type steering and the replacement of the original XK120's lever-arm dampers by the more modern telescopic variety. To help make up for the more heavily front-biased weight distribution, the XK140 was fitted with the uprated front torsion bars used on the Special Equipment version of the XK120. Another SE feature transferred to the XK140 was the uprated, 180-bhp, version of the twin-cam six-cylinder engine required to maintain performance.

## Jaguar XK140 variants

### Jaguar XK140 Fixed Head Coupé

In contrast to the XK120 range, there was a closed version of the XK140 throughout XK140 production; its greater cabin room compared with the XK120 Fixed Head was one of its main attractions.

*Above: The XK140's engine was further forward than the XK120's, but this does not show in a side view.*

### Jaguar XK140 Drophead Coupé

The Drophead differed from the standard Roadster (which was only tonneau-cover-equipped) in being more civilised, having a convertible roof and wind-up windows.

## Specification (1954)

**Engine:** inline six-cylinder, twin-cam
**Bore × stroke:** 83 mm × 106 mm
**Capacity:** 3442 cc
**Maximum power:** 180 bhp
**Transmission:** four-speed manual with optional overdrive, rear-wheel drive
**Chassis:** separate steel frame with box-section side members
**Suspension:** independent front with wishbones and torsion bars; live rear axle with semi-elliptic leaf springs and telescopic dampers
**Brakes:** drums front and rear
**Bodywork:** alloy and steel-bodied Roadster, Fixed Head Coupé or Drophead Coupé
**Maximum speed:** 120 mph (193 km/h)

*Above: The deeper front bumper was one of the main ways of distinguishing the XK140 from the XK120.*

*Below: By the time of the XK140, UK sales required the Fixed Head Coupé to be a permanent part of the range.*

# Jaguar XK150 1957-61

The XK150 is somewhat overshadowed these days for a couple of reasons; it was the end of the XK line and was regarded for a long time as being almost a corruption of that design. It was replaced by one of the most famous of all sports cars, the E-type, which made it look rather old-fashioned.

In truth, by the time it was introduced it *was* an old-fashioned design, but some very worthwhile improvements had been made to keep it competitive. Chief among these was the change to disc brakes, fitted on all four wheels. That was a fundamental difference, but the cosmetic changes were more immediately obvious. The low door line of the XK120 and XK140 had been discarded in favour of a high-waisted look which made the car look, to some, heavier and clumsier. The radiator grille was also considerably wider.

Mechanically, the disc brakes were the main change, although a larger, 3.8-litre, version of the XK engine was later fitted.

On the Fixed Head Coupé, Jaguar

opted for a far larger cabin which made the car look like the company's 1960s' saloons, particularly as by this time the XK had been given a modern wraparound, curved windscreen rather than the 'V' arrangement of the early cars. It was outsold by the Drophead Coupé and

75 per cent of production was exported, making the Fixed Head a very rare sight in Britain.

## Jaguar XK150 variants

### Jaguar XK150S
The final flourish of the XK line was the XK150S, introduced in 1958; The 'S' model was available with either the 3.4-litre or 3.8-litre engine. In both cases, power was increased over the standard engine, to 250 or 265 bhp.

*Left: The XK150 was the last and the most luxurious of the range, but in its final XK150S form it was also very fast indeed, capable of 135 mph.*

*Below: The wider grille, curved windscreen and the far higher door line are the most obvious features distinguishing the XK150 from the earlier XK140 and XK120.*

*Above: The XK150 was heavier than its predecessors but had the advantage of disc brakes, which Jaguar had developed on its Le Mans-winning C- and D-types.*

## Specification (1958 XK150S)

**Engine:** inline six-cylinder, twin-cam
**Bore × stroke:** 87 mm × 106 mm
**Capacity:** 3781 cc
**Maximum power:** 265 bhp
**Transmission:** four-speed manual with optional overdrive, rear-wheel drive
**Chassis:** separate steel frame with box-section side members
**Suspension:** independent front with wishbones and torsion bars; live rear axle with semi-elliptic leaf springs and telescopic dampers
**Brakes:** discs front and rear
**Bodywork:** steel Roadster, Fixed Head Coupé or Drophead Coupé
**Maximum speed (approx):** 135 mph (217 km/h)

# Jaguar Mk VII 1950-61

The Mk VII was the first all-new Jaguar saloon, for it combined the new Mk V-type chassis, the XK twin-cam engine from the XK120, and a massive brand-new four-door saloon shell supplied by Pressed Steel from Cowley.

If Pressed Steel could have completed body tooling earlier, the Mk VII might never have been put on sale. As it was, the Mk VII was a direct replacement for the 'interim' Mk V model, and in one form or another it was to be built for more than 10 years.

Although it was a large and heavy car – the first cars were 196.5 inches long, and weighed nearly 3,900 lb – the Mk VII was also very fast. Because it had the same basic chassis and suspension as the XK120 it handled well, and because its body style was much more aerodynamic than that of the Mk V it had a top speed of more than 100 mph. Very few British saloon cars could reach such speeds, and like all other Jaguars of the day the Mk VII was remarkably cheap at £1,693 when introduced.

The appeal of the Mk VII was not only in its performance, and its style, but in the quality of the interior, which featured leather seat facings, wood on the fascia and the cappings of the doors, and exuded a general 'club-land' aura and atmosphere.

Over the years the specification was consistently improved, and the choices expanded: Borg-Warner automatic transmission became optional in 1953, Laycock de Normanville overdrive in 1954, extra power (as the Mk VIIM) for 1955, while the better-equipped Mk VIII and Mk IX models followed up in the late 1950s.

It was, however, the last 'separate-chassis' Jaguar to remain on sale; its successor, the Mk X of 1961, was an even larger, unit-construction, model. Total production of all types in 10 years was 46,537, of which 20,939 were Mk VIIs.

*Below: With the 3.4-litre straight-six XK engine producing 160 bhp, the Mk VII could reach a top speed of 102 mph.*

## Jaguar Mk VII variants

### Jaguar Mk VIIM

This development of the original Mk VII was made from 1954 to 1957. The engine produced 190 bhp, and detail style changes included relocated fog lamps and larger wrap-around bumpers. Total production was 9,261.

### Jaguar Mk VIII

This was a further development on the Mk VII theme, produced from 1956 to 1959, eventually replacing the Mk VIIM. Power was once again increased, to 210 bhp, and there was a one-piece screen instead of the 'V'-type, as well as optional duo-tone colour schemes. Total production was 6,332.

*Above: The Mk VII was one of the most stately cars Jaguar ever built, and the last to be constructed on the traditional separate chassis. Despite its bulk and width, it had elements of the XK120's styling in the line of the front and rear wings. It also shared much of the mechanical specification of the XK range, including the chassis and suspension.*

### Jaguar Mk IX

The final derivative of the Mk VII was produced from 1958 to 1961. This car had an 87-mm × 106-mm, 3781-cc engine, producing 220 bhp, with four-wheel disc brakes and power-assisted steering. Top speed was 114 mph. Total production was 10,005.

## Specification (1951)

**Engine:** inline six-cylinder, twin-cam
**Bore × stroke:** 83 mm × 106 mm
**Capacity:** 3442 cc
**Maximum power:** 160 bhp
**Transmission:** four-speed manual gearbox with optional overdrive, or three-speed automatic transmission; rear-wheel drive
**Chassis:** separate steel frame with box-section side members
**Suspension:** independent front with wishbones and torsion bars; live rear axle with semi-elliptic leaf springs
**Brakes:** drums front and rear
**Bodywork:** steel four-door five-seater saloon
**Maximum speed (approx):** 102 mph (164 km/h)

## Jaguar C-type 1952-53

Having dabbled with a motor racing programme in 1950, Jaguar then designed a special racing two-seater for the 1951 Le Mans 24 Hours. Because its engine and transmission were based on those of the XK120, it was originally called XK120C (C for Competition), but enthusiasts soon began calling it the 'C-type', and the name stuck.

The new car had a multi-tubular chassis frame, and a body shell shaped with aerodynamic drag reduction in mind, and although there *were* two seats, that on the passenger side was really only fitted to satisfy the regulations. Jaguar built three prototypes in 1951, and amazed the world by winning Le Mans first time out, at an average speed of 93.49 mph.

A limited run of 'production' C-types was then laid down, and deliveries began in 1952. Most of the cars were used by private owners to go motor racing, but a few were used on public roads, where they provided supremely fast, if spartan, transport. In those days racing-sports cars were not as specialised as they became in the 1960s, which meant that C-type motoring was entirely practical provided that the occupants wrapped up well (there was no weather protection of any kind, not even a full-width windscreen) and did not attempt to carry any luggage!

The roadgoing C-type, with 200 bhp, was a remarkably flexible machine, with supple suspension but very little trim and 'comfort equipment', which could nevertheless exceed 140 mph (a remarkable speed for the early 1950s) with ease. The final works cars of 1953, with more power (up to 220 bhp) and featuring disc brakes, were altogether fiercer machines.

The C-type's first Le Mans victory came in 1951 when the Whitehead/Walker driving partnership overcame the second-placed Talbot Lago and the Aston Martin DB2 of Macklin and Thompson. Jaguar repeated the feat in 1953 when the C-types of Rolt/Hamilton and Moss/Walker were first and second, ahead of an American Cunningham.

All in all, including works competition cars, a total of 54 C-types was produced, the last being a rebodied example which Norman Dewis drove at 180 mph in Belgium in 1953.

*Above: With a top speed of over 140 mph, the C-type was an immediate winner on the racetrack.*

*Below: The rear wheels stay upright, indicating that the C-type used a live rear axle, like the XK120.*

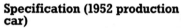

*Above: The C-type was the racing version of the XK120; it used the XK120's mechanical components but in a new tubular steel chassis and with aerodynamic alloy bodywork. Production cars were built the year after the prototype C-type won the Le Mans 24 Hours at its first attempt, averaging 93.49 mph.*

### Specification (1952 production car)

**Engine:** inline six-cylinder, twin-cam
**Bore × stroke:** 83 mm × 106 mm
**Capacity:** 3442 cc
**Maximum power:** 200/210 bhp
**Transmission:** four-speed manual gearbox, rear-wheel drive
**Chassis:** separate steel multi-tubular frame
**Suspension:** independent front with wishbones and torsion bars; live rear axle with 'A' frame, transverse torsion bars and telescopic dampers
**Brakes:** drums front and rear
**Bodywork:** aluminium two-seater open sports-racing car
**Maximum speed (approx):** 143 mph (230 km/h)

# Jaguar D-type 1955-57

To succeed the C-type as a racing-sports car, Jaguar designed the D-type, whose sensual lines later provided the inspiration for the E-type. Like the C-type, the D-type used a much-modified XK engine and front suspension, but almost everything else (including an all-synchromesh gearbox) was specially designed.

Not only did the car have a smooth and wind-cheating shape, with a headrest behind the driver's position, but it had a light-alloy central monocoque which was allied to a complex multi-tubular front frame. The so-called two-seater cockpit was really two single-seat cocoons separated by a body panel, for this was even less of a road car than the C-type had been.

The new D-type narrowly failed to win at Le Mans in 1954, but then succeeded in 1955, 1956 and 1957. As with the C-type, Jaguar then laid down a production run of 'customer' D-types, some of which were actually used on the road. Compared with the C-types, these were still faster, but even less practical, yet could be (and often were) driven to and from race meetings all round the world.

When D-type sales stalled at the end of 1956, Jaguar produced the XKSS, which was ostensibly a road-equipped version of the D-type, but with the same running gear. The XKSS had a full-width screen, a second passenger door, a luggage rack and boot lid and a folding soft top – but it was really still a racing car.

Works D-types were raced with various specifications, including 3.4-litre or 3.8-litre engines, different cylinder heads with fuel injection, and featuring de Dion rear suspension. For 1955 and 1956 the works cars had lengthened noses and modified styling behind the driver's head.

By the time the last car of all was delivered, Jaguar had built 20 works or works-blessed D-types, while a total of 43 D-type and 16 XKSS production cars had also been delivered. In almost every way, the E-type was a spiritual successor to the XKSS.

*Above: Jaguar's roadgoing version of the D-type was the XKSS.*

### Jaguar XKSS

This was a 'road car' version of the production D-type fitted with a second door, a full-width windscreen and a fold-back soft top, plus small bumpers. Only 16 were produced due to a fire at the factory; Jaguar threw all its resources into rebuilding the factory.

## Specification (1955 production car)

**Engine:** inline six-cylinder, twin-cam
**Bore × stroke:** 83 mm × 106 mm
**Capacity:** 3442 cc
**Maximum power:** 250 bhp
**Transmission:** four-speed manual gearbox, rear-wheel drive
**Chassis:** separate steel multi-tubular front frame, bolted to aluminium monocoque centre section
**Suspension:** independent front with wishbones and torsion bars; live rear axle with torsion bars and telescopic dampers
**Brakes:** discs front and rear
**Bodywork:** aluminium two-seater open sports-racing car
**Maximum speed (approx):** 138 mph (222 km/h) with standard axle ratio

*Above: The D-type's aerodynamics were the work of Malcolm Sayer and, given the right axle ratio, made the car very fast, capable of 180 mph.*

*Below: The rear fin was not there just for show; it did improve directional stability on fast tracks such as the long Le Mans circuit.*

# Jaguar 2.4-litre and Jaguar Mk II 1955-69

In 1955 Jaguar's new 2.4-litre saloon started several trends for the Coventry-based company. It was the first 'small' Jaguar to be designed in the post-war years, the first to use a smaller version of the XK engine, and the first to have a unit-construction body shell.

The 2.4 was designed to sell alongside the Mk VIIM and XK140 models, as a smaller and lower-priced car than the big saloon. Although styled by Sir William Lyons, it had rather a 'plain-Jane' reputation, for the looks were not helped by the rather thick windscreen and door pillars, and by the narrow-tracked tail, which hid a live rear axle.

The 2.4 only had 112 bhp, and struggled to reach 100 mph, but its sister car, the 3.4, which was launched in 1957, was a different proposition, with its 120-mph top speed and flashing acceleration.

this was nothing new for British cars of the 1960s.

The design was so successful, in fact, that it was used as the basis for the later S-type and 420 derivatives, with the last of all these types not built until 1969.

*Right: The 2.4-litre Jaguar of 1955 set a style for Jaguar saloons that lasted until the late 1960s.*

### Jaguar 2.4-litre variants

### Jaguar 3.4-litre
This larger-engined car was produced from 1957 to 1959. The engine was of the Mk VIII/XK150 type, with a displacement of 3442 cc and a maximum power output of 210 bhp. The grille was wider, to allow extra air into the radiator. Top speed was 120 mph.

### Jaguar Mk II variants

### Jaguar 2.4-litre Mk II
This had an 83-mm × 76.5-mm, 2483-cc/120-bhp engine. Its top speed was about 100 mph. A total of 25,713 was built before 1967, when the Mk II was replaced by the revised 240, which had the same 'chassis' but simplified trim, furnishing and decorations; 4,446 240s were produced.

### Jaguar 3.4-litre Mk II
This had an 83-mm × 106-mm, 3442-cc/210-bhp engine. Top speed was about 120 mph; 28,666 3.4-litre cars were built before 1967, when the model was replaced by the 340, which had simpler trim and furnishings. 2,800 340s were produced.

### Specification (3.8-litre Mk II)
**Engine:** inline six-cylinder, twin-cam
**Bore × stroke:** 87 mm × 106 mm

**Capacity:** 3781 cc
**Maximum power:** 220 bhp
**Transmission:** four-speed manual gearbox with optional overdrive, or three-speed automatic transmission; rear-wheel drive
**Chassis:** steel unit-construction body/chassis assembly
**Suspension:** independent front with wishbones and coil springs; live rear axle with cantilever leaf springs
**Brakes:** discs front and rear
**Bodywork:** steel four-door four-seater saloon
**Maximum speed (approx):** 125 mph (201 km/h)

*Below: In its day the Jaguar Mk II had everything – sensuous looks as well as excellent performance from a 220-bhp engine which in 3.8-litre form gave a top speed of 125 mph. Despite a live rear axle, the car's handling was considered to be more than adequate.*

*Above: The Mk II version of Jaguar's standard saloon appeared in 1959, made in 2.4-, 3.4- and 3.8-litre form.*

Until disc brakes became optional, neither car was a truly satisfactory machine for fast motoring, and the handling was often criticised for its tail-out habits.

Jaguar took note of these comments, and produced the famous Mk II versions. Jaguar's 'second guess' at the layout of a compact four-door saloon was much more successful than the original, not only in looks, but in dynamic behaviour and in reputation. Starting on the basis of the Mk I cars, Jaguar gave the Mk II much more glass area, a wider rear track, disc brakes as standard, and a choice of three different sizes of XK engine.

The Mk II became Jaguar's most successful 1960s car, particularly in 3.4-litre and 3.8-litre form, where the combination of sheer performance, character and value for money was unbeatable. Compared with the Mk I, the handling was much improved, the car felt more secure, and its internal and external styling was a full step ahead.

As they cars grew older, they acquired a reputation for going rusty, but

# Jaguar S-type 1963-68

The next stage in Jaguar's development of its unitary-construction saloons was to introduce the S-type in 1963. This car had evolved from the famous Mk II layout by being given a lengthened tail (with more stowage space) and independent rear suspension like that of the contemporary E-type.

That meant replacing the old live axle, with its rather simple location and springing medium of semi-elliptic leaf springs, by one of the most advanced rear suspension systems to be seen on any production car of the era. The new suspension featured a pressed-steel carrier or subframe holding the differential and the inboard-mounted rear disc brakes. Individual driveshafts went to cast hub-carriers onto which a long trailing arm was attached. The driveshafts acted as the upper transverse link on each side, while the complementing lower link was a large tubular member with wide-based brackets on each end; in effect the arrangement acted as a

*Below: The S-type, introduced in 1963, was the first unitary-construction Jaguar; in other words, it was built without a separate chassis.*

double-wishbone system. Four concentric coil spring/damper units were used, a pair on each side. All this suspension sophistication was cleverly insulated from the body by bushes chosen to mask road noise and vibration. One way of realising how advanced the S-type's ride was in its day is to recall that in essence that same suspension lived on in the XJ6 and XJ12 of the 1980s.

Other style changes, like the slightly hooded headlamps, were less easy to accept, but there was never any criticism of the new car's handling, nor of its appeal. From the rear, at least, there was a touch of Mk X about the style, though very little of this shape would be carried forward to the next-generation Jaguar, which was the XJ6 of 1968.

In performance terms, and in the size of its cabin, the S-type was nearly identical to the Mk II, but customers found it sufficiently different to be attractive. Because it was a heavier and subtly more up-market car than the Mk II, Jaguar did not sell it as a 2.4 litre, in which form it would have been underpowered.

The S-type gave way to the XJ6 in 1968, after 10,036 3.4-litre engines, and 15,135 3.8-litre cars, had been produced.

## Jaguar S-type variants

### Jaguar 420

This model followed in 1966 and was effectively a 4.2-litre-engined S-type, with a 4235-cc power unit producing 245 bhp, and a different nose style similar to the XJ6 which was to follow.

The front-end change meant that the 420 was, at 187.8 inches, longer than the S-type and rather heavier. Mechanical changes included the switch to an all-synchromesh gearbox and an improved cooling system which operated at higher pressure and also

*Above: As well as unitary construction, the S-type pioneered independent rear suspension in Jaguar saloons, following the E-type's lead.*

featured a viscous-coupling fan rather than one driven direct from the engine. The end result was a very high-class saloon; as *Road & Track* put it in their road test: "When cruising at 100 mph across the desert in overdrive, the most noticeable noise comes from the air-conditioning blower." 9,801 420s were produced.

## Specification (1963 3.4-litre)

**Engine:** inline six-cylinder, twin-cam
**Bore × stroke:** 83 mm × 106 mm
**Capacity:** 3442 cc
**Maximum power:** 210 bhp
**Transmission:** four-speed manual gearbox with optional overdrive, or three-speed automatic transmission; rear-wheel drive
**Chassis:** steel unit-construction body/chassis
**Suspension:** independent front with wishbones and coil springs; independent rear with upper and lower links, coil springs and telescopic dampers
**Brakes:** discs front and rear
**Bodywork:** steel four-door four-seater saloon
**Maximum speed (approx):** 120 mph (193 km/h)

*Below: The 420 was an S-type with a new nose (foreshadowing the XJ6) and a larger, 4.2-litre, straight-six.*

## Jaguar E-type 1961-75

During the 1960s the E-type was one of the most famous sports cars in the world. Not only did it look sensationally fast, and have obvious connections with earlier racing Jaguars, but it was always sold at amazingly low prices. The 1961-model roadsters sold for a mere £2,098.

In the beginning the E-type was intended to be a racing replacement for the D-type, but after Jaguar withdrew from motorsport it was completely re-engineered, and introduced as a road car in 1961. The E-type's structure was a logical development of that pioneered for the D-type, with a steel centre monocoque bolted to a multi-tubular frame chassis which supported the engine and front suspension.

The first cars were sold in open roadster or smoothly-shaped fastback/hatchback coupé forms, had all-independent suspension and 3.8-litre derivatives of the famous XK engine. With only minor engine tuning these cars reached 150 mph, and had acceleration to match.

The E-type's attractions were its performance, its style, and its obvious value for money, but there were failings too. The cabin was cramped, the bodywork

was vulnerable to traffic scrapes, the cooling was marginal and the braking and handling were not perhaps as secure as the top speed suggested.

In the next few years the car improved progressively. From 1964 the engine was enlarged to 4.2 litres and matched to an all-synchromesh gearbox; from 1966 there was also a longer-wheelbase 2 + 2

coupé, and from 1968 the car became 'Series II', with many improvements.

The Series III car of 1971 saw the old XK engine dropped in favour of a brand-new 5.3-litre V12 unit, all cars being built on the longer wheelbase. Performance losses of the 1960s were restored at a stroke, but this was altogether a 'softer' car than the first types had been. Series III cars had wider wheels and flared wheel arches but the same rather slim driving compartment.

E-type assembly ended in 1974, but this was not announced until 1975. A total of 15,496 3.8-litre cars, 41,724 4.2s, and 15,287 V12s were built in this period.

*Above: The first cars were available in open roadster or smooth fastback body styles and were fitted with a 3.8-litre derivative of the famous XK engine. These cars could reach 150 mph, though their handling and braking were perhaps not sufficient to cope with such a high speed.*

*Below: The inline, six-cylinder twin-cam engine, seen here in the Lightweight, was mated to a four-speed manual transmission. The racer's life was terminated when Jaguar withdrew from motorsport.*

*Above: Not only did the E-type look sensationally fast, but it also had obvious connections with earlier racing Jaguars. Indeed, originally it was intended to be a track star and successor to the D-type. It was introduced as a road car in 1961.*

*Below: Lightweight racers were launched by the factory in 1963. Although they never achieved any great racing success in their short careers, they were blindingly fast, with a 0-100 mph time of 10.8 seconds.*

## Specification (1961 3.8-litre)

**Engine:** inline six-cylinder, twin-cam
**Bore × stroke:** 87 mm × 106 mm
**Capacity:** 3781 cc
**Maximum power:** 265 bhp
**Transmission:** four-speed manual gearbox, rear-wheel drive
**Chassis:** steel multi-tubular front chassis frame, bolted to steel centre monocoque
**Suspension:** independent front with wishbones and torsion bars; independent rear with upper and lower links, coil springs and four telescopic dampers
**Brakes:** discs front and rear
**Bodywork:** choice of steel two-seaters, coupé or open roadster
**Maximum speed (approx):** 150 mph (241 km/h)

## Jaguar E-type variants

### Jaguar E-type 4.2-litre

This took over from the 3.8-litre model in 1964, with a new all-synchromesh gearbox. The engine was 92.07-mm × 106-mm, displacing 4235 cc, and producing 265 bhp. From 1966 the E-type 2+2 coupé was introduced, mechanically like other E-types, but with a 9-in longer wheelbase, and 2+2 seating; automatic transmission was optional.

### Jaguar E-type Series II

The Series II was introduced in 1968, powered by the 4.2-litre engine and produced in roadster, 2+2 and coupé forms. It could be distinguished from the earlier cars by the bonnet's larger air intake and the wrap-around rear bumper with larger light clusters.

### Jaguar E-type Series III

The Series III, introduced in 1971, saw the XK engine replaced by the larger, 5.3-litre, alloy V12 engine. The larger engine necessitated a larger bonnet with bigger air intake and grille, while larger

*Below: The Series III was introduced in 1971 and featured the 5.3-litre alloy V12 engine. The wheelbase was extended to 105 inches.*

wheels and tyres saw the wheel arches flared to accommodate them. The V12 cars were equipped with ventilated front disc brakes and built on the longer 105-in wheelbase. The V12 Series III was discontinued in 1975, having been built in roadster and coupé formats.

*Above: The Series II was powered by a 4.2-litre engine and produced in roadster, 2 + 2 and coupé forms. It could be distinguished by the bonnet's larger air intake, the wrap-around rear bumper and larger light clusters.*

*Below: The V12 E-types featured ventilated front disc brakes and larger wheels and tyres. The wheel arches were flared to accommodate them. The last car rolled off the line in 1974 after 13 years in production.*

# Jaguar Mk X 1961-70

To replace the long-running separate-chassis Mk VII/Mk VIIIM/Mk VIII and Mk IX series, Jaguar eventually developed the new Mk X saloon, which had a unit-construction body/chassis and all-independent suspension.

Although the XK engine and transmission choices, and the E-type-derived independent rear suspension, were familiar to Jaguar watchers, the rest of the design was new. It was a very large car indeed – the 120-in wheelbase was the same as that of the old Mk IX, but was matched to an overall length of 202 inches, a width of 76 inches, and an unladen weight of around 4,200 lb.

The style featured four headlamps and a long sweeping 'straight-through' waistline, but the shape was obviously aerodynamically efficient, as the original 3.8-litre cars were capable of 120 mph thanks to a power output of 265 bhp.

The 4.2-litre-engined version, which followed in 1964, was no faster but rather more flexible, while the renamed 420G of 1966 was virtually the same car as before. All these saloons were spacious and well-appointed; a number were equipped with limousine-style divisions.

This was never one of Jaguar's most famous cars, but it carried on in production until 1970 – two years after the XJ6 family had been launched. Total production was 12,977 3.8-litre models, 5,680 4.2-litres and 6,554 badged as 420Gs.

*Below: The interior was typically luxurious in the traditional Jaguar manner, with its leather upholstery and walnut dashboard and door trim.*

### Jaguar Mk X variants

#### Jaguar 420G
This took over from the Mk X in 1966, and remained in production until 1970. Mechanically it was the same as the 4.2-litre Mk X, but there were some detail decoration differences.

### Specification (1964 4.2-litre)
**Engine:** inline six-cylinder, twin-cam
**Bore × stroke:** 92.07 mm × 106 mm
**Capacity:** 4235 cc
**Maximum power:** 265 bhp
**Transmission:** four-speed manual gearbox with optional overdrive, or three-speed automatic transmission; rear-wheel drive
**Chassis:** steel unit-construction body/chassis
**Suspension:** independent front with wishbones and coil springs; independent rear with upper and lower links, coil springs and telescopic dampers
**Brakes:** discs front and rear
**Bodywork:** steel four-door five-seater saloon
**Maximum speed (approx):** 120 mph (193 km/h)

*Above: The Mk X's incredible length and rather bulbous styling meant it was never very popular. It featured four headlamps and a long, sweeping waistline but was aerodynamically very efficient. For such a large car it handled very well.*

*Above: The six-cylinder twin-cam engine was borrowed from the XK. Power output was 265 bhp to give a maximum speed of 120 mph.*

*Below: The levels of comfort and performance made the Mk X very attractive to chauffeurs. Several versions had limousine-style divisions.*

# Jaguar XJ6 1968-86

By the mid-1960s Jaguar had realised that its range was getting too complex, so a brand-new style was developed to replace the Mk II, the S-type *and* the 420 models. This was the XJ6, which was the last new model to be designed by an independent Jaguar company.

Compared with the Mk II/S-type family, the XJ6 was slightly larger, had a more roomy cabin, and along with its new and very attractive style, it was also an astonishingly refined car. Many motoring specialists thought that it was quieter and smoother than the Rolls-Royce or Mercedes-Benz cars of the day. The key to this performance lay in the great attention Jaguar paid to suspension design and to the suppression of noise and vibration generated by the road surface. The rear suspension system was a direct descendant of that used in the E-type, being mounted within a separate cage which was insulated from the monocoque.

The XJ6 was also as perfectly proportioned and elegant as it was refined, and showed the continuing influence of William Lyons, with his unerring eye for good design.

Like previous Jaguars, it was powered by a choice of six-cylinder XK engines, though Jaguar also developed V8 *and* V12 engines as alternatives. The V8 engine was never put into production, but the V12 was later used in the XJ12, E-type and XJ-S.

In an 18-year career, XJ6s were built in an amazing number of different types. The Series II arrived in 1973 (there were two-door versions in this Series only), and the Series III followed, with cabin style revisions, in 1979. Although this type of XJ6 was replaced by a new-generation car in 1986, the V12-engined types carried on into the 1990s.

*Above: The XJ6 was as perfectly proportioned as it was refined. Many people thought it quieter and smoother than a Rolls-Royce or Mercedes. The Series III cars were available with a five-speed gearbox.*

A new model appeared in 1994, superseded in 1998 by the V8 XJ series, with some of the styling cues of the XJ6.

## Jaguar XJ6 variants

### Jaguar XJ6 2.8-litre
In addition to the 4.2-litre, there was also the XJ6 2.8, with a 2792-cc, 180-bhp version of the twin-cam engine. Long-wheelbase models with 4.2-litre engines were built in 1972 and 1973.

### Jaguar XJ6 Series II
In 1973 the Series I was discontinued in favour of the Series II, this model being produced until 1979; there was no 2.8-litre-engined version. An additional 3.4-litre-engined car, with 161 bhp, was added from 1975. From 1974 all cars had longer wheelbases.

### Jaguar XJ6 Series III
In 1979 the Series II was replaced by the Series III, with a restyled cabin on the same basic hull. The 4.2-litre engine got fuel injection, and was rated at 205 bhp. There was a new manual gearbox – with five speeds instead of four; overdrive was no longer available.

The six-cylinder-engined Series III model was discontinued in 1986, being replaced by the new-style XJ6.

## Specification (1968 4.2-litre)
**Engine:** inline six-cylinder, twin-cam
**Bore × stroke:** 92.07 mm × 106 mm
**Capacity:** 4235 cc
**Maximum power:** 245 bhp
**Transmission:** four-speed manual gearbox with optional overdrive, or three-speed automatic transmission; rear-wheel drive
**Chassis:** steel unit-construction body/chassis
**Suspension:** independent front with wishbones and coil springs; independent rear with upper and lower links, coil springs and telescopic dampers
**Brakes:** discs front and rear
**Bodywork:** steel four-door five-seater saloon
**Maximum speed (approx):** 124 mph (200 km/h)

*Below: Total production of the six-cylinder XJ6s (including Daimler-badged versions) numbered 349,352 in an 18-year lifespan. The wire wheels fitted here were an unusual option.*

## Jaguar XJ12 1972–97

The famous single-overhead-cam V12 engine was developed, over a period of years, from a four-cam engine originally designed as a racing unit. The engine was first seen in 1971, to power the Series III E-type sports car, but has featured in saloons and coupés ever since.

The XJ12 of 1972 was effectively an XJ6 with a V12 engine transplant, offered with automatic transmission only. There is no question that this *was* the quietest car in the world at the time, but refinement was also linked to agile road behaviour and a 150-mph top speed!

All XJ12s were thirsty cars – 11-12 mpg was quite normal on earlier types – which meant that sales were badly hit when petrol prices soared. Even so, the XJ12 (sometimes known as the XJ 5.3) has been in production for almost 20 years, the type having evolved through Series I, Series II and Series III, with a limited number of two-door types built from 1975 to 1977.

The 'HE' (or 'High-Efficiency') engine was phased in from 1981, which gave rather better fuel consumption (perhaps 14-15 mpg), but the size – 5.3 litres – has never been changed.

Another feature which has remained essentially unchanged in the XJ12 is the body shell; whereas the XJ6 moved into the new revised shell originally coded the XJ40, the V12 continued in the old-style body, as the V12 engine would not fit. That's an attraction to many who consider the older design to be the more elegant.

The production totals for the first two series of V12-engined saloons (including Daimler-badged cars) was 24,457, although only 4,113 were the Series I type. More than 20,000 Series III cars had been built by 1991.

### Jaguar XJ12 variants

#### Jaguar XJ12 Series II
After a long-wheelbase version of the car was introduced in 1972, the Series I was replaced in 1973 by the new Series II version, which had the same minor style changes as those of the six-cylinder cars, this model being produced until 1979. Longer-wheelbase cars were standardised from 1974, along with fuel injection, giving a power output of 285 bhp.

#### Jaguar XJ12 Series III
In 1979 the Series III cars took over from the Series II, with the same monocoque changes as for the six-cylinder cars. At this point the engine was rated at 299 bhp.

*Above: The big saloon was proven to be the quietest car in the world when introduced in 1972. It was extraordinarily refined but still capable of 150-mph performance. The famous single-overhead-cam V12 engine was originally used in the Series III E-type and has been seen in saloon and coupé Jaguars ever since.*

### Specification (1972 5.3-litre)
**Engine:** V12, single overhead camshaft per bank of cylinders
**Bore × stroke:** 90 mm × 70 mm
**Capacity:** 5343 cc
**Maximum power:** 253 bhp
**Transmission:** three-speed automatic transmission, rear-wheel drive
**Chassis:** steel unit-construction body
**Suspension:** independent front with wishbones and coil springs; independent rear with upper and lower trailing links, coil springs and telescopic dampers
**Brakes:** discs front and rear
**Bodywork:** steel four-door five-seater saloon
**Maximum speed (approx):** 138 mph (222 km/h)

*Above: The XJ12 was effectively an XJ6 with an engine transplant and was supplied only as an automatic.*

*Below: XJ12s were also produced in Daimler form as the Double Six, the name of the famous pre-war Daimler.*

# Jaguar XJ6 and XJ12 Coupés 1975-77

The two-door Jaguar Coupés were a short-lived diversion of the mid-1970s, when all manner of changes were being rung around one theme. The Coupés were effectively two-door saloons, with pillarless styling, all built on the original (shorter) wheelbase of the XJ6/XJ12 types; as with all such Jaguars of the period, they were also sold with Daimler badges.

Mechanically these cars were identical to the normal saloons, which is to say that there was a 4.2-litre XK-engined version, and a 5.3-litre V12 version, this having fuel injection and no less than 299 bhp.

Because these cars were more costly than the saloons, and offered less space and less versatility than the four-door types, they were not commercially successful.

Since the Coupé was smaller and rather more agile than the saloon it was chosen as the basis for Jaguar's assault on the European Touring Car Championship, with cars prepared by Broadspeed. The result was an immensely fast car that looked every inch the part, but it proved unreliable, with braking and cooling problems, and became an embarrassment to the company.

That was very unfortunate, as Broadspeed had made an enormous effort to modify the cars appropriately. The road-going Coupé's body shell was lightened but given reinforced bulkheads front and rear, while a hefty roll cage contributed to the car's torsional stiffness.

Although the suspension followed the road car's format, it differed in having fabricated suspension arms all round,

along with uprights cast in magnesium alloy.

Far larger wheels and tyres were fitted for racing, with 19-in diameter Speedline wheels wearing huge Dunlops – 300-650s at the front and 330-700s at the back. That necessitated some of the bodywork alterations which make the racer look so impressive, those flared glassfibre wheel arches being added by Broadspeed along with the deep front air dam.

They helped the Coupé look even weightier than it was, and despite the body lightening the car was just too heavy, as the brake specification indicates. Despite Broadspeed fitting double twin-pot calipers to massive ventilated front discs, stopping the Jaguar was always a problem, and was compounded by the fact that heat from the inboard rear discs caused some transmission failures. Also, the wheels tended to come off at crucial times, as driver Derek Bell recalled: "I think most of us had a wheel come off at some time. It happened to me in testing."

Supreme outright performance was guaranteed by increasing the standard

Jaguar's 5.3-litre V12 displacement to 5410 cc (the maximum the rules allowed), drastically increasing the compression ratio, changing the cams and making the engine breathe far better. As much as 560 bhp was extracted from the engine but racing a wet-sump unit proved unwise, oil surge being a serious problem on long, fast corners.

The car ran on British Dunlop tyres, for patriotic rather than practical reasons, and they did not help the cause, nor did the British Leyland management. Leyland Cars' managing director claimed that the Jaguar would win the first European Touring Car Championship round in 1976, a claim made before the car had even run!

The Broadspeed car made its racing debut in September 1976 but won no races, despite managing six pole positions. The best it achieved was second place at the Nürburgring when driven by Andy Rouse and Derek Bell.

Not including the racing cars, 10,462 Coupés were built in all, in six-cylinder and V12 form, badged as Jaguars and Daimlers.

*Above: The Coupé was chosen as the basis for Jaguar's assault on the European Touring Car Championship, with cars prepared by Broadspeed. They were incredibly fast, but suffered from braking and cooling problems.*

## Specification (1975 XJ12)

**Engine:** V12, single overhead camshaft per bank of cylinders
**Bore × stroke:** 90 mm × 70 mm
**Capacity:** 5343 cc
**Maximum power:** 253 bhp
**Transmission:** three-speed automatic transmission, rear-wheel drive
**Chassis:** steel unit-construction body/chassis
**Suspension:** independent front with wishbones and coil springs; independent rear with upper and lower links, coil springs and telescopic dampers
**Brakes:** discs front and rear
**Bodywork:** steel two-door pillarless coupé
**Maximum speed (approx):** 140 mph (225 km/h)

*Below: The pretty two-door Coupés were sold in Jaguar and Daimler form but were not commercially successful. Although they were considerably more nimble than the four-door cars, they offered less space inside.*

## Jaguar XJ-S 1975-96

*Left: The original XJ-S was conceived as a replacement of the E-type, although it was larger, heavier and more of a Grand Tourer than the delicate E-type. During its 21-year life it was frequently revised.*

### Specification (1975 XJ-S)

**Engine:** V12, single overhead camshaft per bank of cylinders
**Bore × stroke:** 90 mm × 70 mm
**Capacity:** 5343 cc
**Maximum power:** 285 bhp
**Transmission:** four-speed manual gearbox or three-speed automatic transmission, rear-wheel drive
**Chassis:** steel unit-construction body/chassis
**Suspension:** independent front with wishbones and coil springs; independent rear with upper and lower links, coil springs and telescopic dampers
**Brakes:** discs front and rear
**Bodywork:** steel two-door four-seater coupé
**Maximum speed (approx):** 153 mph (246 km/h)

In the early 1970s Jaguar saw that the E-type would soon die out, and took the major decision not to produce a direct replacement. Instead, for its new sporting car, Jaguar chose to produce a larger, heavier and rather more 'Grand Touring' machine, which it called the XJ-S. Whereas the E-type had its own unique mechanical layout, the XJ-S was another derivative of the successful XJ6/XJ12 theme.

Basically, the XJ-S used a shortened XJ12 platform (the wheelbase, at 102 inches, was nearly 10 inches shorter than that of the XJ12 saloon), with a fuel-injected version of the V12 engine, topped by a new 2 + 2 coupé body.

This shape, although demonstrably more aerodynamically efficient than the much-loved E-type, was bulkier and featured 'flying buttresses' at the rear quarters which were, and still are, controversial.

In original form the XJ-S was a very fast Grand Tourer, not as spacious and not quite as refined as an XJ12, but with supple and very capable suspension, and a character all of its own. Early cars were not at all fuel-efficient, but from 1981 the HE ('High-Efficiency') model not only produced more power, but was more economical.

There was a burst of design activity in the 1980s, first with the launch of an AJ6 (six-cylinder)-engined version

and the arrival of a two-seater Cabriolet body style, while a full Convertible replaced the Cabriolet in 1988.

The design was completely updated in 1991, not only with a styling facelift which featured new side window lines and a different tail, but with a larger six-cylinder engine.

### Jaguar XJ-S variants

#### Jaguar XJ-S HE
This version took over from the original type in 1981, with an engine that produced 299 bhp. An open-top Cabriolet version was added to the range in 1985. The Cabriolet was replaced by a full Convertible in 1988.

#### Jaguar XJ-S 3.6-litre
This was available in two styles – Coupé and Cabriolet – from 1983, with a new twin-cam six-cylinder 3590-cc engine with a bore and stroke of 91 mm × 92 mm, producing 228 bhp. There was a choice of five-speed manual or four-speed automatic transmissions. Top speed was about 141 mph (227 km/h).

#### Jaguar XJ-S – facelifted
The car was given a styling facelift in 1991, with new-profile side windows and tail-lamps. The V12-engined car was mechanically similar to the

previous car. The six-cylinder car had an enlarged engine of 91 mm × 102 mm/3980 cc, producing 223 bhp.

#### JaguarSport XJS-R
This version of the XJ-S featured modified suspension, styling 'dress-up' kits and more powerful engines. In the case of the V12 this was a six-litre unit which, in 1992, produced 333 bhp, giving a top speed near 160 mph.

*Above: The ultimate version of the XJ-S was the Jaguar Sport's XJR-S, which used a larger six-litre, V12 engine producing 333bhp. The boot-mounted spoiler created rear downforce.*

*Below: The Coupé's design was completely revised in 1991, with new side window lines and a wholly different tail; these revisions were shared by the XJR-S.*

## Jaguar XJ220 1992–93

In 1988 Jaguar displayed a prototype supercar, the XJ220, which the Coventry engineers had found time to develop in their spare time!

This car had a sensational mid-engined two-seater coupé style, and not only featured the famous V12 engine, but also four-wheel drive; its top speed was forecast to be 220 mph.

This car, however, had not turned a wheel before the project was handed over to the joint Jaguar/TWR concern, JaguarSport, to see if it could be made into a production car. JaguarSport completely re-engineered it by shortening the wheelbase, abandoning the four-wheel-drive concept, and deciding to use a modified version of the TWR racing twin-turbo V6 engine which was in use at that time rather than the bulky V12 unit.

JaguarSport revealed the new concept (for a car had yet to be built) at the end of 1989, forecasting that the 3.5-litre engine would produce 500 bhp, and that the top speed (where usable) would still be 220 mph. With little doubt, this would make it the fastest car in the world.

JaguarSport also stated that only 350 examples would be built, and received more than 1,200 orders in the next few days! In 1990 and 1991 a new factory was set up at Bloxham, near Banbury, and seven prototypes were constructed as part of the development programme. The first deliveries were due to be made in the spring of 1992, with the production run forecast to be complete by 1994.

The definitive V6 XJ220 was a lot shorter and lighter than the original prototype 'XJ220 4 × 4', but retained the same basic style. The two-seater cabin was sumptuously equipped and air conditioning was standard, while the whole car was as light and as compact as possible. It was intended to be a thoroughly usable roadgoing supercar, in all climates and traffic conditions, though clearly it would excel in wide-open spaces and on fast motorways.

The most frustrating feature of the project was that it was not intended for sale in the USA – it was not thought worth the effort of meeting the safety legislation and exhaust-emission regulations. The XJ220C was a successful racing car, however, and won the GT class in the 1993 Le Mans, only to be disqualified several weeks later on a technical issue.

*Above: Claimed top speed was 220 mph, making this the fastest car in the world – in theory.*

*Below: The chassis was shortened and four-wheel drive dropped from the original concept.*

*Above: The most flamboyant Jaguar in the early 1990s was intended to be a thoroughly usable road-going supercar. When it was unveiled Jaguar received 1,200 orders for a production run of just 350 cars. In 1990 a new factory was set up at Bloxham near Banbury by the joint Jaguar/TWR concern Jaguar Sport.*

### Specification

**Engine:** V6, quad-cam
**Bore × stroke:** 94 mm × 84 mm
**Capacity:** 3498 cc
**Maximum power:** 500 bhp
**Transmission:** five-speed manual gearbox, rear-wheel drive
**Chassis:** aluminium/honeycomb unit-construction body/chassis
**Suspension:** independent front with wishbones and coil springs; independent rear with wishbones and coil springs
**Brakes:** discs front and rear
**Bodywork:** aluminium two-seater coupé
**Maximum speed (approx):** 212 mph (341 km/h)

## Jaguar S-type 1998-present

The S-type was a long time coming. It was common knowledge that a new sports saloon was in the pipeline, a successor to the immortal Mk II and original S-type of the 1960s, and when the new S-type was unveiled at the NEC in 1998, feelings were divided. Some felt it was too much designed by committee, while others thought the mix of traditional styling cues and modern refinement were spot-on. Either way, the S-type was an elegant sports saloon with as many state-of-the-art gizmos that could be accommodated.

It was available with a new all-aluminium 240 bhp 3.0-litre AJ-V6 engine, or the 280 bhp 4.0-litre AJ-V8 unit. The 3.0-litre AJ-V6 motor was designed with the S-type in mind, and was the company's first ever production V6, sharing many features with the V8, including combustion system, cooling system, cylinder head design and valve gear. The 3.0-litre S-type could be specified with a new five-speed Getrag manual gearbox, and a five-speed automatic transmission was available on both 3.0- and 4.0-litre models. Engine and transmission functions were controlled by an electronic powertrain controller. The 3.0-litre V6 manual performed the

*Above: The S-type's dashboard and control console were state-of-the-art; the leather and walnut trim were in keeping with Jaguar's heritage.*

0–60 mph (0-96 km/h) sprint in 6.8 seconds, and 8.0 seconds for the automatic, up to a top speed of 146 mph or 141 mph (235-227km/h) for the automatic. The 4.0-litre automatic could go from 0–60 mph (0-96 km/h) in 6.6 seconds with a top speed of 150 mph (241 km/h).

S-type suspension consisted of a double wishbone set-up not dissimilar to the XK Series, with extensive use of lightweight aluminium componentry

and twin front crossbeams, resulting in an equal 50/50 front-to-rear weight distribution. The specification also included electronic traction control, anti-lock braking and a variable ratio, speed proportional steering systems. Electronic brake distribution and an optional dynamic stability control system linked with the anti-lock braking, traction and steering systems to prevent oversteer. The S-type could also come with Jaguar's CATS electronic adaptive dampers, and it was shod with Pirelli P6000 (16 inch) or P Zero (17 inch) tyres on alloy rims.

The interior was as civilised as could be expected of a Jaguar, featuring leather and walnut trim and upholstery, dual-zone climate control, optional rain sensing wiper, reverse park control system and an integrated satellite navigation system. The S type also debuted voice activated control of all primary audio, phone and climate control functions for hands-free operation, which was available as an option in the UK and USA. Safety features included a collapsible steering column and under-floor plastic fuel tank, while driver and front passenger front and side airbags and pyrotechnic seat belt pre-tensioners

were fitted. As a member of Ford' global family, the S-type was built on th same platform as the Lincoln LS and th AJ-V6 cylinder block was derived from the Ford V6 unit, developed at Jaguar Whitley Engineering Centre in Coventr The S-type was assembled at the Castl Bromwich plant near Birmingham which cost £200 million to redevelop es pecially for S-type production.

### Specification (3.0 V6)

**Engine:** all aluminium V6, 24-valves
**Bore x stroke:** 89 mm x 79.5 mm
**Capacity:** 2967 cc
**Suspension:** independent front, by unequal length wishbones, crossbeams, coil springs, dampers and anti-roll bar; rear, double wishbones incorporating driveshafts acting as upper links, coil springs and dampers, anti-roll bar. Electronic traction control
**Brakes:** ventilated discs with 4-channe ABS
**Body:** all steel monocoque

*Below: While some did not like the S-type's styling, others agreed that it combined styling cues from its 1960 ancestors with up-to-date packaging to make an excellent 'small' Jaguar.*

## Jaguar XK8 & XKR 1996-present

*Above: Although it was widely touted as the long-awaited replacement for the E-type, the XK8 was a more substantial-looking car, despite its elongated cigar-shaped body, and certainly one of the most desirable GT cars on the market. Like its exalted predecessor, the XK8 was available in coupé and convertible format, powered by the all-aluminium 4.0-litre V8 engine.*

The XK8 was Jaguar's first new proper sports car for a whole generation, following on in the tradition of the E-type rather than the more restrained XJ-S. The model was launched at the 1996 Geneva show and won 'Best in Show' award. It was available in two configurations, both of them long and lean – as a convertible and coupé – in normally aspirated form as the XK8 and supercharged as the XKR. The latter was characterised by a rear spoiler, twin louvres on its bonnet and larger wheels. Bodies were constructed and painted at the Castle Bromwich plant and dispatched to Browns Lane for final assembly.

Both versions used the 32-valve, quad-cam all-aluminium 4.0-litre AJ-V8 engine, developed at the Whitley plant, and in normally-aspirated form, the AJ-V8 unit delivered 290 bhp. The supercharged XKR developed 370 bhp, and top speed for both models was lim-ited to 155 mph (249 km/h), with 0-60 mph (0-100 km/h) acceleration figures of 5.2 seconds for the XKR and 6.7 seconds for the XK8. Engines were built at the Jaguar facility within Ford's Bridgend factory in South Wales and final assembly was at Browns Lane. All aspects were monitored by an electronic engine management system, and both engine versions were mated to a five-speed automatic gearbox with torque converter. The engine was located slightly ahead of the front wheel-axis, although weight distribution was fairly even front to rear.

Suspension was fully independent, by double wishbones, coaxial springs and digressive dampers and a cast aluminium cross-beam at the front, with anti-dive geometry, and an anti-roll bar. At the rear were lower wishbones with drive shafts providing the upper links, coil springs, two stage adaptive dampers (on the XKR) and an anti-roll bar, set up to provide anti squat and anti-lift. Brakes were vacuum-assisted discs all round with 4-channel ABS, supported by stability control that was activated by the engine management system, so that if wheelspin was detected, stability control backed off the electronic throttle to maintain vehicle equilibrium. Traction control was administered via the ABS by braking the rear wheels to a point where grip was retained.

Both XK8 variants had the option of CATS (Computer Active Technology Suspension), which was standard on the XKR. This included electronically-sensored adaptive dampers, 18 inch wheels and low-profile, uni-directional front tyres with asymmetric rear tyres. Both models were equipped with speed-sensitive Servotronic power-assisted steering.

Within the cabin, driver and front passenger airbags and front seat-belt pretensioners were standard. The XKs had reinforced floor and door pillars and side-impact door beams, including crumple zones. Interior trim could be specified in two styles, either Classic or Sport. The Classic interior was a combi-nation of traditional sports car features including walnut veneer, leather seats, wood-rim wheel and wooden gear knob, whereas the Sport interior was more modern in concept, with black leather-rim wheel, leather gear knob, grey-stained birds eye maple fascia and seats with cloth facings. Both seats and steering column were electronically adjustable with memory settings. Climate control and a sophisticated hi-fi system were included, with mobile phone facility. The XK convertible models were fitted with a fully automatic hood powered by an electro-hydraulic system, enabling the hood to be fully opened or closed in under 20 seconds and locking into the windscreen header rail automatically. The XK Series was generally viewed as a more affordable alternative to its sibling, the DB7.

### Specification (XK8)

**Engine:** all aluminium V8
**Bore** x **stroke:** 86 mm x 86 mm
**Capacity:** 3996 cc
**Suspension:** independent front, by unequal length wishbones, front crossbeam coil springs, dampers and anti-roll bar; rear, double wishbones incorporating driveshafts acting as upper links, coil springs and dampers, anti-roll bar
**Body:** all steel monocoque

*Left: The supercharged XKR developed 370 bhp, and was equipped with electronically-controlled suspension for sharper handling.*

# Jensen Motors Ltd

**A**lan and Richard Jensen founded the company bearing their name in West Bromwich, near Birmingham, originally to produce bodies for other companies, but launched their first 'own-brand' Jensen model in 1937. Car production was naturally tiny at first, and the new models relied on proprietary engines, transmissions, and even suspension components.

Jensen prospered more by building bodies for other companies, and in post-war years made many thousands of body shells, or body/chassis assemblies, for Austin and Austin-Healey. In the 1960s, too, Jensen undertook complete assembly of the Volvo P1800 sports coupé, and the Sunbeam Tiger.

In the 1950s the company dabbled with a Meadows-engined PW design which never went into series-production, before steadily beginning to build small quantities of fast but rather ponderous sporting coupés like the first-generation Interceptors, followed by cars in the 541 and CV8 families. Like other European carmakers, Jensen later turned to the USA for its engines, fitting Chrysler V8 units from 1960.

Expansion in the 1960s was not matched by profitability, the result being that the Jensen family sold out, and the firm came to be managed by the Norcross group. It was under this ownership that an ambitious new range of cars – the Interceptor and FF models – was developed, the FF being the world's first four-wheel-drive production car using the Ferguson Formula (hence the 'FF' title).

These cars also had very smart Italian-styled bodies for which expensive tooling had to be produced, the result being that the range had to stay in production for a long time to pay back the investment.

By the end of the 1960s Jensen's outside contract work had come to an end with the death of both the Austin-Healey 3000 and the Sunbeam Tiger. To compensate, Interceptor/FF production had been forced up to record levels. Then, in 1970, the company was taken over by a consortium headed by the American Kjell Qvale and Donald Healey.

The result was the launch of the Jensen-Healey marque in 1972, but the 'energy crisis' of 1973-74 hit Jensen very hard, and the company ceased

*Above: The Jensen brothers began building their own cars in 1937, but production was tiny to begin with. This badge dates from the 1950s.*

*Below: By the 1960s, the ambitious Interceptor/FF range of cars was under way. The company logo had been streamlined, too.*

trading in 1976. Small parts of the old company survived into the 1990s, and began manufacture of the Interceptor model on a limited basis. The marque resurfaced at the 1998 Motor Show with a new S-V8 sports car, built in its Reddich factory.

*Left: Jensen built small quantities of fast but rather ponderous sporting cars, like this CV8 from 1965. Like some other European car manufacturers, Jensen turned to the USA for its high-performance engines, fitting Chrysler V8s from 1960 onwards.*

*Below: The Interceptor was undoubtedly the most famous Jensen of them all. Its smart Italian-styled body required expensive tooling and the range had to stay in production for a long time so that the company could recoup its investment. The FF Interceptor was the world's first production car to use the Ferguson Formula four-wheel-drive system. As Jensen's outside contract work building bodies declined, so Interceptor production rose.*

# Jensen Model S 1936-39

The first Jensen-badged car was launched in 1936, a large and heavy model with a variety of exceptionally smart body styles which hid an amalgam of surprisingly mundane mechanical components. These original cars were expensive for their time (the saloon cost £695 in 1937) and ran on a long, 126-in, wheelbase.

Power was by Ford's ubiquitous 3.6-litre side-valve V8, which was matched to its usual three-speed gearbox. In the Jensen application, however, it was also mated to the Columbia two-speed axle. This meant that a total of six forward (and two reverse!) gears was available, the change from 'normal' to 'overdrive' ratios being accomplished by moving a pre-selector lever and dabbing the clutch.

*Below: The Jensen Model S, seen here in 1937 form, was expensive but brisk and exceedingly smart for its day. The original engine was a Ford side-valve V8.*

Suspension was by Ford-type transverse leaf springs front and rear, but as the chassis was perhaps better damped than that of a Ford there were few criticisms of the handling. Although it was outpaced by the more expensive Bentleys and Lagondas of the day, the Jensen was a brisk and exceedingly smart sports saloon which helped to establish the Jensen brothers' reputation as car-makers.

To give the range a bit of variety, Jensen also launched a smaller-engined version in 1938, using the 2.2-litre side-valve Ford V8. Performance was disappointing unless the engine was tuned considerably, but since this usually led to a lack of reliability, the car did not sell very well.

Just before the war Jensen modified the design yet again, this time slotting in an eight-cylinder American Nash engine, which had 120 bhp and gave the car a top speed well into the 90s, but deliveries were still very restricted.

All the original range of Jensens were killed off by the onset of World War II.

## Jensen Model S variants

### Jensen Model H

The Model H was introduced in 1938, with a 4.2-litre straight-eight Nash engine of 79.3 mm × 107.9 mm, giving 4205 cc and producing 120 bhp. The chassis was similar to the original 3½-litre car, but with independent front suspension.

*Above: A three-speed gearbox mated to a two-speed axle meant that a total of six forward and two reverse gears was available to the 1936 Jensen Model S driver.*

## Specification (1936 Model S 3½-litre)

**Engine:** V8, side-valve
**Bore × stroke:** 77.98 mm × 95.25 mm
**Capacity:** 3622 cc
**Maximum power:** 89 bhp
**Transmission:** three-speed manual gearbox and two-speed back axle, rear-wheel drive
**Chassis:** separate steel frame with channel-section side members
**Suspension:** non-independent with beam front axle and transverse leaf springs; live rear axle with Panhard rod, coil springs and telescopic dampers
**Brakes:** drums front and rear
**Bodywork:** five-seater saloon, drop-head coupé or tourer
**Maximum speed (approx):** 80 mph (129 km/h)

*Below: Photographers gather round the stylish four-seater at the Welsh Rally. Jensen later introduced a smaller-engined version, which was too slow to be successful.*

# Jensen Interceptor 1949-57

In the immediate post-war period Jensen proposed to build a new PW (PW standing for Post-War) model, which had a newly-designed 3.8-litre straight-eight Meadows engine, but this was not a success, and only about 15 were built.

The definitive post-war model then evolved, powered by a new Austin 4.0-litre six-cylinder engine; it was called the Interceptor, and went on sale at the end of 1949. The chassis was a rugged new design, while the engine was not only shared with Austin's A125 and A135 models, but was also used in Austin trucks. Like the pre-war models, the Interceptor itself was large and ponderous, for it was 188 inches long, and weighed more than 3,300 lb.

The chassis was essentially that of the Austin 70 (with Austin's approval), suitably modified by lowering the centre cruciform section and also inserting very large tubular longitudinal chassis members attached to the rest of the frame by outriggers. The whole unit was extremely rugged and stiff.

It provided a good basis for the wishbone front suspension (which used the Girling lever-arm dampers as upper members) and the leaf-sprung rear axle. If anything, the suspension was rather too softly sprung for a car with the Interceptor's performance, which came from the robust 3993-cc four-bearing straight-six with its Harry Weslake-designed cylinder head.

Despite its lowly compression ratio of 6.8:1 and single Stromberg carburettor, it produced a useful 212 lb ft of torque at only 2,200 rpm. As that figure implies, the Interceptor's overhead-valve engine was no screamer . . .

*Below: The hand-built Interceptor was available in saloon or convertible styles and was remarkable in its day for offering a top speed of 102 mph as well as fuel consumption of 20 mpg.*

Like its pre-war predecessors, the Interceptor was a hand-built model, with bodies produced by Jensen itself. The style, incidentally, was very like that used by Austin on the A40 Sports – the reason being that Jensen had styled the little Austin and was producing all the bodies!

Because the Interceptor was expensive, it sold only slowly, but it was one of the very first British cars to be offered with Laycock overdrive as an option, and it was also one of the few with a genuine top speed of more than 100 mph. If Jensen built two Interceptors a week it was

delighted – in fact only 25 cabriolets and 52 saloons were produced.

## Specification (1950)

**Engine:** inline six-cylinder, overhead-valve
**Bore × stroke:** 87.3 mm × 111.1 mm
**Capacity:** 3993 cc
**Maximum power:** 130 bhp
**Transmission:** four-speed manual gearbox with optional overdrive, rear-wheel drive
**Chassis:** separate steel frame with box-section side members
**Suspension:** independent front with

*Above: Like the firm's pre-war models, the Interceptor was large and ponderous, the rugged new straight-six engine struggling to propel the car's 3,300-lb body. The engine was also used in Austin trucks.*

wishbones and coil springs; live rear axle with semi-elliptic leaf springs
**Brakes:** drums front and rear
**Bodywork:** steel on wooden frame; five-seater cabriolet or coupé
**Maximum speed (approx):** 102 mph (164 km/h)

## ensen 541 1954-60

*Left: After criticism that the Interceptor was stodgy, Jensen developed the prettier and much faster 541. It was a long-legged and satisfying GT car and sold steadily.*

### Jensen 541 variants

#### Jensen 541R
The 541R of 1957-60 was a more powerful version of the 541, with 150 bhp on some of the cars, and rack-and-pinion steering; 200 were built.

#### Jensen 541S
The 541S of 1960-63 was a replacement for both the 541 and 541R models, widened by four inches, and with the option of a four-speed automatic transmission; 108 were built.

### Specification (1954 541)

**Engine:** inline six-cylinder, overhead-valve
**Bore × stroke:** 87.3 mm × 111.1 mm
**Capacity:** 3993 cc
**Maximum power:** 125 bhp
**Transmission:** four-speed manual gearbox with optional overdrive, rear-wheel drive
**Chassis:** separate steel platform with tubular main side members
**Suspension:** independent front with wishbones and coil springs; live rear axle with semi-elliptic leaf springs
**Brakes:** drums front and rear
**Bodywork:** glassfibre coupé
**Maximum speed:** 112 mph (180 km/h)

*Below: The 541R's distinguishing mark was its pivotting flap above the radiator. This was operated via a lever on the dashboard.*

hen Jensen came to develop a new odel in the 1950s, it reacted strongly to aims that the original Interceptor had een an over-large and somehow stodgy esign. The new 541 was smaller, eeker, and a lot faster.

Shown in prototype form with a metal dy shell, the 541 coupé went on sale th a glassfibre body – one of the first amples of GRP coachwork built by a itish concern – and by any mid-1950s andards it was a very fast car. With a w chassis, but powered by the same ustin engine as the Interceptor, the 541 as an elegant, long-legged and satis-ng GT which sold steadily in spite of rrying a very high price.

The coupé cabin was a four-seater, no more, but most well-to-do owners bought it as a spacious 2+2 machine. Apart from its general style, the 541's unique feature was the pivotting flap in the body shell ahead of the radiator, which was controlled by a cable and a lever on the fascia. For maximum cooling effect the flap could be 'feathered' open, but at high speeds, and to improve the aerodynamics, the flap could be closed completely. It was up to the driver to keep an eye on the temperature gauge!

In nine production years there were major technical advances. From late 1956 Jensen became the first British concern to fit disc brakes to a production road

car, while a year later the original 541 was joined by the faster 541R, which had a more powerful Austin engine and better steering.

The 541R is still an unappreciated car today, for it had a top speed of 124 mph, which put it on a par with Jaguar's XK150 of the day, yet it had more passenger accommodation. Its problem, of course, was that it was still expensive, so sales were limited.

The last of the line, the 541S, was a wider car than the 541R (Jensen literally cut the body moulds and widened the shell that way!) which bridged the gap between the earlier types and the CV8 which was to follow.

## Jensen CV8 1962-66

By the end of the 1950s Jensen, like Bristol, needed more powerful engines to allow its cars to hold their own in prestige markets. The trusty old Austin engine had run out of potential, so Jensen turned to Chrysler of the USA, and bought in their V8s and associated automatic transmissions.

Jensen had no links with Chrysler at the time and any one of the American 'big three' of Ford, GM and Chrysler would have been happy enough to supply their V8 engines and transmissions, as Jensen production was so small that it could not possibly have proved any threat to Corvette or Thunderbird sales.

Jensen wanted real performance, however, and opted for what was considered the best-engineered of the big American V8s – Chrysler's short-stroke six-litre unit allied to Chrysler's own Torqueflite three-speed automatic transmission. Despite its large displacement, the engine was relatively light and compact and, when fitted well back in the CV8's robust chassis, helped give fairly neutral weight distribution.

Yet again the old 541 chassis and style was rejigged, this time with a very fussy nose which incorporated four headlamps positioned slant-fashion, and with other fancy details. The result, the CV8 (standing for Chrysler V8), might have been called 'hideous' by some, or 'different' by others, but there were no criticisms of the performance, for the original model had a top speed of 131 mph, with acceleration to match.

The CV8, like its predecessors, was too expensive to sell fast, especially with those controversial looks, but it found a limited clientele who could not afford an Italian supercar, and wanted something different from an Aston Martin. In 1963,

*Below: All CV8 models featured glassfibre bodies, which is probably why so many of the 461 cars built have survived into the 1990s.*

when the first deliveries were made, the CV8's British price was £3,392, which compared well with the £3,505 asked for an Aston Martin DB4. The problem was that Jaguar's 3.8-litre Mk II saloon cost only £1,557, and most people preferred that tried-and-trusted production model even if it could not match the Jensen's power and performance.

It may not have been as fast, but its all-steel body (ironically in view of how most have now rusted completely away) did not suffer the quality problems associated with the early days of glassfibre construction. That was hampered on the CV8, incidentally, by the difficulty in matching the finish on the aluminium doors with the rest of the glassfibre body.

CV8s were produced in three slightly different types. There were 70 Mk Is, 250

Mk IIs and 141 Mk IIIs made – 461 in all. Because each had a GRP body, most survived into the 1990s, where they were admired as genuine classic cars.

### Jensen CV8 variants

#### Jensen CV8 Mk II and Mk III
The CV8 Mk II took over from the original type in 1963, with a larger V8 engine of 108 mm × 86 mm and 6276 cc/330 bhp, while the CV8 Mk III replaced the Mk II in 1965, with style changes and a dual braking system.

### Specification (1962)
**Engine:** V8, overhead-valve
**Bore × stroke:** 105 mm × 86 mm
**Capacity:** 5916 cc
**Maximum power:** 305 bhp

*Above: The controversially styled CV8 appealed to those people who wanted a distinctive supercar but could not afford an Aston Martin. Top speed was 131 mph.*

**Transmission:** four-speed manual gearbox or three-speed automatic transmission, rear-wheel drive
**Chassis:** steel platform with tubular-section main side members
**Suspension:** independent front with wishbones and coil springs; live rear axle with semi-elliptic leaf springs and telescopic dampers
**Brakes:** discs front and rear
**Bodywork:** glassfibre four-seater coupé
**Maximum speed (approx):** 131 mph (211 km/h)

# ensen Interceptor 1966–90

*Left: The second-generation Interceptor was made of steel and was by far the most numerous Jensen ever built, with 5,577 constructed.*

## Interceptor SP

The Interceptor SP (SP stood for Special Performance) used the 7.2-litre engine, with 385 bhp. Its top speed was 143 mph (230 km/h).

## Specification (1966)

**Engine:** V8, overhead-valve
**Bore × stroke:** 108 mm × 86 mm
**Capacity:** 6276 cc
**Maximum power:** 325 bhp
**Transmission:** four-speed manual gearbox or three-speed automatic transmission, rear-wheel drive
**Chassis:** separate steel platform
**Suspension:** independent front with wishbones and coil springs; live rear axle with semi-elliptic leaf springs
**Brakes:** discs front and rear
**Bodywork:** steel four-seater coupé/ hatchback
**Maximum speed (approx):** 133 mph (214 km/h)

 replace the old GRP-bodied CV8, nsen commissioned a startlingly odern Italian style, which not only atured four seats and a massive hatch ck rear window glass, but was de ned to be produced in pressed steel. e result was the second-generation terceptor, which stayed in production a decade, and was by far the most merous Jensen ever built.

The new car's chassis was a devel ed version of the CV8 layout, and wer was still provided by a massive rysler V8 engine, with a choice of nual or automatic transmission. Later ere was an even more technically vanced version – the four-wheel-drive ' – which is described overleaf.

The new body style was by Touring of lan, but Vignale was contracted to oduce the press tools and assembly s, and actually built the first bodies, ugh this tooling was eventually trans rred to West Bromwich.

Compared with the CV8, the new terceptor was more spacious but no vier, more luxuriously trimmed, and nsiderably more versatile. Its styling pealed to many more people than

before, and it had high performance (the top speed was over 130 mph) and a rugged character to match.

The first Interceptors lacked power-assisted steering and ran on crossply tyres, but by the 1970s the model had pro gressed through Mk II and Mk III and was more suitably equipped. All these cars were thirsty beasts – a typical fuel consumption figure was 14 mpg – which meant that their appeal was severely dented by the upward trend in fuel prices after the first 'energy crisis'.

If the Interceptor had been more fuel-efficient, and if the body had not become known for rusting away, the car might have sold even better. In the end its poten tial customers grew bored with the same styling, and the late introduction of con vertible, coupé and Special Performance alternatives did little to postpone the end.

In nearly 10 years a total of 5,577 Inter ceptors and SPs was produced.

## Jensen Interceptor variants

### Interceptor Mk II and Mk III

The Interceptor Mk II replaced the original Mk I in 1969, with the Mk III

taking over in 1971. Later Mk IIIs had larger, 7.2-litre, engines of 109.7 mm × 95.25 mm, producing 330 bhp; convertible and coupé options were also introduced.

*Above: If the massive Chrysler V8 engine had been more economical, the car may have sold even better.*

*Below: The later Mk III cars were offered in convertible form and are today highly desirable.*

## Jensen FF 1966-71

Jensen showed a prototype four-wheel-drive car in 1965, but the first to go on sale was the pioneering FF of 1966. This was effectively a long-wheelbase version of the new-generation Interceptor allied to the Ferguson four-wheel-drive system.

Ferguson had been working on such systems for some years, but Jensen was the first company to adopt the layout for a production car. Using the new Interceptor as its base, Jensen installed the FF system, which included a front propeller shaft up one side of the engine, and a front final drive to one side of, and ahead of, the engine. This arrangement was also allied to Dunlop Maxaret anti-lock brakes. It was the only automotive application of this system, which had been developed for aircraft.

To squeeze this into the Interceptor's shell, the front wheels had to be moved forward by four inches, but clever styling made this stretch virtually undetectable

*Right: Jensen first applied Ferguson four-wheel-drive technology to the CV8 body in 1965. This was one of the first prototypes.*

– except, that is, for the use of two cooling slots instead of one in the front wing pressings.

The FF was equally as fast – and thirsty – as the rear-drive Interceptor, with the same solid feel, while it had the phenomenal traction which four-wheel-drive lovers now find familiar on so many modern cars.

For the customers of the 1960s, however, it was all too strange, expensive, and difficult to repair, which perhaps explains why only 320 Jensen FFs were produced between 1966 and 1971. Nevertheless the model was upgraded along with the ordinary two-wheel-drive Interceptor, becoming a Mk II in 1969 and a Mk III in 1971.

*Above: The luxurious interior, with its leather and wood panels, carried four people at speeds up to 130 mph.*

*Below: Twin cooling vents on each front wing are the only real clue to the FF's exclusive identity.*

## Specification (1966)

**Engine:** V8, overhead-valve
**Bore × stroke:** 108 mm × 86 mm
**Capacity:** 6276 cc
**Maximum power:** 325 bhp
**Transmission:** four-speed manual gearbox or three-speed automatic transmission, rear-wheel drive
**Chassis:** separate steel platform
**Suspension:** independent front with wishbones and coil springs; live rear axle with semi-elliptic leaf springs and telescopic dampers
**Brakes:** discs front and rear
**Bodywork:** steel four-seater coupé/hatchback
**Maximum speed:** 130 mph (209 km/h)

*Below: The FF engine included a front propeller shaft up one side of the engine and a front final drive to one side of, and ahead of, the powerplant. This system was allied Dunlop Maxaret anti-lock brakes.*

# Jensen-Healey

T his short-lived marque came into existence after Jensen had been taken over by a consortium which included Kjell Qvale (a wealthy motor trader from San Francisco) and Donald Healey. Both had an obvious interest in keeping the Healey name alive Qvale because his business concentrated on selling imported sports cars in the USA (and the Austin-Healey marque had just been killed off). Donald Healey's BMC/British Leyland partnership had finished and he was keen to form another car-building alliance.

The takeover, which took place in 1970, was commercially promising. The Jensen factory in West Bromwich had been used to make tens of thousands of sports cars for other manufacturers during the 1960s (body/chassis units for the Austin-Healey 3000, and complete assembly of Volvo 1800s, then Sunbeam Tigers), so the new management planned to make Jensen-Healeys in large numbers.

In the meantime, production of Chrysler-engined Jensens continued, and it was not until 1972 that the Jensen-Healey went on sale. However, while this soon filled up the factory at West Bromwich, it was always a troublesome project, and by the end of 1975 sales had dropped, the old 'big' Jensens were nearly obsolete, and financial losses mounted.

Early in 1976 Qvale put his British business into liquidation, and no more Jensen-Healeys were produced. There was no concerted attempt to revive the Jensen-Healey, unlike the Chrysler-engined Jensens, so the marque had an effective life of only four years. It was the last production car, incidentally, to carry the famous Healey name.

*Below: The management of the newly-formed Jensen-Healey company planned to make their new sports car in large numbers at the West Bromwich factory. After many different prototypes had been produced, this, the definitive production car, emerged in 1972.*

*Above: Because it was not meant to be a sports car, the Healey name was dropped for the distinctive Jensen GT.*

*Below: The Jensen takeover, by a consortium including Donald Healey, led to the birth of the new marque.*

## Jensen-Healey 1972-76

door cabin. It was about 60 lb heavier than the roadster, but had similar performance, and had 2 + 2 seating and more stowage space.

### Specification (1972 Jensen-Healey)

**Engine:** inline four-cylinder, twin overhead camshafts
**Bore × stroke:** 95.2 mm × 69.3 mm
**Capacity:** 1973 cc
**Maximum power:** 140 bhp
**Transmission:** four-speed manual gearbox (later five-speed manual), rear-wheel drive
**Chassis:** steel unit-construction body/chassis
**Suspension:** independent front with wishbones and coil springs; live rear axle with coil springs, radius arms and telescopic dampers
**Brakes:** discs front, drums rear
**Bodywork:** steel two-seater open sports car, optional hard top
**Maximum speed (approx):** 119 mph (192 km/h)

After British Leyland told the Healey family that the Austin-Healey marque was to be killed off, and that its consultancy arrangements were also to be discontinued, the Healeys – Donald, and his sons Geoff and 'Bic' – began to develop a new model. This, in final form, became the Jensen-Healey sports car.

The original concept used many Vauxhall components, mostly lifted from the Viva GT, but the single-cam engine was not powerful enough when encumbered with USA exhaust-emissions equipment. After casting around Europe for an engine, the Healeys settled on Lotus's brand-new 16-valve type 907 twin-cam unit, and became the first user of a unit which was later adopted for all of Lotus's late-1970s production cars.

To match it, a Chrysler-UK gearbox (as used in the Sunbeam Rapier H120) was chosen, and by the time the car was announced, the only Vauxhall components were the front and rear suspensions and steering, for Jensen produced its own steel body/chassis units.

*Below: The prototype used many Vauxhall components, mostly taken from the Viva GT, but the production car was Lotus-powered.*

The least outstanding feature of the new car was its rather plain-Jane styling, which had gone through several phases before being committed to series-production. In other respects, though, the new two-seater was a brisk, good-handling sports car, which went on sale in the summer of 1972. When its engine was in good health, it had an urgent and high-revving character, with a great deal of potential for tuning.

In the next three years the car's reputation was dented by teething problems associated with the new Lotus engine; but cosmetic style changes, and the introduction of the new Getrag five-speed gearbox in place of the weaker Chrysler unit, all helped.

Sales were never up to expectations (the aftermath of the 'energy crisis' of 1973-74 had much to do with this as the model was never very economical). Another point hampering sales was the appalling quality control; panel fit and finish were poor, and the cars had little corrosion resistance.

When Jensen stopped trading in 1976, the Jensen-Healey marque died, and was never revived. In rather less than four years, 10,926 Jensen-Healeys and 473 Jensen GTs were produced.

*Above: Just 473 GTs were produced. The 2 + 2 estate offered space and performance.*

### Jensen-Healey variants

#### Jensen GT
The GT of 1975-76 was an additional type, with the same basic style and running gear as the Jensen-Healey, but with a 'sporting-estate' type of three-

*Below: The instrument panel was well served with dials; the gearbox was a Chrysler unit.*

# Jowett Cars Ltd

**B**enjamin and William Jowett set up their carmaking business near Bradford, Yorkshire, in 1910, naturally enough calling their cars Jowetts. The marque they created pursued its own very individual path for more than 40 years.

Jowett always built its cars as simply and cheaply as possible, and until he 1930s every Jowett was built with some version of a horizontally-pposed flat-twin-cylinder engine. A flat-four engine was then introduced 1 1936. Changes of shareholding by this time meant that the Jowett family o longer controlled its own destiny, though the company's philosophy of uilding simply-engineered, economical and basically-equipped cars ever deviated.

After World War II the company changed its approach, and aimed igher up the market by commissioning a brand-new design, this being he ultra-modern Javelin, the first the company had ever produced with a ought-in unit-construction steel body shell (by Briggs Motor Bodies of )oncaster), and the first to use a new design of 'flat' four-cylinder engine.

By this time the Jowett family was no longer connected with the

*Above: The Jowett brothers, here with one of their early models, set up shop in Bradford, Yorkshire, in 1910 and built cars for over 40 years.*

business which it founded, and majority control had passed into the hands of Lazards, the London-based merchant bank, who installed George Wansborough as the chairman.

The Javelin saloon design was then followed by the development of the limited-production Jupiter sports car, whose reputation was soon underpinned by some fine performances in races and rallies, notably the Le Mans 24 Hours.

In the early 1950s problems with reliability, particularly of the engines and the gearboxes, led to the Javelin's reputation falling away, and by 1953 the factory was overstocked, and had no choice but to close down its assembly lines.

This was the point at which all development on new models (including the exciting R4 two-seater sports car) was abandoned. Apart from building more Bradford vans, Jowett production soon died away. The factory and the remnants of the business were sold to International Harvester in 1954.

*bove: The Jowett badge was onsiderably less innovative than ome of the Yorkshire company's esigns.*

*Below: The exciting R4 two-seater sports car project was unfortunately abandoned owing to lack of funds in the 1950s.*

## Jowett Javelin 1947-53

winner in the Spa 24 Hours.

Unhappily for Jowett, however, the model was rather too expensive to sell in large numbers, and by the 1950s its engine and gearbox reliability problems were well-known. Not even its high performance and good looks could save its reputation, so Javelin assembly ended in 1953, after a total of 23,307 cars had been produced in six years.

*Left: Considering that it used a compact flat-four engine, the Javelin was a rather upright design but the car was, by British standards, technically advanced for its time.*

### Specification (1947)

**Engine:** flat-four, overhead-valve
**Bore × stroke:** 72.5 mm × 90 mm
**Capacity:** 1486 cc
**Maximum power:** 50 bhp
**Transmission:** four-speed manual gearbox, rear-wheel drive
**Chassis:** steel unit-construction body/chassis
**Suspension:** independent front with wishbones and torsion bars; live rear axle with torsion bars
**Brakes:** drums front and rear
**Bodywork:** steel four-seater saloon
**Maximum speed (approx):** 82 mph (132 km/h)

For its post-war cars Jowett made a new start by appointing Gerald Palmer in 1942, and allowing him a free hand to design a new family car. The result, unveiled in 1946, but going on sale in 1947, was the all-new Javelin.

Except that it used a flat-four engine layout, there were no links with Jowett's past. The new Javelin had smooth and attractive body lines with what we would now call a 'fastback', had torsion-bar independent front suspension, and a chassis-less structure, with the body/chassis units supplied to Bradford by Briggs Motor Bodies of Doncaster.

The new Javelin was technically and visually advanced by almost any British standards, and matched good handling to brisk performance, so it was soon known as a sports saloon, and was regularly used in races and rallies.

The Javelin was good enough to win its class in the 1949 Monte Carlo Rally and, showing its versatility, it was also a class

*Above: A Javelin is chased by two Aston DB2s at a 1954 BARC meeting at Goodwood. Javelins handled well.*

*Below: The smooth and attractive fastback body was supplied by Briggs Motor Bodies of Doncaster.*

## owett Jupiter 1950-54

fter Javelin designer Gerald Palmer ad left the company, and Roy Lunn had ken over, Jowett dabbled with the idea producing a sports car of its own, but ventually awarded a development conact to ERA of Dunstable.

The ERA-Javelin, as it was originally alled, mated tuned-up Javelin running ear and suspension systems (including e steering-column gear change!) to a ew tubular chassis frame which had een designed by ex-Auto Union GP gineer Professor Eberan von Eberorst. This short-chassis machine (the heelbase was only 93 inches) was uneiled in 1949, but went on sale in the ummer of 1950 as the Jupiter.

Clothed in its own distinctive twoeater sports car style, the Jupiter was a st and nimble machine by early 1950s andards. One feature, which was later ken up for the 'frog-eye' Austin-Healey

Sprite, was that the entire bonnet/front wings/nose assembly was hinged at the scuttle and, when lifted, gave excellent access to the engine bay for repairs and maintenance. On the other hand, the original design had a long and sweeping rear in which there was no external opening to the stowage area.

There were two related problems with the Jupiter, however – the bodies were expensive and complicated to build, and as a result the cars were costly. Consequently, sales were slow, even though there were never any complaints about the performance.

During its three-year production life there were many small development changes to improve the design, but one major improvement – from Mk I to Mk IA in 1952 – saw the adoption of an exterior boot lid for the stowage compartment, though the petrol tank was smaller than

*Above: A Jupiter takes part in the 1990 Pirelli Marathon. With its short wheelbase, it was fast and nimble.*

before. A total of 825 fully built-up cars was sold; in addition 75 rolling chassis were equipped with special coachwork by outside coachbuilders.

The successor to the Jupiter would have been the R4, but this was killed off when the company was sold to International Harvester in 1954.

### Specification (1950)

**Engine:** flat-four, overhead-valve
**Bore × stroke:** 72.5 mm × 90 mm
**Capacity:** 1486 cc

**Maximum power:** 60 bhp
**Transmission:** four-speed manual gearbox, rear-wheel drive
**Chassis:** separate steel frame with tubular main and bracing members
**Suspension:** independent front with wishbones and torsion bars; live rear axle with torsion bars
**Brakes:** drums front and rear
**Bodywork:** aluminium and steel two-seater sports car
**Maximum speed (approx):** 88 mph (142 km/h)

*Below: Instruments included a tachometer, speedo and oil temperature and pressure gauges.*

*bove: The entire front body ssembly swung forward, giving reat access to the flat-four engine.*

*Below: The Jupiter's flowing lines were aerodynamically efficient, allowing a good top speed.*

# Lagonda

Wilbur Gunn, the founder of Lagonda, was an American from Springfield, Ohio, who arrived in the UK in 1897. After building air-cooled motorcycles, he turned to car manufacture in 1906, calling them Lagondas. This was a modified version of the name of a stream which had flowed near his hometown in the USA.

Basing his company at Staines, in Middlesex, Gunn first built a series of four-cylinder family cars, but the first sporting Lagonda was the two-litre-engined 14/60 of 1925, which had a twin-high-camshaft engine layout.

For the next 15 years Lagonda built a series of sporting cars of rare distinction which rivalled Bentley for performance and in later years preserved the 'vintage' tradition years after the 1920s had gone and other manufacturers had turned to more modern designs.

Lagonda, like many other independent British concerns, was too small to develop all its own running gear, which is how it came to rely on the Meadows six-cylinder engine for its larger cars at this time, and why it was led to experiment with a German Maybach transmission which featured eight forward gears!

In the 1930s a series of six-cylinder cars, including the massive 4½-litre, were also joined by the complex little four-cylinder Rapier, before the company hit financial trouble in 1935, and the receivers were called in.

A new company, financed by Alan Good and with W. O. Bentley as the technical director, then rose from the ashes of the old, not only reviving and improving the 4½-litre but producing the magnificent V12 model. The Rapier project was sold off, although the design, virtually unaltered, was maintained until 1939.

After World War II W. O. Bentley planned to make an all-new 2.6-litre Lagonda, the LB6. The intention to call it a Lagonda-Bentley was killed off after an expensive court case brought by Rolls-Royce (who successfully claimed that they owned the Bentley trademark), and Lagonda was then

*Above: One of the rarest of Lagondas, this special-bodied racer was built in the 1950s and powered by a 4.4-litre Lagonda V12.*

*Below: The perfect symmetry of the Lagonda badge was helped by the name having seven letters and the middle letter being an 'o'.*

obliged to sell out to David Brown (who had just acquired Aston Martin) before this car could go on sale.

In 1947 David Brown merged Lagonda's interests with those of Aston Martin and developed a bigger factory at Feltham, a few miles from Staines. The result was a reprieve for Lagonda, but a gradual loss of its separate identity. Under new ownership the LB6 went on sale in 1948, its engine also being used in the Aston Martin DB2 family which followed; that engine, in much-developed form, was also used in the race-winning Aston Martin DB3, DB3S and DBR1 two-seaters, the last of which brought Aston Martin the World Sports Car Championship in 1959.

Having taken over Tickford (the coachbuilders) of Newport Pagnell, David Brown then moved Aston Martin and Lagonda assembly to this plant in the late 1950s, closing down the Feltham base, and severing all Lagonda links with south-west London.

Henceforth Lagonda was merely a minor arm of the business, for all later models were based on Aston Martin designs. From the mid-1970s, indeed, Lagonda became solely a model name, not a marque name, in the Aston Martin range, though traditionalists have always insisted on treating it as a separate marque.

*Above: The mid-1950s saw elegant designs like this three-litre four-door saloon model with Tickford bodywork.*

*Below: In 1974 Aston Martin Lagonda produced a four-door lengthened version of the V8, which was given the Lagonda name.*

# Lagonda 3-litre 1929-34

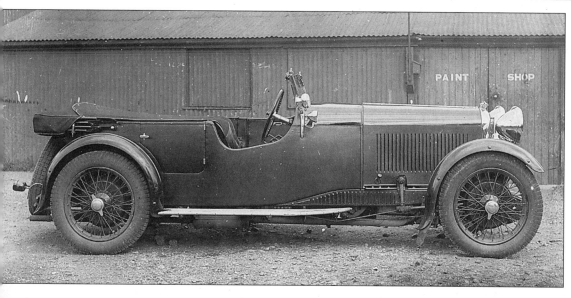

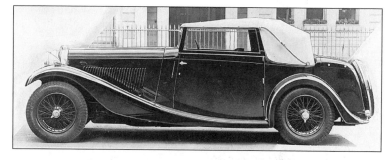

Lagonda's first six-cylinder model was the 2½-litre of 1926, and the 3-litre, introduced in 1929, was a direct descendant of that model.

The 3-litre was a solid but graceful car, built by hand, which rivalled Bentley in many ways in the early 1930s.

Like all such typical British 'vintage' cars, the 3-litre combined a simple chassis frame, on a choice of wheelbase lengths, with a heavy yet lusty six-cylinder engine with seven main crankshaft bearings. This straight-six was a Lagonda-designed unit, built at Staines. Although several different body styles were available, the most familiar derivative was a rakish four-seater tourer on a 129-in wheelbase.

Like its Bentley opposition, the 3-litre tourer was very substantially built (it weighed about 3,400 lb), and cost £1,000, which was about eight times the price of a small family car of the period. On the other hand it was beautifully built and

nicely detailed, and by the standards of the day it was fast and sporting.

In the early 1930s Lagonda responded to a new fashion for 'easy-change' gearboxes, by offering the 3-litre 'Selector Special', which featured a Maybach transmission offering no fewer than eight forward speeds and no less than four reverse ratios. This was heavy, complex and unhappily not reliable. Only about 30 such cars were produced, most of which were later reconverted by Lagonda to more conventional transmissions.

From 1934 the 3-litre was overshadowed by the Meadows-engined 4½-litre, but there was one final attempt to prolong its life in 1935, when the 3½-litre model (with a 3.6-litre version of the Lagonda engine) was offered. This car had 88 bhp and could manage a top speed of 85 mph.

Between 1929 and 1934 a total of 570 3-litres was produced, followed by 65 3½-litre types in 1935.

*Above: This Lagonda 3-litre dates from shortly after the model was first unveiled in 1929. Its solid and upright look was reminiscent of Bentleys of the period and its performance was similar.*

*Above: After the end of 3-litre production in 1934 a 3½-litre variant was introduced, using a 3619-cc version of Lagonda's own straight-six engine which was marginally more powerful, with an extra 8 bhp.*

*Below: The 3-litre's very upright styling looked even more perpendicular when the hood was raised. Considering the car's poor aerodynamics, its top speed of 80 mph was excellent.*

## Lagonda 3-litre variants

### Lagonda 3½-litre
In 1935 the 3½-litre model briefly replaced the 3-litre, with a 3619-cc/88-bhp version of the six-cylinder engine, and with a choice of M45R (4½-litre) bodies.

## Specification (1929)
**Engine:** inline six-cylinder, overhead-valve
**Bore × stroke:** 72 mm × 120 mm, later 75 mm × 120 mm
**Capacity:** 2931 cc
**Maximum power:** 80 bhp (approx)
**Transmission:** four-speed manual gearbox, rear-wheel drive
**Chassis:** separate steel frame with channel-section side members
**Suspension:** non-independent with beam front axle and semi-elliptic leaf springs; live rear axle with semi-elliptic leaf springs
**Brakes:** drums front and rear
**Bodywork:** aluminium and fabric tourer, saloon or limousine
**Maximum speed (approx):** 80 mph (129 km/h)

# Lagonda 4½-litre 1933-39

At the 1933 British Motor Show, Lagonda introduced two outstanding new models, one of them the small-engined Rapier, and the other being the magnificent 4½-litre model. In every way this was the perfect successor to the 3-litre car.

Like the famous vintage Lagondas, the 4½-litre had a simple but solid channel-section chassis frame, and there was a wide choice of different body styles, but the secret of the new car's success was the rugged, reliable and very powerful Meadows 4½-litre engine, the same type which had already proved itself in the 4½-litre Invicta sports car.

The original car was fast, with very firm suspension but – like all large-engined Lagondas – it was expensive, which limited its sales. As the factory at Staines was not equipped for mass-production in any case, this suited everyone except the company's bankers, who saw losses growing in the mid-1930s, and took the company into receivership in 1935.

It was the reborn firm, with W. O. Bentley as its technical director, which got the best out of the 4½-litre, at first in the refined and softer-suspended LG45, and finally in the LG45R Rapide four-seater tourer. The Rapide was lower than other types, more powerful (it was advertised as having 150 bhp, but 130 bhp was nearer the truth), and aggressively styled with exposed flexible exhaust pipes protruding from the sides of the bonnet. A top speed of over 105 mph was certainly possible, yet at £1,050 it was an expensive sports car which sold only slowly.

The final flowering of this excellent design was the LG6, a combination of V12-type chassis (complete with independent front suspension), which had hydraulic brakes, and the Meadows 4½-litre six-cylinder engine and its related transmission. This car carried V12 model body styling (by Frank Feeley) – in a variety of open and closed shapes – on a choice of wheelbases, but by this

time buyers were mesmerised by the V12 Lagonda, and sales fell away before the outbreak of war.

In six years, a total of 410 M45 types, 53 M45R Rapides, 278 Bentley-inspired LG45s, 25 LG45R Rapides and 85 LG6s was produced, many of which survive to this day.

## Lagonda 4½-litre variants

### Lagonda M45

The original 4½-litre was the M45 model of 1933-35, which ran on a 129-in wheelbase chassis, and was offered with a wide choice of bodies. The Meadows engine was very powerful, so every example of this type would exceed 90 mph, the tourers being capable of more than 95 mph.

*Below: The LG45 appeared in a variety of guises, with long and short wheelbases, in touring and sports form. The most powerful was the Rapide of 1937 with 130 bhp and over-100-mph performance.*

*Above: Last of the Lagonda 4½-litre line was the LG6, which had the more flowing lines of the larger-engined V12 models combined with the six-cylinder 4½-litre Meadows engine. It was a short-lived model produced only from 1938 to 1939.*

### Lagonda M45R

The M45R (built only in 1935) was a sporting version of the M45, using a shortened and stiffened chassis, and a more forward-mounted engine, which was tuned to give 119 bhp, while the transmission incorporated a free wheel.

### Lagonda LG45

The LG45 (1935-37) was the redeveloped version of the M45, with a synchromesh gearbox, softer suspension and modern styling.

### Lagonda LG45R Rapide

The LG45R Rapide (1937 only) was the short-wheelbase sports version of the LG45, with 130 bhp and a top speed of over 100 mph.

### Lagonda LG6

Finally, the LG6 of 1938-39 was a combination of the V12 chassis and LG45 running gear, with independent front suspension and V12-type body styles.

### Specification (1937 LG45R Rapide)

**Engine:** inline six-cylinder, overhead-valve
**Bore × stroke:** 88.5 mm × 120.6 mm
**Capacity:** 4453 cc
**Maximum power:** 130 bhp
**Transmission:** four-speed manual gearbox, rear wheel drive
**Chassis:** separate steel frame with channel-section side members
**Suspension:** non-independent with beam front axle and semi-elliptic leaf springs; live rear axle with semi-elliptic leaf springs
**Brakes:** drums front and rear
**Bodywork:** choice of aluminium two-seater or four-seater, open or closed
**Maximum speed (approx):** 105 mph (169 km/h)

# Lagonda V12 1938-40

After joining the reborn Lagonda concern in 1935, W. O. Bentley's first job was to refine and improve the existing 4½-litre model, but his design team then settled down to create the magnificent V12 model. Previewed in 1936, but not actually on sale until the end of 1937, it was one of the finest British cars produced in that period.

Bentley's aim was to produce a better car than the Rolls-Royce Phantom III, with which he had been reluctantly involved after Rolls-Royce had taken over his own Bentley company in the early 1930s. To do this he inspired the birth of an overhead-cam V12 engine, and a new chassis with torsion-bar independent front suspension.

It was a car for the moneyed few, and was available in seemingly infinite variety, with a choice of three wheelbase lengths, at least seven different body styles (including a limousine), and three different rear axle ratios. Chassis prices started at £1,200 (there was no purchase tax or VAT in those far-off days), and complete cars cost between £1,500 and £1,800.

The V12 was an excellent car in every way, technically the equal of the Rolls-Royce, and although a typical saloon weighed about 4,500 lb, it was more powerful and somewhat faster than a Rolls, and could easily reach 100 mph. Most body styles were voluptuous creations inspired by Frank Feeley, and were years ahead of the Rolls-Royce in fashion, if not in grace.

The only thing missing was the final cachet of a model reputation (for Lagonda was not yet seen at the same level as Rolls-Royce), but Lagonda was working on that, and if World War II had not intervened there would have been interesting battles to be seen. An excellent performance in the Le Mans 24 Hours of 1939 saw specially-bodied V12s finish third and fourth, their pace held back, they say, by W. O. Bentley's caution about his new design.

*Above: Lagonda's V12 lived on into the post-war world when this one-off version was produced with the 1954 Le Mans 24 Hours in mind. Here it's being driven by Reg Parnell at Silverstone; it crashed at Le Mans.*

In the end just 189 V12s were made in two years, the jigging and tooling was scrapped during the war, and neither engine nor chassis was ever revived. It was felt that such a luxurious car was out of tune with the austere post-war conditions.

## Specification (1938)

**Engine:** V12, single overhead camshaft per bank of cylinders
**Bore × stroke:** 75 mm × 84.5 mm
**Capacity:** 4480 cc
**Maximum power:** 180 bhp
**Transmission:** four-speed manual gearbox, rear wheel drive
**Chassis:** separate steel frame with channel-section side members
**Suspension:** independent front with wishbones and torsion bars; live rear axle with semi-elliptic leaf springs
**Brakes:** drums front and rear
**Bodywork:** aluminium and wood four-seaters, saloons or drop-head coupés
**Maximum speed (approx):** 100 mph (161 km/h)

*Above: Although the Lagonda V12 engine was a surprisingly compact unit and would have permitted a relatively low bonnet line, Lagonda stylist Frank Feeley retained the very tall upright radiator grille which was a Lagonda hallmark.*

*Below: The flowing lines of Frank Feeley's V12 design could have graced a European exotic like Hispano-Suiza. Unfortunately, few of the 180-bhp, 100-mph, Lagonda V12s were produced before the onset of World War II brought an end to car production.*

## Lagonda Rapide 1961-64

After a three-year gap, the Lagonda name was revived by Aston Martin, to badge a four-door saloon car which was based on the engineering of the modern Aston Martin DB4 coupé. Called the Rapide, which brought back memories of the 1930s, this was very much a personal favourite of Aston Martin's chairman, Sir David Brown, but it sold only slowly, and was dropped after a mere 55 cars had been built in three years.

All the well-proven elements of the DB4 were present under the skin of the new car, except that the massive twin-cam engine was both larger and less highly tuned. Displacement had been increased to just short of four litres by increasing the bore by 4 mm. The change was intended to generate more torque rather than greater power, and to the same end the camshaft profiles were altered. The result was a boost to 265 lb ft at 4,000 rpm, enough to give the heavy luxury saloon the right degree of effortless performance. Other changes from the Rapide included a longer wheelbase

*Right: The Rapide of 1961 had curious front styling which some considered reminiscent of the ill-fated Ford Edsel and others thought had very strong Facel Vega overtones. The protruding headlights were one of the car's more awkward features. Its performance, however, was excellent, with a top speed of 130 mph.*

and de Dion rear suspension using double transverse torsion bars rather than coil springs (along with trailing arms and a Watt linkage for transverse location), to save space and allow adequate room for the rear passengers.

The style itself was of a large and heavy (195.5-in long/3,780 lb unladen weight) four-door saloon, with some elements of Aston Martin construction including the windscreen and some front panels. The front was dominated by the latest interpretation of the Aston Martin grille with four headlamps, two of them 7-in and two of them 5¾-in diameter; cynics pointed out a slight resemblance to Ford's ill-fated Edsel style, which did

nothing for the Rapide's reputation.

This was a fast and roadworthy car, but it was somehow not as graceful as Aston Martin would have hoped. Like previous (and future) 'four-door Aston Martins', it did not sell as well as the coupés, partly because it was much more expensive, so it quietly died away in 1964.

In the mid-1970s Aston Martin dabbled with yet another approach to the long-wheelbase/four-door Aston Martin requirement, but this car, also dubbed Lagonda, was dropped after a mere seven cars had been built.

### Specification (1961)

**Engine:** inline six-cylinder, twin-cam
**Bore × stroke:** 96 mm × 92 mm
**Capacity:** 3995 cc
**Maximum power:** 236 bhp
**Transmission:** four-speed manual gearbox or three-speed automatic
**Chassis:** steel platform
**Suspension:** independent front with wishbones and coil springs; de Dion rear with torsion bars
**Brakes:** discs front and rear
**Bodywork:** four-seater saloon
**Maximum speed:** 130 mph (209 km/h)

## Aston Martin Lagonda 1976-89

Under yet another new management, stylist William Towns (who had shaped the Aston Martin DBS/V8 series) was asked to produce a four-door saloon on a lengthened version of the current Aston Martin platform chassis. This new car, rather clumsily titled Aston Martin Lagonda, was previewed in 1976, although first deliveries were not made until 1978.

The style was in a severe sharp-edged 'origami' fashion, with angular features, being low, wide, and flat, but there was ample seating and luggage space for four wealthy people. Prototypes had ultra-advanced instrumentation, and that proved a mistake on Aston Martin's part. They had, naturally, wanted the Lagonda to be as up-to-date as possible, and to

offer more than the competition. Unfortunately, although the electronic digital displays were years ahead of the rest of the industry, they were both unpopular and terribly unreliable despite Aston Martin's protracted efforts to get the system to work. That was hardly a selling point in a car so expensive, and the electronics were quickly replaced by more conventional analogue dials.

The chassis was closely based on that of the existing Aston Martin V8, but because of the car's size (it was 208-in long), and its unladen weight of 4,400 lb, it was not quite as fast. Its top speed of 143 mph, therefore, was well behind that of its obvious competitor, the Ferrari 400 GT, but it was still an impressive long-distance performer.

Like the Aston Martin from which it was derived the Lagonda was a solid, hand-crafted machine with great character. Its interior featured all the traditional British fittings of leather, fine carpets and wood, while it had stable and predictable handling, as well as restful high gearing.

A more powerful engine, with fuel injection and 309 bhp, was standardised from 1986, and in 1987 the style was re-skinned and subtly 'rounded-off', though the basic proportions were not changed.

### Specification (1976)

**Engine:** V8, quad-cam
**Bore × stroke:** 100 mm × 85 mm
**Capacity:** 5340 cc
**Maximum power:** N/A

**Transmission:** three-speed automatic transmission, rear wheel drive
**Chassis:** steel platform
**Suspension:** independent front with wishbones and coil springs; de Dion rear with coil springs
**Brakes:** discs front and rear
**Bodywork:** aluminium and steel four-seater saloon
**Maximum speed (approx):** 143 mph (230 km/h)

*Below: The Aston Martin Lagonda was a complete contrast to stylist William Towns' previous design for Aston Martin Lagonda, the DBS. Under the sharp edges was a quad-cam Aston Martin V8 engine powerful enough to take the big saloon to beyond 140 mph.*

# Lamborghini

The Lamborghini marque was set up because its founder was frustrated by Enzo Ferrari's attitude to him when he was a customer. That's how the story goes, and the fact is that Lamborghini has been a worthy competitor to Ferrari ever since the first car took to the road.

Ferruccio Lamborghini was already a self-made millionaire – his businesses including the manufacture of tractors and heating and air-conditioning equipment – before he founded the car company which bears his name in 1963.

Although he was not a design engineer himself, Ferruccio Lamborghini knew how to pick the best men and to provide them with the best facilities. To produce cars he chose a 'green-field' site at Sant' Agata Bolognese and commissioned a new factory – not far from Bologna, and relatively close to Italy's supercar centre of Modena – and hired engineers like Italy's Giotto Bizzarrini, Gianpaolo Dallara and Paulo Stanzani to design his first cars.

Like other Italian supercar manufacturers, Lamborghini hired independent design houses to shape its cars, but it was Bizzarrini's magnificent four-cam V12 engine and Dallara's advanced chassis design which gave the early models their sensational character and, for a while, a definite advantage over Ferrari.

The first Lamborghinis were relatively conventional front-engined V12s, but from 1966 the fabulous transverse V12 mid-engined Miura made the headlines, and after that model had been joined by the sleek four-seater Espada saloon, Lamborghini's status in this rarified market was assured. However, it was easier to make a reputation than to make

*Above and right: Lamborghini's bull emblem still appears today on the Diablo. The earlier Miura was named after a Spanish fighting bull.*

profits, but such progress only seemed to be a matter of time.

In 1970 Lamborghini followed the Miura and Espada with a new 'small' model, the mid-engined V8 Urraco, and showed the amazing V12 Countach in 1971. By this time the company seemed to have models to match *every* Ferrari, but as it was not similarly backed by the might of a large concern (Fiat, in Ferrari's case), commercial problems were still holding the firm back.

Early in the 1970s Ferruccio Lamborghini had begun to lose interest in his car company. In 1972 he sold 51 per cent of the business to Georges-Henri Rossetti of Switzerland, and the remaining 49 per cent went to Rossetti's associate, René Leimer, in 1974. Although the Countach was in production by that time, the other models were fading away, for the Urraco had made no impact in the USA, where success would have ensured the firm's security, the decline being such that a mere 16 cars rolled out of the Sant' Agata factory doors during 1978. A contract to develop and produce the BMW M1 had to be abandoned when the money ran out, and Lamborghini went into receivership in 1978.

The Franco-Swiss Mimram brothers (Patrick and Jean-Claude) took control in 1981, and began resuscitating the business, first by producing the Jalpa (which was essentially an improved Urraco), then by creating more powerful and better Countachs, and finally by putting the amazing 4 × 4 V12 LM002 off-road vehicle into production.

In 1987 Chrysler bought control of Lamborghini from the Mimram brothers, announced plans for new models, and hired ex-Ferrari engine designer Mauro Forghieri to develop a new V12 Formula 1 engine, which appeared in 1989. Although Lamborghini engines enjoyed little success in Grands Prix, the company continued its Formula 1 involvement into 1992 with Venturi and Minardi.

The first Chrysler-influenced Lamborghini was the Diablo of 1990 styled by Marcello Gandini. The company was sold to Audi in 1998, and the Diablo's successor, the Canto, appeared in prototype form the same year.

*Above: The 400 GT 2 + 2 was essentially identical to the first Lamborghini of all, the 350 GT.*

*Below: The most famous Lamborghini, the angular and futuristic Countach, replaced the Miura in 1973.*

## Lamborghini 350 GT 1964-66

The very first Lamborghini prototype was shown in 1963, and was a predictable amalgam of front-engined layout, multi-tubular chassis, V12 engine, all-independent suspension and aluminium two-seater coupé coachwork. That first car, however, was not ready for production when unveiled, and the definitive 350 GT, which followed in 1964, differed in many details.

True to his resolve, however, Ferruccio Lamborghini had inspired the birth of a faster and more advanced car than his rival, Ferrari, was making at the time. The major problem, unresolved in the early years, was that his cars had neither a reputation, nor the world-renowned Pininfarina styling, to help them become established with wealthy buyers.

The original Lamborghini, dubbed the 350 GTV, with chassis by Neri & Bonacini and Scaglione-styled body by Sargiotto, was shown at Turin in November 1963, and was seen to be a dramatically-shaped two-seater coupé, but was sufficiently different from a 'classic' Pininfarina profile for the media to be only luke-warm about its prospects.

This was not the first pretender to Ferrari's supercar crown to come from Italy, the media said, nor would it be the last. Was there sufficient financial backing

behind the scheme for it to be treated seriously? Would it even go on sale at all?

Lamborghini himself was quite determined to make a success of his new venture, and passed the style to Carrozzeria Touring of Milan for refinement. He awarded the production contract to Marazzi and deliveries of the renamed 350 GT models began in 1964. The body style was certainly different from those on offer by Ferrari or Maserati at the time, for the lines of the car were sensuous, the large oval headlamps were unique, and the entire package was undeniably distinctive.

The new model was very fast (with a top speed of more than 150 mph), surprisingly nimble, and was immediately seen to have the same (or better) build quality than the Ferraris with which it had to compete. From late 1964, however, Ferrari introduced the 275 GTB, with a new and improved chassis design, so the 350 GT had to struggle (successfully) to make its mark.

Until 1966 the 350 GT was the only production Lamborghini, but in that year it was supplanted by an improved model, the 400 GT 2+2. Although it retained the same wheelbase and chassis, the 400 GT had a larger engine and a reworked Touring body shell into which a '2+2'

*Left: Coachwork company Touring of Milan was awarded the contract to style the first Lamborghini's alloy body; the production contract went to the Marazzi firm.*

seating package had been squeezed. Although the style of the 350 GT was preserved, virtually every panel had been revised; there were four headlamps instead of the twin ovals, and the cabin was larger and more spacious.

Before the original type was replaced by the Islero in 1968, a total of 131 350 GTs, 23 400 GTs, and 224 400 GT 2+2 models was built.

### Lamborghini 350 GT variants

#### Lamborghini 400 GT

The short-lived 400 GT of 1966-67 used an enlarged 3929-cc V12 producing 320 bhp in the 350 GT shell, and with a Lamborghini gearbox in place of the original ZF. Only 23 were made, 20 of them with steel bodies. The top speed was 156 mph.

#### Lamborghini 400 GT 2+2

The 400 GT 2+2 was built between 1966 and 1968 and was a further revision of the original 350 GT, with the same basic chassis and running gear as the 400 GT. At 224, production was almost twice that of the 350 GT.

### Specification (1964)

**Engine:** V12, quad-cam
**Bore × stroke:** 77 mm × 62 mm
**Capacity:** 3465 cc
**Maximum power:** 270 bhp
**Transmission:** five-speed ZF manual gearbox, rear-wheel drive
**Chassis:** separate steel platform with tubular main and bracing members
**Suspension:** independent with unequal-length wishbones, coil springs telescopic dampers and anti-roll bars front and rear
**Brakes:** discs front and rear
**Bodywork:** aluminium two-seater coupé
**Maximum speed (approx):** 152 mph (245 km/h)

*Above: The quad-cam V12 engine produced 270 bhp and gave the 350 GT and 400 GT 2+2 (shown here) maximum speeds of over 150 mph.*

*Below: All-independent suspension helped make the 400 GT's handling nimble, but there was some body roll*

# Lamborghini Miura 1966-73

[I]f only for the Miura and Countach, Lamborghini will be famous as long as cars are known, and discussed. Both were monstrously fast and wickedly attractive mid-engined designs. Apart from their use of the same Lamborghini V12 engine, however, their engineering and general layouts were utterly different.

The very first appearance of the Lamborghini Miura caused a sensation. When the partly-completed rolling chassis was displayed at the Turin Motor Show of 1965, its mechanical design and specification appeared completely impractical. Not only was this the first time that a V12 engine had ever been mounted transversely behind the driver of a two-seater car, but it was the first V12 mid-engined production car – the Ferrari 250LM, after all, had merely been an omologation special.

No-one believed Ferruccio Lamborghini when he promised that the new car, engineered by Dallara and Stanzani, would go into production, but when a complete car, with Bertone styling which

seemed to take some cues from Ford's GT40, was shown at Geneva in 1966, they changed their minds. Initially, it is said, Lamborghini thought that about 20 cars could be sold, but in the end – by 1973 – a magnificent total of 763 Miuras had been produced.

The basis of the new car, called Miura after a breed of Spanish fighting bull, was a steel punt-type chassis, built by Marchesi in Modena, and the transverse engine was the familiar V12 coupled to a new five-speed gearbox.

The extraordinarily compact two-seater was treated to a body shell styled at Bertone by a young man called Marcello Gandini, with help from Giorgetto Giugiaro – two names which are now synonymous with industrial design all over the world.

The shell had many aluminium panels, and was welded to the platform chassis on assembly. It was built so low that pop-up headlamps (which were always exposed to view) were necessary to give proper night-time visibility and to meet

*Left: The Miura was named after a fighting bull, and that image can be seen in the Miura script.*

legal requirements in certain countries. All production cars had the same coupé style, though one open-top convertible was also built for promotional purposes.

For some years the Miura was without question *the* most desirable car in the world, until Ferrari's Daytona came along. As the power was increased from the 350 bhp of the original P400 to the 385 bhp of the SV, so was the chassis improved to match it, for the later cars had wider wheels, stronger suspension and a wider track.

Apart from the front end's strong tendency to lift at high speeds, the Miura was a very reassuring car to drive and, in spite of its compact dimensions, it was also a thoroughly practical car for everyday, high-speed, or long-distance use.

The Miura was discontinued in 1973, to make way for the new Countach, but there are many people who insist that it was dropped prematurely, and that it was a better car than the model which replaced it.

## Lamborghini Miura variants

### Lamborghini Miura P400S

In the fourth year of Miura production the original P400 gave way to the more highly tuned P400S. That had an extra 20 bhp, bringing output up to 370 bhp and taking the top speed over the 170-mph mark.

### Lamborghini Miura P400SV

The final version of the Miura, the SV, had the most power of all – some 385 bhp – along with an excellent torque output of 294 lb ft at 5,750 rpm. Naturally, that made it the fastest of all the Miuras, with a top speed approaching 180 mph. Along with the extra power, some other, more obvious changes were made, such as the wider wheels and tyres and the absence of 'eyebrows' on the headlights.

## Specification (1966 P400)

**Engine:** V12, quad-cam
**Bore × stroke:** 82 mm × 62 mm
**Capacity:** 3929 cc
**Maximum power:** 350 bhp
**Transmission:** five-speed manual gearbox, rear-wheel drive
**Chassis:** separate steel platform
**Suspension:** independent with unequal-length wishbones, coil springs, telescopic dampers and anti-roll bars front and rear
**Brakes:** discs front and rear
**Bodywork:** aluminium and steel two-seater coupé
**Maximum speed (approx):** 170 mph (274 km/h)

*Below: The Miura broke new ground in being the first mid-engined production car. Power output from the familiar V12 engine was 350 bhp, later rising to 370 bhp in the P400S and finally 385 bhp in the SV version. The torque output was also excellent.*

*Above: Extraordinarily compact exterior dimensions were not reflected by a cramped interior, but there was no space behind the driver.*

*Below: Bertone's styling seemed to have taken some cues from Ford's GT40. The alloy body was so low that pop-up lights were required.*

## Lamborghini Islero 1968-69

Lamborghini's follow-up to the 400 GT 2+2 was the short-lived Islero model. It was only in production for two years, during which time 125 GTs were built, followed by 100 of the more powerful GTS models.

Although the rolling chassis was virtually the same, the Islero had a completely new body shell. Earlier Lamborghinis had been styled by Touring, but were built by Marazzi. Now for the new model, Lamborghini commissioned the style *and* the construction of the body shells from Touring.

Compared with the 350 GT/400 GT 2+2, the new Islero had blunter and more angular lines, still with two doors, but this time with more '+2' space in the rear seats, and with headlamps concealed in the daytime behind lift-up flaps. It was a smart, but not a sensationally beautiful, car, and it was always overshadowed by its sensuous stable-

mates, the Espada and Miura.

The original Islero was slightly more powerful than the 400 GT 2+2 had been – 330 bhp against 320 bhp – and the later Islero GTS produced even more, with no less than 350 bhp from its 4.0-litre V12 engine. This was the same output as the mid-engined Miura, and was matched by better brakes and further chassis developments. The GTS also had a redesigned interior, including a completely new dashboard layout.

Like the 400 GT 2+2, the Islero models were always overshadowed by the more attractive styles which surrounded them at Sant' Agata Bolognese at the time, but they were still extremely fast and capable cars which could compete on equal terms with the best front-engined Ferraris.

The last Islero was delivered early in 1970, being replaced by the similarly angular Jarama.

*Above: Production of the Touring-designed and built Islero was short-lived, lasting just two years, during which time 125 GTs were built, followed by 100 of the 20 bhp more powerful GTS model.*

### Specification (1968 GT)

**Engine:** V12, quad-cam
**Bore × stroke:** 82 mm × 62 mm
**Capacity:** 3929 cc
**Maximum power:** 330 bhp
**Transmission:** five-speed manual gearbox, rear-wheel drive
**Chassis:** separate steel frame with tubular main and bracing members

**Suspension:** independent with unequal-length wishbones, coil springs telescopic dampers and anti-roll bars front and rear
**Brakes:** discs front and rear
**Bodywork:** steel 2+2-seater coupé
**Maximum speed (approx):** 158 mph (254 km/h)

*Below: The Islero's rev-counter read up to 8,000 rpm and was unusual in that it showed no red line to warn the driver. Although the car was classified as a 2 + 2, there was reasonable space for two passengers in the back but access was poor.*

*Above: The Islero's 330-bhp version of the V12 engine was more powerful than that in its predecessor, the 400 GT.*

*Below: Although lacking the sensuous lines of the Miura, the Islero was still extremely stylish.*

# Lamborghini Espada 1968-78

Apart from the fact that it was front-, rather than mid-engined, the Espada was almost as much of a masterpiece as the Miura. The chassis had an exciting specification – anything which could combine a 150-mph top speed, a good ride, and four-seater capacity with that marvellously sensual V12 engine had to be – but it was also allied to a splendidly individual fastback body styled by Bertone. At the end of the 1960s, when so many supercars tended to resemble their rivals, the Espada was unmistakable.

The new shape was most influenced by the one-off Lamborghini Marzal 'dream car', although that model's lift-up gull-wing doors were not used in the Espada. The only other supercar remotely to resemble the Espada was the Bertone-styled Alfa Romeo Montreal. For the first time in a Lamborghini there

was genuine accommodation for four, although space in the rear was a little limited. At 15 ft 4 in long, this was also the largest Lamborghini of all.

In some ways the chassis design was like that of the Miura, for Marchesi of Modena constructed the pressed and fabricated steel platform frame, which was stronger and more rigid than the tubular type used on the other front-engined cars.

Naturally, there was coil-spring and double-wishbone independent suspension all round, and in the first Espadas the 4.0-litre V12 developed 325 bhp. Lamborghini's own five-speed gearbox was used; this was so refined it even had synchromesh on reverse gear.

The name Espada was derived from the Italian word 'spada', which means sword. The styling, by Bertone, was still considered controversial by the end of

*Above: The Espada used Lamborghini's V12 engine in four-litre guise, tuned to deliver a maximum of 325 bhp.*

*Below: The extremely individual fastback body seated four and was styled by Bertone, influenced by the Marzal show car.*

the car's 10-year career. Most observers thought it was stunningly attractive, but a few found its wide and rather flattened lines ugly, for it was a very wide car, one of the widest of its day. Most comment was reserved for the sharply cut-off tail, with its vertical louvred glass panel.

The Espada sold very well indeed – a total of 1,217 was made – which made it a commercial as well as a technical success. There were three versions; the original Series 1 model was built between 1968 and 1969, the Series 2 took over in 1970 (with optional power steering, vented disc brakes and 350 bhp), while the Series 3 type (with power steering as standard, a new fascia layout, better suspension and brakes, and – for the first time – an automatic transmission option) followed in 1973.

From 1970 the Espada was joined by its short-wheelbase stablemate, the Jarama, which used the same chassis layout. After that was dropped, however, Lamborghini never again produced a four-seater car.

*Above: A wide transmission tunnel separated the leather-trimmed bucket seats. The instrumentation was very comprehensive, although the ergonomics were hardly perfect; some of the dashboard switches were almost out of reach.*

### Specification (1968)

**Engine:** V12, quad-cam
**Bore × stroke:** 82 mm × 62 mm
**Capacity:** 3929 cc
**Maximum power:** 325 bhp
**Transmission:** five-speed manual gearbox or three-speed automatic transmission, rear-wheel drive
**Chassis:** separate steel platform
**Suspension:** independent with double unequal-length wishbones, coil springs, telescopic dampers and anti-roll bars front and rear
**Brakes:** discs front and rear
**Bodywork:** aluminium and steel four-seater saloon
**Maximum speed (approx):** 150 mph (241 km/h)

# Lamborghini Jarama 1970-78

Like the Islero which it replaced, the front-engined 2+2 Jarama was a car specifically requested by Ferruccio Lamborghini himself. And in common with the Islero, the Jarama's main problem was that it had rather undistinguished, angular, coupé styling.

The name Jarama came from the Spanish motor racing circuit, and from an important centre for fighting-bull breeding. The new car's chassis was a shortened version of that used in the Espada, being a punt-type platform. It carried the same 4.0-litre V12 engine, transmission and other running gear as the Espada.

The Jarama was shorter, but even wider than the massive Espada and its styling was credited to Bertone, whose team was headed by Marcello Gandini.

One recognition point was the partly hooded headlamps, with covers which retracted when the lights were on.

The bodies were built at the Marazzi factory (thus extending the Islero links), and early cars were criticised for poor detail finish and quality problems. Because it was mainly panelled in steel, the Jarama's body shell was surprisingly heavy. *Motor*'s original road test from 1971 highlighted that as a problem: the heavy doors had no stay-open catches, for example, and were inclined to slam on the driver's legs. That was accompanied by other niggling faults such as poor ergonomics with badly placed instruments and controls, and very heavy, unassisted, steering at low and parking speeds.

*Above: Although the Jarama's body used both glassfibre and steel, it was relatively heavy for a performance coupé. Its design is credited to coachbuilders Bertone, where the chief designer at the time was Marcello Gandini – the same man who styled the Miura.*

*Below: Like most Lamborghinis (with the exception of the Countach), the Jarama was named after a Spanish fighting bull – Taurus being the birth sign of company founder Ferruccio Lamborghini. The GTS featured a large bonnet air intake.*

These quibbles, however, paled into insignificance when the car was under way. The Michelin 215/70s, although a modest size by today's standards, were considered to give the Jarama enormous grip. That, coupled to the virtually neutral handling balance, meant the Jarama was a delight to drive very quickly, once the driver had adjusted to the considerable width, and the car cornered quickly without undue drama or any appreciable body roll.

The performance was everything you would expect from Lamborghini's quad-cam V12, with 0-60 mph acceleration taking only 6.8 seconds and 100 mph coming up in 16.4 seconds. Such performance was easily achieved by the driver as the gear change (once warmed up) had an easy action, the clutch was smooth and progressive and the ventilated discs worked very effectively. Care was needed in the wet, however, when the car tended to understeer and the front brakes to lock. The Jarama would cruise without complaint for hours at 130 mph and even then had lots in hand. Its maximum speed of 162 mph was better than that of its rivals and the overall fuel consumption of 11 mpg rather worse, but few complained on that score before the first 'energy crisis'.

The original 400 GT was produced for two years, during which time 177 cars were built, but from 1972 the 400 GTS took over, with a power increase, power steering and some styling changes,

*Above: A total of 327 Jaramas was built – the bodies coming from the Marazzi plant. Production ran in parallel to the far more beautiful Urraco. Automatic transmission was a surprising option in the car's final years.*

which included a big air intake in the bonnet panel. There was also the very rare Jarama 'Targa', which had two removable panels above the front passengers' heads. A total of 150 400 GTS models was built before production ended in 1978, with automatic transmission on offer as an option in the final years.

## Specification (1970)

**Engine:** V12, quad-cam
**Bore × stroke:** 82 mm × 62 mm
**Capacity:** 3929 cc
**Maximum power:** 350 bhp (later 365 bhp on the GTS)
**Transmission:** five-speed manual gearbox or three-speed automatic transmission, rear-wheel drive
**Chassis:** separate welded steel platform
**Suspension:** independent with double unequal-length wishbones, coil springs, telescopic dampers and anti-roll bars front and rear
**Brakes:** discs front and rear
**Bodywork:** aluminium and steel 2+2-seater coupé
**Maximum speed (approx):** 162 mph (261 km/h)

# Lamborghini Urraco 1972-79

*Left: By the mid- to late 1970s, there was constant conflict between management and workers at Lamborghini, a malaise affecting the whole of Italy. That overshadowed the Urraco, which never attained its objective of being a serious competitor to the Porsche 911 and Ferrari Dino.*

Although the Urraco ('young bull') was by no means the 'small' Lamborghini which had been rumoured regularly in the late 1960s, it was the smallest car ever to be put into production at Sant' Agata. Intended as direct competition for cars like the Ferrari Dino, it appealed to an entirely different clientele from those who bought the big V12 cars. It was aimed to sell well in the USA, but that market's reaction to the 'energy crisis' of 1973-74 spoiled that strategy.

In its layout, if not in its engineering – which was all-new – the P250 (the P stood for *Posteriore*, or rear-engined) Urraco was a direct descendant of the Miura, for it was the second mid-engined Lamborghini of the transverse-engined type. In this case, however, it was a smaller and lighter car, with a new engine. Because Gianpaolo Dallara had moved on, to set up his own business, the Urraco was the work of Lamborghini's new chief engineer Paolo Stanzani.

Thanks to its beautifully integrated Bertone styling, the new Urraco looked smaller than it actually was, for although it was only 13 feet long, and the engine was behind the cabin, there was 2+2 seating. Like other early-1970s Lamborghinis, the Urraco had a pressed and fabricated steel platform chassis, and naturally there was all-independent suspension, this time by MacPherson struts front *and* rear.

The original Urraco had a 2.5-litre single-overhead-camshaft engine, but two further versions were later produced, one with a two-litre engine to match special Italian taxation regulations, the other with a larger (three-litre) twin-cam version of the engine. Transmission was by means of an all-indirect

five-speed gearbox which, like that of the Miura, was tucked in behind the transverse engine.

Although the Urraco was a beautiful car, and had a promising specification, it took two years to get it on sale after its initial launch, and it was not the success Lamborghini had expected. Perhaps the company was unlucky because, after potential customers had become aware of early teething troubles, the first 'energy crisis' erupted, Ferrari announced its own V8 Dino models, and the public turned its back on the Urraco.

Lamborghini spent so much time and money investing in facilities to build the Urraco, in trying to improve it, and to sell it, that the expense was a major factor in the company's bankruptcy in 1978. Yet the later versions were fine, fast cars, and the basic design was used to produce both the Silhouette and the Jalpa which followed.

In seven years, 520 P250s, 66 two-litre P200s and 205 three-litre P300 models were built.

## Lamborghini Urraco variants

### Lamborghini Urraco P200
The P200 was built from 1972 to 1976, as an additional model to the P250, fitted with a 77.4-mm × 53-mm, 1994-cc engine producing 182 bhp.

### Lamborghini Urraco P300
The P300 arrived to supplement the P250 model in 1975, but took over completely in 1976 and was built until 1979. It looked the same as the P250, but had a quad-cam 86-mm × 64.5-mm, 2996-cc engine producing 265 bhp. Top speed was 158 mph.

## Lamborghini Silhouette
The Silhouette was a short-lived attempt to produce a more exciting derivative of the mid-engined Urraco. It was in production for only two years (1976-78), and just 52 were built.

Although based on the Urraco, the Silhouette had quite different Bertone styling which included a lift-off Targa top, a two-seater cabin, wider wheels and tyres cowled by flared wheel arches, and altogether more sporty characteristics. Naturally, the Silhouette had the most powerful version of Lamborghini's quad-cam V8, the three-litre 265-bhp unit, which guaranteed a

top speed of no less than 160 mph.

The Silhouette was more expensive than the P300 Urraco and, unhappily for Lamborghini, no better built. Furthermore, it was never officially exported to the USA, where most sales could have been expected.

## Specification (1972 P250)
**Engine:** V8, single overhead camshaft per bank
**Bore × stroke:** 86 mm × 53 mm
**Capacity:** 2463 cc
**Maximum power:** 220 bhp
**Transmission:** five-speed manual gearbox, rear-wheel drive
**Chassis:** separate steel platform
**Suspension:** independent with MacPherson struts front and rear
**Brakes:** discs front and rear
**Bodywork:** steel 2 + 2-seater coupé
**Maximum speed (approx):** 143 mph (230 km/h)

*Above: Gandini made little effort to disguise the car's mid-engined layout. The louvred engine cover was the designer's 'signature'.*

*Below: It's difficult to believe that this car, the Silhouette, was essentially a Urraco under its more flamboyant Bertone body.*

# Lamborghini Countach 1974-88

Along with the Ferrari Berlinetta Boxer, the Lamborghini Countach was one of the most important supercar trendsetters of the 1970s. When the Countach went on sale in 1974, immediately after the 'energy crisis' had erupted across the world, there was an element of defiance in its launch. Lamborghini thought the car was so good it would sell regardless.

The prototype Countach was shown in 1971, but by the time it went on sale the details had changed considerably. The prototype had been called an LP500, and had used a 5.0-litre version of the V12, but by 1974 it had become the LP400, with the engine in its more familiar 4.0-litre guise. LP stood for *Longitudinale Posteriore* (longways rear-mounted), which referred to the engine location.

The Countach replaced the Miura, and although both cars used the same mid-engined V12 they were otherwise completely different. Instead of a transverse engine, the Countach used a longitudinally-mounted engine, though it drove *forward* to a new five-speed gearbox, from which a propeller shaft in the engine sump connected to the final drive at the rear of that sump.

Unlike the Miura's platform frame, the Countach used a complex multi-tubular

chassis, while the body style was once again by Bertone, penned by Marcello Gandini, although body shell construction was by Lamborghini themselves.

Where the Miura had been rounded and sensual, the Countach was sharp-edged and brutal. Its windscreen was very sharply angled, and there was a unique door-opening action, forward and upwards, which posed the problem of how to get out if the worst came to the worst and the car ended up on its roof!

The LP400 was the fastest Lamborghini to be built for a decade, as the diffi-

culty of meeting tightening emission laws (especially for sale in the USA) meant that the power output was gradually eroded. It was not until Lamborghini introduced the LP500S, with a considerably greater displacement, that the 1974 levels were restored.

A total of 150 LP400, 385 LP400S and 325 LP500S models was built – a rate of around 80 cars a year – and this surpassed the figure achieved by the Miura.

## Lamborghini Countach variants

### Lamborghini Countach LP400S
The Countach LP400S took over from the original Countach in 1978. The basic design was the same, but the chassis was retouched to run on wider wheels and the recently-introduced, more grippy Pirelli P7 tyres. This meant that flared wheel arches had to be fitted, and an optional free-standing rear aerofoil section became available.

### Lamborghini Countach LP500S
From 1982 to 1985 the Countach became the LP500S model. It looked the same but was now fitted with an enlarged engine of 4754 cc, producing 375 bhp with far more torque.

### Lamborghini Countach 5000 QV
When Lamborghini launched the *quattrovalvole* version of the Countach in 1985, they boldly stated that it was "the world's fastest production car". The

*Above: Like the Miura, the Countach was far ahead of its time. It also used a derivative of the same quad-cam V12 engine as in the Miura.*

QV's 180 mph top speed was faster than all the opposition – especially the Ferrari Testarossa.

Compared with the previous LP500S, the new car had an even larger engine – 5167 cc against 4754 cc – and 455 bhp instead of 375 bhp. To achieve this big increase, the engineers had developed new four-valves-per-cylinder heads which breathed more deeply than ever before. Around 150 *quattrovalvole* models were built every year, and the final 'Anniversary' edition sold out as quickly as the cars could be produced.

### Specification (1974 LP400)
**Engine:** 60-degree V12, twin overhead camshafts per bank
**Bore × stroke:** 82 mm × 62 mm
**Capacity:** 3929 cc
**Maximum power:** 375 bhp
**Transmission:** five-speed manual gearbox, rear-wheel drive
**Chassis:** separate multi-tubular steel frame
**Suspension:** independent with coil springs front and rear
**Brakes:** discs front and rear
**Bodywork:** aluminium and steel two-seater coupé
**Maximum speed (approx):** 175 mph (282 km/h)

*Above: The Countach was undeniably muscular-looking, with its various scoops, scallops and spoilers.*

*Below: The Anniversary Countach of 1988 celebrated 25 years of Lamborghini production.*

# Lamborghini Jalpa 1982–91

*Left: The Jalpa was one of the new breed of Lamborghinis, made possible by the Mimram brothers' bankrolling of the company. The Countach's angular brother was very well received.*

## Specification (1982)

**Engine:** V8, quad-cam
**Bore × stroke:** 86 mm × 75 mm
**Capacity:** 3485 cc
**Maximum power:** 255 bhp
**Transmission:** five-speed manual gearbox, rear-wheel drive
**Chassis:** steel platform frame, with body welded on at assembly
**Suspension:** independent with MacPherson struts front and rear
**Brakes:** discs front and rear
**Bodywork:** steel and aluminium two-seater coupé
**Maximum speed (approx):** 154 mph (248 km/h)

*Below: A direct descendant of the Urraco, the Jalpa's front end was slightly reworked and the wheel-arch flares were remodelled.*

Here is a mystery: how could the Jalpa, which was not as pretty as the Urraco P300, not as roomy, nor even as powerful, continue to sell for a decade? How could progressive Bertone restyles turn the neat and integrated Urraco 2 + 2 into the less delicately styled two-seater Silhouette, and finally into the Jalpa? Yet it happened and the Jalpa, along with the Countach, kept Lamborghini afloat throughout the 1980s.

The Urraco had died in 1979, and no replacement was offered for three years, while Lamborghini itself was put into administrative receivership by the Italian government. It was only after the Mimrams had injected new finance, and Giulio Alfieri was persuaded to move from Maserati, that the Urraco's direct descendant, the Jalpa, was born.

The Jalpa clearly inherited much from the Silhouette of 1976, with almost identical Bertone styling except for the rear three-quarters. Mechanically the Jalpa

was like the Urraco, except that the engine was enlarged once again – this time from 2996 cc to 3485 cc – and made a lot more flexible, with a considerable torque increase (from 195 lb ft at 5,750 rpm to 235 lb ft at 3,250 rpm). Curiously, however, peak power was actually down by 10 bhp. Jalpa, by the way, was the name for yet another breed of bull, so a time-honoured Lamborghini tradition was continued with this model.

The suspension was reworked, with low-profile Pirelli P7 tyres now on 16-in instead of 15-in wheels. There was also a new fascia layout, new alloy wheels, and subtle changes to the wheel-arch flares and front-end treatment.

This new car was well received, and sold steadily for the rest of the 1980s, though by 1990 it had been built in only small quantities. Major automotive directories had deleted it by 1991, yet Lamborghini still produced it that year.

Whatever the confusion, the Jalpa had

allowed Lamborghini to regain its heavy investment in the original Urraco machinery and tooling, but instead of building a replacement, the company concentrated on the Diablo supercar.

*Below: The Jalpa had a very high performance, with a top speed of 154 mph. The model's long production run helped Lamborghini recoup its investment in the Urraco, from which the Jalpa was derived.*

# Lamborghini LM002 1982-90

In the late 1970s Lamborghini seemed to stagger from crisis to crisis, usually brought on by changes of ownership or by strange policy decisions. In 1977 none could have been stranger than the decision to develop a massive Lamborghini 4×4, which was originally named the Cheetah. That was never put into production, but years after the rear-engined Cheetah had been abandoned, the front-engined LM002 evolved from it.

Like the Countach, which was already in production, the Cheetah was best described as outrageous, and not at all the sort of project that any sane and sensible carmaker would have tackled. It was the result of a contract secured from the American firm Mobility Technology International, which wanted a vehicle to compete for the US Army's High Utility Mobile Military Vehicle (Hum-Vee) programme, for a more powerful and more commodious replacement for the famous Jeep.

This project collapsed in legal and final chaos after only one Chrysler V8-powered prototype had been built, that car eventually being written off in a testing accident. It was not until 1981 that Lamborghini's new owners, the Mimrams, sponsored a new rear-engined 4×4, calling it the LM001, where 'LM' was thought to mean 'Lamborghini-Mimram', or 'Lamborghini-Military', depending on which Sant' Agata personality you were talking to at the time!

This design, to be powered either by Lamborghini's own V12, or by an imported American Motors V8, was no more successful than before, mostly because the rear weight bias made it difficult to steer when being accelerated hard. The Mimrams decided that the solution was to build a *front*-engined version, first named LMA (A for *Anteriore*), but finally called the LM002.

*Below: Surely one of the most eye-catching creations ever to leave the doors of an Italian design house, the LM002 used the same immensely powerful engine as the Countach.*

The front-engined LMA looked surprisingly like the original rear-engined type, in that it had enormous wheels and tyres, very high ground clearance, boxy lines, and a four-door cabin without a roof panel or doors, although it had a more squared-up prow (to enclose the engine and the radiator). By the time sales began, however, the LM series had been equipped with conventional doors and a solid roof panel. There was also an open 'deck' behind the cabin where people, dogs or luggage could be stowed.

The chassis was a solid steel-tube spaceframe, with all-independent suspension and huge 325/65 17-in tyres. To give the LM002 the kind of performance that would outgun any other of the world's 4×4s, Lamborghini used the same 5.2-litre 48-valve V12 which powered the Countach, matching it to a massive ZF gearbox and 'part-time' four-wheel-drive system.

The body could only be described as boxy, for there was really no attempt at styling, or aerodynamics. The LM002 was no less than 72.8 inches high, and the unladen weight was an impressive 5,950 lb, even though many aluminium and GRP panels were used. It was astounding, therefore, that this massive machine could sprint to 60 mph in around 8.0 seconds, and reach a top speed of 125 mph.

The LM002 was tastefully trimmed and equipped, with comfortable seating for four, air conditioning, and every creature comfort. It was a fast although ponderous vehicle on sealed surfaces, but made up for that with superb off-road performance; on sand it was well-nigh unbeatable, and Middle Eastern sales were excellent.

It was also a vehicle of great extremes, for by the end of the 1980s it cost the best part of £100,000, it had a huge fuel tank (more than 60 gallons), a prodigious thirst for petrol (8 mpg was normal), yet it was refined enough to use in large cities. The miracle of it all is that there were enough wealthy, and eccentric, buyers to sustain the demand for so long.

*Above: Despite its military appearance, the LM seated four people in air-conditioned comfort. It had superb off-road ability, making it an attractive buy for very rich Middle Eastern customers. Towards the end of the 1980s, it cost the best part of £100,000.*

## Lamborghini LM002 variants

### Lamborghini LM003

The LM003 was a one-off project with a 3.0-litre turbocharged six-cylinder diesel engine from VM of Italy, though this only had 150 bhp, which meant that the performance was very sluggish.

### Lamborghini LM004

The LM004 was also based on the LM002, but was fitted with an entirely different four-cam Lamborghini V12, unrelated to the passenger-car engines. This had been specially-designed by Stanzani for use in offshore racing boats and luxurious marine cruisers. In LM004 form, it was a 7257-cc unit which produced 420 bhp at 5,200 rpm.

## Specification (1982)

**Engine:** V12, quad-cam
**Bore × stroke:** 85.5 mm × 75 mm
**Capacity:** 5167 cc
**Maximum power:** 450 bhp
**Transmission:** five-speed manual gearbox, high and low ranges; four-wheel drive
**Chassis:** separate steel multi-tubular frame
**Suspension:** independent with double unequal-length wishbones, coil springs telescopic dampers and anti-roll bars front and rear
**Brakes:** discs front, drums rear
**Bodywork:** aluminium and glassfibre four-seater off-road saloon
**Maximum speed:** 125 mph (201 km/h)

# Lamborghini Diablo 1990-present

To replace the Countach, Lamborghini would need to launch an outstanding car; perhaps that was why the Countach stayed in production for so long. It was also going to absorb a great deal of investment capital, and *that* is certainly the reason why a new car – the Diablo – was delayed until Chrysler had control.

The P132 project which became the Diablo actually began, on paper, in 1985. The aim was not only to replace the Countach but to build the world's fastest production car. That meant ensuring a top speed of at least 200 mph, even though no private owner would ever be able to verify it.

Compared with the old Countach, the P132 was larger, heavier and had a bigger engine with a lot more power. It was technically different in many ways too, although it retained the same layout of the gearbox in front of the engine, and a developed version of the same V12 engine used in the Countach. The styling was by Marcello Gandini, who needed to produce several styles before Chrysler's top management was satisfied.

Although a multi-tubular chassis frame was retained, it was very different from that used in the Countach, principally because it had a longer wheelbase and used square-section instead of round-

section tubes. The body shell, as expected, was a complex mixture of steel, light alloy, carbonfibre and other exotic materials.

The gorgeous V12 engine displaced 5729 cc compared with the Countach's 5167 cc. Bore, stroke *and* peak power were all increased, and torque was also much higher than before. For the first

time, all versions of this engine, for all markets, used a Lamborghini fuel injection system; the exciting stack of twin-choke Weber carburettors was consigned to history.

The style of the new car was pure Gandini – in that traces of it could be seen in other cars he was shaping at the same time – and was distinguished by longer and more fluid lines, with big air intakes in the flanks, and an exaggerated front wheel arch which resulted in a shallow and elongated passenger door window shape. Even so, it had a drag coefficient of only 0.31, which was far superior to that of the old Countach.

Unhappily, Gandini was not allowed to tackle the fascia and interior layout, which was credited to Chrysler of Detroit, the result being a two-seater arrangement with swooping curved lines, and a massive centre console.

The new car was launched in January 1990 with the name Diablo, which does not just mean 'devil' as most people thought, but is yet another Lamborghini reference to a legendary fighting bull. Although no independent tests verified that astonishing top-speed claim of 202 mph, a test car was reputed to have reached 210 mph at the Nardo test track, and it certainly looked the part.

By 1999, the face-lifted Diablo range included the SFV and the 4 x 4 VT Coupés and SV and 4 x 4 VT roadsters.

*Above: After an unusually long gestation period of five years, the Diablo swept onto the supercar scene in 1990, claiming to be the world's fastest production car. A test car was reputed to have reached a top speed of 210 mph.*

## Lamborghini Diablo variants

### Lamborghini Diablo VT

When the original rear-drive car was launched, Lamborghini promised that there would also be a Diablo VT, with four-wheel drive and semi-automatic transmission. It has yet to appear.

## Specification (1991)

**Engine:** V12, quad-cam
**Bore × stroke:** 87 mm × 80 mm
**Capacity:** 5729 cc
**Maximum power:** 492 bhp
**Transmission:** five-speed manual gearbox, rear-wheel drive
**Chassis:** separate steel multi-tubular frame
**Suspension:** independent with double unequal-length wishbones, coil springs, telescopic dampers and anti-roll bars front and rear
**Brakes:** discs front and rear
**Bodywork:** aluminium, carbonfibre and steel two-seater coupé
**Maximum speed (approx):** 202 mph (325 km/h)

*Above: The traditional banks of carburettors are nowhere in sight on the Diablo's V12 quad-cam engine. Fuel injection is used in all models.*

*Below: The Gandini-styled body uses a mix of conventional and composite materials to achieve a design even more striking than the Countach.*

# Lanchester Motor Company

**B**ased in Birmingham until its merger with the Daimler company in 1931, Lanchester was one of the pioneering British carmakers. It was set up by the Lanchester brothers – Frederick and George – both of whom were exceptionally skilful engineers. In the beginning Frederick – 'Dr Fred' as he was usually known – was solely responsible for design, with George as his right-hand man.

Like the German Benz cars of the 1880s, the first Lanchesters were not designed as converted horse carriages, but as a new type of machine. Then, and in the next 30 years, Lanchester made their own decisions, followed no obvious trends, but merely produced the best cars that the talented brothers could design and build.

The very first Lanchester car ran in 1895, but production did not start until 1900, the motive power being by an air-cooled horizontally-opposed twin-cylinder engine. The first water-cooled engine was offered in 1902, the first four-cylinder cars in 1904, and the original Lanchester 'six' in 1906.

Lanchester only made two 'supercars' – the Forty of 1919-29 and the short-lived Thirty. These were by no means the most successful vintage Lanchesters, but were the designs which made the most headlines and bolstered the reputation of other models. Both were fast, and very expensive (in the Rolls-Royce class), so they sold only in small numbers,

and were certainly not profitable projects. It was cars like the Twenty-One (a scaled-down version of the Forty) and its descendant, the Twenty-Three, which really kept the company afloat.

During the Depression, which reached its nadir in 1931, Lanchester's bankers withdrew their support at a crucial time, which meant that a merger with another company became inevitable. The Birmingham-based BSA Group (which owned Daimler) came to the rescue and moved Lanchester's operations to Coventry.

Almost immediately there was a rush of new designs, but also a radical shift in strategy, for the Lanchester badge was soon habitually used on smaller-engined and subtly down-market versions of Daimler cars. At one time, too, down-market versions of the Lanchesters were badged as BSAs. Technical features of 1930s Lanchesters included engines with fixed cylinder heads, and fluid-flywheel/preselector transmissions, while the Roadrider De Luxe was also given independent front suspension.

The Lanchester marque struggled on into the mid-1950s. The last car was the stillborn Sprite, after which Lanchester became merely a 'shell' company, one of the assets bought by Jaguar in 1960.

*Below: All early Lanchesters, like this 28-bhp model from 1910, were designed by Fred Lanchester. His brother George acted as his right-hand man.*

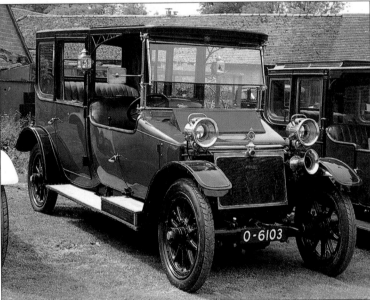

*Above: This 1930 Corsica-bodied drop-head coupé was one of the last Lanchesters built before the Daimler merger in 1931.*

*Below: The Thirty was faster and easier to manoeuvre than previous Lanchesters, but it was too expensive in the Depression.*

# Lanchester Forty 1919-29

The Forty was an engineering masterpiece by vintage standards, built to the highest levels of workmanship and material quality, and priced accordingly. It rivalled Rolls-Royce and Daimler as one of the finest cars of this period, selling in restricted numbers to the gentry, to royalty and to many foreign potentates. The Duke of York (who later became King George VI) is said to have preferred his Forty to all other machines.

Designed by George Lanchester, the new car was a direct descendant of the pre-World War I 38HP and Sporting Forty models. It was big and heavy (up to 5,500 lb with long-wheelbase, limousine coachwork), with a ponderous and stately character. However, although limousines struggled to beat 65 mph, lightened versions with touring bodies could sometimes exceed 80 mph.

On sale for a full 10 years, and still available to special order from 1929 to 1931, this car made no concessions to cost-saving. The original chassis was priced at £2,200, although this was reduced to £1,800 in 1921, just £50 below the price of the equivalent Rolls-Royce 40/50HP. Pundits have described it as a splendid but old-fashioned car, while most agree that it was the high-cost excesses of this design which eventually led to Lanchester's financial collapse.

The whole of this car was designed, and mainly manufactured, 'in-house', including the impressive overhead-camshaft six-cylinder engine (said to have been influenced by the aero engines Lanchester built during World War I), the complex but effective epicyclic gearbox, and the innovative worm-drive rear axle.

Lanchester went on to adopt four-wheel brakes (an interesting hydro-mechanical system) in 1924, just in time to stop Rolls-Royce from claiming such an innovation as its own.

One Forty was extensively modified, tuned, lightened and rebodied, and achieved great things as a Brooklands racing car, with a top speed of more than 100 mph. Many long-distance endurance records were set.

## Specification (1919)

**Engine:** inline six-cylinder, single overhead camshaft
**Bore × stroke:** 101.6 mm × 127 mm
**Capacity:** 6178 cc
**Maximum power:** 100 bhp
**Transmission:** three-speed epicyclic manual gearbox, rear-wheel drive
**Chassis:** separate steel frame with channel-section side members and tubular cross-members
**Suspension:** non-independent with beam front axle and semi-elliptic leaf springs; live rear axle with cantilever leaf springs
**Brakes:** drums at rear (front and rear after 1924)
**Bodywork:** choice of steel or aluminium bodies, three- to eight-seater; open, closed or limousine
**Maximum speed:** 65 mph (105 km/h)

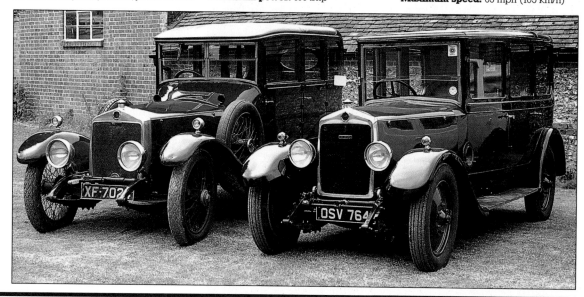

*Right: With many titled patrons, including King George V, the Forty (on the left in the photo) was sold for a decade and reached Rolls-Royce standards of comfort and quality. It was something of a supercar for its day and, in lightened form, also enjoyed racing success.*

# Lanchester Thirty 1928-32

In hindsight one might think that Lanchester's new Thirty was a pragmatic response to the onset of the Depression in 1929. In reality the Lanchester brothers were not possessed of second sight, and had started this design in 1927, well before the economic down-turn.

The chassis layout, and of course the stately bodies which covered it, were solid, spacious and conventional enough, but there was a completely new eight-cylinder engine and, for the first time in many years at Lanchester, a conventional gearbox.

Historians like Michael Sedgwick have described the Thirty as the very best of the vintage 'eights'. The engine, with a cast-iron monoblock atop an aluminium crankcase, had a shaft-driven overhead camshaft in the cylinder head, and there were no fewer than 10 crankshaft main bearings to ensure the unit's smoothness. The gearbox, by comparison, was a simple but rugged sliding-speed four-speeder; and Lanchester's traditional type of worm-drive rear-axle and cantilever-leaf-spring rear suspension was retained.

Lanchester always intended this car to be faster and more agile than the Forty, which it effectively replaced. It was also a lot cheaper than the Forty; on introduction, the chassis price was set at £1,325, and a typical fabric-panelled four-door saloon body cost an extra £450.

The new Thirty certainly achieved the designers' aims, for every model could reach 75 mph, and lightweight versions could reach 90 mph, but it was too expensive for its period, and in three years only 126 cars were sold. Production ended almost as soon as BSA/Daimler had merged with Lanchester.

## Specification (1928)

**Engine:** inline eight-cylinder, single overhead camshaft
**Bore × stroke:** 78.7 mm × 114 mm
**Capacity:** 4440 cc
**Maximum power:** 82 bhp
**Transmission:** four-speed manual gearbox, rear-wheel drive
**Chassis:** separate steel frame with channel-section side members and tubular cross-bracing
**Suspension:** non-independent with beam front axle and semi-elliptic leaf springs; live rear axle with cantilever leaf springs
**Brakes:** drums front and rear
**Bodywork:** choice of five-seater saloon or seven-seater limousine, plus special coachwork
**Maximum speed (approx):** 75 mph (121 km/h)

*Left: The nimble Thirty was made between 1928 and 1932, the rear wheels driving through a conventional, four-speed gearbox. Every car could reach a maximum of at least 75 mph.*

# Lancia

*Right: The Lancia badge has traditionally taken the form of a flag or banner.*

*Below: The Delta Integrale was the perfect continuation of Lancia's sporting heritage, one of the most successful rally cars ever produced, winning both the drivers' and the manufacturers' titles in 1992.*

*Below: The Stratos was a purpose-designed rally machine and won the World Championship three years in a row, between 1974 and 1976. Lancia had to build 500 examples for homologation, and the road cars topped 140 mph.*

V incenzo Lancia, the son of a wealthy Italian soap manufacturer, was apprenticed to the Ceirano car company in 1898, worked for Fiat after Ceirano was taken over, then founded his own carmaking business in 1906. From then until 1956, the Lancia family controlled the firm which bore its name.

Many classic Lancia models used Greek symbols for model names, and until the company finally lost its independence in 1969 the cars were all noted for their advanced and individual technical features. The Lambda of 1923, for instance, was really the world's first production car to have a combined body/chassis structure, and the Aprilia was an economical but advanced family car, while post-war models such as the Flaminia, Flavia and Fulvia were all attractive, mechanically unique, but costly models.

For many years Lancia used a variety of engines with a narrow-angle 'V' layout, and most models had a distinctly sporting character. Until the 1930s, annual production was always very limited, for the Lancia family was more interested in producing 'different' cars which it enjoyed marketing, than in mass-production. That sort of trade, they reasoned, was best left to Fiat.

After World War II, that policy gradually changed, for models such as the Aurelia, then the Flavia and especially the Fulvia, were built in larger numbers than ever before. In the 1950s Lancia also embarked on an ambitious motorsport programme, which culminated in the D50 Formula 1 cars that eventually won the World Championship.

By this time, however, the Lancia family was running out of cash to fund its business, so the Formula 1 programme was abandoned (the cars being handed over to Ferrari), and control of the company passed to the Presenti family, with Professia Fessia taking over from Vittorio Jano as technical chief.

There was further over-ambitious expansion in the 1960s, with the introduction of the complex front-wheel-drive Flavia (mid-size) and Fulvia (small/medium-size) ranges. Each was offered as a saloon *and* with a variety of specially-styled sporting bodies.

Under Cesare Fiorio's direction, Lancia successfully re-entered big-time motorsport. A new assembly factory was built just outside Turin, but although sales rose to new heights the company still was not profitable.

By 1969 Lancia was struggling, so Fiat rescued the business and by the late-1970s all Lancia production cars used Fiat engines and many other components. The Beta models (though rust-prone) sold very well indeed, and the phenomenal mid-engined Stratos had given the company an invincible sporting image.

In the 1980s Lancia was almost totally integrated with Fiat and even cars like the Y10 Delta and Thema, though unique-looking had Fiat running-gear and shared many structural components. During the 1990s Lancia was given the rôle of luxury car producer for the Fiat corporation, with Alfa Romeo making sporting vehicles, Ferrari and Maserati the 'supercars' and Fiat itself the 'bread and butter' vehicles.

## Lancia Lambda 1922-31

The Lambda was a technical masterpiece; not only did it have the clever design of a narrow-angle V4 engine, but it was the first car in the world to use a steel monocoque.

Vincenzo Lancia is said to have been inspired by ship construction, but the new Lambda's form was unique. If by 'monocoque' we mean a combined chassis and body structure, then the Lambda certainly qualifies. Built in the form of an open-topped tube, with cut-outs for the doors and numerous lightening holes, it was quite unlike any other car being sold anywhere in the world at that time.

However, the unique design of the structure dictated the same door profile for all the early versions, which explains

why tourers, saloons and limousines all shared basically the same lower cabin shape and layout. Outer bodywork was usually welded or rivetted to the inner structure.

The engine, gearbox, axles and suspension layout were conventional enough by Lancia standards, for the 'V'-engine concept had been established on earlier designs, as had the sliding-pillar independent front suspension. At the prototype stage, incidentally, Lancia had also experimented with a narrow-angle V6 engine, which was almost certainly a world premiere.

Because the structure was so stiff, and the engine relatively powerful, the Lambda was considered to be years

ahead of its competitors, and though prices were relatively high, this saw Lancia production boom as never before.

This was the first Lancia to be built in several series – no fewer than nine of them – each differing slightly from the last. The most important advances on the original design came with the Series 5 (with a new four-speed gearbox) and the Series 6 (with a modified monocoque with wider door cut-outs and a longer wheelbase).

Series 7 cars, however, had a different chassis construction – really a platform type – and a larger and more powerful engine, while yet more chassis changes and an even bigger engine followed for the Series 8. The original monocoque

layout had been abandoned to allow conventional coachbuilt bodies to be offered by specialists, some of these being particularly handsome and spacious.

In more than eight years, a total of 13,003 Lambdas of all types was built.

### Lancia Lambda variants

#### Lancia Lambda Series 5 to 9

The Series 5 cars were equipped with a four-speed gearbox. The Series 6 cars were given an optional longer wheelbase – 135.8 inches instead of 122.0 – and a modified monocoque with larger door cut-outs. The Series 7 cars had a larger engine, of 79.37 mm × 120 mm and 2370 cc, producing 59 bhp. The Series 8 and 9 cars had an even larger engine, of 2570 cc producing 69 bhp.

### Specification (1923)

**Engine:** V4, single overhead camshaft
**Bore × stroke:** 75 mm × 120 mm
**Capacity:** 2120 cc
**Maximum power:** 50 bhp
**Transmission:** three-speed manual gearbox, rear-wheel drive
**Chassis:** steel unit-construction chassis/inner body
**Suspension:** independent front with sliding pillar and coil springs; live rear axle with semi-elliptic leaf springs
**Brakes:** drums front and rear
**Bodywork:** steel two- or four-seater, open or closed
**Maximum speed (approx):** 68 mph (109 km/h)

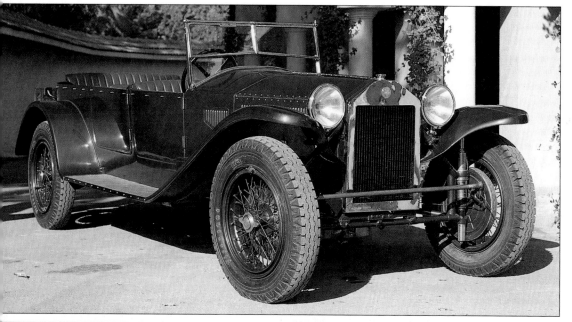

*Left: The Lambda was outdated by the time it was dropped in 1931, but it established Lancia's reputation for producing technically advanced cars, thanks to its combined body/chassis. The Series 8 featured a 2570-cc V4.*

## Lancia Aprilia 1936-49

After the Lambda was dropped in 1931, Lancia produced the Artena and Astura. They were followed by the 1.2-litre Augusta, which was of 'pillarless' construction with a combined body/chassis unit. It was the forerunner of the famous Aprilia model, a small saloon which made almost all other manufacturers' contemporary models look old-fashioned.

The Aprilia stayed true to Lancia traditions by using a narrow-angle V4 engine and vertical-pillar/coil-spring independent front suspension along with independent rear suspension. Its unit-construction four-door saloon body was very smoothly detailed and remarkably aerodynamically efficient.

Another 'first' for the Aprilia was that this was the first Lancia engine to feature part-spherical combustion chambers with opposed valves operated by rockers from an overhead camshaft.

This advanced and appealing model

sold well until the end of the 1940s when it was displaced by the Appia range. To make the design even more attractive to Italy's many coachbuilders, the platform frame needed no saloon bodywork to make it rigid enough.

Because of its shape and chassis, the Aurelia combined speed (80 mph) and fuel efficiency with good roadholding, which helped to give the car a sporting reputation. Even though the outbreak of

war hampered its development when its reputation was still rising, the Aprilia continued to sell very well until the Appia replaced it in 1949.

### Specification (1936)

**Engine:** V4, overhead-valve
**Bore × stroke:** 72 mm × 83 mm
**Capacity:** 1352 cc
**Maximum power:** 47 bhp
**Transmission:** four-speed manual

gearbox, rear-wheel drive
**Chassis:** steel unit-construction body/chassis
**Suspension:** independent front with sliding pillars and coil springs; independent rear with transverse leaf springs
**Brakes:** drums front and rear
**Bodywork:** steel four-seater saloon
**Maximum speed (approx):** 80 mph (129 km/h)

*Right: The pillarless construction of the Aprilia meant that the front doors hinged at the front and the rear doors at the rear.*

# Lancia Aurelia 1950-58

Lancia's Aurelia, launched in 1950, was the first car in the world to use a V6 engine. That in itself was enough to make it a benchmark in motoring history, but the adoption of smooth and trend-setting Pinin Farina styling for the Coupé and Spider models was also important.

As with most Lancias, the engineering of the saloon (which had been directed by the famous ex-GP car designer Vittorio Jano) was also used to form the basis of sporting and more specialised models. In the Aurelia's case, these comprised the GT Coupé (the world's first 'fastback') and the Spider (also known as the America, after its major intended market).

At first, all these cars used a chassis with all-independent suspension which was a development of the Aprilia concept. Naturally the 1.75-litre V6 engine was front-mounted, but the gearbox was in unit with the rear final drive.

The original B20 Coupé appeared in 1951, using a 2.0-litre engine in a short-wheelbase version of the Aurelia saloon's chassis. Not only did it have smooth lines, but it was meticulously detailed, with two-door coachwork, a traditional Lancia-shield shape of grille, and a long, smooth tail. The S2 GTs were more powerful, but it was the S3 and S4 models which really caused a stir, for they both had 2.5-litre V6 engines, while the S4 was given de Dion rear suspension instead of the original swing-axles.

The Coupés proved to be successful class-winning racing cars and potential outright winners in long-distance rallies (such as Monte Carlo in 1954, where Louis Chiron was the driver).

From 1954 the Coupé GT was also joined by the two-seater Spider. Although this shared Series 4 GT running

gear, it had an entirely different structure, for the wheelbase was even shorter than that of the GT. The first 240 cars had an American-style wrap-around windscreen; a revised type was then introduced with a more conventional screen and wind-up windows.

Production eventually ended in 1958 when the Aurelia was replaced by the larger Flaminia. In all, 3,011 Coupé GTs and 1,621 Spiders were produced.

## Lancia Aurelia variants

### Lancia Aurelia Series 1 and 2 GT
The original Series 1 and Series 2 GT types, built until 1953, had two-litre engines with 75 or 80 bhp, and swing-axle independent rear suspension.

### Lancia Aurelia Series 3, 5 and 6 GT
The Series 3 GT of 1953 had de Dion rear suspension, which was then retained to the end of production, while the Series 5 and 6 GTs had 112 bhp instead of 118 bhp.

*Above: Pinin Farina neatly integrated the traditional upright Lancia grille into a very modern-looking design, although that did dictate a high side profile as the wings and doors had to be so deep and the car was rather short.*

## Specification (Aurelia GT2500 Series 4)

**Engine:** V6, overhead-valve
**Bore × stroke:** 78 mm × 85.5 mm
**Capacity:** 2451 cc
**Maximum power:** 118 bhp
**Transmission:** four-speed manual gearbox, rear-wheel drive
**Chassis:** steel platform frame with welded-on body
**Suspension:** independent front with sliding pillars and coil springs; de Dion rear axle with semi-elliptic leaf springs and tubular dampers
**Brakes:** drums front and rear
**Bodywork:** steel and aluminium four-seater coupé
**Maximum speed (approx):** 112 mph (180 km/h)

*Above: When introduced in 1951, the Aurelia Coupé was very advanced indeed and it pioneered the fastback style of body with a smooth shape drawn by Pinin Farina.*

*Below: The combination of an aerodynamic body, independent suspension all round and, eventually, as much as 118 bhp made the Coupé an effective racer.*

# Lancia Flavia Coupé and Zagato 1962-75

*Left: This shape could only be the work of Zagato. No-one else would have attempted such a strange front grille treatment or designed the rear side windows to encroach onto the roof. The body shell of the Zagato versions was all-alloy.*

Like the Aurelia which preceded it, Lancia's new Flavia caused something of a sensation, because it broke so many conventions. It was Professor Fessia's first 'all-new' design for Lancia, one which broke with all the old traditions.

Not only did the new car use a horizontally-opposed engine, but it had front-wheel drive – the first ever to be built in Italy – and it also had four-wheel-disc brakes. The transverse-leaf independent front suspension was interesting, but on the original saloons the steering-column gear change was a great disappointment.

As usual with Lancia, the saloon model was revealed first; this was a stubby and none-too-attractive four-seater, but it was not long before the inevitable Touring, Pininfarina and Zagato sporting versions came along. Naturally these had a floor-mounted gear change.

In fact the Flavia had a very versatile chassis, and the engine proved to be surprisingly robust and tunable. Pininfarina's Coupé was an extremely smart close-coupled four-seater, originally with four headlamps stuck rather awkwardly at the corners of the front wings, while the Zagato offering was a strange-looking device, much more wind-cheating but with multi-curved bodywork, and a complex front grille.

In the car's original form the flat-four engine was a 1.5-litre unit, but 1.8-litre versions became available in 1963 (some with fuel injection), and the full-size 2.0-litre was offered from the spring of 1969, although the Zagato style was discontinued just before it arrived. When the 2.0-litre engine appeared, so did a facelifted version of the Pininfarina Coupé, with a lower, smoother and more integrated nose, this time without a traditional Lancia-type grille. The cabin design, and the car's general proportions, were distinctly reminiscent of Pininfarina's Ferrari 250 GTE/330 GT of the same period, but Lancia found this flattering.

The 2.0-litre Coupé was sold in two forms, one with a 131-bhp carburettor engine, the other with a 140-bhp engine which featured Kugelfischer mechanical fuel injection.

## Specification (2000 models)

**Engine:** flat-four, overhead-valve
**Bore × stroke:** 89 mm × 80 mm
**Capacity:** 1990 cc
**Maximum power:** 131 bhp/140 bhp
**Transmission:** four-speed or five-speed manual gearbox, front-wheel drive
**Chassis:** steel unit-construction body/chassis
**Suspension:** independent front with wishbones and transverse leaf spring; beam rear axle with semi-elliptic leaf springs
**Brakes:** discs front and rear
**Bodywork:** steel four-seater coupé or cabriolet, aluminium two-seater coupé by Zagato
**Maximum speed (approx):** 118 mph (190 km/h)

*Below: A number of Italy's most famous coachbuilders worked on the Flavia chassis. This is a Vignale-bodied convertible from 1963. By that year, the flat-four engine's displacement had risen to 1.8 litres.*

*Below: The Flavia Zagato's lightweight alloy body helped give excellent performance. Unfortunately, it was never used with the later two-litre engine.*

# Lancia Fulvia Coupé 1965-76

Without doubt, the sporting Fulvias were some of the most elegant and successful Lancias ever produced, yet they evolved from a singularly dumpy design. By this time Lancia was accustomed to this process of designing a saloon, then developing prettier, more compact, and more specialised cars from that basic model.

The Fulvia saloon itself was launched in 1963, featuring front-wheel drive (some parts, including the transmission and the disc brakes, being shared with the Flavia), but with a new narrow-angle V4 engine. This had considerable 'stretch' built into it at first, and there was a unique double overhead camshaft (not strictly a twin-overhead-cam layout) where each camshaft looked after inlet (or exhaust, as appropriate) operation in both 'banks' of cylinders.

Lancia styled its own Coupé version of the saloon, launching it in 1965, while Zagato produced the bulkier but actually lighter Sport Coupé a year later. Both models were produced on a short-wheelbase version of the saloon car's underpan, and both had truly sporty characters. They were, however, entirely different in concept, for the Lancia-styled Coupé was almost a four-seater, while the Zagato Sport had only two seats but the advantage of a great deal more stowage area.

Both had free-revving engines, precise steering, reassuring handling, and the sort of urgent character which attracted tens of thousands of customers. The Lancia-built Coupé, in particular, became a formidable competition car. Neither car was substantially restyled over the years; except for a slight change to its four-headlamp nose, the Coupé of 1976 looked the same as that introduced in 1965. In that time, though, there were two big changes. One was that engine displacement was progressively enlarged (from the original 1.2 litres to 1.6 litres) and, with competition in mind, a lightweight HF derivative, complete with aluminium skin panels and less complete trim, was also put on sale. The 1600HF Lusso was a better-trimmed version of the 1.6-litre homologation special.

The 1300HF and 1600HF types were rally-winning cars, for by this time Lancia was determined to become the most successful manufacturer in World Championship rallying. With the Fulvia HFs, and later with the Stratos, this aim was achieved.

Almost 100,000 Coupés were eventually produced, of which 3,690 were 1600HF/Lusso Coupés, and a mere 800 were 1.6-litre Zagato Sports, making the latter a very collectable model.

## Lancia Fulvia Coupé variants

The original Fulvia Coupé was launched in 1965 and the Zagato Sport followed soon afterwards. The Coupé was to be built until 1976, but the Zagato Sport was discontinued in 1972. Original cars had a four-speed gearbox. The standard engine was a small 76-mm × 67-mm, 1216-cc/80-bhp unit, although the 1200HF had 88 bhp.

From 1967 Lancia introduced a 77-mm × 69.7-mm, 1298-cc, engine producing 87 bhp or (in the 1300HF) 101 bhp. In later years the 87-bhp engine was upgraded to 90 bhp. A five-speed gearbox was standardised in the 1970s.

From 1969 Lancia also introduced a 1584-cc engine producing 115 bhp, while the five-speed gearbox, with a relatively low fifth gear to preserve top-gear performance, had become standard.

*Above: Lancia turned the Fulvia Coupé into a very effective rally car with the 1600HF, fitting a 115-bhp version of the compact V4 overhead-cam engine and lightweight alloy panels. This is Kallstrom's car during the 1972 RAC Rally.*

## Specification (1600HF Coupé)

**Engine:** V4, twin overhead camshafts
**Bore × stroke:** 82 mm × 75 mm
**Capacity:** 1584 cc
**Maximum power:** 115 bhp
**Transmission:** five-speed manual gearbox, front-wheel drive
**Chassis:** steel unit-construction body/chassis
**Suspension:** independent front with wishbones and transverse leaf spring; beam rear axle with semi-elliptic leaf springs
**Brakes:** discs front and rear
**Bodywork:** steel (with some aluminium panels) four-seater coupé
**Maximum speed:** 106 mph (171 km/h)

*Above: Despite this extreme cornering angle, the handling and roadholding of the small front-wheel-drive Fulvia was extremely good.*

*Below: Zagato's version of the Fulvia Coupé looked bigger and heavier than the standard car, but its alloy body made it lighter.*

# Lancia Beta 1973-84

*Left: The Beta was produced in a variety of styles, the rarest of which was the Spider with its curious combination of Targa top and hood for the rear of the roof only.*

*Below: Towards the end of its life, the HPE version of the Beta was fitted with a supercharger and marketed as the Volumex. Top speed was 122 mph.*

After Fiat took control of Lancia, the first new model to be developed was the Beta, which combined a version of Fiat's latest twin-overhead-camshaft engine with Lancia's flair for getting a lot out of one single design. It went from concept to production-line status in a mere three years, which was a remarkable achievement in those days before computer-aided design, and did much to restore Lancia's fortunes.

It was almost inevitable that the saloon should also spawn a Coupé and a Spider, for this was a Lancia tradition, but in this case there was also a real innovation, the HPE, or 'High Performance Estate'. Although all Betas soon earned a well-deserved reputation for being rust-prone, Lancia thought it worth developing a further saloon version (the Trevi) and the range stayed in production for more than a decade. Well over 400,000 of

all types were eventually built.

All three sporting types had charms of their own. The Coupé was styled by Lancia, and ran on a shortened version of the front-wheel-drive saloon's floorpan. The Spider featured a unique Targa top and used the same short wheelbase; it was styled by Pininfarina but produced by Zagato, while the HPE was an elegant mixture, clearly inspired by Reliant's Scimitar GTE, with a saloon-length underpan, a Coupé-style front end, and a unique 'sporting-estate' cabin. In many ways the HPE was the most attractive model of all.

Although all cars had the same transversely-mounted twin-cam engine, a five-speed gearbox and front-wheel-drive, they were offered with a multitude of engine displacements over the years from 1300 cc to two litres. As far as sports car fanatics were concerned, the most

desirable of all had 2.0-litre engines, some with fuel injection and a limited number with Volumex supercharging.

## Specification (1980 Beta Coupé 2000)

**Engine:** inline four-cylinder, twin overhead camshafts
**Bore × stroke:** 84 mm × 90 mm
**Capacity:** 1995 cc
**Maximum power:** 119 bhp
**Transmission:** five-speed manual gearbox, front-wheel drive
**Chassis:** steel unit-construction body/chassis

**Suspension:** independent with MacPherson struts and anti-roll bars front and rear
**Brakes:** discs front and rear
**Bodywork:** steel four-seater coupé
**Maximum speed (approx):** 120 mph (193 km/h)

*Below: Although the standard Beta saloon looked uninspiring, it was roomy and comfortable and had much the same dynamic qualities as the sportier Coupé and HPE models. A serious rust scare ended the car's career in Great Britain.*

## Lancia Stratos 1973-75

*Right: The Stratos was a very successful rally car, particularly when driven by Sandro Munari, as here on the 1975 Safari Rally.*

Because Lancia was determined to dominate World Championship rallying in the 1970s, competitions manager Cesare Fiorio persuaded his management to back the development of a 'homologation special' – a car specifically designed with motorsport in mind. The result was the charismatic mid-engined Stratos, which swept all before it in a five-year rallying career.

Although the structure was a simple and rugged pressed-steel monocoque, the engine/transmission package was lifted straight out of the 2.4-litre Ferrari Dino 246. The body was mainly made from lightweight glassfibre mouldings, while Bertone not only styled the model but also manufactured the structures and all the panels for Lancia to use in finishing off the cars.

Until the arrival of various four-wheel-drive Group B cars in the mid-1980s, the Stratos had been the most exciting and the most dominant rally car of all time, which everyone – fans and rivals alike – seemed to respect and admire. To ensure its homologation, Lancia naturally had to offer the Stratos as a roadgoing car, though (like the Group B cars which followed) it was never properly developed for that purpose.

The Stratos was a stubby little coupé, with a tiny cockpit which only just had room for two passengers (the footwells were very cramped, and there was nowhere except wells in the doors to stow anything), yet it had flashing performance, a raucous engine note, and an endearingly urgent character.

In rallying form, it could win on tarmac or in the loose, and it could also be set up as a ground-hugging racer or in high-ground-clearance mode to float across the rocks of the Safari. It was used with 12-valve or 24-valve Ferrari engines, and at times race cars were campaigned with turbocharged engines. There is no question that it was the most effective of all two-wheel-drive rally cars, a point it proved by winning the World Rally Championship for Lancia in 1974, 1975 and 1976.

Between 1973 and 1975 Lancia produced 492 examples of the Stratos, but the limited demand for such cars meant that the last examples were still for sale, at much reduced prices, in 1978. Nowadays, of course, they are highly-prized collectors' pieces.

### Specification (1973)

**Engine:** V6, quad-cam
**Bore × stroke:** 92.5 mm × 60 mm
**Capacity:** 2418 cc

**Maximum power:** 190 bhp
**Transmission:** five-speed manual gearbox, front-wheel drive
**Chassis:** steel monocoque with glassfibre body
**Suspension:** independent front with wishbones and coil springs; independent rear with MacPherson struts and wishbones
**Brakes:** discs front and rear
**Bodywork:** glassfibre two-seater coupé
**Maximum speed (approx):** 143 mph (230 km/h)

*Below: The rally versions featured a battery of powerful lights across the very low nose. The external body panels were made from lightweight glassfibre covering a very strong steel central monocoque.*

*Above: Although principally a rally car, the Stratos was produced in roadgoing form to give mid-engined exhilaration to a lucky few.*

*Below: The whole rear section of the Stratos was hinged to lift up, revealing the Ferrari V6 engine which gave the car 140-mph-plus performance.*

## Lancia Monte Carlo 1975-78, 1980-84

*Right: Despite the shallow rear window, visibility out of this uncompromising wedge shape was good. Early cars were subject to much criticism for their severe braking deficiencies in the wet – a fault which Lancia rectified in 1978.*

The second of the 'Fiat-Lancias' was actually conceived as a Fiat, and only took on a Lancia identity at a late stage of its development. In the beginning Fiat coded it as a 'Fiat X1/20' – in effect it was meant to be a larger X1/9.

By the time it went on sale it was badged as a Lancia Monte Carlo, and the design then changed very little in the next nine years. Like the X1/9, the Monte Carlo was a mid-engined two-seater sports coupé with its own unique steel monocoque, and a lift-off roof panel. As with the X1/9, the engine/transmission was lifted straight out of a front-wheel-drive saloon – in this case the Beta. Other Beta hardware, notably the MacPherson-strut suspension, was also used in its chassis.

Pininfarina not only got the job of styling this stubby little two-seater, but also of building the cars, and Fiat-Lancia obviously had big ideas for this car in the North American market, where it took the name Scorpion (which harked back

*Above: The mid-engined layout and MacPherson-strut suspension all round gave excellent handling.*

*Below: The performance of the Pininfarina-styled sportster did not match its impressive looks.*

to the Abarth badge), but in this form it only had a 1.8-litre 'de-toxed' version of the twin-cam engine which produced a mere 82 bhp.

The Monte Carlo was a pretty little car which handled well, but it was a disappointment at first, as it always looked faster than it actually was, particularly in the Scorpion's case, making the car a flop in North America.

Lancia actually withdrew the car for two years, from 1978 to 1980, while several serious chassis deficiencies (notably wet-road braking) were eliminated, mostly by the rather crude expedient of removing the brake servo and fitting what was termed 'variable-effect brake control'. Other changes saw Marelli electronic ignition added, which gave a slight increase in torque output to 126 lb ft. Even that slight difference appeared to be responsible for a dramatic increase in acceleration, which was improved to the extent that 0-60 mph took only 8.6 seconds rather than 10.0 as before.

Since the Monte Carlo relied on the Beta/Trevi for its hardware, it died off when that range was withdrawn. Lancia

never offered it in supercharged form, which would have helped the performance a bit. Only 7,595 cars were made, though the elements of the cabin lived on as the basis of the Rallye 037 model of 1982.

### Specification (1975)

**Engine:** inline four-cylinder, twin overhead camshafts
**Bore × stroke:** 84 mm × 90 mm
**Capacity:** 1995 cc
**Maximum power:** 120 bhp
**Transmission:** five-speed manual gearbox, front-wheel drive
**Chassis:** steel unit-construction body/chassis
**Suspension:** independent with MacPherson struts and anti-roll bars front and rear
**Brakes:** discs front and rear
**Bodywork:** steel two-seater coupé
**Maximum speed (approx):** 119 mph (192 km/h)

# Lancia Gamma Coupé 1976-84

*Left: The flat-four, single-overhead-cam, 2.5-litre engine was designed specifically for the Gamma. It was a markedly over-square unit which produced 140 bhp, an output barely adequate for the large Coupé.*

This large, but elegant, coupé was a triumph for Pininfarina, which shaped a great car on the most unpromising basis. Lancia's Gamma saloon, launched in 1976, was a lumpy and unrefined car, yet the Pininfarina coupé, which used a shortened version of the floorpan, and the same running gear, was an altogether more satisfactory machine.

Curiously, it was the saloon which had coupé-like fastback styling, while the Coupé had three-box saloon lines.

Fiat had allowed Lancia one last piece of self-indulgence in the 1970s, with the design of the Gamma, for it had no technical links with any other Lancia or Fiat of the period. Before the car was announced, many observers were convinced that it would share the same rear-drive transmission as Fiat's recent 130 models, so there was some surprise when it was launched with front-wheel drive.

It was typical of Lancia that the engine chosen was an all-new horizontally-opposed four-cylinder 'boxer' unit, one which was not really smooth enough to match up to the image the company desired for the Gamma despite the single overhead camshaft per bank of cylinders. That was rather curious, as the engine was an overhead-cam design and great attention had been paid to mount the engine so as to minimise the vibration fed back into the cabin, and two tiny hydraulic dampers were used in addition to four large conventional rubber engine mounts.

The engine was tuned to produce a very good spread of torque, rather than the maximum outright power, and was consequently quite flexible; if necessary a driver could pull away at 800 rpm in fifth. There was sufficient power to give an adequate top speed of slightly over 120 mph, a performance that was complemented by excellent handling and roadholding, courtesy of independent MacPherson-strut suspension all round. That system was compliant enough to provide a comfortable ride and, with precise steering and very effective brakes, the Gamma (at least in Coupé form) was a satisfying car to drive.

The Coupé was large, but its styling was restrained and nicely detailed, with two passenger doors and comfortable seating for four adults. Almost all the cars had 2.5-litre engines, though there was also a 'tax-break' version with an 'under-bored' two-litre engine, sold only on the Italian market.

The Gamma Coupé was in production for eight years, during which time 6,789 examples were built. This figure, incidentally, easily beat that of another large and elegant Pininfarina effort, the Fiat 130 Coupé, which was one of the inspirations behind the Gamma's design.

## Specification (1976)

**Engine:** flat-four, single overhead camshaft
**Bore × stroke:** 102 mm × 76 mm
**Capacity:** 2484 cc
**Maximum power:** 140 bhp
**Transmission:** five-speed manual gearbox or optional four-speed automatic transmission, front-wheel drive
**Chassis:** steel unit-construction body/chassis
**Suspension:** independent with MacPherson struts and anti-roll bars all round
**Brakes:** discs front and rear
**Bodywork:** steel four-seater coupé
**Maximum speed (approx):** 121 mph (195 km/h)

*Above: The Coupé's interior design hardly matched the elegance of the Pininfarina body styling.*

*Below: Pininfarina managed to make what was a very big car look delicate and restrained.*

# Lancia Rallye 037 1982

Like the Stratos, the Rallye 037 was a 'homologation special' – a car built in minimum numbers so that it could be used in motorsport. In this case, only 200 cars had to be built, and this was the number originally laid down by Lancia. Like the Stratos, too, the Rallye was not only an effective, but also a beautiful car, which kept its charm long after becoming obsolete. The low, wide and very sleek style was by Pininfarina, who also produced the cabins of the production cars.

Lancia's Abarth motorsport centre designed the 037 – the number, by the way, was an Abarth project code – as their contender for the Group B category. The homologation regulations also allowed manufacturers to build a further 20 'Evolution' cars, with more specialised equipment, in an effort to produce the ultimate competition car.

Although four-wheel drive had recently been authorised for rallying, when Lancia began designing the 037 in 1980 this did not seem to be necessary. The result was that the 037 was Lancia's ulti-mate expression of a mid-engined/rear-drive car. In some ways it was 'son of Stratos', although there were no common features, except for the choice of a mid-engined/rear-drive installation.

The 037 was like a massive construction kit, designed to be assembled, disassembled, and repaired in double-quick time. To do this, the bare bones of the Monte Carlo's centre section were retained, to which multi-tubular front and rear 'chassis' frames were then fixed. Naturally there was all-independent suspension, adjustable for height, along with four-wheel disc brakes.

The engine was a further development of the 16-valve two-litre Fiat 131 Abarth unit, this time with supercharging. Lancia never gave a convincing reason for its rejection of turbocharging with the 037, but it was to make up for this on the Delta S4 which followed. In 'road car' form the engine produced 205 bhp, making the 037 a smooth and satisfying 140-mph car, though the works competition cars had up to 310 bhp.

The 037 was launched at the end of

1981 and, according to Lancia, all 200 cars were completed in the first half of 1982. As rally cars these models were extremely successful between 1982 and 1985, after which the Delta S4 took over.

Unlike some other Group B cars, the unmodified Rallye 037 was a surprisingly pleasant road car, for it combined flashing performance and excellent handling with a surprisingly good ride, and a nicely-equipped cockpit. Although many of these cars were used in motorsport, a proportion were used on the road in their standard state, and are now looked upon as true Lancia classics.

## Lancia Rallye 037 variants

### Lancia Rallye 037 Evolution E2

For use in motorsport in 1984 and 1985, Lancia built 20 Evolution E2 models, which were fully rally-tuned cars, with 2111-cc/325-bhp engines. None of these were sold as road cars.

*Above: Even roadgoing Rallyes had near-140-mph performance, thanks to Lancia's twin-cam two-litre engine in 205-bhp tune; competition versions produced up to 310 bhp.*

### Specification (1982)

**Engine:** inline four-cylinder, twin overhead camshafts

**Bore × stroke:** 84 mm × 90 mm

**Capacity:** 1995 cc

**Maximum power:** 205 bhp (310 bhp in fully-tuned competition form)

**Transmission:** five-speed manual gearbox, rear-wheel drive

**Chassis:** steel centre-section body/chassis with front and rear tubular subframes

**Suspension:** independent with wishbones and coil springs all round

**Brakes:** discs front and rear

**Bodywork:** glassfibre two-seater coupé

**Maximum speed (approx):** (205-bhp version) 137 mph (220 km/h)

*Above: 200 road cars were built to satisfy homologation rules. They produced 205 bhp in standard form.*

*Below: Looking rather like a stretched, squashed Monte Carlo, the Rallye had incredible road presence.*

## Lancia Delta S4 1985-86

*Left: A Group B Delta S4, driven by Markku Alen, is on its way to victory in the 1986 San Remo Rally. Group B supercars were banned that year after Henri Toivonen was killed.*

### Specification (1985)

**Engine:** inline four-cylinder, twin overhead camshafts
**Bore × stroke:** 88.5 mm × 71.5 mm
**Capacity:** 1759 cc
**Maximum power:** 250 bhp
**Transmission:** five-speed manual gearbox, four-wheel drive
**Chassis:** separate steel multi-tubular frame
**Suspension:** independent with coil springs all round
**Brakes:** discs front and rear
**Bodywork:** glassfibre and Kevlar two-seater hatchback
**Maximum speed (approx):** 140 mph (225 km/h)

Although the Rallye 037 was initially successful in motorsport, it was rapidly overhauled by the four-wheel-drive Audi Quattro. The result was that Lancia decided to cut its losses and design yet another Group B homologation special. The result was the Delta S4, a car which had a short and glamorous career in 1985 and 1986.

Although this car was called a Delta, it had virtually no parts in common with the production car except for the windscreen, the front grille and headlamps, and the same general proportions. Under that GRP skin it was a purpose-built rally car, with a multi-tubular chassis frame, a mid-mounted engine and four-wheel drive. Although it was the same size as the mass-produced Delta hatchback, the S4 was only a two-seater, for the engine filled all the space behind the front seats.

Because Lancia saw how Group B power outputs were racing ahead, the engineers made sure of being competitive by designing a brand-new engine, which featured both supercharging *and* turbocharging. The intention was that the supercharger would provide low-rev boost, while the turbocharger would chime in at higher rpm, there being a complex system of manifolding to ensure that one component did not 'choke' the other.

Lancia unveiled the S4 prototype at the end of 1984, though it was not yet ready to go into production. The fully-trimmed and remarkably civilised road car did not appear until the summer of 1975. As with the 037, Lancia proposed to build only 200 cars, along with a further 20 'Evolution' models for the works rally team to use in World Championship rallies. Their engines produced between 450 and 500 bhp.

Lancia built all the production cars in its San Paulo factory, near Turin. These had fully-trimmed cockpits, and a five-speed gearbox with synchromesh, along with a smart and well-equipped fascia and instrument panel, while there was power-assisted steering and a supple all-independent system. The road car was a semi-civilised, but very fast, machine which steered to an inch.

The rally car made a dramatic debut on the Lombard-RAC Rally of 1985, where it came first and second, while in 1986 it fought a season-long battle with the Peugeot team of 205 T16s. Tragically, Henri Toivonen was killed while driving a Lancia S4 on the Tour de Corse, an accident which led to the banning of the Group B cars and to the premature death of the Delta S4.

*Above: The S4s enjoyed a season-long battle with the Peugeot 205 T16s during 1986. Here Markku Alen leaves a dust trail on that year's Acropolis.*

*Below: Miki Biasion comes down to earth in his S4 on the 1986 Tour de Corse – this was the event in which his team-mate Toivonen died.*

# Lancia Delta 4 × 4 and Integrale 1986–95

Lancia's Delta range of hatchbacks was conceived around the running gear of the Fiat Strada, featuring a transversely-mounted engine and front-wheel drive, but there was a unique pressed-steel five-door monocoque body shell. It was not until 1986, after several other car-makers had produced four-wheel-drive cars, that Lancia launched a four-wheel derivative, afflicting it with the clumsy name of Delta HF 4 × 4.

For 1986, FISA imposed a Group A formula on top-level rallying, whereby 5000 identical cars had to be produced before homologation could be gained. The fact that this two-litre (eight-valve) twin-overhead-cam car, complete with turbocharger, was eminently suitable for the new Group A was dismissed by Lancia as mere coincidence, but rivals were convinced that this had always been a fully-fledged Group A project.

The road car was launched in mid-1986, and the first 5,000 necessary for homologation were completed at the beginning of 1987, though production and sales then continued. By the standards of what was to follow, these were tame machines, with 14-in road wheels and a mere 165 bhp, but with a sophisticated 4 × 4 layout which naturally featured three differentials. Right away this was assessed as a great driver's car, for it was fast and agile, but still civilised. Its top speed was 129 mph.

Lancia made sure that it was a successful rally car – it won its first event (Monte Carlo 1987), and dominated World Championship rallying in all its forms until 1989, when Toyota's Celica GT4 began to beat it on an irregular basis. Even so, three derivatives on, and five years later, it was still good enough to give Juha Kankkunen his third World Championship title, along with yet another Manufacturers' Championship for the Lancia factory.

The first Delta Integrale of 1987-89 had

a 185-bhp version of the twin-cam engine, along with 15-in wheels, and a top speed of 134 mph.

Then, to keep the four-wheel-drive Delta ahead of its rivals in motorsport, Lancia produced a series of updated models, each of which was built in quantities of 5,000 and more. For 1988 and 1989 the HF was replaced by the eight-valve Integrale, which had flared wheel arches to cover larger wheels and a wider track, and in the summer of 1989 it was succeeded by the 16-valve Integrale, which used the latest type of corporate two-litre turbocharged engine, and needed a bonnet bulge to enclose the bulkier and more powerful unit.

What Lancia called the 'final evolution' of the car was launched in late 1991, this having more pronounced wheel-arch bulges to accommodate more wheel movement and a power increase to 210 bhp. Before Integrale faded out, a more extreme evolution appeared, known as Evo II, it featured wider wheel-arches and an aerofoil over the rear of the roof.

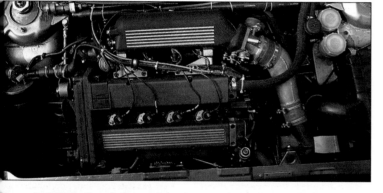

*Above: In 1989 the Lancia Integrale was upgraded with a 16-valve turbocharged two-litre engine which produced 200 bhp.*

*Below: The original Delta Integrale produced 'only' 165 bhp, although the drivetrain was praised by everyone who drove the four-wheel-drive car.*

*Above: Miki Biasion leads home a trio of Deltas on the 1990 Acropolis. Although their performance was only on a par with the Toyota Celica GT4 – the Delta's biggest rival – they were consistently more reliable. Whether running on desert sand or snow and ice, they were invincible.*

## Specification (1991 Integrale 16V)

**Engine:** inline four-cylinder, twin overhead camshafts
**Bore × stroke:** 84 mm × 90 mm
**Capacity:** 1995 cc
**Maximum power:** 210 bhp
**Transmission:** five-speed manual gearbox, four-wheel drive
**Chassis:** steel unit-construction body/chassis
**Suspension:** independent with MacPherson struts front and rear
**Brakes:** discs front and rear
**Bodywork:** steel four-seater hatchback
**Maximum speed (approx):** 137 mph (220 km/h)

## Lancia k Coupé 1998-present

Lancia's 1998 kappa range of well-appointed high-performance saloon cars included the 'k' saloon, Station Wagon and Coupé, and while all of them were well-appointed high-speed carriages, it's the Coupé that falls most comfortably into the league of vehicles we're looking at here. The 220 bhp five-cylinder 2.0-litre turbo 20 valve unit and the 204 bhp 3.0-litre V6 power units would be optimum choice for the Coupé, although the complete set of engines was available throughout the range, apart from the 2.4-litre five-cylinder JTD turbodiesel that was available only in the saloon and Station Wagon. The five-cylinder 2.0 turbo unit superseded the previous four-cylinder 2.0 turbo 16 valve unit, lifting top speed from 145 to 150 mph (235 to 243 km/h ). It didn't suffer from turbo-lag either, thanks to adjustments to timing, the electronic control unit and intake and exhaust valve geometry. It was modified for use in Lancia's more sober cars to make power delivery smoother and more gradual.

Kappa Coupé styling could best be described as state of the art mid-1990s, and not a patch on the exciting Zagato-built Hyena of 1993. That was tossed away in the corporate dustbin, probably because it was based around outgoing Delta Integrale components and conflicted in the market place with Fiat's own Coupé and the Alfa Romeo GTV.

Lancia's k-range was really about available options. In addition to a wide choice of engines, there was a tempting array of high-tech kit, including xenon

*Below: The 'k' Coupé was based on the old Delta Integrale, but the styling was completely contemporary.*

headlamps, Bosch radio navigator – the Lancia k was the first Italian car to be fitted with this device – side airbag and passenger presence sensor, which detected whether the seat next to the driver was occupied and would only allow the front and side airbag to inflate if someone was sitting there. Leather upholstery could be specified, along with electric sunroof. The package could also include a self-adaptive, sequential electronic automatic transmission for the 3.0-litre V6 engine, which included cruise control facility. Controlled dampers were available, while the braking system had been developed in conjunction with Brembo, improving efficiency by 10 per cent, meaning more responsive modular braking, con-

sistent pedal response and greater fade resistance.

Alongside the kappa range was the long-running Dedra series that shadowed the Alfa 155 and available in saloon and estate format. There was also an interesting Integrale 4 x 4 estate version. In the late 1990s, Lancia was also offering the d HPE HF hot-hatch that ran with the old 2.0-litre turbo engine, and the diminutive flat-backed Y model, which came with 1.4-litre and 16-valve 1.2-litre engines. Along with most other European car makers, Lancia also offered a six-seater MPV known as the Z, which was predictably based on the Fiat Ulysse platform. Powered by the turbocharged 2.0-litre petrol engine, it presented the family motorist with a means

of getting the kids to school rather mo[re] swiftly and in greater style than the re[st] of the people carrier market.

### Specifications
### (k 2.0 five-cylinder turbo)

**Engine:** in-line five, front transverse installation
**Bore x stroke:** 82.0 mm x 75.65 mm
**Capacity:** 1998-cc
**Compression ratio:** 10.4 :1
**Gearbox:** five-speed manual or four-speed automatic
**Chassis:** two-door steel monocoque
**Suspension:** front, independent by MacPherson struts, lower wishbones, anti-roll bar; rear, torsion beam, coil springs, dampers, anti-roll bar

# Lea-Francis Cars

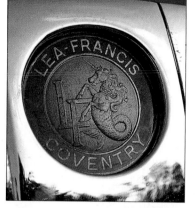

L ike so many of Coventry's pioneering carmakers, Lea & Francis started as cycle manufacturers. Their most prolific car manufacturing period was in the 1920s and 1930s.

At first Lea-Francis models were mainly an amalgam of proprietary components, and most of the cars built at this time used engines produced by Henry Meadows of Wolverhampton (who also supplied power to companies like Frazer Nash).

On the whole, the mixture of components was a harmonious success, and the company's first sports car was the L-Type of 1925, which then evolved into the altogether better P-Type in 1927. The company's outstanding 1920s-style model was the Hyper sports car, which was lighter and more nimble than most of its rivals, and which benefitted from the use of a supercharged Meadows engine.

The original Lea & Francis company got into serious financial trouble after the Depression, and stopped building cars in the early 1930s. The marque was revived by a new company – Lea-Francis Cars Ltd – in 1937, when two entirely new cars were designed by ex-Riley engineer Hugh Rose. These were fitted with advanced new twin-high-camshaft engines whose design owed a lot to the famous Riley motors of the period.

Similar cars, though with more modern styling, were produced after World War II but, once the insatiable post-war demand for cars tapered off, Lea-Francis sales gradually fell away, and the last production models were built in 1953.

For the next few years the company existed, precariously, on sub-contract work, and one final attempt to produce a new sports car in 1960 – the Leaf Lynx – was a humiliating failure and the company eventually closed down. A fourth revival came in the 1980s, when the name and surviving parts were bought by Barry Price. And a prototype was shown at the NEC Motor Show in 1998.

*Left: The Lea-Francis emblem was a common sight in the 1920s, and was then revived in 1937 for the launch of two new cars.*

*Below: Kaye Don follows a Stutz in his Lea-Francis Hyper Sports round a tight bend on the first-ever Ulster Tourist Trophy in 1928. He went on to win the event at an average speed of 64.5 mph. The Hyper's supercharged performance was great for the day.*

## Lea-Francis Hyper Sports 1928-32

*Left: The Hyper Sport's Cozette supercharger endowed the engine with 61 bhp in standard form, although this could be pushed up considerably if the owner fancied taking his car round the racetrack.*

Although the L-Type and P-Type Lea-Francis sports cars were competitive with rival cars such as the Alvis 12/50, they were neither faster nor particularly outstanding. That situation changed with the ultra-sporting Hyper model.

The Hyper was a conventional car, with a none-too-rigid chassis frame, beam axles at front and rear, and rod-operated drum brakes. However, its Meadows engine was fitted with a Cozette supercharger, which endowed it with 61 bhp in standard 'over-the-counter' form; even more power was available if the customer was interested in going motor racing.

It was difficult to provide a truly noticeable style in the 1920s – most sports cars of the period tended to have cycle-type wings, squared-up lines, and similar proportions – but the Hyper was distinguished by a radiator which was sloped back at a rakish angle, this angle being matched by the rear shut line of the lift-up bonnet panels.

Between 1928 and 1930 the factory sup-

ported a sports car racing programme, during which Kaye Don won the 1928 Tourist Trophy race, which was held in Northern Ireland. The Hyper also showed well in the Le Mans 24 Hours. At this time the works Hypers were almost as fast as the 'blown' 1750 Alfas, and if only more money had been available to back the racing programme, they might have changed the face of sports car racing for a time.

*The Autocar* of the day, a magazine inclined to be over-favourable to British cars, thought that the Hyper was "fast, genuinely fast" but insisted that it was also a docile sports car, describing it as suave, although reporting that its engine was quite a lot noisier than a normally-aspirated unit would have been.

### Specification (1928)

**Engine:** inline four-cylinder, overhead-valve

**Bore × stroke:** 69 mm × 100 mm

**Capacity:** 1496 cc

**Maximum power:** 61 bhp (79 bhp for competition use)

**Transmission:** four-speed manual gearbox, rear-wheel drive

**Chassis:** separate steel frame with channel-section side members, and pressed and tubular cross-bracings

**Suspension:** non-independent with beam front axle and semi-elliptic leaf springs; live rear axle with semi-elliptic leaf springs

**Brakes:** drums front and rear

**Bodywork:** aluminium and steel two-seater sports car, coupé or tourer

**Maximum speed (approx):** 85 mph (137 km/h)

*Left: At a time when most sports cars looked very similar, the Hyper Sports could be distinguished – by enthusiasts at any rate – by the subtle slope of its bonnet line. The Autocar went so far as to call its styling suave ...*

# Leyland Motors Ltd

Above: J. E. P. Howey pilots the first Leyland Eight, with its distinctive radiator, at Brooklands in 1923.

Below: The Eight's designer, and famous racing driver, Parry Thomas takes the wheel of his creation.

**L**eyland of Lancashire was already well-established as a truck-maker before it decided to start building expensive cars in the 1920s. It was a short-lived experiment which lasted for only two years. Thereafter Leyland concentrated on trucks again until the 1960s.

By 1920 Leyland was already building the best trucks in the UK (having enjoyed a very successful time supplying vehicles to the British forces during World War I) when it decided to add a car line to its range.

Like the Rolls-Royce 40/50HP model, with which it was meant to compete, this was intended to be 'the best car in the world' regardless of cost – and the price asked reflected this. Chief engineer J. G. Parry Thomas, who was also a racing driver, was delighted to design the car, which certainly delivered everything that was promised.

Unhappily, the British public did not rush to buy the car, so after a mere 18 had been produced, the project was abandoned.

Although Leyland was to go on to become even more famous as a truck and bus builder, and to absorb other commercial vehicle manufacturers like Albion and AEC along the way, this was the only private car to carry the famous badge until the 1970s. Leyland, of course, moved back into the car industry in the 1960s, first by taking over Standard-Triumph, then by absorbing Rover and Alvis, and finally becoming the dominant member of the British Leyland colossus in 1968.

For a time, as British Leyland's future looked promising, there were proposals to call new car models Leyland (instead of Austin, Morris, Rover or whatever), and project codes like LC8 (Leyland Car project no. 8) or LM10 (Leyland Motors project no. 10) found use in the corporate design offices in the UK.

In the end, Leyland chose to use its own marque name on private cars in Australia in the 1970s. The model chosen was a spacious new 'land-cruiser' meant to compete with the native Holdens, and was produced with a choice of six-cylinder or V8 engines. This was not a marketing success, so after British Leyland was nationalised in 1975 the project was abandoned, as was any further plan to use the name on private cars.

## Leyland Eight 1920-22, and 1927

J. G. Parry Thomas was instructed to start designing a Leyland car in 1917, and to make it as perfect as possible; further, he was instructed not to worry about its cost. His assistant in this work was a young man called Reid Railton, who would later go on to develop cars as diverse as the Railton road car, the Napier-Railton Brooklands car, the chassis of the ERA racing car, and the Railton land speed record car; he was also involved in post-war design work with Hudson.

Thomas chose to power this so-called 'perfect car' with a complex new straight-eight cylinder engine, which had an opposed-valve cylinder head and single overhead camshaft with leaf valve springs. It was almost inevitable, therefore, that the new car should simply be named the Eight, the title under which it was to be sold from 1920 to 1922.

The prototype exhibited at the Olympia Motor Show of 1920 was the very first British car to have an eight-cylinder in-line engine, and was listed at £2,500 for the chassis alone. The car, and the design of its chassis, looked so magnificent that the press made a play on the Leyland trademark by dubbing it the 'Lion of Olympia'.

The chassis, though conventional enough in most ways, was nicely detailed, and featured vacuum assistance for the rear brakes (there were no front brakes), along with cantilever quarter-elliptic rear springs linked by an anti-roll torsion bar. There were two

small gearboxes in the steering linkage, and the rear axle design allowed a modicum of positive camber to suit Britain's heavily-cambered roads.

The first car had a lofty and square-rigged open tourer body, complete with a proudly rectangular Leyland radiator, and there were other fascinating 'styling' touches such as the headlamps, with a circular glass section but almost square cowls.

Even though design work had started on the new car three years earlier, it was still not ready to sell to the public, and by the time deliveries began, the chassis price had been lowered to £1,875, while a complete five-seater tourer was listed at £2,700.

Despite the price reduction, and although there were three chassis lengths available, the Eight sold very slowly indeed. It was still the most expensive British car, and went on sale during the post-war slump, so it was no wonder that sales were so low.

Leyland offered the Eight with a variety of bodies, including open tourers, coupés (by Windover) or saloons (by Vanden Plas). Two cars were sold to India, and one went to Michael Collins, the Irish politician who was assassinated in 1921.

When the project was seen to have failed, two chassis were turned into racing cars by Parry Thomas – one for himself to drive, the other for the use of Captain J. E. P. Howey. Thomas eventu-

ally left Leyland in 1922, moved to Brooklands, and transformed his race car into the Leyland-Thomas with a 200-bhp engine; the model went on to enjoy great success in the mid-1920s.

The only Leyland car to survive today is a massive two-seater sports car, now owned by the British Motor Industry Heritage Trust. This was built up from a chassis, and parts, in 1927 by Thomson & Taylor at Brooklands, and had a 200-bhp version of the 7.0-litre engine. In styling, however, it bore no relation to other Eights, all of which were scrapped in the 1930s or 1940s.

### Specification (1922)

**Engine:** inline eight-cylinder, single overhead camshaft
**Bore × stroke:** 89 mm × 140 mm, later 89 mm × 146 mm
**Capacity:** 6967 cc, later 7266 cc
**Maximum power:** 145 bhp
**Transmission:** four-speed manual gearbox, rear-wheel drive
**Chassis:** separate steel frame with tubular and pressed cross-braces
**Suspension:** non-independent with beam front axle and semi-elliptic leaf springs; live rear axle with reversed quarter-elliptic leaf springs and anti-roll bar
**Brakes:** drums rear, no front brakes
**Bodywork:** steel four- or five-seater, open or closed, to choice
**Maximum speed (approx):** 75 mph (121 km/h)

Below: This car is the sole remaining Leyland Eight. The massive two-seater has a 200-bhp seven-litre straight-eight engine.

# Lincoln Motor Co.

**A**fter Henry M. Leland had sold his stake in Cadillac in 1917, he immediately set about founding another car company. This, using the famous name of one of the USA's presidents, was Lincoln, which produced its first model in 1920.

The first Lincoln used a side-valve V8 engine, but it had stodgy styling and did not appeal to American motorists at first, and the faltering business was taken over by Henry Ford in 1922. In the next few years there was little change to the cars, but from the 1930s (and with the arrival of the Model K) Ford transformed Lincoln into a truly prestigious top-line marque, which it has been ever since.

Integration into the Ford product line was slow – Lincoln used its own unique V12 engines until 1940 – and it was only with the launch of the Zephyr range in 1936 (with unit-construction and a simple new V12 engine) that closer links with Ford became obvious.

Lincoln's original Continental of 1940 (which was *not* badged as a Lincoln) showed that a large business in an even larger company could

*Above: The Zephyr, introduced in 1936, was originally conceived as a rear-engined design. Unit-construction meant that the price could be kept down.*

still produce distinctive cars if its management had the will.

From 1946 to modern times Lincoln has always retained its place at the top of the Ford model line as a head-on competitor to Cadillac, although Cadillac has usually outsold Lincoln.

By the 1960s Lincoln used its own V8 engine, which it sometimes shared with other Ford models, and always had a distinctive style of bodywork, but over the years, running gear, chassis, body platforms and even basic body structures gradually came to be shared with other models, in particular the Ford Thunderbird.

From 1961 all Lincolns tended to carry the Continental model name, so if an interloper (such as the Versailles in 1977) crept into the price lists this was usually as an 'entry-level' model, meant to compete with a particular model which Cadillac had launched.

Lincoln's most famous line was the Continental 'Mark' models, which effectively took over from the unbadged Continentals of the 1940s and 1950s. The Mk III of 1968 was a vast four-seater coupé (whose structure and chassis had evolved from that of the contemporary Ford Thunderbird) which became the Mk IV in 1972, the Mk V in 1977, then in down-sized form the Mk VI in 1980. The next generation, dubbed Mk VII, was also Thunderbird-based, and took Lincoln into the 1990s. It showed that even Lincoln had been tempted to follow the new aerodynamic trends of the 1980s.

Lincoln's best-sellers, however, were always the big four-door six-seater Continentals, along with a formal limousine called the Town Car.

*Below: Several generations of Lincolns are shown here. Lincoln and Cadillac were founded by the same man: the stern, patrician Henry Leland. Lincolns have always been characterised by being big, silent, expensive and elegant.*

*Below: For the 1956 model year, Lincoln added seven inches to the Continental's length and three to its width, making it elegantly long and sleek. The stylish wrap-around windscreen was expensive to replace.*

## Lincoln Model K 1930-40

The first Lincoln to be designed completely under the control of Ford was the large and impressive Model K, which made its bow in 1930, and was to be produced in gradually modernised form throughout the 1930s. It showed that Ford was serious about developing a head-to-head competitor to Cadillac, this philosophy never varying throughout the model's long life. Although not built regardless of price, it always carried the best-quality coachwork.

Its basis was a solid but conventionally-detailed new chassis frame, with nine-inch-deep side members, and it was originally offered with a choice of three wheelbases – 145 in, 150 in or 155 in – and with more than 20 coachbuilders' body styles. Prices started at $4,400.

The first Model K used an updated version of Lincoln's 1920s-era long-lasting side-valve V8, but the new chassis had really been developed to accept the all-new 65-degree side-valve V12 which made its debut a year later. This engine had 'vintage-style' construction, with a cast-alloy crankcase topped by two separate cast-iron blocks, and produced a smooth and utterly reliable 150 bhp.

*The Autocar* tested a V12-engined Model K Town Sedan in 1932, a six-seater machine priced in the UK at £1,895, which put it in the Rolls-Royce bracket. This test recorded a top speed of 96 mph, but overall fuel consumption of 10 mpg and a massive weight of 5,936 lb, while describing the Model K as "one of

*Right: The Henry and Edsel Ford-designed Model K sat on a massive 145-in wheelbase chassis and was powered by a modernised 120-bhp V8 engine incorporating a three-piece cast-iron block/crankcase assembly. Advertisements for the model talked of its 'precision-built' quality.*

those exceptional cars", and pointing out that "the whole car is beautifully finished, and the workmanship beneath the bonnet is utterly different from what is usually associated with America..."

Very few V12 cars were on the market in the early 1930s, and because of the Depression, Model K sales were limited to no more than 2,000 a year at first. Prices were slashed for 1933, and a smaller-capacity V12 took over from the old V8 (which was dropped), but it was not until a redeveloped V12 (with aluminium cylinder heads) was launched for 1934 that the Model K's future seemed to be assured.

Even the earliest examples had a freewheel to the gearbox, and servo-assistance to the brakes, while later cars became progressively more refined. Synchromesh was added to the gearbox for 1937, while the engine was given hydraulic tappets. The first major restyle, away from the original and rather upright stance, came for 1936, while for 1937 and later the headlamps were tucked rather awkwardly into the flowing front wings.

By the late 1930s the old-style Model K Lincoln was looking more and more like an automotive dinosaur, especially as it did not have independent front suspension, nor the sleeker styling of its competitors. By this time prices were in the $6,000/$7,000 bracket, like those of Cadillac, which might explain why only 124 cars were built in 1939, and 133 in 1940. The Model K was not revived after World War II.

*Below: Having decided on the length of chassis required – there was a choice of three – buyers could then select from around 20 different body styles, designed by the cream of American coachbuilders. That, plus all the various colours available, meant that practically no two Model Ks were the same.*

### Lincoln Model K variants

#### Lincoln Model KA and KB

The original Model K of 1930 had a V8 engine, of 6306 cc producing 120 bhp. It became known as the KA for 1932, sharing the same basic chassis and body choices as the KB. The V8 engine was discontinued at the end of the 1932 model year. The KA and KB names referred to shorter- or longer-wheelbased V12s for 1933 and 1934, but both reverted to plain Model K from 1935 to 1940. For 1933 an additional V12, of 6255 cc producing 125 bhp, was standard on KA models. For 1934 a substantially revised V12 engine, of 6808 cc, with aluminium cylinders and producing 150 bhp, was standardised. This engine was retained until 1940.

### Specification (1932 V12 KB)

**Engine:** V12, side-valve
**Bore × stroke:** 82.55 mm × 114.3 mm
**Capacity:** 7340 cc
**Maximum power:** 150 bhp
**Transmission:** three-speed manual gearbox, rear-wheel drive
**Chassis:** separate steel frame with channel-section side members, tubular and pressed cross-bracings
**Suspension:** non-independent with beam front axle and semi-elliptic leaf springs; live rear axle with semi-elliptic leaf springs
**Brakes:** drums front and rear
**Bodywork:** steel four-, five-, six- or seven-seater; open, closed and limousine styles, to choice
**Maximum speed (approx):** 96 mph (154 km/h)

# Lincoln Continental Mk III, Mk IV and Mk V 1968-79

For all high-income-bracket Americans, the attraction of the gargantuan Continental 'Mark' models of this period was not what the cars could do, but what they represented. Quite simply, they exuded status, and confirmed the buyer's freedom to choose it instead of opting for practicality, or better roadholding – or a foreign car.

Lincoln's Mk III came along at a time when Cadillac's Eldorado had been rejuvenated, and when the Ford Thunderbird had moved decisively up-market. In all cases the designers offered what was dubbed a 'personal' car – one which was large and heavy, with a vast engine but with no thought of fuel-efficiency. All such cars had enormously long bonnets (someone once said you could land a helicopter on the bonnet of a 'Mark'), with shallow boots, but four-seater interiors which were wide but without a great deal of leg room.

In the beginning, it is said, Ford boss Lee Iacocca started the development of the Mk III with the immortal command: "Gimme a Thunderbird with a Rolls-Royce grille" – and this is what he got. The interior of the first cars had large separate front seats, a wood-grained dashboard, and every possible fitting. There was a choice of 26 exterior colours, 150 lb of sound-deadening insulation, and the equipment included power windows and seats, through-flow ventilation and frameless side windows.

On the other hand it was better not to enquire too much about the roadholding, for all these cars had a very soft ride, tyres whose wet-road grip was negligible, and brakes which were not really adequate for the straight-line performance on offer.

In many ways these 'Marks' were the last of the dinosaurs, for during the 1970s they grew progressively larger, heavier, but slower and no more roadworthy as emissions and safety standards became more restrictive. In 1968 a Mk III had 365 bhp, a 117.2-in wheelbase, and weighed in at 4,740 lb. By 1979, when the last Mk V was produced, the weight had increased to 5,362 lb but the wheelbase had grown to 120.4 inches, and the power had plummeted to a mere 159 bhp – pathetic considering the size of the engine.

The Mk VI which followed for 1980 was an entirely different, smaller, and less impressive machine – 10 inches shorter, 600 lb lighter, and with only a 5.0-litre engine.

## Specification (1968 Mk III)

**Engine:** V8, overhead-valve
**Bore × stroke:** 110.79 mm × 97.79 mm
**Capacity:** 7536 cc
**Maximum power:** 365 bhp
**Transmission:** three-speed automatic transmission, rear-wheel drive
**Chassis:** separate steel frame with box-section side and bracing members
**Suspension:** independent front with wishbones and coil springs; live rear axle with coil springs
**Brakes:** drums front and rear
**Bodywork:** steel two-door four-seater coupé
**Maximum speed (approx):** 130 mph (209 km/h)

*Right: The stand-up bonnet decoration on the Mk III folded flat to avoid pedestrian injury.*

# Lincoln Mk VII 1984-88

After the 'down-sized' Continental of 1982, which was really nothing much more than the Ford Fairmont platform with only a V6 engine, Lincoln produced something far more daring and interesting in the shape of the Mark VII.

It appeared at a time when Ford was switching to a new range of overtly aerodynamic designs and the Lincoln was no exception, with smooth, rounded lines reminiscent of the contemporary Thunderbird and Mercury Cougar. It was clearly aimed at trying to woo back buyers who were opting for expensive imports from BMW and Mercedes, and was more mechanically sophisticated than previous Lincolns, boasting, for example, air springs all round. A compressor maintained air pressure to the 'springs' and sensors were used to monitor ride height and give a constant level, combining previous Lincoln ride standards with handling approaching that of the imports. Other firsts included flush glazed headlights.

The most exciting Lincoln variant was the LSC (Lincoln Sport Coupe) with more conventional but stiffer suspension, cast-alloy wheels, larger tyres, and sufficient power to make it interesting, thanks to the Ford five-litre V8 engine in HO (High-Output) form. By 1986 that unit was producing 200 bhp, thanks to fuel injection, with another 25 bhp on tap by 1988. The LSC was easily the most sporting of all Lincolns, as it was surprisingly agile to drive and had excellent handling. It sold well too, with around 30,000 finding buyers in the car's first season.

## Specification (1988)

**Engine:** V8, overhead-valve
**Bore × stroke:** 101.6 mm × 76.2 mm
**Capacity:** 4950 cc
**Maximum power:** 225 bhp
**Transmission:** four-speed automatic
**Chassis:** unitary-construction
**Suspension:** independent front with MacPherson struts; live rear axle with trailing arms and coil springs; electronic ride height control
**Brakes:** discs all round
**Bodywork:** steel two-door coupé
**Maximum speed (approx):** 135 mph (217 km/h)

*Left: Lincoln took a surprising new direction with the dramatic Mk VII. It was aimed at younger buyers.*

357

# Lotus Cars Ltd

**B** y the time Colin Chapman started his working life with the British Aluminium Company, he was already crazy about cars. Not only did he make (and eventually lose) money by buying and selling cars, but he had also built a two-seater 'special' which he called a Lotus.

The first Lotus production car was the Six of 1953, which had a multi-tubular chassis frame and was always supplied in kit form. This was an 'evenings and weekends' model, built in a stable in Hornsey, north London. During the 1950s Chapman also began designing a number of successful, lightweight, racing-sports cars, soon moved up to producing single-seaters, and eventually bought new premises at Cheshunt on the outskirts of London, where Lotus began building the Elite coupé.

Chapman's early associates included Mike Costin (who eventually joined Keith Duckworth to develop the Cosworth company), Fred Bushell and Peter Kirwan-Taylor, but Chapman was always the technical genius who masterminded all race-car and road-car design until the end of the 1960s, when the business had grown too large for him to do everything.

Between 1960 and 1980 Lotus expanded mightily, not only producing a succession of fine road cars – the Elan, the Elan Plus 2, the Europa and the Esprit and its derivatives – and its own road-car engines, but also becoming one of the most successful of all Formula 1 manufacturers. Jim Clark became World Champion Formula 1 driver, and models like the 25, 33 and 49 were built for him to drive. Lotus also found time to branch out into Indy racing, and most other racing formulas.

*Above: Elan variants: a 1973 Sprint at the front and behind, and from left, a 1964 S1, 1966 S3 and a 1966 26R lightweight factory racer.*

An association with Ford was forged in 1962, one result being that Lotus assembled the Lotus Cortina from 1963 to 1966, another being that the Lotus twin-cam engine was supplied to Ford for the Escort Twin-Cam. The company outgrew its Cheshunt premises in the 1960s and moved to a new factory at Hethel, in Norfolk, in 1966. Two years later, Lotus became a public company.

A new generation of road cars – the Elite, the Eclat and the Esprit – arrived in the mid-1970s, all powered by a new 16-valve engine. Next an engineering consultancy business was set up; as one of its first tasks, Lotus undertook the complete redesign of the new DeLorean DMC12 model with an Esprit-inspired chassis.

At the end of 1982, however, Colin Chapman suddenly died (he was only 54) and the company appeared to be rudderless for a time. Soon after Chapman's death, Lotus became embroiled in fraud investigations connected with Chapman's dealings with John DeLorean, investigations which were still ongoing in the early 1990s.

Until the mid-1980s there was a danger that Lotus would close down. The consultancy business subsidised the car-making side and after General Motors rescued the company a new generation Elan was launched. Lotus went though two further eras in the 1990s. The first was its acquisition by Romano Artioli, under whose auspices the fabulous Elise was put into production. By 1996 the company was controlled by Malaysian car maker Proton, and apart from the Elise and Esprit manufacture, Lotus carried out exclusive consultancy work for clients in the motor industry.

*Above: The original Lotus Seven appeared as a kit car in 1957. It was basic but had superb handling and performance.*

*Below: The new Elan, which appeared in 1989, was compact and rounded, and front-wheel-driven by the 1588-cc 16-valve Isuzu engine.*

# Lotus Seven 1957-73

*Left: The Seven was ideal for racing; this is a Series 1 in the 1961 Wiscombe Park hill climb.*

*Above: At Silverstone in 1961, a Seven is put through its paces; note that the car is road-registered.*

Having established Lotus in the 1950s with a series of racing-sports cars, all of which used multi-tubular spaceframe chassis, Colin Chapman then set out to widen the scope, and appeal, of his business, partly to provide financial backing for his motor racing ambitions. On the one hand he conceived the technically advanced Elite, and on the other he developed the rugged little Seven.

The Seven looked superficially similar to the earlier Six – which is to say that it was a starkly-trimmed and lightweight two-seater open sports car, but it was technically quite different. Like the Six, though, it used a multi-tubular frame, which was clad in an aluminium body shell. There were separate front wings, no doors (only cutaway sides to the body), and wet-weather protection was an afterthought.

Lotus was far too small to build its own drivetrains, so engines, transmissions and axles were all bought-in, proprietary, items. Over the years a wide variety of engines found a home in this car, ranging from the ancient Ford side-valve unit to the aluminium racing-type Coventry Climax powerplant. Front suspension was independent, while the rear axle was controlled by coil springs, radius arms and a Panhard rod.

In every case, the Seven was produced as a kit car; Lotus supplied a body/chassis unit, together with a complete kit of parts, so that the customer could assemble his own car at home. This was done to exploit a loophole in British tax laws – no purchase tax was levied on cars sold in this way.

Like the earlier Six, the Seven made absolutely no concessions to the comfort of driver or passenger, and there was virtually nowhere to stow any luggage – and when it rained, the occupants got wet. On the other hand, by 1950s and 1960s standards it offered amazing road-holding, and could be used in motorsport or as a road car.

The Seven's character was very appealing, even on cars fitted with less powerful engines, and it has been

*Right: Over the years, styling changes have included a roll-over bar and new front wing design.*

likened to a four-wheel motorcycle.

Although hundreds of Sevens were sold in every year of production, Colin Chapman and many of his Lotus colleagues seemed to lose interest in the car after a time. Even so, over the years a few dedicated staff kept updating the design (most notably in 1970 with the launch of the radically different S4, which not only looked different from before, but had a new chassis and a glassfibre body), yet Chapman forced the sale of the entire project in 1973, when Caterham Cars took over the rights to production and sales.

Thereafter the Lotus Seven became the Caterham Super Seven, a model which was extremely successful in the 1990s.

## Lotus Seven variants

### Lotus Seven Series 2
The Series 2 was built from 1960 to 1968. Engine choice (all four-cylinder units) included A-series BMCs, side-valve Fords, and overhead-valve Fords, some tuned by Cosworth; power outputs ranged from 40 bhp to 95 bhp. Front-wheel disc brakes were available from 1962. Typical top speed (with a 90-bhp 1.3-litre Ford-Cosworth engine) was 102 mph.

### Lotus Seven Series 3
The Series 3 was built from 1968 to 1970. Engines were either overhead-valve Fords (1.3-litre or 1.6-litre) or 1.6-litre Lotus-Ford twin-cams. Power options spanned 84 bhp to 125 bhp. All cars had front-wheel disc brakes. The top speed of a 120-bhp model was 107 mph. This model was reborn in the 1970s as the Caterham Super Seven, which still exists in modified form.

### Lotus Seven Series 4
The Series 4 (built from 1970 to 1973) was an evolution of the Series 3, with a newly-designed chassis, but still of multi-tubular design, and with a glassfibre body and quite different styling.

## Specification (1957 S1)

**Engine:** inline four-cylinder, various types – side-valve Ford, overhead-cam Coventry Climax, overhead-valve BMC A-series

**Transmission:** three-speed (with Ford side-valve engine) or four-speed manual gearbox, rear-wheel drive

**Chassis:** multi-tubular steel frame

**Suspension:** independent front with wishbones and coil springs; live rear axle with radius arms and coil springs

**Brakes:** drums front and rear

**Bodywork:** aluminium open two-seater

**Maximum speed (approx):** (with 1.1-litre Coventry Climax engine) 104 mph (167 km/h)

## Lotus Elite 1958-63

*Right: A sleek road car, the Elite could also race, such as here at Silverstone in 1961.*

The sleek Elite was the first Lotus to be conceived entirely as a road car, although naturally it was also a suitable basis for development as a racing-sports car. As one might have expected from the technically adventurous Colin Chapman, its design was quite unconventional, and its style was remarkably advanced for the period.

The Elite was the first car to use a complete monocoque of glassfibre, with only a little local stiffening in steel. All previous cars with glassfibre bodies had used steel chassis frames of one type or another, but for the Elite this heavy item was abandoned completely. However, glassfibre construction brought its own problems, notably the suppression of noise and vibration inside the cabin. Sadly, this car was not anything like as smooth and silky to drive as its appearance suggested.

Power was provided by Coventry Climax, in a variety of engine tunes (though the majority of these 1.2-litre-engined cars had 83 bhp), and was complemented by all-independent suspension and four-wheel disc brakes. It was a remarkably light, fast and fuel-efficient car, with supple roadholding and precise steering; if only the Elite had been more reliable and less expensive, it would surely have sold far better.

The beautiful two-seater fixed-head coupé style was the work of Colin Chapman's associate Peter Kirwan-Taylor, a financier by profession, and featured a sharply-angled windscreen and side glass. The cross-sectional profile was such that the door glasses could not be wound down into the doors to provide ventilation; occupants either had to become hotter as the engine heat filtered through the bulkhead, or the window glasses had to be removed.

Although the first prototype was shown at Earl's Court in 1957, the first deliveries were delayed until 1959, and once the rather different Elan was announced in 1962 this really marked the end for the Elite, with only 988 cars having been built.

Although everyone loved the car's looks, performance and handling, it soon acquired a doubtful reputation for quality and reliability and this, allied to the rather high price (even as a kit car) harmed its sales. A proposal to build late-model Elites with the new Lotus twin-cam engine was abandoned after just one car was produced.

In later years Lotus admitted that it had never made money from the Elite. The model's successor, the Elan, was an entirely different story.

### Specification (1959)

**Engine:** inline four-cylinder, overhead-camshaft
**Bore × stroke:** 76.2 mm × 66.6 mm
**Capacity:** 1216 cc
**Maximum power:** 83 bhp
**Transmission:** four-speed manual gearbox, rear-wheel drive
**Chassis:** reinforced glassfibre unit-construction body/chassis
**Suspension:** independent with wishbones and coil springs front; Chapman struts and lower wishbones rear
**Brakes:** discs front and rear
**Bodywork:** glassfibre two-seater coupé
**Maximum speed (approx):** 118 mph (190 km/h)

*Above: An Elite takes part in the 1961 Tourist Trophy; the car was fast, frugal and great fun to drive.*

*Below: The lines are still right, but the side windows could not be wound down into the doors.*

# Lotus Elan 1962-73

To replace the troublesome Elite, Lotus chose to develop an entirely different type of sports car. In some ways it was more complex, but in others it was far more simple and rugged than the Elite had ever been.

The new car, called the Elan, was open where the Elite had been closed, had a separate chassis instead of relying on glassfibre to provide a monocoque, and had a Lotus-designed engine instead of a bought-in item. It was also a great success, whereas the Elite had been a commercial failure. More than any other single Lotus model, the Elan brought not only respectability, but also profit to this growing carmaker.

Central to the design thinking for the Elan was that it should have a separate, simple, steel chassis – one that Lotus would find easy to make, one that could be developed without heartache, and one that would be straightforward to maintain and repair. Lotus chose to make this as a sturdy steel backbone, with the engine and gearbox mounted at the front end, which was shaped something like a tuning fork, with the seats low down and to either side of it, and with the final drive and rear suspension fixed to the rear.

A feature which only became obvious when the glassfibre body shell was removed was that the rear struts (a modified version of the steerable MacPherson type) were mounted to high outriggers on the frame, which looked weak but were remarkably strong. Another quirk of the design was that there were rubber-based universal joints in the rear driveline, which helped to give the car its well-known 'jack-rabbit' tendencies when the throttle was feathered, then re-applied.

The real design breakthrough was the engine, a new Lotus layout (commissioned from ex-Coventry Climax racing designer Harry Mundy) which was based on the sturdy five-bearing bottom end of the Ford Cortina engine. The aluminium cylinder head was a logical development of the classic 1950s twin-cam racing layout, complete with partly spherical combustion chambers, two valves per cylinder, and twin overhead camshafts. This new Lotus engine was to be the company's mainstay for more than a decade, and would also find a home in three Ford models – the Lotus Cortina Mk 1, the Lotus Cortina Mk 2 and the Escort Twin-Cam.

Right from the start, the new Elan (which could be purchased in kit form or, at a higher price, as a completely built-up car) was a great success. It was tiny, light, fast and economical, and had the most phenomenal combination of agile handling, tenacious roadholding, and an excellent supple ride.

Although this design was gradually developed and improved over the years,

*Left: The little Elan offered the virtues and not the vices of the Elite; this is a 1966 S3.*

it was originally well-known for unreliability, notably from the electrics, and for tendencies such as the headlamps' pop-up mechanism to fail from time to time. Over the years these faults were eliminated, and the small two-seater became a firm favourite.

The best Elans of all were the lusty Big Valve-engined Sprints of 1971-73, particularly the smoothly-detailed fixed-head coupés. In retrospect the least desirable were the Stromberg-carburettor types of 1968-69, but every Elan was a complete generation ahead of its rivals in terms of function and behaviour.

In just over 10 years, a total of 9,659 Elans was produced.

## Lotus Elan variants

### Lotus Elan S2
The S2 (1964-65) was mechanically like the S1, but with better front brakes, optional centre-lock wheels, and a full-width wooden fascia.

### Lotus Elan S3
The S3 (1965-68) featured a fixed-head coupé option, an optional (SE) 115-bhp engine, and framed door windows for the open sports car version.

### Lotus Elan S4
The S4 (1968-71) had style changes including flared wheel arches, a bonnet bulge, and different fascia details.

### Lotus Elan Sprint
The Sprint (1971-73) used the Big Valve engine, with 126 bhp, and a strengthened driveline to suit. Surprisingly, the top speed rose only to 118 mph.

## Specification (1964 S1)

**Engine:** inline four-cylinder, twin overhead camshafts
**Bore × stroke:** 82.55 mm × 72.75 mm
**Capacity:** 1558 cc
**Maximum power:** 105 bhp
**Transmission:** four-speed manual gearbox, rear-wheel drive
**Chassis:** separate steel fabricated backbone frame
**Suspension:** independent with wishbones and coil springs front; Chapman struts and lower wishbones rear
**Brakes:** discs front and rear
**Bodywork:** glassfibre two-seater sports
**Maximum speed (approx):** 115 mph (185 km/h)

*Below: The first Elans of 1962 were far ahead of their time, offering open-top motoring, economy and performance.*

*Below: The Sprint is generally regarded as the most desirable model, thanks to the extra acceleration provided by the 126-bhp Big Valve engine; the drivetrain was strengthened to take the increased torque.*

## Lotus Elan Plus 2 1967-74

The Elan Plus 2, which was announced after Lotus had moved to a new factory at Hethel, near Norfolk, was almost precisely what its model name implied. It combined most of the engineering, and all the qualities, of the two-seater Elan, in a longer wheelbase, with a bigger and more roomy glassfibre coupé body with 2 + 2 seating.

Plus 2s shared the engines, transmissions and basic suspension systems of the Elan two-seaters, but had entirely different chassis and bodies. The chassis, still a backbone of the now-established Lotus type, had a 12-in longer wheelbase, along with a wider track. Every Elan Plus 2 had a fixed-head coupé body, although a few drop-head coupé versions were privately produced by outside coachbuilders.

Like the smaller Elan, the Plus 2 was a fast car which could also be surprisingly economical, and it retained all the road-holding characteristics of the smaller model. On the other hand, its cabin was considerably more roomy, and in many ways it was a more practical machine.

Because it was a heavier car than the Elan two-seater, the Plus 2 was never as

fast, but to counter this Lotus not only fitted Big Valve engines from 1971, but also offered the car with a new five-speed gearbox for the last two years of its life. By this time, too, the kit car alternative had been withdrawn, and in fact most

Plus 2s were completely Lotus-assembled machines.

In 1974 the Plus 2 family was withdrawn, for it was then replaced by the much larger and more expensive second-generation Elite. By this time no fewer than 4,798 Elan Plus 2 models of all types had been built.

*Above: The 126-bhp Big Valve engine was fitted to the Plus 2 from 1971 until production ended.*

*Below: Graceful from any angle, the Plus 2's flowing lines were enhanced by recessed headlights.*

### Lotus Elan Plus 2 variants

#### Lotus Elan Plus 2S
The Plus 2S (1969-71) was a more completely equipped version of the original, sold as a complete car; kit car versions were not available.

#### Lotus Elan Plus 2S 130
The Plus 2S 130 (1971-74) used the Big Valve engine, which produced 126 bhp (rather than the 130 bhp implied by the model name).

#### Lotus Elan Plus 2S 130/5
The Plus 2S 130/5 (1972-74) combined the 126-bhp engine with a new Elite-type five-speed gearbox. Top speed was 120 mph.

*Above: Although the Plus 2 was a foot longer than the Elan, it handled just as well. It also looked very attractive and offered considerably more room, yet the smaller Elan is still more sought-after. This car is a factory-built Plus 2S 130 of 1971. The clumsily-named 2S 130 featured the Big Valve engine.*

### Specification (1968)

**Engine:** inline four-cylinder, twin overhead camshafts
**Bore × stroke:** 82.55 mm × 72.75 mm
**Capacity:** 1558 cc
**Maximum power:** 118 bhp
**Transmission:** four-speed manual gearbox, rear-wheel drive
**Chassis:** separate steel fabricated backbone frame
**Suspension:** independent with wishbones front; Chapman struts, lower wishbones and coil springs rear
**Brakes:** discs front and rear
**Bodywork:** glassfibre 2 + 2-seater coupé
**Maximum speed (approx):** 118 mph (190 km/h)

# Lotus Europa 1967-75

Although Lotus took very little time to bring mid-engined racing cars to a high state of technical excellence, it was several years before Colin Chapman was ready to use the same basic layout in a road car. The problem, in the main, was the lack of an available transaxle (gearbox/transmission) which could be matched to a suitable engine.

Then, in the mid-1960s, Lotus struck an alliance with Renault, the first fruit of which was the mid-engined Europa two-seater, an interesting combination of Lotus engineering and Renault hardware. It was called the Europa – quite simply, because it was initially intended only to be sold in Europe.

Central to the layout was the Renault engine and transaxle, mounted behind the cabin, but with the engine ahead of the driven rear wheels. The engine was a tuned version of that used in the Renault 16 front-wheel-drive hatchback; this car, however, had its engine mounted behind the line of the front wheels – a moment's thought reveals that it was necessary to rejig the transmission so that the Europa was not inflicted with four reverse gears!

Like the Elan models, the Europa had a steel backbone chassis and, as usual on a Lotus, the body shell was made of glassfibre. All cars were built at the new Hethel factory. On the first cars the body was actually bonded to the chassis on assembly, but from 1968, when the Series 2 Europa was launched, this was changed to the usual separate body concept. From the summer of 1969 the Europa finally went on sale in the UK, either in kit form or fully assembled.

In the beginning the Europa was intended as a relatively cheap Lotus; by the standards of other mid-engined cars, the Europa had a simple mechanical specification and rather limited performance. Within four years Lotus had detected a demand for more performance, even if the car needed to be sold at a higher price, so the Renault links were ended and a Lotus twin-cam engine was fitted instead, along with rear style changes to enable the new customers to make their purchase obvious.

*Above: The 1970 two-seat Europa was the first production Lotus to have a mid-mounted engine.*

*Below: The odd bodywork treatment at the rear of this 1971 model turned out to be a styling dead-end.*

Only a year after the Europa Twin-Cam had been launched it moved one step further, to become the Big Valve-engined Special, featuring an optional five-speed gearbox. By 1973 all such cars were being sold as complete cars, and this was the form in which production ended in 1975.

Not only was the Europa a small car, but it had beautifully balanced roadholding allied to a supple ride, so a reliable example was a joy to drive. Unhappily for Lotus, most Europas suffered from irritating little problems, and cars which were neglected soon deteriorated rapidly.

## Lotus Europa variants

### Lotus Europa Twin-Cam

From 1971, the Europa became the Europa Twin-Cam, with the 1558-cc Lotus twin-cam engine of 82.55 mm × 72.75 mm, producing 105 bhp. From 1972 this model became the Europa Special, with the 126-bhp Big Valve engine, an optional five-speed gearbox and a 121 mph top speed.

*Above: The competition derivative of the Europa was the Lotus 47. This is a Gold Leaf-Team Lotus 47 in action at Brands Hatch in 1968. Powered by the Lotus twin-cam engine, the 47 was successful in club racing into the 1970s.*

## Specification (1968)

**Engine:** inline four-cylinder, overhead-valve

**Bore × stroke:** 77 mm × 84 mm

**Capacity:** 1565 cc

**Maximum power:** 82 bhp

**Transmission:** four-speed manual gearbox, rear-wheel drive

**Chassis:** separate fabricated steel backbone frame

**Suspension:** independent with wishbones and coil springs front; lower wishbones, upper lateral links, upper and lower trailing arms and coil springs rear

**Brakes:** discs front, drums rear

**Bodywork:** glassfibre mid-engined two-seater coupé

**Maximum speed (approx):** 109 mph (175 km/h)

## Lotus Elite 1974-82

Lotus began developing a new generation of road cars in the early 1970s, launching two entirely different models – the Elite/Eclat and the Esprit – in the 1974-76 period. Although these cars shared the same type of engine, they were radically different, for the Elite/Eclat types had front-mounted engines, while the Esprit was a mid-engined two-seater.

As was almost traditional by this time at Lotus, these cars all used backbone chassis, allied to glassfibre body shells, but each developed its own distinct character. The Elite (which had been given a notable old Lotus model name, even though there was no mechanical link between the two types) was the first Lotus ever to have a hatchback style, the car having 'almost four-seater' accommodation, a sloping tailgate, and generous stowage room.

Both the Elite and Eclat were produced during the darkest days of the 1970s recession, and at the worst times only half a dozen cars were built per month at the Hethel works, most of them Eclats, with perhaps one Elite a month coming off the line. In terms of the body styling, the cars were perceived by customers as soft, with an almost feminine look.

The Elite was a very fast and nimble car, not only because it had all-independent suspension and the usual miraculous Lotus combination of grip, steering precision and ride, but also because it had a powerful new 16-valve twin-cam two-litre engine. Compared with the old Elan Plus 2, the new Elite was a much faster, much more spacious, and more expensive proposition – in fact it was in an entirely different market sector.

Less than two years after the Elite had been launched, the Eclat was added to the range, this being a modified and cheaper version of the Elite, with a fastback coupé cabin instead of the near-hatchback style of the original. Lotus

*Below: The hatchback Elite was practical, but buyers for it and the fastback Eclat were few during the 1970s recession.*

then confused everyone by marketing several different versions of each car, so that in theory a potential customer could 'design' his own car. These were the first Lotuses where an automatic gearbox option was available – not that many customers chose it.

To make these good cars even better, Lotus upgraded them to '2.2' in 1980, the major improvement being an enlarged and more torquey engine. The Elite, whose styling had never been totally accepted by sports car enthusiasts, was dropped at the end of 1982, by which time 2,398 S1 models and 132 S2.2s had been produced.

### Lotus Elite variants

#### Lotus Elite S2.2
The S2.2 took over from the original model in 1980, with an over-square 160-bhp/2174-cc engine, and a different type of five-speed gearbox. Top speed was 127 mph.

#### Lotus Eclat
The Eclat S1 of 1975 used the same basic running gear as the Elite S1, though some cars used a four-speed gearbox, and there was no automatic transmission option. The body style featured a 2+2 fastback coupé (not hatchback) layout. The Eclat S2.2 of 1980-82 combined Elite S2.2 running gear with Eclat body styling.

*Above: The car's glassfibre body was built in two halves joined along the waist line.*

*Below: The Elite's 'stick-on' type of bumper was phased out when the Excel was designed.*

### Specification (1974)

**Engine:** inline four-cylinder, twin overhead camshafts
**Bore × stroke:** 95.28 mm × 69.24 mm
**Capacity:** 1973 cc
**Maximum power:** 160 bhp
**Transmission:** five-speed manual gearbox or optional three-speed automatic transmission, rear wheel drive

**Chassis:** separate pressed steel backbone frame
**Suspension:** independent with wishbones and coil springs front; trailing arms, lower links and struts rear
**Brakes:** discs front and rear
**Bodywork:** glassfibre 2+2-seater hatchback coupé
**Maximum speed (approx):** 124 mph (200 km/h)

# Lotus Esprit 1976-87

Lotus's master plan for the 1970s included replacing the Europa by a new mid-engined car – a completely new design based around the new 16-valve type 907 engine. Not only was the new car given a fresh name – Esprit – but it was clothed in a body style by the top Italian designer, Giorgetto Giugiaro.

The original concept car for this design was previewed in 1972, but completion of the development had to wait until the new generation of front-engined cars – Elite and Eclat – had been put on sale. Even when the Esprit production car was first shown, in October 1975, it was not yet ready to go on sale, for first deliveries were delayed until the summer of 1976.

The Esprit combined all the expected Lotus virtues – a backbone chassis, all-independent suspension with a remarkably soft ride and pin-sharp steering – along with a unique and unmistakable body, again made from glassfibre. The original cars had normally-aspirated engines, with 160 bhp, but this was merely the start of a development process which was to occupy more than 10 years and produce another 55 bhp.

Between 1976 and 1987 the Esprit was produced in many guises – normally-aspirated and turbocharged, standard or special livery, and in specially-developed USA-market form – though the basic layout and style were never abandoned. There was one major revision to the basic design in 1980, when the engine was enlarged to 2.2 litres, a turbocharged version was introduced, and the chassis and suspension were updated.

All types shared the same compact – some would say cramped – two-seater cabin, where the screen rail always seemed to be close to the passengers' heads, and where the footwells were small. There wasn't much useful luggage space either, but Esprit customers didn't usually worry about that sort of thing. The Esprit's real charm was its very high standards of handling, roadholding and performance, which were a match for many Italian supercars, but at a much lower price.

Final changes, to HC (high-compression) specification, came in 1986-87, just before the long-running original-shape Esprit was finally replaced by a moder-

*Above: The 1983 Esprit Turbo featured the 2.2-litre four-cylinder twin-cam fed through a Garrett T3 turbocharger, giving 210 bhp, 200 lb ft of torque and 150-mph performance. It offered great value for money and was a best-seller.*

nised, smoother-styled, model in 1987. In all that time, more than 4,000 of the original-shape Esprits were produced, sometimes at the rate of more than 500 cars a year, which made it Lotus's most successful model of the period.

## Lotus Esprit variants

### Lotus Esprit S2 and S2.2
The Esprit S2 took over from the original version in 1978, complete with subtle styling revisions, a different instrument cluster, revised seating, and wider-rim wheels. This car, in turn, was replaced by the Esprit S2.2 in 1980, which had a 95.28-mm × 76.2-mm, 2174-cc/160-bhp engine.

### Lotus Esprit S3
Less than a year after the S2.2, the Esprit S3 was introduced, this having the chassis and suspension of the Esprit Turbo (see below), and the optional fitment of the Esprit's 15-in wheels and tyres.

### Lotus Esprit HC
The final normally-aspirated version was the Esprit HC of 1987, which had a 180-bhp version of the 2.2-litre engine.

### Lotus Esprit Turbo
The first turbocharged version of this design was called, logically enough, the Esprit Turbo, and was launched in 1980; this had the 2174-cc engine, but far more power (210 bhp), and a faster top speed of 148 mph. To go with this engine was a revised chassis and suspension layout, together with 15-in wheels and larger brakes, plus body changes including new front and rear spoilers, and NACA ducts in the flanks to channel the required volumes of air into the engine bay.

### Lotus Esprit Turbo HC
For the last year of its life, the Turbo received a revised, High Compression, version of the engine, and became known as the Esprit Turbo HC.

## Specification (1976)
**Engine:** inline four-cylinder, twin overhead camshafts
**Bore × stroke:** 95.28 mm × 69.24 mm
**Capacity:** 1973 cc
**Maximum power:** 160 bhp
**Transmission:** five-speed manual gearbox, rear wheel drive
**Chassis:** separate pressed/folded steel backbone frame
**Suspension:** independent with wishbones, coil springs and anti-roll bar front; radius arms, lower links and struts rear
**Brakes:** discs front and rear
**Bodywork:** glassfibre two-seater coupé
**Maximum speed (approx):** 135 mph (217 km/h)

*Above: This 1982 Esprit Essex Turbo is in the livery of the Essex Petroleum company, who that year sponsored the Lotus Formula 1 team.*

*Below: The Esprit Turbo HC, with its High Compression engine, more boost and bigger Dellorto carburettors, produced 215 bhp.*

## Lotus Excel 1982-92

Early in the 1980s Lotus began casting around for a partnership with a large company, and eventually chose Toyota. In the medium term the intention was to produce a Toyota-engined 'new Elan' (a project which was cancelled), but the first fruit was a revision of the old Eclat design, to use Toyota components, the new car being renamed Excel.

Compared with the Eclat S2.2, the new Excel had a modified backbone chassis and suspension layout, along with a Toyota gearbox, rear axle and other components, though the 2.2-litre engine was left unchanged. The Eclat's body style was altered to be subtly more rounded, to have different side window profiles, and much of the car's rear end was different in detail from what had gone before.

By Lotus standards the Excel was a modest success, with annual sales settling down to around 250-300 a year. Nevertheless the car remained in production throughout the 1980s and into the early 1990s, though it was gradually and inexorably modified and updated. The body shape, in particular, was retouched from time to time, though one always needed to put the new and the old side-by-side to spot the differences.

Body style changes were phased in for 1985, while a new fascia with tilted steering column followed a year later. In the same period the Excel SE appeared, with 180 bhp, different spoilers and a walnut veneer fascia. An automatic transmission option (the SA model) appeared at the end of 1986, at the same time that the HC (High Compression) engine also appeared. Further cosmetic changes, and improved suspension settings, were introduced for 1989, but the Excel of 1992 was still recognisably developed from the original Eclat of 1975.

*Below: With nearly 50/50 weight distribution, the Excel corners flat with a great deal of grip; the rear spoiler reduces lift.*

### Lotus Excel variants

#### Lotus Excel SE and SA

In 1985 the Excel was updated to SE, with the addition of the 180-bhp HC engine and a large rear spoiler; top speed was 131 mph. A year later the Excel SA was launched; its engine was also in 180-bhp tune, but allied to the bought-in German ZF four-speed automatic transmission.

### Specification (1989)

**Engine:** inline four-cylinder, twin overhead camshafts
**Bore × stroke:** 95.28 mm × 76.2 mm
**Capacity:** 2174 cc
**Maximum power:** 160 bhp
**Transmission:** five-speed manual gearbox, rear wheel drive
**Chassis:** separate pressed/folded steel backbone frame
**Suspension:** independent with wishbones, coil springs and anti-roll bar front; radius arms, lower links and struts rear
**Brakes:** discs front and rear
**Bodywork:** glassfibre two-seater coupé
**Maximum speed (approx):** 130 mph (209 km/h)

*Above: This is a 1989 Excel. The series started as a reworking of the Eclat, with new styling giving a masculine, more aggressive look.*

*Below: The 1985 Excel SE had a restyled interior and a more powerful engine delivering 180 bhp and 165 lb ft of torque.*

## Lotus Esprit 1987-present

The original Giugiaro-styled Esprit was a stunning concept when unveiled in the 1970s, but Lotus decided to freshen it up dramatically in the mid-1980s. Neither the finance nor the manpower was available to develop a completely new car, so the existing layout was modernised in all departments, not least in the style.

Compared with the sharp-edged 'origami' style of the original, the lines of the revised car were smoother and more rounded from every aspect, although its skin, remarkably, was never more than half an inch away from the original profile at any point. There was more Kevlar reinforcement in the two-piece glassfibre shell, which was built by Lotus's patented VARI process, and there was a revised cabin with more space than before, though still virtually no in-cabin stowage.

As before, there was a choice of normally-aspirated or turbocharged 2.2-litre engines, though the old-type Citroën gearbox had been ditched in favour of the latest Renault five-speed type as found in the rear-engined

Renault GTA coupé.

The new type was considerably more expensive – by £3,000 for the Turbo – but clearly the customers were happy, as the new style gave an impetus to sales. It handled just as well as before, was more convenient in some ways, and looked

**Above: The Esprit Turbo engine is tested on a rig, with the exhaust manifold glowing red-hot.**

**Below: The restyled Esprit was redrawn with curves and rounded edges but the same dimensions.**

smoother and very much more modern.

In May 1989 Lotus launched the ultimate Esprit, the Turbo SE, where 'SE' stood for Special Equipment. It included some fundamental improvements to both the handling and performance. The front suspension was retuned to improve steering feel and reduce the understeer which had been criticised on the previous model, while the tyre size was increased. Aerodynamic improvements were made too, with a deeper nose section and a separate rear wing. Although by this stage the Lotus engine was tuned to run on unleaded fuel, it was made more powerful through the use of what Lotus called a 'charge cooler', a liquid-to-air intercooler which lowered the intake air temperature, making it denser and helping boost output to no less than 264 bhp at 6,500 rpm. That was used in conjunction with a Garrett TB03 water-cooled turbocharger and changes to the fuel injector system wherein another 'rail' of injectors was fitted to supply more fuel under high-boost conditions. One of the remarkable things about this engine is not just the power, which at 120 bhp per litre is outstanding, but that so much torque is produced at relatively low rpm. To extract 261 lb ft at only 3,900 rpm from 2.2 litres shows just how well Lotus have mastered the art of turbocharging.

For very short bursts, higher boost was allowed, which increased power yet further, to 280 bhp. That meant a top speed in the 160-mph region, good enough to keep pace with the Porsche or

**Above: In 1989 the Esprit Turbo SE was given improved power, brakes, steering and aerodynamics.**

Ferrari competition.

The Esprit had a brief career as a works backed GT1 sports racing car in the 1990s. By 1999, the latest model, the 3.5-litre V8, was favourably compared with the Ferrari 355 and the Porsche 911.

### Lotus Esprit variants

#### Lotus Esprit Turbo SE

Introduced in May 1989, the Turbo SE featured an intercooled engine, and a power output of 264 bhp. This gave the car a 159 mph top speed, with 0-60 mph acceleration in a mere 4.9 seconds.

### Specification (1992 Turbo SE)

**Engine:** inline four-cylinder, twin overhead camshafts
**Bore × stroke:** 95.3 mm × 76.2 mm
**Capacity:** 2174 cc
**Maximum power:** 264 bhp
**Transmission:** five-speed manual gearbox, rear wheel drive
**Chassis:** separate pressed/folded steel backbone frame
**Suspension:** independent with wishbones, coil springs and anti-roll bar front; radius arms, lower links and struts rear
**Brakes:** discs front and rear
**Bodywork:** glassfibre two-seater coupé
**Maximum speed (approx):** 159 mph (256 km/h)

## Lotus Elan 1989-92

The 'new Elan' was the compact new Lotus that every enthusiast was waiting for in the 1980s, but its arrival was long delayed. There were times in the 1980s when it looked as if Lotus would *never* produce a new model to fit within the range below the existing 2.2-litre-engined cars.

Financially, the company nearly foundered after Colin Chapman's death, then stumbled again in the mid-1980s, before General Motors finally took over in 1986. The first 'Elan' project was the rear-drive Toyota-engined M90 of 1982, but this was cancelled in favour of a new rear-drive X100 model in 1985, which would have retained Toyota running gear. After GM took over, this was cancelled, and work began on an all-new M100 project in 1986.

The definitive 'new Elan' turned out to be a front-wheel-drive car (the first Lotus to utilise this system), with a transversely-mounted 1.6-litre 16-valve Isuzu engine

and five-speed transmission; this power pack was chosen for pragmatic reasons – GM was also an Isuzu shareholder.

Not only did the new car have front-wheel drive, but it had a new type of alloy 'raft', or subframe, which insulated the front suspension from the otherwise conventional steel backbone chassis and the steel-reinforced composite platform moulding which formed the base of the shell. Apart from being mounted on that clever 'raft', the front suspension was conventional enough, with upper and lower wishbones, while the rear suspension set-up was a tried-and-tested design essentially lifted from the contemporary Excel, which meant the same arrangement of wide-based links. Significantly, space was left by the designers for the drivetrain that would be needed for a four-wheel-drive version, a model which never appeared.

The car was a short, wide, squat but rounded two-seater, with a vast

windscreen and a tightly packaged two-seater cabin. The hood was a neat arrangement too; when not in use, it folded under a flush-mounted cover to leave an uncluttered profile.

The car was always offered in normally-aspirated (130-bhp) or turbo-charged (165-bhp) form; Lotus's forecast that the majority of sales would be of turbo ('SE') types was soon borne out in the marketplace. The Elan not only handled remarkably well, but also offered good value, for in 1990 when sales began, the SE was priced at £20,325 – which compared favourably with the £26,400 price tag of the current Excel.

The car's superb handling drew accolades immediately, and in a straight line the Elan SE accelerated to 60 mph in 6.5 seconds, and to 100 mph in only 17.5.

Lotus was hoping that the new Elan would help it expand its own business, and although the front-wheel-drive car got off to a slow start, it looked as if it would carry the Lotus badge forward well into the 1990s. Unfortunately, sales in the US were well below expectations and Lotus owners GM ended production in 1992.

*Above: Testers found that the Elan set new standards of front-wheel-drive handling. Autocar & Motor considered that it "bordered on the awesome . . . dry road grip, stability and suspension control are a match for some supercars".*

### Specification (1992)

**Engine:** inline four-cylinder, twin overhead camshafts
**Bore × stroke:** 80 mm × 79 mm
**Capacity:** 1588 cc
**Maximum power:** 130 bhp normally-aspirated or 165 bhp turbocharged
**Transmission:** five-speed manual gearbox, front-wheel drive
**Chassis:** steel backbone frame with additional steel/composite mouldings
**Suspension:** independent with wishbones, coil springs and anti-roll bar on front subframe; upper transverse links, lower wishbones, coil springs and anti-roll bar at rear
**Brakes:** discs front and rear
**Bodywork:** glassfibre two-seater sports car, open or with a detachable hard top
**Maximum speed (approx):** (165-bhp version) 136 mph (219 km/h)

*Above: The styling is functional rather than pretty, and with the hood up the Elan has a 0.34 Cd.*

*Below: The Elan jigs and moulds were sold to Kia and the model resurfaced as the Kia Sport in 1998.*

## Lotus Elise 1996-present

The Elise emerged at a time when Lotus itself was in the crucible of corporate desire. Having been hived off by General Motors to dashing Italian entrepreneur and Bugatti manufacturer Romano Artioli, just as it was being launched ownership of the company passed to Proton. That it came out at all was an achievement, but that it should have emerged as such a cracking little car was doubly commendable.

With the Elise, Lotus was able to productionise several revolutionary ideas in car construction within three years from conception to launch. Conceptually, it reverted to Colin Chapman's basic premise, which was to offer racing car handling at production car prices achieved through light weight and simplicity rather than sheer power. Designers Julian Thomson and Richard Rackham turned to the world of super-sports motorcycles for their inspiration, since that's where performance motoring is at the cutting edge. The chassis was constructed of lightweight aluminium extrusions, bonded together and secured with Ejot fasteners, and made initially by Hydro-Raufoss engineering in Denmark then shipped to Hethel for assembly. Elise GRP body panels were made at Hethel, with two main fore and aft clamshell sections abutting the central nucleus that contained the cockpit and transverse mid-mounted 1.8-litre Rover K-series twin-cam engine. Elise styling was based heavily on sports-racing cars of the 1960s, which stylist Thomson regarded as a halcyon era. The mini-

malist trappings of the Elise shell and interior pointed directly at the race track, and the cockpit was an austere environment indeed. Part of the aesthetic attraction was the juxtaposition of bare aluminium chassis and bright gloss of the glass-fibre bodywork. The Italian brake specialists Brembo produced the silicone carbide metal matrix brake discs, originally designed and made by the Lanxide Corporation in the USA.

The Elise could be raced with very few alterations, and as a result its road manners were impeccable, so that it handled superbly and could be cornered with total accuracy and commitment. Suspension was by double wishbones that were fabricated in-house, with coil springs and monotube dampers all round and an anti-roll bar at the front: the car was originally so light that the anti-roll bar was needed to get some weight into the tyres. Long hours were spent testing the prototypes, honing their brakes and suspension at the Hethel test track and other locations like Nardo, the Neuburgring and Stelvio pass. Damper settings were regarded as crucial, and much of the setting up was undertaken by Lotus chassis experts John Miles, Dave Minter, Steve Swift, and overseen by project manager Tony Shute.

### Variants
### Sport Elise
The Sport Elise was an evolution that could be used as a racing car. To reduce weight even further the Sport

had carbon-fibre clamshells, magnesium wheels, lightweight battery, silencer and rear window glass, bringing its weight down to 650 kg. Options included an FIA approved roll cage, a full four point harness, competition springs, dampers, anti-roll bar, competition Stack instrument pack with data logging facility, a closer ratio gearbox and competition silencers.

### GT1
The GT1 was an Elise-based sports racing-car built to contest long distance sports car races in 1997 like the Le Mans 24-Hours. There were two versions: a road car, required for homologation purposes, and an all-out racing car, powered by a new 6.0-litre normally aspirated engine based on the Lotus developed Chevrolet Corvette motor. Last minute rule changes stymied any realistic chance of success.

### Specification
**Engine:** aluminium four-cylinder Rover K-series
**Bore x stroke:** 80 mm x 89.3 mm
**Capacity:** 1796 cc
**Suspension:** Double wishbones with single coil springs over monotube dampers all round. Lotus-patented uprights of extruded aluminium, made

*Above: The Elise was a ground-breaking sports car, embodying the principles of high performance attained through light weight, responsive steering, superlative handling and a small engine. With its chassis made from bonded aluminium extrusions, metal matrix brake discs and glass-reinforced plastic bodywork, it pioneered some highly innovative new technologies.*

by Alusuisse.
**Brakes:** aluminium/metal matrix ventilated discs, non-servo split hydraulic system, including unique Lotus/AP Racing opposed piston front callipers
**Chassis:** Lotus-designed spaceframe structure of epoxy-bonded sections of aluminium extrusions (built by Hydro Raufos Aluminium) incorporating integral roll-over hoop
**Body:** composite GRP panels with detachable front and rear "clamshells"

*Above: The Elise is a driver's delight, and being small and lightweight, it is responsive with pin-sharp handling and can be cornered with confidence and unerring accuracy.*

369

# Marcos

**W**hen Jem Marsh and Frank Costin got together in 1959 to develop a lightweight racing-sports car in 1959, the result was the birth of Marcos; the name came from the first three letters of each man's name. Because the first cars sold looked odd, and had strange chassis engineering, it was a miracle that the company stayed afloat.

Marsh was the owner of the Speedex Castings & Accessories business in Luton (a small tuning company), while Costin was the famous aerodynamicist who had shaped cars like the Vanwell GP car in the 1950s. The very first few cars, which had complex marine-ply semi-monocoque chassis, weird styling and vast four-piece windscreens, were assembled at Dolgellau, in north Wales, where Costin had family connections.

In the next few years the company held on – just – by moving briefly to Llanberis, then in 1961 to Speedex at Luton, but a more permanent move, to Bradford-on-Avon, followed in 1963. The looks of the original race-bred GT were improved by smoothing out the nose and screen sections, but it

was not until a new model, styled by Dennis Adams, was launched in 1964 that the company began building real road cars.

By this time Frank Costin had dropped out of the enterprise he had helped to found, so Marsh, along with Dennis Adams and financier Greville Cavendish, now looked after Marcos's expansion in the 1960s. Until the arrival of the fast but awkward-looking Mantis in 1970 there were two basic shapes – one the sleek two-seater coupé which was sold with a variety of Ford or Volvo engines and transmissions, the other the dumpy GRP-hulled Mini-Marcos, which was a kit sold to impecunious buyers who relied on used Minis or Mini-Coopers for all the running gear.

Although the Mini-Marcos had zero visual appeal, it sold in large numbers and was profitable, but the project was eventually sold off to Harold Dermott, ultimately to reappear as the redeveloped and much-improved Midas.

Steady expansion at Bradford-on-Avon led to the design of a new steel chassis, a move into the North American market, and to over-confidence. The combination of a move to a big new factory at Westbury, the disastrous launch of the Mantis model, and problems in getting Volvo-engined models approved for sale in the USA led to the collapse of the concern in 1972.

Receivers sold off the remains of the company, but Jem Marsh subsequently bought back all the moulds and jigs for the moribund cars and – eventually – the rights to recommence manufacture.

By the early 1980s, in converted Nissen huts on a rambling trading estate in Westbury, Marsh was ready to go back into business. Continuing its handbuilt tradition, Marcos produced two models in the late 1990s – the Mantis and its LM derivative, and the Mantaray – all of which used a Rover-based V8 engine and were fine cars to drive.

*Below: In the early days, Marcos cars were built one at a time, either by the workforce (here with a Volvo-engined 1800) or by customers.*

# Marcos GT 1960-63

The first Marcos was really a racing model which a few hardy souls used on the road. In its original form it was the ugliest of ugly ducklings, but attention from stylist Dennis Adams finally turned it into a more rounded and acceptable two-seater coupé.

The original design was by Frank Costin, who not only drew on his aircraft industry experience (in particular from his work on Mosquito bombers at De Havilland) but gained inspiration from his love of boats. The chassis of the new car, astonishingly, was effectively a wooden monocoque, using marine ply and spruce, with torsion boxes and local stiffening. This worked very well indeed, for the glassfibre body could be bonded to it, showed little tendency to rot away, and was very light.

It was made with three thin veneers laid with their grains at right angles and bonded with a glue impervious to weather, micro-organisms, steam and boiling water. The frame members were made of spruce, a wood commonly used in musical instruments, and the stressed skin was either mahogany or birch ply between 1.5 mm and 3 mm thick.

The glue was a type which allowed simple clamping of the wooden pieces to be joined, rather than requiring complex jigs, and where wood was joined to glassfibre, Araldite was used. When finished, and treated with Cuprinol wood preservative, the entire assembly weighed just 145 lb, and the whole car

*Below: The GT was one of the few cars with gull-wing doors. The high waistline increased the body's structural rigidity.*

was claimed to weigh a mere 1,008 lb. The high sills of the car, under the gull-wing doors, were basically triangular in shape, and they helped to ensure that the structure was very stiff, although a price was paid in terms of interior space and the ease of getting in and out of the car.

The rest of the car – all the running gear, in fact – relied on bought-in components, notably Ford engines and Triumph Herald front suspension. The rear suspension design featured a live rear axle with twin links on each side running back from the axle, and sprung by long coil springs ahead of the axle. In three years, a mere 29 cars were built, each one different from the last. The styling changed gradually and persistently,

but underneath the same wooden chassis was retained. Racing experience at the time (and later, in the 1970s and 1980s, with Jem Marsh at the wheel) showed that the car had a very effective chassis.

This extremely tentative project merely paved the way for the much more practical Volvo-engined Marcos which arrived in 1964.

## Specification (typical)

**Engine:** inline four-cylinder, overhead-valve
**Bore × stroke:** 81 mm × 48 mm
**Capacity:** 997 cc
**Maximum power:** 39 bhp
**Transmission:** four-speed manual gearbox, rear-wheel drive

*Above: Frank Costin's design for the Marcos GT was influenced by aircraft and boats; even after Dennis Adams' styling revision, the GT still looked rather odd.*

**Chassis:** separate marine-ply wooden frame with large box-section and diaphragm members
**Suspension:** independent front with wishbones and coil springs; live rear axle with coil springs
**Brakes:** drums front and rear, optional front discs
**Bodywork:** wood and glassfibre two-seater coupé
**Maximum speed (approx):** 90 mph (145 km/h)

## Marcos 1800 and 3-litre 1964-71

The sports coupé that made Marcos's reputation was launched at the Racing Car Show of 1964, its two-seater cabin being shaped around the lanky frame of Jem Marsh himself. In gradually developed and improved form, it was to become the mainstay of Marcos for the next three decades.

Like the original Marcos, the new car had a complex wooden chassis, to which the glassfibre body was bonded during manufacture, but this time the shape was beautiful. It was long, low and attractive, with a sharp nose housing four headlamps, and a sweeping tail which ended in a sharply cut-off rear end.

The choice of original engine was a surprise, but on the basis that a larger unit would be more reliable than a smaller, more highly tuned one, Marcos chose the Volvo four-cylinder engine which was already powering the 1800S sports coupés and many other Volvo family cars.

The first batch of cars used independent rear suspension, but this soon proved to wear rapidly and allow the wheels to move in ways not foreseen on the drawing board. Only about 50 such cars were built before a Ford live axle was substituted, and most of the surviving independent-rear-suspension cars

were later converted.

Like most cars from tiny companies, the Marcos 1800 lacked refinement, and its two-seater cabin needed more development of the ventilation, noise insulation, and trim detailing, but the customers never complained about the character, the performance and the general balance.

After the 1800 had made its mark, Marcos then added a whole series of short-run derivatives with Ford four-cylinder engines, and by the end of the decade the design had also been adapted to accept big three-litre engines from Ford and Volvo. Although re-engineered in many ways, this original basic design lived on into the 1980s and 1990s, as the Mantula.

A total of 99 1800s, 82 1500s, and 192 1600 models was built.

The Marcos sports car design finally grew up in 1969, when the marine-ply chassis design was abandoned in favour of a speedily-developed multi-tubular layout, and when two different types of three-litre engine were installed.

Marcos intended the Ford V6-engined cars for sale to UK customers, while the big straight-six Volvo unit (in suitably 'federalised' guise) was meant for sale in the USA. These were the cars that made

up the vast majority of Marcos sales by the time the company struck financial difficulties and had to close down.

Total production was 80 3-litres and 250 Volvo-engined 3-litre types.

### Marcos 1800 variants

#### Marcos 1500
The 1500 model of 1966 and 1967 had a 1498-cc/85-bhp Ford four-cylinder engine, no overdrive and a live rear axle.

#### Marcos 1600
The 1600 model, built in 1967 and 1968, had a 1599-cc/88-bhp Ford four-cylinder engine, no overdrive and a live rear axle. Its top speed was 109 mph. A few cars were made with a highly-tuned 1650-cc Lawrencetune version of this engine.

#### Marcos 2-litre
The 2-litre model, produced in 1970 and 1971, had a 93.67-mm × 72.4-mm, 1996-cc/83-bhp Ford V4 engine, no overdrive and a live rear axle.

### Marcos 3-litre variants

#### Marcos 2½-litre
The 2½-litre (1971 only) was the same basic car as the 3-litre, but was fitted with an overhead-valve straight-six Triumph engine of 2498 cc. Only 11 such cars were produced.

*Above: This 1971 Marcos 2-litre looks little different from the first model launched in 1964. The ultra-low coupé was always a car for people who valued attention more than practicality, and climbing in and out of a Marcos was not easy for old bones.*

#### Marcos Volvo-engined 3-litre
The 3-litre Volvo model (built 1970-71) was also the same basic car, but was fitted with a straight-six Volvo 2979-cc/130-bhp engine. Top speed was 120 mph.

### Specification (Ford V6-engined 3-litre)
**Engine:** V6, overhead-valve
**Bore × stroke:** 93.67 mm × 72.4 mm
**Capacity:** 2994 cc
**Maximum power:** 128 bhp
**Transmission:** four-speed manual gearbox, electrically-operated overdrive; rear-wheel drive
**Chassis:** separate steel multi-tubular frame with box-section main and bracing members
**Suspension:** independent front with wishbones and coil springs; live rear axle with trailing arms, coil springs and telescopic dampers
**Brakes:** discs front, drums rear
**Bodywork:** glassfibre two-seater coupé
**Maximum speed (approx):** 120 mph (193 km/h)

*Above: Low and purposeful, the coupé still looked exciting nearly 30 years after its launch. This model was built towards the end of 3-litre production, when higher quality and performance had boosted the price.*

*Below: In 1965 the Marcos coupé was first offered with Volvo's sturdy 1800 engine, which could stand considerable tuning. Access to it was excellent, thanks to the large forward-hinged bonnet.*

# Marcos Mantis 1971

Except for the awful Mini-Marcos, a kit car powered by BMC Mini components, the Mantis was probably the ugliest Marcos. Compared with the classic two-seaters, the Mantis was larger and more spacious – and not nearly as attractive.

The same basic type of multi-tubular chassis layout was retained, but the car had a longer wheelbase and carried a four-seater body with a very strange style (which was not as originally envisaged by its designer, Dennis Adams). It was these controversial looks, above any other feature, which ensured that the car would not be a success.

There was no reason, surely, for the car to look so awkward, no reason why the headlamps should have protruded quite so crudely or for the windscreen pillars to have been so thick. There was no good styling explanation for the waistline to wobble about so much between the nose and the tail. Everywhere you looked, there were styling elements which simply did not fit together. The large side windows, although a blessing for rear three-quarter vision, were larger than the front side windows and unbalanced the car's side profile. That wasn't helped by the raised sections of the front wings that housed the square headlights. The lights themselves were surrounded by a curiously-shaped chrome trim which only served to highlight the odd lines of the light cutaway.

The chassis marked Marcos's move away from the original wooden type to a steel structure. That was a square-section steel tube affair, square sections being used for ease of welding the joints. The structure was stiffened by welding on steel plates at strategic locations to triangulated joins in the chassis, to create partial box-sections. On top of that was placed the glassfibre body, which was constructed in two large sections, top and bottom. To be fair to Marcos, they joined the two halves in a less obtrusive fashion than Lotus used in later years on the second Elite, which actually made a feature of the join.

The suspension design was far less

*Above: The Mantis's styling seemed wrong from most external angles. The front view was spoiled by the grating over the air intake, which looked like a drain cover.*

radical than the body styling and made use of other manufacturers' parts. The front featured the double-wishbone set-up found on the Triumph Vitesse, but with a longer coil spring/damper unit to give long travel suspension and a compliant ride. The very direct Vitesse's steering rack was used too, with suitably lengthened track-rod ends to accommodate the Mantis's very much wider track. A German Ford live axle was used at the rear, located by a large 'A'-bracket and trailing arms. Again, long-travel coil springs and damper units were used.

Under the skin, in fact, the Mantis was a conventional car by Marcos standards, although there had been considerable vacillation over the engine choice at the prototype stage. The straight-six Volvo three-litre engine was considered, but rejected as too long, and the very first prototype was built with a three-litre Ford Capri V6 before the definitive engine – a fuel-injected Triumph TR6 six-cylinder unit – was finally specified.

Only 33 Mantis cars were produced, all of them being delivered in 1971.

## Specification (1971)

**Engine:** inline Triumph six-cylinder, overhead-valve
**Bore × stroke:** 74.7 mm × 95 mm
**Capacity:** 2498 cc
**Maximum power:** 150 bhp
**Transmission:** four-speed manual gearbox, electrically-operated overdrive; rear-wheel drive
**Chassis:** separate steel multi-tubular frame with box-section main and bracing members
**Suspension:** independent front with wishbones and coil springs; live rear axle with trailing arms, coil springs and telescopic dampers
**Brakes:** discs front, drums rear
**Bodywork:** glassfibre 2+2-seater coupé
**Maximum speed (approx):** 120 mph (193 km/h)

*Above: The cockpit: note the high transmission tunnel, in effect the central chassis member.*

*Below: The Mantis looked more like a firm's carefully disguised prototype than a production car.*

## Marcos Mantula 1983–98

A decade after Marcos assembly had ended, Jem Marsh revived the marque, introducing a 2.8-litre Ford V6-powered version of the old 1960-style two-seater coupé. This, though, was a false start, for the definitive 'new Marcos' was the Mantula, which was launched in 1983. Because Britain's tax regime had changed a lot in that time, the Mantula was only offered as a fully-built-up car rather than a kit.

Compared with the 1960s-style cars, the Mantula had wider wheels and tyres, and more pronounced wheel-arch flares to cover them, along with an integrally moulded-in front spoiler, but its principal innovation was the use of the lightweight Rover 3½-litre V8 engine and matching gearbox, as already used in Morgan Plus 8s and TVRs, and as recently used in the Triumph TR8. These cars were also offered with other engines, notably the 1.6-litre and 2.0-litre overhead-cam Ford 'Pinto' types, and the 2.8-litre Ford V6. Most cars, however, were built with the Rover V8. Two years later the original coupé was joined by an open-top Spider, the first Marcos ever to have been offered in this style.

Both the open car and the coupé had excellent handling, helped by the good balance given by the Rover V8, which was lighter than any of the engines offered in the earlier, basically similar, designs. There were still idiosyncracies, however. The extremely low car dictated a very reclined driving position, and as the seats did not adjust, the pedals had to be moved to suit shorter drivers.

The Mantula – the name of which is derived from 'mantis' and 'tarantula' – impressed road-testers with its road-holding, which had been proven in a

*Below: Two years after the coupé, the Mantula convertible arrived, and very neat it was; most have been sold into sunnier climes.*

lengthy competition career. *Autocar's* reviewer of 1987 described a "handling balance that could best be described as neutral, with beautifully controllable oversteer available on demand from the long-travel throttle pedal . . . the cornering power available from this layout plus the 225-section Yokohama tyres is particularly impressive".

The only two minus points in the Mantula were judged to be the steering (which could be very heavy, although at the same time direct and responsive) and ride quality, with all road irregularities transmitted into the cabin and to the occupants who, of course, were virtually sitting over the back axle. The car was finished to a high standard, but in some ways it could not quite get away from its

*Above: The Mantula was a smooth revision of the three-litre Marcos of the 1960s, but with a powertrain that boosted it into the lower levels of the supercar league.*

kit-car origins.

Performance with the Rover V8 was sensational by any standards: 60 mph in a mere 5.4 seconds, equal to a De Tomaso Pantera and more than a match for most performance cars.

The HP version, launched in 1987, had a 3.9-litre/280-bhp version of the Rover V8 engine, and a claimed top speed of 150 mph. The Mantula's styling and ethos lived on in the Mantaray and Mantis, both V8-engined two seaters. In LM form the Mantis was a Le Mans contender.

### Specification (1985)

**Engine:** V8, overhead-valve
**Bore × stroke:** 88.9 mm × 71.1 mm
**Capacity:** 3528 cc
**Maximum power:** 190 bhp
**Transmission:** five-speed manual gearbox, rear-wheel drive
**Chassis:** separate steel frame with box section main and bracing members
**Suspension:** independent front with wishbones, coil springs and anti-roll bar; live rear axle with trailing arms, Panhard rod, coil springs and telescopic dampers
**Brakes:** discs front and rear
**Bodywork:** glassfibre two-seater coupé or convertible
**Maximum speed (approx):** 137 mph (220 km/h)

# Marmon

*Left: The only Marmon V12 dated from an unsuccessful mid-1930s attempt to revive the marque. The car had a 368-cu in (six-litre) aluminium engine which gave 151 bhp at 3,700 rpm and an impressive 263 lb ft of torque at 1,200 rpm.*

H oward Marmon began making cars in Indianapolis in 1902, and his company remained on the same site until 1933, when car assembly finally ended. Like other independent North American manufacturers, Marmon could only stay in business hile he could source his bodies from outside specialists and while the arket for expensive luxury cars existed. The combined repercussions of ass-production, and of the Depression, finally killed off the marque hen sales plummeted.

The very first Marmons were technically advanced, with air-cooled V4 ngines, and something approaching independent front suspension (it as a complicated system called double three-point suspension). These odels were continued until 1908. After dabbling with a 60-bhp V8, Iarmon then introduced conventional-type four-cylinder units, and by )14 there was also a 9.3-litre 'six'. Marmon also won the very first dianapolis 500 in 1911 with the Wasp.

Throughout the 1920s Marmon began to produce more complicated nd costly cars, the first type not only being an overhead-valve six-ylinder, but also having an aluminium cylinder block. By 1924, however, Iarmon had hired George M. Williams to restore the profitability which s complicated designs had eroded, but he became so distressed by the ew man's liking for staid straight-eight-cylinder cars that he retired in )26, to concentrate on research.

Williams wanted Marmon to became a 'small General Motors', by

offering a whole range of straight-eights, and there were new examples of such engines almost every year in the late 1920s. By the end of the 1920s, when the Depression hit the USA's economy with such terrifying suddenness, there was a range of Marmons priced at between $1,000 and $5,000.

Foolishly, however, Marmon then pressed on with its plan to introduce a true supercar – a V16 machine to match (and, in Williams's view, to beat) the rival model which Cadillac had already introduced. At a time when likely buyers were going bankrupt in droves, this must surely have been a stubbornly ill-considered thing to do. The records show that Cadillac's V16 outsold Marmon's by 10 to one.

Marmon sales, which had peaked at 22,300 units in 1929, dropped to 12,300 in 1930, then fell fast to 5,768 in 1931, and to a mere 1,365 in 1932. In spite of revising the eights, and reducing prices, the business went into terminal decline, and the last cars of all were produced in 1933.

A year later there was an attempt to revive the marque, when the business was purchased by the American Automotive Corporation, which was organised and backed by Harry Miller (the racing-car designer) and Preston Tucker (whose post-war project, the Tucker Torpedo, would become notorious). This effort failed, but not before Howard Marmon had designed a revolutionary V12 car which had a tubular backbone chassis frame, independent front suspension and a de Dion rear. Only one such car was built, which was later consigned to Brook Stevens' museum in Wisconsin, USA, where it remains.

The remnants of the Marmon business were finally liquidated in 1937.

*Below: The V16, with its enormous eight-litre engine, was a brave attempt to take on Cadillac, but few could then afford such super-luxury motoring.*

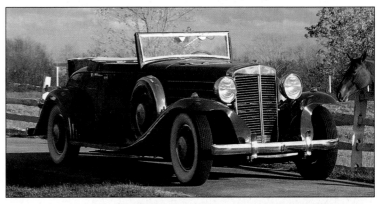

*elow: The V12 was a forward-thinking design, with a separate tubular steel hassis and a stressed steel body, the latter mounted on three rubber blocks.*

## Marmon Sixteen 1930-33

Cadillac had already startled the world by announcing its own V16 in 1930, but Marmon's attempt to match this caused even more astonishment. Cadillac, after all, was part of the giant General Motors Corporation, and could probably afford such a frivolity; Marmon, being small and independent, could not.

Howard Williams had been working on a V16 car for five years before the new car was finally launched in the autumn of 1930. It was the worst possible time to introduce a vast, heavy and costly ($5,200) machine, but Marmon gritted its teeth, and pressed on.

The new car was bigger, heavier and naturally more complicated than any previous Marmon. There were many light-alloy castings and components in the gargantuan eight-litre engine, which weighed 930 lb and produced 200 bhp, making it more powerful and a *lot* lighter than the rival Cadillac.

Even though it had a 145-in wheelbase

and weighed more than 5,400 lb, the new Marmon Sixteen was a very fast car, with an excellent power-to-weight ratio for the period, one which was probably bettered only by the Duesenbergs of the day. Marmon actually guaranteed each Sixteen buyer that his or her car would have been tested at more than 100 mph for two complete laps of the Indianapolis racetrack. One was timed at 111 mph.

Many years later, car collector Bill Harrah test-drove his Marmon Sixteen two-seat convertible on Nevada's Interstate 80 and, on an engine not fully run in, managed an indicated 93 mph. "It handled very well, almost lithely . . . braking is almost too good to believe," he said.

The body styles were massive and elegant, penned by Walter Dorwin Teague Sr, with much help from his son W. D. Teague (who went on to become chief stylist at American Motors). The new cars were very different from previous Marmons, for they had raked

'V'-style radiator grilles, and filler caps were all hidden away under the bonnet, while pressed flares hid the dampers and steering linkages.

In happier times (say, 1928, or even the mid-1930s), the heavyweight battle between Marmon and Cadillac would have been entertaining, but in 1931-33 it was pathetic to see this huge car struggling to stay alive. Nevertheless, the Sixteen was the last Marmon of all to stay in production, though the 86 cars built in the 1933 model year were probably assembled from existing parts. In less than three years, estimated total Sixteen production was only 350 cars.

### Specification (1930)

**Engine:** V16, overhead-valve
**Bore × stroke:** 79.4 mm × 101.6 mm
**Capacity:** 8049 cc
**Maximum power:** 200 bhp

*Above: The stately grille hid an engine which was lighter and more powerful than Cadillac's V16, but although 350 were built up to 1933, the Marmon was outsold 10-to-one b the Cadillac. Peerless also planned and built a prototype V16, but did no risk going into production.*

**Transmission:** three-speed manual gearbox, rear-wheel drive
**Chassis:** ladder frame with channel-section side members
**Suspension:** non-independent front with beam axle and semi-elliptic leaf springs; live rear axle with semi-ellipt leaf springs
**Brakes:** drums front and rear
**Bodywork:** steel coupé or saloon; four five- or seven-seater
**Maximum speed (approx):** 100 mph (161 km/h)

*Above: The V16 Marmon was the height of mobile luxury, and lasted in production for three years; this is a 1931 sedan.*

*Below: The body styling, by Walter Teague and son, exuded wealth and power; note the twin, chromed spare wheel covers, one on each side.*

# Maserati

*bove: The modern face of Maserati, the Biturbo Spyder. Launched in 1984, it d a shorter wheelbase than the coupé and a two-litre V6 with twin turbos.*

I
n the beginning, the Maserati brothers built competitive sports and Grand Prix racing cars from a factory in Bologna; these were driven with great success by the likes of Tazio Nuvolari. The brothers sold their company to Adolpho and Omer Orsi in 37, although they continued to work with the firm until 1947, when they ft to found the OSCA concern.

Under the Orsis' control, the Maserati business was moved to Modena d then began to build a few road cars – the A6, and the A6G and the 3G54 being the first few – but this sideline was still subservient to cing until the fast and glamorous 3500 model was launched in 1957. efore then, in the first 10 years, only 137 Maserati road cars had been oduced.

Thereafter, Maserati changed very quickly, for by the mid-1960s racing r production had ended, and road cars like the Sebring and Mistral ere selling at the rate of hundreds a year. In a very short period aserati had come close to matching Ferrari, and it kept up this running ttle for supercar stardom over the next two decades. In most ways, but ver quite in aura or 'image', Maserati achieved parity.

Further expansion and excitement came with the launch of the V8 00GTs, Quattroportes, Mexicos and Ghiblis, then by the Orsi brothers lling control of the company to Citroën of France. Citroën underwrote

the launch of new cars like the Indy, the Khamsin, and the mid-engined Bora and Merak models, while using a new Maserati-built V6 engine for its own SM coupé, but Maserati's financial problems continued, especially after the 'energy crisis' of 1973-74, and in 1975 Citroën abandoned Maserati to its fate.

At that time the company went into receivership, but shortly thereafter the Argentine-born entrepreneur Alejandro De Tomaso took control, and began to restore the business to health. A few new-type Quattroportes were produced, but the first major new model was the Kyalami, which was a re-engined, facelifted, De Tomaso Longchamps.

De Tomaso had big ideas for Maserati, which was rapidly being combined with the De Tomaso, Innocenti and other marques in his business, for he wanted to build larger numbers of less expensive types. The result was the launch, in 1981, of the two-litre turbocharged Biturbo model, several different variants of which appeared during the 1980s.

The Biturbo's turbocharged V6 engine was eventually enlarged to 2.8 litres, but the styling of 1980s Maseratis was always boxy and uninspired, proposed close links with Chrysler were never formalised, and by the late 1980s Maserati was once again in trouble. Total sales, which had rocketed from 195 cars in 1976 to 6,180 in 1984, slipped back alarmingly in the next few years, to a mere 2,617 in 1989. This was the point at which Fiat bought 49 per cent of the business and by 1998 had taken over, administered a huge cash injection and rationalised production.

*Above: Pre-war Maserati sports cars came in a bewildering variety of body styles; this is a Tipo 4CM-1500, built between 1932 and 1938.*

*Below: Only two of these Tipo 4 V16s were made, in 1929, and only one survived. The engine was two 2.0-litre straight-eights with two crankshafts, gear-linked to a central shaft. This unusual car was capable of 150 mph.*

## Maserati A6 1947-50

Although Maserati had built a handful of road-equipped two-seaters in the 1930s, these were really 'specials' for rich sportsmen, based on the current chassis of its racing cars. The impetus to build road cars came after World War II, when motor-racing activity was very limited, and when Maserati needed to refocus its business to stay alive.

Work on the project started in 1941, and the layout of a new six-cylinder engine was defined by 1943, well before the end of the war, although the first car was not actually road-tested until 1946. Maserati, like its illustrious rival Ferrari, was not capable of building bodies (nor, if the truth be told, interested in doing so), and concentrated on the design of new rolling chassis.

The first real Maserati road car combined a complex new engine with a rugged tubular chassis and a live rear axle. Maserati itself built as much as possible of this running gear, including a brand-new gearbox, and the back axle. However, when the A6 went on sale in 1947, it only had 65 bhp from 1.5 litres, and before long it was clear that more power was needed to make the car attractive enough to sell at such high prices.

Pinin Farina produced the two-seater

bodies, mostly coupés but latterly in optional convertible guise. Just 61 cars of this type were built before an enlarged (two-litre) engine was made available in 1951. With 100 bhp and a lot more torque, this was a more attractive proposition, but in its turn it was overshadowed by yet another new Maserati model, the A6G54, which used the same chassis but had a 150-bhp twin-cam engine.

### Maserati A6 variants

#### Maserati A6G

In 1951 the original A6 was replaced by the A6G type, using the same basic chassis but this time with leaf-spring rear suspension, updated body styles and an enlarged 72-mm × 80-mm, 1954-cc, overhead-cam engine producing 100 bhp. Top speed was 99 mph. Only 16 A6Gs were produced in three years, because the later twin-cam A6G54 was much more attractive, more civilised and significantly faster.

*Right: The attractive Maserati A6SSG sports car gave 100-mph performance from its two-litre engine. The chassis was a complex tubular steel frame, and the classic sports bodywork was styled by Pinin Farina.*

### Specification (1947)

**Engine:** inline six-cylinder, single overhead camshaft
**Bore × stroke:** 66 mm × 72.5 mm
**Capacity:** 1488 cc
**Maximum power:** 65 bhp
**Transmission:** four-speed manual gearbox, rear-wheel drive
**Chassis:** separate steel frame with tubular side members and cross-bracings
**Suspension:** non-independent front with wishbones and coil springs; live rear axle with trailing arms and coil springs
**Brakes:** drums front and rear
**Bodywork:** aluminium and steel two-seater or four-seater, to choice
**Maximum speed (approx):** 95 mph (153 km/h)

## Maserati A6G54 1954-57

The first real Maserati supercar was the A6G54, a long-winded title meaning a 1954 A6G. This was the first Maserati model to have a twin-overhead-camshaft engine, and the first to have a genuine top speed of more than 100 mph.

Except for the use of wider-rim wheels, the chassis was virtually the same as that used in the A6G, but the engine was nothing less than a slightly detuned version of the current six-cylinder Maserati A6GCS/Formula 2

unit. This was the only Maserati road car sold in the 1954-57 period, and was finally displaced by the new, more refined 3500GT model in 1957.

Total production was 60 cars, all of which had special coachbuilders' bodies, with offerings from companies like Allemano, Zagato and Frua, in open or closed forms.

### Specification (1954)

**Engine:** inline six-cylinder, twin-cam

**Bore × stroke:** 76.5 mm × 72 mm
**Capacity:** 1986 cc
**Maximum power:** 150 bhp
**Transmission:** four-speed manual gearbox, rear-wheel drive
**Chassis:** separate steel frame with tubular side and cross-bracing members
**Suspension:** independent front with wishbones and coil springs; live rear axle with semi-elliptic leaf springs
**Brakes:** drums front and rear

**Bodywork:** aluminium and steel two-four-seater, to choice
**Maximum speed (approx):** 118 mph (190 km/h)

*Below: The shape of things to come for Maserati was epitomised by this Frua-bodied A6G54. Only 60 were built between 1954 and 1957, all individually bodied, but they launched Maserati as a maker of supercars and rival to Ferrari.*

# Maserati 3500GT 1957-64

e six-cylinder Maserati 3500GT of 1957 s really the company's first attempt at uxury GT car, and was meant to pro- le direct competition for the Ferrari D GT range. It was also a direct re- acement for the A6G54, which it dis- aced from the assembly workshops in odena.

The chassis and powertrain of the D0GT were all-new, but followed the es of the earlier model, with a 98.4-in 500-mm) wheelbase. Like Ferrari at e time, Maserati considered engines ich more important than advanced assis, which explains why the D0GT's rear suspension consisted of thing more ambitious than a live axle pported by half-elliptic leaf springs, d radius arms.

The 3500GT engine was a detuned rsion of the racing unit which had re- ntly powered the 250F, 300S and 350S odels, and was backed by a ZF gear- x, Alford & Alder front suspension and rling brakes. However, even though s was something of an 'assembled' car, was very fast, and was made even re satisfying by the introduction of nt disc brakes in 1959 and Lucas fuel ection in 1961.

As ever, Maserati had no facility for ilding bodies, so bought in its supplies m Italian coachbuilders. In the begin- ig there was a variety of styles on offer, : as production stabilised, most cars re Touring-bodied coupés or Vignale avertibles.

The 3500GT changed the face of Mas- ati from racing-car to production-car astructor, for in 1958 122 cars were d, and in 1959 no fewer than 200 hich was more than the *total* of old- le A6-derived models built in the first years of road-car production).

Once injected, the 3500 became the D0GTI, with a power output of 235 bhp, d from 1963, when Vignale produced a art 2+2 coupé, the car became own as the Sebring, the name being

taken from the famous American racing circuit. More than 2,000 3500GT/GTI types were built, followed by 438 Sebring models.

Although the Mistral was a short-wheelbase version of this mechanical design, there was no direct replacement for the Sebring, as all future Maseratis had V8 or V6 engines.

## Maserati 3500GT variants

### Maserati Sebring
In 1963 the Sebring coupé was introduced, using the same basic chassis as the 3500GTI, on the same wheelbase but with a Vignale-styled 2+2 coupé body. The chassis featured four-wheel disc brakes, and a five-speed gearbox was standard with Borg-Warner automatic transmission optional. Between 1963 and 1969, a total of 438 cars was built, eventually with three different engines – 3.5, 3.7 and 4.0 litres, producing 235, 245 and finally 255 bhp, which gave a top speed of 146 mph.

## Specification (1957)
**Engine:** inline six-cylinder, twin-cam
**Bore × stroke:** 86 mm × 100 mm
**Capacity:** 3485 cc
**Maximum power:** 220 bhp
**Transmission:** four-speed manual gearbox, optional automatic on late-model cars; rear-wheel drive
**Chassis:** separate steel frame with tubular side and cross-bracing members and pressed-steel reinforcements
**Suspension:** independent front with wishbones and coil springs; live rear axle with semi-elliptic leaf springs
**Brakes:** drums front and rear
**Bodywork:** aluminium and steel two- or 2+2-seaters, coupé (Touring) or convertible (Vignale), plus specials
**Maximum speed (approx):** 130 mph (209 km/h)

*Above: A superbly styled 3500GT coupé is put through its paces. The straight-six engine (top) had fuel injection fitted on middle- and late-series production cars. Note the twin spark plugs.*

*Below: Vignale's attractive 3500GT coupé became known as the Sebring. In original form it had fuel injection, 235 bhp and was capable of nearly 140 mph. It became a best-seller for Maserati during the 1960s.*

## Maserati 5000GT 1959-64

Soon after Maserati had put the 3500GT into series-production, the company withdrew from motor racing following the disastrous loss by fire of their stable of 4.5-litre sports-racers in the final round of the World Sports Car Championship at Caracas in Venezuela. That misfortune was compounded by a huge loss on a machine tool order which was never paid for.

Maserati were left with a small but valuable stock of the V8 engines that had powered the 450S racers, and that prompted the company to build a car suitable for that engine – the 5000GT. It was a combination of that five-litre quad-cam V8 and the chassis used in the last of the 3500GT models, which had the great advantage of front disc brakes.

This was the first Maserati road car to have a V8 engine, and its quad-cam layout was a strong selling point. It made its debut at the 1959 Turin Motor Show and went into production that October. The Maserati chassis were clothed by a number of the top Italian styling houses. The majority of bodies (20) were by Allemano, with another four produced by Touring, two by Frua and one each by Pinin Farina, Michelotti, Monterosa, Bertone and finally a convertible by Vignale.

The first series of cars had Weber 45IDM carburettors and four-speed ZF gearboxes. The improvements made to produce the Mk II model saw Lucas fuel injection replace the Webers (adding an extra 15 bhp to the original 325 bhp), the introduction of a five-speed gearbox and the use of disc brakes all round.

The 5000GT easily rivalled its V12

competition from Ferrari, who were building the Superamerica at the time, and was sold at a similarly colossal price. The 325-bhp V8 powered the 5000GT to over 160 mph, despite a hefty kerb weight of some 3,520 lb (1600 kg).

### Specification (1959)

**Engine:** V8, quad-cam
**Bore × stroke:** 98.5 mm × 81 mm
**Capacity:** 4938 cc

**Maximum power:** 325 bhp
**Transmission:** ZF four-speed manual
**Chassis:** separate steel frame with tubular main and reinforcing members
**Suspension:** independent front with double wishbones and coil springs; live rear axle with semi-elliptic leaf springs and tubular dampers
**Brakes:** discs front, drums rear
**Bodywork:** steel and alloy two-seater
**Maximum speed (approx):** 162 mph (261 km/h)

*Below: The Tipo 103, or 5000GT 'Indianapolis', was styled by Michelotti at Allemano. Note the rectangular headlights, unusual for the period. In all, 32 cars were built*

*Bottom: This 1961 5000GT sports one-off coachwork by Ghia. Such hand-built cars, enormously expensive and very fast, quickly enhanced Maserati's growing international supercar reputation.*

# Maserati Mistral 1963-70

he final derivative of the very success-
l 3500GT chassis was the Mistral, which
as introduced at the Turin Motor Show
1963, and remained in production for
even years.

Compared with earlier 3500-based
hassis, this was a shorter-wheelbase
ersion (94.5 inches instead of 98.4)
hich used square-section main tubes.
he choice of engines was 3.7 litres or 4.0
res. Even with the smaller engine,
ower output was more than respectable
s the 245 bhp generated was sufficient
give a top speed of just over the 150-
ph mark, while the 253 lb ft of torque
uaranteed good acceleration in a car
eighing 2,800 lb. A 0-60 mph time of 8.0
econds could be achieved with suitably
rutal treatment.

The styling for both coupé and con-
ertible versions was a departure from
e Vignale-designed Sebring, and the
odywork was a combination of steel
d aluminium; alloy was used for non-
ad-bearing parts of the structure such
the doors and bonnet and, on the con-
ertible, the boot lid. Neither style was
oduced by Maserati themselves, who
ntracted-out body production to the
urin-based firm of Maggiore.

The new Mistral, by Frua, was more
ounded than the Sebring, wider and
th a far larger glass area. It is interest-
g to note that the coupé was an early
atchback, and it bore a close resem-
ance to the AC 428 of the period –
hich was almost inevitable as that car
as also bodied by Frua.

By comparison with Ferrari's current
o-seaters – the 275 GTB and, later, the
aytona – the Mistral did not have an ex-
ting specification, but it was an honest,
st and likeable supercar. In rather less
an seven years, no fewer than 828
istral coupés and 120 Spyders were
oduced.

## Specification (1963)

**Engine:** inline six-cylinder, twin-cam
**Bore × stroke:** 86 mm × 106 mm
**Capacity:** 3694 cc
**Maximum power:** 245 bhp
**Transmission:** five-speed manual
gearbox or optional automatic
transmission, rear-wheel drive
**Chassis:** separate steel frame with
tubular main members and pressed
reinforcements
**Suspension:** independent front with
wishbones and coil springs; live rear
axle with trailing arms and semi-elliptic
leaf springs
**Brakes:** discs front and rear
**Bodywork:** steel and aluminium two-
seater coupé or spyder, by Frua
**Maximum speed (approx):** 152 mph
(245 km/h)

*Below: Despite the simple rear
suspension, the 245-bhp Mistral
offered wonderful performance, even
if the optional Borg-Warner
automatic gearbox was fitted rather
than the five-speed manual.*

*Above: Wire wheels were standard
on the Frua-styled Mistrals, but on
the Spyder, of which 120 were built,
the hard top was an extra.*

*Below: This four-litre, 2+2
berlinetta's flowing rear-end styling
by Frua influenced many other car
manufacturers.*

# Maserati Quattroporte 1963-70

Starting in 1963, Maserati ushered in the first of a new family of large V8-engined cars, all of which shared the same basic mechanical layout. The 'productionised' version of Maserati's old V8 quad-cam race engine (with chain rather than gear cam drive) was mounted up front, there was a choice of manual or automatic transmissions, and the cars employed a unique front 'half-chassis'. These cars – Quattroporte, Mexico and Ghibli – saw Maserati sales reach new heights, finally matching those of the company's main rival, Ferrari.

Quattroporte means 'four doors' and as the name implies, the Quattroporte was a four-door saloon rather than a sports car. It was the first four-door Maserati and, when it made its debut at the 1963 Turin Show, it was unique among Italian supercars in that respect, indicating that Maserati were trying to create a new slot at the very upper end of the market.

Compared with the 3500GT/5000GT generation the chassis was entirely new, featuring a complex platform arrangement for the main structure with a subframe for the front suspension and engine. Early cars were fitted with a de Dion rear axle, but that was soon discarded in favour of a conventional live axle, albeit one very well located by radius arms.

The original coachwork was by Frua, although when series-production began, the bodies were built by Vignale and seemed to echo some of the styling features found on the earlier Vignale-styled Sebring.

Despite the car's bulk the Quattroporte was an easy car to drive fast, or, thanks to its power-assisted steering, in traffic. No fewer than 679 Quattroportes of this generation were built; the majority of those consisted of the revised type with the live rear axle and semi-elliptic leaf springs. From 1969 a larger, 4719-cc, engine producing 290 bhp rather than 260 bhp was available.

## Specification (1963)

**Engine:** V8, quad-cam
**Bore × stroke:** 88 mm × 85 mm
**Capacity:** 4136 cc
**Maximum power:** 260 bhp
**Transmission:** five-speed manual or three-speed automatic
**Chassis:** central steel platform with tubular steel and box-section subframe
**Suspension:** independent front with double wishbones and coil springs; non-independent rear with de Dion axle and coil springs
**Brakes:** discs all round
**Bodywork:** steel four-door four-seater saloon
**Maximum speed (approx):** 143 mph (230 km/h)

*Above: Early Quattroportes were fitted with a de Dion rear axle which helped the car's handling but was later discarded in favour of a simpler live-axle design.*

*Bottom: The styling, by Frua, of the original Quattroporte was little more exciting than its name, which simply translates as 'four-door'; it was Maserati's first big saloon car.*

*Below: Bulky it may have been, but the big Maserati was still a very brisk performer thanks to 260 bhp from its quad-cam V8 engine, which would take it to over 140 mph.*

# Maserati Mexico 1965-72

The Mexico was essentially a Quattroporte in heavy disguise. Two years after the Quattroporte was launched, Maserati took the four-door saloon's chassis, shortened it by nearly five inches, added a two-door coupé-style body to it and created the Mexico as a 2+2 replacement for the big 5000GT.

The styling, by Vignale, was rather bland, particularly at the rear, which was appropriate in a way as the Mexico used the simpler rear suspension system of a live axle and semi-elliptic leaf springs rather than the de Dion system used in the first of the Quattroportes.

The Mexico was offered with two engine displacements – either 4.7 or 4.2 litres. The larger engine produced 290 bhp and its smaller brother (which had a narrower bore of 88 mm rather than 94 mm) managed 260 bhp.

The 2+2 Mexico fell between two stools; it was neither as spacious nor as practical as the Quattroporte, and within two years it had been completely upstaged by the two-seater Ghibli. After 1968, Mexico sales declined dramatically, but the car was still produced in very small numbers up to 1973, by which time either 260 or as many as 468 examples (depending which source you believe) had been made. If the latter figure is correct, that was a respectable total for a model that never really captured the public imagination. The bulk of Mexico production went to France or Switzerland.

## Specification (1965 4.7-litre)

**Engine:** V8, quad-cam
**Bore × stroke:** 94 mm × 85 mm
**Capacity:** 4719 cc
**Maximum power:** 290 bhp
**Transmission:** five-speed manual or optional three-speed automatic
**Chassis:** main steel platform with separate tubular steel and box-section front subframe
**Suspension:** independent front with double wishbones and coil springs; live rear axle with semi-elliptic leaf springs
**Brakes:** discs all round
**Bodywork:** steel two-door coupé
**Maximum speed (approx):** 158 mph (254 km/h)

*Above right: Vignale's styling of the Mexico, successor to the big 5000GT, was practical if rather uninspired, but as a Grand Tourer the car had few equals.*

*Right: Vignale's rear-end treatment was bland for the day, but car styling has moved progressively towards blandness for three decades, epitomised by the much later Maserati Biturbo.*

*Below: At speed the Mexico behaved well, despite retaining the old live rear axle and leaf springs, a design other performance car builders were transcending.*

# Maserati Ghibli 1967-73

Considering that the Ghibli is one of the all-time supercar greats, it comes as a shock to realise that it was not an original, clean-sheet-of-paper, design but one that owed much to the original Quattroporte high-speed saloon and its shortened two-door brother, the Mexico.

The chassis was a truncated form of that used in the Mexico, which in turn was a shortened version of the Quattroporte's (which apart from anything else indicates what a massive machine the Quattroporte was). By the time the Ghibli appeared, that chassis had been somewhat revised. Just shortening it improved its torsional stiffness, of course, but further box-sections were added to make one of the stiffest chassis ever used on a roadgoing Maserati.

Whereas the Mexico appeared uninspiring, the Ghibli looked terrific, thanks to a brilliant design by the young Giorgetto Giugiaro, then working for Ghia. Its long and low look was partly achieved by removing the wet sump from the familiar quad-cam V8 engine in favour of a dry-sump system. That meant the V8 was more compact and could be mounted low in the engine bay, allowing a low bonnet line. As the Ghibli was intended to be one of the fastest of all supercars, Maserati extracted another 50 bhp compared with the engine in Mexico tune and the Ghibli's 340 bhp gave it sparkling performance, with a 0-60 mph time of 6.6 seconds and a top speed that was theoretically over 160 mph (even though the best recorded road-test figure was only 154 mph).

*Below: Premiered at the Turin Motor Show in 1966, the Ghibli was drawn by the talented Giorgetto Giugiaro, who established a reputation as one of the world's greatest designers.*

That power was fed through a five-speed manual transmission to a traditional live axle sprung on equally traditional semi-elliptic leaf springs. Nevertheless the system worked extremely well, as the axle was well located by radius arms and a Panhard rod to limit transverse movement. The Ghibli's ride quality was exceptional and yet the car cornered fast without drama and with little roll, all the time giving the driver great confidence in the well-balanced chassis.

A good car was made even better when the SS version appeared in 1970. That featured a larger, 4930-cc, version of the V8, the stroke having been lengthened by 4 mm. The additional capacity boosted power output to 355 bhp with over 350 lb ft of torque.

The bulk of the 1,274 Ghiblis produced were coupés, but 125 Spyders were also built. Curiously, the coupé was by far the more elegant design.

*Below: Supremely elegant, the Ghia-styled Ghibli convertible was first unveiled at the Turin Show in 1968.*

## Specification (1967)

**Engine:** V8, quad-cam
**Bore × stroke:** 94 mm × 85 mm
**Capacity:** 4719 cc
**Maximum power:** 340 bhp
**Transmission:** five-speed manual or optional three-speed automatic
**Chassis:** tubular steel chassis with fabricated, tubular and box-section cross-members
**Suspension:** independent front with double wishbones and coil springs; live rear axle with semi-elliptic leaf springs, radius arms and Panhard rod
**Brakes:** discs all round
**Bodywork:** steel two-door coupé or convertible
**Maximum speed (approx):** 154 mph (248 km/h)

*Above: The superb 340-bhp V8 had a large air-box covering the four twin-choke carburettors. Its compression ratio was 8.75:1.*

## Maserati Indy 1969-74

By the late 1960s Maserati had wrung just about every possible combination from the front-engined V8 theme, but the Indy was one of the most successful permutations of all. The Indy was a replacement for the more mundane Mexico and although it was also styled by Vignale it was a far more imposing, crisp, design than the Mexico. It could not quite match the Ghibli's visual appeal, however, being five inches taller for one thing. That extra height was needed to allow the required 2+2 seating and it did not distort the car's looks as much as it might have done as the Indy was the widest Maserati coupé produced up to that time, even wider than the Ghibli.

There was little that was novel in the Indy's mechanical make-up as it was the standard recipe of a quad-cam V8 mounted at the front, driving the rear wheels via a five-speed manual or three-speed automatic transmission and live rear axle with the ubiquitous semi-elliptic leaf springs. Where the Indy did break new ground, however, was in its

chassis construction. Whereas all previous Maseratis had featured a separate chassis, the smart Vignale hatchback body was welded onto the chassis to form a version of unitary construction and a very stiff overall assembly. Because of

the extra stiffening conferred by the steel body, the chassis frame was a simpler construction than that of the Ghibli or the Mexico before it.

The Indy was attractive, practical and very fast, with a top speed in the 160-mph

region. It was also offered with various different engine displacements (4136 cc, 4709 cc and finally 4930 cc) and power outputs from 260 bhp right up to 335 bhp, to maximise its appeal. Consequently, Maserati managed to sell as many as 1,136 cars over five years.

### Specification (1969)

**Engine:** V8, quad-cam
**Bore × stroke:** 88 mm × 85 mm
**Capacity:** 4136 cc
**Maximum power:** 260 bhp
**Transmission:** five-speed manual or optional three-speed automatic
**Chassis:** steel unitary construction
**Suspension:** independent front with double wishbones and coil springs; live rear axle with radius arms and semi-elliptic leaf springs
**Brakes:** discs all round
**Bodywork:** steel four-seater coupé
**Maximum speed:** 156 mph (251 km/h)

*Above: Wider and taller than the Ghibli, the Indy was Maserati's first model with unitary construction.*

*Left: First shown on the Vignale stand at the 1968 Turin Show, the Indy was a four-seat Grand Tourer.*

*Below: The Indy was a big car indeed, weighing 3,484 lb, with a 102-in wheelbase, and being 189.6 inches long and 70.4 inches wide.*

## Maserati Bora 1971-79

To be truly modern, every 1970s Italian supercar manufacturer needed to have a mid-engined two-seater of immense performance in its range. Lamborghini had started the trend with the Miura, and since Ferrari were known to be dabbling with the same layout, Maserati decided to follow suit.

The result was the launch of the V8 Bora in 1971 (and the very closely related V6 Merak which followed one year later in 1972). Because Maserati could not afford the time, nor the investment, to develop its own transaxle, it bought in the robust German ZF unit used by rival manufacturers.

The Bora caused a real sensation when it was introduced at the 1971 Geneva Motor Show, not merely because of its looks but also because its mechanical design had clearly been influenced by Maserati's new owners Citroën. The Bora was the first Maserati to use Citroën's 'no travel' brake-pedal system and it featured the complex Citroënesque hydraulics to power the adjustable seats and pedals. The best that can be said for the brakes is that Citroën were convinced of their merits – many road-testers thought otherwise. Their lack of feel was no problem with relatively slow Citroëns but somewhat of a handicap with a really high-performance car such as the Bora.

The Bora's high performance came courtesy of a quad-cam, light-alloy V8 engine longitudinally mounted behind the cabin with the drive going back to the transaxle, which projected past the rear axle line. The V8 produced 310 bhp, and 339 lb ft of torque at 4,200 rpm, to give excellent acceleration on the way to the car's 160 mph top speed.

The advanced Citroën hydraulics were almost enough to divert attention from another Maserati 'first' – independent suspension all round, with wishbones at the rear – and the hybrid nature of the chassis, which was a tubular and sheet-steel arrangement. Even though the Bora was short (overall length was a mere 173.4 inches), it was beautifully styled by Giorgetto Giugiaro at Ital Design and well packaged with a generous front luggage area and another container behind the engine.

Bodywork was all-steel (although some early cars were in aluminium), welded to form a monocoque, with the engine and transmission on a steel subframe insulated with rubber bushes.

Although the Bora suffered a lack of detail development over the years (thanks to the combination of the 'energy crisis' and the financial traumas caused by Citroën's withdrawal from the company), it was virtually a match for Ferrari's Boxer and in its final 4.9-litre form from 1975 onwards it was a very desirable car indeed. Total Bora production was 571 cars in seven years.

*Right: At the 1971 Geneva Motor Show, where it made its debut, the looks of the Bora created a sensation; the mid-engined car also handled as well as it looked.*

### Specification (1971)

**Engine:** V8, quad-cam
**Bore × stroke:** 93.9 mm × 85 mm
**Capacity:** 4719 cc
**Maximum power:** 310 bhp
**Transmission:** five-speed manual
**Chassis:** tubular and sheet-steel frame
**Suspension:** independent with double wishbones, coil springs and anti-roll bars front and rear
**Brakes:** discs all round
**Bodywork:** steel two-door coupé
**Maximum speed (approx):** 160 mph (257 km/h)

*Above: The well-designed cockpit had full instrumentation, a gear lever close to hand and Citroën-style power-assisted brakes which, although they were very effective, had virtually no pedal movement. Seats were adjusted hydraulically.*

*Below: Balanced in looks and design, the sleek Bora was 45.3 inches high. Performance from the V8 was superb, top speed being 160 mph, and fuel consumption around 17 mpg. Luggage space was minimal, however, with room for just one medium-sized suitcase at the front.*

# Maserati Merak 1972-83

The Merak was effectively a junior version of the Bora and a fine example of some skilful product planning by Maserati. It combined the structure and chassis of the Bora with the V6 engine that Maserati had developed for Citroën to use in their SM. That was allied to the five-speed transaxle from the SM. The most obvious visual difference between the two cars was that the Merak had open 'flying buttresses' at the rear, rather than the glassed-in arrangement on the Bora.

Because the quad-cam V6 was obviously shorter than the V8 engine from which it was developed and which powered the Bora, more space was liberated inside the cabin. Maserati suggested that this made the car a 2+2, but as the rear 'seats' had a base virtually on the floor with vertical backrests, this was straining credulity.

The Citroën SM influence extended to the instrument panel, which was lifted directly from the French car, along with the high-pressure braking system. Since the main difference between the Bora and Merak was the loss of two cylinders, there was little change in weight (the Merak being lighter by only 190 lb or so). That meant a drop in performance as the Merak's V6 produced only 190 bhp to begin with. Instead of the Bora's 6.5-second 0-60 mph time, the Merak took well over nine seconds and could reach 'only' 135 mph.

In the mid- and late 1970s, when even the wealthy appeared to worry about fuel consumption and hesitated to run exceptionally powerful cars, the Merak was an interesting (and cheaper) alternative to the V8 Bora. Long after the Bora was discontinued, the Merak stayed in production; nearly 2,000 were produced in a 10-year period.

## Maserati Merak variants

### Maserati Merak 2000

As its name implies, this was powered by a two-litre engine, which was really too small for what was a fairly heavy car but made sense for taxation purposes in Italy, its only market. Displacement was 1999 cc, with a bore and stroke of 80 mm × 66 mm.

### Maserati Merak SS

An improved version of the Merak was introduced in 1975 with more power (208 bhp) and consequently more performance; the top speed rose to 143 mph. To complement the extra power, it was given wider tyres along with the ZF transmission from the Bora (rather than the SM's unit) while a conventional braking system replaced the Citroën system, and by this time the Citroën dashboard had been exchanged for a Maserati design.

## Specification (1972)

**Engine:** V6, quad-cam
**Bore × stroke:** 91.6 mm × 75 mm
**Capacity:** 2965 cc
**Maximum power:** 190 bhp
**Transmission:** five-speed manual
**Chassis:** tubular and sheet-steel frame
**Suspension:** independent with double wishbones, coil springs and anti-roll bars front and rear
**Brakes:** discs all round
**Bodywork:** steel two-door coupé
**Maximum speed (approx):** 135 mph (217 km/h)

*Top: The most radical departure from the Bora in styling terms was the flying buttresses', which, with a smaller rear window, allowed more ventilation for the mid-mounted V6.*

*Above: The Merak's ferocious front-end aspect bore a strong similarity to that of the Bora. This is a Merak SS, distinguished by the horizontal grille on the bonnet top.*

*Below: The wheelbase and overall length and width of the Merak were identical to those of the Bora, although the shorter V6 engine gave a little more space inside the cockpit.*

# Maserati Khamsin 1974-82

The Khamsin took its name from a sea-sonal wind which blows only in Egypt, and it was designed to replace another model named after a wind, the Ghibli – and to some extent, the Indy. It was the first Maserati to have Bertone styling and the first front-engined car from the Bologna-based company to have inde-pendent rear suspension, with similar unequal-length wishbones and coil springs front and rear.

The styling work was actually done by Bertone's Marcello Gandini, who had been responsible for the highly futuristic Lamborghini Espada, and the Maserati has lasted better in styling terms.

The influences of Citroën control were clear in the design of the Khamsin as well as the Bora/Merak and it too used the high-pressure hydraulic system to power the brakes and assist the steering. In other respects, however, this was a traditional Maserati design with the ex-pected quad-cam V8 engine mounted at the front and driving the rear wheels through a five-speed ZF manual or three-speed Borg-Warner automatic transmis-sion. Power assistance, as on Citroëns, was very strong, and some drivers found it easy to lock the wheels inadvertently. Self-centring, and variable power assist-ance which diminished as the car travelled faster, meant that the steering required only two turns lock-to-lock.

As far as Khamsin customers were concerned, the main innovation was the styling. Bertone had given the car an almost exaggeratedly sharp nose and an equally finely sculpted rear. There was a sharp crease in the side panel that ran from the top of the front wheel arches right to the back of the car and sloped up by the merest fraction at the back, just enough to lighten the look of the rear end. The glass panel fitted below the hatchback was another nice Bertone touch. As *Autocar* commented, the car

*Right: Following Ford's takeover of Ghia, Maserati turned to Bertone to style the Khamsin. The result was angular and purposeful, even though Maserati's claim that it was a 2 + 2 was optimistic.*

was "an unusually clear statement of Italian style and temperament". As with the Merak, Maserati liked to pretend that the Khamsin was a 2+2 even though the rear seat was little more than a padded shelf with virtually no leg space and with very limited head room, so '2 + 1' would have been a more plausible designation.

With a five-litre V8, the Khamsin could hardly fail to be a good performer and could manage the 0-60 mph sprint in eight seconds on its way to a top speed in the 160-mph region. That was allied to well-balanced handling, thanks to a nearly equal weight distribution.

Perhaps if the chassis had been better developed, if the 'energy crisis' had not struck, and if company finances had been on a better footing the Khamsin might have been a success. As it was, sales fell away sharply in the late 1970s and total production was only 421 over nine years. The most successful produc-tion year was the launch year, 1974, when 96 cars were ordered.

## Specification (1974)

**Engine:** V8, quad-cam
**Bore × stroke:** 93.9 mm × 89 mm
**Capacity:** 4930 cc
**Maximum power:** 320 bhp
**Transmission:** five-speed manual
**Chassis:** steel unitary construction
**Suspension:** independent with double wishbones, coil springs and anti-roll bars front and rear
**Brakes:** discs all round
**Bodywork:** steel two-door 2+2 coupé
**Maximum speed (approx):** 160 mph (257 km/h)

*Above: The Khamsin had high performance, safe roadholding and good looks. The glazed panel across the tail, below the hatchback, was unusual but helped rear visibility.*

*Below: The handling of the Khamsin, with its all-independent rear suspension, earned much praise. Citroën hydraulics also operated the headlamps and adjusted the seats.*

# Maserati Quattroporte 1975-present

Towards the end of Citroën's seven-year control of Maserati, the French company began to impose more of its own design ideas. This trend reached its height with the second version of Maserati's four-door saloon, the Quattroporte II.

Although the car was considerably larger than the Citroën SM, it was very closely based on the SM's running gear, with the same engine, transmission and suspension, and that made it rather underpowered. Like the SM, it was equipped with fully-powered steering and brakes and the same self-levelling hydro-pneumatic suspension system, interconnected front to rear.

The styling was by Bertone but it wasn't one of his better efforts. It was actually an update of a design Bertone had proposed to Jaguar for the XJ6. Only five were made before Maserati returned to a more conventional layout for

the next, third-series, Quattroporte. That used a V8 engine driving the rear wheels in traditional fashion.

Just as the front-wheel-drive Quattroporte II had used the SM chassis, the new Quattroporte also borrowed heavily from another model, in this case the De Tomaso Deauville (by this time Maserati had been acquired by De Tomaso). The body was styled by Ital Design and was imposing rather than beautiful. It did, however, offer generous accommodation and four-door convenience, allied to excellent performance with a top speed in the 140-mph region.

After the car had been in slow, steady production for some years, Maserati decided to upgrade the quad-cam V8 engine to a much larger displacement, five-litre, unit with 280 bhp. A much sleeker version was available in 1999, providing a classier alternative to an M3.

*Above: Styled as a luxury family and executive express, the second-series Quattroporte had a five-litre V8 which gave a significant boost to performance. But the car looked tame compared with earlier Maseratis.*

## Maserati Quattroporte variants

### Maserati Royale

In a deliberate echo of Bugatti's largest model, Maserati finally renamed the Quattroporte the Royale, but there was little mechanical change other than an increase in power to 300 bhp, which boosted top speed to 149 mph.

## Specification (1980)

**Engine:** V8, twin overhead camshafts per bank of cylinders
**Bore × stroke:** 93.9 mm × 89 mm
**Capacity:** 4930 cc
**Maximum power:** 280 bhp
**Transmission:** five-speed manual or three-speed automatic
**Chassis:** steel unitary construction
**Suspension:** independent with double wishbones and coil springs front; transverse and longitudinal control arms and coil springs rear
**Brakes:** discs all round
**Bodywork:** steel four-door saloon
**Maximum speed (approx):** 140 mph (225 km/h)

*Above: The Bertone-designed Quattroporte II was a front-wheel-drive V6-engined model based very much on the Citroën Maserati SM.*

*Below: The Quattroporte looked bland but handled well, with 289 lb ft of torque from the alloy five-litre V8.*

## Maserati Kyalami 1976-83

*Left: The Kyalami's styling was well balanced, with room for four in the two-door coupé bodywork, but the car attracted few buyers. The wheelbase was 102 inches and overall length 180.*

After Citroën walked away from Maserati, the company was put on a life-support machine by the Italian government, who in turn passed the problem on to De Tomaso. In De Tomaso's view the logical move was to integrate the two companies, and the first fruit of that was the Kyalami, which could be considered a De Tomaso Longchamps with a Maserati engine.

The front-engined Longchamps was itself the shorter-wheelbase coupé version of the Deauville five-seater saloon with a workmanlike all-independent suspension system, rather angular Frua styling and a very capacious interior with more than adequate rear leg room and head room.

In its Maserati Kyalami guise, however, the model acquired a more distinguished nose along with the Maserati powerplant. Whereas the De Tomaso used an American Ford pushrod V8, the Kyalami was powered by Maserati's customary quad-cam V8 engine, first in 4136-cc then in larger, bored and stroked, 4930-cc form.

The Kyalami's problem was that it was all too obviously a design 'rush job' and something of a mongrel. Although it was superior to the Longchamps, it did not sell well and by the end of the 1970s only 150 had been sold. Sales had dried up completely by 1983. It lived on in another form, however, in that its chassis was the foundation for the last in the line of Quattroportes, which were still on sale in the 1990s.

### Specification (1976)

**Engine:** V8, twin overhead camshafts per bank of cylinders
**Bore × stroke:** 88 mm × 85 mm
**Capacity:** 4136 cc
**Maximum power:** 270 bhp
**Transmission:** five-speed manual or three-speed automatic
**Chassis:** steel unitary construction
**Suspension:** independent with double wishbones and coil springs front and rear
**Brakes:** discs all round
**Bodywork:** steel four-door coupé
**Maximum speed (approx):** 147 mph (237 km/h)

## Maserati Biturbo 1981-93

Following the takeover of Maserati by De Tomaso in 1975, it took six years for a new generation of Maseratis to evolve. That time-span was understandable as the new cars, led by the first Biturbo, were completely different from previous Maseratis.

The chassis layout at least was conventional, with a front-mounted engine driving the rear wheels, but the engine itself was quite different. As the name Biturbo implies, it used twin turbochargers, one for each bank of cylinders on the V6 overhead-cam layout. Its displacement was far less than any Maserati since the days of the A6 range in the 1950s, being only 1996 cc. To make up for that, however, it did have three valves per cylinder (two inlets and one exhaust) to help its breathing and that, coupled with the two small turbochargers, gave an adequate amount of power. Its 180 bhp meant the small coupé could reach a maximum speed of 134 mph – fast, but not outstandingly so.

It was enough to boost Maserati sales; from a mere 550 in 1980, annual production had rocketed to no less than 3,500 by 1989. That was despite the car's overly conservative in-house styling, which made the model look anything but exotic. The Biturbo's looks, and sales, were helped by the development of the Spyder version in 1984, which was given a shorter wheelbase. That was just one of a number of models Maserati produced on the same basic platform. Lengthening the wheelbase allowed the production of a four-door variant, the 425, launched in 1983. That was soon followed by a four-seater coupé called the 228 which appeared very little different from the original Biturbo. The change of name was explained by the fact that it had a larger, bored and stroked 2.8-litre version of the twin-turbo V6 engine producing 250 bhp at 5,500 rpm, with a torque output of 273 lb ft at 3,500 rpm.

By 1988 the original styling was looking even less exciting, and it was dressed up

*Left: The Biturbo engine in stretched 2.8-litre form with, at left, the two pipes rising from the intercoolers and joining before entering the intake manifold over the V6. The finned sections on each side of the manifold are fuel injector rails.*

*Above: The Biturbo range has been continuously developed since its launch in 1981, but the broad look of the cars has remained much the same. The flat front end does little for the aerodynamics, but increased engine power has made them very fast saloons.*

somewhat to produce the Karif, which was very much the mixture as before on a short wheelbase, and powered by the same engine as the Biturbo 228. There was even more to come from the basic design in 1990, when the Racing model appeared with power boosted to 282 bhp, thanks to new four-valve twin-cam heads being fitted to the V6 engine.

With four valves per cylinder, the two-litre Biturbo offered performance figures, according to *Motor Sport* in 1990, "that make Latin, British and Teutonic supercars flinch. In the 0-62 mph stakes it can hold its own with monsters like the Ferrari Testarossa . . . " Only in terms of top speed did the Maserati not fare so well, due in part to the uncompromising front-end aerodynamics.

An option included a four-setting adjustable suspension system, designed in conjunction with Koni, and the geometry of the MacPherson-strut front suspension was refined and improved to ensure a constant parallelism between the steering track rods and lower suspension arms.

On the road, the 24-valve car handled extremely well, as did all the Biturbos, and was very tractable in town. Said *Motor Sport*'s tester: "The impression is very like that of one of the large Japanese bikes . . . by the time the rest of the traffic has let their clutches out, you are already 100 yards down the road." Visually, the model was distinguished from its stablemates by new spoilers and skirts.

*Left: Compared with other Italian supercar builders like Ferrari and Lamborghini, during the 1980s Maserati showed that, in styling terms at least, it preferred to follow the 'sensible' look established by, among others, Ford, BMW and Mercedes-Benz.*

*Below: Bringing the fun back into Maserati motoring, the two-litre Biturbo Spyder was introduced in 1984 and built by Zagato on a short, 94.5-in, wheelbase and offered luxury high-speed open-air performance. Overall length was a mere 159 inches. A variable-torque Sensitork differential was optional.*

*Above: In production terms, the Biturbo proved a very successful and adaptable design for what had been an ailing manufacturer; in 24-valve form it offered true supercar performance.*

## Specification (1982)

**Engine:** V6, overhead-cam, twin-turbo
**Bore × stroke:** 82 mm × 63.5 mm
**Capacity:** 1996 cc
**Maximum power:** 180 bhp
**Transmission:** five-speed manual gearbox
**Chassis:** steel unitary construction
**Suspension:** independent with MacPherson struts and anti-roll bar front, semi-trailing arms and coil springs rear
**Brakes:** discs all round
**Bodywork:** steel two-door four-seater saloon
**Maximum speed (approx):** 134 mph (216 km/h)

## Maserati Shamal 1989–96

The Shamal marked Maserati's return to V8 engines. In this case it was an all-alloy unit with wet cylinder liners, twin overhead cams per bank of cylinders and four valves per cylinder. Bore and stroke dimensions were perfectly 'square' at 80 mm × 80 mm and displacement was 3217 cc, which alone would have generated more power than the smaller V6 engines but, as the V8 followed the lead of the Biturbo range in having twin IHI turbochargers, maximum power was an excellent 318 bhp, allied to a very creditable 319 lb ft of torque. The presence of two turbos, each with its own air-to-air intercooler, helped engine response and there was no need for overall boost pressures to be that high to extract sufficient power, so the Shamal's engine ran on a maximum boost of 7 psi. In line with the 'green' concerns of the early 1990s, and with a view to making the model saleable in the lucrative North American market, the Shamal's twin-turbo V8 was equipped with a catalytic converter. That, allied to electronic engine management and injection, guaranteed low emissions.

The return to the use of a V8 engine was complemented by a resurrection of Maserati's habit of naming their cars after famous winds (Ghibli, Khamsin, Bora), but in this case a not so famous

wind, as Shamal indicated a "hot and strong north-west summer wind from the Mesopotamian plains". The car was hot and strong enough to live up to that name as its twin-turbo V8's over-300 bhp was enough to speed the car to nearly 170 mph, which was faster than the likes of bygone classic Maseratis such as the Ghibli. The 0-60 mph acceleration figure of just over five seconds was also enough to put previous Maseratis in the shade.

The twin-turbo's power and torque was fed to the rear wheels by a Getrag manual gearbox boasting no fewer than six forward ratios (fifth being a 1.12:1 ratio and sixth an 'overdrive' ratio of 0.8:1). That made it one of the very few cars in the world to have a six-speed manual transmission, the most famous other example being the Chevrolet Corvette with a ZF unit. The six-speeder is allied to a Torsen-type limited-slip differential.

Such performance and specification should have been enough to make the Shamal an instant classic but, curiously, demand was not enormous. That may well have had something to do with the styling. Sensibly, in developing the Shamal, Maserati had decided to retain as much of the Biturbo as possible rather than build something totally new. Although they employed Lamborghini Countach designer Marcello Gandini to

style the car, the end result was not that attractive, looking somewhat like a Biturbo on steroids thanks to the bulging wheel arches front and rear which were accentuated by doors in the standard Biturbo position. Gandini incorporated one of his Countach trademarks in the Shamal with the angled top to the rear wheel arches, but Maserati's basic shape could only be altered so far without resorting to a completely new model.

Under those big wheel arches the Shamal used MacPherson struts at the front, and a tubular trailing-arm rear suspension design in conjunction with an adjustable damper system developed by Koni. That was controlled via a button on the console that enabled the driver to choose one of four positions, from very soft to a setting hard enough to be "the perfect solution for drivers who like to get all the sporting soul from the car", as Maserati put it. The system, which was also offered as an option on some Biturbos, was designed automatically to choose setting number two to begin with as that was considered a reasonable compromise for speeds up to 100 mph.

Deliveries for the UK were scheduled to begin in the late summer of 1992, at a projected price of £63,450. But by the time Fiat took over, the charismatic Shamal was gone.

*Above: In 1989 Maserati attempted to revitalise the unadventurous, although clean, styling of the Biturbos in the Shamal, but retained enough of the panels to make it look like a body-kitted, muscle-Biturbo. The more aggressive shape clothed a new four-valves-per-cylinder V8 developed from the V6, which fed its 325 bhp and immense torque through a six-speed gearbox. Performance was well and truly in the supercar league, with just over five seconds needed to reach 60 mph and a maximum speed of over 160 mph.*

### Specification (1989)

**Engine:** V8, overhead-cam, twin-turbo
**Bore × stroke:** 80 mm × 80 mm
**Capacity:** 3217 cc
**Maximum power:** 325 bhp
**Transmission:** six-speed Getrag manual gearbox
**Chassis:** steel unitary construction
**Suspension:** independent with MacPherson struts and anti-roll bar front; semi-trailing arms and coil springs rear; electronically-controlled Koni dampers all round
**Brakes:** servo-assisted ventilated discs all round
**Bodywork:** steel two-door 2 + 2 coupé
**Maximum speed (approx):** 168 mph (270 km/h)

# Maserati 3200GT 1998-present

In spite of a few high spots like the Ghibli Cup and Quattroporte, Maserati floundered in the supercar wilderness for some 15 years, bogged down with Biturbo derivatives and financial crises. But under the protective wing of Ferrari, the backing was available to produce a stunning new coupé, the 3200GT. Originally set to be named the Mistral, Maserati discovered another European manufacturer owned the name, so plumped for the 3200GT designation that connected with the 3500CT of 1957.

When Ferrari took over in 1997, it invested £35 million in Maserati's Modena plant specially to make the 3200GT – although the bodies were painted at Maranello – and hired Giorgetto Giugiaro's Italdesign company to style it. It was another masterpiece, with flowing rounded contours, faired-in headlight clusters, bonnet louvres, flared wheelarches and ovoid grille reminiscent of classic sports racing cars, yet blending in with contemporary aerodynamics and safety requirements. The unusual rear light clusters followed the line of the curvature of the car's bluff tail. The body was in steel, reinforced by tubular frames front and rear that support the engine and suspension. Wind-tunnel testing evolved a 0.34 Cd and constant Cz distribution under varying loads and driving conditions.

The 3200GT was a conventional front-engine, rear-wheel drive layout with two-section aluminium prop-shaft, powered by a new Maserati 3.2-litre 90-degree quad-cam V8 with twin turbochargers, complete with red and silver crackle-finished cam covers and plenum chamber and charismatic embossed Maserati logo. It produced 370 bhp at 6,750 rpm, and drove through a six-speed Getrag gearbox, attaining 0–62 mph (0-100 km/h)in 5.1 second, covered a standing quarter mile in 13 seconds and reached a top speed of 175 mph (281 km/h). Mixed-flow turbines caused the turbochargers to respond 20 percent faster than conventional versions, improving engine flexibility.

Suspension was by double-forged aluminium wishbones front and rear with forged aluminium hub-carriers, with toe-in regulator at the rear to provoke steer-effect. Suspension geometry was designed to provide anti-dive and anti-squat, and anti-roll bars were fitted front and rear. The 3200GT's speed-sensitive power-steering was reminiscent of the Ferrari Maranello, with adjustable dampers and sophisticated Bosch ASR traction control system that could be switched to normal or Sport settings. Normal mode limited slip to a minimum, while Sport allowed 15 percent slippage to permit a modicum of oversteering fun before cutting in. With the ASR switched off, the sky was the limit. Traction control worked in conjunction with the Maserati's Magneti Marelli drive-by-wire throttle linkage and the 4-channel ABS system that operated the Brembo disc brakes, reducing the amount of torque sent to the rear wheels and applying the rear brakes to slow whichever wheel was spinning

*Above: The 3200GT re-established Maserati as a credible manufacturer of luxury sports coupés and placed Neptune's trident firmly back on the 'most wanted' lists of right-thinking car enthusiasts. Styled by Giorgetto Giugiaro's design house, Italdesign, this Maserati combines chunky good looks with sweeping lines and a sporting character on the road.*

*Above: Powered by a 3.2-litre 90-degree V8 with twin turbos, the Maserati 3200GT produces 370 bhp at 6,750 rpm and rushes to 62 mph (100 km/h) in 5.2-seconds, with a top speed of 175 mph (281 km/h). Inside, it's an ergonomic triumph, being spacious and comfortable. Even in the rear, there is sufficient space for adults to travel without feeling*

fastest. The dampers were controlled by a series of electronic sensors, relaying data to actuators on each damper. 14 different damper settings were available. There was also a brake-force distributor, applying virtually 100 per cent braking effort when deceleration exceeded 0.45 g.

The tastefully upholstered cabin interior was much more restrained than previous riotous leather and veneer combinations, and the famous lozenge-shaped clock was absent. Instrumentation was kept to a minimum, and

regular equipment included a Becker hi-fi and climate control. Driving position was totally in keeping with the northern European physique rather than Italianate, and the 3200GT was a genuine four-seater rather than a cramped 2 + 2. There was also a reasonably capacious boot space.

The 3200GT was a serious rival to all major-league players in the supercar segment, rivalling the Porsche 911 for interior space and performance, as well as the Jaguar XKR and dearer Aston Martin DB7. Ferrari's own grand touring

cars were considerably more expensive than the £55,000 Maserati.

### Specification

**Engine:** V8, 4-cam, 32-valve
**Bore x stroke:** 80 mm x 80 mm
**Capacity:** 3217 cc
**Suspension:** independent front and rear by double forged aluminium wishbones with coil springs, adjustable dampers and traction control
**Brakes:** Brembo ventilated discs
**Chassis:** monocoque steel
**Body:** two-door four-seater coupé

# Matra

E ngins Matra first became famous in the 1950s and 1960s in the French aerospace and armaments industries, but then decided to diversify into low-volume sports car production, and into motor racing. In 1964 the company took over the struggling René Bonnet concern, and before long Matra single-seater racing cars became successful, notably when driven in Formula 1 by Jackie Stewart. The company later developed its own V12 racing engine, and a series of successful sports-racing cars.

After building Bonnet-style cars for a few years, at the old Bonnet factory at Champigny-sur-Marne, Matra then established a new factory at Romorantin, in central France, in 1967, using this to build a newly-designed but oddly-styled sports coupé, the Ford-engined M530A. The best that could be said about the M530A was that it was instantly recognisable, but Matra soon realised that it would have to develop a prettier and faster car if it was to expand. To reduce its material costs, and to make technical co-operation easier, it realised that it would also have to forge major and permanent links with larger carmakers.

The result, in the early 1970s, was an alliance with Chrysler-Simca, who took a large stake in the company. The first result was the launch of a new mid-engined car called the Bagheera, which was a smoothly-styled *three*-seater coupé which relied heavily on chassis components from the Simca 1100 family car. Like other manufacturers, before and since, Matra used transverse front-engine components to enable it to produce a transverse-mid-engined sporting car.

The new Bagheera was actually badged as a Matra-Simca, and sold well for the next few years, though Matra became diverted by the development of a chunkily-styled estate car called the Rancho, which looked as if it should have had four-wheel drive, but only ever had its front wheels driven.

The corporate scene changed yet again in 1978, when Chrysler sold out its European interests to Peugeot of France, the result being that Matra-Simca had a new partner. The Chrysler badge soon disappeared from old-style Simca cars, to be replaced by an exhumed Talbot marque name instead.

For the next few years, however, Peugeot allowed what was the old Simca business to carry on developing its own specific models, the result being the launch of a new family car called the Talbot Tagora. It was the Tagora and the established Talbot (previously Chrysler-Simca) Alpine models, therefore, which donated their engines, transmissions and suspension components to the fourth-generation Matra sports car, the Murena, which was launched at the end of 1980.

Early in the 1980s, however, the complicated French automotive scene changed yet again. Matra dissolved its commercial links with Peugeot, setting up a larger and more expansive deal with Renault instead. The result of that sea-change was the launch of the seven-seater Espace 'people-carrier', and an end to Matra's sports car activities.

*Above: Unusual with its three front seats, the innovative Bagheera was still an impressive sports car.*

*Below: Matra took over Bonnet, builders of the Djet, in 1964; this is one of the last, built in 1968.*

*Below: The Matra Murena was essentially an updated Bagheera, with a galvanised chassis and, in 2.2-litre engine form, high performance.*

# Matra Bonnet Djet 1964-68

The Bonnet sports car was originally conceived by René Bonnet in 1961, once he had unscrambled his links with Deutsch, and like the Alpine-Renault with which it competed head-on, it used many existing Renault components including the engine. Once Matra had taken over the financially tottering Bonnet concern in 1964, the car was retitled the Matra Bonnet Djet.

Although the Bonnet Djet looked superficially like an Alpine-Renault, and competed in the same motor-racing classes, it was entirely different under the skin. Unlike the Alpine-Renault, the Bonnet was a *mid*-engined car – that is to say, the engine was behind the seats but ahead of the line of the rear wheels. Both cars used the same Renault R8 type of four-cylinder engines and gearboxes,

*Below: The four-cylinder 1108-cc Renault engine was accessible under a cover behind the two front seats. Maintenance and adjustments were relatively easy, but noise levels were high inside the cabin.*

but in the case of the Bonnet the assembly was turned round through 180 degrees, which significantly improved the weight distribution.

The backbone chassis featured all-wishbone independent suspension which, together with a favourable weight distribution, made this car technically superior (in theory at least) to its rival. The body was a neat and immediately recognisable glassfibre fastback two-seater, distinguished by a large 'goldfish-bowl' type of rear window.

Although the Djet was a capable little car which was fast, economical, and handled very well, it was not at all refined, and suffered from excessive noise levels inside the cabin. Customers were given a choice of Renault-based engines – so that they could decide whether to have a fast, or a very fast, car, and decide whether they wanted to use their Djet on the road or on the track.

Renault engines came either as normal (pushrod overhead-valve) or Gordini-modified (still with overhead valves, but with part-spherical combustion

chambers), and towards the end of the run the fierce and rather special 1.25-litre version was offered (74.5 mm × 72 mm producing 103 bhp), along with a five-speed gearbox.

Matra was not satisfied with this type of car, and this relatively crude image, for long. On the one hand Matra wanted to expand its racing interests (into Formula 2 and eventually into Formula 1), while on the other it wanted to sponsor a more spacious and refined road car. The result was that the original Bonnet factory was closed down in favour of a new plant at Romorantin. Soon after this, the Djet disappeared, in favour of the new Ford-powered M30A.

*Below: A 1967 Djet in French blue. This compact glassfibre sports car was both nimble and economical.*

*Above: The Djet was a driver's car, hence the bucket seats, small steering wheel and fulsome instrumentation.*

## Specification (1964)

**Engine:** inline-four, overhead-valve
**Bore × stroke:** 70 mm × 72 mm
**Capacity:** 1108 cc
**Maximum power:** 72 bhp or 95 bhp
**Transmission:** four-speed manual gearbox, rear-wheel drive
**Chassis:** separate steel frame with central tubular backbone
**Suspension:** independent with wishbones and coil springs front; trailing arms and coil springs rear
**Brakes:** discs all round
**Bodywork:** glassfibre two-seater coupé
**Maximum speed (approx):** (72-bhp model) 99 mph (159 km/h)

## Matra M530A 1967-73

At the 1967 Geneva Motor Show, Matra showed its first in-house design, an angular 2 + 2-seater coupé which was at once practical, relatively cheap to build and certainly distinctive in its looks. This new model, dubbed the M530A, would run for six years before being displaced by the Bagheera. In that time, no fewer than 9,690 examples were built.

The M530A was totally different from the Matra Bonnet Djet, for although it was still a mid-engined car, it had a new chassis, a different engine and transmission, altered suspension, and a totally unique 2 + 2 coupé style. The style itself was flattened rather than sinuous, and had pop-up headlamps, a built-in roll-over bar and a roof panel which could be removed to give open-air motoring.

The new car was built around a fabricated sheet-steel platform chassis, which also supported the steel inner body structure, the whole being clothed in glassfibre body panels. Power was by courtesy of Ford-Germany, who not only provided the 1.7-litre V4 from the Taunus 12M, but that car's transaxle too. Because the Taunus 12M was a front-wheel-drive car, with the engine ahead of the line of the front wheels, making a mid-engined Matra was only a matter of 'moving' the assembly back in space, and driving the rear wheels instead.

The M530A was a well-packaged car, for the engine was compact; this allowed the designers to provide space for luggage in a coffer between the front wheels, and also in a separate compartment behind the rear wheels, above the gearbox.

The M530A took Matra one step further towards its ambition of becoming a major carmaker, but this model was still not fast enough, and certainly not pretty enough, to make a significant impact. Even in post-1969 form, with a 90-bhp engine and a claimed top speed of 109 mph, it was a brisk rather than an outstanding performer.

*Below: The M530A had a glassfibre 2 + 2 body. The styling of the roof, windows and rear end was eccentric.*

The looks could best be described by the French phrase of *jolie laide* (attractively ugly), so after Matra had founded links with Chrysler-Europe (née Simca) in 1969, and the use of a Ford engine became something of a political embarrassment, there was little resistance to designing a replacement with Simca running gear.

### Specification (1967)

**Engine:** V4, overhead-valve
**Bore × stroke:** 90 mm × 66.8 mm
**Capacity:** 1699 cc
**Maximum power:** 73 bhp (90 bhp from mid-1969)
**Transmission:** four-speed manual gearbox, rear-wheel drive
**Chassis:** steel unitary construction platform chassis and inner body structure
**Suspension:** independent with wishbones and coil springs front; struts and coil springs rear
**Brakes:** discs all round
**Bodywork:** glassfibre 2 + 2-seater coupé
**Maximum speed (approx):** (90-bhp version) 109 mph (175 km/h)

*Above: The M530A had distinctive angular looks and a Targa roof, but was not attractive from all angles.*

*Below: The mid-mounted V4 Ford Taunus engine with one carburettor gave a top speed of 109 mph.*

# Matra-Simca Bagheera 1973-80

Having forged links with Chrysler-Europe (or with Simca, if you have chauvinistic tendencies) in 1969, Matra set about using that company's brand names and, eventually, its hardware. The Matra-Simca name was soon applied to the racing-sports cars, and this was also the marque name chosen for a new road car, which was launched in 1973.

It was a direct replacement for the ungainly M530A, and was graced with the name Bagheera, after that notable black panther character from *Jungle Book*. In the story, Bagheera was a sinuous and intelligent beast – and Matra hoped that its new car could develop the same sort of character.

The smart and individual Bagheera was not only a pretty little car, but a technically integrated design which also had one unique selling point – that it featured three-abreast seating. Because of the links with Chrysler/Simca, Matra decided to use as much of the running gear of the front-wheel-drive Simca 1100 as possible. As with the previous M530A sports coupé (and as Fiat was already doing with the X1/9), Matra produced a

mid-engined car by picking up the transverse-engine/transmission/front-drive package of the Simca, moving it back behind the cabin, and driving the rear wheels instead.

The basis of the design was a rather Italian-style chassis, made of many tubes, with sheet steel and box-stiffeners in appropriate places. The whole was covered in a neat, rounded and altogether understated coupé body shell styled by Matra itself, and made from glassfibre.

The cabin layout, in theory, offered three-abreast seating, with the driver on the left having a normal seat, and with a pair, almost a small bench, of seats to his right. It was smart and interesting, but practical only if the prospective occupants were not all broad-shouldered men.

Because of this choice of cabin, Matra had no intention of making a right-hand-drive version of the car, though British entrepreneurs soon discovered that it *was* possible, albeit with considerable difficulty and at high cost, and a few such conversions were sold in the UK.

Like all such cars, the Bagheera's chassis was capable of handling rather more power than it was ever given by Matra; but without a larger engine/transmission transplant being carried out, this was not easy to do. Nevertheless, the Bagheera sold very well indeed. It was always seen as a rather underpowered design, though the 1.4-litre engine (optional from 1977, standard from 1979) helped a little.

For the 1980s Matra decided to build on a good idea by producing a new car – the Murena – which had more powerful engines and a lot more performance. Before then, however, no fewer than 47,802 Bagheeras had been produced. The last few cars were rebadged as Talbot-Matras.

*Left: With three seats, the driver sat at the extreme side of the car. Note the vertical radio and optimistic speedometer, which read to 130 mph.*

*Below: Over the tube and sheet-steel chassis was a rounded coupé shell styled in-house. The low nose necessitated pop-up headlights.*

*Above: The rear view of this well-designed and stylish car hardly reveals the Bagheera's most individual feature: three-abreast seating. This car is from the last year of production, with the 1.4-litre engine; but the Bagheera was always rather underpowered.*

## Specification (1973)

**Engine:** inline four-cylinder, overhead-valve

**Bore × stroke:** 76.7 mm × 70 mm

**Capacity:** 1294 cc

**Maximum power:** 84 bhp

**Transmission:** four-speed manual gearbox, rear-wheel drive

**Chassis:** separate steel multi-tubular frame with sheet-steel and box-section stiffeners

**Suspension:** independent with wishbones, torsion bars and anti-roll bar front; lower wishbones and torsion bars rear

**Brakes:** discs all round

**Bodywork:** glassfibre three-seater coupé

**Maximum speed (approx):** 101 mph (163 km/h)

## Matra Murena 1980-83

The Bagheera had sold well during the 1970s, and when Matra came to design a new model it kept the same basic layout, and some of the same chassis components. The new car, titled the Murena, was also a mid-engined rear-drive coupé, and had that unique three-abreast seating layout, but it had new styling and a lot more performance.

Like the Bagheera it was built at Matra's Romorantin factory in central France, but to reflect the latest moves in corporate ownership (Chrysler had sold out to Peugeot, and all traces of 'Simca' had finally been expunged) it also carried a Talbot tag, though most people simply called it a Matra.

Unlike the Bagheera, the Murena was sold with a choice of engine types – either the old-type 1.6-litre, 80.6-mm × 78-mm/92-bhp, overhead-valve Simca unit (a final 'stretch' of the Bagheera's engine), or the more modern overhead-cam 2.2-litre 'four' as found in the contemporary Talbot Tagora saloon. The chassis retained the old-type Bagheera torsion-bar front suspension, but this time there were MacPherson struts fitted at the rear.

The fastback style was simple and pleasing, and – like many other mid-engined road cars – the roadholding was excellent. In many ways this car was a grown-up version of the Fiat X1/9, or a better-detailed version of the Lancia Monte Carlo, and certainly shared all the advantages of style and packaging, but had the same problem of limited space for anything but people. Because of the three-seater layout it was only ever produced in left-hand-drive form, though a few cars were later converted.

If Peugeot-Talbot had not gone ahead with the speedy rationalisation of its businesses in the early 1980s, the Murena might have lasted longer, but the engines which powered this car were soon rendered obsolete. Matra, in any case, had received an approach from Renault, and the big Espace 'people-carrier' soon took over the factory facilities once occupied by the Murena.

In three years, no fewer than 10,613 Murenas were built, but this was the last Matra-badged road car to have been produced. They should survive longer than the Bagheeras, as the tendency for the chassis (hidden under the glassfibre body) to rust has been overcome thanks to galvanising, for which future collectors will be grateful.

*Left: The styling treatment of the Murena was similar to the Bagheera at the front and sides, but the tail and roof were distinctive.*

### Specification (1980)

**Engine:** inline four-cylinder, single overhead camshaft
**Bore × stroke:** 91.7 mm × 81.6 mm
**Capacity:** 2156 cc
**Maximum power:** 118 bhp
**Transmission:** five-speed manual gearbox, rear-wheel drive
**Chassis:** steel unitary construction chassis and interior body structure
**Suspension:** independent with wishbones, torsion bars and anti-roll bar front; MacPherson struts and lower wishbones rear
**Brakes:** discs all round
**Bodywork:** glassfibre three-seater coupé
**Maximum speed (approx):** 124 mph (200 km/h) or 113 mph (182 km/h) for 1.6-litre model

*Above: The largest engine fitted to the Murena was the 2.2-litre four from the Talbot Tagora saloon.*

*Below: The 2.2-litre Murena was fast and looked purposeful; inside, it retained three-abreast seating.*

# Maybach

Wilhelm Maybach was one of the first great engineers of the motor car age. Born the son of a skilled carpenter in Heilbronn, on the river Neckar in Germany, he was orphaned at the age of 10. At 15 he was apprenticed to the Bruderhaus engineering works, and also studied physics and draughtsmanship. He later studied mathematics and foreign languages and showed a talent for invention.

The altruistic principles of the Bruderhaus organisation didn't exactly go hand-in-hand with business efficiency, and it had to call in outside help to bring profitability. An able young engineer named Paul Daimler was entrusted with this task, and realised Maybach's potential during his two years at Bruderhaus. When Daimler left to become factory manager of the Karlsruhe machine works, he took Maybach with him, and the two men were subsequently recruited by the Deutz gas-engine works in 1872, Daimler as factory manager, and Maybach as chief designer.

Their work on stationary engines convinced them that a smaller, lighter, power source was needed. They left Deutz in 1882 to work on a light internal combustion engine which was fitted to a motorcycle test-bed in 1885 and subsequently to a carriage. Maybach designed a purpose-built motor car in 1889, and production of cars for sale came soon after.

The Daimler cars of the 1890s were heavily-built horseless carriages, but after Gottlieb Daimler's death in 1900 Wilhelm Maybach – encouraged by Daimler's enterprising French agent, Emil Jellinek – created the first truly modern motor car, the Mercedes (which was named after Jellinek's daughter).

After Daimler's death, Maybach's position became increasingly untenable, despite his world-beating designs, which included the Mercedes 60HP, so in 1907 he left to build aero engines for the airship pioneer Graf Zeppelin. In 1912 his son Karl capitalised on the family name by opening an aero-engine factory at Friedrichshafen, not far from the Zeppelin works on Lake Constance.

After World War I, Karl Maybach then turned to engine manufacture, and after that enterprise stalled he began making his own cars, always building spectacularly large luxury models. In the 1920s these all had straight-six power units and, initially, a two-speed pedal-controlled transmission. Wisely, the Maybach firm never laid down its own body plant; like Rolls-Royce, it supplied complete rolling chassis which could then be clothed by specialist coachbuilders.

Wilhelm Maybach died at Christmas 1929, the same year in which his company had followed the worldwide trend towards luxury cars, and had launched the absolutely massive V12, which soon became the Zeppelin model. Some of these cars appeared with rather avant-garde streamlined coachwork, which made them very suitable for high-speed cruising on Germany's new autobahns. Maybach Zeppelins were always very

*Above: The 'M' stood for Maybach and the '12' for the mighty V12 engine, which was used in the Maybach Zeppelin in both 7.0- and 8.0-litre forms.*

expensive, and very rare, and were built in limited numbers up to the outbreak of World War II.

The only concession Maybach made to the less prosperous 1930s was to offer a six-cylinder-engined version of the Zeppelin (the SW range) which was built until the outbreak of war. To their credit, Maybach always distanced themselves from the Nazi party, which perhaps explains why few Maybachs were ever used by high officials.

After the war, in which Maybach's premises were badly damaged, the company abandoned car manufacture completely, and from 1960 its diesel-engine interests (for use in locomotives and ships) were merged with those of Daimler-Benz.

*Below: One of the world's finest cars, this 1938 8.0-litre V12 Maybach Zeppelin Cabriolet Sport features coachwork by Spohn; it was capable of over 115 mph.*

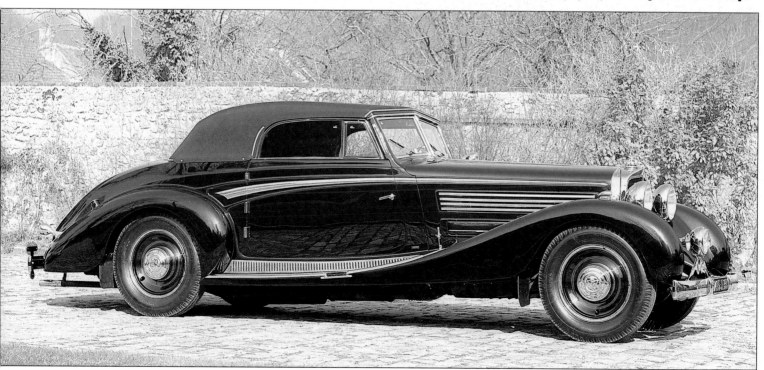

# Maybach W3 and W5 1921-30

The ban on aero-engine manufacture in Germany, which followed the country's defeat in World War I, forced Karl Maybach to look around for a new line of business. Since his company had already built successful marine and motorcycle power units for other concerns, it wasn't too big a step to decide to make car engines too.

Even so, Maybach completely misread the needs of the market; the engine he proposed was a side-valve 5738-cc six-cylinder, a gargantuan power unit quite out of step with the depressed postwar climate. Just one customer was forthcoming – Spyker of Holland, which built luxury cars in tiny numbers. Undaunted by this, Maybach decided to produce his own marque of car; the very first Maybach duly appeared in 1921.

Known as the W3 ('W' standing for *Wagen*, the German for car), it epitomised Karl Maybach's idea that motoring should be foolproof. So that the driver never needed to take his hands from the wheel, the W3 was given a combined starter/accelerator pedal, and its two-speed epicyclic gearbox was also con-

trolled by a pedal (just like the humble Ford Model T, from which Maybach probably took his inspiration). The car was designed to spend most of its time in top gear; depressing the transmission pedal selected an emergency 'mountain gear'.

The W3 was the very first German car to have four-wheel brakes. It also had a dual-choke carburettor (naturally this was of Maybach's own manufacture, having fuel and air jets controlled by the accelerator pedal, to eliminate the conventional float chamber and throttle butterfly), and a partially-boxed chassis frame.

Even in the aftermath of defeat, Germany could still find clients for such a large and extravagant machine. As a consequence, the W3 was always fitted with bespoke bodywork by such top German coachbuilders as Spohn, Glaser, Armbruster, Erdmann & Rossi and Voll-Ruhrbeck.

The W3 was heavy and ponderous, and Karl Maybach wasn't satisfied with it. Even the runaway inflation of Weimar Germany could not constrain his automotive megalomania, and in 1926 he introduced the W5, using the same chassis as the W3, but having a seven-litre engine which gave the car a top speed of 75 mph. At the same time he abandoned his declared aim of flexibility of operation, by co-operating with the ZF gear works to develop the W5 SG model, whose *Schnellgang* auxiliary two-speed overdrive gearbox helped raise the huge car's top speed to 85 mph.

*Below: Upright, imposing and heavy, the W5 was a very expensive car in its day and was always coachbuilt to the highest standards. It was capable of 75 mph with its seven-litre engine, and had been designed by Maybach to be as simple to drive as possible: the Schnellgang epicyclic two-speed auxiliary overdrive gearbox was controlled by pedals.*

*Above: The W5 was a tall car with a high bonnet, yet the great seven-litre straight-six took up nearly all of the underbonnet space. Maybach engines were built to high standards and, being very understressed, proved extremely reliable.*

## Specification (1926 W5)

**Engine:** inline six-cylinder, side-valve
**Bore × stroke:** 95 mm × 135 mm
**Capacity:** 6995 cc
**Maximum power:** 120 bhp

**Transmission:** two-speed epicyclic gearbox (later W5 SG models also had overdrive), rear-wheel drive
**Chassis:** separate steel frame with channel-section main side members, boxed at front and rear
**Suspension:** non-independent with beam front axle and semi-elliptic leaf springs; live rear axle with semi-elliptic leaf springs
**Brakes:** drums front and rear
**Bodywork:** various, to special order
**Maximum speed:** 75 mph (121 km/h)

# Maybach Zeppelin 1929-39

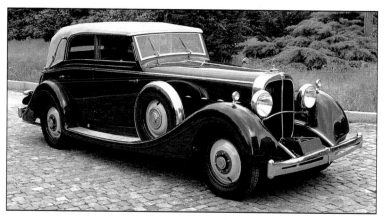

**Left: The height of prestige: the grille of a Zeppelin Cabriolet Sport, powered by an eight-litre V12.**

**Above: A Graber-bodied Zeppelin saloon of 1934. Despite a weight of 2.5 tons, it could reach 100 mph.**

The seven-litre 'six', as used in the W5 model, wasn't grandiose enough for Karl Maybach. In 1929 he launched the 6922-cc V12 DS7 model (where DS7 stood for Double-Six, 7 litres), and quite wrongly claimed that the new engine was derived from the mighty 515-bhp Maybach power units of the airship LZ127 *Graf Zeppelin*, which had just flown successfully round the world.

The new model was an absolutely enormous machine, for with a 147-in wheelbase it was so big that its driver was required to have an omnibus licence!

This was a car that could travel from walking pace up to 100 mph in top gear; its overdrive, which operated on all three forward gears, was engaged by releasing the accelerator pedal, touching a vacuum control button on the steering wheel, then accelerating again. In 1930 this arrangement was displaced by the new *Doppelschnellgang* four-speed gearbox, with overdrive on all forward gears, again with vacuum servo controls on the steering wheel.

This gearbox, by the way, was arranged so that the brave driver could have a choice of four reverse gears too –

though Maybach did not exactly publicise the feature! The same gearbox was used, for a time, in the Lagonda Selector Special.

The double-six V12 engine (which was fitted under a bonnet over seven feet long), was enlarged to 7922 cc in 1931, this new DS8 derivative becoming officially known as the Zeppelin, to commemorate Maybach's contribution to Germany's current engineering triumph (a model airship was displayed on the car's badge bar).

The Maybach Zeppelin was as ambitious a project as its flying namesake. Despite using light-alloy construction, the engine was said to weigh a ton. The completed rolling chassis alone weighed 4,600 lb, and a typical coachbuilt limousine scaled around 7,200 lb. The only German car to weigh more was the second-generation Mercedes-Benz 770 Grosser model of the late 1930s. Naturally the brakes were vacuum servo-assisted, in direct proportion to the car's speed.

These cars were built in tiny numbers

throughout the 1930s, and from the late 1930s they were fitted with *seven*-speed gearboxes of great complexity. Some Zeppelins had full-width Spohn aerodynamic coachwork, which had been designed by Paul Jaray, the same chassis and style being available in the late 1930s with a new six-cylinder overhead-camshaft engine.

Priced at between 40,000 and 42,000 Reichmarks, the DS8 Zeppelin was too expensive even for the market it served – it cost nearly twice as much as a large Mercedes-Benz 540K, for example – and of around 300 Zeppelins ever built, just 12 were delivered in Germany. The rest were exported.

## Specification (1931)

**Engine:** V12, overhead-valve
**Bore × stroke:** 92 mm × 100 mm
**Capacity:** 7977 cc
**Maximum power:** 200 bhp
**Transmission:** three-speed manual gearbox and overdrive at first, four-speed pre-selector (plus overdrive on all gears) from 1930
**Chassis:** separate steel frame with channel-section main side members
**Suspension:** beam axle front and rear, leaf springs all round
**Brakes:** drums front and rear
**Bodywork:** various, to special order
**Maximum speed (approx):** 100 mph (161 km/h)

**Below: The 1934 two-door Zeppelin Cabriolet Sport was built on a short chassis, but was still longer than most limousines. It was a fast car, but the 200-bhp alloy V12 was very thirsty, giving about 10 mpg. A 30-gallon fuel tank was fitted.**

# Mazda

*Right: The stylish Mazda RX-7, launched at the Tokyo Motor Show in 1978 and powered by a twin-rotor Wankel engine, proved decisive in establishing Mazda as a genuine sports car manufacturer and in demonstrating that rotary engines could offer real performance and reliability. RX-7s later were very successful in European and North American racing and rallying.*

Toyo Kogyo of Japan originally manufactured cork products, then expanded into the building of machines, and began making three-wheeler trucks in 1931. But it was not until 1960 that the first Mazda car, the R-360 model, was put on sale.

In the next two decades the Mazda car marque expanded enormously, not just in numbers, but in scope and technology; it was the first (and only) Japanese carmaker to adopt rotary Wankel engine technology, keeping faith with rotary power units to this day.

Except for the limited-production 110S coupé, all early Mazdas were aimed at the family market, many of the products being tiny saloons of the type favoured by Japanese buyers because of taxation concessions. Mazda's love-affair with the Wankel engine then saw this expensive type of powerplant offered as an alternative in several models, such as the RX-3, in the early 1970s.

In the aftermath of the 'energy crisis' of 1973-74, and the movement towards cleaner emissions which followed it, most of the world's Wankel-users abandoned this engine as being too 'dirty' and too thirsty, but Mazda was not willing to lose face and persevered with development. From that day to this, there has always been at least one high-powered Wankel-engined car in the Mazda range.

In the 1970s Mazda forged financial links with Ford-USA and later in the decade the company's image was boosted by the Wankel-powered RX-7 (which was completely redesigned in the mid-1980s). After the 323 model was relaunched as a transverse-engined front-wheel-drive car in 1980 the marketing image began to change perceptibly. Links with Ford were rapidly turned into joint engineering, marketing and manufacturing agreements, often to Mazda's disadvantage.

By the mid-1980s Ford had stopped building cars of its own design in countries like Australia and New Zealand, preferring to let Mazda do the job, producing lightly-restyled and re-engineered models which always carried the Ford badge. Also in the mid-1980s Mazda opened a brand-new factory in Michigan, USA, not only to produce Mazdas for sale in that country, but to build Ford cars which had been developed from Mazda designs. By this stage, Mazda had consolidated its domestic range, and was building large numbers of cars for every market, from tiny micro-models to large limousines.

Then, in the late 1980s, a further change to the image became perceptible. Mazda's interest in worldwide motorsport had been obvious for some time – not only by the financing of big Group C race cars, but by the creation of a rally team based in West Germany. To emphasise their sporting involvement, Mazda then began to introduce a series of technologically complex sporting cars, notably the MX-5 Miata (really a latter-day and more sophisticated interpretation of the MG Midget theme), the MX-3 and the MX-6.

Mazda was the most adventurous of the Japanese car makers and frequently went out on a limb with its styling with cars like the MX6, Xedos and 323. By the late 1990s this confidence appeared to be faltering however.

*Below: The much improved second-generation RX-7 appeared in 1985, with independent rear suspension and the larger 13B 1216-cc rotary engine which in standard form gave 150 bhp at 6,500 rpm and 136 lb ft of torque at 3,000 rpm.*

# Mazda 110S Cosmo 1967-72

Almost at a stroke, the 110S Cosmo gave Mazda the image it required. Produced at a time when Mazda was little-known outside Japan, it immediately made its point.

The Cosmo was certainly different from previous Mazdas, in virtually all respects. Not only did it have unique 'rocket-ship' styling in a long and flamboyant two-seater coupé shape, but it was also the first Mazda to use a Wankel rotary engine. Work began on the style in 1962, and the prototype was put on display at the Tokyo Motor Show in 1964, where it caused a sensation. It was, after all, the world's very first twin-rotor Wankel-engined project, and Mazda made it clear that limited production for the Japanese market was on the way.

Development and proving took time, but sales began in 1967 and continued for five years, during which 1,176 Wankel-powered Cosmos were made. Naturally the car was expensive, but it was also fast, with an astonishingly smooth engine

which impressed in other respects too; at a time when NSU's Wankel engines seemed to suffer from premature wear to rotor tips, the Mazda engine was more long-lived.

Under the skin the chassis was straightforward enough, although Mazda indulged itself with de Dion rear suspension, a feature which it did not continue on later models. Mazda was cautious, and intended to keep all these cars in Japan, but a few were exported, and Britain's *Autocar* magazine actually tested one in February 1968, when it recorded a top speed of 115 mph, and a rather disappointing fuel consumption of 20 mpg.

At 100 mph the car delivered just 14 mpg but, said *Autocar*, "this is the only feature that deters such motoring, since both engine and car are completely happy at this speed and oil temperature was well within its limits". Maximum power in the engine was attained at 7,000 rpm, although it could be revved to 8,000.

*Above: The engine was powerful and smooth, but under a heavy load it sounded rather like a two-stroke. Nevertheless, it would rev freely to 7,000 rpm and yet its response was flexible at low rpm.*

The twin-rotor Wankel was so flexible that the car could be driven from very low speeds in top gear and then accelerate smoothly to its maximum, sounding more turbine-like but hardly increasing in volume as the revs rose. According to *Autocar*, there was "an uncanny lack of vibration and a complete absence of mechanical clatter whatever the engine speed". This was noticeable even in the magazine's acceleration runs, which saw 60 mph reached in 9.3 seconds and 100 mph in 30.6 seconds. The standing quarter-mile took just 17.5 seconds.

One curiosity of rotary engines was that they provided little engine braking, and drivers had to learn to leave a little more time for engine revs to fall before changing gear. Although the handling was considered good, the ride was judged less satisfactory by testers. The engine was mounted well behind the front wheels and a weight distribution of 45/55 was biased to the rear. To those who drove the Cosmo, the success of the later RX-7 came as no surprise.

Hardened pundits like Denis Jenkinson of *Motor Sport* were prepared to be cynical at first, but after a brief test drive he commented that the Cosmo was the "Lotus Elan of Japan", which was high

praise for a carmaker who had never previously produced sports cars. All were agreed that this low, wide, and expensive car was also a very effective machine, holding the road well, and with performance to match.

## Specification (1967)

**Engine:** twin-rotor Wankel
**Capacity:** (nominal) 982 cc, equivalent to 1964 cc
**Maximum power:** 110 bhp
**Transmission:** four-speed manual gearbox, rear-wheel drive
**Chassis:** steel unitary construction body/chassis
**Suspension:** independent front with wishbones and coil springs; non-independent rear with de Dion axle and coil springs
**Brakes:** discs front, drums rear
**Bodywork:** steel two-seater coupé
**Maximum speed (approx):** 115 mph (185 km/h)

*Above: The Cosmo offered good performance, reaching 60 mph in 9.3 seconds, but against it were high price and poor fuel economy.*

*Below: The two-seat GT would pull in top gear from 25 mph as smoothly as an electric train all the way to its excellent top speed of 115 mph.*

## Mazda RX-7 1978-85

In the 10 years since Mazda had introduced its first Wankel-engined car, technology had moved on considerably. The Wankel engine had been offered in a whole variety of Mazda models, but it was not until 1978 that it was married to a smart new 2 + 2-seater coupé, though the '+ 2' seats were very small indeed.

The new car, the RX-7, was aimed squarely at the North American market, where it was sized (and priced) directly against the Porsche 924 and the Triumph TR7. Compared with previous sporting Mazdas, the new RX-7 was a smooth, even rather understated, coupé, with the fashionable wedge nose, flip-up headlamps, a fastback tail and a large lift-up glass-back.

Except for the Wankel engine, on which Mazda had lavished hundreds of thousands of development hours, the rest of the RX-7's chassis was conventional enough. The front suspension was by MacPherson struts, which by this stage were becoming accepted for sports cars, and the rear featured a live axle. The axle was well located, however, with upper and lower trailing arms (the upper ones angled) and a Watt linkage to help lateral location. The original model was let down by details like having rear drum brakes rather than discs and insufficient power to match the looks. The displacement of the small rotary engine was actually equivalent to a 2.2-litre conventional four-stroke engine and on that basis its 100 bhp and 105 lb ft of torque was really inadequate despite the incredible smoothness of the engine and its willingness to rev to very high rpm.

The drawback was soon rectified as an unofficial 'Mk 2' version appeared in 1981, fitted with rear disc brakes and, rather more important, more power –

115 bhp at 6,000 rpm. Power went up yet again when the larger 13B engine was fitted in 1984, giving 135 bhp and allowing a top speed easily over the 120-mph mark. Larger wheels and tyres, along with bigger brakes, were also fitted to complement the larger engine. During all these changes, the shape and style of the RX-7 remained unchanged, as did its character, with the rotary engine having its own unique feel and sound.

Mazda, like Datsun before them, had judged the North American market exactly right, and with the help of the RX-7, Mazda sales boomed as never before. RX-7s were entered with great success in races and rallies in Europe and North America, which further boosted the marque's reputation. In 1981 the Percy/Walkinshaw car won the Spa 24 Hours.

The RX-7 was also a success in other export markets. From late 1983 a fuel-injected turbocharged version was also available (although not in the UK), with 165 bhp at 6,500 rpm and 166 lb ft of torque at 4,000 rpm. The claimed top speed was 137 mph. A second generation RX-7 arrived in 1985 to rival the 944. The third generation RX-7 was a

*Above: The interior of the Elford RX-7 Turbo. Like the body, the styling inside was functional and neat.*

*Below: The clean lines of the RX-7 clothed a daring engine but relatively simple suspension.*

*Above: Rear view of a Vic Elford-tuned RX-7, with turbocharged rotary engine. The Garrett T3, feeding air through an SU HI44 carburettor, produced some 160 bhp. Mazda later built a turbo model but never exported it to Britain.*

fabulous-looking coupé that retained the thirsty Wankel engine, and went out of production in 1998.

### Specification (1978)

**Engine:** twin-rotor Wankel
**Capacity:** (nominal) 1146 cc, equivalent to 2292 cc
**Maximum power:** 105 bhp
**Transmission:** five-speed manual gearbox or optional automatic transmission, rear-wheel drive
**Chassis:** steel unitary construction body/chassis
**Suspension:** independent front with MacPherson struts; live rear axle with upper and lower trailing arms, Watt linkage and anti-roll bar
**Brakes:** discs front, drums rear
**Bodywork:** steel two- or 2 + 2-seater coupé
**Maximum speed:** 115 mph (185 km/h)

# Mazda MX-6 1992-present

In only three years, Mazda changed its public face, and became a much-respected manufacturer of sporting cars. Before 1989 there had been only the Wankel-engined RX-7, but by 1992 no fewer than three other cars – the MX-3, the MX-5 and, now, the MX-6 – had been added to the range. If you then add in the exclusive Eunos Cosmo, that meant the launch of no fewer than five new sporting cars in those three years. It was a remarkable achievement.

The latest car, the MX-6, was less specialised than the other types, in that it was based on the structural platform, suspension and other running gear of a new Mazda family car – the 626 family car – but it was still an exciting machine which threatened to upset the balance of a category headed (in Europe) by the GM Calibra and the two Toyotas – the enlarged MR2 and the Celica.

Not only was this car important on its own, but it was also the mechanical base around which the Ford-USA Probe of 1992 was built. Except in tiny details

(such as wheels and suspension settings), the two cars shared the same 'chassis' and manufacturing centre – the MX-6 was to be built in the USA as well as Japan – though the Probe had its own completely different hatchback cabin.

The MX-6 used an enlarged version of the new all-alloy Type KL Mazda V6 engine, which had first appeared as a tiny 1.8-litre unit in the MX-3 of 1991, and which was now to be used in 2.5-litre displacement in the 626 saloons, and also in the Ford Probe. This was mated to a choice of manual or automatic transmissions, and there was front-wheel drive.

The suspension set-up sounded overly simple, with struts all round, but the MX-6's handling and roadholding showed what such a system could achieve and it was not embarrassed by the power and performance, which was sufficient to give a 0-60 mph time of 7.5 seconds and a standing quarter-mile in 16 seconds on the way to a maximum speed of 134 mph. That made the car fully competitive with the best of its

coupé rivals, such as the Honda Prelude.

At first the MX-6 was only offered with the advanced and complex 165-bhp V6 engine, but as the closely-related new-generation 626 cars were also being built with 16-valve 1.8-litre and 2.0-litre four-cylinder engines, these seemed certain to be added in future years.

*Above: The transverse 60-degree 24-valve V6, with alloy heads and an iron block, is fitted with multi-point electronic fuel injection and mapping, plus a catalytic converter. With a 9.2:1 compression ratio, it produces 165 bhp at 5,600 rpm and 163 lb ft at 4,800 rpm.*

*Left: The MX-6 cockpit features flowing lines throughout; fittings include power-assisted steering, cruise control, electric windows and mirrors, a headlamp height adjuster and full instrumentation. At the left, above the radio, are the plentiful ventilation controls.*

*Below: The two-door, 2 + 2 coupé offers reasonable space at the rear, although tall people have to duck the low roof. Styling is in the new 1990s tradition, with an emphasis on smoothness, curves and aerodynamics, with few appendages, and a tight panel fit.*

## Specification (1992)

**Engine:** V6, twin overhead camshafts per bank of cylinders
**Bore × stroke:** 84.5 mm × 74.2 mm
**Capacity:** 2497 cc
**Maximum power:** 165 bhp
**Transmission:** five-speed manual gearbox or four-speed automatic transmission, front-wheel drive
**Chassis:** steel unitary construction body/chassis
**Suspension:** independent with MacPherson struts front and rear
**Brakes:** discs all round
**Bodywork:** steel 2 + 2 coupé
**Maximum speed (approx):** 134 mph (216 km/h)

## Mazda MX-5 1989-present

The main point about the MX-5 was that it reawakened the motoring masses to the potential of affordable sports car motoring. Mass produced MGs and Triumphs were long-gone, while vehicles like the classic Alfa Spider soldiered on in small volumes, but Mazda's trick was to style the MX-5 like a 1960s Elan and equip it with a reliable drivetrain and running gear. It thus caught the tail end of the classic boom as well as helping to instigate the sports car bonanza of the early 1990s.

Also known in various markets as the Eunos and Miata, the MX-5 was a conventional front-engine, rear-wheel drive two-seater sports car, with steel body and aluminium bonnet, built with expected Japanese competence. It was thus worthy but rather dull, in spite of its Lotus inspired looks. In 1998 a facelifted MX-5 was introduced, offering better performance, comfort and passive safety features such as dual air bags, and its centre of gravity was lowered by storing the battery and spare wheel beneath the boot floor. The main alteration in its appearance was the replacement of the retractable headlamp system with a lightweight fixed design. Styling work was carried out under Tsutomu 'Tom' Matano, chief designer at Mazda's R&D studio in Irvine, California. The front of the new car retained the air intake design while the back end featured the familiar oval rear lamp clusters. These wrapped around more prominently than before, each housing the brake light, indicator, reversing light and rear fog light. On the previous car the fog light was not integrated into the rear light cluster. A separate spoiler behind the air-dam was standard on all models, intended to improve under-floor airflow.

The 1998 versions of the MX-5 were

powered by Mazda's electronic fuel-injected twin-cam 16-valve four-cylinder engines, of 1,839 cc and 140 bhp, and 1,597 cc and 110 bhp. Transmission was via the M-type 5-speed manual gearbox, with short-throw gearlever. The cylinder head was in aluminium and the block was cast iron, and raised-crown pistons lifted its compression ratio, while the sump and radiator were in weight-saving aluminium. Mazda doctored the exhaust system so that it made the sort of noise emitted by a traditional sports car.

The 0–62 mph (0-100 km/h) acceleration time for the 1.6-litre car was 9.7-seconds with top speed of 118 mph (190 km/h), and the 1.8-litre version made 0–62 mph (0-100 km/h) in 8.0-seconds, going up to 127 mph (204 km/h). Fuel consumption for the 1.6-litre was 34.9 mpg and 33.2 mpg for the 1.8-litre. Output and torque were improved over the old model by modifications to the intake and exhaust systems, while the 1.8iS model featured a Torsen limited-slip differential. Suspension was independent all round by unequal length upper and lower wishbones, coil springs, dampers and anti-roll bars, attached to front and rear subframes. The subframes were in turn bolted onto the welded-steel monocoque body shell. Steering was by rack and pinion, power assisted as standard. The MX-5 had disc brakes all round, backed up by four-sensor, three-channel ABS.

A decent, easy to operate soft-top has always been fundamental to every-day sports car motoring, and the MX-5 was certainly an improvement on the old Lotus Elan's, which shredded itself given half a chance. The MX-5's vinyl soft-top was easier to operate, gave good weather protection, and contributed to aerodynamic efficiency. As with the pre-

*Above: The original MX-5 was a founder member of the 1990s soft-top revival, and its classic lines were tweaked in 1998 to include faired-in headlights and a more mature shape, powered by 1.8-litre 16-valve twin-cam engines.*

*Above: The revamped dashboard of the MX-5 was upgraded in quality, yet remained traditional in layout. Revised suspension meant there was plenty of steering feedback, so the model was even more of a treat to drive.*

vious MX-5, a detachable hardtop was optional. The facelifted cars' soft-top was fitted with a heated glass rear window, and dual airbags and seat belts with pre-tensioners were standard. The one-piece moulded instrument panel housed the standard passenger-side SRS airbag in its upper section. The instrument cluster was deeply hooded and housed the speedo and rev counter, flanked by smaller, round fuel-level and coolant-temperature gauges. A four-spoke steering wheel with SRS airbag within the centre pad was standard, although the 1.8iS was fitted with a three spoke leather-rim Nardi wheel. Cockpit ergonomics were improved,

and a so-called retractable 'aero-board' was installed in the 1.8-litre cars to reduce the amount of air flowing from the rear of the car to the front floor during open air driving, which improved the efficiency of the heater.

### Specification (1.8iS)

**Engine:** in-line four-cylinder
**Bore** x **stroke:** 83 mm x 85 mm
**Capacity:** 1839 cc
**Suspension:** independent by double wishbones, coil springs, dampers and anti-roll bars
**Brakes:** discs all round, with ABS
Chassis: monocoque
**Body:** two-door two-seat roadster

# McLaren Cars

*Left: In the early 1990s the world saw a crop of extraordinarily fast supercars with top speeds over the 200-mph mark; the McLaren F1 promised to be the fastest and most spectacular of all.*

McLaren Cars was the brainchild of McLaren Formula 1 designer Gordon Murray. Murray had long had a desire to build the ultimate roadgoing supercar and by the late 1980s had had enough of the F1 world and decided the time was right. The company was launched on 17 March 1989 and soon hired a team of excellent designers and engineers, notably Peter Stevens, the designer of the modern Lotus Elan and the Jaguar XJR-15. With the right staff in place, the company took over Ferrari's Guildford Technical Office (discarded by Ferrari after parting company with their British-based designer John Barnard).

Work on the prototype, which was essentially a rolling test-bed rather than an indication of what the finished car would look like, began in June 1991 and the first car was unveiled at the Monaco Grand Prix in 1992, an appropriate venue to launch a model that according to Gordon Murray himself was "an entirely new starting point for supercars". Production began in 1993 and for the rest of the decade the F1 remained the fastest, most powerful and most expensive production car in the world.

## McLaren F1 1992-present

The F1 is a tour de force of supercar design. Expected to cost around £550,000 when production starts in 1993, it is powered by a 6.1-litre V12 engine specially commissioned from BMW, with individual ignition coils to each cylinder and variable valve timing for the 48 valves. The all-alloy engine is mid-mounted, driving the rear wheels through a transversely-mounted six-speed gearbox. Top speed is expected to be in the 250-mph region thanks to a combination of a weight of only 2,244 lb, a low coefficient of drag and a power output of 550 bhp at 7,000 rpm, not to mention a massive 442 lb ft of torque.

As you would expect from Formula 1 designers, great attention has been paid to the suspension and aerodynamics, and the F1 is the first road car to feature a flap on the rear used to control the movement of the car's Centre of Pressure under braking, thus avoiding the back of the car becoming light under heavy

braking. Murray had intended for the braking itself to be beyond compare, but had to discard the idea of carbonfibre brakes as road use would not get them hot enough to work.

*Right: The 0.34 Cd gull-wing bodywork and composite chassis are made from 94 components of Dyneema fibre. The driving position is absolutely central.*

### Specification (1992)

**Engine:** V12, quad-cam
**Bore × stroke:** 86 mm × 87 mm
**Capacity:** 6064 cc
**Maximum power:** 550 bhp
**Transmission:** six-speed manual
**Chassis:** Dyneema composite
**Suspension:** independent with double wishbones front and rear
**Brakes:** Brembo ventilated discs all round
**Bodywork:** composite material coupé with gull-wing doors and central driving position
**Maximum speed (approx):** 250 mph (402 km/h)

*Below: The race-bred F1 features ground-effects technology, a 550-bhp V12 and 250-mph performance.*

# Mercedes-Benz

**M**ercedes merged with Benz in 1926, to found the German concern which is now thought by many to build the best cars in the world. The three-pointed star emblem was a combination of previous Benz and Mercedes badges, and formed a proud link between one generation and the next.

Car assembly was soon concentrated in Stuttgart, in an increasingly-crowded downtown factory, although the modern Sindelfingen plant was originally only a coachbuilding facility in the 1930s.

Because of Germany's grave economic difficulties in the 1920s and 1930s Mercedes-Benz struggled to survive, and the company's premises were pulverised during World War II, but after 1945 the business expanded steadily, making many series of fine cars and becoming a technical leader in car design.

From the 1920s to the 1990s, Mercedes-Benz usually had one or more sporting cars – sometimes real supercars – on sale, but the vast majority of production has always been of saloon cars, many with smaller-capacity engines. Mercedes-Benz was the first company to offer diesel engines in private cars, establishing a tradition maintained to the present day. It was with only a mild trace of malice that the firm's products soon became known as Stuttgart taxis.

In the 1930s Mercedes-Benz produced cars like the superb 500/540K Cabriolets, and the massive Grosser flagships – to the world an expression of pomp, and a demonstration of effortless technical superiority. Total success in Grand Prix racing added to this reputation, as did the use of features such as all-independent suspension, and a dabble with rear- *and* mid-engined cars.

After 1945 the company slowly and methodically rebuilt its factories, its reputation and its model range. From the 1950s stunning supercars like the 300 SL, allied to another short but successful Grand Prix and racing sports car programme, added spice to the image. Although the company

*Above: The fast SSK, introduced in 1928, was propelled at speeds well over 100 mph by a massive 7.0-litre straight-six with twin-lobe Roots supercharger.*

was never flamboyant in its actions, it had high and low points – such as pioneering features like fuel injection and spaceframe chassis, yet clinging on to outmoded swing-axle rear suspension and drum brakes years after they had been proved obsolete.

For year after year, decade after decade, Mercedes-Benz's main business was in supplying saloons and coupés to the middle and upper classes, with styling and engineering changing only gradually, but there was usually a leavening of the range with sports cars, lavishly equipped roadsters, or outrageously powerful saloons (like the V8-engined 300 SEL 6.3 of the 1960s).

Although Mercedes-Benz produced superb and fast Wankel-engined prototypes in the 1960s and 1970s, it never put engines of that type into production. The main thrust has been to make its cars faster, safer, better equipped, more luxurious and ever more reliable. Because of large and profitable sales (more than 600,000 cars a year would be sold in the late 1980s), and with a thriving truck business, the company remained independent throughout the 1990s, taking over Chrysler in 1998. The ultra-compact A-Class model (1998) took the company into a brand new market.

*Left: Fast and superbly engineered, the 1990 300 SL-24 offered safe, sure handling and up to 134 mph from its three-litre, 24-valve six.*

*Right: The Mercedes-Benz emblem was a combination of Daimler's three-point star and the Benz circle of laurel leaves, symbolising victory.*

*Below: One of the company's most famous products was the 300 SL, available as Roadster and Gullwing coupé. The Roadster had a modified version of the coupé's spaceframe chassis and more sophisticated single-low-pivot rear suspension.*

# Mercedes 35HP and 60HP 1901-06

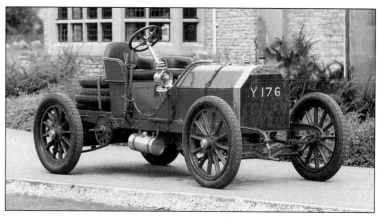

**Above: A splendid 1903 Mercedes 60HP open two-seater. Note the plentiful spare tyres at the rear.**

**Left: In 1908 German driver Christian Lautenschlager won the French GP in the 120HP Mercedes Rennwagen.**

The car which Emil Jellinek requested for use in the Nice Speed Week of 1901, changed the face of motoring, and was really the inspiration for all other Edwardian and Vintage sports cars. At a stroke its designers, led by Paul Daimler, invented the sports car, and helped found a sporting reputation for Mercedes which grew and grew over the coming years.

The first of the range, dubbed 35HP after its rated power output, was one of the first cars in the world to have a simple but rugged frame with channel-section side members, and another innovation was the mounting of the engine directly onto it, rather than to a subframe. Not only was the chassis, suspension and general stance much lower than before, but the engine was further back than was still considered normal.

The engine was a brand-new 6.0-litre water-cooled four-cylinder unit with overhead inlet and side exhaust valves which, by the standards of the day, was much more silent and smooth-running than its rivals. It was backed by a scroll clutch and a separate (mid-mounted) gearbox, which featured a built-in differential and countershaft. Final drive was by exposed chain.

The original car dominated the Nice Speed Week of March 1901, just as Jellinek had hoped it would, and it was not long before larger-engined and more powerful versions of the same basic design were also put on sale. The original 35HP car was joined by the 40HP racing car of 1902, and the sensational 60HP sports *and* racing car arrived in 1903, while the rather less successful 90HP and 120HP racing models followed in 1904 and 1905.

Not only was the 35HP a fast and thoroughly reliable car by any standards, but it was lighter and had better roadholding than any of its rivals. It was, in other words, a layout which set standards for other manufacturers to follow. Look around at most sports cars of the later 1900s, in Europe and in the USA, and you can see what effect the original Mercedes 35HP design had.

## Specification (1903 60HP)

**Engine:** inline four-cylinder, overhead inlet and side exhaust valves
**Bore × stroke:** 140 mm × 150 mm
**Capacity:** 9292 cc
**Maximum power:** 60 bhp
**Transmission:** four-speed manual gearbox, rear-wheel drive
**Chassis:** separate steel frame with channel-section main members and tubular cross-bracing
**Suspension:** non-independent with beam front axle and semi-elliptic leaf springs; live rear axle with semi-elliptic leaf springs – no shock absorbers
**Brakes:** drums on transmission shaft, and at rear
**Bodywork:** aluminium two- or four-seater open tourer
**Maximum speed (approx):** 65 mph (105 km/h)

**Below: This 1903 Mercedes 60HP has more bodywork than the roadster above. The model featured mudguards, space for rear passengers and baskets for luggage. The engine was efficient for the time, and power was delivered to the rear wheels through a spring-operated clutch and a countershaft which turned the two chain sprockets.**

## Mercedes 24/100/140 1924-26

Until Dr Ferdinand Porsche took charge of the technical team at Stuttgart in 1922, most of Mercedes' road car efforts had gone into updating the pre-1914 models, building smaller-engined touring cars, or getting back into motor racing.

Porsche then settled down and inspired the birth of a magnificent new sports car, the 24/100/140, with a new chassis, a six-cylinder overhead-camshaft engine, and an aggressive new style which would be continued, little changed, for the next 10 years. Like the famous 'W. O.' Bentley cars, these truly splendid models typified the glorious era of the Vintage sports car.

As with the Vintage Bentleys, too, the two main attractions of these cars were their engines and their style, for the chassis engineering was basic, and the brakes could not match the performance. The engines had single-overhead-camshaft valve gear, which was very advanced for the period. The engines usually operated as normally-aspirated units, but there was a supercharger at the front of the engine which could be clutched into mesh by pushing the throttle pedal to the very limits of its movement. This optional 'blower' feature was to be used on many Mercedes and Mercedes-Benz models in the next two decades.

The effect of the blower was quite dramatic, as the rather clumsy name of the car indicated. The 24 stood for the taxable horsepower, while 100 was the amount of power produced in normally-aspirated form, and the 140 was the out-

*Below: This supercharged 24/100/140 Mercedes of 1924 is notable for its particularly upright and imposing coachwork. Despite its bulk, when the blower was engaged the car was capable of reaching 90 mph. Note the opening windscreen and separate driver partition.*

put once the supercharger was clutched in briefly to give a short burst of power.

There were several body styles, some closed and some open, but all were rakish, at once bulky but sleek, and carried two quite unmistakeable features – the exhaust pipes which protruded from the side of the bonnet panels, and the 'V'-profile radiator block where the three-pointed Mercedes star was carried on both flanks of the top tank.

The cars were heavy, and the engines low-revving, but by any standards these were very rapid machines indeed. They were also very expensive, which explains why very few were built in this period of roaring inflation. However, once the merger between Mercedes and Benz had taken place in 1926, the design was further developed, and used in the S, SS and SSK models.

*Above: A 15/70/100 touring model of 1924, powered by the four-litre six; the car could be ordered with a normally-aspirated or a supercharged engine. The twin-lobe Roots supercharger became engaged when the throttle was fully depressed.*

### Mercedes 24/100/140 variants

#### Mercedes 15/70/100

In 1924 the sister model to this car was the 15/70/100 model, which had a smaller, 80-mm × 130-mm, 3920-cc/70-bhp (normally-aspirated) or 100-bhp (supercharged) engine.

All descendants of the original car used the same type of engine, with clutched-in supercharging, were badged Mercedes-Benz, and formed the K, S, SS, SSK and SSKL family.

### Specification (24/100/140)

**Engine:** inline six-cylinder, single overhead camshaft
**Bore × stroke:** 94 mm × 150 mm
**Capacity:** 6246 cc
**Maximum power:** 100 bhp
**Transmission:** four-speed manual gearbox, rear-wheel drive
**Chassis:** separate steel frame with channel-section main side members and tubular cross-bracing
**Suspension:** non-independent with beam front axle and semi-elliptic leaf springs; live rear axle with semi-elliptic leaf springs
**Brakes:** drums all round
**Bodywork:** steel or aluminium two-, four- or seven-seater, coachbuilt to choice
**Maximum speed (approx):** 90 mph (145 km/h)

# Mercedes-Benz 30/150/200 Grosser and 770 Grosser 1930-40

*Left: Adolf Hitler was fond of the Grosser, which epitomised the might and arrogance of 1930s Nazi Germany. Here he is being driven past troops for the opening of the Frankfurt–Darmstadt autobahn, in a special open tourer version.*

Naturally the cars were very large and heavy – around 216 inches long and weighing nearly 6,000 lb even *before* the passengers got on board – which explains why the brakes were power-assisted. Almost all these cars were chauffeur-driven, and as there was no such thing as power-assisted steering at that time, the chauffeurs had to be as imposing as the car itself.

To replace the original and outmoded Grosser model, which had become technically obsolete by the late 1930s, Mercedes-Benz introduced a glossy new type in 1938. Like the original, the latest Type 770 Grosser was an enormous and heavy car meant for ceremonial use. Production was strictly limited, and at the prices asked, sales were always tiny.

This sort of car usually sold on its looks, but the new Grosser was technically interesting too. The style was massive, rounded, self-important and somehow florid, so it was no wonder that the majority of deliveries went to Adolf Hitler, Hermann Goering, and the rest of the Nazi leadership. It was this creepy political connection, rather than any other, which tainted the reputation of Mercedes-Benz at this time.

Under the skin of these huge cars, whose wheelbase was nearly 156 inches, and which weighed between 7,600 and 8,100 lb, was a tubular chassis with independent front and de Dion rear suspension, all of which owed much to the latest Mercedes-Benz Grand Prix layouts, while the engine was a more highly-developed version of the optionally-supercharged straight-eight of the original Grosser.

For the latest car, Mercedes-Benz produced a five-speed gearbox (making this the first such application in a road-going car, as opposed to a racing car), and issued firm instructions to limit the use of the supercharger to not more than one continuous minute at a time. Fuel consumption was reputed to fall to below 5 mpg at times.

As most of the cars were fitted with armour-plated bodywork and bullet-proof glass, they were incredibly heavy, and must have been extremely hard work to drive. In every case, of course, the owners sat in the rear seats, while the chauffeur developed his arm and leg muscles.

In this case, Grosser was an absolutely apt title for a car that was over-the-top in every respect. It is no surprise that only 88 were built. Most of the surviving cars change hands for high prices, especially if they can be proved to have a Nazi party connection and been ridden in by the likes of Himmler or Goebbels.

## Specification (1930 30/150/200 Grosser)

**Engine:** inline eight-cylinder, overhead-valve
**Bore × stroke:** 95 mm × 135 mm
**Capacity:** 7655 cc
**Maximum power:** 150 bhp (normally-aspirated) or 200 bhp (supercharged)
**Transmission:** four-speed manual gearbox or six-speed Maybach pre-selector transmission, rear-wheel drive
**Chassis:** separate steel frame with channel-section main side members
**Suspension:** non-independent with beam front axle and semi-elliptic leaf springs; live rear axle with semi-elliptic leaf springs
**Brakes:** drums all round
**Bodywork:** steel four-door five/seven-seater saloon or cabriolet
**Maximum speed (approx):** 100 mph (161 km/h)

In spite of the Depression that had already exploded in the USA, and was about to hit Europe, Mercedes-Benz completed development of a massive new flagship model, launching it as the 30/150/200 Grosser. This was meant to be nothing less than the grandest, the most powerful and (almost by definition) one of the most expensive cars produced anywhere in the world.

It was also very exclusive, for the new straight-line eight-cylinder engine was machined in the tool rooms, and every aspect of the car was hand-built. The

*Below: Outsize in all dimensions, this 1939 Grosser had a factory limousine body and weighed around 8,000 lb. The Nazi leaders (and dictators such as Salazar in Portugal) were very drawn to a car which exuded so much presence, and which reflected the power politics of the day.*

Grosser, as you might expect, was built to order, and in seven years only 117 – mainly saloons or limousines – were produced. Customers included ex-Kaiser Wilhelm II – and Emperor Hirohito of Japan, who bought seven cars, keeping some of them until the 1960s. Until the *next*-generation Grosser arrived at the end of the 1930s, this was also the car chosen by Adolf Hitler and his acolytes for their ceremonial transport.

In this sort of car the coachwork and the style were more important than the technical details, which probably explains why there was nothing unique about the chassis, and why the special new engine was vast, heavy, old-fashioned and ordinary (apart from the 'optional' supercharging, which had been well proven on the early sports cars). The only real novelty was the availability of the six-speed pre-selector Maybach gearbox.

# Mercedes-Benz 540K 1936-40

In the 1930s, Mercedes-Benz completely changed the image of its cars, modernising them and thus broadening their appeal. Therefore, although the eight-cylinder supercharged 380K of 1933, and the more assertive 500K which followed a year later, were the spiritual and actual descendants of the massive 38/250 types, they were entirely different in concept.

The 38/250 had been the apotheosis of a splendidly-detailed Vintage car, while the new 540K family was appropriate to the 1930s. Comfort, refinement and (later) increasingly vulgar styling had taken the place of sheer red-blooded performance.

The new cars retained separate chassis construction, but these were much more rigid, and were distinguished by the use of coil-spring independent front *and* rear suspension, and they used hydraulic brakes. Instead of a vast overhead-cam six-cylinder engine, the new

cars used a newly-developed straight-eight (different from that of the contemporary Grosser model) which had simple overhead-valve operation, but used the now-traditional type of supercharging layout, where the Roots blower was mounted on the nose of the crankshaft, and only came into use when the throttle pedal was fully depressed.

In a mere three years the engine size, and its power, expanded considerably – from 3796 cc to 5401 cc, and from 120 bhp to 180 bhp. If World War II had not intervened, a larger, 5.8-litre-engined, Cabriolet would also have appeared, with a five-speed gearbox as used in the Grosser limousine.

All the cars were sold with a gloriously ornate series of open or closed coachwork, mainly built by Mercedes-Benz at Sindelfingen, but sometimes provided by outside coachbuilders. In many cases the cars had twin spare wheels, one

mounted on each side of the bonnet, and tucked into a recess in the flowing front.

In every way these were the grandest of Grand Tourers, ideal for swishing along the new and ever-expanding network of dual-carriageway autobahns, and no-one seemed to care that the swing-axle rear suspension sometimes provided perilous handling characteristics. It was the image, and the sensation, rather than the handling, which sold cars of this type.

## Mercedes-Benz 540K variants

### Mercedes-Benz 380K

The originator of this family was the 380K sports model of 1933-34, which had a 78-mm × 100-mm, 3822-cc engine that produced 90 bhp (unblown) or 120 bhp (supercharged).

### Mercedes-Benz 500K

The successor to the 380K was the 500K of 1934-36. This was basically the same car, but with an enlarged and more powerful engine of 86 mm × 108 mm and 5018 cc, which produced 100 bhp/160 bhp. The top speed was at least 100 mph. The 540K took over from the 500K in 1936.

*Above: A classic 500K sedanca of 1936, which offered 100-mph performance with its five-litre, six-cylinder supercharged engine, and excellent handling thanks to all-independent suspension. Most of the bodies for these cars were designed and built at the factory; a few were made by outside coachbuilders.*

## Specification (1936 540K)

**Engine:** inline eight-cylinder, overhead-valve
**Bore × stroke:** 88 mm × 111 mm
**Capacity:** 5401 cc
**Maximum power:** 115 bhp (normally-aspirated) or 180 bhp (supercharged)
**Transmission:** four-speed manual gearbox, rear-wheel drive
**Chassis:** separate steel frame with box section main and cross-bracing members
**Suspension:** independent with wishbones and coil springs front; swing-axles and double coil springs per side at rear
**Brakes:** drums all round
**Bodywork:** steel two- or four-seater sports, cabriolet or coupé
**Maximum speed (approx):** 105 mph (169 km/h)

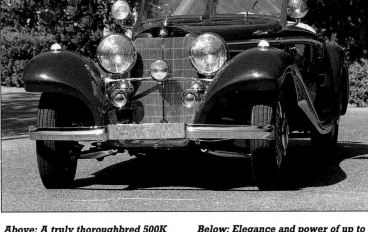

*Above: A truly thoroughbred 500K drop-head, built in 1936. Note the split windscreen and side lights.*

*Below: Elegance and power of up to 180 bhp combined in the shape of the 1936 540K short-wheelbase Roadster.*

# Mercedes-Benz 300 SL Gullwing 1954-63

Mercedes-Benz had not gone on to sell 258 examples of the 300 SL in nine years, it would have been easy to dismiss the design as a magnificent folly, for the engineering was self-indulgent to a degree, it was very expensive, and it cannot possibly have been a profitable project.

On the other hand, there is no question that the 300 SL was the most advanced supercar of its day, one of the fastest and certainly one which sold better than any of its rivals. It was also an unforgettable machine, in style, in layout, and in performance, so in some respects it did a great job for Mercedes-Benz.

The story began in 1951 when Mercedes-Benz, which was recovering rapidly from the ravages of war, decided to get back into motorsport. The object was always to re-enter Grand Prix racing, but the first programme was for racing-sports cars. These used developed versions of the new 300 Saloon model's powertrain, but the sophisticated chassis drew on recent aeroplane construction practice.

The new chassis was a spaceframe, a complex three-dimensional structure in

*Right: The Mercedes SL range was broadened in 1957 with the introduction of the Roadster.*

which there was a mass of small-diameter tubes connecting the major stress points. All the tubes were in tension or compression, but none of them was in torsion or bending. The trade-off was light weight against complexity, or mechanical 'purity' against easy access to the machinery.

To cover this, the company designed a novel body shell. Because the sides of the spaceframe chassis were very high, conventional door openings were not possible. The result was that upward-opening doors were fitted, and because of their shape and articulation these soon became known as 'gull-wing' types.

The 1952 race cars were so successful that the USA distributor for Mercedes-Benz (Max Hoffman) persuaded the company to sell a roadgoing version, stating that he would take 1,000 such cars to sell. This was enough to tip the balance. The productionised version had a fuel-injected version of the engine (which was canted over to help lower the

bonnet line), and the performance was well up to Ferrari standards, though no tester ever achieved the 165 mph top speed which was claimed by the manufacturers.

From 1954 to 1957, Mercedes-Benz built and sold 1,400 Gullwings, all of which had tricky handling because of the use of high-pivot swing-axle rear suspension, and had rather marginal brakes. Even though the cars looked fragile, they proved to be astonishingly durable, as a spate of race and rally victories later proved.

## Mercedes-Benz 300 SL Gullwing variants

### Mercedes-Benz 300, 300 S and 300 Sc

All the major powertrain components – engine, gearbox and final drive unit – of the 300 SL were developed and modified versions of those used in the 300, 300 S and 300 Sc touring cars, although the chassis and body styles were unique to this car.

### Mercedes-Benz 300 SL Roadster

The Mercedes-Benz 300 SL Roadster was introduced in 1957. That had a

modified chassis which allowed the use of conventional front-opening doors. As its name suggests, the car was a convertible, which increased its appeal, as did the presence of an improved 'low-pivot' form of the swing-axle rear suspension which made the car far better-behaved at the cornering limit. The last cars had the advantage of disc brakes.

## Specification (1954 300 SL Gullwing)

**Engine:** inline six-cylinder, overhead-camshaft
**Bore × stroke:** 85 mm × 88 mm
**Capacity:** 2996 cc
**Maximum power:** 215 bhp
**Transmission:** four-speed manual gearbox, rear-wheel drive
**Chassis:** separate steel multi-tubular spaceframe with a multitude of bracing members
**Suspension:** independent with wishbones and coil springs front; swing-axles and coil springs rear
**Brakes:** drums all round
**Bodywork:** aluminium two-seater coupé with gull-wing doors
**Maximum speed (approx):** 150 mph (241 km/h)

*Above: The Roadster's bodywork looked similar, but did not have the coupé's torsional strength.*

*Below: The high-sill, gull-wing doors were functional, and allowed the use of a very strong chassis.*

## Mercedes-Benz 230 SL 1963-71

In 1963 Mercedes-Benz retreated, and made an advance, at one and the same time. The company abandoned the exotic but slow-selling 300 SL, and only partly replaced it with the cheaper, slower, and simpler, and altogether more mass-produced Type W113 230 SL type.

The 230 SL was successor (hardly a replacement) for two cars – the 190 SL and the 300 SL – but was an entirely different type of car from the 300 SL. Not only was it slower, and simpler, but it was more plush, more 'touring', better built and intrinsically easier to maintain.

The new car had individual and very pleasing styling, complete with 300 SL Roadster-type vertical headlamp/side-lamp units at the front, and an optional lift-off hard top with an odd 'pagoda-roof' cross-section, all based on a unitary construction body/chassis which had evolved from that of the underpan, suspensions and powertrain of the W111 'fin-tail' S-Class saloons.

Despite its low-pivot swing-axle independent rear suspension, the new sports model handled remarkably well. It was considerably more refined than any previous sporting Mercedes-Benz, and it went on to be an enormous commercial success.

In eight years the range evolved into three different models, each of which had its own version of the fuel-injected six-cylinder single-overhead-cam engine (which was under constant development by Mercedes), and as ever the clue to engine size was in the model name itself.

The original 230 SL had a four-bearing 2306-cc unit, and was on sale from 1963 to 1966. For 1967 only, it was replaced by the 250 SL, complete with a 2496-cc engine, the same powerplant as that fitted to the contemporary S-Class saloons, with a seven-bearing crankshaft for greater refinement and more silent running. By this time four-wheel disc brakes had been standardised.

The last derivative was the 280 SL of 1968-71; this had a 2778-cc version of the same engine. Through all these changes, however, Mercedes-Benz never altered the style, or the fascia layout, so a 1963 230 SL looked almost identical to the late-model 280 SL.

Those who complain that this family was not *real* sports car material should be reminded that the 230 SL was entered for the toughest of all rallies – Spa–Sofia–

*Above: The 230 SL handled well, and this 1968 drop-head had a roll-over hoop for race use.*

Liège – in 1963 where, driven by Eugen Bohringer, it won outright. A year later the same combination took second place. After such performances, its sporting pedigree was unquestioned.

In 1971 this W113 family was replaced by a new generation of sporting Mercedes-Benz models, the V8-engined W107 range. All in all, production totalled 19,831 230 SLs, only 5,196 250 SLs and 23,885 280 SLs – a total eight-year run of 48,912 cars.

## Mercedes-Benz 230 SL variants

### Mercedes-Benz 250 SL

The 250 SL took over from the original 230 SL for 1967 and a few weeks of 1968. This car had an 82-mm bore × 78.8-mm stroke, 2496-cc/150-bhp engine. Disc brakes were fitted at front and rear. The top speed had been increased to 124 mph.

### Mercedes-Benz 280 SL

The final derivative of the design was the 280 SL, built from 1968 to 1971, which had an 86.5-mm bore × 78.8-mm stroke, 2778-cc/170-bhp version of the six-cylinder engine.

*Below: A 280 SL automatic of 1970; it was faster but looked identical to the 230 and 250 SLs.*

### Specification (1963 230 SL)

**Engine:** inline six-cylinder, single overhead camshaft
**Bore × stroke:** 82 mm × 72.8 mm
**Capacity:** 2306 cc
**Maximum power:** 150 bhp
**Transmission:** four-speed manual gearbox (five-speed manual transmission optional from 1966) or optional four-speed automatic transmission, rear-wheel drive
**Chassis:** steel unitary construction
**Suspension:** independent with wishbones and coil springs front; swing-axles and coil springs rear
**Brakes:** discs front, drums rear
**Bodywork:** steel 2 + 2 roadster with optional lift-off hard top
**Maximum speed (approx):** 121 mph (195 km/h)

*Below: A 1966 230 SL. The styling of the sports models was derived from that of the saloon cars but, while retaining the clean, understated lines, was subtly lighter in mood.*

## Mercedes-Benz 600 1963-81

y the early 1960s Mercedes-Benz had ot only rebuilt its factories, its reputaon, and its model range, but it felt ready nd able to indulge in the design of yet nother prestige model, effectively a escendant of the 1930s-type Grosser odels. The result, launched in 1963, was e massive 600 limousine.

Not only was this the largest and most ophisticated Mercedes-Benz car yet esigned, but it was also meant to be ore than a match for contemporary olls-Royces and Cadillacs. In short, lercedes-Benz wanted it to be the best ar in the world.

The Type 600 was new from end to nd – with an angular but impressive uniry construction body/chassis, a new 8 engine, and all-independent suspenon by pneumatic springs, with self-evelling. Naturally, automatic transmison was standard, there were disc rakes all round, and there was a mass of lectro-hydraulic equipment controlling verything from door locks to seat djustment.

The smallest version (although small is eally a misnomer in this case) was 218 ches long, and weighed 5,445 lb. Even this form the car could carry two eople up front, and five in the rear comartment, and the top speed was at least 0 mph. The larger version had a huge 3.5-in wheelbase, an overall length of 6 inches (over 20 feet), and weighed arly 6,000 lb. Some versions even had

six passenger doors, and it was sometimes said that companies didn't need a boardroom, but could have meetings inside the chairman's limousine instead!

A few, a very few, of these cars were produced as state landaulettes, in which the rear of the steel roof was removed, to be replaced by a folding frame which could then be folded back to allow distinguished occupants to be seen by the public.

The Type 600 was never a strong seller, nor was it ever intended to be so, but it was a wonderful flagship for the company, and of course for West Germany. However, although it sold very well to various Middle East, African and South American heads of state, it never achieved the sheer prestige of a Rolls-Royce.

Annual production peaked at 408 in 1965, but fell away rapidly in the 1970s, by which time the 600 was only being built to special order. In 1973 sales were a mere 82 cars, and after the 'energy crisis' they fell away rapidly to around 40 or 50 a year.

The last 20 cars of all were produced in 1981, by which time 2,190 'ordinary' 600s, 428 long-wheelbase Pullmans and 59 Landaulettes had been built – a grand total of 2,677 600s of all types.

The 600 was never replaced, although the massive V8 engine was later used in two different cars – the 300 SEL 6.3 and the 450 SEL 6.9 sports saloons.

## Specification (1963)

**Engine:** V8, single overhead camshaft per bank of cylinders
**Bore × stroke:** 103 mm × 95 mm
**Capacity:** 6332 cc
**Maximum power:** 250 bhp
**Transmission:** four-speed automatic transmission, rear-wheel drive
**Chassis:** steel unitary construction, two wheelbase lengths
**Suspension:** independent with pneumatic springs and self-levelling front and rear

**Brakes:** discs all round
**Bodywork:** steel five/seven-seater four-door or six-door limousine or landaulette
**Maximum speed (approx):** 130 mph (209 km/h)

*Below: This extremely capacious 1970 Mercedes-Benz 600 stretched limousine was the sort of vehicle in which it was said companies could hold their board meetings. Even in this form the huge 250-bhp car could reach 120 mph with ease.*

# Mercedes-Benz 300 SEL 6.3 1967-72

Perhaps the most exciting, and unexpected, Mercedes-Benz model of the 1960s was the incredible sports saloon which some people called the 'Waxenberger Express' – the 300 SEL 6.3. Erich Waxenberger was the development chief at Mercedes-Benz at the time, and this was something of a personal venture, a model dear to his heart.

By any standards it was a miraculous 'quart into pint pot' achievement, the massive 6.3-litre V8 engine of the Type 600 model being squeezed into the engine bay of a standard six-cylinder 300 SEL. No-one had ever thought that such a transplant would be possible, but it was in fact achieved with the minimum of aggravation.

When this car was introduced in 1967 there had been no pre-launch leaks (Waxenberger had reputedly built the first car himself), so even the German media was astonished. Such was the admiration with which it was received that one German paper then published a cartoon showing Waxenberger struggling away to force a World War II 2,000-bhp Daimler-Benz V12 aero engine into a Mercedes-Benz car, the caption stating: "Grunt . . . it's *got* to go in . . .".

In every way the 300 SEL 6.3 was a classic 'Q-Car', for apart from the use of twinned circular headlamps, one atop the other (instead of the habitual Mercedes-Benz oval units), and the wider wheels and tyres, it was almost impossible to distinguish it from the straight-six model on the road. As you might expect from Mercedes-Benz, it was a totally refined and reliable package, a veritable magic carpet which could be swished rapidly up to 130 mph and beyond.

This monster was a member of the S-Class range which spanned 1965 to 1972, and one which embraced six-cylinder and small V8 engines of 130 bhp to 200 bhp. All were based on the same four-door style, but the 'L' in various model titles stood for 'long wheelbase'. The 300 SEL 6.3, therefore, combined the longer-wheelbase shell, the pneumatic (air-spring) suspension of the 300 SEL, and the massive 250-bhp 6.3-litre engine and matching four-speed automatic transmission of the Type 600 limousine.

It all melded remarkably easily, and worked well, the result being a docile, easy-to-drive, executive package which nevertheless had a top speed of 134 mph. *Road & Track* magazine described it as "merely the greatest sedan in the world", and a total of 6,256 buyers obviously agreed with that verdict.

The 300 SEL 6.3 was not, nor did it ever become, a competition car. However, it *did* give rise to a successor in the next-generation S-Class range – the 450 SEL 6.9.

*Above: It looked almost identical to the standard three-litre 300 SEL, but the twin circular headlamps reveal that this saloon had the tremendous power of the 6.3-litre, 250-bhp V8 shoehorned under the bonnet. It proved a refined but very potent package.*

### Specification (1967)

**Engine:** V8, single overhead camshaft per bank of cylinders
**Bore × stroke:** 103 mm × 95 mm
**Capacity:** 6332 cc
**Maximum power:** 250 bhp
**Transmission:** four-speed automatic transmission, rear-wheel drive
**Chassis:** steel unitary construction body/chassis
**Suspension:** independent with pneumatic springs and self-levelling front and rear
**Brakes:** discs all round
**Bodywork:** steel four-door five-seater saloon
**Maximum speed (approx):** 134 mph (216 km/h)

*Left: The powerplant of the 'Waxenberger Express' was the mighty petrol-injected 6.3-litre V8 from the limousine range. It fitted, just, into a bay designed for a three-litre straight-six.*

*Below: The styling of the 300 range was conservative, clean and harmonious. Virtually identical to its lesser-engined brethren, the 'L' designation on this 300 SEL 6.3 indicated 'long wheelbase'.*

# Mercedes-Benz 350 SL 1971-89

*Left: Fast and effortless to drive, this 500 SL, which looked identical to the 350 SL, was powered by a 4973-cc V8 and had a four-speed automatic gearbox as standard. Maximum speed was 140 mph.*

The 350 SL was the first of what was known in-house at Mercedes as the W107 range, which enjoyed a life of nearly two decades. By any standards, the W107 – which was built as an open roadster, a roadster with a detachable hard top, or a longer-wheelbase fixed-head coupé – was an enormous success for Mercedes-Benz. Over the years, the spread of power was surprisingly limited – from 185 bhp to 240 bhp – although the smallest engine used was a 2.8-litre 'six' and the largest a 5.6-litre V8 for the US market only.

The new Type W107 was a direct replacement for the old 230 SL/250 SL/280 SL Type W113 family. When the new range was launched in 1971, it appeared in both Roadster and SLC Coupé form, sharing just one engine, the modern 3.5-litre V8, but that rapidly became more complex as the years passed. The main influences were the 'energy crisis' of 1973 which led to the rapid development of smaller-engined, more fuel-efficient six-cylinder versions, the USA exhaust-emission regulations (which caused Mercedes-Benz to enlarge the V8 engines to maintain their power output), and the use of larger-capacity, lighter-weight V8s in the 1980s.

Through all this, the basic design never changed. Under the unitary construction body the front and rear suspensions were lifted directly from the middle-size/middle-class 'New Genera-tion' W114/W115 saloons, the engines coming from the corporate parts-bin – the V8 from the modern S-Class saloon, and the various six-cylinder units from the New Generation and S-Class types.

Although the new SLs were definitely sporting – and in some cases were also extremely fast cars – the V8 models were always sold with automatic transmission as a no-cost option (it was standard on the 4.5-, 5.0- and 5.6-litre cars), and that was always a big seller, even in the six-cylinder cars.

Compared with the ousted 230/250/280 SL models, the new 350 SL looked larger (which it was), more muscular, and alto-gether less dainty, though power-assisted steering, power brakes, and carefully-developed controls all helped to make the car exceptionally easy to drive. Even in open, hood-down, condition, customers found the efficient air conditioning a great boon.

Like the previous SLs, this incredibly successful range earned a slightly unfair reputation for lacking real sports car appeal, but that was due to its clientele, who bought prestige rather than performance.

The first major update came in 1974, when the six-cylinder 280 SL appeared. The next came in 1981, when the 350/450 SL gave way to the aluminium-engined 380 SL and 500 SL, and there was a further reshuffle in 1985 when the 280 SL gave way to the 300 SL, and the 380 SL bowed out in favour of the 420 SL. All these changes were made to reflect the advances in engine design made for the Mercedes-Benz saloons, and also to look after the USA market, which was very important indeed to the Stuttgart-based concern.

The last of these cars was finally built in 1989 (18 years after launch), when the new-generation 300/500 SL model took over. Production of SL and SLC types had been in the 15,000 to 20,000 bracket for every one of those years – which meant that over 300,000 cars were produced in all.

## Mercedes-Benz 350 SL variants

### Mercedes-Benz 380 SL

The 380 SL (1980-85) was powered by a 92-mm bore × 71.8-mm stroke, 3818-cc/218-bhp V8 with either a five-speed manual or four-speed automatic transmission. Claimed maximum speed was 127 mph.

### Mercedes-Benz 420 SL

This derivative (1985-89) had a larger 92-mm bore × 78.9-mm stroke, 4196-cc V8 engine producing 218 bhp, linked again with a five-speed manual or four-speed automatic transmission. Claimed top speed was 127 mph.

### Mercedes-Benz 450 SL

Originally called the 350 SL 4.5, this car (1971-80) featured a 92-mm bore × 85-mm stroke, 4520-cc unit producing 225 bhp (later 218 bhp). Only a three-speed, and later four-speed, automatic transmission was available. Top speed was approximately 130 mph.

*Below: The 350 SL was a fast car which handled extremely well, but most owners preferred to drive in a sedate, unstressed manner.*

### Mercedes-Benz 500 SL

This variant (1980-89) was powered by a V8 of 96.5-mm bore × 85-mm stroke, with a displacement of 4973 cc producing 240 bhp. Only a four-speed automatic transmission was available. Top speed was 140 mph.

### Mercedes-Benz 560 SL

Intended for sale in the USA only, the 560 SL (1985-89) had a 96.5-mm × 94.8-mm, 5547-cc/230-bhp V8 engine. A four-speed automatic transmission was offered and claimed top speed was 134 mph.

### Mercedes-Benz 280 SL

This version (1974-85) had a twin-cam 2746-cc/185-bhp six-cylinder engine (rather than a V8) of 86-mm bore × 78.8-mm stroke. Maximum speed was 124 mph.

### Mercedes-Benz 300 SL

With a larger 88.5-mm bore × 82.2-mm stroke, 2962-cc/190-bhp single-overhead-cam six, this model (1985-89) came with either a five-speed manual or four-speed automatic transmission. Claimed top speed was 124 mph, no greater than the slightly smaller-engined 280 SL, but the extra displacement and torque increased its acceleration potential.

## Specification (1971 350 SL)

**Engine:** V8, single overhead camshaft per bank of cylinders
**Bore × stroke:** 92 mm × 65.8 mm
**Capacity:** 3499 cc
**Maximum power:** 200 bhp
**Transmission:** four-speed or five-speed manual gearbox or optional four-speed automatic transmission, rear-wheel drive
**Chassis:** steel unitary construction body/chassis
**Suspension:** independent with wishbones and coil springs front; semi-trailing arms with coil springs rear
**Brakes:** discs all round
**Bodywork:** steel two-seater tourer/cabriolet, with optional lift-off hard top
**Maximum speed (approx):** 126 mph (203 km/h)

## Mercedes-Benz 450 SLC 1971-81

The SLC models were mechanically identical to the two-seater SLs, but had considerably longer wheelbases, by 14 inches. The 'C' part of the title meant Coupé, for these cars all had fixed-head coupé bodywork, allied to more head room, longer doors, and two perfectly viable, if none too roomy, rear seats.

The Mercedes-Benz models of the 1970s had countless improvements in strength, safety and handling, and in 1973 the 450 Series was voted Car of the Year.

The tables show that many of the multifarious engine and transmission options of the enormous SL range were also offered for the SLCs. Although the SLCs were a little heavier than the two-seaters – by around a surprisingly low 110 lb – this did little to affect the performance.

The most interesting version of all the SLC types was the 450 SLC 5.0, another Waxenberger Special developed with motorsport (or higher performance, at least) in mind. Compared with the normal 4.5-litre car, this had aluminium bonnet and boot lid panels, extra spoilers at

front and rear, and a five-litre V8 engine with an aluminium cylinder block which was 95 lb lighter than standard.

This was the car used by the Mercedes works team to win the Round South America Marathon of 1978, the Bandama Rally of 1979, and other events, before the company made an abrupt withdrawal from the sport at the end of the 1980 season. That was a shame as Bjorn Waldegaard had shown what the 450 SLC could achieve. It was tough enough to withstand the pounding of the Ivory Coast and Safari Rallies and help earn Waldegaard the World Championship, but Mercedes feared that, having recruited Walter Rohrl for 1980, expectations would be too high for the car.

A few 'productionised' versions of this model – called the 500 SLC – were made in 1981, but the last of all the SLCs was built at the end of that year. As with the short-wheelbase types, production was very large indeed, large enough that there is no likelihood of these machines ever becoming rare collectors' items.

*Above: A late-production 450 SLC. From the front, the coupé was identical in styling to the SL models, but the longer wheelbase allowed useful seating space for two rear passengers. Depending on engine size, maximum speed was between 130 and 140 mph.*

### Mercedes-Benz 450 SLC variants

#### Mercedes-Benz 350 SLC
The 350 SLC (1972-80) had a V8 engine with a 92-mm bore × 65.8-mm stroke, 3499-cc displacement and 200 bhp. Claimed maximum speed was 130 mph.

#### Mercedes-Benz 450 SLC 5.0
This version (1978-81) was powered by a larger V8 of 97-mm bore × 85-mm stroke, 5025-cc displacement and 240 bhp. Top speed was 140 mph.

#### Mercedes-Benz 500 SLC
This was a short-lived derivative (1980-81) with a V8 engine of 96.5-mm bore × 85-mm stroke, 4973-cc displacement and 240 bhp. Claimed maximum speed was 140 mph.

#### Mercedes-Benz 280 SLC
This twin-cam-engined variant (1974-81) had a 86-mm bore × 78.8-mm stroke, 2746-cc six-cylinder producing 185 bhp. Top speed was 127 mph.

### Specification (1971 450 SLC)
**Engine:** V8, single overhead camshaft per bank of cylinders
**Bore × stroke:** 92 mm × 85 mm
**Capacity:** 4520 cc
**Maximum power:** 225 bhp
**Transmission:** four-speed (later three speed) automatic transmission, rear-wheel drive
**Chassis:** steel unitary construction
**Suspension:** independent with wishbones, coil springs and anti-roll bar front; semi-trailing arms and coil springs rear
**Brakes:** discs all round
**Bodywork:** steel 2+2-seater coupé
**Maximum speed (approx):** 136 mph (219 km/h)

*Above: This 1979 450 SLC, with its coupé styling, epitomised luxury and high performance.*

*Below: The SLC was long and low, and a curiosity of the design was the small louvred rear windows.*

# Mercedes-Benz 450 SEL 6.9 1975-80

Mercedes-Benz announced their new-generation (W116) S-Class saloons in 1972. These were bigger, faster, safer, more comprehensively equipped and altogether better cars than the old range which they replaced. Everyone assumed that there would be a version to supplant the fearsome old 300 SEL 6.3, and this car duly appeared in 1975, with an enlarged 00-type V8 engine.

As you would expect from Mercedes-Benz, almost every aspect of the new cars was different, improved, or merely better than that of the old, in line with the company's philosophy of providing the most comfortable, safest, best-built and most reliable machines possible.

The largest of the original mainstream range was the 450 SEL which, as you might expect from its title, had a 4.5-litre engine (the same V8 as used in the 450 SL roadster), and used the longer of two wheelbases developed for the new range. Smaller-capacity V8s and new-type 2.8-litre twin-cam sixes were also available. All these engines seemed to find their way into the SLs and SLCs of the period.

The 450 SEL 6.9, therefore, was a predictable flagship, which would undoubtedly have appeared earlier if the 'energy crisis' of 1973 had not erupted. Compared with other S-Class models, the new car had virtually no visual clues to its performance, except for a discreet chrome '6.9' badge on the boot lid.

The huge displacement of the nearly seven-litre engine was achieved by enlarging the bore of the biggest V8 from 103 mm to 107 mm, which took the engine capacity up to 6834 cc. At the same time, a special dry-sump lubrication system was also developed. The result was an engine which produced an absolutely effortless 286 bhp, and gave the car an easy 125-130 mph cruising speed.

The suspension on this car was completely hydro-pneumatic (rather like that used on big Citroëns), and was very different from that used under the old-type 300 SEL 6.3. As with the old car, of course, it was always extremely expensive (as much as £30,476 in 1979, when a Rolls-Royce Silver Shadow cost £34,421), so Mercedes-Benz had to work hard to sell 7,380 examples in five years.

*Above: The clean styling of the 450 SEL 6.9 has lasted well. From the front the car was totally identical to the 4520-cc model, but the 6.9 would reach 60 mph in 7.3 seconds, while the 4.5-litre took 9.1 seconds.*

*Left: Only a discreet rear badge identified the 6.9, but the power gained was a very expensive extra: in 1977 a standard 450 SEL cost £14,300, and the 450 SEL 6.9 £22,995. The difference was more than the price of a new 280E saloon.*

*Below: The 6.9-litre car's top speed was 140 mph, and the 4.5-litre's 134 mph. Average fuel consumption was 13.6 and 14.7 mpg respectively. The larger-engined car certainly accelerated quickly, but the price (close to a Rolls-Royce Silver Shadow) made it a slow seller.*

## Specification (1975)

**Engine:** V8, single overhead camshaft per bank of cylinders
**Bore × stroke:** 107 mm × 95 mm
**Capacity:** 6834 cc
**Maximum power:** 286 bhp
**Transmission:** three-speed automatic transmission, rear-wheel drive
**Chassis:** steel unitary construction body/chassis
**Suspension:** independent with hydro-pneumatic springs and self-levelling front and rear
**Brakes:** discs all round
**Bodywork:** steel five-seater saloon
**Maximum speed (approx):** 140 mph (225 km/h)

## Mercedes-Benz 190E 2.3-16 1983–95

*Above: A 1986 Mercedes-Benz 190E 2.3-16. Performance was phenomenal, thanks to the four-valve engine with a light-alloy, twin overhead-cam head developed and built by Cosworth.*

For many years Mercedes-Benz had looked with some envy at the way in which its rival, BMW, had developed a series of ultra-sporting saloons on the basis of less-specialised executive models; Mercedes-Benz had no in-house expertise of its own with which to produce similar results. Then, in 1980, a rally contract with Cosworth changed all that.

Having entered rallying with the 450 SLC 5.0 coupé, Mercedes-Benz then planned to produce a winning, limited-production, homologation special based on the new 190E saloon. Cosworth was hired to produce a 16-valve twin-overhead-cam version of the 190E's engine; the result was the first four-valves-per-cylinder engine to carry the Mercedes-Benz badge.

The directors then cancelled the rally project, which could well have killed off the Cosworth-designed engine. However, at this point Mercedes-Benz then decided to fight for a slice of the expanding 'BMW sports saloon' market. The result was the detuning of the engine, in a successful move to make it more refined and docile, and the launch of a new model with the long-winded title of 190E 2.3-16.

Visually, it appeared to be no more than a 190E four-door saloon, to which spoilers and side skirts had been added, but the chassis had been tightened up to help produce an agile and very pleasing sports saloon, which instantly began to sell well. In some ways this car had the character of a very much more expensive Sierra Cosworth, though because it lacked a turbocharger it was neither as fast nor as extrovert as that extraordinary machine. Indeed, because it retained so much of the normal 190's refinement, the 2.3-16 rarely felt or looked as fast as it

really was. The engine was fed by Bosch K-Jetronic fuel injection, and only when driven hard did engine noise become noticeable, mainly that of air induction during hard acceleration. The car's superb handling was gained, as always, at the expense of stiff suspension giving a rather hard ride.

In the late 1980s it was improved still further, with a larger and more torquey engine, and there was even a limited-production Evolution version produced purely with saloon car racing in mind.

The 1990s generation of new Mercedes-Benz models mostly used four-valves-per-cylinder heads which, though designed by Mercedes-Benz's own team of engineers, clearly leant on the original expertise provided by the British Cosworth company.

### Mercedes-Benz 190E 2.3-16 variants

#### Mercedes-Benz 190E 2.5-16
This version took over in 1988. The engine was basically the same, but with a longer stroke of 87.3 mm, giving 2498 cc and 197 bhp.

#### Mercedes-Benz 190E 2.5-16 Evolution
In 1989 there was also a 500-off 190E 2.5-16 Evolution model, with a slightly shorter-stroke 2490-cc engine, which could be tuned to produce up to 320 bhp in race-developed Group A guise. This car also had a larger front spoiler and other slight aerodynamic changes.

### Specification (1983 190E 2.3-16)
**Engine:** inline four-cylinder, twin overhead camshafts
**Bore × stroke:** 95.5 mm × 80.25 mm
**Capacity:** 2299 cc
**Maximum power:** 185 bhp
**Transmission:** five-speed manual gearbox, rear-wheel drive
**Chassis:** steel unitary construction body/chassis
**Suspension:** independent with wishbones, coil springs and anti-roll bar front; semi-trailing arms, coil springs and anti-roll bar rear
**Brakes:** discs all round
**Bodywork:** steel four-door five-seater saloon
**Maximum speed (approx):** 143 mph (230 km/h)

*Above: The standard 190E with 1.8-litre engine did not have the spoilers or skirts of the faster 190E 2.3-16.*

*Below: The five-seat saloon had real sports performance, yet gave an average fuel consumption of 25 mpg.*

# Mercedes-Benz 500 SL 1989–present

The original 350/450/500 SL family of luxury sports cabriolets sold so well that it remained on the market for 18 years, almost throughout the 1970s and 1980s. To replace it, Mercedes-Benz spent years developing an all-new model, one which was also expected to have a long show-room life.

The only thing the new and old types had in common was the basic layout. Both had open-topped unitary construction bodies, both were spacious two-seaters, and both had front-mounted six-cylinder or V8 engines which drove through automatic transmission (manual transmission was only available with six-cylinder engines) to the rear wheels.

The new SL family, though, was altogether more advanced, more sophisticated, and far more aerodynamically efficient than the older car. The V8 engine had been given twin overhead camshafts per bank, with four valves per cylinder, and variable inlet camshaft timing. Naturally, it was totally 'green' and there was a catalytic converter in the exhaust system.

Its safety features included a roll-over bar which was normally retracted, but which erected itself in a mere 0.3 seconds if its sensors detected sufficiently unusual movements. There was also an optional acceleration skid control which used ABS sensors as part of its mechanism. It was typical of Mercedes-Benz, too, that the erection or lowering of the soft top was completely power-operated, with no fewer than 15 hydraulic pressure cylinders, 11 solenoid valves and 17 micro-switches under the control of a micro-processor.

There were three different models in the new range when it went on sale in 1989, two of them having straight-six engines (one single-cam, one twin-cam with four valves per cylinder) and one having the light-alloy V8. Almost every car was equipped with automatic transmission (although there was a five-speed manual gearbox on the 24-valve six), and a high proportion had the optional heavy lift-off hard top.

One of the perennial problems with open-top motoring was wind buffeting, especially from behind; Mercedes-Benz solved that by including the option of a fine mesh net to fit over the raised roll-over bar, and that practically eliminated draughts. This, coupled with the very powerful heating and air-conditioning systems, ensured comfort in virtually all open-top conditions.

All versions were very heavy (the V8-engined types weighed 4,200 lb), very thirsty (as low as 16 mpg for the V8 car, and only 19 mpg on the 24-valve six), but they were also exceptionally capable. Mercedes-Benz took the view that virtually nothing was impossible, that anything could be included in the specification at a price, and there would always be some customers who would pay, which explains why all the marque's types were very expensive indeed.

On the other hand they were very fast, very stable, very well-equipped, very safe, and extremely well-built. It was no wonder that the major criticism directed at the new cars was that there was a waiting list to buy them.

## Mercedes-Benz 500 SL variants

### Mercedes-Benz 300 SL

At the same time as the V8 model was announced, the car was also made available with a choice of two six-cylinder engines. The 300 SL had a straight-six engine, with a single overhead camshaft, 88.5-mm bore × 80.2-mm stroke, a displacement of 2960 cc and 190 bhp. There was a choice of five-speed manual or four-speed automatic transmission, and the claimed maximum speed was 142 mph.

*Above: A 1990 300 SL-24, with a 231-bhp twin-cam engine. The automatic model had a top speed of 149 mph.*

*Below: The top of the range was the very fast and ultra-sophisticated 500 SL, powered by a quad-cam V8.*

### Mercedes-Benz 300 SL-24

The 300 SL-24 had the straight-six engine from the 300 SL but with twin overhead camshafts. Bore, stroke and displacement were unchanged, but power rose to 231 bhp. Transmissions were five-speed manual or four-speed automatic. Claimed top speed was 149 mph.

### Specification (1989 500 SL)

**Engine:** V8, twin overhead camshafts per bank of cylinders
**Bore × stroke:** 96.5 mm × 85 mm
**Capacity:** 4973 cc
**Maximum power:** 326 bhp
**Transmission:** four-speed automatic transmission (no manual gearbox option), rear-wheel drive
**Chassis:** steel unitary construction body/chassis
**Suspension:** independent with MacPherson struts and anti-roll bar front; multi-link system rear
**Brakes:** discs all round
**Bodywork:** steel two-seater cabriolet or coupé
**Maximum speed:** 157 mph (253 km/h)

*Below: A 300 SL-24. Extremely stylish from any angle, the SL was a subtle evolution from the earlier sports series, more wedge-shaped and curved. Technically it was very advanced and had been designed to offer optimum driving comfort in open, closed and hard-top form.*

## Mercedes-Benz 500E 1990-present

*Left: In the 500E saloon the five-litre V8 gave a 0-60 mph time of 6.3 seconds and an average of 16.5 mpg.*

To build on the appeal of the exciting 190E 2.5-16, complete with its Cosworth-developed engine, Mercedes-Benz then developed an altogether larger, more luxuriously equipped, heavier and faster machine for the 1990s, the 500E. The car was always destined to be built in limited numbers, and was assembled by Porsche rather than Mercedes-Benz at its own Stuttgart-Zuffenhausen factory.

In some ways the new 500E followed the great Waxenberger V8 engine transplant tradition of the 1960s – as represented by cars like the 300 SEL 6.3, or the 450 SEL 6.9 – this time by having the smaller type of V8 engine shoe-horned into the engine bay of the mid-sized W124 four-door saloon. The W124 range normally had inline engines of between 75 bhp and 220 bhp, so the use of a five-litre 326-bhp 32-valve V8 gave the 500E a completely different character. Although the bulky powerplant was an extremely snug fit in what was a small engine bay, the whole package was, as you might expect, immaculately presented and carefully detailed.

The 500E was a tremendously fast and luxurious five-seater saloon in the best Mercedes-Benz tradition, equally as fast as cars like the BMW M5, and just as well-engineered, refined, and reassuring as any other car in the Stuttgart company's massive range.

Externally it looked almost the same as any other middle-size W124 model, except that there were modest wheel-arch flares at front and rear, to accommodate wider wheels and tyres and the wider track. The fascia and instrument panel were as sober as expected, complete with a battery of switches and dials, and with air conditioning as standard.

The five-litre engine was in new-type 500 SL tune, and was matched to a four-speed automatic rather than any manual transmission. This, allied to ASR (Acceleration Skid Control), ABS, and every other safety feature which the engineers could pack into the space, not only ensured an extremely fast car, but one which was completely reassuring in every motoring condition.

It was not merely the car's ability to reach a rev-limited 159 mph, or to sprint to 100 mph from rest in 14.7 seconds which made it so very appealing. The late 1990s generation E class were smart, if not totally state-of-the-art, with the exception of the fast E55 version.

## Mercedes-Benz 500E variants

### Mercedes-Benz 400E
For 1992 Mercedes-Benz produced an appealing halfway-house between the colossally fast 500E and the 300E from which it was developed. Logically enough, this car was fitted with a 4196-cc/268-bhp V8 engine, and was called the 400E. The 400E did not have the flared wheel arches, nor the wider track, of the 500E, but could still reach 149 mph.

### Specification (1992 500E)
**Engine:** V8, twin overhead camshafts per bank of cylinders
**Bore × stroke:** 96.5 mm × 85 mm
**Capacity:** 4973 cc
**Maximum power:** 326 bhp
**Transmission:** four-speed automatic transmission (no manual gearbox option), rear-wheel drive
**Chassis:** steel unitary construction body/chassis
**Suspension:** independent with wishbones, coil springs and anti-roll bar front; semi-trailing arms, coil springs and anti-roll bar rear
**Brakes:** discs all round
**Bodywork:** steel four/five-seater saloon
**Maximum speed (approx):** 159 mph (256 km/h)

*Below: The interior was tasteful and comfortable in plastic and fine wood; leather seats were optional.*

*Below: Flared wheel arches allowed a front and rear track increase of 1.5 inches. With ASR and ABS systems, handling was progressive and safe.*

# Mercedes-Benz SLK 1996-present

With its supercharged engine and folding metal hardtop, the SLK was definitely a car for all seasons. While its 140 mph (225 km/h) top speed was by no means startling for a supercharged sports car, it could turn itself into a weatherproof coupé at the touch of a button. The letters SLK stand for 'sportlich' (sporty), 'leicht' (light) and 'kompact' (compact), with the suffix Kompressor for supercharger. The SLK 230 was powered by a 193 bhp supercharged 2.3-litre 16-valve four-cylinder unit, allied to electronically controlled five-speed automatic transmission with torque converter, while a normally aspirated 136 bhp 2.0-litre engine was also available in some markets.

Suspension was by double-wishbones at the front and a multi-link system at the rear, similar to the set-up used in the C- and E-class. Gas dampers and coil springs were positioned separately so as not to be subjected to any turning stresses. Despite relatively long spring travel at front and rear, the SLK suspension was significantly tauter than on the C-class saloon. ABS-backed ventilated disc brakes were derived from the E-class, augmented by 'Brake Assist', which shortened the stopping distance in critical situations. Having concluded that emergency braking is required, this system activated full brake pressure, virtually halving braking distance from 60 mph, (96 km/h) while the ABS ensured the wheels didn't lock up.

The most remarkable aspect about the SLK was its folding steel Vano roof, which was stowed in the boot and erected by pressing a button on the central console. It consisted of a double-skinned steel roof split into two across the width of the car, with both inner section and exterior panelling of the front half firmly linked and reinforced with a surrounding roof frame. A hydraulic pump in the boot controlled the opening and closing process by five hydraulic cylinders, two operated the Vano roof, two moved the boot lid and another locked the roof at the header rail, all completed in six co-ordinated phases. The bootlid was rear hinged so the roof sections had enough space to fold away, and once the roof was retracted, the boot lid moved forward again to lock on the wheel arches. It was front-hinged to open in the usual manner for loading.

The SLK was said to have the same rigidity and strength as that of a Mercedes saloon. A series of cross members in the front and rear areas of the bodywork and between the A-pillars reinforced the SLK's bodyshell – as well as confirming the maker's reputation for tank-like construction. A multi-part floor assembly with a centre tunnel and side members was made of thick sheet steel, while a bolted-in partition between the fuel tank and the boot was made from die-cast magnesium – half the weight of steel – and the first time Mercedes-Benz had used it as a construction material in standard production. Magnesium was also used in the engine compartment and the cylinder head covers, as was the cover behind the two roll-over bars. The SLK's impact protection was based largely on the Mercedes-Benz C- and E-class energy

*Above: The SLK was one of the most desirable vehicles in the late 1990s. Not only well-made, but with all-weather potential thanks to its unique roof design. The supercharger made it thirsty but it lacked power.*

*Above: At the first sign of inclement weather, SLK occupants could erect the steel Vano roof, operated by hydraulic cylinders in the boot via a button on the dashboard. This unclipped the roof, lowered it into the boot and closed the lid.*

absorption systems, and included a large front cross-member connecting the two side members. Passive safety also included full-size airbags for driver and front passenger, belt tensioners and belt force limiters and optional side airbags. Side impact beams were naturally included as standard. The SLK seats were similar to the C-and E-class, and included their own individual suspension system.

Other standard equipment included two roll-over bars, a draught-stop to fit behind the driver, power-assisted steering, adjustable steering column, air conditioning, electric windows and central locking. The SLK 230 Kompressor ran on 16-inch cast aluminium spoked wheels, and was equipped with a collapsible spare tyre, inflated by an electric air pump supplied with the car.

### Specification (SLK 230 Kompressor)

**Engine:** in-line four-cylinder, supercharged
**Bore x stroke:** 90.9 mm x 88.4 mm
**Capacity:** 2,295 cc
Suspension: independent front by double wishbones, multi-link rear, coil springs and dampers all round
**Brakes:** ventilated discs all round, with ABS and Brake Assist
**Chassis:** monocoque
**Body:** two-door, two seater with folding steel roof

# Mercer Automobile Company

H ere was a short-lived but interesting make of American car named, logically enough, after Mercer County, New Jersey, where the cars were made. It was not a long-lived marque, however, mainly because it was well away from the mainstream of USA's fast-growing motor industry in Detroit.

The thrusting tycoons behind the business were the Roebling family, who had already made their fortune by building New York's Brooklyn Bridge, but they had no previous motor industry experience, and all three of the founding members died before 1918 (one of them, tragically, in the *Titanic* disaster of 1912).

Several different designers were employed, and moved on, over a 15-year period. In the beginning, the specification of the cars was conventional by North American standards, but the marque's reputation was immediately made by the style of one car – the Type 35 Raceabout of 1911 – which had very little bodywork, a monocle windscreen, and a great deal of wind-in-the-hair performance. It was the sort of car which appealed to sporting motorists throughout the country.

The car had a 4926-cc 'T'-head engine, and publicity was gained for the marque by a factory-backed racing team which appeared in races across the country. In 1911 Mercers finished 12th and 14th in the Indianapolis International Sweepstakes. In 1912 the cars came first and second in the Kane County Trophy race at Elgin, Illinois, and then third in the Elgin Trophy race, running against much larger cars. Said Mercer afterwards: "Winning first and second at Elgin was like taking candy from a baby, but to land third overall for the stock car championship with a 300-cu in engine in the big race was some achievement."

Finlay R. Porter designed that first car, but the later Type 22 model (with a more conventional side-valve engine) which followed was drawn up by E. H. Delling, and the Series 4 and 5 types which arrived immediately after World War I were conceived by A. C. Shultz.

Even in the early 1920s, when North American buyers were turning more and more to mass-produced cars from Ford and General Motors, Mercer continued to build individual machines of great charm, but with expensive features (including fixed-cylinder-head engines), and with rather old-fashioned styles.

It was no wonder that the limited demand for the products eventually died away, and the company was never able to repeat its marketing success with anything resembling a descendant to the appealing Raceabout. Conventional Rochester-made overhead-valve engines were made available as an alternative to the antiquated side-valve types in the

*Above: The 1912 Type 35C Mercer Raceabout was designed with rugged, simple bodywork, to be as fast as possible. Such spartan cars were almost always bought by wealthy clients who also had other, more comfortable, cars.*

1920s, but this merely delayed the end.

Production never exceeded 500 units a year – this was tiny, even by the standards of the 1920s – and the last cars were sold in 1925.

The Elcar Motor Car Co. of Indiana attempted to revive the Mercer marque in 1931, using a powerful (140-bhp) straight-eight Continental engine, and claiming a top speed of 100 mph, but this project foundered after a mere two prototypes had been built.

*Below: The Mercer 35J was a stark but striking car, and, fitted with a four-cylinder five-litre 'T'-head side-valve Continental engine, offered thrilling performance along with surprisingly good handling.*

# Mercer Type 35J Raceabout 1911-14

was fitted with bodywork which not only had sides, but also a bench-type front seat. Conventional tourers were also on offer.

## Specification (1911 Type 35J)

**Engine:** inline four-cylinder, side-valve
**Bore × stroke:** 111.1 mm × 127 mm
**Capacity:** 4925 cc
**Maximum power:** 56 bhp
**Transmission:** three-speed manual gearbox, rear-wheel drive
**Chassis:** separate steel frame with channel-section main side members, and tubular and pressed cross-bracings
**Suspension:** non-independent with beam axle and semi-elliptic leaf springs front; live axle with semi-elliptic leaf springs rear
**Brakes:** drums on transmission, and at rear
**Bodywork:** steel open two-seater
**Maximum speed (approx):** 70 mph (113 km/h)

In its day Finlay Porter's stark and very purposeful-looking Raceabout was called the best sports car ever to be made in North America; considering the opposition, this was a remarkable claim. In every way, though, it looked the part.

In effect the Raceabout was an adaption of the original Type 30M Mercer racing car, and very few compromises were made when transforming it for road use. In so-called 'civilised' road car form the chassis carried little more than a radiator, bonnet, cowl and two stark bucket seats, with an exposed petrol tank and the spare wheel behind those seats. There were no doors – in fact there were no sides to the body at all, so the passengers' legs were always exposed.

The only weather protection was for the driver, who was provided with a magnificent but surely ineffective circular 'monocle' windscreen, which was clamped halfway up the steering column. The passenger received no protection of any type. There was no full-width screen, and no way of erecting any soft top – all of which added to the rough charm, and allowed the car to stand out from its rivals.

The engine was a rugged and proprietary four-cylinder side-valve 'T'-head unit from Beaver, built by Con-

tinental; by the standards of the day, it was powerful and high-revving (it peaked at 1,800 rpm). Because the whole car was light (it weighed a mere 2,300 lb) and ran on a very compact 108-in wheelbase, it was fast, even though the braking was rudimentary, with a transmission drum operated by pedal and rear-axle brakes operated by a hand lever.

Naturally the Raceabout was handbuilt by craftsmen, and was expensive, but on the other hand it looked wonderful, and every red-blooded North American male wished he could afford one. More than 500 were produced in four years before it was redesigned and made less desirable, with unwanted addenda such as a hood.

*Right: The 35J's five-litre side-valve engine was not notably efficient, but it offered sufficient torque to drive a lightweight Raceabout at breathtaking speed, and win races.*

*Below: The 35J had no soft top and, on this example, no windscreen, so occupants had complete open-air motoring. Rival raceabout maker Stutz claimed, "There's no car worser than a Mercer". Said Mercer: "You've got to be nuts to drive a Stutz".*

## Mercer Raceabout variants

### Mercer Type 22

The Type 22 of 1915 was a redesigned version of the same chassis, but with an 89-bhp 'L'-head side-valve engine, and

# Merkur

*Right: A Ford in everything but name, Merkur's Scorpio had the 2933-cc, petrol-injected engine which produced 150 bhp and 172 lb ft of torque. It had a top speed of 124 mph and could accelerate to 60 mph in 9.8 seconds. To confuse customers, it looked similar to the Mercury Sable and Ford Taurus.*

Throughout the 1970s Ford of Europe sold tens of thousands of cars to North American customers. The cars were usually built in West Germany and sold in the US through the Ford-USA Lincoln-Mercury dealer chain. In the 1980s the strategy was to build on this success, by developing more specialised cars, and giving such models a special marque name. The result was the launch of the Merkur marque, which was merely Ford under another name.

Deciding *what* to sell in North America was straightforward enough – in the early 1980s Ford decided to 'federalise' the Sierra model – but deciding what to call it was another matter. To quote Ford's Walter Hayes: "There was no point in calling it a Ford, to sell against other Fords. It was too similar in size to their Tempo for that. It was Bob Lutz's idea [Lutz, at the time, was Ford of Europe's president] to call it Merkur, for this is German for Mercury. He was proud of the fact that it was a German-built car, being sold in the USA."

The original Merkur of 1984 was the XR4Ti, a much-changed Sierra XR4i, with a totally different type of engine. Because of the technical changes, and because the body shells also had to be specially strengthened to meet USA legislation, assembly was handled by Karmann of Osnabruck, an independent concern which was also building other Fords, and VW models, at the same time.

The new Merkur XR4Ti was launched in 1984, and soon proved to be a fast car (faster than almost any other Ford or Mercury-badged model currently on sale in the USA), and sold well at first, but a down-turn came in 1987. American customers, it seemed, *were* confused by the name, and by the way the car looked rather like the Tempo/Topaz range, but wasn't developed from it. At the time it was often said that more people would have bought the car if they had really known what it was!

A second so-called Merkur – a federalised version of the Ford Granada/Scorpio – was added to the range for 1987, this being mechanically and visually the same as the European car, except for badging. Here was another confusion, for the Scorpio looked similar to the modern Ford-USA Mercury Sable/Ford Taurus, though the domestic product had front-wheel drive while the Merkur had rear-wheel drive.

By 1989 it was clear that this marketing project did not appeal to the North American public, and was not going to expand any more, so at the end of 1989 Merkur disappeared from the price lists.

## Merkur XR4Ti 1984-89

When Ford of Europe decided to sell a modified version of the Ford Sierra in the USA, it took two strategic decisions – one was to use an engine which had already been developed with USA exhaust-emission regulations in mind, the other was to give the car a new marque name. The result was the Merkur XR4Ti, which was a lineal development of the Ford of Europe XR4i.

The same basic three-door hatchback body style was used, complete with the controversial and purely decorative twin-wing arrangement at the rear. Whereas the European XR4i was powered by a 2.8-litre V6 engine, and a choice of European transmissions, the Merkur XR4Ti was given a complete engine transplant.

The engine was a turbocharged version of Ford-USA's 2.3-litre Lima unit, and one which was already used in the Ford Thunderbirds and the Ford Mustangs of the period. Although this was neither silky-smooth nor refined, it *was* extremely lusty, and in intercooled form it produced no less than 177 bhp.

Like the European Sierra XR4i from which it was developed, the new Merkur was fast, spacious, and (in this form) extremely well-equipped. Features like air conditioning, cruise control and the glass 'moon-roof' (to use Ford's description) were all available. By European standards it had quite a soft ride, but in the USA it was a competitive sporting car, with a great deal of performance; 16,842 were sold in the first full year.

When volume sales began in 1985 the car cost $16,503, which put it squarely in the BMW/Saab/Audi price bracket. *Road & Track's* test summing-up was that the XR4Ti was "the best sedan Ford sells here in the US. It is one of the quickest available and can achieve cornering speeds that few sports cars can match".

On the other hand, the report went on to comment: "What the Merkur XR4Ti needs is more refinement. And a better name wouldn't hurt either."

### Specification (1984)

**Engine:** inline four-cylinder, overhead-camshaft
**Bore × stroke:** 96.04 mm × 79.4 mm
**Capacity:** 2301 cc

**Maximum power:** 147 bhp (automatic) or 177 bhp (manual)
**Transmission:** five-speed manual gearbox or three-speed automatic transmission, rear-wheel drive
**Chassis:** steel unitary construction body/chassis
**Suspension:** independent with MacPherson struts and anti-roll bar front; semi-trailing arms rear
**Brakes:** discs all round
**Bodywork:** steel three-door five-seater hatchback saloon
**Maximum speed (approx):** 120 mph (193 km/h)

*Below: Behind the Merkur badge was the 2.3-litre Lima engine which gave the car a top speed of 120 mph.*

# MG

**T**he MG marque was created by Cecil Kimber in 1923; he was manager of Morris Garages (of Oxford) at the time. Kimber started by asking coachbuilders Raworth to produce six special two-seater bodies for Morris Cowley chassis, following that up by commissioning special coachwork on Morris Oxford chassis, thus fuelling a demand which had to be satisfied by the birth of cars like the MG 18/80. The MG marque – 'MG' stood for Morris Garages – was invented to identify those models. Not even in the early days could it be called independent (for it relied on Morris's goodwill for its survival), and from the mid-1930s it was definitely just one part of a corporation.

The first cars were produced at the Morris Garages premises, but the first MG factory was built by 1927, and the business moved into its famous factory at Abingdon (a few miles south of Oxford) in 1929 where the first of the famous Midgets – the M-Type, was produced. For the next 50 years all MG sports cars were assembled at Abingdon, although by the 1960s the mass-produced MG saloons were assembled at other sites.

Until 1935 MG sports cars grew steadily more complex, with overhead-camshaft engines developed from Wolseley/Morris designs, and the company competed actively in racing and record-breaking. Then, in a corporate upheaval, Lord Nuffield sold the personally-owned MG business to his Nuffield Organisation, and a new policy saw larger, less specialised (but, as it transpired, more commercially successful) models like the T-Series and the S, V and W saloons put on sale.

MG prospered after World War II by producing more and more T-Series sports cars, plus the Y-Type saloons, but after Nuffield merged with Austin to form the British Motor Corporation (BMC), there was yet another change of strategy.

The first BMC MG was the smart MGA of 1955, which used corporate BMC running gear, and within three years the Abingdon factory was also building Austin-Healeys like the small Sprite. MG saloons like the BMC-designed (but Abingdon-built) Z-Series Magnette were followed by less distinguished cars such as the Farina-designed Magnettes and the front-wheel-drive MG 1100s. Although overall MG sales increased, character was steadily lost.

In the 1960s and 1970s MG's reputation was upheld by the new-generation Midget (which was a development of the Austin-Healey Sprite), and by the smart MGB, which itself spawned several larger and more powerful types. These cars were produced for two decades, but when BMC was submerged within British Leyland, the MG marque was not favoured. The Abingdon plant was closed down in 1980 and all MG sports car production came to an end.

The MG marque was revived in the 1980s, though all types were merely modified versions of Austin-Rover family cars. Then the MG RV8 roadster appeared in 1992, which was a false dawn, as waiting in the wings was the Roger Group's biggest surprise, the all new MGF.

*Above: Small, noisy and surprisingly nippy, the MG PA Midget of 1935 had an 847-cc engine, and was based on a contemporary Morris. This car was raced successfully more than half a century later; note the reversed headlamps.*

*Right: The famous octagon badge graced grilles and hub caps on classic British sports cars from 1923 until the Abingdon factory closed in 1980; the logo appeared later on hotter versions of the Austin Montego, Maestro and Metro, and, in late 1992, the MG RV8 sports car.*

*Below: A 1971 MGB roadster. One of Abingdon's most successful models, the B was introduced in 1962, powered by the BMC 1798-cc four-cylinder engine. Sales were brisk, with 23,000 sold in 1963, and 26,542 in 1964. The 2 + 2 coupé MGB GT appeared in 1965. The model continued in production until 1980, and its demise was mourned by enthusiasts like the death of a national hero.*

## MG 18/80 Six 1928-33

JB 855

### MG 18/80 Six variants

#### MG 18/80 Mk II

The 18/80 Mk II was built from 1929 to 1933. Compared with the Mk I, it had a more solid chassis, a four-inch wider track, and 14-in rather than 12-in diameter brakes. The power output was unaltered, and there was a four-speed gearbox with remote-control change, but the Mk II weighed 300 lb more than the Mk I and was slower.

#### MG 18/100 Mk III 'Tigress'

The 18/100 Mk III 'Tigress' was a road-racing version of the Mk II, with 83 bhp as standard, or 95 bhp in full-house racing trim. This type had a special four-seater open sports-tourer style, built to minimum regulations allowed by the AIACR (the forerunner of FISA).

### Specification (1928 18/80 Six)

**Engine:** inline six-cylinder, single overhead camshaft
**Bore × stroke:** 69 mm × 110 mm
**Capacity:** 2468 cc
**Maximum power:** 60 bhp
**Transmission:** three-speed manual gearbox, rear-wheel drive
**Chassis:** separate steel frame with channel-section main side members
**Suspension:** non-independent with beam axle and semi-elliptic leaf springs front; live axle with semi-elliptic leaf springs rear
**Brakes:** drums all round
**Bodywork:** steel two/four-seater tourer or sports saloon
**Maximum speed (approx):** 78 mph (126 km/h)

---

*Above: An expensive car when launched in 1928, the 18/80 was based on the humble Morris Six saloon, but had a special chassis and attractive bodywork. This 1930 Mk II model had the stronger chassis, four gears, larger brakes and a wider track.*

The first MGs had been modified Morris Cowley or Oxford types, but having moved into a new factory in Oxford in 1927, Cecil Kimber inspired the birth of a more specialised model, which was christened the 18/80. This title had little meaning, for although in current British parlance the '18' referred to the 'taxable' horsepower rating, the '80' was a boastful reference to the engine's power output – which was actually only 60 bhp.

Nevertheless, the 18/80 was the first *real* MG sports car. Not only did it have an overhead-camshaft engine (which was shared with the Morris Six family car of the period), but it had a special chassis frame and – most important of all – it had the first of the characteristic MG radiator grilles, and naturally carried the soon to be famous MG octagon-shaped badge.

The 18/80 was a fine but also very pragmatic design. Kimber could (and did) boast about the special frame and the special body styles, and he was proud of the advanced new overhead-camshaft engine, but he conveniently forgot to mention that suspension and axle components were lifted from the Morris Motors 'parts bin'.

MG never built their own bodywork; bodies were produced by Carbodies of Coventry (the descendant of this company became even more famous after the war for building the unique London black taxis). This added to the cost and the first 18/80s were priced at £555, which was a considerable sum for the period, when Britain's economy was being sucked into the Depression.

The 18/80 was well received, especially as it was a fast and nimble car by late-1920s standards, and considering its engine size, but Kimber thought he could do better and the Mk II version was launched only a year later. This not only had a massively stronger chassis frame, but a four-inch wider track, larger brakes and, most importantly, a four-speed gearbox. There was no more power, however, so the Mk II was considerably heavier, and therefore slower, than the original.

MG developed two more specialised types – the Mk I Speed Model (with a light-alloy four-seater touring body), and the Mk III 18/100 'Tigress', which was a five-off variety intended strictly for road racing.

All in all, there were 500 Mk Is, 236 Mk IIs, and just five Mk IIIs, all of which were effectively 'vintage' cars built in the post-vintage era. Sales, no doubt, would have been higher if another newly-launched MG, the cheap-and-cheerful M-Type Midget, had not diverted the public's attention.

*Above: Flanking the smaller gauges were the speedometer and, in front of the driver, the rev-counter.*

*Below: The overhead-cam engine had water, exhaust and inlet manifolds all on one side of the block.*

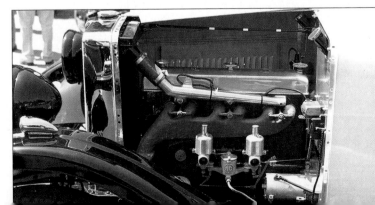

# MG M-Type Midget 1928-32

The first of the MGs that would make the marque truly famous – the M-Type Midget – was launched in October 1928, although volume deliveries did not begin until MG had been moved into the Abingdon factory the following year. Setting a trend for future Midgets, the M-Type leaned heavily on Morris Motors for its running gear, though it had a style and character all its own.

The car that made the M-Type possible was the all-new Morris Minor family car, which was also launched in 1928 with a new four-cylinder overhead-camshaft engine. By this time Wolseley had been added to the Morris empire, and it was that company's experience with overhead-cam engines which inspired the

*Below: Although based on the Morris Minor, the Midget was very distinctive, with its MG grille and boat-tail bodywork (above); the latter contained the spare wheel.*

*Right: The Midget had a simple four-spoke wheel, ammeter, speedometer and water gauge, and a three-speed gearbox.*

birth of this unit.

A closely-related 'straight-six' was conceived at the same time, for use in Morris and Wolseley models. Until 1936 all MG production sports cars would use derivatives of one or other of these types, though Cecil Kimber of MG did his best not to admit it, and tried very hard to make the MG engines visually, if not technically, different from those being used by his supplier!

Mechanically, in fact, the new M-Type Midget was almost pure Morris Minor, but to turn it into a more sporting little car the steering column was re-raked and the individual new MG radiator style was also added. The first bodies were simplicity itself, for they had lightweight wooden – ash and plywood – frames, mainly covered by fabric. The ensemble was completed by cycle-type wings, a neat little 'V' windscreen, and a simple soft top.

To be fair, this car was not fast – especially in its original 20-bhp form, where a realistic top speed was just 60 mph – but it sold briskly for two very good reasons. One was that it had great character (something which MG appeared able to build into any new model at whim), and the other was that it was priced at a mere £175.

At a stroke, therefore, MG had not only introduced a new model, but invented an entirely new class of sports car – cheap and cheerful, but at the time unmatched. It didn't seem to matter that the brakes were not very good, for the car was light (it weighed only about 1,120 lb), and had good handling and roadholding.

MG eventually made considerable improvements to the chassis – notably with

a power boost to 27 bhp (a 35 per cent improvement on the original), and with the fitment of an optional four-speed gearbox. Steel body panels and a Sportsman coupé style were also added, and it wasn't long before these amazing little cars began to compete successfully in motor racing. The phenomenal little C-Type Montlhéry Midget was a direct descendant.

After 3,235 cars had been delivered in rather more than three years, M-Types were finally displaced in 1932 by a new-generation car, called the J-Type.

## MG M-Type Midget variants

### MG C-Type Montlhéry Midget

The C-Type was one of two more specialised Midgets built by MG in 1931 and 1932, and based on the design of the M-Type. The C-Type used a new chassis frame, and a 746-cc version of the game little engine; some cars were supercharged, with a Powerplus 'blower'. This model was universally known as the Montlhéry, and was a very successful racing car in handicap events. Total production was 44 cars, built in 1931 and 1932.

### MG D-Type Midget

The D-Type was a typical MG amalgam of the period. It used a slightly longer-wheelbase version of the C-Type Montlhéry's frame, but had the normal 27-bhp M-Type engine and three-speed gearbox, with a slightly modernised body style; 250 D-Types were built in 1931 and 1932.

## Specification (1928 M-Type)

**Engine:** inline four-cylinder, single overhead camshaft
**Bore × stroke:** 57 mm × 83 mm
**Capacity:** 847 cc
**Maximum power:** 20 bhp
**Transmission:** three-speed manual gearbox, rear-wheel drive
**Chassis:** separate steel frame with channel-section main side members and pressed cross-bracings
**Suspension:** non-independent with beam axle and semi-elliptic leaf springs front; live axle with semi-elliptic leaf springs rear
**Brakes:** drums all round
**Bodywork:** steel two-seater convertible, or closed Sportsman coupé
**Maximum speed (approx):** 60 mph (97 km/h)

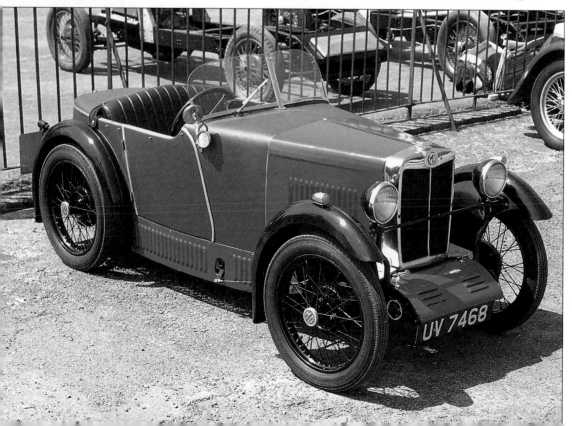

# MG F-Type Magna 1931-32

*Left: A 1932 F-Type Magna. Cecil Kimber, founder of MG, followed the maxim that a sports car should look fast "even when standing still".*

## MG F-Type Magna variants

### MG L-Type Magna

The L-Type Magna of 1933-34 effectively replaced the original F-Type, but had a 1087-cc 41-bhp version of the six-cylinder overhead-cam engine, and the slighter longer-wheelbase chassis from the K-Type Magnettes, but the narrow tracks of the F-Type Magna. This juggling of components (and body styles) was typical of MG at that period. The L-Type was made for just one year, during which time 486 L1s and 90 L2s were produced.

### Specification (1931 F-Type)

**Engine:** inline six-cylinder, single overhead camshaft
**Bore × stroke:** 57 mm × 83 mm
**Capacity:** 1271 cc
**Maximum power:** 37 bhp
**Transmission:** four-speed manual gearbox, rear-wheel drive
**Chassis:** separate steel frame with channel-section main side members
**Suspension:** non-independent with beam axle and semi-elliptic leaf springs front; live axle with semi-elliptic leaf springs rear
**Brakes:** drums all round
**Bodywork:** steel two/four-seater convertible or saloon
**Maximum speed (approx):** 73 mph (117 km/h)

The first of a whole new series of overhead-cam six-cylinder MGs – the F-Type Magna – appeared in 1931 and started a family which eventually included K-Type Magnettes, L-Type Magnas, and N-Type Magnettes. Each was developed from its predecessor, and each used a 1087-cc or 1271-cc version of the six-cylinder Wolseley-based engine.

In many ways the F-Type Magna was the big brother to the small four-cylinder types (M-Type and D-Type Midget), for the engines shared many detail parts along with the same basic layout, the transmissions were similar, and the chassis was merely a long-wheelbase version of the D-Type frame.

This was MG's first attempt at a small six-cylinder car, and it was by no means fully developed. In retrospect it is easy to criticise the narrow, 42-in, track but that was inevitable as the new model used the same axles as the M-Type Midget – and the power output was a disappointing 37 bhp, but as with the M-Types these cars had a character all of their own. MG even managed to hide the fact that the engine (in essence an M-Type plus two cylinders) was the same as that used in the Wolseley Hornet, by adding some sheet-metal 'styling' disguise to each side of the unit.

Another ruse intended to divert customers' minds from the fact of the Wolseley engine was a claim by MG boss Cecil Kimber that one model's (the F-Type's) engine bore and stroke were 57 mm × 84 mm (the stroke 1 mm longer than the Wolseley unit actually had), thereby giving it a capacity of 1286 cc instead of 1271 cc. But despite this, and rather exaggerated power claims, the cars had sufficient character and pace to ensure healthy sales.

The F-Type Magna was well received, and sold well. Apart from the smoothness of its engine, the main attraction was its more spacious coachwork, for the wheelbase was 16 inches longer than that of the M-Type Midget, which allowed the designers to squeeze four seats – in open tourer or closed coupé form – onto the chassis. It was, however, only a praiseworthy first attempt, for the K-Type Magnettes and the later Magnas were faster, more spacious and better-developed models. A total of 1,250 F-Types was built in one year – half of all MG production for that period.

*Below: A 1932 F-Type. The longer wheelbase made the car a four-seater, but space was cramped. Mechanically the car was unadventurous, but in terms of styling it had great character.*

*Below: The cockpit of a 1933 Magna L-Type, which replaced the F-Type and had the 1087-cc engine. The curved fascia design and layout of instruments was typical of MGs until well into the 1950s.*

# MG J1 and J2 Midget 1932-34

*Right: A thoroughly British sports car in every respect, the superb MG J4 Midget was powered by a supercharged, overhead-cam 746-cc engine. The cutaway doors, classic lines and lively performance made it a young man's dream in the 1930s.*

The second-generation Midget, dubbed the J-Type, took over directly from the M-Type in 1932, and was an altogether better car. Not only was it more powerful, and therefore faster, but there was more passenger space, and the styling established an attractive basic layout which would only gradually be changed over the next 20 years.

Here was the archetypal British sports car which every motoring-mad schoolboy sketched on his pad for years to come. It was narrow and rakish, and had cutaway body sides alongside the passengers' elbows, centre-lock wire spoke wheels and an exposed spare wheel. Two big headlamps were mounted proudly at each side of the vertical grille, the windscreen could be folded flat, and weather protection – hood and windscreens – was only marginally effective in severe conditions.

The chassis was narrow (the track was only 42 inches), which made the cockpit very snug indeed, the ride was hard and bouncy, there was no gearbox synchromesh, and there was almost nowhere to stow luggage. In theory these were all disadvantages, but in truth they all added to the car's glamour, and character. Every red-blooded man who could scrape up the necessary £199.50 wanted to own one, and the J-Types certainly established a sports car class which persisted for the next decade and more.

There were two types, both built on the same 86-in wheelbase chassis, which

*Below: This sporting J2 of 1932, with a 939-cc engine and an exposed high-mounted exhaust pipe, raced at Silverstone in 1992. Unlike the J1, the J2 was strictly a two-seater.*

was a direct descendant of the Montlhéry Midget type, as was the engine and the rest of the running gear. The J1 was offered as an open four-seater, or as a closed 'Salonette' coupé, while the ultra-sporting J2 was an open two-seater.

Such was the progress of MG design in the early 1930s that the J-Types lasted for only two years before they were replaced by yet another Midget – the P-Type. In those two years there were 380 J1s and 2,083 J2s built. These may not sound like large numbers in the 1990s but in the context of the car market of the 1930s they were excellent and showed that the Midget had become *the* popular small sports car to own.

## MG J1 and J2 Midget variants

### MG J3 and J4 Midget

The J3 and J4 Midgets (of which 22 J3s and only 9 J4s were produced in 1932 and 1933) were racing derivatives of the J2, with smaller, 57-mm × 73-mm, 746-cc versions of the overhead-camshaft engine to bring them into the 750-cc competition class. Their engines were supercharged, while the J4 had much larger and more effective brakes.

## Specification (1932 J1)

**Engine:** inline four-cylinder, single overhead camshaft

**Bore × stroke:** 57 mm × 83 mm
**Capacity:** 847 cc
**Maximum power:** 36 bhp
**Transmission:** four-speed manual gearbox, rear-wheel drive
**Chassis:** separate steel frame with channel-section main side members and tubular cross-bracing
**Suspension:** non-independent with beam axle and semi-elliptic leaf springs front; live axle with semi-elliptic leaf springs rear
**Brakes:** drums all round
**Bodywork:** steel two/four-seater convertible or coupé
**Maximum speed (approx):** 80 mph (129 km/h)

# MG K-Type and N-Type Magnette 1932-36

*Right: With headlamps taped, a 1934 MG NA races at a 1992 Silverstone meeting, powered by the overhead-cam straight-six. This car has the fold-down windscreen removed.*

That legendary MG historian, Wilson McComb, once wrote: "Few things are more bewildering than the ramifications of the MG Magnette series", which perhaps explains one reason for MG's ability to make profits at this time. In four years Magnettes were produced with three different chassis, four different types of six-cylinder engine, three gearboxes and at least five different body styles. As McComb went on to observe, "the cars were built in such minute quantities that no two of them seemed alike".

Much of the body design work was done by MG founder Cecil Kimber, and in the words of Harold Connolly, the graphic artist who created most of the marque's pre-war brochures, Kimber had "a lovely flair for line, a lovely idea of what the young lad of the village wanted". The appeal of those designs has never waned, and inspired many imitations.

Every Magnette, however, used the same type of simple, hard-sprung and sporting chassis, and one or other further developed version of the six-cylinder engine which had been used in the L-Type Magnas and in the rival Wolseley Hornet. Major changes to the cylinder head, to the camshaft profiles, and to the manifolding, all helped produce a lot more power, and these cars, despite their cramped cabins and relatively expensive price tags, were more attractive than their predecessors.

Although undoubtedly possessing the mid-1930s MG pedigree, these Magnettes were never as successful as the more charismatic four-cylinder Midgets of the day. The name, however, lived on for use in two different types of BMC-designed saloon cars in the 1950s and 1960s.

## MG K-Type and N-Type Magnette variants

### MG K1, K2, KA and K3 Magnette

The first of the breed of Magnettes were the K1 and K2, of which 171 were built in 1932-34. The original cars had a 48-in track, a choice of wheelbase lengths, and a 1087-cc engine producing 39 or 41 bhp. KAs had Wilson pre-selector gearboxes.

The 1933-34 variety of K1 and K2 reverted to the Magna-sized 57-mm × 83-mm 1271-cc engine, with 49 bhp or 55 bhp, and all 85 cars used Wilson pre-selector gearboxes.

The K3 was a sports-racing version of this design, and is described separately.

### MG NA and NE Magnette

The NA took over from the K1 and K2 between 1934 and 1936, and was the best-selling of all the Magnettes.

The NE was a seven-off oddity, with the same chassis as the NA, and had 74 bhp at 6,500 rpm, and was another racing-sports car.

### MG KN Magnette

Finally, there was the KN of 1934 and 1935, 201 of which were produced. This had a longer, 108-in, wheelbase, and the 1271-cc engine was in the same tune as in the NA. It was available generally only as a two-door saloon.

*Above: The MG sports cars were notoriously cramped and narrow, but a longer wheelbase was standard on the MG KN Magnette. This is a 1935 KN Magnette Speed Model Tourer, a model which offered comfortable seating for four.*

## Specification (1934 NA Magnette)

**Engine:** inline six-cylinder, single overhead camshaft
**Bore × stroke:** 57 mm × 83 mm
**Capacity:** 1271 cc
**Maximum power:** 57 bhp
**Transmission:** four-speed manual gearbox, rear-wheel drive
**Chassis:** separate steel frame with channel-section main side members and tubular cross-bracing
**Suspension:** non-independent with beam axle and semi-elliptic leaf springs front; live axle with semi-elliptic leaf springs rear
**Brakes:** drums all round
**Bodywork:** steel two/four-seater convertible or Airline coupé
**Maximum speed (approx):** 81 mph (130 km/h)

*Left: A well-restored 1934 MG NA at speed. MG founder Cecil Kimber always believed in the value of racing as promotion for the marque.*

# MG K3 Magnette 1932-34

*Below: A splendid K3 Magnette with rounded aluminium bodywork, two seats and a supercharged engine. The model was very expensive for the time at £795, and was intended specifically for motorsport.*

*Right: This special single-seater K3 Magnette record car was raced at Brooklands. K3s were very successful in competitions of all kinds during the 1930s, including the Mille Miglia and Ulster TT.*

Although the K3 was one of the amazingly complex K-Type and N-Type family of the early 1930s, its aim in life was absolutely plain. Although based on the production Magnette running gear, the K3 was a highly-tuned machine, intended primarily for use in international motorsport.

For that purpose the ubiquitous six-cylinder overhead-cam engine was given a short-stroke crankshaft, which dropped its capacity to 1087 cc, and slotted it neatly into the 1100-cc capacity class; the engine was also supercharged. All the engines were powerful, but for sprint or short-distance track racing they were boosted still further and made very powerful indeed.

It was with this engine, and with supercharged versions of the four-cylinder Midget design, that MG produced sensational specific power outputs in the 1930s. To harness the power of the K3 engine, MG mated it with the fashionable Wilson-type pre-selector gearbox, which was heavy but reliable, and had already proved itself in other competition cars.

The K3, naturally, was very expensive £795 was a lot of money in early 1930s currency – and because of its stark bodywork, and complete lack of thought for creature comforts, it was not meant to be a versatile machine. It was, however, exactly right for its purpose, and is more of an MG legend in the 1990s than it was 60 years ago.

The 'works' K3 cars excelled themselves in the Mille Miglia of 1933 (finishing first and second in their class, despite consuming large numbers of sparking plugs), while the world's fastest racing driver, Tazio Nuvolari, won the Ulster TT in another K3, and Eddie Hall used another special K3 to win the Brooklands 500 Miles race at the end of the season.

To quote McComb, once again: "The K3 Magnette won so many races that its few failures came as a distinct surprise." One car, George Eyston's specially-streamlined EX135, used a modified K3 chassis and running gear, ensuring that car's reputation for many years to come. A total of 33 K3s (including EX135) was produced, but there was no replacement for this outstanding design.

*Below: Despite the K3's relatively small engine, MG supercharged it to achieve outputs of up to 100 bhp.*

*Above: A famous Brooklands racer, pictured here at the track, this K3 was fitted with special single-seat bodywork. Such cars enormously boosted the marque's reputation.*

## Specification (1932)

**Engine:** inline six-cylinder, single overhead camshaft
**Bore × stroke:** 57 mm × 71 mm
**Capacity:** 1087 cc
**Maximum power:** up to 100 bhp, depending on application
**Transmission:** four-speed pre-selector gearbox, rear-wheel drive
**Chassis:** separate steel frame with channel-section main side members and tubular cross-bracing
**Suspension:** non-independent with beam axle and semi-elliptic leaf springs front; live axle with semi-elliptic leaf springs rear
**Brakes:** drums all round
**Bodywork:** aluminium two-seater convertible
**Maximum speed (approx):** 100 mph (161 km/h)

# MG PA and PB Midget 1934-36

To replace the J-Type Midgets, which had only been on sale for two years, Cecil Kimber's team developed yet another small MG, this time the P-Type. It was yet another development on the original Midget theme, slightly more spacious, slightly more rakishly styled, but still with the same 847-cc overhead-cam engine.

Compared with the J2, the PA had a slightly longer wheelbase, and was much improved in detail. The chassis was sturdier than before, the engine had been given a three-bearing crankshaft, the brakes were much larger and more powerful, and there were long, flowing front wings. The price, too, had increased – the two-seater cost £220, which compared with £199.50 for the J2, and just £185 for the M-Type, which had disappeared only two years earlier.

At this time MG, to be honest, was stuck in a whirlpool of diminishing re-

turns, for as the cars improved (and, make no mistake, the PA *was* a better car than its predecessor), they also became more expensive, and sales dropped. MG production, which had peaked at 2,400 a year in 1932, fell away to 1,300 in 1935.

One of the PA's problems was that although it was charming, it was actually no faster than the J2, so after only 18 months MG revealed the PB, which had an enlarged (939-cc) version of the engine, a closer-ratio gearbox, and, significantly, no increase in the price. The extra 92-cc displacement was achieved by the simple expedient of widening the bore from 57 mm to 60 mm and keeping the long 83-mm stroke the same. The effect was dramatic, as maximum power rose from the humble 35 bhp of the PA to a far more impressive 43 bhp.

By this time, however, Lord Nuffield had transferred ownership of the MG company to his massive Nuffield Organ-

isation, which soon meant that simpler, cheaper-to-build, MG sports cars were on the way. The result was that the PB faded away after less than a year, and the TA took over.

In all, 2,000 PAs and 526 PBs were produced.

*Above: From an era when many cars received bespoke coachwork, this is a special-bodied single-seat MG PA, with polished aluminium wings and a similarly-curved, non-MG grille.*

## Specification (1934 PA)

**Engine:** inline four-cylinder, single overhead camshaft
**Bore × stroke:** 57 mm × 83 mm
**Capacity:** 847 cc
**Maximum power:** 35 bhp
**Transmission:** four-speed manual gearbox, rear-wheel drive
**Chassis:** separate steel frame with channel-section side members and tubular cross-bracing

**Suspension:** non-independent with beam axle and semi-elliptic leaf springs front; live axle with semi-elliptic leaf springs rear
**Brakes:** drums all round
**Bodywork:** steel two/four-seater convertible or Airline coupé
**Maximum speed (approx):** 74 mph (119 km/h)

*Below: A 1934 MG PA in racing guise, with all of 35 bhp, cycle-type wings and no spare tyre.*

*Above: Under-bonnet view of a fast, supercharged P-Type; air was blown through the single carburettor and greatly boosted engine power.*

*Below: In the 1936 MG PB, with its flowing wings and running boards, Kimber had created a style that was the epitome of pre-war roadsters.*

# MG TD Midget 1950-53

To replace the long-running TA/TB/TC models, MG developed a new car which had a modern chassis, with independent front suspension, but a 'traditional' – i.e. old-fashioned – body style. The new car was made available with right-hand or left-hand drive, which was a real innovation for MG and long overdue considering the numbers of cars MG exported.

This was a sound move, for it allowed the company to build on the export reputation newly won by the TC, and the result was that sales of the TD – nearly 30,000 – were far greater than those of any previous MG model.

The TD used the same engine and transmission as the superseded TC, while the chassis was a modified version of that already used in the YA saloon, which had actually been designed just before the war, but had not been put on sale until 1947.

The body style, although chunkier and a bit more spacious than the TC, was clearly an evolution of that style, for the new car still had cutaway doors, clip-on canvas sidescreens, a windscreen which could be folded flat, headlamps mounted on each side of the grille, and long, flowing front wings. Notably, this was the first MG sports car for many years to have pressed-steel disc wheels; in fact wire-spoke wheels were not even optional. This was a strange marketing decision, brought about to save money, for wire wheels were expensive.

The new TD had a softer ride than the TC, and steered and handled well, in part thanks to the new feature of rack-and-pinion steering, which was superior to the old system. The TD's aerodynamics were still awful, however, so there was no more performance than before. That didn't seem to matter, and the TD sold extremely well in export markets, with more than 10,000 cars produced in 1952 alone. A total of 29,664 TDs would

eventually be built.

When MG's designers, led by Syd Enever, began to plan a replacement for the old-style TD, they wanted to produce a smart new car with modern styling, but this project (which became the MGA) was refused the required investment at the time. In a hurry, therefore, the TF was developed, so that in the autumn of 1953 the TD was replaced by a facelifted model with the same chassis but with semi-recessed headlamps and a more rakish tail. After a three-year gap, centre-lock wire-spoke wheels once again became available – but only as optional equipment.

This car sold well, but not well enough, for another year, but it still lacked performance, and the last 3,400 TFs became TF1500s, with an enlarged engine producing 63 bhp instead of 57 bhp. Even before then, however, MG (and BMC, the parent company) had realised that the old-style car was obsolete, and an all-new car, the MGA, was on the way.

The last TF1500 of all was produced in May 1955, although the new MGA was not ready for sale until that September.

*Above: The MG TD had the drivetrain of the TC, plus a new chassis with, for the first time on an MG, independent front suspension, along with restyled wings.*

## MG TD variants

### MG TD Mk II

The TD Mk II was a low-volume-production derivative of the TD, with a more powerful (60-bhp) engine, and different gear ratios.

### MG TF1250

The TF1250 was really a facelifted TD, with a sloping nose and semi-recessed headlamps, and with a more flared tail and a more sloping spare wheel mounting. Centre-lock wire-spoke wheels (not available on TD models) were once again available on TFs. Engine power had been increased to 57 bhp, but there was no significant change in performance. A total of 6,200 TFs was built in 1953 and 1954.

### MG TF1500

The TF1500 was the final derivative of this design. Except that it had a larger-bore, 1466-cc, version of the overhead-valve engine producing 63 bhp, and a top speed of about 85 mph, the basic design was unchanged.

## Specification (1950 TD)

**Engine:** inline four-cylinder, overhead-valve
**Bore × stroke:** 66.5 mm × 90 mm
**Capacity:** 1250 cc
**Maximum power:** 54 bhp
**Transmission:** four-speed manual gearbox, rear-wheel drive
**Chassis:** separate steel frame with box-section main side members, box and tubular cross-bracing
**Suspension:** independent front with double wishbones and coil springs; live rear axle with semi-elliptic leaf springs
**Brakes:** drums all round
**Bodywork:** steel two-seater convertible
**Maximum speed (approx):** 80 mph (129 km/h)

*Above: Launched in 1953, the TF was the last T, and its revamped pre-war bodywork was considered the most attractive by many MG fans.*

*Below: The pleasures of open-air motoring in an MG TD were enhanced by its not being fast enough to cause real discomfort.*

# MGA 1955-62

The 1930s style generation of T-Series MG sports cars had sold so well after the war that the first truly post-war MG did not appear until 1955, 10 years after Abingdon reverted to peace-time activities. The new MGA was worth waiting for; not only did it look extremely smart, but it was also easily the fastest MG so far put on sale.

Work on a new car, coded EX175, began in 1952, at a time when MG proposed to retain the TD/TF type of engine and transmissions in a radical new shape, but this car was never approved for production. The definitive MGA, codenamed the EX182, was developed in 1954-55; although it looked like the EX175, it had an entirely different powertrain.

The new car had a rock-solid chassis frame, with massive bracing behind the passenger bulkhead, and used the TF type of independent front suspension, but this was the only carry-over component. The engine, transmission and rear axle were all developed versions of the new BMC B-Series range. Derided at first by MG die-hards, these proved to be remarkably robust and tunable, and would be used for many years.

The style was smooth and attractive by any standards. At a stroke, it pulled MG out of the 1930s, and into the mid-1950s, which was just as well as the marque now faced major competition from Austin-Healey and Triumph. Although the new roadster body still had clip-on side screens, it was otherwise smooth, shapely and very practical; MG also offered an alternative version, the Coupé, with a steel 'bubble-top' hard top and glass wind-up windows.

Compared with the TF1500 which it replaced, the new MGA was a revelation. It looked a lot better, it had a much higher cruising and top speed, it had a more practical interior and more stowage space, yet it still steered and handled like a real sports car should.

The same basic design served MG well for seven years, and was gradually developed as the engine was enlarged and made more powerful. The special Twin-Cam was not a success, but every other version sold well. Because the chassis was so solid, many MGAs have survived into the 1990s to become cherished classic cars.

All in all, a total of 98,970 pushrod-engined MGA was produced – 58,750 MGA 1500s, 31,501 1600s, and 8,719 of the final 1600 Mk II type.

## MGA variants

### MGA 1600
To replace the original MGA 1500, the MGA 1600 was built from 1959 to 1961. It looked the same, and was mechanically similar, but had a 75.39-mm × 88.9-mm, 1588-cc engine producing a top speed of 101 mph; front-wheel disc brakes were standard.

### MGA 1600 Mk II
The MGA 1600 Mk II of 1961 was the final derivative of the design, with a 76.2-mm × 88.9-mm, 1622-cc engine producing 86 bhp.

## Specification (1958 MGA)
**Engine:** inline four-cylinder, overhead-valve
**Bore × stroke:** 73.02 mm × 88.9 mm

**Capacity:** 1489 cc
**Maximum power:** 72 bhp
**Transmission:** four-speed manual gearbox, rear-wheel drive
**Chassis:** separate steel frame with box-section main side members, cross-braces and scuttle-bracing structure
**Suspension:** independent front with double wishbones and coil springs; live rear axle with semi-elliptic leaf springs
**Brakes:** drums all round
**Bodywork:** steel two-seater convertible (with optional hard top) or coupé
**Maximum speed (approx):** 100 mph (161 km/h)

*Above: Appearing so soon after the TF, the modern-looking MGA came as something of a shock to MG traditionalists, but the car had virtue enough in handling and performance to ensure high sales.*

*Below: An MGA 1600 Mk II, which had the stepped, rather than curved, grille design. Launched in 1961, this model had a new 1622-cc, 93-bhp pushrod engine with a big-valve head, plus a higher final drive ratio.*

# MGA Twin-Cam 1958-60

Even before the MGA had been introduced, BMC had begun to dabble with the development of special twin-overhead-camshaft engines to power the car. At first these were intended for motor racing, and for record attempts, but after the design – by Morris Engines Branch in Coventry – had proved itself to be the best, it was further refined as a production unit. The result was the launch of the MGA Twin-Cam in mid-1958.

Not only did this car have a new and

Above: The MGA Twin-Cam coupé body design was launched in 1956, and looked very attractive. Only badges distinguished the Twin-Cam.

powerful engine, but it was also fitted with disc brakes at front *and* rear, and also used centre-lock Dunlop disc wheels. Thus equipped, here was a car which was not only a lot faster than the normal MGA, but one which had all the chassis reserves needed to turn it into a good racing-sports car.

At the time, however, there was one basic problem – the high-compression engine soon got a reputation for piston burning. Even a redesign in mid-run – to

Below: The Twin-Cam was very fast and had disc brakes. Its engine problems could be avoided by reducing the compression ratio.

lower the compression ratio, and drop the peak power to about 100 bhp – arrived too late to save its name, and it was withdrawn after only two years.

In later years, enthusiasts worked miracles on the specification, so that surviving Twin-Cams are not only better and more reliable than ever they were in the 1950s, but they show just what could have been achieved in the 1960s if MG, and BMC, had persevered.

After the Twin-Cam model was dropped, MG made the best of a bad job by introducing the 1600 (later the 1600 Mk II) De Luxe, which effectively used left-over Twin-Cam chassis, brakes and suspension, but which was powered by the normal MGA overhead-valve pushrod engines of the period.

In all, 2,111 Twin-Cams were produced; they were followed by 395 push-

rod-engined De Luxe models.

## Specification (1958)

**Engine:** inline four-cylinder, twin overhead camshafts
**Bore × stroke:** 75.39 mm × 88.9 mm
**Capacity:** 1588 cc
**Maximum power:** 108 bhp
**Transmission:** four-speed manual gearbox, rear-wheel drive
**Chassis:** separate steel frame with box-section main side members, cross-braces and scuttle-bracing structure
**Suspension:** independent front with double wishbones and coil springs; live rear axle with semi-elliptic leaf springs
**Brakes:** discs all round
**Bodywork:** steel two-seater convertible (with optional hard top) or coupé
**Maximum speed (approx):** 113 mph (182 km/h)

*Below: The chain-driven, twin-cam engine had a 9.9:1 compression ratio and gave 108 bhp, 50 per cent more than the pushrod car. Top speed was 113 mph and acceleration was greatly improved, but the unit was temperamental.*

# MG Midget 1961-79

Once MG abandoned the TF Midget in 1955, their sports cars grew inexorably larger, to the extent that they no longer deserved to carry the Midget badge. From 1961, however, MG went back to their roots by introducing a new family of small Midgets, which were entirely different from the existing MGAs.

The modern Midget story starts with the Austin-Healey Sprite, which had been introduced in 1958, and was always assembled at Abingdon. For 1961 BMC not only decided to restyle the Sprite, but to produce it in two varieties; for the next decade there would be Austin-Healey Sprite and MG Midget versions of the same angular little car.

Like the Sprite, the Midget was tiny, light, but brisk and full of character, with a minimal-sized two-seater cabin, responsive handling and inch-accurate steering. It was no faster, and in many ways no better, than its main opposition, the Triumph Spitfire, which was its keenest rival throughout its career. It did, however, have the incalculable advantage of using an MG badge, and could be sold through experienced MG dealers, especially in North America where the majority of cars were exported.

The design was gradually improved over the years, first by adding front disc brakes, and then by altering the rear suspension, and finally by making the cabin and weather protection more complete and civilised, but each and every Midget retained the cheeky and appealing character which made it so successful.

There is still controversy over the last type – the 1500. Not only did it have a Triumph Spitfire engine and gearbox (both marques having become a part of British Leyland by this time), but to satisfy new USA legislation it was also fitted with large and none-too-stylish black bumpers. In fact the 1500 was not only the

*Above: Here is a 1967 MG Midget, with the 1275-cc engine and capable of 94 mph. Its styling bore a strong family resemblance to the MGB.*

fastest, but also the best-selling Midget of all time, so perhaps the company *had* got it right after all!

The Midget was finally discontinued in 1979, when it was well past its best, and was never replaced. Over 18 years, total Midget production was 226,526 cars, accompanied by a further 129,359 Austin-Healey/Austin-badged cars.

## MG Midget variants

### MG Midget Mk II, III and IV

Improvement of the Midget was a continuous process. From late 1962, the design was updated with a 64.58-mm × 83.72-mm, 1098-cc/56-bhp engine, and with front-wheel disc brakes. The top speed rose to 89 mph.

The Midget Mk II appeared in 1964, with 59 bhp, suspension by semi-elliptic leaf springs at the back instead of the cantilever type, wind-up door windows, and a top speed of 92 mph.

Then came the Midget Mk III of late 1966, with a 70.6-mm × 81.3-mm, 1275-cc/65-bhp engine, and a top speed of 94 mph. This car carried on extremely successfully until late 1974. From late 1969, with no more than cosmetic changes (and, for two years, with rounded instead of squared-off rear wheel-arch cut-outs) the car became known as the Mk IV.

### MG Midget 1500

The final variety was the Midget 1500 of 1974-79, which was fitted with a 66-bhp Triumph Spitfire engine of 73.7 mm × 87.5 mm and 1493 cc, and had a top speed of 101 mph. The style was

altered to feature large energy-absorbing black plastic front and rear bumpers, for the USA market.

## Specification (1961 Midget)

**Engine:** inline four-cylinder, overhead-valve
**Bore × stroke:** 62.9 mm × 76.2 mm
**Capacity:** 948 cc
**Maximum power:** 46 bhp
**Transmission:** four-speed manual

gearbox, rear-wheel drive
**Chassis:** steel unitary construction body/chassis
**Suspension:** independent front with double wishbones and coil springs; live rear axle with semi-elliptic leaf springs
**Brakes:** drums all round
**Bodywork:** steel two-seater convertible with optional hard top
**Maximum speed (approx):** 86 mph (138 km/h)

*Above: At 12 years old, the Midget still sold well; this is a 1973 car showing only minor styling changes.*

*Below: The last cars had rubber bumpers to satisfy the Americans, but still sold better than ever.*

## MGB 1962-80

The best selling MG sports car of all time was the MGB, introduced in 1962 and originally intended to stay in production for about eight years. In fact it remained on the market for almost two decades. When it was new the MGB was a very appealing combination of smart looks, good roadholding, and a simple power-train, and that was all its customers, especially those in the USA, seemed to want.

Even when it was new, though, the specification was strictly conventional. The smooth monocoque body style hid updated versions of the MGA's engine and transmission – the engine had been enlarged to 1.8 litres – which meant that there was a gearbox with a 'crash' first gear, a live rear axle, and rather uninspired performance. Overdrive, however, was a worthwhile innovation, originally optional, but made standard from the mid-1970s.

Within three years the original road-ster style had been joined by a very smart fastback/hatchback GT alterna-tive, which was an extremely versatile and good-looking design, and after five years the model was improved to in-clude a new all-synchromesh gearbox. From then – 1967 – until 1980, a succes-sion of MGBs received no more than cos-metic attention, or updates, mainly in-tended to keep abreast of new legislation in the USA.

The most controversial change of all came at the end of 1974, when the design was severely compromised by the addi-tion of vast black plastic-covered bumpers, front and rear, and the ride height was increased to the detriment of the car's handling and roadholding. These changes were all made necessary by new rules in the USA, but they did nothing for the car's appeal.

If investment capital had been made available, MG's designers would have replaced the MGB during the 1970s, but British Leyland would never grant this, as the rival marque, Triumph, was favoured instead – wrongly, as it turned out. The result was that the MGB fell badly behind the times in its last few years, and it was dropped in 1980, by which time 513,272 cars had been pro-duced, mostly for the US market.

*Above: This 1969 MGB has the sporting yet understated styling of an enduring best-seller.*

### MGB variants

#### MGB Mk II

The Mk II version of the MGB was introduced in late 1967, with a new all-synchromesh gearbox, and optional three-speed automatic transmission; the automatic option was discontinued in 1973. Overdrive was standardised in 1975.

The only significant restyle came in autumn 1974, when the car was given larger black plastic bumpers at front and rear (energy-absorbing for the USA market), while the ride height was raised at the same time.

#### MGC

The MGC of 1967-69 was a derivative of the MGB Mk II, with torsion-bar front suspension and a six-cylinder engine, essentially as used in the Austin-Healey 3000.

#### MGB GT V8

The MGB GT V8 of 1973-76 was a variant of the MGB GT of the period, and was fitted with Rover's light-alloy 3.5-litre V8 engine. There was no factory convertible version.

*Below: The last 'Bs were the limited-edition models with special trim and alloy wheels.*

*Above: From 1975 MGBs had dodgem-like rubber bumpers to satisfy US legislation; they looked heavier than the earlier style (below).*

### Specification (1962 MGB Mk I)

**Engine:** inline four-cylinder, overhead-valve

**Bore × stroke:** 80.26 mm × 88.9 mm

**Capacity:** 1798 cc

**Maximum power:** 95 bhp

**Transmission:** four-speed manual gearbox with optional overdrive, rear-wheel drive

**Chassis:** steel unitary construction body/chassis

**Suspension:** independent front with double wishbones, coil springs and lever-arm dampers; live rear axle with semi-elliptic leaf springs

**Brakes:** discs front, drums rear

**Bodywork:** steel two-seater convertible (with optional hard top) or coupé

**Maximum speed (approx):** 103 mph (166 km/h)

# MGC 1967-69

*Left: The discreet badge indicated that the MGC was powered by the 145-bhp three-litre straight-six.*

By the mid-1960s BMC's Austin-Healey 3000 design was ageing. To replace it the planners originally intended to offer *two* cars – one badged as an Austin-Healey, the other an essentially identical model with an MG badge – but Donald Healey objected and only one version made it to the showrooms. This was the six-cylinder MGC which, by MG's exalted standards, was not a success.

The basis of the new car was a much-modified MGB body shell, with a six-cylinder engine squeezed under the bonnet. It was such a close fit that a new torsion-bar type of front suspension replaced the MGB's coil springs. This sounds straightforward enough – except that the engine was a much-changed version of the old Austin-Healey 3000 unit, and there was also the choice of a new all-synchromesh gearbox, or automatic transmission.

The result was a somewhat unbalanced car, which had a front-heavy weight distribution, needed a bulge in the bonnet to clear the long engine, and had larger-diameter wheels (15-in instead of 14-in) than the MGB.

At the time, the MGC received mixed reactions from the specialist press, but it sold at least as well as the Austin-Healey 3000 had done. Although it looked almost identical to the MGB, it was a much more powerful and higher-geared car. The result was that it had an altogether lazier and relaxed character, which appealed to many.

*Autocar* in 1967 tested the car and commented that the engine had a lack of low-speed torque and was reluctant to rev. The report also criticised the gear ratios, particularly the high-ratio first gear, the large step between second and third (0-60 mph required 10 seconds), and the high-ratio rear axle. Even so, an average fuel consumption of 19 mpg was high. Strong understeer and low-geared steering were also criticised. Compared with the Austin-Healey 3000, which cost £24 more than the MG, the MGC offered slower acceleration and a lower maximum speed. Wire wheels were an optional extra, for £30, as was a recirculating-air heater, for £15.

Undoubtedly it would have sold better if it had handled in a more spritely way, and had been visually more different from the MGB. MG's new owners, British Leyland, found its unique body shell and front suspension awkward and inconvenient to produce in relatively limited

*Above: The big six-cylinder was a tight squeeze and required a wide bonnet bulge and the adoption of torsion-bar front suspension.*

numbers, so after only two years the car was discontinued.

In those two years, 8,999 MGCs – the split between Roadster and GT was almost exactly 50/50 – were produced. No fewer than 4,256 were exported to the USA, and only 3,437 were sold in the UK.

## Specification (1967)

**Engine:** inline six-cylinder, overhead-valve

**Bore × stroke:** 83.34 mm × 88.9 mm

**Capacity:** 2912 cc

**Maximum power:** 145 bhp

**Transmission:** four-speed manual gearbox with optional overdrive, or optional three-speed automatic transmission; rear-wheel drive

**Chassis:** steel unitary construction body/chassis

**Suspension:** independent front with wishbones and torsion bars; live rear axle with semi-elliptic leaf springs

**Brakes:** discs front, drums rear

**Bodywork:** steel two-seater convertible or coupé

**Maximum speed:** 120 mph (193 km/h)

*Above: Power for the MGC came from the heavy cast-iron engine used in the Austin-Healey 3000.*

*Below: Its powerful engine and larger wheels made the MGC a relaxed long-distance tourer.*

## MGB GT V8 1973-76

he last important derivative of the MGB the V8-engined GT version – was the est of all, but despite that it only sold owly. Introduced in 1973, immediately efore the outbreak of the Yom Kippur Var, it was expensive, and was originally een as a gas-guzzling indulgence. It was ever sold in the USA, which was clearly major marketing mistake.

The MGB and the light-alloy Rover V8 ngine could only get together after the ormation of British Leyland, for until 1968 ie two companies were business rivals. privately marketed conversion, by Ken ostello, inspired British Leyland to do s own thing, the result being a very atisfying Grand Touring car.

The new car was effectively an MGB T with a V8 engine transplant, for there ere no changes to the basic structure, the transmission, nor to the suspension yout. The engine was no heavier than ie four-cylinder 1.8-litre unit which it isplaced, but it was more powerful, and

*elow: The V8 was much easier to fit han the MGC six; this engine has pecial finned rocker covers.*

had a great deal more torque, with 193 lb ft at only 2,900 rpm.

According to the published figures, the MGB GT V8 (it was never marketed as an open roadster) was less powerful than the 1960s-style MGC, but it was actually a faster, and no less fuel-efficient, machine. It looked as good as any other MGB, had an identical package, and handled in the same way, but it had an altogether more refined character. *Autocar* characterised it as "MG elegance, Rover smoothness", and commented on the lack of vibration from the drivetrain and how the engine ("for which praise cannot be too high") had moved the MGB GT "into the realms of the fastest European sports cars".

In some respects, though, the qualities of the engine only emphasised some of the dated aspects of the MG, particularly the harsh ride, heavy steering and wind noise, but the combination was a car which offered very tractable performance, with 60 mph in 8.6 seconds, a standing quarter-mile in 16.4 seconds and 100 mph in 25.3. Also impressive was the fact that the V8's fuel consumption of

25 mpg was equal to that of the four-cylinder MGB GT.

Strangely, only 2,591 cars were made, every one of which was sold in the UK. The MGB GT V8 was dropped in 1976, and cynics are convinced that this was done to make way for the Triumph TR8, which was still not ready to go on sale at that time. In contrast to the MGB GT V8, the TR8 (which used the same engine) *was* intended for sale on the North American market. The rationale was that the TR8 could be sold as a convertible while the V8 MG was only produced as a coupé, despite Ken Costello having proved that the convertible body shell could handle the torque. But then British Leyland at this time was full of missed opportunities.

*Below: The coupé body of the 1973 MGB GT V8 was an enduring design, made with help from Pininfarina, and combined sports appeal with practical four-seat accommodation.*

*Above: The MGB GT V8 was able to accelerate to 60 mph in 8.6 seconds, thanks to the well-proven GM/Rover alloy V8. Only 2,591 were built, but in the years since the MGB's demise, the V8 cars have become the most sought-after.*

### Specification (1973)

**Engine:** V8, overhead-valve
**Bore × stroke:** 88.9 mm × 71.1 mm
**Capacity:** 3528 cc
**Maximum power:** 137 bhp
**Transmission:** four-speed manual gearbox with overdrive, rear-wheel drive
**Chassis:** steel unitary construction body/chassis
**Suspension:** independent front with wishbones and coil springs; live rear axle with semi-elliptic leaf springs
**Brakes:** discs front, drums rear
**Bodywork:** steel two-seater coupé
**Maximum speed (approx):** 124 mph (200 km/h)

# MG Metro 6R4 1985-86

*Left: It looked like a Metro on steroids, but the MG Metro 6R4 was very different under the skin, with four-wheel drive and a rear-mounted V6. The rear spoiler led to its 'supermarket trolley' nickname.*

*Below: The three-litre V6 had four valves per cylinder and twin belt-driven cams, very like the 1970s DF Cosworth V8. With 250 bhp and 225 lb ft in basic tune, the car would reach 60 mph in 4.5 seconds.*

Although this Group B rally car project carried an MG badge, it was more truly an Austin-Rover project, loosely based on the Metro style, but with virtually no MG input, and certainly no design influence from Abingdon.

To match the requirements of the new Group B rallying formula, Austin-Rover asked Williams Grand Prix Engineering to design a mid-engined four-wheel-drive car, of which only 200 would need to be built. For marketing purposes the style was based on that of a Metro family car, though there was absolutely no mechanical link between the two cars, and very few common panels; by the time all the slots, bulges and spoilers had been added the result was hideous.

The first prototypes used cut-and-shut V6 versions of the Rover V8 engine, but the production 6R4s used a specially-designed four-cam V6 whose cylinder heads owed a lot to the layout of the Cosworth DFV Formula 1 engine. This three-litre engine was mounted behind the seats, and drove through a complex four-wheel-drive transmission.

Austin-Rover saw this as a potential rally-winner in Group B, and made haste to produce 200 cars in 1985, while the works motorsport department then built 20 Evolution versions with more specialised componentry and a lot more power. There were no compromises towards making this a civilised road car, the result being that this £35,000 machine was sparsely equipped and hard riding, though it was also astonishingly fast and nimble. The car had to be registerable for the road to qualify as a rally car, and a few were, but very high levels of engine noise and transmitted heat deterred all but the hardiest of drivers.

It was, however, an entirely different type of car from, say, the Ford RS200. Whereas enthusiasts bought RS200s for road use, and admired their looks and their versatility, Metro 6R4 sales went only to people who wanted to use them in motorsport.

The debut was the Lombard-RAC Rally in November, and Tony Pond proved the car's value by setting nine fastest stage times, finishing 41 times in the top four places, and coming third overall. The following year, despite some problems with the belt drives, 6R4s achieved high places in international rallies and were driven by the winners of the French and British National Rally Championships.

Because Group B's rallying life was cut short in 1986, and because the 6R4 was already being outpaced by its turbo-charged rivals in rallying, Austin-Rover had to sell off most of the 200 6R4s at very low prices (many for only about £15,000). In later years the cars built up illustrious reputations in rallycross, but few, if any, were regularly used on the road.

## Specification (1985)

**Engine:** V6, twin overhead camshafts
**Bore × stroke:** 92 mm × 75 mm
**Capacity:** 2991 cc

**Maximum power:** 250 bhp (410 bhp in fully-tuned form)
**Transmission:** five-speed manual gearbox, four-wheel drive
**Chassis:** steel multi-tube frame with body panels welded to form unitary construction
**Suspension:** independent with MacPherson struts, lower wishbones and anti-roll bars front and rear
**Brakes:** discs all round
**Bodywork:** aluminium and glassfibre two-door two-seater hatchback saloon
**Maximum speed (approx):** (250-bhp model) 140 mph (225 km/h)

*Below: The MG Metro 6R4 at speed. The front spoiler was designed to smooth air over the bluff front. The short body/long wheelbase meant that no weight overhung the axles.*

# MG RV8 1992–95

hirty years after the MGB made its first ppearance Rover decided the time was pe to re-introduce the model, to cash in n an appeal that had never died.

It was modernised just enough to give some driving appeal for the 1990s and, st as important, the kind of performance that would enable it to live with far ore modern sports cars. To that end over fitted their pushrod ex-Buick and ldsmobile V8 engine which was even ore venerable than the 'B itself. There ad been a V8 version of the MGB efore, but that model was never a great ales success owing to various factors: e fact that a roadster version was never oduced (despite the fact that the man ho showed a V8 MGB was possible, en Costello, produced open versions), d the energy crisis. It was felt that the xtra power and torque of the V8 engine ould really be too much for the open ody, which naturally lacked the torsonal stiffness of the closed car, but as e V8 was in a fairly mild state of tune d the MGB a tough and strong design, at view seemed rather strange. The ew model, the RV8, was designed with che marketing very much in mind so its conomy or lack of it was never an issue, d the coupé-only policy had sensibly en thrown out in favour of an open car.

Whereas the old V8 had been just 3.5 res, the new RV8 had the stretched 3.9-re V8 in 188-bhp and 228-lb ft tune, mplete with catalytic converter. It was ated to Rover's fine five-speed gearox and installed in a body shell built by itish Motor Heritage using a combinaon of old and new pressings. The body as clearly recognisable as an MGB, but s moulded front and rear bumper treat-

*Right: An engine with 40 years of history, the Rover V8 returned to MG in 1992 in 3.9-litre form, with petrol injection, a catalytic converter and 188 bhp. Well-proven in TVRs, Morgans, Range Rovers and the new Pegaso, the high-torque engine gave excellent performance.*

ment plus its bulging wheel arches and moulded sills between the wheels, not to mention the new split-rim style alloy wheels, showed it to be something apart. Although the old MGB's wishbone and lever-arm damper front suspension had been redesigned, it was decided that changing the live rear axle for a modern independent system would be too expensive and that a traditional live axle would be adequate despite the new car's impressive performance, which promised a top speed of 134 mph and the ability to sprint to 60 mph in under six seconds.

No-one could really argue with the performance, which promised to be significantly better than that of the original MGB GT V8 – an increase of 10 mph on the top speed was good, but the improvement in the 0-60 mph time was dramatic. Rover's figures showed that well over two seconds had been taken off the old car's time of 8.6 seconds, and that was a bigger improvement than the extra 466 cc displacement, 27 lb ft of torque and 51 bhp would suggest. The real issue lay with the styling; by common consent the original-style MGB was more attractive than the later, higher, rubber-bumper models, but the new design retained some of the clumsiness of the later car.

The RV8 was scheduled for introduction at the 1992 Birmingham Motor Show and with a price of around £26,500, when the car went on sale in early 1993, the RV8 was a far more expensive proposition than the first MGB. But with

production scheduled to run at only 15 cars a week, the company had more than enough orders. If nothing else, the RV8 served to keep the MG name alive and to whet the appetite for the all new MGF.

## Specification (1992)

**Engine:** V8, overhead-valve
**Bore × stroke:** 94 mm × 71 mm
**Capacity:** 3947 cc
**Maximum power:** 188 bhp
**Transmission:** five-speed manual gearbox, rear-wheel drive
**Chassis:** steel unitary construction body/chassis

*Right: The RV8 was the first MG sports car to carry the octagon badge since the demise of the MGB.*

**Suspension:** independent front with wishbones, coil springs, telescopic dampers and anti-roll bar; live rear axle with radius arms, coil springs and telescopic dampers
**Brakes:** discs front, drums rear; servo-assisted
**Bodywork:** steel open two-seater sports
**Maximum speed (approx):** 134 mph (216 km/h)

*elow: MG had a long and successful istory of old-fashioned styling, and e 1990s RV8, an update of the old 1GB, maintained the tradition.*

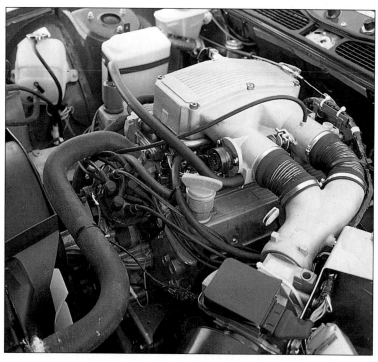

## MGF 1996-present

*Above: The arrival of the MGF in 1996 put the smile back on the faces of MG enthusiasts the world over, for here was a brand-new design in the finest tradi-tions of the marque. It was agile, rode well in a saloon-car sort of way thanks to Hydragas springs, was adequately powerful, especially in VVC variable-valve timing format, and as pretty a sports car as you could wish for. Its good looks were given a facelift in mid-1999. Powered by Rover's lightweight alu-minium 1.8-litre K-series unit, the MGF had a mid-engined layout, yet still provided decent luggage space for a sports car. The driving position was a bit cramped, but the dashboard contained some neat details like the black-on-cream dials. The manual folding soft-top was engineered by Pininfarina, and was quite in keeping with MG motoring from previous eras.*

After a succession of mundane MG-badged BL saloons – and the misguided MGB RV8 – the MGF was a welcome return to core MG values as an affordable two-seater sports car. Launched in 1996, the MGF took the marque through to its 75th anniversary in 1999 as the best selling sports car in the UK. The MGF was quite radical for Rover, being a mid-engined, rear-wheel drive configuration, whereas traditional MGs were invariably front-engine, rear drive. The competition-inspired powertrain layout provided good balance with high levels of grip for optimum handling, and under acceleration, weight transfer onto the driven rear wheels gave outstanding traction, with steering uncompromised by drive torque or front axle weight.

Although simple and efficient, the rounded body-shape of the MGF was restrained, and certainly less extravagant than its drivetrain format might have justified, designed to be functional rather than extrovert. Such understatement was calculated to impress traditional MG customers, and in this sense, Rover had got it just right.

The MGF was available with a choice of two engines, mounted transversely behind the cockpit and ahead of the rear wheels. Base unit was the much-praised 1.8-litre Rover K-series multi-point injection twin-cam engine, which developed 120 bhp at 5,500 rpm and a maximum torque of 165 Nm at 3,000 rpm. This all-aluminium engine was also selected by Lotus for the mid-engined Elise sports

car. The second, more highly tuned version was the 1.8i VVC power unit, which incorporated a unique Variable Valve Control system developed by Rover Group powertrain engineers. This allowed the opening period of the inlet valves to be varied, optimising torque and power output across the entire power band. Transmission was via a five-speed manual gearbox. Through gear acceleration achieved a 0–60 mph(0-96 km/h) time of 8.5 seconds and 7.0 seconds for the 1.8i and 1.8i VVC respectively, with maximum speeds of 120 mph (93 km/h) and 130 mph (209 km/h).

Suspension was by double wishbones front and rear, with tuned steer characteristics and a high ratio steering rack. The MGF's ride and handling balance was derived from Hydragas damper units interconnected front to rear that served as the springing medium, complemented by special dampers and front and rear anti-roll bars. The MGF's progress was retarded by disc brakes all round, and while ABS was standard on the VVC model, it was optional on the 1.8i. The 1.8i VVC was equipped with electric power-assisted steering that was speed and load-sensitive, which had the advantage over a conventional hydraulic PAS system in that pump groan and valve hiss were eliminated. Once again, this was optional on the base model.

The MGF was equipped with a black manual folding-hood, engineered by Pininfarina and made from woven acrylic fabric with a tinted plastic zip-down rear

window. A polymer hard top incorporating a heated rear window and full headlining was also available, converting the MGF into a snug coupé for the winter.

Within the cockpit was a centre console and a radio/cassette player with two speaker system. Door beams and reinforced waist line rails provided side impact protection, while a certain amount of roll-over protection was inherent in the 3 mm steel tube within the windscreen frame. Additional protection was provided by pyrotechnic seat belt pre-tensioners and a 30-litre driver's side airbag on both models, and an 80-litre passenger airbag was optional. The 50-litre fuel tank was isolated in its own steel cage.

Security systems for the MGF were developed in consultation with the British Police Scientific Development Branch, and included normal locking and remote-control locking, which meant immobilisation was automatically engaged thirty seconds after the ignition was switched off and the driver's door

opened. The car was alarmed eve when parked with the hood left dow and the bonnet release was located the boot for added security.

The bodyshells were built by Mot Panels who were Rover's partner in t development of the body design, a the dedicated Rover assembly line corporated advanced manufacturi techniques and equipment, as well a appropriate degree of hand workir The MGF was available in six standa body colours, known as flame red, wh diamond, metallic British racing gree metallic charcoal, amaranth and volcar

### Specification (1.8 VVC)
**Engine:** in-line four-cylinder
**Bore x stroke:** 80 mm x 89.3 mm
**Capacity:** 1798 cc
**Suspension:** independent by double wishbones, Hydragas springs and an roll bars
**Brakes:** discs all round, with ABS
**Chassis:** monocoque
**Body:** two-door two-seat roadster

# Mitsubishi Motor Corporation

**M**itsubishi was already a notable heavy-industry concern before it built its first few cars in 1917. Until 1959, however, it was still a company more concerned with shipbuilding and other heavy industry, and it had been extremely busy during World War II when its most famous product was the Zero fighter.

Serious Mitsubishi car production began in 1959, with mini-cars, and from 1963 the company began building US Jeeps under licence. Expansion was rapid in the 1970s, for by this time Chrysler-USA had acquired a stake in the company and had started selling rebadged Mitsubishis in the USA.

Until the 1980s Mitsubishi concentrated on making a wide variety of small and medium-sized (but only a few large) family cars, but the first smart coupés had also appeared, and the company had also begun supplying engines to Chrysler for use in USA-built cars. The first transverse-engined front-wheel-drive Mitsubishi, the Mirage, appeared in 1978, while 4 × 4 production expanded steadily, and successfully.

A move towards more sporty machines came in 1982, with the launch of the turbocharged Starion, but this was still only a toe-in-the-water exercise. Later in the 1980s the company drew on all its accumulated expertise, to launch complex new cars such as the little Dangan, and the four-wheel-drive, four-wheel-steering Galant VR-4. Next came the major push towards making sports cars and supercars. Mitsubishi collaborated with Chrysler to form a jointly-owned concern known as Diamond Star Motors, which combined Mitsubishi and Chrysler design input and began building sporting cars in a new factory in Illinois, USA.

The first fruit of this project was the Mitsubishi Eclipse, closely followed by the Mitsubishi GTO and 3000GT, both of which were sold alongside various Chrysler Eagle, Dodge and Plymouth-badged models. Mitsubishi was building over 800,000 cars a year by this time, and was extremely profitable and ambitious.

If Chrysler's own finances had not suffered so much in the recession which hit the USA at the end of the 1980s, the Diamond Star business might have prospered even more quickly than it did. As it was, in 1991 Chrysler was obliged to sell its stake to Mitsubishi, which allowed it to become yet another Japanese concern with its own North American assembly plant.

*Above: The Mitsubishi Galant VR-4, introduced in 1987, was a revolutionary design in that it featured both four-wheel drive and four-wheel steering. The advantages of these were soon proved with international rally successes.*

*Right: The Starion Turbo, launched in 1982, was the firm's first attempt on the large North American sports car market. It was fast, especially with the 200-bhp three-valves-per-cylinder engine, which gave a top speed of 143 mph. Later wide-body models, as shown, had the 177-bhp engine, which with the revised bodywork reduced top speed to 133 mph.*

*Below: A real supercar, the 3000GT reached Britain in 1992, and with its twin-turbo, 24-valve, three-litre V6 producing 281 bhp at 6,800 rpm and 300 lb ft of torque at 3,000 rpm, it could hit 60 mph in 6.5 seconds, the quarter-mile in 14.5 seconds, and go on to 153 mph.*

# Mitsubishi Starion Turbo 1982-89

flared wheel arches to cover this change made the styling more meaty than most people wanted. The 177-bhp engine was retained, and the 200-bhp unit was discontinued. With the 177-bhp engine the larger frontal area knocked back the top speed to 133 mph.

Even so, the turbocharged engine was none too flexible (*Autocar* described the engine as having "all the low-down punch of a tortoise . . ."), so as a final update the car was given the options of a four-speed automatic transmission and the larger Mitsubishi engine, a 91.1-mm × 98-mm 2.6-litre (2555-cc) unit with three valves per cylinder and the famous 'Lanchester' balancer-shaft technology. The result was a slower car, with more flexibility than before (output was 150 bhp for some markets, and 191 bhp for the USA), which was enough to keep it selling until the new GTO arrived in 1990.

Until the 1970s Mitsubishi had made a succession of worthy, but conventional-looking machines. Then the company began to change its image. First of all, coupés like the Sapporo appeared, then turbocharged engines and finally, in 1982, the Starion Turbo was launched.

Like most Japanese makers, Mitsubishi were aiming at the vast North American market. If the Starion had a direct competitor it was the new Porsche 944, though it would be some years before the image would catch up with the ambition. The Starion was a front-engined 2 + 2 seater hatchback coupé, with a wedge-nosed style and – at first – a 168-bhp engine.

By this stage all the Japanese carmakers were adept at what could cynically be called 'parts-bin' engineering, but which should be more accurately seen as the resourceful use of existing components. Much of the underside and platform was based on that of the Galant/Sapporo range, and included the suspension assemblies, the gearbox and the rear suspension from those cars. The engine was the turbocharged two-litre unit found in the Colt Lancer Turbo; not only did it have fuel injection but a phenomenal power output for what was really a simple two-valve overhead-cam turbocharged unit.

The new car had clearly been styled after a team of designers had looked closely at what Porsche and Nissan (with the 280Z) were already offering, for it was a chunky and individual-looking coupé, with a well-equipped interior, but with rear seats which were only practical if passengers could find somewhere else to put their legs!

The chassis was well developed; there was power steering, four-wheel disc brakes, and a great deal of performance. A good car became even better in 1984 when a turbocharger intercooler was added to the engine, increasing power to 177 bhp and the top speed to 138 mph. At the same time, an alternative version, with three valves per cylinder, 200 bhp, and an approximate top speed of 143 mph was added to the range. Then in 1986 the chassis was improved with a wider track, although the addition of

*Above: A 1987 Starion Turbo, with the bulbous bodywork that was made necessary by chassis improvements and the resulting wider track; despite the more aggressive look, the revised design actually reduced top speed.*

*Above: The fussy interior featured fingertip switch gear on either side of the leather-rimmed steering wheel.*

*Above: Pentti Airikkala and Ronan McNamee drove their Starion Turbo to a win in the Welsh International Rally of 1988, and had earlier won the Cartel Rally, first round of the British Open Championship.*

*Below: The 1982 Starion Turbo could accelerate to 60 mph in 7.5 seconds and go on to a maximum of 133 mph, with fuel consumption averaging 22 mpg; the EX version, launched in 1985, gave better performance but used more petrol.*

*Above: The Starion radiated character even if the whole package lacked a certain sophistication.*

## Specification (1982)

**Engine:** inline four-cylinder, single overhead camshaft; single Mitsubishi turbocharger (intercooler added for 1984 models)
**Bore × stroke:** 85 mm × 88 mm
**Capacity:** 1997 cc
**Maximum power:** 168 bhp
**Transmission:** five-speed manual gearbox or optional three-speed automatic transmission, rear-wheel drive
**Chassis:** steel unitary construction body/chassis
**Suspension:** independent with MacPherson struts and anti-roll bar front; MacPherson struts, lower wishbones and anti-roll bar rear
**Brakes:** discs all round
**Bodywork:** steel 2 + 2-seater hatchback coupé
**Maximum speed (approx):** 133 mph (214 km/h)

# Mitsubishi Galant VR-4 1987-present

Galant had been a familiar Mitsubishi model name for many years before a new family of medium-sized cars appeared in 1987. Right from the start these cars fell into what we might call the 'Sierra' size class and, like the Sierra, some were a lot more exciting than others.

The basic design featured a transverse-mounted four-cylinder engine (some with only 79 bhp), with front-wheel drive and a choice of transmissions. The most intriguing of all, however, was the VR-4, which featured a 16-valve two-litre twin-cam with a turbocharger and no less than 205 bhp. It could also boast four-wheel drive and Mitsubishi's new feature, four-wheel steering.

Into the 1990s there is still controversy about the worth of four-wheel steering. Is it really necessary in a car with modern chassis dynamics; does the customer even notice it is there? Nevertheless, the 205-bhp 4 × 4 chassis was undoubtedly effective, and at a stroke the comfortable-looking VR-4 became a car combining Sierra RS Cosworth straight-line speed with phenomenal traction.

Naturally it was soon groomed as Mitsubishi's World Rally Championship contender, and by 1990 it had recorded outright victories against the cream of the world's rally teams, with drivers like Ari Vatanen behind the wheel. The Galant won the Ivory Coast event ahead of an Audi Quattro and enjoyed other excellent placings such as fifth on the Safari, fourth and sixth at the New Zealand Rally, and a splendid second and third on one of the greatest of all rallies, the Finnish 1,000 Lakes.

In 1990, with motorsport in mind, an improved version was put on sale, with a larger turbo intercooler, better under-bonnet airflow, and a power increase, to 220 bhp.

Into the 1991 season the Galant did far better when not faced with the all-con-quering Lancia Delta HF Integrales, in their absence winning the Ivory Coast Rally, but by 1992 Japanese technology had moved on further. By the end of the decade the Galant had enough rallying credibility to achieve minor cult status.

*Above: A brilliant performance by Pentti Airikkala and Ronan McNamee in their Galant VR-4 gave them victory in the 1989 RAC Rally, and previously they had won the 1,000 Lakes event, but the title was Lancia's.*

*Above: Compact and powerful, the double-overhead-cam, 16-valve two-litre engine of the 1990 Galant GTi produced an extra 15 bhp over the VR-4. The car, intended for motorsport, had four-wheel drive and four-wheel steering.*

## Specification (1987)

**Engine:** inline four-cylinder, twin overhead camshafts; turbocharger and intercooler
**Bore × stroke:** 85 mm × 88 mm
**Capacity:** 1997 cc
**Maximum power:** 205 bhp
**Transmission:** five-speed manual gearbox, four-wheel drive and four-wheel steering
**Chassis:** steel unitary construction body/chassis
**Suspension:** independent with MacPherson struts and anti-roll bar front; compound axle with torsion tube and trailing arms, coil springs and telescopic dampers rear
**Brakes:** discs all round
**Bodywork:** steel four-door four-seater saloon, or five-door hatchback
**Maximum speed (approx):** 143 mph (230 km/h)

*Below: A 1989 Galant VR-4, with sober saloon styling which hardly expressed the performance and advanced technology underneath; but buyers remained unconvinced of the merits of all-wheel steering.*

## Mitsubishi Eclipse 1989–93

Mitsubishi's links with Chrysler were originally forged at the end of the 1960s, but it was not until the 1980s that jointly-developed models went on sale. The smart three-door Eclipse, launched in 1989, was originally shown as a Chrysler Eagle Talon GSi or a Plymouth Laser, and was built at the new Diamond Star factory in Illinois, though much of its chassis technology was Japanese.

The Eclipse was in fact closely based on the platform, suspension and engines of the new late-1980s generation of Galant models, although the body style – a sleek, smoothly detailed, 2 + 2 hatchback – was all new, and shared with the Chrysler Eagle.

Like the latest Galant, therefore, the Eclipse had a choice of transverse-engined front-wheel-drive or four-wheel drive transmissions, with engines which spanned the whole range from a 1.8-litre/92-bhp unit to a slightly under-square turbocharged 2.0-litre engine which produced 200 bhp.

The Eclipse, in other words, offered almost everything to almost everyone, especially as it was sold at bargain prices in the first model years. At the top of the range Mitsubishi had great hopes for the four-wheel-drive 200-bhp GSX, dubbing it the "poor man's Porsche 959". This claim was certainly far-fetched in some ways (especially in terms of its power-to-weight ratio), but there was no doubting the Eclipse's phenomenal traction, and its roadholding balance. That was achieved through the use of a four-wheel-drive system utilising a central viscous coupling dividing torque equally between the front and rear pairs of wheels, while drive to the rear wheels was fed through a limited-slip differential.

The style was simple, rounded, and extremely attractive; it was what became known in the 1990s as a cab-forward design, with a low and rounded nose, a wing crown line which rose gradually towards the tail, and a generously detailed 'glasshouse' above the waist line.

Chrysler's own financial problems (which included having to sell off its stake in Diamond Star) hid the true worth of this beautifully-balanced design at first, but once it was joined by the new V6-engined Stealth/GTO models, the promise of this co-operation was there for all to see.

*Above: A smooth, aerodynamic coupé with looks very much in tune with 1990s thinking, the Galant-based Eclipse was offered with up to 200 bhp.*

*Above: The 1990 Eclipse GS Turbo, with four-wheel drive and a rear limited-slip differential, gave tremendous traction and performance to match, with fuel consumption between 16 and 31 mpg.*

### Specification (1990 GSX)

**Engine:** inline four-cylinder, twin overhead camshafts; single Mitsubishi turbocharger
**Bore × stroke:** 85 mm × 88 mm
**Capacity:** 1997 cc
**Maximum power:** 200 bhp
**Transmission:** five-speed manual gearbox or four-speed automatic transmission, four-wheel drive
**Chassis:** steel unitary construction body/chassis
**Suspension:** independent with MacPherson struts and anti-roll bar front; compound axle with torsion tube and trailing arms, coil springs and telescopic dampers rear
**Brakes:** discs all round
**Bodywork::** steel 2 + 2 three-door hatchback
**Maximum speed (approx):** 143 mph (230 km/h)

*Left: Identical to the Eclipse, a 1990 Chrysler Eagle Talon proves its all-wheel grip in snow.*

# Mitsubishi 3000GT 1990-present

he second Diamond Star Motors pro-ject (the Eclipse/Chrysler Eagle being he first) was an even more ambitious machine. For Mitsubishi this was meant be a replacement for the long-lived, st, but rather crude Starion, and was an together quicker and more technologi-lly advanced machine. For Chrysler, e new car (produced as a Dodge ealth) was a larger, faster and more ylish addition to the range. Both cars ere to be built in the Illinois factory.

As with the Eclipse, the Mitsubishi and hrysler products shared an identical porpan, and a complex choice of front-ounted transverse engines, transmis-ons and suspensions, but this time ere was an easily-spotted difference 'greenhouse' styling between the itsubishi and Dodge types.

The basis of all the cars was the same alant and Eclipse-based platform, but e engine was a new 24-valve twin-erhead-cam V6 unit which also found a me in Mitsubishi's new large saloon, e Diamante. As with the Eclipse, there as a choice between front-wheel drive four-wheel drive in the USA market,

but for export all cars were to be sold with four-wheel drive.

Both Mitsubishi and Dodge cars looked absolutely stunning, with rounded contours, softly detailed noses, and 2 + 2 seating. In their most highly tuned forms, performance matched their looks; these were extremely fast cars – far too fast, in-deed, to be let out on any public road in the USA, where many of the machines would certainly be sold.

The complex V6 engine could power the 3,800-lb car to a maximum speed of 153 mph, reaching 60 mph along the way in just 5.6 seconds; and with twin turbo-chargers (rather than a single larger unit) being fitted, turbo lag was virtually eliminated.

Cars like this, however, did not sell on their performance, but on their looks and their equipment, both of which were second to none. There was electroni-cally-variable four-wheel steering (of Galant VR-4 type), anti-lock brakes, air conditioning, active aerodynamics (which meant that the tail spoiler altered its angle of attack as the speed rose), and the cars were even equipped

with variable-geometry rear suspension which was sensitive to braking or lift-throttle conditions in cornering. The end result was extremely secure handling; the 3000GT had immense grip, turned into corners sharply and could be powered out of them at very high speeds with no loss of traction. There was a high price to pay for these abilities – some £45,000 in 1999 – but compared with Porsche prices, that seemed a bargain.

*Above: The styling of the 150-mph, four-wheel-drive and four-wheel-steer 3000GT was striking, with vestigial Ferrari Testarossa-like vents ahead of the rear wheels.*

*Below: The lavishly-equipped interior featured an electrically-adjustable driver's seat, with air conditioning as standard, as was a six-CD autochanger in the boot.*

*Left: Despite 300 lb ft of torque from the 24-valve V6 and a 153 mph top speed, the 3,800-lb car accelerated in high gears more slowly than its main rivals. Fuel consumption was high, averaging less than 17 mpg.*

## Mitsubishi 3000GT variants

### Dodge Stealth

The Dodge Stealth of North America, also launched in 1990, was mechanically almost identical to the Mitsubishi, with a broadly similar body, but had different 'greenhouse' styling. It was built on the same assembly lines as the Mitsubishi.

The bottom-of-the range Stealth, however, was quite a different prospect from the 3000GT, with a power output of only 166 bhp.

## Specification (1992)

**Engine:** V6, twin overhead camshafts per bank of cylinders; twin-turbo
**Bore × stroke:** 91 mm × 76 mm
**Capacity:** 2972 cc
**Maximum power:** 300 bhp at 6,000 rpm
**Transmission:** five-speed manual gearbox, four-wheel drive
**Chassis:** steel unitary construction body/chassis
**Suspension:** independent with MacPherson struts and anti-roll bar front; double wishbones, coil springs, telescopic dampers and anti-roll bar rear; electronically-controlled damping
**Brakes:** discs all round
**Bodywork:** steel 2 + 2 two-door coupé
**Maximum speed (approx):** 153 mph (246 km/h)

# Monica

Jean Tastevin was already the successful head of CFPM (Compagnie Française des Produits Metallurgiques), a firm of railway wagon manufacturers from Balbigny, near Lyon in France, when he decided to start making motor cars. Having read about Chris Lawrence's exploits in motorsport, Tastevin contacted him, and suggested a liaison.

The final result was the short-lived Monica, though the end product was not the original machine that Tastevin had conceived. Lawrence was first of all asked to provide a tuned version of the Triumph TR4 engine, but soon persuaded the French industrialist that he should design the whole car!

In 1967 work began in the UK, but the race-tuned Triumph engine was soon abandoned in favour of a special three-litre V8 designed by Lawrence's associate Ted Martin. Shortly, however, the idea of producing a sports car was cancelled, and replaced by a much larger, Grand Touring car concept.

The first prototype was ready in 1968, but it took two further years for the style to be settled upon, and for six prototypes to be made. By 1972, when the prototype was shown at the Paris Salon, Tastevin had taken over the project, Lawrence had faded out of the picture, and the car had been given a name – Monica, after Tastevin's wife.

Even then there was much change in prospect before sales could begin, for the style was altered yet again and, most importantly of all, the troublesome Martin engine was abandoned in favour of a big, heavy, but completely trustworthy Chrysler V8.

Unhappily for Tastevin, the Monica went the same way as its spiritual predecessor, the Facel Vega. There were few French buyers, and few other possible customers for a French-built car with Detroit power. The eruption of the 'energy crisis' in the autumn of 1973 didn't help either.

The result was that very few Monicas were ever produced before the project was halted in February 1975. A smaller company than CFPM would have gone bankrupt in the process, but the railway business could support such a folly, and the company survived an ill-judged and under-developed disaster.

After the Monica episode, the factory at Balbigny reverted totally to producing railway wagons, and although Chris Lawrence later tried to revive the Monica project by contacting Bob Jankel of Panther Westwinds, nothing came of it.

*Above: Following a protracted gestation from 1968, with numerous hitches along the way, the Monica coupé, in its final form, was an extremely attractive four-door design which offered excellent performance and handling and air-conditioned luxury for four adults.*

*Below: Long, low and aerodynamic, the hand-built Monica, named after Jean Tastevin's wife, was powered by a 5.6-litre Chrysler V8, which gave a top speed of around 150 mph and acceleration to 60 mph in 7.7 seconds. Of the 30 or so Monicas built, some 25 were prototypes.*

# Monica 1973-75

*Left: The front, with the low nose and pop-up headlamps, was smoothly aerodynamic and aided downforce – vital in a car capable of 150 mph.*

*Below: The Monica's interior was trimmed in the finest materials, with a veneered fascia and padded leather trim and upholstery.*

The original Monica design was conceived totally by Chris Lawrence, of Lawrencetune fame, and was a front-engined, four-door Grand Touring saloon meant to be in the Facel Vega, Lagonda, Iso Rivolta and Maserati mould. It could not possibly be a Ferrari competitor because it lacked a suitably charismatic engine.

Lawrence based his design on a multi-tubular chassis frame, with a front-mounted engine, and with a de Dion rear axle allied to a Rover P6B differential. He styled the car himself, the first alloy-bodied prototype being built by Lawrencetune, the second by Williams and Pritchard in north London.

In the next four years Jean Tastevin took over responsibility for the car's shape, first by commissioning two French stylists – Robert Collinée and Tony Rascanu – and finally by hiring David Coward to clean up and finalise the four-door shape. Vignale of Italy produced the third prototype in steel; then Airflow Streamlines of Northampton pro-

duced two sets of panels, this time in alloy again.

The muddle – and this is the most charitable way the project can be described – continued with Rolls-Royce being approached to make engine castings (they refused), with Jensen being asked to consider making the body shells, and finally with CFPM being charged with setting up its own facilities, and producing the shells in steel.

All this took time, and with the Martin engine continuing to give trouble, the months slipped by alarmingly fast. Even though the Martin unit was enlarged to 3.4 litres, it was not up to the job, so in the winter of 1972-73 Tastevin ordered the fitment of a Chrysler V8 and its related automatic transmission instead.

The definitive style was shown at Geneva in 1973, at which time the car was seen to have a very torquey, hand-rebuilt, Chrysler engine, and a claimed top speed of around 150 mph. On paper, at least, the specification could match that of its rivals, for there was generous

accommodation, good ride and handling, and air conditioning to keep the (wealthy) customers comfortable.

Even so, sales, which were always slow and garnered one by one, did not truly begin until 1974, by which time the Monica was priced at £14,000 – about the same cost, at the time, as a Lamborghini Espada. Predictably, demand never increased, and Tastevin finally abandoned the project a year later.

The main problem was that the car conceived in 1967 was no longer suitable for sale in 1974 – and the public was always cautious about buying such an expensive hybrid from an unknown manufacturer. Between 30 and 35 Monicas were built.

## Specification (1974)
**Engine:** V8, overhead-valve
**Bore × stroke:** 102.6 mm × 84.06 mm
**Capacity:** 5560 cc
**Maximum power:** 280 bhp
**Transmission:** three-speed automatic transmission, rear-wheel drive
**Chassis:** steel multi-tubular frame, welded to steel body shell on assembly
**Suspension:** independent front with wishbones, coil springs and telescopic dampers; de Dion rear axle with coil springs and telescopic dampers
**Brakes:** discs all round
**Bodywork:** steel four-door four-seater sports saloon
**Maximum speed (approx):** 150 mph (241 km/h)

*Below: The Monica had been intended, like the Facel Vega and Iso Rivolta, to combine the best of coachbuilt styling and interiors with the sheer power of an American V8; the result was a superb performer, but buyers were few.*

# Monteverdi

The Monteverdi story began in Binningen, Switzerland, where Peter Monteverdi's father, Rosolino, had a multi-faceted automobile business. By 1951, when the young Monteverdi built his first car – a Fiat 1100 Balilla-engined special – his father had progressed from being a mechanic to a very well-established motor trader.

The elder Monteverdi died in 1956, leaving the 22-year-old Peter to run the business. Peter soon expanded the company, concentrating on fast GT cars, and shortly took on the Ferrari dealership for north-east Switzerland. In 1957 he began to race, at first in a Ferrari sports car. In 1959 he set up his own-make MBM Formula Junior team, and by the early 1960s the business had also started to sell Rolls-Royces, BMWs and Lancias.

Like many ambitious entrepreneurs, Monteverdi eventually quarrelled with Ferrari and lost the distributorship. Like Ferruccio Lamborghini, Monteverdi then decided to take his revenge by setting up a rival business – the result being the birth of the Monteverdi GT car. Unlike Lamborghini, however, Peter Monteverdi could not draw on a pool of local skilled labour, and he was certainly not able to have his own engines and bodies made in Switzerland.

For the decade in which Monteverdi cars were produced in Switzerland, therefore, the production process involved chassis and bodies being trucked to and from northern Italy, while engines, transmissions and most of the running gear were imported to Binningen for final assembly.

The original Monteverdi car of 1967 was the beautiful fastback 375S – where the '375' referred to the Chrysler engine's power output. Like all subsequent Monteverdi private cars, this had a simple but rigid chassis designed by Peter Monteverdi, but although links were originally forged with the Frua coachbuilding concern, almost all production cars were eventually produced by Fissore of Savigliano.

Like all Monteverdis, the 375S's chassis was fabricated in Switzerland before being sent to Italy. The body shells were hand-beaten by craftsmen at Fissore, mated with the chassis, then the assemblies were returned to Binningen. All painting, wiring and assembly was then carried out there, and Peter Monteverdi is reputed to have test-driven every car before it was delivered to the customer.

In the next few years the Monteverdi marque prospered in a hand-built manner, around what seemed to be a multitude of models, and production never exceeded 60-80 cars a year. In fact there were only two basic chassis designs – one being the front-engined layout which included the 375S, the 375L 2+2, the 375C Cabriolet and the very large 375/4 Limousine, the other being the mid-engined two-seater Hai 450SS type.

Like many such small companies, however, the energy crisis, and the explosion in car-running costs which followed, hit hard at Monteverdi in the mid-1970s. The car side of the business ran down rapidly, and the fast and sleek GTs were soon displaced by the Safari 4 × 4 model. Later Monteverdi produced its own four-door conversion of the Range Rover, but by the mid-1980s the marque had disappeared completely. GT production was measured only in hundreds, and was certainly never enough to perturb the established supercar manufacturers.

Early in the 1990s the Monteverdi name once again flared into the limelight, when the mercurial Swiss bought the bankrupt remains of the Onyx Formula 1 team. Within months, however, he had renamed the team Monteverdi, inexplicably run it into the ground, and disappeared from the motor racing scene.

**Above:** *Attractive, and rather reminiscent of the Ferrari Dino, the Hai 450SS was a mid-engined two-seater which offered tremendous performance and handling. Largely hand-built and very expensive, its sales did not harm the main supercar makers.*

**Right:** *Monteverdi bought the Onyx team with the intention of fielding the ORE-1 and ORE-2 cars in Formula 1, but nothing came of it. This 1991 car, designed by Alan Jenkins and with a specification little changed since 1989, was powered by a Cosworth DFR V8.*

# Monteverdi 375S 1967-77

*Left: Monteverdi's Palm Beach cabriolet of 1975 was powered by the Chrysler 7.2-litre V8. With 375 bhp and enormous torque, it offered effortless performance, but the high price and the 1970s oil crises ensured that sales were minimal.*

*Above: Peter Monteverdi's father had imported Ferraris, Rolls-Royces and other makes; later the son quarrelled with Ferrari and then decided to build his own cars.*

The original Monteverdi production car, badged 375S, was revealed at the 1967 Frankfurt Motor Show, and the first deliveries followed during 1968. Like all subsequent cars from this tiny Swiss concern, the first model had a rugged but simple chassis frame, fabricated from square-section steel tubes.

In many ways the new Monteverdi followed traditions established by Iso Rivolta in Italy, and by Jensen in Great Britain. For power it chose American engines and running gear, while it used Italian expertise and craftsmanship to shape the car.

The engine was Chrysler's famous 7.2-litre Magnum 440 V8, which Jensen was to use in the SP model, but which was more famous for its use in Chrysler New Yorkers and other full-sized saloons and limos of the period. Naturally it was backed by Chrysler's own TorqueFlite

*Below: The Frua- (and then Fissori-) styled 375S was very handsome, and went as well as it looked.*

automatic transmission (not only Jensen, but Aston Martin, also used this gearbox), or a manual option, while the rest of the running gear included Girling brakes, ZF steering, and a Salisbury rear differential.

The original car was styled by Frua, which naturally made it look similar to other contemporary Frua designs such as the AC 428 and the Maserati Mistrale coupés. By the time series-production began, this shape had been revised, and from 1969 production was by Fissore of Italy. This time the front end had been re-shaped, and there was an efficient air-conditioning installation. However, even though the new cars looked wonderful, and were undoubtedly very fast, build quality was often disappointing. In many ways, therefore, Monteverdi was harking back to the Ferrari philosophy of the 1950s, when performance and style took precedence over most other aspects.

Sales of the 375S were always limited, so to give the image a boost Monteverdi asked Fissore to provide a facelift. This

new style, called the Berlinetta, took over in 1972, and in 1975 it was also joined by a convertible type called the Palm Beach, though both models had died out by 1977.

## Monteverdi 375S variants

### Monteverdi 375C Cabriolet

From 1971 Monteverdi also offered a two-seater Cabriolet version, badged 375C and introduced at the Geneva Show. This had the same basic lines as the coupé, was also made by Fissore, and had a fold-down soft top. It was extremely rare.

### Monteverdi Berlinetta

From spring 1972 the original car was displaced by the Berlinetta, a two-seater fastback coupé which used the same basic chassis and body shell as the ousted 375S, but had a new front end style with rectangular headlamps, and used the famous Chrysler Hemi engine of 107.95 mm × 95.25 mm, displacing 6974 cc and producing 390 bhp. At first this was allied to a five-speed ZF gearbox, but from 1973 the familiar Chrysler manual or automatic transmission were also on offer, as was the old-type 7210-cc engine, which had been re-rated at 340 bhp. The top speed of the Hemi-engined coupé was claimed to be 180 mph, which was almost certainly an exaggeration.

### Monteverdi Palm Beach

In 1975 the Palm Beach cabriolet was added to the range. This was effectively a soft-top version of the Berlinetta, and was equally rare.

## Specification (1967)

**Engine:** V8, overhead-valve
**Bore × stroke:** 109.72 mm × 95.25 mm
**Capacity:** 7210 cc
**Maximum power:** 375 bhp (400 bhp optional)
**Transmission:** four-speed manual gearbox or three-speed automatic transmission, rear-wheel drive
**Chassis:** separate steel ladder frame with square-section main side members and cross-bracings
**Suspension:** independent front with wishbones, coil springs and telescopic dampers; de Dion rear axle with coil springs and telescopic dampers
**Brakes:** discs all round
**Bodywork:** steel two-seater two-door fastback coupé
**Maximum speed (approx):** (375-bhp model) 152 mph (245 km/h)

# Monteverdi 375L 2 + 2 1969-75

The second Monteverdi was a longer-wheelbase model than the 375S with 2 + 2 seating, so logically it was dubbed 375L 2 + 2. Making its debut at the Geneva Show in 1969, it featured a 5.9-in longer version of the original chassis and had automatic transmission as standard.

The Fissore-styled 375L 2 + 2 was longer (by 7.5 inches) than the 375S, but typical Italian packaging ingenuity produced a car which looked equally as smooth as the two-seater *and* with 2 + 2 seating. In many ways it resembled the current four-seater Ferrari (the 365 GT 2+2), and theoretically it was competing for the same clientele.

As changes were made to the shorter-wheelbase Monteverdis, they were also applied to the 375L 2+2. In particular, the car became available with the brawny Chrysler Hemi unit as an option.

Sales of 375Ls dried up in 1975, and this 160-mph car was never replaced.

## Monteverdi 375L variants

### Monteverdi 375L Hemi

From 1971 this new derivative was made available – like the original car, but fitted with the Chrysler Hemi engine, of 107.95 mm × 95.25 mm, displacing 6974 cc and producing an enormous 390 bhp. Claimed top speed was 162 mph.

### Specification (1969)

**Engine:** V8, overhead-valve
**Bore × stroke:** 109.72 mm × 95.25 mm
**Capacity:** 7210 cc
**Maximum power:** 340 bhp
**Transmission:** three-speed automatic transmission, rear-wheel drive
**Chassis:** separate steel ladder frame with square-section tubular main side members and cross-bracings
**Suspension:** independent front with wishbones, coil springs and telescopic dampers; de Dion rear axle with coil springs and telescopic dampers
**Brakes:** discs all round
**Bodywork:** steel two-door 2 + 2 coupé
**Maximum speed (approx):** 152 mph (245 km/h)

*Right: The long-wheelbase 375L was a two-door car with comfortable rear seating, and performance as high as 162 mph with the 390-bhp V8.*

# Monteverdi 375/4 1971-77

The third derivative of the front-engined Monteverdi theme was the massive 375/4 model, which had four doors and was built either as a saloon or (with a division) as a limousine.

Compared with the original 375S, the 375/4 had a 26.7-in longer wheelbase. Since the original track dimensions were retained, and the overall length was no less than 209 inches, this made it a long and slim machine, and the Fissore style was elegant, if a touch angular.

Like the other front-engined Monteverdis, this car was available with the Chrysler 440 Magnum, or with the sporty Chrysler Hemi power unit. Naturally, automatic transmission was standard, as was air conditioning and power-assisted steering.

### Specification (1971)

**Engine:** V8, overhead-valve
**Bore × stroke:** 109.72 mm × 95.25 mm
**Capacity:** 7210 cc
**Maximum power:** 340 bhp
**Transmission:** three-speed automatic transmission, rear-wheel drive
**Chassis:** separate steel frame with square-section tubular main side members and cross-bracings
**Suspension:** independent front with wishbones, coil springs and telescopic dampers; de Dion rear axle with coil springs and telescopic dampers
**Brakes:** discs all round
**Bodywork:** steel four-door five-seater saloon or limousine
**Maximum speed (approx):** 140 mph (225 km/h)

*Below: The Fissore-styled 375/4 gave tremendous performance, and with much more space than Ferrari could offer in the 365 GT4 2+2 or 400. The price was prodigiously high, but the few makers, including Rolls-Royce, could rival the degree of exclusivity guaranteed by this rocket-like limousine.*

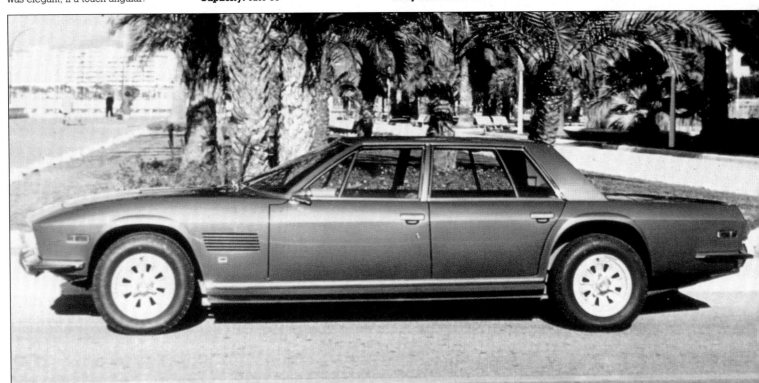

# Monteverdi Hai 450SS/450GTS 1970-76

To follow his established line of sleek front-engined supercars, Peter Monteverdi then astonished the world of motoring by announcing a starkly but brutally attractive mid-engined car, the Hai 450SS.

This car, complete with the seven-litre Chrysler Hemi engine and ZF gearbox, looked every bit as purposeful as the contemporary Lamborghini Miura or the Maserati Bora, even if its maker had no similar reputation to help him sell the cars. The Hai, in fact, was meant to be a truly versatile machine; not only did it have shattering performance, but its cabin was also air-conditioned, and had a great deal of equipment to make the car as comfortable and convenient as possible.

The layout was conceived in 1969, and the first prototype was ready for the 1970 Geneva Motor Show. Monteverdi's stated intention was to produce no more than one Hai every month (assuming the demand was even that high), and to keep investment costs down he wanted to use as many as possible of the components already being used in the front-engined 375-series cars.

The chassis, like those used in the front-engined Monteverdis, and in other Italian supercars of the period, was a solid steel multi-tubular frame, with rectangular-section tubes and suitable cross-bracings. The front suspension was lifted from the 375 models, and much of the de Dion rear suspension layout was also taken from the front-engined cars' design.

The engine, also shared with other Monteverdis, was the Chrysler Hemi unit, built in Detroit. Although this engine produced 390 bhp (DIN), Monteverdi liked to quote its SAE (gross) figure of 450 bhp, a number which gave the car its model name. The 'Hai' part of the title, in-

cidentally, was derived from the German word for shark, while 'SS' merely stood for Super Sports, which it most assuredly was.

The bulky engine, which was almost as wide as it was long, was mounted well forward, and was mated to the same type of ZF gearbox used in Maseratis and De Tomasos. This forward mounting, in fact, required a power bulge in the cabin bulkhead, and the two seats had to be spread wide to accommodate it.

To clothe this exciting, if simple, structure, Monteverdi commissioned Fissore to build the curvaceous bodies, which bore a close stylistic resemblance to the front-engined models. The nose of the Hai was so low, and the wheel 'boxes' so obtrusive that there was no space ahead of the occupants for anything except the large fuel tank and the radiator. When the car was launched, there was no spare wheel in the specification, because the front and rear wheels were of different sizes, but complaints from potential customers soon put a stop to that!

The Hai was always expensive – 82,400 Swiss Francs at launch, which was 10,000Sfr more than a Miura, for instance – but it was always claimed to be phenomenally fast. Certainly its performance matched that of contemporary supercars; in its native Switzerland, *Revue*

*Above: Italian coachbuilders Fissore designed and built the Hai bodies for Monteverdi.*

*Automobile* clocked one at 169 mph.

Despite its extraordinary performance, very few Hais were sold, even after 1973 when the original 450SS became the 450GTS, complete with a slightly longer wheelbase and more roomy cockpit. Potential customers, it seemed, preferred to stand in line for a Miura, a Countach, a Bora or a Boxer.

## Specification (1970)

**Engine:** V8, overhead-valve
**Bore × stroke:** 107.95 mm × 95.25 mm
**Capacity:** 6974 cc
**Maximum power:** 390 bhp
**Transmission:** five-speed manual gearbox, rear-wheel drive
**Chassis:** separate steel frame with square-section tubular main side members and cross-bracings
**Suspension:** independent front with wishbones, coil springs and telescopic dampers; de Dion rear axle with coil springs and telescopic dampers
**Brakes:** discs all round
**Bodywork:** light-alloy mid-engined two-seater coupé
**Maximum speed (approx):** 169 mph (272 km/h)

*Above: Although the engine was rear-mounted, Fissore was able to fit a large rear window in his design.*

*Below: The big mid-mounted seven-litre Chrysler V8 gave a top speed of 169 mph and stunning acceleration.*

## Monteverdi Sierra 1977-78

After the effects of the energy crisis had changed the European motor industry, Monteverdi found its car sales falling away badly. This, no doubt, was made worse by the lack of new models, for there is nothing which bores well-to-do buyers more quickly than familiarity.

To counter this, and to reflect the changing times, the Swiss company produced a new model – the Sierra. This, of course, was years before Ford picked up the same name for a totally different type of car.

Hindsight tells us that Monteverdi got it wrong on almost every count. Although Fissore (by this time financially con-

*Left: Monteverdi's Sierra was really the wrong car at the wrong time. Its styling was forgettable and the model had no real advantages over its main rivals.*

trolled by Monteverdi) produced a new unitary-construction layout, and smaller Chrysler engines were chosen to power it, Monteverdi ignored the two-door coupé style that had served the company so well. Instead he decided to offer the two body styles that had *never* sold well for him – a four-door saloon and a two-door convertible!

The saloon looked much like the BMW 7-Series or Peugeot 604s of the day, while the convertible was a rather amorphous, even angular, machine which was a step back from the late-1960s lines of the 375S and 375L. And although Monteverdi had made some concessions to the changing post-energy crisis world of using smaller engines, their units were not really in tune with the times, being either the 5.2-litre or 5.9-litre pushrod Chrysler V8s producing 168 bhp and 180

bhp respectively – hardly new, fuel efficient powerplants. That, coupled with the cars' unfortunate looks, meant it was no surprise that sales were very low and that the Sierra was dropped after less than two years.

### Specification (1971)

**Engine:** V8, overhead-valve
**Bore × stroke:** 99.31 mm × 84.07 mm
**Capacity:** 5210 cc
**Maximum power:** 168 bhp
**Transmission:** three-speed automatic transmission, rear-wheel drive
**Chassis:** unitary construction steel body/chassis
**Suspension:** independent front with wishbones, coil springs and telescopic dampers; live rear axle with coil springs and telescopic dampers
**Brakes:** discs all round
**Bodywork:** steel four-door four-seater saloon, or two-door four-seater cabriolet
**Maximum speed (approx):** 112 mph (180 km/h)

# Morgan Motor Company

*Above: Morgan's badge design is flexible enough to accommodate the model names from +4 to +8.*

*Left: Morgan really made its name producing sporty three-wheelers. This is a JAP motorcycle-engined trike, although the company later produced a car-engined three-wheeler.*

Since 1935, when the original Morgan sports car was announced, the small Worcestershire-based company has made a comfortable living by staying close to its traditions. In a time when rivals have made frenzied dashes to innovation, to new styles and new mechanical trends, Morgan has stuck with what it knows best. The result is that today's Morgan looks much like its ancestors – and the customers love it.

The Morgan Motor Company was set up in 1910 at Malvern Link, and for the next 25 years it built a variety of three-wheelers, all of which had a single rear wheel. More importantly, they all had sliding-pillar independent front suspension, a feature which has persisted on all subsequent Morgan products.

The three-wheelers had tubular chassis frames until 1933, but a pressed frame with 'Z'-section side members was adopted thereafter, this being another feature which has remained to this day. Three-wheeler popularity was at its zenith in the 1920s, and continued long after the birth of the first Morgan four-wheel sports car, until 1951.

When changes in government taxation led to a dramatic slump in three-wheeler sales in the mid-1930s, H. F. S. Morgan, the company's founder, speedily developed a conventional four-wheel sports car, which was launched at the end of 1935. Because Morgan was, and still is, a small family-financed concern, capital investment had to be marginal, and there were many 'bought-in' items; Morgan has never, for example, built an engine.

The new 4/4 set the pattern to be followed by its descendants, for its chassis had the 'Z'-section side members, there was sliding-pillar

independent front suspension, the body style was that of an open sports car with separate, flowing, front wings, constructed around a wooden skeleton, and all major mechanical items – engine, gearbox, rear axle and brakes – were proprietary units.

By 1930s standards the original Morgan 4/4 was a modern design, but after World War II the company showed no signs of updating, or changing, its range. Even though other sports car makers eventually introduced smooth new styles with more luxuriously-trimmed interiors, with better chassis and more supple suspension, Morgan stuck to its original designs.

Mechanical improvements came steadily – a new type of engine here, a different braking installation there, a change of gearbox one year, of steering gear the next – although the style altered almost imperceptibly. Two-seaters were joined by four-seaters, sports tourers by drop-head coupés, but only the short-lived glassfibre-bodied Plus Four Plus disturbed the traditions – and H. F. S.'s son Peter admitted that it was a mistake.

Take-over offers came, and were rebuffed – most notably from Standard-Triumph in the 1950s, and from Leyland-owned Rover in 1966 but the company carried serenely on. There were times when the demand for anachronistic new Morgans fell away but there were also times when the waiting list for cars reached 10 years.

Peter's son Charles took over the reins in the early 1990s and brought the company up-to-date. Although traditional construction methods held sway, the cars complied with ever-more stringent safety legislation. Other evolutions were in the pipeline including honeycomb aluminium and composite chassis, while certain models had one-piece GRP bodyshells

## Morgan Super Sports 1928-38

*Left: Morgan three-wheelers only offered minimal cockpit room for two people within the very narrow, strictly open body.*

*Below: The three-wheelers' handling was good enough for them to be raced with great verve.*

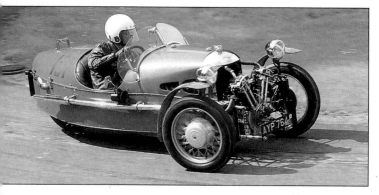

*Below: Placing the engine, in this case a JAP twin, ahead of the Morris Bullnose-like radiator was a styling master-stroke achieved by chance.*

For many years the only models that Morgan built were three-wheelers, and the earliest could hardly be called sports cars; some even had tiller steering. But as the company grew, it produced sportier versions like the Super Sports of the late 1920s, along with Aero variants, distinguished by a tiny tapering tail. The Aero name came from the presence of small aero screens rather than a proper windscreen. The three-wheelers were powered by a number of engines, all built by outside concerns rather than Morgan, and they included JAP, Anzani, Blackburne and Matchless. As these names suggest, Morgan used motor-cycle engines, a V-twin layout being ideal to hang at the front of the car, actually ahead of the radiator.

The Super Sports Aero of the early 1930s was the epitome of the classic Morgan three-wheeler, with very racy looks which masked a tubular central spine (enclosing the propshaft and acting as the main chassis) rigidly connecting the engine to the final-drive housing, from which went double chain drive to the single rear wheel. That wheel was located and sprung by two sets of quarter-elliptic leaf springs, one set on each side of the vestigial rear axle. The front suspension was, inevitably, by the time-honoured Morgan system of sliding pillars.

It was all very basic with no weather protection for the driver, no bumpers front and rear, and only a two-speed transmission. Nevertheless it was light enough that only the single rear brake was foot-operated, while the handbrake worked on the two small front drums. The car's light weight also meant that performance was also sprightly if hardly devastating, and the 1.1-litre JAP engine, for example, in 45-bhp tune could produce a top speed of 75 mph.

*Above: Like all Morgans, the three-wheelers used the company's traditional sliding-pillar front suspension. The JAP V-twin engine was a one-litre overhead-valve unit producing 45 bhp.*

### Specification (1930)

**Engine:** JAP V-twin, overhead-valve
**Bore × stroke:** 85.7 mm × 95 mm
**Capacity:** 1096 cc
**Maximum power:** 45 bhp
**Transmission:** two-speed manual
**Chassis:** tubular steel spine with two supplementary tubular chassis members
**Suspension:** independent with sliding pillars front; twin quarter-elliptic leaf springs rear
**Brakes:** drums all round
**Bodywork:** steel open two-seater
**Maximum speed (approx):** 75 mph (121 km/h)

# Morgan 4/4 1936-50

The original Morgan sports car drew heavily on the company's existing F-Type three-wheeler for its inspiration, though that model was powered by the humble side-valve Ford engine. The new sports car, called the 4/4, used a new version of the frame, complete with 'Z'-section side members, and was powered by a Coventry Climax engine.

The layout of the 4/4 set Morgan standards for years to come. The frame was a simple ladder-style affair, with coil-spring and sliding-pillar independent front suspension, and a beam rear axle mounted above the line of the side members. The gearbox (a Meadows unit) was separated from the engine by a long aluminium tube and the Coventry Climax powerplant was an overhead-inlet/side-exhaust design, one supplied to many other British carmakers of the period.

In the style of the day, it was a markedly over-square design with bore and stroke of 63 mm × 90 mm. With its rather basic valve gear, output was just 34 bhp from the 1122-cc displacement.

There were several design features unique to the Morgan, however, such as its styling, with the distinctive radiator, separate headlamps, and flowing front wings – and the bone-shattering ride of the suspension. The front suspension had to be lubricated by pressing a plunger on the toe-board, thus releasing oil from a reservoir. Careless owners who forgot to do this soon found the front pillars seizing up, but the ride was so hard that they often didn't notice for some time!

The original 4/4 had a wheelbase of 92 inches and a track of 45 inches, which is a little smaller than the modern Plus 8's 98 and 54 inches, though in all other respects the mid-1930s chassis would look familiar today. Right from the start the Morgan became a successful competition car, especially in rallies, where its nimble handling made it ideal for use in driving tests.

Except for a break during the war years, the 4/4 was continued until 1950, although Morgan made many changes to the design in that time. In 1939 an optional engine became available, with a displacement of 1098 cc (62-mm bore and 90-mm stroke) and a power output of 46 bhp. In the same year a 39-bhp/1267-cc overhead-valve Standard engine took over from the Coventry Climax unit, a Moss gearbox replaced the Meadows design, and the original open two-seater was later joined by a four-seater and by a drop-head coupé.

All in all, 824 4/4s were built before the war, and 1,084 examples followed between 1945 and 1950. All post-war examples had the 1267-cc Standard engine; incidentally, this unit was never actually used on a Standard or Triumph model. The replacement for the 4/4 was the long-running Plus 4, with a much larger Standard Vanguard engine.

## Morgan 4/4 variants

### Morgan Le Mans Replica

In 1939 the rare Le Mans Replica was produced, featuring the 1098-cc Coventry Climax engine, and cycle-type front wings.

## Specification (1936)

**Engine:** inline four-cylinder, overhead-inlet and side-exhaust
**Bore × stroke:** 63 mm × 90 mm
**Capacity:** 1122 cc
**Maximum power:** 34 bhp
**Transmission:** four-speed manual, rear-wheel drive
**Chassis:** separate steel frame with 'Z'-section side members and tubular cross-braces
**Suspension:** independent front with sliding pillars and coil springs; live rear axle with semi-elliptic leaf springs
**Brakes:** drums all round
**Bodywork:** steel two-seater open sports car (four-seater from 1937)
**Maximum speed:** 70 mph (113 km/h)

*Above: In 1939 the 4/4 appeared in Le Mans Replica form with skimpy front cycle wings and a 1.1-litre Coventry Climax engine.*

*Below: This 4/4 also dates from 1939 but has more conventional wings and a larger, 1122-cc, four-cylinder engine giving 34 bhp.*

## Morgan Plus 4 1950–present

To replace the 4/4, which was still selling steadily, but was becoming outpaced by its opposition, Morgan developed the Plus 4 model. The familiar chassis, suspension, transmission and styling features were all retained, but with a new and brawnier engine. The wheelbase was four inches longer, the track was two inches wider – and the engine was the 68-bhp 2.1-litre Standard Vanguard wet-liner unit.

From 1954 the Triumph TR2 engine could be ordered as an option to the Vanguard powerplant, with an 83-mm × 92-mm bore and stroke, and a maximum output of 90 bhp from 1991 cc; this was boosted to 100 bhp by 1956. The maximum speed of the 90-bhp car was 96 mph. The last Vanguard-engined car was produced in 1957.

Semi-recessed headlamps were adopted in 1953, and a sloping semi-cowled radiator shell followed a year later. Extra body styles – a two-seater drop-head coupé and a four-seater drop-head coupé – were both available in the 1950s.

Front disc brakes were fitted from 1960, while two years later the 100-bhp 2.2-litre version of the Triumph TR four-cylinder engine (86 mm × 92 mm) was standardised.

Like MG, which also had just replaced the TC with the TD, Morgan decided to build on its strengths, and to keep on supplying the cars its customers wanted. Except that the new Plus 4 was larger, faster, and heavier than the 4/4 which it replaced, the mixture and, more importantly, the character were much as before. By degrees the Plus 4 specification matured with Fiat twin-cam power in 1985, Rover M16 engines in 1988 and the fuel-injected T16 twin-cam coming in 1992. Despite the anachronistic driving position the Plus 4 could still be excellent fun on country roads.

### Morgan Plus 4 variants

#### Morgan Super Sports

A light-alloy-panelled Super Sports type was available from 1961. This had either the 115-bhp/1991-cc or the 125-bhp/2138-cc engine.

*Above: The four-seater drop-head version of the Plus 4 offered greater practicality at the cost of less agreeable styling, with a rather abrupt, upright rear end treatment.*

### Specification (1950)

**Engine:** inline four-cylinder, overhead-valve
**Bore × stroke:** 85 mm × 92 mm
**Capacity:** 2088 cc
**Maximum power:** 68 bhp
**Transmission:** four-speed manual, rear-wheel drive
**Chassis:** separate steel frame with 'Z'-section side members and tubular cross-braces
**Suspension:** independent front with sliding pillars and coil springs; live rear axle with semi-elliptic leaf springs
**Brakes:** drums all round
**Bodywork:** steel two-seater open sports car (four-seater from 1951)
**Maximum speed (approx):** 86 mph (138 km/h)

*Above: The curved grille, which appeared in 1954, gave the Plus 4 a more modern look.*

*Below: The Plus 4 continued Morgan's pre-war designs, but the car was larger overall.*

# Morgan Plus Four Plus 1963-67

*Left: The curved Morgan grille was retained in vestigial form, but the radically different model ultimately drew only 26 buyers.*

*Above: This rear view of a 1964 Plus Four Plus reveals lines which were typical of sports cars of that decade, but not Morgans.*

Since the war Morgan's only real concession to progress was to produce the Plus Four Plus, a car which combined the old-style chassis and running gear with a new and modern style. It was a sales disaster, however, and the experiment was never repeated.

Critics of Morgan's 1930s styling and chassis layout complained long and hard about this (but were they prospective Morgan customers, anyway?) and after some years Peter Morgan decided to placate them. He would not countenance a new chassis with more wheel travel

*Below: From this angle, particularly, the steep bubble-like roof can be seen; the short cabin meant that an opening boot could be fitted.*

and a softer ride, but he was willing to provide a different style.

Racing driver Chris Lawrence was influential in the decision because, highly aware that the pre-war styling and non-existent aerodynamics were slowing his Morgan (in which he had many notable successes), he and partner John Sprinzel produced three hand-built alloy coupés, two of them on a Plus 4 chassis, and with them had several wins.

Peter Morgan saw that the most cost-effective way to produce a modern-looking Morgan would be to use glass-fibre. Designs were drawn up, somewhat like racing cars, and a company called EB Plastics was given the job.

The result was that the virtually unmodified Plus 4 chassis, complete with a

2.2-litre Triumph TR4 engine and transmission, was hidden under a smooth but oddly detailed coupé shell made from glassfibre. It looked different, although it was not all that pretty when viewed from some angles, but was neither as luxuriously trimmed nor as civilised as might have been hoped, although it did have glass sliding windows.

The main stylistic problem with the design was that Morgan were unable successfully to combine all the features they thought desirable. Having a proper boot (a first for Morgan), for example, meant that the cabin had to be abbreviated, producing a curious bubble-top to the car which appeared disproportionately high.

When it went on sale in 1963 the GRP-bodied car cost £1,275, which compared badly with the £816 asked for the existing Plus 4. This, and the car's controversial

shape and character, virtually ensured a poor reception. Only 26 cars were built and Morgan has never been tempted down the same path again.

## Specification (1963)

**Engine:** inline four-cylinder, overhead valve
**Bore × stroke:** 86 mm × 92 mm
**Capacity:** 2138 cc
**Maximum power:** 100 bhp
**Transmission:** four-speed manual gearbox, rear-wheel drive
**Chassis:** separate steel frame with 'Z'-section side members and tubular cross-braces
**Suspension:** independent with sliding pillars and coil springs front; live rear axle with semi-elliptic leaf springs
**Brakes:** discs front, drums rear
**Bodywork:** glassfibre two-seater coupé
**Maximum speed:** 105 mph (169 km/h)

## Morgan Plus 8 1968-present

### Specification (1968)

**Engine:** V8, overhead-valve
**Bore × stroke:** 88.9 mm × 71.1 mm
**Capacity:** 3528 cc
**Maximum power:** 151 bhp
**Transmission:** four-speed manual gearbox, rear-wheel drive
**Chassis:** separate steel frame with 'Z'-section side members and tubular cross-braces
**Suspension:** independent with wishbones and coil springs front; live rear axle with semi-elliptic leaf springs
**Brakes:** discs front, drums rear
**Bodywork:** steel two-seater sports
**Maximum speed (approx):** 124 mph (200 km/h)

*Below: At the front was the old sliding-pillar suspension which gave a notoriously hard ride, but customers never complained.*

By the mid-1960s it was clear that Leyland-Triumph was planning to stop making the famous wet-liner four-cylinder TR engine which Morgan had used for so long. This provided the challenge, and the opportunity, for Morgan to develop a new model.

Various engines were tested, but after Rover had suggested a merger (and been turned down), Morgan then decided to use that company's new light-alloy V8 unit, which had once been fitted to Buick and Oldsmobile 'compacts' in the early 1960s.

As ever, Morgan did not change the basics, so the chassis, the body structure and the style were all familiar to Morgan enthusiasts. To make space for the bulkier engine (which was actually no heavier than the old four-cylinder unit), the wheelbase was stretched by two inches, and the track widened at front and rear.

For the first few years the age-old Moss gearbox was retained, still separated from the engine by a cast-aluminium tube, but it was clear that this would have to be changed soon. Not only was it

an old-fashioned and crude-feeling gearbox with a very 'slow' change and limited synchromesh, but it was costly.

The new car, badged Plus 8 to reflect the type of engine fitted, was a magnificent anachronism, for it had shattering acceleration and amazing flexibility, enormous character but a bone-bruising hard ride, wind-in-the-hair bodywork and awful aerodynamics.

None of the customers seemed to care, and neither did Morgan, who could produce about 150 cars every year. The engine was de-rated to 143 bhp in 1972, then up-rated again to 155 bhp in 1977. Nearly 1,200 had been made by that time, when a five-speed Rover gearbox was finally mated to the V8 engine. Aluminium bodywork had become available in 1975. Rack-and-pinion steering was fitted from 1983, and from 1984 the engine was given fuel injection (at first as an option, later standardised), and up-rated to 193 bhp. By the early 1990s, when a fuel-injected 190-bhp 3.9-litre engine had become available, Plus 8 assembly was fast approaching 4,000, and demand showed no signs of tailing off.

In the early 1990s, for a BBC business programme, ex-ICI chairman Sir John Harvey Jones investigated Morgan and suggested that the Plus 8 was under-

priced. He recommended a price hike to increase profits and to allow new-model investment. Instead the Plus 8 got more powerful, with a 4.6-litre V8 in 1998. Morgan was right to ignore his advice, since residual values remains higher than most and the seven-year waiting list never diminished.

*Below: A true English sports car, the Plus 8 was hand-built exactly like its pre-war ancestors.*

# Morris

*Right: The Mini was one of the most successful designs of all time, still in production more than three decades after its introduction in 1959. It was also an excellent race/rally car, and was easily tuned, as with these three examples: at the front a 1965 Speedwell, then a 1969 Mini-Cooper S and finally a 1986 Janspeed Mini.*

*Below: BMC Special Tuning at Abingdon turned the Mini into an extremely effective race and rally machine.*

**A**lthough one of the great names in the British motor industry, with few exceptions the Morris company steered clear of anything that was at all sporty. Their stock in trade, and a successful one, was the production of cheap family transport.

The firm's first offering was the original Morris Oxford of 1913, a car which cost £180 and was powered by a White and Poppe 1017-cc engine. Although there was little imaginative about their car production, Morris's decision to slash prices in the slump of the early 1920s boosted sales dramatically and firmly established the Morris name. The first contact with anything really sporty came when MG (Morris Garages) used the Morris Minor of 1929 as the basis for the first MG Midget.

The post-war Morris Minor was a very advanced design by Alec Issigonis which boasted rack-and-pinion steering and torsion-bar suspension, and elements of the Minor lived on to be included in the unfortunate Marina model. Production of the Marina showed that Morris (by now part of the large conglomerate that was eventually rationalised to become simply Rover under British Aerospace's control in the 1990s) had reached a very low ebb indeed, and the Marina (and its slightly revamped development, the Ital) was the last model to be badged as a Morris. In between the Minor and the Marina, however, Morris had produced one of the most revolutionary models of all time, the Morris Mini Minor, produced alongside the virtually identical Austin Seven.

*Below: Minis from 1960 and 1990; in three decades the saloon hardly changed, while the open Mini-Moke and booted Wolseley Hornet came and went.*

For the very first time in history, motorists were offered an absolutely tiny full four-seater saloon which had its engine transversely mounted, and which drove the front wheels. The Mini-Cooper of 1961 took that concept a stage further. Not only was it still tiny and agile, but it was also fast, and fun to drive. In many ways the Mini-Cooper was the precursor of all other small sports saloons and hot hatches.

The Mini-Cooper was the result of co-operation between the Mini's designer, Alec Issigonis, and Formula 1 racing constructor John Cooper. The key to a successful project was the nimble front-wheel-drive layout, but Cooper reasoned that a much faster Mini, with better brakes, could be a good racing car. Having built a prototype he handed over his ideas to BMC. Chairman Sir George Harriman was not even convinced that the 1,000 cars needed to achieve homologation could be sold, but he gave the go-ahead anyway – and the demand proved to be enormous.

Throughout the 1960s Mini-Coopers were produced with two badges – Austin and Morris – and all were assembled at the ex-Austin Longbridge plant. Within two years the original type had been joined by the Mini-Cooper S, which was basically the same car, but with a much more specialised and tunable engine, and better brakes.

The Mini-Cooper S became a phenomenally successful racing and rally car. As something of a homologation special, it was gradually given standard equipment (such as twin fuel tanks and an engine oil cooler) which it needed, and in 1964 and 1965 there was even a short-lived 970-cc version to make it suitable for 1.0-litre class competition.

As the Mini was improved, so was the Mini-Cooper, which explains how the cars became 'Mk 2' in 1967, and why the Mini 'Mk 3' (with wind-up windows and different interior trim – but no Austin or Morris badges) followed in 1970.

British Leyland, however, had been formed in 1968, and had no liking for models which carried extraneous names, and for which royalties had to be paid. This explains why the Mini-Cooper was dropped in 1969, and the Mini-Cooper S in 1971, for both cars were still selling extremely well.

It took British Leyland's successor Rover until 1990 to realise that this had been a mistake, and a Mini-Cooper was reintroduced in 1990. It had long since liquidated its production and development costs, so every unit sold was profit. At the close of the decade it was still selling in small numbers.

# Morris Mini-Cooper 1961-69, re-introduced 1990

The first Mini was an 848-cc model with a single carburettor and 34 bhp. It was only 10 feet long, and had a top speed of about 72 mph.

Suspension was independent all round, by rubber cone springs. The combination of hard springing, and the use of rack-and-pinion steering, made it an exceptionally agile little car which, to some eyes, cried out for further development.

The answer was the Mini-Cooper, the result of John Cooper's efforts to transform the original Mini into a useful racing car. The concept was his, but the detail engineering was done by BMC, and the outcome was a one-litre sports saloon which buzzed merrily up to 85 mph – an excellent top speed for that size of car at that period.

The engine was a long-stroke version of the existing A-Series unit, with twin carburettors, better exhaust manifolding, and 55 bhp – which was 62 per cent better than the basic 850 Mini. Lockheed provided small front-wheel disc brakes (actually the smallest in the world at the time) which, although better than the 850's drums, were still alarmingly prone to fade if used very hard.

Everyone who drove a Mini-Cooper loved it, for its combination of verve, spritely handling and sheer character. Everyone came to terms with the rather awkward driving position, and the fairly upright steering wheel position, so the only two complaints were that more performance was still needed, and that the engine was not smooth enough. BMC tackled the engine problem by phasing in a different, shorter-stroke, 998-cc/55-bhp unit for 1964. Also, from September of that year, the suspension was changed, with a pressurised Hydrolastic system (interconnected front to rear) taking over from rubber cones. Those wanting more performance were politely referred to the Mini-Cooper S types, which arrived in 1963. The 'Mk 2' version was introduced in October 1967, with minor trim and decorative changes. An all-synchromesh four-speed gearbox was phased in during 1968.

Although the Mini-Cooper was outgunned by the Mini-Cooper S and was improved only gradually over the years, it sold as well at the end as it had in the beginning. Annual production was 13,916 in 1962, and 13,978 in 1969, the final year. All in all, 99,281 Mini-Coopers were built – an impressive number.

*Above: Here the Rauno Aaltonen/Henry Liddon 1275-cc Mini-Cooper S contests the 1968 Monte Carlo Rally. At right is Paddy Hopkirk with the car in which he and Liddon won the 1964 Monte Carlo event.*

This car was prematurely abandoned in 1969, more for political reasons than because it was no longer popular. Twenty-one years later, Rover tried again, with an updated Mini-Cooper, but the modern car needed a fuel-injected 1.3 litre engine to gain the same effect. By the end of the decade it was still being made at the Longbridge plant.

*Above: A 988-cc 1966 Mini-Cooper 'Mk 1'. Everybody liked the little car, but many wanted more power.*

## Morris Mini-Cooper variants

### Morris Mini-Cooper, re-introduced 1990

In 1990 Rover re-introduced a variant of the Mini called the Mini-Cooper, as a limited-edition model, later converting it to a regular production car. This time round it was equipped with a 61-bhp single-carburettor version of the 1275-cc engine, and had 12-in wheels. A top speed of 92 mph was claimed.

## Specification (1961)

**Engine:** inline four-cylinder, overhead-valve
**Bore × stroke:** 62.43 mm × 81.28 mm
**Capacity:** 997 cc
**Maximum power:** 55 bhp
**Transmission:** four-speed manual, rear-wheel drive
**Chassis:** steel unitary construction body/chassis
**Suspension:** independent with wishbones and rubber cone springs front; semi-trailing arms and rubber cone springs rear
**Brakes:** discs front, drums rear
**Bodywork:** steel two-door four-seater saloon
**Maximum speed (approx):** 85 mph (137 km/h)

*Left: The 1990s saw the re-introduction of the Mini-Cooper, in an attempt to evoke a previous era of fun motoring. The 1990 Mini-Cooper looked like its earlier namesake and, with 61 bhp available from its 1275-cc engine, offered sparkling performance.*

# Morris Mini-Cooper S 1963-71

By the early 1960s BMC was actively involved with the Cooper Car Company in the development of Formula Junior racing engines, which were highly-tuned versions of the familiar A-Series unit. After a number of extremely special types had been produced, including some with re-positioned cylinder barrels, different cylinder heads and short-stroke layouts, John Cooper and BMC's new competitions manager, Stuart Turner, persuaded the directors to put the engines into production.

Like the Mini-Cooper, the appeal of the S lay not only in its performance (which was excellent by mid-1960s standards), but in its miraculous handling, steering, and sheer ability to dodge in and out of tiny gaps. In many ways it was the ideal town car, many examples being used for this purpose and, except on long, straight roads, it had the beating of most larger machines.

Three different engine sizes were eventually put on sale, all of which shared the same cylinder block and cylinder bores, but had different crankshafts and strokes, to give 1071 cc, 970 cc and 1275 cc. It was the 1275-cc version which sold so well, so persistently, and which won so many races, rallies, rallycross events – and hearts – over an eight-year career.

The original Mini-Cooper S was the 1071S, which had a 70.6-mm × 68.26-mm, 1071-cc engine producing 70 bhp and an approximate top speed of 95 mph. This

*Right: Issigonis's simple idea of transversely mounting the engine, with the radiator at the side, made the Mini very compact. With twin SU carburettors the 1275-cc four-cylinder produced 76 bhp in the Cooper S.*

car was made from 1963 to 1964 and total production was 4,005.

Although the S looked almost identical to the Mini-Cooper – indeed, it shared exactly the same body shell, suspension, seating, trim and general layout, it was a faster, stronger and altogether more formidable machine. Not only were the engines more robust, and more tunable (in racing form a 1.3-litre engine could be made to produce 130 bhp), but the brakes were bigger and better. Later types had twin fuel tanks and engine coolers.

The Mini-Cooper S only kept its rub-

*Left: In Cooper S form the Mini – classless, practical and tough – became a real sports car.*

ber cone springs until the summer of 1964, after which it was given the rather softer Hydrolastic suspension, which combined rubber and high-pressure liquid, with interconnection front to rear.

Because the Cooper S was more expensive than the Mini-Cooper – in 1965 a 1275S cost £778, while a Mini-Cooper was only £590 – and because the insurance companies hated it, sales were usually limited to about 4,000 a year – except for the final Mk 3, of which no fewer than 10,075 were sold in the final season.

Like the Mini-Cooper, it was dropped prematurely, with much potential still locked away, in 1971. Total Mini-Cooper S production was 45,679, of which 10,618 were sold with Austin badges, 15,550 with Morris badges, while the 19,511 Mk 3 types had 'Mini' badges.

## Morris Mini-Cooper S variants

### Morris Mini-Cooper 970S

The 970S was a homologation special with a 70.6-mm × 61.9-mm, 970-cc engine producing 65 bhp and giving a top speed of approximately 92 mph. This version was made in 1964 and 1965 and total production, which should have been 1,000 cars to satisfy homologation requirements, was actually only 972. Before September 1964, both this and the original 1071S type were fitted with rubber cone springs, without interconnection as offered by the Hydrolastic system.

### Morris Mini-Cooper 1275S Mk 2 and Mk 3

From October 1967, minor trim and decorative changes turned the 1275S into the Mk 2 version, and during 1968 an all-synchromesh gearbox was standardised.

From March 1970, the car became the Mk 3, with wind-up windows, Mini-Clubman seats and trim, and concealed hinges. Total 1275S production was 21,141 cars.

*Below: Instrumentation was kept to the minimum, and the fascia area doubled as a useful shelf.*

### Morris Mini-Cooper S, after-market conversion

Rover launched a car badged as a Mini-Cooper S in 1991; this was actually an after-market conversion of the re-introduced 1990-style Mini-Cooper with a 1275-cc engine producing 78 bhp. As before, the top speed was 97 mph.

### Specification (1965 1275S)

**Engine:** inline-four, overhead-valve
**Bore × stroke:** 70.6 mm × 81.33 mm
**Capacity:** 1275 cc
**Maximum power:** 76 bhp
**Transmission:** four-speed manual gearbox, rear-wheel drive
**Chassis:** steel unitary construction body/chassis
**Suspension:** independent with Hydrolastic springs and wishbones front; semi-trailing arms with Hydrolastic springs rear; Hydrolastic system interconnected front to rear
**Brakes:** discs front, drums rear
**Bodywork:** steel two-door four-seater saloon
**Maximum speed (approx):** 97 mph (156 km/h)

*Above: Bonnet badges were the only difference between the Morris and less common Austin Mini-Coopers.*

*Below: From the side there was nothing to indicate the Cooper S's performance potential.*

# MVS

F or many years Alpine Renault had a virtual monopoly of sports car production in France, where, unlike the UK, there were very few small-scale manufacturers such as Lotus or TVR, although Matra were making an effort with the excellent mid-engined three-seater Murena. But with only a prosaic overhead-cam 2.2-litre engine, the attractive Murena was no supercar and in the early 1980s a group of enthusiasts decided to do something about the lack of a French contender. MVS (the initials standing for *Manufacture de Voitures de Sport*) was formed in Cholet, near Nantes, with Gérard Godfroy and Claude Poiraud, along with financiers Hervé Boulan and Hervé Lejeune who by this time had attracted the interest of the French racing driver/constructor Jean Rondeau. Rondeau knew all about the small-scale manufacture of very fast cars, his own endurance racers having won his home-town event, the Le Mans 24 Hours, in 1980 after many years of competition.

Jean Rondeau's involvement was useful on many levels; he had the expertise to produce an excellent-handling chassis and he had the workshop facilities in Le Mans to get the project under way. There the first MVS took shape in 1984. It was mid-engined and powered by the 2.2-litre four-cylinder engine used in larger Peugeots such as the 505. Turbocharged, it produced enough power to give the glassfibre-bodied prototype a top speed of 155 mph and a 0-60 mph time in the region of seven seconds – good if not shattering performance, and not really in the supercar league in the 1980s. That performance simply wasn't enough, and the next stage of its evolution was radical, with the Peugeot engine dropped in favour of a modified version of the PRV (Peugeot/Renault/Volvo) V6 overhead-cam alloy unit, while the original MacPherson-strut suspension system was also discarded, to be replaced by the wishbone front and multi-link rear system which would be found on all MVS production models. That heavily-revised model was also developed by racing drivers, in this case by Mauro Bianchi and the rather more famous Jean-Pierre Beltoise, as Rondeau himself had been killed in a road accident, struck by a train on a level crossing in his Porsche 911.

Although MVS appeared to be aiming for the same, rather limited, clientele as Alpine Renault, Renault were happy to supply the same engines and gearboxes as found in their GTA and A610, on the basis that MVS production would be too small to provide serious competition. Production got under way in Cholet with the Venturi 210 in 1987, while a new large factory was being built to open in 1991. As with many such ventures, it took a

*Above: MVS used the French colours of red, white and blue, a hawk and gauntlet, and an aerodynamic term to describe a car built to go like the wind.*

great deal more money and effort to turn what was a good idea into practice and the MVS company had to be rescued by Xavier de la Chapelle's Primwest France business in 1989. Their initial stake of 62 per cent was increased to more than 90 per cent before the car's future was assured.

After initial ideas of using Peugeot's 2.2-litre turbo four were dropped, the MVS used a 200-bhp version of the PRV V6 engine, but by 1990 a 260-bhp version had also been made available. Once a cabriolet version had been introduced (in 1986) the car's medium-term future looked brighter, and after assembly was moved to a new factory at Coueron near Nantes in 1991 it looked to be assured. That same year saw a substantial amount of extra capital injected into the company, bringing total capital to £18.5 million, some 10 per cent of which was held by an outside industrial group, Omnium Europe. With a total staff of 70 in the early 1990s and the promise of a purpose-built 1.2-mile test track, all the ingredients for success were firmly in place, in France at any rate. The Venturi made the short trip across the channel in 1991, where it was up against rivals like the new Renault A610 and the firmly established Lotus Esprit. After its UK debut at the 1991 Motorfair in Earl's Court the specialist British magazines, not to mention the influential TV programme *Top Gear*, gave the car very favourable reports but its high price (just short of £48,000 in 1992) and lack of image might have seen it struggling even in good times, let alone when the British economy was firmly in recession.

By the early 1990s, annual production was around 120, and in 1999, the Venturi Atlantique cost £59,000, but lacked the image of rival Lotus Esprit.

*Below: The Venturi coupé is distinctive, although in the side profile there are Ferrari, Lotus and Renault Alpine influences, but this is more the result of contemporary concepts of aerodynamics than any attempt to copy.*

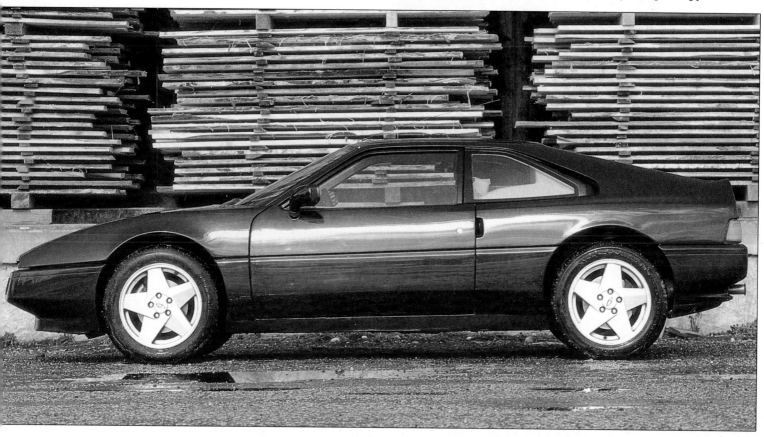

## MVS Venturi 210 1986-present

*Right: Under the composite body is a steel backbone chassis which can be driven on its own; bonded together they form an exceptionally rigid unit.*

Although the new Venturi sports coupé looked rather similar to the Renault Alpine GTA, it had a radically different chassis and layout. The GTA was a true rear-engined design in the traditional Alpine mould, whereas the Venturi's engine was mid-mounted with the engine ahead of the rear axle line, and two seats rather than 2 + 2 seating.

The Venturi made its first appearance at the 1984 Paris Motor Show, launched as a very smart fixed-head coupé with a pressed steel underbody and a glass-fibre body – the result of considerable wind-tunnel work at St Cyr University. Although the end result of a Cd of 0.31 was not outstanding, the designers had made sure the mid-engined car was very stable at high speeds.

The chassis was an interesting structure, possessing a backbone but being essentially a tub onto which was bonded the body, forming a very stiff overall structure. Conventional upper and lower wishbones were used at the front, allied to a rather more complex rear suspension system with five links per side, designed to give excellent handling and roadholding. There was sufficient power to make that worthwhile, thanks to the PRV V6 engine being used in 2458-cc turbocharged form to give an output of 210 bhp (hence the car's name).

Although the Venturi was the equal of its Renault Alpine rival in every respect in export markets, it struggled to overcome its obscure origins and sales were slow. That was despite an ambitious

*Right: The interior is trimmed in a classic combination of walnut veneer and Connolly hides.*

sponsorship deal which saw the Venturi name in Formula 1 with the Venturi Larousse team, in an effort to give the car the high profile it needed.

### MVS Venturi 210 variants

### MVS Venturi 210 Cabriolet
A convertible version of the 210 appeared at the 1986 Paris Motor Show. It featured a very neat roof arrangement with a rear section that folded down flush with the bodywork with the top down and served as a rigid roll-over bar when in place.

### MVS Venturi 260
The 260 was introduced in 1990; as its name suggests, it had 260 bhp, courtesy of a 2849-cc version of the PRV V6 turbo engine. That gave a claimed top speed of 168 mph with 0-60 mph acceleration in a fraction over five seconds.

### Specification (1989)
**Engine:** V6, overhead-cam, turbo
**Bore × stroke:** 91 mm × 63 mm
**Capacity:** 2458 cc
**Maximum power:** 210 bhp
**Transmission:** five-speed manual

**Chassis:** pressed steel underbody with glassfibre/composite body bonded in place
**Suspension:** independent with double unequal-length wishbones, coil springs, telescopic dampers and anti-roll bar front; five-link system with coil springs and telescopic dampers rear
**Brakes:** discs all round
**Bodywork:** glassfibre/composite two-seater coupé
**Maximum speed:** 152 mph (245 km/h)

*Below: With the mid-mounted V6 in 210-bhp tune the sleek Venturi can race to 62 mph in 6.9 seconds. When the turbocharged version is fitted, power output increases to 260 bhp and the 0-62 mph time drops by over a second on the way to a maximum speed of 168 mph.*

# Nacional Pescara

*Above: Juan Zanelli pilots his supercharged twin-cam Nacional Pescara in the 1933 Rabassada Hillclimb in Spain, a year after the company had folded.*

Time after time, governments have backed attempts to found a national motor industry – and time after time they have failed. Spain's Nacional Pescara project was no exception to this rule. At a time when Spain was still a poor country, ruled by a few extremely rich aristocrats and with only 200,000 cars on its roads, the state decided to back a project to produce expensive and complex cars.

The original project was put together by the Marquis Raoul de Pescara, and the car was designed by his brother Enrique, who was aided by the Italian Edmond Moglia. Wifredo Ricard (later to be more famously involved with Alfa Romeo and Pegaso designs) was also credited with some of the work. The company was set up in Barcelona in 1929 (where Hispano-Suiza already had a thriving business), and cars were ready to go on sale in 1930, though a proposal to race cars at Le Mans never came to anything.

The new cars, which exhibited much contemporary Detroit design thinking, were too large and too expensive to sell well in Spain, and were never well enough known to be exported. The onset of the Depression did not help, and this probably explains why a project to have the cars assembled at the French Voisin works at Issy never came to pass either.

The Spanish Revolution of 1931 saw King Alfonso XIII, one of the car's most enthusiastic supporters, removed from the scene, which effectively put paid to its prospects. The result was that the project swiftly died, and no more cars were built after 1932. Like many other such state-backed ventures, this one had lost a great deal of money.

Spain's next 'national car' was the Pegaso of 1951, which was also produced in Barcelona.

## Nacional Pescara Eight 1930-32

Edmond Moglia's newly-designed eight-cylinder Nacional Pescara had clearly been influenced by what American designers in Detroit were thinking, for its conventional chassis supported a straight-eight engine backed by a three-speed gearbox; it also featured a hypoid rear axle, and hydraulic brakes.

The engine, however, was no ordinary straight-eight, for it had nine main bearings, an aluminium crankcase, cylinder block *and* cylinder head castings, and the valves were operated by a gear-driven single overhead camshaft. Originally producing a mere 80 bhp, the engine appeared to have great tuning potential, and so it proved when race-tuned examples followed in later years.

Behind this beautifully detailed power unit, which looked as good as its specification, there was a surprisingly mundane transmission (the three-speed gearbox and the long centre gear lever were pure General Motors), while the chassis was a conventional layout, with half-elliptic leaf springs at front and rear.

*Below: Here Zanelli proves the speed of his Nacional Pescara in a 1931 hill climb near Prague.*

Several different body styles were on offer, and to minimise the weight of the cars the panelling was mainly in electron. The result was that the NP's overall weight was less than that of its rivals, the company claiming that the four-seater saloon weighed in at less than 2,600 lb – an outstanding achievement by the standards of the day.

A twin-cam version was produced for competition only. In supercharged form it produced up to 180 bhp. A stripped-down two-seater, it weighed little more than 1,350 lb and was a successful hill-climb car.

Nacional Pescara originally promised to build a straight-10-cylinder version of the engine, an astonishing 3.9-litre unit which was to be backed with only a two-speed gearbox, though this never progressed further than the drawing board.

If the Spanish Revolution had not disrupted the project, the world of motoring might have seen more, faster and technically more exciting models from the state-backed Nacional Pescara concern. If nothing else, there was always an element of rivalry between this company and Hispano-Suiza (which was in the same city) – and rivalry usually spurs on designers to ever greater efforts.

### Specification (1930 twin-cam)

**Engine:** inline eight-cylinder, twin-cam
**Bore × stroke:** 72 mm × 90 mm
**Capacity:** 2948 cc
**Maximum power:** 125 bhp
**Transmission:** three-speed manual gearbox, rear-wheel drive
**Chassis:** separate steel frame with channel-section main side members
**Suspension:** non-independent with beam axle and semi-elliptic leaf springs front; live axle with semi-elliptic leaf springs and friction dampers rear
**Brakes:** drums all round
**Bodywork:** steel open sports or roadster
**Maximum speed (approx):** 115 mph (185 km/h)

*Below: Estevan Tort lays a strip of rubber at the start of Shelsley Walsh in 1931, a year when Nacional Pescaras dominated hill climbs.*

# Napier

Way back in 1808, while the British Industrial Revolution was still in its infancy, a small precision-engineering business called D. Napier & Son Ltd was set up in London, but by the end of the 19th century its fortunes were declining.

This was the point at which Montague Napier decided to get involved in the fledgling motor industry. His very first product was a two-cylinder engine which S. F. Edge required to be fitted as a replacement power unit for his 1896 Panhard. The result of this tentative project was that Edge set up a car distribution company, which became Napier's sole distributor until 1912.

The original Napiers were large, heavy and fast machines and, with Edge not only acting as a vigorous (not to say vociferous) publicist but also as a racing driver, the marque made many headlines. Soon Edge had a lucky win in the Gordon Bennett Cup race, and by 1903 Napier was building 250 cars a year, which meant that a move from Lambeth to a new factory in Acton, west London, became essential.

Napier then launched the world's first commercially-available six-cylinder car in 1904, soon to be followed by engines with overhead inlet valves. At this time Napier was Britain's most prestigious marque, and not even the arrival of Rolls-Royce could destroy that reputation at first.

Four-cylinder and six-cylinder types were sold for some years, Edge's team of four-cylinder cars actually winning the 1908 Tourist Trophy race. Sales boomed before World War I, by which time the range included a simple twin-cylinder-engined taxicab and new fours and sixes; peak pre-war production was 801 cars in 1911.

By the 1920s Napier was heavily involved in more profitable pursuits than making cars – most famously with an aeroplane engine, the W12 Lion, which had evolved during the 1914-18 conflict, but went on to find many other applications. Napier, in fact, expanded so mightily, and so securely, on the back of aero-engine production that Montague Napier is said to have decided to let motor car manufacture wither on the vine in the 1920s.

By comparison with the peak pre-war period, therefore, when no fewer than 1,800 cars were built between 1909 and 1911, Napier built few cars in the 1920s. Nevertheless, the true vintage Napiers were fine machines, particularly the magnificent 40/50HP models which were launched in 1919 and were built until 1924.

These were large, hand-built and therefore expensive machines, which explains why very few were sold; in five years only 187 were delivered. Napier car production ended at that point, after only 4,258 cars had been delivered.

The Napier story could well have had a different ending. In 1931 the famous Bentley concern was made bankrupt by its creditors, and Napier attempted to buy up the assets. W. O. Bentley was so confident that this rescue would be formalised that he actually began work on a new 'Napier-Bentley' design; both he and Napier were then shattered when Rolls-Royce made a higher bid to the bankruptcy courts, and the project was stillborn.

Above: The six-cylinder 1903 Gordon Bennett Cup racer, in the Napier livery which was later adopted as British Racing Green.

Right: At the turn of the century Napier was regarded as Britain's finest motor car manufacturer.

Below: The Napier Colonial 20HP of 1915 was built to the highest standards, but by then the firm was turning more towards aero-engine production.

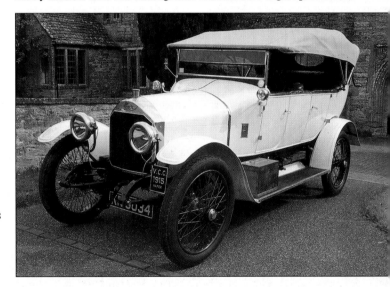

Below: The Napier-Railton, with a 22.3-litre 450-bhp Napier Lion aero engine, was a car designed for use at Brooklands. It was also employed by John Cobb to set numerous long-distance records on the Bonneville salt flats in 1935.

# Napier 40/50HP 1919-24

*Right: Chassis of a 1924 40/50HP, the last Napier. The pressed-channel ladder frame was typical of the period; less so was the superb engine and the high quality of construction. Note the cantilever rear springs.*

Napier's rather half-hearted attempt to match the Rolls-Royce 40/50HP model produced a magnificent failure. At least as well-engineered, and equally as well-built as the Rolls-Royce, it was not enthusiastically marketed by the London-based concern, especially as Napier owned its own coachbuilding company, which meant that the truly upper-crust coachbuilders patronised by Rolls-Royce were rarely allowed to clothe the Napier car.

The prototype was unveiled in November 1919, at the first post-war Olympia Show, but labour problems at Acton delayed deliveries until late 1920. In the end the Napier was abandoned after only 187 had been built; 17 of these were 'Colonial' models with high ground-clearance chassis, and just five others were more sporting short-chassis models. Napier had originally planned to produce 500 examples before abandoning car manufacture altogether.

The 40/50HP was a splendid throwback to Edwardian days, and design was credited to A. W. Rowledge, who had already been responsible for the Lion aeroplane engine. His touch can surely be seen in details of the advanced overhead-camshaft engine, and the aluminium cylinder block and head castings, though the chassis was merely a de-velopment of Napier's pre-war designs. Bodies, usually by Cunard, were generally lofty and stately, which ensured that prices were high and performance limited.

The 40/50HP proves the point about many such cars of the period – that they looked faster than they were. A 40/50HP limousine could weigh at least 5,200 lb and since the aerodynamics were of the barn-door variety, top speeds were under 70 mph, with acceleration (and fuel consumption!) to match. Incidentally, to deal with engine roughness at low speeds, a special low-compression piston was fitted to the sixth cylinder only! Napier rebuilders confirm that a 40/50HP engine *without* this feature is noticeably less smooth.

Only a handful of these impressive supercars seems to have survived. As for the chief designer Rowledge, his reputation was such that Rolls-Royce 'head-hunted' him to join them at Derby, where he stayed until he retired in 1945.

## Specification (1919)

**Engine:** inline six-cylinder, single overhead camshaft
**Bore × stroke:** 102 mm × 127 mm
**Capacity:** 6177 cc
**Maximum power:** 82 bhp
**Transmission:** four-speed manual gearbox, rear-wheel drive
**Chassis:** separate steel frame with channel-section main side members
**Suspension:** non-independent with beam axle and semi-elliptic leaf springs front; live axle with cantilever springs rear
**Brakes:** drums on transmission and rear wheels; no front brakes until 1924
**Bodywork:** coachwork usually by Cunard, with choice of open or closed tourer, saloon and limousine styles
**Maximum speed (approx):** 70 mph (113 km/h)

*Below: A 1921 Napier 40/50HP limousine, very much a stately mobile edifice. The tremendous weight greatly reduced the performance potential and increased fuel consumption, but cars like this were generally owned by clients who valued a measured and uninterrupted driving pace.*

# Nissan Motor Company

eventually lost its market leadership to Toyota.

As far as Europe is concerned, sales of Nissans – as opposed to Datsuns – began in 1983, when the new generation of 'Z-cars', the V6-engined 300ZX range, was launched. At a time when the vast majority of Nissans were boring Micra, Cherry and Sunny family cars, it was the 300ZX and its successors which made enthusiasts smile.

Even as recently as 1988 the 300ZX was Nissan's sole sporting car, but by 1992 the company had not only replaced this with a new-generation model but had also produced smaller-engined, fast and versatile coupés, and a stubby homologation special, the Sunny GTi-R, intended for World Championship rallying.

Nissan, whose cars had been dismissed as dull, boringly styled and technically backward in the mid-1980s, had transformed itself in the early 1990s. Cynics pointed out that change had been sorely needed, but by the late 1990s parallel importers were keen to seize the Skyline GT-R, a blend of high-tech 4WD, four wheel steer, turbopower yet excellent to drive.

*Above: Stig Blomqvist and Benny Melander took fifth place in the 1991 Safari Rally in a 300-bhp, six-speed, turbocharged Nissan Sunny GTi-R.*

Nissan was set up in 1934 to manufacture Datsun cars, taking over that process from the original DAT concern. The first Nissan-badged car was launched in 1937, but most cars continued to be sold as Datsuns until the 1960s.

Nissan had rejuvenated its post-war production lines by manufacturing Austin cars under licence in 1952. Starting with the Nissan Cedric of 1960, however, Datsun and Nissan cars were then built side-by-side in Japan.

By the 1970s many new models were sold as Nissans at home and in some export territories, and as Datsuns only in some markets.

This confusing situation persisted until the early 1980s when the company finally began to phase out the Datsun name. In the UK the company's sporting cars were all Datsuns until 1983, after which the Nissan name took over completely. This name-swapping confusion should not obscure the fact that Nissan grew steadily in the post-war years to become one of the largest car manufacturers in the world. The company's first overseas manufacturing facility (in Mexico) started production in 1966, and mass-production of fine sports cars (such as the Nissan Fairlady, also known as the Datsun 240Z) followed in 1969. By 1972 Nissan had built its 10 millionth car.

By 1980 Nissan/Datsun was building nearly 2,000,000 cars a year, though sales then stuck at this figure throughout the next decade, and Nissan

*Above: The 1991 quad-cam, 24-valve, turbo V6 300ZX could reach 155 mph, and 60 mph in 5.6 seconds.*

*Below: The first 300ZX model appeared in 1983, with lines which echoed Datsun's 280ZX.*

*Below: Unlike buyers of some exotica, owners of Nissans pay for the car, not the badge.*

# Nissan 300ZX 1983-89

The third-generation 'Z-car', badged as a 300ZX in Europe, but also known as the Fairlady Z in Japan and some other countries, was launched in September 1983 as a direct replacement for the previous model, the 280ZX. Not only did the new car have a new, larger and more capacious structure, and had put on weight, but it was powered by an entirely new engine – a 60-degree V6.

The Type VG engine was a technical tour de force, especially as it came from a company whose engines had previously been rather staid and conventional designs. Arranged from the very start to be built in a variety of capacities, and to be installed in various Nissan models, it was 45 lb lighter than the old 2.8-litre 'six'. It was an overhead-camshaft design in which opposed valves were operated by way of hydraulic tappets and cast-aluminium rocker arms.

Eventually this engine also found its way into the Maxima (closely related to the Bluebird saloon), the Leopard Coupé, the Laurel, the Cedric/Gloria and the Terrano 4×4 vehicle. It was typical of the way that Nissan maximised its assets, and it also ensured that the engine was thoroughly dependable in all conditions.

Although at first glance the new Nissan 300ZX was similar to the old 280ZX, it shared no common panels. The floorpans were closely related; the choice of wheelbase – 91.3-in (two-seater) or 99.2-in (2+2-seater) – was the same as before. Equally, there were similarities in the suspension layout, although almost every component had been changed, and the angle of the semi-trailing arms in the rear suspension had been changed from 23 degrees to 18 degrees.

All in all, the 300ZX was a very fast but at the same time very comfortable sporting car. On the one hand the turbocharged versions would cruise easily at 120 mph and more, but on the other hand the interior was very well-furnished, and air conditioning could keep the car cool in hot climates like California where many such cars were sold. The chassis was competent, if not outstanding, for most expert observers found it inferior to that of a Porsche or a Lotus.

In 1989, after a very successful five-year career, this model was replaced by the fourth-generation ZX – and a smaller model, also given the ZX title (200ZX), also appeared.

*Above: This 1989 300ZX, with the 'T-bar coupé hatchback bodywork, offered the pleasures of open-air motoring. Performance was excellent, as were sales.*

## Nissan 300ZX variants

### Nissan 300ZX Turbo

In addition to the normally-aspirated car with its 2960-cc and 160-bhp V6 engine (a unit that was given twin-cam heads, four valves per cylinder and 190 bhp in 1986), Nissan also produced a more potent turbo version of the V6 engine with 228 bhp. That was supplemented on some markets by a smaller, 1998-cc, V6 with a bore and stroke of 78 mm × 69.7 mm and an output of 170 bhp. The top speed of that model was 124 mph. This engine was also improved in 1986 with four valves per cylinder and 180 bhp. On the US market the turbo engine produced only 203 bhp, giving a top speed of 130 mph.

## Specification (1984 300ZX Turbo)

**Engine:** V6, single overhead camshaft per bank of cylinders
**Bore × stroke:** 87 mm × 83 mm
**Capacity:** 2960 cc
**Maximum power:** 228 bhp
**Transmission:** five-speed manual or four-speed automatic transmission, rear-wheel drive
**Chassis:** steel unitary construction
**Suspension:** independent with MacPherson struts and anti-roll bar front; semi-trailing arms and anti-roll bar rear
**Brakes:** discs all round
**Bodywork:** steel two-seater or 2+2-seater coupé, or 'T-bar coupé hatchback
**Maximum speed (approx):** 137 mph (220 km/h)

*Above: The interior was comfortable and well equipped; very effective air conditioning was optional.*

*Below: With its 228 bhp, the 300ZX was very rapid indeed; the chassis was less impressive, however.*

## Nissan Silvia/200SX 1988-present

**Left:** *The 200SX's turbo four-cylinder was very powerful and reliable, and made the car a class leader.*

**Above:** *A 1991 Nissan 200SX, with the smooth styling that has become a hallmark of the 1990s.*

Throughout the 1980s Nissan had sold a car badged as a Silvia, but this was a rather ponderous and angular coupé with little charm. As part of its model rejuvenation process, the company then introduced a new-generation machine which was faster, more technically advanced, and which looked sensually attractive. The new-generation Silvia, also known as the 200SX, had a front-mounted engine and rear-wheel drive, and was formidable opposition for other longer-established two-litre sporting coupés.

Launched in 1988, but not exported until the following year, the new 200SX was intended to be a complete change

from the old model – and it was. There was a brand-new monocoque style, smooth and rounded, with hidden headlamps, hiding an advanced new chassis which included independent suspension all round.

Nissan, by this time, was well advanced with its move to four-valves-per-cylinder technology. Naturally the Silvia's engine had this feature, along with twin overhead camshafts, multi-point fuel injection, a turbocharger, an intercooler and a comprehensive electronic engine management package. The 200SX came with a choice of engines, beginning with a normally-aspirated 2.0-litre unit, of 86 mm ×

86 mm, which produced 140 bhp. There was also a turbocharged version of an enlarged 2.0-litre powerplant with a 'square' bore and stroke of 86 mm × 86 mm, producing 205 bhp. This gave the car an approximate top speed of 143 mph. The chassis featured what Nissan called 'multi-link' suspension geometry, which was also employed on the new-generation 300ZX. The handling was extremely well developed, and the overall package was at least the equal of anything being marketed by Porsche at the time. Here, in fact, was Porsche 944 performance at lower cost, although in the USA Nissan was much more interested in beating Toyota in this market.

This was the best sports car to have come out of Japan for many years; it was only the arrival of cars like the next-generation Nissan 300ZX and the new Mitsubishi Eclipse and 3000GT which redressed the balance.

For rivals the terrifying news was that Nissan was not ready to leave this splendid new car alone, for it received its first front-end facelift in 1991, at which time a normally-aspirated 157-bhp 2.4-litre

engine was also made available for the USA market. No wonder this model, the 240SX, was described as the fastest and the best car in its class.

### Specification (1988 200SX Turbo)

**Engine:** inline four-cylinder, twin-cam
**Bore × stroke:** 86 mm × 86 mm
**Capacity:** 1952 cc
**Maximum power:** 205 bhp
**Transmission:** five-speed manual or four-speed automatic, rear-wheel drive
**Chassis:** steel unitary construction body/chassis
**Suspension:** independent with multi-links, lower wishbones and anti-roll bar front; multi-links and anti-roll bar rear
**Brakes:** discs all round
**Bodywork:** steel 2 + 2 coupé or cabriolet
**Maximum speed (approx):** 143 mph (230 km/h)

**Below:** *The high performance, sleek looks and design quality of the 200SX were offered at a price European firms found hard to beat.*

# Nissan Skyline GT-R 1989-present

A Skyline had figured in Nissan's product range for many years, but the new-generation models, introduced in May 1989, were technically much more advanced than ever before. The basic design was of a front-engined rear-drive car, though a four-wheel-drive option was also developed.

The Skyline's role was that of a medium-large range of cars, larger than the Bluebirds and smaller than the Laurels. What neither of these ranges had, however, was an extremely powerful derivative. These were four-door saloons and two-door coupés, with engines ranging from a 1.8-litre overhead-cam unit to a 2.5-litre twin-cam, while power outputs varied from 91 bhp to 215 bhp. Manual or automatic transmission was available, as was rear-wheel or four-wheel drive. The Skyline GT-R's ambition as the top-of-the-range derivative, however, was nothing less than ousting the Ford Sierra RS500 Cosworth from its pedestal as the world's fastest and most successful racing saloon car. Underneath the Nissan's rather mundane two-door coupé body was a very exciting chassis indeed.

Into the 104.3-in wheelbase of the Skyline platform, Nissan's designers squeezed a magnificent brand-new 2.6-litre six-cylinder engine, mounted con-

ventionally 'north-south', which had four valves per cylinder, twin overhead camshafts, state-of-the-art electronics – and twin turbochargers. The same engine family – in various types, sizes and tunes – soon found a home in other large Nis-

*Below: With electronic, torque-sensing, all-wheel drive the GT-R handled superbly, as here with Matt Neal's car at Silverstone, 1991.*

sans, but in the GT-R its state of tune was phenomenal. With 280 bhp, it easily out-gunned the Sierra's 224 bhp, and it was not long before the Skyline started winning touring car races all round the world.

To match this engine, Nissan not only fitted their ATTESA all-wheel-drive layout, which had electronic front-to-rear sensing of torque requirements, but they also provided four-wheel steering, where the rear-wheel steering angles were set by sensors which measured road speed to see if additional turning was required.

Sales of GT-Rs began in Japan during 1989, although exports were delayed until 1990, and it was immediately clear that Nissan had set new standards among race-pedigree touring cars. Unfortunately for Nissan, however, race regulations were gradually turning away from international Group A competition, where the GT-R's engine could develop well over 500 bhp, and by the early 1990s most of its technical advances were nullified. Even so, it remained a high-performance standard by which all other ultra-fast touring cars were measured.

*Above: The scene is Donington in 1990; leaving the pack, and the Ford Sierra Cosworths, behind is Keith Odor at the wheel of his Nissan Skyline GT-R, a highly-tuned all-wheel-drive coupé.*

## Specification (1990)

**Engine:** inline six-cylinder, quad-cam, twin-turbo
**Bore × stroke:** 86 mm × 73.7 mm
**Capacity:** 2568 cc
**Maximum power:** 280 bhp
**Transmission:** five-speed manual, four-wheel drive
**Chassis:** steel unitary construction body/chassis
**Suspension:** independent with multi-links and anti-roll bars front and rear
**Brakes:** discs all round
**Bodywork:** steel two-door four-seater coupé
**Maximum speed (approx):** 155 mph (249 km/h)

*Below: The GT-R coupé was built for go, not show, as under the simple shell was a superb engine and sophisticated transmission.*

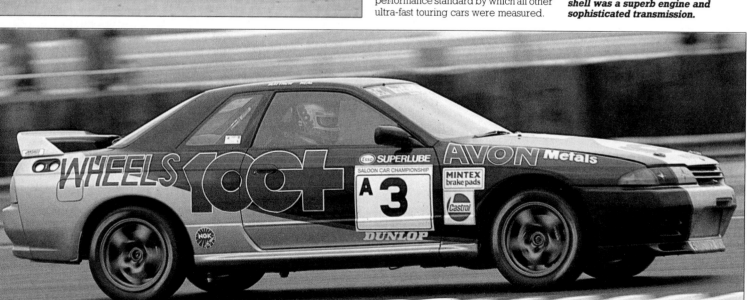

# Nissan 300ZX 1989–94

*Above: With the 300ZX Nissan had created a supercar to challenge the Italian and German marques.*

*Below: Its compact coupé body clothed an impressive array of sophisticated high-technology.*

Nissan's new-generation 300ZX of 1989 was a real supercar; it had been transformed from a Californian 'cruiser' to a taut and nimble sports coupé. Not only was the normally-aspirated version modified to produce more than 220 bhp, but there was a new option of a twin-turbo unit with no less than 280 bhp. At a stroke, the car's power-to-weight ratio had been improved by about 30 per cent.

As with previous 'Z-cars', the latest 300ZX was aimed squarely at the affluent North American market. Compared with the first 300ZX, the latest car had a new platform with a choice of longer wheelbases, and the body was more spacious, smoother, and had a much reduced drag coefficient, claimed to be only 0.31. In spite of this there were almost no weight increases, the two-seater being only 3,219 lb.

The new car's chassis was a real advance, as sophisticated as anything yet developed by European carmakers. Naturally it included ABS brakes, a viscous-coupling differential, and comprehensive electronics.

There was new multi-link coil-spring suspension at front and rear (developed from that of the stillborn mid-engined MID4 project), which was also fitted to the 200ZX/240ZX/Silvia Coupé. The 300ZX also featured Nissan's HICAS system (High-Capacity Actively-Controlled Suspension), which used a computer to adjust rear-wheel alignment and give a degree of four-wheel steering when required. The computer responded to chassis sensors that indicated the car was cornering quickly, by providing a twitch of counter-steer before settling with all four wheels pointing in the same direction. Although the rear-wheel movements were subtle – usually no more than 0.5 degrees – the effect was rather like the rally driver's technique of flicking the steering onto opposite lock before turning into a corner.

The HICAS system was not considered necessary in North America, the 300ZX's main market, and in truth the car felt agile enough without it. For what Nissan considered the more testing environment of Europe, however, HICAS conferred just that extra sharpness of steering response.

The engine, though still the familiar 60-degree V6 with four-valve twin-cam cylinder heads, was much revised, and the most powerful type, a twin-turbo unit, was sensationally potent, at 280 bhp. At a stroke, the new 300ZX was thrust into the Ferrari/Porsche performance league – and looked good enough to match its competition. Not only did this car have a top speed of nearly 160 mph, but it could sprint to 100 mph in 14.5 seconds – tyre-strippingly fast by any standards. *Autocar & Motor* testers thought it had "stunning power, stupendous presence and tremendous dynamic ability". Once the turbo engine really got into its stride, at around 2,700 rpm, the Nissan took off, the engine spinning freely around to the maximum power point of 6,400 rpm.

Inside the car, a wide and full-length centre console almost gave a 'twin-cockpit' feel to the cabin, and although the rear seat was virtually useless when the front seats were pushed well back, the front-seat occupants were cosseted in great comfort, including air conditioning as standard.

It was hard to fault the 300ZX in any fundamental respect. Some critics considered that, at almost six feet, the Nissan was rather too wide for really high speeds along some of Britain's narrower roads and, with a kerb weight of 3,485 lb, it was hardly a lightweight. Nissan were aware of the penalty incurred by incorporating so many sophisticated handling and performance aids, and had even gone to the lengths of making the brake calipers in alloy, in a not altogether successful attempt to keep weight down. Nevertheless, the company had come a very long way from the days of the first 'Z-car', the 240Z.

*Above: Instruments were clear and legible and the fascia design was logical, with controls on the side of the instrument binnacle.*

## Specification (1989)

**Engine:** V6, quad-cam, twin-turbo
**Bore × stroke:** 87 mm × 83 mm
**Capacity:** 2960 cc
**Maximum power:** 280 bhp
**Transmission:** five-speed manual or four-speed automatic, rear-wheel drive
**Chassis:** steel unitary construction body/chassis
**Suspension:** independent with multi-links, lower wishbones and anti-roll bar front; multi-links and anti-roll bar rear
**Brakes:** discs all round
**Bodywork:** steel two-seater or 2 + 2-seater; coupé, 'T'-bar Targa coupé or cabriolet
**Maximum speed (approx):** 155 mph (249 km/h)

*Below: The 300ZX's excellent aerodynamics (the Cd was 0.31) contributed to good performance and reasonable fuel consumption.*

# Nissan Sunny GTi-R 1990–97

For many years Nissan had dabbled with World Championship rallying. Finally, as Group A became established, the company took the plunge, developed a special version of a new-generation Sunny, and launched the GTi-R.

The new-type Sunny/Pulsar range appeared in January 1990, comprising unremarkable transverse-engined front-wheel-drive saloons, hatchbacks and estate cars, but the GTi-R was entirely different. Hidden away under the much-modified skin of a Sunny hatchback was an immensely powerful 220-bhp two-litre engine, allied to four-wheel drive. Nissan made no bones about this being a homologation special with which it intended to take rallying by storm in 1991.

Although rally victories were very difficult to achieve – basically because the stubborn Japanese concern would not use state-of-the-art tyre supplies, and because the turbo intercooler was placed in an inefficient position on top of the engine rather than behind the front grille – the road car was fast, handled well, and had stupendous performance.

The transversely-mounted 220-bhp engine was a highly-tuned version of the same basic unit used in the contemporary Primera, Bluebird and Silvia/200SX models, but in this application it was matched to Nissan's ATTESA (Advanced Total Traction Electronic System All-terrain) transmission, which featured centre and rear viscous-coupling differentials, with an electronically-sensed front/rear torque split.

The front-end style was, shall we say, extrovert, for there was a large grilled scoop on the bonnet above the intercooler, and a big roof-level spoiler at the tail.

Its handling wasn't as delicately balanced as that, say, of a Lancia Delta Integrale or a Ford Escort RS Cosworth, but the chassis generated a huge amount of grip, and there was a great deal of sheer 'go': 0-60 mph in 5.0 seconds is very fast by anyone's standards, as is the ability to sprint to 100 mph in 14.2 seconds. Its in-gear performance was outstanding, too. From 20-40 mph, 30-50 mph and 40-60 mph in top and fourth

gear, the Nissan was quicker than one of its main rivals, the Lancia HF Integrale, and could match the more exotic car even in the 90-110 mph span. This was all accompanied by a hairy-chested engine character and a purpose-built transmission with built-in shunt.

If the 'works' rally cars had worked well – unfortunately they didn't, for despite their 300 bhp they seemed to have what cynics called 'interwarmers' instead of intercoolers – the car's reputation might have been made. As it was, the GTi-R was still the fastest and most agile small car ever to have been made by Nissan, if hardly one of the prettiest.

*Left: The Sunny GTi-R was a compact and well-designed hatchback. Malleable in traffic and yet with 220 bhp on tap, the car's performance was electrifying.*

*Below: The epitome of the 'hot hatch', and evidence of the growing sophistication coming from Japan, the three-door GTi-R had awkward looks which concealed the considerable performance potential.*

*Above: Nissan went into rallying with the Sunny GTi-R very seriously and intended to win, but the car was not quite the equal of the Lancia Deltas and Escort RS Cosworths. Here Stig Blomqvist does his best in the 1991 RAC Rally; he gave an impressive performance until the suspension broke and he was forced to retire.*

### Specification (1990)

**Engine:** inline four-cylinder, intercooler, turbo
**Bore × stroke:** 86 mm × 86 mm
**Capacity:** 1998 cc
**Maximum power:** 220 bhp
**Transmission:** five-speed manual, four-wheel drive
**Chassis:** steel unitary construction body/chassis
**Suspension:** independent with MacPherson struts front and rear
**Brakes:** discs all round
**Bodywork:** steel three-door four-seater hatchback
**Maximum speed (approx):** 140 mph (225 km/h)

# Nissan-Datsun

*Right: This is not a Datsun logo as such but the badge borne by the legendary Z-series sports cars that did so much to vitalise the Japanese company's previously unexciting image. The precise origins of the 'Z' designation seem impossible to pin down.*

The name of 'Datsun' actually evolved because of the complexities of the Japanese language. Sotaro Hasimoto founded the Kwaishinsha Company in 1911 to build motor cars, calling them 'DAT' after the initials of his three backers.

In 1930 a small car, logically called Datson, was born, but as 'son' in Japanese means 'lose' this was rapidly altered to Datsun. Legends are sometimes born in a peculiar way. . . .

By 1937 larger cars were also in production, called Nissans, and in later years there was a great deal of confusion, with some cars marketed as Nissans in one market, and as Datsuns in another. The sports cars covered here are a case in point – for a European/USA Datsun 240Z was a Nissan Fairlady Z in Japan.

We have wriggled neatly out of this by adopting the usual European custom of calling the 'inline'-engined cars Datsuns, while the V-engined cars which followed in 1983 were always known as Nissans, and will be described under that banner.

Nissan-Datsun rapidly built up their business in the 1950s, first of all by building British Austins under licence, then producing Austin-copies of their own, and finally by developing their own ranges.

At first the business concentrated on producing more and more rugged, simple and cheap-to-run family cars and light trucks, but it also dabbled with two dumpy little sports cars in the 1950s. Its first serious sports car was the Fairlady (Type SP310) range of the 1960s. Cynics who think that this was inspired by Britain's MGB should remember that the Fairlady appeared a full year *earlier* than the MGB was ever seen in public.

By 1970 Nissan-Datsun's annual production had rocketed to 900,000 cars a year, and the export business to the USA and Europe was well-established, so the company then made its big move into modern sporting cars with the launch of the famous 240Z.

Almost at a stroke this transformed Datsun's stodgy image, for the 240Z was not only very attractive, but also fast, and had great character. American enthusiasts took this car to their hearts, and it soon became the best-selling sports car in history.

In the next 12 years Nissan-Datsun confirmed itself as Japan's second-largest carmaker. By the early 1980s Nissan was producing 1.8 million cars a year, and the popularity of the sports cars grew alongside this. More than 540,000 of the original 'Z-cars' were built in nine years, and more than 410,000 280ZX-type machines followed in the next five years.

Nothing, it seemed – neither energy crises, fashion changes nor sheer anti-Japanese prejudice – could stop this avalanche. In the next few years, with all cars now firmly badged as Nissans, the advance continued.

*Above: The Datsun S211 was produced in small numbers, from 1959 to 1963, with an 1189-cc four-cylinder engine putting out about 60 bhp. It was a far cry from the later Z-cars, but it was a start . . .*

*Above: The Nissan 300ZX was the 1990s descendant of the Z-car. Twin-turbo versions offered 155 mph supercar performance, but this model is an American-market non-turbo.*

# Datsun Fairlady SP310, SP311 and SR311 1961-69

Although Datsun had already dabbled with open-air motoring in the 1950s, cars like the Sports (DC-3) of 1952, and the Sports of 1959 (S211) never went into long-term series production.

The Fairlady SP310, launched at the Tokyo Motor Show in 1961, was a much more serious project. It pre-dated the MGB and was based on a solid box-section chassis frame with conventional suspension. The SP310 originally used the same running gear as that of the Bluebird family cars of the period, and had the rather unusual feature of being a three-seater. Like Daimler's Conquest roadster, which had been in production a few years earlier, it had two front bucket seats, and a third seat was mounted cross-wise in the rear compartment.

In the next few years the Fairlady roadsters had a fair degree of success in the USA, where they proved to be com-

petitive in certain price classes of motor racing. An official US competition programme was set up in 1967. Very few of the cars were ever exported to Europe, where the rather plain Datsuns encountered stiff opposition from established marques like MG, Alfa Romeo and Fiat.

The original SP310 had a 71-bhp 1.5-litre four-cylinder overhead-valve engine, a four-speed gearbox, drum front brakes, and a three-seater layout; 7,000 examples were sold. After three years, in 1965, the model was updated to become the SP311, with a 90-bhp 1.6-litre engine, a four-speed all-synchromesh gearbox and front-wheel disc brakes; by this time the third seat had been abandoned. This car stayed in production until the end of Fairlady 2000 assembly in 1969.

Two years later, from March 1967, the SR311 model, the Fairlady Sports 2000,

*Above: Sometimes the Japanese companies were ahead of the Europeans, if only in styling. The 1961-69 Fairlady series was very conventionally engineered but pre-dated the similar-looking MGB by more than a year.*

appeared, this car having a brand-new 2.0-litre overhead-cam engine which in some versions produced 145 bhp, this being backed by a five-speed gearbox. These were the Fairlady cars seen in European rallying, but they were never marketed in the UK.

In seven years about 40,000 of these stubby but purposeful little Fairlady cars were produced, most of them being sold in the USA. This was merely a prelude to the mass invasion of the USA by the 240Z, which followed in 1970.

## Fairlady SP310 variants

### Fairlady SR311

In 1967 the SR311 was introduced, with a new two-litre overhead-cam engine and a five-speed gearbox. The car was never marketed in Europe.

### Specification (SR311 Sports 2000)

**Engine:** inline four-cylinder, overhead-cam
**Bore × stroke:** 87.2 mm × 83 mm
**Capacity:** 1982 cc
**Maximum power:** 145 bhp

**Transmission:** five-speed manual gearbox, rear-wheel drive
**Chassis:** separate steel frame with box-section side members
**Suspension:** independent front with wishbones and coil springs; live rear

axle with leaf springs
**Brakes:** discs front, drums rear
**Bodywork:** two-seater sports, optional hardtop
**Maximum speed (approx):** 125 mph (201 km/h)

*Above: Earlier 1.5- and 1.6-litre models were not startling performers, but the post-1967 Fairlady Sports 2000 (SR311) had a two-litre overhead-cam engine that in some versions produced 145 bhp.*

# Datsun 240Z 1970-73

Perhaps Datsun always planned it that way, but there is no doubt that the 240Z arrived on the North American market at exactly the right time. Britain's Austin-Healey 3000 had been dropped at the end of 1967, the MG MGC which was supposed to replace it was not a success, and was dropped at the end of 1969 – while the Datsun Z-car went on sale in 1970.

No-one really knows where the 'Z' part of the title came from. The '240' part of the title, however, referred to the 2.4-litre engine size. This way of identifying the car made it easy to distinguish the various derivatives which followed in the 1970s.

Not only was the 240Z a very attractive car, but it was well-packaged with a fast-back/hatchback cabin. The design was simple but boasted up-to-the-minute engineering, and it had bags of character.

This was the secret of the 240Z's success. No previous Nissan-Datsun could ever have been flattered with the word 'character', nor could it have been called beautiful. The 240Z, and its immediate successors, broke the rules.

The startlingly beautiful style of the 240Z project was conceived by Count Albrecht Goertz, a German designer working mainly in West Germany, and was subsequently modified by Datsun before launch. Like many other graceful sports cars, it had a long and flowing nose, a cabin set well back on the floor-pan, and a stubby tail. There were some touches of the Porsche 911, and some of the Jaguar E-type, in the proportions. The customers, particularly in the all-important American market, loved it.

The body hid a drivetrain which was slightly modified from that of the latest Datsun Laurel/Skyline/Cedric family cars, all of which used one of several versions of the big, heavy, overhead-cam six-cylinder engine. Unlike the cars

which it supplanted, however, the 240Z also had independent front *and* rear suspension, by MacPherson struts in each case.

Driven gently, it was smooth, civilised, and seemingly dead-reliable. Driven hard, it bellowed, and became a real muscle car. Datsun entered it in long-distance international rallies to make their point, and the car rewarded them by winning the East African Safari on two occasions.

North American sales rocketed from 10,000 in 1971 to 52,500 in 1973, the rest of the world having to take second place in the growing queue. During this time demand developed for more space, and more options. The result, launched in 1973, was the larger-engined, though no faster, 260Z – and the addition of a 2+2 body style.

A total of 231,711 240Zs and their Fairlady-badged equivalents was produced.

## Datsun 240Z variants

### Fairlady Z and Z432

In Japan, the Fairlady Z had a 130-bhp/two-litre engine, while the limited-production Fairlady Z432 had a special twin-overhead-cam 160-bhp/two-litre engine which produced 160 bhp in 'street' form, but also had racing applications; only 419 such cars were produced.

### Specification (240Z)

**Engine:** inline six-cylinder, overhead-cam
**Bore × stroke:** 83 mm × 73.7 mm
**Capacity:** 2393 cc
**Maximum power:** 151 bhp
**Transmission:** four- or five-speed manual gearbox, or optional automatic transmission, rear-wheel drive
**Chassis:** unit-construction body/chassis assembly

*Above: The original 240Z undercut Jaguar and Porsche prices and filled the gap left by the end of Austin-Healey 3000 production for the USA. The 240Z was just as powerful as the 'Big Healey' but was far more modern.*

**Suspension:** independent front and rear, each with MacPherson struts
**Brakes:** discs front, drums rear
**Bodywork:** two-seater coupé
**Maximum speed (approx):** 125 mph (201 km/h)

*Above: Standard Z-cars had tacky-looking wheel covers over conventional steel wheels and many owners fitted 'slot mags', which improved the car's appearance dramatically.*

## Datsun 260Z 1973-78

In 1973 the 240Z was dropped, in favour of two closely-related new cars – the 260Z and the 260Z 2+2. Although both cars were based on the layout of the original model, Datsun had done a lot of work to make them even better suited to 1970s motoring conditions.

Both cars received a larger-capacity version of the heavy old six-cylinder engine, although in accommodating the growing problem of meeting North American exhaust-emission regulations, the tune and general character of the engine became 'softer' than before. The 260Z, in fact, was promoted as having more power than the 240Z, but the performance figures proved that it actually had less. This didn't harm the car's reputation, however – the Japanese, as ever, were inscrutable, smiled politely, and merely pointed to the sales figures.

The 260Z looked almost exactly like the 240Z, but the 2+2 version was built on a much longer version of the floorpan, had a more capacious cabin, and squeezed in two extra occasional seats, just ahead of the rear axle. It didn't matter that these were too cramped to carry fully-grown adults, for this was a more practical car which weighed only about 50 lb more than the two-seater. British testers called this larger car ". . . a complete success. It provides enough extra room without losing the visual appeal of the shorter model."

Only two years after the 260Z had been launched in America it was superseded by the 280Z (which was a USA-only

model), this having the 2.75-litre version of the lusty old engine, which had a bit more power and a lot more torque than the 2.6-litre model.

Once again, annual US sales rocketed – in 1975 they passed the 50,000 mark, while in 1977 they reached 69,500. Without the USA, it is certain that this model would not have been viable. It was therefore not surprising that Datsun pressed on with a new design, this eventually appearing in 1978 as the 280ZX.

Between 1973 and 1978, 310,497 260Zs and 280Zs were produced, 230,128 of them being USA-only 280Zs.

### Datsun 260Z 2+2 variants

#### Datsun 260Z two-seater
The other mass-production version of the car was the 260Z two-seater (1973-78), which looked identical to the original 240Z, with a 12-in shorter wheelbase than the 2+2, and only two seats.

#### Fairlady Z 2+2
As with the 240Z, there was a Japanese-only version, called the Fairlady Z 2+2 (1974-78), complete with a 125-bhp/two-litre overhead-cam engine.

#### Datsun 280Z
For sale only in the USA, from 1975-78, was a 149-bhp/2.8-litre version of the two-seater, called the 280Z. This had a larger, fuel-injected engine to compensate for the 'strangulation' effect of exhaust-emission regulations, and a four-speed manual gearbox.

*Above: With the introduction of the 260Z came a stretched 2+2 version with a 12-in longer wheelbase and a different rear side-window line. The extra inches were all added to the cabin area to allow two cramped rear seats, and the change shows in the distance from door to rear wheel arch. That extra length and that reshaped side window spoilt the purity of the original design and also started the Z-car's trend away from a sporting two-seater towards a softer and heavier Grand Tourer style. This trend culminated in the 300ZX of the 1980s, but was reversed with the new 300ZX for the 1990s.*

### Specification (260Z 2+2)

**Engine:** inline six-cylinder, overhead-cam
**Bore × stroke:** 83 mm × 79 mm
**Capacity:** 2565 cc
**Maximum power:** 150 bhp
**Transmission:** five-speed manual gearbox, optional automatic transmission, rear-wheel drive
**Chassis:** unit-construction body/chassis assembly
**Suspension:** independent front with MacPherson struts; independent rear with MacPherson struts
**Brakes:** discs front, drums rear
**Bodywork:** 2+2 coupé
**Maximum speed (approx):** 120 mph (193 km/h)

*Below: For the 260Z, displacement of the six-cylinder engine went up to 2565 cc but US exhaust-emission regulations were biting hard, and even in European form the car was not as fast as its predecessor.*

# Datsun 280ZX 1978-83

Nissan launched the second-generation Z-car in 1978. Except that the existing engine and gearboxes were used, it was almost all new.

Not only was there a new shell and style and a new type of rear suspension but, above all, there was also a new character. The new cars, titled 280ZX and 280ZX 2+2, were longer, wider and heavier than the previous models.

Nissan had carried out intensive market research before finalising the 280ZX, discovering that American customers wanted it to be more of a 'GT' than before, with lots of comfort, power-assisted windows, cruise-control, and everything that would make it what the USA called a 'personal car'.

When the car was launched, Nissan waxed lyrical about its increased size, its softer ride, its 'Grand Luxury' packaging, and its great refinement. The out-and-out sports car fanatics, who complained that it had lost its edge and lost its dynamic appeal, were in the minority.

Even though the 280ZX looked more bulky than the 260Z which it replaced, it was actually more aerodynamically efficient in all respects – drag, lift at speed, and stability in cross-winds.

As before there was a choice of two-seater (ZX) or 2+2-seater (ZX 2+2) styles, the difference now being 7.9 inches in the wheelbase, and nearly 200 lb in unladen weight. Aft of the windscreen the two structures were completely different, but both were roomier than the models they superseded.

The 280ZX used improved versions of the engine and transmissions of the obsolete 260/280Z models, but the new car used a semi-trailing-arm rear suspension which had been lifted straight from the contemporary Datsun Bluebird Type 810 saloon. For the first time, too, this was a Z-car with power-assisted steering, and with four-wheel disc brakes.

In a decade, in fact, the Z-car had lost about 10 mph on top speed, nearly two seconds on the 0-60 mph time, and

5 mpg on fuel economy. You might say that this was not a desirable form of progress, but then Nissan's response was that the 280ZX was a completely different type of car from the original 240Z, and that the car's popularity (measured by its sales) proved the point.

Statistically, they were right – the 280ZX family was in production for only five years, in which no fewer than 414,628 cars of all types were built. In the calendar year 1979, and again in 1980, nearly 72,000 were sold in North America alone.

The 280ZX range, especially in its final 'T-bar' form, continued to sell very well indeed until it was replaced by the V6-engined 300ZX. Not just the engine was new, but so was the badge, for the 300ZX was officially a Nissan, and will be more fully described in a future entry under that company name.

## Datsun 280ZX variants

### Datsun 280ZX two-seater

Parallel with the 2+2 model there was the 280ZX two-seater, which had an 8-in shorter wheelbase and subtly different roof/tail-end styling. USA versions of these cars had 135-bhp (to 1981) or 145-bhp (1981-83) engines.

### Datsun 280ZX Turbo

From 1981 to 1983 there was a 280ZX Turbo (USA sale only), with 180 bhp from its 2.8-litre engine.

### Fairlady Z and Fairlady 280Z-L 2BY2

For sale only in Japan, the two-seater was called a Fairlady Z, with a 130-bhp/two-litre engine, while the 2+2 seater was called the Fairlady 280Z-L 2BY2, with 145 bhp and 2.8 litres.

### 'T-bar' option

As an alternative to the coupé/hatchback style, Datsun also introduced a 'T-bar' derivative, where two roof panels (one over each front seat) could be removed. This car went on sale (two-seater) in 1980 and (2+2) in 1981, and quickly became very popular.

### Specification (European-spec 280ZX)

**Engine:** inline six-cylinder, overhead-cam
**Bore × stroke:** 86 mm × 79 mm
**Capacity:** 2753 cc
**Maximum power:** 140 bhp
**Transmission:** five-speed manual gearbox, optional automatic transmission, rear-wheel drive
**Chassis:** unit-construction body/chassis
**Suspension:** independent front with MacPherson struts; independent rear with semi-trailing arms and coil springs
**Brakes:** discs front and rear
**Bodywork:** two-seater coupé
**Maximum speed (approx):** 112 mph (180 km/h)

*Below and inset below: Bigger, heavier, mushier (but more aerodynamically efficient) than the 'real' Z-cars that preceded it, the 280ZX was designed to be the comfortable GT car that American customers wanted. Two-seater and 2+2 versions were produced and a 'T-bar' roof became an option in 1980-81. Only the straight-six engine (in Bosch fuel-injected, 2753-cc, form as fitted to the last US-spec Zs) and five-speed manual gearbox were retained unchanged from the previous range. A semi-trailing-arm arrangement borrowed from the 810 saloon replaced the old MacPherson-strut rear suspension which had been used since the days of the first 240Z.*

# NSU

This German concern, already noted for its pedal cycles and motorcycles, began producing four-wheelers in 1906, and carried on with all types of engine-driven transport until its last and most famous model, the Ro80 (which brought about the downfall of the company), was finally discontinued in 1977.

The cars were built at Neckarsulm, a relatively small town north of Stuttgart. The business was modest until the 1930s, and expansion into a new factory at Heilbronn (a few miles away from Neckarsulm) was a mistake, but NSU survived by selling off the new plant to Fiat, and carried on in its old premises.

In the aftermath of the slump which hit Europe in 1930, NSU car production came to an end in 1931, although motorcycle assembly continued unabated. The first post-war cars were not built until 1958 and these – like NSU's pre-World War II products – had small, low-powered engines, for cheapness and fuel economy.

The 1960s NSUs featured stubby body styles (clearly inspired by Chevrolet's 'bath-tub' Corvair shapes), along with air-cooled rear-mounted engines. These gradually became larger, more powerful and faster, but none had much in the way of performance.

It was only after NSU formed links with Felix Wankel, to develop the potential of his fascinating new rotary engine, that the cars became more inspired. Even so, NSU was only able to put two Wankel-engined cars on sale before it hit financial troubles and sold out to VW in 1969.

In a conventional piston engine, up-and-down motion of pistons has to be converted to rotary motion of the crankshaft, but in the Wankel layout a complex-shaped rotor circulates inside a housing, effectively taking the combustion chamber to the fuel/air mixture (which is admitted from ports in the housing), and being geared directly to the eccentric, or crankshaft. If only the chambers could have been effectively sealed, manufacturing costs contained and fuel consumption improved, NSU would have had a winner.

The world's first Wankel-powered car was NSU's little Spider, which astonished the world when it went on sale in 1963, but it was the aerodynamically advanced, front-wheel-drive, twin-rotor Ro80 of 1967 which made all the headlines.

Problems with the Wankel engine prompted a change in policy, and NSU was about to launch a piston-engined version of the Ro80, the K70, in 1969, but the merger with VW killed this off. VW then redeveloped the car, badged it as a VW, and put it on sale in 1971. After 1972 the only NSU was the controversial Ro80, which was built in smaller and smaller numbers until 1977, at which point the NSU name was finally abandoned.

*Above: The NSU Wankel Spider, introduced in 1963, was an extremely optimistic attempt to launch a new form of engine onto the market, a small single-rotor Wankel.*

*Below: The NSU Ro80 saloon, which appeared in 1967, was a very revolutionary design both in engine and aerodynamic terms, but rotor wear hurt its reputation.*

## NSU Wankel Spider 1963-66

Dr Felix Wankel began developing his extraordinary rotary engine in the 1950s, but it took him years to persuade a major manufacturer to back his ideas. Although various companies showed interest, NSU was the first to take out a development and manufacturing licence, originally with an eye to using the new engine in motorcycles.

By the early 1960s NSU's management was convinced that it could make a real breakthrough with the rotary engine. Even in single-rotor form the engine was smoother and potentially more high-revving than a normal piston engine, and in twin-rotor guise (to be used in later applications) the engines felt quite astonishingly refined. There was a major problem, however – to cut down the rapid wear-rate of the rotor-tip seals.

To gain experience, and public acceptance for the engine, NSU asked Bertone to style an open Spider on the basis of the existing Prinz underframe, then installed a single-rotor Wankel engine in the tail, with the engine behind the line of the rear wheels. In spite of the rear-biased weight distribution, the handling was perfectly acceptable.

*Autocar's* road-testers were intrigued by the rotary engine, the first they had experienced for any long spell. They thought it felt like a four-stroke flat-twin, found that it idled smoothly at 1,000 rpm (although tending to shake slightly in its mounting if set faster than that) and they detected a rough period at 2,400 rpm. Beyond that, however, it ran with exceptional refinement all the way to the peak engine speed, a high 8,000 rpm. They expected to find the tiny engine lacking in torque and power at low rpm but discovered that the engine pulled very strongly from 2,000 rpm, while maximum-torque rpm was a remarkably low 2,500 rpm.

Poor fuel consumption (along with excessive rotor-tip wear) were the twin Achilles heels of the rotary engine, but neither revealed themselves in the Spider; the overall fuel consumption of 26 mpg *Autocar* recorded was not good, but it was not disastrous, and it was not until NSU launched the bigger and heavier Ro80 that engine wear became a monumental problem.

Although the engine's nominal capacity was 497 cc, the fact that there were effectively twice as many firing impulses per revolution (compared with a normal piston engine) meant that the engine was always seen as a 1.0-litre unit, which meant that it was on a par with current British sports cars like the Triumph Spitfire and the MG Midget. Overall it compared quite well with those cars, actually being quicker over the standing quartermile (if fractionally slower that the 1275S Mini-Cooper S). Its 0-60 mph time of 16.7 seconds sounds painfully slow by today's standards, but it matched its Triumph and MG opposition.

NSU were quite satisfied with the performance and the exposure the car generated, and withdrew it from sale as they prepared to market the far more ambitious Ro80.

Total production of Wankel Spiders was a mere 2,375.

*Above: The tiny rotary engine was at the rear of the car, and its 50 bhp would propel the Spider to over [ ] mph. It worked well, but the problem of engine wear had yet to be solved.*

*Below: Bertone's styling of the Wankel Spider was considered very successful. Only the relative shortness of the bonnet and boot gave the hint that the engine was mounted at the rear.*

*Above: The interior was typical of a 1960s sports car, and the Spider, an effective rival to other small sports cars, would probably have carried on selling well had NSU persevered with it.*

### Specification (1963)

**Engine:** single-rotor Wankel rotary
**Nominal capacity:** 994 cc (actual capacity 497 cc)
**Maximum power:** 50 bhp
**Transmission:** four-speed manual gearbox, rear-wheel drive
**Chassis:** steel unitary construction body/chassis
**Suspension:** independent with wishbones, coil springs and telescopic dampers front; semi-trailing arms with coil springs and telescopic dampers rear
**Brakes:** discs front, drums rear
**Bodywork:** steel two-seater open sports car, optional hard top
**Maximum speed (approx):** 92 mph (148 km/h)

## NSU Ro80 1967-77

Compared with the original rear-engined Spider, the Wankel-engined Ro80 was a much more ambitious project. It was the world's very first Wankel-powered saloon and the first twin-rotor Wankel engined car to go on sale.

NSU, a relatively small company with limited technical resources, very bravely went for an advanced chassis *and* advanced engineering to match the Wankel engine. Even without its revolutionary engine, the Ro80 would have been quite a car. In road manners, in response, and in engineering it was a match for the contemporary big Citroëns; the Wankel engine merely made it technically more interesting.

The twin-rotor engine was nominally a two-litre, and was rated at 115 bhp, and with refinement as much in mind as tech-

nical advance, this was matched to a Fichtel & Sachs three-speed semi-automatic transmission, and to front-wheel drive. The rest of the chassis was similarly inspired, for there was all-independent suspension to give a smooth ride, four-wheel disc brakes to match the performance, and a smooth body style which would not have looked out of place if it had been launched a decade later.

The Ro80 not only looked good, but had excellent road manners, and good performance. The engine had very little low-speed torque, but was incredibly free-revving when wound up, the result being a car that could be driven remarkably quickly. It was one of those rare cars which seemed to become quieter as it went faster.

The problem was that it was too easy to

over-rev the rather delicate engine, so that the Ro80 soon got a well-deserved reputation for rapid rotor-tip seal wear. NSU was faced with mountainous warranty claims for its new invention, but valiantly stood by them, and this was certainly a factor in the financial collapse which followed, and the agreement to a rescue by VW.

Before it was recognised as a real classic, the Ro80 tended to be butchered by second and third owners, usually by the fitment of a Ford V4 or V6 engine, but most survivors now have rotary engines.

Although VW bought NSU in 1969, it kept the controversial Ro80 in production for several years after sales had slowed to a trickle. It was only in 1977 that the very last of the 37,204 cars were produced. The lessons of being pioneers, however, had been learned the hard way; for neither NSU, nor VW, has ever produced another Wankel-engined car.

*Above: The Ro80 was a very brave attempt to create a new sort of car, but the gamble failed and warranty problems broke NSU.*

### Specification (1967)

**Engine:** twin-rotor Wankel rotary
**Nominal capacity:** 1990 cc (actual capacity 995 cc)
**Maximum power:** 115 bhp
**Transmission:** three-speed semi-automatic gearbox, front-wheel drive
**Chassis:** steel unitary construction body/chassis
**Suspension:** independent with MacPherson struts and anti-roll bar front; MacPherson struts and trailing arms rear
**Brakes:** discs all round
**Bodywork:** steel four-door four-seat saloon with hard top
**Maximum speed (approx):** 107 mph (172 km/h)

*Above: The revolutionary Ro80 did not accelerate particularly fast but had a top speed of 107 mph, and with fine aerodynamics and a smooth-running rotary engine it was quiet at speed.*

*Right: The styling of the 1967 Ro80 was, like the engine, ahead of its time, with elements that became common during the 1980s. The rotor-tip problems have now largely been solved by Mazda.*

# Oldsmobile

Ransom Eli Olds started by building an experimental steam-powered car in 1891, then followed up by making single-cylinder petrol-engined dog carts, before launching the amazing Curved Dash Runabout in 1901, which was really the world's first mass-produced car. By then, the copper and timber tycoon S. J. Smith had bought the Olds Gasoline Engine Works for his two sons to run, and so successful was the Curved Dash that in 1904 more than 5,000 of these 1600-cc single-cylinder, 20-mph cars were built.

After 1904 Olds left the company which he had founded, to set up the REO concern, and five years later, in 1909, Oldsmobile became one of the founding companies in the General Motors combine, which went on to become the world's largest motor manufacturer.

By the 1920s, with Alfred P. Sloan in charge of General Motors, Oldsmobile had settled down, immediately below Cadillac and Buick in the corporate pecking order and price structure, and above Pontiac and Chevrolet. For many years Oldsmobiles faithfully followed the GM party line, building ranges of conventional cars; except for the styling excesses of the 1950s and 1960s there was rarely anything out of the ordinary about an Oldsmobile, which regularly occupied fifth or sixth position in the USA's best-sellers' lists.

It was not until 1965 that Oldsmobile's first – and only – true supercar arrived. This was the front-wheel-drive Toronado, a lavishly-dimensioned V8 coupé which was not only a head-to-head competitor with Ford's Thunderbird range for what American product planners called the 'personal car' market, but was also a statement of GM's technological prowess. When tested by the British magazine *Motor* in 1966, the Toronado was the most powerful and most thirsty car ever encountered, but also "proved that front-wheel drive will work extremely well with seven litres".

The Toronado was GM's first front-wheel-drive car, in fact the only front-wheel-drive car in the North American motor industry at the time. The practicalities of corporate planning meant that Oldsmobile was not allowed to keep this design to itself. The result was that the same basic layout was soon adopted for the Cadillac Eldorado.

In the 1960s many Detroit-watchers hoped that the Toronado layout would be the first of several such from Oldsmobile, but they were speedily disappointed. In the 1960s the Toronado had been the most powerful and the most glitzy of all Oldsmobiles, but by the 1980s the model had been down-sized, made less powerful and – some said – had lost its styling appeal. By the early 1990s, in fact, almost every current Oldsmobile had front-wheel drive, of an entirely different type from that invented for the Toronado in the 1960s, and a number of other models had larger and more powerful engines.

In the early 1990s Oldsmobile was established in fourth place in the Detroit sales charts, selling well over 400,000 cars every year.

**Above: The sleek 1970 Oldsmobile Toronado sports coupé was available with a seven-litre V8 which, with a 10.25:1 compression ratio, developed 375 bhp at 4,600 rpm. It was a car with real performance, and standard equipment included Turbo Hydramatic transmission and power steering and brakes.**

**Left: Ransom Eli Olds first built cars in the 1890s, and the firm he founded has the longest history of all the US carmakers.**

**Below: The 1966 Oldsmobile Toronado was a real supercar, with its advanced front-wheel-drive design. It was also extremely fast, with an output of 385 bhp and prodigious torque from the seven-litre V8.**

## Oldsmobile Toronado 1965-present

After the war, and until the 1960s, General Motors cars had all followed the same basic design pattern – conventional chassis engineering, massive and inefficient engines, loads and loads of equipment options, all topped by extravagant styling. The befinned Cadillacs of the 1950s, and the Oldsmobiles which accompanied them, were typical.

Then came the 1960s, the influence of engineer Ed Cole, and a series of technically exciting cars. The ill-starred Chevrolet Corvair was first, and the second wave of compacts from Buick,

Oldsmobile and Pontiac followed. After the arrival of the all-independent-suspension Corvette Stingray, GM's engineers then took a breather, but the new Toronado, launched in 1965, was worth waiting for! It was the first front-wheel-drive American car since the Cord 810/812 of the 1930s.

Up to the mid-1960s American cars in this class had featured V8 engines and rear-wheel drive, but were merely technical updates of models conceived and sold for the previous decade. The new Toronado, which could seat only four in

*Above: The shape of Oldsmobile's Toronado sports coupé was notably clean for 1966. This influential car also both went and handled well, and sales were excellent.*

what was a truly massive coupé shell, nearly 19 feet long, was a complete breakaway from this.

Although the conventional seven-litre Oldsmobile V8 engine was mounted more or less in the standard position, the Hydramatic automatic transmission was placed alongside and below the engine itself. The torque converter was bolted to the rear of the crankshaft, as usual, but drove across to the transmission by a 2-in wide rubber-damped multi-link chain. The transmission was bolted direct to the final drive unit, itself chassis-mounted, and the front wheels were then driven by exposed driveshafts.

Other features, like the perimeter-type chassis frame (which stopped ahead of the line of the rear wheels) and power-assisted everything, were conventional enough, although the style, by David North, was smoother and sleeker than most other GM cars.

Although General Motors had no previous experience of building front-wheel-drive cars, this mammoth coupé was not only fast but surprisingly nimble, and immediately began to sell very well. Priced at $4,812 for the De Luxe version (almost the same price as the contemporary Thunderbird), it was also very good value.

The American car historian Richard Langworth once described the Toronado as: ". . . probably the most outstanding single Olds model of the 1960s. Although the 1968-70 versions were not as clean as the '66 and '67, the Toronado was a landmark creation".

The first cars all had 385 bhp and closed coupé styles, but the engine was boosted to 7.4 litres and 375 or 400 bhp for 1968. By this time the Toronado had been joined in the GM stable by the Cadillac Eldorado, which used the same basic chassis and internal panels but with its own large V8 engine and a far craggier style.

The first generation of Toronado, with a 119-in wheelbase and up to 400 bhp, was built for five years. The next-generation models were larger and heavier, but less powerful, as was the equivalent Cadillac. Styling was gradually sharpened up, and made closer to that of the Cadillac Eldorado during the 1970s. Unlike the Eldorado, however, the Toronado was never available as a convertible. For 1971 Oldsmobile completely rejigged the design, with a 122-in wheelbase and a 7457-cc/350-bhp engine. The power rating plummeted to 250 bhp for 1972 and to 215 bhp for 1975. For 1977 the engine size was cut to 6477 cc/200 bhp.

From late 1978 the down-sizing process began in earnest, with the wheelbase being chopped, and power reduced yet again, to 6577 cc and 190 bhp. As with most so-called American performance cars of the period, increasing emissions-control legislation had taken away most of the performance and destroyed the cars' image. By the time the third-generation Toronado appeared the wheelbase was only 114 inches and engine power was down to a mere 165 bhp. Although the Toronado was still an important part of the Oldsmobile line-up in the early 1990s, it was no longer a supercar like the original.

A total of 143,134 of the first Toronado coupés were produced in five years, while 267,888 second-generation types followed in the 1970-78 period.

*Above: By 1969 the front grille had been revised, but the style remained strong. The seven-litre V8 delivered 375 bhp at 4,600 rpm.*

*Below: In 1969 the $4,812 Toronado shared the distinction of front-wheel drive with only one other car, the two-door Cadillac Eldorado.*

### Specification (1966)

**Engine:** V8, overhead-valve
**Bore × stroke:** 109.2 mm × 101.1 mm
**Capacity:** 6965 cc
**Maximum power:** 385 bhp
**Transmission:** three-speed manual gearbox, front-wheel drive
**Chassis:** separate steel perimeter frame with box-section side member
**Suspension:** independent front with wishbones and torsion bars; beam axle with semi-elliptic leaf springs rear
**Brakes:** drums all round
**Bodywork:** steel four-seater coupé
**Maximum speed (approx):** 130 mph (209 km/h)

# Opel

L ike many other motor manufacturers, Opel did not start by building cars. The five Opel brothers first established a business making sewing machines and bicycles. The original cars were constructed in Germany at Russelsheim, west of Frankfurt, where Opel's main factory is still situated.

Car production began in 1898, but the first model was a failure, and Opel only achieved stability after agreeing to produce licence-built French Darracqs. The factory was completely burned down in 1911, but production resumed in 1912. Until the mid-1920s Opel was independent, and concentrated mainly on building middle-class cars.

In the 1920s the business was taken over by General Motors of the USA, which meant that it became a distant corporate relative of Britain's Vauxhall company, which had also joined the GM empire. For many years, however, the two companies did not co-operate with each other. By 1928 Opel sales had expanded so far that Opel was Germany's largest car manufacturer, with a 37 per cent market share.

During the 1930s Opel countered the Depression (shored up by GM finance) by building more and more small, cheap cars, and became mainland Europe's largest carmaking concern, but during World War II

*Above: An Opel Kadett GT-E in the 1976 Tour of Britain Rally. In rally form the best-selling coupé had a ZF five-speed gearbox and fuel injection.*

the factory was badly hit by Allied bombing, then in 1945 the Russians annexed the old Kadett production facilities as reparations. Opel started building cars again in 1947, and within 20 years had re-established itself as a major manufacturer.

Most of the time Opel, like Vauxhall, has concentrated on building family cars, but with the occasional sporting indulgence. The first such car was the appealing little GT coupé of the 1960s, but there was then a long gap before GM allowed Opel to make a limited-production homologation special for motorsport, the Ascona 400.

From the 1970s GM gradually merged the skills and facilities of Opel and Vauxhall. Although each company continued to use some of its own engines and transmissions until the 1980s, body styles and structures were rapidly rationalised. Opel took over design leadership in Europe, which meant that 1980s and 1990s Vauxhalls were really no more than lightly-disguised Opels. The cognoscenti soon learned to equate a Kadett with an Astra, an Ascona with a Cavalier, and a Carlton with a Rekord.

Like many other European companies of the day, too, Opel not only produced ever-wider ranges of a particular car, but also began investigating more exciting, limited-production machinery. In the 1980s Cosworth Engineering was hired to produce a 16-valve two-litre engine for Kadetts and Asconas, following which Opel developed four-wheel-drive transmissions and a smart coupé body.

Finally, for the 1990s, two truly outstanding new models appeared – one a turbocharged version of the Calibra coupé, the other an extrovert supercar variant of the Omega/Carlton, which was developed and assembled by another GM-owned company, Lotus.

Even so, this never distracted Opel from its main purpose, which was to make and sell as many cars as possible. By the early 1990s at least 600,000 cars were being produced every year, which put Opel on a par with Ford-Germany, though both these companies were a long way behind VW in the German pecking order.

*Above: An Opel Manta in the 1985 RAC Rally; in 1984 Servia and Jordi won the Catalunya Rally in a Manta.*

*Below: In the early 1990s the very top of the Opel range was the fearsomely quick Lotus Omega, with 377 bhp.*

## Opel GT 1968-73

*Above: The GT started as a styling exercise and became an unlikely sports best-seller for Opel – out of character for the company but, with its Opel Kadett running gear, a lively and, when tuned, engagingly fast two-seater. Opel could have developed the theme but never did.*

*Below: The cockpit was plain rather than luxurious, but the driving position was comfortable and engine information was well displayed.*

Like other famous cars which evolved from a striking styling exercise, the Opel GT was a direct descendant of a show special or dream car, one displayed at the Frankfurt Motor Show of 1965. At the time, Opel stated that it had no intention of making such a car in quantity, and that in view of the demand (thought to be limited) it would be uneconomic to do so.

Less than three years later, the company had changed its mind. A new sporting Opel, the GT, was revealed; Opel had got round the economic problems by having body shells tooled and manufactured under contract by Brissoneau and Lotz of France.

The shell was based on the body platform of the Kadett/Olympia saloon, but was then built up from steel pressings into a smart two-seater coupé. There were two versions of this pretty style – 1100 and 1900 – of which the 1897-cc-engined 1900 was much the more popular type. Its output was enough to give a top speed of 115 mph, while the 1087-cc engine's 60 bhp was not sufficient to yield

any sporting performance.

The GT was a great departure for Opel, which, although well on the way to modernising its range, was still thought to make a series of boring, stodgy, but reliable cars in the true General Motors tradition. The GT, however, was a very engaging first step towards a new and more sporting image, a trend which carried on into the 1970s with cars like the Manta, and the smart Rekord and Commodore coupés.

The GT was only ever sold as a two-seater fixed-head coupé, and it is instructive to compare its overall shape with that of the long-running Chevrolet Corvette (another GM car, of course), which had recently been introduced to the public in the form of the Mako Shark show car. Although there were also superficial detail resemblances to the Lotus Elan (such as the pop-up, or rather swivel-up, headlamps, which were actually mechanically-activated) this seems to have been no more than coincidence. British customers for this car were not catered for, as no right-hand-

*Below: The 1900-cc four could be tuned to give superb performance, as with the homologation specials.*

drive version was ever made.

It was the first and – so far – the la[st?] modern two-seater Opel to be put [on] sale. Even though no fewer than 103,3[??] such cars were built in five years, Op[el] never repeated the trick.

## Specification (1968)

**Engine:** inline four-cylinder, overhead-valve
**Bore × stroke:** 93 mm × 69.8 mm
**Capacity:** 1897 cc
**Maximum power:** 90 bhp
**Transmission:** four-speed manual gearbox or three-speed automatic transmission, rear-wheel drive
**Chassis:** steel unitary construction body/chassis
**Suspension:** independent front with wishbones and coil springs; live rear axle with trailing arms and coil springs
**Brakes:** discs front, drums rear
**Bodywork:** steel two-seater fixed-head coupé
**Maximum speed (approx):** 115 mph (185 km/h)

*Right: The GT certainly had eye-catching and successfully balanced looks. The headlamp pods rotated discreetly away when closed.*

# Opel Ascona 400 1979-80

In the 1970s Opel's ambition to become competitive in world-class rallying was frustrated by the lack of a specialised car, until the Ascona 400 was speedily developed as a 'homologation special'. For use in what was known as Group 4, only 400 cars had to be built, which explains the model name. Since the car was considered unlikely to be a profitable project, Opel never set out to make many more than this. In fact, 448 Ascona 400s (all left-hand-drive) were actually produced at the Antwerp factory in rather less than a year.

The 'base car' was the two-door version of the second-generation Ascona saloon, which Opel always knew as the Ascona B, although the running gear of the 400 was entirely different. To make the car handle better at high speeds and, frankly, to give it a more glamorous image, the 400 was fitted with plastic skirts under the doors, a big tail spoiler, and a glassfibre bonnet with vents above the radiator. Road cars were also given a very jazzy colour scheme which featured diagonal stripes of the red, yellow and black elements of the German flag.

The 2.4-litre engine was based on the cylinder block of the Opel diesel, but had a new aluminium head with twin overhead camshafts and four valves per cylinder. Although the original head had been designed in Germany, Britain's Cosworth concern got the job of making it work properly, and of machining and assembling all the cylinder heads. Road cars had Bosch fuel injection and 140 bhp, though rally car engines (with

Weber carbs) produced much more.

To match the engine there was a heavy-duty five-speed Getrag gearbox, a more robust back axle, disc brakes on all four wheels, better suspension and Commodore-type alloy wheels. The car looked purposeful, sounded brawny, and handled very well indeed. At German autobahn speeds it sat down well,

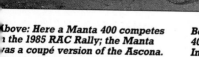

*Above: Here a Manta 400 competes in the 1985 RAC Rally; the Manta was a coupé version of the Ascona.*

*Below: One of the 238 Opel Manta 400s, seen in action in the Manx International Rally of 1986.*

looking and sounding the part.

Right away, in 1980, the works rally car began to win at World Championship level, although its greatest achievement came in 1982, after it had dropped out of production. This was the year in which Walter Rohrl won the World Rally Championship for Opel, in a Rothmans-sponsored car.

## Opel Ascona 400 variants

### Opel Manta 400

To carry the 'homologation special' theme one stage further, Opel launched the Manta 400 in 1981, though its homologated rallying career (as a Group B car) did not begin until mid-1983. The mainstream Manta was a smart two-door coupé version of the Ascona, built on the same platform, chassis and running gear; the Manta 400, therefore, was really a coupé version of the Ascona 400 and used the same 16-valve and five-speed gearbox.

Compared with the Ascona 400, the Manta 400 was lighter, and had a slightly better aerodynamic shape. Like

*Above: The Opel Ascona 400, here at the Nürburgring, was an effective race car as well as rally machine.*

the Ascona 400, it was never meant to be other than the basis for a rally car (for which more than 270 bhp was available), and only 238 were built.

## Specification (1980)

**Engine:** inline four-cylinder, twin overhead camshafts
**Bore × stroke:** 95 mm × 85 mm
**Capacity:** 2410 cc
**Maximum power:** 140 bhp
**Transmission:** five-speed manual gearbox, rear-wheel drive
**Chassis:** steel unitary construction body/chassis
**Suspension:** independent front with wishbones and coil springs and anti-roll bar; live rear axle with trailing arms, Panhard rod and and coil springs
**Brakes:** discs all round
**Bodywork:** steel with glassfibre panels and spoilers; four-seater saloon
**Maximum speed (approx):** 124 mph (200 km/h)

# Opel Lotus-Omega 1990–93

Soon after General Motors bought control of Britain's Lotus concern, it decided to indulge its European subsidiaries. Purely as an image raiser, to produce a phenomenal car with which to impress the opposition, it commissioned Lotus to develop a supercar derivative of the ordinary Opel Omega/Vauxhall Carlton saloon. The result was the four-door four-seater Lotus-Omega/Lotus-Carlton, which was certainly the world's fastest-ever saloon car, with a top speed of more than 170 mph.

The base car, on which the transformation was effected, was GM-Europe's extremely capable Omega/Carlton 24-valve three-litre saloon (itself a series-production model which could reach 146 mph). The Lotus treatment, however, featured a twin turbocharger conversion for the enlarged twin-cam engine, backed by the same *six*-speed gearbox which was then being used on the Chevrolet Corvette ZR-1. Naturally there were suspension and braking changes to suit, along with a full body kit which included wheel-arch extensions, front and rear spoilers and side skirts under the doors.

In every way the Lotus-Omega was an astonishing car, for its true maximum speed was well over 170 mph (magazine testers had to find deserted autobahns in Germany to confirm this), it could sprint up to 100 mph in 11 seconds, and it had the sort of acceleration which left cars like the Ferrari Testarossa gasping.

The main controversy concerned the gearbox, for most testers agreed that sixth gear (which pulled 44.1 mph per 1,000 rpm) was virtually useless, especially in the UK where a speed-limited 70 mph saw the engine turning over at only 1,587 rpm, well below the point at which the turbochargers started working properly. No less than 110 mph was available in third (of six!) gears, and 143 mph in fourth, with the true maximum speed attainable in fifth. Sixth gear, in fact, could only pull 140 mph – worse than that achieved in fourth!

Although all cars were built by Lotus at Hethel in the UK, they were marketed either as Opel Lotus-Omegas or – in the UK only – as Vauxhall Lotus-Carltons. There was no suitable motor-racing or rallying formula for this car to contest, so

it never built up a glamorous image. Because the price was always high (a UK-market car cost £48,000 at first, while by 1992 this had risen to £49,995), and because this colossally fast car could not legally be driven rapidly in many parts of the world, it never sold well. GM originally said that a total of 1,100 cars would be built (of which 440 would be Vauxhall-badged cars for UK buyers), but sales lagged well behind forecasts, and there were suggestions that the project might be killed off prematurely.

The Lotus-Omega/Lotus-Carlton, however, was an amazing and extrovert car – a truly superfluous type of machine to put on sale – which will certainly become a collectors' piece.

*Above: This is no ordinary saloon; the power transfusion at Hethel made the Opel Lotus-Omega into a twin-turbo machine with the speed and acceleration to leave Italian supercars behind.*

*Above: The fascia was similar to that of the standard saloon, but note the speedometer reading to 200 mph, and the six-speed gear lever.*

## Specification (1990)

**Engine:** inline six-cylinder, twin overhead camshafts, twin-turbo
**Bore × stroke:** 95 mm × 85 mm
**Capacity:** 3615 cc
**Maximum power:** 377 bhp
**Transmission:** six-speed manual gearbox, rear-wheel drive
**Chassis:** steel unitary construction body/chassis
**Suspension:** independent with MacPherson struts and anti-roll bar front; semi-trailing arms, coil springs and anti-roll bar rear
**Brakes:** discs all round
**Bodywork:** steel four-door four-seater saloon
**Maximum speed (approx):** 176 mph (283 km/h)

*Above: Lotus developed an engine suitable for both town traffic and all-out autobahn speed.*

*Below: The plentiful spoilers reduced lift and turbulence, vital at speeds over 150 mph.*

# Packard

**Above: During the 1920s and 1930s Packard was associated with the finest in quality; this immaculate 1938 Twelve has town coachwork by Brunn.**

T he first Packards were built (in Warren, Ohio, USA, in 1899) because two brothers – J. W. and W. D. Packard – thought they could produce a better car than one they had just bought. Enthusiasts all round the world, therefore, should thank Winton or inspiring the birth of the Packard motor business.

For many years, particularly in the 1920s and 1930s, well-to-do Americans usted after a Packard almost as much as a Cadillac. In its heyday, ndeed, a Packard was a splendid combination of everything that was ine in motor cars – good looks, fine engineering, high quality and

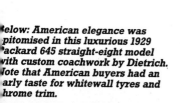

*Right: Although the Packard grille designs changed over the years, all featured the raised centre, as on this 937 model.*

*Below: American elegance was pitomised in this luxurious 1929 Packard 645 straight-eight model with custom coachwork by Dietrich. Note that American buyers had an arly taste for whitewall tyres and hrome trim.*

reliability. It was the equal of Cadillac in every way – except for the vital asset of a massive GM-backed dealer network.

Like many other American cars of the 1900s, early Packards were simply-engineered but large-engined cars, first with four-cylinder and then (from 1911) with straight-six-cylinder engines. Packard moved from Warren to Detroit in 1903, and built all its subsequent cars there. By 1914 it was already one of North America's most desirable marques.

Then, in 1915, Packard's reputation was assured with the launch of the Twin-Six, which was the world's first V12-engined car. This base was built upon in the 1920s and 1930s with a series of straight-eight-engined models which took over from the Twin-Six. Another, new-generation, V12 followed in the 1930s, but the Depression hit Packard hard.

Although the company lost a lot of money in the early 1930s, somehow it survived. Six-cylinder-engined models arrived in 1936, by which time production was about 60,000 cars a year. By 1940 Packard was building 100,000 cars a year, the result of a planned and persistent move gradually down-market by the late 1930s. The firm could see little future for its largest models, the last V12 being produced in 1939. One consequence was that by 1941 Packard was offering a very wide range of outwardly patrician machines with outputs ranging from 100 bhp to 160 bhp, and costing up to $5,595.

Packard built Merlin V12 aero engines and other power units during World War II, but unhappily, after the war Packard never recovered its former pre-eminence. In fact by this time the pre-war body dies of the largest models had been sold off to the Soviet Union (where the Packard-like Zis emerged in 1946!).

Six-cylinder and eight-cylinder engines were continued from 1946, and there were only gradual styling changes until a brand-new shape appeared in 1950. The old side-valve engines (born in the 1930s) were gradually refined and retained until as late as 1954, when a new V8 engine finally arrived. There was a technologically-advanced new range at the same time, but after that Packard's fortunes declined rapidly.

In 1955, at a time when it was still selling 50,000 cars a year, Packard merged with Studebaker (which was selling 115,000). Packard was originally the dominant partner, but soon discovered that Studebaker was in deepening financial trouble, which would soon drag Packard into oblivion. Studebaker-Packard was bought by the Curtiss-Wright corporation in 1956, but the 1958 Packards were no more than modified Studebakers, and the marque shortly died of shame.

## Packard Twin-Six 1915-23

*Below: Sedate but powerful, a 1920 Packard Twin-Six Town Car, with the seven-litre side-valve V12.*

While the rest of North America's motor industry was still debating the merits of six- or eight-cylinder engines for luxury cars, Packard went one better – by launching the world's very first V12-engined car in 1915. Before America entered World War I no fewer than 12,605 such cars were produced, and sales held up well thereafter.

In every way the fabulous Twin-Six was a trend-setter, many years ahead of its day, for it was a long time before other manufacturers started making V12s of their own. The USA's new president, Warren Harding, used just such a car to drive to his inauguration in 1920.

Not only was the engine unique in layout, but it was also the first American unit to use aluminium pistons. The original engines had fixed cylinder heads, although later units were redesigned with detachable heads. The engine was very neatly detailed, with all the porting (inlet and exhaust) concentrated in the centre of the 'V' – which meant that the exhaust pipes were led out behind the centre of the engine, then over the three-speed transmission.

In every way Twin-Sixes were large and impressive cars, for there was a choice of 125-in or 135-in wheelbases, and although the top speed of 70 mph was not outstanding, the engine's flexibility most certainly was, for the car could accelerate smoothly in top gear from no more than 4 mph.

The Twin-Six had noble lines, with an unmistakable shouldered radiator style, and in spite of the mechanical complexities it was not unreasonably priced at between $2,600 and $4,600. Strangely enough, the first cars not only had left-hand drive, but also used a left-hand gear change, though this arrangement was abandoned on later-series cars.

The car did much to enhance Packard's reputation, and when *The Motor* tested one in Britain in 1922 it described the Twin-Six as "Twelve-Cylinder Luxury... a superfine American chassis... In America, the land of its origin, there is probably no more respected large car than the Packard Twin-Six". The testers were most impressed by the engine and wrote: "A top-gear car, at 50 miles an hour it appears to be travelling at about 30 mph, and there is only the suck of air through the carburettor to denote the fact that there is an engine underneath the bonnet at all."

The engine was fitted with a 'fuelizer', a kind of mixture-enriching choke, to give rapid starting in cold weather. The size of the engine and its tremendous torque were what really set the Twin-Six apart from any competitors, and the testers noted that "Perhaps the greatest fascination about the car, however, is its performance at moderately low speeds. When other drivers are changing gear and waiting for the engine to accelerate, the man at the wheel of the Packard merely depresses the accelerator gently and the car surges forward from 5 mph as if it were being pulled by some huge invisible magnet . . . the practiced Packard driver does everything on the accel-

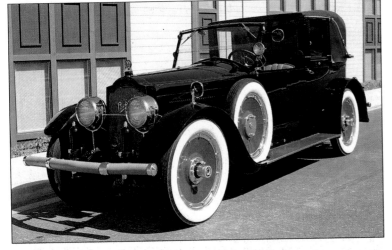

*Above: This chauffeur-driven Packard Twin-Six was built in 1920. Despite its high price, the world's first V12-powered car became a best-seller.*

*Above: The very tall coachwork on this 1920 Packard Twin-Six Town Car made it extremely spacious and comfortable; as it was intended primarily for urban use, aerodynamic factors were of little importance. Note the grand lines of the radiator and the wooden artillery wheels.*

erator and the brake."

At a crossroads at the foot of a hill *The Motor's* driver left the car in top gear and then acclerated up a 1-in-9 gradient achieving 45 mph at the crest of the hill - remarkable performance for the period. With the carburettor tuned to give a top speed of 72 mph the landaulette, with coachwork by Beadle of Dartford, consumed fuel at the rate of 13.5 mpg. Despite light steering the car was heavy on tyres, and a new set of Firestones wa required every 10,000 miles or so.

The car was priced at £1,850 in England in 1922, which made it an expensive machine, but it cost less than other super-luxury cars and did offer a engine of great flexibility in an era when many people were nervous of changing gears.

The Twin-Six was certainly no limited production millionaires' plaything, for before production ended in 1923 (when an eight-cylinder-engined car took over a total of 35,046 had been built.

## Specification (1920)

**Engine:** V12, side-valve
**Bore × stroke:** 76.2 mm × 127 mm
**Capacity:** 6950 cc
**Maximum power:** 90 bhp
**Transmission:** three-speed manual gearbox, rear-wheel drive
**Chassis:** separate steel frame with channel-section main side members
**Suspension:** non-independent with beam axle and leaf springs front; live axle and semi-elliptic leaf springs rear
**Brakes:** drums at rear, no front brakes
**Bodywork:** choice of coachwork, mainly open tourer, with four or five seats
**Maximum speed (approx):** 70 mph (113 km/h)

*Right: The Twin-Six was an effortless car to drive, its huge and flexible engine making gear changes almost unnecessary.*

# Packard Twin-Six/Twelve 1932-39

*Left: During the Depression-hit 1930s there were still buyers for Packard's superb V12.*

## Packard Twin-Six variants

The Twin-Six was renamed the Twelve for 1933, and retained that name until the end of production. For 1935 an enlarged V12 engine, with a bore and stroke of 87.31 mm × 107.95 mm, displacement of 7755 cc and a power output of 175 bhp (complete with aluminium cylinder heads), replaced the original type, and the top speed rose to around 100 mph.

## Specification (1932)

**Engine:** V12, overhead-valve
**Bore × stroke:** 87.31 mm × 101.6 mm
**Capacity:** 7299 cc
**Maximum power:** 160 bhp
**Transmission:** three-speed manual gearbox, rear-wheel drive
**Chassis:** separate steel frame with channel-section side members
**Suspension:** non-independent with beam axle and semi-elliptic leaf springs front; live axle with semi-elliptic leaf springs rear
**Brakes:** drums all round
**Bodywork:** wide choice; saloon, limousine, coupé or convertible
**Maximum speed (approx):** 90 mph (145 km/h)

*Below: A 1936 V12, with alloy cylinder heads and displacement increased to 7755 cc.*

Even though North American industry was in the depths of Depression in the early 1930s, several manufacturers tried to kick-start car sales to rich men by introducing fabulously-engineered new cars. To match Cadillac's V12 and V16 models, therefore, Packard launched a new series of V12 cars, confusingly calling them Twin-Six models yet again, though this title was dropped in favour of Twelve after only one season.

The new engine was, of course, entirely different from the old, for this time it used an odd 67-degree block, and had originally been designed for a front-wheel-drive project (apeing Cord) which was later cancelled. With 160 bhp, it was much more powerful than Cadillac's contemporary V12, and on a par with that company's gargantuan V16 unit.

Although the new V12s were not intended as ultra-high-performance cars, suitably-bodied versions managed to get to almost 100 mph, their most important characteristic being silky-smooth behaviour. At 60-70 mph the cars were almost whisper-quiet, and all featured the lushest, roomiest, and best-equipped of bodywork.

The original cars were enormous and heavy, for they ran on a choice of 142.5-in or 147.5-in wheelbases and weighed more than 5,000 lb. Even though annual sales and production were tiny by American standards, Packard regularly introduced new features, including a vacuum-controlled free-wheel for 1933, a choice of shorter wheelbases from 1934 and a larger and more powerful V12 engine for 1935.

The biggest improvement, however, came for 1937, when a new chassis was introduced, complete with independent front suspension and conventional (instead of Bijur) chassis lubrication. By this time wheelbases had shrunk a little – to a mere 134 or 139 inches – although the cars were still large and heavy by any standards. In this period, too, body styles (which, although individually coachbuilt, all shared the same lofty and patrician radiator shell) had gradually smoothed out, so that without seeing the grille it was often difficult to distinguish a Packard from, say, a Cadillac.

In eight years total production of the V12 models was 5,744. The story goes that by the end of the 1930s 50 per cent of Packard's workforce were producing just eight per cent of the cars – usually no more than 600 to 800 V12s every year. It is no wonder, therefore, that surviving Twelves of the 1930s are now highly-valued collectors' pieces, cosseted by their owners and rarely used except to attend classic car meetings.

*Below: Replete with Hollywood connections and glamour, this Packard LeBaron Runabout Speedster was given to Clark Gable by Carole Lombard.*

## Packard Caribbean 1954-56

In the immediate post-war period Packard's engineering changed slowly and methodically, with every car powered by one or other version of the 1930s-style side-valve straight-eight engine. Automatic transmission was offered from 1949, and the first complete post-war restyle was in 1951.

Then came the launch of the 1955 model-year cars, which not only had a new look, but a new chassis and a new engine. By Detroit standards the style of the new cars was conventional enough, and might have been enough to satisfy customers. For the engineers and for the pundits, however, the big talking points were all mechanical, and hidden away.

The engines were big, heavy, cast-iron V8 units – typical Detroit practice but by Packard standards a quantum leap forward. The suspension was unique – torsion bars, more than nine feet long, connected the front and rear wheels on

*Below: Under the convertible bodywork was a powerful 5.8-litre V8 and an advanced torsion-bar suspension system.*

*Below: An American ideal, the Caribbean offered a soft ride and easy driving with a push-button, electrically-controlled two-speed automatic gearbox.*

each side, with short torsion bars connecting the rear wheels to the frame.

As a front wheel rose after passing over a bump, a reaction was carried over to the rear wheel. In addition there were front and rear anti-roll bars, and a self-levelling control actuated by height-sensitive electric motors connected to the shorter rear-only torsion bars.

In the first model year the Caribbean was only sold as a convertible version of the Patrician saloon and the Four Hundred hard-top coupé – 500 were built at a whopping $5,932 each – but for the 1956 model year it was available as a special series, both as a convertible or a hard-top coupé, with total production of 539 cars. Clearly this was never going to be a profitable project for Packard, but the hard-pressed company thought it needed such a spectacular flagship. For 1956, the last year of Caribbean production, engine size was increased from 5768 cc to 6147 cc, which raised the power output from 275 bhp to 310 bhp. This made it the most impressive variation on the original new Packard line of 1955, which included the Clipper and

*Above: The Caribbean had 1950s styling, with plentiful chrome and striking two-tone paintwork.*

Clipper Custom, built on a similar but shorter wheelbase with power outputs from 225 bhp to 260 bhp.

Nostalgic Packard fans thought the Caribbeans were "real Packards in every sense of the word", a sentiment backed up by a look around the industry in Detroit, which showed that only the Chrysler 300, with 300 bhp, was more powerful than the original Caribbean.

No-one pretended that the Packard handled like a Jaguar, let alone like a Ferrari, but it was attractive to the Americans at which it was aimed. The ride was soft, brake pressures were low (but fade soon set in), and a smooth though fuel-inefficient automatic transmission was standard.

Tragically for Packard, this car's prospects were ruined by the general financial trouble which hit Studebaker-Packard at this time, and it was dropped in mid-1956.

### Specification (1954)

**Engine:** V8, overhead-valve
**Bore × stroke:** 101.6 mm × 88.9 mm
**Capacity:** 5768 cc
**Maximum power:** 275 bhp
**Transmission:** two-speed automatic transmission, rear-wheel drive
**Chassis:** separate steel frame with box-section side members
**Suspension:** independent front with torsion bars; live rear axle with torsion bars; suspension interconnected front to rear, by torsion bars and links, self-levelling at rear
**Brakes:** drums all round
**Bodywork:** steel five/six-seater coupé or convertible
**Maximum speed (approx):** 110 mph (177 km/h)

# Panther

*Right and below: The Panther company grew on the strength of the appeal of its pastiches of pre-war designs such as the Kallista. The badge also had a 1930s look.*

*Below: Panther's first 'production' model was the J72, an expensive creation owing homage to the original SS100 Jaguar.*

R obert Jankel, an artist and an entrepreneur rather than a businessman, set up Panther West Winds in the 1970s to indulge his love for the looks of older motor cars. Based in the Byfleet factory last used by the Cooper Formula 1 team, he gathered together a team of craftsmen to produce new cars which looked old, selling pastiches of sports and sporting cars of a bygone age.

In the 1970s Panther produced an astonishing variety of cars, some successful and some failures, but in no case could anyone congratulate Jankel, the stylist, for having good taste. All the cars, in various ways, were somehow vulgar, and not nearly as elegant as the models whose shapes they set out to ape.

Although Jankel's team produced their own separate chassis, and the bodies were constructed according to traditional coachbuilding methods, the engine, transmission and (eventually) the suspensions were all bought in from the current Jaguar parts bin. The original J72 sports car may have looked somewhat like the old SS100 model of the 1930s, but it was powered by modern and efficient Jaguar running gear.

Successes like the J72 and (to an extent) the huge V12 De Ville saloon were balanced by failures like the early-Ferrari-like FF and the Rio saloon (which was a reskinned Triumph Dolomite Sprint), but in the heady atmosphere of the period, Panther survived. Jankel then set out to expand further, into what we might call the Morgan market, with the Lima sports car. Earlier cars used Vauxhall underpans, but a tubular frame was later adopted.

Because of the financial strain of producing the Lima (and the failure to break into the US market), the original Panther business collapsed at the end of 1979, and was eventually rescued (from the receiver) in 1980 by the Jindo Group of South Korea. The new chairman, Young C. Kim, killed off the old 'pastiche' models, relaunched the Lima as the much-changed though similar-looking Kallista, and pushed ahead with the development of a new car to be called Solo.

The original rear-drive Solo was abandoned in favour of a new Sierra Cosworth-engined four-wheel-drive project, but development was so protracted that by the time the company moved from Byfleet to a new factory in Harlow New Town, costs were out of control and the Solo was priced out of the reach of almost everyone. The project died a rapid death, and chairman Kim left the company.

As the 1990s opened Panther was no longer selling cars, for the old-style Kallista had been dropped to make way for the ill-fated Solo, and there were no signs of new models. Financially the Jindo Group was large enough to support Panther's continuing losses, but the long-term future of the business was certainly in doubt.

*Below: With the Solo, Panther departed completely from its roots and from what it knew best; this was the wrong car at the wrong time.*

# Panther J72 1972-81

*Above: Power for the J72 came from Jaguar's long-established straight-six twin-cam engine, in 3781-cc form with twin SU carburettors.*

The whole secret of designing a pastiche of an older car is to make people think that it is how they remember the original – which may explain some of the success of the J72. Designed originally by Robert Jankel as a one-off machine for his own use, he was persuaded to put it into small-scale production in 1972. Jankel chose the name Panther as a close relative of Jaguar, and 72 denoted the year in which the car had been launched.

The J72 was a rather liberal interpretation of what the famous SS100 sports car of the 1930s might have looked like with a

*Above: Beyond the wood-rimmed steering wheel the Jaguar switch gear and instruments are evident.*

few more years of technical development behind it. Although the two-seater sports car was beautifully constructed (much better, most people agreed, than the first SS100 had ever been), it was not as elegant as the original. However, because it was fitted with a modern Jaguar drivetrain it was faster, more refined and more reliable.

The chassis, designed to be assembled with the minimum of tooling and expertise, was a simple tubular affair, and on the first series of cars there were beam front and rear axles, both properly located by radius arms, Panhard rods and coil springs. The body shell was not only traditionally styled, but traditionally constructed, with light alloy panels on a wooden framework. Jankel drew the necessary coachbuilding skills from craftsmen who had been working for companies like Hooper in west London.

The J72 had an extrovert character, which meant that customers had to like being exhibitionists, and in the first few years Panther seemed to have no difficulty in finding enough of them to keep his factory busy. The combination of light weight but appalling aerodynamics meant that the car had flashing acceleration up to 110 mph, after which it ran out of steam; here, spelt out again, was the Morgan syndrome. The handling, at least, was significantly improved after 1977, when independent front suspension took over from the original beam.

The very first few J72s were fitted with an 87-mm × 106-mm, 3781-cc version of

the Jaguar twin-cam six-cylinder engine, but to extend the performance envelope even further, from 1974 Panther offered the car with Jaguar's single-overhead-cam V12 and its associated automatic transmission. Although this made the car's tyre-stripping performance even more impressive (top speed was 137 mph), it did nothing for the looks, as the wider engine could only be accommodated by adding two large bulges to the sides of the engine bay.

Demand for the J72s held up well until the second energy crisis of 1979 hit hard. Sales had almost died away before

*Above: Elements like the modern seats and side bulges in the bonnet (to accommodate the later V12 engine) detracted from the J72's intended vintage look.*

Panther called in the receiver at the end of 1979. Once the new Korean management arrived, the car was doomed, and the last of all was produced in 1981. A total of 300 J72s had been built, the vast majority with six-cylinder engines.

## Specification (1972)

**Engine:** inline six-cylinder, twin overhead camshafts
**Bore × stroke:** 87 mm × 106 mm
**Capacity:** 3781 cc
**Maximum power:** 190 bhp
**Transmission:** four-speed manual gearbox and overdrive, or optional three-speed automatic transmission; rear-wheel drive
**Chassis:** separate steel frame with tubular main and reinforcing members
**Suspension:** non-independent with beam axle and coil springs front; live axle with coil springs rear
**Brakes:** discs all round
**Bodywork:** aluminium on wooden frame, two-seater open sports car
**Maximum speed:** 114 mph (183 km/h)

*Left: At first glance the J72 looked better from this angle, but closer inspection revealed more jarring aspects, such as the crude side window screen and the side exhaust pipe routed under the running board*

# Panther De Ville 1974-85

After Jankel's J72 had been in production for two years, he decided to expand the Panther range with something entirely different. Instead of a pastiche of a real 1930s sports two-seater, the new product was to be an interpretation of what might have been a massive 1930s saloon.

The result was the gargantuan, vulgar and really rather tasteless De Ville, which may or may not (depending on who was passing an opinion of the car) have had a resemblance to a Bugatti Royale. It was offered as a four-door saloon or a two-door cabriolet, both on the same tubular chassis. The character of this car did not appeal to British enthusiasts, so the majority of all De Villes were exported.

Mechanically and structurally, the De Ville was a strange mixture of modern and obsolete design. The engines, transmissions and suspension systems were all pure modern Jaguar, while the tubular

*Right: Grandest of all the Panther retrospectives was the De Ville, loosely based on the huge Bugatti Royale; once again Panther used Jaguar running gear.*

chassis was simple, but rigid. All this ensured that the car had an acceptable ride, respectable handling, great refinement and good performance.

The body, on the other hand, was carefully built by the same craftsmen who produced the J72s – the same craftsmen who, in previous years, might have been making bodies for Rolls-Royce – yet the style could never look other than strange. It was barrel-sided where a 1930s car would have been flat, it had much smaller-diameter wheels than any real 1930s model, and its massive headlamps actually had smaller headlamps mounted inside them – a deceit all too obvious to even the casual observer.

An alternative six-cylinder-engined version was also available, with the familiar Jaguar XK engine, of 92.05 mm × 106 mm/4235 cc, producing 190 bhp. A four-speed manual gearbox, with overdrive as standard, was also available. The claimed top speed was 124 mph.

Predictably enough (for the De Ville was priced at £21,851 in 1975 when a Rolls-Royce Silver Shadow cost only £14,830, and a Jaguar XJ12 a mere £5,960), it sold very slowly indeed, although the final production total of 60 was quite impressive for such a project.

*Above: Under the large, flexible trunking was Jaguar's overhead-cam 5.3-litre V12 producing 285 bhp.*

*Below: The most obvious Bugatti influence was the incorporation of a horseshoe-shaped radiator grille.*

*Above and right: Standard-size headlights were sunken in outsize chrome housings. If the De Ville looked good from any angle, it was from the rear.*

## Specification (1974)

**Engine:** V12, single overhead camshaft per bank of cylinders
**Bore × stroke:** 90 mm × 70 mm
**Capacity:** 5343 cc
**Maximum power:** 285 bhp
**Transmission:** three-speed automatic transmission, rear-wheel drive
**Chassis:** separate steel frame with tubular main and reinforcing members
**Suspension:** independent with wishbones and coil springs front; trailing links, coil springs and telescopic dampers rear
**Brakes:** discs all round
**Bodywork:** aluminium on a wooden framework; four-door saloon or two-door cabriolet
**Maximum speed (approx):** 137 mph (220 km/h)

# Panther Lima 1976-82

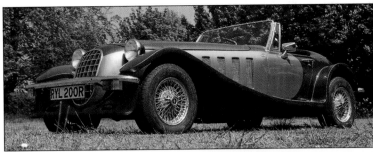

*Above and right: The original design, the Lima, was powered by Vauxhall's 2.3-litre overhead-cam four-cylinder engine which produced a no more than adequate 108 bhp.*

Only four years after the launch of the first Panther, the J72, the business had expanded far enough for Robert Jankel to want to produce a cheaper, faster-selling, sports car. The result was the launch of the Lima – a smaller, nimbler model than any of the previous Panthers.

The new Lima was designed to sell in much higher quantities than the previous cars. With that in mind, the car was laid out around the pressed-steel body platform, suspension and running gear of the Vauxhall Magnum, topped by a glass-fibre body shell. While it retained the flowing, separate, front wings of a 1930s sports car, the chosen shape was not really a pastiche of any other car, for it was more rounded than expected. Those who looked closely could tell that the Lima had MG Midget doors, complete with wind-up windows.

Perhaps the Vauxhall platform was not

*Below: The Lima evolved into the rather more highly developed Ford-powered Kallista.*

*Above: The Kallista was the most successful of all Panthers, in both styling and total sales.*

rigid enough without a steel superstructure welded to it, for the car soon acquired a reputation for being too flexible. Accordingly, Panther then designed a simple, rugged and effective tubular frame in its place, and phased this in from the end of 1978.

Like the contemporary Morgans, which the Lima tried to emulate in some respects, this Panther had a rock-hard ride, awful aerodynamics and a cramped cockpit, but there were enough individualists (masochists?) in the world who liked that sort of thing.

In six years, no fewer than 897 Limas were produced. Once the Korean concern had control, however, the basic design was completely rejigged, a choice of four-cylinder or V6 Ford engines became available, and as the Kallista (with much-modified but still recognisable Lima-type styling) it kept going until

1990, when it was dropped in favour of the futuristic Solo. Even though testers often criticised the car's ride, its seats and its fuel efficiency, it was clearly right for a small sector of the market, for Panther regularly built between 200 and 250 Kallistas a year in the 1980s.

## Panther Lima variants

### Panther Kallista

Following the takeover of Panther by the Korean Jindo Group, the Lima's basic design was much modified, first with the use of a light-alloy shell in place of glassfibre, then with different engines and Ford front suspension.

The result was the launch of the Kallista of 1982-90, which had near-identical styling, but used a wide range of Ford engines, starting with the 96-bhp inline-four, overhead-camshaft, 1598-cc unit. Top speed was approximately 92 mph.

From 1982 to 1988 the 2792-cc overhead-valve V6 was available with 135 bhp or (with injection) 150 bhp. There was the choice of a five-speed manual gearbox or three-speed automatic transmission. Maximum speed with the 150-bhp engine was 109 mph. In 1988 the old 2.8-litre V6 was

replaced by the similar, although slightly larger, 2935-cc unit, again with five-speed manual or three-speed automatic transmission. According to Panther, top speed remained the same

## Specification (1976)

**Engine:** inline four-cylinder, single overhead camshaft
**Bore × stroke:** 97.5 mm × 76.2 mm
**Capacity:** 2279 cc
**Maximum power:** 108 bhp
**Transmission:** four-speed manual gearbox or optional automatic transmission, rear-wheel drive
**Chassis:** separate pressed-steel body platform at first; separate steel chassis frame with square-section tubular main and reinforcing members for 1978-79
**Suspension:** independent front with wishbones and coil springs; live rear axle with coil springs and trailing arms
**Brakes:** discs front, drums rear
**Bodywork:** glassfibre two-seater
**Maximum speed (approx):** 98 mph (158 km/h)

# Panther Solo 1990

Two sports cars, both British, probably hold the record for the lengthiest gestation period of any model; one was the AC 3000ME, the other was Panther's Solo project. Both died soon after they eventually went on sale; neither made any money for their makers.

The first prototype to carry the Solo name was a mid-engined/rear-drive car shown in 1984, while the definitive design was a much more powerful and totally re-engineered four-wheel-drive car first shown in 1987. Deliveries were long delayed, and began haltingly in 1990. Only months later, with demand non-existent, the project was closed down with only 10 cars delivered to customers.

All in all, a total of 26 Panthers – prototypes, crash-test cars, and actual customer cars – was all there was to show for a project which had been heavily hyped from the very beginning. It was a project by which chief executive Young C. Kim's reputation would rise or fall. In the end it fell; Kim was demoted by his own family, and the stylist/engineer Ken Greenley lost a great deal of face.

Kim originally conceived the Solo as a sensibly-priced mid-engined two-seater sports car, but once Toyota launched the MR2 he realised that he could not match it. A major redesign led to the use of a modified version of Ford's Sierra RS Cosworth 4 × 4 running gear, and at its launch in 1987 Panther hoped to retail the car for £25,000, and to produce 100 cars.

The concept was not only sound but also unique, as this was the world's very first mid-engined four-wheel-drive supercar. There is no doubt that the Solo was a stunning-looking two-seater and (in spite of forecasts about the difficulty of cooling the mid-mounted turbocharged engine) it proved to have a very effective chassis. The problem was that the decision to produce a high-tech chassis monocoque – using steel, aluminium honeycomb, carbonfibre and Kevlar – was suicidal. From that day costs soared, production problems increased and even at a 1990 list price of £39,850 (which no potential customer would seriously contemplate) the car was never likely to make money.

Prospective customers got bored of waiting for deliveries which were repeatedly postponed, and when they heard the price they were taken aback. In spite of the remarkable handling, the reliable (if, according to some testers, somewhat agricultural) powertrain and the exclusivity, the Solo could not keep its customers, and the project was killed off. The roughness of the Cosworth engine might have been acceptable in a Sierra, but not in an expensive supercar.

With the cancellation of the Solo, Panther's entire reason for being disappeared, and the company then dropped out of the carmaking business.

*Below: The Solo went through many variations before production; the original concept was for a two-wheel-drive/mid-engined car, but by the time of this late prototype the decision had been made to move the Solo up-market and have it incorporate four-wheel drive.*

## Specification (1990)

**Engine:** inline four-cylinder, twin overhead camshafts
**Bore × stroke:** 90.8 mm × 77 mm
**Capacity:** 1993 cc
**Maximum power:** 204 bhp
**Transmission:** five-speed manual gearbox, four-wheel drive
**Chassis:** composite material unitary construction body/chassis
**Suspension:** independent with MacPherson struts front; double unequal-length wishbones, coil springs and telescopic dampers rear
**Brakes:** discs all round
**Bodywork:** glassfibre/composite two-seater coupé
**Maximum speed (approx):** 144 mph (232 km/h)

*Above: When the Solo finally arrived after an interminably protracted development process, the end result was undeniably a striking design. The car's performance almost matched its looks, but escalating costs had meant that the production Solo was simply too expensive to be a marketable proposition.*

*Below: The Solo had some neat styling details, such as the headlight pods which rotated to hide the lights when not in use. The designer's touch clearly deserted him when it came to the rear of the car, however, with too much body behind the forward-mounted cabin and a clumsy treatment of the side vents.*

# Peerless Motors Limited

**B**ernard ('Bernie') Rodger was a Jersey-born man, an ex-racing mechanic who, while moving from team to team during the 1950s, developed design skills. In 1956 he got together with two ex-racing drivers, John Gordon and James Byrnes, to start a specialist car business. The result was the birth of the Peerless GT car – a good idea never properly developed and, in the end, commercially unsuccessful.

Rodger designed a 2 + 2-seater prototype which was originally called the Warwick (Byrnes owned several successful restaurants close to that historic city), with the currently-fashionable multi-tube frame construction. John Gordon's connection was that he owned Peerless Motors Ltd (which held the Jaguar distributorship for Buckinghamshire) on the Bath Road Trading Estate between Slough and Maidenhead.

The definitive Peerless car was launched in 1958, with assembly taking place in the capacious Peerless Motors building in Slough. The very first car had metal bodywork, but it immediately became clear that quantity production in metal was not feasible. Accordingly, Peerless concluded a deal to have glassfibre shells of an identical style supplied by James Whitson Ltd of West Drayton, Middlesex.

Although Peerless courted publicity by entering a car for the 1958 Le Mans 24 Hours – a successful reliability exercise – sales were always hard to achieve, not least because the GT was rather more expensive than expected, and was fighting for recognition against more established sporting manufacturers such as Jaguar.

The main problem, as so often in such ventures, was a lack of investment capital, which meant that Peerless was very reliant on selling all its cars before they were built, making sure that there was a healthy positive cashflow into the business, and never being caught with too much stock. It was therefore almost impossible to expand the business to make overseas sales (particularly to the USA) viable, and the company finally ran out of money in March 1960.

Not long after this, however, the project was revived under the guise of Bernard Rodger Developments Ltd, when a modified version of the Peerless, renamed Warwick, went into production at Horton, near London's Heathrow airport. Although the Warwick was a much better car, certainly in detail, than the Peerless, it also cost more, the result being that very few were ever built before this business, too, had to be closed down after less than two years of production.

*Above: The Peerless GT lived on after the company died, in the form of the Warwick; this is a 1961 model.*

## Peerless GT 1958-60

The rationale behind Peerless's new venture was to introduce a modestly-priced Grand Touring car that would have high performance, but which could use mass-produced running gear. Because it would have been stupid to attack any of the cars built by the British 'Big Five' in head-on competition, Bernie Rodger was encouraged to create something a bit different.

The solution was not only to develop a 2 + 2 closed coupé, but also to specify a multi-tube chassis frame distinguished by the use of de Dion rear suspension. After flirting with other high-cost alternatives, the team chose to use square-section tubing (easier to weld than the round-section variety), and eventually to use a glassfibre body shell, which was economic to manufacture in the limited quantities envisaged.

The engine, transmission and front suspension were all taken from the Triumph TR3A, then one of the most successful British sports cars, and since the body style was compact and light this ensured a top speed of more than 100 mph.

Even though the first cars suffered from a lack of decent detail build quality – and (like the contemporary Lotus Elite) were soon found to have very noisy interiors – they began to sell slowly, but steadily. A works entry at Le Mans in 1958, when the car was driven by Peter Jopp and Percy Crabb, was remarkably successful, for the Peerless GT finished 16th overall at 83.6 mph, confirming the favourable impressions of stability and performance which the standard cars had already shown.

Already 43 cars had been ordered before Le Mans, and immediately after the race the company began to talk about building 20 a week by the end of that year. There were even high hopes of breaking into the North American market, and selling at least 2,000 cars every year, but such plans were dashed by a lack of investment capital.

The Peerless project, in fact, lasted for only two years, as there were not enough customers ready to pay £1,493 for a car which was rather rough and ready in character, fit and finish. At the time, for instance, a TR3A hard-top cost £1,102, while the Jaguar XK150 Fixed-Head Coupé (which also had rudimentary rear seats) was priced at £1,764.

In two years just 325 GTs were built. In spite of their use of rot-resistant glass-fibre bodywork, very few seem to have survived to this day.

### Peerless GT variants

#### Warwick

The Warwick was an improved version of the Peerless, built only in 1960 and 1961 by the new management team of Bernard Rodger Developments Ltd. In contrast to the Peerless, the Warwick had a one-piece forward-hinged bonnet (Triumph Herald-style) and styling revised in detail.

#### Warwick Buick

There was also a proposed variation of the Warwick, the Warwick Buick, which was to have the light-alloy Buick V8 engine that soon became the Rover V8. Only one car was built.

### Specification (1958 GT)

**Engine:** inline four-cylinder, overhead-valve
**Bore × stroke:** 83 mm × 92 mm
**Capacity:** 1991 cc
**Maximum power:** 90 bhp
**Transmission:** four-speed manual gearbox and optional overdrive, rear-wheel drive
**Chassis:** separate multi-tubular steel chassis
**Suspension:** independent front with wishbones and coil springs; de Dion rear axle with semi-elliptic leaf springs
**Brakes:** discs front, drums rear
**Bodywork:** glassfibre 2 + 2-seater coupé
**Maximum speed (approx):** 103 mph (166 km/h)

*Left: For its time, the Peerless GT was a smooth, uncluttered 2 + 2 coupé shape; the body shell was made in glassfibre over a multi-tube steel chassis and de Dion suspension.*

# Pegaso

T he name Pegaso (after Pegasus, the winged horse of Greek legend) was an appropriate title for the new car marque that Spain's state-owned ENASA organisation set up in 1951. For there was an element of myth surrounding the creation of the marque, about the way that it survived so long on minimal sales, and about the way the final model was reborn in 1992.

ENASA wanted to see a prestige car produced – a real supercar – one which would bring great glory to ENASA and to Spain. Because the status element was all-important (and, frankly, because ENASA was a nationalised concern and did not have to answer to shareholders) the project never needed to be a profitable one. Perhaps that was as well, for the final product was technically complex, and in seven years only about 110 cars were produced – all of them by hand, the vast majority with coachbuilt bodies.

The designer was Wifredo Ricart, who had been involved with an earlier Spanish car, the Nacional Pescara. He had also been technical chief at Alfa Romeo, in Italy, for a period before and during World War II, during which time he had designed the stillborn Type 512 Alfa Romeo Grand Prix car. Ricart was delighted with his Pegaso commission, and laid out what he (and many observers) considered to be the ultimate in automotive design.

At the time, the Z102 was undoubtedly the most technically advanced road car in the world, for it had twin overhead camshafts in each head of its V8 engine, and de Dion rear suspension, at a time when Ferrari was making do with single cams and a beam-axle rear end. Pegaso built everything for the new cars (except the coachwork) at its Barcelona factory, using its extensive tool-room facilities to ensure the highest possible quality.

Prices, of course, were high – the actual cost sometimes appeared to be a function of how much an exclusive customer was willing to pay – for all cars were hand-built in the research departments, and there was usually a long wait between an order being placed and delivery being effected. Some cars had factory-styled coupé shells, but most were delivered as rolling chassis, for completion by outside coachbuilders such as Touring of Milan.

Because of its hand-built nature, a Pegaso would be available with several different engine sizes and tunes, normally-aspirated or supercharged, but even though a three-year warranty was offered, there were very few takers. In seven years only about 110 cars were built, and even when the original, complex Z102 was replaced by a pushrod-engined Z103 in 1955 this did not increase sales.

By the mid-1950s, in any case, ENASA had really lost interest in building cars, as its heavy vehicle sales had increased considerably. Ricart left the company to become president of Lockheed France, and private car assembly was closed down. Visitors to Spain will know, of course, that the Pegaso marque lives on in many commercial vehicles, but there has never again been an attempt to produce a new generation of motor cars.

Even so, ENASA commissioned IAD of Great Britain to recreate the Z103, using modern components, as a marketing tool to coincide with the Barcelona Olympic Games of 1992. That was a sympathetically faithful recreation of one of the few Z103s with Spanish- (rather than Italian-) designed coachwork, in this case by Pedro Serra. The IAD car had a glassfibre rather than alloy skin, and economic reality dictated the use of a Rover V8 pushrod engine.

*Above: The vast majority of Pegasos were bodied by outside coachbuilders rather than by the factory, accounting for the wide variety of designs. This is one of the very few Pegaso-bodied Z102s.*

*Below: Oddest of all the Z102s was this streamlined coupé designed by El Dominicano which was exhibited at the 1952 New York Motor Show. Like all the Z102s, it was driven by a powerful quad-cam V8 engine.*

*Left: Touring of Milan produced the most elegant, and the most numerous, bodies for the Z102, but the cars were still extremely rare; this, for example, is the only one to be imported into Britain, a 1954 Z102B. The combination of alloy engines and alloy bodywork made for lightness, resulting in an excellent power-to-weight ratio.*

# Pegaso Z102 1951-58

Because Wifredo Ricart was not encumbered by the need to produce a profitable machine, he could indulge all his engineering, race-bred, experience in the layout of the new Pegaso car. The result was that the Z102, which made its public debut at the Paris Salon in 1951, was a complex and exciting car which set new standards for the period.

Because the car was always intended to be hand-built, as a method of training the company's apprentices and engineers to the highest possible standards, it was built around what was described as a steel monocoque (although this could more accurately be described as a platform chassis with extra reinforcement) to allow a whole variety of bodies to be fitted. There were pressings and foldings in profusion, all welded together; this meant that an outside coachbuilder's creative efforts were rather limited by the position of the front and rear scuttles, the engine bay panels and the inner wing panels at front and rear – yet there was a surprising variation of open or closed cars built over the period.

Front suspension, by longitudinal torsion bars, was carefully hand-crafted (the bars needed to be precisely ground to produce the correct rate), while the rear suspension, a de Dion layout using transverse torsion bars and with massive finned rear brake drums at each side of the chassis-mounted final drive, was as modern as that of any contemporary Grand Prix car.

It was the jewel-like V8 engine, however, which set the tone for the whole car, for this used light-alloy castings for block and heads, had detachable wet cylinder liners, and featured twin-overhead-camshaft valve gear. A customer could order this unit in one of three engine sizes, with a variety of Weber carburation, and even specify supercharging if necessary. This ensured that there was really no such thing as a standard Z102, and the likelihood of two Pegaso owners meeting each other and finding that they had identical specifications was remote.

In addition to factory-designed and produced two-seater coupés, there were special bodies by coachbuilders like Saoutchik and Touring. The factory only produced 19 shells of its own, the most popular style being the Touring Berlinetta, of which 45 were produced.

In theory the Z102 could have been a successful competition car, but a Le Mans entry in 1953 was cancelled when one of the cars crashed in practice. Another car crashed out of the Mexican Carrera Panamericana when well placed. Road cars were either fast, or very fast, depending on the engine specification chosen. A normally-aspirated 2.4-litre car may have been no quicker than the Jaguar XK120 of the day, but a supercharged 3.2-litre example, with 285 bhp, was on a par with anything that Ferrari or Mercedes-Benz could offer.

The Z103 model, complete with a larger-capacity pushrod V8 engine, was launched in 1955 to provide a less clamorous, but equally powerful, alternative to the four-cam-engined cars, but somehow the magic had been lost and demand was virtually non-existent; only a handful (certainly fewer than 10) of Z103s were ever built.

The Z102 and Z103 were both intriguing designs, but there is no doubt that the cars would have benefitted from a great deal more development and refinement. Even so, surviving examples are so rare today that they command extremely high prices when they change hands.

## Pegaso Z102 variants

### Pegaso Z103

The Z103 model was revealed in 1955, this being effectively the same chassis into which was fitted a much simpler overhead-valve V8 engine, which was offered in various sizes. There was the option of 88 mm × 82 mm/3990 cc, giving 247 bhp; or a bigger-bore, 93-mm × 82-mm/4456-cc unit with 285 bhp. Finally there was a bored and stroked version of 93 mm × 88 mm and 4780 cc; power output was 289 bhp.

*Above: Rarer still than the Z102 was the Z103, introduced in 1955. By this stage Pegaso had dropped their complicated quad-cam V8 in favour of a simpler, overhead-valve, design with displacements of up to 4780 cc.*

*Above: Touring of Milan's Z102 coupé body was a very well-balanced design; its many ornate touches, such as the scallops behind the side windows and the inset rear lights, did not detract from the car's overall look.*

### Pegaso IAD Z103

The IAD Z103 of 1992 was not a recreation but a pastiche, using a Rover V8 engine and an Alfa Romeo 75 de Dion rear axle and transmission.

### Specification (1951 Z102)

**Engine:** V8, twin overhead camshafts per bank of cylinders
**Bore × stroke:** 75 mm × 70 mm/80 mm × 70 mm/85 mm × 70 mm
**Capacity:** 2474 cc/2815 cc/3178 cc
**Maximum power:** 140 bhp/170 bhp/210 bhp – or 275 bhp with 3.2-litre supercharged engine
**Transmission:** five-speed manual gearbox, rear-wheel drive
**Chassis:** steel platform inner chassis structure with body welded in place on assembly
**Suspension:** independent front with wishbones and torsion bars; de Dion rear axle with transverse torsion bars
**Brakes:** drums all round, inboard at rear
**Bodywork:** steel two-seater; various styles, coupé or cabriolet
**Maximum speed (approx):** (2.8-litre/170-bhp model) 140 mph (225 km/h)

*Below: Pegaso followed in the footsteps of Spain's only other two prestige manufacturers, Hispano-Suiza and Nacional Pescara, and at one stage the Z102 was the most expensive sports car in the world.*

# Peugeot

*Above: Peugeot have always had a fine reputation in Africa, one enhanced by their successes in the Paris–Dakar Rally with cars like the 405 T16.*

*Above: The 205 T16 brought Peugeot to the forefront of world rallying during the mid-1980s with wins in the World Rally Championship for Timo Salonen in 1985 and Juha Kankkunen in 1986.*

*Left: Peugeot are one of the oldest motor manufacturers in the world; the company dates back to 1876 and car production to before the turn of the century.*

A lthough Peugeot of France has one of the longest and most distinguished histories in the world's motor industry, it has concentrated almost exclusively on making family cars. The very first Peugeot car was built more than a hundred years ago – in 1889 – but the only model we can truly call a supercar was built in the 1980s.

The Peugeot family business was founded in 1876, and the first car connections came in the late 1880s. Car sales (of machines derived from early Daimler layouts) began in earnest in the 1890s, and before long Peugeot became one of the most significant companies in the fledgling European motor industry. For many years the company also built pedal cycles and motorcycles.

Expansion under Peugeot family control was steady, though never flamboyant, with a move to a new factory at Sochaux, in eastern France, taking place in 1910. By the end of the 1920s the business was concentrated on Sochaux, the famous old De Dion-Bouton business had been taken over, and Peugeot had become one of the three largest French concerns (the others being Renault and Citroën).

By the 1960s Peugeot had set out on the acquisition trail, setting up technical links with Citroën in 1964, and following this with a full-blown takeover in 1974. Four years later, in 1978, Peugeot took over the Chrysler-Europe businesses in France and the UK, soon dropping that name and reviving the old Talbot marque in its place.

Although Peugeot supported a 'works' rally team for many years in the 1970s, this concentrated on endurance events where the company's strong, large cars could perform well. In 1981, however, the British-based Talbot Sunbeam-Lotus team won the World Rally Championship and, with a new Group B category becoming popular, Peugeot then decided to produce a speical car to meet those regulations.

The result was the launch, and spectacular success, of the 205 T16 model, which went on to dominate world-class rallying and, in later manifestations, the world's toughest 'Raid' events. As this car's career came to a close, Peugeot then turned to Group C sports car racing, and after TWR/Jaguar withdrew from this category the V10-engined 905 became the dominant model in this branch of motorsport.

Even so, this was still only an indulgence for what was essentially a sober company. In the early 1990s Peugeot-Citroën was producing 1.5 million cars a year. Peugeot's output was based on only five model ranges, and although engines varied from 954 cc and 44 bhp to 2975 cc and 200 bhp there wasn't a supercar in sight.

*Below: One of the most attractive Peugeots of recent years was the Pininfarina-designed 504 Convertible, available with a 144-bhp V6.*

# Peugeot 205 GTi 1983–91

When Peugeot brought out the 205 in 1983, its main role was as a small family hatchback, but the design was flexible enough for it to be turned into one of the trend-setting hot hatches of the 1980s.

The changes needed to go from family car to sports car consisted of fitting the fuel-injected version of the 1580-cc overhead-cam four-cylinder unit found in the 305 GTi which, in its 205 application, produced an excellent 105 bhp at 6,250 rpm – thanks to features such as the Bosch LE2 Jetronic injection, a high compression ratio of 10.2:1 and a four-into-one exhaust manifold. The more potent engine was matched to a larger, 7.9-in, diameter clutch and a five-speed gearbox with close ratios and a relatively low final drive (giving 18.7 mph per 1,000 rpm in top), for good acceleration.

The suspension was naturally upgraded to deal with the extra power and performance, and the MacPherson-strut/lower-wishbone system at the front was given stiffer springs and uprated dampers, while the anti-roll bar linkage was revised to produce more effect. Revisions were made to the rack-and-pinion steering, the geometry of which was changed to give a larger tyre contact patch under the hard cornering that would be expected with the GTi. At the rear the transverse torsion bars were stiffened, the dampers uprated and the mounting points for the trailing arms strengthened.

Some of the easiest changes were those needed to uprate the wheels, tyres and brakes. More attractive 5½-in x 14-in cast alloys were fitted, complemented by 185/60 R14 Michelin MXVs, while behind the perforated wheels could be found large, 9.7-in diameter, discs at the front and 7.1-in drums at the rear.

These changes transformed the car. Because it was light and aerodynamically efficient, its performance was excellent. It could reach a top speed of 116 mph and cover the 0-60 mph sprint in 8.6 seconds. That compared well with all its rivals; the Renault 5 Turbo took 9.8 seconds, the Vauxhall Astra GTE made it in 9.2 seconds and the MG Metro Turbo some 9.4 seconds.

It was not just on paper that the 205 GTi excelled; when *Autocar* tested the car in 1984 they were impressed by its extremely responsive behaviour coupled to very neutral balance. In fact, if anything, Peugeot had masked a front-wheel-drive car's normal understeering tendency almost too well, as it was possible (when trying very hard) to reach the car's cornering limit and find that it switched suddenly to oversteer, needing a quick response to correct.

The 306 GTI-6 of 1993 was almost as good, but the 206 GTI anticipated in 2000 was expected to be better.

## Peugeot 205 GTi variants

### Peugeot 205 CTi

A couple of years after the GTi appeared, Peugeot broadened its appeal by producing a convertible version. The conversion was by Pininfarina rather than Peugeot themselves and was necessarily a rather compromised design in that there was little room for the hood and it folded rather clumsily at the back, while a hoop at the 'B'-pillar was needed to maintain torsional stiffness. Unusually, however, the convertible gave away little in performance to the

*Above: With the 205 GTi, Peugeot showed that front-wheel drive was no barrier to making a sporting car with excellent handling.*

standard GTi and had the same top speed of 116 mph.

### Peugeot 205 GTi 1.9

To counter increasing competition from Ford, Vauxhall and Toyota, in 1987 Peugeot added a larger-engined version to the range, fitting their 1905-cc engine. This produced considerably more power – 125 bhp

*Below left and below: The GTi was set aside from the more humble 205s by its badging, trim and attractive alloy wheels with low-profile tyres.*

rather than 105 bhp. With more torque (118 lb ft rather than 99 lb ft), acceleration also improved, giving a 0-60 mph time of 7.8 seconds.

## Specification (1984 205 GTi)

**Engine:** inline four-cylinder, overhead-camshaft
**Bore × stroke:** 83 mm × 73 mm
**Displacement:** 1580 cc
**Maximum power:** 105 bhp
**Transmission:** five-speed manual
**Chassis:** unitary construction
**Suspension:** independent with MacPherson struts and anti-roll bar front; trailing arms rear
**Brakes:** discs front, drums rear
**Bodywork:** two-door hatchback
**Maximum speed:** 116 mph (187 km/h)

*Left: In 1987, with competition in the GTi market becoming fiercer, Peugeot introduced a more powerful, 1.9-litre, 205 with 125 bhp.*

# Peugeot 205 T16 1983-84

Although the T16 was designed by a team of Peugeot motorsport engineers, it was conceived by one man – Jean Todt. In the 1970s Todt had become one of the world's most successful rallying co-drivers, then in 1981 he also took over the management of the Peugeot-Talbot sport team in Paris.

Even while a subsidiary team, Talbot (ex-Chrysler) UK was on its way to winning the World Rally Championship. Todt was formulating a plan for a new special rally car. A new category, Group B, was being phased in, and as Audi had already proved that four-wheel drive was essential to be competitive, so Todt urged the birth of an entirely new Peugeot to take on the world at this level.

To meet the Group B regulations, Peugeot had to build a mere 200 cars, and the works team would then be allowed to make 70 much more specialised 'Evolution' versions.

The birth of the project was announced in December 1981, but the prototype was not shown until 1983, following which 200 identical roadgoing cars were produced. Other companies had been known to cheat, but Peugeot not only built the required number of cars, but lined them *all* up for inspection when the count was made in March 1984.

Although the basic silhouette of this new supercar was the same as that of the mass-production front-engined front-wheel-drive 205 model, the resemblance stopped there, for this was a unique and very specialised machine.

In a very rigid pressed-steel three-door monocoque, Peugeot actually installed a new turbocharged engine behind the two seats, transversely positioned, and driving all four wheels. The design was so compact, and so full of machinery, that on the road car there was literally no place for stowage – except on the engine cover, behind the seats.

Apart from the fact that it had a rather noisy cabin at high speeds, the 200-bhp

machine was a perfectly viable, attractive and flexible road car, which could be driven in heavy traffic but was at its best on sweeping, open roads, where its superb balance and traction could be fully enjoyed.

The rally car, which started winning in 1984, and which dominated the Group B category until the end of 1986, was an outstanding machine. Compared with the standard car, most of the running gear was replaced by special components, but the same basic 1.8-litre engine was boosted to give 335 bhp in 1984, and to produce at least 450 bhp by the end of 1986 in E2 form.

Early rally cars did not 'fly' very well over jumps, and there was a weight bias to the right side, but the E2 type of 1985-86 was much improved – mainly because it used a large aerofoil section on the rear of the roof panel, along with front spoilers, and had a less tail-heavy weight distribution.

Although Peugeot speedily sold all 200 road cars, the company was never tempted to make any more, which suggests that this was a necessary rather than a profitable project. The competi-

*Above: The standard 205 was front-engined, but the T16's potent 200-bhp twin-cam was mid-mounted, driving all four wheels.*

*Above: Ari Vatanen in the 1985 Swedish Rally; the following year's event was won by Juha Kankkunen, again in a Peugeot 205 T16.*

tion versions, however, did remarkable things for the marque's reputation, which most assuredly made the investment worthwhile.

In 1987 Peugeot produced the very special 205 T16 Grand Raid derivative, a longer-wheelbase version of the rally car, which proved to be outstandingly successful in long-distance events like the Paris–Dakar Rally. The 405 Grand Raid and the Citroën ZX Grand Raid were both developed from this design. None of these derivatives was ever sold to the public.

## Specification (1983 road car)

**Engine:** inline four-cylinder, twin overhead camshafts
**Bore × stroke:** 83 mm × 82 mm
**Capacity:** 1775 cc
**Maximum power:** 200 bhp
**Transmission:** five-speed manual gearbox, four-wheel drive
**Chassis:** steel unitary construction body/chassis
**Suspension:** independent with double wishbones and coil springs front and rear
**Brakes:** discs all round
**Bodywork:** glassfibre three-door two-seater hatchback
**Maximum speed (approx):** 130 mph (209 km/h)

*Above: Kankkunen in the 1986 1,000 Lakes Rally, won by Timo Salonen's T16, and by other Peugeot T16s in 1984 and 1985.*

*Below: To satisfy homologation requirements a number of roadgoing four-wheel-drive T16s had to be built and sold.*

# Pierce-Arrow

**A**lthough this North American marque was only in existence for 29 years, a period which included the Wall Street Crash and the Depression that followed it, it became one of the most prestigious of all, and its reputation has endured to this day.

George N. Pierce produced the first Pierce car in 1901, a spindly de Dion-powered machine. He introduced a Pierce Great Arrow model in 1904, and then changed the marque name to Pierce-Arrow in 1909. By 1914 three sizes of magnificently-detailed six-cylinder Pierce-Arrows were available, the 66 reputedly being the largest production car of the day in the United States.

By 1915 more than 12,000 cars had been built, and Pierce-Arrow's prestige reputation had been established. The related 38/48/66 models were finally discontinued in 1923, and replaced by smaller-engined cars in the mid-1920s.

By 1928 George Pierce was ailing, and ready to quit business for a quiet life, so he sold his company to Studebaker; Albert Erskine of Studebaker soon became Pierce-Arrow's president. The immediate result was a doubling of annual sales – to 10,000 cars in 1929, just before the Crash – and in the medium term it ensured the existence of a prestige manufacturer in very perilous times.

*Below: The Pierce-Arrow V12 of 1933 was a valiant attempt to attract the wealthy; its body shell was a foretaste of post-war styling.*

*Above: The elegance and straight-line speed of the marque's models was expressed by the sculpted bowman mascot, here on a 1933 V12.*

In the multi-cylinder race which followed the Wall Street Crash, Pierce-Arrow first introduced a side-valve straight-eight, then a V12 in 1931. The old six-cylinder units were dropped in favour of two modern engines which powered all Pierce-Arrows built in the 1930s.

The company suffered badly in the aftermath of the Crash, selling only 2,241 cars in 1932. Ab Jenkins broke many endurance speed records in a modified V12 car in 1932, but Studebaker went into receivership in 1933, following which Albert Erskine committed suicide, and Pierce-Arrow was sold to a group of businessmen and bankers.

In spite of everything, the firm had managed to produce splendid Silver Arrow show cars, and somehow carried on trading for a time, but finally went bankrupt in August 1934. There was yet another corporate rescue, and the cars were restyled for 1936, but only 875 cars were built in 1935, followed by 787 in 1936, and a mere 167 in 1937. The final blow came in the spring of 1938 after just 30 '1938 models' had been assembled, when the sad remnants of the company were sold at auction.

This time there was no attempt at a revival, and one of North America's most famous names was lost for ever. Along with Packard, it had been one of the last great independent carmakers.

*Below: Typical of Pierce-Arrow were large, stately models available with various wheelbases, the longest (such as on this 1932 model) being huge.*

# Pierce-Arrow 66 1910-18

*Right: With its massive 13.5-litre six-cylinder side-valve engine the Pierce-Arrow 66 model was capable of great speed, and (as maximum power developed at only 1,200 rpm) with little strain on the engine.*

The very first six-cylinder engine produced by Pierce was used on a car built for the Glidden Tour of 1906, and this was an obvious candidate to power the original Pierce-Arrows of 1909. In 1910 the largest of such units, a 13.5-litre monster, was used for the 66, which remained on sale throughout America's short involvement in World War I, until 1918.

The 66 was the biggest of a range of side-valve six-cylinder Pierce-Arrows, running on a long, 140-in, wheelbase which was stretched to 147.5 inches in 1913. The engine had three separate two-cylinder cast-iron blocks on an aluminium crankcase, but because of its large and very heavy cast-iron pistons, the unit was a low-revving piece of architecture. After a stretch from an initial 10.6 litres through to 11.7 litres in 1910, the 13.5-litre machine was the largest US private-car engine on sale, its peak power developed at a mere 1,200 rpm. A simple 'T'-head side-valve design, the engine had the distinction of dual ignition, with two sets of spark plugs. Six were triggered by a magneto and the other six by a coil. The driver had the choice of one or the other, or both at once.

Although the chassis was conventional by North American standards, interesting technical details included the use of two types of rear brakes – a foot brake operating externally-contracting shoes, and a hand lever operating different, internally-expanding, shoes. The famous faired-in headlamps (smoothly fixed to the front wings) were introduced in 1913, although bodywork remained formal.

In nine years 1,638 examples of this

largest-ever North American car were produced; a fair proportion found their way to Minneapolis, where the city's fire chief had discovered that he could produce a most satisfactory fire engine by putting a special body on this capable chassis.

The last 66 of these fabulous cars were built in 1918, for by this time even Pierce-Arrow had acknowledged that the market for such super-large and very expensive models had gone.

## Specification (1912)

**Engine:** inline six-cylinder, side-valve
**Bore × stroke:** 127 mm × 177.8 mm
**Capacity:** 13514 cc
**Maximum power:** 80 bhp
**Transmission:** four-speed manual gearbox, rear-wheel drive
**Chassis:** separate steel frame with channel-section main side members, tubular and pressed bracings
**Suspension:** non-independent with beam axle and semi-elliptic leaf springs front; live axle and semi-elliptic leaf springs rear
**Brakes:** rear drums only
**Bodywork:** various coachbuilt styles, open or closed
**Maximum speed (approx):** 70 mph (113 km/h)

*Below: This grand 1914 Pierce-Arrow open tourer has, on the front wings, the faired-in headlamps which were characteristic of the marque.*

# Pierce-Arrow Straight Eight 1928-38

Well before North America's economy overheated, and large-engined cars became difficult to sell at the end of the 1920s, Pierce-Arrow developed a new generation of cars, designed to use the company's new straight-eight engine, a solid nine-bearing side-valve unit which would power Pierce-Arrow cars, pre- and post-Depression, for 10 years.

Pierce-Arrow had sold out to Studebaker before the new model was launched but the Eight was enthusiastically received, and deservedly so. Not

*Below: A 1932 Straight Eight sedan, with coachwork very like the company's first V12 cars of that year.*

only was the engine more powerful than anything which Pierce-Arrow had previously built, but the new chassis was lower-slung, better-handling and lower-priced than its six-cylinder predecessor. The style of the new car was distinctly Pierce-Arrow, looking dignified but neatly detailed, and the company looked forward to prosperity in the 1930s.

The Wall Street Crash changed everything, and the Eight never achieved the sales its specification promised; 6,795 Eights were sold in the 1930 model year and 4,522 in 1931, but buyers then drifted inexorably away. By 1935 (after yet another financial crisis and rescue) only 523 were built in the year and in the last

*Above: A 1930 Pierce-Arrow Straight Eight, featuring sumptuous seven-seater phaeton coachwork.*

full year, 1937, only 121 cars left the factory in Buffalo, New York.

Despite the low-volume production Pierce-Arrow still offered three different engine displacements, although they were not different enough for the rationale to be immediately obvious. The Eight started with a 5991-cc unit which was produced from 1928 to 1935. In 1929 a slightly smaller, 5587-cc, version with a narrower bore was introduced, and that ran until 1931. Produced alongside that was a bigger, 6306-cc, unit with a longer

stroke and the same bore as the original 5991-cc engine. The 6306-cc engine was discontinued in 1931 but was then reintroduced in 1933 and lasted until the end of Pierce-Arrow production in 1938. Power outputs were 115 bhp, 125 bhp and 132 bhp.

During the 1930s the Eight's chassis was shared with that of the V12 model which arrived in 1931, and style improvements applied to one line were always added to the other. Even from remote New York state, Pierce-Arrow always kept an eye on Detroit's styling trends which explains why the 1934 models were more rounded and better equipped, and why the 1936 models had a new cruciform-braced chassis frame with the engine pushed forward in the frame, and with fashionably-rounded body styling.

In its 10 years, however, the Eight gradually fell behind the times, for it never received independent front suspension. The last cars, however, were as well built as the first, and all automotive fanatics mourned the passing of a famous name in 1938.

### Specification (1928)

**Engine:** inline eight-cylinder, side-valve

**Bore × stroke:** 85.85 mm × 120.65 mm

**Capacity:** 5587 cc

**Maximum power:** 115 bhp

**Transmission:** four-speed manual gearbox, rear-wheel drive

**Chassis:** separate steel frame with channel-section main side members, pressed and tubular cross-bracings

**Suspension:** non-independent with beam axle and semi-elliptic leaf springs front; live axle and semi-elliptic leaf springs rear

**Brakes:** drums all round

**Bodywork:** various coachbuilt styles, open or closed, two- to seven-seater

**Maximum speed (approx):** 85 mph (137 km/h)

THE ENCYCLOPEDIA OF CLASSIC CARS

# Pierce-Arrow V12 1931-38

In spite of the horrendous economic climate in the USA in the early 1930s, there was an inexplicable rush to develop and launch large, complex and powerful V12 and V16-engined cars. Faced with such power units from the likes of Cadillac, Lincoln and Marmon, Pierce-Arrow chimed in, launching their excellently-detailed 7.6-litre V12 model in 1931.

This was more of a flagship design and loss-making indulgence than a viable proposition. Pierce-Arrow, like its rivals, made a lot more publicity than sales, for between 1931 and 1938 it only sold 1,812 V12s, as they were very expensive as well as impressive cars. In the model's first year prices started at $3,650, nearly $200 more than that of the V12 Cadillac; to put matters into perspective, prices for the best-selling four-cylinder Ford Model B started at $410.

The chassis was a strengthened version of that already used in the Eight, although there was also an extra-long-wheelbase option. The V12 engine itself was a classic of its type, with an 80-degree 'V' and two cast-iron cylinder

blocks atop a light-alloy seven-bearing crankcase. Although there were conventional side valves, they were operated via hydraulic tappets.

Not even Ab Jenkins' achievements – in setting speed records at the Bonne-ville salt flats in a stripped-out V12 model (112.9 mph for 24 hours in 1932, a figure raised to 127 mph in a repeat run in 1934) – could boost sales, nor could the showing of the sensationally advanced Silver Arrow show cars (of which only five were sold at $10,000 each in 1933).

Original cars had 6.5-litre or 7.0-litre engines, but even with 150 bhp they were not powerful enough to give the desired performance. A 175-bhp 7.6-litre version appeared for 1933, and was used until the end of the run, in 1938.

*Left: The cockpit of one of the five $10,000 Silver Arrow show cars, with beautifully-figured bird's-eye maple trim, even on the windscreen surround, and excellent instrumentation.*

*Below: The Pierce-Arrow Silver Arrow V12, built for the 1933 Century of Progress exhibition in Chicago, was a real show-stopper; designed in a wind tunnel, it was capable of 115 mph. Spare wheels were kept in the front wings, behind the wheels. Note the tiny rear windows.*

*Above: One of the last of the line, this formal-looking 7.6-litre Pierce-Arrow V12 with town coachwork was built in 1937, shortly before the end of production. In that year only 137 cars left the factory.*

## Specification (1933 Silver Arrow)

**Engine:** V12, side-valve
**Bore × stroke:** 88.9 mm × 101.6 mm
**Capacity:** 7566 cc
**Maximum power:** 175 bhp
**Transmission:** three-speed manual gearbox and freewheel, rear-wheel drive
**Chassis:** separate steel frame with box-section side members, channel and tubular cross-bracings, and cruciform bracing
**Suspension:** non-independent with beam axle and semi-elliptic leaf springs front; live axle and semi-elliptic leaf springs rear
**Brakes:** drums all round
**Bodywork:** streamlined saloon
**Maximum speed (approx):** 115 mph (185 km/h)

# Plymouth

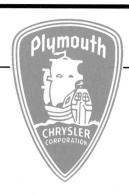

Plymouth

**Above: The Plymouth marque got its name from Plymouth Rock, where the Pilgrim Fathers landed.**

**Left: The bewinged Superbird was a complete departure for the conservative Chrysler division.**

T he name of Chrysler's new low-priced make, introduced in the late 1920s, was suggested by manager Joseph W. Frazer. Plymouth, it was hoped, would remind people of Plymouth Rock, Massachusetts, a port associated with the Pilgrim Fathers, but Walter Chrysler approved the name because he thought it reminded people of Plymouth Binder Twine, a farmers' staple aid!

No matter; Plymouth cars appeared for the first time in 1928, and have been an integral, high-selling, and mundane component of the Chrysler empire ever since. Almost throughout its life the Plymouth marque has represented value for money, which was reflected in its high position – regularly fourth, fifth or sixth – in the North American sales charts, behind Chevrolet, Ford and Chrysler itself.

Whereas Chrysler indulged itself in the mid-1950s building the likes of the very powerful and attractive 300 range, with as much as 375 bhp, Plymouth's most notable offering in the same period was the rather less potent but still impressive Fury. That was the nearest thing Plymouth built to a supercar until the incredible Road Runner Superbird appeared in 1969. Although basically a homologation exercise it was still a sales success, but not one that tempted Plymouth into producing performance cars. That role in the Chrysler empire was reserved for Dodge, a policy which continued into the 1990s, with Dodge making the outrageous Viper, while the sportiest Plymouth model was the 94-bhp Laser coupé.

**Above: More staid than the exotic Superbird, the 1969 Road Runner was still very fast, particularly with the 426-cu in Hemi V8 engine.**

**Below: Like everyone else in the USA in the 1950s, Plymouth went for fins in a big way; these are on a 1957 Fury with a 318-cu in V8 engine.**

# Plymouth Road Runner Superbird 1969-70

*Below: The fastest of the Superbirds had outstanding performance, generated by Chrysler's excellent Hemi V8 with as much as 390 bhp.*

*Above: It may have looked ridiculous, but the tall rear wing on the Superbird was functional, albeit at race rather than road speeds. It was mounted so high partly to allow the boot to open . . .*

Like other North American combines, Chrysler was ruthlessly efficient at exploiting the badge-engineering process, and in cross-breeding models between marques. By the end of the 1960s its Plymouth Road Runner line shared a body shell with the Dodge Charger, providing an ideal opportunity for producing a Plymouth-badged supercar, chiefly as a marketing ploy.

In the 1950s and 1960s Chrysler had an outstanding high-performance V8 engine, the Hemi (the name came from the shape of the combustion chambers), which was successfully used in NASCAR racing. For 1969 Chrysler read the regulations very carefully, realised that to add an aerodynamic advantage to the Hemi's horsepower would produce an unbeatable combination, and duly put the Dodge Charger Daytona on sale.

Plymouth dealers complained that

*Below: The extended nose was a glassfibre addition intended to make the Superbird more aerodynamically efficient, as was the small spoiler.*

Dodge was getting all the headlines, so for 1970 Chrysler relaunched the car virtually without change, this time calling it a Plymouth Road Runner Superbird. As one wag remarked, this was "the same sausage, but a different sizzle . . ."

Like the Charger Daytona, the Superbird hid a relatively ordinary chassis under a stunning exterior. Road cars were offered with the latest 7.2-litre/440-cu in Chrysler V8, with automatic transmission and four-wheel drum brakes as standard. If a customer begged and pleaded, and was prepared to wait, he could have the car built with the expensive 7.0-litre/426-cu in Hemi engine, nominally rated at 425 bhp but capable of a lot more, along with a 'four-on-the-floor' transmission and disc front brakes.

The result was an incredibly brash, but undoubtedly very effective, design. Even in 440-cu in automatic-transmission form this was an extremely fast car, and when race-tuned it was stunning.

Because it was meant to be a NASCAR-winning package, where a high top speed was all-important, the Superbird

had the most extraordinary shape, one almost identical to that of the previous year's Daytona Charger. Somewhere under the skin was the conventional two-door hard-top coupé Road Runner shell, but added to the front was an enormously long wedge-style proboscis, and at the rear there was a massive transverse spoiler, mounted high on pylons above the rear wings; the spoiler, in fact, was higher than the roof line.

All in all, the Superbird was fully 17 inches longer than the conventional Road Runner, which meant that the rare road cars were beasts to park, and very vulnerable to minor accidents.

Chrysler, however, were totally unconcerned by all this, for the Superbird was a race-winner extraordinaire. Competition versions, with fully-tuned Hemi engines, could achieve more than 220 mph, which left the competition trailing. The Daytona 500-winning car of 1970 averaged nearly 150 mph, and during the year the cars won 21 out of the 38 Grand National events.

The Superbird was such an outstanding success that race organisers speedily changed the regulations to ban it. The 'Bird, therefore, was a one-season wonder, both on the tracks and in the showrooms. To meet a more demanding

minimum-production requirement from NASCAR, a total of 1,920 cars had been built, which compared well with the 1968-69 Dodge Charger Daytona, of which only 505 had been produced.

## Specification (1970)

**Engine:** V8, overhead-valve
**Bore × stroke:** 109.73 mm × 92.25 mm
**Capacity:** 7202 cc
**Maximum power:** 375 bhp or 390 bhp
**Transmission:** four-speed manual gearbox or three-speed automatic transmission, rear-wheel drive
**Chassis:** steel unitary construction body/chassis
**Suspension:** independent front with wishbones and torsion bars; live rear axle with semi-elliptic leaf springs
**Brakes:** drums all round or optional front discs
**Bodywork:** steel and glassfibre four-seater coupé
**Maximum speed (approx):** 150 mph (241 km/h)

# Pontiac

The Oakland company of Pontiac, Michigan, had barely been born before it was taken over by General Motors, but there was little corporate rationalisation for the next 20 years. A lower-priced car, the Pontiac Six, was introduced in 1926, and became so popular that Oakland-badged cars disappeared after 1931.

By the 1950s Pontiac's position in the GM 'pecking order' was well established with the marque selling cars that were a little larger, faster and better-equipped than the best-selling Chevrolets. Pontiac settled into sixth place, or thereabouts, in the sales league, competing happily with Ford's Mercury and Chrysler's Dodge marques.

Although Pontiac had no high-performance pretensions before the 1960s, it nevertheless rose to third place in USA sales (behind Chevrolet and Ford), then produced a series of sensationally fast Tempest GTO 'muscle cars'. After building the first GTO and then being chosen to make the Firebird, the sister car to Chevrolet's Camaro, the company's reputation changed progressively. Depending on the model year, the first-generation Firebirds had a wide choice of Pontiac overhead-cam six-cylinder engines (3769 cc and 115-235 bhp, or 4093 cc and 175 or 215 bhp), or V8 engines of 5340 cc/253-285 bhp, 5799 cc/265-325 bhp, or 6558 cc producing 330-345 bhp. The big-engined models set the seal on Pontiac as a producer of high-performance cars.

This was the period in which one John Zachary DeLorean became the Pontiac division's chief, so there was naturally much razzmatazz and image-building at this time. By the 1970s the family cars were more sporting than ever before, and in the 1980s the company's engineers were allowed to indulge themselves by developing the mid-engined Fiero 'commuter car', which was only built for five seasons.

Even in the early 1990s the Firebird was still a very important model in the range, although most Pontiacs were family cars, closely related to Chevrolets and Oldsmobiles. As ever, though, Pontiac's third place in the USA sales charts looked secure, for even in the recession year of 1991 more than half a million Pontiacs left the factory.

*Above: Pontiac's name as a performance carmaker was established in the 1960s with the GTO range; this is a 1968 example. The name was cribbed from Ferrari.*

*Left: High performance was flaunted with the use of extravagant decals like this one, which adorned the bonnet of the Pontiac Firebird throughout the 1970s.*

*Below: In the early 1950s Pontiac had a one-model policy, producing the Chieftain – in sedan, station wagon and convertible form. This is a 1953 model with a side-valve 268-cu in V8 producing 118 bhp at 3,600 rpm.*

*Below: The Pontiac Fiero was described by the company as a 'commuter car', a mid-engined two-seater which evolved into a more powerful sports car.*

*Below: By 1970 the GTO had acquired a more rounded body on a shorter wheelbase to become 'The Judge', with a Ram-Air V8 and rear wing.*

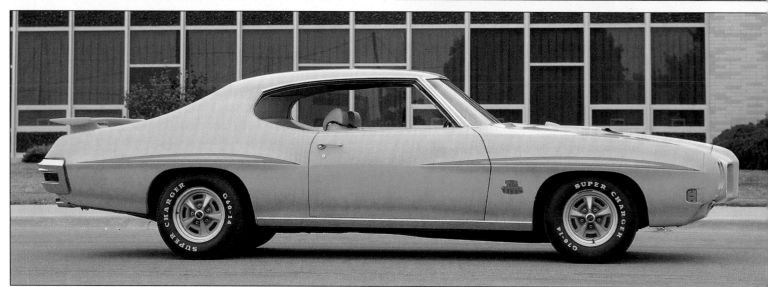

# Pontiac Tempest GTO 1964-67

No sooner had Ford astonished North America with the Mustang – the first of the 'pony cars' – than Pontiac invented yet another exciting series of machines, the 'muscle cars'. The first of the new breed was the Tempest GTO, a car which was to change the face of American motoring in the next few years.

There was nothing intrinsically new about the GTO, except that it crammed a lot of power into a relatively lightweight (by American standards) structure. The straight-line performance was outstanding, and the character was extrovert, to say the least.

The American automotive historian Richard Langworth summarised the original car perfectly. "Equipped with the proper options, a GTO could deliver unprecedented performance for a six-passenger automobile. Of course, it could be ordered in relatively mild-mannered form with automatic transmission, a 335-bhp engine, and so on. Enthusiasts, however, learned to use the option book wisely. The base was a Tempest Le Mans coupé priced at $2,500. The GTO package – floorshift, 389-cu in engine, quick steering, stiff shocks, dual exhaust and premium tyres – cost about $300. The four-speed gearbox cost $188 more. $75 bought a package comprising metallic brake linings, a heavy-duty radiator and a limited-slip differential. And an addi-

*Above: In 1967 the GTO was available with the Ram-Air 400-cu in V8, producing 360 bhp.*

tional $115 would buy a 360-bhp engine. At that point, all you needed was a lead foot and lots of gasoline . . ."

Purists reacted against Pontiac's choice of the GTO name, for they thought it should only be applied to a Ferrari. On the other hand, the Pontiac *was* faster than the Ferrari in a drag race and, as *Car & Driver* wrote: "With every conceivable option on a GTO, it would be difficult to spend more than $3,800. That's a bargain."

By European standards, of course, there was a lot wrong with the GTO, which had poor roadholding, dodgy brakes, and a serious lack of refinement, all allied to awful aerodynamics. And after all, if a car with a nominal 360 bhp (gross) could only reach 120 mph, there must have been formidable obstacles to good airflow.

There was, however, never any complaint about the acceleration. When *Autocar* tested a 1965 model, it recorded 0-100 mph in 18.6 seconds, which was almost up to Jaguar E-type standards – and this from a car which weighed no less than 3,640 lb.

During the 1960s the GTO, along with other related cars from the GM stable,

gradually changed its styling, but there were few major technical changes. The original GTO had been itself a derivative of the mainstream Tempest range, which was introduced in 1963. This was sold in four-door saloon, estate car, coupé and convertible types. The square-rig car of 1964 turned into a more curvaceous machine in 1965, after which there was another re-skin for 1968, and an all-new style for 1970. Until 1967 all these cars were built on a 115-in wheelbase, but this was reduced to 112 inches for 1968. The next-generation, shorter-wheelbase, GTO had a more rounded style, a derivative of GM's latest 'A'-body platform. Introduced in 1967, it was produced until 1971, before GTO became a mere options package in the Le Mans range. It used the same basic types of V8 engine, the largest being a 104.65-mm × 106.9-mm, 7356-cc unit. Peak power of 370 bhp was available in 1970, but output was significantly reduced in 1971 and again in 1972.

On the later, shorter, wheelbase, the hottest GTO was 'The Judge', which had a 366-bhp Ram-Air V8 engine, a three-speed Hurst manual gearbox and a rear spoiler. Only 11,004 of these cars were made, from 1969 to 1971, because by this time the 'muscle car' trend had waned, exhaust-emission controls were on the way in, and dramatic performance reductions were on the horizon.

Model-year sales figures of the original-wheelbase (115-in) cars tell their own story. In the truncated 1964 model year, 32,450 GTOs were built, but this rocketed to 75,352 in 1965. No fewer than 96,946 followed in 1966 and 81,722 in 1967. That made a total of 286,470 in less than four years.

By 1970, though, GTO sales had dropped to 40,149, and a miserable 10,532 followed in 1971. The 'muscle car' craze was over – but the first of the GTOs would always be the most famous of that breed.

## Specification (1964)

**Engine:** V8, overhead-valve
**Bore × stroke:** 103.1 mm × 95.25 mm
**Capacity:** 6362 cc
**Maximum power:** 325-360 bhp
**Transmission:** three-speed or four-speed manual gearbox, optional two-speed automatic transmission; rear-wheel drive
**Chassis:** separate steel frame with box-section main side members and cross-bracings
**Suspension:** independent front with wishbones and coil springs; live rear axle with coil springs and radius arms
**Brakes:** drums all round
**Bodywork:** steel two-door five-seater coupé or convertible
**Maximum speed (approx):** (360-bhp version) 120 mph (193 km/h)

*Above: All GTOs used large cast-iron overhead-valve V8s and four-barrel carburettors.*

*Below: The pillarless GTO was understated and elegant; it was also extremely fast.*

# Pontiac Firebird 1970-81

*Above: The short-lived Trans Am Turbo, with a 210-bhp V8, was not as successful as the normally-aspirated variety. This is a 1980 model.*

Immediately after Ford launched the best-selling Mustang 'pony car', General Motors set out to match it, choosing to produce not one, but two closely-related cars –, the Chevrolet Camaro and the Pontiac Firebird. Chevrolet had design leadership on this project, but because Pontiac's designers were allowed to create unique front-end styles, and to fit their own engines, their development time was more protracted and the Firebird was launched a few months behind the Camaro.

First-generation Firebirds were short-lived by Detroit standards (they were built for less than three years), but the legendary second-generation Firebirds

were a great success – more than a million of all types were sold in their first decade on the market.

The fastest Firebirds of all, called Trans Ams after the American sports-car racing series of the period, were the most glamorous and extrovert of the lot. Although they shared the same compact (cramped, some would say) four-seater coupé shell of all the other Firebirds, with simple live-axle rear suspension, they had the most powerful V8 engines, the tightest suspensions, and the most flamboyant styles.

For tyre-stripping flair and excitement, the Firebird matched anything that Ford's Mustang could offer and, after the Mustang had been down-sized and the Chevrolet Corvette's engines had been emasculated, the mid-1970s Firebird was one of the very fastest cars to remain on sale in emissions-conscious North America.

Many derivatives of the second-generation Firebird were produced, with straight-six, V6 or V8 engines, different transmissions (manual or automatic), various trim packs, coupé or convertible styling, but all based on the same basic structure and 108-in wheelbase. Power outputs and engine sizes were drastically cut back in the 1970s, reflecting the effect of exhaust-emissions legislation.

*Above: In 1972 the Firebird was available with engines ranging from the 250-cu in straight-six to a 455-cu in, 300-bhp V8.*

The least powerful Firebird was a 4.1-litre/100-bhp machine; the most potent were the V8 Trans Ams.

By North American standards, the Trans Am produced its sensational straight-line performance in the most logical way, by providing more of everything. Ferrari or Jaguar offered power from high-revving engines with lots of complicated valve gear and carburation; Pontiac merely provided ultra-large engines – 7.4 litres was typical for the Trans Am – with simple four-barrel carburettors. It was a formula that worked well, and which has ensured that many Trans Ams survive to this day.

Cars like this were just small enough to appeal to export customers, and a number were sold in Europe and the UK, but because they were neither as elegant nor as sumptuously trimmed as their performance rivals from Europe, they attracted a different clientele.

Over the years there were several facelifts, especially around the nose, but the cabin and general package never changed. Production of Firebirds was substantial – in a typical early-1970s year a total of 53,000 would be made, of which

only 2,000 would be Trans Ams. By 197[ ] the balance had shifted completely, wit[ ] 90,000 cars built, 47,000 of which wer[ ] Trans Am models.

## Specification
### (1970 Trans Am)

**Engine:** V8, overhead-valve
**Bore × stroke:** 104.65 mm × 106.93 mm
**Capacity:** 7356 cc
**Maximum power:** 300-345 bhp, depending on chosen options
**Transmission:** four-speed manual gearbox or three speed automatic transmission, rear-wheel drive
**Chassis:** steel unitary construction body/chassis
**Suspension:** independent front with wishbones and coil springs; live rear axle with semi-elliptic springs
**Brakes:** discs front, drums rear
**Bodywork:** steel four-seater coupé
**Maximum speed (approx):** (300-bhp version) 140 mph (225 km/h)

*Above: In 1974 the Firebird was facelifted to incorporate a longer, sharper, nose section. This is a 1978 model with 180 bhp.*

*Below: The rear-wheel-drive Trans Ams of the early 1970s were among the most attractive of all post-war American designs.*

# Pontiac Firebird 1982-92

Replacing the long-running and successful Firebird (and Chevrolet Camaro) of the 1970s was not easy, which is presumably why Pontiac delayed the decision for such a long time. From 1982, however, a pair of all-new cars was introduced, with a 7-in shorter wheelbase, and lighter by about 150 lb. Once again General Motors found a winning formula, as these cars were still selling steadily 10 years after they had been introduced.

General Motors had tapped the current American mood, making the new cars ostensibly a little more economical and a little less extrovert than the old, and although the 'base' car had the heumy old four-cylinder 'Iron Duke' engine, which pushed out a miserable 88 bhp, there were more powerful V6s and V8s which meant it was still possible to order a very rapid Firebird.

Like the older types, the new-generation Firebird was meant to be a car the customer 'designed for himself', by visiting a showroom to browse through the catalogue, to mix and match his options. Even in the first season there were three different engine configurations – straight-four, V6 and V8 (all of which were cross-related in some respects,

with common components). There were engine tune options, brake options, transmission options, instrument options, electrical options, in-car entertainment options; the list was almost endless.

The basic platform was simple in the extreme, being typical GM, for there was still a live rear axle and, like many other GM cars, this was suspended on coil springs, and located by radius arms. The shape, however, was a magnificent creation by Chuck Jordan's stylists, with a long, low, snout, an equally curvaceous

rear, and a glass hatchback.

The most exciting of all these Firebirds were still called Trans Ams (for this racing series was still in existence, and the Firebird was a major player), the original example having a fuel-injected V8 engine, but a mere 165 bhp. Although this was now a 'net' figure, it was a far cry from the thunderous power of the early 1970s – the Firebird's days as an extrovert 'pony car' were apparently over.

GM, however, worked away to improve efficiency without infringing US exhaust-emission laws, so from 1987 a new type of five-litre V8 Trans Am GTA engine, complete with throttle-body fuel injection, arrived. At first rated at 210 bhp, it was soon urged upwards to 235 bhp for 1990. Trans Ams of this type were great image-raisers, although across the length and breadth of the USA only about 10,000 were sold every year.

## Pontiac Firebird variants

Although only one body style – the hatchback/coupé – was sold, this was available with a large variety of engines, trim packs, transmissions and equipment options.

The external style was lightly facelifted for 1985, then again for 1988, and once more for 1991, but the same basic 101-in wheelbase and cabin structure were retained throughout.

The range of optional engines was large indeed, starting with a four-

*Above: The Trans Am was the most powerful of the 1985 Firebird range, with a 205-bhp V8 pushrod engine giving a top speed of 129 mph.*

cylinder of 101.6 mm × 76.2 mm and 2471 cc, producing 88 bhp. That was followed by a V6 of 88.9 mm × 76.2 mm and 2838 cc, producing 135 bhp. Next came a 3128-cc V6 with 142 bhp (from 1990). The V8 range commenced with a 94.89-mm × 88.39-mm, 5001-cc unit, producing from 155 bhp to 208 bhp, depending on model year and application. Finally, there was a 101.6-mm × 88.39-mm, 5733-cc unit, with 210 to 243 bhp, depending on model year and application (from 1986).

## Specification (1987 Trans Am)

**Engine:** V8, overhead-valve
**Bore × stroke:** 94.89 mm × 88.39 mm
**Capacity:** 5001 cc
**Maximum power:** 210 bhp
**Transmission:** five-speed manual gearbox or four-speed automatic transmission, rear-wheel drive
**Chassis:** steel unitary construction
**Suspension:** independent front with wishbones and coil springs; live rear axle with coil springs, radius arms and torque tube
**Brakes:** discs all round
**Bodywork:** steel two-door coupé
**Maximum speed (approx):** 137 mph (220 km/h)

*Above: The first of the third generation of Firebirds was introduced in 1982; this is the top-of-the-range Trans Am type.*

*Below: By 1991 the Trans Am GTA had a longer nose and as much as 243 bhp generated from its five-litre V8, lifting the top speed to 137 mph.*

## Pontiac Fiero 1983-88

*Below: When the original four-cylinder engine was replaced by this V6, performance rose appreciably.*

*Left: The advantage of the Fiero's unique form of construction was that the style could be very easily updated with new plastic panels fitting over the steel frame, transforming the angular original model to this smooth 1985 GT.*

*Right: The Fiero's badge was fractionally more tasteful than the huge Firebird logo Pontiac used on its front-engined coupés.*

During the lean years after the second 'energy crisis', Pontiac developed a sleek little two-seater coupé. To every knowledgeable enthusiast this was a straightforward update of the transverse mid-engined Fiat X1/9's layout, and therefore a sports car, but Pontiac managed to convince itself, and General Motors' higher management, that it was really an energy-efficient two-seater 'commuter car'.

No doubt many people actually did commute in Fieros but many more bought one for use as a sanitised, Americanised, re-statement of the Italian sports car theme. In the end it wasn't surprising that it fell between several stools. The original cars used GM's legendary 'Iron Duke' 2.5-litre overhead-valve four-cylinder engine but were underpowered. Nor were they as spacious as Americans liked, and sales fell away after the first three 'novelty' years. Unlike other GM cars of the period, the Fiero was never produced by any other division and was dropped at the end of the 1988 model year.

Technically the Fiero, dubbed 2M4 by its designers (two-seat, mid-engined, four-cylinder), was very advanced for an American car, for it featured a pressed steel monocoque structure clothed by immensely tough bolt-on plastic (not glassfibre) body panels, a transversely-positioned engine mounted behind the two-seater cabin, four-wheel independent suspension and four-wheel disc brakes.

The body panels were completely rust-resistant (although the inner steel structure was not), and the car certainly looked extremely smart, but early four-cylinder versions were too heavy, with too little power, and could barely keep up with the flow of standard Detroit metal in the daily commuting Grand Prix for which it was ostensibly designed.

Things improved when the corporate GM V6 engine (as already used in cars ranging from the Chevrolet Camaro/Pontiac Firebird to the Cadillac Cimarron) became optional. The first V6 models were badged SEs, but from mid-1985 there was also the Fiero GT, which was given a smoother and more aggressive nose.

Unfortunately, none of this helped boost demand to what General Motors considered to be an acceptable level. Even though the Fiero died from lack of customer interest (Pontiac never even considered exporting it, where it might have had an encouraging reception), those who drove it loved it for its fine roadholding, its brisk performance in V6 form, and its completely different character compared with other GM cars of the period. Even though nearly 190,000 V6s were built, this did not make it a profitable project, and a second-generation Fiero was never developed.

### Specification (1985 GT)

**Engine:** V6, overhead-valve
**Bore × stroke:** 88.9 mm × 76.2 mm
**Capacity:** 2838 cc
**Maximum power:** 135 bhp
**Transmission:** four-speed manual gearbox (five-speed from late 1986) or three-speed automatic transmission, rear-wheel drive
**Chassis:** pressed steel monocoque frame with bolted-on plastic body panels
**Suspension:** independent with wishbones, coil springs and anti-roll bar front; MacPherson struts rear
**Brakes:** discs all round
**Bodywork:** composite plastic two-seater coupé
**Maximum speed (approx):** 118 mph (190 km/h)

*Above: The restyle which brought about the Fiero GT was in response to poor initial sales.*

*Below: After a long gestation period the mid-engined 92-bhp 2.5-litre four cylinder Fiero appeared in 1983.*

# Porsche

*Right: Porsche's name is now synonymous with high performance, thanks to the marque's exploits on the racetrack with cars like the immensely powerful 917, which dominated endurance racing in the early 1970s with power outputs at one stage exceeding 1,000 bhp.*

Although Dr Ferdinand Porsche had a long and distinguished career in Europe's motor industy, it took more than 40 years before the first Porsche-badged cars were made. By that time Ferdinand Porsche was old and ailing; it was his son 'Ferry' Porsche who masterminded the growth of the concern. After 1951, when Dr Porsche died, Ferry Porsche and his sister Louise Piech became joint owners of the company.

One of Dr Porsche's most important projects was the design of the Volkswagen Beetle in the 1930s. This car, which went into production immediately after World War II, was a symbol of Germany's rebirth; when Porsche came to develop his own sports cars at Gmünd, in Austria, he did so on the foundation of the VW's platform and running gear. Then, and for many years, Porsche believed that rear-engined cars, with air-cooled engines, offered the best layout.

The first 52 Beetle-based Type 356 sports cars, all with aluminium bodies, were built at Gmünd from 1948 to 1951, but in 1949 Porsche also opened up in Stuttgart, in a corner of the Reutter coachbuilding works, starting an expansion process which showed no signs of faltering until the end of the 1980s with the onset of worldwide recession.

Until the 1960s Porsche concentrated on building more, and better, versions of the Type 356, while also indulging in motorsport. At the same time the company operated as the design and development centre for VW, producing prototype after prototype in an attempt to replace the Beetle. It was an agreed royalty on VW sales (said to be 5DM – about 50 pence – per car) which helped to make the little firm so buoyant.

During the 1950s most traces of Volkswagen were eliminated from Porsche cars (although the lineage was always obvious), and with the launch of an all-new model, the Type 911, they disappeared completely. For the next decade, at least, Porsche could do no wrong, for 911s were built in ever more powerful and various guises, the motor racing programme was extremely successful, and the company also set up a thriving engineering consultancy business at Weissach, west of Stuttgart.

The marque's growth, it seemed, was unstoppable, but in the early 1970s there were several setbacks. A joint project with Volkswagen, to build sports cars badged as VW-Porsches, was not a lasting success. It also seemed that Porsche could never satisfy VW with its designs for a new small car, the result being that the expensive EA266 project was eventually cancelled, and all such passenger-car links were thereafter severed.

Then came the early 1970s, when Ferry Porsche re-arranged the company's financial structure and retired from front-line management, following which the firm's research facilities expanded enormously. This was also a period in which Porsche decided to develop front-engined

*Above: Unquestionably one of the world's greatest supercars, the 959 was a homologation special designed for Group B racing in the 1980s.*

sports cars. The first of these was intended for Audi-VW, but the project was cancelled. This, though, was good news for Porsche, which bought back the rights, turned the car into the Porsche 924, arranged for it to be built in an Audi factory, and prospered mightily as a result. The front-engined 928 was launched in 1977, originally intended as a replacement for the 911, but the old rear-engined model refused to die.

The 1980s was a troubled decade for Porsche. Although its consultancy business was buoyant – there was Formula 1 engine design success, and much work for companies as diverse as Lada, Seat and Mercedes-Benz – the car product line languished. Although the 911 was substantially re-engineered, and the 944 eventually supplanted the 924, Porsche's 1990s model line was recognisably developed from that of the late 1970s. By this time prices were also extremely high and customers began to drift away in ever-increasing numbers.

Early in the 1990s sales fell dramatically in many countries, and one by one the front engine models were phased out. By the end of the decade, the mid-engined Boxster was in production and the 911 had been reinvented as a sleek water-cooled sophisticate.

*Below: For years Porsche emulated the company that inspired their first products, Volkswagen, by having their own one-model policy with the 911.*

# Porsche 356 1948-55

Although the original Porsche prototype was a mid-engined two-seater roadster, the layout of the famous Type 356 (a project code retained for the car's actual title) settled on the familiar form of the Volkswagen Beetle, which Dr Porsche's bureau had designed for Adolf Hitler in the 1930s. For the next 14 years all Porsche production cars would share the same basic configuration.

The 356 was originally a slow and rather evil-handling machine, but tenacious development – and a certain amount of stubborn pride – eventually saw it changed into a formidable sports car. All 356s used the same basic body/chassis platform as the VW Beetle, which meant that the engine was in the tail, driving the rear wheels. The Porsche came complete with the Beetle's torsion-bar suspension, including a high-pivot swing-axle rear end, while power was provided by an air-cooled horizontally-opposed four-cylinder engine.

The body shape was quite unmistakable, for the lines were rounded but chubby, the headlamps were faired Beetle-style into the front wings, and aerodynamic performance was surpris-

*Below: Early Porsche interiors were sparsely trimmed to save weight, as the four-cylinder cars were not overendowed with power.*

ingly good. Originally there was a choice of coupé or cabriolet styling with 2+2 seating, but a more rakish two-seater Speedster (roadster) soon followed.

A total of 52 cars was hand-built at Gmünd, with aluminium coupé or cabriolet bodies, but from 1949 Porsche began to relocate to Stuttgart, where the coachbuilders Reutter set up production-line facilities for steel body shells, delivering these in larger and larger numbers to the Porsche factory next door.

In the first few years Porsche gradually, but very persistently, began to develop its own components to take over from the original VW running gear, so that by the mid-1950s the engines and gearboxes were much more Porsche than Volkswagen. Most importantly, the engine was gradually enlarged, beefed up, and made more powerful. Several different engine sizes and power outputs were available in the 356. In addition to the 1.5-litre unit, from 1948 to 1955 a 73.5-mm × 64-mm, 1086-cc version producing 40 bhp was offered. That outlived the wider-bore, 75-mm × 64-mm, variant

displacing 1131 cc which also produced 40 bhp. From 1949 to 1955 two similar-displacement engines ran side by side: a 80-mm × 64-mm, 1286-cc version producing 44 bhp and a 74.5-mm × 74-mm, 1290-cc unit producing either 44 bhp or 60 bhp.

If the car had a problem, it was in the handling. A properly-driven Porsche was very fast and nimble, but novices found it difficult to master the combination of swing-axle rear suspension and tail-heavy weight distribution, which could pitch the car into terminal oversteer very suddenly if it was abused.

Compared with many other sports cars of the period, however, the Porsche was better built, more economical and more modern. Although power outputs were modest, the 356s were amazingly successful in motorsport, particularly in rallies, where their strength and traction were so valuable.

After six years of unstoppable success Porsche withdrew the 356, after 7,627 had been built – but only in favour of improved versions of the same design.

*Above: The most sought-after version of the first 356 generation is the Speedster, worth nearly £40,000 in 1993*

## Specification (1950)

**Engine:** horizontally-opposed four-cylinder, overhead-valve
**Bore × stroke:** 80 mm × 74 mm
**Capacity:** 1488 cc
**Maximum power:** 55 bhp
**Transmission:** four-speed manual gearbox, rear-wheel drive
**Chassis:** steel unitary construction
**Suspension:** independent with trailing arms, transverse torsion bars and anti-roll bar front; swing-axles and transverse torsion bars rear
**Brakes:** drums all round
**Bodywork:** steel 2+2-seater coupé or cabriolet, or two-seater Speedster
**Maximum speed (approx):** 87 mph (140 km/h)

*Below: The lines of the Speedster were kept simple, for ease of production and to increase aerodynamic efficiency.*

# Porsche 356A, 356B and 356C 1955-65

*Above: The 356A could be distinguished from the first 356s by the curved glass windscreen. This is one of the 1.6-litre Super Coupé models built up to 1959.*

In the 1950s, as in the decades which followed, Porsche liked to develop each model gradually, and to get the very best out of it before finally replacing it by an entirely new design. The original Type 356 had already been in production for seven years before any significant changes were made; the 356A of the late 1950s, and the 356B/356C models of the early 1960s, were all recognisably developed from the first 356's layout.

The 356A retained the original 356 type of running gear and suspension, although the engine itself was enlarged to 1.6 litres, in which form it was to become the standard unit in future years; a 1.3-litre powerplant was still available, though the smallest engine size of all (1086 cc) had been dropped as long ago as 1951. As far as the 356's fans were concerned, this was great news, but the sceptics wished that the handling could have been improved.

There were important changes to the suspension settings (if not to the basic layout of the swing-axle rear end), and to the body style. Instead of the 'V'-screen there was now a single piece of glass, curved and panoramic, while the interior had also been upgraded, with fully-reclining front seats as standard.

Porsche sales continued to climb, to the extent that Reutter was building 25 body shells a day by 1959. This trend continued when the 356B was introduced in

*Below: The 356B was built between 1959 and 1963 in convertible as well as conventional coupé form.*

1959, for the style had been changed again, with raised and more efficient headlamps, while (from 1960) there was the popular option of a 90-bhp 1.6-litre engine. The 40,000th car was produced early in 1961.

By that time very few VW Beetle parts were still being used, for Porsche's engineers had redeveloped almost every aspect of the chassis, which was now so rugged that it was possible to offer a two-litre twin-cam engine as a high-performance option, and a small-series of Abarth-bodied coupés were also produced.

Finally came the 356C of 1963, a car introduced at the same time as the all-new 911 (then badged 901) was previewed. There were no style changes, but the greatest advance was the adoption of disc brakes for all four wheels.

The last 356s were built in April 1965, just a few months after the 911 went into production. From 1948 to 1965, 76,302 cars of all types were made.

## Porsche 356A variants

### Porsche 356B

The 356B (1959-63) was a direct replacement for the 356A, with the same basic style and range of bodies. The most noticeable change was that

the headlamp position was raised, and there were different bumpers. The 1.6-litre engine became standard, and was rated at 60, 75 or 90 bhp. The approximate top speed of the 90-bhp model was an impressive 111 mph, thanks to its aerodynamic efficiency.

### Porsche 356C

The 356C (1963-65) was the final development of the 356 design, produced for two years only. The 1.6-litre engine remained standard, in 75-bhp or 95-bhp tune, and the car was offered as a coupé or cabriolet.

### Porsche 356 Carrera

The 356A, B and C models were also available in Carrera guise, featuring a special twin-cam-per-bank engine.

## Specification (1955 356A)

**Engine:** horizontally-opposed four-cylinder, overhead-valve
**Bore × stroke:** 74.5 mm × 74 mm
**Capacity:** 1290 cc
**Maximum power:** (1.3-litre) 44 bhp/60 bhp
**Transmission:** four-speed manual gearbox, rear-wheel drive
**Chassis:** steel unitary construction body/chassis
**Suspension:** independent with trailing

*Above: With its uncluttered lines, as much as 111 mph could be achieved in a 356B, like this example.*

arms, transverse torsion bars and anti-roll bar front; swing-axles and transverse torsion bars rear
**Brakes:** drums all round
**Bodywork:** steel 2+2-seater coupé or cabriolet, or two-seater Speedster (roadster)
**Maximum speed (approx):** 95 mph (153 km/h)

*Below: All 356s except the Carrera models were powered by simple overhead-valve air-cooled flat-four engines, a design evolved from that of the VW Beetle but refined, enlarged and made more powerful. By the early 1960s, output of the 1.6-litre version was 90 bhp.*

## Porsche 356 Carrera 1955-65

*Above: The Carrera name was first used on a Porsche as early as 1955, celebrating Porsche's involvement in the Carrera Panamericana race.*

*Left: Competition models could be fitted with removable wire stone guards to give a measure of protection for the headlights.*

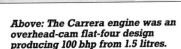

fitted with twin spark plugs per cylinder, giving it eight in all.

Although it was a racing engine – solid and efficient but not meant to be quiet, refined, cheap to build or particularly amenable to low-speed running – Porsche eventually decided to put it on sale, by offering special versions of existing 356 models for use in motorsport. In almost every way these were what we began to call 'homologation specials' in later years, for they were more powerful and less civilised than the cars from which they were developed.

The original type was the Type 356A Carrera, a model known within Porsche as the 1500GS, which had 100 bhp at first, though this rating was improved to 110 bhp two years later. In both cases this transformed a fast sports car into a race- and rally-winning device, and although it was expensive it sold very well.

Later, Porsche enlarged the engine to 1.6 litres/105 or 115 bhp and offered two versions – one called a De Luxe, for customers who did not intend to go

motor racing or rallying; the other being stripped out and lightened, and called the Carrera GT. From 1961 the car was made even more competitive with the offering of a two-litre engine which developed 130 bhp, while race-tuned

*Above: The steel disc wheels had a widely-spaced five-bolt attachment for extra security.*

*Above: The Carrera engine was an overhead-cam flat-four design producing 100 bhp from 1.5 litres.*

versions of that unit were capable of much more horsepower. Disc brakes, thank goodness, had made their appearance by that time, replacing the ineffective drums all round.

In all these cases performance took precedence over refinement, and although the handling of the rear-engined chassis still had to be mastered, the cars were extremely successful, in racing and in rallying. The engine, of course, went on to be used in many Porsche racing cars of the 1950s and 1960s, in the 1.5-litre Formula 1 single-seaters, and in the Type 904 racing sports car.

Production of these specialised cars was always limited. In 10 years there were 700 based on the 356A, and 50 cars based on the 356B/356C styles. Of these, 195 cars had the ultimate 130-bhp two-litre engine.

### Porsche 356 Carrera variants

#### Porsche Carrera GTL

Early in the 1960s a series of 21 lightweight Carrera GTL cars were produced by Carlo Abarth of Turin, which featured lightweight bodies of a better aerodynamic shape. With a two-litre engine producing 135 bhp these cars were capable of 143 mph. (Top speed of the standard-bodied cars was approximately 124 mph.)

### Specification (1955 356A 1500)

**Engine:** horizontally-opposed four-cylinder, twin overhead camshafts per bank of cylinders
**Bore × stroke:** 85 mm × 66 mm
**Capacity:** 1498 cc
**Maximum power:** 100 bhp
**Transmission:** four-speed manual gearbox, rear-wheel drive
**Chassis:** steel unitary construction
**Suspension:** independent with trailing arms, transverse torsion bars and anti-roll bar front; swing-axles and transverse torsion bars rear
**Brakes:** drums all round
**Bodywork:** steel 2+2-seater coupé or two-seater Speedster
**Maximum speed (approx):** 115 mph (185 km/h)

Early in the 1950s Porsche began to develop its own very special engine for motor racing. Although it was still a horizontally-opposed 'boxer' four mounted in the tail, this new unit was a very complex design, with twin overhead camshafts per bank of cylinders (driven by shafts and bevel gears) and a built-up Hirth crankshaft which ran in roller-bearings. To aid combustion the engine was also

*Right: Light weight, good aerodynamics and reasonable power helped give an impressive top speed of 115 mph.*

# Porsche 904 1964

*The 904, left, was succeeded by the more numerous 906 – or Carrera 6 – seen here above, in Jarama, in 1967.*

Was the 904 a racing car, a racing car that could be used on the road, or a specialised road car which was also a successful racing car? The 904 was an early example of a homologation special, for use in Grand Touring car racing. The company was delighted that it also shone in rallies too.

Although the 904 used a highly-tuned version of the existing air-cooled four-cam Carrera engine, it was effectively a new design. Unlike most previous Porsches – road cars or competition cars – it had a mid-mounted rather than a rear-mounted engine, which is to say that the engine was ahead of the line of the rear wheels, rather than in the tail.

It was a squat and purposeful-looking two-seater, the ancestor of several more specialised racing Porsches built later in the 1960s. The 904 had its own personality with its own unmistakable engine sound; for such a fast car it was also amazingly flexible.

To qualify to go motor racing in the Grand Touring category, Porsche would need to build at least 100 cars, so the design was laid out with that in mind. For the first – and only – time on a Porsche there was a separate box-section chassis frame, and the body shell was made from glassfibre mouldings. The spartan trim level did not stop some owners from using their cars on the road, but the 904's next role was that of a rally car, and in this it excelled. The old-type four-cylinder engine was pushed to the very limits of its development – when race-tuned, 180 bhp was available – and right from the start it proved to have performance and great stamina. Two outright racing versions were built: the 904-6 with a Porsche 911-type flat-six engine, and the 904-8 with a flat-eight two-litre unit.

There was no problem in building the necessary number of cars, all of which sold remarkably quickly; the first 100 cars were ordered before assembly

began. For Porsche this was not only a successful but also a profitable programme, for in the end a total of 116 cars was produced. Works cars were soon joined by privately-owned cars, and started winning all round the world – at Sebring, in the Targa Florio, and on other road endurance events.

On the road, the 904's greatest achievement was undoubtedly to finish second in the 1965 Monte Carlo Rally, which was held in blizzard conditions. The driver was Stuttgart restauranteur Eugen Bohringer, and this was a drive which was remembered for years by rallying historians.

## Specification (1964)

**Engine:** flat-four, twin overhead camshafts per bank
**Bore × stroke:** 92 mm × 74 mm
**Capacity:** 1966 cc
**Maximum power:** 155 bhp (180 bhp when race-tuned)

*Above: The 904's quad-cam flat-four was fed by Weber carburettors and produced 180 bhp in race trim.*

**Transmission:** five-speed manual gearbox, rear-wheel drive
**Chassis:** separate steel frame with box-section main side members and cross-bracing
**Suspension:** independent with upper and lower wishbones, coil springs and telescopic dampers front and rear
**Brakes:** discs all round
**Bodywork:** glassfibre two-seater sports coupé
**Maximum speed (approx):** (180-bhp version) 161 mph (259 km/h)

*Below: Racing versions of the glassfibre-bodied 904 were capable of speeds in excess of 160 mph.*

# Porsche 911 2.0, 2.2 and 2.4-litre 1964-73

*Below: The original two-litre Porsche 911; this is one of the first road-test cars from 1964.*

The famous and seemingly immortal 911 model was carefully conceived as a replacement for the original 356. Its market was researched in depth before the design was fixed, the decision being to make a similar type of car, but one which was larger, faster and more luxuriously equipped than any previous Porsche.

Whereas the old 356 had evolved from the VW Beetle, the new car, originally coded Type 901, was totally new. The basic (one might now say traditional) Porsche layout was retained, but every component was new. The air-cooled engine was in the tail, giving a rearward weight bias, the body/chassis unit was a unitary-construction design, there was all-independent suspension, and the car had a cabin with four seats, only two of which were truly comfortable for use on long journeys.

Porsche's decision to stick with the rear-engined, tail-heavy layout was made on the grounds of dogma, for there was no doubt that this brought severe roadholding problems. No matter how loudly Porsche enthusiasts denied it, there was no question that the 911's roadholding was unpredictable at all times, and perilous in some conditions.

The flat-six engine, on the other hand, was a magnificent piece of engineering which went on to be refined, enlarged, redesigned, and further improved in the years which followed.

Although the original model first appeared as a 130-bhp two-litre, with a fastback coupé body, this was only the beginning, for Porsche had every possible derivative up its sleeve. Even with the original two-litre-engined cars, the 130-bhp 911/911 L type was soon joined by the 160-bhp 911 S in 1966 and the 110-bhp 911 T in 1967, and from 1968 all these engines were gradually uprated. In the

*Above: Early 911s were renowned for their tail-heavy handling, thanks to the rear-mounted flat-six engine.*

model's first decade the engine was twice increased in capacity, a semi-automatic transmission was announced, various trim packs were introduced, and a smart Targa convertible body style was also made available.

By 1973, however, this famous car was only getting into its stride, for bigger and more powerful engines, more refined chassis and yet more body styles were on the way.

## Porsche 911 variants

### Porsche 911 S, 911 T and 911 E
Even in the early days the 911 range was confusingly wide, with only slight differences between the models. The first significant change was in 1966 when the 160-bhp 911 S was introduced, while the very next year saw the introduction of the 911 T which was, with 110 bhp, *less* powerful than the original car. The mainstream 911 model was replaced in 1969 by the slightly more powerful (140-bhp rather than 130-bhp) 911 E. A Targa-top version was introduced in 1968, a year before the 911 S was updated with a 170-bhp (rather than 160-bhp) engine.

The first rear mechanical change (other than the steady power increases) came in 1968 when the wheelbase and track were both widened, and flared

wheel arches were incorporated to cover the wider wheels. In 1969 the original two-litre engine was replaced by a 2.2-litre (2195 cc with a bore and stroke of 84 mm × 66 mm) available in various states of tune – 125 bhp for the 911 T, 155 bhp for the 911 E and 180 bhp for the 911 S. A further increase in displacement came in 1973 when the stroke went up to 70.4 mm, to give a displacement of 2341 cc and power outputs of 130, 165 and 190 bhp for the 911 T, 911 E and 911 S respectively.

### Specification (1964-68 2.0)
**Engine:** flat-six, single overhead camshaft per bank of cylinders
**Bore × stroke:** 80 mm × 66 mm
**Capacity:** 1991 cc
**Maximum power:** (911/911 L) 130 bhp; (911 T) 110 bhp; (911 E) 140 bhp; (911 S) 160 bhp/170 bhp
**Transmission:** four- or five-speed manual gearbox, Sportomatic semi-automatic transmission from 1968 on some models; rear-wheel drive
**Chassis:** steel unitary construction
**Suspension:** independent with MacPherson struts, lower wishbones, longitudinal torsion bars and anti-roll bar front; semi-trailing arms, transverse torsion bars and anti-roll bar rear
**Brakes:** discs all round
**Bodywork:** steel 2+2-seater coupé or Targa convertible coupé
**Maximum speed (approx):** (130-bhp version) 131 mph/211 km/h; (160-bhp version) 137 mph/220 km/h

*Above: Variations on a theme with, from the top: a 911 S, a 2.2-litre 911 E and a 2.4-litre, 130-bhp 911 T.*

*Below: A 1969 911 T; at this stage the 911 T had a 2.2-litre flat-six producing a maximum of 125 bhp.*

# Porsche 912 and 912 E 1965-69, 1975-76

*Right: The 912 needed a certain amount of promotional help as it lacked the power and performance of the 911, having only a 1582-cc flat-four engine and an output of 90 bhp. Despite its low power, top speed was an impressive 119 mph.*

*Above: This is the badge which adorned no fewer than 30,745 four-cylinder Porsche 912s in an initial four-year production run.*

There was only one problem with the 911 – it was considerably more expensive than the 356 which it replaced. No sooner had Porsche put the flat-six-engined 911 on sale in 1964 than they looked round for a lower-priced car – something which in the 1990s we would call an 'entry-level' model. The result was the 912, the amalgam of a new structure with an old engine.

The 912 was developed specifically to replace the old 356C model, at similar price levels. Very simply, this merged the new 911 structure, suspension and transmission with the 1.6-litre flat-four engine which had been used in the 356 range for some years.

As a range 'gap-filler' the 912 was a great success, for it introduced sports car buyers all over the world to 911-style motoring, but at a considerably lower price. Depending on the market, both

four- or five-speed gearboxes were available, and although the car lacked the searing acceleration of the six-cylinder 911s, it still had a very creditable top speed of 119 mph. In four years a total of 30,745 912s was produced, making this an extremely profitable extra model in the 911 range. Several years later, when Porsche once again needed to fill a gap in the series, a completely updated version of this car, called the 912 E, was introduced.

The 912 E was needed for the North American market only, where sales of the mid-engined VW-Porsche 914 were to end in 1975, and where deliveries of the new front-engined 924 would not begin until 1977. By modernising the

original 912, Porsche was able to produce a short-lived but satisfactory model which kept the North American pot boiling for a short time. In contrast to the first 912's 1.6-litre engine, the 912 E was powered by a 1971-cc (94-mm × 71-mm) flat-four producing 90 bhp, to give a top speed of 115 mph.

Sales of the 912 E were limited – just 2,099 cars were built.

## Specification (1965 912)

**Engine:** flat-four, overhead-valve
**Bore × stroke:** 82.5 mm × 74 mm
**Capacity:** 1582 cc
**Maximum power:** 90 bhp
**Transmission:** four- or five-speed manual gearbox, rear-wheel drive

**Chassis:** steel unitary construction body/chassis
**Suspension:** independent with MacPherson struts, lower wishbones, longitudinal torsion bars and anti-roll bar front; semi-trailing arms with transverse torsion bars rear
**Brakes:** discs all round
**Bodywork:** steel 2+2-seater coupé or Targa convertible coupé
**Maximum speed (approx):** 119 mph (192 km/h)

*Below: Being built with the same body shell as the 911, there was virtually nothing to distinguish the 912 from its rather more powerful six-cylinder relations.*

# Porsche 911 2.7, 3.0 and 3.2-litre 1973-89

In the 1970s and 1980s the Porsche 911's reputation grew and grew, development continued steadily, and sales never looked like falling away. The body style was gradually modified, the engines were enlarged and made more powerful, and the battle to improve the suspension continued.

Although the car's basic style did not change, Porsche retouched it from time to time, not only to satisfy the engineers' wishes to install ever-wider wheels and tyres, or to fit more sophisticated front and rear spoilers, but to keep ahead of safety-related legislation. A late-1980s 911, therefore, was still recognisably developed from the 1963 variety, but most panels had been changed. Porsche's designers even managed to integrate the heavier bumpers required for the USA onto an old design in a smooth, seamless way which was a world apart from British Leyland's clumsy efforts on the MGB, even though the North American market was just as vital to both companies.

At first the range opened with the standard 911; the best-selling type was the 911 S, and the most sporty was the Carrera SC or Carrera RS, but from mid-1975 the 'mainstream' model was called a Carrera (with a 3.0-litre engine). Following the launch of the 928, from the summer of 1978 the range was rationalised still further, there being a 3.0-litre 911 SC until 1983, after which the car became the Carrera once again, this time with a 3.2-litre engine.

During this period the most astonishing advances made were to the famous flat-six engine, which had started

life as a two-litre unit in 1963. By 1971 this had grown to 2.7 litres, a 3.0-litre powerplant followed two years later (and was standardised from 1977), and the amazing Turbo was given 3.3 litres in 1977. The final, normally-aspirated unit was launched in 1983, with 3164 cc.

The first of the 2.7-litre types produced 210 bhp, but the last of the 1980s-type Turbos were rated at 300 bhp, while the normally-aspirated 3.2-litre unit pro-

*Above: The injected 2.7-litre Carrera engine produced its 210 bhp at 6,300 rpm, which was enough to generate a maximum speed in excess of 150 mph.*

duced 231 bhp. In the intervening years, though, Porsche made sure that *all* engines (not merely those sold in the USA) could run on low-octane (two-star in the UK) and unleaded fuel, and the engines also became progressively more torquey and flexible.

For the 1990s there were further, and

*Above: Great care was taken to make the Carrera as light as possible; stripped RS versions weighed under 2,000 lb, and with wide wheels and stiffer anti-roll bars the Carrera could corner at a lateral g of 0.912.*

equally impressive, enlargements on the way, but these were reserved for a new generation of 911.

The coupé and Targa types had both been available for many years before a third variety, the full convertible, arrived in 1982, while later in the 1980s it was possible to order cars with an even smoother nose which featured hidden headlamps.

As the 1980s passed Porsche continued to improve the chassis in detail, though the limitations of having a heavy engine in the extreme tail could never be ignored. Sales were strong, year in and year out, and any thoughts Porsche might have had of killing off the 911 in favour of the front-engined 928, by this time selling far more slowly than originally envisaged, were forgotten.

There was something about the rear-engined car's character, a combination of searing performance, styling, reputation, and that spine-tingling flat-six engine growl, which could not be duplicated by any other car. Tens of thousands of 911s were built every year, so that total production passed the 250,000 mark in the 1980s.

By the late 1980s, however, Porsche had to face up to a major problem. On the one hand its customers wanted to carry on buying a car which looked like a 911 but on the other they were demanding a much better chassis. What could replace the 911? This was a question Porsche's management regularly asked itself. In the end, it seems, the answer was to be found in a new type of 911. The result, in 1988 and 1989, was the arrival of the Carrera 2 and Carrera 4 family.

## Specification (1973 2.7)

**Engine:** flat-six, single overhead camshaft per bank of cylinders
**Bore × stroke:** 90 mm × 70.4 mm
**Capacity:** 2681 cc
**Maximum power:** 210 bhp
**Transmission:** five-speed manual gearbox, optional four-speed semi-automatic 'Sportomatic' transmission; rear-wheel drive
**Chassis:** steel unitary construction body/chassis
**Suspension:** independent with MacPherson struts, lower wishbones, longitudinal torsion bars and anti-roll bar front; semi-trailing arms, transverse torsion bars and anti-roll bar rear
**Brakes:** discs all round
**Bodywork:** steel 2+2-seater coupé or Targa convertible coupé
**Maximum speed (approx):** 150 mph (241 km/h)

*Above: A 1974 2.7-litre 911 Carrera; the Carrera made its debut in 1972 as a 210-bhp homologation special capable of 0-60 mph in 5.5 seconds. It did not go on general sale until 1973, in which year 100 were exported to the United Kingdom.*

*Right: Apart from its badges, the Carrera could be easily identified by the duck-tail spoiler, which was an integral part of the glassfibre engine cover and drastically reduced rear-end lift, from 320 lb to 93 lb.*

# Porsche 911 (930) Turbo 1975-89

*Below: One of the very first 911 Turbos, from 1975. The large 'whale tail' was functional.*

*Right: By the time of this 1987 model the 911 Turbo had acquired vents ahead of the rear wheels.*

Early in the 1970s turbocharging was still confined to the racetrack. Porsche, who had first used turbocharged engines in CanAm, with 917s, then started racing turbocharged versions of the 911. As so often in the past, the company then decided to start selling a productionised version. The result – launched in 1975 – was the mighty Turbo model.

For well over 10 years the 911 Turbo (which, more properly, held the Porsche project number of 930 and was known as a 930 in North America) was the car by which other makers measured supercar performance. It was an impressive, frightening and extremely fast car with great charisma. On the one hand it had colossal performance and good reliability, but on the other hand it still suffered from the normally-aspirated 911's handling and refinement problems.

The large, three-litre, displacement was chosen for the Turbo version to mask the effect that the low (7.0:1) compression ratio needed for turbocharging would have when the car was not running under boost. Bosch K-Jetronic injection was used in conjunction with a turbo boost pressure of 11.5 psi.

The original three-litre Turbo of 1975-77 had excellent outright performance, with a most impressively even power curve and torque delivery, but the 3.3-litre (with turbo intercooler) which followed it had even more torque and was even more flexible.

Turbos looked similar to ordinary 911s, but had many different touches. Wheel-arch flares were much more pronounced, wheel rims were wider and tyres were larger, the rear spoiler was larger and more flamboyant than ever before, and under the skin there was a robust new four-speed gearbox to cope with the engine's beefy torque. An oil cooler and Bilstein gas dampers were also fitted, while the huge four-pot-caliper, ventilated-disc set-up from the mighty 917 racer was added later. Just to confuse the issue, Porsche eventually offered the 'Turbo look' bodywork as an option on normally-aspirated 911s of the 1980s, and there was another front-end style available for the Turbo which incorporated a lower nose with flip-up headlamps.

For many years the Turbo was only offered as a coupé, but towards the end of its run Targa-topped and convertible versions also became available. Porsche never debased the car by offering it with any form of their Sportomatic clutchless gear change.

In 1978 engine size was increased from three to 3.3 litres (3299 cc to be precise, thanks to a bigger bore and stroke), not to produce yet more performance but to make up for the effect of increasingly stringent emissions laws both in North America and Europe. Inevitably though, the power output rose, from 260 bhp to 300 bhp, and the 3.3 Turbo could travel from 0-60 mph in a fraction over five seconds.

Although there were only 2,873 three-litre Turbos built, well over 10,000 of the enlarged-engine type were produced.

*Above: By the 1980s, engine size had risen to 3.3 litres and power output to 300 bhp, enough to give a top speed of 158 mph.*

*Below: The 1976-model 911 Turbo had the advantage of a fully-galvanised body shell. Its large wheels required flared arches.*

*Below: The intercooler and the large cooling fan below it dominated the Turbo's engine bay.*

In 1989, when the Turbo's imminent demise was announced, there was a rush to buy the last few cars, but there was really no need, for Porsche had a new generation on the way!

## Specification (1975)

**Engine:** flat-six, single overhead camshaft per bank of cylinders
**Bore × stroke:** 95 mm × 70.4 mm
**Capacity:** 2993 cc
**Maximum power:** 260 bhp
**Transmission:** four-speed manual gearbox, rear-wheel drive
**Chassis:** steel unitary construction body/chassis
**Suspension:** independent with MacPherson struts, lower wishbones, longitudinal torsion bars and anti-roll bar front; semi-trailing arms and transverse torsion bars rear
**Brakes:** discs all round
**Bodywork:** steel 2+2 coupé
**Maximum speed (approx):** 150 mph (241 km/h)

## Porsche 924 1975-88

When the new 924 was introduced in 1975, it was only the fourth completely new Porsche to have been put on sale in 27 years. More importantly, it was the very first front-engined Porsche *and* the very first to have a water-cooled engine.

In some ways, however, this car should never have carried a Porsche badge – and in later years there were die-hards who said it did not deserve one. Early in the 1970s VW had asked Porsche to design a new sports coupé as a replacement for the existing VW-Porsche 914. This was allocated project number EA425, and was always intended to use as many VW or Audi parts as possible.

Porsche stuck carefully to its brief, and although it went ahead with the design of a brand-new front-engined monocoque car with neat but unassuming looks, EA425 was always a classic 'parts-bin' job. It was already well on course for announcement when two events conspired to kill it: the 'energy crisis' made VW think twice about such cars, and there was a change of VW's chairman.

In February 1975 the new management, led by Toni Schmucker, decided to wind up the VW-Porsche business, cancelled EA425 and was ready to pay off Porsche for its efforts. Instead, Porsche offered to 'buy back' the design, to rebadge it as a Porsche, and to have it built in a VW-Audi factory. This deal was speedily done, the one-time NSU plant at Neckarsulm was chosen, and what we now know as the Porsche 924 was born.

In some ways this was a real mongrel of a car – part pure Porsche, part Audi and part VW – so it is no wonder that it got a rather puzzled reception. The engine was linked to the rear-mounted gearbox/transaxle by a rigid torque tube. The engine itself was a two-litre four-cylinder VW design, shared with (of all things) the LT van, the transaxle was that of a front-wheel-drive Audi 100 (an Audi automatic transmission was soon to be optional), and there were many recognisable VW parts in the suspension and steering layout.

Once people had accepted the car's origins, it was much easier to be happy about the packaging, the nicely-balanced handling, and the brisk performance. But in its original 125-bhp form this was not a spine-tinglingly fast car like other contemporary Porsches. Its 126 mph top speed was excellent (and said a lot for the aerodynamic properties of the body shell), but 0-60 mph in nearly 10 seconds felt positively pedestrian to some critics. To others, it almost seemed wrong for a Porsche to handle so well, and for novices to be able to drive it so

*Left: By 1986 the 924 had been replaced by the 924 S, with a 2479-cc engine and 150 bhp.*

fast and securely.

Porsche's management, however, did not mind; the 924 was far cheaper than any 911, and the company was soon taking massive orders. Within 26 months the first 50,000 924s had been sold, and many other derivatives were on the way. Not only did Porsche soon reveal a turbocharged version (and an even faster, Carrera development of that car), but the basic design was also used for the 944. Even the 968 of the 1990s was still closely based on the monocoque and general front-engined/rear-transmission mechanical layout of the original 924.

### Porsche 924 variants

#### Porsche 924 S
The 924 S replaced the 924 in 1985 and was built until 1988. The Audi-based engine was discarded in favour of a detuned version of the 944's powerplant, a 100-mm × 78.9-mm, 2479-cc/150-bhp unit. The peak power was uprated, to 160 bhp, from mid-1987. The top speed of the 160-bhp version was 137 mph.

### Specification (1975 924)

**Engine:** inline four-cylinder, single overhead camshaft
**Bore × stroke:** 86.5 mm × 84.4 mm
**Capacity:** 1984 cc
**Maximum power:** 125 bhp
**Transmission:** four- or five-speed manual gearbox, optional three-speed automatic transmission; rear-wheel drive
**Chassis:** steel unitary construction body/chassis
**Suspension:** independent with MacPherson struts, lower wishbones and anti-roll bar front; semi-trailing arms and coil springs rear
**Brakes:** discs front, drums rear
**Bodywork:** steel 2+2 hatchback coupé
**Maximum speed (approx):** 126 mph (203 km/h)

*Above: It was the 924's neutral handling rather than its outright power which suited it for racing.*

*Below: The original 924 of 1975 was powered by a two-litre engine producing 125 bhp, giving 126 mph.*

# Porsche 928 1977–95

Early in the 1970s Porsche decided that it needed to develop a replacement for the 911 model. After a lot of contemplation, internal corporate breast-beating, and technical analysis the post-Ferry Porsche regime elected to make a complete change. The result was the 928, which was completely different from the 911 in every way.

To begin with, it was front-engined and had a water-cooled V8 engine rather than the 911's air-cooled flat-six. The car first appeared in 1977, and although the rear-engined 911 continued alongside it, at that time Porsche managers forecast that the 928 would eventually take over completely as customers deserted the 911, which by that time was a very old design indeed.

Things never worked out that way. The customers, it seemed, always saw the 928 as a completely different type of Porsche, and demand for the 911 stayed stubbornly high. Even from its early years it was the 928 which struggled to stay alive, and by the end of the 1980s very few were being built; a less proud management would have killed it off years earlier.

Even so, the 928 was (and still remains) an excellent supercar, for it was very fast, very safe, very reliable, and very well-engineered. Its style – rounded and, in spite of the badging, rather anonymous – was much less assertive than that of the 911, but it had a more spacious and practical four-seater interior.

*Below: The larger and more luxurious 928 was intended as a replacement for the 911 but lacked that model's popularity.*

*Above: Like the 924 before it, the 928 was front-engined with a rear-mounted transaxle.*

Although it shared its general layout – front-engined, rear-wheel-drive, rear-mounted transaxle, and a torque tube linking engine to transaxle – with the 924, technically everything was new and different. For the 928 there was a new hatchback structure, a new suspension layout, a V8 rather than inline four-cylinder engine, a new five-speed gearbox, and an optional automatic transmission 'borrowed' from Mercedes-Benz.

The big 928 was completely different in character from the 911. That doyen of all Porsche enthusiasts, Denis Jenkinson of *Motor Sport*, once commented that if you got each car into trouble on the road, the 911 washed its hands of the whole affair and left everything to the driver's skill, or lack of it, whereas the 928 effectively said: "Leave this to me, I'll sort myself out!"

Yet it seemed to be difficult for drivers to get enthusiastic about the 928. It was so capable, so secure, so thoroughly competent, that the character was almost dull – remarkable considering the top speed of every 928 was more than 140 mph.

Over the years 928 engines were enlarged, peak power was increased, the performance became even more stupendous, and the general reputation of the car held up well, yet after the early years sales only stumbled along. In the USA especially, very high prices ensured that sales were low.

Even so, the 928 S succeeded the 928, and S2, S3 (USA only), S4, GT and GTS versions all followed. Although 17,710

original-type 928s were built, production then fell away. Each and every car was a limited-production machine – by the late 1980s fewer than 1,000 a year – but each one was a technical masterpiece.

## Porsche 928 variants

### Porsche 928 S
The 928 S, introduced in 1979, was a direct development of the original 928, with an enlarged 97-mm × 78.9-mm, 300-bhp/4664-cc engine. The approximate top speed was 152 mph.

### Porsche 928 S2
From 1983 the 928 S became the 928 S2. A new type of fuel injection (Bosch LH-Jetronic) was featured and peak power rose to 310 bhp, while a new four-speed Mercedes-Benz automatic transmisssion became optional. ABS braking was standardised.

### Porsche 928 S3
For sale only in the USA, the unofficial (in other words, it was not badged as such) '928 S3' was produced for 1985 and 1986. This had a four-valve, quad-cam 4.7-litre V8 with 292 bhp.

### Porsche 928 S4
The 928 S4 took over from 1986 to 1991, complete with a 100-mm × 78.9-mm, 4957-cc engine producing 320 bhp, and a top speed of 160 mph.

### Porsche 928 GT
The 928 GT was a 330-bhp, manual-transmission-only version of the 928 S4.

### Porsche 928 GTS
For 1992 Porsche introduced the 928 GTS, complete with a 100-mm × 85.9-mm, 5397-cc version of the quad-cam V8 producing 340 bhp, and a claimed top speed of 171 mph.

## Specification (1977 928)

**Engine:** V8, single overhead camshaft per bank of cylinders
**Bore × stroke:** 95 mm × 78.9 mm
**Capacity:** 4474 cc
**Maximum power:** 240 bhp
**Transmission:** five-speed manual gearbox or three-speed automatic transmission, rear-wheel drive
**Chassis:** steel unitary construction body/chassis
**Suspension:** independent with MacPherson struts, lower wishbones and anti-roll bar front; 'Weissach' rear axle with semi-trailing arms and transverse torsion bars
**Brakes:** discs all round
**Bodywork:** steel 2+2 hatchback coupé
**Maximum speed (approx):** 142 mph (229 km/h)

*Below: The 928 was continuously improved; this is a 1987 S4, capable of 160 mph and 0-60 mph acceleration in 6.3 seconds.*

## Porsche 924 Turbo and 924 Carrera GT/GTS 1978-82

Only two years after deliveries of 924s began, Porsche revealed a much more exciting derivative, the 924 Turbo, which had 170 bhp and a top speed of 142 mph. Almost at a stroke this dealt with every criticism of the original 924 – it was faster, more specialised, and more sporting – yet because of its higher price it did not sell in similar quantities.

It was typical of Porsche that the engineers were allowed to improve not just the engine, but every aspect of the 924's layout. The engine was a lot more powerful – 170 bhp instead of 125 bhp – and it was complemented by a new Porsche five-speed gearbox ahead of the final drive (instead of an Audi gearbox behind it), and a stronger clutch and

*Above: The 142-mph 924 Turbo could be distinguished by its wheels; the Carrera GTS (right), with its flared arches, was far easier to spot.*

driveshafts. Instead of the 924's disc-and-drum system the 924 Turbo had four-wheel disc brakes, accommodated in larger-diameter wheels.

Not only was there a new spoiler surrounding the rear hatchback, but there were extra air intakes at the front and – most importantly – a prominent air intake duct in the bonnet panel to feed more cold air into the engine bay.

To many critics the 924 Turbo was what the 924 should always have been, and road-testers soon confirmed that it

was a much faster and more capable car than the original model. It was, however, much more expensive than the normally-aspirated 924, which remained in production, so sales were limited to about 3,000 units a year worldwide.

The Carrera GT version of 1980 was nothing more than a 'homologation special', of which only 406 were produced, intended for use in Group 4 racing. It was important, however, because it also introduced the idea of flared wheel arches to the 924 body shell, a feature which would be carried over to the next new Porsche, the 944.

By 1981 the 924 Turbo had been improved yet again, with a 'second-generation' engine developing 177 bhp, but as stories about a forthcoming 944 model spread it became clear that this was just an interim car. While the 944 prospered, the 924 Turbo was discontinued after 12,365 of the cars had been produced in five years.

### Porsche 924 Turbo variants

#### Porsche 924 Carrera GT and GTS
The limited-production 924 Carrera GT

(only 406 cars were built) was available in 1980. This car was based on the 924 Turbo but, with 210 bhp, it had rather more power. The top speed was 150 mph.

The Carrera GTS (59 cars made in 1981) was an evolution version of the Carrera GT, and had 245 bhp.

### Specification (1978 924 Turbo)
**Engine:** inline four-cylinder, single overhead camshaft
**Bore × stroke:** 86.5 mm × 84.4 mm
**Capacity:** 1984 cc
**Maximum power:** 170 bhp (177 bhp from mid-1980)
**Transmission:** five-speed manual gearbox, rear-wheel drive
**Chassis:** steel unitary construction body/chassis
**Suspension:** independent with MacPherson struts, lower wishbones and anti-roll bar front; semi-trailing arms, transverse torsion bars and anti-roll bar rear
**Brakes:** discs all round
**Bodywork:** steel 2+2 hatchback coupé
**Maximum speed (approx):** 142 mph (229 km/h)

*Above: By 1982 the 924 Turbo had 177 bhp (a far cry from the first 924 with only 125 bhp), enough to yield a top speed of over 140 mph.*

*Below: The flared wheel arches of the 924 Carrera GTS provided the inspiration for the later 944. Power output was 245 bhp.*

# Porsche 944 1981-91

Soon after the original 924 went on sale, Porsche began to plan an important new version. This, coded 944 by Porsche, would have an entirely new type of four-cylinder engine, and feature other major changes.

The 944 story really starts with the V8 engine of the 928 model, for Porsche's new four-cylinder engine was effectively one half of this, although such descriptions are always simplistic. The V8 was a 90-degree aluminium single-cam design. The four-cylinder engine used the same cylinder head, valve gear and the same design of pistons and connecting rods. Because its displacement, at 2.5 litres, was large, it also used a 'Lanchester' type of balancer shaft to make it smoother and more refined. Whereas the original V8 had a bore and stroke of 95 mm × 78.9 mm, the new 944's engine measured 100 mm × 78.9 mm.

Porsche took a big gamble by introducing a new model based on the 924; even in 1981, when the 944 made its bow, the 924 was still being criticised for not being 'a real Porsche'. The 944, however, took care of every criticism, for here was a car which had its own dedicated engine, much-modified styling, and real Porsche-type performance.

Porsche customers were convinced, and began ordering 944s in large numbers. The style – really a flared-wheel-arch version of the 924 coupé, like the 924 Carrera GT but much tidier in detail, gave the car a much more aggressive stance, and no-one complained about the performance.

Although it was not a totally refined car to drive – the problem of transmitted road noise into the cabin was never really solved – the 944 was an extremely practical, fast and enjoyable machine which many people could, and did, use for everyday transport. Athough it was not a full four-seater, it was a very practical machine whose cross-country ability was peerless.

As the 1980s progressed Porsche carried on persistently improving the car. Power steering became optional for 1984 and was standardised a year later, a new fascia arrived in 1985, ABS braking was offered for 1987, and for the final year ABS was standardised along with a larger engine with a bore and stroke of 104 mm × 78.9 mm and a displacement of 2681 cc; that was sufficient to generate 165 bhp.

The 944 S and 944 S2 were final derivatives of this long-lived and successful design, both of them having four-valve twin-overhead-cam cylinder heads, and from 1989 a cabriolet version of the S2 went into production. Nevertheless by this time sales were sagging – 924 production had reached 27,460 in 1985, yet by 1990 total four-cylinder Porsche sales had dropped dramatically, to below the 10,000 mark.

In an ideal world, with unlimited capital and resources available, Porsche would then have introduced a brand-new model; but since both were re-stricted, the replacement for the 944, unveiled in 1991, was a much-modified version called the 968.

## Porsche 944 variants

### Porsche 944 S

The 944 S was introduced in 1986 and built until 1990, and had a 2990-cc twin-overhead-cam cylinder head with four valves per cylinder. Peak power was 190 bhp, and automatic transmission was not available.

### Porsche 944 S2

The 944 S2 arrived in 1988, and was built until 1991, and was a direct development of the 944 S, with a 104-mm × 88-mm engine of 2990 cc giving 211 bhp and a top speed of 146 mph. A cabriolet version was also available from 1989.

*Above: In an attempt to widen the 944's appeal, Porsche introduced a drop-head version in 1989.*

### Specification (1981 944)

**Engine:** inline four-cylinder, single overhead camshaft
**Bore × stroke:** 100 mm × 78.9 mm
**Capacity:** 2479 cc
**Maximum power:** 160 bhp
**Transmission:** five-speed manual gearbox or three-speed automatic transmission, rear-wheel drive
**Chassis:** steel unitary construction body/chassis
**Suspension:** independent with MacPherson struts, lower wishbones and anti-roll bar front; semi-trailing arms, transverse torsion bars and anti-roll bar rear
**Brakes:** discs all round
**Bodywork:** steel 2+2 hatchback coupé
**Maximum speed (approx):** 137 mph (220 km/h)

*Below: The 944 was basically a grown-up version of the 924, with a larger, 2479-cc, four-cylinder engine which could almost be considered as half the 928's V8.*

# Porsche 944 Turbo 1985-91

Although Porsche has sometimes been called stubborn, and sometimes too inward-looking in its designing, it has built up a formidable reputation for getting the best out of its models. The 944 Turbo was a perfect example. It failed, however, in one respect – Professor Fuhrmann, Porsche's chief executive, hoped that it would finally oust the 911 (something the 928 had failed to do), but the rugged old rear-engined car stubbornly refused to die!

The transformation, from the original 160-bhp 944 to the 220-bhp 944 Turbo, was done with complete success, the more powerful version being much faster, but equally as well-balanced as the original. Except that it was visually similar to the 924, the 944 Turbo was a supercar in every respect.

Not only did Porsche turbocharge the engine, lowering the compression ratio to 8.0:1 and increasing power initially to 220 bhp, but the engineers reworked every other part of the car to complete an integrated package. Compared with the normal 944, the clutch was larger, the gearbox stronger, and the crownwheel and pinion stronger. The suspension had been reworked, while new brakes with optional ABS, and new alloy road wheels, were fitted.

Not only did the Turbo have a different front end, with more slots to allow extra air into the engine bay, and a larger rear spoiler, but it also had side skirts and a flush-bonded windscreen. Under the car, attempts were made to manage the airflow, and there was a discreet but effective diffuser beneath the tail which helped to promote rear downforce. Inside the car there was a completely new and curvaceous dashboard layout, which would eventually be applied to other 944 models. In 1988 the Turbo's power output was increased to 250 bhp at 6,000 rpm,

*Right: The fast 944 Turbo was to become the basis of the successful German Turbo Cup race series.*

with 258 lb ft of torque being available.

Although the 944 was another expensive Porsche – it cost more, in every market, than the normally-aspirated 911s of the day – it sold steadily. Later models, with the 250-bhp engines first blooded in the Turbo Cup racing series, were even better, faster, more solidly engineered and capable.

The 16-valve twin-cam engine (as seen on 944 S and 944 S2 models) was never turbocharged, and in 1991 all the 944 range was replaced by one new type derived from it – the normally-aspirated three-litre 968 model.

## Specification (1985)

**Engine:** inline four-cylinder, single overhead camshaft
**Bore × stroke:** 100 mm × 78.9 mm
**Capacity:** 2479 cc
**Maximum power:** 220 bhp
**Transmission:** five-speed manual gearbox, rear-wheel drive
**Chassis:** steel unitary construction body/chassis
**Suspension:** independent with MacPherson struts, lower wishbones and anti-roll bar front; semi-trailing arms and coil springs rear
**Brakes:** discs all round
**Bodywork:** steel 2+2 hatchback coupé
**Maximum speed (approx):** 157 mph (253 km/h)

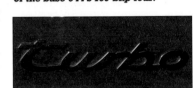

*Below: Eventually offering 250 bhp, the 944 Turbo had a reworked version of the base 944's 160-bhp four.*

*Below: The Turbo's restrained interior layout was destined to be featured in later 944 variants. The horizontally-spoked wheel allowed a perfect view of the instruments.*

*Above: The original 944 Turbo used a water-cooled KKK turbocharger, which helped produce 220 bhp.*

*Below: Revamped bodywork of the Turbo was cleaner, intended to be more aerodynamic than the first 944.*

# Porsche 959 1986-88

*Right: The ultimate luxury race car for the road. Only 200 of Porsche's 450-bhp 959 dream machines were made in a homologation exercise.*

Early in the 1980s motorsport's governing body, FISA, introduced a new category – Group B – for which manufacturers were only obliged to build 200 cars to satisfy homologation requirements. Technically there was a great deal of freedom to exploit the regulations, and before long several manufacturers began to develop new cars. Porsche's project was the four-wheel-drive 959.

The first four-wheel-drive Porsche prototype was shown in 1981, but this was little more than a 911 Convertible mock-up. The true *Gruppe B* prototype – soon to become known by its project number, 959 – was unveiled in 1983.

Most other Group B cars were relatively underdeveloped vehicles – poor road cars but potentially excellent competition cars – but it was typical of Porsche that the 959 was not only the most powerful Group B car of all, but also a thoroughly developed, extremely well-built and comprehensively-equipped machine.

Superficially the 959 looked to be yet another version of the evergreen 911, but although it used some elements of that model's body structure, and the same engine location, the rest of the car was almost brand-new. The engine was a form of the latest turbocharged racing flat-six (as used in the 956/962 racing cars), complete with water-cooled four-valve, twin-cam cylinder heads. A six-speed gearbox and four-wheel drive were standard, with very sophisticated control systems, and the coil-spring/wishbone suspension was utterly different from anything previously seen on a Porsche road car.

Although development cars, of increasing complexity, were used to win the Paris–Dakar Rallies of 1984 and 1986,

*Below: The 959's racing-style suspension and bodywork was designed to give the car zero lift at 200 mph, with a drag coefficient of 0.32.*

the 'Evolution' version of the 959 (with type number 961) was endlessly delayed. Production of the 959 was so late in starting that deliveries did not actually begin until *after* FISA had killed off the Group B rallying category for which the car had been developed, and since no other carmaker was interested in Group B racing the whole *raison d'être* of the 959 evaporated.

Porsche, however, produced all 200 road cars, complete with 450 bhp and a top speed of 190 mph, for which production tooling and components, had been prepared, the result being that a few lucky Porsche enthusiasts enjoyed the fabulous performance and charisma of this magnificent machine.

Only they, and a very few fortunate motoring writers, have ever experienced the phenomenal combination of straight-line performance, traction, handling and sheer capability which was built into the 959. There is little doubt that this was – and in some people's eyes, still is – the best Porsche ever to go on sale.

*Above: The 959's 450-bhp intercooled twin-turbocharged racing flat-six used a six-speed gearbox coupled with a four-wheel-drive system. With a top road speed of approximately 190 mph, this was not a car for beginners . . .*

## Porsche 959 variants

### Porsche 961

The 'Evolution' 959, the 961, was developed purely as a competition car, a considerably lighter and more powerful (but dramatically less refined) version. When fully-prepared, its 2.8-litre engine could produce between 650 and 700 bhp, and the cars weighed about 661 lb less than the road version.

## Specification (1986)

**Engine:** flat-six, twin overhead camshafts per bank of cylinders
**Bore × stroke:** 95 mm × 67 mm
**Capacity:** 2851 cc
**Maximum power:** 450 bhp
**Transmission:** six-speed manual gearbox, four-wheel drive
**Chassis:** steel unitary construction body/chassis with aluminium and composite panels
**Suspension:** independent with upper and lower wishbones, coil springs and telescopic dampers front and rear; electronic height control
**Brakes:** discs all round
**Bodywork:** steel, aluminium and composite 2+2 coupé
**Maximum speed (approx):** 190 mph (306 km/h)

# Porsche 911 Carrera 2 and Carrera 4 1988–98

Looking back, it's easy to brand Porsche's management as extraordinarily stubborn. In 1963, against all trends, it made the 911 rear-engined, and for more than 20 years it turned a deaf ear to criticism of that car's handling and stability. Even when the replacements for the 911 were announced, they were *still* rear-engined, and still looked like 911s.

Using the project code 964, Porsche developed a new type of flat-six rear-engined car, one with a similar rearward bias to the old, but with an almost entirely new structure, floorpan, suspension, aerodynamic package and – most important – the choice of two-wheel drive (Carrera 2) or four-wheel drive (Carrera 4). Although the new car fed on the shape and layout of the old 911 for its inspiration, only 15 per cent of the older model's components – mainly body items – were carried over unchanged.

*Right: Although based on the 911, handling was spectacularly improved using coil springs instead of torsion bars, ABS brakes and, in the Carrera 4, four-wheel drive. The Carrera 2 had two-wheel drive, and was thus lighter than the 4.*

The new car looked similar to the old, except that the detailing of the front and rear ends was smoother than before. The rear spoiler was retractable, not fixed, the bumpers were more integrated, and the drag coefficient had been reduced to a respectable 0.32. The cabin looked familiar to previous 911 owners, but there were many new details and, at last, there was a satisfactory heater/air-conditioning system.

The flat-six engine appeared unchanged, but was much revised – 3.6 litres instead of 3.2 – although still air-

cooled. The four-wheel drive fitted to the Carrera 4 was a simplified and modernised version of that used in the 959 'homologation special', with electronically-sensed anti-slip and torque-transfer arrangements. The major improvement, though, was to the suspension, where coil springs replaced torsion bars all round, and where there was a new type of semi-trailing-link layout at the rear.

Both the Carrera 2 and Carrera 4 handled a lot better than the old type 911 had ever done, although there was strong understeer (particularly with four-wheel drive). There was ABS braking for the first time, and because the enlarged engine was very smooth and torquey it made the new car extremely easy to drive fast, without any drama. The Carrera 2 was actually slightly faster than the Carrera 4 (if only by a couple of miles per hour) as it was around 170 lb lighter and was not burdened by the extra mechanical losses of the Carrera 4's four-wheel-drive transmission.

Thus redesigned, the 911 faced the 1990s with confidence. But would the customers continue to buy a new car which looked so much like the old? In the early 1990s the 911 still accounted for many of Porsche's sales. Then new models appeared in 1998 with updated bodywork based on the Boxster's front end, with larger water-cooled engines.

*Above: As much as 250 bhp came from the familiar air-cooled 3.6-litre flat-six; the Carrera 2's top speed was 158 mph.*

*Below: The 911 Carrera used many of the existing 911's body panels. More radical changes beneath the skin took it into the 1990s.*

## Porsche 911 Carrera 2 variants

### Porsche RS Lightweight

The RS Lightweight was a stripped-out version of the Carrera 2, intended for use on the racetrack, and was mechanically identical to the Carrera 2, though almost all refinement had been lost. Peak power was boosted to 260 bhp, weight was down by 10 per cent, and the top speed was slightly higher, at 161 mph.

### Specification (1988 Carrera 2)

**Engine:** flat-six, single overhead camshaft per bank of cylinders
**Bore × stroke:** 100 mm × 76.4 mm
**Capacity:** 3600 cc
**Maximum power:** 250 bhp
**Transmission:** five-speed manual gearbox or four-speed automatic transmission, rear-wheel drive
**Chassis:** steel unitary construction body/chassis
**Suspension:** independent with MacPherson struts, lower wishbones and anti-roll bar front; semi-trailing arms with coil springs and anti-roll bar rear
**Brakes:** discs all round
**Bodywork:** steel 2+2 hatchback coupé Targa convertible coupé or cabriolet
**Maximum speed (approx):** 158 mph (254 km/h)

## Porsche 911 Turbo 1991-present

*Left and below: Replacing the old, muscular 911 Turbo and its many racing variants, the 1991 Porsche 911 Turbo had a restyled body, with a smoother outline closely resembling the Carrera 2 and 4, and a distinctive fixed rear spoiler.*

ess than a year after the much-loved, ut also much-feared old-style 911 Turbo isappeared from the range, Porsche repared to launch a new version. The ast of the old type had commanded high rices from collectors, who were then ade to look very foolish when a new-eneration car was introduced.

Like the Carrera 2/Carrera 4 models, e 1990s-generation 911 Turbo was a ompletely redeveloped statement of e theme. It was, in fact, exactly the car hich might have been expected, for it ombined an uprated version of the old 11 Turbo's engine, with the new and moother body style of the Carrera Carrera 4, the new underpan and sus-ension of those cars, and with – for the rst time – a five-speed gearbox. In addi-

tion to having a welcome extra ratio (which gave a relaxed 27.8 mph per 1,000 rpm), the new change was also far smoother and more precise than before.

Like the old 911 Turbo, the new car was astonishingly fast. Because the drag coefficient had been reduced and engine power increased, top speed had risen to an astonishing 167 mph, and the 0-100 mph sprint took a mere 11.4 seconds. In fact anywhere you looked along its acceleration graph, the new Turbo was tremendously fast. In third gear it would rocket from 40 to 60 mph in 3.5 seconds, from 50 to 70 in 3.1 seconds, 60 to 80 in 3.0 seconds and 70 to 90 in 3.1 seconds. There was also incredible acceleration in fourth, with the 100-120 mph increment taking just 5.0 seconds and 110-130 a mere 6.0 seconds. Not even the famous Ferrari Testarossa was as quick – and the Porsche, remember, was

almost a four-seater, with every modern feature which Porsche could devise, in-cluding ABS braking, and radically better roadholding than ever before, thanks to revisions to the MacPherson-strut front/semi-trailing-arm rear suspen-sion that included the incorporation of some passive rear-wheel steer.

Distinguishing the new 911 Turbo from the old was easy, for the 1991 model had the new-style body, complete with smoothed-out front and rear bumpers, there was a new type of fixed rear spoiler (Carrera 2 and 4 models featured a retractable spoiler), and a new style of 17-in alloy wheels. Curiously, at a time when other supercar makers were dab-bling with four-wheel drive, and Porsche already had a perfectly viable system, the new 911 Turbo was still only rear-wheel-driven. Nevertheless, although British Porsche enthusiasts were asked

to pay a huge £78,110, a queue quickly grew. The recession soon dulled demand, however, and the price had fal-len to a still high £72,294 by early 1993.

The new 911 Turbo or 993 as it was designated, was rated the word's best all-weather supercar, and would set you back £97,980 in 1999.

### Specification (1991)

**Engine:** flat-six, single overhead camshaft per bank of cylinders
**Bore × stroke:** 97 mm × 74 mm
**Capacity:** 3299 cc
**Maximum power:** 320 bhp
**Transmission:** five-speed manual gearbox, rear-wheel drive
**Chassis:** steel unitary construction body/chassis
**Suspension:** independent with MacPherson struts, lower wishbones and anti-roll bar front; semi-trailing arms with coil springs and anti-roll bar rear
**Brakes:** discs all round
**Bodywork:** steel 2+2 coupé
**Maximum speed (approx):** 167 mph (269 km/h)

*bove: Even with a price tag of 78,110 when introduced in the UK, here was soon a queue for the new orsche 911 Turbo.*

*ight: Capable of 0-100 mph in 11.4 econds, the four-seater Porsche 911 urbo was quicker than a Ferrari estarossa. The 911 Turbo also ported ABS brakes, advanced uspension and a five-speed gearbox. ut, of course, it remained a rear-heel-drive car.*

## Porsche 968 1991–95

By the early 1990s Porsche's business was in deep trouble. Strategy after strategy had been changed, new model after new model had been proposed, then cancelled, and sales continued to fall. The result was that a 1991 release, billed as the new 968 model, was really no more than a third-generation 944, and the design could be traced right back to that of the VW-Audi-based Porsche 924 of the mid-1970s.

The new 968 retained all the best features of the 944 Series 2 it replaced, but introduced major modifications to the three-litre four-cylinder engine, and was built with a different and more rounded front and rear body style. Under the skin the structure was the same as before, which meant that there was still 2+2 accommodation and a versatile but compact hatchback cabin.

Head-on, the 968 looked much like the 928, for it had laid-back, exposed headlamps (which flipped up when in use) and a very smooth aspect. At the rear there were new, carefully-detailed, tail-lamps, a new type of transverse spoiler, and carefully-integrated bumpers. The 968, in fact, was probably the ultimate expression of what Porsche could do with this front-engined chassis.

Development work on the familiar slant-four engine in three-litre form had led to a 240-bhp output, which compared well with the 250 bhp produced by the latest (and larger) 3.6-litre air-cooled flat-six used in the 911. The new engine gave this compact car a top speed of no less than 153 mph, along with extremely creditable fuel efficiency. Porsche's latest feature in the twin-cam cylinder head was a device called VarioCam, which could not only alter the inlet camshaft timing in the mid-rev band, but could also provide improved torque *and* reduced exhaust emissions. Because the 968 also had a new six-speed gearbox it was possible to get up to 24 mpg unless the car was driven very hard.

This was yet another meticulously developed Porsche, produced by the German company's celebrated method of taking almost infinite pains over every small detail of development. Porsche's problem, however, was not to convince customers of its performance and road-holding abilities, but that it was a new model and a better buy than new sports coupés from Japan, particularly the Mazda RX-7 and Mitsubishi 3000GT.

*Above: Launched in the depths of recession, with the survival of Porsche itself under threat, the long-awaited new Porsche – the 968 – turned out to be no more than a revamped 944, with design cues embedded in the 1970s.*

*Left: The smoothed-out rear was given a new transverse spoiler and integrated bumper, with tail-lamp detail, but beneath the shell there's still a 2 + 2 Porsche, along the lines of the old 944.*

*Below: In coupé or cabriolet form, the 968 has a 240-bhp inline four-cylinder twin-cam, using a six-speed gearbox. Porsche paid attention to the 1990s penchant for fuel economy; driven sympathetically, the 968 could achieve 24 mpg.*

### Specification (1991)

**Engine:** inline four-cylinder, twin overhead camshafts
**Bore × stroke:** 104 mm × 88 mm
**Capacity:** 2990 cc
**Maximum power:** 240 bhp
**Transmission:** six-speed manual gearbox or optional four-speed automatic transmission, rear-wheel drive
**Chassis:** steel unitary construction body/chassis
**Suspension:** independent with MacPherson struts, lower wishbones and anti-roll bar front; semi-trailing arms and transverse torsion bars rear
**Brakes:** discs all round
**Bodywork:** steel 2+2 hatchback coupé or cabriolet
**Maximum speed (approx):** 153 mph (246 km/h)

# 911 Carrera 4 1988-present

In 1999, Porsche's Model Range included three versions of the 911 and the Boxster. The most able, if not the most thrilling to drive, was the 911 Carrera 4, which continued the tradition of four-wheel-drive 911 models originating with the 959 in 1986. The first Carrera 4 appeared in 1988 with electronically controlled four-wheel drive, and production of the latest model began in October 1998. It was available in coupé and cabriolet guise, either with six-speed manual gearbox or five-speed Tiptronic S transmission. Engine and transmission were bolted together to form one unit, with double propshafts for permanent four-wheel drive relaying power to all four wheels. Permanent

four-wheel drive with variable power feed to the front axle was provided by a viscous clutch in the front differential. With the Carrera 4, dynamic aids like ABS anti-lock brakes, anti-spin control and the Automatic Brake Differential were somewhat taken for granted, as they were augmented with new PSM Porsche Stability Management, which controlled the car's lateral behaviour. PSM controlled driving stability in bends by intervening with the brakes as required, and influencing engine power regardless of the driver's input. This was a far cry indeed from the raw untamed wilfulness of the original 911.

The Carrera 4 was powered by the latest incarnation of the water-cooled flat-six, in 3.4-litre format, developing 300 bhp, and featuring an electronic accelerator pedal – E-Gas – incorporating a sensor that transmitted signals to the Motronic and operated the throttle butterfly for better engine response. The block and cylinder heads were made of aluminium and contained four overhead camshafts, four valves per cylinder, variable valve timing, hydraulic valve play compensation, a variable intake manifold, integrated dry sump lubrication, double-chamber exhaust system, two metal-based catalytic converters, two oxygen sensors with stereo control. The whole ensemble was monitored by DME (Digital Motor Electronics) engine management for the ignition and electronic injection, with solid-state distributor. Top speed was 174 mph (280 km/h).

All track control arms on the suspension and the two axle subframes inte-

*Above: The Carrera 4 in the late-'90s was based on the front half of the Boxster, and was a longer car as a result. The new water-cooled engine was as responsive as before, dispelling fears that the latest 911s were sanitised editions.*

grated in the body were made of light alloy. The front suspension consisted of MacPherson struts, track control arms, longitudinal arms and coil springs and twin-tube gas dampers, tuned to suit the four-wheel-drive by consistent adjustment of axle geometry and re-adjusted elasticity on the front axle to provide neutral behaviour all the way to extreme speeds. The rear was a multi-link design, with five track control arms, coil springs and monotube gas dampers. Brakes consisted of two-circuit, four-piston aluminium monobloc brake callipers on ventilated discs front and rear axle, with individual circuits per axle, and ABS fitted as standard. A rear spoiler automatically came out at speed, maintaining the 911's poise.

Apart from the full-size frontal airbags for the driver and front passenger, the

latest Side Impact Protection System (POSIP) was fitted as standard, protecting the driver and front passenger around the head, chest, arms and hips, even with the roof down and the side windows fully retracted. The 911 range could be specified with Litronic headlights, special gas-discharge units that illuminated the road ahead more brightly and when main beam was activated, the low-beam headlights remained switched on and moved their own beam up to further improve illumination.

The Carrera 4 could also be ordered with sports seats with reinforced side support, 18 inch turbo-look wheels, shod with 225/40 ZR 18 tyres at the front and 265/35 ZR 18 at the rear, and sports suspension with even firmer and shorter springs, harder dampers and reinforced anti-roll bars.

*Above: The cockpit of the Carrera 4 was an exciting environment, even though Porsche cut corners on interior fittings to save costs.*

# Porsche 911 Carrera coupé 1997-present

Launched at the 1997 Frankfurt Show, the Porsche 911 Carrera coupé used the same 3.4-litre water-cooled six-cylinder boxer engine as the Carrera 4, producing 300 bhp at 6,800 rpm, and six-speed gearbox or optional Tiptronic S transmission. The revised 911 shape had a drag coefficient of 0.30 Cd and weighed a low 1,320 kg unladen, making it one of the lightest cars in its segment. A cabriolet joined the range in spring 1998, and was technically identical to the 911 coupé, except that the bodyshell was particularly stiff and torsionally rigid. The soft-top opened and closed electro-hydraulically at the touch of a button in 20 seconds. It was also available with an aluminium hardtop.

### Specification (Carrera 4)

**Engine:** flat-six
**Bore** x **stroke:** 96 mm x 78 mm
**Capacity:** 3387 cc
**Suspension:** independent front by spring strut axle, track control arms, springs and dampers; multi-link rear with track control arms, springs and dampers
**Brakes:** ventilated discs all round, with two-circuit system, four-piston callipers, ABS and PSM
**Chassis:** galvanised monocoque
**Body:** two-door coupé

*Above: The 1999 Carrera Coupé only served to confirm that the 911 was still the sensible supercar, due to its tactile qualities, aural delights, and classic looks. There was still plenty of magic in the chassis, and traction control, manual transmission and uprated suspension came with the optional sport pack.*

## Porsche Boxster 1996-present

The Boxster was launched in 1996, and in terms of Porsche production cars it was the first mid-engined model since the 914/6 of the late 1960s. Indeed, the very first 356/1 prototype built at Gmünd had its engine in the middle, and the sports racing 550 Spyder followed this principle. Whereas the 911's rear engine location concentrated its weight at the tail, the Boxster's was centralised. Based on an all-steel monocoque shell with galvanised panels, the sleek shape had drag coefficient of 0.31 Cd. It was powered by the 2.5-litre flat-six engine with aluminium crankcase and cylinder head, with four overhead camshafts, four valves per cylinder, and water-cooling and dry sump lubrication. Compression ratio was 11:1, and it produced 204 bhp at 6,000 rpm. Five-speed transmission could be either manual or Tiptronic S, and this option worked in automatic and manual modes, shifting gears in the latter case by means of buttons on the steering wheel. The engine and transmission were bolted together to form one unit, with double drive shafts to the rear wheels. Suspension was by MacPherson struts, aluminium longitudinal and track control arms, and conical springs offset from the dampers. At the rear were MacPherson struts with aluminium longitudinal and track control arms plus tie-rod, and coil springs arranged off-centre from the dampers. The Boxster had an hydraulic/mechani-

cal twin-circuit brake system, with innervented brake discs front and rear. ABS was fitted as standard, with traction control optional, switching to automatic brake differential (ABD) if required.

A number of special features and accessories were available, including sports seats with greater side supports, sports suspension with firmer and shorter springs, harder dampers and reinforced anti-roll bars. Apart from standard 17-inch wheels with tyres measuring 205/50 ZR 17 and 255/40 ZR 17, the Boxster was also available with 18-inch turbo-look wheels, with similar tyre sizes as the 911 Carrera, 225/40 ZR 18 and 265/35 ZR 18.

The Boxster had two luggage compartments, providing 9.1 cu ft carrying capacity. Two front airbags were standard, while side airbags were optional, but steel piping in the windscreen frame and two roll-over bars behind the seats gave a certain amount of protection. The electric roof of the Boxster opened and closed faster than any other roof in the market, at 12 seconds. In 1999 the Boxster was given the same fuel tank as the 911 with 64 litres or 14.1 Imp gallons capacity.

*Above: Launched in 1996, the Boxster was to be the basis for all future Porsche models. Unlike the 911 though, its water-cooled 2.5-litre flat-six engine was mounted amidships, and though in theory this made its handling more predictable than its wayward ancestors, in truth, Porsche had the tail-happy characteristics well tamed by the late 1990s.*

*Above: The basic Boxster has an electric soft-top; lightweight aluminium hardtop is extra. Other cost-options include Tiptronic gearbox, traction control, cruise control, climate control, leather upholstery, and Sport Pack.*

### Specification

**Engine:** flat-six
**Bore x stroke:** 85.5 mm x 72 mm
**Capacity:** 2480 cc
**Suspension:** independent front by spring strut axle, aluminium track

control arms, springs and dampers; multi-link rear with track control arms, tie rod, spring struts, coil springs and dampers
**Brakes:** ventilated discs all round, with

two-circuit hydraulic/mechanical system, four-piston callipers, ABS, optional traction control
**Chassis:** galvanised monocoque
**Body:** two-door two-seat roadster

# Railton Cars

**A**lthough the Railton of the 1930s looked superficially like a traditional British make, this was an illusion caused by the styling. It was actually the first of what a noted historian later called the "Anglo-American sports bastards". The Railton, like several later makes such as Jensen, Bristol and Iso, combined European styling with North American engineering.

The Railton came from the same stable as the Invicta, rising to fame as that company died away. Like the original Invictas, the Railton was built at The Fairmile, Cobham, south-west of London. The first Railton was launched in 1933, although the last pre-war Invicta was built in another factory, in London, in 1935.

Noel Macklin and L. A. Cushman invented the Railton by combining cheap North American running gear with traditional-looking British bodywork and styling; the famous racing-car designer Reid Railton was also involved, although his contribution was minimal. To create the cars, they chose Hudson rolling chassis, contracted out body production to specialists such as Ranelagh and Coachcraft, hired Railton to help carry out the limited number of running changes, and applied his famous name to the finished product.

Even though the Hudson chassis was a conventional Detroit product – its straight-eight engine was a side-valve unit with crude splash-type lubrication for its crankshaft, and there was only a three-speed gearbox – Railton lowered it a little, stiffened the suspension with European Hartford shock absorbers, and offered it with styling which owed much to Invicta themes.

Railton made its debut at the Olympia Show in October 1933, when the cars were priced at a remarkably reasonable £499 (one had to pay £795 for the equivalent Lagonda, or £875 for a 4½-litre Invicta), and in 1934 the company sold a respectable total of 224 cars. In the first year many influential Britons had been dismissive about the idea of hiding American chassis under another name, but by 1935 word of the cars' superb and flexible performance had got round, and 377 chassis left the Cobham works. A further 308 cars, at higher prices, were sold in 1936.

The Light Sports of 1935 made headlines – it was certainly the fastest-accelerating car of its day – but very few were sold, for this was really an aberration. By 1936 Railton was beginning to move towards the traditional

*Above: Railton's most exciting, but most short-lived, car. The 100-mph Light Sports tourer had two seats and the minimum of bodywork. Only a handful were built despite the great publicity generated by the model.*

end of the market, building heavier cars on longer-wheelbase chassis, with more sumptuous coachwork. From 1937 there was an attempt to go down-market with the 2.7-litre Hudson Six chassis, which failed, for only 81 were sold, while the so-called Railton 10 of 1938 and 1939 was no more than a rebodied Standard Flying Ten, which could only achieve an absolute maximum of a hardly sporting 68 mph.

By 1938 Macklin was tiring of the Railton project, in favour of military work on the Fairmile patrol boat. After World War II Hudson took over the production rights, but only 12 cars, built from pre-war parts, were built. The last Railton of all was made in 1948, by which time 1,460 Hudson-engined chassis, and 51 Standard 'miniatures', had been produced.

*Below: The 1936 Railton had an American engine and running gear, with British bodywork. The famous designer Reid Railton lowered the chassis, stiffened the suspension and used traditional English styling.*

# Railton Eight 1933-39

Above: The 1935 Railton Ranelagh saloon. This car had the Hudson inline-eight, with Railton's modified Hudson chassis and bodywork by specialist Ranelagh.

The original Railton was actually previewed as a Railton-Terraplane, for it was directly descended from the American Essex Terraplane, a marque invented by Hudson. The definitive Railton, therefore, used a modified chassis from that American marque, complete with a lazy, low-revving, straight-eight cylinder engine, backed by a three-speed gearbox.

Railton's own modifications produced a chassis which rode and handled in a much firmer way than the original American example, helped by the use of friction-type shock absorbers which could be adjusted from the driver's seat.

Although the original cars looked sporting, in the Invicta manner (complete with rivetted edges to the bonnet panels), their character was completely different. In British sports cars of the period, it was normal to use the indirect gears a lot to extract the best performance; with the Railton, the combination of a torquey eight-cylinder engine and a wide-ratio three-speed gearbox meant a different approach.

Testers were ecstatic, The Autocar stating that "It is the absolute silence and absence of any suggestion of machinery that is so impressive in this car . . .", and claiming that the car was "10 years ahead of its time". Even allowing for the 1930s journalist's love of hyperbole, this was a remarkable tribute for a car which had been developed very rapidly and astonishingly easily.

Right: A straight-eight Hudson-engined 1937 Railton with long wheelbase and Carrington body. The low-revving engine, backed by a three-speed gearbox, resulted in quiet motoring with more than adequate performance.

Early cars had a 4010-cc engine, but this was soon enlarged to 4168 cc, which was then used until 1939. Top speeds, depending on the bodywork chosen, were up to 90 mph, which was excellent for the period, and 0-60 mph acceleration in 10 seconds was outstanding. Railton never mentioned fuel consumption, which was awful – 12-16 mpg was the best that could be expected. That was because, in truth, the engine was a very crude affair. Naturally it was a long-stroke design, with a cast-iron block and head. Designed in 1930, both inlet and exhaust valves were side- rather than overhead-mounted, and the unit's performance resulted from its excellent torque output rather than its mundane maximum power of 113 bhp. Nevertheless, the

Above: The 1936 Hudson engine was a 124-bhp inline-eight with splash-type crank lubrication.

engine was well thought of by Railton customers and in the USA, where it stayed in production until 1954 before being replaced by an overhead-valve unit.

Until 1936 the Railtons competed for the same market which Alvis and Lagonda were already supplying, but after that the design was shifted subtly up-market. Wheelbases were lengthened, heavier and more spacious coachwork was offered, and prices were raised. These were the years in which the customer could specify a tourer, drop-head coupé, saloon or a limousine, ringing any of the 'personalising' changes he might desire.

Each and every Railton Eight had a wide-ratio three-speed gearbox, and a very few were built with Hudson divided-axle independent front suspension. In character they were totally different from their all-British competitors, which may explain why they were never totally accepted. Nevertheless, a sufficient section of the car-buying public was converted, and total production of Eights between 1933 and 1939 was 1,379.

## Specification (1935)

**Engine:** inline eight-cylinder, side-valve

**Bore × stroke:** 76.2 mm × 114.3 mm

**Capacity:** 4168 cc

**Maximum power:** 113 bhp

**Transmission:** three-speed manual gearbox, rear-wheel drive

**Chassis:** separate steel frame with channel-section side members and cruciform bracing

**Suspension:** non-independent with beam axle and semi-elliptic leaf springs front; live axle with semi-elliptic leaf springs rear

**Brakes:** drums all round

**Bodywork:** choice of wood-framed, aluminium-panelled, four- or five-seaters; open or closed tourer, saloon, coupé and limousine

**Maximum speed (approx):** 88 mph (142 km/h), depending on coachwork

# Railton Light Sports 1935

valve eight-cylinder engine and a three-speed gearbox was not very sporting in character. Perhaps this was why *The Autocar's* report emphasised the "soft" nature of the engine, and pointed out that "the car can attain a performance on top gear which rather resembles that which might be attributed to the ideal steam car . . . the absence of need for gear-changing does not detract from the interest . . ."

Even though the Light Sports was spectacular in the extreme – a famous picture showed the test car leaping a distance of 35 feet at the top of the Brooklands test hill – it died soon after birth. Reputedly only two genuine cars were produced, but several seem to have been 'created' since then.

*Left: The spectacular two-seater Light Sports Railton did not sell well, despite its unrivalled performance.*

## Specification (1935)

**Engine:** inline eight-cylinder, side-valve

**Bore × stroke:** 76.2 mm × 114.3 mm

**Capacity:** 4168 cc

**Maximum power:** 113 bhp

**Transmission:** three-speed manual gearbox, rear-wheel drive

**Chassis:** separate steel frame with channel-section side members and cruciform bracing

**Suspension:** non-independent with beam axle and semi-elliptic leaf springs front; live axle with semi-elliptic leaf springs rear

**Brakes:** drums all round

**Bodywork:** aluminium-panelled, wooden-framed, four-seater open sports tourer

**Maximum speed (approx):** 100 mph (161 km/h)

*Below: In 1935, a car that had a 0-60 mph time of 9.8 seconds was a very impressive performer.*

How could it be that such a phenomenally fast four-seater sports car with a price of £878 in 1935 could fail so miserably? Railton's Light Sports, ultra-exclusive at the time, yet now virtually forgotten, got as many British motoring headlines as the XJ220 does today – but it did not sell.

Perhaps it was that the limited clientele for this type of car was not interested in a sports car based on Hudson chassis and engineering? In the same price bracket, after all, they could buy a 4½-litre Lagonda or a 3½-litre Alvis, both of which were traditionally British from bumper to bumper.

Undoubtedly the fastest-accelerating British-market car of its day, the Light Sports was a magnificent failure. It looked fierce and purposeful, and because its body was mainly aluminium and duralumin panels it was much lighter than other Railtons – *The Autocar's* test car weighed a mere 2,203 lb.

This forceful car ran on a 116-in wheelbase, had a top speed of around 100 mph in standard condition and, with only one gear change, it rushed up to 60 mph in 9.8 seconds. More impressive still, it could reach 90 mph in less than 30 seconds, which was an almost unheard-of ability in its day.

The style was even more ferocious than that of other Railtons, for the engine had been moved back in the frame, and there was still a family resemblance to the old-style Invictas. Although it was ostensibly a four-seater, there was still only limited leg room in the rear.

Compared with its competitors, however, the Railton's 16-in wheels looked rather puny – a Lagonda, after all, ran on 18-in wheels, and a 3½-litre Alvis on 19-in wheels – and there is no doubt that this caused some distrust of the Light Sports among traditionalists.

Under the skin the running gear was relatively mundane. As with other Railtons, the Light Sports was based on the chassis of current Hudson models, so the combination of a lazy, low-revving, side-

# Reliant Motor Company

*Left: A rally version of the early 1960s Sabre 6; the Sabre was Reliant's first four-wheeler.*

When the Reliant Scimitar GTE was at the height of its fame in the 1970s, Reliant's publicists were happy to obscure the company's origins. There was no marketing advantage, after all, in trying to sell the world's first "high-performance estate car" as a descendant of the nasty series of unstable three-wheeler economy cars.

Reliant was founded in Tamworth (north-east of Birmingham) by Tom Williams in 1935, its first product being the single-front-wheeled Reliant van. Glassfibre bodywork was adopted in 1956, but the very first four-wheeler Reliant, the Sabre, was not launched until 1962. From that day to this, Reliant has continued to build two entirely different types of car – the three-wheelers (and occasionally a four-wheeler derivative of the tiny-engined economy cars), and a series of sporting cars.

The original Sabre had evolved in connection with Sabra of Israel, and was an ungainly machine which combined a separate chassis with a Ford engine and transmission, and an Ashley Laminates body shell. Even though the company rapidly improved the car, and offered it with a more powerful engine, it was not a success. A short-lived rallying programme only confirmed that it was uncompetitive in many respects, its suspension proving unsuitable for the rigours of rallying.

From 1964, however, Reliant's fortunes began to soar. Not only had the company designed its own competent little alloy four-cylinder engine for the economy cars, but it launched an attractive new sports coupé, the Scimitar GT. The key to this car's success was its styling by Ogle Design, hired to develop the shape of the next generation of Reliant products.

There was great expansion in the 1960s and 1970s. The Hodge Group (controlled by Sir Julian Hodge) took control in 1962, and the Preston-based Bond business was absorbed in 1969. One immediate result was the birth of the wedge-styled Bond Bug three-wheeler, but this was a 'flower-power' aberration. The Bond name, in fact, disappeared in the early 1970s, and the Preston end of the Reliant empire was closed down.

The Scimitar GTE, introduced in 1968, was a great success, and was a best-seller until the 1980s, though the style was virtually unchanged in all that time. This was literally the high point of Reliant's reputation, and influence, for links with Israeli and Turkish companies did not mature as well as the company had hoped, and several attempts to replace the GTE/GTC models were cancelled at the development or styling stages.

Looking for expansion, Reliant decided to move down-market by producing a smaller sports car, but the new Scimitar SS (launched in 1984) was ungainly and initially underpowered.

In the meantime there had been several changes of management and control, and the company eventually began assembling the new Metrocab taxicab. Unhappily, the company's financial fortunes fluctuated alarmingly throughout the 1980s, the design rights of the GTE/GTC were sold off to the Japanese-owned Middlebridge concern in 1987, the SS1 had to be completely restyled to make it acceptable, and in 1990 the receivers were called in.

In 1991 Hoopers bought the Metrocab project, and the remnants of the Reliant business were rescued from receivership by Beans Industries.

*Above: A combination of sports car and estate, the Reliant Scimitar GTE was available with Ford 2.5- or 3.0-litre V6 engines. When Princess Anne bought one, its commercial success was ensured.*

*Right: By the time Reliant were producing the restyled ST Turbo version of Michelotti's unfortunate Scimitar SS1 design the company was in dire straits, with the receivers just around the corner.*

# Reliant Scimitar GT 1964-70

By late 1963 Reliant was fully aware of the shortcomings of the original Sabre sports cars, and decided to try again, with an entirely different model. A new car, coded SE4, was developed, with a graceful new body style from Ogle Design of Letchworth.

Apart from its use of the same Triumph-derived independent front suspension units, the chassis was a sturdy new design. As with the Sabre 6, the controversial aspect of the rear suspension was that its twin longitudinal Watt linkages gave very precise location of the axle, but were fixed in such a way that an enormous anti-roll resistance was set up as the wheels moved up and down.

The engine was still the familiar Ford Zephyr/Zodiac six-cylinder unit, backed either by the Ford four-speed gearbox and overdrive, or (rarely) by a ZF four-speed gearbox of the type used in the Sabre 6, and the original Lotus Elite; the

*Below: The early Scimitar GT had a controversial rear suspension set-up, but once this had been modified, the car sold well.*

last ZF-box cars were produced when stocks ran out in 1966.

This time there were absolutely no complaints about the body style, for the Ogle Design team had produced a variation of a shape they had originally developed for a Daimler SP250 show car, which took the form of a distinctive two-seater coupé with a great deal of extra space behind the seats and which really made no pretence of being rear-seating.

Right from the start the new car, called the Scimitar GT, was a great success, and once the rear suspension location was revised to cut out the anti-roll resistance problems, by using twin trailing arms and a transverse Watt linkage, it became very popular indeed. By the time 59 cars of the original design had been produced, Ford had unveiled its new V6 engines and it became clear that Reliant must soon follow suit. Sure enough, in the autumn of 1966 the SE4 gave way to the SE4a with the more powerful and very torquey three-litre V6 Ford engine fitted. Producing 136 bhp, it gave the car a top speed of 121 mph.

The Scimitar GT achieved everything

*Above: The 1965 Ogle-designed Scimitar GT was a distinctive shape, based on a Daimler show car.*

the Sabre 6 had not. It looked good and handled well, it was comfortable and nicely detailed, and it was an excellent long-distance Grand Touring car, with all this backed by virtually bomb-proof Ford engines.

From the summer of 1967 an alternative 2.5-litre V6-engined Scimitar with a lower top speed of 113 mph was also put on sale, though this was not a great success and only 117 were produced. From the end of 1968, too, the Scimitar GT was overshadowed by the popular new GTE, but production continued steadily until 1970, by which time a total of 590 three-litre V6 GTs had been built.

## Specification (1965)

**Engine:** inline six-cylinder, overhead-valve
**Bore × stroke:** 82.5 mm × 79.5 mm
**Capacity:** 2553 cc
**Maximum power:** 120 bhp
**Transmission:** four-speed manual

gearbox with overdrive, or non-overdrive ZF four-speed gearbox; rear-wheel drive
**Chassis:** separate steel frame with box-section side members and cross-members
**Suspension:** independent front with coil springs and wishbones; live rear axle with coil springs and twin Watt linkages; later rear suspension had radius arms and a transverse Watt linkage
**Brakes:** discs front, drums rear
**Bodywork:** glassfibre two-seater coupé
**Maximum speed (approx):** 117 mph (188 km/h)

*Below: Original GTs had an inline six-cylinder 2.5-litre pushrod Ford engine producing 120 bhp.*

## Reliant Scimitar GTE 1968-86

Although only a modest carmaker, Reliant's designers invented one of the most powerful concepts of all – the high-performance 'sporting estate car'. When the Scimitar GTE appeared in 1968, it was a real 'first' – combining sports coupé behaviour with a really capacious cabin.

The GTE concept evolved around a series of influences. One was that Reliant's managing director Ray Wiggin wanted to replace the existing Scimitar with a more capacious model, while another source of inspiration was undoubtedly the Lamborghini Espada which had just been unveiled.

Not only did the glassfibre-bodied GTE have a new style, but it also ran on a new ladder-type chassis with an 8-in longer wheelbase than the Scimitar GT, and the track was wider, by four inches at the front and three inches at the rear. The cabin was cleverly designed, with rear seat squabs which could be folded forward, and the result was that Reliant advertised a 'seats-up' luggage capacity of 19 cubic feet, but with the seats down that figure rose to a remarkable 36 cu ft. This sort of practicality, backed by the

Ford V6 engine and related gearbox and running gear, made the GTE very appealing, and it immediately began to sell well. By 1972 no fewer than 50 Scimitar GTEs were being made each week, and total production was around 2,500 in 1974 and the same again in 1975.

The same basic design stayed in production for the next 18 years. In all that time there were only two major changes. In 1975 Reliant introduced the SE6 variety, which looked superficially the same, but had a 4-in longer wheelbase, and was three inches wider. Then, in 1980, the GTE design was re-engineered to use Ford's German-built 2.8-litre V6, and for the first time a convertible model (the GTC) became available.

By this time, however, demand for Scimitars was well past its peak, and production slumped to no more than two or three cars a week in the early 1980s. The last car of all was produced at Tamworth in November 1986 (it was destined to be Princess Anne's seventh successive GTE), making a total of 15,273 hatchback coupés and 443 GTC convertibles built in a period of 10 years.

*Above: Developed from the GTE, the Scimitar GTC convertible had a 2.8-litre Ford V6 engine.*

*Below: This 1974 Scimitar GTE had a three-litre Ford V6; a 2.5-litre V6 was an option, too.*

### Reliant Scimitar GTE variants

#### Reliant Scimitar GTE SE6/SE6a
The SE6/SE6a derivative, introduced in 1975 to replace the SE5 type, was mechanically similar, but had a 4-in longer wheelbase and a 2.5-in wider track, improving both its carrying capacity and its handling and roadholding.

#### Reliant Scimitar GTC convertible
The use of a traditional separate chassis made it easy for Reliant to develop a convertible version of the Scimitar, something which was only done after the appeal of the GTE had begun to wane. The GTC, introduced in 1980, did little to revive the model, as by this time the basic design was outdated. The convertible, known within Reliant as the SE8b, was powered by the engine found in the last of the fixed-head cars, the 2792-cc Ford V6, which produced 135 bhp.

*Above: Launched in 1968, the Ogle-designed Reliant Scimitar GTE had considerable luggage capacity combined with sporting performance and a winning appearance.*

### Specification (1968 GTE)
**Engine:** V6, overhead-valve
**Bore × stroke:** 93.7 mm × 72.4 mm
**Capacity:** 2994 cc
**Maximum power:** 138 bhp
**Transmission:** four-speed manual gearbox with optional overdrive, or optional three-speed automatic transmission; rear-wheel drive
**Chassis:** separate steel frame with box-section side and reinforcing members
**Suspension:** independent front with wishbones and coil springs; live rear axle with coil springs
**Brakes:** discs front, drums rear
**Bodywork:** glassfibre four-seater hatchback coupé
**Maximum speed (approx):** 119 mph (192 km/h)

# Reliant Scimitar SSI 1984-89, 1992-93

**Above: The 1986 Scimitar 1800 Ti used a Nissan turbo engine, which made it suitable for the US market.**

**Below: The SS1 was Italian designer Michelotti's swansong but it was an unsuccessful design in all respects.**

**Above: Unfortunately, the interior styling was no improvement over the fussy, toy-like exterior.**

style, by Michelotti of Turin, was not very graceful in detail. Michelotti, the previous master (particularly with 1950s and 1960s Triumphs such as the Herald and elegant Stag), had not produced a pretty design, and this undoubtedly hampered the car's reception.

The original models used Ford's cheap, but rather undistinguished, CVH engines, and with only 69 bhp there is no doubt that the four-speed 1.3-litre version's performance was disappointing. The 96-bhp 1.6-litre car, at least, had a 100 mph top speed, but this was still not at the limit of the chassis's capability, which endowed the SS1 with excellent handling and roadholding.

To counter this lack of performance Reliant moved swiftly, launching a new version, complete with a turbocharged Nissan 1.8-litre engine, in 1986. The Nissan unit was chosen because it was very powerful and already certified for sale in the USA, although Reliant's ambitions in that direction went unrealised.

At a stroke the little Scimitar was transformed from a rather slow 'ugly duckling' to an altogether more desirable sports car, although the model's looks always held back its sales. Only 230 SS1s were sold in 1987, 186 in 1988, and less than 100 in 1989. Perhaps the Nissan-engined machine would have sold better if the facelifts proposed by William Towns had been adopted, but by this time the Reliant Group's finances were in disarray, and the company collapsed into receivership in 1991.

The Scimitar project was rescued by Beans Industries (a long-time major supplier to Reliant) who invested in the new tooling needed to put a facelifted car on sale in 1992. This version, named the Scimitar Sabre, had a different nose, while other parts of the style were cleaned up, and the 135-bhp Nissan engine was retained. It was still a 130 mph machine which Beans hoped would sell during the 1990s. Sadly, their aspirations were unfulfilled.

## Specification (1987 1800 Ti)

**Engine:** inline four-cylinder, single overhead camshaft, turbocharged
**Bore × stroke:** 83 mm × 83.6 mm
**Capacity:** 1809 cc
**Maximum power:** 135 bhp
**Transmission:** five-speed manual gearbox, rear-wheel drive
**Chassis:** separate steel frame with pressed and fabricated backbone main members, multi-tubular outriggers and bracings
**Suspension:** independent with wishbones and coil springs front; semi-trailing arms and coil springs rear
**Brakes:** discs front, drums rear
**Bodywork:** glassfibre two-seater, optional hard top
**Maximum speed (approx):** 127 mph (204 km/h)

**Below: The 130-mph, Nissan-engined model was facelifted by William Towns as Beans Industries, rescuer of a bankrupt Reliant company in 1991, attempted to market the car anew for the 1990s.**

y the end of the 1970s Reliant could see at the popularity of the big V6-engined cimitars was on the wane, so thoughts erefore turned to the development of a ew and smaller sports car. After a eriod of protracted study and development, during which Tony Steven's Reant-engined Cipher project and Vauxall's two-seater Equus prototype were onsidered, the company launched its own machine in 1984. It was intended to take over from the old-type Scimitar on the same assembly lines in Tamworth, and Reliant must have been hoping for enhanced sales.

Compared with the old Scimitar, the new design was smaller, lighter and, visually, considerably less distinguished than before. The wheelbase was short, there was significant overhang, and the

# Renault

A lthough Renault was not the first French company to start selling cars, it rapidly became the largest and most important of them. Three brothers – Louis, Marcel and Fernand Renault – built their first prototype in 1898, and in 1900 nearly 200 cars were sold. Thereafter, expansion was swift and sure.

Although Renault soon started building racing cars – Marcel Renault was himself a successful driver for a short time, and it was a Renault which won the very first Grand Prix in 1906 – its production cars tended to be conventional family machines. Between the wars, like Fiat in Italy, and Austin and Morris in Britain, Renault widened its range considerably. Although it did not produce a tiny-engined runabout at this time, it built cars as vast as the eight-cylinder seven-litre Reinastella, and as mundane as the one-litre Juvaquatre.

After World War II, when Louis Renault was accused of collaborating with the occupying German authorities, the company was nationalised, and completely changed its image. For many years the business concentrated on building small, cheap, rear-engined cars like the 4CV and the Dauphine, but it wasn't long before the French tuning expert, Amédée Gordini, began producing faster versions of these appealing machines.

By the 1960s the firm was much the largest French car company and began to expand its range. Not only did it introduce the extrovert rear-engined 8 Gordini (which became a successful rally car), but it also began developing an entirely new range of front-engined/front-wheel-drive models. At the same time, it supplied engines, transmissions and other running gear to specialists like Alpine and Matra-Bonnet, which rapidly helped Renault to establish a more sporting image.

A works competition department originally concentrated on building

*Above: The 1925 Renault 40CV, with its 9.1-litre engine, power output of 45 bhp and stylish looks, became a favourite with Paris society.*

racing-sports cars, but by the mid-1970s it was also involved in the Formula Renault single-seater series, and the first F1 Renault appeared in the late 1970s. This was the decade in which Renault also took control of Jean Redélé's Alpine company, the result being the launch of larger and faster Alpine-Renault coupés (the latter types with V6 engines), eventually followed by the far faster GTAs, which were built for Renault at the Alpine factory in Dieppe.

In the 1970s and 1980s Renault grew so large that it developed links with other car companies, notably Peugeot of France, Daf of Holland (which was soon absorbed by Volvo), and Volvo of Sweden, although a marketing tie-up with Chrysler in North America was a failure. The corporate V6 engine which was used in various Renault, Peugeot and Volvo models also found a home in cars as diverse as the Renault GTA, the DeLorean DMC-12 coupé, and the French MVS Venturi.

Although Renault was very large, it was not always very profitable, and for some years the French government had to dig deeply, and regularly, into its coffers to balance the books. With the company's image at heart, however, there always seemed to be money to develop quirky low-production models like the mid-engined Renault 5 Turbo (a successful 'homologation special' of the 1980s) and the all-conquering Formula 1 engine of the early 1990s.

Its most prominent sports-orientated cars of the 1990s were the Clio Williams, the Sport Spider, a competition car built for the road, and the Laguna saloon which was 1997 BTCC winner in the hands of Alain Menu.

*Left: Renault's small, twin-cylinder AX was adapted for use in taxis in London and Paris.*

*Below: By the 1990s Renault's image was totally modern, with cars like the three-litre, 250-bhp A610.*

# Renault R8 Gordini 1964-70

*Left: Renault engaged competition-car specialist Gordini to inject sporting life into its mundane R8.*

*Left: The R8 Gordini was far better-equipped with instruments than the rather spartan standard model.*

There is a difference between a 'go-faster' saloon and a serious rally-special. Renault had dabbled with faster versions of its small cars in the 1950s, and in much-modified form such machines, based on the 4CV and Dauphine layouts, were sometimes successful in rallies. But the first true Renault rally-special was the R8 Gordini of 1964.

Viewed with hindsight, this was a totally predictable project. Britain's Ford and BMC companies had produced the world's first 'homologation specials' (the Mini-Cooper S and the Lotus-Cortina) in 1963, and had started winning races and rallies all round the world. Renault set out to match them.

The result was the conversion of the R8 family saloon into a fiercely competitive limited-production car. Although the rear-engined R8 was somewhat larger than the Mini-Cooper S, it was light, it had four-wheel disc brakes as standard, and it had excellent traction on loose surfaces, or snow and ice.

In standard form the R8 had a 956-cc engine which produced a mere 42 bhp. After being worked on by Amédée Gordini, and equipped with a complete new aluminium cylinder head, this became an 1108-cc engine with no less than 95 bhp. Even though it was not a very re-

fined car, it was undoubtedly fast, with a top speed of 106 mph, and an extrovert character to match. R8 Gordinis were usually painted in a bright blue, with a pair of nose-to-tail white stripes which were supplied to the dealer as rolls of tape, for 'optional' fitment.

The French loved it, thousands were built every year, and before long the R8 Gordini became a competitive rally car *and* a trendy little machine for rushing round cities. Its tail-heavy weight distribution, allied to the use of swing-axle rear suspension, meant that the road car tended to oversteer considerably when pressed hard. Extensively-prepared rally cars with lowered and firmer suspension, plus wider wheels, were extremely effective.

The original car did its job, but only two years later Renault produced a Mk II version, the 1300, which was even more effective, especially in the Group 1 (or 'unmodified') sporting categories. The

engine was enlarged to 1255 cc which, with twin-choke Weber carburettors, produced 103 bhp. A five-speed gearbox was fitted, and this must have been the *only* car in the world to have two widely separate fuel tanks – one behind the seats, as with all other R8s, the other on the floor of the front luggage compartment, with separate fillers.

The supplementary tank was used to help improve the weight distribution, there were larger built-in extra driving lamps at the front to help night-time vision in motorsport, and with a 0-80 mph acceleration time in about 20 seconds, this was a serious little machine.

By 1968 the Gordini's reputation was past its peak, but Renault persevered with it as a road car until 1970.

## Renault R8 Gordini variants

### Renault Gordini 1300
From 1966 the Gordini 1300 took over from the R8, with an enlarged engine of 74.5 mm × 72 mm, giving a displacement of 1255 cc and a power output of 103 bhp. A five-speed gearbox was fitted. The car's approximate top speed was 106 mph.

## Specification (1965 R8)

**Engine:** inline four-cylinder, overhead-valve
**Bore × stroke:** 70 mm × 72 mm
**Capacity:** 1108 cc
**Maximum power:** 95 bhp
**Transmission:** four-speed manual gearbox, rear-wheel drive
**Chassis:** steel unitary construction
**Suspension:** independent with wishbones and coil springs front; swing-axles and coil springs rear
**Brakes:** discs all round
**Bodywork:** steel four-seater saloon
**Maximum speed (approx):** 106 mph (171 km/h)

*Right: The 1967 Gordini 1300 had an excellent power output of 103 bhp, and a five-speed gearbox.*

## Renault 5 Turbo 1980-85

*Left: The mid-engined Renault Turbo was a competitive rally car; it won the Monte Carlo Rally in 1981.*

In the late 1970s Renault, whose cars had been outpaced in top-flight rallying for some years, decided to attack the dominant Fords, Fiats and Lancias with a specially-designed car. The result was the birth of the eclectic mid-engined 5 Turbo model.

Renault developed this car in an entirely logical way. For marketing purposes the new model had to look like an existing Renault. To give the best possible combination of handling and trac-tion, it needed the engine behind the seats. To give better performance than its competitors, it needed a more power-ful engine. When all these considera-tions were blended, the decision was made to produce a new mid-engined chassis topped by a body shell based on the standard front-engined Renault 5, with a turbocharged 1.4-litre engine.

Under the skin was an entirely new floorpan but with the familiar 1397-cc overhead-valve engine mounted ahead of the line of the rear wheels, driving those wheels through a five-speed trans-axle. In effect, Renault had taken a front-engined/front-wheel-drive installation and moved it bodily back by several feet!

The engine was actually a turbo-charged version of the existing front-engined 5 Gordini unit, while the trans-axle was that of the much larger front-wheel-drive Renault 30. New suspen-sion, four-wheel disc brakes, and careful attention to engine bay airflow com-pleted an intriguing package.

Because Renault already had an ex-cellent record for building competition cars there was never any doubt that the new car would work. But would it sell? In fact the 5 Turbo was an object lesson in building an 'homologation special' which was also a pleasant road car. With its chunky proportions – the ultra-wide rear track and the rear-wheel drive were emphasised – and its purposeful charac-ter, it looked appealing, and although its engine needed revving before the turbocharger effect appeared, it was nevertheless a flexible car to drive.

Although the engine was behind the seats, it was well insulated from the cabin and the car was surprisingly civilised to drive. It was nimble, an ideal machine for rushing around towns, and on the open road it could cruise easily at 100 mph.

Renault soon turned it into an excellent rally car – Jean Ragnotti won the Monte Carlo Rally of 1981, the Tour de Corse of 1982, and won the Tour de Corse again in 1985, with the Maxi 5 Turbo.

Although Renault had originally only needed to build 400 5 Turbos to make the new car eligible for international motor-sport, demand was so strong that several thousands were produced, and they con-tinued to be successful rally cars until the end of the 1980s.

*Above: The Turbo was designed by Heuliez to keep as much of the original 5's looks as possible.*

### Renault 5 Turbo variants

#### Renault Maxi 5 Turbo
In 1984-85, Renault produced a special version of the mid-engined car, called the 5 Turbo 1430. The engine size was enlarged to 77 mm × 77 mm, giving 1434 cc, and producing approximately 180 bhp. Only 200 were built, as the basis of a Group B rally car which was homologated as the Maxi 5 Turbo. The works cars, with engines enlarged to 1527 cc, produced up to 350 bhp.

### Specification (1980 5 Turbo)
**Engine:** inline four-cylinder, overhead valve, turbo
**Bore × stroke:** 76 mm × 77 mm
**Capacity:** 1397 cc
**Maximum power:** 160 bhp
**Transmissiion:** five-speed manual gearbox, rear-wheel drive
**Chassis:** steel unitary construction
**Suspension:** independent with coil springs and wishbones front and rear
**Brakes:** discs all round
**Bodywork:** aluminium, steel and glass fibre mid-engined two-seater hatchback
**Maximum speed (approx):** 124 mph (200 km/h)

*Above: The rear of the 5 grew over half a foot, to 58 inches, to cover the Turbo's greatly increased track.*

*Below: In 1982 steel panels, suitable for mass-production, were used on the Renault 5 Turbo 2.*

## Renault 5 GT Turbo 1987–92

*Above: A 1988 Renault 5 GT Turbo. When tested by Autocar in 1987, it was described as "easily the fastest small hatchback money can buy".*

*Below: The performance potential of the Renault 5 GT Turbo could be greatly extended, and this soon led to the racetrack; here driving in the rain, Tony Smith's Car leads the pack in a close-fought 1988 event.*

Renault were not first on the scene with a turbocharged road car; that honour fell to the Saab 99 Turbo, but the French company were more concerned with turbocharging than almost any other manufacturer. At one stage in the 1980s turbo versions of the Renault 5, Renault 18 and Fuego were all on offer.

The original Renault 5 was first and foremost an economy runabout but turbocharging transformed its performance, if not its refinements or ultimate driveability. What it did prove was that adding even a simple turbo installation to a car as basic as the R5 would produce tremendous performance.

In the late 1980s the time came to revise the whole R5 range and that car enabled the company to produce a far more refined version of the R5 GT Turbo. Although Renault 5s old and new looked surprisingly similar, the car had been comprehensively re-engineered. The old car, despite its front-wheel drive, had a longitudinally-mounted engine; that was moved through 90 degrees to make it transverse-engined like the vast majority of front-drive cars.

What was retained for the Turbo was the old pushrod engine with its cast-iron block, wet liners and alloy head. Although only an overhead-valve design it had hemispherical combustion chambers, thanks to long rocker arms across the head, and thus efficient breathing. As before, a Garrett turbo was used but this time the T2 blower had the advantage of an intercooler. With a compression ratio of 7.9:1 and a maximum boost pressure of 10.3 psi, as much as 120 bhp was extracted from the small, 1397-cc, engine. The torque output was excellent too, at 121 lb ft at 3,750 rpm.

*Right: It looked like an ordinary small family hatchback, light and economical, but the Turbo badges denoted that it was more than a match for serious sports cars.*

When such power was coupled with a very light body shell (kerb weight was a mere 1,889 lb), the performance could hardly fail to be outstanding, and the tiny Turbo was capable of a maximum speed of 120 mph while being able to reach 60 mph in 7.3 seconds and 100 mph in 23.2 seconds. In-gear acceleration was, with the understandable exception of the 20-40 and 30-50 mph times in top, very good too, 40-60 mph taking only 4.3 seconds in third gear.

With a power-to-weight ratio of 119.4 bhp/ton, the performance of the 1988 model more than impressed the *Autocar* road-testers, who found "acceptable low levels of turbo lag, with the boost gauge

*Above: The car's appeal was further enhanced when Radbourne Racing introduced a convertible.*

beginning to move at 2,000 rpm . . . and up to its maximum by 3,000 rpm". The car was deemed "a master at overtaking on A- and B-roads. It is possible to take opportunities denied to most other cars in safety, so long as the turbo is on full boost prior to making the manoeuvre". Despite such performance, average fuel consumption was still 28.4 mpg.

The car's chassis had been revised somewhat to make the model more manageable, although the revisions were more like fine-tuning rather than fundamental changes. The end result was a

car that was fun, fast, safe and controllable. The pace of change in the industry counted against the R5 GT Turbo, however; in the early 1990s Renault's new Clio proved more than a match for it in all respects – performance, handling and, crucially to some customers, build quality. And it managed that with just a normally-aspirated, 16-valve, engine, albeit with a larger displacement of 1764 cc.

### Specification (1987)

**Engine:** inline four-cylinder, overhead-valve, turbo
**Bore × stroke:** 76 mm × 77 mm
**Capacity:** 1397 cc
**Maximum power:** 120 bhp
**Transmissiion:** five-speed manual gearbox, front-wheel drive
**Chassis:** unitary construction
**Suspension:** independent front with MacPherson struts and anti-roll bar; semi-independent rear with twisting beam axle, four trailing arms, transverse torsion bars and anti-roll bar
**Brakes:** discs all round
**Bodywork:** steel hatchback
**Maximum speed (approx):** 120 mph (193 km/h)

## Renault Sport Spider 1995-1999

Designed by Patrick Le Quément and built at the Alpine Renault factory at Dieppe, the uncompromising mid-engined Renault Sport Spider was essentially a competition car built for the road. Like the Lotus Elise, its chassis was made from aluminium extrusions and produced at the Hydro Raufoss plant in Denmark. Unlike the Elise, which used an epoxy-resin bonded chassis, the Sport Spider's was welded of thicker gauge metal, which made it quite a lot heavier than the Lotus. The purposeful outer panels were made of composite and GRP, which was a medium that Alpine specialised in. However, the Sport Spider was futuristically styled. Its front structure was designed to prevent wheel intrusion in the event of impact – it was to all intents and purposes a racing car – and a degree of protection was afforded by the side beams. A roll-over bar completed the safety angle.

The Sport Spider's engine and gearbox combination was the 150 bhp 2.0-litre 16-valve F7R unit of the Mégane Coupé, which could power it from 0–62 mph (0-100 km/h) in 6.9 seconds and cover 400 metres from a standing start in 14.2 seconds. Short gear ratios permitted a top speed of 134 mph (215 km/h). Its mid-engine configuration provided excellent weight distribution and traction, coupled with 16-inch alloy wheels with 225/50 rear tyres and 205/50 front tyres to give outstanding road-holding when cornering hard. Suspension was the motorsport-derived double wishbone set up all round, allied to coil springs and dampers, with bushless ball-joints and adjustable ride height. The hubs, brake discs and callipers were all sourced from the Alpine A610, retarding the Sport Spider's

*Above: Conceived as a racing car for the road, the Sport Spider came without the windscreen, relying on aerodynamics to protect the cockpit. A GRP body and welded, extruded-aluminium chassis made it stunning to look at and to drive.*

progress most efficiently.

The interior of the cockpit was just as austere as the Elise, and the car was marketed without a windscreen or roof, although a screen version was available, and relied on aerodynamics to avoid buffeting. The dashboard featured an aluminium bar and three round instruments including water temperature and

oil pressure gauges and a rev counter, while a central pod set in the top of the dash housed a digital speedometer, distance recorder and fuel gauge. Recaro bucket seats and a leather-trimmed steering wheel were fitted.

### Variants

A one-make racing championship, the **Elf Renault Sport Spider** Cup began in 1996, and ran for three seasons at top European circuits. In race trim, there was an uprated engine and straight-cut six-speed non-synchromesh box, wider wheels and tyres, dashboard adjustable brake balance, stiffer suspension settings,

race roll-cage, lower ride height – already adjustable on the standard production car – and full-harness belts. A Spider Le Mans coupé version using the 550 bhp V6 turbo unit from the Safrane ran at Le Mans in 1996.

### Specification
**Engine:** transverse four-cylinder, 16-valve F7R
**Capacity:** 1998 cc
**Gearbox:** manual, five-speed (road-going)
**Suspension:** double wishbones front and rear, coil springs and dampers
**Brakes:** ventilated discs front and rear
**Chassis:** welded aluminium extrusions composite panels

## Renault Sport Clio V6 1998-present

Launched at the Paris and Birmingham motor shows in 1998 was Renault Sport's follow up to the Clio Williams and R5 Turbo, the Clio V6 24V. But whereas the late-model Clio Williams was a hotted-up hatchback, the new Clio was a full-blown mid-engined missile in the manner of its R5 predecessor. At the heart of the Clio was the transverse-mounted 280 bhp 24-valve V6 L7X motor, sourced from the Laguna V6, linked to a manual five-speed gearbox. Performance figures included a top speed of over 150 mph (241 km/h) and acceleration from 0–62 mph (0-100 km/h) in less than six seconds.

This Clio V6 was developed for a one-make race series, but with a view to a restricted production run of roadgoing models. Work was carried out by Renault Sport chassis and engine technicians who had worked on Renault's F1 engine programme, and Renault Design produced the dramatic interior and exterior.

In 1999 Renault Sport launched its Clio Trophy series, replacing the European Championship for the Renault Sport Spider. While the roadgoing version provided levels of com-

fort, safety and equipment associated with top-range models, in race trim it was appropriately spartan inside. Being mid-engined, there were only two seats, and the air intakes for the engine revealed it to be fundamentally different from the regular Clio. The front spoiler and extended wings and wheelarches gave a dramatic appearance, and while the body shell, bonnet, roof and rear hatch were from the Clio II, everything else consisted of composite panels made by MOC, who also made the Espace F1, a carbon-fibre Espace with F1 engine and chassis. The cabin was upholstered in leather and Alcantara, with a specific instrument pack with white-faced dials, and minimal luggage compartment between the seat backs and the engine compartment.

New longerons and cross-members were installed to support the engine and transmission assembly and suspension members. Front and rear suspension systems were new, although they employed many standard production parts. The increased wheelbase and wider track front and rear, placed the wheels at the four corners of the car, while spring and damper rates

were specially calibrated. The Clio's 17-inch alloy wheels were shod with 7.5-inch wide tyres at the front and 8.5 inch at the rear. Brakes consisted of four ventilated discs with diagonal-split hydraulic circuit and servo plus ABS and EBV electronic brake distribution control.

### Specification
**Engine:** V6 24-valve
**Capacity:** 2946 cc
**Gearbox:** manual, five-speed
**Brakes:** ventilated discs, 300 mm front and rear
**Chassis:** steel monocoque with composite panels

*Above: This pocket rocket was designed to provide the basis for a one-make race series. It had composite panels and was powered by the 280 bhp V6, mid-mounted like the R5 Turbo of the 1980s, with a top speed of 150 mph.*

# Riley

The Riley family founded its industrial dynasty in Coventry in the 19th century by making and using weaving machinery, then turned to building pedal cycles before producing their original prototype car in 1896. There were motor tricycles from 1900, and series-production of three-wheel Tricars began in 1903, but the first true Riley car was not sold until 1906.

For the next 32 years Riley was one of Coventry's most important carmakers, gradually building up a reputation for producing sporting cars. Before World War I Rileys mostly had V-twin engines, the first side-valve four-cylinder model not arriving until 1913.

From 1919 a recognisable Riley style began to develop. A new range of cars was launched in 1919; these were the first Rileys to have the 'V'-style radiator which became so famous, and it was from this 11HP base that the first true sporting Riley, the Redwinger, was developed.

The big breakthrough came in 1926 when the first of an excellent and advanced series of engines, designed by Percy Riley, was launched. Between 1926 and 1938 several different engine families were developed, all of which shared the same basic layout: a part-spherical combustion chamber, opposed lines of inlet and exhaust valves, and twin camshafts, one on each side of the cylinder block, operating the valves by way of pushrods and reversed rockers.

The first of these engines powered the Nine and lasted until the Nuffield takeover in 1938. It was followed by related six-cylinder units in the early 1930s, a larger 'four' of 1.5 litres in 1935, a V8 (for the closely-related Autovia) in 1937, and finally the 2½-litre 'Big Four' in 1937.

Once the last of the side-valve models had been built in 1928, one or other of these remarkable, and expensive-to-build, modern engines was used in every Riley model for the next 28 years. By the 1930s the company seemed to have different factories dotted all around Coventry – some for building engines, others for making bodies, and another for final assembly of cars, and the influence of the independently-financed business was at its height.

During the 1930s, however, the Riley management became dazzled by the expensive glamour of sports cars and motor racing. Although the 9HP-engined models (notably the Kestrels) were always the best-sellers,

*Above: The Riley RM series was launched after World War II, though styling was pre-war; the elegant 2443-cc Roadster appeared in 1948.*

the company produced many other six-cylinder and Big Four-engined cars, most of which sold slowly.

Although sports cars like the Brooklands Nine, Lynx, Imp, MPH and the Sprite were always praised for their looks and their specification, they never contributed much to profits. The racing programme, while wonderful for morale, did little to boost sales, and not even a link with the ERA racing team (whose engines were based on the contemporary six-cylinder Riley units) could reap a harvest.

The company's finances fell into disarray in 1937, a receiver was appointed in 1938, and the firm was taken over by Lord Nuffield later that year, eventually to be integrated into the Nuffield Organisation, then into BMC, the British Motor Corporation.

Immediately after World War II, Riley introduced the graceful 1½-litre and 2½-litre RM models, but final assembly was moved to the MG factory at Abingdon from 1949, and from the mid-1950s Rileys became no more than rebadged BMC models.

The last (and, ironically enough, best-selling) Rileys of all were badge-engineered, transverse-engined, front-wheel-drive cars based on the BMC Mini and 1100 designs, but after the formation of British Leyland, the Riley name was dropped in 1969.

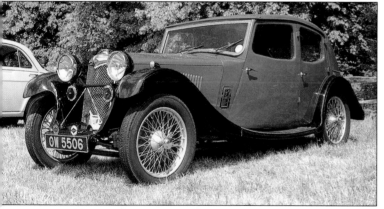

*Above: A 1935 9HP Riley Kestrel, with fastback bodywork and a reputation for nimble performance.*

*Below: This 1951 Riley RM Roadster featured torsion-bar front suspension and a 90-bhp twin-cam engine.*

*Above: The sports 1934 Riley MPH, based on the 1933 TT racing cars, enhanced the Riley name (left).*

# Riley MPH 1934-35

*Above: The 1458-cc straight-six of a 1934 Riley MPH was a remarkably efficient and race-proven engine.*

Riley first showed its inline six-cylinder engine (which was a direct development of the Nine 'four') in 1928, and in 1932 it introduced the Brooklands Six, which was a racing-sports car with a 108-in wheelbase. A year later Riley raced the TT models, which had shortened versions of the frame, and it was this 'building block', with a 97.5-in wheelbase, which formed the base of the whole series of sporting machines – the MPH and Sprite road cars, the TT Sprite and the Racing Six two-litre models.

The MPH of 1934 was probably the most beautiful of all Riley's mid-1930s machines. When it was new it was expensive and rare, but almost all the 17

cars built have survived to this day. The basic style was like that of the Imp (the centre section of the two bodies *was* the same), but the bonnet and front wings were even longer and more sinuous, and the rear wings were flared most gracefully. There was even an Alfa-like 'fin' on the spare wheel cover. The overall effect, if not the price, was irresistible, which caused most observers (especially Riley fans) to drool over the looks.

The MPH, of course, was a fast and powerful model, for it was equipped with Riley's latest six-cylinder engine. In a production run of little more than a year – the MPH was dropped in favour of the Sprite at the end of 1935 – no fewer than three different engine displacements were available. There was the 1458-cc output for those wanting a sub-1½-litre competition car, 1633 cc for 'normal' use, and 1726 cc which was straight out of the 15/6 saloon.

Sadly, the MPH was a commercial failure, for few people were prepared to pay £550 for such a car, even though it could reach about 85 mph, while sounding magnificent and feeling utterly safe. Accordingly the basic design was re-jigged, the new 1½-litre four-cylinder engine was fitted instead, and with a good deal of detail reworking of the body shell (which included making the

cockpit a bit more spacious) the Sprite was conceived. Most Sprites had the 'waterfall' type of front grille, and all had different front and rear wings which gave more coverage of the wheels.

After the MPH, the main attraction of the Sprite was its lower price – £425 – yet it still sold only slowly. No production records survive, but it is likely that between 50 and 70 Sprites were actually built, only five of them being assembled in the final year, 1938. This, therefore, was the last true Riley sports car, for the BMC Rileys which followed were usually saloons or drop-head coupés – elegant, but not sporting.

## Riley MPH variants

### Riley Sprite

The Sprite (1935-38) was a re-engined and redeveloped version of the MPH, with box-section chassis side members, and with detail revisions to the styling. Some cars were fitted with a fencer's-mask type of radiator grille. Its engine was an inline-four, of 69 mm × 100 mm and 1496 cc, producing 60 bhp. That proved sufficient to give a top speed of approximately 80 mph.

*Above: A 1934 MPH. The price was high, which is why so few Riley enthusiasts could afford one, and only 17 were built. The styling, regarded as Riley's best, was influenced by contemporary Alfas.*

## Specification (1934 MPH)

**Engine:** inline six-cylinder, overhead-valve

**Bore × stroke:** 57 mm × 95.2 mm/ 60.3 mm × 95.2 mm/62 mm × 95.2 mm

**Capacity:** 1458 cc/1633 cc/1726 cc

**Maximum power:** 70 bhp (approx) for 1726-cc engine

**Transmission:** four-speed manual or four-speed pre-selector gearbox, rear-wheel drive

**Chassis:** separate steel frame with channel-section main side members

**Suspension:** non-independent with beam axle and semi-elliptic leaf springs front; live axle with semi-elliptic leaf springs and torque tube rear

**Brakes:** drums all round

**Bodywork:** aluminium and steel two-seater sports car

**Maximum speed (approx):** 85 mph (137 km/h)

*Above: The spartan good looks and high price of the MPH soon led to the launch of the Sprite (below), less expensive but with 80-mph performance.*

## Riley Imp 1934-35

*Above: This Riley Imp is being raced more than 50 years after it was built. The 1087-cc engine had a great deal of tuning potential and the car's handling was excellent.*

The story of Riley's smart little Imp began with the Brooklands Six of 1932, a racing-sports car on a 108-in wheelbase which had a new chassis whose side members swept *under* the line of the back axle tubes. This new frame was shortened in wheelbase for the MPH/Sprite models and further truncated – to 90 inches – for a new roadgoing sports car called the Imp, to emphasise its truly diminutive nature.

Although founder Victor Riley did not believe that his engines could be highly tuned, he soon had numerous examples to prove him wrong, produced both within his factory competitions department and by private racing enthusiasts. The highest recorded output for a one-litre, three-bearing Nine engine was 183 bhp at 7,400 rpm, achieved with a very high supercharger boost; this sort of power, in a light, short-wheelbase model like the Imp, would result in phenomenal performance and acceleration, if not engine longevity. The outcome was that the Riley name became synonymous with British sporting success.

Three new Riley sports cars – the Imp, MPH and Sprite – were all conceived and developed at the same time, in 1933, the development engineer being Donald Healey. It was no coincidence that these cars all bore distinct visual similarities to the latest Alfa Romeos (which were *the* fashionable sports cars of the day), or that after Donald Healey moved to Triumph his stillborn Dolomite Straight Eight looked very much the same, although lacking the Alfa Romeo's perfect proportions.

By any standards the Imp was a graceful little car, for it had the fashionable long-bonnet/short-tail style, long-flowing front wings, cutaway doors, a fold-down screen and, of course, it had the famous hemi-head Riley Nine engine.

On the other hand, its chassis was really far too sturdy for the job, the engine only produced about 40 bhp, and acceleration was further hampered on some cars by the use of the heavy ENV-type four-speed pre-selector gearbox. The Imp also had an almost absurdly cramped cockpit, so much so that many owners never fitted the removable side screens, which got in the way of the driver's elbows!

It didn't help that the manual-transmission Imp cost £298 in 1934, which was not competitive with the latest MGs from Abingdon, though no-one could complain about the car's handling, or about its smart and attractive style.

Between 150 and 200 Imps were made in a production life of little over a year, but many of them survived into the modern era, where they are now regarded as typical (and highly desirable) British sports cars of the period.

### Specification (1934)

**Engine:** inline four-cylinder, overhead-valve

**Bore × stroke:** 60.3 mm × 95.2 mm

**Capacity:** 1087 cc

**Maximum power:** 40 bhp (approx)

**Transmission:** four-speed manual or four-speed pre-selector gearbox, rear-wheel drive

**Chassis:** separate steel frame with channel-section main side members

**Suspension:** non-independent with beam axle and semi-elliptic leaf springs front; live axle with semi-elliptic leaf springs and torque tube rear

**Brakes:** drums all round

**Bodywork:** aluminium and steel two-seater sports car

**Maximum speed:** 70 mph (113 km/h)

*Right: The 1932 Brooklands Six was the car which led to the development of the Imp. The six-cylinder engine, with supercharging or multiple carburettors, could be tuned to deliver up to 300 bhp.*

# Rolls-Royce

**H**enry Royce was a Manchester-based electrical engineer who bought a French Decauville car in 1903, was disappointed in several of its design and construction features, and decided to start building cars himself.

Within months he sold an early Royce car to the Hon. C. S. Rolls, who was so impressed that by the end of 1904 a new business partnership had been agreed, and the cars were henceforth called Rolls-Royces. From that day until the end of his life, Henry Royce dedicated himself and his workforce to designing and building the best cars in the world – and for a long time they succeeded.

The car which made the company famous was the 40/50HP (more commonly called the Silver Ghost), a dignified six-cylinder machine which went on sale in 1906, and from 1908 was built in a new factory in Derby. This would be the home of Rolls-Royce motor cars for the next 30 years.

Before long the firm had to survive without the day-to-day presence of its founders, for in 1910 Rolls was tragically killed, in an aeroplane accident, and after a serious operation Royce was persuaded to move to a better climate, where he continued to design cars, but let a professional manager (Claude Johnson) run the business for him.

Before World War II Rolls-Royce never built the elegant coachwork which clad its cars, merely supplying rolling chassis, complete with the characteristic radiator shell, to approved coachbuilders.

The business expanded rapidly between 1910 and 1940. The company began producing powerful and reliable aero engines, and an ultimately unsuccessful attempt was made to develop a branch of the concern in Springfield, USA. Most importantly, the firm bought up the remains of Bentley Motors in 1931, the first 'Rolls-Bentley' then appearing two years later.

After having designed a splendid series of cars in the 1920s and 1930s, Sir Henry Royce died in 1933. By this time the 40/50HP had given way to the Phantom family, the 'small' 20HP model had started a new line, the V12 Phantom III was on the way, and production had expanded to more than 1,000 cars a year.

By the time war broke out in 1939, Rolls-Royce had effectively become an aero-engine manufacturer which also produced a few cars. After the war, during which the famous Merlin V12 had been such an important powerplant, and the first gas turbine engines had been developed, this trend continued further.

Car assembly was moved to Crewe, to a modern factory which had originally produced Merlin aero engines, and for a time far more Bentleys than Rolls-Royces were made. The new Silver Wraith was soon followed by the Silver Dawn (the first-ever Rolls-Royce to have

*Above: The Silver Spirit was launched in 1980; this is a 1988 model. Its 6.75-litre V8 gave 119-mph performance, and the boxy styling was a mix of old and new.*

a factory body shell), the Silver Cloud series followed in 1955, and at long last in 1965 the first of the monocoque models, the Silver Shadow, took over.

By this time the Bentley marque had slipped back into the shadows, and Rolls-Royce expanded rapidly until 1971, when financial troubles in the aero-engine business saw the company go bankrupt. Car production continued, and in due course this was floated off as a separate concern. Before the Silver Spirit succeeded the Silver Shadow in 1980, Vickers had bought the car company. Production reached 4,000 in the late 1980s, in 1998 Rolls-Royce was sold to Volkswagen. Engine suppliers BMW own the name and will establish a new Rolls-Royce company in 2003.

*Above: The Silver Ghost really was the world's best car; this is a 1915 model, bodied by Hamshaw.*

*Below: A Barker-bodied Phantom I (left) and a 1934 Thrupp and Maberley-bodied Phantom II.*

## Rolls-Royce 40/50HP Silver Ghost 1907-25 (1921-26 in the USA)

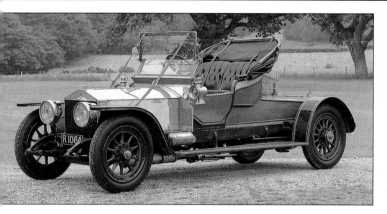

*Above: This 1911 40/50HP is a replica of the car in which Henry Rolls, a keen flyer, carried his balloon.*

Strictly speaking, there was only one Silver Ghost – the car built up by Rolls-Royce on the 13th chassis, with a silver-painted touring body and silver-plated fittings, and given that name by the company in 1907. Its more conventional title is 40/50HP, which denotes the engine type and power rating, but the Silver Ghost nickname refuses to die.

The new car was conceived by Henry Royce in 1905 as a complete redesign of the earlier Thirty model. Whereas the Thirty's engine had suffered from all kinds of vibration and technical problems, the new 40/50HP unit was silent, re-fined and almost totally reliable. It was a meticulously-detailed and low-revving side-valve unit with a very sturdy crank-shaft, which seemed to be vibration-free. Since Henry Royce did not believe that his customers knew or cared about horsepower ratings, he never quoted the unit's output, thus establishing a Rolls-Royce tradition which has persisted to his day.

The 40/50HP model was an enigma, whose reputation was built on legend. Although it was no more than technically up-to-date when announced, and was virtually obsolescent by the time it was dropped nearly 20 years later, it always *seemed* to perform better, and in a more refined manner, than any of its contemporaries.

The chassis layout was conventional, with the big side-valve six-cylinder engine taking up the front third of the frame, and at first there was a peculiarly Edwardian type of rear suspension, where the axle was sprung on half-ellip-tic leaf springs which were themselves supported by a transverse leaf spring. To make space for a large passenger com-partment there was a choice of wheel-bases – 135.5 inches or 137.5 inches – and the original cars were equipped with artillery-style wooden spoke wheels.

It was with this car that the Rolls-Royce reputation of building "The Best Car in the World" was founded. While the engineering of rival cars from Napier, Lanchester or perhaps Mercedes-Benz could match it, nothing could surpass the workmanship and care taken in the 40/50HP's construction.

At this time Rolls-Royce did not build coachwork, the rolling chassis being supplied to coachbuilders who could

provide an almost infinite variety of dig-nified styles, all of which shared the same long, low bonnet, and were fronted by what became the famous radiator shell, whose proportions were inspired by the buildings of ancient Greece. A really well-equipped 40/50HP would weigh as much as 5,000 lb, and top speed rarely exceeded 60 mph.

At no time was the 40/50 a design leader, but it was persistently improved over the years, not least in the engine, transmission, braking and suspension departments. It was very expensive, and new cars were invariably tended by a full-time chauffeur with a heated motor house and workshop at his disposal. It was, in other words, the best car for the richest owners, who expected the best possible behaviour.

In the 1920s Rolls-Royce tried to tap the growing wealth of North America by set-ting up a factory at Springfield, Massa-chusetts, where the 40/50HP was also built. A total of 6,173 chassis was built in Britain, and a further 1,703 in the North American factory, where the last 40/50 of all was produced in 1926.

### Specification (1907)

**Engine:** inline six-cylinder, side-valve
**Bore × stroke:** 114.3 mm × 114.3 mm
**Capacity:** 7036 cc
**Maximum power:** N/A
**Transmission:** four-speed manual gearbox, rear-wheel drive
**Chassis:** separate steel frame with channel-section main side members, tubular and pressed cross-bracings
**Suspension:** non-independent with beam axle and semi-elliptic leaf springs front; live axle with cantilever leaf springs and transverse leaf spring rear
**Brakes:** foot-operated drum at rear of gearbox, hand-operated drums at rear wheels
**Bodywork:** wide choice of five- to seven-seater coachwork, open or closed
**Maximum speed (approx):** 60 mph (97 km/h), depending on coachwork fitted

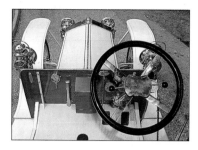

*Above: The driving position in Silver Ghosts was high, as on this very early 1907 example; the elevated posture intimated exalted status, and also gave excellent visibility.*

*Below: This 1914 40/50HP Silver Ghost has touring coachwork typical of the period. Designed to be used almost entirely in top gear, most Silver Ghosts were chauffeur-driven; note the rear windscreen.*

*Below: The original Silver Ghost, the 13th 40/50HP built, was painted silver with plated fittings. Its seven-litre engine (right) was in effect two three-cylinder units.*

# Rolls-Royce Phantom I 1925-29 (1925-31 in the USA)

*Right: The replacement for the long-lived Silver Ghost was the Phantom I. This example was built in 1926 and fitted with extravagant polished aluminium tourer bodywork by Barker, a coachbuilder with a long association with the marque.*

Although the 40/50HP Silver Ghost was a fine and successful machine, it was long overdue for replacement by the mid-1920s. Rolls-Royce, however, was a traditionally-minded company with a traditional clientele, so almost every element of its replacement, the New Phantom, was predictable.

Titled the New Phantom at first (but Phantom I after it was discontinued), the new model even shared the same chassis as the older car, though it had a brand-new overhead-valve six-cylinder engine, a smooth and utterly discreet 7.7-litre unit. Rolls-Royce, in fact, had not spent money developing a new chassis because it did not think that the customers would look under the skin! In any case, the style of the new cars was almost exactly like that of the old, because the same independent coachbuilders were producing bodies on the same-wheelbase chassis as before.

The New Phantom was not the fastest car in the world, nor the best-handling, but according to Sir Henry Royce's orders it was still built to the highest possible standards. It was certainly the most elegant, and refined, British car of the period, if perhaps no longer "The Best Car in the World", an honour which could be fought over by the likes of Hispano-Suiza and Cadillac.

*Above: This 1928 Phantom I was built in the USA. American clients, even then, tended to be more style-conscious than British ones; note the low roof and whitewall tyres.*

Each New Phantom, in one of two wheelbase lengths, took shape at the Derby factory, alongside the 20HP model, in a complex which also built aero engines, and when it was in the complete 'rolling chassis' form, with radiator and passenger bulkhead/scuttle in place, it would then be delivered to the coachbuilder of the customer's choice. Rolls-Royce was always discreet but liked to control the choice of coachbuilders, and particularly the choice of individual body style, but sometimes an extravaganza slipped through its net. A customer would begin discussions with the coachbuilder months before the chassis was ready; between six months and a year might elapse between a car being ordered and the new machine being delivered, which complicated this unofficial monitoring.

The new engine was certainly more powerful (but Rolls-Royce never revealed its power output), and because the Hispano-Suiza type of brake servo had been adopted, the New Phantom was also one of the most secure of 1920s machines. It was also very expensive – the chassis price was £1,850, and a complete car cost about £2,500 – but for this, Rolls-Royce gave a three-year guarantee on the chassis and running gear.

This model was only produced for four years in the UK, but it was also built in the USA, at the Springfield factory, where assembly persisted until 1931. In total, 2,212 cars were built at Derby, and another 1,225 in the USA.

## Specification (1925)

**Engine:** inline six-cylinder, overhead-valve
**Bore × stroke:** 107.9 mm × 139.7 mm
**Capacity:** 7668 cc
**Maximum power:** N/A
**Transmission:** four-speed manual gearbox, rear-wheel drive
**Chassis:** separate steel frame with channel-section main side members, pressed and tubular cross-bracings
**Suspension:** non-independent with beam axle and semi-elliptic leaf springs front; live axle with cantilever leaf springs rear
**Brakes:** drums all round
**Bodywork:** wide choice of five- to seven-seater coachwork, open or closed
**Maximum speed (approx):** 80 mph (129 km/h), depending on coachwork

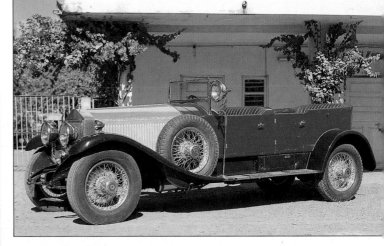

*Left: A short-wheelbase Phantom I roadster by American coachbuilder Brewster, made in 1927. Rolls-Royces were built in the USA until 1931.*

*Above: This 1926 Phantom I open tourer was given plain, unadorned coachwork by Barwani. Note the extra driving light.*

# Rolls-Royce Phantom II 1929-35

By the end of the 1920s the public, and the media, knew all about Rolls-Royce – or thought they did. On the surface they saw a company with patrician attitudes, selling expensive cars to rich people. What they did not see, under the skin, was the ongoing battle between Sir Henry Royce, the traditionalist, and some of his staff who would have liked to produce more exciting new cars.

The Phantom II, which took over from the New Phantom in 1929, was a typical example. As far as the adoring public – and, to be fair, most of the clientele – was concerned, here was a typical Rolls-Royce. It was more of the same – more refinement, more space, more (unstated) power, and naturally more prestige.

Critics were rarely given the chance to publish their opinions which, in the case of the Phantom II, were that it was not nearly as smooth, as advanced or as technically modern as some of its rivals. On the one hand, the Rolls-Royce fanatic David Scott-Moncrieff wrote that it was a magic carpet, wafting you silently",

*Below: Built in 1933 in America, this elegant 7.7-litre Phantom II convertible features Henley roadster bodywork by Brewster.*

whereupon John Bolster (who would later come to love his old Silver Ghost with great fervour) responded by calling this "arrant nonsense . . . the Phantom II was an even rougher car than the Isotta-Fraschini".

Customers made up their own minds,

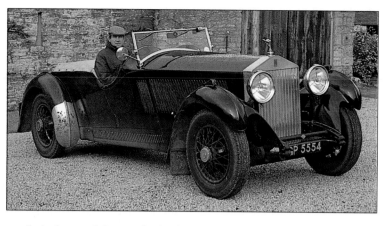

usually in favour of the car, for in six Depression-ridden years 1,672 Phantom IIs were built. Compared with the New Phantom, there was an all-new chassis, the gearbox was in unit with the 7.7-litre overhead-valve engine, and features such as flexible engine mountings, a synchromesh gearbox, and damper settings adjustable from the driver's seat were all fitted during the life of the car.

Body styles, in the main, were mere developments of late 1920s designs, for the famous radiator was as lofty as ever, but styling changes saw more flowing front wings, along with more rounded and 'streamlined' tails added as the years passed by. As ever, Rolls-Royce did not build its own coachwork.

The most exciting Phantom IIs of all were the 280 Continental types, which used the shorter of the wheelbases (144 inches instead of 150), higher overall gearing, different gear ratios, stiffened suspension, and lowered and more sporting four-seater saloon coachwork. There was no more power than with the standard cars, but Continentals were rather lighter (*The Autocar's* test car of 1932 weighed 5,488 lb) and handled that important bit better.

Even though the Phantom II was very large, and very heavy, it was undoubtedly a magnificent machine, beautifully

*Above: This owner-driver Phantom II, dating from 1931, has a Carlton Carriage Tourer body. Performance was not sporting, but progress was smooth.*

built and tested, and with an unbeatable presence. While other concerns producing very large cars went under during the Depression, or changed their marketing strategies, Rolls-Royce swept serenely, and profitably, on.

## Specification (1929)

**Engine:** inline six-cylinder, overhead-valve
**Bore × stroke:** 108 mm × 139.7 mm
**Capacity:** 7668 cc
**Maximum power:** N/A
**Transmission:** four-speed manual gearbox, rear-wheel drive
**Chassis:** separate steel frame with channel-section main side members and tubular cross-bracings
**Suspension:** non-independent with beam axle and semi-elliptic leaf springs front; live axle with semi-elliptic leaf springs rear
**Brakes:** drums all round
**Bodywork:** wide choice of steel or aluminium coachwork, open or closed
**Maximum speed (approx):** 90 mph (145 km/h), depending on coachwork

*Above: A sedate-looking Phantom II of 1930 with an all-weather body; the double-skin hood was very draught-free and waterproof.*

*Below: Note the eye-catching polished and painted coachwork, by the British firm Thrupp and Maberley, on this 1934 Phantom II.*

# Rolls-Royce Phantom III 1936-39

*Far right: Although both the chassis and engine were new, Phantom IIIs were often given coachwork little different from that of earlier models, as with this Thrupp and Maberley-bodied limousine.*

*Right: Phantom IIIs such as this 1938 model usually weighed more than 2½ tons. The 7.3-litre V12 was certainly powerful enough to ensure effortless progress, but steering required strong arms.*

By the time Sir Henry Royce died, in 1933, his design team had produced the first of many V12 aero engines. Work had also begun on a new-generation Phantom car – the Phantom III – so it was natural that the same engine layout was chosen. This was the first V12 model to go into series-production in Britain.

The Phantom III was the most complex *and* the most troublesome car Rolls-Royce had so far developed, and very few seem to have survived to this day. One innovation – that of independent front suspension – was overdue but thoroughly reliable when launched, but the other principal one – the massive engine – gave endless detail trouble.

As far as most wealthy customers were concerned, the Phantom III was merely a larger, heavier and slightly more expensive improvement on the dear old Phantom II, for there was the graceful continuity of body styles, the same noble radiator as ever, and the new car was apparently even more silent and discreet than before.

The engine, so tenderly developed, was a 7.3-litre V12 with overhead valves and hydraulic tappets. Although the bore and stroke were the same as those of the existing 3.7-litre 20/25HP model, there was virtually no connection between the two designs. The new unit leaned heavily on the latest aero-engine layouts – the racing R-Type and the Merlin – for V12 experience, for it featured light-alloy castings and wet cylinder liners. The hydraulic tappets, a feature first seen in Detroit, had been adopted to add refinement, but in old age these persistently clogged up owing to impurities in the engine oil.

The only way to describe the Phantom III is with superlatives. Up to that time it was the most successful Rolls-Royce ever put on sale, and also the heaviest. At around 6,000 lb a Phantom III weighed at least three times as much as an average small family saloon of the period, yet could reach more than 90 mph, so an average fuel consumption of 10 mpg was considered normal.

A British customer paid between £2,500 and £2,800 for a sumptuously-bodied Phantom III (only a Hispano-Suiza or a Grosser Mercedes-Benz cost more than this), and expected the best. He got a car with a modern chassis and a silent, torquey and advanced engine. His running costs may have been stratospheric, but he also got enormous prestige. In the late 1930s there was no more exclusive way of motoring than in a Phantom III, and although the chauffeurs had to work hard to look serene (for there was no power-assisted steering, nor automatic transmission at this stage of a Rolls-Royce's life), the ambience of the car was unbeatable.

Because the wheelbase was no less than 142 inches, and the rear track 61 inches, there was a vast amount of space in the rear seats for the owner to recline, for in those days few wealthy customers troubled to drive their own Phantom IIIs. Although Rolls-Royce was beginning to spend more hours on aero-engine work than on cars at this stage, there was still time for 710 Phantom IIIs to be produced in less than four years, before war broke out and killed off this amazing machine.

## Specification (1936)

**Engine:** V12, overhead-valve
**Bore × stroke:** 82.5 mm × 114.3 mm
**Capacity:** 7338 cc
**Maximum power:** N/A
**Transmission:** four-speed manual gearbox, rear-wheel drive

**Chassis:** separate steel frame with box section main side members and pressed cruciform cross-bracings
**Suspension:** independent front with wishbones and coil springs front; live axle with semi-elliptic leaf springs rear
**Brakes:** drums all round
**Bodywork:** wide choice of steel five- to seven-seater coachwork, open or closed
**Maximum speed (approx):** 90 mph (145 km/h), depending on coachwork fitted

*Above: A 1938 Phantom III with graceful saloon bodywork by Hoope. The all-alloy V12 was later estimate to deliver between 165 and 180 bhp; Rolls-Royce did not reveal output fo any of its models.*

*Left: This Phantom III is fitted with limousine de ville bodywork by Vanden Plas and has a division between chauffeur and passengers. Despite the heavy appearance, performance and roadholding were vast improvement on earlier cars.*

# Rolls-Royce Silver Wraith 1947-59

Well before the end of World War II, Rolls-Royce had begun to plan a completely new range of cars. These were known as the 'rationalised' models, and would share a new chassis, but were built in various wheelbase lengths. There was also to be a new range of engines – four-cylinder and inline-eight.

It was all very different from the 1930s, and it was signalled by the move of car assembly from Derby to the modern ex-aero-engine 'shadow' factory at Crewe. After 1945 Derby would concentrate on producing gas turbine aero engines in much larger numbers.

For the time being there was to be an even bigger emphasis on building Bentleys instead of Rolls-Royces; the company had decided to standardise the design of *all* its cars, and quite soon it was also planning to produce a model with a standard, factory, body style.

The first post-war Rolls-Royce, though, went only halfway down this road. Called the Silver Wraith, it had little in common with the pre-war Wraith, except for the famous radiator, and for the very high standard of build. Like the pre-war cars, Rolls-Royce only completed it to the rolling chassis stage, after which the body was built at one of the few surviving UK coachbuilders – Park Ward, Hooper, H. J. Mulliner, and Freestone and Webb being the most prominent.

*Right: A 1949 Silver Wraith with limousine body by Hooper. Following pre-war custom, two-colour paint schemes were common, but the yellow here was probably not original.*

*Below: Another 1949 Silver Wraith touring limousine. At this period the model's wings were gradually being faired into the bodywork.*

The Silver Wraith was built on two wheelbase lengths – 127 inches at first, or 133 inches from mid-1951 – with the latest six-cylinder engine, which featured overhead inlet but side exhaust valves. Although the bore and stroke were identical to the Wraith, few other parts were shared, and the new unit would be produced until 1959.

The Silver Wraith was Rolls-Royce's flagship for 12 years, and although not as powerful (or as large) as before, it was the direct successor to the Phantom III. It was big and heavy (complete cars rarely weighed less than 5,000 lb), and, although a few horrible aberrations slipped through, the usual coachwork was a large, lofty and dignified limousine, an owner-driver saloon, or a magnificent cabriolet or landaulette. The interiors were fitted out in top-quality materials, with the usual range of cocktail cabinets, extra rugs, subdued cabin lighting and – in a few cases – an onboard television set.

No-one bought a Silver Wraith for its performance, as its top speed, even if you persisted, was rarely more than 90 mph and it might take 20 seconds to glide unobtrusively up to 80 mph from rest. Instead the car sold to customers (mainly companies, governments or large and ostentatious civic bodies) who wanted to demonstrate their wealth or emphasise their social standing.

By the late 1950s, when the engines had been enlarged as far as possible and when automatic transmission became standard, the Silver Wraith was an automotive dinosaur. Nevertheless, it sold steadily until replaced by the new V8-powered Phantom V in 1959.

In 12 years 1,444 cars were sold on the 127-in wheelbase, and a further 639 followed on the 133-in wheelbase. On average, that was about 150 cars every year – a slow, but exclusive, business. Because of their ultra-solid construction, most of these cars have survived to this day.

## Specification (1947)

**Engine:** inline six-cylinder, overhead inlet and side exhaust valves
**Bore × stroke:** 88.9 mm × 114.3 mm
**Capacity:** 4257 cc
**Maximum power:** N/A
**Transmission:** four-speed manual gearbox, rear-wheel drive
**Chassis:** separate steel frame with channel-section side members and pressed cruciform cross-bracings
**Suspension:** independent front with wishbones and coil springs; live rear axle with semi-elliptic leaf springs
**Brakes:** drums all round
**Bodywork:** wide choice of aluminium and steel five- to seven-seater coachwork
**Maximum speed (approx):** 85 mph (137 km/h), depending on coachwork

*Above: This 1951 Silver Wraith has bodywork by Park Ward. After the war, Rolls-Royce's clients tended to order less diverse designs from the firm's regular coachbuilders.*

*Right: There were exceptions, of course, as with this Inskip-bodied 1946 Wraith; the Rolls-Royce chassis and grille were certainly adaptable, but clearly not to everything ...*

# Rolls-Royce Phantom IV 1950-56

If a supercar has to be exclusive, then the Phantom IV certainly qualifies. Mere money was not enough to buy such a car; in 1950s Britain it was as close to a motoring unicorn as could be found.

Even though Rolls-Royce could not indulge itself as much in the 1950s as it had between the wars, there was still time for one piece of hand-built whimsy. It made no commercial sense, and it was made in tiny numbers, but it was a magnificent folly. This was the Phantom IV, an eight-cylinder car so rare, and so exclusive, that only 18 were produced in six years. All of them went to members of the British Royal Family, or to Heads of State in other countries.

There was no Rolls-Royce precedent for a car like this. Even though it had always produced expensive machines in limited numbers, the company always had what businessmen called 'the bottom line' in mind. A new model, in other words, could be exotic, but it also had to be profitable.

But not the Phantom IV. Except for its front and rear suspension, and the transmission (all of which were shared with the Silver Wraith), almost everything else was special – and never used on another Rolls-Royce.

The chassis might have *looked* like that of the Silver Wraith, but had a con-siderably longer wheelbase – 145 inches, instead of 127 or 133 inches. The engine might have shared the same bore, stroke, pistons and valve gear as that of the Silver Wraith, but it was a straight-eight, not a straight-six. The bodies – all 18 of them – had ultra-spacious cabins, most of them with unique styles.

The hand-built Phantom IV was the fastest, largest, heaviest, most expensive *and* most exclusive of all Rolls-Royces. The very first car was delivered to HRH Princess Elizabeth in 1950 (two years before she became Queen), and was one of the Royal 'fleet' for many years after that. The last was delivered to the Shah of Iran in 1956.

Each and every body was individually styled and detailed. There were nine limousines, three saloons, two cabriolets, a sedanca de ville, a state landaulette (for the Queen), a special Franay-bodied car – and a delivery wagon! The last was Rolls-Royce's own development chassis which was put to good use until 1963.

Only two of the cars originally had automatic transmission (though the Queen's two cars were later converted). The H. J. Mulliner coachbuilding concern produced nine of the bodies, and Hooper built seven. The British Royal Family collectively bought five cars, but the ruler of Kuwait and Spain's dictator

*Above: The ultra-exclusive Phantom IV, very much a pre-war design, was imposing in a way unmatched by modern cars.*

General Franco bought three cars each.

In the beginning, incidentally, a Phantom IV was only delivered on the understanding that it would never be sold on by the first owner, but returned to the Rolls-Royce factory.

## Specification (1950)

**Engine:** inline eight-cylinder, overhead inlet and side exhaust valves
**Bore × stroke:** 88.9 mm × 114.3 mm
**Capacity:** 5675 cc
**Maximum power:** N/A
**Transmission:** four-speed manual gearbox, rear-wheel drive
**Chassis:** separate steel frame with channel-section main side members and pressed cruciform cross-bracings
**Suspension:** independent front with wishbones and coil springs; live rear axle with semi-elliptic leaf springs
**Brakes:** drums all round
**Bodywork:** choice of aluminium/steel seven-seater limousine or drop-head coupé coachwork
**Maximum speed (approx):** 95 mph (153 km/h)

# Rolls-Royce Silver Cloud 1955-65

For the first 10 post-war years, Bentley had completely overshadowed Rolls-Royce, but with the launch of the Silver Cloud all that changed. Ten times more Mk VI/R-Type Bentleys than Silver Dawns had been sold, but the new Silver Cloud range comfortably outsold the Bentley S-Series cars which were produced alongside it.

In many ways the Silver Cloud, which also inspired the Phantom V that followed, was the last of the Rolls-Royce dinosaurs. Even in 1955 it was new, but old at the same time. To the traditionalists it was still enough that a new Rolls-Royce had all the old virtues, but under the elegant skin the running gear was already obsolescent. With only one major update in the whole period, it was a miracle that the Silver Cloud sold so well for a decade. There was still a separate chassis, still four-wheel drum brakes, still the ancient but trustworthy mechanical servo, and still a live rear axle. The engine was a further development of the Silver Wraith type, and the transmission was an improved version of that used in the Silver Dawn – certainly there was nothing to surprise or interest the technical pundits.

Nevertheless, this was a larger and more impressive model than the Silver Dawn. The wheelbase was three inches longer, the track two inches wider, the overall weight up by about 400 lb, and there was a large and more spacious body. As with the Silver Dawn, the lofty but graceful shell was produced by Pressed Steel of Cowley; its sister model the new S-Series Bentley shared the same shell, except that it used a unique radiator style.

In four years no fewer than 2,238 4.9-litre Silver Clouds were built, before Rolls-Royce finally unveiled its new aluminium V8 engine. This unit, which had been in development for some years, was more powerful, but no less smooth than the old 'six', and would power all new Rolls-Royce and Bentley models for the next 30 years or more.

By this time the Silver Cloud design had advanced in many details. The longer-wheelbase type had arrived in 1956, and power-assisted steering came along in the same year, as did air conditioning. The 6.3-litre V8, which produced about 200 bhp (though the company never admitted to anything, or boasted about it), made a good car even better.

As *The Autocar*'s testers put it: "Every year 'The Best Car in the World' gets a little better", but by 1965, when the last cars of all were produced, the design was thoroughly out-of-date. Every Silver Cloud had been a pleasure to drive; that is, if one took account of its bulk and weight. With the V8 engine the car could swish up to about 115 mph, although it took 34 seconds to reach 100 mph from rest. As for fuel consumption, a typical Rolls-Royce owner rarely worried about such trifles, but if you bothered to measure it, 12 mpg was about average!

No fewer than 7,248 Silver Clouds with 'standard steel' coachwork were produced in 10 years, before the monocoque Silver Shadow range took over.

*Left: High-waisted and very long, the late-1950s Silver Cloud was the acme of prestige and luxury, especially the convertible model.*

## Rolls-Royce Silver Cloud variants

### Rolls-Royce Silver Cloud II

This model replaced the Series I, was built from 1959 to 1962, and had a 90-degree overhead-valve V8 engine of 104.1 mm × 91.4 mm, and 6230 cc. Peak power output was never quoted. The car's maximum speed was approximately 113 mph.

### Rolls-Royce Silver Cloud III

This model took over from the Series II, and was built from 1962 to 1965. Except for a different front-end style (four paired headlamps instead of two headlamps), and a more powerful engine (though this level was never quoted), it was virtually the same car as before, although styling was much updated and simplified. The approximate top speed was 116 mph.

### Specification (1955)

**Engine:** inline six-cylinder, overhead inlet and side exhaust valves
**Bore × stroke:** 95.2 mm × 114.3 mm

**Capacity:** 4887 cc
**Maximum power:** N/A
**Transmission:** four-speed automatic, rear-wheel drive
**Chassis:** separate steel frame with box-section main side members and cruciform cross-bracings
**Suspension:** independent front with wishbones and coil springs; live rear axle with semi-elliptic leaf springs
**Brakes:** drums all round
**Bodywork:** steel five-seater four-door saloon, with optional limousine or special coachwork
**Maximum speed (approx):** 106 mph (171 km/h)

*Above: A 1964 Silver Cloud III, with the twin headlamps, angled as on the Bentley Continental, and more power from the V8. Its much cleaner lines signalled that body styling had moved into the present day; note the blade-like rear wings, which were universal on cars of that period.*

# Rolls-Royce Phantom V 1959-68

*Above: A vivid two-tone Phantom V of 1963 – very long, very spacious and almost entirely hand-built.*

Even in the very late 1950s, Rolls-Royce still saw a demand for huge and stately cars with massive limousine coachwork. Introduced in 1959, the new Phantom V was a natural successor to the Silver Wraith and, for that matter, to the very exclusive Phantom IV. It was larger, heavier, and even glossier, yet just as elegant and just as carefully hand-built as any of its predecessors. In the first years a choice of body styles was available from the few surviving Rolls-Royce-approved coachbuilders.

To make such choices available, Rolls-Royce used a separate chassis layout once again – essentially an ultra-long-wheelbase version of the Silver Cloud II design, complete with the brand-new 6.3-litre V8 engine and automatic transmission. Because the Phantom V's wheelbase was 145 inches (the same as the Phantom IV), all the bodies were extremely spacious.

Soon, however, it became apparent that the world *had* changed considerably. Although Hooper and James Young

offered some remarkably elegant saloons or sedanca de ville styles, the vast majority of cars ordered were equipped with the lofty seven-seater limousine coachwork by Park Ward, who by the mid-1960s had merged with H. J. Mulliner.

This was, of course, an enormous car which (depending on options fitted) sometimes weighed up to 6,000 lb. Much of the time it would be seen gliding around towns and cities, or carrying out official, mayoral or chairman's duties, often at low speeds.

It was a car which Rolls-Royce had developed to be at ease when creeping along in processions, when moving sedately from head office to airport, or from townhouse to country estate, which explains why so much thought had gone into the automatic transmission, the power-assisted steering – and to the low-speed ride. Even so, these cars could exceed 100 mph, but the fuel costs were horrendous – less than 10 mpg was likely in certain conditions.

It was typical of Rolls-Royce's priorities that the chauffeur's seat was quite cramped, and because of the division-fitting there was no adjustment. Rear-compartment passengers had acres of lounging room, though the foldaway 'occasional' seats could hardly be called luxurious.

Demand for these cars was steady at first, but gradually fell away. A total of 832 Phantom Vs was built in nine years before the near-identical Phantom VI (with better air conditioning, and a Silver Shadow-type engine) took over in 1968. A mere 311 Phantom VIs were produced before the change-over to a 6.8-litre engine followed in 1978, after which only about 10 cars were built every year until assembly at Willesden faded away in 1992.

This was the last, and the grandest, of the separate-chassis Rolls-Royce models.

### Rolls-Royce Phantom V variants

#### Rolls-Royce Phantom VI

From late 1968 the Phantom V was replaced by the Phantom VI, which was mechanically identical, but had

better and more comprehensive equipment. Only limousines and landaulettes were available. From 1978 the specification was updated, with the 101.1-mm × 99.1-mm/6750-cc engine, allied to three-speed automatic transmission.

### Specification (1959 Phantom V)

**Engine:** V8, overhead-valve
**Bore × stroke:** 104.1 mm × 91.4 mm
**Capacity:** 6230 cc
**Maximum power:** N/A
**Transmission:** four-speed automatic, rear-wheel drive
**Chassis:** separate steel frame with box-section main side members and pressed cruciform cross-bracings
**Suspension:** independent front with wishbones and coil springs; live rear axle with semi-elliptic leaf springs
**Brakes:** drums all round
**Bodywork:** steel and aluminium five-to seven-seater limousine, with optional landaulette and other coachwork to special order
**Maximum speed (approx):** 101 mph (163 km/h)

*Right: The Phantom V, dominated by its tall grille, could be driven very smoothly at walking pace in processions but the 6.3-litre V8 had the torque to give rapid acceleration to over 100 mph.*

# Rolls-Royce Silver Shadow 1965-80

Stung by the criticism of its old-fashioned cars in the 1950s, Rolls-Royce struck back in the mid-1960s with a totally new design. Except for its rather elephantine handling there could be no complaints about this new car, for after two years of production the *only* item still common with that of the old Silver Cloud III was the engine.

The Silver Shadow was eventually launched in 1965, with a boxy but carefully-detailed style which had no links with previous Rolls-Royce shapes, with a new monocoque construction, new suspension, new braking systems and – for export-only at first – a new transmission.

In the late 1950s Rolls-Royce knew that several million pounds would have to be invested in the tooling for a new project and the directors took two huge decisions. One was to plan to keep the new design in production for a very long time indeed – the other was to endow it with a monocoque structure.

For a company with an annual output of fewer than 2,000 cars a year, this was an enormous gamble, but such was Rolls-Royce's standing that the Pressed Steel Company was delighted to take on such a low-volume project. Getting on for 30 years later, many of those panels were still being pressed at Swindon.

With the Silver Shadow, Rolls-Royce laid down its strategy for the period.

There would be one new wide-ranging generation of cars, eventually to be built as a saloon, coupé or convertible. Because it had a monocoque construction, this meant that Britain's surviving coachbuilders would find it almost impossible to produce special styles.

Although this was still a Rolls-Royce which was meant to glide rather than to rush, to sweep rather than to judder, to be silent rather than to be extrovert, and to be swift but utterly sure, Rolls-Royce gave it an extraordinarily advanced specification. It was a car which could cruise at 100 mph (and many owner-drivers – for chauffeurs, as a breed, were almost extinct by this stage – did just that), in comfort and in silence.

The four-door monocoque shell was conventional, as was the now-familiar aluminium V8 engine, but there was all-independent suspension complete with self-levelling controls, four-wheel disc brakes, a new type of General Motors automatic transmission – and enough complex hydraulics to make a Citroën designer envious.

Although the company no longer boasted of building "The Best Car in the World", it still endowed the new cars with the finest trim and furnishing details – wood, top-quality carpet and leather – and sought to make driving a totally stress-free business.

Before long the Silver Shadow was selling faster than any previous Rolls-Royce, a whole series of careful modifications and updates saw it command its market for 15 years, and by the late 1970s annual production was around 3,300.

Even after the Silver Shadow was displaced by the new Silver Spirit in 1980, the complex platform and all the running gear lived on in the new model, and with the company not planning to replace the Silver Spirit before the mid-1990s, the basic 'chassis' was to have a life of at least 30 years, easily a record for Rolls-Royce.

In 15 years a total of 30,059 Silver Shadow saloons was built, not to mention all the coupés, convertibles, Corniches, Camargues – and Bentleys – which were based on them.

## Rolls-Royce Silver Shadow variants

### Rolls-Royce Silver Shadow II and Silver Wraith II

From 1977 the design was updated and dubbed the Silver Shadow II, with rack-and-pinion steering, many detail changes and (from 1980) with Bosch fuel

*Above: A Silver Wraith II (left) with the long wheelbase, and a Silver Shadow II which, for the USA, had a fuel-injected V8.*

injection for sale in California, where emissions regulations were strictest.

At the same time the long-wheelbase version of the car was officially named the Silver Wraith II.

## Specification (1965 Silver Shadow)

**Engine:** V8, overhead-valve
**Bore × stroke:** 104.1 mm × 91.4 mm
**Capacity:** 6230 cc
**Maximum power:** N/A
**Transmission:** three- or four-speed automatic, rear-wheel drive
**Chassis:** steel unitary construction
**Suspension:** independent with double wishbones and coil springs front; semi-trailing arms and coil springs rear; self-levelling all round
**Brakes:** discs all round
**Bodywork:** steel five-seater four-door saloon
**Maximum speed (approx):** 115 mph (185 km/h)

*Above: The informative dashboard of a 1976 Silver Shadow Mk I was faced in fine veneer and hide.*

*Below: The Silver Shadow had a well-balanced and understated design which lasted well for 15 years.*

# Rolls Royce Corniche 1971-93

**Above: The epitome of luxury in 1975 was the two-door, five-seat Rolls-Royce Corniche convertible, beautifully trimmed and with a sensuous curve to the body sides. It looked simpler than the saloon, but much work had been done to strengthen the monocoque.**

Although the Corniche was unveiled in 1971, for the first five years, cars of that shape were sold merely as coachbuilt two-door Silver Shadows. Since that time, however, there has always been a Corniche in the Rolls-Royce range, built either on the basis of the Silver Shadow, or the Silver Spirit platform which developed from it. Naturally, there was a Bentley version of this car, too.

Because the Silver Shadow was of unitary construction, it was economically almost impossible for any traditional coachbuilder to construct special bodywork for the new platform. James Young tried it, with a two-door saloon style, but lost money on every one of the 50 cars (35 Rolls-Royce and 15 Bentley-badged machines) produced.

Even before the Silver Shadow was revealed, Rolls-Royce decided to solve this problem by involving its subsidiary, Mulliner Park Ward, where a consider-able amount of investment went into new welding and assembly facilities. Operating out of a Willesden (London) factory, this coachbuilder would accept an in-complete body platform from Pressed Steel, strengthen the underside, construct two-door body shells – coupé or drop-head coupé – and send them on to Crewe for finishing off.

The result was that a smart new, curvaceous two-door saloon was launched in March 1966, and the convertible version followed in the autumn of 1967. The introduction of the Corniche, which had a 10 per cent more powerful engine, was delayed until the spring of 1971, making it the first new Rolls-Royce to be brought out after the traumatic financial collapse of the parent company.

Except in detail, the Corniche always shared the same complex running gear as the Silver Shadow, usually getting major innovations a few months before they were applied to the saloon. When changes were being made to the under-pan and suspension ready for the forth-coming Silver Spirit, they were actually phased in on Corniche models a year earlier.

Apart from using the same nose and bonnet panels as the saloon, most of the Corniche's body was new, with a more graceful aspect to the side and the tail. Two, longer, doors were fitted, but access to the rear seats was not as easy as in the saloon. Electric seat adjustment, window lifts, and full air conditioning were naturally standard – it was even arranged so that the power convertible top could not be moved unless the automatic transmission selector level was in 'neutral' and the handbrake on.

Because of the way it was built, the time involved (20 weeks from the start of build to releasing a car to the distributor), and the limited numbers produced, the Corniche was always much more expensive than the saloon. In 1971, for instance, a Corniche convertible cost £10,270, while a Silver Shadow was priced at 'only' £7,600.

After the Silver Shadow gave way to the Silver Spirit in 1980, the last of the Corniche two-door coupés was produced in 1981, but Corniche convertible production continued unabated. By the early 1990s Corniche prices *started* at £159,997, compared with the £96,144 asked for a Silver Spirit. In a recession-struck world, it was no wonder that sales had fallen away considerably, that the London facility had been closed down, and that the body assembly lines had been moved to Crewe.

By the mid-1980s more than 2,800 Corniche convertibles had been delivered, but by the early 1990s only around 100 were being produced every year.

## Specification (1971)

**Engine:** V8, overhead-valve
**Bore × stroke:** 104.1 mm × 99.1 mm
**Capacity:** 6750 cc
**Maximum power:** N/A
**Transmission:** three-speed automatic, rear-wheel drive
**Chassis:** steel unitary construction
**Suspension:** independent with double wishbones and coil springs front; semi-trailing arms and coil-springs rear; self-levelling all round
**Brakes:** discs all round
**Bodywork:** steel two-door five-seater fixed-head coupé or convertible
**Maximum speed (approx):** 120 mph (193 km/h)

**Above: Named after Nice's coast roads, the Corniche was perfect for 'being seen in' in warm climes.**

**Below: With the hood erected progress was quiet, but broad rear panels obscured visibility.**

## Rolls-Royce Camargue 1975-85

The third major derivative of the Silver Shadow model, coded 'Delta' in its formative years, was not revealed until 1975, and signalled an important departure for Rolls-Royce; it was the first factory-built car to use an Italian-styled body.

Although the new car, called Camargue, was only a two-door model, it was still built on the same 120-in platform as the Silver Shadow, and was a full four-seater. It was the first Rolls-Royce to be given a new generation of fascia design and to be equipped with integrated split-level air conditioning.

The bulky, clumsy style was by Pininfarina, who clearly had a great deal of difficulty in combining the severe lines of the traditional radiator with their own ideas for the body. Those with an eye for styling cues claim that the Camargue's features were derived from a special T-Series Bentley built for James Hanson (later Lord Hanson) in 1968, and from the rather more elegant Fiat 130 Coupé. The Camargue had much the same bulk as the Corniche two-door coupé, yet the two cars looked strikingly different; the Corniche had elegant lines whereas the Camargue was slab-sided.

Camargues went on sale in 1975, slowly at first, then specially built to order, and they seemed to satisfy a slightly different market from the Corniche. Although Rolls-Royce never considered the Camargue to be a 'sporting' model, it was always tacitly understood that it was somewhat more rakish than other Rolls-Royces. Even so, its performance and handling were almost the same as any other car in this family.

*Above: Pininfarina tried hard, but the Italian coachbuilders could not blend their own ideas with the upright grille (right), and the Camargue thus looked like a foreign-bodied experiment.*

The Camargue was strictly a four-seater, as the leather rear seat was designed with two individual cushions and back rests, and for a time it was famous for being the most expensive British car of all. When launched in 1975, a Camargue sold for £29,250 – at a time when a Silver Shadow cost £15,462, and a Mini 850 was a mere £1,184.

Part of the expense was in the complicated way of producing the cars. From 1978 Pressed Steel Company would supply partly-built chassis platforms to Motor Panels of Coventry, who would then complete the body shells. These were then delivered, one at a time, to Crewe, where they went through the same rust-proofing and painting sequence before being diverted to a special department for completion.

By the early 1980s a Camargue cost £83,122, and sales were down to a mere 20-25 cars a year, which was not even profitable by Rolls-Royce standards, so after 531 cars had been built the Camargue was discontinued.

*Above: The Italian rear of this 1982 Camargue did not convey Rolls-Royce grandeur. Note the lack of door trim.*

*Below: A 1978 Camargue, with the earlier metal door trim designed to lighten the slab-sided effect.*

### Specification (1975)

**Engine:** V8, overhead-valve
**Bore × stroke:** 104.1 mm × 99.1 mm
**Capacity:** 6750 cc
**Maximum power:** N/A
**Transmission:** three-speed automatic, rear-wheel drive
**Chassis:** steel unitary construction
**Suspension:** independent with wishbones and coil springs front; semi-trailing arms and coil springs rear; self-levelling all round
**Brakes:** discs all round
**Bodywork:** steel four-seater coupé
**Maximum speed (approx):** 120 mph (193 km/h)

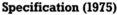

# Rolls-Royce Silver Spirit 1980-98

Rolls-Royce finally retired the Silver Shadow range in 1980, after a distinguished 15-year career, and replaced it with a slightly larger, heavier and more rounded car called the Silver Spirit. The new model was mechanically very familiar, with a modified version of the Silver Shadow's platform, and with developed variations of the same V8 engine, transmission, suspension and complicated electrical and high-pressure hydraulic systems.

Project SZ, as it was initially known, was born in 1969, but there was never a hurry to displace the profitable Silver Shadow. New air-conditioning systems were introduced (on the Camargue) in 1975, power-assisted rack-and-pinion steering followed on Silver Shadows in 1977, and a redeveloped rear suspension system, with new components and revised semi-trailing arm angles, was introduced in 1979 on the Corniche, all in

*Above: The Silver Spirit's flat, cluttered fascia contained plenty of information and warning lights.*

*Below: The model looked rather ponderous, but its torque gave the Silver Spirit brisk acceleration.*

preparation for the Silver Spirit.

Although styling studies leading to the Silver Spirit shape actually began in 1972, the 'energy crisis' of 1973 held things up for a time, and Fritz Feller did not finalise the design until 1977. Following customary Rolls-Royce practice, Project SZ covered a range of cars, with the conventional saloon also intended to spawn a longer-wheelbase version, the Silver Spur, and with Rolls-Royce *and* Bentley badges both scheduled for use.

The new body was slightly more spacious, marginally heavier, and a little more rounded than before. Since most of the equipment and furnishings – leather, wood, carpet, the silky switch operation and complex control layouts – was the same as before, the media made much of one new detail. On safety grounds, the 'Spirit of Ecstasy' mascot, mounted atop the radiator shell, was arranged to retract when struck by a blow from the sides or the top! It was an intriguing little detail – and one which Mercedes-Benz eventually copied, more than 10 years later.

Although Rolls-Royce was buffeted from several directions in the early 1980s – not least by the British recession – the Silver Spirit continued to sell well. At first it was little faster, no more economical and certainly no more nimble than the Silver Shadow, but in the mid- and late 1980s a whole series of development changes added to its appeal. In 1986 Bosch fuel injection was standardised for all markets (instead of merely for the USA, where exhaust-emission regulations demanded it), and at the same time ABS brakes were introduced. Sophisticated automatic ride-height controls were added in 1989, and as recently as 1992 the latest type of GM four-speed automatic transmission was standardised. An exhaust catalyst had arrived some years earlier, so even the thirsty Silver Spirit was as environmentally-friendly as possible.

Suspension rates and damper and

*Above: A 1987 Silver Spirit; the straight-line styling of this range was discreet and reserved.*

anti-roll bar settings were continually fussed over, the result being that the early 1990s Silver Spirit, while looking like the original 1980 model, was a better car in all departments. By the end of the 1980s Bentleys were assuming much more prominence at Crewe, which meant that sales of Silver Spirit cars fell back somewhat. At its peak, more than 1,500 Silver Spirits had been built every year, but this figure fell below 1,000 cars a year in the early 1990s. Even so, well over 10,000 Silver Spirits had been produced in the 1980s.

In 1998, a replacement finally appeared as the £155,000 BMW-engined Silver Seraph. With 322 bhp, it was capable of 140 mph but in a Rolls Royce, who's looking at the speed?

## Rolls-Royce Silver Spirit variants

### Rolls-Royce Silver Spur

This was a longer-wheelbase (by four inches) version of the Silver Spirit, with the extra length arranged to give more rear leg room, and was available from the start of production in 1980-81. The unladen weight was increased by about 60 lb. The Bentley equivalent was badged as the Mulsanne L.

### Rolls-Royce Touring Limousine

This was a much longer derivative of the Silver Spirit, still in the same basic style, but with a division between front and rear seats, and with a much enlarged rear compartment. Compared with the Silver Spirit, the Touring Limousine's wheelbase was increased from 120 inches to 148.5 inches.

### Specification (1980 Silver Spirit)

**Engine:** V8, overhead-valve
**Bore × stroke:** 104.1 mm × 99.1 mm
**Capacity:** 6750 cc
**Maximum power:** N/A
**Transmission:** three-speed automatic, rear-wheel drive
**Chassis:** steel unitary construction
**Suspension:** independent with wishbones and coil springs front; semi-trailing arms and coil springs rear; self-levelling all round
**Brakes:** discs all round
**Bodywork:** steel four-door five-seater saloon
**Maximum speed (approx):** 125 mph (201 km/h)

# Rover

I n the 1990s Rover's name covers every car produced by what used to be known as British Leyland, but until the 1960s it was an independent marque. Except for a brief period in the 1950s and 1960s, Rover built a series of conventional family cars, whose performance was well outside the supercar league.

Rover started life when James Starley set up a company to make bicycles in Coventry in the 1880s. Rover then progressed to building motorcycles in the early 1900s, and began selling cars in 1904. By 1914, and the outbreak of war, Rover was already a respected maker of cars and motorcycles, but the last two-wheeler was built in 1924.

By trying to make too many cars, too cheaply, in the late 1920s, Rover almost bankrupted itself, but a change of management and of marketing approach saved the company. From the 1930s to the 1960s Rover was in the safe and sensible control of Spencer Wilks and his brother Maurice.

By 1939 Rover was well known for building solid, high-quality, middle-class machinery, and its future was secured, though the Wilks family was more interested in fine furnishings than in high performance. During World War II Rover built or managed several aero-engine factories, and took on development of the very first gas turbine engines (which had been designed by Frank Whittle), but eventually this pioneering work was transferred to Rolls-Royce in Derby.

After the war Rover concentrated its car production at Solihull (originally one of the wartime factories), and introduced the famous Land Rover. In the next 20 years the company produced not only a series of gracious, well-built, but totally uninspiring cars, but also a growing mountain of Land Rovers – and a series of experimental gas turbine cars, the first to be built anywhere in the world.

Even though gas turbine engines were notoriously expensive and thirsty power units at that time, Rover's wartime experience of jet engines led a small team, which included Spencer King, to start work on gas turbine cars. Between 1950 and 1961 no fewer than five different types were built, and developed, but in spite of their advanced specification none ever came close to going into production.

Rover bought up Alvis in 1965, but by merging with Leyland in 1966-67 the marque lost its independence. Accordingly, Rover became a constituent member of the new British Leyland group in 1968. There were fast Rovers, and outstanding 4 × 4 Rovers, in the years that followed – all powered by the company's own V8 engine – and one splendid prototype, the mid-engined P6BS, which was cancelled after the first car had been assembled.

By the end of the 1980s, British Leyland had been sold to British Aerospace. Rover emerged as the sole survivor; it was acquired by BMW in 1992. First fruits of the new ownership were the revival of the MG marque in the MGF, the land Rover Freelander, excellent new engines and in 1999 the Rover 75. Profitability remained a problem however.

*Above: JET 1 was a gas turbine car built in 1950; it could reach 152 mph, but drank fuel at the rate of 5 mpg.*

*Left: The Rover logo decorates the honeycomb grille of this Rover 16/20HP, a sporting model launched in 1907 with variable-profile camshafts.*

*Right: The Viking longship badge was once associated with sober, solidly-built family cars; today it is featured on a range spanning from hatchbacks to supercars.*

*Left: Here the Walkinshaw/Percy Rover SD1 is in front in the 1985 European Touring Car Championship race at Donnington. The fuel-injected V8 Rover proved a strong contender.*

*Below: The 1992 two-litre turbo Rover 2220 Coupé was an adequately built family supercar, with a top speed of 149 mph and acceleration 0–60 mph in 6.3 seconds. Its Honda-led influences were clearly visible.*

# Land Rover 1948-present

Land Rover? A Supercar? Well, yes. If you've ever watched a trial or hill-rally, you'll know just how versatile a Land Rover is, thundering up near-vertical gullies and escarpments and edging down again without falling off. Anything that can survive an endurance event like the Camel Trophy has to be a supercar. It's become such an institution that you'll find a Land Rover pretty much anywhere in the world, and it celebrated its fiftieth anniversary in 1998.

In 1947 Rover took advantage of the need for a utility vehicle and the surplus of aluminium from the wartime aircraft industry and set up a production line at its new Solihull factory.

The Land Rover production line was, and still is, like a giant Meccano set, and the vehicle is based on a massive box-section steel-ladder chassis, to which three separate units of body panels were fitted. Original 50 bhp power unit was sourced from the Rover P3 saloon, with reduction gearbox giving a second set of ratios. The prototype was unveiled at the Amsterdam Motor Show in April 1948, and the vehicle became an instant hit with the farming community, and an export boom began to places where regular roads were lacking.

Subsequent evolutions were designated Series II – the original Land Rovers being retrospectively known as Series Is, built from 1948–1954, and the Series IIA ran from 1962–1971, the Series III from 1972–1984, and the more civilised Ninety (which became the current Defender in 1990) appeared in 1983. Among these basic evolutions were a whole host of specification and detail changes, including long and short

*Above: The Land Rover Defender was at home in any walk of life. Powered by the 2.5-litre turbodiesel engine, and available in 90-inch or 110-inch long-wheelbase with different body configurations including the County station wagon.*

wheelbase models, four and six cylinder petrol engines, bigger diesel engines, hard and soft-tops, along with variants for military and special applications. These included the forward control models like the Series IIB and V8-powered 101 that provided greater carrying capacity. Possibly the most significant development was the adoption of the turbodiesel TDi engine, which trans-

formed the performance and economy of the model. Apart from offerings from Jeep, the Austin Gypsy and military Champ, nothing came close to matching the ability of the basic Land Rover.

### Specification (Ninety TDi)
**Engine:** in-line four-cylinder diesel
**Capacity:** 2494 cc
**Bore x stroke:** 90.47 mm x 97 mm

**Gearbox:** permanent four-wheel drive, manual five-speed with step-down ratios
**Suspension:** live axles front and rear, coil springs and dampers, rear A-frame; optional self-levelling at rear
**Brakes:** dual-circuit servo-assisted, discs front, drums rear.
**Chassis:** box-section steel with aluminium panels

# Range Rover 1970-present

A more civilised Land Rover model came out in June 1970, with long-travel coil spring suspension with a rear ride levelling unit and retarded by four-wheel disc brakes, and powered by the new aluminium Rover V8 engine. This of course was the Range Rover, which went on to become a design icon. What was so remarkable about the Range Rover was its Jekyll and Hyde persona, as it could scale the rough stuff with the aplomb of its rustic sibling, yet cruise the blacktop like a limousine.

Increasingly luxurious Range Rover models became available, and developments included automatic transmission that made the transition to off-road easier for customers used to creature comforts, and pioneered a new market segment – the luxury 4 x 4. Emissions legislation led to fuel-injection being added to the V8 engine in 1985, with top speed rising to over 100 mph (161 km/h) for the first time. When Range Rovers were first exported to the US in 1987, air-conditioning, cruise-control and automatic transmission were standard.

What can be seen as a development of the Range Rover was the avant-garde Discovery, introduced in three-door form at the Frankfurt Show in 1989. As well as the Rover V8 engine, it was also

*Above: The Range Rover was equally as capable off road as it was on smooth blacktop. It could scale near-vertical cliffs yet was an imperturbable motorway cruiser.*

powered by the new 2.5-litre Garrett turbocharged, intercooled, direct-injection 200 TDi diesel engine. With the addition of a five door version the following year, and a facelift in March 1994, the Discovery gave Land Rover greater presence in the leisure sector, and it rapidly became the benchmark vehicle.

The BMW take-over of the Rover

Group in 1994 coincided with the launch of a new Range Rover, based on a new chassis and driveline with heavily revised V8 engines and a turbocharged BMW 2.5-litre six-cylinder diesel unit. State-of-the-art electronics controlled everything from the security system to the air suspension system and traction control. The new larger body was a monocoque design made in a new pro-

duction facility, and it served to consolidate Range Rover's position as class leader in the luxury 4WD sector. The original model continued to be produced as the Range Rover Classic until 1996.

To pick up on the market for small leisure off-roaders, Land Rover came out with the Freelander model in September 1997 at the Frankfurt Motor Show. It looked the part especially in three-door format and was almost as versatile as the Defender and Range Rover, thanks to its electronic Hill Descent Control (HDC), which used ABS for controlled descents of steep inclines.

### Specification (Range Rover V8)
**Engine:** aluminium V8 petrol
**Capacity:** 4554 cc
**Gearbox:** automatic sport/manual four-speed, with transfer box and viscous coupling
**Suspension:** electronic air suspension with variable ride height
**Brakes:** discs all round, four-channel ABS, electronic traction control.
**Chassis:** box-section steel ladder-frame
**Body:** zinc-coated steel semi-monocoque with aluminium panels

## Rover Turbine T1 1950

Rover's interest in gas turbine cars stemmed from the secret pioneering work done on prototype jet engines for aircraft during World War II. Between 1940 and 1943 Rover slaved to turn Frank Whittle's dreams into reality, and this experience was turned towards motor cars after the war.

When work started in 1946, Rover did not know if such engines could become economically viable in cars. The very first gas turbine-engined Rover – T1, as it

*Above: The car raced to 152 mph, its gas turbine engine producing 230 bhp. The power unit took up most of the car's rear (below).*

was known internally, or JET 1 as it was popularly named in the 1950s – was a world 'first' in every sense of the word. It was always intended to be a test car, and not to go into production, even on a small scale, in that state.

Gas turbine engines, which have no parts in reciprocal motion, are inherently very smooth, though they run at very high speeds and high temperatures, which means that rare and costly materials have to be used in their construction. As far as motor cars were concerned, designers had to balance cost against the potential huge power outputs which could be developed.

Work on gas turbine engines began at Rover in 1950, with Frank Bell in charge, and with Spencer King as his youthful assistant. The first engine ran early in 1947, but several different layouts were drafted before the T8 type was born in 1949. Although the popular press dubbed it a jet engine, it did not rely on jet thrust for its power. It was, in fact, more closely related to turbo-prop engines, as used in aircraft, where the power is developed at the output shaft.

The engine fitted to the first prototype could produce up to 230 bhp, but was restricted to a mere 100 bhp at first, and ran on cheap aviation-type kerosene. There was a single-stage centrifugal compressor (which revved up to 40,000 rpm), and the axial power turbine revved up to 26,000 rpm. Although the engine also acted as its own clutch or torque converter, naturally a step-down gearbox was needed!

To handle the new engine, Rover then developed a radically different version of its conventional P4 passenger car chassis. The gas turbine engine was mounted not at the front, but just ahead of the rear axle, driving the rear wheels through a step-down gearbox and a conventional propeller shaft. There was no clutch, and no conventional gearbox.

A smart two-door open tourer shell was fitted, making the Rover one of the

*Above: July, 1952, and RAC officials stand by as Spencer King prepares to drive Rover's JET 1, the world's first gas turbine car, as fast as possible on the Jabbeke motorway in Belgium. It never ran so quickly again.*

first mid-engined road cars ever built. Even so, it was not a stylish shape, all the model's charisma coming from its performance and its specification rather than from its looks.

JET 1 first ran in 1950, but a great deal of test work lay ahead before Rover fitted a 230-bhp engine in 1952, to allow the car to reach an RAC-observed 152 mph on the Jabbeke highway in Belgium, with Spencer King behind the wheel. In this tune the engine 'idled' at 13,000 rpm on the compressor shaft, and overall fuel consumption was about 5-6 mpg. At this stage there was obviously a lot more to come from gas turbine engine design, but Rover preferred to direct this work to another type of car, and JET 1 was never driven as fast again.

JET 1 proved that gas turbine engines were technically practical, if not yet economically viable. After Rover finished with it, the car found an honoured place in London's Science Museum display, where it rests to this day.

### Specification

**Engine:** single-stage gas turbine with centrifugal compressor
**Maximum power:** 100 bhp (later 230 bhp for record-setting purposes)
**Transmission:** forward and reverse gears, rear-wheel drive
**Chassis:** separate steel frame with box-section main side members and pressed cross-bracings
**Suspension:** independent front with wishbones and coil springs; live rear axle with semi-elliptic leaf springs
**Brakes:** drums (later discs) all round
**Bodywork:** steel two-door open two-seater
**Maximum speed (approx):** (230-bhp version) 152 mph (245 km/h)

# Rover Turbine T3 1956

Rover's second-generation gas turbine car was a much more serious project than the first. Not only was there a new type of engine, but the chassis, driveline and styling were new from end to end. Spencer King and his 'packaging' expert Gordon Bashford produced an advanced and thoughtfully-detailed machine. Compared with JET 1 and its descendants, here was a car which could have been a perfectly practical road car if further developed.

Unfortunately, by this time there was neither much money for T3's construction, nor time to allocate a team of designers to do the job. King and Bashford (with some input from Peter Wilks) therefore tackled the design as an evenings and weekends job, using Bashford's dining-room table as the drafting board. The style, as with other one-off Rovers, came from Spencer King himself.

Although T3, as a rear-engined car, was unique as far as Rover was concerned, there were several pointers to technical themes still in Rover's future – one of which was the use of de Dion rear suspension with fixed-length driveshafts and a sliding joint in the de Dion tube, the other being a layout for the independent front suspension in which the top wishbones fed loads direct into the scuttle.

The basis of the car was a fabricated steel frame, suitably stiffened by light-alloy honeycomb, while the smart two-seater coupé body was glassfibre.

The gas turbine engine was a new two-shaft 110-bhp design, designated 2S/100, which was matched to four-wheel drive – a real innovation in the British motor industry. Four-wheel Dunlop disc brakes (then at the experimental stage with many of Britain's carmakers) were also fitted, inboard at front and rear.

Observers boggled at the turbine engine's vital statistics and habits, for here was a unit which did not 'light up' until the compressor turbine shaft was revolving at 15,000 rpm, and which 'idled' at 20,000-25,000 rpm. Peak power was developed at 52,000 rpm, at which speed the power unit was still completely smooth. Such engine speeds meant that an overall step-down ratio of 28.92:1 was needed!

Although T3 was practical, it was still not economically viable. Compared with JET 1, there had been a dramatic improvement in fuel economy – from 5 mpg to around 13 mpg – but this was still not acceptable. The major improvement had come from the use of a heat exchanger, which helped to 'recycle' waste exhaust heat, of which there was a great deal in this type of engine.

Rover was beginning to realise that the cost of building gas turbines was never likely to fall to piston-engine

*Above: The glassfibre-bodied Rover Turbine T3 would have been a superb 105-mph road car, if not for the enormous cost of its engine and the fuel it consumed.*

levels. At the time the company admitted that it cost as much to make just one turbine disc as it did to build a complete six-cylinder P4 piston engine.

Apart from its economic problems, T3 was a fast, practical, stylish and well-handling car. The company never intended to put it into production as the price would have been horrendous, but in most other respects it was a viable and attractive machine. Only one car was built, which survives to this day.

## Specification

**Engine:** single-stage gas turbine with centrifugal compressor and heat exchanger
**Maximum power:** 110 bhp
**Transmission:** forward and reverse gears, four-wheel drive
**Chassis:** separate steel frame with fabricated and pressed main and reinforcing members, some in aluminium honeycomb
**Suspension:** independent front with wishbones and coil springs; de Dion rear axle with coil springs
**Brakes:** discs all round
**Bodywork:** glassfibre two-seater coupé
**Maximum speed (approx):** 105 mph (169 km/h)

# Rover Turbine T4 1961

Although Rover had realised that automotive gas turbines were still far too expensive to put into series-production in the 1960s, the company built two fascinating project cars in that period. One was the Rover-BRM racing-sports car, which appeared at Le Mans in 1963 and 1965, the other being an entirely practical road car, the T4, the two sharing the same type of engine.

Although few realised it at the time, the T4 saloon was not a totally unique design, for it used a modified version of the monocoque style and structure which

was to form the basis of the forthcoming Rover 2000; the front suspension of that car was actually arranged to allow space for the bulky turbine power unit. Even so, this was not merely a re-engined prototype, for Spencer King and Gordon Bashford had developed an entirely new driveline for this final gas turbine car.

The T4 was yet another solution of the problem of matching gas turbine power to a car chassis; T1 had been mid-engined with rear-wheel drive, and T3 had been rear-engined with four-wheel drive, while T4 had a front engine and

front-wheel drive.

The newly-developed 2000 structure and front suspension was used almost unchanged, but instead of a sturdy four-cylinder two-litre piston engine there was a 2S/140 gas turbine which had a regenerative heat exchanger, produced 140 bhp, and was claimed to give between 16 and 20 mpg.

This was matched to front-wheel drive (with a simple forward-and-reverse transmission), while at the rear swing-axle independent suspension was used. The huge volume of exhaust gases was

routed through capacious ducts in what was really the propeller-shaft tunnel.

The T4 was undoubtedly the fastest of Rover's roadgoing gas turbine cars, for it could accelerate to 60 mph in no more than eight seconds (as rapidly as the later V8-engined version of the Rover 2000), although when the driver floored the throttle while the car was cruising there was still a lot of what we would now call turbo lag.

Undoubtedly the T4 handled well, looked good, and was certainly very fast, but the problem of making the engines at the right price was insuperable. In 1961 Rover bosses suggested that T4 *could* be put on sale in the mid-1960s if there was a demand for it – but that it would cost £3,000-£4,000 at a time when the Rover 2000 was available for £1,265.

*Left: The bodywork was almost a prototype of the Rover 2000, but this 120-mph model was the last of the company's turbine experiments.*

## Specification

**Engine:** single-stage gas turbine with centrifugal compressor
**Maximum power:** 140 bhp
**Transmission:** forward and reverse gears, front-wheel drive
**Chassis:** steel unitary construction
**Suspension:** independent with wishbones and coil springs front; swing-axles and coil springs rear
**Brakes:** discs all round
**Bodywork:** steel four-door saloon
**Maximum speed (approx):** 120 mph (193 km/h)

# Rover P5B 1959-1973

Here's another British institution that in its day was beloved of elderly aunts and uncles, and indeed, was one of Her Majesty's favourites. The P5B was a direct descendent of the P5, launched in 1959 as Rover's first unit-construction design, and a coupé version appeared in 1963 with a cut-down roofline. The quantum leap occurred in 1967 when Rover clinched a deal with Buick to use the American manufacturer's all-aluminium 3.5-litre V8 engine, and the P5B was born. It was instantly faster, lighter, more economical and handled better, yet still provided that elusive combination of pace with tradition, luxury and style.

The rumbling V8 and its three-speed automatic transmission provided relaxed, effortless progress, while occupants lounged in leather armchairs within. All cars had loathsome Rostyle wheels – nothing that a nice set of Minilites wouldn't cure, if a little racy for the P5B – but not a lot changed during the car's production run. An automatic choke fitted post-1968 proved problematic, and inertia reel seat belts were fitted from 1969. The Rover V8 was fed by twin SU carbs and could turn a respectable 110 mph (177 km/h) and get to 60 mph (96 km/h) in 12.4-seconds, which seems slow until you consider this was a hefty car. Suspension consisted of wishbones and laminated tor-

*Above: The P5B was a dependable car, something between a family saloon and limousine. Leather and walnut gave it a palatial interior. It had the light-weight 3.5-litre Rover V8 engine which was powerful, though hardly frugal.*

sion bars with dampers and anti-roll bar at the front, and the live rear axle was supported by good old-fashioned semi-elliptic leaf springs and dampers. Brakes were discs at the front and drums at the rear, and power steering was standard fitment.

The P5B remained in production alongside the P6 2000 and 3500 models until it was phased out in 1973. Today, its main drawbacks as a usable classic are corrosion and high fuel bills, plus the assumption of bystanders that ownership somehow confers upper class status.

**Variant:**

**Rover P5B Coupé**
This was exactly the same specification as the saloon, but with a lowered roofline, and consequently seen by some as more desirable.

**Specification**
**Engine:** V8
**Capacity:** 3528 cc
**Gearbox:** three-speed automatic
**Suspension:** front, independent by wishbones, laminated torsion bars, dampers, anti-roll bar; rear, live axle with semi-elliptic leaf-springs, dampers
**Brakes:** discs front, drums rear
**Chassis:** four-door steel monocoque

# Rover 75 1999-present

The Rover 75 was introduced at the 1998 Birmingham NEC Motor Show and was the first Rover to be designed wholly 'in-house' for over two decades. It was also the first to emerge under BMW's ownership of the Rover Group, the result of a £700-million investment programme that included a brand new factory in Oxford. The pundits were quick to heap praise on the 75, to the detriment of the Jaguar S-type launched at the same time, largely because it was felt that the Rover's styling was innovative, rather than derivative in the case of the Jaguar.

The 75 was designed under the supervision of Richard Woolley, Studio Director at Rover Cars Design department, and Wyn Thomas, Chief Designer, Interiors. They were careful to include styling cues from past eras to please the marque's traditional audience, including touches of chrome on the door mirrors, bumper, body-side inserts and the sill finisher, along with the rear number plate surround that doubled as a spoiler. Inside, traditional materials like chrome, soft leather and real wood were used. Equipment included an integrated telephone, choice of two navigation systems, 'concert hall' audio system and automatic air conditioning. The bodyshell was more than twice as rigid as the outgoing Rover 600, and had a drag coefficient of 0.29 Cd.

The 75 was powered by a range of K-series petrol engines, including the KV6 quad-cam 24-valve units, available in 1.8-, 2.0- and 2.5-litre format. The 2.0-litre engine developed 150 bhp and the 2.5-litre version produced 175 bhp,

*Above: Unveiled at the 1998 NEC Motor Show amid speculation about Rover's future under BMW rule, the 75 was an excellent design that promised to re-establish the company's fortunes as a purveyor of quality mid-range cars.*

and it could also be ordered with the 115 bhp BMW common rail 2.0-litre CDT diesel unit. At launch, the 75 was the only transverse engined front wheel drive car to offer a fully electronic JATCO five-speed automatic gearbox, while a Getrag five-speed manual gearbox was also available.

Front suspension was by MacPherson struts, mounted on a perimeter frame, with a subframe mounted Z-axle at the rear, with springs and dampers all round. The all-disc brake system included the

latest four-sensor ABS and Electronic Brake force Distribution (EBD) set-up.

Ironically, just as Rover was poised to make a comeback after its days in the stylistic doldrums with Honda-inspired products, BMW was in the throes of a top-level personnel shake-up, which threatened the future of the entire Rover Group. With a starting price of just under £20,000 in the UK, the 75 presented a real threat to BMW's own 3-series as well as other class leaders like Alfa Romeo and Audi.

**Specification (KV6)**
**Engine:** transverse V6, 24-valve KV6
**Capacity:** 2.5-litre
**Gearbox:** five-speed manual, five-speed electronic automatic
**Suspension:** front, MacPherson struts, L-shaped lower arms on subframe, dampers, anti-roll bar; rear, Z-axle, coil springs, dampers, anti-roll bar
**Brakes:** discs front and rear, Bosch 4-channel, EBS, ABS; electronic traction control available
**Chassis:** four-door monocoque

# Rover Vitesse 1983-86

Rover may never have made a sports car, but in the early 1980s they showed what could be done with their main luxury saloon car by transforming the SD1 into a real BMW competitor, in the shape of the Rover Vitesse.

The original SD1 was introduced in 1977 as a large four-door hatchback powered by Rover's ex-GM all-alloy V8 engine in rather basic tune, producing just 155 bhp at 5,250 rpm and 198 lb ft of torque at 2,500 rpm. The chassis specification was rather basic, with MacPherson struts at the front and the rear having a simple live axle. Nevertheless, it soon became clear that the car could handle considerably more power without compromising its handling or roadholding in the least. It took six years, however, before Rover produced the right performance package. The most important

*Below: The Vitesse was large, but agile and very fast. Some said the SD1 shape was influenced by the Ferrari Daytona.*

change was to give the engine more power, and this was done by discarding the rather restrictive twin SU carburettors in favour of Bosch L-Jetronic fuel injection. That was allied to some re-profiling of the inlet ports to give better gas flow and an increase in compression ratio from 9.25:1 to a high 9.75:1. That proved sufficient to boost the power output to a far more impressive 190 bhp at 5,280 rpm, while torque was also improved, to 220 lb ft at a rather high 4,000 rpm.

Good though the standard chassis was, it was improved to cope with the extra power by fitting larger, alloy, wheels with low-profile tyres, the final choice falling on 6.5-in × 15-in wheels with 205/60 VR15 tyres. The body was lowered by around an inch and the spring rates increased by 20 per cent. Attention was paid to making the Vitesse stop better too, with larger, four-pot, calipers being fitted to the vented front discs (although drums were retained at the rear). Those brakes had been develop-

*Above: The aerodynamic Vitesse, with a drag coefficient of 0.36, could be distinguished from more humble models by its alloy wheels and rear spoiler.*

ed during the car's very successful competition career. Its combination of a very tunable engine and excellent handling made the Rover a favoured mount in the British Touring Car Championship for many years.

Vitesses could be distinguished by those special, spoked, alloy wheels and a large spoiler on the rear hatch; the latter provided useful downforce and also helped reduce the drag coefficient to 0.36. Combined, all those changes went to produce a fast car, one capable of a top speed of 135 mph and 0-60 mph acceleration in 7.6 seconds. The 0-100 mph sprint took 20.7 seconds and the standing quarter-mile could be covered in 15.9 seconds. Naturally, with all that torque available, the in-gear figures were very good too, with 30-50 mph and 40-60 mph in third taking only 5.2 and 4.9 seconds respectively. Fuel consumption, at 21.8 mpg, was better than with the slower Rover 3500S.

By the time the Vitesse appeared, it was already an old design, and at £14,950

it was only £1,000 cheaper than the more sophisticated Jaguar XJ6 4.2. Still, it certainly proved there was lots of life left in the SD1.

## Specification (1983)

**Engine:** V8, overhead-valve
**Bore × stroke:** 88.9 mm × 71.1 mm
**Capacity:** 3528 cc
**Maximum power:** 190 bhp
**Transmission:** five-speed manual gearbox, rear-wheel drive
**Chassis:** unitary construction
**Suspension:** independent front with MacPherson struts and anti-roll bar; live rear axle with trailing arms, Watt linkage and coil springs
**Brakes:** discs front, drums rear
**Bodywork:** steel four-door hatchback
**Maximum speed (approx):** 135 mph (217 km/h)

*Below: The Walkinshaw/Percy Vitesse was one of many used to great effect in the European Touring Car Championship, as here at Donington in 1985.*

# Saab (Svenska Aeroplan Aktiebolaget)

A s endless adverts in the 1980s and 1990s stressed, Saab was first and foremost an aircraft manufacturer rather than a car-builder. The Svenska Aeroplan Aktiebolaget – to give Saab its full original name – began developing their first car in the 1940s, while the rest of Europe was still engaged in the war. The prototype appeared in 1947 (the year which coincidentally saw the first Saab jet fighter), but it was another two years until it went into production as the Saab 92. It was designed by Sixten Skasten and, as befitted an aircraft company, was a very aerodynamic design and of unitary construction; it also had front-wheel drive. Such advanced features were a little negated by its powerplant, however. Saab did not consider it a viable proposition to make their own engines and relied initially on a version of the pre-war German DKW two-stroke twin, a small low-powered engine of just 764 cc.

By 1955, the car had changed into the Saab 93 and had a three-cylinder two-stroke of 748 cc. Further evolution brought the Saab 96 in 1960, a car which made its fame in rallying with Erik Carlsson, winning the RAC in 1960, 1961 and 1962 and the Monte Carlo Rally in 1962 and 1963. As the Saab 96 grew up, its three-cylinder two-stroke was replaced by a German V4 and then the long-lived design was superseded by the far more advanced 99, which first appeared in 1969 and used a development of the inline four-cylinder, overhead-cam Triumph engine. Saab stressed that over the years they themselves carried out a lot of work on this engine to bring it to the standard they required.

Saab had a brief diversion into sports car production with a range of glassfibre-bodied Sonnets, with either the three-cylinder two-stroke or the V4, but soon reverted to the bread-and-butter of saloon cars. In 1968 Saab merged with the Scania-Vabis truck company, and the late 1960s and 1970s saw steady progress and development of the 99 range, with a larger-displacement, 1985-cc, Saab-built derivation of the Triumph overhead-cam engine appearing in 1972. Fuel injection was later added to power the EMS model, which was followed by the 99 Turbo. By 1978 the 99 was rather long in the tooth, but it was developed, rather than totally discarded, to produce the longer 900 model which was to last to the 1990s in various forms. Up to and including the 900, all Saabs had been odd-looking vehicles, but that changed with the advent of the 9000 in 1984 – which was initially part of a collaborative venture between Saab, Lancia (with the Thema), Fiat (with the Croma) and Alfa Romeo (with the 164) – but by the time the various models appeared, the links were tenuous. By the time of the 900, Saab had developed a twin-cam 16-valve head for their four-cylinder engines, and as the 1980s progressed they brought out a 2.3-litre version. Saab never felt rich enough to develop anything other than a four-cylinder engine, and such financial and marketing constraints eventually spelled the end of the company's independence as General Motors took a stake in 1991.

*Above: A 1977 Saab 96L; its rounded styling was still very like that of the original 1949 Saab 92.*

*Below: The 1993 Saab 900 Turbo 16S; Saab was one of the first companies to market turbo cars.*

*Below: The experimental Saab EV-1 was built in 1985 and debuted at the Los Angeles Motor Show. Its tuned 16-valve turbo engine developed 285 bhp, gave a top speed of 186 mph and did 0-60 mph in 5.4 seconds.*

## Saab 99 Turbo 1978-80

*Left: The front-wheel-drive 99 had first appeared in 1968, and was a well-proven model before Saab fitted a turbocharger.*

*Above: The 99 Turbo was rugged enough for rallycross; this is Will Gollop's car at Snetterton.*

### Specification (1978)

**Engine:** inline four-cylinder, overhead-cam, turbo
**Bore × stroke:** 90 mm × 78 mm
**Capacity:** 1985 cc
**Maximum power:** 145 bhp
**Transmission:** four-speed manual gearbox, front-wheel drive
**Chassis:** unitary construction
**Suspension:** independent front with wishbones, coil springs, telescopic dampers and anti-roll bar; beam axle with trailing links, Panhard rod, coil springs and telescopic dampers rear
**Brakes:** discs all round
**Bodywork:** steel two-door hatchback
**Maximum speed (approx):** 120 mph (193 km/h)

*Below: The 99 had a very rigid body shell and durable suspension. With 174 lb ft of torque it offered tremendous acceleration, but fuel consumption was heavy.*

To Saab went the distinction of marketing the first production turbo car in Europe (the world's first had been a version of the Chevrolet Corvair). The turbo installation was, however, added not to a new model but to one already 10 years old. The 99 had been introduced in 1968, with a 1.7-litre Triumph/Saab overhead-cam engine and a modest power output. The engine was mounted longitudinally at the front, but turned through 180 degrees compared with conventional practice so the camshaft drive was towards the back of the car's huge engine bay, which was easily accessible under a large forward-hinging one-piece front section. The combination of front wishbones and a dead-beam rear axle gave excellent handling and road-holding, and the car was made steadily more powerful, principally through the

introduction of the 99 EMS in 1975. That had a 1985-cc version of the engine with Bosch fuel injection and a maximum output of 110 bhp. Adding a turbocharger, as Saab did in 1978, produced the ultimate 99. The compression ratio was dropped to 7.2:1 to allow for the Garrett T3 turbo, a larger clutch was fitted, gear ratios were made higher, and different alloy wheels were fitted, along with harder pads for the four-wheel disc brakes. Spoilers were added front and rear, and the end result was an impressively fast and very stable car.

Turbocharging made an already smooth engine far smoother, as well as greatly increasing its power, which went up to 145 bhp at 5,000 rpm, while maximum torque was an even more impressive 174 lb ft at 3,000 rpm. As the figures indicated, Saab had gone for maximising

torque rather than outright power with their turbo installation, making the engine feel almost like a larger six-cylinder. Its performance was excellent; a figure of 9.1 seconds for the 0-60 mph sprint may not be outstanding today, but it was in 1978, while the in-gear acceleration times were excellent. Although the effects of the boost could be felt from as low as 1,800 rpm, the Turbo did feel initially sluggish until well into its stride compared with the EMS, but that impression soon evaporated as the revs climbed. About the only drawbacks to the car, which was superbly built, strong, safe and well equipped (even having a heated driver's seat), were the fuel consumption, which could easily average below 20 mpg, and the price, which was slightly higher than its main rivals (at £7,850 in 1978).

# Saab 9000 Turbo 1985–97

## Saab 9000 Turbo variants

### Saab 9000CS

After Saab had built their largest-displacement engine so far, it made sense to offer that in turbocharged form, too. The larger, 2.3-litre, engine of the 1990 9000CS was given an intercooled turbo allied to traction control for the front wheels, which now had to deal with an output of 200 bhp at 5,000 rpm, along with an excellent torque figure of 244 lb ft at just 2,000 rpm – emphasising again that Saab liked to give its turbo the attributes of larger, normally-aspirated engines. The extra power and torque brought the 0-60 mph time down to eight seconds, and 0-100 mph acceleration to 21.4 seconds. Top speed was unchanged from the two-litre car, although the tuned Aero model of 1993, which was the spiritual successor to the Carlsson, could reach 149 mph.

With Saab's reluctance to make anything other than four-cylinder engines, it was inevitable that the 9000 went the same route as the 99 and 900 before it and received turbocharging to boost its power and performance dramatically.

The 9000 had appeared in the mid-1980s and broke new ground for Saab in several ways, in starting out as a collaborative venture (although the degree of co-operation between Saab, Fiat, Lancia and Alfa Romeo was far less than first envisaged), in being an executive-size car and, thanks to the input of Ital Design, in being attractive if perhaps slightly bland.

With Saab never having built a rear-drive car, the 9000 predictably had front-wheel drive (despite its size) and originally power came from a twin-cam four of 1985 cc. Unlike the 99 and 900, the 9000 had its engine mounted transversely rather than longitudinally. Nevertheless, the engine could trace its ancestry back, if rather tenuously, to the Triumph-inspired unit used in the 99. Great strides had been made since then, however, and the 9000 could boast an output of 130 bhp. The addition of another eight valves and a Garret turbocharger in 1985 was enough to transform the car. It gained another 45 bhp over the normally-aspirated car and a corresponding increase in performance to give

*Below: A 9000 Turbo tackles the Swedish snow. Saabs were renowned for their reliability in adverse conditions, which they proved in many rallies.*

a top speed of 137 mph and a 0-60 mph time of 8.3 seconds.

In the late 1980s Saab decided to stress the turbo car's performance even more and cash in on one of the company's great assets, the name of rally driver Erik Carlsson. The limited-edition Carlsson model made a fine-handling car even better with slight revisions to the MacPherson-strut front and beam-axle rear suspension, stiffening the spring and damper settings to suit the extra power of 220 bhp.

Even this did not satisfy some critics who felt a car of that size should have more than just two litres, even if the engine was an intercooled 16-valve turbo, and size was increased to 2.3 litres.

## Specification (1989 9000 Turbo)

**Engine:** inline four-cylinder, twin-cam, 16-valve, turbo
**Bore × stroke:** 90 mm × 78 mm
**Capacity:** 1985 cc
**Maximum power:** 175 bhp
**Transmission:** five-speed manual gearbox, front-wheel drive
**Chassis:** unitary construction
**Suspension:** independent with MacPherson struts and anti-roll bar front; beam axle with trailing arms, coil springs and telescopic dampers rear
**Brakes:** discs all round
**Bodywork:** steel hatchback
**Maximum speed (approx):** 137 mph (220 km/h)

*Below: The 9000 Aero had higher trim levels, bigger wheels, more power and 149-mph performance.*

## Saab 9-3 Turbo Sport 1998-present

Saab's sporting flagship for the end of the decade was the Saab 9-3 Turbo Sport, introduced in 1998. It was available as a three-door model, described as a coupé, a five-door saloon and convertible, and was distinguished from regular cars in the range by a 200 bhp 2.0-litre turbocharged engine, a unique leather interior, sports-pack bodywork and a certain amount of chassis tuning. Uprated suspension settings and recalibrated shock absorbers were applied to all three models.

Despite its GM floorpan, Saab's restrained styling was sufficiently individualistic to make the cars stand out from the herd. This was matched under the bonnet by Saab's tried and tested transverse-mounted front-drive turbo engine, which delivered mid-range performance efficiently via a five-speed box. The 9-3 Turbo Sport accelerated

*Right: By 1999 Saab had made 1000 changes to its 900 model, including chassis improvements that made the 9-3 a car with superb handling. There were three body styles: five- or three-door, and cabriolet; and four engine options including a diesel. The best performer was the 2.0-litre Turbo S three-door model that recalled the days of the original.*

from 40-60 mph (64-96 km/h) in fourth gear in less than six seconds, while top speed was 146 mph (239 km/h) and 0-60 mph (0-96 km/h) took 6.9 seconds.

In common with all Saab turbocharged engines, the Turbo Sport unit had a typically flat torque curve and provided strong pulling power between 2,000 rpm and 4,000 rpm. Saab's 32-bit Trionic engine management system controlled boost pressure, fuel injection, and ignition timing for each cylinder. Maximum boost was regulated to 1.0 bar and peak power of 200 bhp was developed at 5,500 rpm. Counter-rotating balancer shafts made for smoother running, in addition to intercooling and direct ignition, which eliminated distributor and plug leads.

The 9-3 Turbo Sport's cabin featured a uniquely-styled leather-clad interior with seats upholstered in black or beige

'pebble grain' leather. Equipment included automatic climate control, dual front airbags, two-phase side airbags, electrically-adjustable headlamps with wash/wipe and steering-wheel-mounted audio controls.

A number of body styling features distinguished the Turbo Sport from the rest of the Saab 9-3 range, including deeper front and rear bumpers and scalloped sill extensions. The rear spoiler and door mirrors were colour-coded, and the whole ensemble was set off by 16-inch, three-spoke alloy wheels, shod with 205/5ORW tyres.

### Specification
**Engine:** in-line four-cylinder
**Bore x stroke:** 90 mm x 78 mm
**Capacity:** 1,985 cc
**Gearbox:** five-speed manual; optional four-speed, electronic automatic with three driving programmes
**Suspension:** front, MacPherson struts, gas dampers and anti-roll bar; rear, H-formed, twist-beam rear axle, inner and outer anti-roll bars, coil springs and gas dampers.
**Brakes:** power-assisted disc brakes all round, ventilated at the front; ABS with electronic brake force distribution (EBD).
**Chassis:** steel monocoque

## Saab 9-5 Griffin 1998-present

The most luxurious car ever produced by Saab, the 9-5 Griffin, was launched in 1998. It was powered by the 200 bhp 3.0-litre V6 Ecopower engine with automatic transmission, which was the world's first asymmetricall tubocharged engine, meaning that the Garrett GT17 turbocharger was driven by exhaust gasses from one bank of cylinders to charge all six. Boost pressure was regulated to a mild 0.25 bar and the boost control system operating via the electronic throttle eliminated the need for a wastegate. The turbocharger housing was part of the exhaust manifold, instead of being a separate casting. The engine monitoring was by the T.7 Trionic management system, incorporating an electronic 'drive-by-wire' throttle, and power was fed to the front wheels via an electro-hydraulically controlled, four-speed automatic Aisin Warner transmission with three separate modes: 'normal', 'sport' and 'winter'. A switchable electronic traction control system was also incorporated, utilising the ABS. Peak torque was available between 2,100 rpm and 4,200 rpm, while maximum power was 200 bhp at 5,000 rpm. Suspension by MacPherson struts with gas dampers, and anti-roll bar at the front, with a multi-link set up at the rear incorporating a rubber-suspended central beam, one longitudinal and two transverse link arms for each wheel, spring struts with gas dampers and anti-roll bars.

The Griffin's sumptuous leather interior included the first electrically-ventilated front seats offered in a production saloon, 'after-heating' which kept the interior warm without the engine running, and armchair-like electrically-adjustable leather seats. There was also dual zone automatic climate control, heated front seats and, would you believe, a cooled glove-box. Thus cosseted, occupants could entertain themselves with the 200 watt, nine-speaker Harman Kardon hi-fi system. A 'smart' volume control automatically compensated for changes in background noise level and remote controls were fitted to the steering wheel.

You'd have to keep a good look out to spot one though. Griffin badges behind each front wheel-arch, 16-inch alloy wheels and a twin chromed exhaust tailpipe were the only visual clues to the most opulent Saab yet produced.

### Specification
**Engine:** V6, four overhead camshafts, four valves per cylinder
**Bore x stroke:** 86 mm x 85 mm
**Capacity:** 2962 cc
**Transmission:** four-speed, electronically controlled automatic
**Brakes:** power-assisted discs all round, ventilated in front; ABS with electronic brake force distribution (EBD)
**Suspension:** front, MacPherson struts with gas dampers, anti-roll bar; rear, multi-link type, rubber-suspended central beam, one longitudinal and two transverse link arms each side, spring struts with gas dampers and anti-roll bars.

*Below: The 9-5 was agile and handled well. The Griffin was a scorcher with 200 bhp from its 3.0-litre V6 Ecopower engine with asymmetric Garrett turbo.*

# Salmson

*Left: The British Salmson badge recalled the parent French firm's flying origins and the radial engines it built during World War I. In 1910 the company had built a helicopter, but it did not fly.*

*Right: A 1927 Salmson VAL3. The model, launched in 1925, was a more robust version of the Type AL cycle-car, and had semi-elliptic front suspension.*

T he Paris-based Salmson concern had already made its name as a maker of aircraft engines before it began to build cars. As a carmaker it was most popular between the wars, and like many other French manufacturers it then died slowly in the 1950s.

Salmson aero engines figured strongly in World War I military aircraft, but as demand for these naturally slumped in 1919 Salmson took out a licence to build GN cars instead. The first true Salmson designs followed in 1921, but the company carried on building aero engines.

During the 1920s Salmson grew up, its models developing from the spidery GN cycle-car layout to more substantial four-cylinder sports cars. By the mid-1920s the first twin-cam Salmson engine had appeared (and was used in the cycle-car Grand Prix) and had been adopted for road cars, which made this marque one of the most technically advanced in the world.

The fashion for small French sports cars flared briefly in the late 1920s and vanished almost as rapidly as it had appeared. Like other French companies, Salmson then made a rapid change of policy by turning to more luxurious machines. Six-cylinder twin-cam cars were produced, and by the end of the 1930s these 1.6-litre models had been joined by 2.3-litre cars.

For a time in the 1930s Salmson even branched out into British manufacture, the so-called 12HP British Salmson having a 1.5-litre engine, and being assembled at Raynes Park, Middlesex, with its mechanical equipment mainly imported in kit form from France, but this business fizzled out before the outbreak of World War II.

Until France was overwhelmed by the German invasion of 1940, Salmson carried on making military aircraft engines, but for the next five years the factories operated unwillingly on behalf of the German conquerors. Remarkably, after 1945 the company was still financially

sound, and rapidly returned to making cars once again, with models based on pre-war designs.

Briefly, after the war, there was a demand for such exotically-specified cars, and about 1,000 Salmsons were sold in 1950 alone. By the early 1950s the economic realities had sunk in – very few such cars could be exported, and French customers preferred to buy small Renaults or larger front-drive Citroëns rather than exotic and possibly temperamental sports coupés. Salmson was therefore forced to introduce a more conventional touring car, the Randonnée, but in a real gesture of defiance the 2300S coupé was then launched in 1953.

Students of style will realise that the coupé design later influenced the shape of the original Facel Vega, although production shells were actually made by the coachbuilders Chapron. Although the 2300S, and its roadster derivative, were fine and fast Grand Touring machines, they sold very slowly indeed, for the French probably realised that the underpinnings (like the electro-magnetic pre-selector gearbox) were very old-fashioned.

By the mid-1950s the end was already in sight. The G72 sports coupé of 1953 did not sell well, Renault took over the factory in 1956, and the very last Salmson of all was built early in 1957.

*Left: A 2.6-litre British Salmson Tourer, one of the last built in 1939 at the firm's Raynes Park factory. Pre-war, a variety of body styles were fitted to Salmson chassis.*

*Below: The 2590-cc twin-cam six-cylinder engine, introduced in 1937, was unique to the British Salmson factory; French legislation effectively stifled the demand for larger engines.*

## Salmson Grand Sport 1923-30

Salmson's pretty little Grand Sport models were amazingly advanced for the period, for at a time when most other cars – large and small – had side-valve engines the Salmsons were fitted with small high-revving twin-overhead-camshaft units. These were, in fact, the world's very first twin-cam road cars.

The Grand Sport models made their appearance in 1923, four years after the very first Salmson-badged cars had appeared, and were really the forerunners of a short-lived series of small-engined French sports cars. With a relatively long wheelbase of 104 inches, but absolutely no overhang (or bumpers!), it set a style soon copied by others. At the time no other country was building such machines – it was not until MG developed the first M-Type Midgets that there was any real competition.

Except for its engine, the Grand Sport was utterly conventional; the flexible ladder-style chassis was short, with the rear axle cantilevered off the back by quarter-elliptic leaf springs, and there were no rear brakes – but this was normal for the period.

The twin-cam engine was undoubt-edly inspired by other famous French racing engines of the period, including the pioneering Peugeot GP units. Like them, and in common with many other units which followed, it was produced in cast-iron, part-spherical combustion chambers were used, and there was a 90-degree angle between the line of valves. Strangely enough, only a two-main-bearing crankshaft was used at first, though a three-bearing crank was standardised before the end of the 1920s.

The original engines developed a mere 36 bhp. This, and the fact that there was only a three-speed gearbox (with a cone clutch), limited the little car's performance, but the chassis was nimble and, by the standards of the day, this was an exciting little car.

The height of the Grand Sport's career was in 1927, when the cars finished second and third at Le Mans (behind the three-litre Bentley which won the race). Production and sales were always limited – even though France had some of the best roads in 1920s Europe, its motor industry was relatively small – and in eight years only about 2,700 twin-cam-engined Salmsons were made.

### Specification (1923)

**Engine:** inline four-cylinder, twin overhead camshafts
**Bore × stroke:** 62 mm × 90 mm
**Capacity:** 1087 cc
**Maximum power:** 36 bhp
**Transmission:** three-speed manual gearbox, rear-wheel drive
**Chassis:** separate steel frame with channel-section main side members and tubular cross-bracings
**Suspension:** non-independent with beam axle and semi-elliptic leaf springs front; live axle with quarter-elliptic cantilever leaf springs, torque tube and radius arms rear
**Brakes:** drums at rear, no front brakes
**Bodywork:** aluminium-panelled two-seater
**Maximum speed (approx):** 70 mph (113 km/h)

*Above: A 70-mph 1923 Salmson Grand Sport; examples of the twin-cam racer came second and third at Le Mans in 1927.*

## Salmson 2300 1953-57

Although Salmson began making 1930s-style cars again immediately after World War II, using the same chassis and the twin-overhead-camshaft engines which had made the marque so famous, the first true post-war model was the Randonnée touring car of 1951.

Although this had a redeveloped engine, which featured more light-alloy castings and a 110-lb weight-saving, it was not a success, for it was a bulky four-door, high-quality saloon which the French public could not afford.

Then, in 1953, Salmson made what would be its final model, a true *Grand Routière* in miniature, this time in then-fashionable shape of a fastback

*Below: The 2300 was possibly the best Salmson ever, but French politicians successfully killed off the builders of such exotica.*

coupé. Even eight years after the war, France was still recovering, and was austerity-stricken, so this smart indulgence, with a claimed top speed of 100 mph, received a lot of attention.

Although the engine was a slightly enlarged version of the Randonnée type, with 105 bhp – which made it comparable to the contemporary Jaguar XK unit – there was a brand-new chassis, and the French-made Cotal electro-magnetic gearbox was standard. Although the designers may have looked at what Jaguar was doing, the 2300's torsion-bar front suspension was very much in the Salmson traditions.

The coupé shell, whose lines predicted those which would shortly appear on the larger Facel Vega coupés, was made by Chapron, and shortly it was joined by a smart roadster version whose style had surely been influenced by the latest Ferrari barchettas.

By early 1950s standards the 2300, especially in roadster form, was a fast car, but although it was successful in French rallies it was too expensive to sell widely. Further, potential customers could clearly see that there was old-fashioned engineering under the modern styles.

*Above: The 2300 coupé was fast and attractive, with styling points shared by the Facel Vega, early Ferraris and the Pegaso.*

This, then, was the last – and possibly the best – Salmson sports car of all, but only 227 were made in five years. Renault took over the Billancourt works in 1956, and car assembly closed down completely in 1957.

### Specification (1953)

**Engine:** inline four-cylinder, twin overhead camshafts
**Bore × stroke:** 84 mm × 105 mm
**Capacity:** 2327 cc
**Maximum power:** 105 bhp
**Transmission:** four-speed pre-selector electro-magnetic gearbox, rear-wheel drive
**Chassis:** separate steel frame with box-section side members
**Suspension:** independent front with wishbones and torsion bars; live rear axle with cantilever leaf springs and torque tube
**Brakes:** drums all round
**Bodywork:** steel two-door four-seater fastback coupé
**Maximum speed (approx):** 100 mph (161 km/h)

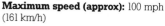

# Shelby American Inc.

**B**efore he became a legendary figure in North America's motor industry, Texan-born Carroll Shelby had several earlier careers. During World War II he was a flight instructor; he also operated a dump-truck business, then raised chickens immediately afterwards, but he rose to fame as a racing driver.

Soon after driving the winning Aston Martin with Roy Salvadori at Le Mans in 1959 he retired with a heart ailment, and shortly struck a deal with Ford-USA and AC of Great Britain to build exotic, low-production sports cars. After recruiting a few like-minded engineers and managers – there was no shortage of either breed in California – Shelby set up Shelby American Inc. and based it at Venice (a district of Los Angeles).

Shelby American was always a very compact business, which did not design new cars, but rather inspired, modified or improved a series of others. For that reason there are purists who insist that Shelby is not a marque of its own, but such people are invariably shouted down by thousands of Cobra and GT500 fans.

The car-marketing business began in 1962, when Shelby himself visited AC in Thames Ditton with a promise of V8 engine supply from Ford-USA, and persuaded AC to develop a car which he called the Shelby American Cobra, but which the rest of the world has always known simply as the AC Cobra.

Hundreds of these cars were sold successfully in the USA before Shelby then turned directly to Ford-USA, to inspire, develop, and then sell a series of much-modified versions of the Ford Mustang, called Shelby GT350s and GT500s. By comparison with the hand-built Cobras, many more of these cars were sold, for the production process was easier. Starting in 1965 Ford supplied partly-completed Mustangs to Venice, where a small workforce completed the transformation into seriously fast road cars which were also highly suitable for racing saloons, or even as dragsters.

Although Carroll Shelby himself could no longer race at top level, he attracted large financial support from Ford-USA, and from Goodyear, to allow him to set up SCCA and World Sports Car Championship teams. Shelby won the American SCCA Manufacturers Championship in 1963, 1964 and 1965 with Cobras, but the biggest triumph of all was the trouncing of Ferrari to win the World Manufacturers' Championship in 1965, with the brutally effective Daytona Cobra.

Demand for GT350s and GT500s was at its height in 1969, but by the beginning of 1970 the American love affair with 'pony cars' – which had enormous performance and extrovert styling – was fading, and Ford

*Right: The Shelby badge graced some of America's most famous performance cars, created by Carroll Shelby (below), who is shown with the Shelby AC Cobra 427 and the Shelby Mustang GT350.*

decided to run down its direct involvement with North American motorsport. The result was that these charismatic cars were dropped early in that calendar year.

During the 1970s Carroll Shelby turned to other, non-automotive, business ventures, but he returned in 1982, founding links with Lee Iacocca at Chrysler. Before the end of that decade his name was appearing on various Chrysler Corporation products, including a 16-valve twin-cam engine which was actually designed and developed by Lotus in the UK. As in the 1960s, batch-production of much-modified cars – Dodges this time – was carried out in California.

In 1960 Shelby underwent a successful heart transplant operation, and carried on, indefatigably, in business. Thirty years after starting the Cobra business, he built up a new series of these cars, thus provoking the anger of the Cobra's modern builder, Brian Angliss.

*Below: "Designed to be designed by you" was Ford's slogan for the Mustang, and referred to the many options. The Shelby GT350 was the ultimate option, with far more power and better handling than the standard cars.*

# Shelby GT350 1965-70

Purists might say that these cars were no more than modified Ford Mustangs, but most American motor historians and performance fans agree that the GT350 was truly a Shelby. From 1965 to 1970 they were the fastest and most desirable of all derivatives of this famous model.

Carroll Shelby's success with the AC

*Above: A four-barrel carburettor and high-lift camshaft resulted in prodigious power and torque.*

*Left: Shelby's Mustangs had the twin-stripe livery; this is one of the Hertz rental models.*

Cobra led Ford-USA to ask him to race Mustangs in the Sports Car Club of America (SCCA) racing series, the objective being to defeat the Chevrolet Corvettes which were currently so dominant. To make sure that these 'production sports cars' had the highest possible performance, Ford agreed that Shelby should assemble a limited number at the Venice plant, in California, alongside the Cobras.

Starting on the basis of the brand-new fastback hard-top Ford Mustang, Shelby's engineers developed machines which were the equal of the fastest Corvettes, with more power, greater strength and better roadholding. Shelby began with a blue-striped white Mustang (supplied from a Ford factory with the new 4.7-litre V8 engine).

By adding a high-rise camshaft, a four-barrel carburettor, and free-flow exhaust manifolds, the horsepower was pushed up to 306 bhp – making this easily the most powerful Mustang of the day. Tuning enabled it to produce 350 bhp (later 400 bhp) in racing form. This was matched to a Borg-Warner T10 'four-on-the-floor' manual gearbox, and a beefy Ford Galaxie-type rear axle.

All this was complemented by bigger and better brakes, Koni shock absorbers, high-ratio steering and special 15-in alloy wheels, along with a glassfibre bonnet (which included a fresh-air scoop), while the rear seat was removed and the spare wheel was strapped into that position instead.

Although the GT350 was conceived as a racing car, most were sold for normal road use, with 1965 prices starting at a mere $4,547. A total of 4,115 original-shape GT350s was produced between 1965 and 1968, which included the optional models with a 350-bhp Paxton super-charged engine, before a restyle for 1969-70 began to destroy the original 'built-for-racing' pedigree; this was the point at which a convertible body style was made available. Hertz Rent-a-Car got in on the act in 1966 by ordering 936 GT350s painted black with gold striping, the main mechanical difference being the use of automatic transmission.

Because Shelby GT350 assembly was moved back to a Ford factory in 1968, and because Ford's need for 'racing road cars' had evaporated by the end of the 1960s, customers were reluctant to pay a big premium for Mustangs which did not seem to have the same pedigree as before, so sales dropped away – 1,657 were built in 1968, and 1,279 in 1969, but only 315 1970 models (which were really leftover 1969 cars) followed.

In 1968 the engine size was increased to 4941 cc, with 250 bhp or (super-charged) 350 bhp. For the 1969 and 1970 model years, engine capacity was increased again, to 5765 cc, giving 290 bhp.

Although the original GT350 was an extremely popular limited-production model, the demand for which often stretched Shelby to its limits, it was a harsh-riding car which seemed to attract wild drivers. Before long the insurance rates asked spiralled out of all proportion, which effectively killed off the model's attraction.

*Above: A 1966 Shelby GT350; the compact 'personal' Mustang was one of Ford's best-sellers.*

*Above: The cockpit and fascia of a GT350 incorporated more instruments than the standard car.*

## Specification (1965)

**Engine:** V8, overhead-valve
**Bore × stroke:** 101.6 mm × 72.9 mm
**Capacity:** 4727 cc
**Maximum power:** 290 or 306 bhp, to choice
**Transmission:** four-speed manual gearbox, rear-wheel drive
**Chassis:** steel unitary construction
**Suspension:** independent front with wishbones and coil springs; live rear axle with semi-elliptic leaf springs and radius arms
**Brakes:** discs front, drums rear
**Bodywork:** steel two-seater fastback coupé
**Maximum speed (approx):** (306-bhp version) 124 mph (200 km/h)

## Shelby GT500 1967-70

In the autumn of 1967, when Ford first offered the large-block Galaxie-type 6.4-litre V8 engine, Shelby immediately adopted it as a means of selling more cars, and also added the even larger version of that engine, the same basic 7.0-litre unit that was being fitted to some AC Cobras and AC 428 models of the period.

The new Shelby GT500 was an entirely different type of Mustang. Instead of having a relatively high-revving small-block V8 which could be further tuned for racing, it had a larger and altogether lazier unit. At the expense of considerably more front-end weight, this gave the much-modified Mustang a lot more torque than before. At the same time Shelby assembly was moved out of California, back to the very same production lines as those occupied by the more mundane 'mainstream' Mustangs.

To keep the insurance companies happy, Shelby and Ford not only advertised the 7.0-litre engine as having 355 bhp when in fact it had about 400 bhp, but also offered a smaller 6.4-litre/335-bhp version. The Shelby cars received a considerable facelift, which featured a new bonnet and nose, and a built-in roll bar for the convertible.

By 1968 the visual image of the Shelby Mustang had changed considerably – the new car being larger, and more luxuriously equipped than ever before. Luxury options like automatic transmission, air conditioning and tinted glass now outweighed performance features. For 1968 only there was a GT500KR, where KR stood for 'King of the Road'; this car had the 400-bhp Cobra Jet 428-cu in V8, with a four-barrel Holley carburettor which pumped air into those vast cylinders at the rate of 735 cubic feet a

minute. Weight had by this time crept up to 3,700 lb.

By 1969 the Shelby Mustang craze was past its peak, and one has to say that Carroll Shelby himself was no longer as interested in a project which was becoming dominated by accountants and product planners rather than racing drivers. The later cars were mechanically closer to the specification of a mainstream Mustang than ever before. Like the GT350 before it, the GT500's accident record and the resultant rise in insurance rates helped to kill it off.

A total of 1,442 GT500s and 1,351 GT500KRs was built in the 1968 model year, 1,871 GT500s followed in 1969, and a mere 286 GT500s were produced in the winter of 1969-70. Over the next few years Mustangs got larger, heavier and more completely equipped, which made them quite unsuitable for performance conversions.

### Specification (1967)

**Engine:** V8, overhead-valve
**Bore × stroke:** 107.4 mm × 101 mm
**Capacity:** 7016 cc
**Maximum power:** 400 bhp

*Above: This 1969 GT500 convertible offered wind-in-the-hair excitement at up to 120 mph.*

**Transmission:** four-speed manual gearbox, rear-wheel drive
**Chassis:** steel unitary construction
**Suspension:** independent front with wishbones and coil springs; live rear axle with semi-elliptic springs
**Brakes:** discs front, drums rear
**Bodywork:** steel four-seater fastback coupé, or four-seater convertible
**Maximum speed:** 120 mph (193 km/h)

*Below: The view that most other drivers got of a GT500 was the flat Kamm tail with twin stripes.*

*Above: The 1967 Shelby GT500 was a real 'muscle car', which many were inclined to drive too fast.*

*Below: The King of the Road, the GT500KR, had it all in 1968: looks, handling and 400 bhp.*

# Squire

*Above and right: As rare as the Bugatti Royale, Squires were attractive but very expensive.*

**S**quire was very much a one-man marque. At school Adrian Squire had been obsessed with the idea of building his own sports car, and to the highest possible standards. After finishing school he became an apprentice at Bentley before moving on to MG. With this experience behind him, he attracted the attention of a wealthy friend from his school days, Jock Manby-Colegrave, who provided the backing for Squire's dream.

A workshop was set up at the top of Remenham Hill between Henley-on-Thames and Marlow where Squire, then aged just 21, and Manby-Colegrave were joined by Reginald Slay. At 27 Slay was the oldest man in the venture, and he was put in charge of selling the new car.

Unfortunately, while Squire toiled to make the model as good as it could possibly be, he had no idea of cost control, and there was no way his car could be produced at a competitive price. By the time Squire decided to try marketing a less expensive version with cheaper bodywork, the writing was already on the wall. In all, only seven customers had been attracted . . . in two years. The original Squire company was wound up in 1936, although after that three more cars were completed. Adrian Squire himself was killed in an air raid in Bristol in 1940, aged only 30. He was survived by nearly all his cars, nine of which still exist.

## Squire 1935-36

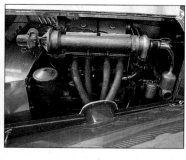

*Left: The supercharged Anzani engine was unreliable, but when it ran well (right) as here at Oulton Park in 1935, the car was fast.*

With his limited resources, Adrian Squire could not make his own engines and used an Anzani four-cylinder twin-cam of 1.5 litres. It was fitted with a Roots-type supercharger running at 1.5 times engine speed with a maximum boost of 10 psi. That was claimed to be enough to give 110 bhp at 5,000 rpm, which in turn should have guaranteed a top speed of 100 mph; indeed, a certificate was supplied with each car testifying to its having achieved that speed at Brooklands. The acceleration was in keeping with that; when *Motor Sport* tested a car they managed an excellent 0-60 mph time of 13 seconds.

Unfortunately, the Anzani engine proved thoroughly unreliable, thanks to poor design in the cooling system, while the boost pressure turned out to be too much for the cylinder-head gasket.

There were some faults in the chassis

The Squire appeared in two wheelbase lengths, and although the longer wheelbase made for a far more elegant car (particularly with Vanden Plas bodywork), the majority of the few cars made were short-wheelbase models. Although the Squire looked a conventional sports car in the mid-1930s style, it was designed to have the best equipment and running gear available. To that end it had huge brakes in a finned alloy casting, a front axle in forged Hiduminium, a four-speed Wilson pre-selector gearbox and a twin-cam engine.

too, which was prone to fracture at certain points, and often at inconvenient moments, such as in the BRDC 500-Mile Race at Brooklands after 54 laps when the car was leading its class.

All such problems might have been overcome, showing the Squire to be the fine-handling, fast sports car Adrian Squire had envisaged when he first drew its outline as a 16-year-old schoolboy. As it was, the combination of design faults and a very high price (which was far in excess of the cost of MGs or Aston Martins and approaching that of a Bugatti Type 55 or Alfa Romeo 1750) brought the model's downfall.

### Specification (1935)

**Engine:** inline four-cylinder, twin-cam, supercharged
**Bore × stroke:** 69 mm × 100 mm
**Capacity:** 1496 cc
**Maximum power:** 110 bhp
**Transmission:** four-speed Wilson pre-selector gearbox
**Chassis:** pressed steel channel
**Suspension:** non-independent with beam axle and semi-elliptic leaf springs front; live axle with semi-elliptic leaf springs rear
**Brakes:** drums all round
**Bodywork:** open sports
**Maximum speed (approx):** 100 mph (161 km/h)

*Left: The model's looks epitomised 1930s British roadsters; the grilles were distinctively raked.*

# SS Cars Ltd

I n 1922 a young man named William Lyons forged a partnership with William Walmsley in Blackpool, a business move which eventually led to the birth of the Jaguar marque. The original firm produced the Swallow sidecars for motorcycles, but by the late 1920s Lyons had directed his artistic talents to shaping special bodies for cars.

The very first Swallow-bodied car was an Austin Seven, which went on sale in 1927, speedily followed by Morris, Fiat, Swift, Swallow and Wolseley types. The company outgrew its Blackpool premises in 1928, so it was moved to Foleshill, Coventry, where expansion continued. There, in the early 1930s, Lyons conceived the idea of building a car, which he badged as an SS. Like every car he ever influenced, it was a real beauty.

No-one has ever defined what the initials 'SS' actually stood for – Standard Swallow, Swallow Sidecars, Swallow Sports all being mentioned – but within months this no longer mattered because the marque had become accepted. SS Cars Ltd was therefore set up as a natural successor to Swallow Coachbuilding, and spent the next 14 years expanding rapidly.

In 1935 Lyons bought out his partner's financial interests, and floated SS Cars on the stock market. In 1935 the Jaguar model name was chosen and the very first SS-Jaguar car was produced. The first 100-mph model (the SS100) soon followed, and the company's first all-steel saloon body shell appeared in 1938.

Because SS was a very small and modestly-capitalised business at first, it could only afford to design its own bodywork, and had to buy in the complete rolling chassis from a more established carmaker. For the first four years, therefore, all the mechanical items were bought from Standard of Coventry. The SS1 (six-cylinder) and SSII (four-cylinder) models were both closely related to the Standards of the day.

With the birth of the SS1, Lyons immediately established the marque as a builder of beautiful cars which also represented remarkable value for money. As the years unfolded, more and more people flocked to buy these elegant machines which seemed to offer more performance at a lower cost than any of their rivals. SS Cars built 776 cars in 1932, and 1,720 in 1935, but this rocketed to 5,378 in 1939, by which time other middle-class marques like Alvis, Riley and Triumph had lost many of their traditional customers.

*Above: This was a car with pace and grace at a very low price: a proud owner poses with his SSII tourer, surrounded by admirers, at the 1935 Blackpool Rally.*

Lyons invited William Heynes to become his chief engineer in 1935, which soon led to the birth of the all-new SS-Jaguar chassis, and he also recruited Harry Weslake to develop a new range of overhead-valve engine conversions on the basis of Standard blocks. These features, along with with sleek body styles developed by Lyons himself, made SS-Jaguars highly desirable.

During World War II, when the company produced many military aircraft parts for Whitley, Stirling and Mosquito bombers and for Meteor jet fighters, along with Spitfire and Lancaster components and thousands of special trailers, the team also designed a totally new twin-overhead-camshaft engine which was destined to take over completely from the Standard/Weslake types of the 1930s.

Immediately after the war, by which time the 'SS' initials had acquired sinister connotations, the business was renamed Jaguar Cars Ltd, and the pre-war SS-Jaguar saloons were sold for another three years with Jaguar badges. The first new post-war Jaguar, the Mk V saloon, had styling links with the SS-Jaguar past and used SS-Jaguar six-cylinder engines, but once the XK120 sports car and the Mk VII saloons went on sale all technical links were lost.

HFC 862

*Below: There is uncertainty over what 'SS' signified, but grim wartime associations saw it dropped after 1945 and replaced by the name Jaguar.*

*Left: A 1937 SS drop-head tourer, with the 3.5-litre, 125-bhp straight-six, an engine which gave the car effortless high-speed cruising. By this stage the bodies were all steel, rather than coachbuilt, enabling the firm to keep prices very low.*

# SS1 1932-36

In looks and in character, if not in performance, the SS1 of 1932 was a supercar, the original ancestor of all Jaguar cars. Under the skin there was a specially-designed chassis, but all the running gear – engine, transmission, axle and suspension – was supplied by the Standard Motor Company, whose factory was on the other side of Coventry. Two versions of the new model were immediately offered, with 2.0-litre and 2.5-litre versions of the same six-cylinder side-valve engine.

The original 1932-model SS1s were more stylish than practical, for they had long bonnets only partly filled by engines, with a small four-seater cabin, and were sold as two-door coupés or open cars. Perhaps there was more show

*Below: This long, low SS1 coupé, which looked more French than British, has the perfect lines that characterised SS. After the model's 1931 Motor Show debut, the Daily Express said the SS1 had the "£1,000 look for £310".*

than go at this stage – but since the car cost only £310 when its looks outranked those of £1,000 models from other manufacturers, there were few complaints.

Then, after only one year, came the first big step forward, as a longer-wheel-base chassis was combined with a larger cabin, with sweeping wing lines and significantly more powerful engines. It was the start of a programme which saw a variety of bodies, including a 'streamlined' Airline saloon and the limited-production SS90 sports car, put on sale – all at amazingly low prices.

The SS90, which used a short-wheel-base 'cut-and-shut' version of the SS1 chassis with a rakish two-seat roadster body, was really the prototype for the SS100 that would follow, but its performance was limited by the side-valve engines, and very few were produced. Even though later SS1 models had aluminium cylinder heads, the engines were always conventional side-valve units.

For the next three years SS1s sold in increasing numbers, to those buyers who wanted to cut a dash at the golf club but

*Below: A four-seat, two-door SS1, with a fabric-covered roof. Despite the length of the bonnet it housed an unexceptional side-valve powerplant.*

did not want to spend a fortune at their garage. Rival marques such as Riley and Triumph were so alarmed by the success of the SS that they started vigorous whispering campaigns against the cars' reliability, style and clientele; luckily, this was quite ineffective.

The second-series models of 1933-36 had more powerful and larger engines, initially with 48 and 62 bhp and then in 1934 with larger-displacement, 2143-cc and 2664-cc, engines and 53 and 68 bhp. By 1935, output of these two engines had been increased to 62 and 70 bhp, and the Airline 'streamlined' saloon and the SS90 model were available on the 1935 version of the chassis.

After only four years William Lyons, by this time in sole control of the business, decided to introduce a completely new range of cars with overhead-valve engines, which he proposed to call SS-Jaguars, and the SS1s were phased out. Total production was 4,254 cars, which included 24 SS90s.

*Above: The Thirties look was epitomised in the SS1, with its upright grille, swooping wings, long bonnet and huge headlamps.*

## Specification (1932)

**Engine:** inline six-cylinder, side-valve
**Bore × stroke:** 65.5 mm × 101.6 mm
**Capacity:** 2054 cc
**Maximum power:** 45 bhp
**Transmission:** four-speed manual gearbox, rear-wheel drive
**Chassis:** separate steel frame with channel-section main side members and pressed cruciform bracings
**Suspension:** non-independent with beam axle and semi-elliptic leaf springs front; live axle with semi-elliptic leaf springs rear
**Brakes:** drums all round
**Bodywork:** wooden-framed, steel and aluminium-panelled four-seaters; drop-head coupé or coupé
**Maximum speed (approx):** 70 mph (113 km/h)

# Stanley

The Stanley brothers were identical twins, Francis E. and Freelan O., who turned to building cars in 1897 after selling their photographic dry-plate business to Eastman Kodak. Their first model, like all the Stanleys to come, was steam-powered and the design worked so well that Francis Stanley beat all comers in a race during the first motor show held in New England.

His race success prompted a flood of orders, and the Stanleys began building a batch of 200 cars; these were to appear as Locomobiles, however, as the Stanley model was bought by a consortium for some $250,000. The injection of so much capital enabled the Stanleys to perfect their design; there was no rush, as part of the deal stipulated that they should not make a rival model until May 1900. By 1901 they were ready with the new Stanley, which was powered by a twin-cylinder steam engine geared directly to the back axle. The boiler was mounted beneath the seat, where it stayed until moved to the front of the car (under what looked like a conventional bonnet) from 1904.

Compared with early petrol engines, steam power was very well developed by this time and Stanley Steamers were capable of excellent performance. With wind tunnel-developed, boat-like bodywork, one managed over 127 mph in 1906 along the beach at Daytona, driven by Fred Marriott. The engine was very light, weighing only 185 lb, and its boiler could withstand pressures of 1,000 psi. The whole car weighed just 160 lb and maximum power was around 120 bhp at a mere 800 rpm. Its 127-mph speed record wasn't recognised, but an earlier maximum of 121.57 mph stood as the official land speed record. The following year, an improved model was estimated to be doing over 190 mph when it took off and crashed, injuring but not killing Marriott. The point had been proved.

Roadgoing Steamers were quick, too, the fastest being capable of around 75 mph, which was more than adequate – as was, originally, their limited range. Unfortunately, when there was an epidemic of foot-and-mouth disease in New England in 1914, many of the plentiful roadside

*Above: A 1910 Stanley Steamer, with front-mounted boiler; in its day this design was as powerful, efficient and reliable as petrol-driven cars.*

horse troughs were removed in an attempt to keep the outbreak under control. At a stroke, a ready source of water for the Steamers was removed and more expensive models were developed with condensers rather than a constant-loss water system. That change cut production down from a reasonable 743 in 1914 to only 126 in 1915. Although this bounced back to 500 by 1917, the Stanley brothers were bought out in May 1918 and the marque suffered badly in the post-war slump. Another takeover occurred in 1924 – by the Steam Vehicle Corporation of Allentown, Pennsylvania – but the business ceased trading in 1927. The steam age was well and truly over.

## Stanley EX 1904-14

The EX was the second-generation Stanley model and was recognisably a car rather than a motorised buggy. The boiler had been moved from under the seat to beneath the bonnet. This also had the advantage of moving the burner away from the driver, which made for more reassuring travel. The boiler was safe to a pressure of 650 psi and gave no trouble as long as the water level was not allowed to fall either too low, when performance would drop right off and the engine would stop, or too high, causing the engine to prime. The consequence of that was to send incompressible water into the engine, destroying it.

The rest of the car was very simple, with beam axles front and rear on full elliptic leaf springs, and with brakes on the rear wheels only. A variety of body styles were offered, the most exciting and sporting of which was the curiously-titled Gentleman's Speedy Roadster, which could just about be considered a rival for the likes of the Mercer Raceabout and Stutz Bearcat. One major drawback, however, was that the car's range was restricted to around 50 miles, necessitating plentiful water supplies all along any proposed route.

### Specification (1908)

**Engine:** horizontal single-acting twin-cylinder, steam-powered
**Bore × stroke:** 76.2 mm × 101.6 mm
**Maximum power:** 30 bhp
**Transmission:** direct drive to rear axle

**Chassis:** wooden frame with tubular steel underframe
**Suspension:** non-independent with beam axle and full elliptic leaf springs front; live axle with full elliptic leaf springs rear
**Brakes:** drums at rear only
**Bodywork:** two- or four-seat tourer or raceabout
**Maximum speed (approx):** 60 mph (97 km/h)

*Below: In the high-pressure boiler of a Stanley Steamer, the radiator acted as a steam condenser.*

*Left: Here a 1914 Stanley Steamer takes off, 75 years after it was built. The twin-cylinder engine gave speeds of up to 60 mph.*

# Studebaker

**S**tudebaker had one of the longest histories of any American make, going back to a highly successful wagon and carriage factory founded by brothers Henry, Clem and John Studebaker at South Bend, Indiana, in 1852. In 1900 they began to build bodies for electric cars, and the first petrol-engined model came out in 1904, based on a 16 hp two-cylinder General Automobile chassis. Studebaker took over Everitt-Metzger-Flanders of Detroit in 1910, and thus gained several other car-making plants in Detroit, as well as EMF's Canadian factory.

*Above: The Avanti was a futuristic-looking coupé. When Studebaker ended production, two dealers maintained production in part of the Studebaker plant, with bodies made by Molded Fiberglass of Ashtabula, Ohio.*

During World War I, large numbers of Studebaker trucks, gun carriages and staff cars were supplied to the French, British, US and Russian military. Studebaker's last four-cylinder car was made in 1919, and for most of the 1920s it produced side-valve sixes of up to 5.8-litres. Models included the Light Six roadster, the Big Six seven-seater saloon, and the Erskine light car. Top of the range was the President Eight of 1928, designed by chief engineer Barney Roos and powered by a 100 bhp 4.9-litre straight-eight engine, and available in five body styles.

*Above: By the mid-1950s American cars had gone fin-crazy, and the Silver Hawk of 1956 was no exception. Predictably, bumpers and radiator grilles were heavily chromed. This was one of stylist Raymond Loewy's last designs for Studebaker before he went freelance.*

In 1928 Studebaker acquired Pierce-Arrow, which lasted until Studebaker went into receivership in 1933. Apart from Pierce-Arrow cars, the merger bore fruit in a line of Studebaker-Pierce Arrow trucks, with Studebaker's car model range including the six-cylinder Dictator and Commander, and the 5.4-litre President Eight. Studebaker finances were hit by the Depression and a merger was proposed with the truck maker White Motor Company. After a messy bankruptcy, Studebaker was saved by selling off Pierce-Arrow and by 1935 the company was solvent again. Trucks and commercials became increasingly profitable, and Studebaker output included coaches and fire-engines.

Another small Studebaker, the 78 bhp 2.8-litre Champion, appeared in 1939 and went on to become one of its most successful models, helping to bring the company back to profitability. Wartime output included 6 x 4 and 6 x 6 medium- and heavy-duty trucks, amphibious Weasels and Wright Cyclone aircraft engines, amounting to over 210,000 vehicles and 63,789 aero engines between 1942 and 1945.

In 1947 Studebaker launched its 3.8-litre Commander, 2.8-litre Champion and Regal models with the radical wraparound rear window look, styled by Raymond Loewy and Virgil Exner, although beneath the futuristic bodies there lurked conventional engineering. Possibly the most radical was the 1950 Champion Starlight Coupé, featuring a space-age rocket-ship nose and aircraft cockpit rear window. The Cyclops look of the 1950 Commander was a highlight for Donald Sutherland at a stock-car track in the movie Steelyard Blues.

*Above: By the mid-1950s, Studebaker was in trouble. A merger with Packard did little for either firm and Packards disappeared in 1958. The Golden Hawk coupé sold fairly well into the early 1960s but was dropped along with the Avanti in 1963.*

By this time, the Studebaker truck line extended from a range of half-ton pickups to truck-tractors capable of hauling 12-ton trailers. During the Korean War, Studebaker made the J-47 turbo jet engines at its Chicago and New Brunswick factories. In the late 1940s and early 1950s it had 11 overseas assembly plants, as well as a new production facility at Hamilton, Ontario.

But as the post-war boom evaporated, the market became more competitive, and Studebaker sales fell dramatically, despite Loewy's attractive new designs for 1953, fitted with overhead-valve V8 engines. The following year Studebaker merged with Packard, and the combine was acquired by the aircraft manufacturer Curtiss Wright in 1956. Packards became badge-engineered Studebakers in 1957 and were dropped altogether in 1958. The roller-coaster of fortune climbed again in 1959 with the introduction of the compact budget-priced Lark model, while the high performance Golden Hawk and 124 mph (199 km/h) glass-fibre Studebaker Avanti coupé did well for a short while. The Chevrolet-powered Daytona and Cruiser models were built at the Canadian factory. But things were on the slide, and the Golden Hawk and Avanti were dropped. The Ontario plant closed in 1966, and the Corporation then merged with the Wagner Electric and Worthington Corporation to form Studebaker-Worthington in 1967, and was absorbed by the McGraw Edison Company in 1979.

# Studebaker Commander Coupé 1947-1956

When Studebaker hired Raymond Loewy to design its post war cars, it produced some of the most memorable cars of that era. Among them was the Commander, which evolved into a sleek, almost Italianate coupé in its 1953 guise, with rounded contours and twin grilles almost resembling a moustache either side of the beak-front bonnet. It was a big car by European standards, being 17 ft long and 5 ft 11 in wide. Track was 4 ft 9 in at the front and 4 ft 8 in at the rear, with a 10 ft wheelbase, so there was a fair amount of space beyond the wheels.

The Commander was powered by a 3.8-litre overhead valve V8 engine with a twin-choke Stromberg carburettor, set relatively far back in the chassis, and driving through a Borg Warner automatic gearbox and two-section propshaft to a regular Salisbury hypoid rear axle. While a certain amount of performance was absorbed by the automatic transmission, it was compensated for by swift clutch-less gear-changes under full power. That was 120 bhp, at 4,000 rpm. Top speed was in excess of 100 mph (161 km/h), returning an average fuel consumption of 20 mpg. Its range on a full 15-gallon tank was thus about 300 miles (482 km) at a steady 60 mph (96 km/h).

Suspension was a familiar competi-

tion-derived double wishbone, coil spring and damper set-up at the front, and at the rear were semi-elliptic leaf springs that were particularly wide yet very thin, with telescopic dampers. It was characterised by a relatively robust, if at times alarmingly noisy ride but, could soak up pot-holed and irregular road surfaces with equanimity. Probably the Commander's weakest point was its brakes, which were Wagner-Lockheed hydraulic drums, and faded under repeated heavy usage. Wheels were of the steel disc bolt-on variety, usually shod with 7.10 x 15 Firestone Whitewall tyres, which were prone to wear rapidly if the car was habitually driven fast.

The Commander had an excellent reputation for reliability as well as being entertaining to drive, even by motoring enthusiasts. It had power steering, and in its day it had a driving position that was second to none, with excellent all-round visibility – thanks to its panoramic rear window – and could effortlessly outperform many more exalted thoroughbreds. The coupé interior had a bench front seat, which allowed a third person to be accommodated, albeit on the cramped side because of the gearbox location, and head and legroom was somewhat restricted for passengers in the rear. The boot space wasn't

*Right: The Commander made Studebaker stylist Raymond Loewy a household name, while the New York Museum of Modern Art hailed it as one of the ten most significant designs in the history of the automobile – which was quite an accolade. Powered by a 3.8-litre o.h.v. V8 engine, and producing 120 bhp, the Commander could reach speeds of over 100 mph. At 17 ft long and 5 ft 11 wide, the car could transport five passengers with ease – with three abreast on its bench front seat. Sadly for its many fans, despite the Commander's striking good looks, production difficulties held back sales.*

all that it seemed from the outside, being rather shallow and irregular in shape, and while it was fine for hold-all type luggage, big suitcases were defeated.

Cars like the Commander made stylists like Raymond Loewy household names in the USA. He worked at Studebaker for 15 years, from 1940–1955, and New York's Museum of Modern Art went as far as to describe his 1948 model as one of the ten most significant design concepts in the history of the automobile. Although the Studebakers of the late-1940s and early-1950s were undoubtedly his best known work, among his other creations was the lettuce-green Lincoln Continental Derham 'port-hole' of 1941, which featured gold-plated bumpers, and a number of one-off prototypes on Jaguar XK-140, BMW 507, Lancia B20 and Cadillac Eldorado chassis

Although their shapes reflected a concern with aerodynamic efficiency – and the Lancia coupé even had an aerofoil on its roof in 1960 – their luxurious interiors ruled out any prospect of competition motoring. The merger with Packard spelled the end of Loewy's time at Studebaker, and the Commander's successor was the be-finned and glitzed-up Golden Hawk coupé.

## Specification

**Engine:** o.h.v. push-rod V8.
**Bore x stroke:** 85.73 mm x 82.55 mm
**Capacity:** 3812 cc
**Transmission:** Borg-Warner automatic
**Brakes:** Wagner-Lockheed hydraulic drums
**Suspension:** front, double wishbones, coil springs and dampers, anti-roll bar; rear, semi-elliptic leaf-springs, dampers
**Body:** two-door coupé

# Stutz

H arry C. Stutz was the enthusiast behind the cars which bore his name, but the very first Stutz racing cars were built by the Ideal Motor Car Company of Indianapolis. Perhaps this title was a touch over-confident, for the company name was changed in 1913 when road car production began. The first of a series of Stutz sports cars – the Bearcat speedster – was launched in 1914.

The Bearcat was probably the most famous of all American sports cars for some years, and was as effective as it was distinctive, for the low-slung chassis and the primitive bodywork were later copied by several rival concerns.

In the early days the Bearcat had to compete head-on with the Mercer, but neither company ever perturbed Detroit, as their annual production was very low. Even though Stutz also began building touring cars as well as a limited number of Bearcat sports cars, annual production was a mere 759 cars in 1913 – a figure which rose to 2,207 in 1917.

The firm lost its founder in 1919, when Harry C. Stutz left his company to set up another marque, HCS, which was a short-lived concern leaving no imprint on the world. During the 1920s the Stutz marque gradually began making more and more conventional cars, moving the gearbox forward from the rear axle position to a more conventional location, and before long the business also began to manufacture its own engines.

A change of management followed in 1926 when Frederick E. Moskovics took over as president, and the Belgian designer Paul Bastien (who had inspired the birth of the two-litre Metallurgique) arrived to develop a new series of eight-cylinder models, the Vertical Eights.

These cars were unconventional, and much more advanced than contemporary mass-production Detroit models, for they had overhead-cam engines, hydraulic brakes and an underslung worm-drive rear axle, along with centralised chassis lubrication. To boost their image, Stutz developed racing versions which competed at Le Mans.

At the end of the 1920s Stutz reacted to North America's financial gloom by introducing a range of cheaper cars called Blackhawks, though these were soon balanced by the launch of the fabulous twin-cam DV32 (dual-valve) models with which Stutz hoped to compete against the 12-cylinder and 16-cylinder machines recently put on sale by Cadillac, Lincoln and

*Right: Stutz had the advantage of being based in Indianapolis – very handy for the famous 500, which helped in the development of cars like this 1918 Roadster (below).*

even the smaller Marmon company.

Predictably, however, Stutz's high-priced cars suffered badly during the American Depression, and sales fell rapidly away. In 1932 the small company lost $315,000, followed by nearly $500,000 in 1933 and then $250,000 in 1934, so its future was always in doubt. Stutz then tried to balance the books by building light delivery vans with rear-mounted engines (these were called Pak-Age Cars) in 1936, but this only delayed the final collapse.

A mere six cars were built in 1934, and even though the same types were listed into 1936, there were no further sales. Stutz went out of business in 1938, when the Pak-Age project was taken over by the Diamond T Truck Company.

Such was the reputation held by Stutz, however, that a 'new' Stutz company was set up in 1970 to build cars, fitted with modern Pontiac V8 engines and styled by Virgil Exner, but there was no real link with the old classic concern.

*Left: After Harry Stutz left Stutz he founded another marque, HCS (his initials), but the venture soon ended.*

*Right: The legendary Barney Oldfield was a Stutz driver, but he did not figure in the 1913 team line-up (below) of Merz, Anderson and Herr.*

## Stutz Bearcat 1914-17

The original racing Stutz models inspired the birth of a new Stutz roadgoing sports car, although the style and the general character were clearly influenced by the success of the Mercer Raceabout, for the new Stutz, called the Bearcat, resembled it visually, and sought to invade the same market.

Like the Raceabout, the Bearcat was a large-engined, rough-and-ready sports model, with the very minimum of weather protection and fittings. There was a low-slung chassis and a big and slow-turning proprietary engine (a 6.4-litre side-valve 'T'-head four-cylinder Wisconsin unit) which produced only 60 bhp at a leisurely 1,500 rpm.

There was a special three-speed gearbox mounted in unit with the rear axle, but this was the limit of the technical innovation in a frame which naturally had no front brakes, and whose suspension was by simple semi-elliptic leaf springs.

The style was simple, rakish, and attractive to a certain class of buyer, who needed to be masochistic as well as rich.

*Right: Despite its appalling aerodynamics, the 6.4-litre Bearcat could reach a top speed of 80 mph with considerable ease.*

Apart from the angular bonnet, the front wings and the simple covers over the rear wheels, there was precious little bodywork – no doors, no flanks and no windscreen.

The sharply-raked steering column pointed to two totally exposed seats which were close to the line of the rear axle, and the only weather protection for the driver was a small 'monocle' screen clamped to the column ahead of the steering wheel; the passenger had no protection at all.

One reason for the car's fame was the performance of a team of racing cars called the White Squadron in the USA in 1915. These cars had special 16-valve overhead-camshaft 4.8-litre engines, which bore no relation to the Wisconsin units, though the customers didn't seem to notice this. 'Cannonball' Baker also

used a Bearcat to break the unofficial Atlantic–Pacific speed record by a large margin in 1916, which was a great publicity stunt for Stutz.

In spite of its reputation, however, the starkly-equipped Bearcat was only built until 1917, after which North American buyers turned to more serious things.

### Specification (1914)

**Engine:** inline four-cylinder, side-valve
**Bore × stroke:** 120.6 mm × 139.7 mm
**Capacity:** 6388 cc
**Maximum power:** 60 bhp
**Transmission:** three-speed manual gearbox, rear-wheel drive
**Chassis:** separate steel frame with channel-section main side members, tubular and pressed cross-bracings
**Suspension:** non-independent with beam axle and semi-elliptic leaf springs front; live axle with semi-elliptic leaf springs rear
**Brakes:** drums at rear, no front brakes
**Bodywork:** steel and aluminium two-seat roadster
**Maximum speed (approx):** 80 mph (129 km/h)

*Below: The steering column (with an advance/retard mechanism) could be lethal in a crash.*

*Above: Wooden-spoked wheels with demountable rims were a notable Bearcat feature.*

*Below: Bucket seats were all that held the intrepid driver in place; note the fuel tank behind the seats.*

# Stutz DV32 1931-34

*Right: It was the 4.9-litre Vertical Eight which ran from 1926 to 1934 that made the development of the Stutz DV32 possible.*

In the mid-1920s Stutz's new owner, Charles Schwab, enticed Fred Moskovics away from Marmon to become the company's president. It was under his leadership that the famous Vertical Eight family of Stutz cars was born, and in one form or another these ran from 1926 to 1934, when the last Stutz production cars were delivered.

The original models had 4.9-litre eight-cylinder single-overhead-camshaft engines producing no less than 115 bhp – which made them among the fastest of North America's production cars of the period – and the most notable in the 1920s range was the Black Hawk sports car. Cars of that type raced at Le Mans in 1928, and proved to be as fast (if not quite as durable) as the 4½-litre Bentley which won the race.

For 1931, however, Stutz defied the North American Depression by producing a real supercar. Unlike Cadillac and Marmon, Stutz did not have the resources (or the technical bravery) to produce a large new 'V' engine. Instead its engineers elected to produce a complex derivative of the existing Vertical Eight unit, after testing a supercharged version of it.

The new car was called the DV32, and appeared in 1931. It was an outstanding design by the standards of the day. The inline eight-cylinder engine was a 5.3-litre unit which used a sturdy cast-iron cylinder block, with no fewer than nine crankshaft main bearings. On top of that block was a brand-new cast-iron cylinder head, emulating Duesenberg in having twin overhead camshafts and four valves per cylinder. Eight cylinders, with four valves each, gave a total of 32 valves – hence the DV32 title, which stood for Double-Valve, 32 valves.

Another of the DV32's special features

*Below: Based on a shortened Vertical Eight chassis, the DV32 weighed as much as 4,000 lb. That made its 100-mph performance from 156 bhp all the more impressive.*

*Right: Although nothing like as famous as the Bearcat, the Vertical Eight was one of the very finest American pre-war cars.*

was its transmission. Although it had four forward ratios, first gear was really meant as an emergency ratio, and could only be actuated by lifting a lock-out device on the gear lever itself. Other advanced features included the one-shot chassis lubrication system, while the brakes were hydraulic, with vacuum-servo power assistance.

The DV32 was an expensive car. In 1931, at a time when almost every North American car buyer was cutting back on his expenditure, the chassis price alone was $3,200, and by the time a coachbuilt body from the likes of LeBaron or Fleetwood had been fitted, the on-the-road cost was about $5,000 – as much as the V12-engined Cadillac of the day.

The chassis was an updated version of the Vertical Eight unit, and was available with a 134.5-in or 145.1-in wheelbase. Even though a typical DV32 weighed about 4,000 lb, the cars could usually beat 100 mph in sporting-bodied form, and there was no doubt that they were carefully built and well finished.

In addition to the standard DV32, there was a shorter-wheelbase version called the Super Bearcat which had lightweight

two-seater or four-seater open bodywork on a 116-in wheelbase.

Unfortunately, the DV32 was too expensive and too specialised to sell in

early-1930s USA, and even though a rugged new Muncie three-speed gearbox, with optional freewheel, appeared for 1932, the car gradually died away. By 1934 Stutz's life as a carmaker was over, with just six cars being produced that year. An attempt was made to revive the marque in 1936 but it proved abortive.

## Specification (1931)

**Engine:** inline eight-cylinder, twin-cam
**Bore × stroke:** 85.7 mm × 114.3 mm
**Capacity:** 5277 cc
**Maximum power:** 156 bhp
**Transmission:** four-speed manual gearbox, rear-wheel drive
**Chassis:** separate steel frame with channel-section main side members, channel and tubular cross-bracings
**Suspension:** non-independent with beam axle and semi-elliptic leaf springs front; live axle with semi-elliptic leaf springs rear
**Brakes:** drums all round
**Bodywork:** variety of open or closed individually-styled coachwork, two- or five-seater
**Maximum speed (approx):** 100 mph (161 km/h)

# Subaru

*Right: The Subaru SVX, a four-wheel-drive luxury coupé with performance of up to 144 mph, received the highest praise when tested in 1992 by Autocar & Motor, who found it to be "better than a Jaguar XJ-S". The engine was a quad-cam 226-bhp 3.4-litre flat-six.*

*Below: How it all began, with the tiny Subaru 360s, shown here on the production line in 1962. These were powered, economically but not quickly, by a 360-cc air-cooled, two-stroke twin which was rear-mounted and drove the wheels through a three-speed gearbox. Suspension was all-independent.*

*Above: The Subaru Leone Grand Am 1600 saloon, one of the Leone range which was launched in 1971. The first cars had 1200-cc engines, and by the late 1970s 1361-cc and 1595-cc fours were available. During the 1980s the range was increased to include four-wheel-drive models with 1800-cc motors, some turbocharged.*

*Right: The straight- and chamfered-edge styling of the 1986 Subaru four-wheel-drive XT Turbo was utterly different from the company's curvy 1990s offerings. This two-door sports coupé was powered by a 1781-cc, 135-bhp turbocharged flat-four driving all four wheels through a five-speed gearbox and two-speed transfer box.*

ubaru came late to the world of supercar manufacturers; it was not until the 1990s that the SVX model granted it entry. The car company's roots go back to 1953 when Fuji Heavy Industries was created out of a group of smaller companies that had been part of the Nakajima Aircraft Company producing wartime aircraft.

It was not until 1958, however, that the business produced its first car, the Subaru 360, which was a tiny mini-car powered by a rear-mounted air-cooled two-stroke twin. The transmission was only three-speed, but the 360 did have independent suspension all round. Progress was slow, and it was not until well into the 1960s that four-speed transmissions were introduced to the range. By 1968 Subaru had produced its first proper car; that was powered by a 997-cc four-cylinder engine, later increased to 1088 cc in 1970, and then 1300 cc.

The long-lived Leone range started in 1971, and that saw engine size increase to 1595 cc by the end of the decade before four-wheel drive was introduced in the 1980s. Subaru did not forsake mini-cars though, and the Rex range of the 1970s featured a 544-cc four-stroke which was even turbocharged and made to power all four wheels in some models. Such cars were clearly of no interest on the European market, particularly given import restrictions that made Japanese manufacturers unwilling to export such low-cost models. It was not until the very capable four-wheel-drive estates of the 1970s that Subaru began to make an impact on the UK market. They had definite character, with features such as a robust flat-four engine, and proved very rugged.

The company began to change its image in the 1980s by introducing performance models. Like the estate, the XT coupé was flat-four-powered and had four-wheel drive, but its 1.8-litre engine was turbocharged to produce 135 bhp. The model's styling was quirky, to say the least, and its chassis was criticised, but Subaru built on this foundation and began to produce some far more capable cars. In the 1990s the profile was heightened with the rallying exploits of Colin McRae in the Legacy RS Turbo and Impreza Turbo, which inherited the Integrale's crown, and achieved cult status through World Rally Championship victories in 1995–97. By the late 1990s, the Impreza STi 22B was the one to have.

# Subaru SVX 1992–96

## Specification (1992)

**Engine:** flat-six, quad-cam, 24-valve
**Bore × stroke:** 96.9 mm × 75 mm
**Capacity:** 3319 cc
**Maximum power:** 226 bhp
**Transmission:** four-speed automatic gearbox, four-wheel drive
**Chassis:** unitary construction
**Suspension:** independent with MacPherson struts and anti-roll bar front; MacPherson struts, trailing links, transverse links and anti-roll bar rear
**Brakes:** discs all round
**Bodywork:** two-door four-seater
**Maximum speed (approx):** 144 mph (232 km/h)

*Left: The most unusual styling feature was the 'window within a window'; only the smaller section of the front windows wound down.*

*Below: With a flat-six, a wide track, wide tyres and four-wheel drive, handling and grip were exceptional in all conditions.*

In 1992 Subaru demonstrated that their extensive rally experience had not been wasted; it enabled them to build a car with an extremely impressive blend of performance, handling and roadholding. The performance came from a horizontally-opposed engine; that was normal enough for Subaru, but the difference was that this was their first flat-six, and an outstanding one too. With a displacement of 3319 cc, four cams and four valves per cylinder, not to mention a variable intake system, its output was high: 226 bhp at 5,600 rpm and 228 lb ft of torque at 4,800 rpm. Such power was required, as the SVX was heavy (3,600 lb) owing to the equipment packed under the aerodynamic Giugiaro-styled shell with a drag coefficient of 0.29. The only transmission on offer was a four-speed automatic coupled to four-wheel drive and what Subaru called 'Active Torque Split', or traction control. That, as well as anti-lock brakes and electrically-operated doors, locks, mirrors, driver's seat and sunroof, all increased the weight.

*Above: The 3.3-litre six was very smooth and had a variable intake valve system to improve response.*

Performance was nonetheless excellent, with a top speed of 144 mph and the ability to reach 60 mph in 8.7 seconds and 100 mph in 23.2 seconds. The standing quarter-mile took a mere 16.7 seconds and the engine's impressive pulling power enabled it to go from 30 to 70 mph in only 7.9 seconds. The handling fully matched the performance, *Autocar & Motor* finding it "superbly well balanced no matter what the conditions". In fact the magazine's road-testers regarded it highly enough to choose it over the likes of the four-litre XJ-S, Nissan 300ZX or Mitsubishi 3000GT, and at £27,999 in Britain it had the advantage of being cheaper than its rivals.

*Right: The SVX was a high-speed Grand Tourer rather than a true sports car, and was fitted with a four-speed automatic gearbox only. The handling was matched by a comfortable and quiet ride.*

# Sunbeam

J ohn Marston's Wolverhampton-based company, which had been producing pedal cycles in the 1890s, built prototype Sunbeam cars in 1899 and 1901 before beginning to sell Sunbeam-Mabley models with the short-lived diamond-pattern wheel layout in 1901.

The company's great days began in 1909 when the celebrated designer Louis Coatalen joined the firm from Hillman, and it was not long before the first Sunbeam racing cars were built. Sunbeam's independence was then lost in 1920 when the company joined the Anglo-French alliance of Sunbeam, Talbot and Darracq (STD), after which the group's operations expanded rapidly.

A Sunbeam (driven by Sir Henry Segrave) won the French Grand Prix in 1923, and the Spanish GP in 1924, which led to Coatalen's racing ambitions getting all out of proportion, for a large loan was needed to bankroll the next models, and the inability to repay this was to cause STD's financial downfall 10 years later.

In the 1920s Sunbeam built a series of fine and conventional six-cylinder and eight-cylinder touring cars, the 3-Litre model being a high-performance indulgence which reflected the thinking in Sunbeam's racing department.

By the early 1930s, though, the British economic slump hit hard at Sunbeam's fortunes, and even the small-engined (and cheaper) Dawn was a commercial failure.

In 1935 the STD combine ran into serious financial difficulties, which resulted in the Rootes Group buying up Sunbeam and Talbot. Production of old-type cars soon ceased, and in 1938 the first of a series of Rootes-engineered Sunbeam-Talbot models appeared. Without exception these were Hillmans or Humbers in more fashionable styles, though by the early 1950s the 90 saloons, and the Alpine sports cars, had established their own reputations. A determined works competition programme further helped to boost the image.

The Talbot half of the marque title was dropped in 1954, after which Sunbeam production expanded considerably. The 1950s and 1960s variety were either sporting saloons and coupés (Rapiers) based on Hillman Minx structures, or smart two-seater sports cars (Alpines) which used a shortened version of the same chassis/underpan.

This was the period in which Sunbeam once again became a successful sporting marque – in rallies and endurance races – and there was even time for Rootes to produce the Tiger sports car, with a Ford-USA V8 shoehorned into the Alpine's monocoque structure.

Chrysler took over Rootes in the 1960s (then sold out to Peugeot in 1978), which ensured the degeneration of the Sunbeam name into merely an up-market version of the Hillman/Chrysler family car ranges. There was even a rear-engined sports coupé called a Sunbeam Stiletto, which was based on the Hillman Imp family car. At the end of this period Sunbeam was only a model, and not a marque, title – for a series of three-door hatchback models based on the Hillman/Chrysler Avenger.

At the end of the 1970s Peugeot ditched the Chrysler name which it had inherited, and resurrected Talbot in its place. Sunbeam flared into sporting prominence again in 1979 as the Talbot Sunbeam-Lotus model went on to win the World Rally Championship for Makes in 1981. The last of these Sunbeam-Talbot cars were produced in 1981, although the last so-called pure Sunbeams (the Rapiers) had been phased out some years before, in 1976.

*Above: The straight-six twin-cam Sunbeams dominated the 1923 French GP; this is K. L. Guinness's car.*

*Above: Sunbeam's 1912 Coupe de l'Auto racer was a 85-bhp 3.0-litre four capable of 84 mph.*

*Below: The 95-mph Alpine of the mid-1950s was a competitive rally car despite being overweight.*

*Left: The Sunbeam Alpine produced in the 1960s was a direct competitor to the MGB and was a far more civilised design. It was the last Sunbeam of any real note, but the name (below) lived on as a model title rather than a marque.*

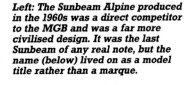

# Sunbeam 3-Litre 1925-30

Under Louis Coatalen, Sunbeam and Talbot were always liable to produce technical extravagances, none being more outrageous than the Sunbeam 3-Litre. This car featured a perfectly mundane chassis, powered by what was effectively a detuned racing engine.

The noted motoring historian Michael Sedgwick once described this car as having a chassis unworthy of its engine, and there is no doubt that it needed more stability when driven hard. The big and heavy engine was mounted well forward, there was a long wheelbase with a relatively narrow track, and the rather rudimentary location of the rear axle (by cantilever leaf springs) did not help.

When testing the car in 1925, *The Autocar* described this model as "something quite out of the ordinary. It is frankly and peculiarly a car for the enthusiast, and it is as near to a racing car as it is possible to go". Of course, that was by the standards of the mid-1920s, and the 3-Litre was on a par with Bentley's equally outstanding 4½-litre model.

Coatalen's engineers, who had also developed a series of fine racing

*Above: The 3-Litre got its name from the superb 2916-cc straight-six twin-carb, twin-cam engine which produced 120 bhp at 3,800 rpm.*

*Right: It may have been built for racing, but the chassis of the 3-Litre did not match the huge engine.*

engines, produced a new power unit for this car, a bulky inline-six. The iron cylinder block and head were cast together, and there were twin overhead camshafts with an opposed valve angle of 90 degrees. This unit was the very first twin-cam to be put on sale in the UK.

Coatalen certainly intended the engine to be sturdy and reliable, as there was a seven-bearing crankshaft, the lower end castings were solid in the extreme, and there was a massive dry-sump lubrication system. What was strange, therefore, was that the four-speed gearbox was so mundane (although, like the Bentley, there was a right-hand gear change, to the right of the driver's seat) and that the chassis was so thoroughly conventional.

Even so, in a road test published in 1925 *The Autocar* still found itself able to write that "To handle the 3-Litre Sunbeam is really to experience to the full the enormous difference that there is between such a machine and the ordinary touring car, and there is no doubt that this car is a wonderful and thrilling mount . . . it is probably the fastest three-litre sports car at present in existence."

All this performance, and character, carried a high price tag, which may explain why so few Sunbeam 3-Litres were sold. At a time when popular cars like the Bullnose Morris cost £170, a 3-Litre was priced at £1,125. Even so, this could

hardly have been profitable to Sunbeam – Bentley's 6-litre, for instance, cost £1,995 at the same time.

A supercharged version was briefly marketed in 1928, but sales were always very limited, and the last example of all was produced in 1930.

*Above: The radiator cap-mounted temperature gauge. The car itself (left) was a rather more delicate construction than rivals like the massive 4½-litre Bentley.*

## Specification (1925)

**Engine:** inline six-cylinder, twin-cam
**Bore × stroke:** 75 mm × 110 mm
**Capacity:** 2916 cc
**Maximum power:** 120 bhp
**Transmission:** four-speed manual gearbox, rear-wheel drive
**Chassis:** separate steel frame with channel-section main side members and tubular cross-bracings
**Suspension:** non-independent with beam axle and semi-elliptic leaf springs front; live axle with cantilever leaf springs rear
**Brakes:** drums all round
**Bodywork:** aluminium and fabric (Weymann) four-seater; saloon or sports tourer
**Maximum speed (approx):** 90 mph (145 km/h)

# Sunbeam Alpine 1959-68

*Right: The clean, feline lines of a 1963 Sunbeam Alpine Series III GT, with detachable hard top.*

For its second-generation Sunbeam Alpine, Rootes started from an altogether more promising base line. In the mid-1950s a completely new range of Hillman Minx family cars was developed, from which the smart two-door coupé/convertible Sunbeam Rapier evolved, followed by the short-wheelbase Hillman Husky estate car.

To develop a new sports car, Rootes then cannily combined the engine and transmission of the Rapier with the short-wheelbase underpan of the Husky, topped it all off with a very smart finned two-seater open body, and called the result the Sunbeam Alpine. Even in its original form this 1.5-litre machine was faster, more nimble and altogether more attractive than the old 2.3-litre Alpine of 1953-55.

The new Alpine was compact and ideally suited for sale in export markets, where it competed head-on with successful models like the MGB, the Triumph TRs and the Austin-Healey 3000. The Alpine was less powerful than those cars, but was always nicely trimmed and equipped. In general it gave a softer ride, but had good road-holding and a capable character.

Die-hards sometimes mocked the

*Above: This works Alpine was among those which ran in the 1963 Le Mans 24 Hours. The last model was the Series IV (below), without fins.*

Alpine because of its rather feline good looks, and for its use of features like wind-up windows (which were adopted before the opposition took them up), but this was usually because of envy. Race-prepared Alpines competed with honour at the Le Mans 24 Hours and other endurance events, and it needed little engine tuning for the cars to be capable of well over 100 mph.

In nine years the design was steadily improved, with larger and more torquey engines, with an all-synchromesh gearbox from 1964, and with a facelift (including the cropping of the original fins) for Series IV and Series V versions. Each new type was that significant bit better than the last. In 1964 the car also spawned an important derivative, the V8-engined Tiger. During the early 1960s, too, a heavier hatchback coupé version, the Harrington Alpine, was produced by the Sussex-based coachbuilding concern, though these cars were only built in small numbers.

In later years Chrysler management insisted that the Alpine was never a profitable venture, but the sales figures were impressive – 11,904 SIs, 19,956 SIIs, 5,863 of the short-lived SIIIs, 12,406 SIVs

and 19,122 of the final Series V models.

The Alpine was the last open-top two-seater sports car produced by the Rootes/Chrysler combine.

## Sunbeam Alpine variants

### Sunbeam Alpine Series II

Produced from 1960 to 1963, this replaced the original Series I type, the principal difference being a larger, 81.5-mm × 76.2-mm, 1592-cc/80-bhp four-cylinder engine.

### Sunbeam Alpine Series III

This model supplanted the Series II in 1963, and lasted only one year. There were two stages of engine tune – 82 bhp for the sports car, and 77 bhp for the GT (hard-top) type.

### Sunbeam Alpine Series IV

This appeared in 1964, and again lasted only one year. The fundamental difference was a restyling exercise which eliminated the high rear fins, which by this time were out of fashion in both the USA and UK. Automatic transmission became an option but was not popular.

### Sunbeam Alpine Series V

Introduced in 1965 and running until 1968, this replaced the IV, with an 81.5-mm × 82.55-mm, 1725-cc/92-bhp engine. Automatic transmission was no longer available. Top speed was 100 mph.

## Specification (1959)

**Engine:** inline four-cylinder, overhead-valve
**Bore × stroke:** 79 mm × 76.2 mm
**Capacity:** 1494 cc
**Maximum power:** 78 bhp
**Transmission:** four-speed manual gearbox with optional overdrive, rear-wheel drive
**Chassis:** steel unitary construction with 'X'-braced chassis reinforcement
**Suspension:** independent front with wishbones and coil springs; live rear axle with semi-elliptic leaf springs
**Brakes:** discs front, drums rear
**Bodywork:** steel two-seater sports
**Maximum speed (approx):** 98 mph (158 km/h)

*Below: A 1961 Series II car with the high fins. The Alpine combined good looks and civilised manners.*

# Sunbeam Tiger 1964-67

suddenly a clash of commercial and marketing interests. When the Chrysler V8 could not be persuaded to fit into the same engine bay, it became apparent that the Tiger's very existence was threatened, and only a limited number of the improved Tiger IIs were built in 1967 before the model was dropped.

## Sunbeam Tiger variants

### Sunbeam Tiger II

The Tiger II was made briefly in 1967. This had a larger 101.6-mm × 73-mm/4727-cc V8 engine, producing 200 bhp. Approximate top speed was 122 mph, but only 571 of the cars were built, compared with a production run of 6,495 for the original model.

### Specification (1964)

**Engine:** V8, overhead-valve
**Bore × stroke:** 96.5 mm × 73 mm
**Capacity:** 4261 cc
**Maximum power:** 164 bhp
**Transmission:** four-speed manual gearbox, rear-wheel drive
**Chassis:** steel unitary construction with 'X'-braced chassis reinforcement
**Suspension:** independent front with wishbones and coil springs; live rear axle with semi-elliptic leaf springs
**Brakes:** discs front, drums rear
**Bodywork:** steel two-seater sports
**Maximum speed:** 117 mph (188 km/h)

*Below: A works Tiger at Le Mans, with special fastback bodywork and a much-tuned Ford V8.*

Following the success of the hairy-chested AC Cobra, Carroll Shelby turned his attention towards enacting a similar V8 engine transplant in a quantity-production sports car, settling on the Sunbeam Alpine. After Shelby American had built a prototype in 1962, and demonstrated it to Rootes, the project was taken up by the factory, and went on sale less than two years later.

The Tiger used the same basic structure and style as the Alpine Series IV (which is to say that it lacked the earlier cars' tail fins), but was powered by the modern 4.2-litre V8 engine from Ford-

USA, driving through a different and stronger gearbox and axle. Rack-and-pinion steering had also been adopted, along with Panhard-rod location of the rear axle.

In some ways the Tiger was a wolf in sheep's clothing, for except for discreet chrome striping on the flanks it looked identical to the altogether less powerful Alpine. There were two fundamental design problems at first – wheels and tyres which were too small for the performance, and brakes which were only marginal for the job.

As an understated road-burner, at once cheaper and much more civilised than the AC Cobra, the Tiger was a qualified success, and it sold steadily in North America. It also went on sale in the UK

*Left: The veneered fascia of the Tiger, a car which externally (below) revealed little of its prodigious power and performance.*

from mid-1965, though few cars were sold there. Buyers found that it had a great deal of effortless performance which, combined with the typically soft ride of an Alpine, made an appealing package.

When the car was conceived, Rootes was an independent company, and a commercial link with Ford-USA looked logical enough. However, by the time sales began in 1964 Chrysler had taken a financial stake in Rootes, and there was

# Talbot

T his is a marque which really had several distinctly different lives – first as an independent concern in London, later as a subsidiary of the Rootes Group, and finally as a 're-invented' marque controlled by Peugeot of France.

In the beginning Clément-Talbot Ltd was set up in 1903, with the aid of finance provided by the Earl of Shrewsbury, to import French Clément cars into Britain, but by the end of that year the cars were being rebadged as Talbots. Within two years British-designed Talbots were on the market, and by the outbreak of World War I Talbot had established itself, with a modern factory in North Kensington. A racing Talbot was the first to cover more than 100 miles in an hour – at Brooklands in 1913.

In 1919 the company was absorbed by the French-based Darracq organisation, one result being the launch of a Talbot-based one-litre Darracq, which eventually became the 10/23HP Talbot model. Darracq also absorbed Sunbeam in 1925, which caused the foundation of the STD combine. By that time Talbot's reputation was on the slide, but Georges Roesch, who had been the company's chief engineer since 1916 before briefly moving to Sunbeam and Talbot-France, returned and single-handedly inspired a revival, with the development of a new series of six-cylinder cars, the largest having 3.0-litre or 3.4-litre engines.

The 'Roesch-Talbots' all had efficient and high-revving engines, and were gradually made more powerful in a long and distinguished career which lasted until 1937. Cars like the 75, 90, 105 and 110 were all indecently fast, powerful and well-engineered, although as prices and service costs were always high, sales were limited. Talbot spent far too much money on works racing and rallying programmes, but success brought much favourable publicity.

When the STD combine collapsed in 1935, Talbot's business was taken over by the Rootes Group and the old Roesch-Talbot models were milked of their remaining appeal. Then a new marque – Sunbeam-Talbot – was launched and Hillman and Humber chassis were clothed in stylish new bodies. Talbot hung on as a jointly-advertised marque at Rootes until 1954, after which it was dropped and Sunbeam cars carried on alone.

Rootes was taken over by Chrysler in the 1960s, and that might have been the end of the Talbot story if Peugeot had not then bought Chrysler-Europe in 1978. As a consequence the Chrysler name had to be abandoned, so within a year the Talbot name was revived. Existing Chrysler models were rebadged, the change being heavily advertised, and a number of new Talbot models then came on the scene.

Talbot Sunbeam, Samba and Horizon hatchbacks all sold in large

*Above: The Stig Blomqvist/Bjorn Cederberg Talbot Sunbeam-Lotus in the 1982 Scottish Rally; the car had won the 1981 World Rally Championship.*

numbers in the early 1980s, but the big Granada-sized Tagora was a failure. One ex-Chrysler model which achieved great (if brief) fame as a Talbot was the Sunbeam-Lotus hatchback, a fast and rugged homologation special which was good enough to win the World Rally Championship in 1981.

The revived Talbot, however, was always the least successful of marques in the Peugeot stable, and could not compete against Citroën, which was also in the group. By the mid-1980s the marque was laid to rest, with the British and French factories rapidly being converted to build Peugeot and Citroën models instead.

*Below: Fast and very masculine-looking, this 1931 Roesch-Talbot 105 Sports was originally fitted with a three-litre six-cylinder engine which, when supercharged, produced an excellent 138 bhp.*

# Roesch-Talbot series 1930-37

*Above: In 1931 this 105 raced in the TT, Brooklands Double 12, Brooklands 500 and Irish GP.*

Georges Roesch was a Swiss-born engineer who had learned his craft in the French motor industry before moving to Britain to become Talbot's chief engineer in 1916. After a short period with Sunbeam, in Wolverhampton, and at the French Talbot concern, he returned to London in 1925.

At that time the British Talbot company was struggling, with almost non-existent sales and very uninspired cars. Roesch's job was to revitalise the business. His first new car, the 14/45HP, was launched in the autumn of 1926, and established a remarkable pedigree which was unbroken for a decade.

The chassis, like all subsequent Roesch designs, was conventional enough, not outstanding in any department, but the new six-cylinder engine was superb. At first it had only four main bearings and 1665 cc, but as a limited-production engine it could be given frequent and successful redesigns which eventually resulted in a seven-bearing crankshaft, a displacement of 2969 cc in the 105 model, and no less than 3377 cc in the 110 derivative.

This was the period in which the cars were built at Barlby Road, North Kensington, in limited quantities, with a whole variety of body styles, many of which were provided from the Darracq works in Acton.

The engine was nominally a simple single-carburettor overhead-valve design, but was brilliantly detailed, with very light and efficient valve gear. The most powerful version of the 110 engine developed more than 160 bhp, and allowed a specially-bodied car to lap the Brooklands banking at 140 mph.

Talbot raced and rallied with great distinction from 1930 to 1934, its cars noted for their refinement and reliability as much as for their great pace, in an era when other racing cars were turning to supercharging and the use of multiple carburettor installations. This was

*Above and below: A works 105 which won its class at Le Mans in 1931, coming third overall; it also raced in the TT and at Brooklands.*

Roesch's policy, which certainly frustrated the works teams and held back the cars from outright victories, but the publicity spin-off was obvious.

Most Roesch-Talbots carried model names which approximated to their engine power outputs (and Roesch was an honest engineer, rather than a hyped-up publicist). There was a rush of such cars in the early 1930s – the 70/75 in 1930, the new 90 (a car with a successful competition record) in the same year, and the 105 in 1931. The low-compression three-litre 95 came in 1932 and the most powerful type, the 110, appeared in 1934.

Unhappily for Roesch, whose heart was broken by political events inside the company which followed in 1935, the Rootes takeover meant that his cars' famous pedigree was speedily lost, as more and more Humber components were fitted.

The last Roesch-Talbot being prepared before the dead hand of Rootes took over would have established a new pedigree, for it would have had all-independent suspension, but by this time Barlby Road was ill-equipped to build modern designs. Roesch also found time to design a magnificent new straight-eight-cylinder, 4½-litre, engine for an aborted Rootes 'Sunbeam' in 1936.

The 70 and 75 models were the most numerous (2,757 were produced in five years), as there were only 216 90s, 806 95s, 335 105s and 154 110s built.

## Roesch-Talbot variants

### Roesch-Talbot 70/75

The 70/75 (1930-35) had a 69.5-mm × 100-mm/2276-cc version of the straight-six. It was originally the 70 but was renamed 75 after only the first 119 chassis had been built!

### Roesch-Talbot 90

The 90 (1930-33) had a high-compression variant of the 75's 2276-cc engine. This was a sporting car, and the model was raced. Later changes included shorter-wheelbase chassis.

### Roesch-Talbot 95

The 95 model (1932-35) used a low-compression version of the 2969-cc 105 engine, in a longer (120-in) wheelbase frame. Later cars had double-drop frames and a pre-selector gearbox option, for this model was intended to wear formal saloon coachwork.

### Roesch-Talbot 105

This was the third most numerous of the range, introduced in 1931 with the 2969-cc version of the engine, producing 100 bhp.

### Roesch-Talbot 110

The 110 (1934-37) had a 80-mm × 112-mm/3377-cc engine, which actually produced 120 bhp. Even with a 120-in wheelbase below the Airline saloon coachwork, this true Grand Touring model had a top speed of at least 95 mph. Both double-drop frames and pre-selector gearboxes were standard.

## Specification (1931 105)

**Engine:** inline six-cylinder, overhead-valve
**Bore × stroke:** 75 mm × 112 mm
**Capacity:** 2969 cc
**Maximum power:** 100 bhp
**Transmission:** four-speed manual gearbox, rear-wheel drive
**Chassis:** separate steel frame with channel-section main side members, pressed and tubular cross-bracings
**Suspension:** non-independent with beam axle and semi-elliptic leaf springs front; live axle with semi-elliptic leaf springs rear
**Brakes:** drums all round
**Bodywork:** choice of steel and aluminium four-seaters; saloons, tourers or sports cars
**Maximum speed (approx):** 85 mph (137 km/h)

*Below: Roesch's six-cylinder 105 engine was very compact owing to its staggered-cylinder design.*

## Talbot Sunbeam-Lotus 1979-81

*Right: The Talbot Sunbeam-Lotus, seen here in action in the 1984 Manx Rally, was, for a homologation special, a best-seller.*

Just before Chrysler-Europe was sold to Peugeot it had approved the development of a compact and powerful hatchback model with which the works team could go rallying. In the words of team boss Des O'Dell: "To beat the Escorts they said we had to build a better Escort, so that's what we did!" Launched in March 1979 with the title of Chrysler Sunbeam-Lotus, it actually went on sale later in the year as the Talbot Sunbeam-Lotus.

By late-1970s standards the new machine was light, compact, and relatively simple, so Georges Roesch would undoubtedly have approved, even if this model was neither as elegant nor as refined as he would no doubt have liked. It was a limited-production homologation special designed for a purpose – to be the basis of a very fast and very strong car to attack the special stages of the World Rally Championship.

It was Chrysler/Talbot Motorsport, rather than the company's design engineers, which inspired its layout, the first prototype actually being cobbled together at Coventry before O'Dell even approached his directors for approval. The basis of the car was the three-door Chrysler/Talbot Sunbeam hatchback (the underpan of which was a shortened version of the Hillman/Chrysler Avenger), into which a 16-valve twin-cam Lotus engine was inserted. Backed by

*Above: Guy Frequelin and Jean Fauchille sail their Talbot through the 1982 RAC Rally.*

the five-speed ZF gearbox, with a stronger back axle and suitably beefed-up suspension and brakes, it was a ready-made rally contender.

To gain Group 4 homologation, only 400 cars needed to be built, which would easily have been possible in a one-year run, but Peugeot's planners saw a larger market for the 150-bhp road car, and aimed for a longer run than this. The result was that no fewer than 2,308 such cars were produced in less than two years (of which 1,184 went to British buyers), which made the Sunbeam-Lotus a very genuine production car. Its main rivals – Ford's Escort RS1800 and Vauxhall's Chevette HS – had never remotely approached such figures.

Production cars were partly built at the Sunbeam hatchback plant in Scotland

before being transported to Lotus in Norfolk for completion. In standard form the 2.2-litre engines produced 150 bhp, but up to 250 bhp was available in works rally car tune, and this was enough to make them competitive at World Rally Championship level, where they also proved to be remarkably reliable.

The road cars were nimble and fast, if a little uncivilised, for like other rival models of this type their refinement was compromised to make them suitable for tuning and modification; the ZF gearbox, surely, would never have been fitted had it not been the type which O'Dell's team deemed to be most suitable for motorsport.

In a short works rallying career which lasted three seasons, the cars rapidly became winners, and in 1981, after the road

*Below: Private teams also raced the Talbot; this is the Brookes/Bryant car in the 1980 RAC Rally.*

cars had actually been discontinued, Talbot won the World Rally Championship for Makes, and the team's most successful driver, Guy Frequelin, finished second in the drivers' series.

This, however, was also the end of the team's rally programme, for the car had already dropped out of production, and for motorsport the Peugeot management had already turned its attention to the development of a four-wheel-drive rally supercar, the 205 T16.

### Specification (1979)

**Engine:** inline four-cylinder, twin-cam
**Bore × stroke:** 95.25 mm × 76.2 mm
**Capacity:** 2174 cc
**Maximum power:** 150 bhp
**Transmission:** five-speed manual gearbox, rear-wheel drive
**Chassis:** steel unitary construction
**Suspension:** independent front with MacPherson struts; live rear axle with coil springs and radius arms
**Brakes:** discs front, drums rear
**Bodywork:** steel four-seater hatchback
**Maximum speed (approx):** 121 mph (195 km/h)

*Left: The Frequelin/Todt Talbot is captured in action on the 1980 RAC Rally, in which it finished third; the car won in 1981.*

# Tatra

**W**ith its origins in wagon and railway rolling stock manufacture in Nesselsdorf, northern Monravia, in 1850, Tatra's first prototype was the Benz-powered President, built in 1897. Principal engineers were Dr Edmund Rumpler, Leopold Svitak and Hans Ledwinka. Having worked on steam-engined cars, Ledwinka returned to Nesselsdorf in 1905 and created the 3.3 litre o.h.c S-model, volumes were small however, particularly when the company reverted to railway wagon production.

By 1918 Nesselsdorf was part of the new state of Czechoslovakia and the town was renamed Koprivnice, while the vehicles were called Tatras after the local mountain range. After a sojourn at Steyr, Ledwinka returned in 1923 and promptly put his revolutionary Type 11 car into production. It was characterised by a 12 hp flat-twin air-cooled engine, swing axle and backbone chassis. Between 1923 and 1930, 11,070 units were made of this and the similar Type 12, which had four-wheel brakes. A commercial derivative was also produced, of which 7,500 became post office vans, and other Tatra commercials of the period included a small range of six-wheelers and 6 x 6 heavy-duty trucks, most of which used central backbone chassis and independent suspension and air-cooled engines. In 1923 Tatra merged with railway rolling stock maker Ringhoffer of Prague, and its Bohemia coachworks built special bodies for Tatra, as did Sodomka, which became the Karosa bus firm, a subsidiary of the Renault V.I. truck division. During the 1930s, railway locomotives with 18-cylinder air-cooled engines were made alongside cars and commercials. In 1932, output was 3,334 cars, making it not far behind Skoda the market leader.

Then in 1934 the amazing Tatra Type 77 was introduced, a streamlined saloon with rear-mounted air-cooled V8 engine. While the front was similar to the VW Beetle, the long roof and arched rear quarters were extraordinary. Doors were hinged at the central pillar, rear wheels were covered by spats, the windscreen was in three sections, and the driving position was in the middle. The Type 77 evolved into the fin-tailed Type 87, which was popular with masochistic motoring enthusiasts. Around this time, a small rear-engined prototype designated the V570 appeared, displaying marked similarities to the 1938 Volkswagen Type 38 that became the Beetle. It was powered by the 25 bhp flat-four engine that featured in the (front-engined) Type 57 that came out in 1931. After World War II, Ringhoffer Tatra sued Volkswagen for alleged patent infringement,

*Right: Tatras were unusual looking cars to say the least, and one of the most notable quirks of the Type 77A was its centrally mounted Cyclopean headlight. Extra spot-lamps made this particular car somewhat over-endowed.*

*Above: Like the VW Beetle, the horns were located in the front panel, while on the original Type 77A of 1935 (below), the horn occupies the central position. Note the central-hinged doors, recessed door handles and front quarter-light windows.*

and in 1967 judgement went against VW and Tatra was awarded DM3-million damages.

During the war, Tatra came under the control of the German Army, and built military vehicles with a range of four-, six-, eight- and 12-cylinder air-cooled diesel engines with inter changeable components. One of the most notable was the Type 111 six-wheel truck that appeared in 1944, and over the next 20 years, some 35,000 units were built.

Post-war car production revived the Type 57 and a four-cylinder version of the streamlined Type 77. However, the communist regime that took over in Czechoslovakia incarcerated anyone seen as a German sympathiser, and Hans Ledwinka was locked up for six years. When released he returned to his native Austria and subsequently ran a design consultancy in Munich. Unlike Dr Ferdinand Porsche who was freed after two years and

went on to greater things, Ledwinka remained largely unknown and died almost penniless aged 89 in 1967.

His inspiration was not neglected, however, and his successor Dr Julius Mackerle instigated the replacement of the pre-war designs in 1948 with the T600 Tatraplan. This was another streamlined saloon with a rear-mounted 2.0-litre engine, with a frontal aspect like a Standard Vanguard, even though its engine was at the very back. The nationalised company put most of its efforts into building heavy-duty commercials from this point, and car production was in limited volumes, many of which were used exclusively by state officials. The six-wheel T111 truck was replaced by the similar T138 in 1962, of which 45,000 units were built during the following decade.

In 1957 the rotund V8-powered T603 four-door saloon car was introduced, and this was updated with Vignale styling in 1975 to become the 165bhp T613. A measure of the imbalance between truck and car manufacture is revealed by the production figure for 1969, which amounted to about 4,000 units in total, of which a mere 250 were cars. Thereafter, truck production rose to 7,000 vehicles a year in the 1970s, augmented via a development loan from the International Investment Bank to 14,000 units in the early 1980s. Apart from the mid-1980s T700 V8 model, Tatra's most notable products were forward control 4 x 4, 6 x 6 (twin-steer) and 8 x 8 military and civilian trucks and truck-tractors for hauling up to 300 tons gross train weight (GCW) or for cross-country haulage. From 1990, its designer was British design consultant Tim Bishop,

*Above: The new Tatra T-700 comes with a heavy-duty air-cooled, eight-cylinder engine on the rear axle. Indirect fuel injection gives the cars a sports character.*

who penned a new T800 model, but Tatra was beset by the legacy of its country's former rulers' marketing sloth, and by 1999 car production had ceased altogether.

# Tatra T603 1956-1975

The rotund shape of this extraordinary saloon was curious enough, but it was also a product of the automotive cul-de-sac penetrated by the Beetle and Porsche 911. Like these two better-known paragons of post-war motoring, the Tatra's unburstable 2.5-litre V8 engine was mounted behind the rear wheels. From 1964, this characterful-sounding power unit shrank slightly to 2.4 litres but rose in output to 98 bhp, and the model became known as the T2-603. The o.h.v. V8 was fed by a pair of twin-choke Jikov (Solex) carbs, and drove through an all-synchromesh four-speed gearbox with column shift. Since two types of cylinder-head were produced during the model's lifetime, it paid to know whether to fit short- or long-reach plugs. The T2-603's prodigious weight (3,240 lb) mitigated against a high top speed – it ran out of

puff at 105 mph (169 km/h), and could make 0–60 mph (0-96 km/h) in 14 seconds, and an overall fuel consumption of 23 mpg was probably better than you'd expect. Its performance shouldn't be dismissed lightly, as T2-603s finished a spectacular 1-2-3 in the arduous Marathon de la Route rally in 1966.

Suspension was independent at the front by MacPherson struts, trailing arms, coil springs and telescopic dampers, with a swing axle at the rear and coil springs and telescopic dampers. It had a servo assisted Jaguar-pattern disc brakes all round from 1970, having previously been stopped by drums. By 1956 when it was launched, Tatra had given up on the backbone chassis and the T603 was a 16ft 7in long all-steel monocoque. There were huge overhangs ahead of and behind the axles, meaning that it had

a relatively short wheelbase, and there were air scoops for the air-cooled engine in both rear wings. The back window was a big panoramic two-pane affair, and the rear wings ended in fins that were fashionable in the late 1950s. Its twin headlight arrangement was set in an ovoid chrome-rimmed front panel that was suggestive of a flying saucer.

Inside the spartan cabin were black vinyl seats – a generous bench in the front – with cloth or velour inserts. Instrumentation was of the period, a long ovoid speedo mimicking the shape of the external front panel. Switchgear was unique and neatly set out, with a big black two-arm Bakelite steering wheel

with chrome horn ring. Beneath the rubber floor matting was sound-insulating foam rubber, and therein lay the Tatra's Achilles heel, because as we know only too well today, it traps water and corrosion is the inevitable result.

## Specification (Tatra T603)
**Engine:** V8, rear-mounted
**Capacity:** 2.4 litres
**Suspension:** independent front by MacPherson struts, trailing arms, coil springs, telescopic dampers; rear, swing axle, coil springs, telescopic dampers
**Brakes:** drums until 1970, discs thereafter
**Chassis:** all-steel monocoque

*Below: Introduced in 1957, the T-603 was a round, four-door saloon car with unusual styling. It clearly echoes the classic Porsche and Beetle profiles of the same time.*

# Toyota Motor Company

T oyota is now the largest single carmaker in the world. It has taken fewer than 50 years to reach that position since car production started in 1936. The Toyota Motor Company was actually founded in 1937, a year after the prototype Model AA had been created. That was a 3389-cc six-cylinder car modelled on the Chrysler Airflow. The early days of production yielded no indication of the company's future prowess, as military output took priority during the war and Japan's subsequent economic recovery was protracted. An attempt was made to collaborate with Ford in 1950 to lessen the technology gap between Japan and the USA but nothing came of it, although that same year Toyota opened their export department, targetting South East Asia, Latin America and the Caribbean.

The first signs that Toyota would play a part on the world stage came in 1956 when a Crown model was driven from London to Tokyo by two journalists, a 30,000-mile trip that took eight months. Two years later a Crown Deluxe became the first Japanese car to take part in an international rally, the Round Australia Rally, and it finished third in the foreign car class in the 10,000-mile event. The way had been paved for the massive export drive to come over the next decades. Exports to the USA began in the late 1950s but were halted in 1960 as the cars were unsuited to American conditions. It was a valuable lesson learnt and Toyota resumed North American exports in 1965 with a far more suitable range and the scene was set for the US to become Toyota's biggest market. By 1962 the millionth Toyota had been built and the rear-drive Corolla introduced; by 1969 a million Corollas alone had been made.

The company's first overseas base, the Calty Design Research Centre in Newport Beach, was opened in 1973 and by May 1986 Toyota had opened its first US-based car plant, at Georgetown, Kentucky. By 1965 exports to the UK had begun, but there was nothing sporty about the early Corollas supplied. Exports to Germany, Italy and France also started in 1970-71. Toyota had by this stage built its first sports car, the Sports 800, which appeared at the 1964 Tokyo Motor Show. This was a tiny 790-cc model with a twin-cylinder engine and a power output of just 45 bhp. Its front-end treatment hinted at what was to come: the impressive and exclusive 2000GT of 1967, with its 150-bhp two-litre twin-cam six-cylinder engine. This was Japan's first supercar to have the handling and looks to match its performance, but although it was raced under the direction of Carroll Shelby in the USA, sales were slow.

After the 2000GT, Toyota concentrated on building its sales of more practical family cars, although models like the lift-back Celica twin-cams of the late 1970s showed that the promise of the earlier twin-cam engines was being fulfilled even if handling left a huge amount to be desired compared with European rivals. This did not stop Toyota's inexorable rise, built on successive generations of the Corolla, which became the world's best selling model. By 1999 the curvaceous Celica was in its sixth incarnation, but it wasn't as hard-edged as before. And by now the mid-engined MR2's bodywork was almost 10 years old.

*Above: The Corolla 1100 Sedan of 1967 may have been unsuitable for the American market, but it sold well in Japan and poorer countries.*

*Above: The sleek Toyota Celica Cabrio of the late 1980s was expensive, but capable of 125 mph.*

*Below: Toyota Carina GTis became very effective saloon racers in the British Touring Car Championship.*

*Below: The Toyota 2000GT, launched in 1967, was Japan's first supercar. It was powered by a 150-bhp twin-cam which gave 130-mph performance.*

# Toyota 2000GT 1967-70

*Below: The styling of the 2000GT was individual, yet inspired by the best Italian creations.*

*Right: Handling was superb, thanks to the equal weight distribution and all-independent suspension.*

The 2000GT project started in 1963 with a group of engineers being set up under chief engineer Jiro Kawano to study the best of the world's existing sports cars and to produce a rival to demonstrate just what Toyota were capable of.

Power for the new model came from the company's first twin-cam six-cylinder engine, which was based on the existing block from the Crown saloon but with a new twin-cam head built by Yamaha. The result was an excellent 150 bhp from two litres. This advanced unit was fitted in a backbone chassis which showed that Toyota had made a very intense study of Colin Chapman's Lotus Elan, as the same system was used. The suspension featured double unequal-length wishbones at front and rear, and disc brakes were fitted all round. Although the technical specification was impressive, it was the car's styling that really set it apart. It had all the ornate fussiness which characterised oriental cars of the early 1960s yet, despite that, had an overall elegance which few cars matched. That was not the only feature which distinguished this model from other contemporary Japanese cars; the unique 2000GT actually handled in keeping with its performance, and it was capable of a top speed of 128 mph and of reaching 60 mph in 10.0 seconds and 100 mph in 24.

Carroll Shelby – creator of the AC Cobra and the GT350 and GT500 Mustangs – was given the task of boosting the car's, and Toyota's, image on the increasingly important US market by running a racing team in SCCA Production Class C. Shelby improved the suspension with Koni dampers and stiffer springs and managed to finish second in the championship, behind the Porsche 911, with four wins. Notwithstanding such performances, the 2000GT did not catch on with customers and only 337 were sold, despite the car having the boost of an appearance in the James Bond film *You Only Live Twice*.

## Specification (1967)

**Engine:** inline six-cylinder, twin-cam
**Bore × stroke:** 75 mm × 75 mm
**Capacity:** 1988 cc
**Maximum power:** 150 bhp
**Transmission:** five-speed manual gearbox
**Chassis:** separate folded steel backbone
**Suspension:** independent with double unequal-length wishbones, coil springs, telescopic dampers and anti-roll bars front and rear
**Brakes:** discs all round
**Bodywork:** steel two-door two-seater coupé
**Maximum speed (approx):** 128 mph (206 km/h)

*Left: Chromium light surrounds were typical of Japanese styling, but in other respects the model transcended its origins.*

*Below: Only 337 2000GTs were sold, but this was Japan's first sign of interest in the sports car market; much more was to come.*

# Toyota MR2 1984-present

Before the MR2, there had been only two affordable, mass-produced, mid-engined sports cars; first was the Fiat X1/9, followed – just before the MR2 – by the Pontiac Fiero. As with the Fiat and Pontiac, Toyota used an engine/transmission package taken from one of their front-engined/front-wheel-drive models and moved it to behind the two-seater cabin to drive the rear wheels. In that respect it broke no new ground; the difference lay in the quality of that engine, and the level of design and engineering input, all of which combined to make the MR2 a quantum leap over the admittedly smaller and cheaper Fiat and the underpowered Fiero.

The first indication that Toyota were going to introduce a mid-engined sports car came at the 1983 Tokyo Motor Show. There the reaction to the company's SV-3 show car was so positive that the MR2 project was completed in time for production in 1984. During its development, under a team led by Seiichi Yamauchi, Toyota had bought and evaluated all the relevant mid-engined cars on the market – the X1/9, Matra Murena, Lotus Esprit, and even a Ferrari 308 GTBi; the lessons from all were quickly learnt.

*Above: The 154-bhp, fuel-injected two-litre four-cylinder engine of the second-generation MR2.*

The MR2's power came from a compact fuel-injected four-cylinder twin-cam engine with four valves per cylinder and an impressive power output of 122 bhp from just 1587 cc, along with 105 lb ft of torque. The engine was also designed to rev highly – maximum power came in at 6,600 rpm – and very freely. The design target was for it to rev

*Above: A first-series 1985 Toyota MR2, a light and compact twin-cam sports car capable of 120 mph.*

from its 800-rpm idle to a 7,500-rpm maximum in less than a second, and that was duly achieved. Such power and response guaranteed good performance in a car weighing only 2,300 lb, and in European trim it could reach 120 mph and took just eight seconds to hit 60 mph. The rationale for making the MR2 mid-engined, though, was not good straight-line performance but excellent handling, and that was one of the car's outstanding features, achieved with a surprisingly simple suspension system of MacPherson struts all round. Toyota also strived to make the MR2 as user-friendly as possible and drivers felt completely at home in the car within minutes of first driving it. This had the effect of making people think that the car was even better than it was. This was illustrated by one magazine's comparison of the front-drive Corolla GTi hatchback, with the same engine, against the MR2 in acceleration, roadholding and handling around a skid pan and on the Castle Combe racetrack. The testers found that the MR2 felt far better, but the timing gear showed there was nothing in it... Nevertheless, the MR2 was an instant classic which was steadily made more powerful before being replaced by a second-generation car in 1990. By then the original MR2 was six years old and it was time for a change

away from the unfashionable sharp lines to the now almost universal rounded look. Toyota retained the MR2's mid-engined configuration but made the car larger in all dimensions. Overall length was increased by 10 inches, the wheelbase by over three inches and the track by an inch. Naturally, the bigger model was heavier too, by over 200 lb. That was counteracted by a larger, two-litre engine producing 158 bhp at 6,000 rpm, along with 140 lb ft of torque at 4,400 rpm. That was enough to give a top speed just below 140 mph and a 0-60 mph time of 7.2 seconds. The turbocharged version produced even more power, 225 bhp at 6,000 rpm, and had a maximum speed of 150 mph.

## Specification (1984)

**Engine:** inline four-cylinder, twin-cam
**Bore × stroke:** 81 mm × 77 mm
**Capacity:** 1587 cc
**Maximum power:** 122 bhp
**Transmission:** five-speed manual gearbox
**Chassis:** unitary construction
**Suspension:** independent with MacPherson struts and anti-roll bars front and rear
**Brakes:** ventilated discs front, solid discs rear
**Bodywork:** steel two-door two-seater sports coupé
**Maximum speed (approx):** 120 mph (193 km/h)

*Above: A 1989 MR2; the bulkier, curved bodywork made this model less agile than the first-series cars.*

*Above: The MR2 cabin was trimmed to a high standard, and the seats were particularly supportive.*

*Left: Toyota studied several mid-engined cars before finalising the MR2; the result was excellent handling and ease of driving.*

# Toyota Celica GT-4 1986-present

There has been a Celica in the Toyota line-up since the early 1970s, when the cars were front-engined with rear-wheel drive. A whole series of restyled Celicas then followed, still rear-wheel-driven, before Toyota embraced the transverse-engined, front-wheel-drive approach in the mid-1980s.

The new-generation Celica GT model

*Below: Sainz's rallying successes inspired the launch of the Celica Turbo 4WD Carlos Sainz Limited Edition model; the name was ponderous, but the car was fast.*

*Below: The second-series Celica GT-4 appeared in 1990, with the curvaceous styling which was fashionable at that time.*

*Above: Carlos Sainz, the brilliant Spanish rally driver, in his Celica GT-4 in the 1989 RAC Rally; he drove his six-speed, four-wheel-drive car superbly and took second place.*

appeared in 1985; that was followed in 1986 by the best Celica produced so far – the GT-4, with four-wheel drive and a turbocharged engine which produced no less than 182 bhp. In road form the car could perhaps be criticised for being a little too heavy, but rally versions proved extremely competitive, with a power output of 285 bhp at 6,800 rpm. The GT-4 was adopted by Ove Andersson's Toyota Team Europe for World Championship rallying in 1988 and was winning events by 1989. The team built successfully on those early victories and their Spanish driver Carlos Sainz became World Rally Champion in 1990. During that season Sainz tackled 11 rallies, winning four and never finishing any lower than fourth. With such results, it was no surprise when he took the championship. The car he drove was a complicated device with a six-speed gearbox and three differentials, with viscous couplings front and rear. Its complex design paid off in 1990, but the 1991 season was tougher and Sainz suffered accidents and mechanical failures, finally having to concede the

championship to Juha Kankkunen.

Not only was the GT-4 fast, reliable and a superb car to drive, but it was elegant too. Unfortunately, that elegance was to disappear with the introduction of the second-generation GT-4 in 1990. The trend then was for far more rounded shapes and Toyota tried, unsuccessfully, to convince a sceptical press on the car's launch that its contours were inspired by the female form. That aside, the new model offered the same mix of turbocharged engine and four-wheel drive and gave Carlos Sainz his second World Rally Championship, in 1992, ahead of Lancia driver Juha Kankkunen. The roadgoing versions of the GT-4 were obviously rather less potent than the rally car, but could still achieve a top speed of 135 mph and sprint to 60 mph in only 8.2 seconds.

## Specification (1986)

**Engine:** inline four-cylinder, twin-cam, turbo
**Bore × stroke:** 86 mm × 86 mm
**Capacity:** 1998 cc

*Above: Sainz, who became World Rally Champion in 1990, here negotiates the water in the Sutton stage of the 1991 RAC Rally, on his way to third place. That season he won five rallies: Monte Carlo, Portugal, the Tour de Corse, New Zealand and Argentina, with a second place in the Acropolis Rally and finishing second in the World Drivers' Championship.*

**Maximum power:** 182 bhp
**Transmission:** five-speed manual gearbox, viscous couplings and Torsen differential; four-wheel drive
**Chassis:** steel monocoque unitary construction
**Suspension:** independent with MacPherson struts, lower control arms and anti-roll bars front and rear
**Brakes:** ventilated discs front, solid discs rear
**Bodywork:** steel two-door four-seater hatchback coupé
**Maximum speed (approx):** 135 mph (217 km/h)

# Triumph

**L**ike many other famous carmakers, Triumph started by building bicycles, in Coventry, then progressed to even greater fame making motorcycles, but did not start selling motor cars until 1923. Although Triumph remained independent until 1939, it was thereafter owned by a succession of different concerns before the marque was finally laid to rest in 1984.

From 1923, for the first 10 years under Siegfried Bettman's control, Triumph built a series of conventional cars, but more sporting models appeared after Donald Healey became the company's technical chief in 1933. The Dolomite Straight-Eight was a magnificent folly, but a whole series of Glorias, Vitesses and later-model Dolomites sold well until the company's finances collapsed in 1939.

Standard bought up the business in 1944, and before long Triumph became that company's sporting arm. Vanguard-based Roadsters and Renowns built foundations and the quaintly-styled Mayflower kept the name alive, but it was the compact two-litre TR2 sports car of 1953 which changed the marque's image completely.

Within 10 years Triumph had stolen the limelight from Standard, for the last car of that name was built in 1963. By that time not only had the TR2 grown up into the more civilised TR4, but the Triumph Herald family car had appeared, the small Spitfire sports car had been launched, and the big Triumph 2000 had taken over from the Standard Vanguard.

In the meantime Leyland had absorbed Standard-Triumph, and in the next few years the Vitesse, 1300, GT6, and six-cylinder TR5 sports cars were launched. It was a period during which the design engineers, led by that great character Harry Webster, had turned product-planning and 'building-block engineering' into a fine art, juggling chassis, engines and body styles with great skill.

The company became highly profitable, and a fierce sales battle with Rover ended only when Leyland took over that firm as well! Triumph's motorsport programme included successful forays to the Le Mans 24 Hours, while in the USA the Spitfires outsold the rival Sprites and Midgets, which did great things for morale.

Leyland grew into British Leyland in 1968, after which Triumph introduced the TR6, the Stag sports car and the Dolomite range of saloons. This was the period in which Lord Stokes, still proud of what Triumph had achieved for him in the 1960s, favoured the marque instead of preserving MG, the result being that the Abingdon name withered on the bough as new Triumph cars proliferated.

At the same time as British Leyland had to be nationalised to keep it in business (in 1975), the monocoque TR7 appeared, but this was the high point of the marque's reputation and influence. A vast new factory had

*Above: The TR7, introduced in 1975, saw service in rallies and races. In standard form the two-litre four gave 105 bhp and a top speed of 110 mph.*

already been opened up in Liverpool, which was where the TR7 was originally built, but this venture was never a success.

By the end of the 1970s Leyland Cars was in such horrendous financial trouble that model after model was discontinued, and factory after factory had to be closed down. The Liverpool operation was abandoned, and then car assembly in Coventry also finished, so the last sporting Triumphs, the TR7/TR8 range, ended their days at the Rover plant at Solihull.

In the frantic early-1980s era of BL, when links were forged with Honda of Japan, the very first of these joint ventures was a UK-modified Honda Ballade, which was cynically badged as the Triumph Acclaim saloon, but this had no meaning to Triumph traditionalists, and after only three years the model was retired along with the Triumph name.

*Below: The TR2 was launched in 1953 because Standard chief Sir John Black wanted some of MG's export sales, as Triumph's world badge (right) suggested. With its 90-bhp, two-litre engine the TR2 could reach a top speed of 103 mph and yet was cheap to buy and run. Sales were boosted by a 120-mph demonstration on the Jabbeke road in Belgium.*

## Triumph TR2 1953-55

Under Standard's ownership, Triumph took years to re-establish its reputation, for all traces of the original company's heritage had been expunged in the takeover of 1944. The Roadster and Renown models were limited-production machines, and the Mayflower had unique, ostensibly modern 'razor-edge' styling, although it was powered by a side-valve Standard engine.

Standard's chief, Sir John Black, was jealous of the post-war success of MG and Jaguar, particularly in export markets, and wanted to build successful sports cars, but after he failed to take over Morgan he instructed his designers to produce something to beat it.

Budget and unit-cost targets were ambitious and the original bob-tailed Project 20TS model of 1952 (later retrospectively dubbed TR1 by all *except* Standard-Triumph) needed a complete chassis and styling redesign, and a lot of development, before it became the rugged, reliable and fast TR2 sports car.

The public took its time to accept this as a desirable new model – for there was no sporting heritage behind it – but after works-backed cars started to win, or at least to perform creditably, in races and rallies, the tide changed. Everyone seemed to like the styling, and what later became known as the 'side-screen' TR was also a snug and remarkably weatherproof 100-mph machine when the optional hard top was specified.

The original TR2 might have been a somewhat unruly car, with twitchy handling and a raucous exhaust note, but it was strong, reliable and quite amazingly economical. The optional overdrive transmission was extremely popular, giving owners the choice of no fewer than seven forward speeds. Limited

*Above: A 1952 publicity picture of the new Triumph TR2, which was to be launched at the 1953 Geneva Motor Show. The two-seater was powered by the two-litre Standard-Vanguard engine, and its 100-mph performance soon endeared it to enthusiasts.*

wheel movement, hard suspension and a tendency for the rear wheels to hop about, owing to very limited rear suspension travel, were soon accepted as TR2 habits.

Because it was faster, more modern-looking and more rugged than MG's TF, more suitable for rallying *and* a lot cheaper than the Austin-Healey 100, the TR2 soon made its mark among enthusiasts. Export sales built up steadily, and after two years 8,628 cars had been built.

On the Jabekke highway in Belgium a TR2 was driven at 120 mph, and in 1954 came a win in the RAC Rally; also in that year a TR2 made good progress at Le Mans, finishing 15th. In the French Alpine Rally TR2s won the manufacturers' prize, and a TR2 also claimed a Coupe des Alpes.

Standard-Triumph then began upgrading the specification, a process which brought about the TR3 and lasted until 1962. The improvement on the original TR2 had come quickly; during the course of its brief two-year life it was given overdrive, centre-lock wire wheels, a hard top and radial tyres.

*Above: TR2s proved to be true sports cars, and in 1954 they finished 1-2 in the RAC Rally; Gatsonides also won a Coupe des Alpes.*

*Below: Its competition successes soon established the TR2 as a real rival to MGs and Austin-Healeys. Sales soared in the USA.*

### Specification (1953)

**Engine:** inline four-cylinder, overhead-valve
**Bore × stroke:** 83 mm × 92 mm
**Capacity:** 1991 cc
**Maximum power:** 90 bhp
**Transmission:** four-speed manual gearbox with optional overdrive, rear-wheel drive
**Chassis:** separate steel frame with box-section main side members; cruciform, pressed and tubular cross-bracings
**Suspension:** independent front with wishbones and coil springs; live rear axle with semi-elliptic leaf springs
**Brakes:** drums all round
**Bodywork:** steel two-seater open sports car, optional hard top
**Maximum speed (approx):** 103 mph (166 km/h)

# Triumph TR3 1955-62

*Left: From the side, at least, there was little to distinguish this 95-bhp TR3 from a TR2.*

*Right: Clear and simple: the fascia of a TR3, with the central speedometer and rev-counter.*

## Specification (1959 TR3A)

**Engine:** inline four-cylinder, overhead-valve
**Bore × stroke:** 86 mm × 92 mm
**Capacity:** 2138 cc
**Maximum power:** 100 bhp
**Transmission:** four-speed manual gearbox with optional overdrive, rear-wheel drive
**Chassis:** separate steel frame with box-section main side members and cruciform cross-bracing
**Suspension:** independent front with wishbones and coil springs; live rear axle with semi-elliptic leaf springs
**Brakes:** discs front, drums rear
**Bodywork:** steel two-seater open sports car
**Maximum speed (approx):** 102 mph (164 km/h)

The TR3 was very much the mixture as before, but sufficient improvements had been made to the TR2 design to justify calling it a new model. The two cars could be distinguished most easily by the grille; the TR2's extremely deep recess had been closed off with a new, almost flush grille. Behind it, the rugged two-litre wet-linered engine had been improved, thanks to a more efficient inlet port design complemented by larger SU carburettors. The increase in power was hardly dramatic – 5 bhp to be exact – but it helped offset the TR3's slightly greater weight.

Further breathing improvements later on increased power yet again, to 100 bhp at 5,000 rpm. That was sufficient to give a top speed of over 100 mph, far in excess of the small family saloons of the day, along with 0-60 mph acceleration in 12.5 seconds, which was equally outstanding in its class. Such performance made the next improvement to the car a vital one; the front drum brakes were replaced by Girling discs (along with more advanced rear drums), making the TR3 the first production car with discs. It was a popular move indeed; sales in 1956 had totalled 4,726 in the US market, but rose to just over 10,000 in 1957.

## Triumph TR3 variants

### Triumph TR3A

As with the 'TR1', the TR3A, launched in 1958, was a retrospective title; originally to Triumph it was just a continuation of the TR3. There were clear differences, the most obvious of which was the switch to the full-width radiator grille with the indicators inset. For the first time external door handles were standard, as was a locking boot lid. A more important change came in 1959 when the engine displacement was increased significantly, to 2138 cc from 1991 cc. The smaller engine continued as the standard powerplant. Total TR3A production was 58,236.

### Triumph TR3B

The 3B was the end of the line for the first-generation Triumph and really just a way of moving unsold TR3As on the US market. By this time the TR4 had gone into production and its new synchromesh four-speed gearbox was fitted to the TR3B, along with the larger, 2.2-litre, engine. Despite its being only an interim model and really quite obsolete, 3,331 TR3Bs were sold, all in 1962.

*Above:* **Motor magazine commented that the 1955 model had "shortcomings but no vices; the TR3 offers a great deal at a modest price".**

*Below:* **The TR3A had the wide grille, door handles, and the 2.2-litre engine tuned to 100 bhp; exports soared to 300 per week.**

# Triumph TR4 1961-67

*Right: TR4s could be fitted with a Surrey top which featured a removable centre panel.*

Standard-Triumph took ages to decide on the shape, form and specification of the second-generation TR. Between 1957 and 1961 several different styles, two wheelbases, independent rear suspension, an automatic transmission option, a six-cylinder engine and even a detuned racing twin-cam four-cylinder engine were all investigated. Visually, however, all projects were linked to the same young Italian – Giovanni Michelotti – who had been hired as a consultant stylist.

In the end the company opted for the simple mechanical route, but a completely new style. The new car, called the TR4, was given a slightly widened version of the TR3's chassis, complete with the more precise system of rack-and-pinion steering; there was a choice of 2.0-litre or 2.2-litre engines (though the smaller engine was very rare), and a new all-synchromesh four-speed gearbox was standardised.

The Michelotti body style was brand-new and both smart and innovative. Not only was there more space in the cabin, but wind-up windows were standardised and there was a simple form of face-level ventilation. The optional hard top was a two-piece type, with a removable roof panel, and an extra fabric 'Surrey top' could also be ordered to fill the aperture thus provided.

Although the body was modern and attractive compared with the TR3, there had been little improvement to the running gear. The new gearbox and steering gear were well-liked, but testers still complained about the hard suspension and bumpy handling, and wished there was more performance.

In 1965, therefore, Standard-Triumph introduced the TR4A to replace the TR4. This car had a brand-new chassis with longer-travel independent rear suspension of the same basic type as used in the Triumph 2000 saloon. Once again the North American dealers asked for, and were given, a different specification, with a live rear axle; in some parts of the USA up to half of all orders were for this slightly cheaper, and simpler, type.

The larger, 2138-cc, engine was now standard and had been slightly tuned compared with the TR4 to produce a maximum of 104 bhp rather than 100 bhp. The extra power helped give the independent-rear-suspension model a maximum speed of 109 mph.

This was the final TR to use the old-style 'wet-linered' four-cylinder engine, which was at its limit, so the TR4A's replacement had a six-cylinder engine. The result, unveiled in 1967, was the TR5/TR250. Total TR4 production was 40,253, while 28,465 TR4As were built between 1965 and 1967.

## Specification (1961)

**Engine:** inline four-cylinder, overhead-valve
**Bore × stroke:** 86 mm × 92 mm
**Capacity:** 2138 cc
**Maximum power:** 100 bhp
**Transmission:** four-speed manual gearbox with optional overdrive, rear-wheel drive
**Chassis:** separate steel frame with box-section main side members; cruciform, pressed and tubular cross-bracings
**Suspension:** independent front with wishbones, coil springs and telescopic dampers; live rear axle with semi-elliptic leaf springs
**Brakes:** discs front, drums rear
**Bodywork:** steel two-seater open sports car, optional hard top
**Maximum speed (approx):** 102 mph (164 km/h)

*Above: The 2.2-litre four can still be highly tuned for modern club sports car racing.*

*Below: Michelotti's ornate styling was a complete departure from the mechanically-similar TR3.*

# Triumph Spitfire 1962-80

*Above: A 1968 Spitfire Mk 3. The model had many virtues; it was reliable and cheap to run.*

Soon after work began on a new, small Standard-Triumph saloon in 1957 – the Triumph Herald – a sports car derivative was proposed. The new saloon was to be built on a separate chassis (a real anachronism, this, but Standard-Triumph was currently without a major body supplier and had to find a cost-effective solution), so a short-wheelbase frame was also suggested for a sports car.

The new saloon went on sale in 1959, with a 948-cc Standard Ten type of engine, but the new sports car, codenamed 'Bomb' but eventually called the Spitfire, did not appear until the end of 1962, by which time a larger 1147-cc engine had been standardised.

Like the Herald the Spitfire had a remarkably tight steering lock (kerb to kerb in 24 feet was a world record, matched only by London taxicabs), and it also had independent rear suspension by swing-axles and a transverse leaf spring, but this arrangement produced a very high roll centre, and gave all the promise of wheel tuck-under in enthusiastic cornering, not to mention roll oversteer. Overdrive soon became op-

tional, which gave the Spitfire a sales advantage over its arch-rivals, the Austin-Healey Sprite and MG Midget, which it never lost.

The style, by Michelotti, was curvaceous and attractive, with a one-piece bonnet and front wing assembly which could be swung up to give unrivalled access to the engine bay, steering and front suspension. Wind-up windows and a roomy cockpit made this a very appealing package, which immediately began to sell very well.

The Spitfire soon had its fans, but a good number of detractors. The model's fans loved the relatively soft ride, the performance and the good looks, while the detractors hated the handling characteristics and the rather squeaky, leaky, body shell. Even so, more than 20,000 cars were built in the first full year, and in North America the Spitfire was always a great success.

In an 18-year career the Spitfire progressed through five different types, three different engine sizes, and one complete facelift/reskin. Eventually, with the launch of the Mk IV, the suspension was radically improved, and the last major complaint was therefore quelled. The solution was remarkably simple; the transverse spring was retained but the

way in which it pivotted was changed, eliminating a lot of its tail-happy behaviour at a stroke.

To the end of its days, the Spitfire was a faster *and* faster-selling car than the Sprite/Midget models which were its major rivals, but it is the Midget which seems to have more followers today. Strange, isn't it? But can 314,342 customers have been wrong?

## Triumph Spitfire variants

### Triumph Spitfire Mk 2

The first significant change to the Spitfire came with the Mk 2 of 1965, which looked virtually identical to the Mk 1 but had more lavishly-trimmed seats, a vinyl-covered dash rather than painted metal, and carpets rather than rubber mats. With 67 bhp the Mk 2 was slightly more powerful than the original. There were also some tuning kits available to boost performance further, but they were rare.

### Triumph Spitfire Mk 3

For the Mk 3, Triumph introduced a larger, 1296-cc, engine with a bore and stroke of 73.7 mm × 76 mm and a power output of 75 bhp (but only 68 bhp in the USA).

### Triumph Spitfire Mk IV

This model was facelifted, its most notable feature being its much smarter, squared-off tail. It started life with the 1296-cc engine and lasted until 1974 but in 1973, for the North American market, it was given the larger, 1493-cc, four-cylinder engine with a bore and stroke of 73.7 mm × 87.5 mm but a power output of only 57 bhp owing to the effect of emissions controls.

### Triumph Spitfire 1500

From 1974 the 1493-cc engine was standardised for all markets to produce the 1500 model. The power output stayed at a meagre 57 bhp in the USA, but in other markets a slightly more potent 71 bhp was available. That was enough to give a top speed of 100 mph. The 1500 was the final Spitfire and was produced until 1980.

### Specification (1962)

**Engine:** inline four-cylinder, overhead-valve

**Bore × stroke:** 69.3 mm × 76 mm
**Capacity:** 1147 cc
**Maximum power:** 63 bhp
**Transmission:** four-speed manual gearbox with optional overdrive, rear-wheel drive
**Chassis:** separate steel frame with box-section backbone main members, boxed and pressed cross-bracings
**Suspension:** independent with wishbones, coil springs, telescopic dampers and anti-roll bar front; swing-axles and transverse leaf spring rear
**Brakes:** discs front, drums rear
**Bodywork:** steel two-seater open sports car, optional hard top
**Maximum speed (approx):** 92 mph (148 km/h)

*Below: The launch of the 1962 Spitfire (inset) created much interest, and the car was to have an 18-year career during which it underwent only minor body and engine changes.*

# Triumph GT6 1966-73

During the 1960s Standard-Triumph's engineers, led by Harry Webster, performed miracles with a limited budget and resources. In particular they wrung every possible combination out of the available engines and transmissions. The GT6's origins lay in the first Triumph Herald family car, which had a separate chassis, and which was powered by a four-cylinder engine. There was also a straight-six engine which could *just* be fitted into the Herald's frame, creating the Vitesse. As the Spitfire used all the same hardware at the front end of its chassis, the engineers decided to see if a six-cylinder engine transplant could be done once again. It could – and the result was the smooth and refined little GT6.

Although the car looked as if it was no more than a Spitfire with an engine transplant and a steel roof, there was more to the combination than it seemed. Not only was the engine installation new, but there was a new all-synchromesh gearbox, along with a beefier back axle. The engine came from the Triumph 2000 (and was a smaller version of that intended for the TR5). It was long and mounted well forward, which did little for the weight distribution and the handling balance, while the interior was trimmed in an altogether more up-market manner than the Spitfire. The overall gearing was high, and in many ways there was something of the 'mini-E-type' about the model's character.

The body featured a rear lift-up hatchback, which was practical *and* smart, though there was never any question of trying to squeeze '+ 2' seats under the sloping roof. It was the same shape as

**Above: Three generations of GT6s, hatchbacks powered by the very smooth two-litre six: from left are a Mk 1, Mk 2 and Mk 3.**

Triumph's Spitfire race cars at Le Mans and elsewhere, but the road car style came first and the racing one followed.

Because they used simple swing-axle rear suspension, the first GT6s did not handle very well, but Triumph solved that for the Mk 2 by fitting lower-wishbone suspension (while retaining the transverse leaf spring), and two years later the GT6 became even better when it adopted all the Spitfire Mk IV's facelift panels and a cut-off tail, to become the Mk 3 model.

Although the GT6 was faster, quieter and arguably more elegant than the MGB GT, it never sold as well. Although it sold steadily for some years, problems centred around new legislation in the USA killed it off at the end of 1973. By that time a total of 41,253 GT6s had been produced, which made it a profitable, if not a sensational, project for British Leyland.

**Above: One of the very last GT6s, sold in 1974; the rear roof line was very attractive, but sales never matched the Spitfire's.**

**Above: GT6s soon appeared in races, especially with the improved rear suspension.**

**Below: The GT6 was really a Spitfire with a larger engine and roof, making it more practical and bodily more rigid.**

## Triumph GT6 variants

### Triumph GT6 Mk 2
The Mk 2 (badged GT6 Plus in North America) was built from 1968 to 1970 and had a 104-bhp engine (95 bhp in North America), with independent rear suspension by lower wishbones and a transverse leaf spring. The approximate top speed was 107 mph.

### Triumph GT6 Mk 3
The Mk 3 (1970-73) had a facelifted body like that of the contemporary Spitfire. From 1973 the rear suspension reverted to swing-axles and a transverse leaf spring. Depending on the model year, US-market cars had engines of between 76 bhp and 90 bhp.

## Specification (1966)

**Engine:** inline six-cylinder, overhead-valve
**Bore × stroke:** 74.7 mm × 76 mm
**Capacity:** 1998 cc
**Maximum power:** 95 bhp
**Transmission:** four-speed manual gearbox with optional overdrive, rear-wheel drive
**Chassis:** separate steel frame with box-section backbone main side members, boxed and pressed cross-bracings
**Suspension:** independent with wishbones and coil springs front; swing-axles and transverse leaf spring rear
**Brakes:** discs front, drums rear
**Bodywork:** steel two-seater hatchback
**Maximum speed (approx):** 106 mph (171 km/h)

# Triumph TR5 and TR6 1967-76

The third-generation TR was developed to deal with two requirements – one being the need to replace the old four-cylinder engine, the other being to meet the new exhaust-emission regulations which were currently being imposed in North America.

The new car, entitled TR250 in North America, where most sales were certain to be gained, and TR5 in the rest of the world, was launched just as the Austin-Healey 3000 went out of production, so the new Triumph instantly took on the Big Healey's guise. Although it was 14 years since the original TR2 had gone on sale, and Triumph sports car technology had advanced by leaps and bounds, the latest model was now seen to lack the refinement and finesse demanded of modern machinery.

In essence it was still the same technology as the original TR2, and that was hardly modern when the first TR had

been built.

The TR5/TR250 looked almost identical to the TR4A, but was fitted with a 2.5-litre six-cylinder engine of the same family as that found in the GT6 sports car, the Vitesse and the 2000 family saloons. For North America it was in a relatively 'soft' state of tune, but for the rest of the world it had Lucas fuel injection and 150 bhp.

Although fuel injection is now fitted to reduce emissions as well as increase performance in the 1960s, the Lucas mechanical system, although giving more power, was poor on emissions – so much so that the cars for the vital American market had to make do with twin Stromberg carburettors and lacked the power of the 150-bhp European model, with just 104 bhp at 4,500 rpm. Torque output was not so badly affected, although at 143 lb ft rather than 164 for the injected car it was significantly down. It

made a change in the acceleration and outright performance, adding a couple of seconds to the 0-60 mph time and giving a top speed of 107 mph rather than the impressive 120 mph of the injected model.

With carburettors or injection, the TR150/TR5 was a far more impressive car than the old TR4A, and yet there was relatively little to distinguish the two. The restyle that should have accompanied the new engine had not taken place. When it did, the result was the TR6. Michelotti's design had been significantly revamped by the German coachbuilders Karmann. Operating within a strict timetable and budget, they had grafted on a new flat rear and made the front of the car look far more modern, doing away with the old-fashioned grille. There was no budget for significant mechanical improvements, but the TR6 was given far larger wheels and tyres to compensate for its handling deficiencies.

By 1970, therefore, the TR6 was being seen as the last of the Triumph dinosaurs, with a ride now seen as hard and a character considered old-fashioned. Even so, it continued to sell very well. In all, some 14,825 were sold in 1973, the year UK models were actually detuned to 124 bhp. Sales even continued for more than a year after the monocoque

*Above: The Triumph TR5 was a manly British sports car which gave performance without frills.*

TR7 was introduced in 1975.

As many as 8,484 TR250s, 2,947 TR5s, and no fewer than 91,850 TR6s were produced, which made this the most successful type of TR so far built. Even so, the TR7, in spite of its controversial reputation, would exceed these figures.

## Specification (TR5)

**Engine:** inline six-cylinder, overhead-valve
**Bore × stroke:** 74.7 mm × 95 mm
**Capacity:** 2498 cc
**Maximum power:** 150 bhp
**Transmission:** four-speed manual gearbox with optional overdrive, rear-wheel drive
**Chassis:** separate steel frame with box-section main longitudinal members, pressed and tubular cross-bracings
**Suspension:** independent with wishbones, coil springs and telescopic dampers front; semi-trailing arms, coil springs and telescopic dampers rear
**Brakes:** discs front, drums rear
**Bodywork:** steel two-seater open sports car, optional hard top
**Maximum speed (approx):** 120 mph (193 km/h)

*Above: The Karmann-styled TR6 was an adroit facelift of the TR5, transformed at front and rear.*

*Below: The 2.5-litre six could give more than 150 bhp, and TR6s are still raced with enthusiasm.*

# Triumph Stag 1970-77

*Left: Styled by Michelotti, the Stag was a class above Triumph's other models but was marred by its underdeveloped overhead-cam V8 engine.*

### Specification (1970)

**Engine:** V8, single overhead camshaft per bank of cylinders
**Bore × stroke:** 86 mm × 64.5 mm
**Capacity:** 2997 cc
**Maximum power:** 145 bhp
**Transmission:** four-speed manual gearbox with optional overdrive (later standardised), or optional three-speed automatic transmission; rear-wheel drive
**Chassis:** steel unitary construction
**Suspension:** independent with MacPherson struts front; semi-trailing arms and coil springs rear
**Brakes:** discs front, drums rear
**Bodywork:** steel four-seater convertible, optional steel hard top
**Maximum speed (approx):** 115 mph (185 km/h)

In the late 1960s Standard-Triumph was so profitable that its owners, Leyland Motors, agreed to a wide-ranging expansion scheme of new models. Even though Leyland soon acquired Rover, and thus their excellent V8 engine, it was decided to revitalise Triumph by developing a new range of powerplants – a slant-four-cylinder and a related 90-degree V8. The slant-four was used in several models (including the TR7), and the V8 in just a single car – the Stag.

Although it had its contemporary critics, in hindsight one can see that the Stag was so nearly a great car. It looked good, had an exciting specification, and was extremely practical – yet it did not sell as well as it should have. After seven years, and 25,877 examples, the model was laid to rest.

Three factors, only one of them self-inflicted, hurt the Stag in the 1970s. One was the unstoppable collapse of British Leyland's corporate reputation (along with that of the cars which it made); another was the gradual loss of sales in the USA, and the third was the well-publicised reliability problems of the V8 engine.

The Stag itself had an attractive four-seater monocoque based on a shortened and much-modified version of the 2000/ 2/5PI saloon's underpan, and was sold as a convertible with an optional steel hard top. The passengers were protected by a large and permanently fixed 'T'-bar roof (which did nothing for the car's looks when the hard top was lifted off and the soft top folded back), but in hard-top form the Stag looked very smart indeed.

It was a fast and seductively smooth car, for it combined the appeal of a V8 engine with Michelotti-inspired looks, a top speed of 115 mph, and a soft but secure ride and handling package. Many of the cars had automatic transmission and later cars had alloy wheels as standard, the result being a model which could so easily have been superior to its European rivals.

Early in the car's life, however, it became clear that engines often suffered from blown cylinder-head gaskets and cooling problems, which were expen-

sive to put right. British Leyland considered the obvious engine change, to the light-alloy Rover V8, but in the end nothing was done, and when the Speke factory closed the Stag (whose bodies had always been built there) died with it. The long-wheelbase 'TR8 hatchback' (the Lynx) which should have replaced the Stag was never put on sale.

*Below: The Stag was a four-seater; the fabric roof folded neatly behind the rear seats.*

*Below: The padded 'T'-shaped roll bar served multiple purposes, supporting the soft top and increasing the car's rigidity.*

# Triumph TR7 1975-81

Once Lord Stokes had taken over as chairman of British Leyland, it became clear that he favoured the Triumph marque – at the expense of MG. The result was that MG was never allowed to develop replacements for its Midget or MGB models, whereas Triumph was encouraged – and financed – to produce a new range of 'corporate' sports cars for the mid-1970s.

By that time the old separate-chassis TR design was obsolete, so the engineers and product planners started again, in a multi-million investment programme. Not only was the structure and choice of engines of these cars to be new, but they were also intended to be built away from Coventry, at a new factory at Speke, near Liverpool.

The planners' master-plan included a choice of four-cylinder and V8 engines, manual and automatic transmissions, coupé and convertible body styles – and even a long-wheelbase hatchback type, although that car, codenamed Lynx, was never put into production.

The new car had a rigid, short-wheelbase monocoque structure, with a style

*Right: The TR7 had a very rigid shell and was able to handle a lot of power; here are Tony Pond and Fred Gallagher competing in the snow on the 1977 RAC Rally.*

(actually from the old BMC studio at Longbridge) which featured a long, wedge-shaped nose and a short, high tail.

In the beginning there were fears about future US legislation that might ban soft-top cars, so it was only designed in fixed-head form.

The original type was called the TR7, and its engine, transmission, suspension and steering all had much in common with a projected new medium-sized Triumph saloon, but this rationale was later destroyed when that project was cancelled. The use of MacPherson-strut front suspension and a well-located live rear axle was a complete change from that of the old TR6, but it certainly gave the new machine a much more supple ride.

The TR7's engine was an enlarged version of the overhead-camshaft type

already fitted to the Dolomite saloons (and was a close blood-relative of the V8 engine fitted to the Stag), while the four-speed gearbox and rear axle also came from the same source. In this form the car was clearly undergeared, but once a five-speed option (as fitted to the large Rover SD1 hatchbacks) became available, that problem was solved.

If the TR7's build quality had been better, if the styling had been less extrovert, and reliability higher, the TR7 might have prospered – but none of these problems were solved. A long strike at Speke caused assembly to be closed down for five months, then moved to Coventry (and later to Rover's modern plant at Solihull), and it also resulted in the more powerful 16-valve Sprint version being cancelled after only a handful of prototypes had been built.

Although a convertible version of the TR7 was introduced in 1979, the wedge-styled TR's reputation could not be saved. By 1981, when the V8-powered TR8 should have gone on sale in the rest of the world, a recession was causing worldwide sales to slump and the car's fate was sealed.

The TR7 was really killed by a thousand small cuts, and in many people's

opinions this was unjust, as a properly-built example was better in all respects than its rivals – if, that is, you could come to terms with the styling. In spite of the trendy criticism levelled at the TR7, it sold better than any other TR model – 112,368 were produced in six years.

## Specification

**Engine:** inline four-cylinder, overhead-cam
**Bore × stroke:** 90.3 mm × 78 mm
**Capacity:** 1998 cc
**Maximum power:** 105 bhp
**Transmission:** four-speed manual gearbox with optional (later standard) five-speed gearbox, or optional three-speed automatic transmission; rear-wheel drive
**Chassis:** steel unitary construction
**Suspension:** independent front with MacPherson struts and anti-roll bar; live rear axle with coil springs, telescopic dampers, radius arms and anti-roll bar
**Brakes:** discs front, drums rear
**Bodywork:** steel two-seater hard-top coupé, or (from 1979) two-seater convertible
**Maximum speed (approx):** 109 mph (175 km/h)

*Above: With lights aplenty, it's Pond and Gallagher again, negotiating high water in the 1980 RAC Rally.*

*Below: The TR7 styling received few accolades, but what hurt the car more was poor build quality.*

## Triumph TR8 1980-81

*Below: The TR8 was, like the late TR7s, offered in coupé and soft-top forms, but sales were low.*

*Right: The convertible was very attractive, but scuttle shake and body twisting were commonplace.*

The TR7 had been designed from the outset to take the all-alloy Rover V8 engine, and even before the TR8 was launched the four-cylinder TR7 was using the fine Rover five-speed gearbox. Transforming the TR7 into the TR8 was thus quite simple. Various changes were made to suit the bigger engine and larger output – such things as a more efficient radiator, bigger front disc brakes and larger wheel cylinders in the rear drum brakes, power-assisted steering and a higher final drive ratio – but in essence the roadgoing TR8 was a V8 TR7. Even the bonnet on the TR7 had been made with a raised section to accommodate the V8. The rally TR8 was an altogether fiercer proposition, but it was not an ideal shape for a rally car and

*Below: Only a handful of TR8s were sold in the UK, and are now highly collectable. Many TR7s have subsequently been converted.*

despite its power it achieved very little.

With the Rover V8 engine weighing no more than the iron-block slant-four in the TR7, the TR8's performance was much improved, and with no penalty in handling. Indeed, the only handling problem was one shared by both the TR7 and TR8; it was not the old-fashioned live rear axle but the soft spring, damper and bush rates which dulled the car's responses. As the TR7 and TR8 were so similar, there was a small but thriving business in the UK converting one to the other, and they were often given the stiffer suspension settings the car needed. The result was a very impressive sports car, capable of over 130 mph with ease and with a 0-60 mph time of 8.5 seconds even in its detuned North American form. Unfortunately, it was still let down by the poor quality control of the original car.

Although the TR8 was a far nicer car to drive than the TR7, by the time it went into production Triumph's reputation had

sunk too far and the marque itself, let alone the car, was on the way out. The vast majority of the 2,497 TR8s made were for the North American market, but there was a very small number of right-hand-drive models which escaped on to the UK market.

### Specification (1981)

**Engine:** V8, overhead-valve
**Bore × stroke:** 88.9 mm × 71 mm
**Capacity:** 3532 cc
**Maximum power:** 133 bhp (US spec)
**Transmission:** five-speed manual gearbox
**Chassis:** steel unitary construction
**Suspension:** independent front with MacPherson struts, lower wishbones and anti-roll bar; live rear axle with trailing arms, anti-roll bar, coil springs and telescopic dampers
**Brakes:** discs front, drums rear
**Bodywork:** steel two-seater coupé or convertible
**Maximum speed (approx):** 135 mph (217 km/h)

*Below: The cockpit was roomy and well designed, and the seats very supportive. Power steering was not really necessary and some drivers found it too light.*

# TVR

I n a little over 40 years, TVR of Blackpool has had several different owners and it's a miracle that the marque's character has been preserved, virtually intact, through that period. The 1950s TVRs were out-and-out sports cars with tubular chassis, glassfibre bodies, engines and transmissions from larger manufacturers; 1990s models are the same mixture but with far greater power and performance.

The story began in Blackpool with Trevor Wilkinson, a special builder who eventually decided to start making cars in greater numbers. The first 'Wilkinson special' had taken shape as early as 1949, but it was not until 1954 that the first TVR-badged model appeared; the TVR name was a contraction of Trevor. The new marque was tiny, extremely poorly-financed and ill-equipped, and for some years it existed from hand-to-mouth in an old wheelwright's shop. Even though in 1956 the business moved into a redundant brickworks at Layton, on the outskirts of Blackpool, production and sales built up only slowly and it was not until the first Grantura was launched in 1958 that the company became nationally known. Around 500 Granturas, with a variety of engines, were built in the next four years at a time when the firm's finances rocked from crisis to crisis.

By 1962 the Grantura Mk III had been launched and sales to the USA had built up following the introduction of the V8 Griffith, despite the ongoing money problems which saw Trevor Wilkinson leave the

*Above: The potent 150-mph Griffith of 1963 was a combination of the Grantura body and a 4727-cc small-block Ford V8; it could reach 60 mph in 5.7 seconds.*

company in 1962, but when Grantura Engineering (who had taken over TVRs) collapsed in 1965 the remains of the business were bought by Arthur and Martin Lilley. That proved a turning point for TVR; under the Lilleys it went from strength to strength and moved into its current premises in 1970. The M-series and Taimar models, along with the very fast Turbo, sold well and not even a serious fire in 1975 could hold back the company. Annual production soared to around 350 by the late 1970s.

The next generation of TVRs, the sharp-edged Tasmin series followed in 1980 and after a sticky patch when exports languished sales picked up. TVR owner and enthusiast Peter Wheeler took control from Martin Lilley in 1982, and steadily expanded the business. Ford V6, then Rover V8 engines were fitted and the body's sharp lines were rounded off. Wheeler then inspired the rebirth of a cheaper, simpler convertible – the TVR S.

During the 1990s, new models came out almost every year, even if they didn't make it beyond prototype stage. TVR was small enough and imaginatively innovative to try anything. Star cars were the Griffith, Chimaera and Cerbera, and the outrageously powerful Speed Twelve with TVR's own AJP modular engine in 7.7-litre form taking it to 240 mph.

*Above: The Tasmin, built in convertible and coupé form from 1980 to 1988, first had a Ford V6, then Rover's lighter V8 engine in 3.5-litre form.*

*Below: Action from the 1992 Tuscan Challenge Series round at Snetterton. The Tuscan was, like the Griffith, fitted with a highly-developed version of the Rover V8 engine with 320 bhp and almost untameable performance.*

# TVR Grantura Mk III and Vixen 1962-73

*Below: A 1962 Grantura Mk III, built by Grantura Engineering, powered by the MGB 1798-cc motor.*

*Right: The Grantura was a very attractive fastback, but access to the spare wheel was awkward.*

The first really 'mature' TVR was the Grantura Mk III of 1962, a developed version of the first rather stubby two-seater with a more rigid chassis under its glass-fibre bodywork. What really set it apart from the earlier models was its new and vastly improved suspension. The first TVRs had used VW Beetle-type trailing-link suspension, but for the Mk III that was replaced by a coil spring-and-wishbone design in 1960s racing tradition.

The Mk III was like its predecessors, though, in being an out-and-out sports car, one which put comfort, convenience and refinement a long way behind in the search for roadholding, straight-line performance and character. It had a short – perhaps too short – wheelbase, a cramped cabin and poor ventilation, but it still had great appeal.

Developed versions of this car were on sale for 10 years, during which time the Grantura evolved smoothly into the Vixen range. The Mk III had a sharply-sloping tail with no external access, which meant that the spare wheel had to be unloaded over the seats and through the rather small doors. Although TVR restyled the rear of the car in 1964, with a squared-off tail and new rear lights, there was still no rear access, and nor was there in the later Vixens.

Power for the Mk III Grantura came from the 86-bhp, 1622-cc MGA engine or, more commonly, the larger 1798-cc MGB engine, but there were a few models fitted with the Coventry Climax FWE 1216-cc overhead-cam unit, which produced 83 bhp. By 1964 some 90 Mk III Granturas had been built and it was time for a replacement, in the form of the Grantura 1800S with a slightly restyled rear, better trim and different gearing.

This proved more popular and 210 were built before the Vixen replaced the Grantura range in 1967.

The Vixen was virtually the same car as the Grantura except for a change in engine and gearbox, the package from the Cortina GT replacing the MGB unit. The new engine was a 1599-cc overhead-valve four producing 88 bhp. Like the Grantura, the Vixen was steadily improved, particularly with the arrival of the S2 in 1968, which was given a wheelbase lengthened by 4.5 inches, allowing larger doors to be fitted and giving more space inside the car. Not surprisingly, the S2 proved more popular than the first Vixen: 438 were sold compared with 117 of the earlier model. The final version of the Vixen was the 1300, essentially the S2 with a Triumph Spitfire engine; only 15 were built.

*Left: Rear view of a 1973 Vixen, with the Kamm tail and longer wheelbase. Note the Vixen's larger doors and windows (above).*

*Below: Sturdy and compact, the TVR Vixen made an excellent competition car, able to handle much power – as TVR discovered.*

## Specification (1962 Grantura Mk III)

**Engine:** MGB inline four-cylinder, overhead-valve
**Bore × stroke:** 80.3 mm × 88.9 mm
**Capacity:** 1798 cc
**Maximum power:** 95 bhp
**Transmission:** four-speed manual gearbox with optional overdrive, rear-wheel drive
**Chassis:** steel multi-tubular frame with four-tube backbone section and outriggers
**Suspension:** independent all round with wishbones, coil springs and telescopic dampers
**Brakes:** discs front, drums rear
**Bodywork:** glassfibre two-seater coupé
**Maximum speed (approx):** 108 mph (174 km/h)

# TVR Griffith and Tuscan 1963-70

*Above: A 1970 4.7-litre TVR Tuscan races at Silverstone in 1992. It was a short-wheelbase car (left) with enormous power.*

### Specification (1963 Griffith 400)

**Engine:** V8, overhead-valve
**Bore × stroke:** 101.6 mm × 72.9 mm
**Capacity:** 4727 cc
**Maximum power:** 271 bhp
**Transmission:** four-speed manual gearbox, rear-wheel drive
**Chassis:** multi-tubular steel backbone
**Suspension:** independent with wishbones, coil springs and telescopic dampers; twin coil spring/damper units at rear
**Brakes:** discs front, drums rear
**Bodywork:** glassfibre two-seater coupé
**Maximum speed (approx):** 164 mph (264 km/h)

*Above: A 1967 Tuscan with the Ford V8 tuned to deliver 378 bhp and shattering acceleration.*

Like the AC Cobra which preceded it, and the Sunbeam Tiger which soon followed, TVR's Griffith was a sports car transformed by being given a Ford-USA V8 engine transplant. The Griffith owed more to the Cobra than the more civilised Tiger in being a raw-boned bruiser with tyre-stripping performance, and it took a year for the necessary refinement and reliability to be added to the basic concept.

The original model was inspired by Jack Griffith, an American motor trader who installed a mighty 4.7-litre thin-wall Ford V8 into a Grantura Mk III body and chassis in 1962. He liked it so much that he became obsessed with its potential and approached TVR to build replicas. The result was that TVR's North American distributor, Dick Monnich, backed the project and allowed Griffith to put his name on the cars, the first models going on sale in 1963. The cars were delivered to the USA without the Ford engine and gearbox, which were

installed by TVR's distributor.

The original Griffiths, known as Griffith 200s, suffered cooling and braking problems but these were addressed in the rather better-developed Griffith 400 (which featured the cut-off tail of the later Granturas). The Griffith 400 was fitted with a thermostatically-controlled Kenlow fan allied to a larger radiator.

The Griffith looked like a Grantura, except for the big bulge in the bonnet and the wider tyres, but its performance was in a different league. The car was so fast that probably no magazine test ever achieved a true top speed when measuring its performance.

TVR's relationship with Jack Griffith was shattered by a long dock strike in 1965, after which Grantura Engineering collapsed and production of the V8 cars was interrupted after 300 Griffiths had been built. This wasn't the end of the line, however, for in 1967 the Griffith reappeared under a different name, Tuscan. The Tuscan V8 was also built in longer-wheelbase form on the Vixen chassis and with the Vixen body, and was known as the Tuscan V8 SE.

The final evolution of the line was

known as the wide-body Tuscan V8 – just seven were made in 1970 – and that allied the long wheelbase of the SE with a wider body which was more practical and fore-shadowed the M-series cars.

*Above: A 1965 Griffith 200, which was effectively the Grantura III with the Ford V8 shoehorned in.*

*Below: The Griffith was short and light, and with such power that on-limit handling required care.*

*Above: The bonnet bulge was necessary to clear the V8's twin-choke Holley carburettor.*

# TVR 3000M and Taimar 1972-79

By 1972 the Grantura and its Vixen evolution had been pensioned off to be replaced by a new range, the M-type cars. Even these, however, were evolutions of the earlier designs rather than totally new creations. Indeed, it was possible for the older-style bodies to be fitted on the new M-type chassis, something which TVR actually did in the interim change-over period of 1972-73.

The 'M' in the car's name came from Martin Lilley's christian name, and there was enough that was new in the car to warrant a new model name. Lilley's small development team had made it better in all respects than the old cars. The wheelbase stayed the same 90 inches as before and the front and rear track were almost the same, but the backbone chassis – complete with four longitudinal tubes arranged in box formation down the centre of the car – was far more robust than before. The engine bay was roomy enough to accommodate three quite different engines – inline-fours, V6s and the straight-six from the Triumph TR6. As ever, the two seats were mounted far apart and low down on either side of the massive propshaft tunnel.

Although the new body retained the windscreen, door assemblies and rear window of the last of the old shells, the

*Right: The convertible was both attractive and rigid; this 1979 3000M has the three-litre Ford V6.*

rest of the body was new. Its shape was recognisably derived from that of the wide-bodied Tuscan V8 SE of 1968-70 and there was still no rear access. Luckily, the spare wheel had migrated from the boot to the engine bay.

Here was what some observers described as the first 'grown-up' TVR, with more space, and greater refinement and style than before. It was also rather better-built, and increasing sales began to reflect that. The original M coupé was only the first of a series of cars built on that chassis, such as the Taimar hatchback version in 1976. These two models were then supplemented by the convertible in 1978. This was an instant success (and was revived in modified form 10 years later), and sold well in the USA. Although the convertible's chassis and front end were the same as on the 3000M/Taimar, the cabin and rear were entirely new and there was, at last, an opening boot.

Assembly of the M-range of cars ended in 1979 as the factory was geared up for the next generation of TVRs, the many and varied Tasmin models.

*Above: A 1976 1600M with the 86-bhp four-cylinder Ford engine; such was the car's lightness that acceleration was rapid to 105 mph.*

*Below: A TVR 3000M with a sunroof and non-standard split-rim wheels. The spare wheel was now stored in front of the engine.*

## TVR 3000M variants

### TVR 1600M

This smaller-engined model was fitted with a four-cylinder overhead-valve Ford engine with a bore and stroke of 81 mm × 78 mm, a displacement of 1599 cc and a power output of 86 bhp, which was enough to give a top speed of 105 mph. The 1600M was produced in two spells, from 1972 to 1973 and then from 1975 to 1977; 148 were built in all.

### TVR 2500M

As its name suggests, the 2500M was fitted with a 2.5-litre engine, the 2598-cc overhead-valve straight-six from the Triumph TR6. It had a power output of 106 bhp and higher performance than the 1600M, with a top speed of 109 mph. The bulk of these models was sold in North America, where the Triumph engine was a familiar unit. Production ran from 1972 to 1976 and totalled 947.

### TVR Turbo

The Turbo was built in three forms – on the standard 3000M base, as the Taimar hatchback and as a convertible – and was extremely rare. Only 63 in all were made: 20 of the 3000M type, 30 Taimar Turbos and 13 convertibles. TVR turned to the respected Warwickshire-based tuning company Broadspeed for expertise in the conversion, and Broadspeed converted the Ford three-

litre V6 themselves and shipped the units to Blackpool. The installation looked complex but worked very well, boosting power some 67 per cent to as much as 230 bhp. That made all the Turbo versions very fast; the top speed of around 140 mph would have been higher if the final drive ratio had been higher.

### TVR Taimar

The Taimar was built from 1976 to 1979 and was a hatchback derivative of the 3000M; powered by the Ford three-litre V6 engine, 395 were made.

### TVR convertible

With its separate chassis construction, it was easy to turn the 3000M into a convertible and this was duly done, but only from 1978 to 1979.

### Specification (1972 3000M)

**Engine:** V6, overhead-valve
**Bore × stroke:** 93.67 mm × 72.4 mm
**Capacity:** 2994 cc
**Maximum power:** 138 bhp
**Transmission:** four-speed manual gearbox, optional overdrive
**Suspension:** independent with wishbones, coil springs and anti-roll bar front; coil springs and wishbones rear
**Brakes:** discs front, drums rear
**Bodywork:** glassfibre two-seater coupé or convertible
**Maximum speed:** 139 mph (224 km/h)

# TVR Tasmin 1980-85

When the new-generation TVR, the Tasmin, appeared in January 1980 it swept away all the 1970s M-type models at a stroke. It was still recognisably a TVR but it was new in virtually every respect – new chassis, new body and a different Ford V6 engine. For TVR and managing director Martin Lilley it was a major investment which would need steady sales for a number of years to pay off. Fortunately for the company, the venture was a great success.

Building on the long-established TVR theme, the Tasmin featured a four-tube backbone chassis and a glassfibre body. Both chassis and bodies were produced on fairly simple tooling at Blackpool but TVR still went outside for engines, transmissions and other elements of the running gear. The engine was an easy choice – the fuel-injected 2.8-litre Ford V6 fitted to the 2.8i Capri, which gave 160 bhp. The Tasmin had a four-inch longer wheelbase than the previous model but it still looked short in relation to the car's wide track. The chassis was

adaptable and served as the base for a variety of models: the initial hatchback coupé, a two-seater convertible and a +2 convertible. The wedge-shaped styling of all the models was the work of Oliver Winterbottom, who had previously styled Jaguar and Lotus models.

In refinement, equipment and appeal the Tasmin was the best TVR yet, but because it was also rather more expensive sales took time to build. More than 300 M-type models had been made in 1979 but only 144 Tasmins were sold in 1980. By 1985, however, when the V8 model had been introduced, production was running at record levels of 500 cars a year. Although the Tasmin name was dropped in the mid-1980s, the basic design lived on, refined, improved and facelifted as necessary.

The fitment of a lower-powered engine (the overhead-camshaft four-cylinder Ford Pinto) was only a diversion, as was a turbo V6 prototype, before the logical step was taken to use the Rover V8 engine, at first in standard 190-bhp fuel-injected form but then in larger and larger displacements with more and more power.

## Specification (1980)

**Engine:** V6, overhead-valve
**Bore × stroke:** 93 mm × 68.5 mm
**Capacity:** 2792 cc
**Maximum power:** 160 bhp

*Above: The straight-edge wedge styling was radically new for TVR, and very much in tune with 1980s fashion. The distinctive bonnet louvres (below) aided cooling.*

**Transmission:** five-speed manual gearbox, rear-wheel drive
**Chassis:** multi-tubular steel backbone
**Suspension:** independent with wishbones and coil springs front; lower transverse links, radius arms and coil springs rear
**Brakes:** discs all round
**Bodywork:** glassfibre two-seater coupé
**Maximum speed (approx):** 133 mph (214 km/h)

*Above: Colin Blower's 1981 Tasmin convertible in the 1982 Lucas CAV Sports Car Race at Silverstone.*

*Below: The convertible was a natural development; note the changes to the door and bonnet line.*

## TVR 350i 1983-91

The 350i was recognisably derived from the original Tasmin and shared its sharp-edged styling. The car had been transformed, however, by fitting the ubiquitous Rover V8 engine, in fuel-injected form and in 190-bhp Rover Vitesse tune. That was enough to give the car an excellent top speed of 136 mph which, given the car's short wheelbase, was enough for most people as the car could be tricky indeed at the limit, although the handling was worlds better than that of its predecessor. Aimed squarely at the American export market, the 350i's power was proved with a standing quarter-mile figure of less than 15 seconds and a 0-60 mph time of 5.1 seconds. Nevertheless, TVR embarked on a programme of making the cars even more powerful and faster. The first step was the creation of the 390SE, which used the enlarged Rover V8 in 3.9-litre form with engine modifications carried out by the well-known saloon-car racer Andy Rouse. The extra displacement and tuning resulted in a power output of 275 bhp and a top speed of 140 mph. That was just the beginning as the V8 was

stretched again, this time by only a few cc to 3947 cc, enough to prompt another change in model name, to 400SE. There was seemingly no limit to what could be done to the engine and by 1986 its stroke had been increased enough to give a displacement of 4282 cc, prompting a further change in name to 420SE. With maximum power now over 300 bhp, the TVR was even more of a challenge than before. By this time TVR themselves were building the engines and in race tune they could produce 385 bhp.

Just two years after the 420SE, the numbers went up again and the car became the 450SE in 1988, this time with a bored and stroked version of the V8 with a 4441-cc displacement and 320 bhp. The extra power had inevitably improved the performance and gave a top speed, for the brave, of 144 mph.

By this stage the coupé body had died

*Right: Prodigiously fast, this 1984 420SEAC ex-works racer achieved many successes. It has a highly-tuned 4.2-litre V8 and a curved body of Aramid Composites.*

from lack of demand and almost all the cars were the more attractive convertibles. Most striking of these were the 420 and 450SEAC types with more advanced bodies with composite panels (the 'AC' in the title stood for Aramid Composites) which had a rounded front and rear, moulded sills and a rear spoiler.

There was still some variation in the design to come, with TVR launching a new-generation Tuscan; this limited-production racing model appeared in the Tuscan Challenge race series and proved beyond all doubt that they had too much power for the chassis. The cars' spectacular antics were understandably popular with the crowds, though.

*Below: The low and wide 420SEAC racer in action, with power levels only for expert hands.*

### Specification (1991 450SEAC)

**Engine:** V8, overhead-valve
**Bore × stroke:** 94 mm × 80 mm
**Capacity:** 4441 cc
**Maximum power:** 320 bhp
**Transmission:** five-speed manual gearbox, rear-wheel drive
**Chassis:** steel multi-tubular backbone
**Suspension:** independent front and rear with wishbones, coil springs, telescopic dampers and anti-roll bars
**Brakes:** discs all round
**Bodywork:** glassfibre and Kevlar two-seater convertible
**Maximum speed (approx):** 143 mph (230 km/h)

*Below: A modern classic, the 390SE Series 2. TVR always moved slowly with styling changes, but the softer contours worked well.*

*Above: The 390SE, tuned by Andy Rouse, offered 275 bhp and 140 mph; the angular look was aerodynamic.*

*Below: A 350i at speed; note the raked screen and the raised side windows, to reduce wind buffeting.*

# TVR S 1986–94

*Right: The sleek, composite-bodied TVR S was one of the few 1980s cars still built over a separate chassis. It was powered by engines ranging from 2.8 to 3.9 litres.*

When TVR launched its new convertible model in 1986 it came as a real surprise to enthusiasts, as the company had spent some time moving steadily up-market building increasingly expensive cars. In doing so, a hole had been created in the product range and TVR filled it by effectively going back a whole decade and re-introducing a simple two-seater.

Although the S had a new multi-tubular chassis with semi-trailing-arm rear suspension, its body was actually a modernised and widened version of the 3000M convertible of the 1970s with a new windscreen, wind-up windows and a more rigid and modern design of folding soft top. Instead of the big Rover V8 which was then being fitted to the 350i and 390i models, TVR opted for the Ford V6, the 2.8-litre injected version with 160 bhp, which gave a more than adequate top speed of 128 mph. When Ford replaced that engine with the slightly larger but very similar 2.9-litre version, TVR followed suit in 1988 with the S2 model, which had 170 bhp.

On the road the TVR S offered fine handling and a comfortable ride. With near 50/50 per cent static weight distribution, cornering was neutral, and thanks to a weight of just under a ton and a low centre of gravity, there was little body roll. The weight at the rear also gave the S good traction, with excellent acceleration on dry surfaces; the clutch could safely be dropped at 3,500 rpm without provoking wheelspin.

The convertible roof comprised two hard roof panels, which could be stored in the boot, and a fold-down rear fabric section with window:

The S was considerably cheaper than the 1980s-style Tasmin-derived convertibles and before long deservedly became the company's best-seller. It handled well, was fast and had enormous character. The S2 was revamped in 1990 to become the S3 with slight body and trim changes and a more modern fascia. In the process the S moved away from its entry-level role somewhat, costing £21,029 in 1993, a 62 per cent increase from its original price.

TVR could not resist the temptation to make the S even faster and introduced the Rover V8 engine as an option, which maintained sales until the S range was phased out in 1994.

*Left: A 1988 TVR S with the 2933-cc Ford V6. The roof could be folded down, as shown, or the rear section (with window) left up, for reduced wind buffeting.*

*Below: This 1987 TVR S was a car that stressed character rather than aerodynamics. As a result, the breathtaking acceleration slowed a little at speeds near 100 mph.*

## Specification (1991 V8 S)

**Engine:** V8, overhead-valve
**Bore × stroke:** 94 mm × 71.12 mm
**Capacity:** 3947 cc
**Maximum power:** 240 bhp
**Transmission:** five-speed manual gearbox, rear-wheel drive
**Chassis:** separate multi-tubular steel frame with four-tube central backbone and outriggers
**Suspension:** independent with wishbones and coil springs front; semi-trailing arms and coil springs rear
**Brakes:** discs all round
**Bodywork:** glassfibre two-seater convertible
**Maximum speed (approx):** 146 mph (235 km/h)

*Above: The five-speed TVR S was praised for its steering response. The fascia was trimmed in padded vinyl, with a speedometer and rev-counter at the centre, and oil, water and fuel gauges at the side.*

# TVR Griffith 1992-present

*Below: Clearly inspired by the best 1960s designs, the Griffith body, styled by human eyes and not by a computer, was much admired.*

*Below: On the road the 160-mph Griffith had tremendous grip and mild, flat cornering. From any angle the two-seater showed clean lines. The hand-laid glassfibre bodies were fully finished before being fitted to the chassis.*

The Griffith was first shown to an admiring public at the Motor Show at Birmingham's NEC in 1990. Then it was little more than a rebodied V8 S, but it was so attractive that it was almost inevitable it would be transformed from show car to production car. The eye-catching styling was the work of TVR boss Peter Wheeler himself along with engineer Peter Ravenscroft, achieved not with the help of computer-aided design but by whittling away at full-size blocks of foam to arrive at the right shape. The most noticeable styling features were the scalloped doors, a treatment repeated in the bonnet. This conveniently removed the shut-line problems faced by glassfibre car builders, and in both cases these spaces acted as exit vents for engine-bay air. The car's smoothness was emphasised by a lack of bumpers and door locks. The roof was again a simple folding rear section, with window, and a rigid centre section which could be stowed in the boot. The chassis was a typical TVR multi-tube design, with four longitudinal tubes forming a deep transmission tunnel frame, and a complex triangulated array of cross-members and outriggers; the whole was well protected with a polyester coating.

It didn't take TVR long, however, to establish that the new car, which was intended to have a power output to match its looks, would need some chassis development. In the end it kept the V8 S's 90-in wheelbase and the usual multi-tubular backbone chassis with its substantial propshaft tunnel, but took the rear suspension from the fearsome Tuscan racer (though with softer springs, dampers and bushes). Compared with the V8 S, the Griffith had a wider track and far larger wheels with 7-in wide rims holding enormous 215/50 ZR15s at the front and 225/50 ZR16s on the rear. It needed such rubber wear, as even the basic engine was a 240-bhp version of the old V8 and there were 250-bhp and 280-bhp options on offer. The performance of the 280-bhp car was stunning, with a 0-60 mph time of 4.7 seconds and the ability to cover the standing quarter-mile in an outstanding 13.2 seconds, while the top speed was over 160 mph. Performance like that required fuel at the rate of 19 mpg.

Initially there was a handling problem brought about by difficulties with the Tuscan-derived independent rear suspension, but that was addressed and the car took its rightful place among the ranks of British supercars. In the words of *Autocar & Motor*'s delighted road testers: "The Griffith is so close to being a world-beater that it hurts... nothing for the money seems close."

*Above: At speed on smooth roads the Griffith felt safe and very controllable, and with power and performance exceeding that of cars several times the price.*

## Specification (1992)

**Engine:** V8, overhead-valve
**Bore × stroke:** 94 mm × 71.2 mm
**Capacity:** 3947 cc
**Maximum power:** 240 bhp
**Transmission:** five-speed manual gearbox, rear-wheel drive
**Chassis:** multi-tubular steel backbone
**Suspension:** independent front and rear with wishbones and coil springs
**Brakes:** discs all round
**Bodywork:** glassfibre two-seater convertible
**Maximum speed (approx):** 161 mph (259 km/h)

## Variants:

In 1993 the TVR Power/Rover V8 was bored out to 5.0 litres and fitted in the Griffith 500. The Griffith-derived Tuscan Speed Six was shown at the 1997 Earl's Court Show powered by a 4.0 litre AJP straight-six engine.

*Left: The TVR-tuned 4280-cc Rover V8 was mounted low and well back in the chassis. It gave a potent 280 bhp and 305 lb ft of torque.*

*Below: Smooth and uncluttered, the Griffith was a supercar with refinement, and after the launch TVR's order books were soon full. External door locks were obviated by a remote locking key and a dashboard sensor.*

## Chimaera 1993-present

Along with the larger-capacity Griffith 500, the hunkier Chimaera went into production in 1993, and helped consolidate TVR's position as the most prolific of Britain's independent car manufacturers. The same year the 90-degree TVR Power/Rover V8 was bored out to a full 5.0-litres, when output rose to 350 bhp with maximum torque of 350 lb/ft, and that was immediately fitted in the Griffith 500. A 4.0-litre Chimaera V8 on full song produced 235 bhp at 5,500 rpm, or 260 lb/ft of torque at 4500 rpm, accompanied by the most glorious sound track, redolent of its racing Tuscan siblings. The Chimaera was also available with 4.3- and 5.0-litre versions of the TVR Power/Rover V8 unit, allied to the Borg Warner T-55 five-speed synchromesh gearbox. Any of the engine options was powerful enough to propel the Chimaera beyond 150 mph (241 km/h), and the 5.0-litre option took it on to over 160 mph (99 km/h).

The Chimaera was unveiled at the Birmingham NEC in 1992, and while the Griffith was a sleek, elongated egg shape with few intrusions into its flowing lines, the Chimaera was another matter, for it was full of drama, with sculpted air intakes and niches vying for prominence with the slashes down the bonnet. The Chimaera was clearly longer than the Griffith, and much of that extra volume was in the boot space, which made it a slightly more practical car.

Like all TVRs, the fibreglass-bodied Chimaera was constructed around a multi-tubular backbone chassis with independent wishbone suspension all round. Gas dampers and coil springs, plus anti-roll bars, were fitted front and back, and it was slowed by servo-assisted dual-circuit 240 mm ventilated discs at the front and 250 mm discs at the rear. Prodigious grip was provided by 205/60ZR x 15 and 225/55ZR x 16 Bridgestone RE71 tyres.

The wraparound dashboard and scuttle topography of the Chimaera was not so different from the Griffith, with yellow-faced dials with black numbers. Standard interior equipment included electric windows, radio/cassette player, central locking, Personal leather-rim wheel, adjustable pedal box, leather seat facings, an ice detector, and a microwave alarm system. At the 1996 Motor Show TVR showed a subtly revised Chimaera with a fresh nose and tail to bring it into line with the Cerbera, while the controls also included much of the high quality aluminium switchgear from the 2 + 2 model.

The 4.3-litre Chimaera was at its most enthralling over a mixture of fast undulating A-roads, and unlike many sports cars, its interior stayed warm and dry in the rain. It could be driven with just its Targa top removed, or with the rear header retracted completely. Significantly, in the late 1990s, the Chimaera was TVR's best-selling model.

*Above: The Chimaera was a wonderful mix of classic styling cues from the halcyon days of the 1950s sports car. It exemplified TVR's tried-and-tested tubular steel chassis and fibreglass body construction, allied to competition-derived double wishbone suspension all round and storming Rover V8 powerplants that ranged from 4.2- to 5.0-litres.*

### Specification (4.0-litre)
**Engine:** aluminium V8, rear drive
**Bore x stroke:** 94.0 mm x 71.0 mm
**Capacity:** 3950 cc
**Compression ratio:** 9.8:1
**Chassis:** multi-tubular steel, fibreglass body

**Suspension:** front, independent by upper and lower wishbones, coil springs, dampers, anti-roll bar; rear, independent by upper and lower wishbones, coil springs, dampers, anti-roll bar
**Brakes:** ventilated discs all round

## Cerbera 1994-present

The Cerbera was the first TVR coupé to be built since 1989, and the first two-plus-two since the 280i 2 + 2 Coupé wedge of 1985. It was built on a new chassis, similar in design to the Griffith and Chimaera, but six inches longer. In addition, it had a built in steel roll-cage, hidden within the roof pillars of the closed fibreglass bodywork. The suspension was of a similar layout to the rest of the range, but set up especially for the heavier, longer wheelbase car. Just as significantly, the Cerbera was fitted with the company's own 4.2 litre AJP8 engine. This compact 75-degree, lightweight all-aluminium unit had a single camshaft per bank and two valves per cylinder, but an unusual firing order. It developed 350 bhp at a relatively high 6,500 rpm, and 320 lb/ft of torque at 4500 rpm. The Cerbera could top 160 mph (99 km/h), and travel from 0–60 mph (0–96 km/h) in 4.2 seconds. As befitted its bigger chassis, it had wider tyres than the Chimaera, with 225/45ZR x 16 Bridgestones at the front, and 235/50ZR x 16s at the rear.

While the interiors and dashboards of the Griffith and Chimaera were refreshingly different, the Cerbera's was something different again. There was even more of the wraparound feel to the cabin, with plenty of flowing curved shapes. The main dials had black figures on white clocks and were housed in a binnacle ahead of the driver, while the clock and fuel gauge were located in a separate pod underneath the steering column. The wiper, horn and headlight dip control buttons were located in the two-spoke steering wheel, with the stereo and speaker occupying the centre console. The doors had no handles, but release buttons situated in the door pocket and on the key fob. There was no ignition key, and the engine was started and stopped by a pair of ignition buttons beneath the steering wheel. The rear seats were best occupied by children although the front passenger seat could slide further forward than normal, thereby freeing up a substantial amount of extra legroom for the passenger sitting directly behind.

At the 1997 Earl's Court Show, TVR unveiled the Tuscan Speed Six, while a potential successor to the Cerbera was the awesome 12-cylinder 7.7-litre V12 powered Speed Twelve, capable of a towering 240 mph (386 km/h).

### Specifications
**Engine:** AJP8 alloy V8, 16-valve, rear drive
**Bore x stroke:** 86.0 mm x 88.0 mm
**Capacity:** 4280-cc
**Compression ratio:** 10.0:1
**Chassis:** multi-tubular steel, fibreglass body
**Suspension:** front, independent by upper and lower wishbones, coil springs, dampers, anti-roll bar; rear, independent by upper and lower wishbones, coil springs, dampers, anti roll bar
**Brakes:** ventilated discs all round

*Left: Designers Damian McTaggart and Nick Coughlan expanded on the Chimaera theme to produce the Cerbera, TVR's first 2 + 2 coupé since 1985. Based on a chassis extended by 6 inches, the Cerbera was powered by TVR's own 4.2-litre AJP V8 engine. The interior was as innovative in form as the exterior.*

# Vauxhall Motors Ltd

T he very first Vauxhalls were actually produced in Vauxhall in London in 1903, but the company then made a move to Luton in 1904 and have been based there ever since. Although Vauxhall was taken over by the North American giant, General Motors, in 1925, it produced cars as an independent business for the first 20 years.

All early Vauxhalls had large engines, were produced in small quantities, and were relatively costly; it was not until the 1920s that the company regularly built more than 1,000 cars a year. With Brooklands star Percy Kidner as one of the firm's executives, and with Laurence Pomeroy (Sr) as the genius behind the engine design, it was no wonder that the Edwardian company won sports car races and even built splendid, though little-used, racing engines.

One result was the birth of the Prince Henry sports car of 1911, and the 30/98 models which followed it, but after GM had taken stock in the late 1920s it began to convert Luton into a mass-production concern, and there would be no more sporting Vauxhalls for 50 years. By the end of the 1930s Vauxhall had pioneered monocoque construction in the UK, and had become a member of the British 'Big Six'; Bedford, an important player in

the commercial vehicle business, had also been founded, and subsequently developed into a market leader.

For 30 years after World War II Vauxhall produced a series of increasingly transatlantic-looking family cars, including the hideous but successful Victor range, followed in the 1960s by the Viva, its first truly small car.

By the 1960s, too, component-sharing with another GM subsidiary, Opel of West Germany, had become common and from the mid-1970s new-car design leadership was passed to the German concern. At first Vauxhall was allowed to have individual styling of its new models, but by the 1980s all such pretence had faded away, and Vauxhalls were no more than Opels in very light disguise.

Once GM had dropped its ban on participation in motorsport in the 1970s Vauxhall could begin to develop more exciting cars once again, the result being cars like the Magnum/Firenza coupés, and the Chevette HS/ HSR types of the 1970s, both of which did great things for the marque's reputation, which had had no competition lustre for over half a century.

By the early 1990s Vauxhall and Opel were so far integrated that cars with either badge were being built in the UK, in Germany and in Spain, with engines travelling round the world from Australia. The company's cars had become increasingly complex and beautifully styled, the engines in particular getting more and more advanced with every season. Cosworth helped to provide the first four-valve twin-cam cylinder heads in the mid-1980s, but GM itself developed four-wheel-drive systems, a smart body style for the Calibra, and the Carlton/Opel Omega was good enough to form the basis of Lotus's phenomenal 170-mph twin-turbo saloon model.

By this time GM-Europe challenged Ford-Europe for sales leadership in several markets with models like the Vectra, the Corsa-based Tigra and the Astra with Lotus-tuned suspension providing interest in the late 1990s.

*Right: The griffin badge was from the crest of a Norman knight who once owned land at Luton.*

*Below: Vauxhall moved into a new performance era with the likes of the 146-mph Carlton GSi of 1989.*

# Vauxhall 30/98 1913-27

*Left: The 30/98 was a 4.2-litre tourer capable of nearly 100 mph, and of cruising easily at 80 mph – great performance for the day. 30/98s proved very successful in hill climbs and other events.*

Even before the Prince Henry model had passed its peak, Vauxhall was persuaded to build a larger sprint car for Joseph Higginson of Autovac, and replicas were soon put on sale. Aimed to follow other Vauxhall ranges called A, B, C and D-Type, the new car was called the E-Type, and carried the badge of '30/98'.

The true ancestor of the 30/98 was the original sporting Vauxhall, the C-Type 'Prince Henry' model of 1911-15. Fifty of the original three-litre versions, and 190 of the definitive four-litre types, both with rugged side-valve engines, were built in four years, all of them with smart styling and better performance than most cars of the period.

The first 30/98 was launched in 1913; it was larger, heavier *and* faster than the Prince Henry model, mainly because it had a 90-bhp 4525-cc side-valve engine. With a top speed of 80-85 mph, it was faster than all its rivals, though the braking (by a hand lever only to the rear wheels) was not capable of keeping this in check. It differed from the later 30/98 in having a fixed-cylinder-head engine, a multi-plate clutch and a straight-bevel rear axle.

Right from the start the stripped-out version was guaranteed to be capable of 100 mph, a phenomenal speed for the time. This made the original 30/98 the Jaguar E-type of the Edwardian period, as it was so very much quicker than almost all its rivals, so the original catalogue description was apt, to say the least. It was, however, an expensive car (the chassis price alone was £900), so there were few takers before 1914.

The origins of the 30/98 name are obscure, but possibly the 30 denoted the horsepower developed at 1,000 rpm (a figure important for RAC taxation purposes), and the 98 may have referred to the claimed maximum power output at 3,000 rpm.

Series-production of the 30/98, with its simple but effective side-valve engine, got under way in 1919. It was a fast and heavy machine, with good roadholding by the standards of the day, and very impressive performance. At first the price was too high – £1,670 – but even when reduced to £1,300 in 1921 it still had to fight on equal terms with the new and much-hyped 3-litre Bentley. Nevertheless, a total of 283 E-Types was built before the car was redesigned in 1922.

The main change for the new series of cars was that the engine was converted to an overhead-valve configuration and, thanks to its shorter stroke, it also revved faster than before; this probably explains the new type number of OE, for 'O' surely stands for 'overhead-valve engine'. By this time Pomeroy had left Vauxhall, but since the renowned Harry Ricardo had become a consultant Vauxhall's engine developments were in safe hands.

Although the new engine produced 115 bhp at 3,300 rpm, and the chassis had been stiffened, the car was still only supplied with rear-wheel brakes at first, which left it technically behind Bentley for a time. The cable-operated front brakes which followed in 1923 were better, but only a partial solution to the problem. By that time the 30/98 was a very fast car by any 1920s standards.

Even so, the 30/98 was never one of Vauxhall's fastest-selling models. By 1925, when General Motors took over the business, it was only truly in batch-production, with cars being made as and

when new orders were received.

In 1926, though, the finest and best of all the 30/98s was announced, and made in small numbers. For £950 (chassis alone), the customer was offered a car with a 120-bhp engine and hydraulic brakes on all four wheels. Like its predecessors, the revised model was sturdy but heavy, remarkably fast (the top speed was about 95 mph, and 80 mph cruising speeds were normal where there was space), but expensive to buy and maintain.

By then, however, motor industry technology had begun to catch up with the 30/98, which was widely seen as being a much-developed Edwardian-type sports car that was falling behind the times, and it was having to compete with more sophisticated six-cylinder-powered models from Sunbeam and Bentley.

The last of the 313 OE 30/98s was built in 1927, and traditionalists were sad to see that Vauxhall never again built a car of that type, as General Motors' policy was to begin turning Vauxhall into a mass-production company.

## Specification (1913)

**Engine:** four-cylinder, overhead-valve
**Bore × stroke:** 98 mm × 140 mm
**Capacity:** 4224 cc
**Maximum power:** 120 bhp
**Transmission:** four-speed manual gearbox, rear-wheel drive
**Chassis:** separate steel frame with channel-section side members; separate subframe supporting engine
**Suspension:** non-independent with beam axle and semi-elliptic leaf springs front; live axle with semi-elliptic leaf springs rear
**Brakes:** drums all round
**Bodywork:** aluminium four-seater open tourer
**Maximum speed (approx):** 95 mph (153 km/h)

*Above: The 120-bhp overhead-valve engine of a 1914 Prince Henry, which was the precursor of the 30/98.*

*Right: The Prince Henry model of 1915 was a fast tourer.*

# Vauxhall Chevette 2300 HS 1976-80

For many years General Motors' policy forbade its subsidiary companies from entering 'works' cars in motorsport, but this ruling crumbled in the 1970s, allowing the birth of Dealer Team Vauxhall, which soon began to enter cars in races and rallies. This was the period in which Ford's Escort RS1600 and RS1800 models were dominant in British motorsport, so when DTV persuaded Vauxhall to produce high-performance 'homologation specials' these aped the Escort's layout.

The first effort, the Firenza 'droopsnoot' of 1973, was not a success, for it was too large and too heavy and did not handle very well. To follow it up, Vauxhall then carried out a similar transplant operation on the smaller Chevette hatchback, which not only matched the Escort RS1800 in design philosophy, but also provided a very fast and exciting road car for those who did not want to commit their cars to competition.

The Chevette 2300 HS (HS, perhaps, stands for High-Speed, though Vauxhall never spelt this out) was successful on all counts, for it was a rally winner almost from the start. The car was based on the humble three-door hatchback Chevette, which was itself a clone of the Opel Kadett of the period; this model was normally made only with a modest 1.3-litre engine and was not a promising competition car. Fortunately, the engineers found it possible to fit a derivative of Vauxhall's 2.3-litre four-cylinder engine, installed at an angle of 45 degrees, and this was matched to a German Getrag five-speed gearbox. A heavy-duty GM rear axle, special wheels, tyres, aerodynamic aids and suspension settings produced a transformed machine which had a top speed of 115 mph in standard form.

The engine was unique to the HS, for it had a special 16-valve twin-cam cylinder head which Vauxhall had developed, but which Cosworth subsequently made in quantity. It was this engine, or rather the lack of it in the first 'works' rally cars, which provided so much controversy.

The original car was built by DTV for use on the 1976 RAC Rally well before series-production had begun, and featured a Lotus Esprit-type of cylinder

head along with a ZF gearbox. Although Vauxhall had plans to introduce the production car in 1977, the launch was delayed, and the competition programme went ahead in any case. The rally cars soon began winning, and everyone assumed that a Lotus head and the ZF gearbox would be part of the road car's specification!

When pre-production cars, seen in the spring of 1978, were found to have their own brand of head, and the Getrag gearbox, this caused a great deal of confusion. At this point the motorsport authorities stepped in, and demanded that the rally car should use production components, just as the regulations required. This caused something of a hiatus in competition progress, though the production car certainly benefitted from the wide publicity which followed.

A total of 400 HS models were produced (which was the minimum needed for homologation to be achieved), and their high price ensured that it took a

long time for them to be sold. With an eye to making competition cars more competitive, the HSR derivative was then put on sale, with more power and better roadholding, though it now seems that these were not new cars, but merely conversions of unsold old stock.

*Above: The sale of HS Chevettes to the public was surrounded by controversy over the engine head and gearbox, but sales were good.*

*Above: The Chevette 2300 HS was a compact but mundane-looking hot hatchback capable of 115 mph.*

## Vauxhall Chevette 2300 HS variants

### Vauxhall Chevette 2300 HSR
To make the basic HS even more suitable for use in motorsport, DTV persuaded Vauxhall to offer a limited number of HSR types at the end of 1979, these having a more powerful (150-bhp) engine, a twin-plate clutch, revised rear suspension (with twin upper radius arms added) and wider-rim wheels. A glassfibre bonnet, front and rear wheelarch flares and underdoor sills were all fitted to make a good car look even better. Only 50 HSRs were built, and at £7,146 they were far more expensive than the HS had ever been.

### Specification (1976 2300 HS)
**Engine:** four-cylinder, twin-cam
**Bore × stroke:** 97.5 mm × 76.2 mm
**Capacity:** 2279 cc
**Maximum power:** 135 bhp (240 bhp in fully-tuned rally form)
**Transmission:** five speed manual gearbox, rear-wheel drive
**Chassis:** steel monocoque
**Suspension:** independent front with wishbones, coil springs and anti-roll bar; live rear axle with coil springs, radius arms, torque tube and Panhard rod
**Brakes:** discs front, drums rear
**Bodywork:** steel three-door four-seater hatchback
**Maximum speed (approx):** (135-bhp version) 115 mph (185 km/h)

*Left: Penti Airikkala, winner of many rallies and the 1979 RAC Rally Championship, in the DTV/Castrol Chevette 2300 HS, with a 16-valve, twin-cam engine. The HS was effective in rallies, and the 400 HS road cars were very fast.*

# Volkswagen

The original air-cooled rear-engined four-seater 'people's car' was designed by Professor Ferdinand Porsche at Adolf Hitler's request, and it was the German *Führer* who gave it the obvious name of Volkswagen (German for 'people's car'). Mass-production of this strangely-styled machine (which soon attracted the nickname of 'Beetle', was due to start around 1940, but the outbreak of World War II put a stop to that.

After the war, the ruins of the business were offered to various Western carmakers (all of whom rejected it, and regretted it in the years that followed). In the meantime, however, the Allies oversaw the rebuilding of the factory at Wolfsburg, put the Beetle into production, and eventually handed over the project to the West German state. Only 1,785 cars were produced in 1945, and 10,020 in 1946, but the first 'million-car year' came as early as 1961, and more than two million cars were built in 1971. It was not until the 1960s that control passed into the hands of private investors, where it has remained ever since.

In the next 30 years the Beetle became world-famous, and in ever-developing, reliable and versatile form it went on to become the world's best-selling car. The Ford Model T's previous record total (of around 15 million) was surpassed in 1972. Beetles were eventually built in other countries, and the 20-millionth example was produced in the last of those factories, in Mexico, early in the 1990s.

The longevity of the Beetle was almost VW's downfall in the end. Porsche, under contract and getting a royalty on sales, produced prototype after prototype of proposed replacement cars, but all were rejected. Other air-cooled models *were* built and sold – the 1500 and the 411 among them – but not even the purchase of Audi, and of NSU, could get Volkswagen out of a rut in the early 1970s, when Beetle sales began to die away. A diversion to produce sports coupés jointly with Porsche was only an indulgence, and was never repeated when Porsche replaced the 914SC with the Porsche 924 design.

A completely new approach to design – featuring water-cooled engines, front-mounted and driving the front wheels – finally took over in the mid-1970s, the result being the birth of the famous Polo, Golf, Passat and Scirocco ranges, most of them with an Audi equivalent.

It did not take long for VW to reconfirm its position as the best-selling German marque, and once again to be recognised as one of the world's most successful motor businesses. The first truly exciting Volkswagen was the Golf GTI of the mid-1970s, a design which led to the launch of many related derivatives including the Scirocco and Corrado coupés. Even after this, VW was never tempted to produce a range of high-performance supercars, although the V6 VR6 engine of 1992 was an achievement as was the five-cylinder unit introduced in 1998.

*Above: The two-litre, 16-valve Corrado, a fast Golf-based coupé model launched in 1988, was capable of 126 mph. The supercharged G60 type could reach 137 mph, and the VR6 accelerated to 60 mph in 6.4 seconds and went on to 145 mph.*

*Below: The Golf GTI appeared in 1974 and was the original 'hot hatch', combining performance and practical motoring; this is a 1983 1.8-litre limited-edition Campaign model, in special trim with metallic paintwork and extra equipment.*

*Above: The Volkswagen badge is based on the crest of Wolfsburg, the town where the first factory was sited. From the late 1940s the name became synonymous with practical everyday cars; and, in the mid-1970s, with performance too.*

*Below: A 1947 Volkswagen. The people's car, with a rear air-cooled engine, was designed before World War II and then, post-war, was built until the early 1990s.*

## Golf V5 1998-present

Golf GTIs were pretty much taken for granted in the 1990s. The VR6 powered by the Corrado six-cylinder engine was a special case, however, being something of a Q-car, a wolf in sheep's clothing. But that went out of production in 1997, and its successor was the Golf V5, which appeared late in 1998.

The V5 was used as the model to debut Volkswagen's new 150 bhp 2,324-cc five-cylinder engine, derived from the VR6 motor, but with one cylinder less. It contrived to provide the smooth torque and power associated with a six-cylinder unit while being just as compact as a traditional four-cylinder engine. The cylinders were arranged in one bank of two and one of three, set at a narrow 15-degree angle, necessitating only one

cylinderhead. The V5's two-stage inlet manifold provided a high, flat torque curve that rose to 151-lb/ft at 3,200rpm, with 90 per cent of this maximum available in the rev-band from 2,300 rpm to 5,300 rpm. Peak power was delivered at 6,000 rpm and acceleration from 0-62 mph (0-100 km/h), with the car loaded to half payload, took 8.8 seconds with a top speed of 134 mph (215 km/h). Fuel consumption averaged 30.4 mpg. Transmission was a four-speed unit with VW's 'dynamic shift programme' that adjusted its change up or down points according to how the car was being driven.

The Golf V5 cabin was equipped with fully electronic 'Climatronic' air conditioning, driver's and front seat passenger airbags, front seat-mounted side impact

*Above: The V5 engine put some sparkle into the Golf range, making it the most intriguing of the plethora of trim and power options. The 150bhp V5 engine was derived from the VR6, taking the new model to 134 mph (216 km/h).*

airbags, electric windows on all four doors, electrically heated and adjustable door mirrors, and an eight-speaker factory-fitted RDS radio-cassette system. There was a multi-function trip computer, Isofix child seat mounting points, front and rear centre armrests, leather covered three-spoke steering wheel, sports seats with a choice of five upholstery colour combinations, and remote control central locking with an alarm. There was a central rear seat three-point seat belt and three rear head restraints, height and reach adjustable steering column, height adjustable driver's and

front seat passenger's seats, and a dust and pollen filter. The comprehensive trim package was intended to convey the impression of travelling in a much more expensive car – the V5 cost £19,720 in the UK at launch – and included such niceties as subtle blue back-lighting for the instruments, and a glove-box lid with a silicone damper unit. It was one of the first small saloons to be offered with a factory-fitted satellite navigation screen, which also governed the in-car stereo system.

The specification extended to front fog lights and darkened rear light lenses, anti-lock brakes with electronic brake-force distribution, and the V5 ran on 6.5J x 16 'Montreal' alloy wheels with anti-theft wheel bolts. It was finished off with colour-coded bumpers, side strips and door handles.

### Specification
**Engine:** five-cylinder V5
**Bore x stroke:** 81.0 mm x 90.2 mm
**Capacity:** 2324 cc
**Compression ratio:** 10.0:1
**Chassis:** steel monocoque, four-door
**Suspension:** front, independent by MacPherson struts, lower wishbones, anti-roll bar; rear, torsion beam trailing arms, track stabilising wheel location, coil springs, dampers, anti-roll bar

*Left: The new curvaceous styling enhanced the VW range of cars, and the Golf V5 came with a comprehensive spec.*

## Beetle Rsi 1999-present

The original Beetle outlived all other cars, staying in production in South America some 60 years after its debut. The concept can't have been too far wide of the mark, and Volkswagen elected to bring it bang up to date with a new version for the new millennium. There can be no doubt about the seriousness of their intentions, as development cost DM1-billion. First design proposals were drawn up in 1991 at its Simi Valley studio near Los Angeles, and the Concept 1 prototype was shown in 1994 at Detroit and Geneva. Revised versions of the 'New Beetle' appeared in 1996, and production of 600 units a day was scheduled at VW's Puebla plant in Mexico, with initial deliveries taking place in spring 1999.

Several powertrain options were available, allied to five-speed manual and four-speed automatic transmissions. The New Beetle could be powered by the 115 bhp 2.0 litre petrol engine, the 90 bhp turbocharged, direct-injection diesel 1.9 TDi, as well as the latest five-cylinder 150 bhp 2.3 litre V5 unit. But the question is, where are they situated? Unlike the original Beetle, which as everyone knows, had its flat-four engine mounted behind the rear wheels, the modern incarnation was based on a Golf floorpan and therefore had its transverse power-unit situated up front, with front-wheel drive. So those rotund curves – steel shell with plastic wings, and doors kicked out at the bottom to imitate running boards – serve as a superficial retro-pastiche rather than a faithful reworking of the ancient rear-engined model. No torsion-bars to be found here. Instead, suspension was by

MacPherson strut with lower wishbones up front, and torsion crank axle with track-stabilising wheel location, coil springs and separate dampers, with anti-roll bars front and back. Brakes were discs all round, ventilated at the front, with ABS, EBS and ESP (Electronic Stability Programme). A far cry from the aged ancestor.

The rest of the specification was entirely modern too, and included anti-lock brakes, driver and front seat passenger airbags, front side airbags, power steering, electric front windows, electrically heated and adjustable door mirrors, remote control central locking and alarm, air conditioning, 16 in alloy wheels and, bizarrely, a flower vase. The latter affectation was intended to evoke 1960s

*Above: It may resemble its ubiquitous forebear externally, but that's where the similarity ends. The New Beetle is based on the Golf floorpan, with three engine options ranging from 2.0-litre and 2.3-litre V5 petrol engines to 1.9Tdi, mounted, significantly, in front and driving the front wheels.*

kitsch, along with the prominent round instrument dial and Gamma radio, which was another period pastiche.

### Specification (2.0-litre petrol)
**Engine:** in-line four, front transverse installation
**Bore** x **stroke:** 82.5 mm x 92.8 mm
**Capacity:** 1984 cc
**Compression ratio:** 10.5:1
**Gearbox:** five-speed manual or four-speed automatic
**Chassis:** two-door steel monocoque, plastic wings

**Suspension:** front, independent by MacPherson struts, lower wishbones, anti-roll bar; rear, torsion crank axle, track stabilising wheel location, coil springs, dampers, anti-roll bar

*Below: The New Beetle was styled at VW's Californian design studio, and in profile the Rsi version displays the rounded contours of its sleeker cousin the Audi TT. Whether the rearwing is any more than a styling feature is a moot point.*

# Volkswagen Golf GTI 1974-present

*Below: A 1989 Golf GTI, with the 1.6-litre engine and five-speed gearbox. Although launched with little fuss, the fine-handling, lively Golf GTI became a best-seller.*

The completely new Golf – a small/medium front-wheel-drive car, with its front engine transversely mounted – was unveiled in 1974 and, in many different guises, immediately took over from the ancient air-cooled Beetle. At first, though, Volkswagen had no plans to produce a high-performance version – indeed, the company had no experience, or market reputation, with such machinery – and the release of the 1.6-litre GTI at the 1975 Frankfurt Motor Show was a low-key affair.

Once on the market, however, it was clear that with the fuel-injected five-speed GTI, VW had single-handedly invented a new automotive category – that of the 'hot hatchback'. Compared with its base models, and with every other hatchback, the GTI was faster and handled better; it was also beautifully built. In addition it had an eager character, the sort of desirable and extremely saleable attribute which cannot be

bottled, but which usually transforms a worthy car into an altogether exceptional one. Like the Peugeot 205 GTi of the 1980s, the Golf GTI was to be *the* standard-setter for years to come, and there would be many inferior copies.

The GTI used a flexible but powerful derivative of the new overhead-camshaft four-cylinder engine which had been launched for the Scirocco/Golf models, the engine being mated to a new five-speed front-wheel-drive transmission. The suspension – all-independent with a 'torsion-beam' rear end which many other manufacturers would copy in subsequent years – was supple but always in control, and the youngbloods now easing themselves out of two-seater coupés flocked to buy the GTI in huge numbers.

*Above: A 1981 Golf GTI. The body styling was unremarkable but practical and well balanced, giving the Golf a classless appeal.*

*Left: The petrol-injected engine of a 1985 Golf.*

## Volkswagen Golf GTI variants

### Volkswagen Golf GTI Mk 2, G60 and Golf Rallye

The GTI Mk 2 was built from 1983 to 1991, with a new, longer-wheelbase body shell, and with a choice of 81-mm x 86.4-mm/1781-cc engines – an eight-valve single-cam with 112 bhp, or a 16-valve twin-cam with 129 bhp – and four-wheel disc brakes. From 1986 the 160-bhp supercharged version, called the G60, went on sale, followed in 1988 by the Golf Rallye, which had four-wheel drive. The top speed of the 160-bhp cars was about 130 mph.

### Volkswagen Golf GTI Mk 3

The GTI Mk 3 was introduced in 1991, with a yet larger and heavier body shell. Engines had cylinder dimensions of 82.5 mm × 92.8 mm, giving 1984 cc, with 115-bhp (eight-valve) or 150-bhp (16-valve twin-cam) tunes. The supercharged and four-wheel-drive Rallye versions had both been dropped. In addition, there was a 174-bhp VR6-engined version which could reach 140 mph.

## Specification (1976 GTI)

**Engine:** four-cylinder, single overhead camshaft
**Bore × stroke:** 79.5 mm × 80 mm
**Capacity:** 1588 cc
**Maximum power:** 110 bhp
**Transmission:** five-speed manual gearbox, front-wheel-drive
**Chassis:** steel monocoque
**Suspension:** independent with MacPherson struts front; trailing arms and torsion beam rear
**Brakes:** discs front, drums rear
**Bodywork:** steel three-door or five-door four-seater hatchback
**Maximum speed (approx):** 108 mph (174 km/h)

*Left: With time the Golf gained larger and more curvaceous bodywork; this is a 1991 Golf GTI Mk 3.*

# Volkswagen Corrado 1988–96

*Right: The Corrado VR6 was a 145-mph, two-door coupé powered by a 190-bhp three-litre narrow-angle V6.*

To understand the market covered by the Corrado hatchback in the 1990s, one has to go back to 1974, and the launch of a Giugiaro-styled hatchback called the Scirocco. This was the sporty three-door version of the brand-new Golf, built on VW's behalf by Karmann, which gave the company a marketing boost when it needed it most. The Scirocco was given a new body in 1981, and there was eventually a wide choice of four-cylinder transverse engines, but even in the late 1980s it was still being built on the original Golf floorpan which had been out of production for years.

To supplement the Scirocco but not, Volkswagen insisted, to replace it, a new Karmann-built hatchback was developed, the smoother and more capable Corrado. Mechanically, its layout looked rather familiar, although on this occasion it was built around the larger and more spacious Golf Mk 2 floorpan and running gear.

Like the Scirocco, and like the entire Golf GTI range, the Corrado was meant to combine high performance with VW's very high reliability and build-quality reputation. The result, surprisingly, was that it was not seen as a very exciting

*Above: The Corrado's performance was aided by a traction control system on the front wheels, linked to the disc brakes.*

*Below: Autocar & Motor described the Corrado as "the fastest front-wheel-drive production car we've yet come across".*

machine; the ride, handling and general behaviour were refined rather than sporty, and predictable rather than being untamed.

Early cars had 16-valve versions of VW's four-cylinder engine, one being the supercharged *G-Lader* type which the engineers preferred to the turbo boost system chosen by almost every other European carmaker. In 1991, when the Golf GTI Mk 3 cars were launched, a two-litre engine was introduced, but at the same time came the real surprise,

which transformed the car's character. For its top-of-the-range flagship, Volkswagen installed the exciting new narrow-angle (15-degree) V6 engine and this, with 190 bhp and loads of torque, quite electrified those who drove it.

The new engine had always been meant for a multitude of uses at VW, for it was as light and compact as possible and designed with front-wheel-drive applications in mind (almost immediately after announcement, it was fitted in a variety of Golf, Vento and Passat models) but when matched to the Corrado chassis the result was dramatic. There were no styling changes, merely discreet VR6 badges, to give the game away, the outcome being that the brisk Corrado was turned into an immensely fast and capable machine.

Not only was the Corrado VR6 faster and considerably cheaper than cars like the BMW 325i Coupé with which it was in competition, but it also handled extremely well, was splendidly built and finished, and was a very satisfactory car to drive hard. Testers could find no flaws in its performance – and as far as VW and the customer was concerned, the only problem was that it looked little different from the smaller-engined models.

By a long way, though, in the early 1990s this was the best, fastest and most satisfying car which the mighty Volkswagen group had yet produced.

*Above: The VR6's transverse double-overhead-cam V6, with an alloy head and cast-iron block. With a 10:1 compression ratio, it developed 190 bhp at 5,800 rpm and 181 lb ft at 4,200 rpm. Fuel was supplied via Bosch-Motronic injection and there was fully-mapped ignition.*

*Above: The Corrado's drag coefficient was an excellent 0.31. The high tail meant that the rear seats were spacious enough for two adults.*

### Specification (1992 VR6)

**Engine:** 15-degree V6, twin overhead camshafts
**Bore × stroke:** 82 mm × 90.3 mm
**Capacity:** 2861 cc
**Maximum power:** 190 bhp
**Transmission:** five-speed manual gearbox, front-wheel drive
**Chassis:** steel monocoque
**Suspension:** independent with MacPherson struts and anti-roll bar front; trailing arms, torsion bars and anti-roll bar rear
**Brakes:** discs all round
**Bodywork:** steel three-door four-seater hatchback
**Maximum speed (approx):** 145 mph (233 km/h)

# Volvo

The Volvo name is Latin for 'I roll', and was originally a reference to ball bearings. The company was founded by Assar Gabrielsson, born in 1891 in Korsherga, and Gustaf Larson, born near Örebro in 1887. After graduating from the Stockholm School of Economics, Gabrielsson became sales manager of Svenska Kullagerfabriken (SKF), which made ball bearings, hence the connection with Volvo. Larson graduated from Örebro Technical Institute in 1911 and worked for British engine manufacturers White & Poppe of Coventry, going on to work for SKF and Nya AB Galco of Stockholm in 1920. The two men met up and elected to start their own automotive business over a crayfish dinner at Stockholm's Sturehof restaurant in 1924. The scheme was that all the main components would be of their own design, but produced under contract by outside suppliers.

While Volvo cars are abundant today, it was clear from the outset that a motor manufacturer in Sweden could not survive by building cars alone, and commercial vehicle manufacture would support the production of cars. The design for 'Truck Model 1' was completed nearly six months before the first car rolled off the Hisingen Island assembly line at Gothenburg, and Volvo production was sustained by heavy trucks until the late 1940s.

*Above: Production of the PV444 began in 1944, but sales did not start until after 1947. The series was a huge commercial success, and spawned estates, vans and pick-ups as well.*

The first production car was the PV4 of 1927, designed by Larson and engineer Henry Westerberg, while Gabrielsson persuaded SKF to fund the project. Its 1,944 cc four-cylinder engine was built by marine engine specialist Pentaverken (which it later took over), and in 1929 the PV650 3.0-litre six-cylinder series appeared.

Volvo introduced its streamlined model, the PV36 Carioca in 1935, powered by the 3,670 cc engine and fitted with an all-steel body and independent front suspension. Volvo car production reached 2,834 units in 1939, and Sweden's neutrality enabled production to continue throughout World War II. But material shortages kept output down to just 99 cars in 1942. Two years later, Volvo came out with the PV444, a 1,414-cc ohv four-cylinder unit-construction model, which went on sale in 1947. From this point, Volvo built more cars than commercials per year, and production increased annually up to 1973. The PV444 series included estates, vans, pickups and the PV544 derivative, and production lasted until 1965, and the P210 estate to 1969, with a total in excess of 500,000 units. These included 67 fibreglass P1900 sports cars based on the PV444, styled in the USA in 1957 by Glaspar, which built the prototype Kaiser Darrin.

Successor to the PV444 was styled by Volvo's young designer Jan Wilsgaard. The P120 series began in 1956 with the 121 saloon, fitted with the 1,583 cc or 1,778 cc four-cylinder engines derived from the PV544, which remained in production until 1965. The 121 was known as the Amazon, but the name was dropped after Kreidler motorcycles claimed it. The Amazon enjoyed a fair amount of success on the race circuit as well as in rallying, being robust and well made. Another sports car, the P1800 coupé, was launched in 1961, based on Amazon running-gear. The styling was begun by Ghia and finished off by Frua in Italy. Volvo did not have the capacity to build bodies and after agreements with Karmann in Germany

fell through these were built by Pressed Steel in Scotland and the cars assembled from kits by Jensen in England. This arrangement lasted only until early 1963, when Volvo was able to move all production to Sweden, where it continued until 1973 as the fuel-injected 1800ES sports-estate derivative.

In 1959, Volvo started work on a new facility at Torslanda with government backing, which was opened in 1964. Volvo opened its first overseas assembly plants in Canada and Belgium. The 140 series was introduced in 1966 using Amazon running-gear, which was dropped along with the donor model in 1970, by which time the 140 series was well established. The 140's basic shape was regularly updated, evolving into the 240 line in 1974, and still visible in the mid-1990s as the 940/960 series.

In 1972 Volvo acquired a one-third share in the Dutch company DAF's car division, which was increased to 75 per cent in 1975. By 1978, Volvo had reduced its stockholding to 55 percent, falling to 30 per cent in 1985. Another joint venture enterprise was with Peugeot and Renault through Société Franco-Suedoise des Motors PRV in 1971 to develop the 2.7-litre V6 PRV Douvrin engine, launched in 1974 in the new 260 series Volvo. By 1981, the Volvo group was by far the largest company in Scandinavia, with interests ranging from cars, trucks, buses, and boat and aero-engine production to oil exploration and shipping. Early in 1982, the angular 760 series of luxury cars came out, powered by a 2.8-litre V6, a six-cylinder Volkswagen-built diesel and a turbocharged 2.3-litre four. An Electronic Traction Control system was introduced in 1985 as an option on sporting models, and the Bertone-styled and built 780 Coupé was unveiled at the 1985 Geneva Show. This was a two-door version of the 760, initially aimed at the American market. The antique dealers' delight, an estate car version of the 760, was also introduced in 1985, followed in 1986 by the 480ES, a front-drive sports hatch powered by a 1.7-litre Renault engine, and built in Holland.

Arguably Volvo's best car since the Amazon was the 850 series that appeared in 1991. The 850 GLT was powered by a transverse five-cylinder engine, coupled with a live rear axle and new side impact protection system — or SIPS as it was touted. The GLE followed a year later, and the estate version came out in 1993. The model with most performance was the turbocharged T-5R variant, boasting 240 bhp. Now the old Uddevalla and Kalmar plants closed, with 850 production taking place at Torslanda. Fastest and strongest production Volvo ever was the 250 bhp 850 R.

Collaboration between Volvo and Mitsubishi at the Born plant in the Netherlands, bore fruit in the S40, which was based on the Charisma floorpan. The Volvo model contrived to be more charismatic than its sibling, exemplified by Rickard Rydell winning the 1998 British Touring Car Championship in a TWR-prepared S40.

TWR's involvement with Volvo blossomed in 1996 with the specialised C70 coupé and cabriolet models, built at a new AutoNova plant at Uddevalla, and the same year the 850 series was succeeded by the S70 and V70. The executive-class S80 made its debut in 1998.

*Below: The 1997 S70 was the welcome successor to the familiar 850. The collaboration with TWR also led to the development of the C70, which had much in common with the S70, including similar safety features.*

## Volvo P120 1956-1970

The Amazon debuted in Stockholm in September 1956 as the P121/P122, followed in October the same year at the London Motor Show. It was Volvo's first four-door saloon to be manufactured in large volumes, featuring a unit construction bodyshell powered by the 60 bhp 1.6-litre B16A engine. The design came from the new styling department, headed by Jan Wilsgaard, and although reminiscent of prevalent US shapes, the lines were restrained, elegant and, ultimately timeless. One interesting new feature was the duo-tone colour finish, which was highly fashionable at the time. The Amazon name was reserved for the Swedish market, since the German motorcycle and moped manufacturer Kreidler had prior claim, and everywhere except Sweden it was known as the 120 Series – 121 or 122, depending on the version.

Even back in the mid-1950s Volvo recognised the importance of safety, which was evident in front safety belt anchorage points, padded dashboards and sun visors. The P120 had three-point safety belts from 1959, the first time belts were standard fitment in a volume-produced model. It was shod with Firestone 5.90 x 15 tubeless tyres. In August 1961, the now legendary

75 bhp B18 engine was introduced in the P120 Series, and the sports version, the B18D with twin SU carburettors, developed 90 bhp. The Volvo 122S, popularly known as the Amazon Sport was introduced on the American market in the same year, which was a significant step in Volvo's marketing strategy, since it helped lay the foundations of Volvo's future success in the USA. In 1962, the model range was extended to include an estate version, designated the P220. One of these was driven by Robert Redford in the movie 'All the President's Men', and one of the estate's most practical features was its split rear tail-gate.

Improvements included disc brakes on the front wheels, ergonomically designed seats with a wider range of adjustments, and a triangular-split dual circuit-braking system. Front-seat head restraints were one of the final advances before production ended.

By 1970, the less comely Volvo 140 Series had made its appearance and taken over as Volvo's volume production car, and after 667,323 Amazons had been produced, it was time for the model to bow out. On 3rd July 1970, the Amazon epoch came to an end after almost fifteen years of success. About 60 percent of all Amazons made were ex-

ported, and today these cars are justifiably sought after by classic enthusiasts who recognise the virtues of durability, practicality and ease of maintenance.

### Specification (Volvo 122S)

**Engine:** Volvo B16B in-line four-cylinder
**Bore x stroke:** 79.4 x 80.0 mm
**Capacity:** 1583-cc
**Transmission:** 4-speed
**Suspension:** front, wishbones, coil

*Below: The classic family car. The P120 series was Volvo's first four-door saloon to be produced in large numbers. The innovative duo-tone styling was extremely contemporary.*

## Volvo P1800 1961-1972

Volvo's P1800 sports coupé had the reputation for being both attractively styled as well as durable, well built and refined. Perhaps no wonder then that it was chosen to star alongside the suave Roger Moore in the TV series *The Saint* (Moore also drove one in his private life.) Launched at the Brussels Show in 1960, the two-seater P1800 was powered by Volvo's new B18B engine. Initially the body was made at the rate of 150 units a week by Pressed Steel at Linwood in Scotland and assembled and trimmed by Jensen Motors at West Bromwich, using British components

like Lucas lamps and electrical equipment, Smiths instruments and Girling brakes. However, Jensen had to carry out so much rectification work on the bodies that it proved an impractical proposition, and production was transferred to Gothenburg.

The P1800 was powered by the 1,780-cc five-bearing, twin-carburettor engine, which sported a polished valve cover. Handling-wise, it tended to understeer initially, but judicious use of the throttle brought the back end out on wet roads, making cornering behaviour quite predictable.

Interior of the two-seater body was upholstered in plastic material that matched the red leather seats and black fascia trim, and there were big wind-down side windows. A short gear lever protruded from the transmission tunnel. Instrumentation was housed on two levels, and included an overdrive switch (found only on Swedish market cars) flanked by two-speed heater fan, two-speed wash-wipe switch, with, pullout light switch and ignition-key and starter. The dipswitch was floor-mounted, while there was provision on the dashboard for a radio, and three

projecting Smiths dials housed the clock, fuel and oil pressure gauges. Ahead of the driver were speedo and rev-counter. Under the scuttle were toggles for the fresh-air intake, flanked by switches for map-light and interior lamps, ventilation and heating levers and a mixture control toggle for the twin SU HS6 carburettors. The boot was capacious for a two-seater, with extra luggage space behind the seats, and seat belts were standard equipment.

In its final incarnation, the P1800 was turned into a sports estate, following purpose-built precedents like the Scimitar GTE and Jensen-Healey GT, and prefiguring the second generation Lotus Elite. It was very much a car of its time, and was as well made as ever.

### Specification

**Engine:** in-line 4-cylinders, push-rod ohv, 100 bhp at 5500 rpm
**Compression ratio:** 9.5 :1
**Bore x stroke:** 84 mm x 80 mm
**Capacity:** 1780 cc
**Transmission:** 4-speed plus overdrive
**Suspension:** front, wishbones, coil-springs, anti-roll bar; rear, rigid axle, coil-springs, radius arms, Panhard rod
**Brakes:** servo-assisted Girling discs front, drums rear
**Tyres:** 165 x 15 Pirelli Cinturato, bolt-on steel disc wheels

*Left: An early P1800 with cow-horn bumpers. The distinctive styling was up-to-the-minute and very popular.*

# Volvo 850 1991-1996

The Volvo 850 GLT was launched in June 1991, promoted as featuring a transverse in-line five-cylinder engine, delta-link rear axle that combined a live rear axle with independent suspension, integrated side impact protection system – SIPS – and self-adjusting seat-belt reels. Equally merit worthy were the 850's more rounded contours, making it by far the best-looking Volvo since the Amazon. Despite these worthy features, the new model had to battle against European recession and face stiff competition in the USA. The 850 GLE was launched in summer 1992, followed in February 1993 by the 850 Estate that featured a retractable safety net for the folding rear seat and central rear armrest that doubled as a small child seat. Probably its most prominent external feature was the vertical tail lamp cluster. The Volvo 850 Turbo appeared in August 1993, fitted with Volvo's most powerful engine to date, rated at 225 bhp, with maximum torque of 300 Nm at only 2,000 rpm.

It was at this point that Volvo went racing again. Following in the tyre tracks of the 242T - the two-door turbo version of the 240 saloon with electronic traction control - which was extremely successful in European Touring Car racing in the mid-1980s, the Oxfordshire-based TWR organisation campaigned a pair of 850 Estates in the BTCC in 1994 with Rydell and Lammers driving. In 1995 the TWR

Volvo 850 saloons of Harvey and Rydell did much better, with the Swede achieving third place in the BTCC points table. Rydell and Burt drove the saloons again in 1996, but for 1997, TWR went over to the more compact new S40 model, with which Rydell took the title in 1998.

TWR proprietor Tom Walkinshaw had vast personal racing experience, from Formula Atlantic and Capris to Jaguars and Rover Vitesses. Apart from European Touring Car success with the XJ-S in 1984, TWR Jaguar XJRs were World Sportscar champions in 1987, 1988 and 1991, and won twice at Le Mans and the Daytona 24-Hours. More recently he masterminded Benetton's World Championship victories in 1994 and 1995, as well as holding technical control of Ligier in 1995. TWR acquired a major stake in the Arrows F1 team in 1996. Apart from its prowess on the track, TWR built the XJ220 Jaguar supercars at its Bloxham factory from 1992, and designed and engineered the Aston Martin DB7 in 1993. There was also a deal with GM in Australia to create

*Right: The Volvo racing team of Rydell and Burt in action at the 1996 British Touring Car Championships at Snetterton. This was the last time the 850 saloon was used: in 1997 the new compact S40 was in action to take the title.*

niche-model Holdens. TWR ran General Motors' Holden Commodore V8s in events like the Bathurst 1000. A joint venture with Volvo in 1995 saw TWR producing C70 coupé and cabriolet models from a purpose-built plant at Uddevalla.

## Specification (Volvo 850 BTCC racer)

**Engine:** Volvo Motorsport five-cylinder in-line, transverse installation, 20-valve, DOHC, dry-sump unit. Alloy block, alloy head.
**Bore x stroke:** 83 mm x 73.9 mm
**Capacity:** 1999-cc
**Output:** 290bhp at 8500 rpm

**Transmission:** front-wheel drive, six-speed Xtrac gearbox, transverse mounting
**Suspension:** front, TWR-fabricated McPherson struts, Ohlins gas damper units, anti-roll bar; rear, Delta-link, semi-independent trailing arms, anti-roll bar, coil springs, gas dampers.
**Brakes:** hydraulically assisted dual circuit ventilated discs, AP 8-piston callipers front, Brembo 2-piston callipers rear. Carbon metallic pads
**Chassis:** TWR-built, seam-welded, four-door right-hand-drive 850 GLT monocoque, welded-in tubular roll cage; splitter & rear wing to FIA spec

# Volvo C70 1997-present

The C70 Coupé made its debut at the Paris Motor Show in autumn 1996, followed a year later by the C70 Convertible version. The two-door four-seater models were manufactured at the AutoNova plant in Uddevalla, Sweden, in a joint venture between Volvo and TWR, and evolved under head of design Peter Horbury. Conceptually, the C70 recalled the Bertone-built 262C coupé of 1977 but, more significantly, launched Volvo into Mercedes-Benz CLK territory.

Both C70 models were developed by TWR according to Volvo's specifications, and the results are among the best looking designs in their individual segments, especially in coupé format. You might even go so far as to say that it's the best-looking Volvo ever made. Up to

the top of the doors, they are identical, and the convertible's soft-top can be raised or lowered electrically in under half a minute.

The C70 Coupé is built along the same lines as the Volvo S70, powered by a transverse-mounted five-cylinder turbocharged engine with front-wheel drive and five-speed manual gearbox or four-speed automatic. There was a choice of engines: either a 240 bhp 2.3-litre turbo with a torque of 330 Nm, or a 193 bhp 2.5-litre light-pressure turbo of 270 Nm. The C70 turbo T5 with manual gearbox could reach 60 mph (96 km/h) from a standstill in 6.9 seconds. No problems with performance, then. And chassis development and suspension tuning was expertly carried out

by TWR, manifest in above average handling and roadholding. There were three chassis settings to choose from, including lowered suspension and, fundamentally, the coupé was more sports orientated, while the convertible's emphasis was more on comfort. All models were supplied with 16-, 17-, or 18-inch wheels.

The S70's safety features were also inherent in the C70, including the beam structure, SIPS and side airbags, plus the belt system with tensioners. The convertible contained Volvo's Roll-Over Protection System consisting of robust roll-over bars that automatically sprang up behind the heads of the rear-seat passengers in the event of an inversion. The reinforced A-pillars and windscreen

header rail performed the same function for the front-seat occupants.

The interior was upholstered with a blend of wood and aluminium trims and leather and fabric materials. The C70 also had a sophisticated factory-fitted audio installation with ten speakers as standard and was the first car in the world to provide Dolby Surround ProLogic sound system. Principal markets for the C70 were identified as North America, Germany, Italy, the UK and Japan.

## Specification (T5)

**Engine:** in-line 5-cylinders, transverse-mounted, front-drive
**Capacity:** 2.3-litres
**Transmission:** five-speed manual, four-speed automatic
**Suspension:** front, independent by MacPherson struts, coil springs, damper units, anti-roll bar; rear, independent Delta-link, semi-trailing arms, anti-roll bar, coil springs, dampers
**Brakes:** discs, ABS with EDB
**Wheels:** 17-inch Canisto alloy wheels.
**Chassis:** two-door steel monocoque

*Left: The S70 was one of the best-looking Volvos ever produced, and the convertible was just as stunning. Nowhere near as boxy as earlier Volvos, the S70's sensational looks caused a stir at its launch in 1997, and it was given rave reviews by the motoring press.*

# Westfield Sports Cars Ltd

*Right: Produced in the West Midlands, Chris Smith's Lotus-inspired performance cars sell well in Britain and Japan.*

*Below: Based on the Lotus Seven, but changed for copyright reasons, the ordinary Westfield SEi was fitted with a Ford four-cylinder engine.*

Westfield was founded at the beginning of the 1980s, by a West Midlands classic car dealer, Chris Smith, who insists that, at the time, he had no wish to become a specialist car constructor. As it happened, he had a customer from the USA who spotted the remains of a sports-racing Lotus XI chassis of the 1950s lying forgotten in Smith's back garden, and persuaded him to build it up into a replica.

Smith, himself no mean engineer, found that the old frame was too badly rusted to be restored, so he constructed a Lotus look-alike which had a significantly different multi-tube chassis, powered it using an MG Midget engine and transmission, and clothed it in a glassfibre replica of the sleek Lotus body shell.

The customer then backed out of the deal when the first car had been finished, but a Lotus dealer saw the result and liked it so much that he persuaded Smith to set up a small company to build these machines – called Westfields – in small but significant quantities. The first car was delivered in 1982, and following enthusiastic test reports in *Road and Track* and *Autoweek* he secured an American order for 20 vehicles.

The next step was to build a second model, also Lotus-based. Smith based it on the Lotus Seven, which Lotus had made from 1957 to 1973, but which had been out of production for years. As with many such cars of the period, Westfield provided a chassis/body unit, along with an instruction book, leaving the customer to buy his own engine and other running gear.

The Westfield Seven, complete with an aluminium body shell, was an instant success, but unhappily it was a little too close to the original design, and legal wrangles followed. The company which had secured the continuing design and manufacturing rights to the Lotus – Caterham – sued Smith, who was therefore obliged to re-engineer *his* Seven completely, making substantial design changes, and fitting it with a somewhat restyled glassfibre two-seater body, though the Lotus Seven heritage was still clear.

The result was the launch of the Westfield SE and SEi, which had independent rear suspension, and which was so popular that more than 1,000 such cars were sold in 1988. By the early 1990s sales had settled down to about 600 cars a year, with some cars being delivered in kit form, others delivered ready to roll. Many were exported.

## Westfield SE 1988-93

As a result of the acrimonious and costly dispute with Caterham over design rights, Westfield was obliged to re-engineer its small two-seater to make it less like the Lotus/Caterham Seven. The result was still a stark open two-seater with minimal trim, appointments and weather protection, but one which had its own distinctive character and engineering details.

In particular, the Westfield SE had independent rear suspension by double wishbones, which gave it even greater traction than its Caterham rival – and Westfield had ambitions to provide the SE with a still wider choice of engines. To keep the 'entry-level' prices down as far as possible, Westfield always tried to offer a standard car fitted with the cheapest and most reliable Ford four-cylinder engine it could find, and even in 1990 this meant that a body/chassis kit was available for no more than £1,250, though finished cars cost up to 10 times that much.

The basic design featured a multi-tube spaceframe chassis, with square-section tubing, a layout which ensured that (like the Caterham Seven) there were no doors. The body, mainly of glassfibre, featured cycle-type front wings which turned with the wheels. There was a hood, and side screens, of sorts, but true Westfield enthusiasts tried never to use them, as they spoiled the lines! Headlamps, the spare wheel *and* the driver's elbow were all exposed to the weather, but Westfield motoring was so explosively exciting that no-one complained.

By 1991 Westfield offered the SEi with a choice of engines, which included Ford's new Zeta twin-cam, and with a normally-aspirated version of the Ford Sierra/Escort RS Cosworth unit, but the most outrageous version of all was the SEiGHT, into which Chris Smith had somehow persuaded a modified Rover V8 to fit. This required extra-wide wheels and tyres, and a heavy-duty rear axle to match, the result being a two-seater roller skate which weighed only 1,520 lb, and which could accelerate to 100 mph in a mere 10.5 seconds if a 273-bhp engine was fitted. This was Porsche 911 Turbo performance, but without the enormous German prices.

This was unquestionably a dramatic machine, for which Westfield charged £20,888 if a 273-bhp race-prepared engine was fitted, or £17,579 with the standard 3.5-litre Rover instead. This was no car for the faint-hearted, as its character was something akin to a fighter aircraft which never got off the ground. The ride was hard, the steering direct and inch-accurate, and the noise from the engine quite blood-curdling, but it always felt safe and there was a huge incentive for the driver to go faster, and faster, and faster...

That, after all, is what supercar motoring is meant to be about, and although Westfield only set out to build two such cars every week, they were happy with the car's reputation.

### Specification (1991 SEiGHT)

**Engine:** Rover V8, overhead-valve
**Bore × stroke:** 94 mm × 71 mm

*Above: The SEiGHT had 273 bhp and weighed only 1,520 lb; the result was a minimalist machine which could leave a Ferrari Testarossa behind, until a lack of aerodynamics slowed it at 100 mph and above.*

**Capacity:** 3946 cc
**Maximum power:** 273 bhp
**Transmission:** five-speed manual gearbox, rear-wheel drive
**Chassis:** separate multi-tube frame
**Suspension:** independent with wishbones, coil springs and anti-roll bar front; wishbones and coil springs rear
**Brakes:** discs all round
**Bodywork:** glassfibre two-seater open sports car with cycle-type wings
**Maximum speed (approx):** (273-bhp engine) 140 mph (225 km/h)

# Zagato

*Right: The Zagato name has long been synonymous with light, aerodynamic and distinctive car bodywork. Ugo Zagato had worked during World War I in an aircraft factory, where he pioneered the use of lightweight metal skinning, a technique ideal for sporting cars.*

**U**go Zagato set up his coachbuilding works in Milan in 1919, and by the late 1920s had become one of Italy's most famous specialist stylists and producers of sporting bodywork. From that day to this, Zagato has been one of Italy's most prominent coachbuilding concerns, and there has always been a member of the Zagato family at the helm of the company.

Northern Italy, of course, has had a distinguished coachbuilding tradition for centuries, so when Ugo Zagato took up a trade he decided to become a coachbuilder. After training in Germany, and working in the Pomilio aircraft factory during World War I, he struck out on his own.

Before long Zagato of Milan was famous for its light and strikingly stylish bodies on Alfa Romeos (many of which won important motor races), and this business was expanded to include Fiat work in the 1930s. During World War II, the factory was destroyed by Allied bombing, and new premises were built on the northern edge of Milan in 1946.

In the 1950s and 1960s Zagato coachwork, always ultra-light and usually outrageously styled, became a feature on many cars, not least the Fiat 8V, various 'double-bubble' Abarth coupés, the Alfa Romeo Giulietta SV and SZ, the Aston Martin DB4 GT Zagato, the Alfa Romeo TZ, the Lancia Flaminia and Fulvia Coupés and the Alfa GT 1300 Junior Zagato. All the time the company was expanding, and a lot of business was done with Ferrari, Jaguar, Lamborghini, Maserati and other less exotic concerns, but financial control was often shaky.

Before Ugo Zagato died in 1968, to be succeeded by his sons Elio and Gianni, the business had been moved to yet another factory, this one close to the autostrada into Milan. During the 1970s the company seemed to lose its edge, and slipped back compared with Pininfarina, Bertone and especially Ital Design. Zagato made a design comeback in the 1980s, by styling the Aston Martin Vantage Zagato coupé and spider, and 50 per cent of the business was bought by Victor Gauntlett and Peter Livanos of Aston Martin fame.

Even though the cars styled by Zagato in the latter part of the 20th century were sometimes described as clumsy and even ugly, their brutal character and (some say) awkward planes and shapes appealed to a small but defined clientele: the Aston Martin was matched by the Maserati Birturbo Spyder, the Alfa Romeo SZ by a pair of Nissan 300ZX show cars. A real breakthrough seemed likely following the launch of the smoothly-detailed Hyena Coupé, which was not only based on an excellent chassis but which had a style everyone seemed to love. In 1998 Zagato styled the Diablo's replacement for Lamborghini, the P147.

## Zagato Hyena 1992–93

The rebirth of Zagato, a coachbuilding company which had struggled to survive in the 1980s, was completed in January 1992, when the company chose the Brussels Motor Show to launch a smooth new coupé which it called the Hyena.

Here was a machine which combined a great chassis, a shape which almost everyone seemed to admire, and a great deal of high-tech engineering content. Zagato stated that it would like to build and sell this car on its own, rather than selling the rights to the manufacturer on whose chassis it was based, and there was talk of 60, 70 or maybe 90 examples being produced.

If prices could be kept in check, the Hyena looked very promising, for it was built on the extremely famous and

*Below: A production run of just 75 Zagato Hyenas was planned, with a possible larger run of cars built in less exotic materials.*

*Right: Styled by Marco Pedracini, the Hyena was intended to look like the animal. Light, smooth and with hints of retro-styling, it offered significantly more performance than the standard Delta HF Integrale.*

capable base of Lancia's four-wheel-drive Integrale HF, a machine which had been dominant in World Championship rallies for many years. The show car featured an aluminium two-seater body shell, with the spare wheel sitting on the rear floor, in full view through the sloping rear window.

With Lancia's fine chassis, which included ABS braking, OZ rally-style wheels, and Pirelli P Zero tyres, the Hyena also took weight-saving to great lengths, which explains why the bumpers, sills and door panels are constructed from Kevlar, while much of the stripped-out interior was finished in carbonfibre. This way, Zagato claimed, the Hyena weighed 441 lb less than it would otherwise have done.

Zagato described the new machine as looking "functional and innovative"; it featured a squashed Lancia grille, flared wheel arches, and almost a complete lack of drag-raising detail. The front end, naturally, was full of slats to help keep the turbocharged Lancia's engine and intercooler at the right temperatures.

The company gave the go-ahead to this exciting new car in mid-1992, but corporate politics disallowed the supply of Integrale parts and the project foundered with just 26 units built.

### Specification (1993)

**Engine:** four-cylinder, twin overhead camshafts
**Bore × stroke:** 84 mm × 90 mm
**Capacity:** 1995 cc
**Maximum power:** 210 bhp
**Transmission:** five-speed manual gearbox, four-wheel drive
**Chassis:** steel/aluminium/carbonfibre monocoque body/chassis assembly, using Lancia Integrale floorpan
**Suspension:** independent with MacPherson struts front and rear
**Brakes:** discs all round
**Bodywork:** aluminium/carbonfibre two-seater Coupé
**Maximum speed (approx.):** 145 mph (230 km/h)

# Index